Recent Advances
in Aquatic Mycology

Recent Advances in Aquatic Mycology

Edited by E. B. GARETH JONES
Reader in Biological Sciences, Portsmouth Polytechnic

A Halsted Press Book

John Wiley & Sons
New York

Published in the U.S.A. by
Halsted Press, a Division of
John Wiley & Sons, Inc.,
New York.

Library of Congress Cataloging in Publication Data
Jones, Evan Benjamin Gareth, 1937-
   Recent advances in aquatic mycology.
   "A Halsted Press book."
   1. Aquatic fungi. I. Title.
QK617.8.J65   589'.2'0916   74-27179
ISBN 0-470-29176-1

Produced by UNEOPRINT by Unwin Brothers Limited, The Gresham Press, Old Woking, Surrey, England

Contents

Preface

Erratum

The date at the end of the preface should read 'August 1975.' Substantial references up to 1973, and significant new references up to 1974 and 1975, have been added in proof stage.

Traditionally mycologists have devoted most of their time to the study of terrestrial fungi. However, in the 1940s, mycologists became increasingly interested in aquatic fungi especially E. S. Barghoorn, J. N. Couch, R. Emerson, W. Höhnk, C. T. Ingold, J. S. Karling, D. H. Linder and F. K. Sparrow. In 1961, Johnson and Sparrow in their book *Fungi of Oceans and Estuaries* gave a comprehensive account of the fungi known at that time. However, a comparable volume has not been available for the freshwater fungi.

In recent years, aquatic fungi have received considerable attention. Evidence of this is seen by the seven sessions devoted to aquatic fungi at the First International Mycological Congress held in Exeter in 1971. Dr. C. H. Dickinson (in an account of the Congress published in the Bulletin of the British Mycological Society) observed that 'there was so much interest in these fungi (aquatic) that there could have been an entire section of the congress given over to their taxonomy, biology and ecology'. Indeed, the idea for this volume grew from the success of the aquatic fungi sessions of the First International Mycological Congress.

Man's concern with environmental aspects may also account for the increased interest in aquatic organisms. Pollution of streams, rivers and local shores is common, therefore the role of microfungi in these situations is important. Recent research suggests that aquatic fungi may play a key role in the productivity of streams, estuaries and oceans.

This volume has two aims. Firstly to bring information on freshwater and marine fungi together in one volume. Aquatic microbiology is a subject of considerable interest, but the coverage of aquatic fungi in recent texts has been fragmentary and totally inadequate. Furthermore, advances in marine mycology since Johnson and Sparrow's (1961) book more than justify a further review.

The secondary purpose of this book is to review work on aquatic fungi over the past 12 years, to evaluate the available information and to highlight areas requiring further study. A wide spectrum of topics are reviewed, such as morphology, ultrastructure, spore cytochemistry, systematics, physiology, ecology, as well as more specialized aspects, for example: oil degradation, sewage fungi, protein production by aquatic fungi, fungal diseases of animals and the role of fungi in the breakdown of pesticides. In keeping with the growing concern over environmental matters, many chapters emphasize the role of fungi in the ecology of aquatic habitats.

For convenience, the volume is divided into two sections. Section I deals with the marine fungi whilst Section II is devoted to freshwater fungi, Trichomycetes and Actinomycetes. Every effort has been made to present a balanced account within each section.

References up to 1972 and those known to be in press have been included. Significant new contributions are briefly summarised or listed in addenda to chapters.

My thanks are due to the contributors for their helpful collaboration in producing this volume, and especially to my past and present research students for all their help. Finally, my sincere thanks to Mrs Kay Kelsey and Miss Linda Ayling for their invaluable help in the preparation of the typescript of this volume.

E. B. Gareth Jones
1st August 1973

SECTION I: MARINE FUNGI

A. Ascomycetes, Fungi Imperfecti and Basidiomycetes

1 Lignicolous and Algicolous Fungi

E. B. GARETH JONES

1.1 Introduction

A variety of substrates in the sea are available for colonization by fungi (Table 1.1). This chapter will be concerned primarily with those fungi found growing on wood

Table 1.1 Estimated number of species of marine fungi known to colonize different substrates in the sea

	Phycomycetes	Ascomycetes	Basidiomycetes	Fungi Imperfecti
Lignicolous	3	91	2	36
Free floating	10	50	8	—
Polyurethane	—	3	—	1
Sediments, mud, soil, dunes	35	20	—	180
Algae	70 + 32*	50	—	14
Animals	19	5	—	5
Decaying leaves of terrestrial plants	3	2	—	9
Decaying leaves of marine Angiosperms	2	6	1	30

* Doubtful species.

This chapter is dedicated to my teacher and mentor Dr. Irene M. Wilson, who introduced me to this fascinating group of fungi, for her advice and encouragement at all times.

(and other cellulosic materials) and marine algae. Marine fungi on mangroves and hydrocarbons are discussed respectively by Newell (Chapter 2) and Ahearn and Meyers (Chapter 4), while Fell (Chapter 3) considers the ecology of the free floating yeast population of the sea.

Only a few of these higher marine fungi will be illustrated here, and the reader is referred to the beautifully illustrated *Icones Fungorum Maris* of Kohlmeyer and Kohlmeyer (1964-1969).

1.2   Lignicolous Fungi

Some 300 fungi have been described as marine (Jones and Irvine, 1971) but only 132 have been recorded on wood. Over the past decade the early taxonomical work has been consolidated, and revisions of certain groups have been possible (Kohlmeyer, 1972 a).

The methods used for collecting marine lignicolous fungi are well documented (Johnson and Sparrow, 1961; Meyers, 1971; and Jones, 1971b). Test panels (6 x 3 x 1 inches) of *Fagus sylvatica* L. (beech), *Pinus sylvestris* L. (Scots pine) or *Ochroma lagopus* (balsa) are arranged in strings and submerged in the sea from rafts. Test blocks are removed every 4 to 6 weeks, placed in polythene bags, sealed and returned to the laboratory. Fouling organisms are scraped off and the blocks washed in sterile seawater. They are then incubated on a layer of sterile *Kleenex* tissues in sterile plastic boxes. The panels are examined immediately on arrival and at regular

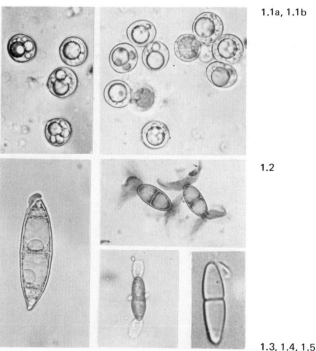

1.1a, 1.1b

1.2

1.3, 1.4, 1.5

Fig. 1.1 (a) and (b).   Hyaline, non-appendaged ascospores of an undescribed Pyrenomycete (x666). **Fig. 1.2.** *Halosphaeria maritima.* Appendaged ascospores (x666). **Fig. 1.3.** *Haligena spartinae.* Ascospore with apical appendage (x666). **Fig. 1.4.** *Halosphaeria torquata.* Ascospore (x666). **Fig. 1.5.** *Halosphaeria hamata.* Apical appendage to ascospore (x666).

intervals throughout the incubation period. Jones (1971 b) has described the methods used for the isolation of marine fungi. The Fungi Imperfecti grow and fruit readily in culture while the Basidiomycetes and Ascomycetes are more fastidious. However, many can be induced to fruit on balsa or birch wood in Kirk's medium (Kirk, 1969).

Timber groynes, rope and driftwood are also colonized by marine fungi. These substrates should be collected and incubated as described above. However, care must be exercised in referring to all the fungi present as marine, because many may be airborne terrestrial fungi.

1.2.1 Ascomycetes

Kohlmeyer and Kohlmeyer (1971 a) list 71 lignicolous Ascomycetes while Jones and Irvine (1971) estimate 91. New species continue to be described (Schmidt, 1969; Jones and Le Campion-Alsumard, 1970 a; Kohlmeyer and Kohlmeyer, 1971 b; and Schaumann, 1972 a, 1973), while others (Jones and Irvine, unpublished) remain to be described (Fig. 1.1). All the major divisions of the Ascomycetes, with the exception of the Discomycetes, have marine representatives.

Two marine Plectomycetes have been described, *Amylocarpus encephaloides* Currey and *Eiona tunicata* Kohlm. Both have cleistothecia, deliquescing asci and appendaged ascospores.

The following families of the Pyrenomycetes have marine representatives: Erysiphaceae (?), Halosphaeriaceae, Hypocreaceae, Polystigmataceae and Sphaeriaceae. The majority belong in the Halosphaeriaceae, originally established by Müller and von Arx (1962) and validated and amended by Kohlmeyer (1972 a). Table 1.2 lists the genera and species accepted by Kohlmeyer (1972 a), and the spores of some of these are illustrated in Figs. 1.2 to 1.9. All members of this family are marine, have deliquescing asci and most of the species have appendaged ascospores.

The Hypocreaceae have only two marine lignicolous species: *Halonectria milfordensis* Jones and *Hydronectria tethys* J. et E. Kohlm. while the Erysiphales are represented only by *Crinigera maritima* Schmidt.

The majority of the Loculoascomycetes belong in the family Pleosporaceae with such well known terrestrial genera as: *Pleospora, Leptosphaeria, Sphaerulina* and *Didymella*. Other genera: *Paraliomyces, Kymadiscus, Manglicola* and *Pontoporeia* have only marine species.

1.2.2 Basidiomycetes

Only two marine Basidiomycetes have been described from submerged wood: *Digitatispora marina* Doguet and *Nia vibrissa* Moore et Meyers. They have respectively branched and appendaged basidiospores, lack sterigmata and are passively released into the surrounding water (Figs. 1.10-1.16). In *N. vibrissa*, the spore is attached to the basidium by a peg-like structure or pedicel.

1.2.3 Fungi Imperfecti

Kohlmeyer and Kohlmeyer (1971 a) list 51 marine Deuteromycetes and 36 of these are lignicolous (Figs. 1.17-1.24). The majority belong in well known terrestrial genera *(Alternaria, Camarosporium, Dendryphiella, Diplodia, Humicola, Monodictys, Stemphylium* and *Sporidesmium)*, while others appear to be exclusively marine *(Asteromyces, Cirrenalia, Cremasteria, Orbimyces,* and *Zalerion)*.

3

Table 1.2   List of genera and species of the family Halosphaeriaceae (after Kohlmeyer, 1972 a).

Genus	Species
Carbosphaerella	*pleosporoides* Schmidt; *leptosphaeroides* Schmidt.
Ceriosporopsis	*calyptrata* Kohlm; *cambrensis* Wilson; *circumvestita* (Kohlm.) Kohlm.; *halima* Linder; *longissima* Kohlm.; *tubulifera* (Kohlm.) Kirk.
Chadefaudia	**marina* Feldmann; **corallinarum* (Crouan et Crouan) Müller et von Arx; **gymnogongri* (Feldman) Müller et von Arx; **polyporolithi* (Bonar) Müller et von Arx; *balliae* Kohlm.
Corollospora	*comata* (Kohlm.) (Kohlm.; *cristata* (Kohlm.) Kohlm.; *intermedia* Schmidt; *lacera* (Linder) Kohlm.; *maritima* Werdermann; *pulchella* Kohlm., Schmidt et Nair; *trifurcata* (Höhnk) Kohlm.; *tubulata* Kohlm.
Haligena	*elaterophora* Kohlm.; *spartinae* Jones; *unicaudata* Jones et Le Campion-Alsumard; *viscidula* Kohlm.
Halosphaeria	*appendiculata* Linder; *cucullata* (Kohlm.) Kohlm.; *hamata* (Höhnk) Kohlm.; *maritima* (Linder) Kohlm.; *mediosetigera* Cribb et Cribb; *pilleata* (Kohlm.) Kohlm.; *quadricornuta* Cribb et Cribb; *quadriremis* (Höhnk) Kohlm.; *salina* (Meyers) Kohlm.; *stellata* (Kohlm.) Kohlm.; *torquata* Kohlm.; *trullifera* (Kohlm.) Kohlm.
Lentescospora	*submarina* Linder.
Lignincola	*laevis* Höhnk.
Lindra	*inflata* Wilson; †*marinera* Meyers; †*thalassiae* Orpurt Meyers, Boral et Simms.
Lulworthia	*fucicola* Suth; *grandispora* Meyers; **kniepii* Kohlm.;
Maireomyces	**peyssoneliae* Feldmann.
Nais	*inornata* Kohlm.
Nautosphaeria	*cristaminuta* Jones.

Rejected genera: *Samarosporella; Torpedospora*
* Algicolous species
† On marine Angiosperms only

1.2.4   Colonization of timber in the sea

Higher marine fungi have been reported from 50 or more countries (Table 1.3). Jones (1968 a, 1971 a) has indicated that the majority are cosmopolitan in their distribution, although a few appear to be restricted to warmer waters.

Brooks *et al.* (1972) have shown that timber removed from the sea is initially colonized by marine fungi. Although they report softening of the wood, they do not describe the decay pattern, i.e. soft, white or brown rot. Observations by Jones (unpublished) and Furtado (unpublished) suggest that bacteria as well as fungi are active in the decay of wood in the sea. Similar observations have been made by Kohlmeyer (1969 d).

Brooks *et al.* (1972) examined driftwood collected between rocks and submerged only at low tide. For detailed ecological work, it is important to submerge test blocks

4

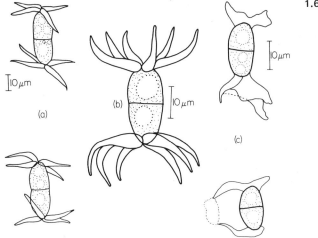

Fig. 1.6. Ascospores of three species of *Halosphaeria:* (a) *H. quadriremis;* (b) *H. stellata;* and (c) *H. maritima.*

free of microbial attack, then the process of colonization can be followed accurately. This procedure has been followed by Byrne and Jones (1974), Jones (1968 a), Jones *et al.* (1972), and Meyers (1971). Tables 1.4 and 1.5 list fungi recorded on beech and Scots pine test panels submerged at Newton Ferres and Port Erin, UK. Some fungi appear on a number of the panels: (*Dendryphiella salina* (Suth.) Pugh et Nicot, *Monodictys pelagica* (Johnson) Jones, *Zalerion maritimum* (Linder) Anastasiou, and *Lulworthia sp.,* while others are infrequent *(Alternaria maritima* Suth, *Culcitalna*

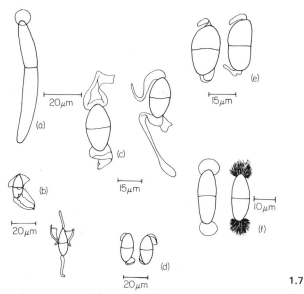

Fig. 1.7. Ascospores of *Halosphaeria* species to show range in ascospore appendages: (a) *H. cucullata;* (b) *H. appendiculata (= R. ornata);* (c) *H. pilleata;* (d) *H. hamata;* (e) *H. trullifera* and (f) *H. gallerita.*

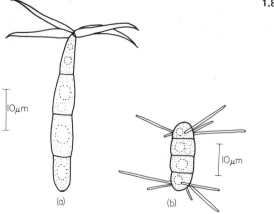

Fig. 1.8. Ascospores of *Torpedospora radiata* (a) and *T. ambispinosa* (b).

achraspora Meyers et Moore, and *Nautosphaeria cristaminuta* Jones). Table 1.6 lists the total number of fungi recorded at three testing sites by Byrne and Jones (1974). This allows a comparison between different test sites and shows that *Monodictys pelagica, Zalerion maritimum, Ceriosporopsis halima* Linder, and *Lulworthia* spp. are common marine fungi. *Asteromyces cruciatus* Moreau et Moreau ex Hennebert, *Sporidesmium salinum* Jones, *Haligena unicaudata* Jones et Le Campion-Alsumard, *Halosphaeria circumvestita* Kohlm. *H. tubulifera* Kohlm., and *Nais inornata* Kohlm., occur only rarely.

In Table 1.7, the frequency of occurrence of some British marine lignicolous fungi are presented. The most common species are *Zalerion maritimum, Ceriosporopsis*

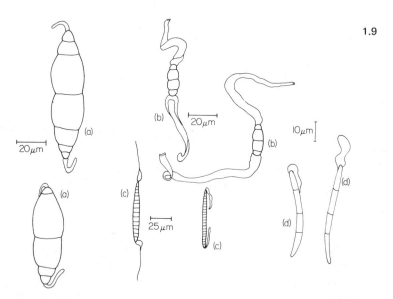

Fig. 1.9. Ascospores of *Haligena* species: (a) *H. spartinae;* (b) *H. elaterophora;* (c) *H. viscidula* and (d) *H. unicaudata.*

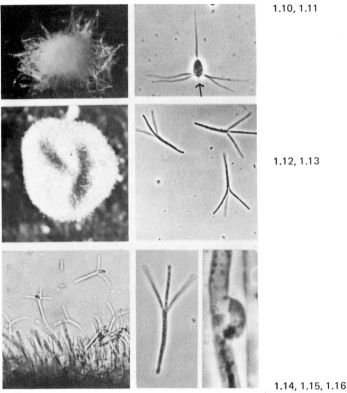

1.10, 1.11

1.12, 1.13

1.14, 1.15, 1.16

Fig. 1.10. *Nia vibrissa.* Developing sporophore (x3). **Fig. 1.11.** *N. vibrissa.* Basidiospore with one apical and four lateral appendages. Pedicel (arrowed) (x333). **Fig. 1.12.** *N. vibrissa.* Mature basidiocarp (x4). **Fig. 1.13.** *Digitatispora marina.* Three branched basiospores (x470). **Fig. 1.14.** *D. marina.* Section of the hymenium with basidia and basidiospores (x166). **Fig. 1.15.** *D. marina.* Tetraradiate basidiospore (x666). **Fig. 1.16.** *D. marina.* Clamp connection on hypha in culture (x666) (photo. K. Fazzani).

halima and *Lulworthia* spp. The observations of Poole and Price (1972) at Chatham, England support these results, although *Lulworthia* spp. were surprisingly absent.

These appear to be commonly occurring species not only at the country level (Jones, 1972) but also on a world level, as Jones (1971) and Jones *et al.* (1972) have shown. The latter conducted a test at 18 sites round the world, and the most frequently recorded species were *Cirrenalia macrocephala* (Kohlm.) Meyers et Moore (present on 45% of the blocks), *Zalerion maritimum* (32%), *Lulworthia floridana* Meyers (25%), *L. purpurea* (Wilson) Johnson (16%), *Dendryphiella salina* (16%), *Ceriosporopsis halima* (15%) and *Humicola alopallonella* Meyers et Moore (13%).

The frequency of occurrence of species in relation to the 18 testing sites revealed that *C. macrocephala* was found in 80% of the sites, *L. floridana* in 50%, *H. alopallonella* in 45%, *C. halima* in 40% and *D. salina* in 35%. Some of the fungi were only recorded once, e.g. *Trichocladium achraspora* (Lisbon), *Haligena viscidula* Kohlm., (Abidjan), *Halosphaeria appendiculata* Linder, (Langstone), *Halosphaeria maritima* (Linder) Kohlm (Lisbon) and *Orbimyces spectabilis* Linder (Abidjan).

Successional patterns of fungi on wood submerged in the sea have been reported by Meyers (1954), Meyers and Reynolds (1960), Johnson and Sparrow (1961), and

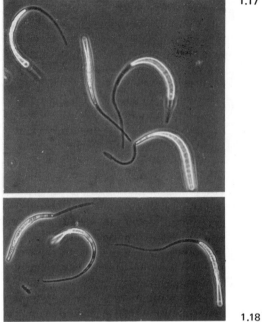

1.18

Fig. 1.17-1.18. Conidia of an undescribed hyphomycete isolated from *Fucus* and *Laminaria* fronds (x333) (photo. J. Haythorn).

1.20

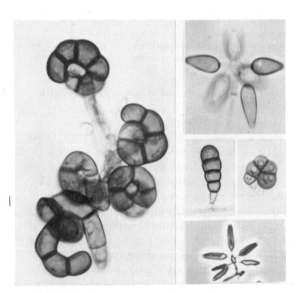

1.21, 1.22

1.19, 1.23

Fig. 1.19. *Zalerion maritimum.* Helicoid conidia (x666). **Fig. 1.20.** *Asteromyces cruciatus.* Group of conidia (x666). **Fig. 1.21.** Conidium of an undescribed *Cremasteria* (x400). **Fig. 1.22.** *Cirrenalia macrocephala.* Conidium (x400). **Fig. 1.23.** *A. cruciatus.* Group of conidia (x366).

1.24

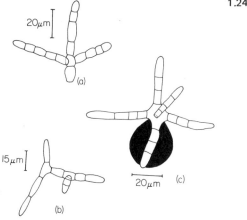

Fig. 1.24. Conidia of (a) *Clavariopsis bulbosa;* (b) *Varicosporina ramulosa;* (c) *Orbimyces spectabilis.*

Table 1.3   List of countries where lignicolous marine fungi have been collected

Country	Author	Number of fungi recorded
Aden	Jones (1968 b)	4
Algeria	Kohlmeyer (1963 a, b, d)	3
Antarctica	Tubaki and Asano (1965)	1
Argentina	Malacalza and Martinez (1971)	6
Australia	Cribb and Cribb (1954, 1956, 1960 a, b) Jones *et al.* (1972)	20
Bahamas	Kohlmeyer and Kohlmeyer (1971 b)	9
Belgium	Kohlmeyer (1959) Kohlmeyer and Kohlmeyer (1964-69)	5
Brazil	Kohlmeyer and Kohlmeyer (1971 b)	5
British Honduras	Meyers (1954, 1957)	3
Bulgaria	Kohlmeyer (1959, 1963 c)	3
Cameroon	Jones *et al.* (1972)	4
Canada	Hughes (1968) Neish (1970) Jones *et al.* (1972)	50
Canary Isles	Kohlmeyer (1967)	17
Chile	Hughes and Chamut (1971)	14
Cuba	Meyers (1957)	3
Denmark	Kohlmeyer (1968 c)	15
Fiji	Kohlmeyer (1968 a)	1
France	Kohlmeyer (1962, 1963 b, c) Jones *et al.* (1972) Jones and Le Campion-Alsumard (1970 a, b)	34
Germany	Kohlmeyer (1963 b) Schaumann (1968, 1969, 1972 a, b, 1973) Schmidt (1967, 1969)	47

Country	Author	Number of fungi recorded
Greece	Jones *et al.* (1972)	4
Guatemala	Kohlmeyer and Kohlmeyer (1971 b)	8
Haiti	Meyers (1957)	1
Hawaii	Kohlmeyer (1969 a)	26
Hungary	Kohlmeyer (1967)	1
India	Kohlmeyer (1959) Kohlmeyer, Schmidt and Nair (1967) Jones (1968) S. Raghu Kumar (1971) (unpublished)	26
Ivory Coast	Jones *et al.* (1972)	17
Italy	Jones *et al.* (1972) Kohlmeyer (1959)	18
Japan	Tubaki (1966, 1968, 1969)	25
Iceland	Cavaliere (1968)	25
Liberia	Kohlmeyer (1968 a, d)	20
Libya	Kohlmeyer (1963 d)	1
Malaysia	Jones *et al.* (1972)	5
Mexico	Kohlmeyer (1968 a 1971 b)	21
Mozambique	Kohlmeyer (1968 a)	1
New Zealand	Jones *et al.* (1972)	9
Norway	Jones *et al.* (1972)	11
Pago Pago	Kohlmeyer (1968 a)	2
Panama Canal Zone	Meyers (1957) Ritchie (unpublished)	2
Philippines	Kohlmeyer (1968 a)	1
Portugal	Jones *et al.* (1972)	7
Puerto Rico	Kohlmeyer (1968 a)	2
Russia	Kohlmeyer (1967)	1
Singapore	Jones (1968 b)	3
South Africa	Kohlmeyer and Kohlmeyer (1971 b) Jones *et al.* (1972)	9
Spain	Kohlmeyer (1963 b)	24
Sweden	Henningson (unpublished)	34
Tahiti	Meyers (1957)	1
UK	Jones (1962, 1963 a, b, 1968 a, 1971 a) Jones *et al.* (1972) Byrne and Jones (1974) Wilson (1951, 1954, 1956)	55
USA	Anastasiou (1963) Johnson (1956) Meyers (1957, 1968) Kohlmeyer (1960, 1961, 1963 c, 1968 a, 1971 c) Johnson and Sparrow (1961) Shearer (1972) Jones *et al.* (1972)	95

Country	Author	Number of fungi recorded
Venezuela	Kohlmeyer and Kohlmeyer (1971 b)	3
Virgin Islands	Kohlmeyer (1968 a)	1
West Indies	Meyers (1957)	2
Yugoslavia	Kohlmeyer (1962, 1963 b)	6

Jones (1963 b, 1968 a). Johnson (1967) maintains that marine fungi do not show a succession pattern, but that succession is an expression of different fruiting times, rather than replacement of one species by another. Jones (1963 b) has shown that temperature does affect the colonization rate of the Ascomycetes, *Ceriosporopsis halima, Lulworthia purpurea, L. floridana* and *L. rufa* (Wilson) Johnson. Perithecia do not develop on six week test blocks until the seawater temperature is about 14°C. Meyers and Reynolds (1960) have shown that *Lulworthia* species attack test blocks at temperatures of 5°C and less, but require a long period for fruiting, for example, 100-200 days.

Jones (1968 a) suggests that certain fungi show a preference for beech wood, e.g. *Halosphaeria appendiculata, Nautosphaeria cristaminuta* and *Halosphaeria hamata* (Höhnk) Kohlm., while other fungi prefer Scots pine,*Humicola alopallonella, Cirrenalia macrocephala* and *Ceriosporopsis circumvestita* (Kohlm.) Kohlm. Johnson *et al.* (1959) found that *Ceriosporopsis* spp. and *Lulworthia* sp. colonized certain timbers (balsa, white pine and yellow poplar) while others were sparsely colonized or not at all (e.g. mahogany, black cherry, narra and prima vera).

The studies of Gold (1959), Hughes (1960), Johnson (1967), Schaumann (1968) and Shearer (1972) have been concerned with the colonization of wood in estuaries. Gold using basswood and sycamore panels as bait, established six sites of various salinities in the Newport river estuary, North Carolina. Three distinct groups of fungi were recognized as a result of this study, those fungi being found only on wood in full seawater, i.e. *Ceriosporopsis halima, Lulworthia* sp., *Mycosphaerella* sp., *Pleospora* sp. and *Sphaerulina orae-maris* Linder; those only found on wood in fresh-water, *Leptosphaeria albopunctata* (West.) Sacc., *Metasphaeria australiensis* Cribb et Cribb, *Macrophoma* sp., *Phoma* sp., *Stagonospora* sp., and *Sphaerella* sp.; and those found on wood over the whole salinity range from freshwater to seawater, *Ceriosporopsis cambrensis* Wilson, *Leptosphaeria salinas L. discors* (Sacc. et Ell.) Sacc. et Ell., *Lignincola laevis* Höhnk, *Piricauda pelagica, Torpedospora radiata* Meyers and *Trichocladium* sp.

The distribution of *Ceriosporopsis cambrensis* is interesting since it exhibited the 'Phoma' pattern reported by Ritchie (1957, 1959). This species was recorded from seawater only when the water temperature was 25-30°C. As the temperature decreased, so the salinity at which the fungus was recorded also decreased; for instance at 70°C it did not occur at salinities above 15°/₀₀. *Torpedospora radiata* showed a similar, if not more marked, response. At 5°C and below, this species was only recorded from fresh-water.

Gold limited his study to recording the occurrence of reproductive structures on the surface of the wood immediately removed from water. Hughes (1960); in a study of the Neuse-Newport estuary, North Carolina, using seven testing stations, employed an incubation technique (Johnson *et al.,* 1959) for wood blocks, and therefore recorded a

TABLE 1.4 The colonization by fungi of beech (B) and Scots pine (SP) test blocks submerged at No. 2 site, Newton Ferrers. (after Byrne and Jones, 1974).

	8		16		24		32		40		48		56		Total	
	B	SP	B	SP	B	SP	B	SP	B	SP	B	SP	B	SP	B	SP
Fungi Imperfecti																
Alternaria maritima	—	—	*	—	—	—	—	—	—	—	—	—	—	—	1	0
Cirrenalia macrocephala	—	—	—	—	—	*	—	*	—	*	—	*	—	*	0	5
Culcitalna achraspora	—	—	—	—	—	—	—	—	—	*	—	—	—	—	0	1
Dendryphiella salina	—	—	*	—	—	—	—	—	—	—	—	—	*	—	2	0
Dictyosporium pelagicum	—	—	—	—	—	—	—	—	—	*	—	—	—	*	0	2
Humicola alopallonella	—	—	—	—	—	—	—	—	—	—	—	*	—	*	0	2
Monodictys pelagica	*	—	—	—	—	—	—	—	—	—	—	—	—	—	1	0
Zalerion maritimum	—	*	*	*	—	*	—	*	—	—	—	*	—	*	1	6
Ascomycetes																
Ceriosporopsis halima	—	—	—	—	*	—	*	*	—	*	—	*	—	*	2	4
Corollospora maritima	*	—	—	—	—	—	—	—	—	—	—	—	—	—	1	0
Halosphaeria appendiculata	*	—	*	—	*	—	*	—	*	*	*	—	*	—	7	1
H. circumvestita	—	—	—	—	—	—	—	—	—	—	—	*	—	—	0	1
Lignincola laevis	—	—	*	—	—	—	*	—	—	—	—	—	—	—	2	0
Lulworthia sp.	*	*	*	*	*	*	*	*	*	*	*	*	*	*	7	7
Marinospora calyptrata	—	—	—	—	—	—	—	—	—	—	*	—	—	—	1	0
Remispora hamata	—	—	*	—	*	—	—	—	*	—	*	*	—	—	4	1
R. maritima	*	—	*	—	*	—	—	—	—	—	—	—	*	—	4	0
Basidiomycetes																
Digitatispora marina	—	—	—	—	—	—	*	—	—	—	—	—	*	—	2	0
Total	5	2	8	2	5	3	5	4	3	6	4	7	5	6	35	30

TABLE 1.5   Fungi on beech (B) and Scots pine (SP) test blocks submerged in the sea at Port Erin.   (after Byrne and Jones, 1974).

Test started 11 October 1968; test completed 12 September 1969.

	6		12		18		24		30		36		42		48		Total	
	B	SP	B	SP	B	SP	B	SP	B	SP	B	SP	B	SP	B	SP	B	SP
Fungi Imperfecti																		
Asteromyces cruciatus	—	—	—	—	—	—	*	—	*	—	—	—	—	—	—	—	2	0
Cirrenalia macrocephala	—	—	—	—	—	—	—	—	—	*	—	—	—	*	—	—	0	2
Dendryphiella saline	*	—	—	*	—	—	*	—	*	—	*	—	*	—	—	—	5	1
Dictyosporium pelagicum	—	—	—	—	—	—	*	*	*	—	—	—	—	—	—	—	2	1
Humicola alopallonella	—	—	—	*	*	—	—	*	—	—	—	—	—	—	—	—	1	2
Monodictys pelagica	*	—	*	—	*	—	*	—	*	—	*	*	*	—	—	—	7	1
Sporidesmium salinum	—	—	—	—	*	—	—	—	—	—	*	—	—	—	—	—	2	0
Zalerion maritimum	—	*	*	*	*	*	*	*	*	*	*	*	—	*	—	*	5	8
Ascomycetes																		
Ceriosporopsis halima	—	—	—	—	—	—	*	—	—	—	—	—	—	—	*	—	2	0
Corollospora comata	—	—	—	—	—	—	—	—	*	—	*	—	—	—	—	—	2	0
C. maritima	—	—	*	—	*	—	*	—	*	—	*	—	*	—	*	—	7	0
Halosphaeria appendiculata	—	—	—	—	—	—	—	—	—	—	—	—	—	—	*	—	1	0
Lulworthia sp.	—	—	*	—	*	—	*	*	*	*	*	*	*	*	*	—	7	4
Nautosphaeria cristaminuta	—	—	—	—	—	—	—	—	—	—	—	—	*	—	—	—	1	0
Remispora maritima	—	—	—	—	—	—	—	—	—	—	—	—	*	—	*	—	2	0
Basidiomycetes																		
Digitatispora marina	—	—	—	—	—	—	—	—	—	—	—	—	—	—	*	—	1	0
Total	2	1	4	3	6	1	8	4	8	3	7	3	6	3	6	1	47	19

TABLE 1.6 Number of times fungus present at each test site and percentage frequency of occurrence (after Byrne and Jones, 1974).

	Port Erin in the sea 88		Port Erin storage tanks 88		Langstone in the sea 77		Langstone storage tanks 77		Newton Ferrers No. 2 site 77		Newton Ferrers No. 1 site 44		Newton Ferrers Kitley site 88		4949		Total 98	%
	B	SP	B	SP	B	SP	B	SP	B	SP	B	SP	B	SP	B	SP		
Fungi Imperfecti																		
Alternaria maritima	—	—	—	1	—	—	—	—	1	—	1	—	—	—	3	—	3	3
Asteromyces cruciatus	2	—	—	—	—	—	—	—	—	—	—	—	—	—	2	—	2	2
Cirrenalia macrocephala	—	2	—	—	—	2	1	1	—	5	—	2	5	—	1	17	18	19
Culcitalna achraspora	—	—	—	—	—	1	1	1	1	—	1	—	—	—	1	4	5	5
Dendryphiella salina	5	1	3	—	—	—	—	—	2	—	—	—	1	—	11	1	12	12
Dictyosporium pelagicum	2	1	2	1	—	4	3	4	—	2	—	—	—	1	4	5	9	9
Humicola alopallonella	1	2	1	—	—	—	6	4	—	2	—	—	—	—	5	12	17	18
Monodictys pelagica	7	1	7	3	—	—	—	—	1	—	1	—	1	—	23	9	32	33
Sporidesmium salinum	2	—	—	—	—	—	—	—	—	—	—	—	—	—	2	—	2	2
Zalerion maritimum	5	8	8	8	—	5	6	6	1	6	—	3	—	8	20	44	64	65

Basidiomycetes

Species	Counts
Digitatispora marina	— 2 · 1 — · 2 — · 2 — · 2 — · 1 1 · 6 — · 6 · 6
Nia vibrissa	2 — · 1 1 · 3 — · 3 · 3

Ascomycetes

Species	Counts
Ceriosporopsis halima	6 3 · 2 — · 4 3 · 2 4 · 2 4 · 2 1 · 4 4 · 20 15 · 35 · 36
Corollospora comata	– 1 · 2 — · 2 — · 2 · 2
C. maritima	6 2 · 7 — · 1 1 · 1 — · 1 — · 1 — · 17 3 · 20 · 21
C. trifurcata	3 — · 1 1 · 3 — · 3 · 3
Haligena unicaudata	1 — · 1 — · 1 — · 1 — · 1 · 1
Halosphaeria appendiculata	3 — · 7 — · 4 — · 8 — · 8 — · 23 — · 23 · 24
H. circumvestita	1 — · 1 — · 1 — · 1 1 · 2 · 2
H. tubulifera	2 — · 2 — · 2 — · 2 · 2
Lignincola laevis	8 7 · 7 6 · 4 3 · 8 7 · 2 — · 2 — · 2 · 2
Lulworthia sp.	8 7 · 7 4 · 7 7 · 1 — · 3 — · 41 34 · 75 · 76
Marinospora calyptrata	5 — · – 1 · 1 — · 5 · 5
Microthelia maritima	– 1 · 1 · 1
Nautosphaeria cristaminuta	3 — · 1 — · 4 — · 4 · 4
Nais inornata	1 — · 1 — · 1 · 1
Remispora hamata	3 — · 1 — · 4 1 · 10 1 · 11 · 11
R. maritima	2 — · 2 — · 4 — · 5 — · 15 — · 15 · 16

TABLE 1.7 The percentage occurrence of some British lignicolous marine fungi

Fungi present	1958-60 *		1960-65†		1969-71‡	
	Times present 60	%	Times present 266	%	Times present 98	%
Common Fungi Imperfecti						
Zalerion maritimum	44	73	198	74	66	65
Humicola alopallonella	–	–	48	18	17	18
Monodictys pelagica	–	–	38	14	32	33
Ascomycetes						
Lulworthia purpurea	32	53	165	62	75	76
L. rufa	–	–	55	21	–	–
L. floridana	–	–	81	31	–	–
Ceriosporopsis halima	26	43	117	44	35	36
Occasional Fungi Imperfecti						
Dictyosporium pelagicum	–	–	15	6	9	9
Cirrenalia macrocephala	2	3	27	10	18	19
Dendryphiella salina	9	15	13	5	12	12
Sporidesmium salinum	–	–	21	8	2	2

Ascomycetes

Halosphaeria hamata	8	14	16	6	11	11
Lulworthia fucicola	—	—	10	4	—	—
Halonectria milfordensis	—	—	24	9	—	—
Ceriosporopsis cambrensis	28	47	25	9	—	—
Halosphaeria appendiculata	9	15	28	11	24	25
Ceriosporopsis circumvestita	—	—	30	11	2	2

Infrequent
Fungi Imperfecti

Trichocladium achrospora (Meyers et Moore) Dixon	—	—	2	0.8	5	5
Asteromyces cruciatus	—	—	1	0.4	2	2
Alternaria maritima Linder	7	12	1	0.4	3	3
Stemphylium maritimum Johnson	8	13	1	0.4	—	—

Ascomycetes

Ceriosporopsis calyptrata	—	—	1	0.4	5	5
Halosphaeria torquata	—	—	2	0.8	—	—
Halosphaeria maritima	—	—	—	—	15	16
Halosphaeria mediosetigera	—	—	1	0.4	—	—
Nautosphaeria cristaminuta	—	—	6	2.3	4	4
Corollospora maritima	9	15	5	1.9	20	21

* Data from Jones (1962, 1963 a, b)
† Data from Jones (1968 a)
‡ Data from Byrne and Jones (1974)

greater number of fungi. The incubation technique allows for the production of fruiting structures from mycelium present, but not sporulating on the wood, at the time of removal from the water. The efficacy of this method is well documented (Jones, 1962, 1963 b, 1968 b; Tubaki, 1966).

Hughes recorded a total of 72 species, but limited his critical ecological studies to seven of these. In contrast to the findings of Gold, Hughes found only two species which occurred over the whole salinity range, i.e. *Cirrenalia macrocephala* and *Phoma* sp. *Lignincola laevis* was the only species to exhibit the *'Phoma'* pattern, the distribution of this species with regard to salinity being a function of the temperature extant at the collection time.

Hughes made many hydrographical measurements throughout the period of the study, but found that variations in dissolved oxygen content, pH and nitrate and phosphate concentrations of the water, had no apparent effect on the distribution of species within the estuary. Certain terrestrial species were found on wood in the fresh to brackish water portions of the estuary, i.e.*Nectria penicilloides, Pseudoeurotium indicum, Leptosphaeria fuscella, Taeniolella rudis* and *Endoxyla cirrhosa*.

Schaumann (1968) recorded the fungi on fixed wooden structures such as pilings, piers and wharves at 13 stations of various salinities in the Weser estuary, West Germany. As a result, 40 species were noted and, in a manner similar to that of Gold, were divided into groups, according to the range of salinities at which they were recorded. Two species *Cirrenalia macrocephala* and *Monodictys pelagica* were found to be holeuryhaline, that is, to be tolerant of the whole salinity range of 0-30$^{\circ}/_{oo}$. Certain species were found to be euryhaline (tolerating 3.5-30$^{\circ}/_{oo}$) i.e. *Dictyosporium pelagicum,* (Linder) Hughes, *Halosphaeria appendiculata, H. mediosetigera* Cribb et Cribb, *Leptosphaeria orae-maris* Linder, *Lignincola laevis, Marinospora calyptrata, Remispora hamata, R. maritima,* and two species stenohaline (tolerating only 20-30$^{\circ}/_{oo}$) i.e. *Zalerion maritimum* and *Corollospora maritima* Werden. This worker also regarded three species as brackish water inhabitants (tolerating only 5-20$^{\circ}/_{oo}$) i.e. *Humicola alopallonella, Leptosphaeria discors* and *Remispora pilleata* Kohlm

Johnson (1967) noted that the lignicolous fungi he collected in the Neuse-Newport estuary were predominantly of terrestrial origin (73%). However, the majority of these were from water of less than 18$^{\circ}/_{oo}$ salinity (81%) while only 12% were recovered from whole estuary, i.e. 0-34$^{\circ}/_{oo}$. Shearer (1972) has shown that the majority (60%) of the fungi she collected on test panels in the Chesapeake Bay area were only recorded once. The number of Ascomycetes (ratio with Fungi Imperfecti) increased with increasing salinity, and the total number of fungi collected decreased with increase in salinity. Shearer concluded that salinity was the most important single factor affecting the distribution of fungi in the Patuxent river.

Few studies have been concerned with the distribution of fungi in deep waters. Kohlmeyer (1968 e) reports on an *Ophiobolus* type species on a test panel recovered from 1615 m. after three years' submergence. A further fungus was briefly described (but not named) from driftwood recovered from 3710 m depth in the Gulf of Panama (Kohlmeyer, 1969 d). Jones and Le Campion Alsumard (1970 a, b) recorded four fungi growing on polyurethane panels submerged at various depths (see Section 1.4.1 and Table 1.9).

Although considerable information is now available for the occurrence of lignicolous marine fungi, the exact climatic distribution of certain fungi is doubtful. The following are cosmopolitan in their distribution: *Cirrenalia macrocephala, Ceriosporopsis halima, Corollospora maritima, Lulworthia* spp., *Monodictys pelagica, Torpedospora radiata* and *Zalerion maritimum.* Many workers regard *Halosphaeria quadricornuta* Cribb et Cribb (Jones 1968 a, Kohlmeyer 1968 a, Hughes and Chamut 1971) and *Varicosporina ramulosa* Meyers et Kohlm. (Kohlmeyer and Kohlmeyer 1971 b) as warm water species. Meyers (1968) regards *C. macrocephala* as subtropical, although this species is known from temperate climates, whilst he considers *Humicola alopallonella* to be a cold water species. However, Jones (1968 b) has collected the latter from the tropics.

1.3 Algicolous Fungi

The first accounts of marine algicolous fungi were made by Rostrup (1889), Church (1893), Jones (1898), Reed (1902), Rosenvinge (1906), Cotton (1908) and Lind (1913). Sutherland (1915 a, b, c; 1916 a, b) in a series of papers, reported on the fungi he found growing on algae in the Solent and Scotland. Unfortunately, he does not appear to have deposited any type material, so that few of his fungi can be identified with certainty. Many of the fungi he collected may have been of terrestrial origin.

1.3.1 Ascomycetes

The first detailed accounts of marine algicolous fungi were made by Dr. Irene M. Wilson and her students (Wilson and Knoyle, 1961; Webber, 1967). These were followed by the more extensive studies of Kohlmeyer (1968 b; 1971 b; 1972 a, c; 1973 a), and Kohlmeyer and Kohlmeyer (1972 a, b). A comparison of the literature on lignicolous and algicolous marine fungi indicates that the latter have only recently attracted the attention of mycologists. A taxonomical revision of these fungi and a re-description of many taxa is urgently required, while new species await description (Figs. 1.17–1.18).

Table 1.8 lists some of the marine fungi known to grow parasitically or saprophytically on algae. Forty eight Ascomycetes are listed but only seven of these are known to grow on substrates other than algae. Unlike the marine lignicolous Ascomycetes, few appear to have appendaged ascospores. Many of the fungi listed in Table 1.8 can be placed in well known families, e.g. Halosphaeriaceae *(Chadefaudia, Corollospora)*, Hypocreaceae *(Orcadia)*, Polystigmataceae *(Phycomelaina)*, Mycosphaerellaceae *(Didymella, Mycosphaerella)*, Pleosporaceae *(Pleospora, Leptosphaeria, Didymosphaeria* and *Thalassoascus)*, while others cannot satisfactorily be assigned to any family, e.g. *Trailia*, which has operculate asci (Kohlmeyer, 1972 a), and *Turgidosculum* (Kohlmeyer and Kohlmeyer, 1972 b).

TABLE 1.8   Algicolous marine fungi and their hosts.

Fungi	Algal host	Author
Alternaria maritima Suth.	*Laminaria* sp. *L. saccharina* (L.) Lamour. *Fucus spiralis*	Sutherland (1916 a) UK
Chadefaudia balliae Kohlm.	*Ballia callitricha* (Agardh) Kützing	Kohlmeyer (1973 a) Australia
Ch. corallinarum (Crouan et Crouan) Müller et von Arx	*Corallina mediterranea* Aresch. *C. officinalis* L. *Epilithon membranaceum* (Esp.) Heydr.	Kohlmeyer (1963 b, 1967, 1972 a) Kohlmeyer and Kohlmeyer (1971 a)

TABLE 1.8 (contd)

Fungi	Algal host	Author
	Halimeda opuntia (L.) Lamour. *H. tuna* (Ellis et Solander) Lamour. *Jania rubens* (L.) Lamour. *J. longifurca* Zanard. *J. corniculata* Lamour. *Lithophyllum tortuosum* (Esper.) Foslie *Pseudolithophyllum* sp. *Udotea petiolata* (Trev.) Boergesen *Dermatolithon pustulutum* (Lamour.) Foslie *Sargassum* sp.	Algeria, France, USA, Yugoslavia, Greenland, Bahamas
Ch. gymnogongri (Feldmann) Müller et von Arx	*Gigartina intermedia* Suringar *Gymnogongrus norvegicas* (Gunn.) J. Ag. *Galaxaura* sp. *Laurencia concinna* Mont. *L. succisa* Cribb *L. heteroclada* Harv. *L. flexilis* Setch. *L. tenera* Tseng. *L. pymaea* Bosse *Ptilonia australasica* Harv.	Kohlmeyer (1972 a) Kohlmeyer and Kohlmeyer (1971 a) Cribb and Herbert 1954 (1960 a) Australia, Algeria
Ch. marina Feldmann	*Rhodymenia palmata* Grev.	Feldmann (1957) Kohlmeyer (1962, 1972 a) Kohlmeyer and Kohlmeyer (1971 a) France
Ch. polyporolithi (Bonar) Müller et von Arx	*Polyporolithon* sp.	Kohlmeyer (1972 a) Kohlmeyer and Kohlmeyer (1971 a)
Corollospora maritima Werden	*Fucus vesiculosus* L. *Macrocystis* spp. *Sargassum* sp. *Ceramium* sp.	Meyers and Scott (1967) Schmidt (1967) Haythorn (unpublished) Tubaki (1969) Germany, USA UK, Japan
C. intermedia Schmidt	*Fucus vesiculosus*	Schmidt (1969) Schaumann (1972) Germany

TABLE 1.8 (contd)

Fungi	Algal host	Author
C. pulchella Kohlm., Schmidt et Nair	Fucus vesiculosus Laminaria sp.	Kohlmeyer, Schmidt, and Nair (1967) Haythorn (unpublished) India, Germany, UK
Cladosporium algarum Cooke et Massee	Laminaria flexicaulis Laminaria sp. Pelvetia sp.	Sutherland (1916 a) UK
Crinigera maritima Schmidt	Fucus vesiculosus	Schmidt (1969) Germany
*Dendryphiella arenaria Nicot	Sargassum sp.	Nicot (1958) USA, France
*D. salina (Suth.) Pugh et Nicot	Chondrus crispus (L.) Stakh. Ceramium rubrum Agardh. Ectocarpus sp. Fucus spiralis L. F. serratus L. Furcellaria fastigata Lamour. Laminaria saccharina Laminaria sp. Ulva sp.	Jones (unpublished) Sutherland (1916 a) Haythorn (unpublished) Kohlmeyer (1971 c) UK, USA
Didymella fucicola (Suth.) Kohlm.	Fucus vesiculosus Fucus sp.	Sutherland (1915 b) Kohlmeyer (1968 b, 1971 c) UK, USA
D. magnei Feldmann	Rhodymenia palmata	Feldmann (1958) France
Didymosphaeria danica (Berlese) Wilson et Knoyle	Chondrus crispus Lyngb.	Wilson and Knoyle (1961) Kohlmeyer (1971 c) Denmark, France, UK, USA
D. pelvetiana Suth.	Pelvetia canaliculata Dcne. et Thur.	Sutherland (1915 b) UK
*Diplodina laminariana Suth.	Laminaria sp.	Sutherland (1916 a) UK
*Epicoccum mariti- mum Suth.	Laminaria sp.	Sutherland (1916 a) UK
Guignardia alaskana Reed	Prasiola sp.	Reed (1902) USA
G. gloiopeltidis Miyabe et Tokida	Gloiopeltis furcata (Post. et Rupr.) J. Ag.	Miyabe and Tokida (1948) Japan

TABLE 1.8 (contd)

Fungi	Algal host	Author
G. prasiolae (Winter) Lemmermann	*Prasiola* sp.	Lemmermann (1901) Germany
G. ulvae Reed	*Ulva* sp.	Reed (1902) USA
Haloguignardia decidua Cribb et Cribb	*Sargassum daemellii* Grunow	Cribb and Cribb (1956, 1960 b) Kohlmeyer (1971 b) Australia
H. irritans (Setchell et Estee) Cribb et Cribb	*Cystoseira osmundacea* (Menzies) Ag. *Halidrys dioica* Gardner	Cribb and Cribb (1956) Australia
H. longispora Cribb et Cribb	*Sargassum* sp.	Cribb and Cribb (1956) Australia
H. oceanica (Ferdinandsen et Winge) Kohlm.	*Sargassum chamissoni* Kützing *S. hystrix* var. *fluitans* Börg. *Sargassum* sp.	Kohlmeyer (1971 b, 1972 c) Sargasso Sea, USA
H. tumefaciens (Cribb et Herbert) Cribb et Cribb	*Sargassum* sp. *S. fallax* Sond. *S. globulariaefolium* Agardh. *S. sinclairii* Hook et Harv. *S. decipiens* (Br. er Turn.) J. Ag. *S. daemelii*	Kohlmeyer (1971 b) Cribb and Cribb (1956, 1960 b) Australia
Lindra thalassiae Orpurt, Meyers, Boral et Simms	*Sargassum* sp.	Tubaki (1969) Sargasso Sea, Japan
Lulworthia fucicola Suth.	*Fucus* sp. *F. vesiculosus*	Sutherland (1916 b) UK
L. kniepii Kohlm.	*Pseudolithophyllum expansum* (Phil.) Lemoine *Lithophyllum tortuosum* (Esper.) Foslie *Porolithon onkodes* (Heydr.) Foslie	Kohlmeyer (1967, 1969 a) Canary Islands, France, Hawaii, Italy
*Macrosporium laminarianum Suth.	*Laminaria* sp.	Sutherland (1916 a) UK
*M. pelvetiae Suth.	*Pelvetia canaliculata*	Sutherland (1915 a) UK
Maireomyces peyssoneliae Feldmann	*Peyssonelia* sp.	Feldmann (1940 a) Algeria

TABLE 1.8 (contd)

Fungi	Algal host	Author
Melanopsamma cystophorae (Cribb et Herbert) Meyers	Cystophora retroflexa (Labill.) J. Ag.	Meyers (1957) Australia, USA
*Monodictys austrina Tubaki	Isolated from algae	Tubaki and Asano (1965)
*Monosporium maritimum Suth.	Laminaria sp.	Sutherland (1916 a) UK
Mycaureola dilseae Maire et Chemin	Dilsea edulis Stackh.	Maire and Chemin (1922) France
Mycosphaerella ascophylli Cotton	Ascophyllum nodosum (L.) Le Jol. A. mackaii (Turn.) Cotton Pelvetia canaliculata	Webber (1967) Kohlmeyer and Kohlmeyer (1972 a) Russia, UK, USA
Nectriella laminariae Eriksson	Laminaria sp.	Eriksson (1964) Norway
Ophiobolus laminariae Suth.	Laminaria sp.	Sutherland (1915 c) UK
Orcadia ascophylli Suth.	Fucus sp. F. vesiculosus Ascophyllum nodosum Pelvetia canaliculata	Sutherland (1915 c) Kohlmeyer (1968 b) UK
Pharcidia pelvetiae Suth.	Pelvetia canaliculata	Sutherland (1915 a) UK
Phycomelaina laminariae (Rostrup) Kohlm.	Laminaria longicruris de la Pyl. L. saccharina (L.) Lamour. L. digitata (L.) Edmons. Alaria esculenta (L.) Grev. Laminaria sp.	Kohlmeyer (1968 b, 1971 c) France, Norway UK, USA Iceland, Greenland
*Phoma laminariae Cooke et Massee	Laminaria sp.	Sutherland (1916 a) UK
Pleospora laminariana Suth.	Laminaria sp.	Sutherland (1916 b) UK
P. pelvetiae Suth.	Pelvetia canaliculata	Sutherland (1915 a) UK

23

TABLE 1.8 (contd)

Fungi	Algal host	Author
Plowrightia pelvetiae Fraguso	*Pelvetia* sp.	Fraguso (1919) Spain
Rosellinia laminariana Suth.	*Laminaria* sp.	Sutherland (1916 b) UK
*Septoria ascophylli Melnik et Petrov	*Ascophyllum nodosum*	Melnik and Petrov (1966)
*S. dictyotae Oudemans	*Dictyota* sp.	Oudemans (1894)
*Sphaceloma cecidii Kohlm.	*Sargassum natans* (L.) J. Meyen *S. fluitans* *S. hystrix* var *fluitans* *S. chamissoni* *Halidrys dioica* *Cystoseira osmundaceae*	Kohlmeyer (1972 c) USA
Sphaerulina codicola Dawson	*Codium* sp.	Dawson (1949) Mexico USA
*Sporotrichum maritimum Suth.	*Laminaria* sp.	Sutherland (1916 a) UK
*Stemphylium codii Zeller	*Codium mucornatum*	Zeller (1918)
Stigmatea pelvetiae Suth.	*Pelvetia canaliculata*	Sutherland (1915 a) UK
Thalassoascus tregoubovii Ollivier	*Cystoseira fimbriata* (Desf.) Bory. *C. abiermarina* (Turner) C. Ag. *C. discors* C. Ag. *Aglazonia chilosa* Falkenb. *A. parvula* (Grev.) Zanard. *Dilophus fasciola* (Roth) Howe *Zanardina collaris* Crouan.	Kohlmeyer (1963 b, 1967) Algeria France
Trailia ascophylli Suth.	*Ascophyllum nodosum* *Fucus* sp.	Kohlmeyer (1968 b) UK, USA
Turgidosculum ulvae (Reed) J & E Kohlm.	*Ulva vexata* Setch. et Gard.	Kohlmeyer and Kohlmeyer (1972 b) USA
Varicosporina ramulosa Meyers et Kohlm.	*Hypnea charoides*	Kohlmeyer (1969 a) Tubaki (1969) Japan

TABLE 1.8 (contd)

Fungi	Algal host	Author
Zignoella calospora Patouillard	Castagnea chordariaeformis	Patouillard (1897) Spain
Z. cubensis Hariot et Patouillard	Stypocaulon scoparium Kütz.	Hariot and Patouillard (1904) Cuba
Z. enormis Patouillard et Hariot	Stypocaulon scoparium	Patouillard and Hariot (1903) Spain
Z. valoniopsidis Cribb et Cribb	Valoniopsis pachynema (Mart.) Boerg.	Cribb and Cribb (1960 a) Australia

The following algae frequently support fungi, e.g. Fucoids (*Fucus* spp.), Kelps *(Laminaria* spp.*)*, *Sargassum* spp., *Pelvetia canaliculata*, *Laurencia* spp. and *Rhodymenia palmata*. However, little quantitative work has been undertaken to examine the role of fungi in the decomposition of cast seaweed. Little is known of the distribution and occurrence of marine fungal pathogens. The most detailed studies to date are those of Wilson and Knoyle (1961) and Webber (1967). Kohlmeyer (1971 b, 1973 a) and Kohlmeyer and Kohlmeyer (1972 a, b) have considered the different types of fungal/algal associations, but no experimental work has been attempted.

1.3.2 Fungi Imperfecti

Sixteen imperfect fungi have been recorded on seaweeds, most of them as saprophytes, e.g. *Dendryphiella arenaria*, *D. salina*, *Alternaria maritima* and *Monodictys austrina* Tubaki et Asano. Many of the species (Fungi Imperfecti) listed in Table 1.8 were described by Sutherland (1916a) and have not been collected since or are doubtful marine species. Algicolous hyphomycetes have received little attention in recent years. Haythorn (unpublished) finds that species most frequently isolated from seaweeds are *Dendryphiella salina*, *Asteromyces cruciatus* and *Alternaria maritima*. A new species found growing on *Laminaria* and *Fucus* fronds is illustrated in Figs. 1-17—1.18.

1.3.3 Spathulosporales

Cavaliere and Johnson (1965) described an interesting Pyrenomycete *(Spathulospora phycophila)* parasitizing the red alga *Ballia callitricha* (C. Agar.) Kützing from Australia. Kohlmeyer (1969 e) re-examined this material and noted that the perithecia were covered by dark, septate, thick-walled, curved hairs which at their tips were forked and bearing one or two phialides. In 1973, Kohlmeyer demonstrated a clear relationship between *Spathulospora* and the Laboulbeniales. A new family and order has been created for *S. phycophila* and four new species described: *S. adelpha* Kohlm., *S. antarctica* Kohlm., *S. calva* Kohlm. and *S. lanata* Kohlm.

These fungi are dark with crustose thalli that cover the host and peg-like cells penetrate the algal cells. Trichogynes and antheridia are produced on the thalli often surrounded by sterile, brown, thick-walled hairs. The ascocarps are formed singly or in pairs on each thallus, remain superficial, and the ascocarp wall is thick and two layered. Paraphyses are not produced but periphyses line the neck canal. The asci are thin-walled, 8-spored, clavate to fusiform and deliquesce early in development.

Hyaline, one-celled ascospores with apical appendages are produced. The five species described by Kohlmeyer (1973) are all parasitic, elongate cells penetrating the host cell and frequently completely filling the cell with mycelium.

Kohlmeyer examined over 100 *B. callitricha* plants and a third of these were found to be infected by *Sapathulospora* species. *S. adelpha* was the most frequent (17) while *S. phycophila* was the least frequent (three). Some of these species appeared to be restricted in their distribution. *S. antartica* was found on *Ballia* from South America and the Falkland Islands while *S. adelpha*, *S. calva*, *S. lanata* and *S. phycophila* are found only on the plants from the Southwest Pacific.

1.4   Other Substrates

1.4.1   Polyurethane

Fig. 1.25. Polyurethane plates on removal from the sea showing dense fouling by polychaete worms, sea anemones and algae. **Fig. 1.26.** Polyurethane panel mounted in a creosoted wooden frame, with the fouling organisms removed and showing areas attacked by marine fungi (arrowed).

Jones and Le Campion-Alsumard (1970 a, b) have reported four fungi growing on polyurethane covered metal panels submerged in the sea at Nice, France (Figs. 1.25–1.31). They are the Ascomycetes *Corollospora maritima, Haligena unicaudata, Lulworthia purpurea* and the imperfect fungus *Zalerion maritimum*. The polyurethane layer was 3 mm deep and fungal mycelium was found to a depth of 1 mm within the polyurethane. The perithecia, at first located within the polyurethane, rapidly increased in volume causing the surface layers to split and tear (Figs. 1.28–1.29).

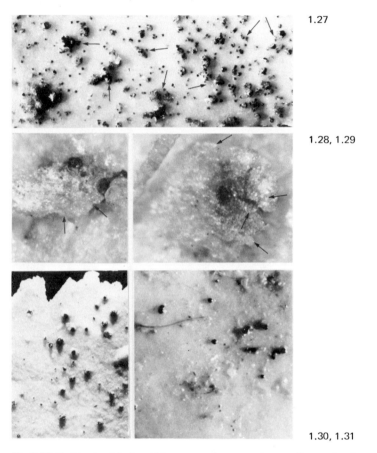

1.27

1.28, 1.29

1.30, 1.31

Fig. 1.27. Perithecia of *Lulworthia purpurea* in groups (arrowed) emerging from polyurethane (x4). **Figs. 1.28-1.29.** Perithecia of *Haligena unicaudata* emerging and fragments of polyurethane pushed to one side (arrowed) (x66). **Fig. 1.30.** Perithecia of *H. unicaudata* breaking through the polyurethane (x5). **Fig. 1.31.** Perithecia of *Corollospora maritima* were found only on the surface of the polyurethane (x5).

Table 1.9 presents information on the distribution of these fungi with depth. No fungi were found on panels submerged at 47 and 67 m. However, fungi were present on the wooden frames holding the panels at these depths. Most of the marine fungi collected on wooden panels are known from the superficial layers of the sea (Johnson *et al.,* 1959; Jones, 1971 a). Their absence from the polyurethane panels could be explained on the grounds of exclusion due to heavy animal fouling.

Twenty six panels were exposed and all but one were colonized by fungi. The degree of attack varied from panel to panel as can be seen from Table 1.10.

1.4.2 Animals

Pathogenic fungi of marine animals have been discussed by Alderman (Chapter 9). However, a number of Ascomycetes and Fungi Imperfecti have been reported from Teredinid tubes, Balanid shells, Hydrozoan and Annelid tubes, Molluscan shells and calcareous algae (Table 1.11). Many of these are common on timber and mangrove wood, e.g. *Cirrenalia pygmea* Kohlm., *Halosphaeria salina*, *H. quadricornuta*, *Humicola alopallonella* and *Lulworthia* sp., while *Abyssomyces hydrozoicus* Kohlm. is known only from Hydrozoans.

1.4.3 Decaying Leaves of terrestrial Plants

Studies of fungi growing on leaves in freshwater are extensive (Ingold, Chapter 13) but

TABLE 1.9 Distribution of marine fungi with depth.

Depth (m)	Zalerion maritimum	Corollospora maritima	Lulworthia purpurea	Haligena unicaudata	Bacterium
47					
67					
80	*		*		
86	*		*		
87	*	*	*		
106		*			
126	*	*			
127			*		
130				*	
134			*		
180		*			
187				*	
210			*	*	*
230					
237				*	*
280		*		*	
287				*	*
330			*	*	
337				*	*
380			*	*	*
387					*
430				*2	*
437				*	
487					*
537					*
Total	4	5	8	12	9

TABLE 1.10   Marine fungi present on the polyurethane panels of ladder No. 3 (20 October 1964 to 6 July 1967.) submerged at Nice (after Jones and Le Campion-Alsumard, 1970).

Depth (m)	Upper surface of panel	% cover	Lower surface of panel	% cover
47	mycelium present	—		
67	mycelium present	—		
87	Zalerion maritimum			
	Corollospora maritima	20	L. purpurea	25
	Lulworthia purpurea			
127	L. purpurea	5	mycelium present	—
187	Haligena unicaudata	10	H. unicaudata	30
237	H. unicaudata	70	H. unicaudata	40
			bacteria	60
287	H. unicaudata	25	H. unicaudata	70
	bacteria			
337	H. unicaudata	25	H. unicaudata	10
	bacteria		bacteria	many
387			bacteria	
437	H. unicaudata	5	H. unicaudata	5
487	bacteria	60	bacteria	50
			mycelium present	50
537	bacteria	50	bacteria	90
	mycelium present	50		

little attention has been devoted to their fate in the marine environment. Anastasiou and Churchland (1969) have investigated the colonization of *Prunus laurocerasus* L. and *Arbutus menziesii* Pursh leaves submerged in the sea at Vancouver. Fourteen species occurred on the 750 leaves examined, the most common being *Zalerion maritimum* (on 59% of leaves), *Papulospora halima* Anastasiou (27%) and *Nowakowskiella elegans* (Nowak.) Schroeter (8%). A new phycomycete, *Phytophthora vesicula* Anastasiou et Churchland occurred on 71% of the leaves. Collections were made only over a 4 week period and further observations may have yielded more fungi.

The intertidal Angiosperm *Spartina* supports a very diverse fungal flora (Table 1.12). Sivanesan and Manners (1970) have shown that the fungi of the subterranean parts and rhizosphere of *Spartina townsendii* agg. to be typically 'soil fungi', while Apinis and Chesters (1956) listed a number of marine fungi (12) as well as many terrestrial species. Jones (1963 a) observed generic dissimilarities between the fungi on decaying stems of *Spartina* floating in the sea and those on wood in the sea. *Leptosphaeria* spp., *Pleospora* spp. and *Sphaerulina pedicellata* Johnson are all very common on *Spartina* culms. Meyer *et al.* (1970) suggest that yeasts may also be active in the degradation of *Spartina* as well as a number of Fungi Imperfecti, e.g. *Fusarium* spp., *Phoma* spp. and *Nigrospora* sp. *Spartina* is an ideal plant for studying the change in fungal flora from the aerial inflorescence with *Claviceps purpurea* (Fr.) Tul., to the inflorescence stem and

TABLE 1.11   Marine fungi in calcareous and chitinous substances.

Substrate	Fungus	Author
1 *Mollusc shells*		
Ostrea edulis	*Ostracoblabe implexa*	Alderman and Jones (1971)
shell fragments.	unidentified	Höhnk (1967)
Mytilidae shells and others.	various—unidentified	Cavaliere and Alberte (1970); Cavaliere and Markhart (1972)
2 *Teredinid tubes*	*Halosphaeria quadricornuta* *Halosphaeria salina* *Cirrenalia pygmea* *Humicola alopallonella* *Periconia prolifica*	Kohlmeyer (1969 b)
3 *Shells of Balanids*	*Pharcidia balani*	Kohlmeyer (1969 b)
4 *Calcareous algae* *Lithophyllum* *Pseudolithophyllum*	*Lulworthia kniepii*	Kohlmeyer (1969 b)
5 *Hydrozoan tubes* Stony coral hydrozoan tubes	*Abyssomyces hydrozoicus* Kohlm. Fungal mycelium	Kohlmeyer (1972 b)
6 *Annelid tubes* *Chaetopterus variopedatus*	*Lulworthia* sp.	Kohlmeyer (1972 b)

leaves with *Cladosporium* spp. and *Phoma* spp., to the decaying lower leaves and stems with a number of marine fungi.

Kohlmeyer and Kohlmeyer (1971 a) have reported *Varicosporina ramulosa*, *Halocyphina villosa* Kohlm. et Kohlm. and *Nia vibrissa* from *Spartina alterniflora* Loisel, while Apinis (1963) has noted the occurrence of thermophilous fungi on *Ammophila arenaria* (L.) Link, *Spartina* sp., *Agropyron pungens* (Pers.) Roem. et Schult. and *A. junceiforme* (A. et D. Love) A. et D. Love. Schmidt (1969) has recently described a new hyphomycete from *Phragmites communis* Trin., namely, *Cirrenalia fusca* Schmidt.

Gessner, *et al.* (1972) have shown that the first fungus to colonize *S. alterniflora* is *Sphaerulina pedicellata*, followed by species assignable to the genera *Leptosphaeria*, *Haligena*, *Pleospora* and *Lulworthia*. Other micro-organisms derive nutrients from this fungal biomass, e.g. bacteria, nematodes and acarid mites also graze on the mycelium.

A number of maritime plants (e.g. *Ammophila, Halimione, Juncus, Salicornia, Scirpus, Suaeda, Triglochin* and *Typha*) are colonized by marine fungi, for example *Asteromyces cruciatus, Camarosporium metableticum* Trail, *Dendryphyiella arenaria, D. salina, Alternaria maritima, Cirrenalia fusca, Stemphylium triglochinicola* Sutton et Pirozynski, *Monodictys pelagica* and the Ascomycetes *Phaeosphaeria ammophilae*

TABLE 1.12   Some marine fungi on decaying *Spartina* leaves and stems.

Fungi	Austwick 1950	Lloyd (1954)	Johnson (1956)	Goodman (1959)	Jones (1962 1963, unpublished)	Apinis and Chesters (1956)	Total
Fungi Imperfecti							
Alternaria maritima	*	–	–	*	*	–	3
Asteromyces cruciatus	–	–	–	–	*	–	1
Cladosporium herbarum	*	*	–	*	–	–	3
Dendryphiella salina	–	–	–	–	*	–	1
Dictyosporium toruloides	–	–	–	–	*	–	1
Monodicty putredinis	–	–	–	–	*	–	1
Phoma spp.	*	*	–	*	*	–	4
Stemphylium maritimum Johnson	–	–	–	–	*	–	1
Ascomycetes							
Ceriosporopsis halima	–	–	–	–	–	*	1
Haligena elaterophora	–	–	–	–	–	*	1
H. spartinae	–	–	–	–	*	*	2
Halosphaeria hamata	–	–	–	–	*	*	2
Leptosphaeria albopunctata (West.) Sacc.	–	–	*	–	*	–	2
L. discors (Sacc. et Ellis) Sacc. & Ellis	*	–	*	*	*	*	5
L. halima Johnson	–	–	*	–	–	–	1
L. macrosporidium Jones	–	–	–	–	*	–	1
L. marina Ellis et Everhart	–	–	*	–	–	*	2
L. maritima (Cke. et Plowr.) Sacc.	–	–	*	–	–	–	1
L. orae-maris Linder	–	–	*	–	–	–	1
L. pelagica Jones	–	–	–	–	*	*	2
L. typharum (Desm.) Karsten	*	–	–	*	*	*	4
Lulworthia medusa	*	*	–	*	*	*	5
Lignincola laevis	–	–	–	–	*	*	2
Gnomonia salina Jones	–	–	–	–	*	–	1
Pleospora herbarum (Fr.) Rabenhorst	*	*	–	*	*	*	5
P. pelagica Johnson	–	–	*	–	–	–	1
P. spartinae Ellis et Everhart	–	–	–	–	–	*	1
Sphaerulina pedicellata Johnson	–	–	–	–	*	–	1

This is not a complete list of species found on *Spartina*. Jones (unpublished) has collected some 80 species growing on the culms of *Spartina*.

(Lasch.) J. et E. Kohlm., *Didymosamarospora euryhalina* Johnson et Gold, *Lepto-sphaeria albopunctata, L. discors, L. marina* Ellis et Ev., *L. maritima* (Cooke et Plow-right) Sacc., *Pleospora gaudefroyi* Patouillard, *P. triglochinicola* Webster, *Haligena spartinae* Jones and *Halosphaeria hamata* (Kohlmeyer and Kohlmeyer, 1971 a).

1.4.4 Decaying Leaves of Marine Angiosperms

Meyers *et al.* (1965) have investigated the fungi occurring in the leaves of the marine Angiosperm *Thalassia testudinum* König. The dominant species were: *Labyrinthula* sp., *Lindra thalassiae* Orpurt, Meyers, Boral et Sims, *Hormodendron* sp., *Cephalo-sporium* sp. and *Dendryphiella arenaria.* A further 26 species were observed, many of these occurring only as single isolations.

Meyers (1969) has described a second species of *Lindra* from *Thalassia,* namely, *Lindra marinera* Meyers and suggests it may be active in the degradation of *Thalassia* leaves. Enzymatic studies of *L. marinera* and lignicolous marine Ascomycetes (Meyers and Scott, 1968) suggest that isolates of *Lindra* have less cellulolytic activity than do representatives of the *Lulworthia* complex.

Varicosporina ramulosa has also been isolated from *Thalassia testudinum* as well as the leaves of *Zostera marina* L. (Meyers and Kohlmeyer, 1965). A number of marine fungi have been reported as growing on *Zostera,* e.g. *Corollospora maritima, Phoma* sp. (Kohlmeyer, 1966 b) *Halosphaeria quadricornuta* (Cribb and Cribb, 1956) *Pontoporeia biturbinata* (Hughes and Chamut, 1971) *Lulworthia* spp. and *Ophiobolus maritimus* Suth. (Kohlmeyer and Kohlmeyer, 1971 a).

1.4.5 Pulp mill effluents

Churchland and McClaren (1972) have investigated the effects of whole pulp mill effluents on the growth of *Zalerion maritimum,* while Poole (1971) has studied the role of soil fungi in the decomposition of cellulose in the Medway estuary. Churchland and McClaren showed that caustic effluents alone would not support the growth of *Z. maritimum.* When the caustic effluent was added to a basal medium, the fungus grew, but acidic bleach plant effluent decreased the growth of the organism. They conclude that *Z. maritimum* is not an effective decomposer of caustic effluent and that acidic bleach plant effluent was toxic, even when nutrients were added.

Churchland and McClaren (1973) further investigated the fungi occurring on wood panels at and near to a kraft pulp mill outfall and compared this with an area not directly affected by pulp mill effluent. They found that fungi grew poorly on baits at the mill. *Phialophora fastigiata* (Lagerb. and Melin) Conant was isolated exclusively from the pulp mill station while *Monodictys pelagica* (Johnson) Jones was isolated more frequently from the mill than from control sites. *Zalerion maritimum* was iso-lated less frequently from the mill than from control sites. They show that salinity and pH were lower at the pulp mill than at the control and suggest that this may be res-ponsible for the observed distribution of the fungi.

1.4.6 Arenicolous Fungi

Brown (1958) and Nicot (1958 a, b) have both isolated fungi from sand dunes, and some of these have been reported from other substrates, e.g. *Asteromyces cruciatus* and *Dendryphiella arenaria.* However, Kohlmeyer (1966 b) was the first to examine foam samples collected along shores. Table 1.13 lists some of the fungi he found present in marine foams.

TABLE 1.13   Arenicolous marine fungi.

Fungi	
Ascomycetes	
Corollospora comata	Kohlmeyer (1966 b)
C. lacera	Kohlmeyer (1966 b)
C. maritima	Kohlmeyer (1966 b, 1968 b, 1969)
C. trifurcata	Kohlmeyer (1966 b, 1968 a, 1969 a)
Lindra marinera	Kohlmeyer (1971 b)
Basidiomycetes	
Nia vibrissa	Kohlmeyer and Kohlmeyer (1971 b)
Fungi Imperfecti	
Alternaria sp.	Kohlmeyer (1966 b)
Asteromyces cruciatus	Kohlmeyer and Kohlmeyer (1971 a)
Dendryphiella arenaria	Kohlmeyer (1966 b)
Varicosporina ramulosa	Kohlmeyer (1966 b, 1969 a)
Near *Spartina alterniflora* stands	
Leptosphaeria discors	Kohlmeyer (1966 b)
Lignincola laevis	Kohlmeyer (1966 b)
Metasphaeria australiensis	Kohlmeyer (1966 b)
Pleospora pelagica	Kohlmeyer (1966 b)

1.5   Developmental Studies

Developmental studies of the marine Ascomycetes have been concerned with (1) the development of the centrum and (2) the development of ascospores and appendages. The latter is considered by Kirk in Chapter 6 and will only be briefly discussed here. Doguet (1962, 1967) has also considered the development of the basidiocarps of two marine Basidiomycetes, while little attention has been devoted to the development of the spores of marine Fungi Imperfecti.

Detailed observations on the structure and life histories of bitunicate marine fungi are available for *Didymosphaeria danica* (Berlese) Wilson et Knoyle (Wilson and Knoyle, 1961); *Leptosphaeria discors* (Wagner, 1965) and *Mycosphaerella ascophylli* Cotton (Webber, 1967). All have normal pseudothecial development, and spermogonia have been reported for each species. Webber showed that in *M. ascophylli*, infection of the host occurs by egg-borne ascospores and egg-borne hyphae. He also suggests that infection of the host sporeling (*Ascophyllum nodosum* (L.) Le Jol.) may be necessary for the growth and survival of the sporelings. Kohlmeyer (1966 a, 1968 d, 1969 c) and Kohlmeyer and Kohlmeyer (1965) have described a number of bitunicate fungi from mangroves. The isolation, sporulation and observation of their life histories would be most interesting, especially *Helicascus kanaloanus* Kohlm. This fungus has thick-walled young asci and is obviously bitunicate but it also possesses an additional wall layer which covers the lower quarter of the ascus.

The early systematics of the so called unitunicate marine fungi was based mainly on ascospore morphology and the structure of the mature perithecia. Wilson (1954, 1956) was the first to describe in detail the immature fruiting bodies of the fungi she worked with and proceeded to show that changes occur in ascocarp morphology as they mature. Kohlmeyer (1960, 1961), and Kohlmeyer and Kohlmeyer (1966) followed her example and illustrated the internal organization of perithecia they were describing. Wilson (1965) continued her study of *Ceriosporopsis halima* and described the development of binucleate ascogenous tissue, croziers and asci. However, fertilization was not observed.

Cavaliere (1966 a, b, c) and Cavaliere and Johnson (1966 a, b) have examined the ascocarp morphology of a wide range of genera, including, *Amphisphaeria, Amylocarpus, Ceriosporopsis, Corollospora, Gnomonia, Halosphaeria, Leptosphaeria, Lignincola, Lindra, Lulworthia, Pleospora, Remispora* and *Sphaerulina*. In the first paper in this series, Cavaliere (1966 a) defines some of the terms used and describes six venter wall types commonly found in marine Pyrenomycetes. He considers the genus *Lindra* distinct from *Lulworthia* only on the basis of spore morphology.

Cavaliere (1966 b) was of the opinion that in *Corollospora* the perithecial wall structure, centrum structure and spore morphology were all variable. The only common feature was the carbonaceous nature of the mature perithecia. He also observed different developmental stages within the genus *Halosphaeria,* e.g. in *H. circumvestita* and others, the centrum contained a dome of cells while in *H. tubulifera* the hymenial layer was flat. Utricular cells were reported from *H. circumvestita, H. torquata* and *H. tubulifera* but were absent in *H. appendiculata* and *H. mediosetigera.* He also observed differences in perithecial wall structure and in the morphology and origin of spore appendages. Cavaliere and Johnson (1966 a) noted that in *Remispora* the following characters were common to all the species: soft and membranous perithecia, asci arise on a dome of pseudoparenchymatous cells, utricular cells present, ascospores all two celled (at the time) and that spore appendages were formed by epispore fragmentation. However, Kohlmeyer (1972 a) reduces *Remispora* to synonymy with *Halosphaeria.*

In their final paper (Cavaliere and Johnson, 1966 b), they considered the stability of various characters used in the identification of species. Ascocarp colour and texture were considered too variable and venter shape was dependent on the nature of the substrate. Neck length was also too variable but the presence of periphyses was considered a useful character. Venter wall was of doubtful usefulness. Two types of centrum development were observed, a dome shaped mass of pseudoparenchymatous cells or a basal hymenial layer. However, these were dependent on the number of ascogonia fertilized. Utricular cells were present only during early stages of development and were not considered useful in the delimitation of species. The presence or absence of paraphyses was considered to be significant taxonomically.

Spore appendages were considered to have developed in four ways (1) by direct growth or exudation from the spore or spore wall: *Halosphaeria tubulifera, Corollospora maritima,* (2) epispore fragmentation, e.g. *Halosphaeria mediosetigera, Remispora maritima,* (3) deposition of ascus cytoplasm onto the mature spores, e.g. *Halosphaeria circumvestita,* and (4) a combination of deposition and growth.

Lutley and Wilson (1972 a) have shown that, in *Ceriosporopsis halima,* the terminal appendages grow out from apical caps of the epispore and are contained within the spore membrane and are supported internally by a fine fibrillar network (Fig. 1.32). An outer exospore, which merges with the epispore and contains acidic polysaccharides in irregular chambers (Fig. 1.33-1.35) surrounds the spore and forms a sheath at the base of each appendage.

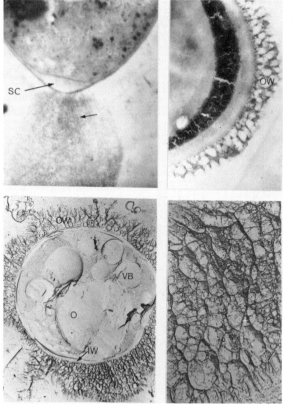

Fig. 1.32. *Ceriosporopsis halima.* Electron micrograph of ascospore to show skeletal elements (arrowed) of the appendage with the episporic spore cap (SC) (x16 000). **Fig. 1.33.** *C. halima.* T.S. of ascospore to show wall layers (x5100). **Fig. 1.34.** *C. halima.* Frozen-etched mature spore showing cytoplasmic components and wall layers (OW: outer wall [epispore and exospore] IW: inner wall of spore mesospore) (x5100). **Fig. 1.35.** *C. halima.* Frozen-etched replica from a fracture tangential to the spore through the outer wall layer (x10 000).

Lutley and Wilson (1972 b) have also examined the development of spore appendages in *Halosphaeria appendiculata, Torpedospora radiata* and *Corollospora maritima.* The appendages of the former appear to be outgrowths of the epispore. *T. radiata* appendages contain a series of longitudinally parallel fibrils comparable to those of *Ceriosporopsis halima* (see Fig. 6.28). The appendages of *C. maritima* (Fig. 1.36) are formed in an entirely different way from those mentioned above. The terminal appendage is formed as an extension of the spore itself and later becomes surrounded by the mesospore forming a spine. The apical caps and the equatorial appendages grow out of the epispore at fixed and separate sites and are reported as differentiating at a very early stage in development. Lutley and Wilson (1972 b) do not agree with the views of Johnson (1963 b) that the appendages of *C. maritima* are cytoplasmic remnants. Unpublished work by K. Fazzani (Portsmouth Polytechnic) shows that the lateral appendages in *C. maritima* are variable in morphology and are probably formed by fragmentation of the outer layer of the spore wall (Fig. 1.37). This is in agreement with the views of Kohlmeyer (1966 c) Figure 1.38 shows an apical spine with an apical

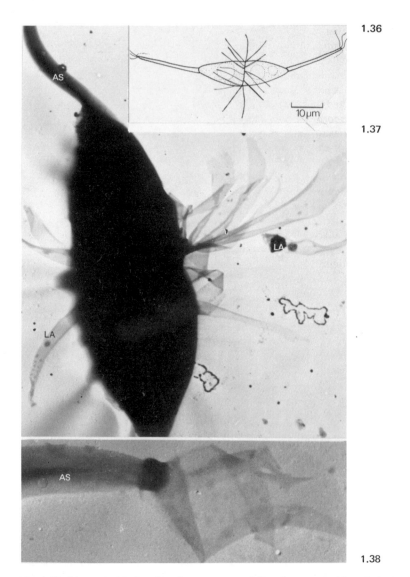

Fig. 1.36. Camera lucida drawing of an ascospore of *Corollospora maritima*. Apical and lateral appendages represented as thin fibres or hair-like projections. **Fig. 1.37.** Ascospore of *C. maritima* (direct shadow preparation) with apical spine (or thorn) (AS) and lateral appendages (LA). The latter are strips of wall material often variable in size. (×3333) (photo. K. Fazzani). **Fig. 1.38.** Apical spine (AS) of *C. maritima* ascospore with an apical cap as described by Kohlmeyer, 1966 c. (×8000) (photo. K. Fazzani).

cap. The tip of the spine is electron dense and Kohlmeyer (1966 c) has shown that this region becomes heavily stained with phloxine and aniline blue.

Johnson (1963 a-e) in a series of papers has investigated the devlopment of spore appendages in the genera *Amylocarpus, Ceriosporopsis, Corollospora, Halosphaeria, Herpotrichiella, Remispora* and *Torpedospora.* These are based on light microscopy and differential staining. Kirk (Chapter 6) has shown the need for careful histochemical work in interpretating the origin of spore appendages. The observations of Lutley and

Wilson (1972 a, b) show that much information can be derived by the use of the electron microscope. Fazzani (unpublished) has shown that in *Corollospora maritima* the equatorial appendages are not thin parallel strips of material as so frequently illustrated (Fig. 1.36) but rather irregular sheets of wall material (Fig. 1.37).

Kohlmeyer (1972 a) has undertaken a revision of the family Halosphaeriaceae. Thirteen genera are accepted, but *Torpedospora*, *Samarosporella* and *Didymosamarospora* are excluded. *Remispora* is reduced to synonymy with *Halosphaeria* due to the lack of clear distinction in venter wall structure, centrum development and spore morphology. Many will not concur with this as the genus *Halosphaeria* will now contain a very wide assemblage of species.

Lignicolous marine fungi have been studied for nearly 30 years, and mycologists should now be able to assign them to families and define generic limits. However, further accurate information on ascocarp and ascospore appendage development is still required. Algicolous marine Ascomycetes are in a more confused state, frequently due to lack of type material and sporulating cultures. The only ultrastructure study to date has been that of Lutley and Wilson (1972 a, b), although a number are in progress (Fazzani, personal communication).

1.6   Spore Liberation, Transportation and Settlement

Ingold (1971) and Gregory (1961) have shown that considerable information is available on the dispersal of spores in terrestrial fungi, and that methods for these studies are well developed (Davies, 1971). In aquatic habitats we know very little of spore dispersal, especially in the marine environment. However, aquatic fungi appear to be world wide in their distribution.

The spores of the higher marine fungi are of three types: appendaged (often mucilaginous) spores, e.g. Ascomycetes (Figs. 1.3-1.9); branched spores as in the Basidiomycetes *Digitatispora marina* and *Nia vibrissa* as well as some Fungi Imperfecti (Figs. 1.10-1.16 and 1.24) and non-appendaged spores, e.g. Fungi Imperfecti and Ascomycetes (Fig. 1.19-1.23). The spores must undergo a series of stages—spore formation, liberation and transportation—prior to actual settlement, and this has often to be accomplished in turbulent waters.

In the marine Ascomycetes, some 60% have appendaged ascospores. These are frequently stated to be mucilaginous or gelatinous in texture e.g. *Ceriosporopsis halima*, *Pleospora gaudefroyi* and *Phycomelainia laminariae*, while in *Corollospora maritima*, *C. lacera* and *C. comata*, the appendages appear as hair-like projections of the spore (*cf* Figs. 1.36-1.37). Kohlmeyer (1969 c) states that in *Lentescospora submarina* the spores are covered by a sheath which retracts to form an apical cap with radiating striae present within the caps. Similarly, in *Phycomelainia laminariae* (Kohlmeyer, 1968 b), the young spores are covered by a gelatinous sheath which later separates around the septum and finally only covers the apices of the spore. In distilled water these appendages swell and finally dissolve, while in seawater they remain intact, even after the spores have germinated. Lutley and Wilson (1972 a, b) have shown that what appear to be no more than mucilaginous appendages do have an internal skeletal system of parallel fibrils, e.g. in *C. halima* and *Torpedospora radiata* (Figs. 1.32; 6.28).

It has been suggested that these appendages help (1) to keep spores afloat by offering increased resistance to settlement; (2) to entangle and attach the spores to suitable substrates or (3) to catch unorganized eddy diffusion currents. However, no quantitative experimental work has been carried out to test these ideas or to determine the time it takes a spore to settle and attach itself to a substrate or how effective the adhesion is. While some appendages may have an adhesive function it is doubtful if the appendages of *Amylocarpus encephaloides, Corollospora maritima, Herpotrichiella ciliomaris* and *Nautosphaeria crista-minuta* have such a function. However, they may help to entangle spores to suitable substrates.

If spores are to colonize their substrate successfully, they must be capable of rapid germination and penetration. Spores have been reported as germinating within 24 hours of seeding agar plates (Lutley and Wilson, 1972 a), but detailed information is again lacking. Byrne (1971) has shown that temperature affects the germination of marine fungi, especially low temperature; e.g. in *Asteromyces cruciatus* 75% germination occurred after 18 hours at 25°C but only 55% germination after 48 hours when grown at 10°C. Most of the fungi tested had a high percentage germination, with the exception of *Torpedospora radiata.* These high germination rates may explain why these fungi are so successful in colonizing freshly submerged timber in the sea.

There are no figures available for the numbers of spores of marine fungi present in seawater. Millipore filtration techniques have proved disappointing as large volumes have to be filtered and even then the counts are low. This is not surprising considering the size of the oceans and the limited substrates available for colonization. However, timber placed in the sea is soon colonized by a variety of species, even at depths of 437 m (Jones and Le Campion-Alsumard, 1970 a, b).

A number of the marine Fungi Imperfecti have branched conidia, e.g. *Clavariopsis bulbosa, Clavatospora stellatacula* Kirk, *Orbimyces spectabilis* and *Varicosporina ramulosa.* Others have long curved spores *(Sporidesmium salinum)* or coiled conidia *(Cirrenalia fusca, C. pygmea, C. tropicalis* and *Zalerion maritimum).* In *Asteromyces cruciatus* a number of conidia are borne on short pedicels. These are rarely dispersed singly but rather as aggregates of conidia (Figs. 1.20 and 1.23). Fazzani (personal communication) has shown that the aggregates are more efficiently trapped than single conidia. Ingold (1966, 1971) has pointed out the advantages of the tetraradiate spore to freshwater fungi. Undoubtedly the branched spores of marine fungi help in impaction, possibly to keep the spores suspended longer in the water and to carry the spores along in water currents.

Non-appendaged spores are also found in the sea, e.g. *Dendryphiella salina, Humicola alopallonella* and *Monodictys pelagica.* The success of *D. salina* in colonizing a variety of substrates in the sea shows that the non-appendaged nature of its conidia is no drawback to life in this environment.

Spore liberation has been documented for a number of marine Ascomycetes and these can be considered under four headings. The first type is used by *Chaetosphaeria chaetosa* Kohlm., which has a unitunicate ascus. The ascus becomes turgid as the result of increased osmotic pressure, the wall is stretched and this leads to the rupture of the ascus resulting in the explosive release of ascospores. Few marine Ascomycetes release their spores in this way as the surrounding water may offer too much resistance for the successful dispersal of the spores. Kohlmeyer (1972 a) has shown that, in *Orcadia ascophylli,* the ascus has an operculum, but he did not observe spore discharge.

The second mechanism is the passive discharge of asci from ascocarps and the subsequent active release of the spores. This method is rarely found in the marine Ascomycetes but has been reported for *Gnomonia marina* Cribb et Cribb (Cribb and Cribb, 1956). This is similar to that reported by Ingold (1971) for *Ceratocystis* and *Ceratostomella.*

The third mechanism is characteristic of many marine Ascomycetes, especially members of the Halosphaeriaceae. The ascus wall is extremely thin (Lutley and Wilson, 1972 a, b) and is structurally quite different from the unitunicate asci of some terrestrial genera (Greenhalgh and Evans, 1967). The ascus wall breaks down and liberates the spores into the centrum. When mature, the tip of the neck opens, seawater may enter the ascocarp and the mucilage around the spores or in the centrum swells. This probably helps to expel the spores up the neck and out of the ostiole into the surrounding water (Lutley and Wilson, 1972 a; Wilson, 1954; Jones, 1962, 1964). If the ascospores are appendaged, any mucilage around the spore expands and dissolves, and the appendages then stretch out.

Amylocarpus encephaloides and *Eiona tunicata,* both cleistothecial forms, have deliquescing asci and appendaged ascospores. This suggests that the deliquescing ascus has been evolved in the marine Ascomycetes more than once, e.g. in the Plectomycetes and Pyrenomycetes. In the sea, this seems an ideal way of releasing ascospores. All that is required is the release of the spores from ascocarps. An explosive mechanism is of limited use owing to the greater viscosity of water as compared with that of air. It is therefore significant that no glycogen has been found in the epiplasm of maturing asci of *Ceriosporopsis halima* (Lutley and Wilson, 1972 a).

Kohlmeyer and Kohlmeyer (1972 b) have described the mode of spore release in *Turgidosculum ulvae* which has thin-walled deliquescing asci releasing ascospores which accumulate in the centrum. At low tide the algal host dries out and the ascocarp becomes compressed, squeezing out ascospores and mucilage through the ostiole. These accumulate at the tip of the short neck and are washed away by the incoming tide. A gelatinous pulvillus develops and prevents penetration of water into the perithecium. In *T. ulvae,* the asci develop at irregular intervals so that the above process is repeated many times.

The bitunicate ascus has an active method of spore discharge and is well illustrated in *Didymosphaeria danica* (Wilson and Knoyle, 1961). The ascus wall consists of an outer rigid layer (ectoascus) and a very thin inner extensile one (endoascus). Just before discharge the ectoascus ruptures apically (sometimes subapically) and water is absorbed, with the result that the endoascus elongates very rapidly up the neck of the pseudothecium, soon projects through the ostiole and bursts, squirting its ascospores into the air or water. The effectiveness of this method must be very much reduced when the fungus is continuously submerged, owing to the increased viscosity of water. Johnson (1956 b) and Wagner (1965) have reported on ascus dehiscence in *Leptosphaeria discors* which is similar to that of *D. danica.* Kohlmeyer (1969 a) has made similar observations for *Helicascus kanaloanus* which differs in having an additional wall layer which covers the lower portion of the ascus. In a recent study (Jones, 1968 a), 970 recordings of marine fungi were made on 266 test panels submerged for up to 120 weeks in the sea. Of these, only 12 recordings were of bitunicate species (*Pleospora* sp. (two recordings), *Leptosphaeria orae-maris* (nine) and *Microthelia maritima* (one)). However, intertidal substrates, e.g. mangroves, *Spartina* culms and driftwood are frequently rich in bitunicate fungi (Kohlmeyer and Kohlmeyer, 1965, 1971 a, b).

1.7   Evolution of the Higher Marine Fungi

Various hypotheses have been formulated to explain the origin of marine fungi, especially the Ascomycetes. This problem is bound up with the evolution of the terrestrial Ascomycetes and Basidiomycetes from a primitive ancestor, there being two main schools of thought regarding their origin. De Bary (1884) suggested they arose from the phycomycetes through a Mucoraceous fungal type while Sachs (1874) and Bessey (1942) hold the view they arose from algae that had some of the characteristics of the simpler Florideae.

If one accepts the first theory, that the Ascomycetes arose from terrestrial ancestors, then the marine and freshwater occurring Ascomycetes must be secondarily adapted to the aquatic environment, and the production of appendaged spores a consequential and advantageous development. Jennings (1973) believes that the properties of the outer membranes of marine fungi appear to be very much like those of their terrestrial counterparts; namely

(1)   the presence of a pump which is highly specific for potassium in the external medium and which is responsible for removing sodium ions from the cell and the absence of any pump capable of taking in sodium;

(2)   low passive permeability to sodium ions and anions, with these latter ions being pumped into the mycelium for the most part at low rates

The Floridean theory has been re-examined and modified by Denison and Carroll (1966), based on the knowledge of marine-occurring Ascomycetes, not generally known to exist when the theory was conceived. These authors suggest that the primitive Ascomycetes evolved as Pyrenomycetes saprophytic on wood, with membranous to carbonaceous unilocular perithecia, not embedded in stromata. After the development of airborne ascospores, these ancestral types then spread to dead and dying wood on the shore, and thence to other saprophytic and parasitic niches on the land. This suggests that the evolution of the high fungi has taken place since the Silurian, Devonian or even the Carboniferous.

Kohlmeyer (1973) favours the Floridean theory but does not accept the lignicolous Ascomycetes as the ancestral types. He believes they were Ascomycetes parasitic on living algae and suggests that the Spathulosporales may form such a link group. These fungi are parasitic on members of the Ceramiales *(Ballia)*, an order which contains adelphoparasites (Feldman and Feldman, 1958). Adelphoparasites are colourless parasitic red algae which are closely related systematically to their hosts and possibly derived from them by mutation. The sequence of events suggested is as follows:

red algae →	red algae → parasitized by adelphoparasites	*Spathulospora* → type parasitizing red alga	Pyrenomycete → parasitizing alga	saprophytic → Pyrenomycete	terrestrial Pyrenomycete-on the evolution of active discharge asci

The sexual reproductive mechanism in the Spathulosporales closely resembles that of the red algae Ceramiales: both have spermatia, trichogynes, and thalli that are compact and multicellular, a protective pericarp to surround the developing spores, and the presence of choline sulphate (ester). The latter appears to be absent in the lower fungi (Catalfomo *et al.,* 1972).

Although the Floridean theory is held by many to be the most plausible, with regard to the available information, many marine mycologists tend towards the concept that the marine Ascomycetes are secondarily adapted to this environment. Wilson (1960) considers that they display no particularly primitive characters and cannot accept the Floridean hypothesis. However, she recognizes that these fungi have probably inhabited the sea for a relatively long time; long enough to have evolved new genera and species. Ritchie (1960) also holds the view that marine-occurring Ascomycetes are derived from freshwater forms by way of intermediate terrestrial ancestors. Certainly a large number of the marine Ascomycetes are secondary marine forms, e.g. the Loculoascomycetes, *Laboulbenia marina* Picard and *Helicascus kanaloanus,* to name a few. One aspect is of special interest with regard to marine Ascomycetes, namely the number of forms with deliquescing asci, e.g. *Eiona tunicata* (Eurotiales), *Halosphaeria appendiculata* and other members of the Halosphaeriaceae, *Crinigera maritima* Schmidt (Erysiphales), and *Spathulospora adelpha* (Spathulosporales). Deliquescing asci are not restricted to the marine environment and are to be found amongst freshwater and terrestrial Ascomycetes. So this may not be a primitive feature but an adaptation to environmental conditions.

The marine Basidiomycetes, *Digitatispora marina* and *Nia vibrissa,* are almost certainly secondary marine forms. They belong to two quite distinct groups of the Basidiomycetes—the Aphyllophorales and the Gasteromycetes respectively. Both release their basidiospores passively as the basidia do not produce sterigmata. The freshwater Basidiomycetes reported by Ingold (1961), Shaw (1972) and Nawawi (1973) also release their spores passively but lack basidia.

New marine fungi continue to be described as techniques for their isolation and growth are developed. The estuarine mycoflora has only been studied briefly and there is much scope for further work in this field.

Acknowledgements

It is a pleasure to thank the following for all their help: Miss J. Haythorn, Messrs. K. Fazzani and J. Irvine for allowing me to refer to their unpublished work and for supplying Figs. 1.1-1.2, 1.15-1.18 and 1.36; Drs. M. Lutley, I. M. Wilson and the British Mycological Society for permission to use Figs. 1.32-1.35; Miss S. Hopkins for photographic assistance, and the Natural Environment Research Council for providing grants for some of the research work mentioned above.

References

ALDERMAN, D. J., and JONES, E. B. G. (1971). 'Shell disease of oysters.' *Fisheries Investigation* 16, 1-16.

ANASTASIOU, C. J. (1963). 'Ascomycetes and Fungi Imperfecti from the Salton Sea.' *Nova Hedwigia,* 6, 243-276.

ANASTASIOU, C. J., and CHURCHLAND, L. M. (1969). 'Fungi on decaying leaves in marine habitats.' *Can. J. Bot.,* 47, 251-257.

APINIS, A. E. (1963). 'Thermophilous fungi in coastal grasslands.' In *'Soil Organisms'* (Eds. J. Doeksen and J. van der Drift). North Holland Publ. Co., Amsterdam, 427-438.

APINIS, A. E., and CHESTERS, C. G. C. (1956). 'Ascomycetes of some salt marshes and sand dunes.' *Trans. Br. mycol. Soc.,* 47, 419-435.

AUSTWICK, P. K. C. (1950). Report on investigations into the cause of dying-out of *Spartina townsendii* Groves in Lymington Harbour, Hants. Unpublished Report to the Director, Royal Botanic Gardens, Kew.

de BARY, A. (1884). 'Vergleichende morphologie und biologie des pilze, mycetezoen und bacterien.' Liepzig, Wilhelm Engelmann.

BESSEY, E. A. (1942). 'Some problems in fungous phylogeny.' *Mycologia,* 34, 355-379.

BROOKS, R. D., GOOS, R. D., and SIEBURTH, J. McN. (1972). 'Fungal infestation of the surface and interior vessels of freshly collected driftwood.' *Marine Biology,* 16, 274-278.

BROWN, J. C. (1958). 'Soil fungi of some British sand dunes in relation to soil type and succession.' *J. Ecol.,* 46, 641-664.

BYRNE, P. J. (1971). 'The physiological responses of some marine, freshwater and terrestrial fungi to salinity.' Ph.D. Thesis, University of London.

BYRNE, P. J., and JONES, E. B. G. (1974). 'Lignicolous marine fungi.' *Veröff. Inst. Meeresforsch. Bremerh.* (in press).

CATALFOMO, P., BLOCK, J. H., CONSTANTINE, G. H., and KIRK, P. W. (1972). 'Choline sulphate (ester) in marine higher fungi.' *Marine Chemistry,* 1, 157-162.

CAVALIERE, A. R. (1966a). 'Marine Ascomycetes: Ascocarp morphology and its application to taxonomy. I *Amylocarpus* Currey, *Ceriosporella* gen. nov., *Lindra* Wilson.' *Nova Hedwigia,* 10, 387-398.

CAVALIERE, A. R. (1966 b). 'Marine Ascomycetes: Ascocarp morphology and its application to taxonomy. II Didymosporae.' *Nova Hedwigia,* 10, 399-424.

CAVALIERE, A. R. (1966 c). 'Marine Ascomycetes: Ascocarp morphology and its application to taxonomy. IV Stromatic species.' *Nova Hedwigia,* 10, 438-452.

CAVALIERE, A. R. (1968). 'Marine fungi of Iceland: a preliminary account of Ascomycetes.' *Mycologia,* 60, 475-479.

CAVALIERE, A. R., and ALBERTE, R. S. (1970). 'Fungi in animal shell fragments.' *J. Elisha Mitchell scient. Soc.,* 86, 203-206.

CAVALIERE, A. R., and JOHNSON, T. W. (1965). 'A new marine Ascomycete from Australia.' *Mycologia,* 57, 927-932.

CAVALIERE, A. R., and JOHNSON, T. W. (1966 a). 'Marine Ascomycetes: Ascocarp morphology and its application to taxonomy III A revision of the genus *Lulworthia* Sutherland.' *Nova Hedwigia,* 10, 425-437.

CAVALIERE, A. R., and JOHNSON, T. W. (1966 b). 'Marine Ascomycetes: Ascocarp morphology and its application to taxonomy. V. Evaluation.' *Nova Hedwigia,* 10, 453-461.

CAVALIERE, A. R., and MARKHART, A. H. (1972). 'Marine fungi of Iceland: calcareophilous forms.' *Surtsey Progress Report,* VI, 1-3.

CHURCH, A. H. (1893). 'A marine fungus.' *Ann. Bot.,* 7, 399-400.

CHURCHLAND, L. M., and McCLAREN, M. (1972). 'The effect of kraft pulp mill effluents on the growth of *Zalerion maritimum.' Can. J. Bot.,* 50, 1269-1273.

CHURCHLAND, L. M., and McCLAREN, M. (1973). 'Marine fungi from a kraft pulp mill outfall area.' *Can. J. Bot.,* 51, 1703-1710.

COTTON, A. D. (1908). *'Notes on marine Pyrenomycetes.' Trans. Br. mycol. Soc.,* 3, 92-99.

CRIBB, A. B., and CRIBB, J. W. (1956). 'Marine fungi from Queensland II'. *Univ. Queensland Papers, Dept. Botany,* 3, 97-105.

CRIBB, A. B., and CRIBB, J. W. (1960 a). 'Marine fungi of Queensland III'. *Univ. Queensland Papers, Dept. Botany,* 4, 39-44.

CRIBB, A. B., and CRIBB, J. W. (1960 b). 'Some marine fungi on algae in European Herbaria.' *Univ. Queensland Papers, Dept. Botany,* 4, 45-48.

CRIBB, A. B., and HERBERT, J. W. (1954). 'Three species of fungi parasitic on marine algae in Tasmania.' *Univ. Queensland Papers, Dept. Botany,* 3, 9-13.

DAVIES, R. A. (1971). 'Air sampling for fungi, pollens and bacteria.' In *Methods in Microbiology* (Ed. C. Booth). Academic Press, London, vol. 4, 367-404.

DAWSON, E. Y. (1949). 'Contributions toward a marine flora of the Southern California Channel Islands.' I-III. Allan Hancock Found. Publ. Occas. Pap. 8, 1-57.

DENISON, W. C., and CARROLL, G. C. (1966). 'The primitive Ascomycete: A new look at an old problem.' *Mycologia,* 58, 249-269.

DOGUET, G. (1962). *'Digitatispora marina* n.g. n.sp. Basidiomycete marin.' *C. r. hebd. Séanc. Acad. Sci.,* Paris, 254, 4336-4338.

DOGUET, G. (1967). *'Nia vibrissa* Moore et Meyers, remarquable Basidiomycete marin.' *C. r. hebd. Séanc. Acad. Sci., Paris,* 265, 1780-1783.

ERIKSSON, O. (1964). *'Nectriella laminariae* n.sp. in stipes of a *Laminaria.'* *Svensk Bot. Tidskr.,* 58, 233-236.

FELDMANN, G. (1957). 'Un nouvel Ascomycete parasite d' une algue marine: *Chadefaudia marina.'* *Revue gén. Bot.,* 64, 104-152.

FELDMANN, G. (1958). *'Didymella magnei,* nouvelle espèce de pseudospheriale marine.' *Revue gen. Bot.,* 65, 414-417.

FELDMANN, J. (1940). *'Maireomyces,* Nouveau genre de Pyrenomycete marin.' *Bull. Soc. Hist. Nat. Afr.,* 31, 163-166.

FELDMANN, J., and FELDMANN, G. (1958). 'Recherches sur quelques Floridées parasites.' *Revue gén. Bot.,* 65, 49-124.

FRAGOSO, R. G. (1919). 'Anotaciones micologicas'. *Mem. Revl. Soc. Espan. Hist. Nat.,* 11, 77-123.

GESSNER, R. V., GOOS, R. D., and SIEBURTH, J. McN. (1972). 'The fungal microcosm of the internodes of *Spartina alterniflora.'* *Marine Biology,* 16, 269-273.

GOLD, H. S. (1959). 'Distribution of some lignicolous Ascomycetes and Fungi Imperfecti in an estuary.' *J. Elisha Mitchell scient. Soc.,* 75, 25-28.

GOODMAN, P. J. (1959). 'The possible role of pathogenic fungi in 'die-back' of *Spartina townsendii* agg.' *Trans. Br. mycol. Soc.,* 42, 409-415.

GREENHALGH, G. N., and EVANS, L. V. (1967). 'The structure of the ascus apex in *Hypoxylon fragiforme* with reference to ascospore release in this and related species.' *Trans. Br. mycol. Soc.,* 50, 183-188.

GREGORY, P. H. (1961). *The Microbiology of the Atmosphere.* Plant Science Monographs. Leonard Hill (Books) London. 251 pp.

HARIOT, P., and PATOUILLARD, N. (1904). 'Description de champignons honveaux de l'herbier du museum.' *Bull. Soc. mycol., Fr.,* 20, 61-65.

HÖHNK, W. (1967). 'Über die submerren pilze an der rumänischen Schwarz maerküste nahe constanza.' *Veröff. Inst. Meeresforsch. Bremerh.,* 10, 149-158.

HUGHES, G. C. (1960). 'Ecological aspects of some lignicolous fungi in estuarine waters.' Ph.D. Thesis, Univ. Florida, Tallahassee.

HUGHES, G. C. (1968). 'Intertidal lignicolous fungi from Newfoundland.' *Can. J. Bot.,* 46, 1409-1417.

HUGHES, G. C., and CHAMUT, P. S. (1971). 'Lignicolous marine fungi from southern Chile, including a review of distribution in the southern hemisphere.' *Can. J. Bot.,* 49, 1-11.

INGOLD, C. T. (1961). 'Another aquatic spore-type with clamp connections.' *Trans. Br. mycol. Soc.,* 44, 27-30.

INGOLD, C. T. (1966). 'The tetraradiate aquatic fungal spore.' *Mycologia,* 58, 43-56.

INGOLD, C. T. (1971). *Fungal Spores: Their Liberation and Dispersal.* Clarendon Press, Oxford, 302 pp.

JENNINGS, D. H. (1973). 'Cations and filamentous fungi: Invasion of the sea and hyphal functioning.' In *Ion Transport in Cells* (Ed. W. P. Anderson). Academic Press, London, 323-335.

JOHNSON, T. W. (1956 a). 'Marine fungi. II Ascomycetes and Deuteromycetes from submerged wood.' *Mycologia,* 48, 841-851.

JOHNSON, T. W. (1956 b). 'Ascus development and spore discharge in *Leptosphaeria discors,* a marine and brackish water fungus.' *Bull. mar. Sci. Gulf Caribb.,* 6, 349-358.

JOHNSON, T. W. (1963 a). 'Some aspects of morphology in marine Ascomycetes: *Halosphaeria,* Linder. ' *Nova Hedwigia,* 6, 67-81.

JOHNSON, T. W. (1963 b). 'Some aspects of morphology in marine Ascomycetes: *Corollospora* Werdermann.' *Nova Hedwigia,* 6, 83-93.

JOHNSON, T. W. (1963 c). 'Some aspects of morphology in marine Ascomycetes: *Amylocarpus* Currey, *Herpotrichiella* Petrak, and *Torpedospora* Meyers.' *Nova Hedwigia,* 6, 157-168.

JOHNSON, T. W. (1963 d). 'Some aspects of morphology in marine Ascomycetes: *Ceriosporopsis* Linder.' *Nova Hedwigia,* 6, 169-178.

JOHNSON, T. W. (1963 e). 'Some aspects of morphology in marine Ascomycetes: *Remispora* Linder.' *Nova Hedwigia,* 6, 179-198.

JOHNSON, T. W. (1967). 'The estuarine mycoflora.' In *Estuaries* (Ed. G. H. Lauff) Amer. Assoc. Adv. Sci. Publ. 83, 303-305.

JOHNSON, T. W., and SPARROW, F. K. (1961). *Fungi in Oceans and Estuaries.* J. Cramer, Weinheim 668 pp.

JOHNSON, T. W., FERCHAU, H. A., and GOLD, H. S. (1959). 'Isolation, culture, growth and nutrition of some lignicolous marine fungi.' *Phyton. Internat. J. expt. Bot.,* 12, 65-80.

JONES, E. B. G. (1962). 'Marine fungi.' *Trans. Br. mycol. Soc.,* 45, 93-114.

JONES, E. B. G. (1963 a). 'Marine fungi 2: Ascomycetes and Deuteromycetes from submerged wood and drift *Spartina.*' *Trans. Br. mycol. Soc.,* 46, 135-144.

JONES, E. B. G. (1963 b). 'Observations on the fungal succession on wood test blocks submerged in the sea.' *J. Inst. Wood Sci.,* No. 11, 14-23.

JONES, E. B. G. (1964). '*Nautosphaeria cristaminuta* gen. et sp. nov. A marine Pyrenomycete on submerged wood.' *Trans. Br. mycol. Soc.,* 47, 97-101.

JONES, E. B. G. (1968 a). 'The distribution of marine fungi on wood submerged in the sea.' In *Biodeterioration of Materials.* (Eds. J. J. Elphick and A. H. Walters) Elsevier, vol. 1, 460-485.

JONES, E. B. G. (1968 b). 'Marine fungi.' *Curr. Sci.,* 37, 378-379.

JONES, E. B. G. (1971 a). 'The ecology and rotting ability of marine fungi.' in *Marine Borers, Fungi and Fouling Organisms of Wood* (Eds. E. B. G. Jones and S. K. Eltringham), O.E.C.D. Paris, 237-258.

JONES, E. B. G. (1971 b). 'Aquatic Fungi.' In *Methods in Microbiology.* (Ed. C. Booth), Academic Press, vol. 4, 335-365.

JONES, E. B. G. (1972). 'The decay of timber in aquatic environments.' *British Wood Preserving Association, Annual Convention,* 1-18.

JONES, E. B. G., and LE CAMPION-ALSUMARD, T. (1970 a). 'Marine fungi on polyurethane covered plates submerged in the sea.' *Nova Hedwigia,* 19, 567-590.

JONES, E. B. G., and LE CAMPION-ALSUMARD, T. (1970 b). 'The biodeterioration of polyurethane by marine fungi.' *Int. Biodetn. Bull.*, 6, 119-124.

JONES, E. B. G., and IRVINE, J. (1971). 'The role of fungi in the deterioration of wood in the sea.' *J. Inst. Wood Sci.*, 5, 31-40.

JONES, E. B. G., KÜHNE, H., TRUSSELL, P. C., and TURNER, R. D. (1972). 'Results of an International Cooperative Research Programme on the biodeterioration of timber submerged in the sea.' *Material u. Organismen*, 7, 93-118.

JONES, H. L. (1898). 'A new species of Pyrenomycetes parasitic on an alga.' *Bull. Oberlin Coll. Lab.*, 9, 3-4.

KIRK, P. W. (1969). 'Isolation and culture of lignicolous marine fungi.' *Mycologia*, 61, 174-177.

KOHLMEYER, J. (1959). 'Neufunde holzbesiedelnder meerespilze.' *Nova Hedwigia*, 1, 77-98.

KOHLMEYER, J. (1960). 'Wood-inhabiting marine fungi from the Pacific Northwest and California.' *Nova Hedwigia*, 2, 293-343.

KOHLMEYER, J. (1961). 'Pilze von der nördlichen Pazifik-Küste der USA.' *Nova Hedwigia*, 3, 85-91.

KOHLMEYER, J. (1962). 'Halophile pilze von den ufern Frankreiche.' *Nova Hedwigia*, 4, 389-420.

KOHLMEYER, J. (1963 a). 'Zwei neue Ascomyceten gattungen auf *Posidonia* rhizomen.' *Nova Hedwigia*, 6, 5-13.

KOHLMEYER, J. (1963 b). 'Repartition de champignons marins (Ascomycetes et Fungi Imperfecti) dans la Méditerranée.' Rapports et Procésverbaux des réunions de la C.I.E.S.M.M., 17, 723-730.

KOHLMEYER, J. (1963 c). 'Parasitische und epiphytische pilze auf meersalgen.' *Nova Hedwigia*, 6, 127-146.

KOHLMEYER, J. (1963 d). 'Fungi marini novi vel critici.' *Nova Hedwigia*, 6, 297-329.

KOHLMEYER, J. (1966 a). 'Neue meerespilze an mangroven.' *Ber. dt. bot. Ges.*, 79, 27-37.

KOHLMEYER, J. (1966 b). 'Ecological observations on arenicolous marine fungi.' *Z. allg. Mikrobiol.*, 6, 95-106.

KOHLMEYER, J. (1966 c). 'Ascospore morphology in *Corollospora*.' *Mycologia*, 68, 218-288.

KOHLMEYER, J. (1967). 'Intertidal and phycophilous fungi from Tenerife (Canary Islands).' *Trans. Br. mycol. Soc.*, 50, 137-147.

KOHLMEYER, J. (1968 a). 'Marine fungi from the tropics.' *Mycologia*, 60, 252-270.

KOHLMEYER, J. (1968 b). 'Revisions and descriptions of algicolous marine fungi.' *Phytopath. Z.*, 63, 341-363.

KOHLMEYER, J. (1968 c). 'Danische meerespilze (Ascomycetes).' *Ber. dt. bot. Ges.*, 81, 53-61.

KOHLMEYER, J. (1968 d). 'A new *Tematosphaeria* from roots of *Rhizophora racemosa*.' *Mycopath. Mycol. appl.*, 34, 1-5.

KOHLMEYER, J. (1968 e). 'The first Ascomycete from the deep sea.' *J. Elisha Mitchell scient. Soc.*, 84, 239-241.

KOHLMEYER, J. (1969 a). 'Marine fungi of Hawaii including the new genus *Heliascus*.' *Can. J. Bot.*, 47, 1469-1487.

KOHLMEYER, J. (1969 b). 'The role of marine fungi in the penetration of calcareous substances.' *Am. Zool.*, 9, 741-746.

KOHLMEYER, J. (1969 c). 'Ecological notes on fungi in mangrove forests.' *Trans. Br. mycol. Soc.*, 53, 237-250.

KOHLMEYER, J. (1969 d). 'Deterioration of wood by marine fungi in the deep sea.' In *Materials Performance in the Deep Sea*. Special Technical Publ. 445, 20-30. Amer. Soc. for Testing and Materials.

KOHLMEYER, J. (1969 e). 'Perithecial hairs with phialides in *Spathulospora phycophila.' Mycologia,* 61, 1012-1015.

KOHLMEYER, J. (1971 a). 'Ein neuer Ascomycet auf Hydrozoen im Südatlantik.' *Ber. dt. bot. Ges.,* 83, 505-509.

KOHLMEYER, J. (1971 b). 'Fungi from the Sargasso Sea.' *Marine Biology,* 8, 344-350.

KOHLMEYER, J. (1971 c). 'Annotated check-list of New England marine fungi.' *Trans. Br. mycol. Soc.,* 57, 473-492.

KOHLMEYER, J. (1972 a). 'A revision of Halosphaeriaceae.' *Can. J. Bot.,* 50, 1951-1963.

KOHLMEYER, J. (1972 b). 'Marine fungi deteriorating chitin of hydrozoa and keratin-like annelid tubes. *Marine Biology,* 12, 277-284.

KOHLMEYER, J. (1972 c). 'Parasitic *Haloquiqnardia oceanica* (Ascomycetes) and hyperparasitic *Sphaceloma cecidii* sp. nov. (Deuteromycetes) in drift *Sargassum* in North Carolina.' *J. Elisha Mitchell scient. Soc,* 88, 255-259.

KOHLMEYER, J. (1973 a). *(Chadefaudia balliae,* a new species of Ascomycetes on *Ballia* in Australia.' *Mycologia,* 65, 244-248.

KOHLMEYER, J. (1973 b). 'Spathulosporales, a new order and possible missing link between Laboulbeniales and Pyrenomycetes.' *Mycologia,* 65, 614-647.

KOHLMEYER, J., and KOHLMEYER, E. (1965). 'New marine fungi from mangroves and trees along eroding shorelines.' *Nova Hedwigia,* 9, 89-104.

KOHLMEYER, J., and KOHLMEYER, E. (1966). 'On the life history of marine Ascomycetes: *Halosphaeria mediosetigera* and *H. circumvestita.' Nova Hedwigia,* 12, 189-202.

KOHLMEYER, J., and KOHLMEYER, E. (1971 a). *Synoptic Plates of Higher Marine Fungi.* 3rd Ed. Cramer, Lehre, 68 pp.

KOHLMEYER, J., and KOHLMEYER, E. (1971 b). 'Marine fungi from tropical America and Africa.' *Mycologia,* 63, 831-861.

KOHLMEYER, J., and KOHLMEYER, E. (1972 a). 'Is *Ascophyllum nodosum* lichenised?*Botanica mar.,* 15, 109-112.

KOHLMEYER, J., and KOHLMEYER, E. (1972 b). 'A new genus of marine Ascomycetes on *Ulva vexata* Setch et Gard.' *Bot. Jb. Syst.,* 92, 429-432.

KOHLMEYER, J., SCHMIDT, I., and NAIR, N. B. (1967). 'Eine neue *Corollospora* (Ascomycetes) aus dem Indischen Ozean und des Ostsee.' *Ber. dt. bot. Ges.,* 80, 98-102.

LEMMERMANN, E. (1901). 'Die parasitischen und saprophytischen pilze der algen.' *Ab. Naturwiss. Ver. Bremen.,* 17, 185-202.

LIND, J. (1913). *Danish Fungi as Represented in the Herarium of E. Rostrup.* Copenhagen.

LLOYD, L. S. (1954). 'Fungi on *Spartina townsendii.'* Thesis, University of Wales, Aberystwyth.

LUTLEY, M., and WILSON, I. M. (1972 a). 'Development and fine structure of ascospores in the marine fungus *Ceriosporopsis halima.' Trans. Br. mycol. Soc.,* 58, 393-402.

LUTLEY, M., and WILSON, I. M. (1972 b). 'Observations on the fine structure of ascospores of marine fungi: *Halosphaeria appendiculata, Torpedosporo radiata* and *Corollospora maritima.' Trans. Br. mycol. Soc.* 59, 219-227.

MAIRE, R., and CHEMIN, E. (1922). 'Un nouveau Pyrénomycète marin.' *C. r. hebd. Séanc. Acad. Sci., Paris,* 175, 319-321.

MALACAIZA, L., and MARTINEZ, A. (1971). 'Ascomycetes marinos de Argentina.' *Bot. Soc. Argentina Botanica,* 14, 57-72.

MELNIK, V. A., and PETROV, Y. E. (1966). 'De specie nova fungi in alga marina *Ascophyllum nodosum* (L.) Le Jolis. (Phaeophyceae) inventa notula.' *Nov. Sist. Niz. Rust.,* 211-212.

MEYERS, S. P. (1954). 'Marine fungi in Biscayne Bay, Florida 2. Further studies of occurrence and distribution.' *Bull. mar. Sci. Gulf Caribb.,* 3, 307-327.

MEYERS, S. P. (1957). 'Taxonomy of marine Pyrenomycetes.' *Mycologia,* 49, 475-528.

MEYERS, S. P. (1968). 'Observations on the physiological ecology of marine fungi.' *Bull. Misaki Marine Biol. Inst. Kyoto Univ.,* 12, 207-225.

MEYERS, S. P. (1969). 'Thalassiomycetes XI. Further studies of the genus *Lindra* with a description of *L. marinera,* a new species.' *Mycologia,* 71,486-495.

MEYERS, S. P. (1971). 'Isolation and identification of filamentous marine fungi.' In *Marine Borers, Fungi and Fouling Organisms of Wood.* (Eds. E. B. G. Jones and S. K. Eltringham). O.E.C.D. Paris, 89-113.

MEYERS, S. P., and REYNOLDS, E. S. (1960). 'Occurrence of lignicolous fungi in Northern Atlantic and Pacific marine localities.' *Can. J. Bot.,* 38, 217-226.

MEYERS, S. P., NICHOLSON, M. E., MILES, P., RHEE, J. S., and AHEARN, D. G. (1970). 'Mycological studies in Barataria Bay, Louisiana and biodegradation of oyster grass, *Spartina alterniflora, Louisiana State Univ. Coastal Studies Bull.,* 5, 111-124.

MEYERS, S. P., and KOHLMEYER, J. (1965). '*Varicosporina ramulosa* gen. nov. sp. nov., and aquatic hyphomycete from marine areas.' *Can. J. Bot.,* 43, 915-921.

MEYERS, S. P., and SCOTT, E. (1967). 'Thalassiomycetes. X. Variation in growth and reproduction of two isolates of *Corollospora maritima.' Mycologia,* 59, 446-455.

MEYERS, S. P., and SCOTT, E. (1968). 'Cellulose degradation by *Lulworthia floridana* and other lignicolous marine fungi.' *Marine Biology,* 2, 41-46.

MEYERS, S. P., ORPURT, P. A., SIMMS, J., and BORAL, L. L. (1965). 'Thalassiomycetes VII. Observations on fungal infestation of turtle grass, *Thalassia testudinum* König.' *Bull. mar. Sci. Gulf Caribb.,* 15, 548-564.

MIYABE, K., and TOKIDA, J. (1948). 'Black-dots disease of *Gloiopeltis furcata* Post et Rupr. caused by a new ascomycetous fungus.' *Bot. Mag. Tokyo,* 61, 116-118.

MÜLLER, E., and von ARX, J. A. (1962). 'Die gattungen der didymosporen Pyrenomyceten.' *Beitr. kryptogamenflora Schwerz,* 11, 1-922.

NAWAWI, A. (1973). 'Two clamp-bearing aquatic fungi from Malaysia.' *Trans. Br. mycol. Soc.,* 61, 521-528.

NEISH, G. A. (1970). 'Lignicolous marine fungi from Nova Scotia.' *Can. J. Bot.,* 48, 2319-2322.

NICOT, J. (1958). 'Quelques micromycètes des sables littoraux.' *Bull. Soc. mycol. France,* 74, 223-235.

NICOT, J. (1958). 'Une moisissure arénicole du littoral Atlantique: *Dendryphiella arenaria* sp. nov.' *Revue mycol.,* 23, 87-99.

OUDEMANS, C. A. J. A. (1894). 'Ouer twee nog oubekende fungi: *Septoria dictyotae* en *Ustilago vuyckii.' Versl. Zittingen wisen nat. Afd. kon. Akad. Wet.,* 3, 54-57.

PATOUILLARD, W. (1897). '*Zignoella calospora'. J. Bot.,* 11, 242.

PATOUILLARD, W., and HARIOT, P. (1903). 'Une alque parasitée par une Sphériacee, *J. Bot,* 17, 228.

POOLE, N. J. (1971). 'A study of the cellulose decomposing soil fungi of the Medway area of Kent'. Ph.D. Thesis, University of London.

POOLE, N. J., and PRICE, P. C. (1972). 'Fungi colonizing wood submerged in the Medway estuary.' *Trans. Br. mycol. Soc.,* 59, 333-335.

REED, M. (1902). 'Two new ascomycetous fungi parasitic on marine algae.' *Univ. Calif. Publ. Bot.,* 1, 141-164.

RITCHIE, D. (1957). 'Salinity optima for marine fungi affected by temperature.' *Am. J. Bot.,* 44, 870-874.

RITCHIE, D. (1959). 'The effect of salinity and temperature on marine and other fungi from various climates.' *Bull. Torrey Bot. Club,* 36, 367-373.

RITCHIE, D. (1960). 'The evolution of salinity tolerance in fungi.' *Trans. NY Acad. Sci.,* 23, 138-140.

ROSENVINGE, L. K. (1906). 'Meddelelser fra den botaniske forening 1. *Leptosphaeria marina* Rostr.' *Bot. Tidsskr.,* 27, 33-35.

ROSTRUP, E. (1889). 'Mykologiske Meddelelser.' *Bot. Tidsskr.,* 17, 228-237.

SACHS, J. (1874). *Lehrbuch der Botanik. vierte, umgearbeitete Auflage.* Liepzig, Wilhelm Engelmann.

SCHAUMANN, K. (1968). 'Marine hohere pilze (Ascomycetes und Fungi Imperfecti) aus dem Weser-Ästuar'. *Veröff. Inst. Meeresforsch. Bremerh.,* 11, 93-118.

SCHAUMANN, K. (1969). 'Über marine hohere pilze von holzsubstraten der Nordsee Insel Helgoland.' *Ber. dt. bot. Ges.,* 82, 307-327.

SCHAUMANN, K. (1972 a). '*Biconiosporella corniculata* nov. gen. et. nov. spec. ein holzbesiedelnder Ascomycet des marinen litoralis.' *Veröff. Inst. Meerforsch. Bremerh.,* 14, 23-44.

SCHAUMANN, K. (1972 b). '*Corollospora intermedia* (Ascomycetes, Halosphaeriaceae) vom sanstrand der Insel Helgoland (Deutsche Bucht).' *Veröff. Inst. Meerforsch. Bremerh.,* 14, 13-22.

SCHAUMANN, K. (1973). '*Brachysporium helgolandicum* nov. sp., ein neuer Deuteromycet auf treibborke im Meer.' *Helgolander wiss. Meersunters,* 25, 26-34.

SCHMIDT, I. (1967). 'Über das vorkommen mariner Ascomyceten und Fungi Imperfecti in des Ostzee und einigen angrenzenden boddengewasseru'. *Natur. Naturschutz Mecklenburg,* 5, 115-126.

SCHMIDT, I. (1969). '*Corollospora intermedia,* nov. spec., *Carbosphaerella leptosphaerioides,* nov. spec. und *Crinigera maritima,* nov. gen., nov. spec., 3, neue marine pilzarten von der Ostseekuste.' *Natur. Naturschutz Mechlenburg,* 7, 5-14.

SHAW, D. E. (1972). '*Ingoldiella hamata* gen. et sp. nov., a fungus with clamp connections from a stream in north Queensland.' *Trans. Br. mycol. Soc.,* 59, 255-259.

SHEARER, C. A. (1972). 'Fungi of the Chesapeake bay and its tributaries. III The distribution of wood inhabitating Ascomycetes and Fungi Imperfecti of the Patuxent river.' *Am. J. Bot.,* 59, 961-969.

SIVANESAN, A., and MANNERS, J. G. (1970). 'Fungi associated with *Spartina townsendii* in healthy and 'die-back' sites.' *Trans. Br. mycol. Soc.,* 55, 191-204.

SUTHERLAND, G. K. (1915 a). 'New marine fungi on *Pelvetia.*' *New Phytol.,* 14, 33-42

SUTHERLAND, G. K. (1915 b). 'Additional notes on marine Pyrenomycetes.' *New Phytol.,* 14, 183-193.

SUTHERLAND, G. K. (1915 c). 'New marine Pyrenomycetes.' *Trans. Br. mycol. Soc.,* 5, 147-155.

SUTHERLAND, G. K. (1916 a). 'Marine Fungi Imperfecti.' *New Phytol.,* 15, 35-48.

SUTHERLAND, G. K. (1916 b). 'Additional notes on marine Pyrenomycetes.' *Trans. Br. mycol. Soc.,* 5, 257-263.

TUBAKI, K. (1966). 'Marine fungi from Japan. Lignicolous.' *Trans. mycol. Soc. Japan,* 8, 5-10;

TUBAKI, K. (1968). 'Studies on the Japanese Marine fungi. Lignicolous group II.' *Pub. Seto. Mar. Biol. Lab.,* 15, 357-372.

TUBAKI, K. (1969). 'Studies on the Japanese marine fungi lignicolous group (III), algicolous group and a general consideration.' *Am. Rep. Inst. Fermentation Osaka,* 4, 12-41.

TUBAKI, K., and ASANO, I. (1965). 'Additional species to fungi isolated from the Antarctic materials.' *Jap. Sci. Reports., Biology,* 27, 1-12.

WAGNER, D. T. (1965). 'Developmental morphology of *Leptosphaeria discors* (Saccardo and Ellis) Saccardo and Ellis.' *Nova Hedwigia,* 9, 45-61.

WEBBER, F. C. (1967). 'Observations on the structure, life history and biology of *Mycosphaerella ascophylli.' Trans. Br. mycol. Soc.,* 50, 583-601.

WILSON, I. M. (1951). 'Notes on some marine fungi.' *Trans. Br. mycol. Soc.,* 34, 540-543.

WILSON, I. M. (1954). *'Ceriosporopsis halima* Linder and *Ceriosporopsis cambrensis* sp. nov.: two marine pyrenomycetes on wood.' *Trans. Br. mycol. Soc.,* 37, 272-285.

WILSON, I. M. (1956). 'Some new marine pyrenomycetes on wood or rope: *Halophiobolus* and *Lindra.' Trans. Br. mycol. Soc.,* 39, 401-415.

WILSON, I. M. (1960). 'Marine fungi: A review of the present position.' *Proc. Linn. Soc. Lond.,* 171, 53-70.

WILSON, I. M. (1965). 'Development of the perithecium and ascospores of *Ceriosporopsis halima.' Trans. Br. mycol. Soc.,* 48, 19-33.

WILSON, I. M., and KNOYLE, J. M. (1961). 'Three species of *Didymosphaeria* on marine algae: *D. danica* (Berlese) comb. nov., *D. pelvetiana* Suth., and *D. fucicola* Suth.' Trans. Br. mycol. Soc., 44, 55-71.

ZELLER, S. M. (1918). 'Fungi found on *Codium mucronatum.' Publ. Puget Sound Mar. Stai, Univ. Wash.,* 2, 121-125.

2 Mangrove Fungi: The Succession in the Mycoflora of Red Mangrove (*Rhizophora mangle* L.) Seedlings*

STEVEN Y. NEWELL

2.1 Introduction

2.1.1 Previous Studies

The study of mangrove fungi has progressed along two avenues of research. One of these has been the approach of Kohlmeyer (citations below) who has conducted extensive searches for fungi inhabiting the woody tissues of mangroves. He has restricted his work to those species of higher marine mangrove fungi (*sensu* Kohlmeyer

---

*Based on portions of a dissertation submitted in partial fulfilment of the requirements for the Ph.D. degree, University of Miami, Rosenstiel School of Marine and Atmospheric Science. Contribution from the University of Miami, Rosenstiel School of Marine and Atmospheric Science, Miami, Florida 33149.

and Kohlmeyer, 1971 b, cf, Section 2.4.6.) which can be directly observed in their fruiting stages without the use of any cultural techniques. As a consequence, his excellent, meticulous studies deal with those species which produce fruiting bodies (basidiocarps, ascocarps or pycnidia) and those hyphomycetes which produce determinate, stable holoblastic conidia. Kohlmeyer contributed his first major taxonomic and distributional study of marine mangrove tissue-inhabiting fungi in 1965 (Kohlmeyer and Kohlmeyer, 1965), then published several others in following years, including a compilation with notes on ecology (1969 a). He has since added new information on mangrove fungi from Hawaii (1969 b) and from tropical America and Africa (Kohlmeyer and Kohlmeyer, 1971 a). The 1969 a and 1971 a papers should be consulted for tables listing the marine mangrove fungi, their substrates and their geographical collection areas. Cribb and Cribb (1955, 1956) have conducted studies in Australia similar to those of Kohlmeyer.

The second approach to the study of mangrove fungi has involved strictly cultural work with fungi which can be isolated from sediments beneath mangrove stands. Several of these studies, as a consequence of their nutrient agar culturing methods, deal only with the higher fungi plus Zygomycetes. Swart (1958, 1963) examined the culturable mycoflora of mangrove soils in eastern Africa. Rai *et al.* (1969) sampled mud from Indian mangrove swamps. Lee and Baker (1972 a, b) investigated the soil microfungi of a Hawaiian mangrove swamp. Two papers, by Stolk (1955) and Pawar *et al.* (1967), include descriptions of new species (of Eurotiaceae and *Phoma*, respectively) cultured from mangrove muds. As might be expected, the lists of species of fungi reported by these authors include none of those studied by Kohlmeyer (except, perhaps, *Phoma* spp., and a *Robillarda* sp. and *Periconia* sp. reported by Swart (1958) which conceivably could have been *R. rhizophorae* Kohlm. and *P. prolifica* Anastasiou, both listed by Kohlmeyer (1969 a) as marine mangrove fungi). No attempts were made, other than laboratory experimentation with physiology, to differentiate between active and inactive members of the mycoflora reported (granted, this is a difficult proposition, as discussed in detail by Gray and Williams (1971)). Consequently, Kohlmeyer (1969 a) has declined to include the species involved as members of the mangrove mycocommunity (= mycological community).

Occurrence and physiology of lower fungi (namely ectoplasmic-net fungi (*sensu* Perkins, 1972) and Chytridiomycetes) from mangrove sediment in Brazil were studied by Ulken (1970, 1972). Her distribution work was done by baiting of aqueous samples with sterile pine pollen.

The object of the present study was to determine what species of fungi constitute the mycocommunities which occur on and within autochthonous mangrove habitat material as it is degraded from living organic material through dead organic debris to particulate organic detritus. The study programme was designed along the lines of the established succession study methods of investigators such as Kendrick and Burges (1962; substrate: pine needles), Hering (1965; substrate: oak forest leaves), Frankland (1966; substrate: bracken fronds), and Hudson (1962; substrate: sugar cane; general review in 1968). Having determined the nature of a succession of fungi in a maritime-marine environment, it was intended to relate this to the general pattern of terrestrial fungal successions (Garrett, 1963; Hudson, 1968; Ruscoe, 1971), and to what little is now known about fungal successions in freshwater (Pugh and Mulder, 1971; substrate: cattail leaves; Taligoola *et al.*, 1973; substrate: reed leaves and culms) and marine environments (Jones, 1963, 1968; Meyers, 1953, 1954; Meyers and Reynolds, 1960: all dealing with non-autochthonous woody materials; Meyers *et al.*, 1965: dealing with blades of a marine grass).

2.1.2 The Mangrove Substrate

The substrate chosen for this study was seedlings of the red mangrove (*Rhizophora mangle* L.) (Figs. 2.1-2.3). The red mangrove is common to undeveloped tropical marine coastlines in the Americas (Long and Lakela, 1971), and is the dominant tree in the Saline Mangrove Province (Craighead, 1971) of South Florida. The red mangrove distribution extends from below the mean low tide level to several miles inland in some localities (Davis, 1940; Craighead, 1971). The tree is well adapted for life as a halophyte. Its tissue fluid solute concentration is higher than that of seawater, while the xylem sap is nearly free of salts; a freshwater supply is acquired via an ultrafiltration system in the root cell membranes and the actively maintained high tissue fluid solute concentration permits production of turgor (Scholander, 1968).

The seedlings of the red mangrove are viviparously produced; the fruits germinate while still on the tree to produce the long (up to 46 cm) pendant seedlings (La Rue and Muzik, 1954; Gill and Tomlinson, 1969). Seedlings are produced year round, but bulk seedling fall occurs in June, July and August (Davis, 1940; Argo, 1963). The great majority of the seedlings fail to take root (Egler, 1948), and the number of seedlings set adrift in southeastern Florida coastal waters has been estimated to run into the millions (Stephens, 1969). Most, if not all, either sink to the bottom after 30 days or less or become entrapped within the maze of proproots in the littoral zone of red mangrove swamps.

Except for those few which establish themselves, red mangrove seedlings contribute organic material to the detritus based food web of southern Florida's estuaries, as is documented for other sources (leaves, twigs, etc.) of mangrove detritus (Heald and Odum, 1969, 1974). As has been demonstrated for detritus based food webs in other environments (Darnell, 1964; Newell, 1965; Adams and Angelovic, 1970; E. P. Odum, 1971), Heald and Odum showed that the food web of the Florida Bay estuarine ecosystem is based largely on plant detritus (mostly of red mangrove origin) and attendant microbes (fungi, bacteria and protozoa). The microbes convert the refractory detrital material of plant origin into microbial biomass, thereby nutritionally enriching the detrital particles for the detritivores at the base of the food web (E. P. Odum, 1971). Kaushik and Hynes (1971) have demonstrated that the fungi are the main agents of this phenomenon in aquatic environments. Thus an important effect of this study is to clarify the understanding of the pattern of fungal contribution to this process.

2.2 Materials and Methods

2.2.1 Selection of Seedlings

Over 1000 mature, healthy seedlings were hand picked from *Rhizophora mangle* trees in southern Florida in late October 1970. The criteria for maturity were the appearance of the fused cotyledonary collar (Fig. 2.1), and the ease of separation of the seedlings from the collar, indicating the onset of natural abscission (Bowman, 1917; Argo, 1963; Gill and Tomlinson, 1969). No seedlings were used which were less than 10 cm long, since seedlings less than 5 cm long are unable to root readily (La Rue and Muzik, 1954).

The seedlings were divided into three sets. One set was not treated prior to placing in the field. One set was weighed (wet) and marked by loosely attaching plastic numbered tags with rubber bands. The third set was given uniform artificial injuries.

2.1

2.2, 2.3

2.4

Figs. 2.1-2.4 *Rhizophora mangle* L. **Fig. 2.1.** Seedlings protruding from fruits—the cotyledonary collar can be seen as the light area between the hypocotyl and the fruit of the seedling in the foreground, **Fig. 2.2.** A successfully rooted, first-year seedling—most seedlings suffer the fate of the two decaying seedlings at its base, **Fig. 2.3.** A young tree with characteristic proproots, **Fig. 2.4.** Dead and decaying pre-injured seedlings which were sampled by cork borer discing. The bar represents 2 cm.

These injuries were administered by removing with a cork borer a 2.0 cm^2 (surface area) disc of tissue including epidermis inward through cortex to the vascular tissue (Fig. 2.4).

The injured set was prepared because it was discovered during collection of seedlings that many of the seedlings were naturally injured before or shortly after their fall from the parent trees. The agents of these injuries, which occurred most often on the radicle (that portion of the seedling covered by brown cork tissue), include rodents, crabs, beetles and perhaps other animals. Injuries of this type do not kill the seedlings; La Rue and Muzik (1954) found that even cutting 5 cm lengths from the radicles of seedlings did not prevent them from rooting.

2.2.2 Establishment of Stations

Station sites were chosen such that a range of hydrographic conditions characteristic of coastal waters of southeastern Florida would be represented. Only three of these stations were sampled throughout the study period; the remaining five were lost at intervals during the study period due to unforeseen difficulties with human interference. Fortunately, the three stations which persisted (numbers 2, 5 and 7; Fig. 2.5 and 2.6) were representative of three of the most common types of degradation sites of seedlings in southeastern Florida, namely intraswamp sites in the eastern and Florida Bay Saline Mangrove Provinces (stations 2 and 7, respectively) where many are trapped among the mazes of *Rhizophora* proproots, and extra-estuarine sites (station 5) into which many are washed via tide flux (Davis, 1940; Stephens, 1969; and personal observations) and sink to the bottom. Data from mid-estuary sites and supralittoral sites were incompletely gathered.

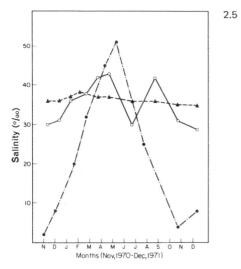

2.5

Fig. 2.5. Salinity for stations 2, 5 and 7. Values are readings (refractive salinometer) taken during each collection trip. The highest salinity values at stations 2 and 7 are probably not reached every year, for 1971 was a drought year in South Florida. ○ —— ○ = station 2; ▲ --- ▲ = station 5; ● · --- ● = station 7.

Nylon mesh bags (mesh size 4 mm x 4 mm) were used to contain the experimental seedlings at station sites. Three bags of seedlings, one for each experimental set (weighed -marked, injured, and uninjured), were tied with nylon cord to anchors or mangrove roots at each station. The bags were submerged at all times. Seedlings were allotted to the bags at random, so that no station would have a preponderance of seedlings from any one of the parent trees.

It must be noted that the use of mesh bags (or other similar traps) in experiments of this kind, though widely practised, has been criticized by Wiegert and Evans (1964).

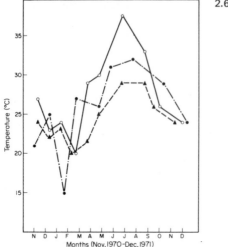

Fig. 2.6. Temperature for stations 2, 5 and 7. Values are readings taken during each collection trip. ○ —— ○ = station 2; ▲ --- ▲ = station 5; ● --- ● = station 7.

They found, in their study of disappearance of dead plant material in an old field, that containing the material in plastic screen mesh bags caused a marked decrease in the rate of breakdown with respect to that which occurred in unbagged material. They attributed this to disturbance of natural stratification and to restriction of availability of the material to soil invertebrates and decomposers. Whether or not these considerations apply to the present study is uncertain, for it is not practicable to study the progress of decay of uncontained seedlings in the mangrove environment, with its high rate of water flux. However, the mesh size (4 mm) of the nylon bags used in the present study was larger than that (2.5 mm) used by Heald and Odum (1974), who found that their 2.5 mm mesh bags allowed as much detritivore grazing as 1.5 cm mesh bags in their study of red mangrove leaf degradation.

2.2.3   Collection and Processing of Seedlings

Collection   Six seedlings were collected at approximately monthly or two-monthly intervals from each bag of injured and uninjured seedlings and returned to the laboratory in sterile plastic bags (Nasco Whirl-Pak). The seedlings were treated with a combination of sampling observation methods similar to those of many of the fungal succession studies reviewed by Hudson (1968). The methods are closest to a combination of those used by Kendrick and Burges (1962) and Hering (1965) but include modifications and additions as described below. A flow diagram for the sampling procedures is given in Fig. 2.7.

The three seedling 'levels' referred to below are herein defined as follows: radicle + rootlets—that portion of the seedling within approximately 5 cm of the radicle tip which is covered by brown cork tissue, and the rootlets which eventually emerge from the radicle tip; upper hypocotyl + epicotyl—that portion of the seedling within approximately 2 cm of the tip of the hypocotyl, and the small epicotyl at its tip; mid-hypocotyl—that portion of the seedling between the 'upper hypocotyl' and 'radicle'.

Disc plating   Sterile cork borers were used to cut discs (Fig. 2.4) of epidermis plus cortex tissue (cut through to the vascular tissue layer) from the three levels (mid-

56

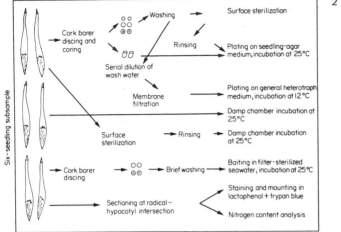

Fig. 2.7. Flow diagram for the sampling observation procedures used.

radicle—2.0 cm² disc; mid-hypocotyl—2.0 cm² disc; upper hypocotyl—1.1 cm² disc)
on two of the six seedlings from each bag. These discs were given a preliminary wash
(5 seconds agitation by hand) in glass vials of 11 ml sterile seawater (15°/oo salinity)
then washed thoroughly (1 min agitation by hand) in a second vial of 11 ml sterile
seawater (15°/oo). The water from this final wash was stored at 2° C for later treatment
(within 5 hours).

The seedling discs were taken from the final wash and submersed in a 1:10,000
HgCl₂ solution in 5% ethanol for surface sterilizing (1 min agitation by hand). After
rinsing in sterile deionized water (three changes, 1 min hand agitation in each), the
discs were placed on plates of a mangrove seedling-agar medium (MSA medium).
This medium consisted of 4% whole, finely ground dried mangrove seedlings plus 2%
agar in seawater of 15°/oo salinity. Chloromycetin (a Parke-Davis chloramphenicol
preparation) was added at 0.02% to prevent bacterial growth. The salinity of 15°/oo
was chosen: (1) because it fell at about the midpoint of the range of salinities encountered at the experiment stations; (2) for the purpose of most effective comparison
with the study of red mangrove leaf mycoflora (Fell and Master, 1973) which involved
the use of media of 15°/oo salinity; and (3) because obligately marine fungi will grow
and fruit on media of this salinity (Jones *et al.,* 1971).

In addition to seedling discs, a 5 mm length of 0.6 mm diameter cylindrical core was
taken longitudinally by cork borer from the pith tissue at upper radicle level of each
disced seedling. These were placed on the MSA plates with the discs, so that each plate
had the three discs and one pith core from each seedling. These plates (referred to
hereafter as 'disc plates') were incubated at 25° C and observed at 3 days and then at
2 week intervals (a maximum of 4) for appearance and development of fungi.

Filtration and plating of wash water   The final seawater wash from the disc treatments was used to enumerate washable (removable from the discs by washing) viable
elements of fungi (including yeasts) and bacteria present on disc surfaces. These
surfaces included interior as well as exterior portions of seedlings, and so bacterial
numbers may well have reflected viable elements washed from interior tissues in decayed seedlings, for in these seedlings bacteria and protozoa often invaded the pith
tissues.

The final wash water from the disc washings was serially diluted in sterile seawater ($15°/oo$) to 1:100. The final wash and the 1:100 dilution water (10 ml and 9 ml respectively) were aseptically filtered through cellulose ester membrane filters (Millipore Corp.) of pore size 0.45 μm. The filters were transferred to plates of a general heterotroph isolation medium (2.3% Difco Nutrient Agar, 2.0% glucose, 0.1% yeast extract, and 0.2% Difco agar, in seawater of $15°/oo$ salinity). These plates, hereafter referred to as 'wash plates', were incubated at $12°C$ in order to retard over-growth by filamentous fungi. Two sets of the isolation medium were used; one set with 0.02% chloromycetin was used with the undiluted wash water for observation of fungi, and one set without the added antibiotic was used for enumeration of bacteria from the 1:100 diluted samples.

In retrospect, it seems that the use of the $12°C$ incubation temperature in combination with the relatively high glucose concentration in the wash plate technique was unfortunate. These two factors may have prevented the development of some fungi, especially in the face of competition from sugar fungi (Cochrane, 1958, pp. 85-86; Kohlmeyer, 1969; Dickinson and Kent, 1972). Therefore, tabulation of frequencies of fungi are presented (Table 2.2) both including and excluding the wash plate data, and effects of the selectivity of the wash plate method can also be examined by reference to Table 2.5.

Induction of fruiting   All colonies of filamentous fungi which did not fruit on original isolation plates (disc plates and wash plates) were transferred to plates of MSA medium with 0.1% yeast extract added. These plates had an autoclaved sterilized disc (2 cm^2, taken from mid-radicle) from a fresh seedling placed on the surface of the gelled agar prior to inoculation. Following inoculation, these 'sporulation plates' were incubated for 3 to 5 days in the dark at $25°C$, then transferred to a $21°C$ incubator under long wave ultraviolet light as prescribed by Booth (1971), where they remained until fruiting structures appeared (or for a maximum of 90 days).

Damp chamber incubation   Two seedlings from each subsample were incubated in baking dish damp chambers (Meyers and Reynolds, 1958; Johnson *et al.*, 1959). These seedlings received no pre-treatment prior to incubation other than agitation in ambient water to remove adherent sedimentary particles. The dishes were sealed with clear tape and incubated at $25°C$. They were examined after 30 days for fruiting fungi.

The long incubation period prior to examination is contrary to Hudson's (1968) recommendation. He felt that only a 2 day incubation should be used, because otherwise some metabolically active fungi might fruit and disappear, and fungi which were only present as casually occurring spores might be allowed to develop. Examination of a few of the chambers throughout this study during the first week of incubation and again at 30 days indicated that no species had disappeared which had originally been present. Those which appeared after 30 days were species which required longer periods to produce recognizable mature stages (e.g. Ascomycetes such as *Keissleriella blepharospora* J. et E. Kohlm. and *Lulworthia* spp.).

Seedlings from the damp chamber observations were tested for viability at each collection period. After having been incubated in damp chambers for 30 days, those which were not obviously dead and decayed were placed upright in partial sunlight in glass containers with freshwater reaching to about mid-radicle level. Seedlings were considered viable if they were able to produce roots and leaves and non-viable if they became brown and withered.

Baiting from discs in sterile seawater   The final two seedlings from each subsample were subjected to cork borer discing, but in this case, 2.0 cm² discs of epidermis plus cortex were taken from two levels (mid-radicle and mid-hypocotyl). They were washed briefly (10 seconds agitation by hand) in 10 ml of sterile seawater and placed in covered glass dishes (5 cm diam) with 20 ml of filter-sterilized seawater (15°/∘∘) containing 0.05% each of penicillin G and streptomycin sulphate. The dishes were then baited with a small amount of autoclave-sterilized, dried, ground seedling powder and incubated at 25°C. Both baits and submerged discs were observed at 10 days and 30 days for the development of lower fungi. These samples are referred to hereafter as 'baited dishes'.

A mid-study methodology change   After the April-May 1971 collection period, all but stations 2, 5 and 7 had been lost. Therefore, in order to maintain a large enough number of observations per collection period to retain validity of results, each of the sampling methods except damp chamber was performed in triplicate. Also, collections were made every other month rather than monthly to avoid exhaustion of the supply of experimental seedlings in the field. Instead of tripling the damp chamber samples, an additional method was initiated, namely surface sterilization prior to damp chamber incubation (Fig. 2.7). The seedlings involved were the disced ones used for preparation of the disc plates. They were surface sterilized and rinsed as in the disc plate method, and incubated as in the untreated-seedling damp chamber method. Since the experimental regime differed between the November-May and the June-December periods, results for these portions of the study period are presented separately in Table 2.5.

Dry weight change, nitrogen analysis and staining of sections   Dry weight change determinations were made on two seedlings from each of the bags of pre-weighed and tagged seedlings. Original dry weight was determined by reference to a regression of original dry weight on original wet weight which had been performed on a 30 seedling sample. The regression was linear and highly significant ($p = 0.001$); the value with 95% confidence interval for dry weight at mean wet weight was 10.10 ± 1.22 g. The values of dry weight change for injured seedlings shown in Fig. 2.25 were determined by reference to another linear regression ($p = 0.01$), of dry weight on seedling length (dry weight at mean seedling length with 95% confidence interval = 8.09 ± 2.50 g).

Nitrogen-content analyses were conducted on a Perkin-Elmer Elemental Analyzer Model 240. Analytical samples were obtained by taking 3 mm thick cross-sections of seedlings at the uppermost radicle level, drying the sections to constant weight at 104°C, and grinding the dried sections to a fine powder. Four seedlings from each collection and from each of three stations (numbers 2, 5 and 7) were sectioned. The seedlings were stored at −40°C prior to processing.

Four seedlings from each collection and from each of the three stations were also sectioned at the uppermost radicle level at 25 μm thickness. These sections were mounted in lactophenol plus trypan blue stain (0.2% w/v) and examined for the presence of fungal structures. The trypan blue staining method (Boedijn, 1956) has been used to study extent of fungal invasion of plant tissues (Ruscoe, 1971), but dematiaceous structures are not stained. In red mangrove seedling sections, unstained intracellular dematiaceous structures were often difficult to identify as fungal in nature, and some heavily stained structures were of dubious fungal origin. Therefore, uninvaded tissue and tissue known to be invaded by members of the seedling mycoflora were stained and compared to ascertain which commonly seen structures did represent fungal tissue.

Frequency calculations and statistical treatments   Frequency of occurrence figures

(Tables 2.2 and 2.5) were computed as follows: number of recorded occurrences/ number of possibilities for occurrence, x 100. One possibility for occurrence was allotted for each wash plate (undiluted sample), one for each disc plate, and one for each seedling in damp chamber. The baited dish results were not included, since the baited dishes were intended only for recording of lower fungi, only ectoplasmic-net fungi among the lower fungi were regularly recorded from baited dishes, and these fungi (*Thraustochytrium* sp. and *Labyrinthula* sp.) were not recorded by any other method. Consolidation of records for the other methods was done because the selectivity of each method quite possibly over- or underemphasized the impor-tance of some species; in combining data from the methods, the occurrence fre-quencies were hopefully brought into perspective. The effect of combining the records can be perceived for individual species by reference to Table 2.5 which presents separated occurrence frequencies among methods and injured versus unin-jured sets of seedlings.

Relative occurrence frequencies are reported for major taxa (Fig. 2.19). Relative occurrence frequency equals the number of records of the members of the taxon/ the total number of records of fungal species, x 100. Again, records from the baited dish results were not included.

Statistical methods used were as follows: one-tailed testing of difference among frequencies—chi square test of two independent samples; testing of difference among totalled numbers of occurrences—chi square one sample test. Both of these non-parametric tests were from Siegel (1956). Minimum significance level used was $\alpha = 0.05$. Normalization of numbers of occurrences was conducted in reporting of numbers of occurrence where numbers of observations were unequal, so that comparison of the figures could be readily made. These adjusted figures were not statistically tested, and the numbers of observations are reported wherever figures have been adjusted.

The rationale for the methodology   The use of the four different fungal sampling observation methods was adopted in order to avoid some of the drawbacks of some previous studies. Johnson (1967) and Hudson (1968) have pointed out that some reported successions are not the result of successive phases of colonization, but merely the result of differing times required for fruiting of fungi which were all mem-bers of one contemporary community. Johnson was referring to reported marine fungal successions and Hudson to terrestrial studies which relied on direct observa-tional techniques. Instead of direct observation alone, direct observation after damp chamber incubation was used in the present study. so that not only those fungi which were fruiting at the time of collection were recorded, but also those which had colonized but not fruited. Since some of these non-fruiting colonizers might not have been able to fruit in damp chamber in competition with species better established in the substrate, agar-culturing of surface sterilized seedling portions was used to permit their detection.

Hudson (1968) pointed out the advantage of this sort of technique in this regard, but also added that fungi which produce sclerotia or other dormancy structures could also be detected after their active role in the fungal community had ceased. *Cladosporium herbarum* (Pers.) Link was given as an example of a species which was probably culturally detectable after completion of its active role in the fungal succes-sion on beech leaves (Hogg and Hudson, 1966). In the present study, by contrast, records of *C. cladosporioides* (Fr.) de Vries (= *C. herbarum* according to some authors (de Vries, 1952)) declined in frequency with time just as rapidly from agar culturing of seedling discs as from damp chamber incubation of seedlings (Table 2.5).

The remaining two methods, wash plates and baited dishes, served respectively to bring out changes in frequency of occurrence of surface limited fungal and bacterial propagules and of fungi which could only develop in submerged water culture.

2.3   Results

As a prelude to this section, two factors which blur or deter from full comprehension of the succession image must be brought out. Firstly, a large degree of variation in rate of senescence and time of death of seedlings was observed within and among stations as well as within and between the injured and uninjured sets of seedlings. Thus the heterotrophic succession did not occur in as well defined stages as might have been the case if all seedlings (or all seedlings of a given set) had senesced and died approximately simultaneously. Second, because of unforeseen difficulties with field conditions, a shortage of experimental seedlings brought about termination of the succession study before seedlings at all stations had reached the stage of breakdown to particulate detritus. In order to have recorded the mycosere as completely as possible, the seedling mycocommunities should have been monitored to the particulate detritus stage, when all seedling material would have joined either sediment or suspended organic matter.

The succession image described in the following paragraphs was synthesized by combining the separate occurrence results from the experimental station sites, from the different sampling methods, from the different levels on seedlings from which samples or observations were taken, and from the injured and uninjured sets of seedlings. Each of these factors influenced the results obtained; combining the data from each part of the experimental regime yielded a comprehensive, integrated image of the seedling mycosere (= mycological sere, or fungal succession).

2.3.1   The Mycoflora

From the 460 wash plate, disc plate and damp chamber sampling observations, and the 95 baited dish sampling observations conducted during the 13 month study period, 947 occurrences of fungi (excluding yeasts) were recorded, representing 84 species of fruiting fungi. Only 1.3% of the occurrences were of strains which could not be induced to produce sexual or vegetative structures which would lead to their identification. The 84 species, listed in Table 2.1, were aligned among major taxa as follows: hyphomycetes—42 species; Sphaeropsidales—19 species; Ascomycetes—13 species; Melanconiales—3 species; Oömycetes—3 species; ectoplasmic-net fungi—2 species; Zygomycetes—1 species; Basidiomycetes—1 species. Many of these species were recorded very infrequently and only a relatively small group (25 species) exhibited a frequency of occurrence of 5% or greater during more than one sampling period. This latter group will be referred to hereafter as the 'prevalent fungi'. Ectoplasmic-net fungi, recorded exclusively by the baited dish method, are treated separately (Table 2.4).

The prevalent fungi are listed in Table 2.2, along with their frequencies of occurrence at each collection period, which are tabulated both including and excluding wash plate occurrences. This separate computation is presented because: (1) of the nature of the selectivity of the wash plate method, explained in Materials and Methods; and (2) for those fungi for which growth on wash plates was not precluded, the reader can detect occurrence frequency contributions from seedling

TABLE 2.1   The species of fungi recorded from red mangrove seedlings in the present study.

	Number recorded [a]	Time of recording [b]
Hyphomycetes		
Acremonium sp.[d]	5	PO, 2nd (SL)[c]
Alternaria alternata (Fr.) Keissler	21	see Table 2.2
Aspergillus niger V. Tiegh.	4	PR&PO, 1st
Aspergillus ornatus Raper, Fenner et Tresner	4	PO, 1st & 2nd
Aspergillus repens de Bary	13	see Table 2.2
Aspergillus terreus Thom	1	PO, 2nd
Aureobasidium pullulans (de Bary) Arnaud	7	see Table 2.2
Cephalosporium spp. (2?)	21	see Table 2.2
Chalara sp. (hyaline)	1	PO, 2nd
Cirrenalia pseudomacrocephala Kohlm.	2	PO, 2nd
Cladosporium cladosporioides (Fr.) de Vries[e]	110	see Table 2.2
Cladosporium sp.	22	see Table 2.2
Culcitalna achraspora Meyers et Moore	1	PO, 2nd
Curvularia sp.	2	PR&PO, 1st & 2nd (SL)
Cylindrocarpon sp.	2	PO, 1st
Dendryphiella salina (Suth.) Pugh et Nicot	4	PO, 1st & 2nd (SL)
Flagellospora sp.[f]	20	see Table 2.2
Fusarium sp.	9	PO, 1st (SL) & 2nd (SL)
Geniculosporium sp.	1	PO, 2nd
Gliomastix spp. (2?)	7	PO, 2nd
Haplobasidion sp.	3	PO, 1st
Harposporium baculiforme Drechsler	1	PO, 1st
Humicola fuscoatra Traaen	6	see Table 2.2
Hyalodendron sp.	1	PO, 2nd
Nigrospora sp.	3	PR&PO, 1st
Paecilomyces sp.	7	PO, 1st
Papulospora halima Anastasiou	6	PO, 2nd
Penicillium roseopurpureum Dierckx	10	see Table 2.2
Penicillium steckii Zaleski	42	see Table 2.2
Periconia prolifica Anastasiou	1	PO, 1st
Scolecobasidium humicola Barron et Busch	1	PO, 2nd
Scytalidium sp.	4	PO, 2nd
Septonema sp.[f]	23	see Table 2.2
Sporothrix sp.[g]	4	PO, 1st
Trichoderma viride Pers.	16	see Table 2.2
Tritirachium sp.	1	PO, 2nd
Verticillium sp.[d]	5	PO, 2nd (SL)
Zalerion varium Anastasiou[f]	38	see Table 2.2
Zygosporium gibbum (Sacc., Rouss. et Bomm) Hughes	1	PR
Zygosporium masonii Hughes[f]	10	see Table 2.2

	Number recorded[a]	Time of recording[b]
Melanconiales		
Colletotrichum sp.	13	see Table 2.2
Cryptosporiopsis sp.	1	PO, 2nd
Pestalotia sp.[f,h]	135	see Table 2.2
Sphaeropsidales		
Coniothyrium sp.	1	PO, 2nd
Cytoplea sp.	13	see Table 2.2
Cytospora rhizophorae Kohlm.	15	see Table 2.2
Cytosporina sp.	15	see Table 2.2
Dendrophoma sp.	4	PO, 1st & 2nd
Dothiorella sp.	2	PO, 1st
Macrophoma sp.	1	PR
Micropera sp.	4	PO, 1st & 2nd
Naemosphaera sp. I	3	PO, 1st & 2nd
Naemosphaera sp. I!	7	see Table 2.2
Naemosphaera sp. III	7	PO, 1st & 2nd
Phlyctaena sp.	3	PO, 1st & 2nd
Phoma sp. I	8	see Table 2.2
Phoma sp. II	16	see Table 2.2
Phoma sp. III	1	PO, 1st
Phomopsis sp.	3	PO, 2nd
Phyllosticta sp.	1	PR
Rabenhorstia sp.	6	PO, 1st & 2nd
Robillarda rhizophorae Kohlm.	1	PO, 1st (SL)
Ascomycetes		
Anthostomella sp.[i]	3	PO, 2nd
Botryosphaeria sp.[j]	22	PO, 1st & 2nd
Chaetomium sp.	1	PO, 2nd
Keissleriella blepharospora J. et E. Kohlm.	21	see Table 2.2
Leptosphaeria maritima (Cooke et Plowr.) Sacc.	2	PO, 2nd (SL)
Leptosphaeria sp.	1	PR
Lophiotrema littorale Speg.[k]	1	PO, 1st
Lulworthia grandispora Meyers[f,l]	101	see Table 2.2
Lulworthia medusa var *biscaynia* Meyers[l]	17	see Table 2.2
Nectria sp.[m]	2	PO, 2nd (SL)
unidentified species (2 Sphaeriales, 1 Plectascales)		
Oŏmycetes		
Phytophthora vesicula Anastasiou et Churchland	5	PO, 2nd

	Number recorded[a]	Time of recording[b]
Phytophthora sp.	1	PO, 2nd
Pythiogeton utriforme v. Minden	8	PO, 1st & 2nd
Zygomycetes		
Rhizopus stolonifer (Ehrenb. ex Fr.) Vuill.	2	PO, 1st & 2nd
Basidiomycetes		
Ceratobasidium sp.	3	PO, 2nd
Ectoplasmic net fungi		
Thraustochytrium sp.[f]	29	see Table 2.4
Labyrinthula sp[f]	16	see Table 2.4

[a]Number of records during the 13 month study period.

[b]Time during which observations were recorded.

[c]PR = pre-abscission; PO = post-abscission; 1st = Nov. 1970, through May, 1971; 2nd = Jun. 1971, through Dec. 1971; (SL) = from supralittoral sites only.

[d]One of the imperfect states of the *Nectria* sp. recorded at supralittoral sites.

[e]So designated because the conidiophores had few or no geniculations.

[f]See Figs. 2.10 - 2.18.

[g]It is quite possible that this was one of the conidial forms of *Zygosporium masonii*, in view of Wang and Baker's report from Hawaii (1967) and unpublished results of Fell and Master with *Z. masonii* from red mangrove leaves from Trinidad, W. I.

[h]Not readily identifiable, because of differences and variability in conidium size and coloration, with any of the five species listed from *Rhizophora mangle* by Guba (1961).

[i]Not *A. rhizophorae* or *A. rhizomorphae*.

[j]Corresponds to the description of *B. ribis*, except that the *Dothiorella* pycnidial state has much smaller pycnoconidia.

[k]A tentative identification; the isolate corresponds to the description of *L. littorale*, except that the slit-like opening of the ascocarp is unclear in culture.

[l]Except in a few instances, a clear, bipartite separation of ascospore size was exhibited in the *Lulworthia* strains encountered in this study. The larger ascospore group had very long ascospores (> 500 μm, as long as 750 μm), and the smaller ascospore group had appendages as described by Meyers (1957) for *L. medusa* var *biscaynia*. Therefore, the two sets of strains are listed as above, since controversy still exists regarding taxonomy of *Lulworthia* spp. (Kohlmeyer, 1968), in spite of Cavaliere and Johnson's (1966) reduction of the members of the genus to synonymy with *L. medusa* (Ell. et Ev.) Cribb et Cribb.

[m]Not *Hydronectria tethys* Kohlm.

surface propagules as distinguished from occurrence frequency contributions which were more likely to represent metabolically active fungal elements. A more complete presentation of the effects of method selectivity on the succession results is given in Table 2.5, and these are brought out in following paragraphs for the principal members of each seedling fungal community. It must be kept in mind that disparate frequencies among records from different sampling methods are not necessarily translatable into conclusions about the degree of activity in the field of given species. For example, fungi which occur with high frequency in damp chamber and at low frequency or not at all on disc plates may be incapable of growth or fruiting on agar plates (especially in competition with other fungi) even though they were not killed by surface sterilization (specific examples are *Keissleriella blepharospora* and *Septonema* sp.).

2.3.2   The Mycosere

The mycosere of red mangrove seedlings, presented in numerical detail in Table 2.2, occurred in four recognizable though intergrading seral stages. The frequencies of occurrence for species representative of these stages are presented graphically in Figs. 2.8 and 2.9. Some of these fungi are depicted in Figs. 2.10-2.18. Relative frequency of occurrence for the mycoseral representatives of major fungal taxa is presented in Fig. 2.19.

First seral stage   The first seral stage encountered was that of the fungal inhabitants of seedlings on the parent trees, in November 1971. These included a group of common primary phylloplane hyphomycetes, represented in Fig. 2.8 by *Cladosporium cladosporioides,* and an acervular fungus, *Pestalotia* sp. (Fig. 2.10). In addition to *C. cladosporioides*, a second *Cladosporium* species, *Alternaria alternata* (Fr.) Keissler, *Zygosporium masonii* Hughes (Fig. 2.11), *Penicillium steckii* Zaleski, and *Aureobasidium pullulans* (de Barry) Arnaud were the prevalent hyphomycetous members of this seral stage. At this time, 20% of the sampling observations yielded no fungi (Table 2.3), and stained microtome sections of seedlings showed no apparent fungal structures internal to the seedling epidermis (Fig. 2.20). Seedlings were all healthy and had a mean nitrogen content of 0.45% (Fig. 2.24). Only *A. alternata, Cladosporium* sp. and *Pestalotia* sp. exhibited occurrence frequencies on disc plates (i.e. after surface sterilization) equivalent to those in damp chamber or on wash plates. *Z. masonii* occurred only in damp chamber, while *C. cladosporioides, P. steckii* and *A. pullulans* showed markedly higher frequencies in damp chamber and/or wash plates than on disc plates (Table 2.5).

Second seral stage   During the first two months of seedling residence in the water at experimental stations, the second mycoseral stage took form. This mycocommunity consisted of all of the members of the pre-abcission community plus several new prevalent species (Table 2.2). The total number of species encountered rose from 16 pre-abcission species to 27 species after one month in the water, and the number of prevalent species rose from 7 to 16. The principal member of the new group of prevalent seedling fungi was *Septonema* sp. (Fig 2.8 and 2.12) which had markedly higher frequency in damp chamber than elsewhere (Table 2.5); other members of this group were *Aspergillus repens* de Barry, *Cephalosporium* sp., *Colletotrichum* sp., and *Phoma* sp. I. None of these had been recorded on pre-abscission seedlings. The pre-abscission fungi, with the exception of *Cladosporium* sp., maintained their original occurrence frequencies through the first month in the water, and then declined after the second through fifth months. This decline was the least marked in *Pestalotia* sp., which had shown an increase ($p = 0.10$) in occurrence frequency during the first month in the water, before going into the decline. As a consequence of its relatively slow decline in frequency, *Pestalotia* sp. was the most prevalent member of the second seral community.

TABLE 2.2 Percentage frequency of occurrence for the prevalent[a] species of the red mangrove seedling mycoflora[b]

	Nov 1970		Dec		Jan		Feb		Mar-Apr		Apr-May		Jun-Jul		Aug-Oct		Dec 1971		Σ[c]	
	+Wd	-Wd	+W	-W	+W	-W	+W	-W	+W	-W	+W	-W	+W	-W	+W	-W	+W	-W	+W	-W
Hyphomycetes																				
Cladosporium																				
cladosporioides	53	50	57	52	16	13	22	3	26	13	7	4	3	0	11	2	8	3	24	19
Penicillium steckii	4	6	27	12	5	3	16	0	10	3	7	0	0	0	5	2	2	0	9	4
Zalerion varium	0	0	0	0	5	0	0	0	5	0	7	7	9	12	16	18	33	40	8	9
Septonema sp.	0	0	9	21	16	3	2	3	2	3	0	0	0	0	0	0	0	0	5	6
Cladosporium sp.	18	19	7	7	5	10	8	2	2	10	0	0	0	0	2	2	2	3	5	5
Alternaria alternata	7	8	9	10	14	0	4	5	5	0	0	0	0	0	2	2	0	0	5	5
Flagellospora sp.	0	0	0	0	0	0	0	0	0	0	0	0	2	2	14	16	21	28	4	5
Trichoderma viride	0	0	3	3	0	0	0	0	0	0	0	0	6	4	7	8	12	15	4	4
Cephalosporium sp.	0	0	7	8	2	3	2	3	0	3	0	0	6	8	5	6	2	0	3	3
Aspergillus repens	0	0	7	8	5	5	6	5	2	5	3	4	2	2	0	0	0	0	3	3
Zygosporium masonii	7	8	7	8	2	3	2	3	0	3	0	0	0	0	0	0	0	0	2	3
Penicillium roseopur-pureum	0	0	0	0	0	0	0	0	0	0	0	0	2	0	9	10	8	10	2	2
Aureobasidium pullulans	7	3	0	0	0	0	0	0	0	0	3	0	0	0	2	0	6	3	2	1
Humicola fuscoatra	0	0	0	0	0	0	0	0	2	2	7	7	0	0	0	0	6	8	1	2

Melanconiales

Pestalotia sp.	44	36	53	52	39	30	33	21	29	29	20	16	16	8	6	5	29	27
Colletotrichum sp.	0	0	5	7	5	0	0	5	7	4	0	0	2	2	0	0	3	3

Sphaeropsidales

Phoma sp. II	0	0	0	0	7	4	5	2	0	0	6	8	2	2	10	8	4	4
Cytospora rhizophorae	0	0	1	2	0	2	3	7	7	7	11	12	2	2	0	0	3	4
Cytosporina sp.	0	0	0	0	0	0	0	2	3	4	6	8	14	16	2	3	3	4
Cytoplea sp.	0	0	3	3	5	2	3	7	7	4	2	2	4	2	0	0	3	3
Phoma sp. I	0	0	5	7	0	0	0	0	0	0	2	2	5	4	0	0	2	2
Naemosphaera sp. II	0	0	0	0	0	0	0	0	0	0	0	0	7	0	6	0	2	0

Ascomycetes

Lulworthia grandispora	0	0	3	3	11	20	25	27	36	36	22	28	32	36	58	73	22	25
L. medusa var biscaynia	0	0	1	2	2	2	3	2	0	0	9	12	13	14	0	0	4	4
Keissleriella blepharo-spora	0	0	0	0	0	0	0	0	0	0	9	12	11	12	17	23	5	5
number of observations	45	36	75	60	44	50	40	42	31	28	65	50	56	50	52	40	460	393

a Prevalent = occurring at 5% or greater frequency during at least two collection periods.
b Listed by major fungal group, in decreasing order of overall occurrence frequency.
c Overall occurrence frequency, November 1970 through December 1971.
d +W = frequency including wash plate records; —W = frequency excluding wash plate records.

TABLE 2.3   Number[a] of observations yielding no fungi

	Nov 1970	Dec	Jan	Feb	Mar- Apr	Apr- May	Jun- Jul	Aug- Oct	Dec 1971	%Σ[b]
Wash plates	1	3	0	1	0	2	5	0	1	16
Disc plates	8	0	0	0	1	2	0	0	0	5
Damp chambers	0	0	1	0	1	0	0	0	0	1
%Σ[c]	20	4	2	2	5	13	8	0	2	6[d]

a The actual numbers; no adjustment performed.
b Percent of total number of observations per method.
c Percent of total number of observations per collection period.
d Percent of total number of observations, all methods and collection periods.

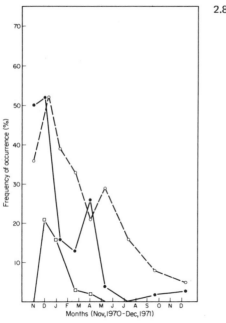

2.8

Fig. 2.8. Percentage frequency of occurrence for representative members of early stages of the red mangrove seedling mycosere. ● — ● = *Cladosporium cladosporioides;* ○ --- ○ = *Pestalotia* sp.; □ — □ = *Septonema* sp.

During the early portion (December-February 1971) of this second mycoseral stage, seedling sections still showed no advance in fungal invasion interior to the seedling epidermal layer; only 10% of damp chamber sampled seedlings were non-viable; no significant amount of dry weight was lost (Fig. 2.25); and nitrogen content of seedlings did not significantly increase (Fig. 2.24). After February, the decline in frequency of both the pre-abcission community members and the new species of the second mycoseral stage were reflected in a significant increase in samples which yielded no fungi from March to May (Table 2.3). Normalized numbers of occurrences of fungi reached their lowest (102) during this same period.

After March 1971, fungal hyphae and pseudoparenchymal tissue began to be detectable within a few cells of the cork tissue at the radicular ends of seedlings. Fungal tissue was also present in few to many cells of the cortex of injured seedlings (Fig. 2.21), particularly at the extra-estuarine site (station 5) where boring isopods had extensively damaged all experimental seedlings. The seedling cuticle had begun to crumble and scale where it covered cork tissue. Concurrent with the appearance of and increase in fungal tissue within seedling tissue, a rapid rise in nitrogen content began to take place in injured seedling samples, while a much slower rise occurred in uninjured seedlings (Fig. 2.24). After February, nearly all injured seedlings (except at station 2) had rapidly suffered senescence and death; they had softened and turned brown. The interiors of these seedlings were penetrated via the wound scar by bacteria, protozoa, nematodes and other meiofaunal organisms. Uninjured seedlings remained green and firm, with only 10% being non-viable after damp chamber incubation.

Third seral stage   As the second mycoseral stage phased into the third, two other prevalent fungal species, *Lulworthia grandispora* Meyers and *Zalerion varium* Anastasiou, made their appearance and began their rise to dominant frequency. At first these two species were found only on dying or dead portions of still viable seedlings, such as injured rootlets, the wound cork formed in injury holes, and dead epicotyl tissue. As many seedlings senesced and died, these fungi and some co-members of the third mycoseral community extended their areas of attack to all

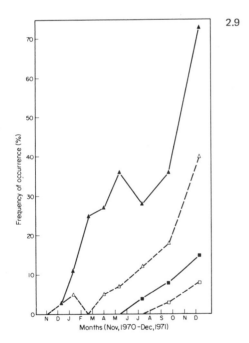

2.9

Fig. 2.9. Percentage frequency of occurrence for representative members of late stages of the red mangrove seedling mycosere. ▲ — ▲ = *Lulworthia grandispora;* △ --- △ = *Zalerion varium;* ■ — ■ = *Trichoderma viride;* □ --- □ = *Phytophthora vesicula.*

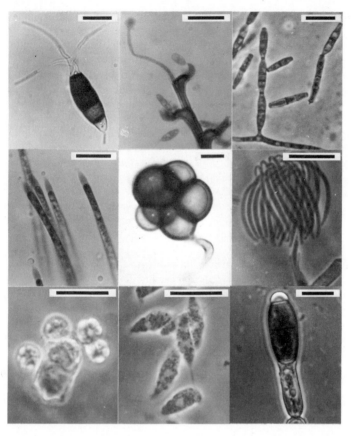

Figs. 2.10-2.18. Photomicrographs of some of the fungi encountered in the present study. **Fig. 2.10.** *Pestalotia* sp., an acervuloconidium, bright field. **Fig. 2.11.** *Zygosporium masonii,* conidiophore and conidia, bright field, lactophenol, trypan blue. **Fig. 2.12** *Septonema* sp., conidial chains, phase contrast. **Fig. 2.13.** *Lulworthia grandispora,* ascospore tips with hyaline appendages exuding droplets, lactophenol, trypan blue. **Fig. 2.14.** *Zalerion varium,* conidium, bright field. **Fig. 2.15.** *Flagellospora* sp., phialide and phialoconidial head, bright field, lactophenol, trypan blue. **Fig. 2.16.** *Thraustochytrium* sp., small sporangia with differentiated zoospores, on powdered seedling bait, phase contrast. **Fig. 2.17.** *Labyrinthula* sp., 'spindle' cells, phase contrast. **Fig. 2.18.** *Phragmospathula* sp., conidium on conidiophore, phase contrast. The fungi in Figs. 2.10 through 2.17 are members of the red mangrove seedling mycosere. The species in Fig. 2.18 is one of five which were observed on submerged red mangrove wood growing with well known marine mangrove fungi (such as *Hydronectria tethys*) and which are not included in the Kohlmeyers' lists of marine mangrove fungi (1969 a, 1971 a, 1971 b). The bar in each photograph represents 10 μm.

parts of the seedling external to the vascular tissues. A division point between the second and third mycoseral stages might be set at April-May 1971 when *L. grandispora* replaced *Pestalotia* sp. as the most prevalent species of seedling fungi, and *Z. varium* eclipsed *C. cladosporioides* as the most prevalent hyphomycete (Figs. 2.8 and 2.9).

Other prevalent species involved in this group of dead seedling invaders appeared after May. These included *Flagellospora* sp., *Lulworthia medusa* var. *biscaynia* Meyers, and sporadically appearing *Humicola fuscoatra* Traaen and *Cephalosporium*

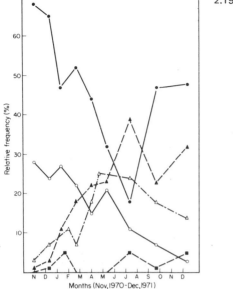

Fig. 2.19. Relative percentage frequency for major fungal groups involved in the red mangrove seedling mycosere. ● —— ● = hyphomycetes; ○ —— ○ = Melanconiales; ▲ --- ▲ = Ascomycetes; △ --- △ = Sphaeropsidales; ■ --- ■ = Oömycetes (excluding ectoplasmic-net fungi).

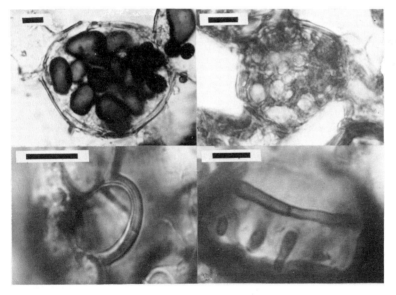

Figs. 2.20-2.23. Photomicrographs of microtome sections of cortex cells of red mangrove seedlings. **Fig. 2.20.** A healthy, uninvaded cell full of starch grains (stained in Gram's iodine solution). **Fig. 2.21.** A cell in which the interstices between starch grains have been filled by fungal hyphae (in lactophenol + trypan blue). **Fig. 2.22.** A larger magnification of a cell as in Fig. 2.21, showing a hypha surrounding a starch grain. **Fig. 2.23.** Dematiaceous hyphae growing within a cell emptied of contents. The bar in each photograph represents 10 μm.

sp. Still present at relatively high though declining frequency was *Pestalotia* sp., which often occurred as large patches of acervuli on brown and rotting seedlings. At this time, *Pestalotia* sp. showed its most marked decline in disc plate and damp chamber frequencies (Table 2.5). The other pre-abscission and first mycoseral members of the seedling mycoflora, if present at all, were recorded almost exclusively from wash plates or damp chamber. The new principal species of the dead seedling fungi of the third mycoseral community, however, showed significant gains in both disc plate and damp chamber frequencies; all of them occurred to a small extent or not at all on wash plates (Table 2.5).

During the third mycoseral stage, *Pestalotia* sp. also still occurred on uninjured and/or still viable seedlings. It was joined in this habitat by several species of pycnidial fungi, and by the Ascomycete *Keissleriella blepharospora,* all of which either appeared for the first time or showed increased frequencies during the progress of the third mycoseral stage. The principal members of the pycnidial group were *Cytosporina* sp. and *Cytospora rhizophorae* Kohlm.; others were *Phoma* sp. I and II. *Cytoplea* sp., which occurred throughout the study period on both injured and uninjured seedlings, was restricted on injured seedlings to those which were not brown and rotted. *Naemosphaera* sp. II, the only remaining prevalent pycnidial seedling fungus, was observed only on wash plates. *K. blepharospora* was virtually limited to damp chambers; *Cytosporina* sp. was significantly more frequent on disc plates than elsewhere, while *C. rhizophorae* was only slightly more common in damp chamber than on disc plates.

As the third mycoseral stage progressed, more and more uninjured seedlings lost viability. During the period from June to December 1971, 50% of those tested were non-viable (the ratios of viable to non-viable seedlings were tested between the first and second halves of the study period, November 1970-May 1971 versus June 1971-December 1971, and $0.05 > p > 0.01$); senescence of this seedling set was continuing apace as some of the third mycoseral fungi extended their invasion of uninjured tissue. Some of the uninjured seedlings died and became brown and rotted. In many injured and a few uninjured seedling cross sections, fungal hyphae and pseudoparenchyma were present in over half of the cortex cells (Figs. 2.22-2.23); all cross sections of both injured and uninjured seedlings contained a few cortex cells full of fungal tissue. The cuticle was entirely lost from the cork tissue, and fascicles of hyphae were observed to penetrate the cork tissue, reaching to the upper cortex. Chloroplasts were disintegrating in many of the uninjured seedling cross-sections, and the cuticle was yellowed and torn where it covered mid-hypocotyl tissue. By October 1971, some seedlings of the injured set were nothing more than a shell, the pith having disintegrated; in these seedlings, nearly all cortex cells contained fungal tissue and even the sclerenchyma bundles were invaded and lysed by fungal hyphae. Uninjured seedlings had lost an average of about 15% of their original dry weight by October 1971, whereas injured seedlings had lost about five times as much dry weight (Fig. 2.25). By December 1971, the mean nitrogen content of uninjured seedlings had increased to about 0.7%, while that of injured seedlings had tripled, to about 1.1% (Fig. 2.24).

Fourth seral stage   In the last two collections of the study period, in October and December 1971, the dominant members of the third mycoseral community all showed marked increases in frequency (Fig. 2.9) except for *Pestalotia* sp. and the pycnidial group (Figs. 2.8 and 2.19). Numbers of samplings yielding no fungi decreased from the peak of April-May (Table 2.3), and the normalized number of

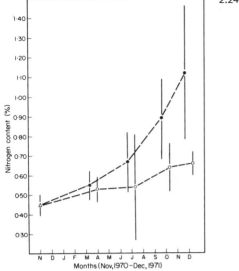

2.24

Fig. 2.24. Mean percentage nitrogen content of red mangrove seedlings during the progress of the mycosere. The vertical bars represent 95% confidence intervals. △ = seedlings sampled before submergence; ● --- ● = injured seedlings; ○ --- ○ = uninjured seedlings.

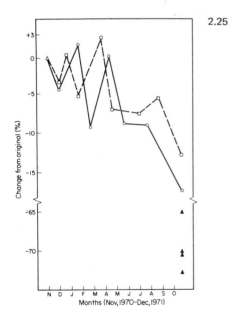

2.25

Fig. 2.25. Dry weight change of red mangrove seedlings during the progress of the mycosere. Each point represents a mean of three determinations, except for ▲ which represent single determinations. △ = seedlings before submergence (original dry weight); □ --- □ = uninjured seedlings, station 2; ○ —— ○ = uninjured seedlings, station 7; ▲ = injured seedlings, station 7.

73

occurrences for all seedling fungi jumped to over 200 in October. It was during this time that the onset of a postulated fourth mycoseral stage took place. The principal new member of this fourth mycocommunity was *Tirchoderma viride* (personal communication) (Fig. 2.9); it was accompanied by *Penicillium roseopurpureum* Dierckx. Both of these species occurred on seedlings in an advanced stage of decay, i.e. on seedlings which seemed near disintegration into particulate detritus. Both *T. viride* and *P. roseopurpureum* were more frequent in damp chamber than on wash plates, and neither occurred on disc plates.

Other species of possible importance   Ectoplasmic-net fungi were observed only in the baited dishes. Oõmycetes such as *Pythiogeton utriforme* v. Minden and *Phytophthora vesicula* Anastasiou et Churchland were observed more frequently in damp chambers and/or on disc plates. Therefore, records from the baited dishes were kept only for the ectoplasmic-net fungi. This was perhaps an unfortunate circumstance, for it was noted that many of the principal higher fungi also developed with regularity and could be recognized in these dishes, including *Cladosporium cladosporioides, Pestalotia* sp., *Cytospora rhizophorae, Lulworthia grandispora* and *Zalerion varium.*

As Table 2.4 shows, *Thraustochytrium* sp. was the only seedling fungus which may have had a fundamentally seasonal rather than successional occurrence pattern. It occurred most frequently in December 1970, and December 1971, when temperatures and salinities were at their lowest. It was as frequent on uninjured as on injured seedlings, and was not significantly more common at station 7 than station 2 ($p > 0.10$); occurrences were recorded only at stations which were adjacent to stands of red mangrove trees, and were absent from mid-estuary and extra-estuarine stations.

Labyrinthula sp. exhibited a different pattern. It increased in frequency as the mycosere progressed, reaching a peak in December, 1971. It was significantly more frequent at station 5 than elsewhere ($p < 0.01$) and was slightly more common from injured than from uninjured seedlings.

TABLE 2.4   Percentage frequency of occurrence for ectoplasmic net fungi[a].

	Dec 1970	Jan	Feb	Mar-Apr	Apr-May	Jun-Jul	Aug-Oct	Dec 1971	Σ[b]
Thraustochytrium sp.	40	33	30	22	14	7	27	53	31
Labyrinthula sp.	7	0	0	0	14	20	20	53	11
Number of observations	15	12	10	9	7	15	15	12	95
			S2[c]	S5	S7		IN[d]	UN[d]	
Thraustochytrium sp.			40	0	57		31	30	
Labyrinthula sp.			11	50	0		15	5	
Number of observations			28	14	28		52	43	

a 'Ectoplasmic-net' is used in the sense of Perkins, 1972.
b Overall frequency, December 1970 through December 1971.
c S2 = station 2; S5 = station 5; S7 = station 7.
d IN = injured seedling set; UN = uninjured seedling set.

A group of species of possibly consequential but uncertain position in the seedling mycosere includes those which occurred with relatively high frequency (approximately 10% or more) in only one collection period; two of these species occurred only at the very end of the experimental period (December 1971). These were the bulbil forming marine sterile fungus *Papulospora halima* Anastasiou, and the Oömycete *Phytophthora vesicula.* Both species were recorded only from advanced decay seedlings; *P. halima* was observed on both disc plates and in damp chamber, while *P. vesicula* occurred only in damp chamber.

Species with relatively high frequencies at points other than the end of the study period were the tropical Ascomycete, *Botryosphaeria* sp., and the Oomycete *Pythiogeton utriforme. Botryosphaeria* sp. had peak frequency (26%) in June-July 1971, after having appeared at less than 5% frequency from February through April. *P. utriforme* appeared sporadically (December 1970 and January 1971) at less than 5% frequency, then peaked at 8% in June-July, 1971. Both *Botryosphaeria* sp. and *P. utriforme* appeared in damp chamber and on disc plates.

Fungi whose occurrence frequencies were less than 5% but came only at the end of the study period were *Gliomastix* sp., *Cirrenalia pseudomacrocephala* Kohlm., *Scolecobasidium humicola* Barron et Busch, *Culcitalna achraspora* Meyers et Moore, *Geniculosporium* sp. and *Anthostomella* sp. All of these species occurred in damp chamber and/or on disc plates.

The succession in major fungal groups When examined on a major taxon basis, the succession image emerges as in Fig. 2.19. Prior to abcission (November 1970), hyphomycetes and Melanconiales were strikingly numerically dominant. After the seedlings were placed in marine and estuarine waters, both hyphomycetes and Melanconiales began decreasing in relative frequency despite the addition of some new hyphomycete species of the second mycoseral community. By July 1971, Ascomycetes and Sphaeropsidales of the third mycoseral community had gained numerical dominance. As the third mycoseral stage progressed, the hyphomycetes and Ascomycetes of this community of senescent and dead seedling attackers became the dominant groups, the pycnidial fungi declining in frequency as the remaining viable seedlings reached or approached death. Neither Oömycetes (excluding ectoplasmic-net fungi) nor Zygomycetes formed a major portion of the fungal occurrences during the study period.

2.3.3   The Effect of Pre-Injury

Injured and uninjured seedling sets did not show much difference in mycocommunities during November-May 1971 (Table 2.5). Only *Alternaria alternata* was significantly more common on uninjured than on injured seedlings, and *Aspergillus repens* was significantly more common on injured seedlings. During the period June-December 1971, *Cytosporina* sp. and *Keissleriella blepharospora* were significantly more common on uninjured seedlings, and *Zalerion varium* and *Lulworthia medusa* var *biscaynia* were significantly more common on injured seedlings. Although *Flagellospora* sp. and *Cytospora rhizophorae* were more common on uninjured seedlings, neither was significantly so ($p > 0.10$). Both were significantly more common at station 2, where both injured and uninjured seedlings were largely viable until the end of the study period. *Flagellospora* sp., like *Lulworthia grandispora*, was common on dead parts of viable seedlings. As a consequence, both species, although most common on dead seedlings, were also present on viable seedlings, and did not occur at significantly different frequencies between the injured and unin-

TABLE 2.5 Differences in occurrence frequency among the separate parts of the experimental regime for representative members of the mycoseral communities: among methods and among injured-uninjured seedling sets.

	WP[a] NM[c]	DP NM	DC NM	WP JD	DP JD	DC JD	SD JD	IN[b] NM[3]	UN NM	IN JD	UN JD
Cladosporium cladosporioides	61	16	43	21	1	0	6	34	32	5	7
Pestalotia sp.	44	46	30	31	9	6	18	42	32	16	13
Cladosporium sp.	5	6	3	2	2	0	0	5	5	2	1
Alternaria alternata	0	7	8	0	1	0	6	4	13	2	0
Zygosporium masonii	0	0	8	0	0	3	0	4	3	0	1
Septonema sp.	0	2	17	0	0	0	0	8	12	0	0
Penicillium steckii	22	7	16	10	1	3	6	18	12	3	5
Cytosporina sp.	0	2	0	0	16	3	3	1	1	4	15
Cytospora rhizophorae	0	3	2	2	2	6	9	4	2	2	6
Keissleriella blepharospora	0	0	0	0	1	50	21	0	0	7	19
Lulworthia grandispora	2	6	25	2	27	56	56	19	12	31	32
L. medusa var biscaynia	0	2	2	0	8	12	21	2	2	15	1
Zalerion varium	0	2	2	5	20	21	12	2	2	21	8
Flagellospora sp.	0	0	0	0	16	18	18	0	0	10	18
Trichoderma viride	0	0	2	5	0	3	35	2	0	6	9
Penicillium roseopurpureum	0	0	0	2	0	15	12	0	0	7	2
Number of prevalent[d] spp.	8	16	19	15	17	14	16	20	18	22	20
Number of occurrences, total[e]	188	175	269	195	209	321	359	263	209	272	261
Number of observations	41	122	124	42	102	34	34	130	113	124	88

a WP = wash plates; DP = disc plates; DC = damp chamber; SD = surface sterilized, damp chamber.
b IN = injured seedling set; UN = uninjured seedling set.
c NM = November 1970 through May 1971; JD = June 1971 through December 1971.
d Prevalent = occurring at 5% or greater frequency during at least two collection periods.
e Proportionally adjusted, for all species of fungi recorded.

jured sets. Neither *Trichoderma viride* nor *Penicillium roseopurpureum* were significantly more common on either seedling set. This was probably a consequence of the fact that these two species were just beginning to occur at relatively high frequency at the very end of the study period, when seedlings of both sets had reached death.

2.3.4   Effects of Station Location and Sampling Level

Both station location and level of seedling sampling or observation led to definite differences in recorded occurrences of members of the seedling mycoflora. For instance, *Zalerion varium* and *Flagellospora* sp. occurred in approximately the same position in the seedling mycosere, but *Z. varium* occurred only at station 7 and *Flagellospora* sp. only at station 2. Correspondingly, the two lulworthias from seedlings, *L. grandispora* and *L. medusa* var. *biscaynia,* colonized dead portions of seedlings, but *L. grandispora* was largely limited to the inshore stations (2 and 7), while *L. medusa* var *biscaynia* was recorded nearly exclusively from station 5, offshore.

Comparison of records of members of the seedling mycoflora from different levels of seedlings showed that most members of the early mycoseral stages were significantly more frequent from radicle + rootlets than elsewhere. This became less obvious as the mycosere progressed, and was not evident during the onset of the fourth mycoseral stage. Another notable fact was that pith tissues yielded very few records of fungi.

Further effects of station location and sampling observation level are discussed by Newell (1974).

2.3.5   Colony Counts: Bacteria, Yeast and Filamentous Fungi

A check was kept during the study period of the progress of bacterial and yeast colonization of seedlings. Table 2.6 shows that numbers of washable, viable elements of bacteria were not significantly different when compared between November and May 1971, and June and December 1971. Bacterial numbers were, however, significantly greater from injured seedlings than from uninjured ones during both parts of the study period. This followed at least in part from the fact that the washable elements were obtained from cork borer discs which included pith tissue on one side, and many injured seedlings had been extensively internally colonized by bacteria.

Numbers of washable viable elements of fungi other than yeasts were greater during the period November-May, 1971, than from June to December 1971, but not significantly so ($p > 0.05$). Also, significance could not be shown for these fungi between injured and uninjured sets, although they seemed more nearly equal during June to December 1971 ($p = 0.50$) than during November to May 1971. Yeasts, although more common than bacteria on pre-abcission seedlings, occurred only sporadically on seedlings after submergence. Large, short lived blooms of *Rhodotorula rubra* (Demme) Lodder and *Debaryomyces hansenii* (Zopf) Lodder et Kregervan Rij occurred during submergence.

2.4   Discussion

2.4.1   Mycosere Resumé

A resumé of the mycosere of red mangrove seedlings is presented in Table 2.7. The four communities or mycoseral stages are outlined. First were the pre-abscission superficial invaders, including a group of universally ubiquitous plant-surface

TABLE 2.6 Comparison of numbers of washable viable elements[a] of filamentous fungi, yeast and bacteria from red mangrove seedlings.

	Range	M[c]	p[d]	Range	M
	NMAS vs JDAS[b]				
Filamentous fungi	0-600	5	0.12	0-110	3
Yeasts	0-6	0	−	0-20 130	0
Bacteria	0-2939	36	0.48	0.23 490	28
	NMIN vs NMUN[e]				
Filamentous fungi	0-600	2.5	>0.05	0-265	5
Yeast	0-6	0	−	0-6	0
Bacteria	0-3885	74	<0.05	0-1140	10
	JDIN vs JDUN[f]				
Filamentous fungi	0-23	3.5	0.50	0-110	2.5
Yeasts	0-410	0	−	0-20 130	0
Bacteria	1-1395	40	0.04	0-23 490	13.5

a As recorded on wash plates; filamentous fungi and yeasts were from undiluted samples (10 ml) and bacteria were from samples diluted to 10^{-2} (9 ml).
b Testing was between viable elements from all seedlings collected November 1970 through May 1971 (NMAS) and those collected June 1971 through December 1971 (JDAS).
[c]M = median.
[d]p = probability as tested by the Mann-Whitney U Test (Siegel, 1956).
[e]NMIN = injured seedlings, November 1970 through May 1971; NMUN = uninjured seedlings, November 1970 through May 1971; see footnote b.
[f]JDIN = injured seedlings, June 1971 through December 1971, JDUN = uninjured seedlings, June 1971 through December 1971; see footnote b.

mycoinhabitants, *Cladosporium* spp. (*C. cladosporioides* was the most prevalent species of this community), *Alternaria alternata, Aureobasidium pullulans, Zygosporium masonii,* a common tropical plant-surface hyphomycete, and a species of common plant-invading acervular fungi, *Pestalotia* sp.

Species of *Pestalotia* have often been associated with plant diseases (Guba, 1961), and *Pestalotia* sp. from red mangrove seedlings was well established subcuticularly at least, as evidenced by its high frequency of occurrence after surface sterilization. There was no evidence, however, that any of the early colonizing species had penetrated into seedlings as deeply as the vascular tissues, as was suggested for them in Pugh and Buckley's (1971) study of sycamore leaf colonization. Also, whether a succession might have occurred within the group of pre-abscission superficial invaders, as Pugh and Buckley (1971) and Pugh and Mulder (1971) have found, was not determined, since fungal colonization of very young, emerging seedlings was not investigated.

The second mycocommunity was that of the post-abscission superficial invaders. It included the pre-abscission community, with *Pestalotia* sp. assuming numerical dominance, plus some new members, principally *Septonema* sp. and *Thraustochytrium* sp. from the marine and estuarine environment. During the onset of this mycoseral stage, no new progress in invasion of subepidermal seedling tissues was

TABLE 2.7 A resumé of the red mangrove seedling mycosere.

Date	Nov 1970	Dec	Jan	Feb	Mar	Apr	May	Jun	Jul	Aug	Oct	Nov	Dec 1971	1972 ———→
Seedling location	pre-abscission, ——→		post-abscission, estuarine subsurface environment											
Seedling condition	mature, healthy ——→		all viable ——→				viable-senescent-dead ——→				senescent-dead ——→			dead
Mycoseral species	Cladosporium cladosporioides Pestalotia sp. Cladosporium sp. Alternaria alternata Zygosporium masonii Aureobasidium pullulans		Pestalotia sp. C. cladosporioides Septonema sp. Penicillium steckii A. alternata Aspergillus repens Thraustochytrium sp.				in viable-senescent seedlings: Keissleriella blepharospora, Cytosporina sp, Cytospora rhizophorae, Pestalotia sp., Thraustochytrium sp.				in senescent-dead seedlings: Lulworthia grandispora ——→, Zalerion varium ——→, Flagellospora sp. ——→, L. medusa var biscaynia ——→, Pestalotia sp., Labyrinthula sp. ——→, Thraustochytrium sp. ——→			Trichoderma viride Penicillium roseopurpureum Papulospora halima Phytophthora vesicula
Mycoseral stages	pre-abscission, superficial invaders		post-abscission superficial invaders								subepidermal invaders, in dead and living tissue			decayed tissue invaders
Analogous stages*	weak parasites + common and restricted primary saprophytes						secondary saprophytes stage I: Ascomycetes and Deuteromycetes							secondary saprophytes stage III: 'soil' fungi

* From Hudson's (1968) generalized terrestrial mycosere.

79

made. As in preabscission seedlings, fungal hyphae were penetrating the cuticles of seedlings, especially over cork tissue, but did not appear to have gained entry to the cortex. Fungi were largely limited in distribution on seedlings to the radicular portion, except for *Pestalotia* sp., which was also common on the upper tips of seedlings.

The third mycocommunity, the subepidermal invaders, was made up of two sub-communities, one inhabiting dead seedlings or dead seedling parts, and the other inhabiting living seedling parts. The dead seedling subcommunity made its first appearance on dead rootlets, epicotyls and wound cork of living but senescent seed-lings, and progressed to attack on all parts of dead seedlings. The second subcommun-ity inhabited living tissue of viable seedlings. Both subcommunities invaded cortex tissue of seedlings; fungal hyphae and pseudoparenchyma were formed within seedling tissue. Invasion of the whole length of seedlings took place, one group of fungi ad-vancing the full degradation of dead seedlings in conjunction with bacteria and meio-fauna, and the other group draining away the viability energy and/or reducing the effectiveness of mechanical protective devices (e.g. cork tissue, cuticle, etc.).

The dead seedling fungal subcommunity paved the way for bacterial and meio-faunal entry to the spongy, starch laden pith tissues by breakdown of wound cork or dead cortex tissue. The living seedling subcommunity probably increased the rate of senescence of seedlings and paved the way for attack by the dead seedling subcommunity. Marine fungi (see Kohlmeyer and Kohlmeyer, 1971b) were among the principal members of these subcommunities (*Lulworthia* spp. and *Zalerion varium* in dead seedling tissue, *Cytospora rhizophorae* and *Keissleriella blepharo-spora* in tissue of living seedlings), along with *Flagellospora* sp. in the dead seedling group, *Cytosporina* sp. in the living seedling group, and *Pestalotia* sp., still present though declining in frequency, in both groups. *Labyrinthula* sp. and *Thrausto-chytrium* sp. may also have been important members of this community—*Laby-rinthula* sp. in the dead-seedling subcommunity and *Thraustochytrium* sp. in both subcommunities.

As the third mycoseral stage progressed and seedlings which had died early in this period reached an advanced stage of decay, with fungal tissue invading even the sclerenchyma of seedlings, members of a postulated fourth mycocommunity appeared. This was the decayed tissue invaders; in addition to the members of the dead seedling subcommunity of the third mycoseral stage, other species involved were principally *Trichoderma viride* and *Penicillium roseopurpureum,* with *Papulaspora halima* and *Phytophthora vesicula* possibly also included. This fourth community can only be postulated, for the study period ended before the majority of seed-lings in estuarine environs had reached an advanced stage of decay. As might be expected, the newly appearing species of this community showed no limitations of distribution along the lengths of the remains of seedlings.

2.4.2 Comparison with Terrestrial Mycoseres

The mycosere of red mangrove seedlings is not unlike the generalized mycosere on plant remains above terrestrial soils assembled in a thoroughgoing review by Hudson (1968), although there are distinct differences. The aspect of timing of mycocommunities with respect to condition of substrate is perhaps the most notable difference.

The pre-abscission superficial invaders are comparable to a combination of Hudson's first mycoseral stage ('weak parasites', on living tissue) plus a portion of his second mycoseral stage, the 'common primary saprophytes'. In Hudson's scheme, the common primary saprophytes are those cosmopolitan phylloplane hyphomycetes which colonize living tissue but reach peak density after host tissues have begun to senesce. This group includes *Cladosporium cladosporioides, Alternaria tenuis* Nees et personal communication (= *A. alternata,* according to Ellis, 1971), *Aureobasidium pullulans, Epicoccum nigrum* Link, and *Botrytis cinerea* Pers. ex Pers., with *Curvularia* spp. and *Nigrospora* spp. common in tropical climes. Only the first three of these were prevalent members of the pre-abscission superficial invaders; *Nigrospora* sp. and *Curvularia* sp. were only infrequently isolated from seedlings, and *B. cinerea* and *Epicoccum* sp. were never isolated from the experimental seedlings. In place of these was *Zygosporium masonii,* which can be isolated from the foliage of many species of tropical plants (Ellis, 1971).

As Ruscoe (1971) found in his study of fungal colonization of beech leaves in New Zealand, and Dickinson (1965) found with *Halimione* leaves, the common primary saprophyte group was active on seedlings prior to abscission, distinctly before senescence. Evidence for their activity on seedlings, other than their persistence after surface sterilization, is the fact that their frequencies were undiminished after a full month of seedling residence in flowing seawater. Thus, in contrast to Hudson's generalized scheme, the common primary saprophytes on seedlings were active coincidentally with the weak parasites, which on seedlings were principally represented by *Pestalotia* sp. *Pestalotia* sp. is designated as a weak parasite rather than one of the common primary saprophytes because of its frequency of occurrence after surface sterilization, which was much higher than those of the common saprophytic hyphomycetes. As with the weak parasites of Hudson's scheme, and those of Ruscoe (1971) and Kendrick and Burges on pine needles (1962), *Pestalotia* sp. caused no evident disease symptoms.

In contrast to other less independent plant parts, red mangrove seedlings are fully viable when cast off by the parent plant. Senescence does not take place until after the seedlings have passed from an aerial maritime environment into an estuarine or marine underwater environment. During the period of full viability in the saline environment, a second community of common primary saprophytes, the post-abscission superficial invaders, emerged. This is understandably in contrast with Hudson's general scheme, which deals with successions on plant parts which are dead when they pass from aerial to soil surface environments.

With the advent of seedling senescence, rather than increasing in frequency as do the common primary saprophytes in Hudson's scheme, the superficial invaders declined in frequency. They became virtually absent from seedlings before half of the seedlings had reached non-viability. They were replaced, rather than joined, by the group (the living tissue subepidermal invaders) of seedling fungi which were comparable either to Hudson's restricted primary saprophytes or to his weak parasites. In Hudson's scheme, both of these groups coexist with the common primary saprophytes.

Whether the living tissue subepidermal invaders of seedlings are comparable to the restricted primary saprophytes or the weak parasites hinges upon whether the tissue which they invade is living and healthy, or senescent. Kohlmeyer and Kohlmeyer (1971 a) have suggested that *Cytospora rhizophorae,* of the living tissue subepidermal invaders, is a parasite or perthophyte in living red mangrove roots and seedlings, possibly causing die-back, and Kohlmeyer (1969 b) stated that *Keissleriella blepharospora* inhabits cork tissue of seedlings and proproots without damaging the plants.

Both of these species are documented by Kohlmeyer (1969 a; Kohlmeyer and Kohlmeyer, 1971 b) as restricted to growth in tissues of the red mangrove. In any case, the distinction between the weak parasite and primary saprophyte categories is difficult to make (Hudson, 1971) and is perhaps even invalid (Last, 1971).

It is interesting to note that *Keissleriella blepharospora* made its first appearance with mature ascospores shortly after bulk seedling fall had taken place. Hogg and Hudson (1966) noted that some Ascomycetes involved in the mycosere of terrestrial tree leaves have ascospore release timed with the availability of new substrate for colonization or contamination. This may also be the case with *K. blepharospora.* It may have colonized the experimental seedlings much earlier than the time of its first recording, for it grows very poorly in agar culture (MSA medium).

During this same time period, because seedling death times were not reasonably simultaneous as they were in those successions which Hudson reviewed, the dead tissue subepidermal invaders of seedlings, which are comparable to Hudson's 'secondary saprophytes', rose to prevalent frequency. In Hudson's scheme, the secondary saprophytes either invade plant tissues only after they have died, or they begin activity only after death of host tissues which they have occupied inactively for some time. The dead tissue subepidermal invaders occupied a secondarily saprophytic role in the seedling mycosere, and they were not present until after the death of the tissues that they invaded.

Hudson included several subgroups within his secondary saprophytes. Ascomycetes and Fungi Imperfecti were involved in the earliest subgroups, and it is these two major taxa which are represented in the dead tissue subepidermal invaders of seedlings. Following these in most successions are Basidiomycetes. Higher Basidiomycetes are rare in the marine environment, and so it is not unexpected that these fungi played no role in the seedling mycosere. However, because the seedling mycosere may not have reached conclusion at all stations at the termination of the present study, it cannot be ruled out that Basidiomycetes might eventually have appeared, for Kohlmeyer and Kohlmeyer (1971 b) have reported *Nia vibrissa* Moore et Meyers, a marine Gasteromycete, from *Rhizophora mangle* tissue.

The final stage in Hudson's generalized succession involves the appearance of a group of soil inhabiting fungi, which are largely surface restricted. These include *Penicillium* spp., *Trichoderma* spp., and members of the Mucorales. It is this group which is comparable to the decayed tissue invaders of the seedling mycosere. In both the generalized succession and the seedling mycosere, these fungi are associated with highly degraded material. *Trichoderma viride* and *Penicillium roseopurpureum* of the seedling mycosere are well known soil fungi, and both of these genera are very common in mangrove sediments (Lee and Baker, 1972 a). If, as postulated, the appearance of these two genera did signify the beginning of a fourth seedling mycoseral stage, then a significant difference between the seedling mycosere and the generalized succession is the absence of the Mucorales in the seedling mycosere. Both Swart (1958) and Lee and Baker (1972 a) found that members of the Mucorales could only be isolated at high frequency from mangrove soils of low salinity. Unless they were destined to appear after *Trichoderma* and *Penicillium,* after the end of the study period, then the Mucorales probably play no role in the more saline portions of mangrove ecosystems.

2.4.3   *Comparison with the Mycosere on Red Mangrove Leaves*

Perhaps replacing the Mucorales on seedlings in their niche as late participators in mycoseres were Oömycetes in the form of *Phytophthora vesicula,* which appeared to have begun a rise in frequency at the end of the study period (Fig. 2.9), coincident with *T. viride* and *P. roseopurpureum*. In this connection, it is interesting to note that, in the succession of fungi on red mangrove leaves (Fell and Master, 1973), *P. vesicula* was one of the most prevalent and earliest invaders once the leaves had reached the estuarine waters. This was also the case with non-autochthonous leaf material in British Columbian marine waters (Anastasiou and Churchland, 1969). In both of these cases, the substrate material was non-living when it was submerged, in contrast to the seedling material. On the red mangrove leaves, after peaking in frequency during the first week of submergence, *P. vesicula* gave way to other fungi, including *Lulworthia* sp. It may be that this position of *P. vesicula* in the leaf succession corresponds to that of Mucorales in successions on dung and compost where they are the earliest to appear (Hudson, 1968). Hudson suggests that the uniquely early appearance of Mucorales in these successions is partly a consequence of the presence of readily available carbohydrates; this factor may also be partially responsible for the early appearance of *P. vesicula* on leaves in the saline watery medium of mangrove swamps, where soluble carbohydrates would immediately become available and where Mucorales may play no role.

Other aspects of note in comparison of the red mangrove leaf and seedling succession, follow: (1) the pre-abscission communities were much the same, with *Cladosporium, Alternaria, Aureobasidium, Zygosporium* and *Pestalotia* numerically dominant, but in the leaf succession *Phyllosticta* and *Nigrospora* were also prevalent; (2) upon submergence, following *Phytophthora vesicula* colonization, *Trichoderma, Aspergillus, Penicillium, Fusarium, Cephalosporium,* and *Verticillium* peaked in frequency, while the pre-abcission community members all declined in frequency except for *Pestalotia,* as was the case with seedlings; (3) late in the leaf succession (35 days was late in this case, as leaves, in general, were much more rapidly converted to detrital particles than seedlings), *Lulworthia* reached its peak frequency (25%), which was much lower than the level it had reached on seedlings; (4) in a small sampling of very old (176 days) leaf remnants, *Trichoderma* had reached nearly 100% frequency (Fell and Master, unpublished data), indicating that it was prominent in the latest part of the leaf mycosere, as it may have been in the seedling mycosere.

Thus the mycosere on leaves was distinctly different from that on seedlings, probably largely due to timing and physical location of the leaves during senescence and death. Because the leaves were much more quickly degraded than seedlings after entering the water, the leaf mycosere was an accelerated version of the seedling mycosere, with the addition of an early Oōmycete invasion phase, reduced frequency of *Lulworthia* and *Zalerion,* and absence of the other subepidermal invaders of seedlings, with the exception of *Pestalotia,* which played a major role in both mycoseres as a weak parasite capable of maintaining activity beyond senescence of host tissue.

It must be added here that the relatively low number of records of *Lulworthia* and *Zalerion* from leaves may have been a consequence of methodology. Fell and Master (1973) used nutrient agar (Difco Cornmeal Agar and a powdered leaf agar) culturing of discs taken from leaves, both with and without surface sterilization. *Lulworthia grandispora* from seedlings was recorded only half as frequently from cultured discs as from damp chamber incubation of whole seedlings, and recently Fell and Master (unpublished data) have found that *L. grandispora* and *Zalerion varium,* along with *Cirrenalia pseudomacrocephala,* can be recorded quite regularly on red mangrove leaves when these are incubated in sterile seawater.

2.4.4 Comparison with other Maritime and Marine Mycoseres

These two fungal successions occurring in estuaries are difficult to compare with other studies of successions in marine environments. Dickinson (1965) found, in his study of fungal colonization of leaves of a salt marsh shrub (*Halimione portulacoides* (L.) Aell.) that a characteristic primary saprophyte mycocommunity occurred on green and yellow leaves, just as Fell and Master (1973) had found for red mangrove leaves. There were some differences. Dickinson found *Dendryphiella salina* (Suth.) Pugh et Nicot colonizing green leaves of *H. portulacoides,* whereas Fell and Master did not find this fungus until leaves had entered the water. This is probably attributable to the fact that even the green *H. portulacoides* leaves were subject to periodic tidal inundation. It is notable that *D. salina* played no part in the red mangrove seedling mycosere. Another difference between the *H. portulacoides* and *Rhizophora mangle* leaf successions was that Oömycetes were not recorded from *H. portulacoides* leaves, but these leaves were subject to periodic immersion, so that Oömycetes may have been prevented from effective colonization. The remainder of the *H. portulacoides* mycosere is unknown, for Dickinson carried his study of *H. portulacoides* leaf colonization no further than the yellow leaves.

Other attempts at determining patterns of fungal colonization of substrates in the marine environment have dealt with activities of fungi on wood of non-maritime origin. The exception is Meyers *et al.* (1965), a study of fungal 'infestation' of *Thalassia testudinum* König (turtle grass) blades. Meyers *et al.,* however, conducted their study for a period of only 9 months, and did not observe a fungal succession. They used nutrient agar culturing of pieces of the grass blades which had been washed in only two changes (10 minutes each) of sterile seawater.

Jones' (1963, 1968) and Meyers' (1953, 1954, 1960) reports of fungal colonization patterns on non-autochthonous wood were largely limited in scope to records of those species of fungi recognized as indigenously marine. Fungi known to be active in terrestrial and freshwater environments were not included in their reports, although Siepmann and Johnson (1960), Hughes (1960), Kirk (1972) and Master (unpublished data) have demonstrated that many of these fungi (e.g. *Aspergillus* spp., *Penicillium* spp. and *Trichoderma* spp.) are present and may well have active though not necessarily primary roles in wood decomposition in marine environments. The pattern of succession of marine fungi appears (Jones, 1963, 1968) to involve an early phase of largely hyphomycete colonization (e.g. *Zalerion maritimum* (Linder) Anastasiou, *Dendryphiella salina, Humicola alopallonella* Meyers et Moore) followed by phases of largely Ascomycete colonization (e.g. *Lulworthia* spp., *Ceriosporopsis halima* Linder among the early Ascomycetes, *Corollospora maritima* Werder. and *Halosphaeria* spp. among the later Ascomycetes). Both *Lulworthia grandispora* and *Zalerion varium* were early colonizers of dead red mangrove seedling tissue, but *H. alopallonella* and *Cirrenalia pseudomacrocephala* did not appear until late in the seedling mycosere, along with *Trichoderma viride* and *Penicillium roseopurpureum* of the decayed tissue invaders.

2.4.5 Comparison with Freshwater Mycoseres

Pugh and Mulder's (1971) study of fungal colonization patterns on *Typha latifolia* L. (cattail) blades in England revealed the nature of a partially aerial, partially freshwater fungal succession. A typical common and restricted primary saprophyte (plus weak parasite?) flora was involved in the colonization of green leaves, and these increased in frequency at senescence (except *Aureobasidium pullulans*) as in Hudson's scheme, and in contrast to the red mangrove seedling mycosere. One notably unique aspect of this portion of the *T. latifolia* mycosere is that a Zygomycete (*Mortierella hygrophila* Linnemann) was present at high (20%) frequency on green leaves and became absent on moribund leaves. A typical early secondary saprophyte flora (including *Leptosphaeria* spp. and *Phoma typharum* Sacc.) reached peak frequency on moribund leaves, but these were not followed by the typical late secondary saprophytes (Zygomycetes plus 'soil fungi'). Instead nematophagous hyphomycete species were dominant on decayed *T. latifolia* blades in the aquatic litter. Also, in contrast to the red mangrove leaf mycosere, no phase of Oömycete colonization of dead blades was recorded when these fell into the water.

Taligoola *et al.* (1973) have recently published reports of the fungal colonization patterns on *Phragmites communis* Trin. (a reed). The study area was near to that used in Pugh and Mulder's *T. latifolia* study. No clear determination of age of the sampled dead *P. communis* parts (culms and leaves) was reported by Taligoola *et al.,* while Apinis *et al.* sampled only submerged portions of standing (living?) culms. Taligoola *et al.* do not give the number of observations made in calculating their frequencies, and they state that only pieces of culms and leaves which showed the presence of fungi were collected. It is thus difficult to define clearly the *P. communis* mycosere, but the following points are salient in comparison with the *T. latifolia* and *R. mangle* mycoseres.

A typical common plus restricted primary saprophyte flora (including *Cladosporium herbarum* (Pers.) Link et S. F. Gray and *Alternaria tenuis)* inhabited living aerial portions of *P. communis*. The common and restricted primary saprophytes persisted for some time after submergence of dead *P. communis* parts, then were replaced by other fungi including strictly aquatic fungal species; this is similar to the *R. mangle* seedling mycosere, in which strictly marine species replaced early colonizers after a period of their persistence. *Dictyuchus monosporus* Leitgeb (a saprolegniacean Oömycete) was frequently recorded during the early portion of the *P. communis* mycosere, corresponding to the early Oömycete (in the form of *Phytophthora* spp.) colonization phase of marine and estuarine leaf mycoseres, and in contrast to the *T. latifolia* mycosere, in which *D. monosporus* was only infrequently recorded, and then only on the leaf sheaths. During the latest monitored stage of the *P. communis* mycosere, fungi characteristic of the pond sediment mycoflora (*Fusarium* sp., *Mucor* sp.) made their appearance, as was the case in the *R. mangle* mycoseres (except that, notably, Zygomycetes were present in the freshwater *P. communis* mycosere), but contrary to the *T. latifolia* mycosere in which nematophagous hyphomycetes dominated the late mycoseral stages. Further careful studies of freshwater mycoseres on plant debris are needed to compare with the *T. latifolia* and *P. communis* mycoseres.

2.4.6   Comparison with the Mycoflora of Mangrove Wood

Just as were the wood colonization studies of Jones and Meyers (cited above), the studies of Kohlmeyer (review 1969 a) and Kohlmeyer and Kohlmeyer, (1971 a) of fungi occurring on red mangrove wood are restricted to those species which he considers to be 'marine'. By his definition (Kohlmeyer and Kohlmeyer, 1971 b), in order to be categorized as marine, a fungus must develop and reproduce in the marine habitat. His application of this definition has excluded those fungi which produce very small, delicate and easily detachable conidia which are very difficult, if not impossible, to detect by direct observation of substrate material without the use of incubation or culturing techniques. Some of the prevalent fungi on red mangrove seedlings are difficult to detect even *with* the use of incubation techniques because of their tiny and delicate conidiogenous structures (a good example from the seedling mycosere is *Flagellospora* sp. (Fig. 2.15). Other fungi which are excluded are those which do not produce their characteristic conidiogenous structures in marine subsurface growth, but which produce other propagules (e.g. I have observed thallic arthroconidia production during growth in seawater of species which produce pycnidia in agar culture), and/or which are active in the marine environment but have their characteristic propagules arriving from outside the marine environment. Thus, Kohlmeyer's definition of a marine fungus effectively eliminates consideration of those fungi which would be categorized by Park (1972) as inactive 'transients' in his discussion of ecology of aquatic microbes, *but* it also eliminates fungi in Park's 'indweller', 'migrant' and 'versatile' categories which have definite but differing degrees of activity in the subsurface marine environment.

Among those higher fungi described by Kohlmeyer as marine occupants of woody red mangrove tissue are three of the subepidermal invaders of the red mangrove seedling mycosere, namely *Lulworthia grandispora*, *Keissleriella blepharospora* and *Cytospora rhizophorae*. *Zalerion varium* was also reported, on indeterminate mangrove wood in Guatemala. The *Phoma* sp. and *Macrophoma* sp. reported from *Rhizophora mangle* by Kohlmeyer may or may not correspond to one or more of the *Phoma* spp. recorded from red mangrove seedlings in the present study. *Lulworthia* sp. was the most frequently encountered fungus from mangrove tissues by Kohlmeyer (20% of collections) and *L. grandispora* was the most common species encountered on dead red mangrove seedlings in the present study. *K. blepharospora* was cited by Kohlmeyer as an important component of the woody tissue red mangrove mycoflora, and it was also very common on old but viable red mangrove seedlings. Two other species cited as abundant or important by Kohlmeyer from red mangrove wood did not appear on seedlings. These were *Leptosphaeria australiensis* Cribb et Cribb (15% of Kohlmeyer's collections) and *Didymosphaeria enalia* Kohlm. Of the remaining 13 species (*Phoma* sp. and *Macrophoma* sp. excluded) recorded by Kohlmeyer from *R. mangle,* only one, *Robillarda rhizophorae,* was found on red mangrove seedlings, and this species was recorded only from a station site which was often emersed.

In limited forays into South Florida's mangrove swamps, I have collected on decaying *R. mangle* roots six of Kohlmeyer's reported species of fungi from *R. mangle* (*D. enalia, D. rhizophorae* J. et E. Kohlm., *Hydronectria tethys* J. et E. Kohlm., *Kymadiscus haliotrephus* J. et E. Kohlm., *L. australiensis* and *Halocyphina villosa* J. et E. Kohlm. Of these, *D. enalia, H. tethys* and *L. australiensis* were very common) and four other marine species (three Ascomycetes, *Thaxteria* sp., *Lophiosphaeria* sp. and an unidentified species, and a dematiaceous hyphomycete, *Phragmospathula* sp. Fig. 2.18 which have not been described by Kohlmeyer) which were not encountered on the experimental red mangrove seedlings. All of these were isolated and grown in single ascospore or conidium culture (MSA medium) except *H. villosa,* the conidia of which would not germinate. None of these wood-inhabiting species produced culture forms which could be identified with those of the fungi of the seedling mycoflora. Thus, seedlings, leaves (on which only *Lulworthia* spp. and *Z. varium* among Kohlmeyer's reported fungi from *R. mangle* were recorded), and wood of red mangroves all appear to harbour quantitatively and qualitatively unique mycoflorae.

2.4.7   Comparison with Mangrove Habitat Sediment Mycoflorae

Examination of the lists of fungi present in saline mangrove swamp sediments (Swart, 1958; Rai *et al.,* 1969; Lee and Baker, 1972 a) reveals that these are largely representative of typical soil mycoflorae, except that Basidiomycetes and Zygomycetes are absent or very infrequent. Another exception is that *Pestalotia* spp. are common in sediments of those swamps which include *Rhizophora* spp., but absent in those which do not. This is not surprising in view of the prevalence of *Pestalotia* sp. on green leaves and seedlings of *R. mangle,* and its persistence in fallen and dead leaves and seedlings. The other common component genera of the sediment and seedling mycoflorae are two of the genera most common in mangrove sediments, *Trichoderma* and *Penicillium;* and these appeared on seedlings at a late stage in the seedling mycosere, just as do the soil fungi involved in terrestrial plant debris mycoseres (Hudson, 1968).

Ulken (1970, 1972) listed several lower fungi from South American mangrove swamp sediments. Among them were four species of *Thraustochytrium* (*T. proliferum* Sparrow, *T. pachydermum* Scholz, *T. multirudimentale* Goldstein and *Thraustochytrium* sp.) and *Schizochytrium aggregatum* Goldstein et Belsky. The other fungi recorded by her from mangrove swamp sediments were Chytridiales, namely a *Rhizophydium* sp. and *Phylctochytrium mangrovii* Ulken (referred to as *Rhizophydium keratinophilum* Karling in her 1970 paper, and described as *P. mangrovii* in her 1972 paper). *Labyrinthula* was not reported.

On red mangrove seedlings both *Thraustochytrium* sp. (no attempt was made to identify this to species, following the example of Clokie, 1970) and *Labyrinthula* sp. were common. *T. pachydermum* and *P. mangrovii* were not baited from red mangrove seedlings, but have subsequently been baited (on boiled blades of grass, *Sporobolus virginicus* (L.) Kunth) from water of South Florida red mangrove habitats, *T. pachydermum* especially frequently (Newell, unpublished data). *Thraustochytrium* sp. exhibited a seasonal distribution, being baited from seedlings most commonly in the months of lowest temperatures and salinities. The reason for its restriction to those stations adjacent to stands of red mangrove trees is unknown; species of *Thraustochytrium* have been isolated from inshore shallow to offshore deep (> 100 m) water (e.g. Sparrow, 1969), and they show affinity for a diversity of solid substrates (Clokie, 1970). The use of mangrove seedling powder as a bait may have limited the number of species of *Thraustochytrium* which could be recorded.

Labyrinthula sp. occupied a position in the seedling mycosere alongside the dead tissue subepidermal invaders. It is not only a saprophyte but also capable of phagocytosis of bacteria and yeast (I have seen *Labyrinthula* sp. with many empty hulls of yeast cells gathered within its ectoplasmic net) and may have increased in frequency with the inflated populations of prey organisms on dead seedling tissue.

Acknowledgements

I wish to acknowledge gratefully the guidance and advice of Dr. J. W. Fell who encouraged me throughout the execution of this research, and I thank Dr. J. Kohlmeyer, whose contagious enthusiasm for the study of the marine fungi gave me the incentive to undertake this project, Mr. I. M. Master, who provided indispensable help with field work and invaluable consultation regarding laboratory operations, Adele Tallman, who provided advice, especially regarding the preparation of illustrations and Ingrid Hunter, who handled much of the work with yeast identifications.

This work was supported in part by a National Science Foundation Graduate Fellowship, by the Atomic Energy Commission, and by the Coca-Cola Export Corporation.

References

ADAMS, S. M., and ANGELOVIC, J. W. (1970). 'Assimilation of detritus and its associated bacteria by three species of estuarine animals.' *Chesapeake Science,* 11, 249-254.

ANASTASIOU, C. J., and CHURCHLAND, L. M. (1969). 'Fungi on decaying leaves in marine habitats.' *Can. J. Bot.,* 47, 251-257.

APINIS, A. E., CHESTERS, C. G. C., and TALIGOOLA, H. K. (1973). 'Microfungi colonizing submerged standing culms of *Phragmites communis* Trin.' *Nova Hedwigia,* 23, 473-480.

ARGO, V. N. (1963). 'Root growth claims soil from sea. Mangrove spreads by unique adaptation.' *Nat. History,* 72, 52-55.

BOEDIJN, K. B. (1956). 'Trypan blue as a stain for fungi.' *Stain Technol.,* 31, 115-116.

BOOTH, C. (1971). *The Genus Fusarium,* Commonwealth Mycological Institute, Kew, Surrey, 237 pp.

BOWMAN, H. H. M. (1917). 'Ecology and physiology of the red mangrove.' *Proc. Am. phil. Soc.,* 56, 589-672.

CAVALIERE, A. R., and JOHNSON, T. W. (1966). 'Marine Ascomycetes: ascocarp morphology and its application to taxonomy. III. A revision of the genus *Lulworthia* Sutherland.' *Nova Hedwigia,* 10, 425-437.

CLOKIE, J. (1970). 'Some substrate relationships of the family Thraustochytriaceae.' *Veröff. Inst. Meeresforsch. Bremerh.,* 12, 329-351.

COCHRANE, V. W. (1958). *Physiology of Fungi,* John Wiley & Sons, Inc., New York, 524 pp.

CRAIGHEAD, F. C. (1971). *The Trees of South Florida. I. The Natural Environments and their Succession,* Univ. Miami Press, Coral Gables, Fla., 212 pp.

CRIBB, A. B., and CRIBB, J. W. (1955). 'Marine fungi from Queensland, I.' *Univ. Queensland Papers Dept. Botany,* 3, 77-81.

CRIBB, A. B., and CRIBB, J. W. (1956). 'Marine fungi from Queensland. II.' *Univ. Queensland Papers Dep. Botany,* 3, 97-105.

DARNELL, R. M. (1964). 'Organic detritus in relation to secondary production in aquatic communities.' *Verh. int. Ver. Limnol.,* 15, 462-470.

DAVIS, J. H. (1940). 'The ecology and geologic role of mangroves in Florida.' *Papers Tortugas Labs.,* 32, 307-412.

DE VRIES, G. A. (1952). *Contribution to Knowledge of the Genus Cladosporium Link ex Fr.,* Hollandia Press, Baarn, 121 pp.

DICKINSON, C. H. (1965). 'The mycoflora associated with *Halimione portul-acoides.* III. Fungi on green and moribund leaves.' *Trans. Br. mycol. Soc.,* 48, 603-610.

DICKINSON, C. H., and KENT, J. W. (1972). 'Critical analysis of fungi in two sand-dune soils.' *Trans. Br. mycol. Soc.,* 58, 269-280.

EGLER, F. E. (1948). 'The dispersal and establishment of red mangrove, *Rhizophora,* in Florida.' *Caribb. Forester,* 9, 299-310.

ELLIS, M. B. (1971). *Dematiaceous Hyphomycetes,* Commonwealth Mycological Institute, Kew, Surrey, England. 608 pp.

FELL, J. W., and MASTER, I. M. (1973). 'Fungi associated with the decay of man-grove (*Rhizophora mangle* L.) leaves in south Florida.' In *The Belle W. Baruch Library in Marine Science. I. Estuarine Microbial Ecology* (Eds. L. H. Stevenson and R. R. Colwell), Univ. S. Carolina Press, Columbia, 455-466.

FRANKLAND, J. C. (1966). 'Succession of fungi on decaying petioles of *Pteridium aquilinum.' J. Ecol.*, 54, 41-63.

GARRETT, S. D. (1963). *Soil Fungi and Soil Fertility*, Pergamon Press, Oxford, 165 pp.

GILL, A. M., and TOMLINSON, P. B. (1969). 'Studies on the growth of red mangrove *(Rhizophora mangle* L.).' *Biotropica*, 1, 1-9.

GRAY, T. R. G., and WILLIAMS, S. T. (1971). 'Microbial productivity in soil.' In *Microbes and Biological Productivity* (21st Symposium of the Soc. for Gen. Microbiol., Eds. D. E. Hughes and A. H. Rose), Cambridge Univ. Press, London, pp. 255-286.

GUBA, E. F. (1961). *Monograph of Monochaetia and Pestalotia*, Harvard Univ. Press, Cambridge, Mass., 342 pp.

HEALD, E. J., and ODUM, W. E. (1969). 'The contribution of mangrove swamps to Florida fisheries.' *Proc. Gulf and Caribb. Fish. Inst.*, 22, 130-135.

HEALD, E. J., and ODUM, W. E. (1975). 'The role of detritus in a South Florida estuary. II. Production and breakdown of vascular plant material.' *Ecology* (in press)

HERING, T. F. (1965). 'The succession of fungi in the litter of a lake district oakwood.' *Trans. Br. mycol. Soc.*, 48, 391-408.

HOGG, B. M., and HUDSON, H. J. (1966). 'Microfungi on leaves of *Fagus sylvatica*. I. The microfungal succession.' *Trans. Br. mycol. Soc.*, 49, 185-192.

HUDSON, H. J. (1962). 'Succession of microfungi on aging leaves of *Saccharum officinarum.' Trans. Br. mycol. Soc.*, 45, 395-423.

HUDSON, H. J. (1968). 'The ecology of fungi on plant remains above the soil.' *New Phytol.*, 67, 837-874.

HUDSON, H. J. (1971). 'The development of saprophytic fungal flora as leaves senesce and fall.' In *Ecology of Leaf Surface Microorganisms* (Eds. T. F. Preece and C. H. Dickinson), Academic Press, London, 447-456.

HUGHES, G. C. (1960). 'Ecological aspects of some lignicolous fungi in estuarine waters'. Ph. D. Dissertation, Florida State Univ., Tallahassee, Fla.

JOHNSON, T. W. (1967). 'The estuarine mycoflora.' In *Estuaries* (Ed. G. H. Lauff), Amer. Ass. Adv. Sci., Washington, D. C., 303-305.

JOHNSON, T. W., FERCHAU, H. A., and GOLD, H. S. (1959). 'Isolation, culture, growth and nutrition of some lignicolous marine fungi.' *Phyton*, 12, 65-80.

JONES, E. B. G. (1963). 'Observations on the fungal succession on wood test blocks submerged in the sea.' *J. Inst. Wood Sci.*, 11, 14-23.

JONES, E. B. G. (1968). 'The distribution of marine fungi on wood submerged in the sea.' *In: Biodeterioration of Materials* (Eds. A. H. Walters and J. J. Elphick) Elsevier, Barking, England, 460-485.

JONES, E. B. G., BYRNE, P., and ALDERMAN, D. J., (1971). 'The response of fungi to salinity.' *Vie et Milieu*, Suppl. 22, 265-280.

KAUSHIK, N. K., and HYNES, H. B. N. (1971). 'The fate of the dead leaves that fall into streams.' *Arch. Hydrobiol.*, 68, 465-515.

KENDRICK, W. B., and BURGES, A. (1962). 'Biological aspects of the decay of *Pinus sylvestris* litter.' *Nova Hedwigia*, 4, 313-342.

KIRK, P. W. (1972). 'Seasonal distribution of marine lignicolous fungi in the lower Chesapeake Bay.' *Am. J. Bot.*, 59, 667.

KOHLMEYER, J. (1968). 'Marine fungi from the tropics.' *Mycologia*, 60, 252-270.

KOHLMEYER, J. (1969 a). 'Ecological notes on fungi in mangrove forests.' *Trans. Br. mycol. Soc.*, 53, 237-250.

KOHLMEYER, J. (1969 b). 'Marine fungi of Hawaii including the new genus *Helicascus.' Can. J. Bot.,* 47, 1469-1487.

KOHLMEYER, J., and KOHLMEYER, E. (1965). 'New marine fungi from mangroves and trees along eroding shorelines'. *Nova Hedwigia,* 9, 89-104.

KOHLMEYER, J., and KOHLMEYER, E. (1971 a). 'Marine fungi from tropical America and Africa.' *Mycologia,* 63, 831-861.

KOHLMEYER, J., and KOHLMEYER, E. (1971 b). *Synoptic Plates of Higher Marine Fungi (3rd Edition),* J. Cramer, Lehre, 87 pp.

LA RUE, C. D., and MUZIK, T. J. (1954). 'Growth, regeneration and precocious rooting in *Rhizophora mangle.' Papers Mich. Acad. Sci., Arts and Letters,* 39, 9-29.

LAST, F. T. (1971). 'Introduction.' In *Ecology of Leaf Surface Microorganisms* (Eds. T. F. Preece and C. H. Dickinson), Academic Press, London, pp. xv-xvii.

LEE, B. H. K., and BAKER, G. E. (1972 a). 'An ecological study of the soil micro-fungi in a Hawaiian mangrove swamp.' *Pacific Sci.,* 26, 1-10.

LEE, B. H. K., and BAKER, G. E. (1972 b). 'Environment and distribution of microfungi in a Hawaiian mangrove swamp.' *Pacific Sci.,* 26, 11-19.

LONG, R. W., and LAKELA, O. (1971). *A Flora of Tropical Florida,* Univ. of Miami Press, Coral Gables, Fla., 962 pp.

MEYERS, S. P. (1953). 'Marine fungi in Biscayne Bay, Florida.' *Bull. mar. Sci. Gulf Caribb.,* 2, 590-601

MEYERS, S. P. (1954). 'Marine fungi in Biscayne Bay, Florida. II. Further studies of occurrence and distribution.' *Bull. mar. Sci. Gulf Caribb.,* 3, 307-327.

MEYERS, S. P. (1957). 'Taxonomy of marine Pyrenomycetes.' *Mycologia,* 49, 457-528.

MEYERS, S. P., and REYNOLDS, E. S. (1958). 'A wood incubation method for the study of lignicolous marine fungi.' *Bull. mar. Sci. Gulf Caribb.,* 8, 342-347.

MEYERS, S. P., and REYNOLDS, E. S. (1960). 'Occurrence of lignicolous fungi in Northern Atlantic and Pacific marine localities.' *Can. J. Bot.,* 38, 217-226.

MEYERS, S. P., ORPURT, P. A., SIMMS, J., and BORAL, L. L. (1965). 'Thalassiomycetes VII. Observations on fungal infestation of turtle grass, *Thalassia testudinum* König.' *Bull. mar. Sci. Gulf Caribb.,* 15, 548-564.

NEWELL, R. (1965). 'The role of detritus in the nutrition of two marine deposit feeders, the prosobranch *Hydrobia ulvae* and the bivalve *Macoma balthica.' Proc. zool. Soc. Lond.,* 144, 25-45.

NEWELL, S. Y. (1974). 'The succession in the mycoflora of red mangrove (*Rhizophora mangle* L.) seedlings.' Ph.D. Dissertation, Univ. of Miami, Coral Gables, Fla.

ODUM, E. P. (1971). *Fundamentals of Ecology* (3rd Edition), W. B. Saunders, Philadelphia, 574 pp.

PARK, D. (1972). 'On the ecology of heterotrophic microorganisms in freshwater.' *Trans. Br. mycol. Soc.,* 58, 291-299.

PAWAR, V. H., MATHUR, P. N., and THIRUMALACHAR, M. J. (1967). 'Species of *Phoma* isolated from marine soils in India.' *Trans. Br. mycol. Soc.,* 50, 259-265.

PERKINS, F. O. (1972). 'The ultrastructure of holdfasts, "rhizoids", and "slime tracks" in Thraustochytriaceous fungi and *Labyrinthula* spp.' *Arch. Mikrobiol.,* 84, 95-118.

PUGH, G. J. F., and BUCKLEY, N. G. (1971). 'The leaf surface as a substrate for colonization by fungi.' In *Ecology of Leaf Surface Microorganisms* (Eds. T. F. Preece and C. H. Dickinson), Academic Press, London, pp. 431-446.

PUGH, G. J. F., and MULDER, J. L. (1971). 'Mycoflora associated with *Typha latifolia.' Trans. Br. mycol. Soc.,* 57, 273-282.

RAI, J. N., TEWARI, J. P., and MUKERJI, K. G. (1969). 'Mycoflora of mangrove mud.' *Mycopath. Mycol. appl.,* 38, 17-31.

RUSCOE, Q. W. (1971). 'Mycoflora of living and dead leaves of *Nothofagus truncata.' Trans. Br. mycol. Soc.,* 56, 463-474.

SCHOLANDER, P. F. (1968). 'How mangroves desalinate seawater.' *Physiologia Pl.,* 21, 251-261.

SIEGEL, S. (1956). *Nonparametric Statistics for the Behavioral Sciences,* McGraw-Hill, New York, 312 pp.

SIEPMAN, R., and JOHNSON, T. W. (1960). 'Isolation and culture of fungi from wood submerged in saline and fresh waters'. *J. Elisha Mitchell scient. Soc.,* 76, 150-154.

SPARROW, F. K. (1969). 'Zoosporic marine fungi from the Pacific Northwest (USA).' *Arch. Mikrobiol.,* 66, 129-146.

STEPHENS, W. M. (1969). 'The mangrove. A tree that makes land.' *Oceans,* 2, 51-55.

STOLK, A. C. (1955). *'Emericellopsis minima* sp. nov. and *Westerdykella ornata* gen. nov., sp. nov.' *Trans. Br. mycol. Soc.,* 38, 419-424.

SWART, H. J. (1958). 'An investigation of the mycoflora in the soil of some mangrove swamps.' *Acta bot. neerl.,* 7, 741-768.

SWART, H. J. (1963). 'Further investigation of the mycoflora in the soil of some mangrove swamps.' *Acta bot. neerl.,* 12, 98-111.

TALIGOOLA, H. K., APINIS, A. E., and CHESTERS, C. G. C. (1973). 'Microfungi colonizing collapsed aerial parts of *Phragmites communis* Trin. in water.' *Nova Hedwigia,* 23, 465-472.

ULKEN, A. (1970). 'Phycomyceten aus der Mangrove bei Cananéia (São Paulo, Brasilien).' *Veröff. Inst. Meeresforsch. Bremerh.,* 12, 313-319.

ULKEN, A. (1972). 'Physiological studies on a Phycomycete from a mangrove at Cananéia, São Paulo, Brazil.' *Veröff. Inst. Meeresforsch. Bremerh.,* 13, 217-230.

WANG, C. J. K., and BAKER, G. E. (1967). *'Zygosporium masonii* and *Z. echinosporum* from Hawaii.' *Can. J. Bot.,* 45, 1945-1952.

WIEGERT, R. G., and EVANS, R. C. (1964). 'Primary production and the disappearance of dead vegetation on an old field in southeastern Michigan.' *Ecology,* 45, 49-63.

3 Yeasts in Oceanic Regions

JACK W. FELL

3.1 Introduction

Marine occurring yeasts were first observed by Fischer and Brebeck (1894); subsequently, reports have appeared sporadically in the literature. Reviews of these efforts have been presented by Kriss *et al.* (1967), van Uden and Fell (1968) and Morris (1968). Largely because of the difficulties and expense of undertaking deep sea expeditions, a great majority of the research has been devoted to estuarine and other inshore regions, a topic that has been discussed by van Uden (1967). This chapter, therefore, will concentrate on yeasts from oceanic regions, with some emphasis on our recently completed research in Antarctic and near Antarctic regions.

3.2 Methods of Collection

Offshore sampling presents two problems: aseptic collection from considerable water depths, and simultaneous collection of sufficient ancillary data to identify the physical and biological characteristics of the water. Some of the early techniques used non-sterile samplers. Willingham and Buck (1965) compared several of these samplers (the van Dorn sampler, the Nansen bottle, the Niskin 5 litre polyvinyl chloride sampler and the Niskin (1962) sterile biosampler). Water samples were collected at two oceanic stations, the comparative counts of yeasts and filamentous fungi clearly demonstrated contamination by the non-sterile samplers. We have run similar tests, and the results agree with those of Willingham and Buck.

Because of the general low quantitative level of yeasts in offshore waters it is necessary to sample 1-2 litres of water; therefore the various small bacteriological water samplers usually are not applicable to this work. The Niskin biosampler has the advantage that it collects approximately 2 litres of water in a sterile polyethylene bag, and the feature of opening and closing at the sampling depth. The disadvantages are the

* Contribution from Rosenstiel School of Marine and Atmospheric Science, University of Miami, 4600 Rickenbacker Causeway, Miami, Florida 33149.

difficulties in handling and the infrequent malfunctions. The latter can be recognized by the use of attached reversing thermometers (Niskin, 1964) to indicate the collection depth.

It is of paramount importance in deep water sampling synoptically to obtain physical data, particularly temperature and salinity in order to ascertain the water mass from which the sample was collected. Also of interest are various parameters such as concentrations of NO_3, NO_2, trace metals, phosphates, oxygen, chlorophylls, and organic and inorganic carbon. Samples of this sort require considerable amounts of water, more than is available in the Niskin biosampler. In addition, considerable effort is required to analyse these factors. Our policy has been to coordinate our programme with hydrographic studies. The biosamplers are placed on the hydrographic wire at 2 metres below the bottles used for physical and chemical collections. While there is some resulting error, the results appear to be within the realm of accuracy for the techniques used. The depths usually sampled are: 2, 10, 25, 50, 100, 150, 200, 400, 600, 800, 1000 m and every additional 250 m to the bottom.

A generally accepted method of isolating yeasts from the water samples is by membrane filtration. Because sterile room conditions are often impossible to obtain on board ship, it is difficult to filter the water and avoid contamination by airborne fungi. We have alleviated this problem by draining the water directly from the sampler to the filter apparatus (Fig. 3.1). The amount of water sampled is dependent on the productivity of the particular region, although duplicate samples of 500-1000 ml are usually required. The membranes are then transferred to agar dishes in the sterile chamber (Fig. 3.1) which also helps reduce contamination.

3.1

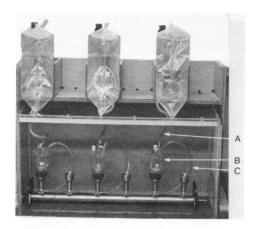

Fig. 3.1. Filter hood for Niskin biosamplers. Water is drained through (A) #13 needle and autoclavable polyvinylchloride tubing into (B) the filter bowl. Tube (C) attaches to a three-way valve at the base, this evacuates the filter bowl and increases the rate of drainage. When the bowl is filled to the desired amount, the valve position is changed to filter the water through the membrane. The entire filter apparatus is autoclaved, in separate sections, prior to use. The hood has a plexiglas front (not shown) with access hand holes.

A variety of media have been used, most of which are similar to those used for isolation of terrestrial yeasts (Morris, 1968). As all media, by their very nature, are selective, it is highly likely that a considerable portion of the yeast community is ignored with the present techniques. One of the critical variables is the addition of bacterial inhibitors to the isolation medium. Acidification of the medium is a standard practice and lactic acid has been used in some studies. However, Phaff (personal communication) cautions against the use of this acid as it may inhibit the growth of some yeasts. HCl is considered to be preferable. Seshadri and Sieburth (1971), in an evaluation of various yeast media, demonstrated higher yeast counts at pH 7.0 than at 6.0 and 8.0. Lactic acid was used as the inhibitor; therefore, it was not ascertained whether the yeast inhibition was due to lactic acid or to the pH. The use of lowered pH has not been a consistently effective method of bacterial inhibition.

Meyers et al. (1967 a), during a study of yeasts from the Black Sea, observed an abundance of bacterial colonies (*Micrococcus* sp.) on their acidified (lactic acid, pH 4.3-4.5) nutrient agar, and they reported some difficulty in distinguishing the bacterial and yeast colonies. We observed similar results in Antarctic waters. A bacterium tentatively identified as *Vibrio* sp. (Wiebe, personal communication) was not inhibited by HCl (pH 4.5) and often formed yeast-like colonies. Use of antibiotics is a more successful technique. Seshadri and Sieburth (1971) tested penicillin G potassium, streptomycin sulphate, chlorotetracycline HCl and chloramphenicol, singly and in combinations. From their results they recommended chloramphenicol (100 mg/litre of media). The adequacy of this amount will depend on the bacterial load. We often find that this level is insufficient. Buck (personal communication) reports that 300-400 mg/litre is often necessary to inhibit bacteria, and he has not observed any mycostatic effects up to 1000 mg.

Seshadri and Sieburth (1971) experienced difficulty in distinguishing white yeast colonies against the white background of the membrane filter. To overcome this they added (100 mg/litre) 2,3,5-triphenyl tetrazolium chloride (TTC) at pH 7.0 to the isolation medium. The yeast hydrogenates the colourless tetrazolium salt to triphenylformazan and the yeast colonies become red. The authors found that at higher levels (500 and 1000 mg/litre) TTC could inhibit yeast growth. In commenting on this problem, Buck (personal communication) reports the successful use of black filters to contrast the white yeast colonies.

The incubation temperature is important and dependent, to some extent, on the study area. Varying between species, the maximal temperatures for growth range from 15 to 46°C. In estuarine regions, many of the yeasts are animal and sewage associated forms with maximal growth temperatures above 37°C. In contrast, most marine yeasts have maximal growth temperatures below 30° C, and those from Antarctic waters are often 15°C. As optimal growth temperature is slightly less than the maximum, we incubate offshore samples at 12°C. It is quite possible that lower temperatures, such as 5°C, and prolonged incubation periods might be preferable. As an example of this type of problem, during one of the Antarctic cruises on the USNS *Eltanin,* 170 samples were processed by the standard filtration technique and the filters placed on agar media in tightly sealed plastic Petri dishes. This appears to reduce evaporation but allows gas exchange. Incubation took place at 12°C and the plates were returned to Miami, under refrigeration, and maintained there at approximately 5°C. Yeast colonies were visible during the first 2-3 weeks of incubation. Additional colonies after this time period were rare and no others were observed at the end of 2½ months. Fourteen months later the plates were examined and 20% of the samples had new yeast colonies that ranged in count from 1-12/litre of seawater (Fig. 3.19).

3.3   Taxonomy of Marine Occurring Yeasts

During the past 23 years the number of descriptions of new yeast species has increased in a nearly geometric fashion. In 1952, when Lodder and Kreger-van Rij's first taxonomic treatise was published, there were 27 genera and 166 species. When the second edition became available (Lodder, 1970) the number of genera rose to 39 with 363 species. In the past three years there have been descriptions of an additional 110 species, including four new genera.

In most cases, the criteria for separation of yeast genera are based on morphological characteristics with some emphasis on biochemical tests. Species separation employs both morphological and biochemical determinations. The morphology includes methods of vegetative reproduction, shapes of vegetative cells and ascospores, presence or absence of clamp connections, teliospores, ballistospores, etc., while the physiology includes the ability of the organisms to grow on 32 individual carbon compounds as the sole source of carbon, the fermentative capabilities with 11 carbohydrates, the utilization of nitrogen compounds, vitamin requirements as well as several other tests.

This seemingly bewildering nature of yeast taxonomy has had a tendency to discourage research in yeast ecology. However, yeast taxonomy is not as difficult as it might seem, and it is probably not as confusing as many of the other fungal groups. While the worker should be aware of the new descriptions that are being published, most of them are of little concern to the marine mycologist as they are often from studies in highly specific terrestrial locales or the result of taxonomic revisions. As most offshore regions have a limited diversity of species it is possible to devise short cuts to eliminate the use of large numbers of physiological tests. Taxonomy of inshore yeasts is somewhat more difficult as there is a large diversity of species, i.e. a mixture of those from terrestrial runoff with the estuarine and marine forms. Most of the species, however, are easily recognized organisms.

3.3.1 Ascomycetous Yeasts

The ascomycetous yeasts belong to the family Saccharomycetaceae of the Endomycetales. According to Lodder (1970) there are 22 genera and 169 species. Based on the number of species the largest genera are *Saccharomyces* (41 spp), *Pichia* (35 spp), *Hansenula* (25 spp), *Kluyveromyces* (18 spp), *Endomycopsis* (10 spp) and *Debaryomyces* (8 spp). There are nine monotypic genera.

Sexuality among these yeasts consists of a system with a single locus and two alleles. The result is that progeny from a single parental cross consist of two mating types (a and $\propto$). Both homothallic and heterothallic conditions exist and further differences in life cycles are usually distinguished by the duration of the haplo- and diplo-phases. In some genera brief dikaryophases have been reported.

Ascomycetes usually are not prevalent in offshore waters. The most important genera are *Debaryomyces* and *Metschnikowia*, although species of *Hansenula*, *Hanseniaspora*, *Kluyveromyces*, *Saccharomyces* and *Pichia* have been reported. *Debaryomyces* consists of species with cells that are spherical or short and oval with pseudomycelium that is primitive to absent. These vegetative cells are usually haploid and conjugation generally takes place between the mother cell and the bud. The resulting spores (1-4 per ascus) are warty walled. Nitrate is not assimilated. *Debaryomyces hansenii* (Zopf) Lodder et Kreger-van Rij is the only species in the genus that is abundant in marine waters, although *D. vanriji* (van der Walt et Tscheuchner) Abadie, Pignal et Jacob has also been reported.

Metschnikowia is a distinctive genus; it produces an elongate ascus with needle shaped asci. The sexual mechanisms in the genus are not completely understood. However, most of the species are heterothallic except for *M. bicuspidata* (Metschnikoff) Kamienski var *biscuspidata* which is exclusively homothallic. Two of the species, *M. pulcherrima* Pitt et Miller and *M. reukaufii* Pitt et Miller, are usually terrestrial, whereas the remaining members of the genus, *M. bicuspidata* (varieties *biscuspidata, australis* Fell et Hunter, *californica* Pitt et Miller and *chathamia* Fell et Pitt), *M. krissii* (van Uden et Castelo-Branco) van Uden and *M. zobellii* (van Uden et Castelo-Branco) van Uden are all from marine sources. Taxonomic separation is based on the number of spores per ascus as well as the organisms' ability to ferment and assimilate certain carbon compounds. Nitrate is not assimilated.

3.3.2 Basidiomycetous Yeasts

The marine occurring basidiomycetous yeasts consist of three genera: *Leucosporidium, Rhodosporidium* and *Sporobolomyces.* Other basidiomycetous genera are *Filobasidium, Bullera* and *Sporidiobolus* (Olive, 1968; Lodder, 1970). The genus *Leucosporidium* is the perfect stage of certain species of *Candida,* while *Rhodosporidium* is the sexual state of several species of *Rhodotorula. Sporobolomyces* is an asexual genus and some of the members have been assigned to the perfect genera *Aessosporon* and *Sporidiobolus.* The separating feature of *Leucosporidium* and *Rhodosporidium* is the production of visible carotenoid pigments in *Rhodosporidium. Sporobolomyces* is distinguished by the production of ballistospores.

The affinity of *Leucosporidium* and *Rhodosporidium* to the Basidiomycetes (Ustilaginales) is based on their smut-like life cycles. The heterothallic life cycle consists of conjugation of haploid yeast cells of opposite mating types, followed by the formation of a dikaryotic mycelium with clamp connections and the development of large, thick walled teliospores. Karyogamy takes place in the teliospore, which germinates to produce a promycelium. Meiosis takes place with the subsequent formation of haploid sporidia.

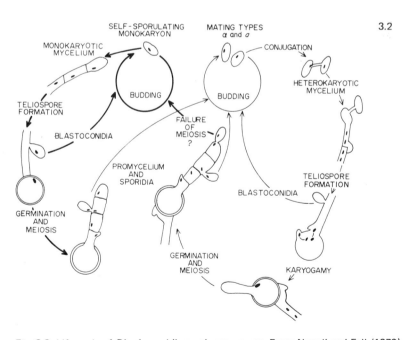

Fig. 3.2. Life cycle of *Rhodosporidium sphaerocarpum.* From Newell and Fell (1970).

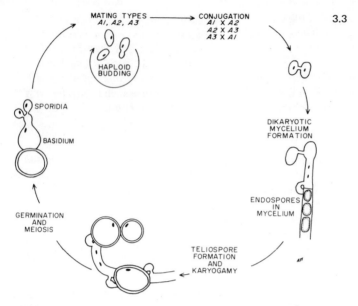

Fig. 3.3. Life cycle of *Rhodosporidium infirmo-miniatum.* From Fell *et al.* (1973).

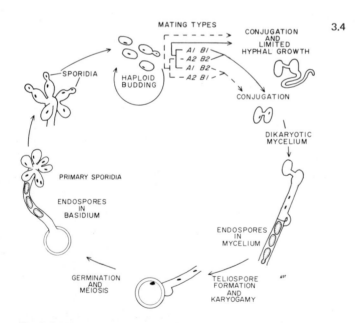

Fig. 3.4. Life cycle of *Rhodosporidium bisporidiis.* From Fell *et al.* (1973).

Three different sexual compatibility systems have been reported (Fell *et al.,* 1973): (1) *Rhodosporidium toruloides* Banno, *R. sphaerocarpum* Newell et Fell, *R. malvinellum* Fell, Hunter et Tallman and *R. diobovatum* Newell et Hunter are bipolar and biallelic; the system consists of one locus with two alleles which results in two mating types (Fig. 3.2). (2) *R. infirmo-miniatum* Fell, Hunter et Tallman is bipolar multiple allelic; there is a single locus, and in this particular case, three alleles. Consequently, there are three mating types, each being fully compatible with the other two mating types (Fig. 3.3). (3) *R. bisporidiis* Fell, Hunter et Tallman and *R. dacryoidum* Fell, Hunter et Tallman are tetrapolar. The system has two loci; mating competence is determined by compatibility factors of two series, A and B. There are four mating types (Fig. 3.4), and the dikaryon is established when the mates have different A and B factors.

Additional research in our laboratory has indicated that *Leucosporidium scottii* Fell, Statzell, Hunter et Phaff, which originally was described as bipolar, biallelic, is tetrapolar; also *L. antarcticum* Fell, Statzell, Hunter et Phaff, described as a homothallic species, has a heterothallic system which has not been completely characterized.

The presence of multiple allelic bipolar and tetrapolar compatibility systems in these yeasts strengthens the hypothesis of the yeast-Basidiomycete relationship rather than a linkage with the Ascomycetes. The compatibility system in the Ascomycetes is strictly bipolar, biallelic, whereas all three systems are found in the Basidiomycetes. As discussed in a detailed review by Koltin *et al.* (1972), the basidiomycetous incompatibility systems have an ecological advantage by reducing inbreeding and promoting outbreeding. The result is genetic heterogeneity which enhances adaptability to new environments and survival under changing conditions.

In addition to heterothallism, homothallism (Fig. 3.5) is prevalent among these yeasts. Banno (1967) described homothallism in *Rhodosporidium toruloides* as resulting from a delay in meiosis in sporidial development. The yeast cells are uninucleate and they develop directly into dikaryotic mycelium with clamp connections. Meiosis takes place during formation of the mycelium. Teliospores that develop on the mycelium germinate to produce promycelia with both heterothallic and homothallic sporidia.

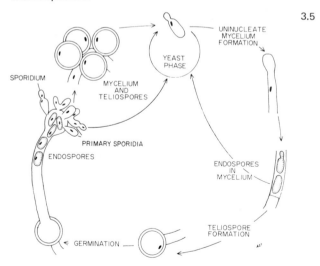

3.5

Fig. 3.5. Life cycle of *Rhodosporidium capitatum.* From Fell *et al.* (1973).

In the majority of the homothallic species *(Leucosporidium frigidum* Fell, Statzell, Hunter et Phaff, *L. gelidum* Fell, Statzell, Hunter et Phaff, *L. nivalis* Fell, Statzell, Hunter et Phaff, *L. stokesii* Fell, Statzell, Hunter et Phaff*)* the uninucleate, presumably diploid, cells give rise to mycelium that remains uninucleate and lacks clamp connections. The teliospores develop and germinate to produce promycelia and sporidia. In one case, *Rhodosporidium sphaerocarpum* (Newell and Fell, 1970) the sporidia are heterothallic, while in *R. capitatum* Fell, Hunter et Tallman the resulting progeny are homothallic. In several species the ploidy of the sporidia has not been determined and it has not been ascertained if meiosis takes place in the teliospore.

Leucosporidium and *Rhodosporidium* are taxonomically separated on the single characteristic of the presence of visible carotenoid pigments. While this is a striking and useful character in distinguishing the red pigmented *Rhodosporidium* and its imperfect stage *Rhodotorula,* this may have limited phylogenetic significance. In looking at the genera as a group, and ignoring the carotenoid pigments, it is possible to separate two groups on different bases. One group, which includes *Leucosporidium gelidum, L. frigidum, Rhodosporidium capitatum, R. infirmo-miniatum,* and *R. bisporidiis,* utilizes inositol as a sole source of carbon and produces extracellular starch compounds. In addition they produce basidia that are one-celled with terminal sporidia. The two closely related families of the Ustilaginales, Ustilaginaceae and Tilletiaceae, are separated by this particular characteristic. The Ustilaginaceae have septate promycelia with lateral basidiospores, whereas the Tilletiaceae have nonseptate promycelia with terminal sporidia. This would suggest that the inositol positive species belong to the Tilletiaceae.

In contrast, the other species group, consisting of *Leucosporidium scottii, Rhodosporidium dacryoidum, R. diobovatum, R. malvinellum, R. sphaerocarpum* and *R. toruloides* do not utilize inositol, do not produce starch and have a septate promycelium with lateral and terminal sporidia, suggesting a relationship to the Ustilaginaceae. At present these distinctions are of informative rather than systematic value. The study of basidiomycetous yeasts is still in its infancy, and it would seem preferable to delay any taxonomic decisions until more information becomes available.

The genus *Rhodotorula* is extremely widespread in freshwater, terrestrial and marine environments, so that the taxonomy of the group is important in assessing its ecology. The perfect state of two or possibly three species of *Rhodotorula* has been discovered. *Rhodotorula glutinis* (Fres.) Harrison is the most significant, due to its ubiquity in nature. *R. glutinis* is comprised of three or possibly more sexual species: *Rhodosporidium diobovatum, Rhodosporidium sphaerocarpum* and *Rhodosporidium toruloides* have the same carbon assimilation pattern as *R. glutinis;* however, the sexual species do not intermate and the morphology of the teliospores is distinctly different for each of the species. Other sexual species also probably exist in the *Rhodotorula glutinis* complex, as the majority of the *R. glutinis* isolates from terrestrial and aquatic environments do not mate with the marine species.

A similar situation exists with *Cryptococcus (Rhodotorula) infirmo-miniatus* (Okunuki) Phaff et Fell which consists of three species that differ in their sexual cycles. *Rhodosporidium bisporidiis* has a tetrapolar compatibility system, *Rhodosporidium infirmo-miniatum* is multiple allelic bipolar and *Rhodosporidium capitatum* is homothallic. The three species have the same carbon assimilation spectrum but do not intermate.

Rhodosporidium dacryoidum appears to belong to the *Rhodotorula minuta-R. pallida* complex. The systematic difference between the two imperfect species is based on melezitose utilization: *R. minuta* (Saito) Harrison is melezitose positive and

R. pallida Lodder is melezitose negative. *R. dacryoidum* has the same carbon and nitrogen spectrum as the imperfects except that melibiose utilization ranges from negative to weak or latent positive. Neither *R. minuta* nor *R. pallida* mate with *R. dacryoidum*, suggesting the existence of another species group.

Sporobolomyces is an asexual genus that is considered to be basidiomycetous due to the formation of ballistospores. Nine species are in the genus and their separation is based on the standard physiological tests. *S. hispanicus* Pelaez et Ramirez, *S. odorus* Derx, *S. pararoseus* Olson et Hammer, *S. roseus* Kluyver et van Niel and *S. salmonicolor* (Fischer et Brebeck) Kluyver et van Niel have all been isolated from oceanic regions. Van der Walt (1969) reported the sexual state of *S. salmonicolor* for which he established *Aessosporon salmonicolor* van der Walt. The life cycle as postulated by van der Walt has three distinct features: homothallism, lack of a mycelial dikaryophase, and presence of ballistospores. The yeast phase cells are either diploid or haploid; both phases reproduce asexually with ballistospores and buds. The ballistospores are normally uninucleate and van der Walt concluded that these spores are not basidiospores but function as dispersal agents. Mating tests of haploids failed to reveal any morphological changes indicative of heterothallism, and van der Walt concluded that the organisms are homothallic with diploidization by fusion of the haploid nucleus of a cell with its bud. Diploidization occurs directly from the haplophase without the intervention of a mycelial dikaryophase. Teliospores develop from the diplophase, and meiosis is presumed to take place in the teliospore, which germinates to a promycelium with buds, or to a mycelium. The sporidial colonies are considered to be haploid, in some instances diploid cells are produced from the teliospore by mitosis. As far as we are aware, there have not been any confirmatory studies of van der Walt's proposed life cycle.

Bardoni *et al.* (1971) observed a heterothallic sexual bipolar, biallelic cycle in *Sporobolomyces odorus*. Following conjugation of opposite mating pairs, a dikaryotic mycelium with clamp connections formed. Teliospores developed that germinated directly into dikaryotic mycelium. In some instances promycelial-like structures were observed, but did not produce viable progeny. Bandoni *et al.* (1971) suggested that they had synthesized *Sporidiobolus johnsonii* Nyland. However, *S. johnsonii* is a homothallic species with a carbon spectrum that is distinct from *S. odorus*, indicating that *Sporobolomyces odorus* and *Sporidiobolus johnsonii* are separate species.

3.3.3 Asexual Yeasts

The imperfect genera belong to the Cryptococcaceae. There are 13 genera, of which seven are found in marine environments and are easily recognized by their morphological characteristics. The *Cryptococcus* species all utilize inositol, most species produce starch, and mycelium formation is negative or rudimentary; *Torulopsis* species do not produce mycelium or produce a very rudimentary mycelium, inositol is not utilized; *Candida* species all produce extensive mycelium; *Trichosporon* species develop mycelium with arthrospores; *Rhodotorula* consists of the red pigmented (carotenoid) species that do not assimilate inositol. *Sterigmatomyces* daughter cells are borne on a sterigma-like structure, whereas *Sympodiomyces* conidia develop sympodially on a conidiophore.

The guanine-cytosine content of the DNA is used as indication of the relationship of yeast species to the Ascomycetes or Basidiomycetes. *Cryptococcus*, *Rhodotorula*, *Trichosporon*, *Sterigmatomyces* and certain species of *Candida* and *Torulopsis* are considered to be Basidiomycetes (Meyer and Phaff, 1970; Nakase and Komagata, 1968) due to a molar percent G-C content greater than 50. Other species, lower than 50%, are considered related to the Ascomycetes.

The majority of the species are differentiated by their fermentative and assimilatory capacities with the various carbon compounds and by their ability to utilize NO_3. *Candida* has 81 species, 24 are marine; *Torulopsis,* 36 species, seven marine; *Cryptococcus,* 17 species, five marine; *Trichosporon,* eight species, one marine; *Rhodotorula,* nine species, seven marine; *Sterigmatomyces,* two species, both marine; *Sympodiomyces,* one species, marine.

3.4 Ecology of Marine Occurring Yeasts

There have been several explorations to oceanic regions in the past 20 years and these will be discussed on a regional basis. Kriss *et al.* (1967) summarized the Russian oceanic research for 1954-1959. During that period considerable microbiological research was conducted in the Arctic, Greenland Sea, Indian Ocean, Antarctic Ocean, Central Pacific, Norwegian Sea and North Atlantic. During these cruises 263 stations were occupied, water was collected at standard hydrographic depths and approximately 4000 samples were examined. Subsamples of 30-50 ml were membrane filtered and the membranes placed on a nutrient agar with tryptic hydrolysate of fish meal. Kriss *et al.,* plotted the species distributions with vertical transects. The results indicated that yeasts are extremely sparse in the oceans. Certain potential errors are inherent in the techniques of Kriss and his co-workers. The use of Nansen bottles has been demonstrated by Willingham and Buck (1965) to be a poor choice for a microbiological collecting device due to a high level of fungal contamination. Also the examina-

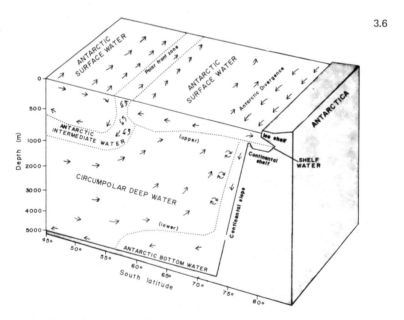

Fig. 3.6. Schematic representation of the water masses in the Antarctic and subantarctic. From Gordon and Goldberg (1970).

tion of a small volume presents difficulties; yeasts are generally found in small concentrations in the open ocean, 1-10/litre is not uncommon; therefore, a 30-50 ml sample would not be representative of the existing populations. Finally, the medium was not selective for yeasts; bacterial competition could have caused an underestimation of the yeast counts. While it seems necessary to criticize the methods of Kriss and his co-workers, it must be remembered that their research was among the first attempts to ascertain the presence of yeasts in the ocean. Some of their field work (Kriss and Novozhilova, 1954) was undertaken in 1951, before the advent of many of our present techniques, which still require improvement.

Also included in this discussion is a summation of a programme that we have recently completed in southern oceanic regions adjacent to the Antarctic. The purpose of the study was to examine the relationship of yeast distributions to the specific water masses in the Antarctic, southern Pacific and southern Indian Oceans. This region is particularly suited for this type of study due to the fairly small changes in temperature and salinity from surface to bottom waters and due to the relative freedom from terrestrial influences. The southern oceans have the water mass structure depicted in Fig. 3.6. The papers of Gordon (1967, 1971) and Gordon and Goldberg (1970) should be consulted for a detailed discussion of this region. The yeast populations in these water masses were examined during six cruises of the USNS *Eltanin* (Fig. 3.7). *Eltanin* Cruise 23 consisted of four transects across the Antarctic Convergence in the vicinity of 56S to 64S, 94W to 131W during April-May 1966. Cruise 24 was a study of the subtropical convergence, 35S-45S, 125W-150W, July-August 1966. Cruise 26 was off New Zealand in the Tasman Sea, November-December 1966. Cruise 27 was a transect from the Ross Sea to Australia, 45S-78S, 147E-180E, January-February 1967. Cruise 35 was in the southern Indian Ocean, 38S-60S, 117E-133E, August-September 1968. Cruise 38 was from the Antarctic ice shelf to Australia, 40S-64S along 150E, March-May 1969.

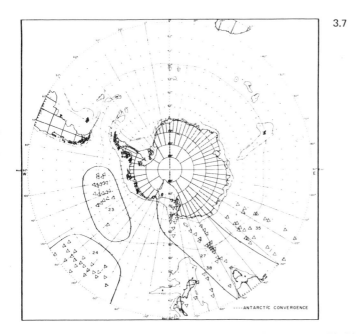

3.7

Fig. 3.7. Station locations for yeast collections during *Eltanin* cruises 23, 24, 26, 27, 35 and 38.

Specific details of the individual station sites of *Eltanin* Cruises 23, 24, 26 and 27 were presented by Jacobs and Amos (1967); Cruise 35 by Jacobs *et al.* (1970) and Cruise 38 by Jacobs *et al.* (1972).

Co-ordinated biological-hydrographic data were collected by placing Niskin samplers 2 m below the Nansen bottles that were used for collecting physical and chemical information. The hydrology was evaluated by using the data published by Jacobs and his co-workers. Temperature-salinity (T-S) diagrams were prepared and the boundaries of the water mass estimated from the information presented by Gordon (1971). The species distributions were plotted on the T-S diagrams with an overlay of the water mass boundaries.

Several of the yeast binomials, as presented in the various ecological papers, are now considered to be synonyms. For uniformity, we have used the nomenclature as presented by Lodder (1970). A few exceptions are made for ecological purposes. Van Uden and Buckley (1970) placed *Candida natalensis* van der Walt et Tscheuschner in *Candida sake* (Saito et Ota) van Uden et Buckley and *Candida polymorpha* Ohara et Nonomura in *Candida diddensii* (Phaff, Mrak et Williams) Fell et Meyer. These conclusions have been questioned by Meyer and Phaff (1970) based on G-C content of the DNA. As *C. natalensis, C. polymorpha* and *C. diddensii* are easily differentiated on physiological properties (differences in rhamnose and erythritol assimilation) we have accepted the taxonomic criteria of Fell and Meyer (1967).

3.4.1 Indian Ocean

Bhat and Kachwalla (1955) collected surface water samples 2-6 miles off the coast of India with sterile glass bottles. They did not give further physical collection data. Eighty isolates of yeasts were obtained from 17 samples; of the 74 isolates that were identified (Table 3.1), 26 were *Candida tropicalis* (Cast.) Berkhout. The authors concluded that *C. tropicalis* is probably one of the most common species of marine yeasts.

TABLE 3.1 Yeasts collected from the Indian Ocean.

Bhat and Kachwalla (1955)

Candida guilliermondii (Cast.) Langeron et Guerra
C. membranaefaciens (Lodder et Kreger-van Rij) Wickerham et Burton
C. tropicalis (Cast.) Berkhout
Cryptococcus sp.
Rhodotorula sp.
Torulopsis candida (Saito) Lodder
T. glabrata (Anderson) Lodder et de Vries
Trichosporon sp.
Debaryomyces hansenii (Zopf) Lodder et Kreger-van Rij
Saccharomyces chevalieri Guilliermond
S. italicus Cast.
S. rosei (Guilliermond) Lodder et Kreger-van Rij

Kriss *et al.* (1967)

Rhodotorula glutinis (Fres.) Harrison

104

R. rubra (Demme) Lodder
Torulopsis holmii (Jorgenson) Lodder

Anton Bruun Cruise (Fell, 1967)

Species	Water masses *
Candida albicans (Robin) Berkhout	CW
C. diddensii (Phaff, Mrak et Williams) Fell et Meyer	AI, ArS, IE, CW, UD, RS (47%)†
C. guilliermondii (Cast.) Langeron et Guerra	CW
C. parapsilosis (Ashford) Langeron et Tallice	ArS, IE, UD
C. polymorpha Ohara et Nonomura	ArS, IE, CW, AI, UD (23%)
C. rugosa (Anderson) Diddens et Lodder	IE
C. tenuis Diddens et Lodder	ArS, RS, IE, UD (6%)
C. tropicalis (Cast.) Berkhout	IE, CW
C. vini (Desmazières ex Lodder) van Uden et Buckley	CW
Candida sp.	CW, AI, UD (28%)
Cryptococcus albidus (Saito) Skinner	RS
Rhodotorula aurantiaca (Saito) Lodder	CW, AI, UD
R. glutinis (Fres.) Harrison	ArS, IE, CW, AI, UD (14%)
R. graminis Di Menna	ArS, UD
R. pallida Lodder	IE, AI
R. rubra (Demme) Lodder	ArS, RS, IE, CW, AI, UD (46%)
Sporobolomyces hispanicus Polaez et Ramirez	ArS, RS
S. odorus Derx	RS, ArS, IE (28%)
Sterigmatomyces halophilus Fell	CW, IE
S. indicus (Fell) Fell	IE, AI
Debaryomyces hansenii (Zopf) Lodder et Kreger-van Rij	IE, AI, CW
Hanseniaspora uvarum (Niehaus) Shehata, Mrak et Phaff	CW
Pichia fermentans Lodder	CW
Saccharomyces cerevisiae Hansen	IE, CW, AI

---

* ArS Arabian Sea	RS Red Sea	IE Indian Equatorial
CW Central Water	AI Antarctic Intermediate	UD Upper Deep Circumpolar Water

†Frequency of occurrence in positive samples. Other species were less than 5%.

In the summary of the Russian oceanic research, Kriss *et al.* (1967) reported the results of the 1956-7 Indian Ocean expeditions from Africa to Antarctica, Antarctica to Asia and along the Antarctic Coast. At the 67 stations sampled, only three species of yeasts were isolated, *Rhodotorula glutinis* at two stations, *R. rubra* (Demme) Lodder and *Torulopsis holmii* (Jorgensen) Lodder at separate locations.

Fell (1967) collected yeasts during a cruise (August-September, 1963) of the *Anton Bruun,* in the Indian Ocean at 16 stations on a transect at 60E from 12N to 41S at depths of 0-2000 m. Collections were made with Niskin biosamplers, following the methods previously discussed. Sixty five percent of the 179 water samples were positive for yeasts. Concentrations ranged from 1-513 cells/litre with an average concentration for positive samples of 36/litre. Quantitatively, the populations were most dense in the Somali Current, which is a region of upwelling, in Antarctic intermediate waters and in some of the surface waters. Yeasts were few in number in the Red Sea, Arabian Sea, Equatorial and Central waters. Twenty five species were isolated (Table 3.1), but 19 were considered to occur infrequently as they were isolated in less than 10% of the positive samples. The remaining species were separated into three ecological groups: (1) *Rhodotorula rubra* and *Candida diddensii* were present in all of the water masses; (2) *C. polymorpha* and *R. glutinis* were widely distributed but apparently absent from Red Sea water (this is a high salinity, low oxygen water mass that flows into the Indian Ocean); (3) Species restricted either to northern waters (12N-22S) *(Sporobolomyces odorus)* or to southern waters (22S-41S) *(Candida* sp. and *R. aurantiaca* (Saito) Lodder. Three species, *Candida albicans* (Robin) Berkhout, *C. tropicalis,* and *C. vini* (Desmazières et Lodder) van Uden et Buckley, considered to be human or animal associated yeasts, were isolated in surface

TABLE 3.2   Yeasts isolated from the South Indian Ocean (*Eltanin* cruise 35).

Species	Water masses*
Candida parapsilosis (Ashford) Langeron et Talice	AS
C. polymorpha (Ohara et Nonomura)	AI
Candida sp.	SA
Cryptococcus albidus (Saito) Skinner	CW
Cr. laurentii (Kufferath) Skinner	AS
Cr. macerans (Frederiksen) Phaff et Fell	SA
Rhodotorula glutinis (Fres.) Harrison	SA
Rhodotorula sp.	AI, SA
Sporobolomyces salmonicolor (Fischer et Brebeck) Kluyver et van Niel	LD
Sympodiomyces parvus Fell et Statzell	WAS, SA (9%)†
Torulopsis austromarina Fell et Hunter	AS, UD, AI (55%)
T. norvegica Reiersol	AS
Trichosporon cutaneum (De Beurm., Gougerot et Vaucher) Ota	CW
Debaryomyces hansenii (Zopf) Lodder et Kreger-van Rij	AI, PF (5%)
Rhodosporidium bisporidiis Fell, Hunter et Tallman	LD, SA
R. capitatum Fell, Hunter et Tallman	AS
R. dacryoidum Fell, Hunter et Tallman	AS
R. malvinellum Fell, Hunter et Tallman	AS, AI, SA (5%)

*AB Antarctic bottom   AI Antarctic intermediate AS Antarctic surface
 CW Circumpolar water   LD Lower deep   PF Polar front
 RS Ross Sea   SA Subantarctic   SPG South Pacific Gyre
 UD Upper deep   WAS Warmed Antarctic
                             surface

†Frequency of occurrence in positive samples. Other species were less than 5%.

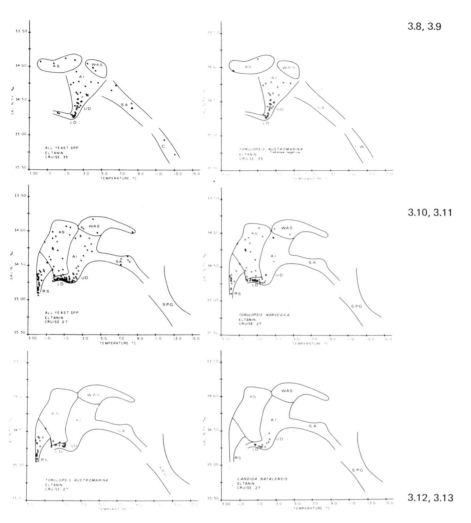

3.8, 3.9

3.10, 3.11

3.12, 3.13

Figs. 3.8-3.13.
Legend:

AB	Antarctic bottom water	RS	Ross Sea water
AI	Antarctic intermediate water	SA	Subantarctic water
AS	Antarctic surface water	SPG	South Pacific Gyre
CW	Central water	UD	Upper deep circumpolar water
LD	Lower deep circumpolar water	WAS	Warmed Antarctic surface water

waters at only one station, suggesting that they may have originated from ship-board contamination or from local bird populations.

Yeasts, as observed during *Eltanin* Cruise 35 (Table 3.2), were sparse in the Antarctic sector of the Indian Ocean. From a total of 393 water samples at 22 stations only 15% contained yeasts with an average of 1/litre and a maximum of 3/litre. The majority of the yeasts were in upper deep circumpolar water, central water and Antarctic intermediate water, although yeasts were observed in the other water masses (Fig. 3.8). *Torulopsis austromarina* was the only abundant species; it was found (46S-58S) at 1-5°C in lower and upper deep circumpolar waters and in Antarctic intermediate waters (Fig. 3.9). This species was also in the Indo-Pacific (Cruise 27, Fig. 3.12, and Cruise 38, Fig. 3.17), usually at water temperatures less than 3°C. The Cruise 35 organisms differed from the Indo-Pacific isolates by the inability to utilize trehalose. In all other taxonomic characteristics the organisms appeared to be identical. Utilization of trehalose is an important diagnostic character in the genus *Torulopsis* (van Uden and Buckley, 1970), which suggests the ecological separation of two physiologically similar species or races. We noted a similar situation in the results from the *Anton Bruun* cruise in the Indian Ocean. *Candida diddensii* was ubiquitous in all of the water masses sampled, whereas a closely related *Candida* sp., that differed on the inability to utilize trehalose, was found only in the southern Indian Ocean (22S-41S) (Fell, 1967).

3.4.2   Indo-Pacific

Eltanin 27, a transect from the Ross Sea to 48S, had a total of 30 stations and 344 water samples; 37% were positive with an average of 14/litre (Fig. 3.10, Table 3.3). *Torulopsis norvegica* Reiersol (Fig. 3.11), averaged 30/litre with a range of 1-200/litre, and was found in all of the water masses with temperatures lower than 5°C. *T. norvegica* was restricted to a narrow geographical zone (151E-175W) southward from the polar front (53S-77S). This species has not been reported previously from marine environments and it would be interesting to compare G-C content of the DNA with the strains from human and animal sources.

Other prevalent species from *Eltanin* 27 were *Torulopsis austromarina* (Fig. 3.12) in Ross Sea and lower deep circumpolar waters (64S-78S, in quantities of 1-4/litre, average 1/litre) and *Candida natalensis* (Fig. 3.13) from lower and upper deep circumpolar waters (1-15/litre, average 3/litre).

Eltanin 38, a transect along 150E, consisted of 18 stations which were in the same vicinity as many of the Cruise 27 stations. A total of 368 samples were taken, 32% contained yeasts at an average of 3/litre and a range of 1-23/litre. The greatest concentrations were repeatedly in the upper 25 m at the southernmost stations (64S) where numbers ranged from 6 to 23/litre. In the remaining stations, concentrations were 1-12/litre. Yeasts (Table 3.3) were distributed (Fig. 3.14) throughout the study area with the exception that they were not isolated from the temperature zone of approximately 4-6.5°C in the warmed Antarctic surface waters. Yeasts were rarely isolated in the central waters and the highest temperature region of Subantarctic waters. The prevalent species had fairly distinct distribution patterns.

C. natalensis (Fig. 3.15) from Cruises 27 and 38 appears to be restricted to a narrow longitudinal zone. The only report from outside this area was of one during Cruise 23 (Table 3.5). The distribution of *C. natalensis* in the Indo-Pacific, was 149E-177E, 50S-64S, from the polar front southward, at 245-3755 m in lower and upper deep circumpolar waters. Population densities were 1-6/litre, average 2/litre.

Leucosporidium antarcticum (Fig. 3.16) was isolated from all of the water masses of temperatures less than 2°C, but was restricted to one location (64S, 150E) which was adjacent to the pack ice. Population densities were 1-22/litre averaging 9/litre. The majority of the isolations were from the upper 100 m, although the species was obtained at 3000 m. The species was not found farther northward (62S) in areas free from ice. The only other report was from waters adjoining the Antarctic peninsula (Fell *et al.*, 1969) which also had abundant sea ice.

TABLE 3.3 Yeasts from the Indo-Pacific (*Eltanin* Cruises 27 and 38).

Species	Water masses†	
	Cruise 27	Cruise 38
Candida intermedia (Ciferri et Ashford) Langeron et Guerra	AS	—
C. natalensis van der Walt et Tscheuschner	LD, UD (9%)*	LD, UD
C. polymorpha (Ohara et Nonomura)	LD	—
C. scottii Diddens et Lodder	LD	—
C. valida-like	AS	—
Candida spp.	LD, UD	—
Cryptococcus albidus (Saito) Lodder	AS, RS	—
Cr. laurentii (Kufferath) Skinner	LD	—
Cr. laurentii var. *magnus* Lodder et Kreger-van Rij	—	SA
Rhodotorula aurantiaca-like	SPG	—
R. glutinis (Fres.) Harrison	AS	AS, SA
R. minuta (Saito) Harrison	AS	—
R. pilimanae Hedrick et Burke	AS	—
R. rubra (Demme) Lodder	AS, WAS	AS, SA, AB, LD (5%)
Rhodotorula sp.	SA	—
Sympodiomyces parvus Fell et Statzell	AI, WAS, SA (6%)	SA, WAS, AI (14%)
Torulopsis austromarina Fell et Hunter	RS, LD (25%)	AS, WAS, UD, LD (18%)
T. norvegica Reiersol	AS, WAS, AI, RS, LD, UD, (49%)	—
T. vanderwaltii-like	AS	—
Torulopsis sp.	LD, AI	LD, UD
Trichosporon cutaneum (De Beurm., Gougerot et Vaucher) Ota	AS, WAS	—
Debaryomyces hansenii (Zopf) Lodder et Kreger-van Rij	AS, AI	LD
Leucosporidium antarcticum Fell, Statzell, Hunter et Phaff	—	AS, AB, LD, UD
Rhodosporidium capitatum Fell, Hunter et Tallman	WAS	—
R. dacryoidum Fell, Hunter et Tallman	LD	LD
R. malvinellum Fell, Hunter et Tallman	—	LD

* Frequency of occurrence in positive samples. Other species were less than 5%.   † As per Table 3.2.

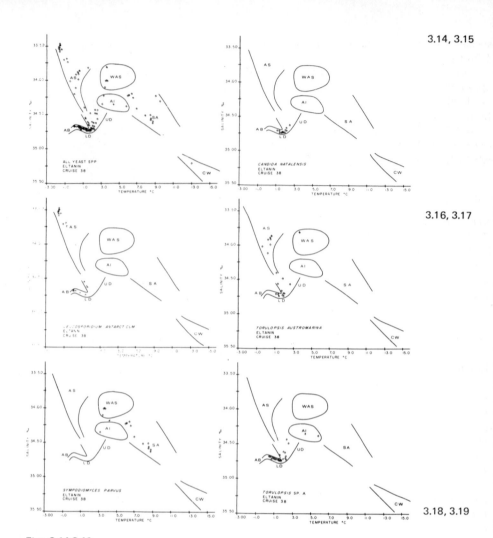

Figs. 3.14-3.19.
Legend:

AB	Antarctic bottom water	RS	Ross Sea water
AI	Antarctic intermediate water	SA	Subantarctic water
AS	Antarctic surface water	SPG	South Pacific Gyre
CW	Central water	UD	Upper deep circumpolar water
LD	Lower deep circumpolar water	WAS	Warmed Antarctic surface water

Torulopsis austromarina, also isolated during Cruise 27, inhabited lower and upper deep circumpolar waters (Fig. 3.17) in concentrations of 1/litre, in the region 57S-64S, which is south of the polar front.

Sympodiomyces parvus Fell et Statzell (Fig. 3.18) is a more northerly species inhabiting warmed Antarctic surface waters in the vicinity of the polar front and northward into the Antarctic intermediate and subantarctic waters. Apparently, the species is not capable of inhabiting the underlying deep waters. *S. parvus* was also isolated from Cruises 23, 27 and 35 (Tables 3.2, 3.3, and 3.5). In all instances the species maintained the same distribution pattern. Concentrations ranged from 1-3/litre, averaging 1/litre.

As discussed in the methods section, isolates of *Torulopsis* sp. A (Fig. 3.19) appeared after prolonged incubation at 5°C. Although many of these cultures were viable, they were extremely difficult to maintain in culture and they have not been identified. Occurrences were in lower and upper deep circumpolar waters.

A distinct difference between Cruise 27 and 38 was the absence of *Torulopsis norvegica* during Cruise 38, although several of the stations were in the same region where *T. norvegica* had been in dense concentrations during Cruise 27.

3.4.3   Pacific Ocean

Van Uden and ZoBell (1962) studied a region in the Torres Strait, which is between Australia and New Guinea. Some of the water samples were taken several miles from land, others over coral reefs. Samples were obtained with sterile 1-litre glass stoppered bottles. Although the authors did not state the number of collections, they were not able to find yeasts in water from the Coral Sea, from the open channels of the Torres Strait or in water over sandy or rock bottoms around Thursday Island, which is also in the Torres Strait. In contrast, they examined sixty-five 200 ml samples over coral and algal growth, 45 contained yeasts at an average of 11 cells/ 200 ml, the largest count was 126/200 ml. The authors experienced difficulty in maintaining the cultures and consequently they only identified 12 representative isolates, six of which were black yeasts (Table 3.4).

Shinano (1962) examined yeast distributions on four cruises, two of which were in the Bering Sea and Aleutian Region, one was east of Japan Proper Island and one cruise was south of Japan Proper Island and into the East China Sea. Eighty-one stations were occupied with a total of 801 samples collected with a J-Z sampler. One hundred and fifteen samples contained yeasts (Table 3.4). Cell counts were greatest from depths of 0, 100-150 and 750 m and yeasts were present to 3000 m. *Rhodotorula rubra* and *R. glutinis* were the most abundant species in the study.

Van Uden and Castelo-Branco (1963) made four vertical casts to 500 m off the coast of San Diego. Eleven of the 24 samples were negative for yeasts, the remainder had counts less than 20/100 ml with the exception of two samples with total counts of 101 and 419/100 ml. *Rhodotorula glutinis* (Table 3.4) was in nine of the samples at 2-367/100 ml, while the black yeasts were 1-52/100 ml. *Cryptococcus albidus* (Saito) Skinner was at three locations, surface −500 m, 1-5/100 ml; *Kluyveromyces bulgaricus* (Santa Maria) van der Walt, one location, 100 m, 9/100 ml; and *Candida rugosa* (Anderson) Diddens et Lodder, one location, 50 m, 1/100 ml.

Steele (1967), in the course of studying fungi from the Hawaiian and Phoenix Islands, reported a predominance of *Aureobasidium pullulans* (De Bary) Arnaud and *Rhodotorula* sp. in intertidal and offshore waters. Yeasts were considerably less abundant in sands than in water samples.

In a survey (Kriss *et al.,* 1967) of 63 stations (33N-41S, 170E-187E) to depths of 10 000 m, only one yeast isolate, *Saccharomyces kloeckerianus* van der Walt (400 m, 18S, 174W) was collected. In a separate study (Kriss and Novozhilova, 1954; Novozhilova, 1955) a survey was made at 15 stations in the deep water regions of the Okhotsk Sea and the Pacific Ocean. Water was sampled to 4800 m with Nansen bottles. The majority of the stations were 60-140 miles from land. Yeasts were in 14% of the samples, the concentrations were variable, ranging from 28 to 4710/litre. The majority of the organisms were in the upper 35 m. Three sampling techniques used wort agar media:

TABLE 3.4   Yeasts isolated from the Pacific Ocean.

Van Uden and Zobell (1962)

Candida marina van Uden et ZoBell
C. reukaufii (Gryss) Diddens et Lodder
Torulopsis maris van Uden et ZoBell
T. torressii van Uden et ZoBell
Kluyveromyces aestuarii (Fell) van der Walt
Pichia farinosa (Londner) Hansen

Shinano (1962)

Candida reukaufii (Gruss) Diddebs et Lodder
C. solani-like
Cryptococcus albidus (Saito) Skinner
Cr. albidus var *diffluens* (Zach) Phaff et Fell
Rhodotorula glutinis (Fres.) Harrison
R. minuta (Saito) Harrison
R. rubra (Demme) Lodder
Sporobolomyces salmonicolor (Fischer et Brebeck) Kluyver et van Niel
Torulopsis candida (Saito) Lodder
T. dattila (Kluyver) Lodder
T. sphaerica (Hammer et Cordes) Lodder
Saccharomyces chevalieri Guilliermond

Kriss *et al.* (1967)

Saccharomyces kloeckerianus van der Walt

Novozhilova (1955)

Candida pulcherrima (Lindner) Windisch
Rhodotorula aurantiaca (Saito) Lodder
Sporobolomyces salmonicolor (Fischer et Brebeck) Kluyver et van Niel
Torulopsis candida (Saito) Lodder

Van Uden and Castelo-Branco (1962)

Candida rugosa (Anderson) Diddens et Lodder
Cryptococcus albidus (Saito) Skinner
Rhodotorula glutinis (Fres.) Harrison
Kluyveromyces bulgaricus (Santa Maria) van der Walt

membrane filtration of 30-40 ml of water, pour plates with 0.5 ml mixed in agar medium at 45°C, and spread plates with 0.5 ml. The counts were extrapolated to one litre.

They also made direct examinations by filtering 20-30 ml of water and fixing the filter in formalin vapour, staining with carbolic erythrosin, drying and clearing in Canada balsam. The entire surface of the filter was examined microscopically. With this technique, yeasts were detected in more samples than by the culture technique, viz. 30% vs. 14%. Membrane techniques are successful for the direct observation of

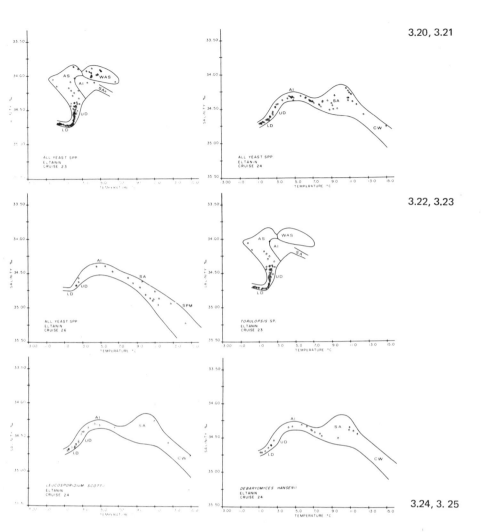

Figs. 3.20-3.25.
Legend:

AB	Antarctic bottom water	RS	Ross sea water
AI	Antarctic intermediate water	SA	Subantarctic water
AS	Antarctic surface water	SPG	South Pacific Gyre
CW	Central water	UD	Upper deep circumpolar water
LD	Lower deep circumpolar water	WAS	Warmed Antarctic surface water

pure yeast cultures (Miller and Kingsley, 1961), however, it has been our experience with seawater samples that it is difficult to differentiate a resting yeast cell from the great variety of plant and animal material that is also in the water sample.

The four species (Table 3.4) from the Okhotsk Sea and the Pacific Ocean were *Torulopsis candida* (Saito) Lodder, which was abundant in the upper 1000 m throughout the study area; *Sporobolomyces salmonicolor* was less frequent, but also in the upper 1000 m; *Candida pulcherrima* (Lindner) Windisch was prevalent in the upper 500 m, but also at one location at 2500 m, and *Rhodotorula aurantiaca* was rarely encountered.

113

TABLE 3.5 Yeasts isolated from the Pacific Ocean (*Eltanin* Cruises 23, 24 and 26).

Species	Water masses†		
	Cruise 23	Cruise 24	Cruise 26
Candida curvata-like	AS	—	—
C. intermedia (Ciferri et Ashford) Langeron et Guerra	—	SA	—
C. natalensis van der Walt et Tscheuschner	LD	—	—
C. parapsilosis (Ashford) Langeron et Tallice	LD	AI, SA	AI, SA (10%)
C. polymorpha (Ohara et Nonomura)	LD, SA	SA	LD
C. rhagii-like	LD	—	—
C. sake Diddens et Lodder	LD, UD	—	—
C. scottii Didden et Lodder	WAS	SA	SA, SPG
Candida spp.		UD	—
Cryptococcus albidus (Saito) Skinner	WAS	AI, UD	SPG
Cr. albidus var *diffluens* (Zach) Phaff et Fell	AI	AI, SA	—
Cr. hungaricus (Zsolt) Phaff et Fell	WAS	—	—
Cr. infirmo-miniatus (Okunuki) Phaff et Fell	WAS	UD	—
Cr. laurentii (Kuffer) Skinner	WAS, LD (8%)*	AI, LD, UD, SA (10%)	—
Cr. laurentii var *flavescens* (Saito) Lodder et Kreger-van Rij	WAS	SA	—
Rhodotorula glutinis (Fres.) Harrison	WAS	UD	—
R. minuta (Saito) Harrison	WAS	—	—
R. pilimanae Hedrick et Burke	—	AI	—
R. rubra (Demme) Lodder	WAS	AI, UD, SA (9%)	AI

114

Species			
Rhodotorula spp.	WAS	—	—
Sympodiomyces parvus Fell et Statzell	AI, WAS, SA, CW (5%)	—	—
Taphrina-like	—	SA	—
Torulopsis sp.	LD, UD, AS, AI (56%)	—	—
Debaryomyces hansenii (Zopf) Lodder et Kreger-van Rij	WAS, LD, SPG (7%)	LD, UD, AI, SA (32%)	AI, SA, SPG, (11%)
D. vanriji (van der Walt et Tscheuschner) Abadie, Pignal et Jacob	LD	—	—
Leucosporidium scottii Fell, Statzell, Hunter et Phaff	WAS, LD	LD, UD, CW, AI, SA (32%)	UD, AI, SA, SPG (46%)
Rhodosporidium bisporidiis Fell, Hunter et Tallman	WAS, AB, LD	LD	—
R. dacryoidum Fell, Hunter et Tallman	WAS, LD, UD	SA, LD	—
R. infirmo-miniatum Fell, Hunter et Tallman	WAS, LD	—	—
R. malvinellum Fell, Hunter et Tallman	WAS, LD	SA	CW

*Frequency of occurrence in positive samples. Other species were less than 5%.
† As per Table 3.2.

2110

There were three *Eltanin* cruises in the Pacific. *Eltanin* 23 (Fig. 3.20) was a 20 station study of the Antarctic convergence in which 417 samples were examined; 31% contained yeasts (Table 3.5) with an average for the positive samples of 4/litre and a range of 1-145/litre. Cruise 24 (Fig. 3.21, Table 3.5), at the subtropical convergence, had 22 stations and 455 water samples; 18% were positive, none exceeding 20/litre, with an average of 2/litre. Cruise 26 (Fig. 3.22, Table 3.6), in the Tasman Sea, had only seven stations; 22% of the 130 samples were positive with an average concentration of 1/litre, in a range of 1-14/litre.

The most prevalent yeast during *Eltanin* 23 was an undescribed species of *Torulopsis* (Fig. 3.23). The occurrences were concentrated in the lower and upper deep circumpolar waters and Antarctic surface waters, 45S-54S. This same species was also observed in Cruise 27 in Antarctic intermediate and lower deep circumpolar waters and in Cruise 38 (Table 3.3) in lower and upper deep circumpolar waters. *Torulopsis* sp. apparently has an unusual nutritional requirement, as the organism did not grow on any of the standard carbon test media (Wickerham, 1951) even when supplemented with 0.1% yeast extract and 3.5% NaCl. Morphologically the colonies are white, smooth and creamy; they develop after 7-10 days on malt agar at 12°C. Additional testing procedures will have to be devised for the taxonomic characterization of this species.

The most abundant species during Cruise 24 were *Leucosporidium scottii* (Fig. 3.24) and *Debaryomyces hansenii* (Fig. 3.25). *L. scottii* was also abundant during Cruise 26 (Table 3.5).

3.4.4 Black Sea

Meyers *et al.* (1967 a) examined yeast distributions at 21 stations along the periphery of the Black Sea. A total of 174 samples were collected with Niskin biosamplers from surface waters to a depth of 2000 m. Eighty four of the samples were positive for yeasts, and concentrations ranged from less than 5/litre to 150/litre with an average count of less than 10/litre. Most of the yeasts (Table 3.6) were found in the upper waters although positive samples were obtained at 2000 m. The prevalent species were *Debaryomyces hansenii, Rhodotorula rubra, R. glutinis* and *C. diddensii*. All of these species were widely distributed in the Black Sea, although *D. hansenii* was most abundant below 100 m. Other abundant species were *Cryptococcus laurentii* (Kufferath) Skinner, *Cr. albidus* and *Candida guilliermondii* (Castellani) Langeron et Guerra. Meyers *et al.* noted that their isolates of *Cr. infirmo-miniatus* produced

TABLE 3.6   Yeasts isolated from the Black Sea and North Sea

Species	Frequency of occurrence (%)
Yeasts isolated from the Black Sea (Meyers *et al.*, 1967 a).	
Candida diddensii (Phaff, Mrak et Williams)	
Fell et Meyer	49
C. guilliermondii (Cast.) Langeron et Guerra	13
C. parapsilosis (Ashford) Langeron et Talice	5
C. polymorpha (Ohara et Nonomura)	7
C. tropicalis (Cast.) Berkhout	5
Candida sp.	1
Cryptococcus albidus (Saito) Skinner	15

Species	Frequency of occurrence (%)
Cr. infirmo-miniatus (Okunuki) Phaff et Fell	2
Cr. laurentii (Kufferath) Skinner	17
Rhodotorula glutinis (Fres.) Harrison	27
R. graminis Di Menna	1
R. minuta (Saito) Harrison	5
R. pilimanae Hedrick et Burke	1
R. rubra (Demme) Lodder	42
Sporobolomyces pararoseus Olson et Hammer	1
S. roseus Kluyver et van Niel	1
Taphrina sp.	4
Torulopsis sp.	3
Debaryomyces hansenii (Zopf) Lodder et Kreger-van Rij	42
Hansenula jadinii (A. et R. Sartory, Weill et Meyer) Wickerham	1
Unidentified	7

Kriss and Novozhilova yeasts isolated from the Black
Sea (1954)

Candida pulcherrima
Sporobolomyces salmonicolor
Torulopsis candida

Yeasts isolated from the North Sea (Meyers et al., 1967 b)

Candida diddensii (Phaff, Mrak et Williams) Fell et Meyer
C. krusei (Cast.) Berkhout
C. lipolytica (Harrison) Diddens et Lodder
C. obtusa (Dietrichson) van Uden et Do Carmo-Sousa ex van Uden et
    Buckley
C. silvicola Shifrine et Phaff
C. tenuis Diddens et Lodder
C. tropicalis (Cast.) Berkhout
C. zeylanoides (Cast.) Langeron et Guerra
Rhodotorula pilimanae Hedrick et Burke
R. rubra (Demme) Lodder
Sporobolomyces roseus Kluyver et van Niel
Debaryomyces hansenii (Zopf) Lodder et Kreger-van Rij
Hanseniaspora uvarum (Niehaus) Shehata, Mrak et Phaff
Hansenula californica (Lodder) Wickerham.

'melanospores' (i.e. teliospores), suggesting that their isolates were Rhodosporidium capitatum. Meyers et al. concluded that the most distinctive aspect of the Black Sea yeast populations was the low density, since only six samples contained more than 20/litre. Probably as a reflection of the high H_2S concentrations in lower levels of the Black Sea, less than 25% of the samples below 100 m yielded yeasts, and these represented the same species as found in upper waters.

Kriss and Novozhilova (1954) and Novozhilova (1955), in the Okhotsk Sea and Pacific Ocean report, occupied seven stations in the Black Sea. Yeasts were observed by the colony count method in 40% of the samples and in 56% by direct count. Colony counts ranged from 29 to 2081/litre and direct counts from 50 to 21 800/ litre. As pointed out by Meyers *et al.* (1967 a), Kriss and Novozhilova's technique of extrapolating the number of yeast cells in a litre using a 0.5-40 ml sample, is subject to considerable error. *Sporobolomyces salmonicolor* was the most prevalent species and was in greatest concentrations in the upper 300 m although isolates were obtained to 1750 m. *Torulopsis candida, Candida pulcherrima* and *Rhodotorula aurantiaca* were also isolated, mostly in the upper 200 m. Kriss and Novozhilova's data indicate large concentrations to 2000 m.

3.4.5   North Sea

Meyers *et al.* (1967 b) examined a series of 12 stations southeast and west of Heligoland for a three year period. Water samples were collected one metre below the surface with a modified ZoBell sampler. Yeasts were in a frequency of 99% at all of the stations. The population densities ranged from less than 10/litre to more than 3000/litre. Maximal densities, mainly *Debaryomyces hansenii,* were at two stations west of Heligoland during the summers of 1964 and 1965. The authors suggested a possible correlation with a dinoflagellate, *Noctiluca,* bloom. The numbers of yeast cells increased with the decline and death of *Noctiluca* cells, although there was insufficient evidence to propose a definitive relationship. The predominate organism in the study area was *Aureobasidium pullulans.* Among the yeasts (Table 3.6), *Debaryomyces hansenii* was the most prevalent species and was frequently in concentrations in excess of 2000/litre at three stations southeast of Heligoland. At these stations there did not appear to be any relationship to *Noctiluca* blooms.

Intensive studies were directed to a station 'Kabeltone' which was between Heligoland and adjacent Sandy Island in a channel with a strong tidal current. The current precluded influences of the island on the collection site. Collections were monthly, or more often, for three years. Seventy two samples were collected, and 71 had yeast concentrations from 2 to 582/litre with approximately 50% of the samples over 50/litre. Several population density peaks were observed through the year. Similarly, in examining samples at 1½ hourly intervals over a 12 hour period there was considerable variability between samples, viz. 8-60/litre. The authors were not able to correlate the peaks with particular hydrographic or seasonal conditions.

Subsequent to this study, Meyers *et al.,* in the same publication, reported a change in the mycoflora SE of Heligoland, which they attributed to flood conditions of the Elbe. Under these conditions, the yeast communities consisted of *Candida lipolytica* (Harrison) Diddens et Lodder, *C. silvicola* Shifrine et Phaff, *C. tenuis* Diddens et Lodder, *Cryptococcus infirmo-miniatus, Rhodotorula graminis* Di Menna, *Sporobolomyces roseus* and *Hansenula californica* (Lodder) Wickerham.

3.4.6   Atlantic Ocean

Kriss *et al.* (1967) reported four yeast isolates at four stations in the North Atlantic, two isolates of *Rhodotorula rubra* (Demme) Lodder and two of *Torulopsis candida.* All four isolates were along 30W between 58N-65N and at 100-1000 m.

Capriotti (1962), as part of a study of yeasts in the Miami, Florida region, collected water samples in the Gulf Stream with the non-sterile van Dorn bottles. The water depths ranged from 50 to 300 m. The organisms isolated were *Aureobasidium pullulans, Rhodotorula glutinis, Candida* sp. and *C. parapsilosis* (Ashford) Langeron et Talice. Capriotti also studied waters 3 miles east of Bimini, Bahamas, at water depths of 50-300 m. This was possibly an error as the area east of Bimini is a shoal bank that does not exceed 8-10 m. Capriotti was probably west of Bimini, on the edge of the Gulf Stream. The species were *Rhodotorula rubra, R. minuta* (Saito) Harrison var. *texensis* (Phaff, Mrak. et Williams), *Rhodotorula* sp. and *Candida* sp. Nineteen of the 36 samples did not contain yeasts. In the other 17 samples, yeasts, including *Aureobasidium pullulans,* ranged from 2 to 120/100 ml.

3.4.7   Other Regions

Kriss *et al.* (1967) rarely encountered yeasts in the Norwegian Sea and the Arctic Ocean. In the Arctic Ocean the species were *Saccharomyces rosei* (Guilliermond) Lodder et Kreger van Rij, *Cryptococcus albidus* var. *aerius,* and *Sporobolomyces roseus.* Isolations were to 4000 m. In the Norwegian Sea, *Debaryomyces hansenii, Cr. albidus* var. *aerius* (Saito) Phaff et Fell, *Saccharomyces kloeckerianus* and *Sporobolomyces roseus* were all isolated above 1000 m.

In the Greenland Sea, Kriss observed a considerable density of yeast populations, particularly from 1000 to 3040 m, where *S. roseus* was isolated in thousands per 50 ml. Other species were *Torulopsis dattila* (Kluyver) Lodder, *T. holmii, Rhodotorula glutinis, R. rubra,* and *Saccharomyces kloeckerianus.*

3.5   Summary and Conclusions

The study of yeasts in the ocean has been valuable to general yeast biology, as we have gained considerable knowledge of the basidiomycetous yeasts, their life cycles, the genetics of mating incompatibility systems and their prevalence in nature. Ecologically, for all marine occurring yeasts, we have some indications as to the quantitative levels of the standing crop and the distribution patterns of certain species. From this information, it should be possible to follow changes in environmental conditions, through alterations in yeast community structures. In contrast, there is very little information available on the specific role of these yeasts.

Yeast cell counts for oceanic waters usually average in the five to tens of cells per litre. As a basis for comparison, van Uden (1967) reported that the estuaries of Portugal contained 118-1228/litre. Exceptions to these low numbers of oceanic yeasts occur, and the most noticeable was in the North Sea (Meyers *et al.,* 1967 b) where populations maintained densities of more than 3000/litre in conjunction with *Noctiluca* blooms. Maximal population densities in other regions were rarely found to exceed 500/litre. In the Antarctic, peaks of 200/litre occurred southward from the Polar Front in a rather narrow longitudinal zone in the Indo-Pacific. Owing to a lack of accompanying biological data, it is not possible to determine the reason for these particular high population densities. In the Indian Ocean (Fell, 1967), increased population densities related to the productivity of the region and, in particular, corresponded with increased concentrations of invertebrates, although causal relationships were not determined.

Distribution of the individual species vary from those that appear ubiquitous to those that appear limited by geographical or hydrographical conditions. *Debaryomyces hansenii,* and the imperfect stage *Torulopsis candida,* have been isolated from all of the oceanic regions irrespective of water mass. The observed quantities are usually

1-40/litre with the exception in the North Sea of *Noctiluca* blooms. The reason for the success of this organism is not apparent, although species of *Debaryomyces* are widely associated with food brines due to their high salt tolerance and ability to assimilate a large number of carbon compounds (Walker and Ayers, 1970). Norkrans (1966) tested 13 species of *Candida, Cryptococcus, Rhodotorula* and *Torulopsis* and four species of *Debaryomyces, Pichia* and *Saccharomyces* for their salinity tolerance. She found that they could all, except one strain of *Cryptococcus laurentii*, grow at $34^\circ/\circ\circ$. Most strains grew at considerably higher concentrations, and *D. hansenii* grew at 24% NaCl. Studies of the genera *Torulopsis* (van Uden and Vidal-Leiria, 1970) and *Candida* (van Uden and Buckley, 1970) demonstrated maximum salinity tolerances varying from 1 to 22% NaCl, which is far above concentrations found in the ocean. Hence, salinity *per se* is not the key to *D. hansenii's* successful colonization of marine environs. Norkrans (1966) demonstrated that strains of *Rhodotorula glutinis, Rh. rubra* and *Debaryomyces hansenii* were capable of surviving in seawater for 120 days, whereas strains of *Saccharomyces cerevisiae* Hansen, *Candida parapsilosis, Pichia fluxuum* (Phaff et Knapp) Kreger-van Rij and *Cryptococcus albidus* were either unable to survive or had a low percentage of survivors. The utilization of a wide range of carbon compounds, which is not unique to *D. hansenii,* plus the survival during 'times of hardship', could possibly be part of the reason for the ubiquity of this species.

Other species that are also widely dispersed, but which have not been recorded as frequently as *D. hansenii,* are *Cryptococcus albidus, Candida polymorpha* and *Rhodotorula glutinis.*

Several species exhibited distinct limitations in their distributions. *Leucosporidium antarcticum* inhabits regions of the Antarctic adjacent to the pack ice. *L. scottii* was found in all of the water masses from 74S-35S in the Pacific Ocean to 158E, but not east into the Indian Ocean nor at sites inhabited by *L. antarcticum. Sympodiomyces parvus* was isolated from a wide geographical range at the polar front northward into Antarctic intermediate and subantarctic waters. *Torulopsis norvegica* was restricted to a narrow geographical zone in the Indo-Pacific south from the polar front. *Candida natalensis* was in lower and upper deep circumpolar water over a two year period, indicating that certain species can be consistent members of the mycoflora; in contrast *T. norvegica* was not found after the same time period. Other species prevalent in specific areas were *Sporobolomyces odorus* in the northern Indian Ocean and *Saccharomyces roseus* in the Greenland Sea.

Torulopsis austromarina has two geographically separated, physiologically distinct varieties; the trehalose positive variety inhabited Indo-Pacific regions, whereas trehalose negative strains were found in the Indian Ocean sector of the Antarctic. A similar situation existed in more northern waters of the Indian Ocean. During the *Anton Bruun* Cruise, *Candida diddensii* inhabited all of the water masses whereas a trehalose negative variety was restricted to southern regions of the study area.

An assumption is that any particular area will have a specific diversity of species, some species are ubiquitous, others peculiar to the region, and still others rare, possibly chance inhabitants. With continued study of a particular region, the alterations in community structure should be predictable, fluctuating with such events as seasonal cycles and plankton blooms. Intrusion of polluted materials should be apparent. Van Uden (1967), in his review of the yeast flora of estuaries, considered two groups of yeasts. First, those such as *Debaryomyces hansenii* that occur in marine and estuarine regions, and second, those that are in estuaries but rarely in the open ocean. The latter group included *Candida tropicalis, C. krusei* (Cast.) Berkhout and *C. parapsilosis,* present in the digestive tract of man and warm-blooded animals, and species such as *C. intermedia*

(Ciferri et Ashford) Langeron et Guerra, *C. catenulata* Diddens et Lodder, *C. vini* and *C. zeylanoides* (Cast.) Langeron et Guerra from vegetables and inanimate terrestrial substrates. Subsequent studies by Combs *et al.* (1971) in Long Island Sound and by Spencer *et al.* (1970) in an aquatic environment (South Saskatchewan River) have shown many of the same 'pollution-indicating species'.

The various studies of offshore environments have confirmed van Uden's observations: while these 'pollution organisms' can be isolated in offshore environments, it is a rare occurrence. In contrast, Bhat and Kachwalla (1955) reported that *Candida tropicalis* was regularly encountered, which suggests heavy pollution of that area of the Indian Ocean. If this is correct, additions of pollutants, such as untreated sewage at ocean outfalls or dumping of oil wastes, should alter the yeast community structure, resulting in high densities of specific pollution indicators.

The role of yeasts in the ocean is generally unknown. The most significant studies have centred on the genus *Metschnikowia*. Initially, *Metschnikowia* was found as a parasite of *Daphnia* (Metschnikoff, 1884). The host would ingest the asci, and the needle-shaped spores would be liberated, penetrate the body wall and germinate. The first culture studies were by van Uden and Castelo-Branco (1961). Two species of *Metschnikowia* were repeatedly isolated from marine substrates along the coast of La Jolla, California. *M. zobellii* was recorded from seawater in quantities of 2-58/100 ml, fish gut contents 25-5730/ml, and the surface of the giant kelp 520-39 200/g. *M. krissii* was isolated from seawater, 1-57/ml. Both species were experimentally pathogenic to *Daphnia*. Seki and Fulton (1969) found that 5% of the specimens of the copepod *Calanus plumchrus* Marukawa from the Straits of Georgia, were infected by *M. krissii*. Yeasts in the surface waters ranged from 30 to 109/100 ml, depending on the sampling date, and approximately 40% of these were *Metschnikowia*. These yeasts were present in the copepods at 0.4×10^5/g dry weight. Similarly, Fize *et al.* (1970) found *Metschnikowia* sp. as a parasite on the copepod *Eurytemora velox* (Lilljebord) G. Brady.

Apparently *Metschnikowia* is a near-shore organism. Seki and Fulton (1969) encountered the highest concentrations of the yeast when the Straits of Georgia were strongly influenced by freshwater inflow from the Nanaimo River. The other marine isolations were: along the California coast (van Uden and Castelo-Branco, 1961, 1963); along the French coast (Fize *et al.*, 1970); in the vicinity of the South Shetland Islands; and in tide pools and a freshwater lake emptying into the ocean at Chatham Island, NZ (Fell and Hunter, 1968).

The majority of the yeasts in the ocean are probably general saprophytes. Other suggested relationships are based on rather weak evidence. Terrestrial heterobasidiomycetes are mostly parasites of plants and often cause destruction of commercially important crops. Whether or not they have similar roles in the ocean has not been determined. While the yeasts may not be parasites, the distribution limits of *Leucosporidium antarcticum* and *L. scottii* suggest a specific activity, as does the limited distribution of other species such as *Candida natalensis*, *Torulopsis austromarina* and *Sympodiomyces parvus*. In some cases the distributions could be temperature dependent, as a few species have a tendency to be psychrophilic. The *Torulopsis* sp. from the *Eltanin* studies has a maximum growth temperature of 12-15°C, *L. antarcticum*, 17°C, and *T. austromarina*, 18-21°C. Temperature and salinity are probably not primary factors in determining distributions, however, since most yeasts have wide temperature and salinity tolerances. With the exception of low-temperature yeasts, most marine yeasts grow at 24°C in laboratory tests. Sodium chloride requirements are rare among fungi and there is no evidence, to our knowledge, to indicate that a 2°/oo salinity difference, a maximum observed in most oceanic regions, is sufficient to inhibit or stimulate yeast growth. The limited distributions could be due to nutrition, the yeasts operating as saprophytes or parasites dependent on a specific group or groups of marine plants or animals.

Acknowledgements

The Antarctic research was supported by the National Science Foundation through the Offices of Biological Oceanography and Antarctic Research. Technical assistance in the laboratory studies was provided by Ingrid L. Hunter and Adele S. Tallman.

References

BANDONI, R. J., LOBO, K. J., and BREZDEN, S. O. (1971). 'Conjugation and chlamydospores in *Sporobolomyces odorus.' Can J. Bot.,* 49, 683-686.

BANNO, I. (1967). 'Studies on the sexuality of *Rhodotorula.' J. gen. appl. Microbiol.,* 13, 167-196.

BHAT, J. V., and KACHWALLA, N. (1955). 'Marine yeasts off the Indian Coast.' *Proc. Indian Acad. Sci.,* 41, 9-15.

CAPRIOTTI, A. (1962). 'Yeasts of the Miami, Florida area. III. From sea water, marine animals and decaying materials.' *Arch. Microbiol.,* 42, 407-414.

COMBS, T. J., MURCHELANO, R. A., and JURGEN, F. (1971). 'Yeasts from Long Island Sound.' *Mycologia,* 63, 178-181.

FELL, J. W. (1967). 'Distribution of yeasts in the Indian Ocean'. *Bull. mar. Sci. Gulf Caribb.,* 17, 454-470.

FELL, J. W., and HUNTER, I. L. (1968). 'Isolation of heterothallic yeast strains of *Metschnikowia kamienski* and their mating reactions with *Chlamydozyma wickerham* spp.' *Antonie van Leeuwenhoek,* 34, 365-376.

FELL, J. W., and HUNTER, I. L. (1974). *'Torulopsis austromarina* sp. nov. A yeast isolated from the Antarctic Ocean.' *Antonie van Leeuwenhoek,* 40, 297-306.

FELL, J. W., and MEYER, S. A. (1967). 'Systematics of yeast species in the *Candida parapsilosis* group.' *Mycopath. Mycol. appl.,* 32, 177-193.

FELL, J. W., HUNTER, I. L., and TALLMAN, A. S. (1973). 'Marine basidiomycetous yeasts (*Rhodosporidium* spp. n.) with tetrapolar and multiple allelic bipolar mating systems. *Can. J. Microbiol.,* 19, 643-657.

FELL, J. W., STATZELL, A., HUNTER, I. L., and PHAFF, H. J. (1969). *'Leucosporidium* gen. nov. The heterobasidiomycetous stage of several yeasts of the genus *Candida.' Antonie van Leeuwenhoek,* 35, 433-462.

FISCHER. B., and BREBECK, C. (1894). 'Zur morphologie, biologie and systematik der Kahmpilze, der *Monilia candida* Hansen und des Soorerrezers.' *C. Fischer: Jena.*

FIZE, A., MANIER, J. F., and MAURAND, J. (1970). 'Sur un cas d'infestation du copepode *Eurytemora velox* (Lillj) par une levure du genre *Metschnikowia kamienski.' Annals. Parasit. hum. comp.,* 45, 357-363.

GORDON, A. L. (1967). 'Structure of Antarctic waters between 20°W and 170°W.' In *Antarctic Map Folio Series, Folio 6,* Am. Geogr. Soc., New York.

GORDON, A. L. (1971). 'Oceanography of Antarctic waters.' *Antarctic Research Series,* 15, 169-203.

GORDON, A. L., and GOLDBERG, R. D. (1970). 'Circumpolar characteristics of Antarctic waters.' In: *Antarctic Map Folio Series, Folio 13,* Am. Geogr. Soc., New York.

JACOBS, S. S., and AMOS, A. F. (1967). 'Physical and chemical oceanographic observations in the Southern Oceans.' In: *Technical Report No. 1-Cu-1-67,* Lamont Geological Observatory of Columbia University, Palisades, N.Y.

JACOBS, S. S., BRUCHHAUSEN P. M., and BAURER, E. B. (1970). *ELTANIN Reports Cruises 32-36, 1968, Hydrographic Stations, Bottom Photographs, Current Measurements,* Lamont-Doherty Geological Observatory of Columbia University, Palisades, N.Y.

JACOBS, S. S., BRUCHHAUSEN, P. M., ROSSELOT, F. L., GORDON, A. L., AMOS, A. F., and BELLIARD, M. (1972). *ELTANIN Reports, Cruises 37-39, 1969; 42-46, 1970, Hydrographic Stations, Bottom Photographs, Current Measurements, Nephelometer Profiles,* Lamont-Doherty Geological Observatory of Columbia University, Palisades, N.Y.

KOLTIN, Y., STAMBERG, J., and LEMKE, P. E. (1972). 'Genetic structure and evolution of the incompatibility factors in higher fungi.' *Bact. Rev.,* 36, 156-171.

KRISS, A. E., and NOVOZHILOVA, M. I. (1954). 'Are yeast organisms inhabitants of seas and oceans?' *Mikrobiologia,* 23, 669-683.

KRISS, A. E., MISHUSTINA, I. E., MITSKEVICH, I. N., and ZEMTSOVA, E. V. (1967). *Microbial Populations of Oceans and Seas,* St. Martin's Press, N.Y. 287 pp.

LODDER, J., and KREGER-VAN RIJ, N. J. W. (1952). *The Yeasts. A Taxonomic Study.* N. Holland Publ. Co., Amsterdam, Holland, 713 pp.

LODDER, J. (1970). *The Yeasts.* N. Holland Publ. Co., Amsterdam, Holland, 1385 pp.

METSCHNIKOFF, F. (1884). 'Uber eine Sprosspilzkrankeit der Daphnien. Beitragzar Lehre uber den Kampg der Phagocyten gegen Krankheitserreger.' *Virchows Arch.,* 96, 177.

MEYER, S. A., and PHAFF, H. J. (1970). 'Taxonomic significance of the DNA base composition in yeasts.' In *Recent Trends in Yeast Research* (Ed. D. G. Ahearn) Georgia State University, Atlanta, Ga., 1-29.

MEYERS, S. P., AHEARN, D. G., and ROTH, F. J. (1967a). 'Mycological investigation of the Black Sea.' *Bull. mar. Sci.,* 17, 576-596.

MEYERS, S. P., AHEARN, D. G., GUNKEL, W., and ROTH, F. J. (1967 b). 'Yeasts from the North Sea.' *Marine Biology,* 1, 118-123.

MILLER, J. J., and KINGSLEY, V. V. (1961). 'A membrane filter mounting method and spore stain for *Saccharomyces.'* *Stain Tech.,* 36, 1-4.

MORRIS, E. O. (1968). 'Yeasts of marine origin.' *Oceanogr. Mar. Biol. Ann. Rev.,* 6, 201-230.

NAKASE, T., and KOMAGATA, K. (1968). 'Taxonomic significance of base composition of yeast DNA.' *J. gen. appl. Microbiol.,* 14, 345-357.

NEWELL, S. Y., and FELL, J. W. (1970). 'The perfect form of a marine-occurring yeast of the genus *Rhodotorula.'* *Mycologia,* 62, 272-281.

NISKIN, S. J. (1962). 'A water sampler for microbiological studies.' *Deep Sea Research,* 9, 501-503.

NISKIN, S. J. (1964). 'A reversing thermometer mechanism for attachment to oceanographic devices.' *Limnol. Oceanogr.,* 9, 591-594.

NORKRANS, B. (1966). 'Studies on marine occurring yeasts: growth related to pH, NaCl concentration and temperature'. *Arch. Mikrobiol.,* 54, 374-392.

NOVOZHILOVA, M. (1955). 'The quantitative characteristics, species composition and distribution of yeast-like organisms in the Black Sea, the Sea of Okhotsk and in the Pacific Ocean.' *Trud. Inst. Mikrobiol.,* 4, 155-195.

OLIVE, L. S. (1968). 'An unusual new heterobasidiomycete with *Tilletia*-like basidia.' *J. Elisha Mitchell scient. Soc.,* 84, 261-266.

SEKI, H., and FULTON, J. (1969). 'Infection of marine copepods by *Metschni-kowia* sp.' *Mycopath. Mycol. appl.,* 38, 61-70.

SHESHADRI, R., and SIEBURTH, J. M. (1971). 'Cultural estimation of yeasts on seaweeds.' *Appl. Microbiol.,* 22, 507-512.

SHINANO, H. (1962). 'Studies on yeasts isolated from various areas of the North Pacific.' *Bull. Jap. Sci. Fisheries,* 28, 1113-1122.

SPENCER, J. F. T., GORIN, P. A. J., and GARDNER, N. R. (1970). 'Yeasts isolated from the South Saskatchewan, a polluted river.' *Can. J. Microbiol.,* 16, 1051-1057.

STEELE, C. W. (1967). 'Fungus population in marine waters and coastal sands of the Hawaiian Line and Phoenix Islands.' *Pacific Science,* 21, 317-331.

VAN DER WALT, J. P., and TSCHEUSCHNER, I. T. (1957). 'Three new yeasts.' *Antonie van Leeuwenhoek,* 23, 184-190.

VAN DER WALT, J. P. (1969). 'The perfect and imperfect states of *Sporobolomyces salmonicolor.' Antonie van Leeuwenhoek,* 36, 49-55.

VAN UDEN, N. (1967). 'Occurrence and origin of yeasts in estuaries.' In *Estuaries* (Ed. G. H. Lauff), AAAS Wash. Publ. 83, 306-310.

VAN UDEN, N., and BUCKLEY, H. (1970). 'The genus *Candida.'* In *The Yeasts* (Ed. J. Lodder), N. Holland Publ. Co., Amsterdam, 893-1087.

VAN UDEN, N., and FELL, J. W. (1968). 'Marine yeasts.' In *Advances in the Micro-biology of the Sea* (Eds. M. Droop and E. J. F. Wood), Academic Press, New York, pp. 167-201.

VAN UDEN, N., and CASTELO-BRANCO, R. (1961). *'Metschnikowiella zobelli* sp. nov. and *M. krissii* sp. nov., two yeasts from the Pacific Ocean pathogenic for *Daphnia magna.' J. gen. microbiol.,* 26, 141-148.

VAN UDEN, N., and CASTELO-BRANCO, R. (1963). 'Distribution and population densities of yeast species in Pacific water, air, animals and kelp off Southern California.' *Limnol. Oceanogr.,* 8, 323-329.

VAN UDEN, N., and VIDAL-LEIRIA, M. (1970). 'The genus *Torulopsis.'* In *The Yeasts* (Ed. J. Lodder), N. Holland Publ, Co., Amsterdam, 1235-1308.

VAN UDEN, N., and ZOBELL, C. E. (1962). *'Candida marina* nov. spec., *Torulopsis torressii* nov. spec. and *T. maris* nov. spec., three yeasts from the Torres Strait.' *Antonie van Leeuwenhoek,* 28, 275-283.

WALKER, H. W., and AYRES, J. C. (1970). 'Yeasts in spoilage organisms.' In *The Yeasts 3: Yeast Technology* (Eds. A. H. Rose and J. S. Harrison), Academic Press, N.Y., pp. 463-528.

WICKERHAM, L. J. (1951). 'Taxonomy of yeasts' *U.S. Dept. Tech. Bulletin,* 1029, 1-56.

WILLINGHAM, C. A., and BUCK, J. D. (1965). 'A preliminary comparative study of fungal contamination in non-sterile water samples.' *Deep-Sea Research,* 12, 693-695.

4 Fungal Degradation of Oil in the Marine Environment

D. G. AHEARN and S. P. MEYERS

4.1 Introduction

Moulds and yeasts are widespread in oceans and estuaries (Johnson and Sparrow, 1961; Meyers et al., 1967 a, b; Ahearn et al., 1968), commonly associated with algal hosts (Kohlmeyer, 1968), plankton and macro algal blooms (Seki and Fulton, 1969), salt marsh vegetation (Meyers et al., 1970), and upwellings, current boundaries and other regions rich in organic compounds (Fell, 1967; van Uden and Fell, 1968). In particular, surface slicks and discrete animal and plant microhabitats frequently yield high fungal populations that may comprise a significant portion of the total microbial biomass. In general, concentrations of marine occurring fungi are highest in littoral zones affected by terrestrial runoff and lowest in subsurface neritic regions (Table 4.1). Implications of such distinctive distributional patterns have been discussed elsewhere (Ahearn, 1973; Meyers and Ahearn, 1973), especially the incidence and activities of fungi in response to the varied input of concentrations of organic substrates within the aquatic ecosystem. Increasing pollution of these areas in all likelihood will continue to affect

TABLE 4.1 Percent frequency of selected moulds and yeasts in estuarine and offshore waters*

Species	Estuarine 10-40‰	Marine 34-36‰
Cladosporium sp.	97	53
Penicillium sp.	80	9
Cephalosporium sp.	49	5
Fusarium sp.	23	< 1
Aureobasidium pullulans	72	67
Candida tropicalis	48	< 1
Candida parapsilosis – complex	25	15
Total samples	67	222

* Samples from the Florida and Louisiana regions of the southeastern United States, (adapted from Ahearn et al., 1968; Ahearn, 1972).

the ecology of the marine mycota, especially species patterns and successions and the association of this biota with animal and plant hosts.

In recent years there has been considerable interest in the accelerated addition of petroleum products into the environment from cultural pollution. The discharge of shipboard petroleum wastes, oil shipping disasters, pipeline breaks, and oil-containing effluents from urban and industrial sites may significantly affect the energy exchange and overall productivity of marine ecosystems. Impact upon economically valuable food webs is of particular concern. In addition, hydrocarbons of plant origin (Clark and Blumer, 1967), or oils from natural seeps, are normally available in the oceans as sources of metabolizable compounds for micro-organisms. Plant oils are chemically comparable to various long chain high molecular weight fractions of petroleum (Davis, 1967). It has been estimated (Button, 1971) that marine algae and phytoplankton produce approximately 10^{13} g of hydrocarbon per year. Similarly, vast marshland regions, characterized by profuse vegetative growth, are noteworthy sources of an array of plant hydrocarbons as well as other organic molecules. Implications of the latter compounds in hydrocarbon utilization are noted subsequently.

4.2 Breakdown of Oil in the Sea

A brief discussion of oil breakdown in seawater is in order, especially in view of the numerous proposals to enhance or accelerate biodegradative activities via nutrient fertilization and/or application of microbial inocula. Upon entering the aqueous environment, oil forms a thin, occasionally monomolecular, surface slick, goes partially into solution and the more volatile fractions rapidly evaporate. Owing to the vast areas and volumes of the sea involved, the production of water-soluble compounds may be especially important in regard to biodegradation. Furthermore, depending on the type of oil and the sea state, the oil may be partially emulsified. Abiotic as well as biotic emulsification processes are of fundamental importance in the total oil biodegradative activity. Processes of weathering, i.e. photochemical reactions, auto-oxidation, etc., and microbial attack, aid in the rapid breakdown and conversion of the paraffinic fractions of oil. The less volatile, more viscous, asphaltene oil fractions are generally recalcitrant, and depend on a balance of nutrients and growth factors for effective biodegradation. Organic substrates, other than those of petroleum origin, are significant, since breakdown of many of the complex aromatic components of oil may be via co-oxidation reactions, i.e. concomitant oxidation of a non-growth substrate during growth of a micro-organism on a utilizable carbon and energy source. However, as observed by Gibson (1971), the initial reactions in microbial oxidation of many aromatic hydrocarbons are still not well defined.

Evidence from various investigators suggests that microbial degradation of oil in the marine environment, particularly that in offshore regions, is affected by limiting amounts of essential nutrients, especially nitrate and phosphate salts (Atlas and Baratha, 1972; Robichaux and Myrick, 1972). As noted by Zobell (1969), other limiting factors for biodegradation may include restricted substrate assimilation capacity of the extant microbial population, presence of toxic substances in crude oil, lack of both sufficient aeration and adequate dispersion, and suboptimal temperatures. Furthermore, levels of essential vitamins, i.e. biotin and thiamine, may be critical, especially for various fungal species. Thus, an understanding of the physiological requirements of hydrocarbonoclastic fungi is basic to elucidation of their role in oil breakdown, and certainly to any proposed application of such organisms as specially prepared inoculum to induce and enhance such processes.

126

4.3 Assimilation of Petroleum Fractions by Fungi

The ability of various fungal taxa to assimilate alkanes and alkenes from C_9 to C_{18} has been well documented. The primary oxidation of straight chained alkanes by *Candida lipolytica* (Harrison) Diddens et Lodder and *C. tropicalis* (Castellani) Berkhout has been shown to occur at the terminal methyl group (Klug and Markovetz, 1971). The resulting primary alcohol is sequentially oxidized to an aldehyde, to a carboxylic acid and then, most probably metabolized by beta oxidation. The alcohol dehydrogenases, of which there may be two for *C. tropicalis,* appear to be NAD dependent (Lebault et al., 1970, 1971). Alkenes appear to be first oxidized at either the saturated end or at the site of the double bond to form a diol. Aromatic compounds are probably converted to phenols and eventually to a dicarboxylic or carboxylic acid and other substituents, depending on the aromatic compound (Davies and Hughes, 1968).

Possible toxicity of hydrocarbon fractions to fungal growth has been discussed by various workers and recently has been evaluated by Gill and Ratledge (1972). The latter investigators examined the toxicity of *n*-alkanes, *n*-alk-1-enes, *n*-alka-1-ols and *n*-alkyl-1-bromides toward two species of *Candida (C. tropicalis* and *C. sp.)* and *Saccharomyces carlsbergensis* Hansen, and observed that small amounts, i.e. 5-10%, of 'potentially deleterious compounds' need not affect the growth of such micro-organisms on petroleum hydrocarbons.

Nyns et al. (1968) and Markovetz et al. (1968) demonstrated that a variety of filamentous fungi assimilated various hydrocarbons. Scheda and Bos (1966) found varied utilization of *n*-decane, *n*-hexadecane and kerosene by representatives of *Pichia, Debaryomyces, Candida* and *Torulopsis.* Markovetz and Kallio (1964) and Klug and Markovetz (1967) implicated strains of *Candida, Debaryomyces, Hansenula, Rhodotorula* and *Trichosporon* as hydrocarbon utilizers. Other references similarly document the broad hydrocarbonoclastic activities of yeasts. Considerable effort in this regard has been directed toward development of yeast protein from petroleum for human and animal consumption (Kihlberg, 1972). Elsewhere, species of *Candida* have been isolated from aircraft fuel storage facilities, as have various moulds, notably *Cladosporium (Amorphotheca) resinae* (Lindau) de Uries from jet fuel systems.

Little data exist on the ability of fungi to degrade compounds shorter than C_9 or the more complex aromatic hydrocarbons. Zajic et al. (1969) reported the growth of a species of *Graphium* in a mineral salts medium with natural gas as the source of carbon. Recently, our laboratory has examined several yeast like fungi capable of growth on vapours of octane and octene (Berner et al., 1971) and various aromatic compounds (Ahearn et al., 1971). A variety of fungi are known to attack aromatic compounds (Nyns et al., 1968; Bollag and Geissbuhlen, 1972), but specific information on fungal attack on cyclic hydrocarbons in crude or refined oils is lacking. Moreover, the processes and particular micro-organisms involved in biodegradation of the asphaltene fraction of oil are unknown.

4.4 Hydrocarbons and Fungal Ecology

The effects of hydrocarbons on fungal ecology in aquatic regions have received only cursory attention. Turner and Ahearn (1970) reported increased populations of hydro-carbonoclastic yeasts in a freshwater stream after the accidental discharge of waste oil from an asphalt refinery into the stream. Yeast populations increased within the five day period following the spill from an initial 30-200 colony forming units (cfu)/ml to 10^4-10^5 units/ml. Species patterns as well as total yeast concentrations were notably affected by the enrichment of the aquatic system by the oil intrusion. Cerniglia and Perry (1972), using an oil enrichment procedure, isolated species of *Penicillium* and *Cunninghamella* from marine sediments and water, and reported the ability of these fungi to degrade a paraffinic base crude oil. Le Petit *et al.* (1970) examined the distribution of hydrocarbon utilizing yeasts in littoral marine areas of the coast of France. Isolates of *Candida lipolytica* and *C. tropicalis* which utilized gas oil were isolated regularly from an area influenced by an oil refinery, but these species were not obtained from a non-polluted zone. These researchers concluded that yeasts, under natural conditions, were of minor importance in the elimination of hydrocarbons from the sea.

Ahearn and Meyers (1972) noted the selective effect of oil on developing yeast populations in estuarine marshlands. The predominant yeasts in the sediments of the *Spartina alterniflora* Loisel salt marshes adjacent to Barataria Bay, Louisiana, are species of the ascosporogenous genera *Kluyveromyces* and *Pichia*. Representatives of these genera, i.e. *K. drosophilarum* (Shehata, Mrak et Phaff) van der Watt and *P. spartinae* Ahearn, Yarrow et Meyers, exhibited negligible growth on hydrocarbon substrates. After three months of periodic controlled enrichment of the field plots with Louisiana crude oil, the dominant species were found to be hydrocarbonoclastic strains of *Trichosporon* and *Pichia* (Table 4.2). Ahearn *et al.* (1971) examined yeasts from various marine habitats and tested representatives that grew on Louisiana crude oil and its distillates as sole sources of carbon. Species capable of utilizing hydrocarbons were in highest concentrations in the proximity of an offshore spewing oil well. *Debaryomyces hansenii* (Zopf) Lodder et Kreger-van Rij, *Candida parapsilosis* (Ashford) Langeron et Talice and *Rhodotorula glutinis* (Fres.) Harrison generally present in concentration of less than 10 c.f.u./100 ml, were the predominant species in oil-free areas. In the vicinity of the aforementioned well, yeast populations ranged from 500 to over 1000 c.f.u./100 ml, comprised mainly of isolates of *Trichosporon* and *Rhodosporidium* sp. Although oil intrusion from the leaking well continued unabated over a four week period, yeast populations gradually decreased in number after an apparent initial growth stimulation by the oil. In laboratory tests, isolates from the oil slicks exhibited good growth when supplied with Louisiana crude oil and its distillates as sole carbon sources.

In marshland studies, *Pichia ohmeri* (Etchells et Bell) Kreger-van Rij, *Trichosporon* sp., and *Rhodotorula* sp. developed in apparent response to the oil enrichment. Selected representatives of *Pichia* and *Trichosporon* demonstrated emulsification capabilities. Certain of the *Trichosporon* strains were oilphilic, eventually filling the interior of the oil globules and exhibiting a filamentous growth consisting of short bulbous hyphae. The *Trichosporon* sp. utilized a wide spectrum of hydrocarbons, including aromatics (Ahearn *et al.*, 1971), but were relatively slow growing. Rates of oxygen uptake on a substrate of 1.5% Louisiana crude oil were significantly higher for yeasts that showed an initial growth response upon addition of the oil to the field plots. Nevertheless, the assimilation and emulsification of oil and the rate of oxygen consumption by the marshland yeasts were approximately 50% of that recorded for isolates of *Candida tropicalis* and *C. lipolytica* from the chronically polluted site of the asphalt refinery. The *Candida* isolates exhibited oxygen uptake of about 400 mg/litre at 20°C with crude oil as a substrate. Strains of *C. lipolytica* and *C. tropicalis* readily metabolized crude oil in seawater in laboratory tests, but only *C. tropicalis* could be established in estuarine test plots. Our explorations indicate that *C. lipolytica* is rarely found in

TABLE 4.2   Effects of oil on marshland yeast populations*

Species	Percentage of total population† Before oil	After oil	Oxygen consumption (mg/litre)
Pichia spartinae	20-30	<10	10
P. saitoi	20-30	<10	24
Kluyveromyces drosophil- arum	10-25	<10	14
Pichia ohmeri	<10	25-30	215
Trichosporon sp.	<10	15-30	65
Rhodotorula/Rhodospori- dium	<10	25-30	—
Cryptococcus sp.	<15	<10	—
Sporobolomyces sp.	<15	<10	—
Mean population	9000‡	18 300	

* Adapted from Ahearn and Meyers (1972).
† Based on colony differences and use of selective agar (Meyers et al., 1971).
‡ Colony forming units per centimetre of sediment.

the marine environment, although we have isolated this species from surface slicks in the North Sea (Meyers, et al., 1967 b). Although C. lipolytica produces extracellular lipases and proteinases, it has a markedly restricted carbohydrate assimilation compared to C. tropicalis. Moreover, C. lipolytica grows poorly or not at all at temperatures above 30°C. These factors may explain the apparent rarity of these species in lipid hydrocarbon rich ocean slicks. In studies of oil biodegradation (Cook et al., 1973) in freshwater aquaria, addition of C. lipolytica and C. tropicalis was observed to stimulate populations of predator protozoans markedly. Turner and Ahearn (1970) also noted rapid development of protozoa on the hydrocarbon utilizing yeasts. Selective predation of yeasts by herbivores in surface slicks may be ecologically significant, as has been shown for mycetophagous marine nematodes (Meyers and Hopper, 1973).

Candida tropicalis also is rarely encountered in open ocean waters. However, this species may be commonly found in inshore areas, particularly those directly influenced by urban runoff. Ahearn et al. (1968) and Fell et al. (1960) noted a restricted distribution for C. tropicalis in Biscayne Bay, Florida. Subsequently, Ahearn (1973) reported that in Biscayne Bay and in freshwaters of Georgia, C. tropicalis rarely occurred in waters with a BOD of less than 3 mg/litre or in areas remote from urban sewage. Waste oils constitute a significant carbon source in sewage effluents and harbour waters. Nevertheless, C. tropicalis was not found in high densities among occasional oil slicks near Miami, Florida, or Grand Isle, Louisiana. Although C. tropicalis typically utilizes hydrocarbons, we have not observed rapid utilization and emulsification of crude oil by strains of C. tropicalis from sites free of chronic oil pollution.

4.5   Summary and Conclusions

Biodegradation of hydrocarbon compounds has been well demonstrated for a considerable number of physiologically diverse micro-organisms, including many taxa of yeasts and moulds. Emphasis on development of microbial protein from petroleum has stimulated considerable research into the species *C. lipolytica* and its mode of attack on the varied constituents of petroleum. The recent review by Kihlberg (1972) discusses production of single cell (yeast) protein from hydrocarbon substrates, notably *n*-paraffin and gas oil. Ecological studies have largely involved analysis of the response of terrestrial fungi to intrusion of oil into soils and associated strata. Jones and Edington (1968) in their survey of hydrocarbon-oxidizing micro-organisms noted the importance of moulds (and yeasts) in such activities. Significantly less information is available on the marine mycota and its response to oil intrusion into the estuarine and neritic environment. The need for such data is apparent.

As noted in our work and that of other investigators, hydrocarbonoclastic yeasts are widespread in the neritic environment and may occur in high densities in surface slicks. However, the rate of degradation and emulsification of crude oil by commonly marine occurring yeasts, mainly strains of *Rhodotorula, Debaryomyces,* and members of the *C. parapsilosis* complex, is relatively slow compared with yeasts from aquatic sites chronically polluted with oil.

Following enrichment of the oceanic site by catastrophic oil disasters, there is evidence that growth of certain of the indigenous yeasts of surface slicks are selectively stimulated. Equally noteworthy is the observation that sustained increase in yeast biomass does not occur, even though ample organic substrate in the form of oil is readily available. The reasons for this lack of a yeast 'bloom' are not immediately apparent, although various considerations have been posed in this review. A combination of field and laboratory studies are needed to supply further pertinent information on the subject.

Hydrocarbonoclastic moulds, mainly species of *Cladosporium* and *Cephalosporium* also occur in marine habitats, but their relationship to natural slicks or cultural oil pollution is unknown. Cooney and Walker (1973) have noted significant hydrocarbon utilization by the fungus, *Cladosporium (Amorphotheca) resinae.* This organism, a constituent of the normal soil mycota, may on occasion be isolated from marine and estuarine waters. However, of far greater interest are the aforementioned marine occurring cladosporia and cephalosporia and their apparent cosmopolitan distribution in marine environments. Evidence to date indicates comparatively low oil assimilating capacities by cladosporia from oil-enriched sediments and water, but the picture is by no means complete. Studies are needed on the response of representative taxa of the marine mycota to oil breakdown (both biotic and abiotic) products and to fungal population densities in association with hydrocarbonoclastic bacteria at sites of active biodegradation.

Considerable interest is being shown in selection of microbial species which, when introduced into oil-contaminated environments, can effectively accelerate the degradation of oil. Among microbial candidates selected have been various moulds and yeasts. However, at present no single micro-organism, or combinations, are known to be capable of completely degrading crude oil.

Acknowledgements

The support of ONR Contract NOOOH-71-C-0145 (Georgia State University) and EPA Project 18080 GDT (Louisiana State University) in the development of these studies is readily acknowledged.

References

AHEARN, D. G. (1973). 'Effects of environmental stress on aquatic yeast populations'. Bella W. Baruch Symposia in Marine Science. *Estuarine Microbial Ecology.* Univ. South Carolina Press.

AHEARN, D. G., and MEYERS, S. P. (1972). 'The role of fungi in the decomposition of hydrocarbons in the marine environment'. In *Biodeterioration of Materials* (Eds. A. H. Walters and E. H. Hueck-van der Plas) Applied Science, London; vol. 2, pp. 12-18.

AHEARN, D. G., ROTH, F. J., Jr., and MEYERS, S. P. (1968). 'Ecology and characterization of yeasts from aquatic regions of South Florida'. *Marine Biology,* 1, 291-308.

AHEARN, D. G., MEYERS, S. P., and STANDARD, P. G. (1971). 'The role of yeasts in the decomposition of oils in marine environments'. *Dev. Industr. Microbiol.,* 12, 126-134.

ATLAS, R. M., and BARTHA, R. (1972). 'Degradation and mineralization of petroleum in sea water: Limitation by nitrogen and phosphorus'. *Biotechnol. Bioeng.,* 14, 309-318.

BERNER, N. H., JONES, R. G., and STANDARD, P. G. (1971). 'The assimilation of hydrocarbon vapors by yeasts'. *Bull. Ga. Acad. Sci.,* 29, 101.

BOLLAG, J. M., and GEISSBUHLEN, H. (1972). 'Biochemical transformation of pesticides by soil fungi'. *CRC Critical Reviews Microbiol.,* 3, 35-58.

BUTTON, D. K. (1971). 'Petroleum—biological effects in the marine environment'. In *Impingement of Man on the Oceans.* (Ed. D. W. Hood), John Wiley and Sons. pp. 421-429.

CERNIGLIA, C. E., and PERRY, J. J. (1972). 'Crude oil degradation by microbes isolated from marine environments'. *Abst. Ann. Meeting Amer. Soc. Microbiol.,* p. 72.

CLARK, R. C., Jr., and BLUMER, M. (1967). 'Distribution of *n*-paraffins in marine organisms and sediment'. *Limnol. Oceanogr.,* 12, 79-87.

COOK, W. L., MASSEY, J. K., and AHEARN, D. G. (1973). 'The degradation of crude oil by yeasts and its effect on *Lesbistes reticulatus'. Louisiana State University,* Center for Wetland Research, Publ. No. LSU-SG-7301, 279-282.

COONEY, J. J., and WALKER, J. D. (1973). 'Hydrocarbon utilization by *Cladosporium resinae'. Louisiana State University,* Center for Wetland Research, Publ. No. LSU-SG-7301, 25-32.

DAVIES, J. A., and HUGHES, D. E. (1968). 'The biochemistry and microbiology of crude oil degradation'. In *Biological Effects of Oil Pollution on the Littoral Communities.* (Eds. J. D. Carthy and D. R. Arthur) Field Studies Council, London, pp. 139-144.

DAVIES, J. B. (1967). *Petroleum Microbiology.* Elsevier Publ. Co., New York. pp. 604.

FELL, J. W. (1967). 'Distribution of yeasts in the Indian Ocean'. *Bull. mar. Sci.,* 17, 454-470.

FELL, J. W., AHEARN, D. G., MEYERS, S. P., and ROTH, F. J., Jr. (1960). 'Isolation of yeasts from Biscayne Bay, Florida and adjacent benthic areas'. *Limnol. Oceanogr.,* 5, 366-371.

GIBSON, D. T. (1971). 'The microbial oxidation of aromatic hydrocarbons'. *CRC Critical Reviews Microbiol.,* 1, 199-223.

GILL, C. O., and RATLEDGE, C. (1972). 'Toxicity of n-alkanes, n-alk-l-enes, n-alkan-l-ols and N-alkyl-l-bromides towards yeasts'. *J. gen. Microbiol.,* 72, 165-172.

JONES, J. G., and EDINGTON, M. A. (1968). 'An ecological survey of hydro-carbon-oxidizing microorganisms'. *J. gen. Microbiol.,* 52, 381-390.

JOHNSON, T. W., Jr., and SPARROW, F. K., Jr. (1961). *Fungi in Oceans and Estuaries.* J. Cramer, Weinheim. pp. 668.

KIHLBERG, R. (1972). 'The microbe as a source of food'. *A. Rev. Microbiol.,* 26, 427-466.

KOHLMEYER, J. (1968). 'Revisions and descriptions of algicolous marine fungi'. *Phytopath. Z.,* 63, 341-363.

KLUG, M. J., and MARKOVETZ, A. J. (1967). 'Degradation of hydrocarbons by members of the genus *Candida.* I. Hydrocarbon assimilation'. *Appl. Microbiol.,* 15, 690-693.

KLUG, M. H., and MARKOVETZ, A. J. (1971). 'Utilization of aliphatic hydro-carbons by microorganisms'. *Adv. Microbiol. Physiol.,* 5, 1-43.

LEPETIT, J. N'GUYEN, M. H., and DEVEZE, L. (1970). 'Etude de l'intervention des levures dans la bio-degradation en mer des hydrocarbures'. *Annls. Inst. Pasteur, Davis,* 118, 709-720.

LEBAULT, J. M., ROCHE, B., DUVNJAK, Z., and AZOULAY, E. (1970). 'Isolation and study of the enzymes involved in the metabolism of hydrocarbons by *Candida tropicalis'. Arch. Mikrobiol.,* 72, 140-153.

LEBAULT, J. M., LODE, E. T., and COON, M. J. (1971). 'Fatty acid and hydro-carbon hydroxylation in yeast: Role of cytochrome P-450 in *Candida tropicalis'. Biochem. Biophys. Res. Comm. UB.,* 42, 413-419.

MARKOVETZ, A. J., and KALLIO, R. E. (1964). 'Assimilation of alkanes and alkenes by yeasts'. *J. Bact.,* 87, 968-969.

MARKOVETZ, A. J., CAZIN, J., and ALLEN, J. E. (1968). 'Assimilation of alkanes and alkenes by fungi'. *Appl. Microbiol.,* 16, 487-489.

MEYERS, S. P., and AHEARN, D. G. (1973). 'Implication of yeasts and yeast-like fungi in marine processes'. *Veröff. Inst. Meeresforsch. Bremerh.,* (in press).

MEYERS, S. P., and HOPPER, H. E. (1973). 'Nematological-microbial interrelation-ships and estuarine biodegradative processes'. Bella E. Baruch Symposia in Marine Science. *Estuarine Microbial Ecology.* University of South Carolina Press.

MEYERS, S. P., AHEARN, D. G., and ROTH, F. J., Jr. (1967 a). 'Mycological investi-gations of Black Sea'. *Bull. mar. Sci.,* 17, 576-596.

MEYERS, S. P., AHEARN, D. G., GUNKEL, W., and ROTH, F. J., Jr. (1967 b). 'Yeasts from the North Sea'. *Marine Biology,* 1, 118-123.

MEYERS, S. P., NICHOLSON, M. L., RHEE, J., MILES, P., and AHEARN, D. G. (1970). 'Mycological studies in Barataria Bay, Louisiana, and biodegradation of oyster grass, *Spartina alterniflora'. Louisiana State University Coastal Studies Bull.,* 5, 111-124.

NYNS, E. J., AUQUIERE, J. P., and WIAUX, A. L. (1968). 'Taxonomic value of the property of fungi to assimilate hydrocarbons'. *Antonie van Leeuwenhoek,* 34, 441-457.

ROBICHAUS, T. J., and MYRICK, H. N. (1972). 'Chemical enhancement of the biodegradation of crude-oil pollutants'. *J. Petrol. Technol.,* 24, 16-20.

SEKI, H., and FULTON, J. (1969). 'Infection of marine copepods by *Metschnikowia* sp.'. *Mycopath. Mycol. appl.,* 38, 61-70.

SCHEDA, S. and BOS, P. (1966). 'Hydrocarbons as substrates for yeasts'. *Nature,* **211, 660.**

TURNER, W. E. and AHEARN, D. G. (1970). 'Ecology and physiology of yeasts of an asphalt refinery and its watershed'. In *Recent Trends in Yeast Research* (Ed. D. G. Ahearn) Spectrum, monograph Series in the Arts and Sciences. Georgia State University, Atlanta., pp. 113-123.

VAN UDEN, N., and FELL, J. W. (1968). 'Marine yeasts'. In *Advances in Microbiology of the Sea* (Eds. M. R. Droop and E. J. F. Wood). Academic Press, London, vol. 1, 167-201.

ZAJIC, J. E., VOLESKY, B., and WELLMAN, A. (1969). 'Growth of *Graphium* sp. on natural gas'. *Can. J. Microbiol.,* 15, 1231-1236.

ZOBELL, C. E. (1969). 'Microbial modification of crude oil in the sea'. *Proc. Joint Conference on Prevention and Control of Oil Spills,* A.P.I., F.W.P.C.A., Dec. 15-17, New York, A.P.I. Publications, New York, 317-326.

5 Physiology of the Higher Marine Fungi

E. B. GARETH JONES and P. J. BYRNE

5.1 Introduction

Early work on the physiology of marine fungi has been summarized by Johnson and Sparrow (1961) and the results discussed by them are not treated here. The fungi most intensively investigated have been those found on wood, and it is natural that the physiological work has concentrated on the degradation activities of these organisms (Jones, 1971; Meyers, 1971). A number of investigations have been concerned with the salinity requirements of marine fungi and discussions of 'What is a marine fungus?' (Ritchie, 1960; Tubaki, 1969; Byrne, 1971; Jones et al., 1971).

5.2. Temperature

Most of the fungi investigated (Table 5.1) showed optimum growth in the range 10-20°C, although a number appear to grow well at temperatures below 10°C. None appeared to require temperatures above 30°C, although Ahearn et al. (1970) and Fell and Phaff (1967) have shown that the yeasts *Pichia spartinae* Ahearn, Yarrow et Meyers and *Cryptococcus lactativorus* Fell et Phaff can grow at temperatures of 37°C. The results of Barghoorn and Linder (1944) indicate that marine fungi have high temperature requirements (25-30°C) but the results of Tubaki (1969) and Jones and Irvine (1972) suggest they have a lower temperature requirement.

Meyers and Simms (1967) have shown that *Lulworthia floridana* Meyers (Ims 190, Ims 384, Ims 490), *Lindra thalassiae* Orpurt, Meyers, Boral et Sims and *Torpedospora* sp. all produce perithecia at 25 and 30°C but require a longer time and have a reduced yield at 20°C. There was no sporulation at 15°C. *Halosphaeria mediosetigera* Cribb et Cribb produced perithecia only at 20°C. Meyers and Reynolds (1960) have shown that *Lulworthia* spp. took 100 to 200 days to fruit on submerged wood when water temperatures were 0-15°C. In contrast, where

TABLE 5.1   The effect of temperature on some marine Ascomycetes and Fungi Imperfecti

Fungus	Author	Optimum temperature for growth (°C)			
		Below 10	10-20	20-30	Above 30
Ceriosporopsis halima Linder	Barghoorn and Linder (1944)	—	—	*	—
Corollospora maritima Werder.		—	—	*	—
Lulworthia salina (Linder) Cribb et Cribb		—	—	*	—
Phialophorophoma littoralis Linder		—	—	*	—
Zalerion maritimum (Linder) Anastasiou		—	—	*	—
C. halima Linder	Tubaki (1969)	—	*	—	—
C. maritima Werder.		—	*	—	—
C. trifurcata (Höhnk) Kohlm.		*	*	—	—
Gnomonia longirostris Cribb et Cribb		*	—	—	—
Leptosphaeria discors (Sacc. et Ellis) Sacc. et Ellis		*	*	—	—
Lindra thalassiae Orpurt, Meyers, Boral et Simms		*	*	—	—
Lignincola laevis Höhnk.		—	*	—	—
Halosphaeria maritima (Linder) Kohlm.		*	*	*	—
H. quadri-remis (Höhnk) Kohlm.		*	*	*	—
Sphaerulina albispiculata Tubaki		*	*	—	—
Torpedospora radiata Meyers		*	—	—	—
Cirrenalia macrocephala (Kohlm.) Meyer et Moore		—	*	—	—
Clavariopsis bulbosa Anastasiou		*	*	—	—
Dendryphiella arenaria Nicot		*	*	—	—
D. salina (Suth.) Pugh et Nicot		—	*	—	—
Humicolla alopallonella Meyers et Moore		—	*	—	—
Monodictys pelagica (Johnson) Jones		—	*	—	—

Nia vibrissa Moore et Meyers		—	—	*	*
Orbimyces spectabilis Linder		—	—	*	*
Zalerion maritimum (Linder) Anastasiou		—	—	*	—
Asteromyces cruciatus (Moreau et Moreau) ex Hennerbert	Jones and Irvine (1972)	—	*	—	—
Lulworthia sp.		—	—	*	—
Corollospora cristata (Kohlm.) Kohlm.		—	—	*	—
Dendryphiella salina (Suth.) Pugh et Nicot.		—	—	*	—
Sterigmatomyces halophilus Fell	Fell (1966)	—	*	—	—
Metschnikowia bicuspidata var. zobelli Fell et Hunter.	Fell and Hunter (1968)	—	*	—	—
M. bicuspidata var australis Fell et Hunter.		—	*	—	—
Leucosporidium scottii Fell, Statzell, Hunter et Phaff.	Fell et al. (1969)	—	*	*	—
L. antarticum Fell, Statzell, Hunter et Phaff		—	—	—	*

water temperatures approached 30°C, *Lulworthia* sp. sporulated on test panels within 10 days following exposure. This is in agreement with the observations of Jones (1963 a).

Doquet (1968) has shown that the marine Gasteromycete *Nia vibrissa* Moore et Meyers fruits readily between 15 and 20°C, but there appears to be a correlation between temperature and salinity.

Byrne (1971) has shown that temperature affects the germination of marine fungi, especially low temperature (Table 5.2). Spores of *Torpedospora radiata* Meyers, did not germinate at 10°C but were able to do so at 15 to 25°C. Similar results have been reported by Kohlmeyer (1966). Ascospores of *Corollospora maritima* Werder and *Dendryphiella salina* (Suth.) Pugh et Nicot germinated equally well at temperatures from 10 to 25°C (Byrne, 1971). Kohlmeyer and Kohlmeyer (1966) report similar temperature requirements for the germination of *Ceriosporopsis circumvestita* (Kohlm.) Kohlm. ascospores. They suggest that this low temperature requirement may explain why this species is not found in tropical or sub-tropical regions.

TABLE 5.2   Spore germination of some marine fungi at different temperatures.

	Temperature (°C)						
	10 hours (%)		15 hours (%)		20 hours (%)		25 hours (%)
Torpedospora radiata							
Meyers	NG		42	(40)	18	(28)	18 (42)
Corollospora maritima							
Werder	42	(100)	24	(100)	18	(85)	18 (98)
Zalerion maritimum							
(Linder) Anastasiou	48	(60)	24	(60)	18	(88)	18 (95)
Asteromyces cruciatus							
(F. et Mme Moreau)							
ex Hennbert	48	(55)	42	(60)	18	(70)	18 (75)
Dendryphiella salina (Suth.)							
Pugh et Nicot	48	(80)	24	(88)	18	(86)	18 (78)

N G = No germination after 72 hours.

The two imperfect fungi *Asteromyces cruciatus* (F. et Mme Moreau) ex Hennebert and *Zalerion maritimum* (Linder) Anastasiou preferred higher temperatures for conidial germination. Similar results have been reported by Kohlmeyer and Kohlmeyer (1966) for *Halosphaeria mediosetigera,* and Kohlmeyer (1968 a) states that ascospores of *Halosphaeria quadricornuta* Cribb et Cribb will not germinate at 20°C but do so at 28° C (within a few hours). Kohlmeyer suggests that this may explain why this species is apparently confined in its distribution to warm waters. However, Johnson and Sparrow (1961) state they have found this species in North Carolina at water temperatures of 8 to 12°C.

Fell (1965) compared the temperature tolerance of deep seawater yeasts with those from warm estuarine waters and showed that marine forms grew at 5°C with maximum growth between 26 to 30°C. Estuarine forms did not grow at 5°C and required higher temperatures for maximum growth.

5.3 Light

Little is known of the effect of light on the fruiting of marine Ascomycetes and Fungi Imperfecti. Kohlmeyer (1968 b) attributes the lack of fruiting structures of marine fungi at a depth of 1615 m, off the coast of California to the constant darkness of this environment and the low temperatures prevailing. Jones and Le Campion-Alsumard (1970) report abundant perithecia of *Haligena unicaudata* Jones et Le Campion-Alsumard at depths of 437 m, and Kirk (1969) states that illumination has no apparent effect on the fruiting of marine fungi. Jones and Ward (1973) have shown that septate conidia are produced by *Asteromyces cruciatus* under two main conditions: when grown on corn meal agar and under continuous black light (Table 5.3). *Coprinus alkalinus* Anastasiou, isolated from wood submerged in alkali lakes, is strongly light sensitive and no basidiocarps are produced when cultures are kept in the dark (Anastasiou, 1967).

TABLE 5.3 Percentage septation of *Asteromyces cruciatus* conidia after 5 days' growth at 21°C.

Number of septa formed	5% malt agar	Glucose/yeast extract agar	Modified Kirk medium	Corn-meal agar
Continuous light (2500 Lux)				
1	0	0	0.6	0.3
2	0	0	0	0.1
12 h light/ 12 h darkness				
1	0	0	0.5	0
Total darkness				
1	0	0	0	0
Continuous black light				
1	2.3	5.1	9.2	12.2
2	0.8	1.8	3.0	4.2
3	0.4	0.4	1.2	2.8
4	0	0.2	0.3	0.8
5	0	0.2	0.3	0.2
6	0	0	0	0.1
7	0	0	0	0.1
Total septate spores	3.5	7.7	14.0	20.4

5.4 Hydrogen Ion Concentration

Barghoorn and Linder (1944) showed that some of the higher marine fungi exhibited a double pH peak for growth, e.g. *Microthelia maritima* (Linder) Kohlm. (4.4 and

TABLE 5.4 Effect of THAM concentration on growth and pH change with various inorganic nitrogen sources (initial pH 7.5)

Fungus	THAM mM	Observed	NH_4Cl	NH_4NO_2	$(NH_4)_2 SO_4$	$(NH_4)_2 CO_2$	KNO_3	KNO_2
Halosphaeria mediosetigera	0	mg mycelium	40	44	36	59	91	111
		final pH	*1.9*	*2.2*	*2.5*	*7.0*	*7.7*	*7.7*
	10	mg mycelium	61	64	53	76	87	93
		final pH	*2.2*	*2.8*	*2.6*	*7.3*	*7.8*	*7.9*
	30	mg mycelium	99	101	102	80	93	99
		final pH	*2.4*	*3.1*	*3.0*	*7.5*	*7.8*	*7.8*
	50	mg mycelium	88	80	83	80	78	92
		final pH	*4.4*	*5.9*	*4.8*	*7.6*	*7.8*	*7.7*
Trichocladium achrasporum	0	mg mycelium	35	39	37	28	45	41
		final pH	*2.1*	*2.3*	*2.1*	*6.1*	*7.5*	*7.2*
	10	mg mycelium	51	55	57	25	52	46
		final pH	*2.6*	*2.6*	*2.9*	*7.4*	*7.8*	*7.7*
	30	mg mycelium	59	57	63	27	54	47
		final pH	*6.0*	*6.1*	*6.5*	*7.6*	*7.9*	*7.8*
	50	mg mycelium	49	38	45	29	37	32
		final pH	*7.0*	*7.1*	*7.1*	*7.5*	*7.8*	*7.7*
Humicola alopallonella	0	mg mycelium	33	35	33	23	38	36
		final pH	*2.0*	*2.1*	*2.0*	*6.3*	*7.4*	*7.3*
	10	mg mycelium	49	52	52	20	49	40
		final pH	*2.5*	*2.8*	*2.6*	*7.3*	*7.6*	*7.6*
	30	my mycelium	52	50	57	23	49	40
		final pH	*6.5*	*6.4*	*6.4*	*7.6*	*7.7*	*7.7*
	50	mg mycelium	46	35	41	26	34	31
		final pH	*7.1*	*7.2*	*7.2*	*7.5*	*7.7*	*7.7*

8.4) and *Lulworthia opaca* (Linder) Cribb et Cribb (5.2 and 8.4). Jones and Irvine (1972) found a similar response in the fungi they tested, one pH peak occurring in the acidic range (6.0-6.6) and the other in the neutral to alkaline range (7.0-8.0).

Sguros and Simms (1963 a) and Meyers and Hoyo (1966) investigated the effect of pH on the growth of four fungi in the presence of the buffer tris (hydroxymethyl) aminomethane (THAM). They found that growth increased with increasing amounts of THAM, thus raising the pH of the medium above inhibitory levels (see Table 5.4). Sguros and Simms also showed that increasing concentrations of THAM were toxic but that the response varied from species to species. Meyers and Hoyo (1966) noted that conidium production in *Varicosporina ramulosa* Meyers et Kohlm., was affected by the pH of the medium. At low concentrations of THAM (0-0.03 M) mycelial cysts were formed but conidia were produced at 0.05-0.10 M THAM.

Holligan and Jennings (1972) have shown that in *Dendryphiella salina,* the loss of the polyols mannitol, arabitol and glycerol appeared to be related directly to the fall in pH of the medium.

5.5 Salinity

Studies of the salinity tolerances of marine fungi have preoccupied many mycologists, as can be seen from the following papers (Borut and Johnson, 1962; Jones, 1963 b; Jones and Jennings, 1964, 1965; Meyers and Simms, 1967 and Jones, *et al.,* 1971). The results can be conveniently divided into groups under the following headings:

5.5.1   The Effect of Salinity on the Vegetative Growth of Fungi

The results of growth studies using fungi isolated from substrates in the sea are shown in Table 5.5. The optimum salinity for growth varies from 10% seawater for *Dendryphiella salina* (Jones, 1963 b) to 100% seawater for *Lulworthia floridana* (Jones, 1963 b), *Orbimyces spectabilis* Linder, *Varicosporina ramulosa* (Meyers and Hoyo, 1966), *Lindra thalassiae* (Meyers and Simms, 1965), and *Corollospora maritima* (Meyers and Scott, 1967; Byrne, 1971). Twenty two of the 28 fungi grew better in seawater than in a distilled water medium, but only in the case of *L. thalassiae* (spore-inoculated cultures) and *L. floridana* (Meyers and Simms, 1965) was growth severely inhibited in the latter medium.

Certain anomalies emerge when comparing the results of different workers. The *L. floridana* isolate used by Jones (1963 b) exhibited a higher optimum for growth than that of Meyers and Simms (1965). These results are not however wholly ambivalent, since a number of factors may affect the salinity tolerances of various fungi. The method of inoculation has been shown by Meyers and Simms (1965 and Table 5.5) to affect the subsequent tolerance of *L. thalassiae.* Variation in growth between isolates of *C. maritima,* using identical experimental procedures (Meyers and Scott, 1967) resulted in different salinity optima for growth.

The three isolates of *D. salina* used by Byrne (1971) exhibited optimum growth at relatively high salinities, i.e. 60-70% seawater. This contrasts with the isolate employed by Jones (1963 b) and the arenicolous species *D. arenaria* Nicot (Meyers, 1968 b) which both exhibited maximum growth at 10 and 20% seawater.

Growth experiments in relation to salinity have also been carried out using typically terrestrial fungi, and this approach is valid as it may explain why these fungi do not occur in the sea. Some of the results reported are summarized in Tables

TABLE 5.5 Responses of marine fungi to salinity

Author	Fungus	Salinity for optimum growth as % SW	Growth distilled water as % of optimum	Growth in seawater as % of optimum	Increase or decrease in SW (%)
Ritchie (1959)	Zalerion sp.	90	72	96	
Jones (1963 b)	Dendryphiella salina	10	60	75	
	Cremasteria cymatilis	50	70	70	
	Lulworthia floridana	100	31	100	
	Sporidesmium salinum	50	98	72	
Sguros and Simms (1964)	Trichocladium achrasporum	60	58	58	
	Halosphaeria mediosetigera	20	57	42	
Meyers and Hoyo (1965)	Orbimyces spectabilis	80-100	18	100	
	Varicosporina ramulosa	20-100	52	100	
Meyers and Simms (1965)	Lulworthia floridana	60	5	95	
	Halosphaeria mediosetigera	20	66	43	
	Lindra thalassiae (Spore inoc.)	100	0	100	
	Lindra thalassiae (Myc. inoc.)	80	33	97	

		80	74	42	
Meyers and Scott (1967)	*Corollospora maritima* IMS 604	80	74	42	
	Corollospora maritima IMS 607	100	100	59	
Meyers (1968 b)	*Dendryphiella arenaria*	20	78	67	
Byrne (1971)	*Asteromyces cruciatus*	90	81.5	27.8	+ 192.7
	Cirrenalia macrocephala	80-60	72.7	16.5	+ 340.3
	Corollospora maritima	100	100	76.9	+ 50.0
	Dendryphiella salina PP5	70	75.8	86.2	− 12.0
	Dendryphiella salina PP255	60	80.7	34.3	+ 135.3
	Dendryphiella salina PP263	60	61.3	20.4	+ 200.0
	Diplodia orae-maris	50	75.4	70.9	+ 6.3
	Lulworthia sp.	80	94.8	57.1	+ 65.0
	Monodictys pelagica	60	87.2	19.2	+ 354.5
	Paecilomyces periscinus	50	84.6	65.9	+ 28.5
	Varicosporina ramulosa	70-50	76.9	16.2	+ 373.0
	Zalerion maritimum	90	89.7	9.7	+ 821.1

143

TABLE 5.6 The responses of terrestrial fungi to salinity

Author	Fungi	Optimum salinity for growth, as % SW	Growth in DW as % of optimum	Growth in SW as % of optimum	Increase or decrease in SW (%)
Byrne (1971)					
	Mucoraceae				
	Zygorhynchus moelleri Vuill.	10	78.7	13.0	− 83.5
	Phycomyces blakesleanus Burgett	10	78.3	18.9	− 75.9
	Mucor hiemalis Wehmer	20	41.2	31.4	− 23.8
	Absidia glauca Hagem	30	42.8	35.2	− 17.7
	Ascomycetes				
	Nectria haematococca Berk. et Br.	0	100	46.8	− 53.1
	Chaetomium globosum Kunze PP117	0	100	2.6	− 97.4
	Neurospora crassa Shear et Dodge	10	99.3	8.3	− 91.6
	Loramyces macrospora Ingold	10	97.6	45.8	− 53.1
	Gelasinospora retispora Cain	10	74.5	28.6	− 61.5
	Sordaria fimicola (Prob.) Ces. et de Not.	10	66.3	33.7	− 49.1
	Pyronema domesticum (Sow.) Sacc.	20	92.5	24.6	− 73.3
	Podospora setosa (Winter) Niessl	20	61.6	35.2	− 42.8
	Chaetomium globosum Kunze R27B	20	58.0	2.7	− 95.2
	Melanospora damnosa	30	77.0	44.0	− 42.8
	Loramyces juncicola Weston	30-40	74.2	43.1	− 41.8
	Fungi imperfecti				
	Tricladium splendens Ingold	0	100	8.7	− 91.3
	Heliscus lugdunensis Sacc. et Therry	10	95.8	73.0	− 24.2
	Stachybotrys atra Corda	10	47.2	69.4	+ 47.0

Myrothecium verrucaria (Albertini et Schweinitz) Ditmar	20	88.4	65.7	− 25.6
Phoma sp.	20	88.4	67.3	− 23.8
Macrophoma sp.	20	34.0	23.4	− 31.3
Wardomyces anomala Brooks et Hansford	30	82.7	67.3	− 18.7
Aspergillus niger van Tiegh.	40	36.0	49.3	+ 36.7
Doratomyces stemonitis Corda	50	44.6	59.2	+ 32.6
Penicillium notatum Westling	100	36.6	100	+173.1
Ritchie (1959) *Aspergillus flavus* Link	80	67	96	
Chaetophoma sp.	30	96	85	
Curvularia sp.	75	82	95	
Mucor spinescens Lendner	30		56	
Ritchie (1961) *Phoma herbarum*	65	81	91	
Jones (1963 a) *Chaetomium globosum* Kunze	30	96	38	
Trametes versicolor L. ex Fr.	10	100	6	
Kirk (1967) *Allescheria boydii* Shear	25	89	45	
Meyers (1968 b) *Hormodendron* sp.	40	97	97	
Cephalosporium sp.	60	43	85	
Swart (1963) *NaCl conc.(%)*				
Aspergillus niger van Tiegh.	2	53	94	
Pythium sp.	2	60	60	
Absidia sp.	1	47	71	
Fusarium A.	0	100	85	
Fusarium B.	2	53	94	

145

TABLE 5.7 Growth responses of terrestrial fungi to distilled water/seawater media.

	Species	Increase/decrease of growth in SW compared with that in DW (%)	Species	Increase/decrease of growth in SW compared with that in DW (%)
Borut and Johnson (1962)	Aspergillus niger van Tiegh.	− 13.3	Jones (1963 b) Robillarda phragmitis Cunnell	− 43.9
	Gliocladium fimbriatum Link	0	Chaetomium globosum Kunze	−164.2
	Penicillium janthinellum Biourge	− 13.1	Trametes versicolor L. ex Fr.	−312.0
	Paecilomyces puntoni (Vuill.) Nann	− 18.0	Phytophthora cryptogea Pethybridge et Lafferty	−125.0
	Cunninghamella blakesleana Lendner	0	Pythium ultimum Trow	−127.2
	Zygorhynchus moelleri Vuill.	− 3.3	Coniophora puteana (Fr.) Karst	−533.3
	Trichoderma lignorum (Tode) Harz	0	Mucor mucedo Auct.	− 54.5
	Curvularia pallescens Boedijn	− 13.6	Thamnidium elegans Link	− 47.0
Gray, Pinto and Pathak (1963)	Phoma sp.	71.9	Pullularia sp.	40.5
	Cephalothecium sp.	31.5	Stemphylium sp.	65.9
	Cylindrocephalum sp.	88.3	Verticillicladium sp.	40.7
	Geomyces sp.	74.1	Epicoccum sp.	32.3
	Linderina sp.	56.0	Myrothecium sp.	7.6
	Sepedonium sp.	− 34.0	Spegazzinia sp.	33.3
	Spicaria sp.	18.0	Heterocephalum sp.	30.9
	Tritirachium sp.	178.5	Rhizopus sp.	40.9
	Bispora sp.	43.8	Collybia sp.	39.4
	Brachysporium sp.	29.4	Morchella sp.	13.2
	Cladosporium sp.	85.9	Hormiactella sp.	− 20.0
	Curvularia sp.	64.1		

5.6 and 5.7. The optimum salinity for growth ranged from distilled water for an isolate of *Fusarium* (Swart, 1963), *Tricladium splendens,* Ingold, *Nectria haematococca* Berk. and Br. and *Chaetomium globosum* Kunze (Byrne, 1971) to 80% seawater for *Aspergillus flavus* Link (Ritchie, 1959) and 100% seawater for *Penicillium notatum* Westling (Byrne, 1971). Of the 39 fungi listed, 26 (66%) grew better in distilled water than in seawater media.

The results of Byrne (1971) fall into two main categories depending on their salinity tolerances. Firstly, the Mucoraceous and Ascomycetous species, whose optimum salinity for growth does not exceed 30% seawater (Fig. 5.1). Growth in distilled water media was good, and the percentage growth of that at the optimum never fell below 40% and in most cases was well above 60%. In contrast, growth in seawater media as a percentage of that at the optimum, showed a marked decrease.

The second group, the Fungi Imperfecti, show a much broader tolerance to high saline conditions. Of the ten species investigated, four grew better on 100% seawater than on distilled water media. Of the 39 species listed in Table 5.7, 21 (54%) grew better in seawater. Most of these are Fungi Imperfecti and would therefore support the observations of Byrne (1971).

5.5.2   Reproduction in relation to salinity

The effects of seawater dilutions on reproduction of marine fungi has only been investigated in a few species, and some of these results are summarized in Table 5.8. Eight Ascomycetes produced mature perithecia in distilled water media while *Lindra thallassiae* and *Halosphaeria appendiculata* Linder produced immature perithecia. The latter produced mature perithecia at all salinities except distilled water. Kirk (1967) using both marine and clinical isolates of *Allescheria boydii* Shear found a wide tolerance to salinity. Although there was some variation between isolates, where reproduction occurred at all, most were able to produce mature cleistothecia and develop conidia over the whole range of salinities.

The hyphomycete *Varicosporina ramulosa* produced normal conidia between 20 and 100% seawater but, at salinities below 20% seawater, malformed conidia, chlamydospores and cysts were formed (Meyers and Hoyo, 1966). In *Dendryphiella salina,* salinity had little effect on sporulation while in *Asteromyces cruciatus* maximum spore production occurred between 60 and 90% seawater.

Siepman (1959 a, b) and Byrne (1971) are the only investigators to examine the effect of salinity on the reproduction of terrestrial fungi. Since reproduction may play such a major role in controlling the distribution of fungi within certain environmental extremes, it is surprising this aspect has not been more fully investigated.

Byrne (1971) investigated the effect of salinity on the fruiting of a number of terrestrial Mucoraceae, Ascomycetes and Fungi Imperfecti. *Mucor hiemalis* Wehmer and *Absidia glauca* Hagem were able to produce asexual spores over the whole range of salinities with maximum production of spores at 10% and 30% seawater respectively. In both cases, increasing salinities caused a decrease in zygospore production and the total inhibition above 60% seawater in *M. hiemalis.*

Table 5.9 presents some results on the effect of salinity on the fruiting of selected terrestrial Ascomycetes. In no case were ascospores produced at salinities above 60% seawater, and in the case of *Neurospora crassa* it was as low as 20% seawater. Byrne (1971) also noted that the time required for the production of perithecia increased with increasing salinities. Increasing salinities had a pronounced

TABLE 5.8   Reproductive responses of marine fungi to seawater dilutions.

Author	Fungus	Seawater (%)										
		0	10	20	30	40	50	60	70	80	90	100
Meyers and Reynolds (1959 a)	*Humicola alopallonella*	**										***
	Piricauda arcticoceanorum	*****										0
	Culcitalna achraspora	**										****
	Zalerion sp.	*										***
	Stachybotrys atra	*****										*
	Alternaria sp.	*****										0
Meyers and Hoyo (1966)	*Varicosporina ramulosa*	Cysts		*	*	*	*	*	*	*	*	*
Kirk (1967)	*Allescheria boydii* (ASEX)	*	*	*	*	*	*	*	*	*	*	*
	Allescheria boydii (SEX)	PAS					PAS					PAS
Meyers and Simms (1967)	*Lulworthia floridana*	–		PAS	PAS	PAS	PAS	PAS	PAS	PAS		PAS
	Lulworthia sp. (IMS 384)	–		PAS	PAS	PAS	PAS	PAS	PAS	PAS		PAS
	Lindra thalassiae	P		PAS	PAS	PAS	PAS	PAS	PAS	PAS		PAS
	Halosphaeria mediosetigera	PAS		PAS	PAS	PAS	PAS	PAS	PAS	PAS		PAS
	Torpedospora radiata	PAS		PAS	PAS	PAS	PAS	PAS	PAS	PAS		PAS
Byrne (1971)	*Lulworthia* sp.	PAS	PAS	PAS	PAS	PAS	PAS	PAS	PAS	PAS	PAS	PAS
	Ceriosporopsis halima	PAS	PAS	PAS	PAS	PAS	PAS	PAS	PAS	PAS	PAS	PAS
	Corollospora maritima	PAS	PAS	PAS	PAS	PAS	PAS	PAS	PAS	PAS	PAS	PAS
	Halosphaeria appendiculata	P	PAS	PAS	PAS	PAS	PAS	PAS	PAS	PAS	PAS	PAS
	H. hamata	PAS	PAS	PAS	PAS	PAS	PAS	PAS	PAS	PAS	PAS	PAS
	Microthelia maritima	PAS	PAS	PAS	PAS	PAS	PAS	PAS	PAS	PAS	PAS	PAS
	Dendryphiella salina	*	*	*	*	*	*	*	*	*	*	*
	Asteromyces cruciatus	*	*	*	*	*	*	*	*	*	*	*

P: perithecia   A: asci   S: spores   –: no sporulation

Other symbols taken from references   *: sporulation of hyphomycetes   ****: heavy sporulation of ascomycetes

148

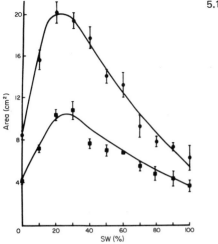

Fig. 5.1. The effect of salinity on the vegetative growth of *Mucor hiemalis* (•) and *Absidia glauca* (■) (temperature: 20°C; yeast glucose agar; time: 3 days).

effect on the number and average size of perithecia produced (Fig. 5.2 a, b). The salinity at which the maximum number of perithecia were produced varied from 10 to 40% seawater, but in each case the largest perithecia were produced in distilled water media. Thus, in general, low salinities maintained relatively few large perithecia, at the optimum salinity a large number of medium sized perithecia and higher salinities produced few small perithecia.

Byrne (1971) has shown that in the freshwater hyphomycetes *Heliscus lugdunensis* Sacc. et Therry and *Tetracladium setigerum* (Grove) Ingold, sporulation was severely inhibited at low salinities (30 and 10% seawater respectively) but no malformation of the conidia was observed. This finding substantiates ecological observations which have demonstrated a paucity of these organisms in waters affected to any extent by the sea (Jones and Oliver, 1964; Eaton and Jones, 1971 a, b). Byrne also studied the sporulation of four terrestrial hyphomycetes and in each case spores were produced over the whole range of salinities. Only in *Wardomyces anomala* Brooks et Hansford was spore production inhibited to any extent by salinity.

5.5.3   Germination of spores in relation to salinity

Very little information is available concerning the germination of fungal spores in relation to salinity. Meyers and Simms (1965) reported that ascospores of *Lindra thalassiae* failed to germinate on distilled water while the spores of five marine fungi tested by Byrne (1971) all germinated in distilled water (Fig. 5.3). Borut and Johnson (1962) have shown that the eight terrestrial fungi they studied all germinated well in distilled water (45-100%) but only poorly in full seawater, with the exception of *Cunninghamella blakesleeana* Lendger (22%) and *Curvularia pallescens* Boedijn (95%). Byrne (1971) reported the inhibition of spore germination with increased salinity in three terrestrial and two freshwater fungi he tested (Fig. 5.3).

TABLE 5.9 The effect of salinity on the sporulation of terrestrial Ascomycetes (after Byrne, 1971).

	Salinity (%)										
	DW	10	20	30	40	50	60	70	80	90	100
Chaetomium globosum Kunze	PAS(9)	PAS(9)	PAS(9)	PAS(9)	PAS(9)	PA(11)	PA(15)	P(17)	—	—	—
Gelasinospora retispora Cain	PAS(2)	PAS(2)	PAS(2)	PAS(2)	PAS(2)	PAS(2)	P(3)	P(3)	—	—	—
Neurospora crassa Shear et Dodge	PAS(2)	PAS(2)	PAS(3)	PA(4)	P(6)	—	—	—	—	—	—
Sordaria fimicola (Rob.) Ces. et de Not.	PAS(2)	PAS(2)	PAS(2)	PAS(2)	PAS(3)	PAS(3)	PAS(4)	PAS(5)	P(7)	P(8)	—

P: perithecia   A: asci   S: spores   —: no fruiting   ( ): days taken to form perithecia   DW: distilled water

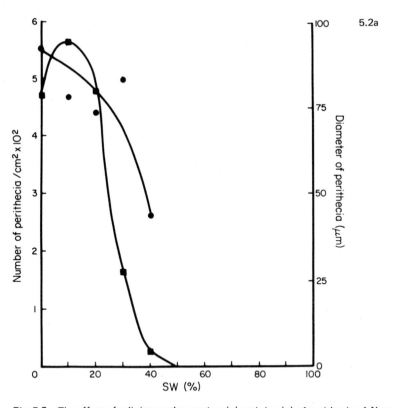

Fig. 5.2a. The effect of salinity on the number (■) and size (●) of perithecia of *Neurospora crassa*.

The salinity requirements of a large number of marine fungi have now been determined and this enables us to make a few generalized statements (Fig. 5.4). It is interesting therefore that in considering the physiological responses of terrestrial and marine fungi to increasing salinities, it can be seen there is good correlation with the observed distribution of these fungi under natural conditions. Typically marine fungi exhibit a broad tolerance to salinity while the terrestrial fungi are inhibited by higher salinities, especially their reproduction and spore germination. Thus, the statement of Jones and Jennings (1964) can be extended 'the reduced vegetative growth, *reproduction and spore germination* terrestrial fungi under saline conditions may be *factors* in maintaining the fungus flora of the sea distinct from that of non-marine habitats'.

5.6 Cation and Anion Requirements

The effect of varying the ionic content of the medium on the growth of selected marine and terrestrial fungi has been investigated by Sguros and Simms (1964), Jones and Jennings (1965) and Allway and Jennings (1970, a, b). Sguros and Simms have demonstrated a partial requirement for Na^+, K^+, Ca^{++} and Mg^{++} and SO_4^{--} by *Halosphaeria mediosetigera* and *Trichocladium achrasporum* (Meyers et Moore)

151

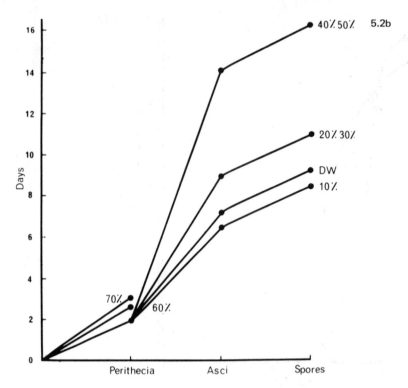

Fig. 5.2 b. The effect of salinity on the reproduction of *Gelasinospora retispora*.

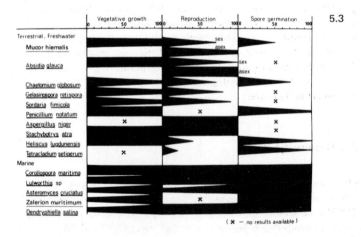

(✗ — no results available)

Fig. 5.3. Physiological responses of fungi to salinity.

152

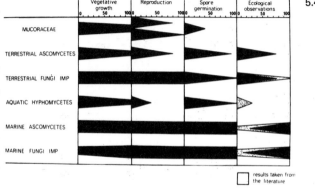

Fig. 5.4. Physiological and ecological responses to salinity of various fungal groups.

Dixon. In no case was the normal seawater quantity of any particular salt required for maximal growth. These authors noted that the inhibitory effect of Na^+ at certain concentrations was reversed by increasing K^+ concentrations above 1.0 mM.

Jones and Jennings (1965), conducting similar experiments with *Dendryphiella salina,* demonstrated a growth stimulation at low concentrations of sodium chloride, with inhibition of growth at concentrations above 100 m-equiv. Na^+. This inhibitory effect was countered by the addition of calcium ions (25 m-equiv. Ca^{++}). Potassium appeared to play a key role in this relationship and a simple relationship between potassium content and dry weight production was established for all cases studied, e.g. *Asteromyces cruciatus, Corollospora maritima, Zalerion maritimum, Lulworthia medusa* (E11. et Ev.) Cribb et Cribb, *Mucor mucedo* Auct., *Sporidesmium salinum* Jones and *Trametes versicolor* L. ex Fr. (see Table 5.10). In certain instances, other ions were more effective than Ca^{++}, e.g. strontium ions were more effective for *Chaetomium globosum* and an unnamed isolate p. 188. Magnesium and barium ions can also have the same effect.

The role of these ions on the uptake of glucose and the carbohydrate metabolism of *D. salina* has been investigated by Allaway and Jennings (1970, a, b). Sodium ions caused a decrease in glucose uptake, which was overcome by the addition of 10 mM Ca^{++}. The primary effect of sodium and calcium is thought to be on the mycelial potassium content and any effect on the rate of glucose uptake is a consequence of changes in the potassium content. These workers also found that the ability of the fungus to retain mannitol and arabitol inside mycelium was dependent on the cations present in the medium (Table 5.11). Sodium ions increase permeability while calcium decreases it.

Jones and Jennings (1965) suggested that sodium exerts its influence on growth by a stimulation of potassium efflux while calcium can remove this stimulation. Allaway and Jennings (1970 b) have provided a metabolic basis for the above hypothesis. They believe that high concentrations of sodium reduce growth through a reduction of the potassium content of the mycelium which in turn reduces the rate of glucose breakdown, rate of respiration and the loss of important metabolities. Calcium counteracts the effect of sodium by not only preventing the loss of potassium but also metabolites.

TABLE 5.10 The dry weight production of fungi over different intervals of time in media to which has been added sodium, either alone or in combination with magnesium, calcium, strontium, barium or potassium (bivalent cations 25 m-equiv.; potassium 50 m-equiv.; sodium as indicated).

	Growth period (days)	Dry weight (mg)					
		Na^+ alone	Na^+ and Mg^{2+}	Na^+ and Ca^{2+}	Na^+ and Sr^{2+}	Na^+ and Ba^{2+}	Na^+ and K^+
Na^+, 400 m-equiv.							
Asteromyces cruciatus F. et Mme Moreau	3	57.5	63.8	70.6	48.2	54.0	49.0
Corollospora maritima Werder.	13	51.1	70.2	74.5	61.9		58.5
Dendryphiella salina (Sutherl.) Pugh et Nicot	4	24.9	81.6	75.7	64.2	46.4	0
Helicoma maritimum Linder	14	0	0	14.5			0
Lulworthia medusa (Ell. et Ev.) Cribb et Cribb	10	0.9		58.9			0.8
Mucor mucedo Auct.	6	37.6	48.3	56.0	45.0		35.1
P188 (unnamed imperfect fungus)	11	201.8	231.4	249.3	297.8		211.8
Sporidesmium salinum Jones	5	0.8	35.8	37.9			11.6
Trametes versicolor L. ex Fr.	7	28.2		81.2			37.8
Na^+, 600 m-equiv.							
Chaetomium globosum Kunze	7	35.6	49.5		94.0	47.9	57.5
Na^+, 2.5 equiv.							
Asteromyces cruciatus	6	6.9		36.4			
Dendryphiella arenaria Nicot	7	0.4		21.2			

TABLE 5.11   The loss of mannitol and arabitol into the experimental solution expressed as a percentage of the total mannitol and arabitol in the system (after Allaway and Jennings, 1970).

Experimental solution	Total sugar alcohol in the system (%)	
	Mannitol loss	Arabitol loss
No added ions	60.0	82.7
200 mM NaCl	84.6	90.2
200 mM NaCl + 10 mM CaCl$_2$	10.9	34.0
200 mM KCl	60.6	80.0
200 mM KCl + 10 mM CaCl$_2$	20.3	53.3
10 mM CaCl$_2$	15.9	57.0

5.7   Nutrition

5.7.1   Carbon requirements

There is an enormous variation in the range of carbohydrates utilized by the higher marine fungi (Table 5.12). However, since the work of Barghoorn and Linder (1944) and Johnson et al. (1959), little new work is available on the carbon requirement of lignicolous fungi, with the exception of their ability to degrade wood. The fungi listed in Table 5.12, with the exception of two yeasts, are able to utilize cellobiose. Meyers et al. (1970) have shown that yeasts are present in high numbers in Spartina alterniflora Loisel rhizosphere and sediments. Although these yeasts are not able to break down cellulose, they are able to compete for the cellobiose and are extremely important in the turnover of materials in marshlands.

Ahearn et al. (1962) examined the assimilation of carbon and nitrogen by marine and terrestrial strains of Rhodotorula and found no differences ascribable to environmental conditions. Van Uden and Fell (1968) calculated the number of carbon compounds assimilated by marine and terrestrial yeasts. They found that marine forms, on average, utilized 19.2 compounds while non-marine forms assimilated on average 12.8 compounds. They attribute the greater variability of the marine forms to their need to utilize any nutrients available in an environment where nutrient supplies are often critical. These observations are supported in a more recent study of Ahearn et al. (1968).

Chesters and Bull (1963 a-c) examined a large number of fungi for laminarin hydrolyzing enzymes. Dendryphiella salina, Halosphaeria mediosetigera, Trichocladium achrasporum, Zalerion xylestrix and Corollospora maritima all produced laminarinase, but only in low amounts, while Lulworthia sp. appeared to be inactive. They conclude that bacteria and actinomycetes are the most prolific colonizers of cast seaweeds, whereas fungi, from a range of marine habitats, had very low laminarinase activity and were relatively unimportant in the breakdown of cast weed.

The ability of yeasts and filamentous fungi to degrade petroleum products is well documented (Komagata et al., 1964). Meyers and Ahearn (1970) report rapid growth of Endomycopsis (Candida) lipolytica Wickerham on the petroleum distillates they investigated, and this was best when natural seawater was used. This topic is discussed further in Chapter 4.

TABLE 5.12   Carbon sources assimilated by marine fungi

		Hexoses				Pentoses		
Fungi	Authors	Glucose	Galactose	L-sorbose	L-rhamnose	D-xylose	L-arabinose	D-arabinose
Kluyveromyces aestuarii Fell	Fell (1961)	*	*	*	0	*W	0	0
Lulworthia floridana Meyers	Meyers (1966)							
IMS 190		*	*	0	0	*	*	—
IMS 384		*	*	*	*	*	*	—
Sterigmatomyces halophilus Fell	Fell (1966)	*	*	*W	0	*	*	0
Corollospora maritima Werder	Meyers and							
IMS 604	Scott (1967)	*	*	*	0	*	*W	—
IMS 607		*	*	*	0	*	*	—
Cryptococcus lactativorus Fell et Phaff	Fell and Phaff (1967)	*	0	*	0	*	0	0
Leucosporidium scottii Fell, Statzell, Hunter et Phaff	Fell, Statzell Hunter and Phaff (1969)	*	*	*	*	*	0	0
L. antarcticum Fell, Statzell, Hunter et Phaff		*	*W	0	0	0	0	0
Rhodosporidium sphaerocarpum Newell et Fell	Newell and Fell (1970)	*	*	*	0	*	*	*
Rh. dinoboratum Newell et Hunter	Newell and Hunter (1970)	*	*	*	0	*	*	*
Pichia spartinae Ahearn, Yarrow et Meyers	Ahearn, Yarrow and Meyers (1971)	*	0	*	0	0	0	0

*: positive   *W: weak growth   0: no growth   —: not tested

Tubaki (1969) has shown (Table 5.13) that *Dendryphiella arenaria*, *Varicosporina ramulosa* and *Lindra thalassiae* all grew well on laminarin, while carrageenin was less favourable and sodium alginate supported the moderate growth of *D. arenaria* only.

The ability of marine fungi to degrade cellulose was first reported by Barghoorn and Linder (1944) when they observed soft rot cavities in sectioned wood. These observations have been confirmed by Kohlmeyer (1958 a, b), Becker and Kohlmeyer (1958) and Jones (1962). Table 5.14 lists the marine fungi known to cause soft rot decay of wood, degrade cordage and utilize cellulose foil under laboratory conditions. The ability of the following fungi to degrade cellulosic materials has been well documented: *Ceriosporopsis halima* Linder, *Corollospora maritima*, Halo-

Galactosides			Alpha glucosides							Alcohols				
Lactose	Raffinose	Melibiose	Maltose	Sucrose	Melezitose	Trehalose	Cellobiose	Inulin	Soluble starch	Ethanol	Glycerol	D-mannitol	D-sorbitol	i-inositol
*	*	0	*	*	*w	*	*	0	0	*	*	*	*	0
0	0	—	*	0	—	*	*	—	*	—	—	0	—	—
0	0	—	*	0	—	*	*	—	*	—	—	*	—	—
0	0	0	0	0	0	*	*w	—	—	*	*	*	0	0
—	0	—	*w	*	—	*	*	—	*	—	—	*	—	—
—	0	—	*	*	—	*	*	—	*	—	—	*	—	—
0	0	0	0	—	0	0	0	0	0	*	*	0	0	*
*	*	0	*	*	*	*	*	0	0	*	*	*	*	0
0	0	0	0	0	0	0	0	0	0	0	*	0	0	0
0	*	0	*	*	*	*	*	*	0	*	*	*w	*w	0
0	*	0	*	*	*	*	*	*	*w	*	*	0	—	0
—	0	0	*	*	*	*	*	0	0	*	0	*	*	0

TABLE 5.13   Utilization of polysaccharides by marine fungi (after Tubaki, 1969).

Fungi	Laminarin	Carrageenin	Na alginate	Cellulose	Glucose seawater
Dendryphiella arenaria	3	1	1	1	3
Varicosporina ramulosa	3	2	1	1	2
Lindra thalassiae	3	1	1	2	3

Growth: 1: scanty   1: moderate   2: good   3: luxuriant

TABLE 5.14 The ability of marine fungi to utilize various cellulosic materials.

	Soft rot attack			Cellulose foil, Kohlmeyer (1958 b, 1960, 1962, 1966)	Cordage, Meyers et al. (1960); Meyers and Reynolds (1963); Meyers (1968)
	Wood, Jones (1962) and (unpublished)	Wood, Johnson and Sparrow (1961)	Wood, Kohlmeyer (1958 a, 1963)		
Ascomycetes					
Ceriosporopsis calyptrata	—	—	*	—	—
C. circumvestita	—	—	—	* (strong)	—
C. halima	—	*	—	* (weak)	*
Corollospora comata	—	—	*	0	—
C. cristata	—	—	*	—	*
C. maritima	* (25.7%)†	*	*	* (strong)	—
Halosphaeria appendiculata	*	—	*	* (weak)	—
H. mediosetigera	—	—	*	* (weak)	*
H. hamata	—	—	*	* (weak)	—
H. quadri-remis	—	—	*	—	*
H. salina	—	—	—	—	—
H. stellata	—	—	—	0	*
Lignincola laevis	—	—	—	—	*
Lulworthia floridana F190	—	—	—	—	*
F483	—	—	—	—	* (weak)
F484	—	—	—	—	* (weak)
F485	—	—	—	—	* (weak)
F487	—	—	—	—	*
F497	—	—	—	—	*
F496	—	—	—	—	*
F507	—	—	—	—	*
F511	—	—	—	—	*

L. opaca	—	—	*	*	—
L. purpurea	* (9.8%)†	—	*	*	—
Microthelia maritima	*	0	—	—	—
Nautosphaeria crista-minuta	—	* (strong)	—	—	—
Pleospora gaudefroyi	—	0	—	—	—
Torpedospora ambispinosa	—	—	—	*	—
T. radiata	—	—	*	—	*
Fungi Imperfecti					
Cirrenalia macrocephala	—	—	*	—	—
Cremasteria cymatilis	*	—	—	*	* (weak)
Trichocladium achrasporum	*	—	*	—	*
Humicola alopallonella	* (16.8%)†	—	—	*	—
Monodictys pelagica	*	* (weak)	—	—	—
Zalerion maritimum	—	—	—	—	*
Z. raptor	—	—	—	*	*
Z. xylestrix	—	—	—	—	—
Alternaria maritima	0	—	—	—	—
Dendryphiella salina	0	—	—	—	—
Stemphylium maritimum	0	—	—	—	—

*: soft rot attack.　—: not tested.　0: unable to soft rot wood.　†: weight loss of beech after 18 weeks.

sphaeria appendiculata, H. mediosetigera, Lulworthia spp., *Cirrenalia macrocephala* (Kohlm.) Meyers et Moore and *Monodictys pelagica* (Johnson) Jones.

Meyers (1968 b), Meyers and Scott (1968) and Meyers *et al.* (1972) have shown that marine fungi can cause weight loss of cellulose (as solka floc). *Lulworthia floridana* showed a 50% weight loss of cellulose after three weeks, while in *Dendryphiella salina* there was a 54% weight loss within 6 days which rose to 88% weight loss by 21 days. Meyers (1968 a) demonstrated that different isolates of *Lulworthia* degraded cellulose at different rates. Isolate IMS 600 produced a weight loss of 25% in 15 days, while comparable activity by IMS 615, 190 and 619 required 19, 22 and 35 days respectively. The *Lindra* species tested showed weak activity producing only 15% weight loss after 42 days. Meyers has also shown that pH and salt concentration has an effect on the degradation of cellulose; e.g. in *D. salina* a maximum weight loss of 65% was observed after 7 days in a medium with 2% sodium chloride with only 32% weight loss in media made up with distilled water.

Meyers and Reynolds (1959 a, c; 1963), and Moore and Meyers (1962) have determined the amount of reducing sugar present in cellulose broths. Some 15 species

TABLE 5.15   The effect of temperature, pH and salinity on protein production by marine fungi grown on a cellulose/urea medium.

(a) Temperature Fungi	pH	10	15	20	25	30°C	
Asteromyces cruciatus	6.0	16.3	22.7	22.1	**61.3**	38.5	
Cladosporium herbarum	6.4	8.7	**14.4**	10.2	10.2	9.8	
Corollospora cristata	6.2	6.9	**17.7**	12.3	13.0	13.1	
Dendryphiella salina	6.6	16.1	**28.2**	26.6	21.6	21.2	
Lulworthia sp.	6.6	1.8	10.1	**13.7**	9.6	9.8	
(b) Salinity		0	10	25	50	75	100% Seawater
A. cruciatus	6.0	**37.9**	19.6	16.4	18.3	16.6	15.3
C. herbarum	6.4	33.7	58.9	**61.5**	50.0	56.4	55.1
C. cristata	6.2	95.8	**128.6**	72.4	88.6	89.9	60.8
D. salina	6.6	48.3	**64.3**	23.1	22.8	22.3	24.8
Lulworthia sp.	6.6	33.1	**47.9**	44.3	10.9	11.2	9.3
(c) pH	5.6	6.2	6.6	6.8	7.0	7.4	7.6	8.4
A. cruciatus	10.8	14.9	18.7	–	30.7	–	8.0	7.5
C. herbarum	44.8	63.9	–	58.1	35.7	29.9	18.2	31.5
C. cristata	121.0	146.8	127.7	99.5	–	–	121.9	65.5
D. salina	28.2	61.0	61.4	–	–	19.9	39.8	42.3
Lulworthia sp.	10.0	13.3	15.5	11.6	8.3	10.8	8.3	5.0

All mg protein per 50 ml medium.

have been investigated and all produced reducing sugar, the amount varying from 0.075 to 0.150 mg sugar per millilitre with a maximum at less than 0.3 mg/ml. However, Meyers *et al.* (1972) have concluded that the marine fungus *D. salina* exhibits poor Cx activity compared with the terrestrial species *Trichoderma viride* Pers. and *Pestalotiopsis westerdijkii.* This is surprising as marine fungi soon colonize wood and can cause appreciable cellulose digestion under laboratory conditions. *D. salina* is infrequently collected on timber (Jones, 1972), and has not been shown to cause soft rot of wood. However, this fungus is frequently isolated from algae (Jones, unpublished) and therefore may not be a good species for use in cellulolytic studies.

Jones and Irvine (1972) have investigated the utilization of cellulose (solka floc) by four marine fungi when they determined the amount of fungal protein produced. They found that nitrogen sources, pH, temperature and salinity all affect the rate of cellulose utilization (Table 5.15).

5.7.2 Nitrogen requirements

The nitrogen requirements of some marine yeasts are summarized in Table 5.16. The ability of marine yeasts to utilize amines is interesting and significant considering their widespread occurrence in marine organisms (Ahearn *et al.,* 1970; Meyers *et al.,* 1970; Meyers and Nicholson, 1970). *Pichia spartinae* can assimilate: methylamine, dimethylamine, ethylamine, diethylamine, triethylamine, propylamine, butylamine, methylethylamine, ethylenediamine, choline, histidine, B-alanine and urea. None of the amines served as a carbon source for growth. Meyers and Nicholson (1970) state that isolate FST 119 of *P. spartinae* cannot utilize betaine, but Meyers *et al.* (1970) report the same isolate as capable of reduced growth on this compound.

Meyers and Hoyo (1966) note that the replacement of NH_4NO_3 by asparagine in a basal medium containing glucose and yeast extract enables good sporulation of *Varicosporina ramulosa.* In *Corollospora maritima* the addition of asparagine to media containing glucose and xylose aided perithecial formation but when added to cellulose, trehalose, fructose and mannitol fruiting was checked.

Jones and Irvine (1972) determined the effect of nitrogen (as urea, potassium nitrate, ammonium nitrate and ammonium chloride) on the utilization of cellulose by four marine fungi. Urea was the most favourable nitrogen source for all the fungi tested, especially *Corollospora cristata* (Kohlm.) Kohlm. and *Dendryphiella salina.* Sguros and Simms (1963 a) have shown that in the case of *Halosphaeria medioseti-gera, Trichocladium achrasporum* and *Humicola alopallonella* Meyers et Moore the addition of ammonium nitrate to the medium caused acidic conditions which inhibited growth. The addition of potassium nitrate and nitrite had the converse effect. However, all the fungi utilized the nitrate, nitrite and ammonium sources tested.

Proteolytic acitivity has been demonstrated in 13 out of 14 marine filamentous fungi tested by Pisano *et al.* (1964). Eight of these contained measurable quantities of glutamic acid and alanine which may serve as sources of microbial food for other organisms (Table 5.17).

5.7.3 Vitamin requirements

Ahearn *et al.* (1962) did not find any differences in the vitamin requirements of the marine and terrestrial strains of *Rhodotorula* they tested. Fell (1961) reports the requirement for niacin by *Kluyveromyces aestuarii* Fell while two varieties of *Metschnikowia bicuspidata* (Metschnikoff) Kamienski have a requirement for biotin

TABLE 5.16   Growth requirements of some marine yeasts.

		KNO₃	Tryptophan	KNO₂	Splitting urea	Vitamin free medium	Niacin	Thiamine	Biotin
Kluyveromyces aestaurii	Fell (1961)	0	0	−	−	0	*	−	−
Sterigmatomyces halophilus	Fell (1966)	*	−	−	−	−	−	*	−
Cryptococcus lactivorus	Fell and Phaff (1967)	0	−	0	−	0	−	*	−
Metschnikowia biscuspidata var australis	Fell and Hunter (1968)	0	−	−	−	−	−	*	*
var zobelli		0	−	−	−	−	−	*	*
Leucosporidium scottii	Fell et al. (1969)	*	−	−	0	*	−	−	−
L. antarcticum		*	−	−	0	*	−	−	−
Pichia spartinae	Ahearn et al. (1970)	0	−	−	*	0	−	−	−
Rhodosporidium dioboratum	Newell and Hunter (1970)	*	−	−	*	*	−	−	−
R. sphaerocarpum	Newell and Fell (1970)	*	−	−	*	0	−	*	−
R. malvinellum	Fell (1970)	*	−	−	−	0	−	*	−

*: positive.   −: Not tested.   0: no growth.

(Fell and Hunter, 1968). Five yeasts are listed in Table 5.16 as having a requirement for thiamine. Sguros and Simms (1963 b) have shown that the lignicolous Ascomycete, *Halosphaeria mediosetigera* has an absolute requirement for 5-10 μg thiamine per litre and a partial or transient requirement for biotin. Tubaki (1969) has shown that 13 of the 38 strains he studied had a requirement for thiamine. Thiamine or biotin alone were ineffective in promoting fruiting in *Lindra thalassiae,* however, a mixture of these two at 1.0 μg% produced vigorous sporulation.

5.8   Sporulation

Kohlmeyer and Kohlmeyer (1971) listed 135 marine Ascomycetes, yet few of these have been shown to sporulate under laboratory conditions. Meyers and his co-

TABLE 5.17 Maximal yields of gelatinase, production of glutamic acid and alanine by marine fungi (after Pisano *et al.* (1964)).

Fungi	Gelatin liquefaction (units/ml)	Amino nitrogen (mg/ml)	Period of maximum enzyme activity (h)	Glutamic acid (mg/ml)	Alanine (mg/ml)
Ascomycetes					
Ceriosporopsis halima	37	0.33	288	0.62	0.40
Corollospora maritima	43	1.77	240	0.73	0.33
Halosphaeria mediosetigera	57	0.13	96	1.28	0.26
Lulworthia floridana					
IMS190	7	0.00	96	–	–
IMS405	25	0.08	48	–	–
IMS503	38	0.53	240	0.84	0.36
Torpedospora sp.	6	0.20	24	0.86	0.44
T. radiata	29	0.95	144	0.84	0.26
Fungi Imperfecti					
Cremasteria cymatilis	0	–	–	–	–
Humicola alopallonella	29	0.63	96	0.26	0.21
Orbimyces spectabilis	27	0.00	288	–	–
Trichocladium achrasporum	34	0.98	192	0.99	0.48
Zalerion raptor	26	0.75	240	–	–
Z. xylestrix	27	0.85	192	–	–

workers have been pre-eminent for their work on the growth and reproduction of marine Ascomycetes. In contrast, most of the Fungi Imperfecti have been grown successfully in culture.

Meyers and Hoyo (1966) have shown that nutrient levels, salinity and pH all affect the sporulation of *Varicosporina ramulosa*. The latter have already been discussed in Section 5.4 and 5.5.2. These workers demonstrated that the addition of asparagine to a medium containing glucose (0.5%) and yeast extract (0.1%) greatly stimulated sporulation. Good sporulation was also obtained on a medium containing 1% glucose and 0.1% yeast extract. Jones and Ward (1973) have shown that light and nutrient levels affect the degree of septation of conidia of *Asteromyces cruciatus* (see Section 5.3).

Meyers and Reynolds (1959 b) were the first to consider the reproduction of marine Ascomycetes and obtained good sporulation of *Lulworthia grandispora* Meyers, *L. medusa, L. floridana, Ceriosporopsis halima* and *Corollospora maritima* on various wood flours incorporated into seawater yeast extract agar. These and *Torpedospora radiata, Halosphaeria quadricornuta* Cribb et Cribb, *H. salina* (Meyers) Kohlm. and *Lignincola laevis* Höhnk, all produced perithecia on balsa wood in flasks of yeast extract broth, which was then transformed to aquaria of aerated seawater.

Factors affecting reproduction of Ascomycetes include salinity, temperature, pH, growth substances and nutritional levels. Fruiting in *Lindra thalassiae* does not occur at salinities below 25% seawater or at concentrations of yeast extract above 0.1% (Meyers and Simms, 1965). Similarly, addition of 0.1 and 1.0% glucose to the 0.1% yeast extract medium inhibited perithecial development. This fungus would not develop in a medium containing cellulose but the addition of 0.1% yeast extract or 10% *Thalassia* epiphyte extract or 2 μg% thiamine and biotin produced mature perithecia. Another species of *Lindra (L. marinera* Meyers) fruits readily on a variety of carbohydrates with 0.25% yeast extract added (Meyers, 1969).

Meyers (1966) reports considerable variability in the reproduction of various isolates of *Lulworthia floridana*. Isolate IMS 548 produced mature perithecia on 11 different carbohydrates at 25°C, while IMS 190 only fruited on arabinose and trehalose. By raising the temperature to 30°C, perithecia were produced on media containing xylose, fructose, mannose, glucose, cellobiose, trehalose, starch and cellulose.

Meyers and Simms (1967) have shown that one isolate (IMS 604) of *Corollospora maritima* fruited readily on a variety of media, while in a second isolate (IMS 607) reproduction only occurred on arabinose and cellulose media with 25-50% seawater after 50 days' incubation. Table 5.18 lists the species that have been known to sporulate under laboratory conditions, while the effect of temperature and salinity on fruiting have been discussed in Sections 5.2 and 5.5.2 respectively.

Marine ascosporogenous yeasts fruit readily under laboratory conditions (Ahearn *et al.*, 1968). However, the heterobasidiomycetous yeasts have specific requirements for sporulation. Fell *et al.* (1969) grew *Leucosporidium* spp. at 12°C on either malt agar or corn meal agar, and teliospores were formed after 1 to 3 weeks. Agar discs containing teliospores were then placed in sterile distilled water and incubated at 12°C for 2 to 10 weeks. Teliospores were then streaked on to 2% agar (in distilled water), and incubated at 5 or 12°C. After one week teliospores germinated to give rise to promycelium and spores. Modifications of this technique have been used by Fell (1970), Newell and Hunter (1970) and Newell and Fell (1970) for other species.

TABLE 5.18 Marine Ascomycetes and Basidiomycetes that fruit under laboratory conditions

Fungus	Meyers and Reynolds (1959 b)	Meyers and Simms (1967)	Byrne (1971)	Kirk (1967, 1969)	Meyers (1966, 1969) Meyers and Scott (1967)
Ceriosporopsis halima	*	–	*	–	–
Corollospora maritima	–	–	*	*	*
Halosphaeria appendiculata	–	–	*	–	–
H. hamata	–	*	*	*	–
H. mediosetigera	*	–	–	–	–
H. salina	*	–	–	–	–
H. quadricornuta	*	–	–	–	–
Lignincola laevis	*	–	–	–	–
Lindra marinera	–	–	–	–	*
L. thalassiae	–	*	–	–	–
Lulworthia floridana	*	*	–	–	–
IMS190 IMS525					
IMS384 IMS543		384*			
IMS400 IMS600A					*
IMS490 IMS605		490*			
IMS503					
L. grandispora	*	–	–	–	–
L. medusa	*	–	–	–	–
Lulworthia sp.	–	–	*	*	–
Microthelia maritima	*	–	*	–	–
Torpedospora radiata	*	*	–	–	–
Basidiomycete	–	–	–	–	–
Nia vibrissa	–	–	*	–	–

*: Positive   –: not tested

165

5.9 Interrelationships with Other Organisms

The higher marine fungi have always been considered as organisms active in the deterioration of various substrata in the sea, and little attention has been given to their possible role in the nutrition of other organisms. The destructive nature of marine borers has been well documented and known for some considerable time. However, it was only in 1959 that marine fungi were implicated in the nutrition of marine fungi (Kampf *et al.*, 1959).

5.9.1 Fungi and marine borers

Marine wood borers belong to the Molluscs and the Crustaceae. The former includes 20 genera and 86 species, the most well known genus being *Teredo* (the shipworm) (Turner, 1971). The wood boring Crustaceae comprise six genera and 39 species with *Limnoria* (the gribble) as the best known genus (Kühne, 1971).

Marine fungi may help the borers in one of two ways. Firstly, they may condition the wood prior to borer settlement and subsequent burrowing, thus making penetration by the borers easier (Schafer and Lane, 1957; and Lane, 1959).

Secondly, the borers may obtain nutrients from wood cellulose indirectly by means of the secretion of cellulases by the fungi, or obtain protein, vitamins and other nutrients by directly ingesting fungal mycelium. These hypotheses have been discussed recently by Becker (1971), Eltringham (1971) and Jones and Irvine (1971). However, little new work has been forthcoming over the past 10 years. Cutter and Rosenberg (1972) have suggested that fungi carry out the initial breakdown of cellulose of the wood, followed by marine bacteria. However, the presence of fungi in the gut of *Teredo* has yet to be conclusively demonstrated.

The role of marine fungi in the nutrition of these two groups of animals may be different and it is incorrect to consider them together, as many workers have done in the past. Clearly, the exact role of micro-organisms in wood borer digestion remains in dispute, and further work along the lines suggested by Eltringham (1971) is required.

5.9.2 Fungi and nematodes

In 1963, Meyers *et al.* noted nematodes feeding on fungi associated with decayed materials. This led Meyers and his co-workers to carry out a number of interesting experiments in the laboratory and in the field (Meyers *et al.*, 1964; Hopper and Meyers, 1966; Meyers and Hopper, 1967).

Meyers *et al.* (1964) investigated the growth and reproduction of *Aphelenchoides* sp. (isolated from the turtle grass *Thalassia testudinum* Konig) when offered the mycelium of a number of marine fungi (Table 5.19). *Dendryphiella arenaria* and *Halosphaeria mediosetigera* were good in supporting animal growth, while others (*Cladosporium herbarum* (Pers.) Link, *Stachybotrys* sp. and *Aspergillus luchuensis* Inui) failed to do so. Hopper and Meyers (1966) and Meyers and Hopper (1967) have shown that significant numbers of nematodes are to be found associated with decaying materials, e.g. cotton cellulose filters, sediments, *Spartina aterniflora* culms and rhizomes. Nematodes found associated with fungi include *Metoncholaimas scissus* Wieser and Hopper, *Monhystera parva* Bastian, *Chromadora macrolaimoides* Steiner, *C. nudicapitata* Bastian, and *Pontonema problematicum* Chitwood, to mention only a few.

166

TABLE 5.19 Development of the Nematode, *Aphelenchoides* sp. on mycelia of various fungi (after Meyers *et al.* (1964)).

	Age of mycelium (days) *	Weight of mycelium (mg)	Total number of nematodes	Percent of animals in mat	Utilization factor (No. of animals/mg mycelium)
Ascomycetes					
Halosphaeria mediosetigera	6	37	99 820	65%	2 698
Lulworthia floridana	9	19	19 830	79%	1 044
Fungi Imperfecti					
Dendryphiella arenaria	5	35	83 286	58%	2 379
Zalerion xylestrix	6	32	98 640	65%	3 083
Trichocladium achrasporum	6	29	69 896	62%	2 410
Helminthosporium sp.	4	37	89 510	90%	2 419
Alternaria sp.	4	27	48 945	85%	1 813
Cladosporium herbarum	3	58	<1 000	—	<50
Stachybotrys sp.	4	16	<1 000	—	<100
Aspergillus luchuensis	4	69	3 100	87%	<50

* Grown on 25 mm glass fibre disc.

167

TABLE 5.20 Metabolites of marine fungi

Ascomycetes	Choline-sulphate	Choline	Ergosterol	Mannitol	Oleic acid	Palmitic acid	Linoleic acid	Caproic-caprylic acid	Palmitoleic acid	Myristic acid	Stearic acid	Arachidonic acid	Behenic acid	Linolenic acid	Cysteine
	Kirk *et al.* (1973)														
Ceriosporopsis halima Linder	—	—	1	—											
Corollospora lacera (Linder) Kohlm.	1	—	—	2											
C. maritima Werder.	1	1	1	1	1	1	1	1	1	1	1	1	1		
C. trifurcata (Höhnk) Kohlm.	1	—	1	2								1	1	—	—
Haligena elaterophora Kohlm.	1	—	1	2											
Halosphaeria appendiculata Linder	1	—	—	2											
H. hamata (Höhnk) Kohlm.	1	—	1	2											
H. mediosetigera Cribb et Cribb	1	—	1	2											

Leptosphaeria oraemaris Linder	1	—	—	—	—	—	—	—	—	—	—	—	—	2
Lignincola laevis Höhnk.	1	—	1	—	—	—	—	—	—	—	1	—	—	—
Nais inornata Kohlm.	1	—	1	—	—	—	—	—	—	—	1	—	—	—

Fungi Imperfecti:

Trichocladium achrasporum (Meyers et Moore) Dixon	1	—	1	1	1	1	—	1	—	—	—	—	—	—
Zalerion maritimum (Linder) Anastasiou	1	—	1	1	—	1	—	1	—	—	1	—	—	1
	1	—	—	1	—	—	—	—	—	—	—	—	—	—
Dendryphiella salina (Suth.) Pugh et Nicot. — Allaway and Jennings (1970) Holligan and Jennings (1972)	1													

1: present   2: presence tentative   —: negative

5.10 Metabolites of Marine Fungi

In recent years considerable interest has been shown in the secondary metabolites of marine fungi, with a view to their application and use in medicine and other applied industries. Kirk and Catalfomo (1970) believe they may be ideal for industrial fermentations 'in which the oceans can provide an inexpensive source of water and nutrients'. Table 5.20 lists some sugar alcohols, amines, sterols and triglyceride fatty acids found present in some common marine fungi.

It is significant that most of the fungi listed contained ergosterol. Kirk *et al.* (1973) have speculated as to the role of ergosterol from marine fungi in the metabolism of marine invertebrates and vertebrates. The association between marine fungi and animals has already been discussed above (Section 5.9). The presence of these secondary metabolites may be important in these associations but needs to be further investigated.

References

AHEARN, D. G., ROTH, F. J., and MEYERS, S. P. (1968). 'Ecology and characterization of yeasts from aquatic regions of South Florida.' *Marine Biology,* 1, 291-308.

AHEARN, D. G., ROTH, F. J., and MEYERS, S. P. (1962). 'A comparative study of marine and terrestrial strains of *Rhodotorula.*' *Can. J. Microbiol.,* 8, 121-132.

AHEARN, D. G., YARROW, D., and MEYERS, S. P. (1970). '*Pichia spartinae* sp. n. from Louisiana marshland habitats.' *Antonie van Leeuwenhoek,* 36, 503-508.

ALLAWAY, A. E., and JENNINGS, D. H. (1970 a). 'The influence of cations on glucose uptake by the fungus *Dendryphiella salinae.*' *New Phytol.,* 69, 567-579.

ALLAWAY, A. E., and JENNINGS, D. H. (1970 b). 'The influence of cations on glucose transport and metabolism by, and the loss of sugar alcohols from, the fungus *Dendryphiella salina.*' *New Phytol.,* 69, 581-593.

ANASTASIOU, C. J. (1967). 'Two species of *Coprinus* from alkali lakes.' *Can. J. Bot.,* 45, 2213-2222.

BARGHOORN, E. S., and LINDER, D. H. (1944). 'Marine fungi: their taxonomy and biology.' *Farlowia,* 1, 395-467.

BECKER, G. (1971). 'On the biology, physiology and ecology of marine wood-boring organisms.' In *Marine Borers, Fungi and Fouling Organisms of Wood.'* (Eds: E. B. G. Jones and S. K. Eltringham.) O.E.C.D. Paris, 304-326.

BECKER, G., and KOHLMEYER, J. (1958). 'Deterioration of wood by marine fungi in India and its special significance for fishing craft.' *J. Timber Dryers and Preservers, India,* 4, 1-10.

BORUT, S. Y., and JOHNSON, T. W. (1962). 'Some biological observations on fungi in estuarine sediments.' *Mycologia,* 54, 181-193.

BYRNE, P. (1971). 'The physiological responses of some marine, freshwater and terrestrial fungi to salinity.' Ph.D. Thesis, University of London.

CHESTERS, C. G. C., and BULL, A. T. (1963 a, b, c). 'The enzymatic degradation of laminarin. 1. The distribution of laminarinase among micro-organisms. 2. The multicomponent nature of fungal laminarinases. 3. Some effects of temperature, pH and various chemical reagents on fungal laminarinases. *Biochem. J.,* 86, 28-31, 31-38, 38-46.

CUTTER, J. M., and ROSENBERG, F. A. (1972). 'The role of cellulolytic bacteria in the digestive processes of the shipworm. II. Requirements for bacterial cellulases in the digestive system of teredine borers.' In *Biodeterioration of Materials.*

(Eds. A. H. Walters and E. H. Hueck-van der Plas) Applied Science, London, 42-51.

DOGUET, G. (1968) *'Nia vibrissa* Moore et Meyers, Gasteromycète marin. 1. Conditions générales de formation des carpophores en culture.' *Bull. Soc. mycol. Fr.,* 84, 343-351.

EATON, R. A., and JONES, E. B. G. (1971 a, b). 'The biodeterioration of timber in water cooling towers. 1. Fungal ecology and the decay of wood at Connah's Quay and Ince. 2. Fungi growing on wood in different positions in a water cooling system.' *Material und Organismen,* 6, 51-80, 81-92.

ELTRINGHAM, S. K. (1971). 'Marine borers and fungi'. In *Marine Borers, Fungi and Fouling Organisms of Wood'* (Eds. E. B. G. Jones and S. K. Eltringham) O.E.C.D., Paris, 327-338.

FELL, J. W. (1961). 'A new species of *Saccharomyces* isolated from a sub-tropical estuary'. *Antonie van Leeuwenhoek,* 27, 27-30.

FELL, J. W. (1965). 'Bionomics and physiological taxonomy of marine occurring yeasts.' Ph.D. Dissertation, University of Miami.

FELL, J. W. (1966). *'Sterigmatomyces,* a new fungal genus from marine areas. *Antonie van Leeuwenhoek,* 32, 99-104.

FELL, J. W. (1970). 'Yeasts with Heterobasidiomycetous life cycles.' In *Recent Trends in Yeast Research.* (Ed. D. G. Ahearn). *Georgia State University,* 49-66.

FELL, J. W., and HUNTER, I. L. (1968). 'Isolation of heterothallic yeast strains of *Metschnikowia* Kamienski and their mating reactions with *Chlamydozyma* Wickerham spp.' *Antonie van Leeuwenhoek,* 34, 365-376.

FELL, J. W., and PHAFF, H. J. (1967). 'Three new yeasts: *Cryptococcus dimennae, Cryptococcus kutzingii* and *Cryptococcus lactativorus* spp. n. *'Antonie van Leeuwenhoek,* 33, 464-472.

FELL, J. W., STATZELL, A. C., HUNTER, I. L., and PHAFF, H. J. (1969). *'Leucosporidium* gen. n., the heterobasidiomycetous stage of several yeasts of the genus *Candida.' Antonie van Leeuwenhoek,* 35, 433-462.

GRAY, W. D., PINTO, P. V. C., and PATHAK, S. G. (1963). 'Growth of fungi in seawater medium.' *Appl. Microbiol.,* 11, 501-505.

HOLLIGAN, P. M., and JENNINGS, D. H. (1972). 'Carbohydrate metabolism in the fungus *Dendryphiella salina.* II. The influence of different carbon and nitrogen sources on the accumulation of mannitol and arabitol.' *New Phytol.,* 71, 583-594.

HOPPER, B. E., and MEYERS, S. P. (1966). 'Aspects of life cycle development of marine nematodes.' *Helgol. wiss. Meersunters,* 13, 444-449.

JOHNSON, T. W., and SPARROW, F. K. (1961). *Fungi in Oceans and Estuaries.* J. Cramer, Weinheim. 688 pp.

JOHNSON, T. W., FERACHAU, H. A. and GOLD, H. S. (1959). 'Isolation, culture, growth and nutrition of some lignicolous marine fungi.' *Phyton Internat. J. Exp. Bot.,* 12, 65-80.

JONES, E. B. G. (1962). 'Marine fungi 1'. *Trans. Br. mycol. Soc.,* 45, 93-114.

JONES, E. B. G. (1963a). 'Observations on the fungal succession on wood test blocks submerged in the sea.' *J. Inst. Wood Science,* No. 11, 14-23.

JONES, E. B. G. (1963 b). 'The effect of cations on certain marine fungi' Ph. D. Thesis, University of Leeds.

JONES, E. B. G. (1971). 'The ecology and rotting ability of marine fungi.' In *Marine Borers, Fungi and Fouling Organisms of Wood.* (Eds. E. B. G. Jones and S. K. Eltringham). O.E.C.D., Paris, 237-258.

JONES, E. B. G. (1972). 'The decay of timber in aquatic environments.' *British Wood Preserving Association, Annual Convention*, 1-18.

JONES, E. B. G., and LE CAMPION-ALSUMARD, T. (1970). 'The biodeterioration of polyurethane by marine fungi.' *Inter. Biodeter. Bull.*, 6, 119-124.

JONES, E. B. G., and IRVINE, J. (1971). 'The role of fungi in the deterioration of wood in the sea.' *J. Inst. Wood Science*, 5, 31-40.

JONES, E. B. G., and IRVINE, J. (1972). The role of marine fungi in the bio-deterioration of materials' in *Biodeterioration of Materials* (Eds. A. H. Walters and E. H. Hueck-van der Plas). Applied Science, London, 422-431.

JONES, E. B. G., and JENNINGS, D. H. (1964). 'The effect of salinity on the growth of marine fungi in comparison with non-marine species.' *Trans. Br. mycol. Soc.* 47, 619-625.

JONES, E. B. G., and JENNINGS, D. H. (1965). 'The effect of cations on the growth of fungi.' *New Phytol.*, 64, 86-100.

JONES, E. B. G., and OLIVER, A. C. (1964). 'Occurrence of aquatic hyphomycetes on wood submerged in fresh and brackish water.' *Trans. Br. mycol. Soc.*, 47, 45.48.

JONES, E. B. G., and WARD, A. W. (1973). 'Septate conidia in *Asteromyces cruciatus*'. *Trans. Br. mycol. Soc.* 61, 181-186.

JONES, E. B. G., BYRNE, P., and ALDERMAN, D. J. (1971). 'The response of fungi to salinity.' *Viet et milieu*, 22, 265-280.

KAMPF, W. D., BECKER, G., and KOHLMEYER, J. (1959). 'Versuche über das auffinden und den befall von holz durch larven der bohrmuschel *Teredo pedicellata* Qutrf.', *Z. angew. Zool.*, 44, 257-283.

KIRK, P. W. (1967). 'A comparison of saline tolerance and sporulation in marine and clinical isolates of *Allescheria boydii* Shear.' *Mycopath. Mycol. appl.*, 33, 65-75.

KIRK, P. W. (1969). 'Isolation and culture of lignicolous marine fungi.' *Mycologia*, 61, 174-177.

KIRK, P. W. and CATALFOMO, P. (1970). 'Marine fungi: the occurrence of ergosterol and choline'. *Phytochemistry*, 9, 595-597.

KIRK, P. W., CATALFOMO, P., BLOCK, J. H., and CONSTANTINE, G. H. (1973). 'Marine fungi: their chemico-ecological significance.' (in press).

KOMAGATA, K., NAKASE, T., and KATSUYA, M. (1964). 'Assimilation of hydro-carbons by yeasts, preliminary screening.' *J. gen. appl. Microbiol., Tokyo*, 10, 313-321.

KOHLMEYER, J. (1958 a) 'Holzzerstorende pilze im meerwasser.' *Holz Roh-Werkstoff.*, 16, 215-220.

KOHLMEYER, J. (1958 b). 'Beobachtungen über Mediterrane meerespilze sowie das vorkommen von marinen moderfaule-erregern in aquariumszuchten holzzerstorender meerestiere.' *Ber. dt. bot. Ges.*, 71, 98-116.

KOHLMEYER, J. (1960) 'Wood inhabitating marine fungi from the Pacific north west and California.' *Nova Hedwigia*, 2, 293-343.

KOHLMEYER, J. (1962). 'Uber *Pleopsora quadefrayi:* Patouillard.' *Willdenenowia*, 3, 315-324.

KOHLMEYER, J. (1963). 'The importance of fungi in the sea.' In *Symposium on Marine Microbiology* (Ed. C. H. Oppenheimer) Charles C. Thomas, Springfield, Illinois, 300-314.

KOHLMEYER, J. (1966). 'Ecological observations on arenicolous marine fungi'. *Z. allg. microbiol.*, 6, 94-105.

KOHLMEYER, J. (1968 a). 'Marine fungi from the tropics.' *Mycologia*, 60, 252-270.

KOHLMEYER, J. (1968 b): 'The first Ascomycete from the deep sea.' *J. Elisha Mitchell scient. Soc.*, 84, 239-241.

KOHLMEYER, J., and KOHLMEYER, E. (1966). 'On the life history of marine Ascomycetes: *Halosphaeria mediosetigera* and *H. circumvestita'. Nova. Hedwigia*, 12, 189-202.

KOHLMEYER, J., and KOHLMEYER, E. (1971). *Synoptic Plates of Higher Marine Fungi.* (3rd ed.). J. Cramer, Lehre.

KÜHNE, H. (1971). 'The identification of wood-boring Crustaceans'. In *Marine Borers, Fungi and Fouling Organisms of Wood'.* (Eds. E. B. G. Jones and S. K. Eltringham). O.E.C.D., Paris, 65-88.

LANE, C. E. (1959). 'The general histology and nutrition of *Limnoria.'* In *Marine Boring and Fouling Organisms.* (Ed. D. L. Ray), University of Washington Press, 35-45.

MEYERS, S. P. (1966). 'Variability in growth and reproduction of the marine fungus, *Lulworthia floridana.' Helgol. wiss. Meeresunters,* 13, 436-443.

MEYERS, S. P. (1968 a). 'Observations on the physiological ecology of marine fungi.' *Bull. Misaki mar. Biol. Inst., Kyoto University,* 12, 207-225.

MEYERS, S. P. (1968 b). 'Degradative activities of filamentous marine fungi.' In *Biodeterioration of Materials.* (Eds. A. H. Walters and J. J. Elphick), Elsevier Publishing Co. Ltd., London, 594-609.

MEYERS, S. P. (1969). 'Thalassiomycetes XI. Further studies of the genus *Lindra* with a description of *L. mariner,* a new species'. *Mycologia,* 61, 486-495.

MEYERS, S. P. (1971). 'Developments in the biology of filamentous marine fungi.' In *Marine Borers, Fungi and Fouling Organisms of Wood.* (Eds. E. B. G. Jones and S. K. Eltringham), O.E.C.D., Paris, 217-236.

MEYERS, S. P., and HOPPER, B. E. (1967). 'Studies on marine fungal/nematode associations and plant degradation.' *Helgol. wiss. Meeresunters,* 15, 270-281.

MEYERS, S. P., and HOYO, L. (1966). 'Observations on the growth of the marine hyphomycete *Varicosporina ramulosa.' Can. J. Bot.,* 44, 1133-1140.

MEYERS, S. P., and NICHOLSON, M. E. (1970). 'Amine utilization by yeasts.' In *Recent Trends in Yeast Research:* (Ed. D. G. Ahearn) Georgia State University, 93-105.

MEYERS, S. P., and REYNOLDS, E. S. (1959 a). 'Growth and cellulolytic activity of lignicolous Deuteromycetes from marine localities.' *Can. J. Microbiol.* 5, 493-503.

MEYERS, S. P., and REYNOLDS, E. S. (1959 b). 'Effects of wood and wood products on perithecial development by lignicolous marine Ascomycetes.' *Mycologia,* 51, 138-145.

MEYERS, S. P., and REYNOLDS, E. S. (1959 c) 'Cellulolytic activity in lignicolous marine Ascomycetes.' *Bull. mar. Sci. Gulf Caribb.,* 9, 441-455.

MEYERS, S. P., and REYNOLDS, E. S. (1960). 'Occurrences of lignicolous fungi in northern Atlantic and Pacific marine localities.' *Can. J. Bot.,* 38, 217-226.

MEYERS, S. P., and REYNOLDS, E. S. (1963). 'Degradation of lignocellulose material by marine fungi.' In *Symposium on Marine Microbiology.* (Ed. C. H. Oppenheimer) Charles C Thomas, Springfield, Illinois, 315-328.

MEYERS, S. P., and SCOTT, E. (1967). 'Thalassiomycetes. X. Variation in growth and reproduction of two isolates of *Corollospora maritima.' Mycologia,* 59, 446-455.

MEYERS, S. P., and SCOTT, E. (1968). 'Cellulose degradation by *Lulworthia floridana* and other marine lignicolous fungi.' *Marine Biology,* 2, 41-46.

MEYERS, S. P., and SIMMS, J. (1965). 'Thalassiomycetes VI. Comparative growth studies of *Lindra thalassiae* and lignicolous Ascomycete species.' *Can. J. Bot.,* *43, 379-392.*

MEYERS, S. P., and SIMMS, J. (1967). 'Thalassiomycetes IX. Comparative studies of reproduction in marine Ascomycetes.' *Bull. mar. Sci. Gulf Caribb.,* 17, 133-148.

MEYERS, S. P., FEDER, W. A., and TSUE, K. M. (1963). 'Nutritional relationships among certain filmentous fungi and a marine occurring nematode.' *Science,* 141, 520-522.

MEYERS, S. P., FEDER, W. A., and TSUE, K. M. (1964). 'Studies of relationships among nematodes and filamentous fungi in the marine environment.' *Dev. in. Indust. Microbiol.,* 5, 354-364.

MEYERS, S. P., CHUNG, S. L., and AHEARN, D. G. (1972). 'Biodegradation of cellulosic substrates by marine fungi.' In *Biodeterioration of Materials.* (Eds. A. H. Walters and E. H. Hueck-van der Plas). Applied Science, London, 121-128.

MEYERS, S. P., PRINDLE, B., and REYNOLDS, E. J. (1960). 'Cellulolytic activity of marine fungi. Degradation of ligno-cellulose material.' *Tappi,* 43, 534-538.

MEYERS, S. P., NICHOLSON, M. L., RHEE, J., MILES, P., and AHEARN, D. G. (1970) 'Mycological studies in Barataria Bay, Louisiana and biodegration of oyster grass, *Spartina alterniflora.'* *Coastal Stud. Bull.,* 5, 111-124.

MOORE, R. T., and MEYERS, S. P. (1962). 'Thalassiomycetes III. The genus *Zalerion.'* *Can. J. Microbiol.,* 8, 407-416.

NEWELL, S. Y., and FELL, J. W. (1970). 'The perfect form of a marine occurring yeast of the genus *Rhodotorula.'* *Mycologia,* 62, 272-281.

NEWELL, S. Y., and HUNTER, I. L. (1972). '*Rhodosporidium diobovatum* sp. n., the perfect form of an asporogenous yeast (*Rhodotorula* sp.)'. *J. Bact.,* 104, 503-508.

PISANO, M. A., MIHALIK, J. A., and CATALANO, G. R. (1964). 'Gelatinase activity by marine fungi.' *Appl. Microbiol.,* 12, 470-474.

RITCHIE, D. (1959). 'The effect of salinity and temperature on marine and other fungi from various climates.' *Bull. Torrey bot. Club,* 86, 367-373.

RITCHIE, D. (1960). 'The evolution of salinity tolerance in fungi.' *Trans. N.Y. Acad. Sci.,* 23, 138-140.

RITCHIE, D. (1961). 'Effects of cultural variation on cell size in a marine fungus.' *Biol. Bull. mar. biol. Lab., Woods Hole,* 120, 85-91.

SCHAFER, R. D., LANE, C. E. (1957). 'Some preliminary observations bearing on the nutrition of *Limnoria.'* *Bull. mar. Sci. Gulf Caribb.,* 7, 289-296.

SGUROS, P. L. and SIMMS, J. (1963 a). 'Role of marine fungi in the biochemistry of the oceans. II Effect of glucose, inorganic nitrogen and tris (hydroxymethyl) aminomethane on growth and pH changes in synthetic media.' *Mycologia,* 55, 728-741.

SGUROS, P. L., and SIMMS, J. (1963 b). 'Role of marine fungi in the biochemistry of the oceans III. Growth factor requirements of the Ascomycete *Halosphaeria mediosetigera.'* *Can. J. Microbiol.,* 9, 585-591.

SGUROS, P. L., and SIMMS, J. (1964). 'Role of marine fungi in the biochemistry of the oceans IV. Growth responses to seawater inorganic macroconstituents.' *J. Bact.,* 88, 346-355.

SIEPMAN, R. (1959 a). 'Ein betrag zur saprophytischen pilz flora des wattes der Wesermündung. Systematischer tiel.' *Veröff. Inst. Meeresforsch. Bremerh.,* 6, 213-281.

SIEPMAN, R. (1959 b). 'Ein bietraf zur saprophytischen pilz flora des wattes der Wesermündung. Zweiter tiel. *Veröff. Inst. Meeresforsch. Bremerh.*, 6, 283-301.

SWART, H. J. (1963). 'Further investigations of the mycoflora in the soil of some mangrove swamps'. *Acta. bot. neerl.,* 12, 98-111.

TUBAKI, K. (1969). 'Studies on the Japanese marine fungi lignicolous group (111), algicolous group and a general consideration.' *Annual report, Institute for Fermentation, Osaka,* 4, 12-41.

TURNER, R. D. (1971). 'Identification of marine wood-boring molluscs.' In *Marine Borers, Fungi and Fouling Organisms of Wood.'* (Eds. E. B. G. Jones and S. K. Eltringham). O.E.C.D., Paris, 17-64.

VAN UDEN, H. and FELL, J. W. (1968). 'Marine yeasts.' In *Advances in Microbiology of the Sea.* (Eds. M. R. Droop and E. J. F. Wood), Academic Press, vol. 1, 167-201.

6 Cytochemistry of Marine Fungal Spores

PAUL W. KIRK, Jr.

6.1 Introduction

The ascospores of marine fungi commonly produce conspicuous ornamentations having ecological and taxonomic significance (Figs. 6.1-6.7). These structures facilitate flotation and attachment of the spores (Kohlmeyer and Kohlmeyer, 1966), and may perform other functions not yet recognized. Considerable diversity in the number, insertion, and texture of the ornamentations is invaluable for separating species of marine Ascomycetes, particularly those having hyalodidymous ascospores (Kohlmeyer and Kohlmeyer, 1971). Likewise, the microscopic cytochemistry and the mode of origin of these structures are generally regarded as fundamental criteria in taxonomic delimitations at the generic level (Cavaliere and Johnson, 1966; Kohlmeyer, 1972).

The application of cytochemistry to the systematics of marine Ascomycetes was suggested by Johnson (1963 a, d) when traditional morphological techniques failed to define the nature and origin of certain spore ornamentations. Johnson (1963 a-d) and Johnson and Cavaliere (1963) stressed the fundamental taxonomic value of these characteristics, while Kohlmeyer (1960) examined the centrum morphology. It should be noted, however, that despite their different emphases, both investigators expressed the view that good characteristics of every kind should be utilized in generic classification (Kohlmeyer, 1962, 1966; Cavaliere and Johnson, 1966). The latter two authors placed much importance on the presence or absence of paraphyses and pseudoparaphyses, and Kohlmeyer (1972) relied heavily upon the cytochemistry and development of spore ornamentations in defining *Ceriosporopsis, Corollospora,* and *Halosphaeria.* Wilson (1965) made the first use of cytochemical methods in marine mycology, and though her results on the development of spore ornamentations in *Ceriosporopsis halima* Linder were inconclusive due to lack of controls, this helped to stimulate further study and the refinement of techniques. Kirk (1966) tested the effectiveness of numerous cytochemical methods under rigorously controlled conditions, while investigating the chemical development of spores and their ornamentations in eight marine Pyrenomycetes. His recommendations on laboratory procedure, plus major findings on the ascospores of *C. halima* and other species, were later confirmed through the combined use of cytochemistry and electron microscopy (Lutley and Wilson, 1972 a, b). Others have made incidental contributions to the cytochemistry of marine Pyrenomycete ascospores, showing that histochemical

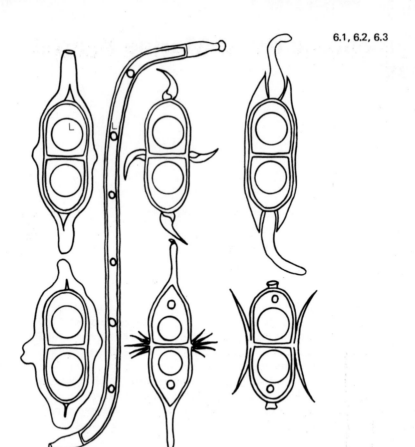

6.1, 6.2, 6.3

6.5   6.4, 6.6, 6.7

Fig. 6.1 *Ceriosporopsis tubulifera* ascospore showing apical mucilaginous processes within spore sheath. **Fig. 6.2** *Halosphaeria appendiculata,* apical and lateral membranous processes. **Fig. 6.3** *C. halima,* and **Fig. 6.4** *Ceriosporopsis circumvestita,* apical mucilaginous processes within spore sheath. **Fig. 6.5** *Lulworthia* sp., scolecosporous ascospore with apical mucilage pouches. L, lipid guttules. **Fig. 6.6** *Corollospora maritima,* apical spines and flexuous equatorial fibrils. **Fig. 6.7** *Halosphaeria mediosetigera,* membranous exosporic fragments.

stains including metachromatic ones are useful to resolve the spore ornamentations (Kohlmeyer, 1971; Tubaki, 1967, 1968).

Three factors have been of fundamental importance to the successful completion of cytochemical studies demonstrating phyletic unity among the diverse spore ornamentations in this group of fungi. First, species representing every textural type of ornamentation can be induced to complete their sexual cycles normally in the laboratory (Kirk, 1966, 1969). These types are the spore sheath, true spine, and flexuous, membranous, or mucilaginous processes on didymosporous spores, and apical mucilage pouches on scolecosporous spores in the genus *Lulworthia* (Figs. 6.1-6.7). Developmental stages of all are readily available for cytochemical and electron microscopic investigations. Second, much morphological similarity among the ascocarps of these species shows them belonging to a natural family, the Halosphaeriaceae (Kohlmeyer, 1972). On this basis it can be postulated that the different types of spore ornamentations comprise a phyletic series, containing primitive and derived

178

forms which should be distinguishable by the techniques of experimental morphology
Third, the large, hyaline ascospores are very amenable to cytochemical analysis.
Many functional groups and classes of substances are readily detectable (Table 6.1).

TABLE 6.1   Microscopic cytochemical tests applicable to ascospores*.

Test	Object	Controls
dinitrofluorobenzene reduced by TiCl$_3$	total protein	trypsin digestion
rosindole	wall protein; tryptophan	trypsin digestion
Benzapyrene/caffeine	total lipid	methanol/HCl extraction
silver bromide	unsaturated lipid	methanol/HCl; performic block
periodic acid/Schiff	total bis-glycol carbohydrate	amylase digestion
IKI	glycogen, dextrin	amylase digestion
azure A in solution of electrolytes	RNA; possibly DNA	trichloroacetic (TCA); RNAse
Feulgen/Schiff	DNA	TCA; perchloric block
Schiff reagent	free sugar and lipid aldehyde	ethanol *vs.* water extraction
lead sulphide	polyphosphate; volutin	TCA; NaHCO$_3$ extraction
Van Wisselingh	chitin	2% acetic; NaOCl; birefringence
alcian or toluidine blue at pH 2.5	acidic mucins	TCA; methylation/ saponification

* Consult Kirk (1966) for references and specifications.

6.2   Techniques

This chapter will not attempt to describe the many methods and pitfalls of cytochemistry that apply to research on sporogenesis. Persons unfamiliar with histochemical reactions should first consult a suitable introductory text such as Jensen's
(1962), and then Kirk's (1966) critical appraisal of methods used to fix and characterize the major chemical constituents of ascospores. Tests on unfamiliar material
should be very carefully controlled and should include checks on the controls themselves. When possible, determinations should be based upon at least two tests involving different chemical mechanisms. It may be necessary at times to pair a highly
specific test whose mechanism is understood with an empirical one having sufficient
sensitivity to resolve cytological details. The tests listed in Table 6.1 have both desirable traits and are recommended as being some of the most reliable for investigating the chemical development of endogenous reserves, spore walls, and ornamentations. Each of these components of the ascospores will be discussed in turn.

6.3 · Endogenous reserves

Figures 6.8-6.10 depict the accumulation and utilization of endogenous reserves during ascospore development and germination in *Halosphaeria mediosetigera* Cribb et Cribb, but the events typify those in all species studied (Kirk, 1966; Lutley and Wilson, 1972 a, b). In general, the description of these events based entirely upon cytochemical data is consistent with other chemical findings on the spores and hyphae of higher fungi (Cochrane, 1958; Zalokar, 1965; Madelin, 1966; Sussman and Halvorson, 1966). During development (Fig. 6.8) glycogen becomes less abundant while neutral oil accumulates within the spores. Schiff-positive, alcohol-soluble substances (SPAS) occur prominently around the oil globules. It appears that glycogen is being transformed into oil, and SPAS consists of intermediary metabolites including acetate. Further research is needed to identify SPAS and indicate its distribution in other groups of fungi. Only freshly prepared smears should be examined for the presence of SPAS, as the spores deteriorate in air and within a few days produce other Schiff-positive, lipoidal compounds around the periphery of the guttules. The oil globules show little unsaturation during spore development, dormancy, or germination, and probably contain triglycerides like those in the mycelium of higher marine fungi (Block, *et al.,* 1973). Because these lipids are mobile in fixatives and organic staining solutions, their true distribution is shown best by fluorescent vital dyes (Kirk, 1970). Most oil coalesces into guttules in the mature spores (Figs. 6.1-6.7, 6.9).

Lipids showing a high degree of unsaturation occur only within a narrow band surrounding the guttules (Fig. 6.9), where Kirk (1966) suggested there may be an accumulation of mitochondria. Electron microscopy has revealed numerous ovoid bodies around the guttules which do not resemble typical mitochondria in that cristae are lacking (Lutley and Wilson, 1972 a, b), although the possibility that these structures may be immature or specialized mitochondria involved with fat metabolism has not been ruled out. Additional study to determine the nature and function of ovoid bodies, including their relation to unsaturated lipids and SPAS, should have general biological significance.

Glycogen is sparse and SPAS generally lacking in the mature, dormant spores, but volutin bodies consisting mostly of acidic polyphosphates, RNA, and protein are

6.8, 6.9, 6.10

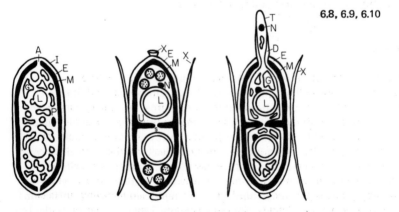

Fig. 6.8-6.10 *H. mediosetigera,* developing, mature, and germinating ascospores, respectively. A: apical ectodesma; D: endospore; E: epispore; G: glycogen; I: investing membrane; L: lipid guttule; M: mesospore; N: nucleus; P: plasmalemma; S: septal pore; T: germ tube; U: unsaturated lipid surrounding guttule; V, volutin; X, exosporic fragment.

abundant (Fig. 6.9). The use of histochemical stains in conjunction with selective extraction techniques has found acidic reactions within the spores to be due almost entirely to phosphates, and those in the walls and ornamentations to uronic acids and other carboxylated carbohydrates. The ascospores of marine fungi do not produce sulphated mucins.

The ascospores have no constitutive dormancy, but germinate readily in various seawater solutions. Several chemical changes can be observed prior to the emergence of germ tubes. The loss of volutin and simultaneous increase in RNA content are readily seen using cytochemistry (Kirk, 1966; Lutley and Wilson, 1972 a). This is in accordance with other chemical evidence that the volutin is utilized in nucleic acid synthesis (Harold, 1966). Glycogen and SPAS reappear, and both substances remain abundant while oil is being utilized within the germinating spores. The guttules become perceptibly smaller as germination progresses. Late in germination the nucleus divides, and one daughter nucleus remains near the major guttules while the other migrates into the germ tube (Fig. 6.10).

6.4 Ascospore wall

The ascospore walls in the Halosphaeriaceae, excluding the ornamentations, conform to a uniform pattern of chemical and morphological development (Kirk, 1966; Lutley and Wilson, 1972 a, b). With the possible exception of the initial delimitation of spores within the ascus, this pattern agrees well with other published reports on ascospore development and composition (Madelin, 1966; Bartnicki-Garcia, 1968; Carroll, 1969). Apparent discrepancies are due to a lack of uniform terminology for the different layers of the spore wall. Here the terms endospore, mesospore, and epispore are used to designate the three inner layers (Figs. 6.10 and 6.11) which are present and homologous in all Halosphaeriaceae that have been examined. The epispore and mesospore arise in centripetal succession between an investing membrane and the plasmalemma (Fig. 6.8). At maturity the rigid epispore contains chitin, numerous carboxyl groups removable by glucuronidase, and protein that is richer in tryptophan and poorer in arginine than the spore cytoplasm. The mesospore is pliant and unreactive, probably consisting mostly of beta (1-3) glucans. This layer becomes swollen but is not removed by alkali, chitinase, or almond emulsin. The endospore is prominent only during germination (Fig. 6.10) and is continuous with the germ tube. This form of germ tube development can no longer be considered typical only of the Zygomycetes, as Hawker (1966) and Bartnicki-Garcia (1968) suggested. Chemically the chitinous endospore resembles the epispore, but is less acidic. Both layers become melanized in older germinated spores.

In didymosporous spores a septum is formed, mainly by inward development of the mesospore (Fig. 6.9). Lutley and Wilson (1972 a) found no pore in this septum, although Kirk (1966) claims to have observed one occasionally in dormant and germinating ascospores. It seems possible that, since the formation of a septum is one of the last and apparently least critical events to occur in ascosporogensis, the presence or absence of a septal pore could be a variable feature dependent upon the degree of completion of this developmental process. The size and extent of the septum are quantitative characteristics which may, like the number of septa, show considerable variation in some genera and species of marine Ascomycetes (Kirk, 1966; Kohlmeyer et al., 1967; Kohlmeyer and Kohlmeyer, 1971).

Structures occurring in the outer, exosporic position (Figs. 6.10 and 6.11) account for the great diversity of spore ornamentations in the didymosporous

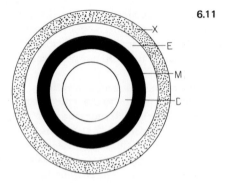

6.11

Fig. 6.11 Schematic representation of laminated wall of germinating ascospore. D: endospore; E: epispore; M: mesospore; X: exosporic layer.

Halosphaeriaceae (Kirk, 1966; Lutley and Wilson, 1972 a, b). This is also the case in yeast ascospores (Kawakami, 1960). The term 'exosporic' is used rather than exospore, because not all structures occurring in this superficial position seem to be homologous. This point is to be developed in subsequent paragraphs, but first it is necessary to explain how the outer two layers of the spore wall appear to be nourished during development.

There is no evidence that structural polysaccharides occurring in the exosporic position are deposited upon the epispore by the ascus cytoplasm, or that they are synthesized and extruded by the spore cytoplasm as others have suggested (Johnson, 1963 a, b, d; Wilson, 1965; Cavaliere and Johnson, 1966). Cytochemical studies suggest that neutral, non-structural polysaccharides produced within the spore are transported through minute ectodesmata to the two outer layers of the wall, and there converted by enzymes into chitin and carboxylated derivatives. The intense dinitrofluoro-benzene-TiCl$_3$ stain has revealed fine proteinaceous strands traversing the mesospore, connecting the outer wall layers with the glycogen-rich plasmalemma in immature spores. These strands, the ectodesmata, are most distinct in the apical walls of *H. mediosetigera* ascospores (Fig. 6.8). Even at maturity, when the ectodesmata are no longer evident, these spores are fragile at the apices. Ectodesmata have been noted also in the apical and lateral walls of ascospores in other species, usually at the base of conspicuous ornamentations which they probably nourish. Electron microscopic confirmation of ectodesmata in the ascospore wall is lacking, although protein has been found associated with a system of pores in the walls of *Neurospora* hyphae (Manocha and Colvin, 1967). It is uncertain whether the ectodesmata in fungal spores consist of unit membranes, or are accumulations of amorphous enzyme protein and associated substrates being transported through the wall. It is well known that enzymes occur in the walls of fungal spores and hyphae (Sussman, 1957; Aronson, 1965; Bartnicki-Garcia, 1968; Cheung and Barber, 1971). Cytochemical methods reveal much protein and glycogen or dextrins in the developing epispore and contiguous ornamentations, and generally lesser amounts in the mature, chitinized structures. This situation is somewhat comparable to the utilization of glycogen within growing hyphal tips (Zalokar, 1965). The simplest explanation for the cytochemical data is the occurrence of enzymes and substrates in the outer layers of the ascospore wall, bringing about the *in situ* polymerization of structural polysaccharides.

6.5 Spore ornamentation

Figures 6.12-6.20 summarize the ontogeny and some possible phyletic relationships of three different textural types of ornamentations in the didymosporous Halosphaeriaceae. These types are the membranous (Figs. 6.13-6.16) and mucilaginous (Figs. 6.17-6.20) exosporic processes, and the spore sheath (Figs. 6.18 and 6.20). Immature stages are shown at the left, and corresponding mature stages to the right. The vertical sequence of drawings is thought to represent a major evolutionary trend in this group of fungi, brought about by adaptive changes in the synthetic capacity of the spore surface. This sequence is not intended to suggest actual lines of descent of the species pictured, but merely how these fundamental kinds of ornamentations may have originated within the Halosphaeriaceae. Stippling in the ornamentations denotes the presence of sufficient dissociable carboxyl groups to cause metachromatic staining in a 0.1% solution of toluidine blue in 3% acetic acid. Stippled circles within the mature spores represent volutin, which also stains metachromatically in this solution, but is distinguishable from acidic carbohydrates by numerous

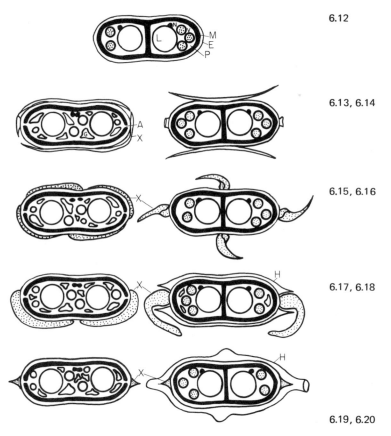

6.12

6.13, 6.14

6.15, 6.16

6.17, 6.18

6.19, 6.20

Fig. 6.12 *Lignincola laevis* mature ascospore. Figs. 6.13 and 6.14, *H. mediosetigera;* Figs. 6.15 and 6.16 *H. appendiculata;* Figs. 6.17 and 6.18 *C. halima;* Figs. 6.19 and 6.20 *C. tubulifera,* immature and mature ascospores, respectively. A: apical ectodesma; E; epispore; G: glycogen; H: spore sheath; L: lipid guttule; M: mesospore; N: nucleus; P: plasmalemma; V: volutin; X: exosporic fragment or process (stippled indicates metachromatic staining in toluidine blue).

methods (Kirk, 1966). Blackened objects denote nuclei, clear circles oil globules, and clear irregular areas glycogen vacuoles.

The ascospore of *Lignincola laevis* Höhnk exemplifies the presumed ancestral condition (Fig. 6.12). This species occurs as commonly as most members of the family on wood in seawater, although the ascospore shows no morphological adaptation to this environment. It lacks ornamentations, but the wall sometimes appears slightly thicker than in other marine fungi. Whether the exospore is lacking, or may be fused imperceptibly with the epispore, remains to be determined. A more basic problem having no immediate solution, is whether the ancestral Halosphaeriaceae evolved from terrestrial Pyrenomycetes, or from the red algae. This perennial question is beyond the scope of the present chapter, and the reader is referred only to some of the more recent chemical and morphological evidence, which seems to support the red algal hypothesis (Denison and Carroll, 1966; Kohlmeyer, 1973; Catalfomo *et al.*, 1973).

The membranous ornamentations in *H. mediosetigera* (Figs. 6.13-6.14) are considered representative of an unspecialized condition, possibly derivable from the *L. laevis* type of ascospore by the elaboration and fragmentation of an exospore. The mature ornamentations are mostly neutral chitin containing little residual glycogen and protein. These structures are indistinguishable from the epispore until late in development, when chitin becomes detectable using the Van Wisselingh test. Their eventual separation from the epispore seems to result, not merely from pressure exerted by the enlarging spore, but also from the uneven deposition of chitin within the exosporic fragments. Apparently these fragments are discontinuously distributed over the surface of the epispore during development, as are the ornamentations on *Neurospora* ascospores (Sussman and Halvorson, 1966). One can envisage ornamentations like those in *H. mediosetigera* having originated from a marine fungus with ribbed ascospores, but none has been described in the Halosphaeriaceae. Perhaps scanning electron microscopy of these ascospores might reveal rib-like structures previously overlooked. It is surprising that this popular technique has not been applied to the ascospores of marine fungi, if only to supplement descriptions of the conspicuous ornamentations.

In their detailed studies of ascospore development in *Halosphaeria appendiculata* Linder, Johnson and Cavaliere (1963) and Kirk (1966) referred to this species as *Remispora ornata* Johnson et Cavaliere. However, Kohlmeyer (1971) has presented indisputable evidence that these taxa are synonymous. The ornamentations in *H. appendiculata* (Figs. 6.15-6.16) represent a degree of specialization intermediate between that in *H. mediosetigera* (Figs. 6.13-6.14) and *C. halima* (Figs. 6.17-6.18). As in *H. mediosetigera,* the membranous ornamentations appear to originate as exosporic fragments, becoming elevated as a partial result of the deposition of chitin. Kirk (1966) obtained a strongly positive Van Wisselingh test plus birefringence at the base of these ornamentations, which Lutley and Wilson (1972 b) interpreted as thickenings in the epispore. Probably chitin is the principal material causing membranous ornamentations to become stiff and enrolled in the Halosphaeriaceae, but the amount deposited shows graded variation between the epispore and the contiguous ornamentations. In addition to chitin, the mature ornamentations in *H. appendiculata* contain dissociable carboxyl groups, much protein that is rich in tryptophan, and glycogen or dextrins. At pH 2.5, the structures stain with alcian blue and show toluidine blue metachromasia. This alcianophilia is not destroyed by trypsin or alpha amylase, but is by methylation of the carboxyl groups. An affinity for basic dyes is restored to the methylated materials by saponification and mild acid hydrolysis. Hot water or alkali diminish basophilia and mild acid hydrolysis enhances it, suggesting that the carboxyl groups on the structural polysaccharide may become involved in lactam internal esters. Esters of this type might form in a carboxylated derivative of chitin containing amino as well as acidic groups.

The apical processes on *C. halima* ascospores (Figs. 6.17-6.18) have the same chemical characteristics of *H. appendiculata* ornamentations, except that chitin is lacking. Owing to the absence of this polysaccharide, the processes have a mucilaginous rather than membranous texture. They are easily distensible, and dissolve in distilled water unless fixed with formalin, basic dyes, or cetylpyridinium chloride. Apparently the carboxyls complex readily with cations, in addition to forming lactam esters. The effect of cations in seawater on the solubility of these acidic mucopolysaccharides has not been investigated, although such information may have ecological and taxonomic implications.

Despite having different textures, the acidic processes on *C. halima* and *H. appendiculata* ascospores develop in a similar manner. The processes can be interpreted as modified exosporic remnants comparable to those on the *H. mediosetigera* ascospore. Each structure grows outward from a point of attachment on the epispore (Figs. 6.15 and 6.17), obtaining nourishment through ectodesmata as does the *H. mediosetigera* exospore (Fig. 6.13). Although the *C. halima* processes usually grow straight out from either end of the spore (Fig. 6.3), they sometimes develop pressed to one side (Fig. 6.17), closely resembling the apical processes on immature *H. appendiculata* spores (Fig. 6.15). This resemblance is most striking when the ornamentations are stained red and the spores blue in toluidine blue solution. In *C. halima* the processes become elevated by the development of a spore sheath (Fig. 6.18), rather than by deposition of chitin within the structures. The existence of numerous tubules in the acidic processes of *C. halima* and *H. appendiculata* was predicted on the basis of cytochemical data (Kirk, 1966), and has been confirmed by electron microscopy (Lutley and Wilson, 1972 a, b). Parallel fibrils noted in the former were not observed in mature ornamentations of the latter. However, in order to compare the ultrastructure of ornamentations in these two species, additional studies are needed of the immature stages occurring prior to the completion of the mesospore. Digesting the fixed ornamentations with the purest grade of trypsin causes loss of glycogen as well as protein, whereas alpha amylase removes only the glycogen. Acidic mucopolysaccharides accumulate around the tubules in the ornamentations, but are not found in the spore cytoplasm. This evidence suggests strongly that the tubules transport raw materials from the cytoplasm and transform them into chitin and mucopolysaccharides. This being the case, slight changes in the enzymic constitution of these tubules could markedly affect the texture and staining properties of the ornamentations, by determining the relative amounts of neutral and acidic polysaccharides accumulated.

It may be possible to characterize some of the biochemical reactions that are thought to occur in the different types of ornamentations. Many enzymes have been identified in the cytoplasm of fungal hyphae and spores by cytochemical methods (Roth and Winkelmann, 1960; Zalokar, 1965). Although enzyme cytochemistry is difficult to interpret in tenuous fungal walls, it should not be in the relatively expansive spore ornamentations of marine fungi. Moreover, these spores may be useful in cytochemical studies to confirm that *in situ* polysaccharide synthesis occurs in the walls of higher fungi. Such studies might focus on the cytochemical detection of enzymes affecting the uridine-diphospho-glucosyls, which presumably are important in the conversion of dextrins into chitin and its derivatives (Aronson, 1965; Bartnicki-Garcia, 1968). This approach may locate reaction sites more precisely than could macrochemical methods, whose accuracy is dependent upon the scrupulous separation of the walls from cytoplasm.

The most fundamental difference between *H. appendiculata* and *C. halima* ascospores is that the latter produces a spore sheath late in development, after the apical processes have been initiated (Figs. 6.17-6.18). The sheath is continuous around the spore except for pouches at either end which contain the mucilaginous processes. Both types of ornamentations are exosporic in position, but the sheath is thought to be a new derivative of the epispore, unrelated to the exosporic material from which other ornamentations were derived. It grows outward from the epispore by the deposition of polysaccharides around a network of proteinaceous tubules (Kirk, 1966; Lutley and Wilson, 1972 a). These tubules are inserted homogeneously over the surface of the epispore, rather than issuing from a few apical and lateral ectodesmata, as in other ornamentations. Chemically the spore sheath and apical processes in *C. halima* are similar but not identical. The former stains less intensely with basic dyes owing to a greater proportion of neutral polysaccharides. In addition to glycogen and acidic polysaccharides, this structure probably contains beta (1-3) glucans. The sheath is mostly soluble in hot trichloroacetic acid solution, whereas the apical processes are not. Lutley and Wilson (1972 a) located chitin in unspecified parts of the sheath, and Kirk (1966) did, but only in the denser part forming the base of the apical pouches.

The ascospores of *Ceriosporopsis tubulifera* (Kohlm.) Kirk (Figs. 6.19-6.20) are strikingly similar morphologically and chemically to those of *C. halima* (Figs. 6.17-6.18). The former has a somewhat smaller ratio of length to width, and produces much smaller apical mucilaginous processes. However, these acidic processes grow out as in *C. halima,* becoming enclosed within apical pouches of the spore sheath. The sheath is more extensive in *C. tubulifera* and is inflated around the equator of the spore. Rarely a small amount of metachromatic material resembling the apical mucilage occurs laterally on the epispore, within the inflated equatorial portion of the sheath. This could be a vestigial ornamentation derived from lateral exosporic fragments like those in *H. appendiculata* (Fig. 6.16). If this can be confirmed, it is but one of many indications that the genera *Ceriosporopsis* and *Halosphaeria* are closely related. When first described, *C. tubulifera* and a very similar fungus, *C. circumvestita* (Kohlm.) Kohlm. (Fig. 6.4), were thought to belong in *Halosphaeria* (Kohlmeyer, 1960). However, later studies have shown the ascospores and ascocarps to differ only in minor respects from those of *C. halima* (Kohlmeyer and Kohlmeyer, 1964-1969, 1966; Cavaliere, 1966 a, b; Kirk, 1966; Kohlmeyer, 1971). Placing much importance on cytochemical evidence, Kohlmeyer (1972) redefined *Halosphaeria* to contain mainly the membranous type of ornamentation stiffened by chitin, and included in *Ceriosporopsis* those species producing mucilaginous processes within a spore sheath. Although additional cytochemical and electron microscopic studies are needed to clarify the position of intermediate forms such as *Halosphaeria torquata* Kohlm., Kohlmeyer's (1972) classification of marine Pyrenomycetes is the most natural to date, taking into account the total known ascocarpic, ascosporic and ecological characteristics of these fungi.

In summary, the diversity of spore ornamentations in the *Ceriosporopsis-Halosphaeria* complex is thought to exemplify the fundamental biological principle, that speciation within a given family usually involves the modification of existing structures rather than the creation of entirely new ones. The chemical and morphological evidence reviewed here suggests that chitinous exosporic fragments like those in *Halosphaeria* gave rise to the mucilaginous processes, which have become greatly elongated in *Ceriospropsis longissima* Kohlm. and rudimentary in *C. circumvestita.*

186

The spore sheath is interpretable as an episporic elaboration, less primitive than the exosporic structures it envelops. This view is supported by the relatively late appearance of the sheath during ascosporogenesis in *C. halima* and *C. tubulifera* (Kirk, 1966). Furthermore, one can easily envisage the gradual envelopment of functional or vestigial mucilaginous processes by a spore sheath, but not the reverse sequence; that is, not the processes arising within and penetrating the completely formed sheath.

The ascospores of *Corollospora maritima* Werdermann (Figs. 6.21-6.23) are not in the mainstream of the foregoing discussion. *Corollospora* as defined by Kohlmeyer (1972) is a natural genus having no outstanding links with *Ceriosporopsis,* and few with *Halosphaeria.* Most species produce carbonaceous ascocarps having a subiculum for attachment to sand grains and calcareous matter. The ascospores show much variation in size and septation, but usually produce equatorial and apical ornamentations by the rupture of a thin exospore during spore expansion (Kirk, 1966; Kohlmeyer, 1966; Kohlmeyer *et al.,* 1967; Lutley and Wilson, 1972 b). The girdle of flexuous processes on *C. maritima* ascospores consists mostly of chitin or other neutral polysaccharides, rather than residual ascus cytoplasm as Johnson thought (1963 b). The growth of a spine from either end of the spore early in development (Fig. 6.21) ruptures the exospore before much chitin can be deposited in it (Fig. 6.22). None is deposited in the apical fragments, but the equatorial ones stiffen somewhat when chitin becomes detectable in the epispore (Fig. 6.23). The cytoplasm contracts into the main body of the spore when the epispore becomes chitinized, leaving only an occasional small oil globule or proteinaceous core as evidence of its having extended into the spines. The *C. maritima* epispore is richer in tyrosine during development than in the other species studied, which probably explains its being more melanized at maturity. The epispore is also more basophilic than others, adsorbing Sudan black B, azure A, and ruthenium red even though controlled cytochemical tests reveal no lipids, RNA, or pectins. Removing uronic acids from the wall reduces this non-specific staining.

6.21, 6.22, 6.23

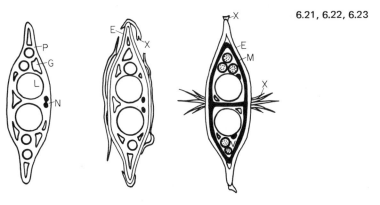

Figs. 6.21-6.23 *C. maritima* ascospore development. E: epispore; G: glycogen; L: lipid guttule; M: mesospore; N: nucleus; P: plasmalemma; V: volutin; X: exosporic fragments.

Cytochemical studies on the apical mucilage pouches of scolecosporous *Lulworthia* ascospores (Fig. 6.5, 6.24-6.26) have shed light on the function and the taxonomic significance of these ornamentations (Kirk, 1966). Early in development, glycogen within the apices of the spores is transformed into periodic acid Schiff (PAS) positive mucilage (Fig. 6.24). This material is mucoprotein or a neutral polysaccharide resemb-

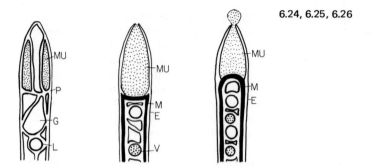

Figs. 6.24-6.26 *Lulworthia* ascospore development and mucilage discharge. E: epispore; G: glycogen; L: lipid guttule; M: mesospore; MU: mucilage (stippled not metachromatic); P: plasmalemma; V: volutin.

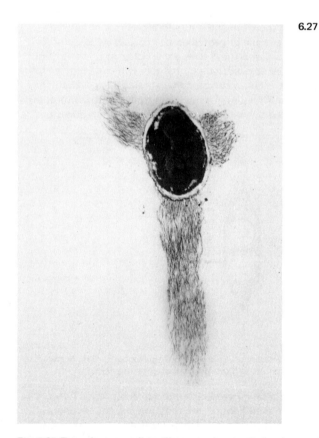

Fig. 6.27 *Torpedospora radiata.* Electron micrograph showing parallel fibrils in spore ornamentations. From Lutley and Wilson (1972 b) in the *Transactions of the British Mycological Society.*

ling dextran, depending upon the species of *Lulworthia*. As in other ascospores of the Halosphaeriaceae, the epispore forms prior to the mesospore. The epispore becomes chitinized throughout the entire length of the spore, and forms the wall of the apical pouches (Fig. 6.25). The mesospore fails to develop within the pouches, probably as a result of their becoming engorged with mucilage. However, the mesospore forms below the pouch, and appears either concave (Fig. 6.25) or convex (Fig. 6.26) in optical cross section, depending upon the internal pressure of the spore. The spore acts as an osmometer, and placing it in a hypotonic solution causes the pliant mesospore to expand and discharge the apical mucilage (Fig. 6.26). Constricting the spore achieves the same result. It is probably of adaptive significance that the germinating spores transform glycogen into osmotically active sugar, causing the spore to swell and discharge mucilage, which secures attachment to substrata. Possibly a somewhat similar mechanism may occur in *Corollospora tubulata* Kohlm. Although marvellous adaptations for marine fungi, these osmometric apical pouches have limited value as quantitative taxonomic characters due to their variable length. Speciation in *Lulworthia* constitutes a major problem in marine mycology which Kohlmeyer summarizes (1972).

There are no cytochemical studies of the ascospores in *Torpedospora radiata* Meyers, but Lutley and Wilson (1972 b) have published an electron micrograph of the mature spore, which provides an excellent demonstration of the occurrence of parallel tubules within the ornamentations (Fig. 6.27). There seems no doubt that such structures could transport and polymerize polysaccharides. Despite its superficial similarity to the Halosphaeriaceae, Kohlmeyer (1972) excludes this species from the family.

6.28

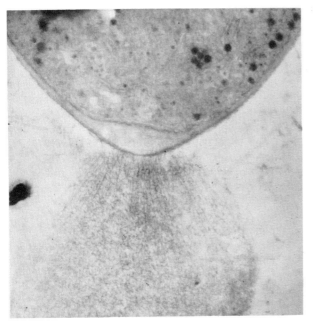

Fig. 6.28 *Ceriosporopsis halima.* Electron micrograph showing fibrillar structures in spore ornamentations. From Lutley and Wilson (1972 a) in the *Transactions of the British Mycological Society.*

The chemical composition and elaborate ultrastructure of certain spore ornamentations (e.g. Figs. 6.27 and 6.28) raises some questions concerning their ecological importance. In addition to their generally recognized roles in flotation and attachment, might some facilitate spore release from the perithecium by imbibing water, or produce enzymes and antibiotics which favourably modify the microenvironment for initial growth of the germ tube? What selective pressures have favoured the enlargement of apical mucilaginous processes in *C. longissima,* as opposed to the spore sheath in *C. circumvestita*? Since these two kinds of ornamentations differ chemically and morphologically, could they not, working in combination with other characteristics of the fungi, help in filling different available niches? How do the solubilities of the different polysaccharides, and hence their functional efficiencies in organelles of dispersal, differ under various combinations of salinity and temperature? Have some ornamentations neutral or negative survival value within the present environment of the fungi, being produced merely as a by product of essential metabolic activities? Such intriguing questions are much too academic and technically difficult to warrant investigation at this time. Nevertheless, the answers could provide much insight into evolutionary processes and relationships in the Halosphaeriaceae.

Acknowledgements

This work was supported in part by a grant from the Old Dominion University Research Foundation. I wish to thank Dr. Martin Lutley and Dr. Irene M. Wilson for Figs. 6.27 and 6.28. Special thanks go to Dr. T. W. Johnson for all his help and support.

References

ARONSON, J. M. (1965). 'The cell wall.' In *The Fungi: an Advanced Treatise,* (Eds. G. C. Ainsworth and A. S. Sussman), Academic Press, London, vol. I, pp 49-76.

BARTNICKI-GARCIA, S. (1968). 'Cell wall chemistry, morphogenesis, and taxonomy of fungi.' *Ann. Rev. Microbiol.,* 22, 87-108.

BLOCK, J. H., CATALFOMO, P., CONSTANTINE, G. H., and KIRK, P. W. (1973). 'Triglyceride fatty acids of selected higher marine fungi.' *Mycologia,* 65, 488-491.

CARROLL, G. C. (1969). 'A study of the fine structure of ascospore delimitation in *Saccobolus kerverni.*' *Arch. Mikrobiol.,* 66, 321-339.

CATALFOMO, P., BLOCK, J. H., CONSTANTINE, G. H., and KIRK, P. W. (1973). 'Choline sulfate (ester) in marine higher fungi.' *Marine Chemistry,* 1, 157-162.

CAVALIERE, A. R. (1966 a). 'Marine Ascomycetes: ascocarp morphology and its application to taxonomy. I. *Amylocarpus* Currey, *Ceriosporella* gen. nov., *Lindra* Wilson.' *Nova Hedwigia,* 10, 389-398.

CAVALIERE, A. R. (1966 b). 'Marine Ascomycetes: ascocarp morphology and its application to taxonomy. II. Didymosporae.' *Nova Hedwigia,* 10, 399-424.

CAVALIERE, A. R., and JOHNSON, T. W. (1966). 'Marine Ascomycetes: ascocarp morphology and its application to taxonomy. V. Evaluation.' *Nova Hedwigia,* 10, 453-461.

CHEUNG, D. S. M., and BARBER, H. N. (1971). 'Uredospore wall proteins of wheat stem rust: localization and enzymic activities.' *Arch. Mikrobiol.,* 77, 239-246.

COCHRANE, V. W. (1958). *Physiology of Fungi.* Wiley, New York, 524 pp.

DENISON, W. C., and CARROLL, G. C. (1966). 'The primitive Ascomycete: a new look at an old problem'. *Mycologia,* 58, 249-269.

HAROLD, F. M. (1966). 'Inorganic polyphosphates in biology: structure, metabolism and function.' *Bact. Rev.,* 30, 772-794.

HAWKER, L. E. (1966). 'Germination: morphological and anatomical changes.' In *The Fungus Spore* (Ed. M. F. Madelin), Butterworths, London, 151-161.

JENSEN, W. A. (1962). *Botanical Histochemistry.* Freeman, San Francisco, 408 pp.

JOHNSON, T. W. (1963 a). 'Some aspects of morphology in marine Ascomycetes: *Halosphaeria* Linder.' *Nova Hedwigia,* 6, 67-81.

JOHNSON, T. W. (1963 b). 'Some aspects of morphology in marine Ascomycetes: *Corollospora* Werdermann.' *Nova Hedwigia,* 6, 85-93.

JOHNSON, T. W. (1963 c). 'Some aspects of morphology in marine Ascomycetes: *Amylocarpus* Currey, *Herpotrichiella* Petrak and *Torpedospora* Meyers.' *Nova Hedwigia,* 6, 157-168.

JOHNSON, T. W. (1963 d). 'Some aspects of morphology in marine Ascomycetes: *Ceriosporopsis* Linder.' *Nova Hedwigia,* 6, 169-178.

JOHNSON, T. W., and CAVALIERE, A. R. (1963). 'Some aspects of morphology in marine Ascomycetes: *Remispora* Linder.' *Nova Hedwigia,* 6, 179-198.

KAWAKAMI, N. (1960). 'Electron microscopy on Ascomycetes. Investigations of fine structure and classification of sporogenous yeasts.' *Mem. Fac. Eng. Hiroshima Univ.,* 1, 207-237.

KIRK, P. W. (1966). 'Morphogenesis and microscopic cytochemistry of marine pyrenomycete ascospores.' *Beihefte Nova Hedwigia,* 22, 1-128.

KIRK, P. W. (1969). 'Isolation and culture of lignicolous marine fungi.' *Mycologia,* 61, 174-177.

KIRK, P. W. (1970). 'Neutral red as a lipid fluorochrome.' *Stain Tech.,* 45, 1-4.

KOHLMEYER, J. (1960). 'Wood-inhabiting marine fungi from the Pacific Northwest and California.' *Nova Hedwigia,* 2, 293-343.

KOHLMEYER, J. (1962). 'Halophile Pilze von den Ufern Frankreichs.' *Nova Hedwigia,* 4, 389-420.

KOHLMEYER, J. (1966). 'Ascospore morphology in *Corollospora.' Mycologia,* 58, 281-288.

KOHLMEYER, J. (1971). 'Annotated check-list of New England marine fungi.' *Trans. Br. mycol. Soc.,* 57, 473-492.

KOHLMEYER, J. (1972). 'A revision of Halosphaeriaceae.' *Can. J. Bot.,* 50, 1951-1963.

KOHLMEYER, J. (1974). 'On the definition and taxonomy of higher marine fungi.' In *Symposium in Marine Mycology* (Ed. A. Gaertner), Veröff. Inst. Meeresforsch. Bremerh. Suppl. 5, 263-286.

KOHLMEYER, J., and KOHLMEYER, E. (1964-1969). *Icones Fungorum Maris,* Cramer, Lehre, vol. I. tbl. 1-90.

KOHLMEYER, J., and KOHLMEYER, E. (1966). 'On the life history of marine Ascomycetes: *Halosphaeria mediosetigera* and *H. circumvestita.' Nova Hedwigia,* 12, 189-202.

KOHLMEYER, J., and KOHLMEYER, E. (1971). *Synoptic Plates of Higher Marine Fungi,* (3rd edition) Cramer, Lehre, 87 pp.

KOHLMEYER, J., SCHMIDT, I., and NAIR, N. B. (1967). 'Eine neue *Corollospora* (Ascomycetes) aus dem Indischen Ozean und der Ostsee.' *Ber. dt. bot. Ges.,* 80, 98-102.

LUTLEY, M., and WILSON, I. M. (1972 a). 'Development and fine structure of ascospores in the marine fungus *Ceriosporopsis halima.'* *Trans. Br. mycol. Soc.*, 58, 393-403.

LUTLEY, M., and WILSON, I. M. (1972 b). 'Observations on the fine structure of ascospores of marine fungi: *Halosphaeria appendiculata, Torpedospora radiata* and *Corollospora maritima.'* *Trans. Br. mycol. Soc.*, 59, 219-227.

MADELIN, M. F., Ed. (1966). *The Fungus Spore.* Butterworths, London, 338 pp.

MANOCHA, M. S., and COLVIN, J. R. (1967). 'Structure and composition of the cell wall of *Neurospora crassa.'* *J. Bact.*, 94, 202-212.

ROTH, H. L., and WINKELMANN, R. K. (1960). 'Histochemical technic for macroscopic study of fungi.' *J. invest. Derm.*, 35, 353-359.

SUSSMAN, A. S. (1957). 'Physiological and genetic adaptibility in the fungi.' *Mycologia*, 49, 29-43.

SUSSMAN, A. S., and HALVORSON, H. O. (1966). *Spores, their dormancy and germination.* Harper and Row, New York, 354 pp.

TUBAKI, K. (1967). 'Studies on the Japanese marine fungi. Lignicolous group. II. *Publ. Seto Mar. Biol. Lab.*, 15, 357-372.

TUBAKI, K. (1968). 'On Japanese lignicolous marine fungi.' *Bull. Misaki Mar. Biol. Inst. Kyoto Univ.*, 12, 195-202.

WILSON, I. M. (1965). 'Development of the perithecium and ascospores of *Ceriosporopsis halima.'* *Trans. Br. mycol. Soc.*, 48, 19-33.

ZALOKAR, M. (1965). 'Integration of cellular metabolism.' In *The Fungi: an Advanced Treatise,* (Eds. G. C. Ainsworth and A. S. Sussman), Academic Press, London, vol. I, 377-426.

SECTION I: MARINE FUNGI

B. Lower Fungi

7 The Phycomycetes: Morphology and Taxonomy

T. W. JOHNSON, Jr.

7.1 Introduction

In their compilation on marine and estuarine fungi, Johnson and Sparrow (1961) provided general comments, evaluated the status of knowledge, and suggested possible future trends for research on these organisms. They gave no summary account of the systematics of the marine fungi, but certain conclusions are evident in their treatment. These are: (1) definite trends in taxonomy of the lower fungi (phycomycetes) had been established prior to 1960; (2) only relatively few approaches to collection and culture had been emphasized, and (3) the systematics of some taxa was far from settled. Moreover, their systematic account made clear another aspect, namely, the apparent paucity of species and the scarcity of techniques for their discovery and isolation.

Two problems were evident in dealing taxonomically with marine and estuarine phycomycetes. First was the perennial one of the nature of these minute organisms themselves: refractory toward growth, evanescent in development, and fragmentary in their appearance (to say nothing of the disagreements among taxonomists as to the proper disposition of some taxa). A second was that of establishing or at least maintaining some degree of respectability for marine mycology: which fungi were marine and which were not?

An insight into the meaning and complexity of the latter problem was to be found, for example, in the results of a study by Scholz in 1958. At least six species, all of them freshwater fungi (if previous accounts were to be believed), reproduced in freshwater, seawater, and in NaCl solutions. By a different means, Harder and Uebelmesser (1955) had uncovered a somewhat similar pattern in nature: the occurrence of freshwater fungi in marine habitats. The ecological implications of such findings are considerable; the impact on taxonomy is substantial.

A combination of the two aforementioned problems provides some rather revealing figures about numbers of marine phycomycetes. Among all the aquatic phycomycetes treated by Sparrow in 1960, 61 species (in the classes Chytridiomycetes, Hyphochytridiomycetes, Plasmodiophoromycetes, and Oömycetes) were considered to be marine.

193

One year later, Johnson and Sparrow accepted 59 species as being characteristically from marine, estuarine, and salt pool habitats, and relegated another 38 taxa to the doubtful or excluded category.

Allowing for the personal conviction factor in taxonomy, one can account for approximately 70 species of marine phycomycetes discovered since the first one came to view something over a century ago. This rather meagre showing reflects, perhaps, more of the mycologist's lack of suitable collecting and culturing techniques than of his failure to come to grips with taxonomic problems. Repeatedly, Johnson and Sparrow called attention to the narrow variety of usable methods. They also testified vigorously to the usual failure of the well known baiting techniques (Sparrow, 1960, among others) as methods for collecting marine phycomycetes. In part, this point has been discounted by studies since 1960.

The account by Johnson and Sparrow did not presage a great surge of effort to solve the mycological riddles of the seas. The decade of the sixties did, however, see substantial advances in the taxonomy and morphology of certain groups of marine phycomycetes. These areas in particular sustained the most notable changes: the occurrence of species in saline soils; the use of gross, pure, or unifungal isolation techniques for collection and identification of fungi; the association of fungi with phytoplankton and marine animals, and the nature of the curious (and problematical) organisms in marine shell fragments.

7.2   Fungi in Saline Soils

It has been repeatedly demonstrated that tide-inundated and spray-washed coastal soils harbour some aquatic fungi which are identified classically with freshwater habitats. Conversely (Sparrow, 1968 a, for example), some ostensible marine fungi occur in saline habitats far removed from the oceans. The implications afforded by these fungi that fail to recognize ecological boundaries have a profound influence on the taxonomy of aquatic fungi where habitat and substratum may figure heavily in species concepts. One major contribution to the knowledge of zoösporic fungi in saline soils was made in the decade of the sixties.

Booth (1969) collected a large number of chytrids (on pine pollen and cellophane) from saline soils at 115 stations in the British Columbia region. The sampling sites represented one or the other of two environmental regimes: soils constantly saline (homoiohalomorphic) and those periodically saline (poikilohalomorphic).

From nearly one half of the stations, Booth collected representatives of the genus *Thraustochytrium.* These he generally left unidentified, finding their taxonomy difficult to perform meaningfully save under strictest conditions of axenic culture. A number of ostensible freshwater species occurred in both homoio- or poikilohalomorphic soils, or in one or the other. *Chytridium citriforme* Sparrow was found only in a constantly saline soil; *Chytriomyces hyalinus* Karling, normally collected on insect exuviae or on chitinous baits, occurred in both soil environmental types. *Rhizophydium,* notably, had representatives with similar occurrence patterns, but Booth also collected species of *Phlyctochytrium* and *Rhizophydium* that had been found by others in 'halomorphic' soils.

The observations by Booth are particularly revealing when compared with those of other investigators. Booth found *Phlyctochytrium reinboldtae* Persiel in poikilohalomorphic soils, yet Sparrow *et al.* (1965) recovered it from non-saline soil in northern Michigan. The same species was collected by K. L. Howard (unpublished) in non-saline, pasture soils in Iceland. On Heimaey (Iceland), he also found *P. palustre* Gaertner in pasture soil. While Gaertner's species was previously known only in saline habitats, Booth collected it both in homoio- and poikilohalomorphic soils. Booth additionally commented on the similarity of *P. palustre* to *P. semiglobiferum* Uebelmesser, and the difficulty encountered in identifying them. To be sure, Howard identified his specimens with Gaertner's species only with some hesitation. Booth's study and Howard's observations leave little doubt that habitat type is not applicable to taxonomy of some chytridiaceous fungi. The collection by Booth of *Septosperma rhizophidii* Whiffen *ex* Seymour on *Rhizophydium chytriomycetis* Karling, certainly de-emphasizes a further taxonomic adjuvant used widely in the past, that of host ranges.

Booth (1969) was forced into the taxonomic retreat of listing some provisional identifications. Specimens assigned tentatively to *Phlyctochytrium,* for example, did not discharge spores, and others did not have discernible rhizoidal systems. Without knowledge of these features, Booth could not identify the fungi confidently. Booth's study does provide observational information that may be of value when applied to such taxonomic puzzles as the relationship of *Olpidium pendulum* Zopf to *O. maritimum* Höhnk and Aleem, and *Phlyctochytrium palustre* to *P. semiglobiferum.*

Two additional papers by Booth (1971 a, b) contain pertinent observations on occurrence and taxonomy of aquatic fungi in saline habitats. These papers assuredly confirm the general nature of the results he reported in his earlier (1969) account.

7.3 Phycomycetes, Phytoplankton and Animals

In the general biological account of their book, Johnson and Sparrow (1961) dealt with various associations of fungi with other segments of the marine biota. There was, they noted, an obvious scarcity of information on phycomycetes and marine algae, and several unsolved problems were evident when the accumulated knowledge of fungus-animal relationships was explored. Advances in these two general areas have been few but not without some meaning.

7.3.1 Fungi and marine and estuarine phytoplankton

The number of known species of fungi in marine phytoplankters is far below that in freshwater plankton. Johnson (1966 a, b; 1967) explored this aspect of marine mycology, looking specifically for planktonic algae invaded by chytridiaceous and oömycetous species.

At best, the results of Johnson's studies merely confirmed what prior literature had already shown, namely, that there was an apparent paucity of species, and that among these the absence of developmental stages often made identities uncertain. While he found so called freshwater species in saline habitats their discovery was not a new event. Johnson found *Rhizophydium marinum* de Wildeman to be conspecific with *R. globosum* (Braun) Rabenhorst, but was unable to identify with confidence species of *Phlyctidium.* Monocentric fungi on species of *Rhizosolenia,* he noted (1967), presented difficult taxonomic problems. Only two of eight species were identified. The remaining fungi were described, and their taxonomic affinities explored. None of the fungi on *Rhizosolenia* (Johnson, 1967), *Melosira,* or *Navicula* (Johnson, 1966 a) produced resting spores. The characteristics of such cells, if they are formed at all, are essential for proper taxonomic decisions.

Johnson did not culture the fungi he collected nor, indeed, did he attempt to collect fungi by even the most primitive of culture methods. His contribution was largely in providing notes on fungal morphology: information that could prove useful in future studies. He certainly failed to uncover a diverse and abundant mycoflora associated with marine phytoplankton.

That we must still turn in our taxonomy of marine phycomycetes to as yet unsettled supraspecific taxa is illustrated also by Drebes' paper (1968). He found it necessary—because generic limits are not agreed upon—to establish a new genus, *Lagenisma*, for a *Lagenidium*-like fungus in a marine diatom. There are recognizable characters of *Lagenidium* (differentiated antheridium, persistent thallus, and large, but few planonts, among other features), but these need to be evaluated along with features of allied genera to determine which, if any, are stable enough for dependable taxonomy.

7.3.2 *Dermocystidium*

Sudden outbreaks of mortality or unexplained population declines in commercially valuable organisms are well documented. Time and again such outbreaks have led to rapid, indeed, almost frantic, efforts to detect cause and formulate remedy. Biological oceanography is not without its example, in this case, warm weather mortality of oysters (gaping disease) and the associated organism, *Dermocystidium marinum* Mackin, Owen et Collier (1950). An undercurrent of dissatisfaction with the taxonomy of the alleged causal agent existed even in the early studies (1950-1955) on oyster mortality. Research emphasis was rightfully directed more at explaining the disease and identifying the factors accompanying its onset, continuation, and eventual decline than at placing the agent in its proper taxonomical niche. Attention was focused in the 1960s on the organism itself and continued efforts on postmortem epidemiology became less prominent.

Dermocystidium marinum had been variously placed, based on interpretations of its scanty morphological expressions, among the sporozoa or the phycomycetes. The organism produced hypnospores (F. O. Perkins and Menzel, 1967), and these thick walled cells (containing a large vacuole and a peripheral nucleus) cleaved endogenously to produce a number of non-motile cells. These products, it was known, could bring about infection of oysters. It remained for F. O. Perkins and Menzel (1966) to demonstrate that the hypnospore produced a discharge papilla through which laterally biflagellate, heterokont planonts (zoöspores) emerged. Inasmuch as released planonts failed to fuse, that is, were not gametic, the hypnospore clearly functioned as a sporangium and not as a gametangium. Subsequently (1967), F. O. Perkins and Menzel established through electron microscopy that the anterior flagellum was of the tinsel type (stichoneme) and the second of the whiplash type. Thus, available evidence all but assured a phycomycetous 'home' for the organism.

In its method of thallus cleavage *Dermocystidium marinum* obviously recalls *Schizochytrium aggregatum* Goldstein et Belsky, though there are some conspicuous differences. Nevertheless, this parallelism between the two was an additional lever to force the oyster pathogen into a fungal niche. On the other hand, *D. marinum* has some characteristics that are difficult to equate with the usual nature of sporangia in the aquatic fungi. The planonts, formed successively and slightly asynchronously within the hypnospores, begin motility 1½-2 days prior to release. A most remarkable time span unheard of among the other zoösporic fungi!

Because they observed plasmodia, amoeboid stages, and the gliding of cells along mucoid tracks in cultures of *Dermocystidium marinum,* Mackin and Ray (1966) placed the organism in the genus *Labyrinthomyxa*. This assignment F. O. Perkins (1969) accepted, tentatively citing one chief reservation in doing so. The organism he cultured (for a study of ultrastructural details) while like that seen by Mackin and

Ray, did not form any cytoplasmic or extracellular extensions that could be termed tracks or rhizoids. His hesitation in accepting the name change seems justified by the fine structure of the so called vegetative portions of the organism from oysters. A subsequent account (Chapter 11) details the cytology of this organism. Suffice it to say that F. O. Perkins found lomasomes in the cells of the organism from oysters *(Labyrinthomyxa = Dermocystidium)*, a clue to the possible alliance of the oyster pathogen with the true fungi rather than with the protozoans. Moreover, cell walls were present in all vegetative stages, a feature of almost universal occurrence among the fungi but not among the animal groups.

The proper taxonomic niche for *Dermocystidium* (or *Labyrinthomyxa*) *marinum* depends very particularly on whether or not the organism does in fact produce 'tracks' or 'slimeways' and gliding cells. This was emphasized by F. O. Perkins in 1969, and, in part, was followed up in a paper published in 1972. He characterized the ultra-structural nature of the extracellular extensions of five organisms: two species of *Labyrinthula, Thraustochytrium motivum* Goldstein, *Schizochytrium aggregatum,* and an unnamed form, T-20, resembling *S. aggregatum* and some species of *Labyrinthula. Dermocystidium* (or *Labyrinthomyxa*) *marinum* was not included in this account by F. O. Perkins, yet its position could not be established precisely without convincing demonstration of any labyrinthuloid affinities it might have. In an earlier paper, F. O. Perkins (1968) had shown that a *Labyrinthomyxa* very much like the oyster pathogen but parasitizing the clam, *Macoma balthica* L., produced laterally biflagellate planonts. These motile cells, like the ones in many fungi (including thraustochytriaceous ones; F. O. Perkins, 1972) and *Labyrinthula,* had a tinsel type anterior flagellum. The 1968 and 1972 studies of F. O. Perkins leave unsolved the question of the correct niche for the oyster pathogen, but they do open new avenues for speculative taxonomy.

From an interpretation of electron micrographs, F. O. Perkins (1972) concluded that holdfasts, rhizoids, and tracks have the same basic fine structure, that is, possessing a unit membrane continuous with the plasmalemma, containing membrane limited cisternae and a fibrogranular ground substance, and originating from one or more organelle complexes located near the cell surface. The rhizoidal system of *Thraustochytrium motivum* and *Schizochytrium aggregatum,* then, was merely an ectoplasmic net structurally like the extracellular track of *Labyrinthula.* This system in these alleged fungi is functionally unlike that of the system (net) in *Labyrinthula.* In the labyrinthulas studied (F. O. Perkins, 1972) and the organism T-20 (seemingly intermediate between *Labyrinthula* and *Schizochytrium*), the tracks are involved in motility of 'vegetative' cells. No such function can be attributed to the rhizoids in *Thraustochytrium* and *Schizochytrium.* Comparative ultra-structure of the ectoplasmic net in thraustochytrids and labyrinthulids is detailed by F. O. Perkins (1973). Studying electron microscope preparations of spores from a *Thraustochytrium* species (near *T. motivum* in its characteristics), Kazama (1972) detected a complexity of electron dense and transitional structures in the kineto-some flagellar base region unlike that of any fungi (or protozoans or algae) that have been examined.

It is an inescapable conclusion that the study by F. O. Perkins (1972) has fundamental implications in the genus *Labyrinthula* itself. The cells of *L. minuta,* he found, are not encased in the strands of the tracks (or net). Other labyrinthulids, however, exhibited gliding motility within the strands. He suggested that *L. minuta* and the unnamed T-20 probably had to be assigned to a new genus.

Nearly simultaneous with the appearance of the paper by F. O. Perkins and

Menzel (1966) on the motile spores of *Dermocystidium marinum* was the publication by Goldstein and Moriber (1966) on *Dermocystidium* sp. This organism is a free living one in contrast to *D. marinum* with its association with animal tissue. The unnamed *Dermocystidium,* described from pure culture, produced a spherical thallus containing a large, eccentric vacuole. Like *D. marinum,* the thallus of *Dermocystidium* sp. cleaved into sub-units, but the products were non-motile, and could themselves undergo successive cleavage.

The two strains of *Dermocystidium* sp. isolated by Goldstein and Moriber were also used by Poyton (1970 a) in his study on *Hyalochlorella marina* Poyton (Figs. 7.9, 7.10). He concluded that *Dermocystidium* sp. could not be retained in that genus, but had to be assigned to his new one, *Hyalochlorella.* The single representative, *H. marina,* grows preferentially (Poyton, 1970 b) on marine algae, but is also found free floating (Fig. 7.9). Poyton was unable to find more than 0.01% of the sporangia with vacuoplasts—a feature prominently displayed in *Dermocystidium* sp. (*sensu* Goldstein and Moriber). Liberation of cells by ecdysis, also a characteristic of the organism studied by Goldstein and Moriber, was not a part of the developmental pattern of isolates assigned to *H. marina. Hyalochlorella* is regarded (Poyton, 1970 a) as the colourless analogue of species in the alga genus *Chlorella.* In terms of morphology, at least, Poyton concluded that the Goldstein and Moriber strains had closer similarities to *Prototheca* than to *Dermocystidium.*

In an orderly fashion Goldstein and Moriber (1966) argued for a saprolegniaceous ancestry for *Dermocystidium.* Their reasoning was based chiefly on the theory of evolved simplification. They proposed that the inability to produce motile spores and rhizoids (as in some of the Thraustochytriaceae and Ectrogellaceae) could have led to a *Dermocystidium*-like entity. Sparrow (1958) hypothesized the derivation of Thraustochytriaceae and Ectrogellaceae from a filamentous, saprolegniaceous ancestor precisely by a reduction process. The close structural similarity in the planont of *D. marinum* (F. O. Perkins and R. W. Menzel, 1967) to that of biflagellate phycomycetes lends weight to a supposition of an ancestry among the fungi, but is not of itself conclusive proof of a progression either to or from fungi.

Miss Ulken (1968 b) has collected in a seawater-peptone-yeast extract medium an organism that seems indistinguishable from the unnamed *Dermocystidium* isolated by Goldstein and Moriber. Their specimens would not grow on pollen (*Pseudotsuga* or *Liquidambar*); in contrast, Miss Ulken's formed sporangia and non-motile cleavage products on pine pollen.

The whole spectrum of labyrinthuloid and thraustochytriaceous groups, together with *Dermocystidium marinum* (= *Labyrinthomyxa marina,* = *Dermocystidium* sp. Goldstein and Moriber, = *Hyalochlorella marina* Poyton) needs to be characterized fully before their systematic position is tinkered with in any serious fashion. Much of the accumulated knowledge on the structure of these organisms is traceable to F. O. Perkins, and he has shown exemplary caution in interpreting the taxonomic implications of his work. He has stated only that the thraustochytriaceous and labyrinthuloid organisms probably could be placed in a single family. He noted that the ectoplasmic net is not characteristic of the rhizoids of other fungi (*Phylctochytrium* species, for instance), nor is successive bipartition of the sporangial protoplast typical of fungi ordinarily classified as aquatic phycomycetes. Consequently, F. O. Perkins concluded, the placement of thraustochytriaceous fungi and the labyrinthulas into any known order of phycomycetes is 'highly questionable'. Certainly the comparison among these organisms in selected characteristics (F. O. Perkins, 1972, Table 1) is by itself a strong but not deciding argument for removing the thraustochytriaceous fungi from

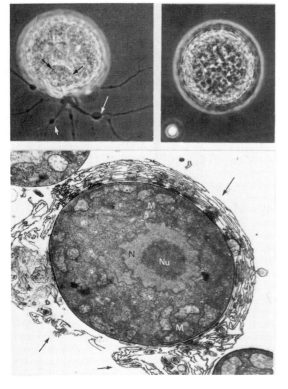

7.2

Fig. 7.1. Thraustochytrium kinnei. Extramatrical sporangium with a basal rudiment (arrowed) and intramatrical rhizoidal system with characteristic swellings (arrowed). Phase contrast (x666) (photo. D. J. Alderman, Portsmouth Polytechnic). **Fig. 7.2. T. kinnei.** Young sporangium showing the multilamellate nature of the sporangial wall (arrowed), nucleus (N), nucleolus (Nu) and mitochondria (M). Electron micrograph (5693) (x 17 300) (photo. J. L. Harrison, Portsmouth Polytechnic). **Fig. 7.3. Althornia crouchii.** Phase contrast micrograph of a free floating thick walled sporangium (x333) (photo, D. J. Alderman, Portsmouth Polytechnic).

their current position in the Saprolegniales. One should not lose sight of the very obvious fact that the Thraustochytriaceae itself is not a satisfactorily coherent taxon as a subsequent section (7.4) will show. It is also well to recall that the obvious differences of opinion concerning the taxonomic niche for the oyster pathogen—with the thraustochytriaceous fungi or the labyrinthulids—have been based on differing interpretations of the significance of some closely parallel structural features (Amon and Perkins, 1968).

7.3.3   Fungi and Calcareous Shell Deposits

Two types of fungus-animal shell associations were explored and reported on during the 1960s. One of these associations is the shell disease of the common edible oyster, *Ostrea edulis* L.

Althornia crouchii Jones et Alderman (1971) is a monocentric fungus producing free floating, globose sporangia with thick, laminar walls and biflagellate planonts (Figs. 7.3-7.5). *Ostracoblabe implexa* Bornet et Flahault (Alderman and Jones, 1967, 1971) is mycelial in general vegetative aspect (see Chapter 9 for description and illus-

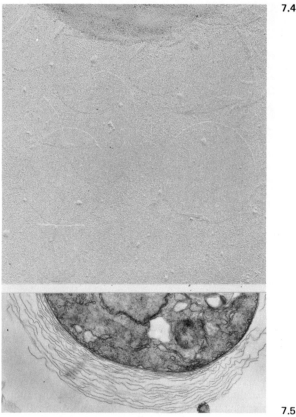

7.5

Fig. 7.4. A. crouchii. Detached thin unornamented membranes from the sporangial wall. Electron micrograph (GJ19) (x27 000) (photo. E. B. G. Jones, Portsmouth Polytechnic). **Fig. 7.5. A. crouchii.** Section of part of a sporangium to show the thick sporangial wall made up of membranes. Electron micrograph (GJ64) (x12 000) (photo. E. B. G. Jones, Portsmouth Polytechnic).

trations). Both were isolated from diseased oysters at the 'wart stage'. Jones and Alderman (1971) were uncertain of the relationship of *A. crouchii* to *O. implexa,* the former having appeared in cultures of the latter, but Alderman (communication) is assured that they are different fungi with no connection to one another. This is supported further by recent fine structure observations.

The small planonts of *Althornia crouchii* possess heterokont flagella, one tinsel (recalling *Thraustochytrium* species) and the second of the whiplash type. Thin, round or oval membranes (Jones and Alderman, 1971) surround the planonts, and the sporangia which arise from these motile cells as well (Fig. 7.4). The sporangium wall is mucilaginous, but the fungus apparently need not settle on or attach to a suitable substratum prior to germination. Internally, both the planonts and the sporangia contain numerous mitochondria, tubular cristae, and well developed dictyosomes.

In its gross morphological simplicity, *Althornia crouchii* presents a considerable taxonomic problem that is complicated rather than relieved by the fine structure (Jones and Alderman, 1971) of the organism. Like *Labyrinthula* and *Dermocystidium marinum, A. crouchii* has tubular cristae, but like *Thraustochytrium,* produces well developed dictyosomes. As Jones and Alderman point out, the transparent membranes suggest the well known scales on certain algae. Such membranes—giving the multilaminar aspect to the sporangium—are found in other organisms assigned to the Thraustochytriaceae (Fig. 7.2; also Chapter 11). Unlike species in the Haliphthoraceae, A. crouchii does not have a mycelial thallus, and it does not form rhizomycelium (or rhizoids) as do members of Thraustochytriaceae.

The systematic position of Althornia crouchii remains unresolved. While its planonts are saprolegniaceous (though, of course, much smaller than is usual among these fungi), and it has morphologically simple counterparts among the Saprolegniales, its position there is not assured. Neither, for that matter, is the position of the thraustochytrids, and it seems likely that these fungi shall have to be settled into a respectable niche before A. crouchii can be assigned to some suprageneric taxon with confidence.

Ostracoblabe implexa is a particularly troublesome taxonomic enigma. Organisms under this name have been considered to be the hyphal component of the lichen Arthopyrenia sublitoralis (Leight) Arn by Santesson. Bornet (one of the authors of O. implexa) subsequent to describing the organism viewed it as the fungal element of another lichen, Verrucaria consequens Nyl (Johnson and Sparrow, 1961). The hyphae illustrated by Alderman and Jones (1967, Fig. 1) are Pythium-like in general aspect, and the intercalary chlamydospores certainly do not rule out a pythiaceous affinity.

Some attention has been given to the problematic organisms—perhaps they are fungi—found in shell fragments from marine animals. Johnson and Sparrow (1961) were unable to satisfy themselves on a taxonomic position for these entities, some of which had been described and named in the 1930s by Zebrowski (Johnson and Sparrow, 1961).

Cavaliere and Alberte (1970) collected shore-deposited shell fragments and reexamined some representatives of shell-boring organisms that Zebrowski earlier (1936) had placed in the Cladochytriaceae. Unable to formulate a respectable conclusion about the nature of the various borings, Cavaliere and Alberte emphasized the apparent cosmopolitan distribution of similar appearing borings.

Among the 'microboring organisms' found by R. D. Perkins and Halsey (1971) in carbonate components of relict continental margin sediments were non-septate filaments bearing spherical, terminal, sporangium-like swellings. In thin section carbonate pieces, these filaments were much like those of phycomycetous organisms, an appearance confirmed in remarkable three dimensional plastic 'models' prepared by a special carbonate etching technique. Non-septate filaments were found in calcareous fragments of echinoderms, corals, coralline algae, barnacles, serpulids, and foraminifers, but were most abundant in bits of molluscan shell.

It has been suggested (R. D. Perkins and Halsey, 1971) that fungi are in large part responsible for erosion of skeletal carbonate in sediments, and thus for removing the carbonate fraction. Confirmation of the supposed fungal nature of the filaments in shell fragments must await development of culture techniques for isolation. Pending this, too, the taxonomy of the organisms will continue to remain unsettled. The media used by Alderman and Jones (1971)—successful in isolating fungi from shells of living animals—offers some positive prognosis for culturing organisms from shell fragments. The hyaline, coenocytic filaments uncovered in the preparations by R. D. Perkins and Halsey are more than vaguely reminiscent of the fungus reported and photographed by Alderman and Jones (1967). There still remains the haunting recollection that shell-boring marine algae exist in calcareous deposits. These shall have to be ruled out unequivocably before most of the organisms that have been reported as fungi can be accepted as such.

7.4 The Thraustochytriaceae

As Sparrow perceptively remarked (1968 b), one of the major advances in marine mycology in the decade beginning in 1960 was the discovery of the widespread occurrence of thraustochytriaceous fungi in ocean waters, in sediments and coastal sands, and on surfaces of algae and organic detritus. Save for a report of *Thraustochytrium globosum* Kobayashi et Ookubo and *Japonochytrium marinum* Kobayashi et Ookubo in 1953, and an account of *T. proliferum* Sparrow by Johnson in 1957 (Johnson and Sparrow, 1961), thraustochytriaceous fungi had not been seen since Sparrow described the type species in 1936. In 1961, four species in two genera (Johnson and Sparrow, 1961) were known. A decade later, nine more species and one additional genus, *Schizochytrium* Goldstein and Belsky (1964), had been added to the family. It is by no means certain, however, that *Schizochytrium* can be included in the Thraustochytriaceae.

The taxonomic excitement brought about by the discovery of new thraustochytriaceous species effectively suppressed an equally significant development, namely, their culture in natural and artificial media. The species described by Sparrow (1936) and by Kobayashi and Ookubo (1953) were discovered fortuitously by the tedious process of scanning surfaces of marine algae for chytridaceous fungi. Johnson and Sparrow (1961) maintained that this procedure was a necessary one if chytrids and other zoösporic fungi were to be discovered. Vishniac (1956) had, however, clearly demonstrated the prevalence of free living chytridiaceous fungi in ocean waters by the use of semiquantitative and selective plating techniques. When seawater was plated on a selective medium, Vishniac (1955) recovered *Thraustochytrium proliferum,* a fungus previously found only by direct examination of suitable marine algae. It remained for Goldstein (1963 a) employing other culture media, and for Gaertner (1966) using pollen baiting methods, to uncover an abundant and diversified thraustochytriaceous mycoflora of the oceans. Johnson and Sparrow (1961) had almost parenthetically predicted that Vishniac's culture method would be found to be the most suitable way for obtaining these fungi, yet without hesitation they held out little if any hope for substantial yields through baiting techniques.

7.4.1 Thraustochytrium *and* Japonochytrium

The research on *Thraustochytrium,* compressed within a short span of years, has followed the usual progression of developments expected in the evolution of modern systematic mycology. Species have been described (Goldstein, 1963 a, b, c; Ulken, 1965; Gaertner, 1967 a; Schneider, 1967), morphological variations noted (Goldstein, 1963 a, b, c; Ulken, 1969; Gaertner, 1970, for example), questions of species validity proposed (Booth and Miller, 1968), and the spectre raised of natural versus artificial media (pollen or nutrient agars) as the proper substratum to use in describing characters (Booth and Miller, 1968; Gaertner, 1972).

The generic concept of *Thraustochytrium* naturally enlarged as new species were added (Sparrow, 1968 c). Originally, the genus was based on a species having internally proliferating sporangia that released non-flagellated spores by dissolution of the sporangial wall. Subsequently, however, the limits were broadened (not without some reservation) to include otherwise obviously thraustochytriaceous fungi with no proliferation, and ones in which spore release was effected through one or more pores or fissures in the sporangial wall. Some newly discovered species produced spores that were motile on discharge, and these fungi, of course, were in obvious contradiction to the type species, *T. proliferum* Sparrow, with its much delayed motility. Were one inclined to do so, then, species of *Thraustochytrium* with motile spores (at release) could be removed from the genus. Goldstein's observation (1963 c) that spore motility in *T. roseum* Goldstein could be suppressed in culture argues against splitting the genus solely on such a character.

On the basis of very extensive culture studies on four species of *Thraustochytrium*, Booth and Miller (1968) demonstrated variability in some major characteristics ordinarily employed as taxonomic criteria: sporangium size and colour, wall thickness, method of discharge, and nature of the rhizoidal system. At most, they argued, two species complexes (embracing the four taxa they had identified and examined) could be recognized. Schneider's (1967) *T. striatum* also was questioned (Sparrow, 1969) because of some variations detected in the spore discharge pattern. Moreover, there is suggestive evidence at hand that *T. aggregatum* Ulken may not be a valid taxon. Specimens (allegedly of this species) on pine pollen baited in samples of coastal waters of Iceland often show aggregates of small sporangia that seem to be nothing more than dwarf forms of *T. globosum* or perhaps of *T. roseum.*

Species concepts in the Thraustochytriaceae recently have been looked at with a more critical and encompassing view than when species were first described. Moreover, the use of nutrient agars as culture media (Goldstein, 1963 a, b, c; Ulken, 1965; Booth and Miller, 1968, for example) have demonstrated the wide ranges of variations one can expect within individual taxa. Some species of the genus, however, can only be identified with great difficulty from such agar cultures. This has led Gaertner (1972) to argue that pollen probably should be used as the substratum if the thraustochytrids are to be characterized in such a manner that they may be subsequently recognized again.

The genus *Thraustochytrium* encompasses 11 named species, with some additional specimens (Sparrow, 1969) yet to be identified precisely. Gaertner (1972) believes that these species segregate into three groups: those in which the sporangia proliferate, those without proliferation, and those (one known species) in which the sporangium deliquesces before the planonts or their rudiments are cleaved. Konno (1969) also recognized three groups of fungi within the genus. Booth and Miller (1968), on the other hand, were able to detect only 'species complexes' among some of the taxa, and it is patently true that some specimens collected in Icelandic coastal waters defy any attempts at identification.

The species of *Thraustochytrium* have been sorted out in various patterns (Sparrow, 1968 c; Gaertner, 1972), but the limits thus set do not encompass the characteristics of many actual specimens (Johnson, unpublished). While there do appear to be basic similarities and differences among groups of species in the genus, the distinctions are not always clear cut, and a few taxa have to be placed in more than one morphological group. It is in any case true that a cursory examination of the literature on *Thraustochytrium* is of little value in the practical matter of identification. Unfortunately, a detailed analysis of that same literature, with actual specimens at hand, only facilitates identification for a few well marked species. It is impossible, therefore, to provide a fully inclusive summary of the genus, and predictions of relationships on the basis of published taxonomic accounts are certain to be of short duration. An overall view of the genus (tinged, of course, with personal views) is possible, but such a general view must be understood to be devoid of any evolutionary significance.

Four species, *Thraustochytrium proliferum, T. aureum* Goldstein, *T. motivum,* and *T. multirudimentale* Goldstein, have a single sporangium type in which there is a basal proliferation body (more than one in *T. multirudimentale*). The manner in which the spores are released, and the nature of the spores at discharge (motile or not) constitute the chief distinctions among the species. Five taxa, *T. roseum, T. globosum, T. visurgense* Ulken, *T. striatum* (Figs. 7.6-7.8) and *T. aggregatum,* produce thin-walled sporangia like those of the previous species, but none has a basal proliferation body. Again, the manner of spore discharge, and the condition of those spores at release are characteristics that in various combinations seem to delimit these five species from one another. In *T. globosum* and *T. striatum,* for example, and in individuals of the aggregate sporangia of *T. aggregatum,* dissolution of the sporangium wall effects release. *Thraustochytrium visurgense* stands out among the species in a very prominent feature, namely, exogenous cleavage of the planonts. Booth and Miller (1968), however, have shown this spore behaviour to be inconsistent among isolates of the species.

The remaining two named species, *Thraustochytrium pachydermum* Scholz and *T. kinnei* Gaertner, produce thick-walled sporangia, and it might be expected that they are accordingly very easily separated from the foregoing two groups of taxa. Both species have been shown to form thick- and thin-walled sporangia (Gaertner, 1970, 1972). Because its sporangia lack a basal proliferation body, *T. pachydermum* naturally aligns with the cluster of species that includes *T. globosum* and *T. roseum.* The sporangium of *T. kinnei* (Figs. 7.1, 7.2) possesses a basal proliferation body, and therefore this species would seem assignable to the group of taxa containing *T. proliferum, T. aureum,* and others. Neither *T. pachydermum* nor *T. kinnei* is precisely defined, however, and thus their position in the genus remains obscure. It is certainly true that in *T. kinnei* the release of spores after separation of a thickened apical segment of the sporangium is not a feature that occurs consistently among individual thalli.

It is quite evident that limits of the taxa in *Thraustochytrium* are not adequately placed, and identification of species is thus severely hampered. In part, this problem in identity can be minimized, but only by the use of pure cultures (or at least unifungal ones) such that all developmental stages of the fungi can be traced. Identifications based on specimens in any other culture conditions are certain to be doubtful if not in direct error.

Allied to *Thraustochytrium* by a superficial similarity in gross morphology is *Japonochytrium* with its single species, *J. marinum* Kobayashi and Ookubo. This species evidently occurs only in Pacific waters, though this is by no means certain. Sparrow (1968 b) reported it from Hawaii, but did not comment on it. The apophysis seems to set the species (and genus) off from *Thraustochytrium,* but Sparrow (1968 c) regarded the presence of an apophysis in *J. marinum* of importance only at the species level. Certainly in its discharge pattern, the fungus does not digress significantly from *T. aureum.* To consider *Japonochytrium* within *Thraustochytrium,* however, would require that internal proliferation be accepted as a character of subgeneric value only.

Ecological work of substance and merit is being done using thraustochytriaceous fungi as indicators (Gaertner, 1967 b; 1968 a, b, for example) and this is discussed further in Chapter 12. It is to be hoped that the taxonomy of the fungi so used is properly founded.

7.4.2 Schizochytrium

One of the most remarkable organisms discovered during the decade of the 1960s is *Schizochytrium aggregatum* (Goldstein and Belsky, 1964). Among the most widely

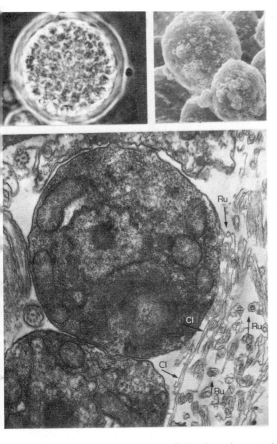

7.6, 7.7

7.8

Fig. 7.6. Thraustochytrium striatum. Fully cleaved sporangium with a thick wall. Phase contrast (x1000) (photo. D. J. Alderman, Portsmouth Polytechnic). **Fig. 7.7. T. striatum.** Scanning electron micrograph to show the rough nature of the walls of 24 hour sporangia. Wall material is sloughing off (x2000) (photo. J. L. Harrison, Portsmouth Polytechnic). **Fig. 7.8. T. striatum.** Section through zoospores and a portion of the sporangial wall. The sporangial wall is fragmented with 'cross linked' portions of wall material (Cl) and 'rolled up' fragments (Ru). (Electron micrograph (5098) (x25 000)

distributed species in the oceans—found where seawater and detritus samples are baited with pollen—*S. aggregatum* has the motile spores of the phycomycetes, but a successive thallus cleavage pattern unlike any fungus. The successive partitioning of the thallus results in an indefinite number of spore producing sporangia.

Though *Schizochytrium aggregatum* is easily recognized, it is unlikely that the taxonomy of the genus is settled. Gaertner (1972), for example, refers to specimens that are probably additional species of the genus, and Booth and Miller (1969) describe an isolate of *S. aggregatum* that differs from the original circumscription of the species in some important respects. The suprageneric position of *Schizochytrium* is still open to debate, and its supposed relationship to labyrinthuloid organisms (F. O. Perkins, 1972) needs to be confirmed or otherwise laid to rest.

7.5   Other Taxa

By the simple—and classical—expedient of baiting samples, Miss Ulken (1968 a, c) demonstrated anew that chytridiaceous fungi are abundant in marine sediments. New taxonomic problems are certain to arise as further exploration of the sediment inhabiting aquatic fungi is undertaken.

It would be unjust to the future taxonomy of *Dermocystidium* to ignore the discovery of *Aplanochytrium kerguelensis* by Bahnweg and Sparrow (1972). This monocentric fungus was isolated into pure culture, but also grew on sterilized pine pollen. It is clearly chytridiaceous in general aspect in that it produces a rhizoidal system and a monocentric thallus (Fig. 7.11). Its nonmotile spores result from progressive cleavage within the sporangium. The species superficially resembles *Dermocystidium* sp. of Goldstein and Moriber (1966), save that it produces rhizoids while the *Dermocystidium* does not. Bahnweg and Sparrow cite as an additional difference the growth of *A. kerguelensis* on pollen. This characteristic of type of substratum may well fade into obscurity as a taxonomic criterion.

The production of aplanospores allies *Aplanochytrium kerguelensis* to *Dermocystidium* sp. rather than to *Thraustochytrium,* but the multilamellate wall (Fig. 7.12) recalls the latter genus. Progressive cleavage of cytoplasm into endogenous spores or spore bearing units is not without some taxonomic consequence. In this respect, *A. kerguelensis* is not far removed from T-20 (F. O. Perkins, 1972) and *Schizochytrium.* Are the rhizoids of *A. kerguelensis,* like those of the thraustochytriaceous fungi which F. O. Perkins (1972) examined, merely strands of an ectoplasmic net? If so, the *Aplanochytrium* has undeniable labyrinthuloid affinities as well.

By using an agar-seawater medium containing glucose, gelatin hydrolysate, and liver and yeast extracts, Fuller and his associates (1964) were able to isolate filamentous phycomycetes (along with thraustochytrids) from surfaces of marine algae. The fungi isolated were all previously known as inhabitants of animal tissue: *Lagenidium callinectes* Couch from ova of *Callinectes sapidus* Rathbun, *L. chthamalophilum* Johnson from ova of *Chamalus fragilis* Darwin, *Haliphthoros milfordensis* Vishniac from egg cases of *Urosalpinx cinerea* Say, and *Atkinsiella dubia* (Atkins) Vishniac from ova, zoeae and prezoeae of *Pinnotheres pisum.*

Fuller and his group were able to characterize rather fully the growth and development of these allegedly parasitic fungi. They demonstrated that *Haliphthoros milfordensis* is holocarpic (the entire thallus converting into motile spores) and for the first time were able to trace and characterize the stages in spore cleavage and release in *Atkiensiella dubia.* For this latter species, they found dimorphism in the planonts (primary and secondary spores) a feature of considerable import in relating the fungus to existing supraspecific taxa. Aronson and Fuller (1969) determined the cell wall structure and chemistry in *A. dubia.* The affinities of the species to Oömycetes is borne out by the cell wall properties: large quantities of glucans along with smaller amounts of cellulose I.

Fuller *et al.* (1964) demonstrated beyond question the importance of culturing (or attempting seriously to culture) marine phycomycetes on natural or defined nutrient media for more complete morphological characterization. The significance of this achievement, however, should not overshadow a point of equal taxonomic impact, namely, the occurrence of a single species of fungus on widely differing substrates, and its ability to shift from a parasitic to a saprobic existence. Host and type of nutrition consequently lose meaning as taxonomic characters.

Readily overlooked among mycological literature, but of considerable importance

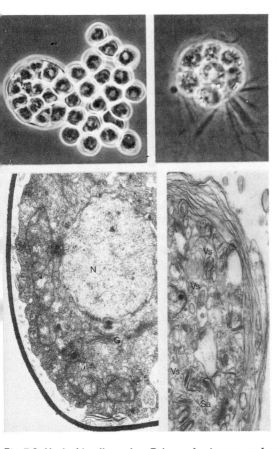

Fig. 7.9. Hyalochlorella marina. Release of aplanospores from a free floating sporangium. Phase contrast (x800) (photo. D. J. Alderman, Portsmouth Polytechnic). **Fig. 7. 10. H. marina.** Section of a portion of a sporangium showing a nucleus (N), mitochondria (M) and Golgi dictyosome (G). The sporangial wall is thick, rigid and composed of an electron dense amorphous material. Electron micrograph (6439) (x17 000) (photo. D. J. Alderman, Portsmouth Polytechnic). **Fig. 7.11. Aplanochytrium kerguelensis.** Cleaved sporangium with rhizoidal system. Phase contrast (x600) (photo. G. Bremer, Portsmouth Polytechnic). **Fig. 7.12. A. kerguelensis.** Section of part of a young sporangium showing a sagenogenetosome (Sa) like structure, vesicles containing membranes (VS) and the multilamellate nature of the sporangial wall. Electron micrograph (7136 (x27 000) (photo. G. Bremer, Portsmouth Polytechnic).

in helping to define which organisms should rightfully be considered marine fungi, is a paper by Galt and Whisler (1970) on *Thalassomyces marsupii Kane*. This organism has been variously assigned to the algae, fungi and protozoans, the decisions being made largely on the weight applied to particular morphological features. Galt and Whisler (1970) discovered the motile stage of *T. marsupii:* flagellated spores surrounded by a pellicle (not a cell wall), and equipped with one trailing and one circumferential flagellum. This evidence appears to confirm the suspected non-fungal nature of the parasite, and suggests a taxonomic position for it among the Dinoflagellates. The motile spores of *T. marsupii* have neither a sulcus nor a girdle, characters shared with the parasitic rather than the free living Dinoflagellates.

7.6 Evaluation of Recent Advances

The decade of the 1960s was not a distinguished period of great strides in the description of new species of marine phycomycetes; the number added was few, indeed. There were, however, two major advances that clearly characterize the period. First, investigators turned to such essential adjuvants to taxonomy as cytology and physiology, and thus discarded the tradition of gross morphology alone in characterizing their fungi. This trend may have led to taxonomic decisions that will fail the test of time, but the value of such an approach was established. Second, it has been demonstrated conclusively that while gross culture methods are needed for collecting marine phycomycetes, pure culture techniques assist materially in characterizing taxa, and are necessary for definitive taxonomic analyses. In commenting on the search for aquatic fungi, Sparrow (1934) emphasized that investigators faced 'a very real problem in endeavouring, first, to find sporangia which have not already discharged their zoospores in the interval between collection and examination, and secondly to provide conditions in the laboratory favourable for the development and discharge of these sporangia'. With the union of classical baiting techniques and modern culture methods formulated in the 1960s, the two problems stated by Sparrow are not as prejudicial to further progress as might be supposed.

References

ALDERMAN, D. J., and JONES, E. B. G. (1967). 'Shell disease of *Ostrea edulis* L.' *Nature,* 216, 797-798.
ALDERMAN, D. J., and JONES, E. B. G. (1971). 'Physiological requirements of two marine Phycomycetes, *Althornia crouchii* and *Ostracoblabe implexa.' Trans. Br. mycol. Soc.,* 57, 213-225.
AMON, J. P., and PERKINS, F. O. (1968). 'Structure of *Labyrinthula* sp. zoospores.' *J. Protozool.,* 15, 543-546.
ARONSON, J. M., and FULLER, M. S. (1969). 'Cell wall structure of the marine fungus, *Atkinsiella dubia.' Arch. Mikrobiol.,* 68, 295-305.
BAHNWEG, G., and SPARROW, F. K. (1972). *'Aplanochytrium kerguelensis* gen. nov. spec. nov., a new phycomycete from subantarctic marine waters.' *Arch. Mikrobiol.,* 81, 45-49.
BOOTH, T. (1969). 'Marine fungi from British Columbia: monocentric chytrids and chytridiaceous species from coastal and interior halomorphic soils.' *Syesis,* 2, 141-161.
BOOTH, T. (1971 a). 'Occurrence and distribution of zoosporic fungi and some Actinomycetales in coastal soils of southwestern British Columbia and the San Juan Islands.' *Syesis,* 4, 197-208.
BOOTH, T. (1971 b). 'Occurrence and distribution of some zoosporic fungi from soils of Hibben and Moresby Islands, Queen Charlotte Islands.' *Can. J. Bot.,* 49, 951-965.
BOOTH, T., and MILLER, C. E. (1968). 'Comparative morphology and taxonomic studies in the genus *Thraustochytrium.' Mycologia,* 60, 480-495.
BOOTH, T., and MILLER, C. E. (1969). 'Morphological development of an isolate of *Schizochytrium aggregatum.' Can. J. Bot.,* 47, 2051-2054.
CAVALIERE, A. R., and ALBERTE, R. S. (1970). 'Fungi in animal shell fragments.' *J. Elisha Mitchell scient. Soc.,* 86, 203-206.

DREBES, G. (1968). 'Lagenisma coscinodisci gen. nov. spec. nov., ein Vertreter der Lagenidiales in der marinen Diatomee Coscinodiscus.' Veröff Inst. Meeresforsch., Bremerh., Suppl. 3, 67-69.

FULLER, M. S., FOWLER, B. E., and McLAUGHLIN, D. J. (1964). 'Isolation and pure culture study of marine Phycomycetes.' Mycologia, 56, 745-756.

GAERTNER, A. (1966). 'Vorkommen, Physiologie und Verteilung "Mariner niederer Pilze" (Aquatic Phycomycetes).' Veröff. Inst. Meeresforsch., Bremerh., 2, 221-236.

GAERTNER, A. (1967 a). 'Ökologische Untersuchungen an einem marinen Pilz aus der Umgebung von Helgoland.' Helgoländer wiss. Meeresunters., 15, 181-192.

GAERTNER, A. (1967 b). 'Niedere mit Pollen köderbare Pilze in der südlichen Nordsee.' Veröff Inst. Meeresforsch., Bremerh., 10, 159-165.

GAERTNER, A. (1968 a). 'Niedere, mit Pollen köderbare marine Pilze diesseits und jenseits des Island-Färöer-Rückens im Oberflächenwasser und im Sediment.' Veröff. Inst. Meeresforsch., Bremerh., 11, 65-82.

GAERTNER, A. (1968 b). 'Die Fluktuationen mariner niederer Pilze in der Deutschen Bucht 1965 und 1966.' Veröff. Inst. Meeresforsch., Bremerh., 3, 105-120.

GAERTNER, A. (1970). 'Beobachtungen über die Sporulation der dickwandigen Sporangien von Thraustochytrium kinnei Gaertner.' Veröff. Inst. Meeresforsch., Bremerh., 12, 321-327.

GAERTNER, A. (1972). 'Characters used in the classification of thraustochytriaceous fungi.' Veröff. Inst. Meeresforsch., Bremerh., 13, 183-194.

GALT, J. H., and WHISLER, H. C. (1970). 'Differentiation of flagellated spores in Thalassomyces ellobiopsid parasite of marine Crustaceae.' Arch. Mikrobiol., 71, 295-303.

GOLDSTEIN, S. (1963 a). 'Development and nutrition of new species of Thraustochytrium.' Am. J. Bot., 50, 271-279.

GOLDSTEIN, S. (1963 b). 'Morphological variation and nutrition of a new monocentric marine fungus.' Arch. Mikrobiol., 45, 101-110.

GOLDSTEIN, S. (1963 c). 'Studies of a new species of Thraustochytrium that displays light stimulated growth.' Mycologia, 55, 799-811.

GOLDSTEIN, S., and BELSKY, M. (1964). 'Axenic culture studies of a new marine phycomycete possessing an unusual type of asexual reproduction.' Am. J. Bot., 51, 72-78.

GOLDSTEIN, S., and MORIBER, L. (1966). 'Biology of a problematic marine fungus, Dermocystidium sp. I. Development and cytology.' Arch. Mikrobiol., 53, 1-11.

HARDER, R., and UEBELMESSER, E. (1955). 'Über marine saprophytische Chytridiales und einige andere Pilz vom Meeresboden und Meeresstrand.' Arch. Mikrobiol., 22, 87-114.

JOHNSON, T. W. (1966 a). 'Chytridomycetes and Oömycetes in marine phytoplankton.' Nova Hedwigia, 10, 579-588.

JOHNSON, T. W. (1966 b). 'Fungi in planktonic Synedra from brackish waters.' Mycologia, 58, 373-382.

JOHNSON, T. W. (1967). 'Monocentric fungi on species of Rhizosolenia from saline habitats.' Mycopath. Mycol. appl., 32, 281-290.

JOHNSON, T. W., and SPARROW, F. K. (1961). Fungi in oceans and estuaries. J. Cramer, Weinheim, 668 pp.

JONES, E. B. G., and ALDERMAN, D. J. (1971). 'Althornia crouchii, gen. et sp. nov., a marine biflagellate fungus.' Nova Hedwigia, 21, 381-399.

KAZAMA, F. (1972). 'Ultrastructure of *Thraustochytrium* sp. zoospores.' *Arch. Mikrobiol.*, 83, 179-188.

KOBAYAS, H. I. Y., and OOKUBO, M. (1953). 'Studies on marine Phycomycetes, I. *Bull. Nat. Sci. Mus. (Tokyo)*, 33, 53-65.

KONNO, K. (1969). 'Studies on Japanese lower aquatic Phycomycetes. II. On *Thraustochytrium* collected from a sea weed.' *Trans. mycol. Soc. Japan*, 10, 9-13.

MACKIN, J. G., OWEN, H. M., and COLLIER, A. (1950). 'Preliminary note on the occurrence of a new protistan parasite. *Dermocystidium marinum* n. sp., in *Crassostrea virginica* (Gmelin).' *Science*, 111, 328-329.

MACKIN, J. G., and RAY, S. M. (1966). 'The taxonomic relationships of *Dermocystidium marinum* Mackin, Owen, and Collier.' *J. Invert. Path.*, 8, 544-545.

PERKINS, F. O. (1968). 'Fine structure of zoospores from *Labyrinthomyxa* sp. parasitizing the clam *Macoma balthica.*' *Chesapeake Sci.*, 9, 198-208.

PERKINS, F. O. (1969). 'Ultrastructure of vegetative stages in *Labyrinthomyxa marina* (= *Dermocystidium marinum*), a commercially significant oyster pathogen.' *J. Invert. Path.*, 13, 199-222.

PERKINS, F. O. (1972). 'The ultrastructure of holdfasts, "rhizoids", and "slime tracks" in thraustochytriaceous fungi and *Labyrinthula* spp.' *Arch. Mikrobiol.*, 84, 95-118.

PERKINS, F. O. (1973). 'Observations of thraustochytriaceous (Phycomycetes) and labyrinthulid (Rhizopodea) ectoplasmic nets on natural and artificial substrates— an electron microscope study.' *Can. J. Bot.*, 51, 485-491.

PERKINS, F. O., and MENZEL, R. W. (1966). 'Morphological and cultural studies of a motile stage in the life cycle of *Dermocystidium marinum.*' *Proc. natn. Shellfish. Assoc.*, 56, 23-30.

PERKINS, F. O., and MENZEL, R. W. (1967). 'Ultra-structure of sporulation in the oyster pathogen *Dermocystidium marinum.*' *J. Invert. Path.*, 9, 205-229.

PERKINS, R. D. and HALSEY, S. D. (1971). 'Geologic significance of microboring fungi and algae in Carolina Shelf sediments.' *J. Sediment Petrol.*, 41, 843-853.

POYTON, R. O. (1970 a). 'The characterization of *Hyalochlorella marina* gen. et sp. nov. a new colourless counterpart of *Chlorella.*' *J. gen. Microbiol.*, 62, 171-188.

POYTON, R. O. (1970 b). 'The isolation and occurrence of *Hyalochlorella marina.*' *J. gen. Microbiol.*, 62, 189-194.

SCHNEIDER, J. (1967). 'Ein neuer Phycomycet aus der Kieler Bucht (*Thraustochytrium striatum* spec. nov.).' *Kieler Meeresforsch.*, 23, 16-20.

SCHOLZ, E. (1958). 'Über niedere Phycomyceten aus Salzböden und ihr Verhalten in Salzlösungen.' *Arch. Mikrobiol.*, 30, 119-146.

SPARROW, F. K. (1934). 'Observations on marine Phycomycetes collected in Denmark.' *Dansk bot. Ark.*, 8, 1-24.

SPARROW, F. K. (1936). 'Biological observations on the marine fungi of Woods Hole waters.' *Biol. Bull. mar. bid. Lab., Woods Hole*, 70, 236-263.

SPARROW, F. K. (1958). 'Interrelationships and phylogeny of the aquatic Phycomycetes.' *Mycologia*, 50, 797-813.

SPARROW, F. K. (1960). *Aquatic Phycomycetes* (2nd Edition). Univ. Michigan Press, Ann Arbor, 1187 pp.

SPARROW, F. K. (1968 a). 'Physoderma hydrocotylidis and other interesting Phycomycetes from California.' *J. Elisha Mitchell scient. Soc.*, 84, 62-68.

SPARROW, F. K. (1968 b). 'On the occurrence of the ¬hraustochytriaceae.' *Veröff. Inst. Meeresforsch., Bremerh.*, 11, 89-92.

SPARROW, F. K. (1968 c). 'Remarks on the Thraustochytriaceae.' *Veröff. Inst. Meeresforsch., Bremerh.,* Suppl. 3, 7-17.

SPARROW, F. K. (1969). 'Zoosporic marine fungi from the Pacific Northwest.' *Arch. Mikrobiol.,* 66, 129-146.

SPARROW, F. K., PATERSON, R. A., and JOHNS, R. M. (1965). 'Additions to the phycomycete flora of the Douglas Lake region. V. New or interesting fungi.' *Pap. Michigan Acad. Sci., Arts, Ltrs.,* 50, 115-123.

ULKEN, A. (1965). 'Zwei neue Thraustochytrien aus der Aussenweser.' *Veröff. Inst. Meeresforsch., Bremerh.,* 9, 289-295.

ULKEN, A. (1968 a). 'Einige Beobachtungen über das Vorkommen von uniflagellaten Phycomyceten (Chytridiales) in der Wesermündung.' *Veröff. Inst. Meeresforsch., Bremerh.,* Suppl. 3, 59-66.

ULKEN, A. (1968 b). Über zwei marine niedere Pilze vom Meeresboden der Nordsee.' *Veröff. Inst. Meeresforsch., Bremerh.,* Suppl. 3, 71-74.

ULKEN, A. (1968 c). 'Über die Isolierung von Phycomyceten aus Süsz- und Brackwasser.' *Mitt. Internat. Verein. Limnol.,* 14, 256-260.

ULKEN, A. (1969). 'Morphologische Variationen einiger mariner Thraustochytrien.' *Ber. dt. bot. Ges.,* 81, 375-379.

VISHNIAC, H. S. (1955). 'Marine mycology.' *Trans. N. Y. Acad. Sci.,* 17, 352-360.

VISHNIAC, H. S. (1956). 'On the ecology of the lower marine fungi.' *Biol. Bull. mar. biol. Lab., Woods Hole,* 111, 410-414.

ZEBROWSKI, G. (1936). 'New genera of Cladochytriaceae.' *Ann. Mol. Bot. Gärd.,* 23, 553-564.

Addendum

From p. 203. Bahnweg and Sparrow (1974, *Am. J. Bot.* 61, 754-766) described four new *Thraustochytrium* species. These have not been treated in this chapter.

8 The Present Status of Classification in Biflagellate Fungi*

F. K. SPARROW

Biflagellate zoospores, the criterion laid down for the fungi to be discussed here, are found in two classes, namely, the Plasmodiophoromycetes and Oömycetes.

8.1 Plasmodiophoromycetes

The modern concept of the Plasmodiophoromycetes might be said to have started with the work of Cook (1926) Ledingham (1939), Couch, Leitner and Whiffen (1939), Pendergrass (1948) Goldie-Smith (1954), Kole (1954) and Miller (1958), when it was shown beyond any doubt that along with the endophytic plasmodial and clustered resting spore stages, and the peculiar protozoan-like promitoses, these fungi also possessed an independent endophytic, thin-wall zoosporangial stage. The unequally laterally biflagellate zoospores, however, rather than having the forward flagellum of the tinsel and the rear one of the whiplash type, as in all other 'biflagellates', in some species of the family have both of the whiplash type and in others the long trailing one whiplash, the other blunt. The situation prevailing in the various genera is given in Karling (1968).

It is clear that on the basis of the peculiar type of nuclear division and zoospore flagella we have here a very unique assemblage of organisms which stands apart from other biflagellate groups, but resembles them in having a thin walled zoosporangial stage, like true 'phycomycetes,' the all inclusive taxon apparently coined by de Bary for all coenocytic sporangial fungi.

8.2 Oömycetes

Oömycetes is a rather unsatisfactory and old fashioned term, hoary with tradition, often used for the remainder of the biflagellates. Unsatisfactory, since many of its members lack the 'oö . . ' and since, perhaps the most clear cut instance of oögamy known in the fungi is to be found in *Monoblepharis* with its animal like egg and motile sperm. *Monoblepharis* is, of course, a Chytridiomycete, and a 'Uniflagellate'. Oömycetes should be put to rest !

*Presented at the First International Mycological Congress, Exeter, England, 1971.

Oömycetes, according to Aronson (1965), Bartinicki-Garcia (1966) and others have walls composed of 'glucans with beta (1 − 3) and beta (1 − 6) -linked polymers with small amounts of cellulose one present in poor crystalline state'. These investigators and Aronson *et al.* (1967) and Cooper and Aronson (1967), have demonstrated by biochemical and optical means that cellulose is in fact a minor but distinctive constituent. Lin and Aronson (1970) have also found chitin present in certain of the Leptomitaceae. a condition more normal in fungi in general. Prior to zoospore formation in Oömycetes, there is a large central vacuole which usually disappears before final cleavage and discharge. Zoospores may be of the 'anteriorly', or 'laterally' biflagellate type, or both types may be present, as in *Saprolegnia*. The forwardly directed often shorter flagellum is of the tinsel, or 'Flimmer' type, the posteriorly directed one, of the whiplash or Peitschen type. Somewhat finer and shorter 'hairs' on the latter type of flagellum have been observed (Manton *et al.*, 1951; Desjardins *et al.*, 1969). The great majority of Oömycetes have only the laterally biflagellate type of zoospores. The homology of this spore among all Oömycetes is to my mind, however, open to question.

As stated, and implicit in the name, a high type of oögamy is supposed to be present. The male gamete, however, is not free swimming, but always conveyed by a structure—often a tube, sometimes a mere pore in the wall—to the female gamete within its gametangium. That is, both gametes might be said to be 'endothallic'. Discrete oöspheres are usually, but not always, formed. The zygotes become heavy walled, their contents undergo changes which result in the resistant oöspore stage of the Oömycete, and we have a structure—the oöspore—capable of protecting against vicissitudes of the environment the genetic materials of the organism. As is well known and thoroughly modern, some female gametes have liberated themselves from mere male dependency, and form their oöspores parthenogenetically.

There is a growing body of evidence (Sansome, 1961, 1963, 1971) that gametic rather than zygotic meiosis occurs in some Oömycetes (Saprolegniaceae and Peronosporaceae) and that the vegetative body is, in fact, a diploid structure. At all events, the oöspore at maturity exhibits a highly characteristic disposition of its materials which it maintains with some constancy in various groups.

For the purposes of this paper I have grouped the Oömycetes into 2 series or galaxies:

(1)   The *Saprolegnian* galaxy, with dimorphic (diplanetic) zoospores, i.e. primary and secondary zoospores or their equivalents formed 1-several eggs lacking periplasm, and oospores usually with a peripheral reserve globule.

(2)   *Peronosporacean* galaxy, with monomorphic zoospores of the so called laterally-biflagellate type only; periplasm usually present in the single egg, and the oöspore bearing a centrally disposed reserve body.

The first family of the Saprolegnian galaxy, the Saprolegniaceae is familiar to you, and it is in this group of mycelial fungi that zoospore dimorphism and oogamy are strongly displayed as in *Saprolegnia* itself.

The second family, the Ectrogellaceae, are simple holocarpic forms almost certainly reduced and adapted for an endoparasitic life in the cramped quarters of diatom cells. *Saprolegnia*-like and *Achlya*-like zoospore discharge are known among the species, but sexual reproduction has not been well authenticated.

Perhaps to be segregated here into a separate family (recently termed the Leptolegniellaceae by Dick, 1971) is the small but interesting group of saprophytes, primarily on keratin, probably also holocarpic, and represented by such forms as *Leptolegniella keratinophila* Huneycutt, *Leptolegniella exospora* Kane, *Brevilegniella keratinophila* Dick etc., which have simple thalli and zoospore discharge reminiscent of the Saprolegniaceae. Instead of oögonia, however, they develop hyphal enlargements in which numerous small asexual resting structures with thick, refractive endospore walls are formed. It is possible that species of *Aphanomycopsis* belong here, too.

The third family which I call provisionally here the Atkinsiellaceae is composed at present of *Atkinsiella dubia* (Atkins) Vishniac a marine fungus found by Miss Atkins on eggs of pea-crab in Great Britain. I have isolated it from crab eggs and it has been found by others in a more emancipated state associated with marine vegetation, and cultivated on various laboratory media. *Atkiensiella* is indeed a remarkable organism and well deserves the generic identity given it by Helen Vishniac (1958). It has a sort of 'junk-heap' appearance (and reminds one of the old wheeze concerning the camel; that it 'looked like something put together by a committee'). It is strongly saccate when given room to develop and bears numerous 'smokestack'-like discharge tubes which are very broad in relation to the size of the zoopores discharged through them. The myriads of primary zoospores formed successively, not simultaneously, in the thallus, come to rest and encyst within. From the cysts emerge the secondary zoospores which escape through the broad precociously opened tubes. *Atkinsiella* is said to be holocarpic but I have found that rhizoids or holdfasts can be formed (Sparrow, 1973a).

The fourth family—Eurychasmaceae—contains a single fungus *Eurychasma dicksonii* (Wright) Magnus, which is closely related to *Atkinsiella* but is evidently strongly reduced by a parasitic existence in cells of brown seaweeds. From a glance it is easy to spot the resemblances with *Atkinsiella* and its broad discharge tubes. In *Eurychasma,* however, a neat net is formed by the cysts of the primary zoospores. Like *Atkinsiella,* the secondary zoospores emerge from cysts and escape through the broad early opened discharge tubes. No sexuality has thus far been found in either of these families, a point I will discuss later.

The next family, the Leptomitaceae, while allied to the Saprolegniaceae by its strongly dimorphic zoospores and lack of periplasm in its oöspheres, differs from the Saprolegniaceae in several respects. It contains the genera *Leptomitus, Apodachlya* and *Apodachlyella.* Dick (1969) has recently pointed out in *Apodachlya* the peculiar organization of the oöspore contents, bearing as it does, several reserve bodies. The unique presence of chitin in the walls has been ascertained by Lin and Aronson (1970). The characteristic jointed body combined with the presence in the cytoplasm of 'cellulin discs' (of hexosamine according to a verbal report by Aronson) have long been recognized as unique.

Several features unite the remainder of the biflagellate fungi which I have placed in the 'Peronosporacean galaxy'. Foremost of these is the strictly monomorphic, biflagellate, 'secondary zoospore'; termed 'secondary', because it has always been considered homologous with the zoospore emerging from the cyst of the primary zoospore of the Saprolegniaceae. Another is the almost universal formation of only a single female gamete in the gametangium. Furthermore, the resultant oöspore bears a large globule, centrally disposed (not peripherally as in *Saprolegnia*) in the protoplasm, and a lateral pellucid vacuole. Returning to non-sexual reproduction, attempts have been made in the past to detect traces of the primary zoospore in the Peronosporacean galaxy and to homologize structures or zoospore actions with it. For example, the vesicle of *Pythium,* and the predischarge and post-discharge movements and subsequent quiescent periods of the zoospores of *Olpidiopsis,* have been suggested as harking back to a primary zoospore stage. To me these seem futile exercises in credulity. For my part I suspect these fungi arose from laterally biflagellate mono-morphic stock, *wholly distinct* from dimorphic zoosporic ancestoral groups.

The Peronosporales consists of the Rhipidiaceae, Albuginaceae, Peronosporaceae.

The Rhipidiaceae with basal apparatus, more or less segmented thallus and pedicellate reproductive organs, I believe is more allied to the Peronosporaceae than the Leptomitaceae. It consists of *Sapromyces, Rhipidium, Aqualinderella, Araios-pora* and *Mindeniella.* There is no chitin in the walls, no cellulin granules and absolutely no evidence for the existence of a primary zoospore. There is a single egg with conspicuous periplasm which, as in the Albuginaceae and Peronosporaceae condenses upon the wall of the oöspore in a characteristic fashion or pattern. There is a single well defined antheridium and fertilization tube and the reserve body of the oöspore is central. The segmented thallus is a vegetative character seen in other groups of both biflagellate and uniflagellate fungi.

I would like to suggest, only suggest, that the Rhipidiaceae with these aforemen-tioned characters, may have closer affinities with the parasitic Albuginaceae than is usually considered.

In the Pythiaceae and Peronosporaceae we again have strongly monomorphic zoospores. In *Pythium,* as indicated, these are completely matured within a well defined vesicle formed from wall material at the apex of a sporangial discharge tube. In *Phytophthora, Pythiogeton* and *Diasporangium* there is a quickly evanescent vesicle, or this may be wholly lacking, when zoospores are discharged. *Phytophthora* and *Trachysphara* (a *Phytophthora* with suppressed zoospore formation) have the remark-able amphigynous antheridia.

I need not dwell on the Peronosporaceae. The downy mildews are too well known and I have nothing to add here other than to agree with their relationship to the other families of the Peronosporales.

I wish to consider now in very brief and arbitrary fashion the Lagenidiaceae, Olpidiop-sidaceae, Sirolpidiaceae, all holocarpic, and the Thraustochytriaceae, Dermocystidiaceae and Labyrinthulaceae. Conjectures as to relationships within these families and between them are hampered by a variety of factors, foremost of which in the last four is a lack of information on sexuality and life cycles. Furthermore, the minuteness of the zoospores in many species resulting in disagreements as to body shape, lengths of flagella, etc., lack of cytological information where sexuality is known, etc., are crippling, since all these are of considerable importance in detecting affinities.

The Lagenidiaceae as it now stands defies generalizations. In the classic species of *Myzocytium* and *Lagenidium* parasitic in algae and in pollen grains, beautifully portray-ed by Zopf (1884), we had a tidy group with jointed thalli and with reproductive pro-cesses reminding us of pythiaceous fungi. All this is now changed, and we find in *Lagenidium* alone, fungi with a 1-cell *Olpidiopsis*-like body, to ones with hyphal systems scarcely distinguishable from species of *Pythium.* Processes resulting in resting struc-tures vary. There may be conjugation by way of a simple pore in the mutual wall of two like-sized contiguous cells, or ones which employ a fertilization tube to convey the contents of a well defined antheridial branch into the receptive structure. The latter may not even have an oosphere differentiated. Furthermore, in certain species as *Lagenidium destruens* Sparrow (parasitic in hyphae of *Achlya*), there is no sexuality. Ordinary vegetative segments of the thallus simply contract their contents into one or more pro-toplasmic masses which then become surrounded by a thick wall.

In the Lagenidiaceae there is also widespread divergence in the method of zoospore formation. Thus, in *Myzocytium microsporum* (Karling) Sparrow (in rotifers) zoospores emerge from the sporangium fully formed. In *Myzocytium zoophthorum* Sparrow (in

216

rotifer eggs) they are partly, sometimes wholly, delimited within the sporangium and emerge surrounded by a vesicle, which like *Phytophthora* at once disappears. In others, such as *Lagenidium rabenhorstii* Zopf (in algae) they are fully formed and matured outside the sporangium in a vesicle at the tip of the discharge tube, like a species of *Pythium*. As a group, no correlation seems to exist between type of zoospore formation, degree of development of the thallus and specialization of sexual organs.

The Olpidiopsidaceae stands in many ways close to the Lagenidiaceae. Species of *Olpidiopsis* may resemble 1-celled species of both *Myzocytium* and *Lagenidium*. *Rozellopsis*, is distinguished by completely filling the host hyphae and by informing heterokont zoospores. *Petersenia*, another genus of the family is in essence a tubular contorted *Olpidiopsis*.

The Sirolpidiaceae, in which I would include *Haliphthoros* of Vishniac (1958), is at the moment exclusively marine. Its members are holocarpic, filamentous, highly vacuolate in the vegetative phase and have a strong tendency for the body to be subdivided into subthalli of varying lengths. In turn, the contents of subthalli may become wholly converted by successive divisions into great numbers of biflagellate zoospores. These, while discharged individually, are often ill-formed and seem, like marsupials, to have been born in an embryonic condition, that is, before their time. They may individually undergo a series of gyrations after discharge which much resembles that of *Pythium* zoospores during their formation in the vesicle, including the rocking motion associated with flagellum maturation and the sort of final, happy, expectant trembling, at dispersal, familiar to all students of *Pythium*. The mature spore is similar to the laterally biflagellate type of the Peronosporaceae, perhaps in some genera more rotund, others more lean and *Olpidiopsis*-like. Flagellar length in living spores is difficult to detect, as always. Most zoospores appear to be almost isokont.

Thus far, no well defined, thick-walled resting structures have been convincingly demonstrated in the Sirolpidiaceae. Nor with the miniscule investigation accorded them, has any sexuality. This recalls the situation found in the marine Saprolegniales. I will refer to this later.

To me, the most interesting morphological feature of the Sirolpidiaceae is their 'generalized' nature. They are informal creatures without specialized sporangia or possibly even holdfast systems. Any part can vegetate, be unbranched or halfheartedly branched, fragment into sub-thalli which may remain dormant, or become wholly asexually reproductive, and form swarms of zoospores. In this holocarpy, because of fragmentation, subthalli assume an independent existence and zoospore production by various sub-thalli from a single thallus may occur successively over a long period of time. They are not all *simultaneously* converted into zoosporangia. These sub-thalli may often be spherical and the resultant body with a more or less developed discharge tube may closely resemble an *Olpidiopsis*. Further, under conditions of abundant oxygen, such bodies may give rise to long hyphal structures.

The details of the zoospore formation in both *Sirolpidium* and *Haliphthoros* have occupied me a great deal lately and it is an interesting and unique process.

Haliphthoros is strongly mycelioid and quickly forms an extensive thallus on media. Like *Sirolpidium* it soon gives rise by fragmentation to sub-thalli. Zoospores form successively in sub-thalli as in *Sirolpidium,* and sometimes also, as in *Sirolpidium,* spherical 'gemmae' are produced. Again, there is no sexual reproduction.

Lagenisma, a parasite of marine diatoms recently described by Drebes (1966) from Helgoland, may belong in this family. The contents of its tubular branched body are completely and simultaneously converted into myriads of small isokont laterally biflagellate zoospores. No fragmentation has been reported by Drebes or more recently by Gotelli (1971), and perhaps it should be left in the Lagenidiaceae where Drebes put it, or possibly near *Petersenia* in the Olpidiopsidaceae.

The Thraustochytriaceae and Dermocystidiaceae are, like the Sirolpidiaceae, exclusively marine and seemingly lack sexuality. *Thraustochytrium* species have now been found in all the principal ocean masses of the world, and as we improve our quantitative methods, I am sure will be demonstrated in sufficient numbers to be considered significant factors in detritus decomposition in the marine ecosytem. Although I first encountered them as saprophytes on marine algae they have subsequently been discovered on a variety of materials, even submerged plastic rods. Morphologically, they resemble monocentric, epibiotic, chytrids. They are eucarpic with a 'rhizoidal' system of varied extent. Zoospores are either matured within the sporangium or outside, which suggests they should go under the taxonomic knife. I can only speculate upon their affinities at this time. Species of *Thraustochytrium* have laterally biflagellate, small zoospores cleaved in a sporangium. No evidence of a primary zoospore has thus far been discovered and these fungi seem to be strictly monomorphic. In some species, they do not assume motility until after discharge when flagella develop. The motile spore does not, however, as in the saprolegnian *Thraustotheca,* emerge from a cyst. In others, the spores are completely matured within the sporangium and swim away after bursting or deliquescence of the sporangium wall, or emerge through a pore. Some species maintain a basal sterile rudiment of protoplasm from which, as in *Saprolegnia* and also certain species of *Pythium,* a new sporangium grows by 'internal' or 'precurrent proliferation'. These biflagellate zoospores have the forward longer flagellum of the tinsel, the posterior directed one of the whiplash, type. The wall has had no expert attention. Asexual resting spores have been reported once by Johnson (1957), who found them to occupy the same position on the thallus as the sporangium and to have a conspicuous central globule and thickened wall. This resembles the Peronosporacean, not Saprolegniacean oöspore.

Two other genera of the family have thus far been described. The first of these, *Japonochytrium* is much like *Thraustochytrium* except that there is a subsporangial endobiotic swelling. *Schizochytrium* Goldstein and Belsky is indeed a puzzler. When I saw and drew colonies of this organism in 1934 I supposed it was some sort of schizoid yeast. Successive bipartitioning of the thallus rudiment and growth of parts with relentless mathematical precision results, as Goldstein and Belsky (1964) have shown, and as has been noted in certain other marine organisms, notably *Labyrinthomyxa* (Perkins and Menzel, 1966) in a heap of stuff resembling groups of dyads and tetrads with strings attached one for each segment. Each of the segments may function as a sporangium and liberates a few laterally biflagellate zoospores. This organism which Dr. Goldstein intends, I hope, to put into a family of its own, defies ordinary definition and he has fled understandably to the chlorosphaeracean algae in his distress.

The Thraustochytriales (Sparrow, 1973b) certainly seem to be an isolated group of reduced forms probably not allied to either the Saprolegniaceae or Peronosporaceae. Sporangial discharge and internal proliferation in *T. proliferum,* for example, appears saprolegniaceous, but no cysts of primary zoospores are found. Furthermore, the zoospores themselves in contrast to other biflagellates appear to have the longer flagellum directed anteriorly. Then, too, the holdfast system ('rhizoids') seems peculiar. According to Perkins (1972) it arises from an organelle similar to that forming the slime track of *Labyrinthula,* i.e. to his 'ectoplasmic nets' (see Chapter 11).

At the moment it is hard to choose relationships here until additional evidence on ultrastructure, wall composition, sexuality, resting stages, life histories, etc., is forthcoming. If, for example, there is an undoubted *Thraustochytrium* with anteriorly biflagellate zoospores and dimorphism, and resting spores with peripheral disposition of the reserve globules, then we will have to reconsider previous suggested affinities with Saprolegnians (Goldstein, 1973).

The Dermocystidiaceae include *Aplanochytrium* of Bahnweg and Sparrow (1972) and ? *Hyalochlorella* (Poyton, 1970). The group of organisms which have been described at one time or another under the name *Dermocystidium,* presents to me at this point in our knowledge a rather confused and complex picture of relationships. They include: *Dermocystidium marinum* Mackin, Owen et Collier (now placed in *Labyrinthomyxa marina* (Mackin, Owen et Collier) Mackin et Ray (Mackin and Ray, 1966); *Labyrinthomyxa marina* (Perkins and Menzel, 1966); *Dermocystidium* sp. of Goldstein *et al.* (1964), Goldstein and Moriber (1966) and now placed in *Hyalochlorella marina* Poyton by Poyton (1970). Perhaps this is best expressed by Goldstein and Moriber (1966) in their paper on a free living *Dermocystidium:* 'The complex of organisms grouped in and near the genus *Dermocystidium* constitutes a heterogeneous assortment of morphologically simple forms whose superficial resemblance undoubtedly results from convergence rather than a common phylogeny'.

The specifics of the *Dermocystidium-Labyrinthomyxa* complex will undoubtedly be forthcoming by students of this group. I am sure the evidence from morphology, E. M. and even physiology will be focused on this fascinating problem. Meanwhile, temporarily, I will associate the Dermocystidiaceae with the Thraustochytriaceae with the thought that we may find that we may be dealing here with several wholly distinct groups both from fungi and algae.

The staggering but pleasing prospect of having to accommodate *Labyrinthula* in the biflagellate fungi certainly should give us all a thrill! Indeed, the pyriform swarmers as depicted by Amon and Perkins (1968) and Perkins and Amon (1969) with lateral, oppositely directed flagella, the anterior one with mastigonemes along opposite sides, the posterior of the whiplash type, and shorter, certainly seem fungal. Only the greater length of the anterior flagellum and the presence of a basal, pigmented stigma seem discordant. The latter may indicate an algal relationship.

The main ideas brought forward here are contained in Table 8.1. Not all genera are included.

Before closing this survey of biflagellate fungi I wish to add a word concerning the strange lack of sexuality and resting spores we find in marine groups, particularly the Atkinsiellaceae, Sirolpidiaceae, Thraustochytriaceae and even Dermocystidiaceae.

These apparent woeful sexual and morphological shortcomings might be explained in several ways. Perhaps it is due to the admittedly small amount of investigation thus far given marine zoosporic fungi, and in fact, both sexuality and resting spores will be turned up any minute. We should call to mind that in the fairly common chytridiomycete, *Gonapodya,* approximately 80 years elapsed from the time of its description until its sexuality and resting spores were found.

On the other hand, the relatively constant aquatic conditions prevailing in the normal marine environment, with no sudden or seasonal drying up, as in a freshwater pond or in soil, would present little need for thick-walled resistant bodies such as oöspores. Perhaps there were never any such structures in these groups, or perhaps they were lost in the eons of time spent in that relatively placid environment—the sea. That these fungi have *no* means of enjoying the fruits of sexual reproduction, I doubt very

TABLE 8.1   Chart of suggested interrelationships in the 'Biflagellatae'.

Saprolegnian galaxy

I Eurychasmales
1. Atkinsiellaceae
   Atkinsiella
2. Eurychasmaceae
   Eurychasma
   Eurychasmidium
   ? *Ectrogella*
   eurychasmoides

II Saprolegniales
1. Saprolegniaceae
   Saprolegnia
   Achlya
   Pythiopsis
   Isoachlya
   Leptolegnia
   Aphanomyces
   Aphanodictyon
   Brevilegnia
   Thraustotheca
   Aplanopsis
2. Leptolegniellaceae
   Leptolegniella
   Brevilegniella
   Aphanomycopsis
3. Ectrogellaceae
   Ectrogella
   Pythiella
4. Leptomitaceae
   Leptomitus
   Apodachlya
   Apodachlyella

Peronosporacean galaxy

III Lagenidiales
1. Lagenidiaceae
   Lagena (Lagenocystis)
   Lagenidium
   Myzocytium
2. Olpidiopsidaceae
   Rozellopsis
   Olpidiopsis
   Petersenia
   Pseudosphaerita
3. Sirolpidiaceae
   Sirolpidium
   Haliphthoros
   ? *Lagenisma*

V Thraustochytriales*
1. Thraustochytriaceae
   Thraustochytrium
   Japonochytrium
2. Schizochytriaceae
   Schizochytrium
3. Dermocystidiaceae
   ? *Aplanochytrium*
   ? *Hyalochlorella*
4. *Althornia*

IV Peronosporales
1. Rhipidiaceae
   Sapromyces
   Rhipidium
   Aqualinderella
   Mindeniella
2. Albuginaceae
   Albugo
3. Pythiaceae
   Zoophagus
   Pythium
   Pythiogeton
   Diasporangium
4. Peronosporaceae
   Basidiophora
   Plasmopara
   Peronoplasmopara
   Sclerospora
   Bremia
   Peronospora

VI Labyrinthulales
1. Labyrinthulaceae
   Labyrinthula
   Labyrinthomyxa

* Sparrow, F. K. (1973b). 'Mastigomycotina'. in *The Fungi* (Eds. G. C. Ainsworth, F. K. Sparrow and A. S. Sussman) Academic Press, New York, vol. 4B, 61-73.

much. Their neighbours and sometimes, indeed, their hosts, the seaweeds, have certain-
y not led a monastic life, nor have they felt the need of a durable resting stage.

We must not forget that despite over a century and a half of increasingly intensive
work on marine algae, only relatively recently have well known discordant entities
been linked up in the life cycles of single species. Here the heteromorphic life cycles
of the kelps come first to mind. Furthermore, few would have guessed at the situation with respect to the well known marine genera of green algae, *Halicystis* and *Der-
besia*, i.e. that they are one organism.

Should we be surprised, then, if one of our more enterprising workers soon discovers,
to use a hypothetical example, that *Thraustochytrium*, and *Sirolpidium* or *Haliph-
thorols*, are phases of one organism?

References

AMON, J. P., and PERKINS, F. O. (1968). 'Structure of *Labyrinthula* zoospores.'
J. Protozool., 15, 543-546.

ARONSON, J. M. (1965). 'The cell wall.' In *The Fungi* (Eds. G. C. Ainsworth and
A. S. Sussman) Academic Press, New York, vol. 1, 49-76.

ARONSON, J. M., COOPER, B. A., and FULLER, M. S. (1967). 'Glucans of
Oomycete cell walls'. *Science*, 155, 332-335.

BARTNICKI-GARCIA, S. (1966). 'Chemistry of hyphal walls of *Phytophthora.'*
J. gen. Microbiol., 42, 57-69.

COOK, W. R. I. (1926). 'The genus *Ligniera* Maire and Tison.' *Trans. Br. mycol.*
Soc., 11, 196-213.

COOPER, B. A., and ARONSON, J. M. (1967). 'Cell wall structure of *Pythium
debaryanum.' Mycologia*, 59, 658-670.

COUCH, J. N., LEITNER, J., and WHIFFEN, A. (1939). 'A new genus of the
Plasmodiophoraceae'. *J. Elisha Mitchell scient. Soc.*, 55, 399-408.

DESJARDINS, P. R., ZENTMYER, G. A., and REYNOLDS, D. A. (1969). 'Electron
microscopic observations of the flagellar hairs of *Phytophthora palmivora*
zoospores.' *Can. J. Bot.*, 47, 1077-1079.

DICK, M. W. (1969). 'Morphology and taxonomy of the Oomycetes, with special
reference to Saprolegniaceae, Leptomitaceae and Pythiaceae'. *New Phytol.*, 68,
751-775. (1971). 'Leptolegniellaceae Fam. nov.' *Trans. Br. mycol. Soc.*, 57, 417-425.

DREBES, G. (1966). 'Ein parasitischer Phycomycet (Lagenidiales) in *Coscinodiscus'.*
Helgoländer wiss. Meeresunters., 13, 426-435.

GOLDIE-SMITH, E. K. (1954). 'The position of *Woronina polycystis* in the Plasmodiophoraceae.' *Am. J. Bot.*, 41, 441-448.

GOLDSTEIN, S., and BELSKY, M. (1964). 'Axenic culture studies of a new marine
phycomycete possessing an unusual type of asexual reproduction.' *Am. J. Bot.*,
51, 72-78.

GOLDSTEIN, S., and MORIBER, L. (1966). 'Biology of a problematic marine fungus,
Dermocystidium sp. I. Development and cytology'. *Arch. Mikrobiol.*, 53, 1-11.

GOTELLI, D. (1971). '*Lagenisma coscinodisci,* a parasite of the marine diatom
Coscinodiscus occurring in the Puget Sound, Washington'. *Mycologia*, 63, 171-174.

JOHNSON, T. W. Jr. (1957). 'On the marine phycomycete *Thraustochytrium
proliferum'. Trans. Br. mycol. Soc.*, 40, 292-294.

KARLING, J. S. (1968). *The Plasmodiophorales.* Hafner, New York (2nd Edition).
256 pp.

KOLE, A. P. (1954). 'A contribution to the knowledge of *Spongospora subterranea* (Wallr.) Lagerh., the cause of powdery scab of potatoes.' *Tijdschr. Plziekt.*, 60, 1-65.

LEDINGHAM, G. A. (1939). 'Studies on *Polymyxa graminis*, n. gen., n. sp., a plasmodiophoraceous root parasite of wheat.' *Can. J. Res. Ser. C,* 17, 38-51.

LIN, C. C., and ARONSON, J. M. (1970). 'Chitin and cellulose in the cell walls of the Oomycete *Apodachlya* sp.' *Arch. Mikrobiol.,* 72, 111-114.

MACKIN, J. G., and RAY, S. M. (1966). 'The taxonomic relationships of *Dermocystidium marinum*, Mackin, Owen and Collier'. *J. Invert. Path.,* 8, 544-545.

MANTON, I., CLARKE, B., and GREENWOOD, A. D. (1951). 'Observations with the electron microscope on a species of *Saprolegnia.*' *J. exp. Bot.,* 2, 321-331.

MILLER, C. E. (1958). 'Morphology and cytology of the zoosporangia and cystosori of *Sorosphaera veronicae'. J. Elisha Mitchell scient. Soc.,* 74, 49-64.

RAO, V. M., and ARONSON, J. M. (1970). 'Cell wall structure of *Sapromyces elongatus'. Mycologia,* 62, 531-541.

PENDERGRASS, W. R. (1948). 'A new member of the Plasmodiophoraceae.' *J. Elisha Mitchell scient. Soc.,* 64, 132-134.

PERKINS, F. O. (1972). 'The ultrastructure of holdfasts, "rhizoids", and "slime tracks" in the thruastochytriaceous fungi and *Labyrinthula* spp.' *Arch. Mikrobiol.,* 84, 95-1

PERKINS, F. O., and AMON, J. P. (1969). 'Zoosporulation in *Labyrinthula* sp., an electron microscope study.' *J. Protozool.,* 16, 235-257.

PERKINS, F. O., and MENZEL, R. W. (1966). 'Morphological and cultural studies of a motile stage in the life cycle of *Dermocystidium marinum.' Proc. natn. Shellfish Assoc.,* 56, 23-30.

POYTON, R. O. (1970). 'The characterization of *Hyalochlorella marina* gen. et sp. nov a new colourless counterpart of *Chlorella', J. gen. Microbiol.,* 62, 171-188.

SANSOME, E. (1961). 'Meiosis in the oogonium and antheridium of *Pythium debaryanum* Hesse.' *Nature,* London, 191, 827-828. (1963). 'Meiosis in *Pythium debaryanum* Hesse and its significance in the life-history of the biflagellatae.' *Trans. Br. mycol. Soc.,* 46, 63-72. (1971). 'Meiosis in the Oomycetes.' Abstr. I Intern. Mycol. Congress, Exeter, p. 83.

VISHNIAC, H. S. (1958). 'A new marine phycomycete.' *Mycologia,* 50, 66-79.

ZOPF, W. (1884). 'Zur Kenntniss der Phycomyceten. I. Zur morphologie und biologie der Ancylisteen und Chytridiaceen.' *Nova Acta Acad. Caesar. Leop. Carol.,* 47, 143-236.

References added in Proof

BAHNWEG, G. and SPARROW, F. K. (1972). *Arch. Mikrobiol.,* 81, 45-49.

GOLDSTEIN, S. (1973). *Ann. Rev. Microbiol.* 27, 13-26.

GOLDSTEIN, S., BELSKY, M. M. and CHOSAK, R. (1969). *Mycologia,* 61, 468-472.

PORTER, D. (1973). *Veröff. Inst. Meeresforsch. Bremerh.* Suppl. 5, 19-44.

SPARROW, F. K. (1973a). *Arch. Mikrobiol.,* 93, 137-144.

9 Fungal Diseases of Marine Animals

D. J. ALDERMAN

9.1 Introduction

Diseases of marine animals have been encountered by scientific investigators over at least the last 100 years, and a significant proportion of these have conclusively been shown to be due to fungi. The number of taxa involved is quite small and the majority are phycomycetes, but Ascomycetes and Fungi Imperfecti are known. The exact taxonomic status of the majority of recognized pathogens is by no means agreed, and the best known species are in no way excepted from this. Thus it has been felt advisable to arrange this chapter in terms of host and substrate rather than in an orderly taxonomic series of fungi. In addition to the known and established fungal pathogens there are a number of organisms which have been very inadequately described and whose existence must be regarded as doubtful, certainly in the form described, but the number of such organisms is not great, and reflects the situation in marine pathology as a whole.

The difficulties involved in the investigation of marine zoonoses should not be understated, and it is these which are only too often responsible for the inadequate information available. The major hurdle in any such investigation is inevitably the difficulty of obtaining fresh, living material of infected host. All too often reports are received of diseased material destroyed without investigation. Amongst zoologists, therefore, the work of Daphne Atkins stands out as a shining example. Not only did she recognize fungal infection of her animals, but her studies resulted in a clear description of three very interesting new marine phycomycetes. Her type material, deposited at the British Museum and now in the Herbarium of the Royal Botanic Gardens, Kew, is still in reasonable condition and it has been possible to make new photomicrographs of all three genera for inclusion in this chapter. Unless living material and cultures can be made available, disease investigations are necessarily limited. Without them it is not possible to show (by artificial infection) that the fungus is a true pathogen, nor can many of the myriad of other details which one would like to know be understood.

So poorly are the majority of fungal diseases known that they have been recorded only from one or two sites, and often only once or over a short period. It is thus impossible to make any coherent statements regarding the geographical distribution of the fungi concerned except in a few fairly limited cases. For example, the distribution of the oyster parasite *Labyrinthomyxa marina (Dermocystidium marinum)* (Mackin, Owen et Collier) Mackin et Ray, is limited to the Eastern and Gulf States coasts of North America and, in the northern parts of its range, has been clearly shown to be temperature limited, requiring $25°C$ for effective spread. There is a wealth of detailed information compiled on this organism over a period of 20 years, but, invaluable though it is in showing the effect of a pathogenic fungus on a susceptible population, it is limited to *L. marina* from those areas of America in which there are active research laboratories. Little or nothing is known of this pathogen in Mexican waters or of the effects of reported related pathogens on other molluscs of less commercial significance. A similar situation exists with *Ostracoblabe implexa* Bornet et Flahault which is a parasite in the shells of European oysters. There is very good evidence of the post World War II distribution of this disease in North Atlantic coastal waters, and again it has been shown that the northern extension of the disease is temperature dependent $(19°C)$. We have knowledge of shell disease in *Crassotrea angulata* Lmk. outside Portugal only where it is grown commercially. Nor is there any information available from the Mediterranean (apart from the French coast) where susceptible hosts exist. A third example is the *Ichthyophonus* disease of fish and illustrates some of the problems associated with diseases of highly mobile marine organisms. Here much less is known of the disease, but there are considerable indications that it is one which is responsible for periodic major epizootics of herring in the western North Atlantic. Outside the North Atlantic area no real records exist.

The distribution of nearly all other fungal diseases is limited to the area in which the original investigator found them, and therefore, has no real significance beyond indicating the wide gaps in our knowledge.

To conclude this introduction, the cautionary point should be made that relatively few fungal diseases have been conclusively proved to have a significant effect on natural populations. Many of the organisms described below are quite probably only facultative parasites at the most, but those which have been proved to have significant effects are of considerable importance and make investigation of all fungal diseases worth while.

9.2   Diseases of Fish

9.2.1   *Ichthyophonus*

This genus of fish parasites consists of one well known organism, *Ichthyophonus hoferi* Plehn et Mulsow (1911) and the poorly known congeneric *Ichthyophonus gasterophilum* Caullery et Mesnil (1905 a, b). This is a genus which has been the subject of considerable nomenclatural confusion. *Ichthyophonus gasterophilum* was originally described as *Ichthyosporidium gasterophilum* in the same taxon as *Ichthyosporidium phymogenes* (now recognized as a protozoan) by Caullery and Mesnil. Neither was designated as type species. *Ichthyophonus hoferi* was subsequently described by Plehn and Mulsow (1911) and shown to be a fungus. Sprague (1965) has ably collated the subsequent confusions and his recommendation as to the use of *Ichthyophonus* Plehn et Mulsow for the fungus and *Ichthyopsoridium* Caullery et Mesnil for the protozoan is followed here.

It seems probable that *Ichthyophonus hoferi* is itself a complex of related forms. Reichenbach-Klinke (1954, 1955) assembled a list of over 80 species of fish found to be infected, both from marine and freshwater habitats. The most detailed description from freshwater is of infections of rainbow trout and salmon by Dorier and Degrange (1960). The best known marine infestations are of the herring *Clupea harengus* L. (Sindermann, 1963, 1970).

In the herring, the organism is both enzootic (1%) and epizootic (25%, many of which were acute). Sindermann (1963, 1970) has identified six epizootics in western North Atlantic waters since 1898 and suggests that the disease is a very significant control of herring populations. Infestation is systematic, affecting particularly viscera and musculature. Internally foci of infection appear as small white nodules of encapsulated fungus which, in acute cases, are accompanied by massive tissue invasion, necrosis, and death (Figs. 9.1 to 9.7).

Despite the numerous reports of the organism in marine fish, only two detailed investigations have been made—in mackerel (*Scomber scombrus* L.) by Sproston (1944) and in herring by Sindermann and Scattergood (1954). These two investigations produced two quite different suggested life cycles.

Sindermann and Scattergood (1954) describe heavy walled spores (Figs. 9.1 and 9.5) germinating to produce hypha-like structures (Figs. 9.2 and 9.6) which invade the host tissues. Cysts are formed which develop into the spores. Sproston (1944) reported fusion between the 'hyphal bodies' suggesting sexual reproduction, whilst Reichenbach-Klinke (1956 a) found conidia-like bodies.

Isolation and culture of *Ichthyophonus hoferi* was reported by Plehn and Mulsow (1911), Fish (1934), Forster (1941), and Sindermann and Scattergood (1954). The latter carried out successful experiments over periods of over 14 months. Isolation was in a Sabouraud dextrose medium plus 1% beef serum. Optimum growth occurred at 10°C with a range from 3 to 20°C. Spores germinated to give club-shaped hyphae in which the cytoplasm aggregated at the tip. From photomicrographs (Sindermann and Scattergood, 1954) it would seem that, in young stages at least, cytoplasmic continuity was maintained by thin strands of protoplasm stretching back and connecting the aggregates at the tips. After initial rapid growth the hyphae tended to round off at the tip with numerous irregular segmentations and some of the tips in older cultures would round up to form large quiescent 'spores'. Except for some external dimensions, development in culture was thus much as that seen in the fish.

Certainly this is an organism which will greatly repay further study. At the moment it is a taxonomic orphan which has never been formally described. Apart from the 'spores' of Sindermann and Scattergood, and the conidia of Reichenbach-Klinke, no reproductive structures are known. It seems certain that it is a complex of fungal parasites rather than one species, and new hosts continue to be found, both fish (Hendricks, 1972) and calanoid copepods (Sindermann, 1970).

9.2.2 Other Fish Diseases

Apart from *Ichthyophonus hoferi,* fungus infestations of marine fish are *apparently* quite uncommon if published records are any true indication. Anadromous fish infected by freshwater fungi, such as *Saprolegnia parasitica* Coker (Aleem *et al.,* 1953) may return to the sea with these fungi on them. Although such infestations may per-

Figs. 9.1 to 9.7 *Ichthyophonus hoferi* Plehn et Mulsow infecting various tissues. Specimens loaned by J. Buchanan.

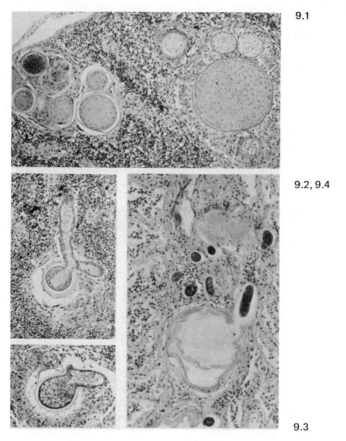

9.1

9.2, 9.4

9.3

Fig. 9.1 Encapsulated cysts in host tissue (x 66). Figs. 9.2 and 9.3 Germinating cysts with club-shaped mycelial outgrowths (x 100). Fig. 9.4 Hyphal stages in gill tissue (x 66).

sist while the fish is in the sea, extension of the infection is unlikely and the infesta-tion is often cured. Thus these cannot be regarded as marine diseases.

Cycloptericola marina Apstein (1910) was described from white epithelial masses on the stomach wall of the lumpfish *Cyclopterus lumpus L.,* but lacking a re-discovery no real understanding of the organism is possible from the author's brief description. *Cladosporium* was identified by Reichenbach-Klinke (1956 b) in *Gadus morhua* L. and two brackish water *Hyphessobrycon* species, but little is known of this organism under marine conditions and the degree of parasitism is uncertain.

A specimen of *Gadus morhua* has been examined at Portsmouth and found to be infected with *Phoma* mycelium, but since the specimen was frozen, isolation was not possible and the infestation could not be shown to be prior to death.

9.3 Disease of Invertebrate 'Hard Tissue'

Included in this section are a number of diseases affecting two basic types of tissue, the

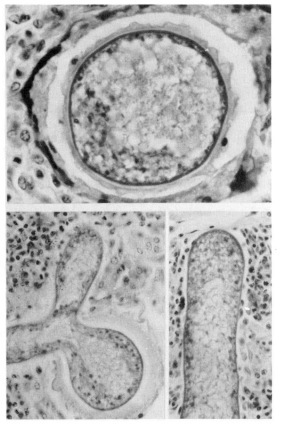

9.5

9.6, 9.7

Fig. 9.5 Encapsulated cyst (x 400). **Fig. 9.6** Germinating cyst (x 400). **Fig. 9.7** Close-up of hyphal tip (x 400).

hard calcified shells of molluscs (including in this instance corals and barnacle tests) and the keratinaceous exoskeletons of crustaceans. Both are similar in that the disease causing fungi attack the horny proteins of the shell matrix and exoskeleton, and the separation made is between sedentary hosts and those capable of active locomotion in the adult.

9.3.1   Fungal infections of sedentary hosts

The shells of all molluscs, tests of barnacles and coral skeletons contain a matrix of organic material, for the most part tanned proteins, and it is these that are attacked by the fungi.

Ostracoblabe implexa *Bornet et Flahault*   *Ostracoblabe implexa* Bornet et Flahault (1889) is a mycelial phycomycetous fungus which has recently been shown to be the cause of shell disease in oysters in European waters (Alderman and Jones, 1971).

The disease was first recognized as early as 1878 by the Montauge brothers, and since then many investigations have been made. Shell disease is mentioned in all major reviews of shellfish published since the beginning of this century: Ranson (1943), Korringa (1952), Yonge (1960) and Galtsoff (1964). When the disease was first recognized in Holland, a number of possible causes were suggested. Hoek (1902) even suggested that 'fungi-like *O. implexa'* might be the cause of the symptoms found, but this suggestion does not seem to have been based on the examination of diseased shell (Korringa, personal communication). Dolfus (1921) recorded *O. implexa* as growing on oyster shells but did not link it with shell disease which he mentions separately. Korringa (1951) was the first to establish the true nature of the disease and to make observations on its epizootiology. He was, however, unable to isolate the pathogen. Subsequently the fungus was isolated and referred to *Ostracoblabe implexa* by Alderman and Jones (1971).

O. implexa is endemic in coastal waters throughout Western Europe but only attacks oysters in a way severe enough to produce visible symptoms under certain well defined conditions. The known distribution of the disease is given in Fig. 9.8. The recognition of shell disease symptoms in newly imported Portuguese oysters has led to the addition of Portugal to the areas shown in Alderman and Jones (1971). Reports of shell disease from outside this area are few (Durve and Bal, 1960; Galtsoff, 1964) and it remains to be proven that the symptoms have the same cause.

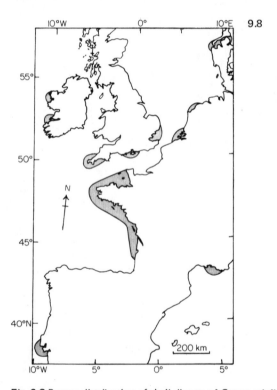

Fig. 9.8 Proven distribution of shell disease of *Ostrea edulis* L. and *Crassostrea angulata* Lmk.

O. implexa was described from the shell of an oyster by Bornet and Flahault in 1889. In a subsequent paper describing mycelium from the shell of *Purpura lapillus* (1891), Bornet redescribed the fungus as a marine lichen *Verrucaria consequens* Nyl. Subsequent redefinitions of that taxon have led to the inclusion by Santesson (1939) and Feldman (1937) amongst others of *O. implexa* amongst

228

synonyms for the lichen *Arthropyrenia* Leight. Alderman and Jones (1971) found that the fungus responsible for shell disease in oysters was identifiable with the original 1889 description of *Ostracoblabe implexa* and that there were no grounds for retaining it under *Arthropyrenia.*

Symptoms of the disease

The syndrome is confined to the shell of the oyster. Both *Ostrea edulis* L. and *Crassostrea angulata* Lmk. have been found infected, but only *O. edulis* has been observed to be heavily attacked. *O. implexa* is a shell boring fungus which obtains nutrient from the organic matrix of the shell. The growth of the fungus within the shell does no harm to the living tissues until the mycelium reaches the inside of the shell. When it grows between the living mantle tissues of the oyster and the shell, it sets up an irritation of the living tissues. Especially in *O. edulis,* there is a normal response to any irritation of the mantle—this is the laying down of additional shell with a very much higher protein content—sometimes almost 100% conchiolin. This horny protein is an ideal nutrient for *O. implexa* which can then grow faster and the situation becomes self-perpetuating.

The visible symptoms in the shell progress from the formation of small white spots which mark the first penetration of the fungus (Fig. 9.9) through clouds of these spots (Fig. 9.10 and 9.12) and increasing conchiolin warts (Fig. 9.11-9.15) and finally extreme deformation of the shells (Figs. 9.15 and 9.16).

Ostracoblabe implexa has a straight mycelium 2 μm in diameter. At intervals (40 μm to 100 μm) the mycelium bears swellings (4 x 6 μm) termed by Alderman and Jones (1971) 'pro-chlamydospores' (Figs. 9.18, 9.20, 9.21). Despite quite extensive investigations, no fruiting structures have been found for this fungus. Electron microscope investigations of the pro-chlamydospores have shown that they contain a nucleus closely appressed to one of the walls (Fig. 9.23). Septa are formed only in senescent or dying mycelium (Fig. 9.19), and chlamydospores form from the pro-chlamydospores at low temperatures (5°C) Fig. 9.24. It is not possible to make any positive statement about the taxonomic position of this fungus at present but the fungus is placed in the phycomycetes because of its coenocytic mycelium.

In thin sections of shell, the mycelium is characteristically very straight with the pro-chlamydospores occurring at regular intervals. When growing in the conchiolin wart material it is more irregular, but still easily identifiable (Fig. 9.20). *O. implexa* can be grown in culture from diseased oyster shell quite easily. If pieces of conchiolin from diseased oysters are incubated in sterile seawater in the presence of penicillin and streptomycin (0.5 g/litre each), the fungus will grow out of the conchiolin slowly. The resultant weft of mycelium can be transferred into a dilute seawater peptone and yeast extract broth. Pieces of infected shell placed in a similar broth with added antibiotic will also normally yield viable isolates of *O. implexa* (Fig. 9.22). Cultures on agar slopes (peptone 1 g, yeast extract 1 g, seawater 1 litre and 12 g agar) have remained viable for five years, and when such stocks are inoculated into fresh media growth takes place from the chlamydospores.

The effect of shell disease on oyster populations has been extensively discussed (Korringa, 1951; Alderman and Jones, 1971 and Sprague, 1972). Its most severe effects are thought to have been in the early 1930s in Holland where very severe mortalities have been attributed to the disease. Korringa (1951 and personal communication) found that the cause of the outbreak was the increased use of old shell for settlement of the oyster larvae. This old shell harboured considerable reserves of the fungus and

9.9, 9.10

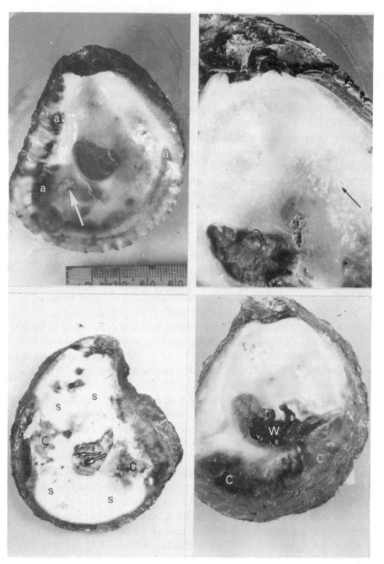

9.11, 9.12

Fig. 9.9 Early shell disease white spots (arrowed). The surrounding dark patches (a) are caused by algae penetrating the shell. **Fig. 9.10** Close-up of white spots. Many of the spots may be seen to have dark centres (arrowed). **Fig. 9.11** This oyster shows spot clouds (s). To the right and left of the adductor muscle the shell is being covered with a dark layer of thin conchiolin (C). In the adductor attachment areas are small round knobs of conchiolin (arrowed). **Fig. 9.12** This oyster has a large conchiolin wart (W) on the adductor muscle attachment, together with extensive conchiolin sheets (C) radiating to the margins of the valve.

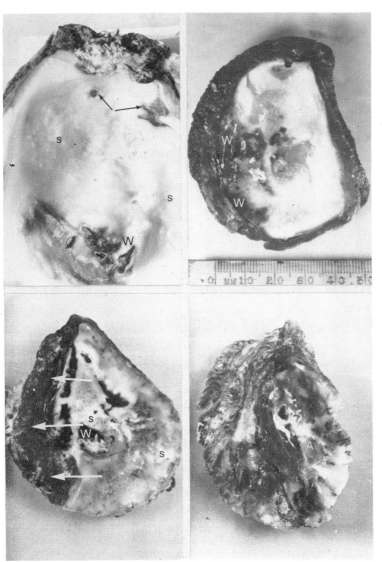

Fig. 9.13 The adductor muscle attachment of this oyster has been converted largely into a raised boss of conchiolin which has subsequently become partially covered with more calcified shell layers (W). The shell also shows a very well developed spot cloud(s) and small warts developing near the hinge *(maladie de la charnière)* (arrow). **Fig. 9.14** In this oyster, the development of the disease (W) has resulted in considerable distortion of one margin of the valve. **Fig. 9.15** Severe distortion and thickening of the shell margin *(maladie de la charnière)* occurred in this oyster as a result of strong fungal activity along the edges and hinge of the valve (arrows). The adductor is warted (W) but there are relatively few white spots in the interior of the valve(s). **Fig. 9.16** This valve represents an extreme example of shell distortion. The actual space available for the meats in this shell is very restricted and the adductor (A) is so diseased that the oyster could be opened with the fingers.

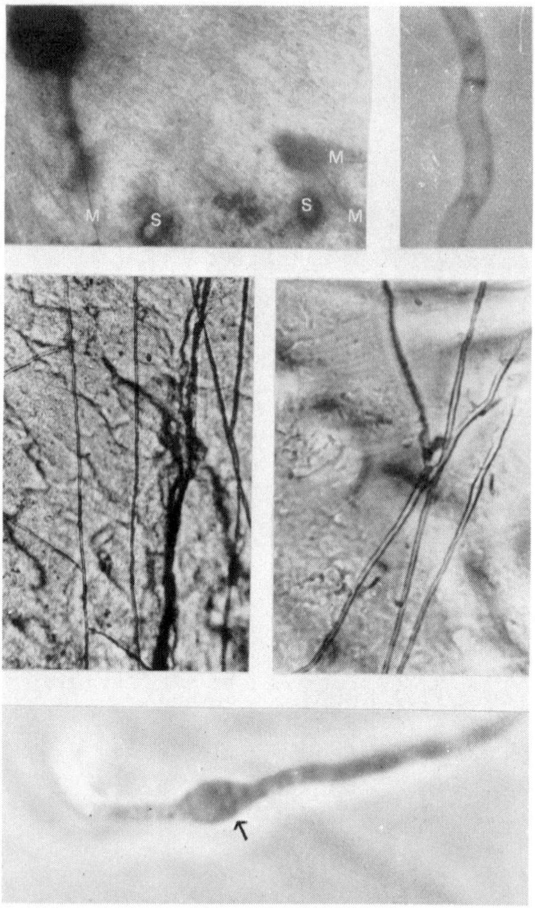

9.17, 9.19

9.18, 9.20

9.21

Fig. 9.17 Sections of diseased shell at the white spot stage. The dark patches are the white spots (S) from which fine mycelium (m) radiates (x 27). Fig. 9.18 Section of diseased oyster shell showing typical features of the mycelium within the shell. The mycelium is straight and one oblique branch is shown. The arrow indicates a chlamydospore-like structure. This oyster was infected artifically (x 66). Fig. 9.19 Decalcified preparation showing a short piece of dead mycelium with septum (x 1000). Fig. 9.20 Section of shell disease wart showing mycelium with a chlamydospore-like structure (x 333). Fig. 9.21 Decalcified preparation of diseased shell to show living mycelium with chlamydospore-like structure (arrowed) (x 800).

young oysters growing on these shells were infected very early, succumbing to the disease rapidly. Alderman and Jones (1971) have confirmed that the younger an oyster is the more susceptible it is to shell disease. The remedy exercised in Holland was the large scale removal of old shell from the oyster beds, the shell being disposed of in areas of shifting sand. This is a very expensive method of control only suitable where young animals are being attacked on productive beds. It is also possible to render young oysters immune to the attack of *O. implexa* for some time by dipping them in a mercuric salt solution. However, with the present state of opinion with regard to mercury in the environment, this is a method which requires critical examination.

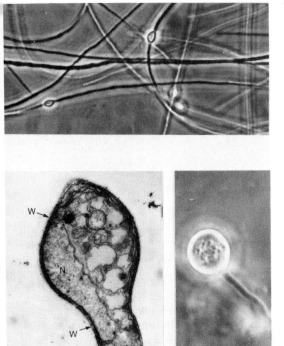

9.22

9.23, 9.24

Fig. 9.22 Pure cultures on yeast/peptone broth of the shell disease fungus *Ostracoblabe implexa* (x 270). **Fig. 9.23** Electron micrograph showing the ultrastructure of prochlamydospore. (N) nucleus, (W) cell wall (x 6666). **Fig. 9.24** Chlamydospore formed on mycelium held at 5°C for three weeks (x 600).

O. implexa is a very slow growing organism but the relative rate in culture increases rapidly above 20°C (Fig. 9.25), which corresponds well with Korringa's suggestion that infection of oysters is insignificant unless water temperatures exceed 20°C for two weeks. Similar results were reported from field experiments by Alderman and Jones (1971).

Lithopythium gangliiforme *Bornet et Flahault.* In the same paper in which Bornet and Flahault described *Ostracoblabe implexa (q.v.),* they also described *Lithopythium gangliiforme,* another shell inhabiting fungus.

The description is incomplete in that only a vegetative mycelium was reported. There is no evidence of any disease produced by this fungus which consists of a horizontal network of interlaced filaments 2.0 to 3.5 μm wide and sometimes profusely branched. The older mycelium seems to develop oval or spherical dilations which may be single or in groups of up to six, and septa were observed at the bases of branches and of the dilations. In a subsequent paper, Bornet (1891) suggested a similarity between *L. gangliiforme* mycelium and that of a marine lichen *Verrucaria calciseda* Bachmann, but was unable to show this conclusively.

Marine 'Lichen' complexes, and other fungal shell infestations. The confusion which has arisen over *Ostracoblabe implexa* and *Lithopythium gangliiforme* in relation to marine lichens of the genera *Arthropyrenia* and *Verrucaria* has already been mentioned.

233

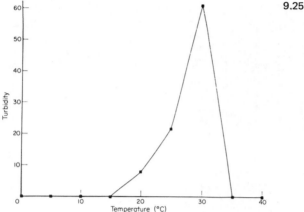

Fig. 9.25 Growth of *Ostracoblabe implexa* at different temperatures for four days, showing in particular the rapid increase in growth rate above 20° C. Medium: yeast extract-peptone seawater broth.

Numerous lichens of these and allied lichen complex, are recorded growing on calcified animal shells all over the world without causing any deleterious effects.

However, in some areas the invasion of barnacle tests and limpet shells by a fungus *Didymella conchae* Bonar (1936) is reported by Girant (1936) to cause such severe pitting and disfiguration of the test as to cause taxonomic confusion between the limpet species *Acmaea digitalis* Eschscholz and *A. persona* Eschscholz. This fungus is now regarded (Santesson, 1939) as synonymous with the mycobiont of *Arthropyrenia sublittoralis* (Leighton) which also includes *Epicymatia balani* Winter (Feldman, 1937). This latter has also been reduced to synonymy with Bonar's *Didymella* as *D. balani* (Winter) J. Feldman, by Feldman (1954), who in this case was probably referring to the mycobiont alone, ignoring the lichen-complex aspect.

There are numerous other earlier reports of fungi from marine animal shells—for example Carpenter (1845), Queckett (1952), Rose (1855), Lacaze-Duthiers (1874), Wedl (1859), Kolliker (1859, 1860), Stirrup (1872), Duncan (1876), and Topsent (1887 a, b). As Johnson and Sparrow (1961) indicate, reports of this age 'defy systematic treatment'. In 1937 Porter and Zebrowski published an account of 'lime loving' moulds from calcareous fragments of beach sands, and Johnson and Anderson (1962) examined similar shell fragments and found in a discarded *Anomia simplex* d'Orbigny shell a fungus assigned tentatively to *Edogone* sp., but there was no evidence of material damage to the host such as is found in oyster shell disease.

Fungi on Hydrozoan tubes   Kohlmeyer (1970) recently described a new Ascomycete growing on and in chitin of a hydrozoan which was itself growing on a stony coral (neither identifiable) from the S. Atlantic. The fungus *Abyssomyces hydrozoicus* Kohlmeyer produced ascomata attached to the hydrozoon tubes by vegetative hyphae. Since only fixed material was available, Kohlmeyer was uncertain whether the fungus was a saprophyte or a parasite, but believed that some parts of the hydrozoon at least were alive when they were infested by the fungus.

9.3.2   Fungal Infection of Exoskeletons

A form of fungal parasitism closely related in type with infestations of mollusc shells is the infection of Crustacean exoskeletons. There is, however, less information available on this subject, and possibly this reflects the greater difficulties involved in work on a population of more mobile animals.

Crustacean shell disease   Burn-like lesions on the exoskeletons of commercial crustaceans have been long known and are normally attributed to chitinoclastic bacteria (Rosen, 1970). Central European workers of freshwater crustaceans (Mann and Pieplow, 1938 and Schaperclaus, 1954) however, recorded the presence of fungi in the lesions.

On marine crustaceans, shell disease is characteristically in the form of dark brown to black stains and depressions in the exoskeletons (Fig. 9.28). Most investigators, as summarized by Rosen (1970), concluded that chitinoclastic bacteria were responsible, but three recorded that fungi were involved.

Figs. 9.26 to 9.28 Shell disease of the crawfish *Palinurus vulgaris Fabr.*

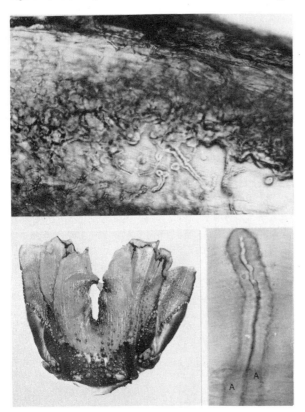

Fig. 9.26 Crude vertical section of infected crawfish exoskeleton showing depth and type of mycelial penetration (x 166). **Fig. 9.27** Close-up of fungal hypha—the area of altered exoskeleton (A) is probably due to enzymes from hypha (x 666). **Fig. 9.28** Crawfish telson with shell disease (↗).

Gordon (1966) reported that burn-like markings on crabs from tanks at Burnham on Crouch were due to fungal attack. However, no identification of the organism involved was made, and similar crabs from the same source have not shown fungal invasion.

In recent years a high incidence of burn spot-like disease has been found amongst Irish Sea Crawfish, *Palinurus vulgaris* Fabr. (Alderman, 1971). Material examined showed only bacteria, but a Cornish crawfish held in tanks at Portsmouth which developed very similar lesions was infected by a fungus. The disease took the form of brown irregular markings on the surface which spread laterally and began to show surface erosion. In a fairly short time the largest lesion on the tail fan had completely penetrated the non-calcified chitin (Fig. 9.28) and the living tissues were exposed, quickly developing a bacterial necrosis. This was treated with penicillin and streptomycin and the animal survived for two months, but then died suddenly. Post mortem examination showed that whilst the animal remained in superficially good condition, there were widespread foci of bacterial necrosis throughout its tissues. Examination of the brown spot lesions did not however, indicate a bacterial origin. Thin sections of exoskeleton showed clearly that a mycelial fungus had invaded (Figs. 9.26, 9.27) and that the brown colouration was the result of the digestive action of the fungus. No fruiting

Figs. 9.29 to 9.32 Gill and hepatopancreas of *Carcinus maenas* invaded by the fungus *Periconia proli.*

9.29

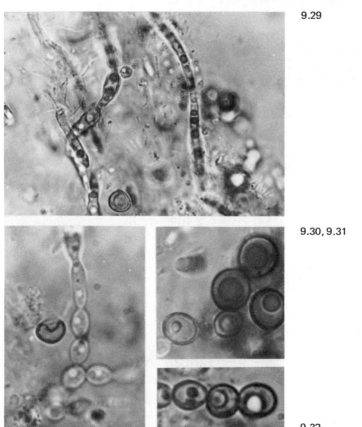

9.30, 9.31

9.32

Fig. 9.29 Fungus Mycelium in hepatopancreas (x 333). Figs. 9.30 to 9.32 Aleurospores of *P. prolifica* (x 666).

bodies were to be found, and since the animal died suddenly, only preserved material was available and no cultures were made. It was thus not possible to compare them with Sordi's (1958) *Ramularia brachialis* and *Didymaria palinum* from the gills of the same species.

More recently, some crabs (*Carcinus maenas* L.) from the Dorset coast have been found with a different type of infestation. The syndrome consisted of 'burn-spots' on the surface of the exoskeleton and scattered hard black nodules about 4 mm in diameter in the hepatopancreas. Much of the gills and nearby hepatopancreatic tissue of one specimen was found to be infested by a mycelium which by the nature of the conidia and aleurospores produced, has been tentatively identified as *Periconia prolifica* Anastasiou (Figs. 9.29 to 9.32). This is the first identification of this organism on animal substrate. Since the history of the specimen between fishing and fixation is known to have included a period of refrigeration, the possibility that the fungus infection is a secondary one must be recognized.

Whilst it is probably unrelated to the erosive burn spot disease, the mottling or leopard lobster disease of *Homarus americanus* (Milne Edwards) is also thought to be of fungal origin. Herrick (1895, 1911) figured a section of lobster with disease in which there were numerous small spherical bodies lying under the exoskeleton. Sindermann (1970) records that diseased animals are 'characterised by yellowish splotches on an otherwise dark green exoskeleton' with 'areas of necrosis in underlying tissues' and 'numerous subspherical heavy walled bodies 30-60 μm in diameter'. Sindermann's tentative conclusion is that a chytrid-like fungus might be involved, but no isolations have yet been successful.

9.4   Diseases of Invertebrate Eggs and Larval Forms

There are a relatively large number of fungi known to infect the eggs and larval forms of marine invertebrates. The original descriptive work in this field was that of Daphne Atkins on infections of *Pinnotheres,* which is not itself a commercially valuable organism, although it is significant in its effects on host molluscs. The importance of the larval parasites in the future lies in the field of aquaculture. Rearing of shellfish under artificial conditions is already a commercial proposition and under these 'vitro' conditions larval diseases become important. The crowded rearing tanks are ideal sites for mass infestation with various parasites and facultitative parasites, which may be unimportant in the wild, and losses could be severe. It must, however, be noted that the only documented case so far is that of *Sirolpidium zoophthorum* Vishniac (Vishniac, 1955).

9.4.1   Lagenidiales

Three members of the Lagenidiales have been found as parasites of marine animals: *Lagenidium chthamalophilum, Lagenidium callinectes* and *Sirolpidium zoophthorum.*

Lagenidium callinectes *Couch*   This fungus was first recognized by Newcome in 1941 (Sandoz, Rogers and Newcome, 1944), and was formally described by Couch (1942). Rogers-Talbert (1948) carried out an ecological investigation on its effects on *Callinectes sapidus* Rathbun, whilst Johnson and Bonner (1966) found it on the ova of the barnacle *Cheloniba patula* Rathbun. Fuller *et al.* (1964) successfully isolated the fungus from algal surfaces, whilst Bland and Amerson (1973) isolated it from blue crab eggs.

The description (modified after Couch) is as follows: a branching mycelial fungus developing within the egg or young larva of the crab with hyphae 5-12 μm in diameter which are sparingly septate (Figs. 9.33, 9.36). The zoospores are formed in a gelatinou protoplasmic mass in a vesicle which is up to 100 μm in diameter lying at the end of a discharge tube which projects through the host wall. Zoospores are differentiated within the vesicle and are active within it, escaping by the rupture of the vesicle. Bland and Amerson (1973) were able to follow the development of zoosporangia in pure culture. They found that conversion of the thallus from vegetative mycelium to asexual reproduction could be induced by depletion of nutrients. If a thallus was transferred to seawater from nutrient media, 12 hours would elapse before the first zoospores were released, and after 48 hours nearly all the vegetative mycelium would have been converted. Cytoplasm accumulates in 'units' in extramatrical hyphae (120–140 x 14–23 μm) which have hyaline tips (Fig. 9.37). This tip expands rapidly as the cytoplasm flows in, in units, each of which is attached to its fellows by a fine cytoplasmic thread (Fig. 9.38). The tip is thus formed into a gelatinous vesicle in which the units of cytoplasm fuse and round up. This expansion occupies between 5 and 30 minutes and the vesicle (in Bland and Amerson's isolates) is about 60 μm in diameter (Figs. 9.39 to 9.50). Flagella may differentiate before cytoplasmic units reach the vesicle, or not until cleavage begins. The last cytoplasmic units may not enter until after cleavage has begun, and uncleaved remnants may remain. The protoplasmic thread connecting the units of cytoplasm is broken when the last unit enters the vesicle. Cleavage takes about 7 minutes and the zoospores escape three min-utes later by rupture of the distal end of the vesicle. The zoospores are pyriform, 9 x 12 μm with two laterally attached flagella, the anterior is a tinsel, and the pos-terior a whiplash (Fig. 9.34). Bland and Amerson report a positive attraction of the zoospores towards crab eggs. Their isolates differed from the original description of Couch in having abundant extramatrical hyphae and long discharge tubes, but they regard these as cultural and nutritional variations.

Rogers-Talbert (1948) found that whilst there was a constant level of infection of eggs of *C. sapidus* in Chesapeake Bay, infection of the egg mass was rarely other than peripheral without apparent effect on the remaining eggs. However, under laboratory conditions, the spread of the fungus and its effect was more pronounced. This must, therefore, be of some significance to any attempted intensive artificial culture. Rogers-Talbert found *L. callinectes* on crabs at salinities between 5 and 30°/oo whilst Johnson (1970) records it from a crab found in a freshwater pond.

Bland (personal communication) finds the fungus to be common in North Caro-lina waters. Between 1 April and 1 June 1972 he found 95% of ovigerous crabs to be infected, the rate declining thereafter, until by mid-July no infected crabs were found.

Lagenidium chthamalophilum *Johnson*   Johnson (1958, 1960) found this organism attacking eggs and embryos of the barnacle *Chthamalus fragilis* Darwin, eggs of the associated barnacle *Balanus amphitrite* Darwin not being attacked under natural conditions.

The description (after Johnson, 1958) is as follows: The hyphae are stout, 10-18 μm in diameter, non-septate and branched with numerous small vacuoles giving a foamy appearance. The sporangia normally are formed within the host by segmentation of the vegetative hyphae, and have a pre-formed vesicle at the end of a stout discharge tube. Within this laterally biflagellate zoospores (8–10 x 7–8 μm) are cleaved. Dis-charge is by the deliquescence of the vesicle wall. Oögonia, when observed, were 19-47 μm in diameter formed on intramatrical hyphae and contained one, rarely two, oospores 18-25 μm in diameter. Antheridia have not been observed.

The zoospores swim for 10 to 15 minutes and were recorded settling on and attacking ova without rounding up, and a foot-like hyphal rudiment is rapidly formed which penetrates the ovum wall. Johnson (1958) was unable to determine whether the embyro itself was attacked. The fungus grows well on seawater agar with glucose 1.1% and yeast extract 0.05%. Johnson (1960) was also able to examine the influence of salinity and temperature on infection ability and found the optimum to be 0-22°C, and a salinity of 34%.

Balanus amiphitrite could not be infected under normal conditions, but prior freezing or 15°C and salinities of 56% would permit infection. As Johnson (1960) states, these phenomena remain to be explained.

Sirolpidium zoophthorum *Vishniac*   In 1954, Davis *et al.* reported the presence of a fungus infesting clam and oyster larvae (*Venus* and *Crassostrea*) grown under artificial conditions. Subsequently Vishniac (1955) isolated the organism (using antibiotics) and described it as a new species, *Sirolpidium zoophthorum.*

On the settlement of zoospores, the cysts enlarge slowly to 7-10 μm diameter, then elongate in the form of a tube of the same dimension. A conspicuous vacuole is characteristic of thalli over 40 μm long. Further elongation is accompanied by septation which forms individual cells 42-98 μm long, and by branching. By the third or fourth day on a dry agar surface, the thallus forms a dense structure with swollen terminal cells. Zoosporulation was induced by Vishniac by placing a drop of seawater on such a thallus when one or more of the terminal cells would produce a discharge tube 5 μm wide and up to 140 μm long through which the zoospores swim. The zoospores are biflagellate, heterokont, 2 x 5 μm in size and monoplanetic.

Older thalli which have not sporulated may develop long (over 600 μm) tapering, branching mycelial extensions from some cells which Vishniac refers to as 'rhizoidal extensions'. The possession of such extensions and the fact that although all cells may produce zoospores, not all actually *do* so, makes it difficult to regard *S. zoophthorum* as truly holocarpic. Brown coloured 'resistant' cells 40-90 μm in diameter and also thick-walled 'gemmae' are sometimes formed. On dry plates thalli may be formed which are olpidioid, spherical, about 30 μm in diameter. Cell contents may also 'pull away' from the original wall and form new spherical cells. It is this character in particular which led Vishniac to regard the parasite as a species of *Sirolpidium.*

Vishniac obtained good growth of *S. zoophthorum* when 1.0 to 3.5% NaCl was present in the growth medium. The fungus would not grow without NaCl, but seemed unaffected by the absence of KCl. Glucose and soluble starch appeared to be the most available carbon sources and amino acid requirements were apparently complex. There is a distinct requirement for thiamine hydrochloride.

The fungus was found to be responsible for significant mortalities of bivalve larvae under laboratory conditions, but no work has been carried out to quantify these findings or to establish the host range.

9.4.2   Saprolegniales Saprolegniaceae

Leptolegnia marina *Atkins*   During the course of many years work on *Pinnotheres pisum* L. in *Mytilus edulis* L., Atkins found a number of parasitic marine fungi. *Leptolegnia marina* was first found in 1929, but without any sexual stages was not fully identified. Subsequent re-examination of original material and the discovery of more infected crabs enabled Atkins to identify the fungus fully.

Figs. 9.33 to 9.37 and 9.39 to 9.50 Stages in the life history of *Lagenidium callinectes,* reproduced from *Mycologia* by permission of the authors and editors.

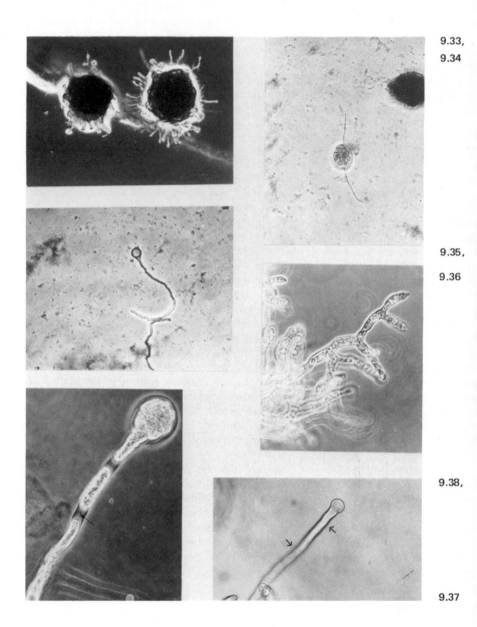

9.33,
9.34

9.35,
9.36

9.38,

9.37

Fig. 9.33 *L. callinectes* growing out on to agar from eggs of *Pinnotheres* (x 25). **Fig. 9.34** Zoospore of *L. callinectes* (x 500). **Fig. 9.35** Spore germinating on agar surface (x 500). **Fig. 9.36** Vegetative hyphae growing in seawater (x 1250). **Fig. 9.37** Gelatinizing tip (arrowhead) of extramatrical hypha (x 875). **Fig. 9.38** Cytoplasmic discharge into expanding hyphal tip (x 875). Note thread connecting cytoplasmic units (arrowheads).

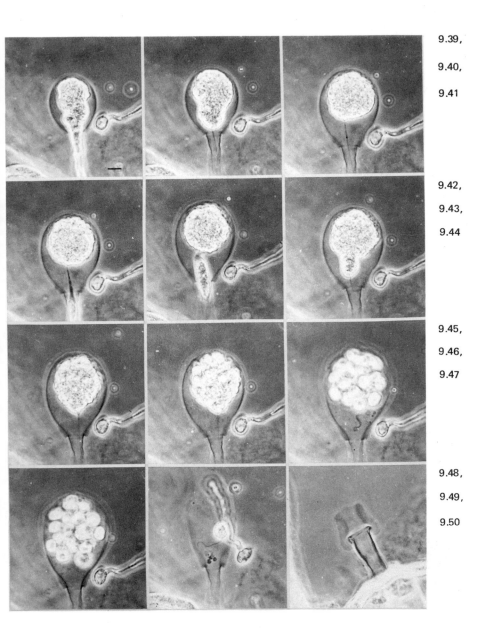

9.39,
9.40,
9.41

9.42,
9.43,
9.44

9.45,
9.46,
9.47

9.48,
9.49,
9.50

Figs. 9.39 to 9.44 Cytoplasmic discharge. **Figs. 9.45 to 9.48** Sporogenesis. **Fig. 9.49** Spore discharge. **Fig. 9.50** Vesicle collapsed around hyphal tip.

Leptolegnia marina has been found to be parasitic not only on the body, eggs and embryos of *Pinnotheres pisum* L., but also on the body of *P. pinnotheres* L., and from two lamellibranchs, *Barnea candida* L. and *Cardium echinatum* L. *L. marina* is recorded from crabs from Devon and Cornwall and from Conway, North Wales.

The mycelium is freely branched and mainly intramatrical, 7.5-20 μm (−40) in diameter (Figs. 9.51 to 9.53). Filamentous, sometimes proliferous sporangia are formed within the host from unchanged hyphae. There are several rows of pyriform zoospores, 8-14 μm in size escaping through short side branches formed on the sporangium. The zoospores are biflagellate and probably diphasic, the primary zoospores swimming for up to 1 hour, encysted spores being 6-11 μm. Oogonia are formed in host tissues on short side branches or diverticula of the hyphae and are spherical, pyriform or oval, thin walled, smooth, 17-30 μm (−37 μm) with a slight beak where the hypogynous antheridium attaches. The single oospores completely fill the oogonia.

Figs. 9.51 to 9.53 *Leptolegnia marina* Atkins (type material) in *Pinnotheres.*

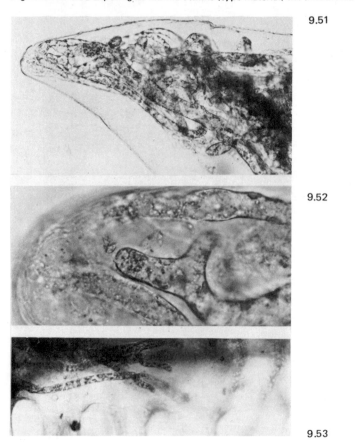

9.51

9.52

9.53

Fig. 9.51 Mycelium in gill leaflet (x 100). **Fig. 9.52** Close-up of hyphal tip (x 400). **Fig. 9.53** Mycelium ramifying along base of gill (x 100).

External symptoms of the attack of *Leptolegnia marina* usually consist of the development of opaque white patches on the chitin of body and abdomen (especially the gill chambers), or by opaqueness of the gills. These white patches are the fungal mycelium. Attack is normally along the roof of the gill chamber from where the gills and mouth parts may be invaded as well as the body of the crab. Sexual stages were found in only one of more than 1000 diseased specimens. Crabs infected with *L. marina* were found at all periods of the year, but that producing oospores was taken in August. Information on the true pathogenicity of *L. marina* is lacking, but under laboratory conditions the length of time before death has varied from eight to 57 days (exceptionally, 78 days). It seems certain that a proportion of, if not all, the crabs were infected under natural conditions.

Johnson and Sparrow (1961) are doubtful whether this organism is correctly placed in *Leptolegnia*. The development of more than one row of zoospores per sporangium is uncharacteristic, and the branched sporangia tend to indicate relationships to *Leptolegniella*. Indeed Dick (1971) includes *Leptolegnia marina* in *Leptolegniella*. However, for the purposes of this non-taxonomic review it seems advisable to follow Johnson and Sparrow and retain Atkins species in *Leptolegnia* until all the species, marine and freshwater alike are studied comparatively.

Leptolegnia baltica *Höhnk et Vallin*   Vallin (1951) reported the occurrence of mass mortalities of the copepod *Eurytermora hirudenoides* (Nordquist). The fungal hyphae were branched, both intra- and extramatrical and were between 5.0 and 20 μm wide. The sporangia were both terminal and intercalary, and formed by conversion of the mycelium. The sporangia produced a single row of laterally biflagellate, oval to elongate planonts (9–) 11 (–16) μm in diameter. Some of these sporangia were similar to those of *Leptolegnia* de Bary, and others of those of *Leptolegniella* Huneycutt. The terminal oogonia were found on small side branches with lateral diclinous antheridia. Like *L. marina* Atkins, this organism shows some features intermediate between *Leptolegnia* and *Leptolegniella*.

9.4.3 Saprolegniales Haliphthoraceae

The Haliphthoraceae was erected by Vishniac (1958) to contain a new filamentous holocarpic genus together with *Atkinsiella dubia* (Atkins) Vishniac, a redescription of *Plectospira dubia* Atkins. The inadequately described *Synchaetophagus balticus* may also belong here, but since Apstein (1911) did not describe flagellation of the zoospores it remains a *nomen dubium*. The description of the Haliphthoraceae, after Vishniac is as follows: They are filamentous, branching holocarpic fungi with large mono or diplanetic zoospores which are produced within the thallus. There is no known mode of sexual reproduction.

Haliphthoros milfordensis *Vishniac*   Vishniac (1958) found this fungus infecting the eggs of the oyster drill *Urosalpinx cinerea* Say, and was able to isolate it into pure culture.

The vegetative growth is in the form of an extensive branched filamentous mycelium 10-13 (–25) μm wide with cytoplasm which is at first granular and later vacuolate. After some time (5 to 7 days at 25°C) thick-walled gemmae with dense, non-vacuolate protoplasm are formed in the mycelium. Sexual reproduction was not observed by Vishniac but zoosporulation could be induced by placing small pieces of stock culture in sterile seawater which was changed every two or three days. Zoospore formation, when it occurred, was at seven days and was not influenced

by temperature but would occur only at salinities above 60% seawater. Zoosporulation took place by the transformation of the entire contents of the thallus into
zoospores which were amoeboid, laterally biflagellate and reniform and about 9 μm
long. Single exit tubes about 400 μm long and about 7 μm wide were formed through
which the zoospores swam. The swarming period may exceed 48 hours before the
zoospores encyst. Germination takes place by means of a thin hair-like filament
which develops to normal hyphal width on encountering a suitable food source.

Vishniac did not describe the effect of *Haliphthoros milfordensis* on the eggs of
Urosalpinx, but Atkins managed to infect eggs of *Pinnotheres* with the isolate. In
some nutritional studies, Vishniac showed that the fungus was obligately marine,
neither gemmae nor zoospores being formed in the absence of NaCl. Growth at 0.5%
and 1.0% NaCl was grossly abnormal. KCl was also necessary for gemma production
and normal vegetative growth. Equimolar concentrations of glucose and sodium
glutamate were needed as a carbon source for good growth.

Figs. 9.54 to 9.58 Infected eggs of *Pinnotheres* with *Atkinsiella dubia* (Atkins) Vishniac (type
material).

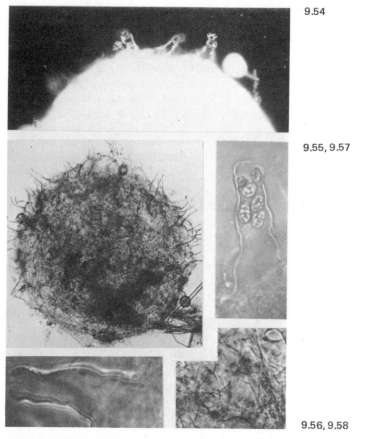

9.54

9.55, 9.57

9.56, 9.58

Figs. 9.54 to 9.57 Discharge tubes on surface of infected egg. **Fig. 9.54** Dark field (x 132).
Fig. 9.55 Bright field (x 132). **Fig. 9.56** Phase contrast (x 660). **Fig. 9.57** Showing encysted
zoospores (x 666). **Fig. 9.58** Mycelium within infected egg (x 666).

244

Atkinsiella dubia *(Atkins) Vishniac*   This fungus was originally discovered by Atkins parasitizing eggs of *Pinnotheres pisum* and *Gonoplax* sp., and was artificially induced to attack developing eggs of *Trypton* sp., *Crangon vulgaris* L. *Palemon serratus* (Pennant), *Macropodia* sp. and *Portunus depurator* L.

The mycelium is stout, up to 50 μm wide (Figs. 9.55, 9.58), its growth soon becoming irregular, with inflated bulbous branches 100 μm wide acting as sporangia, and eventually the whole of the thallus becomes used up in spore formation. Discharge tubes (normally one or two) 50-400 μm long and 10-30 μm wide develop on the sporangia, and pyriform flagellated zoospores are formed within the sporangia and efferent hyphae and move sluggishly within before encysting as spherical 7-8 μm cysts (Fig. 9.57). The zoospores are diphasic and those of the second swimming stage normally escape down the discharge tubes, most of which by this time, have developed flaired open ends (Figs. 9.54, 9.56).

Thin walled gemmae-like bodies 100 μm in diameter are recorded with dense finely granular contents, but sexual reproduction was not observed. The fungus was originally placed by Atkins in *Plectospira* Dreschler, but with the discovery of *Haliphthoros milfordensis* a new genus, *Atkinsiella,* was erected by Vishniac in the new family Haliphthoraceae.

Fig. 9.59 to 9.60 *Pythium thallassium* (type material) in eggs of *Pinnotheres.*

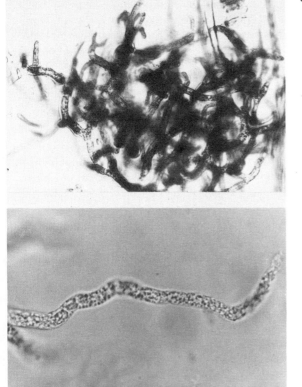

9.59

9.60

Fig. 9.59 Mycelial mass within egg (x 167). **Fig. 9.60** Young hyphal tip (x 666).

245

More recently Aronson and Fuller (1969) studied the structure of the cell wall of *Atkinsiella dubia*. They found that the cell wall consisted of about 80% polysaccharide (mainly glucan) and 14% protein and was not dissimilar to the walls of other Oömycetes. Electron microscopy of wall specimens showed microfibrillar and amorphous regions.

9.4.4   *Peronosparales Pythiaceae*

Pythium thalassium *Atkins*   *P. thalassium* was detected by Atkins (1955 a, b) infecting the eggs of *Pinnotheres pisum*. The mycelium is mostly intramatrical with the intramatrical hyphae being much branched, 5-20 μm in diameter (Figs. 9.59 and 9.60). The frequently proliferous sporangia are filamentous, formed from direct conversion of the vegetative hyphae. The zoospores are laterally biflagellate, 15 μm long, cleaved in an evanescent vesicle. Spherical or pyriform asexual resting bodies 25-50 μm in diameter which germinate by hyphae are also recorded.

Atkins found the fungus on eggs of *P. pisum* and was able to infect further eggs by laboratory transmission. Artificial infection of *Crangon vulgaris, Leander serratus, Portunus depurator* and *Macropodia* sp. was also achieved. Despite a number of attempts to induce sexual reproduction, this was not observed. Johnson (1970) regards the taxonomic status of the fungus as being in doubt. The only other well known marine *Pythium* is *P. marinum* Sparrow, from which it differs in habit and mode of branching, greater number and size of zoospores and growth on animal substrate. Atkins was unable to isolate *P. thalassium* in pure culture owing to associated bacteria, so that the significance of these three characters was not tested. As Johnson and Sparrow (1961) suggest, other aspects of Atkins description may also have been as a result of poor nutrient conditions, but examination of type material does not indicate that this was the case.

9.5   Diseases of Soft Tissues of Adult Invertebrates

The only well known fungal diseases which fall into this category are those belonging to the *Labyrinthomyxa* or *Dermocystidium* group of diseases. Also included is the wasting disease of sponges and the infection of Ascidian 'kidney', neither of which have been properly investigated.

9.5.1   Labyrinthomyxa *and allied organisms*

In *Labyrinthomyxa marina* (Mackin, Owen et Collier) Mackin et Ray we have the only well known example of what seems to be a widespread group of marine organisms generally thought to have fungal associations. There is great need of further work on this group to establish their true nature and relationships since the present state of the literature is highly confused. As yet only the one species *L. marina* is at all well defined and this is considered first.

Labyrinthomyxa marina   Despite the fact that the disease which it causes is one of the best, if not the best, known marine disease, *Labyrinthomyxa marina* remains an outstanding problem in mycological terms. Neither its life cycle or its taxonomic status is as yet well understood. Although Johnson and Sparrow (1961) made an extensive review of the literature on this organism, so much work has been done in the last decade that a further extensive re-examination is valid.

In the spring of 1948 large scale mortalities of the American oyster *Crassostrea virginica* Gmelin on the Louisiana coast of the USA occurred. The causitive organism was identified by Mackin, Owen and Collier (1950) in the host; the organism was provisionally identified as *Dermocystidium marinum,* which was the first marine record of a member of *Dermocystidium* Perez (1908). Ray, (1952 b) developed a diagnostic technique which enabled large scale rapid tests for infection. The Ray technique consists of incubating excised pieces of oyster tissue (gill, mantle, heart and rectum) in fluid thioglycollate medium in the presence of penicillin and streptomycin at 25°C. After two days' incubation, the fungus where present becomes apparent in the form of large (up to 100 μm) spherical cells which stain blue-black with Lugol's iodine. The cause of this staining reaction has still not been finally identified and seems to be specific to *D. marinum* of oysters of the US Eastern and Gulf coasts. In 1966, Mackin and Ray redescribed *D. marinum* as *Labyrinthomyxa marina* as a result of investigations into its life history. However, no full description of this work has so far been published and the situation remains unsettled. Sindermann (1970) states 'the change in generic name does not seem justified on the basis of evidence presented'. Perkins, who has previously accepted, with reservations, *L. marina* in a number of publications, has in this book reverted to *Dermocystidium.* Nevertheless, for the rest of this section the organism will be referred to as *L. marina.*

Certain stages of *L. marina* in the host oyster tissue have been well established, and Mackin and Boswell (1956) constructed a developmental pattern based on their observations. Perkins (1969) and Perkins and Menzel (1966, 1967) in a detailed re-examination of the organism at the fine structure level presented a life cycle which was both more extensive and yet less complex. This is the life cycle presented below.

The most common and easily recognizable stage in oyster tissues sectioned and stained in haematoxylin-eosin is that known as the 'mature thallus' which is a spherical cell (3) 5-7 (10) μm in diameter with a large acentric vacuole giving the cell a 'signet ring'-like appearance (Figs. 9.61 to 9.64). Within the vacuole is usually one vacuoloplast which contains large amounts of electron dense material. From such mature thalli two types of development are possible. By fragmentation of the vacuole and increase in cytoplasmic mass followed by karyokinesis and synchronous cytokinesis to form 8, 16 or 32 celled sporangia (Figs. 9.61 and 9.62). These are released by lysis of the host cell, in the form of individual aplanospores and spread the infection within the host.

The second type of development possible for the mature thallus stage is hypnospore formation. This has been observed to occur in *L. marina* in *C. virginica* only rarely under natural conditions (Perkins, 1969), although Valuilis and Mackin (1969) have frequently observed natural hypnospore formation in a related *Labyrinthomyxa* in the clam *Macoma balthica* L. The hypnospore or prezoosporangium can be difficult to distinguish from the mature thallus, but generally has a larger vacuole, lacks the vacuoloplast and is markedly larger (15-100 μm) (Fig. 9.65). It is this stage which develops in thioglycollate in the Ray test for *L. marina,* where the great majority of mature thalli develop into hypnospores. The term hypnospore was originally coined for this stage because it was thought to be an overwintering stage. Perkins (1966), showed that hypnospores die in a week at 10°C. These cells where they do occur naturally are found only in dead or dying oysters and it seems that some product of tissue lysis is necessary to initiate their formation.

Perkins and Menzel (1966) were able to induce zoosporulation in hypnospores of *L. marina.* The hypnospores were produced by incubation in thioglycollate, the remaining oyster tissues digested away in 0.25% trypsin (6-8 hours) in artificial seawater and

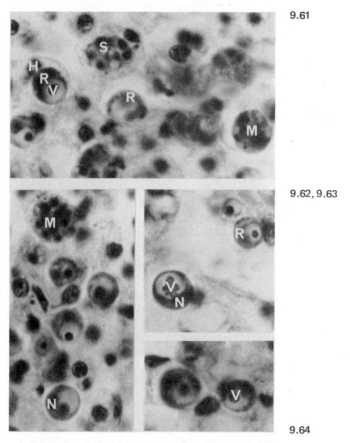

9.61

9.62, 9.63

9.64

Figs. 9.61 to 9.64 Stages of *Labyrinthomyxa marina* (Mackin, Owen et Collier) Mackin et Ray in the tissues of *Crassostrea angulata* Gmelin. (Haematoxylin-eosin) (all x 2000). R: signet ring stages; V: vacuoloplast; H: host cell nuclei; N: *Labyrinthomyxa* nucleus; M: multinucleate plasmodium; S: multicellular 'sori'.

removed by repeated filtrations, re-suspensions and centrifugations. The resultant suspension in seawater consisted of hypnospores—spherical cells about 100 μm in diameter with a large vacuole occupying $^4/_5$ ths of the cell. The cell wall is thick and refringent, and on one side the cytoplasm 'bulges' into the vacuole indicating the location of the nucleus which, prior to the first cleavage, is greatly enlarged. An area of hyaline cytoplasm becomes apparent next to the cell wall early in development, this enlarges, the wall beneath ruptures, and the hyaline structure is extruded, plugging the pore formed by the wall rupture (Fig. 9.66). Before cleavage the protoplast contracts and forces most of the vacuolar fluid into the area between it and cell wall. This resultant dense protoplast then cleaves by means of a very regular bipartition which remains nearly synchronous for some time (Fig. 9.67). The cleavage products become motile, at first slowly, then more rapidly over two days (Fig. 9.68) until the plug in the pore of the cell wall ruptures and the zoospores swim out (Fig. 9.69). The zoospores are biflagellate with laterally attached anterior tinsel flagellum (9-16 μm long) and posterior whiplash (6-10 μm) (Fig. 11.5f). The tinsel flagellum has mastigonemes on one side only and swims with a jerking motion by moving the an-

Figs. 9.65 to 9.69 Stages of sporogenesis in *L. marina.*

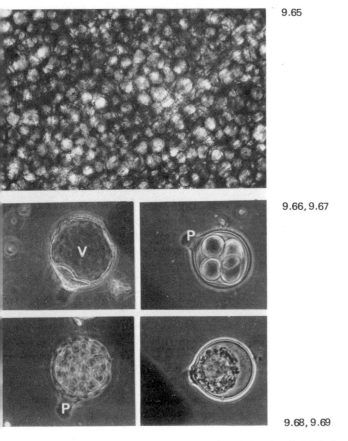

9.65

9.66, 9.67

9.68, 9.69

Fig. 9.65 Enlarged hypnospores after thioglycollate incubation (x 167). **Fig. 9.66** Sporangial pore initiation (x 333). **Fig. 9.67** Four celled stage (x 333). **Fig. 9.68** Zoospores swimming within sporangium (x 333). **Fig. 9.69** Empty sporangium (x 333). V-vacuole. P-plug.

terior flagellum in a 'rowing'-like manner. Perkins and Menzel (1966) produced infections in oysters with these zoospores, but were unable to continue the cycle in vitro; an obligately parasitic stage is apparently an essential part of the life cycle. It seems probable that the planonts are zoospores rather than isogametes.

The preceding description of *L. marina* has been based entirely on the work of Perkins (1969) and Perkins and Menzel, (1966, 1967). Valuilis and Mackin have observed zoospore production in an unidentified species of *Labyrinthomyxa* without the necessity for thioglycollate culture. Mackin and Ray (1966) in their redescription of the genus described very briefly plasmodial stages with labyrinthuloid motile cells in 'mucoid tracks'. The problems arising from this description are considered in the next section.

The pathological effects of *L. marina* were extensively studied in the years following its discovery, and the most detailed summary is that of Mackin (1962). Diseased oysters may often be recognized by their shrunken meats. In light infections parasite cells are generally to be found in the gut epithelium. Heavy infections which cause gross tissue destruction lead to invasion of all tissues: leydig tissues, gut, arterial walls, heart and muscle are all susceptible. The destruction appears to be brought about by the lysis of the parasitized cells rather than by production of any exotoxin. The normal tissue damage reactions of oyster occur as established by Pauley and Sparks (1965).

There have also been very many publications concerned with the epizootiology of *L. marina*. These works all depend on the use of the Ray technique for estimation of degree of infection. Ray (1966 a, b) re-examined his technique (Ray, 1952 a, b) because of reports received of negative results for *L. marina* in the Gulf of Mexico area. He established that these negative results were due to omission of dextrose from the medium. As a result of this re-examination he recommended the use of 200 units mycostatin and 200 μg of chloromycetin per millilitre of fluid thioglycollate medium with dextrose in place of the penicillin streptomycin, and incubating in the dark at room temperature for a week. Tissues are then flooded with Lugol's iodine and examined under a low power objective.

The most recent study of the effect of *L. marina* on oysters is that of Quick and Mackin (1971) who showed that *L. marina* still had continuous distribution along the Florida coastline. Previous work (Andrews 1955, 1965; Mackin, 1951, 1956, 1962, Sindermann, 1970, Perkins; 1966) had shown the presence of infected *C. virginica* from Connecticut southwards to the Gulf of Mexico. Rosenfield (1969) also records Ray test positive cultures from the Far East (unspecified).

Such work on incidence of disease has shown that *L. marina* is basically a summer disease reaching its maximum in August-September (Mackin, 1962; Quick and Mackin, 1971) and generally requiring 25°C for high infection rates to develop (Andrews and Hewatt, 1957). Salinity has been shown to be important and infection is depressed in low salinity waters (Ray, Mackin and Boswell, 1953; Mackin, 1956) or completely absent (Andrews and Hewatt, 1957). Johnson and Sparrow (1961) give a good review of this work.

Allied organisms   There are reports of *Labyrinthomyxa marina*-like organisms (the Aransas Bay organism) with a labyrinthuloid gliding stage which seem to confirm the reports of Mackin and Ray (1966), but until full details are published it is not possible to determine what significance should be placed upon these reports. Mackin and Ray (1966) appear to believe that *Schizochytrium* Goldstein is wrongly placed in the Thraustochytriaceae but Perkins (1972 and Chapter 11) has shown that the Thraustochytriaceae and Labyrinthulales are probably very closely linked. The presence of an apparently unique organelle in both, the sagenogenetosome and many other ultrastructural similarities make this group of organisms (including *Schizochytrium*) much more closely related to each other than they are to *L. marina*. The structure of the zoospore and vegetative stages of *L. marina* is that of a quite distinct organism and, until extensive investigations, particularly into fine structure, are made on the stages reported by Mackin and Ray (1966) and Schlict (1969), the possibility that more than one organism is involved cannot be excluded.

Quick (1972) described provisionally a new species of *'Thraustochytrium'* parasitic in *C. virginica*. Investigations in Europe into various oyster diseases have frequently led to the isolation of various *Thraustochytrium*-like fungi, but these have never been regarded as parasitic. Quick's organism, therefore, adds yet another to the complex of forms around *Thraustochytrium*, *Labyrinthula* and *Labyrinthomyxa* which require further investigation.

The fungus described provisionally by Goldstein and Moriber (1966) as *Dermo-*

cystidium sp. has recently been transferred to a newly erected taxon, *Hyalochlorella,* by Poyton (1970). This organism presents morphological similarities to some stages of *L. marina,* but its fine structure is sufficiently different to allow its exclusion from close relationship. Whether Poyton is correct in allying it to *Chlorella* remains to be seen.

Investigations by Franc and Arvy (1969, 1970) and Comps (1969) into a disease of Portuguese oysters, *Crassostrea angulata,* in France led to their describing a presumed pathogen *Thanatostrea polymorpha* Franc et Arvy. Franc and Arvy felt that this organism might be allied to either *Labyrinthula* or *Labyrinthomyxa marina,* but considerably more information is needed on this organism before it can be regarded as established.

We have then, a definite group of organisms similar to *Labyrinthomyxa marina* which make up a coherent group, but which lack definite details of certain aspects of their life cycle. These details are required to be established before any really worthwhile statements about their taxonomic position can be made. Many of the other organisms which have been suggested by their authors as being related to the main *Labyrinthomyxa* group must be regarded for the present as of doubtful status. Until sufficient information becomes available it would seem wisest to consider them separately from *Labyrinthomyxa marina.*

9.5.2   Microcell disease

Microcell disease or Denman Island disease is another possible fungal disease whose true nature is uncertain. It has been observed in *Crassostrea gigas* from British Columbia, in hatchery *Ostrea edulis* in Connecticut and in European oysters planted in California. An organism resembling some stages of 'slime moulds' (labyrinthulids?) has been isolated, but viruses have also been suggested (Rosenfield, 1969).

9.5.3   Mycelial disease

This is an obscure disease reported by Mackin (1962) in *Crassostrea virginica* in Texas and Louisiana. A 'mycelium' was found on mantle, palps and gills and penetrating into the internal organs. This organism is possibly an Actinomycete rather than a fungus. Rosenfield (1969) also records a similar disease from Chesapeake Bay and says that oysters from Portugal (*Crassostrea angulata*), examined at the Bureau of Commercial Fisheries Laboratory, Oxford, Maryland, had similar 'mycelial' structures (see *Thanatostrea polymorpha* above).

'Thraustochytrium inglei'   Quick (1972) in a paper presented to the Society for Invertebrate Pathology meeting, Minneapolis, 1972, described a species of *Thraustochytrium, T. inglei,* which was parasitic on *Crassostrea virginica* in Florida waters. From the brief description given in the abstract, this seems to present some similarities to the organism T-20 described by Perkins (1972) also from oysters, but without any imputation of parasitism. Species of *Thraustochytrium* and *Schizochytrium* may readily be isolated from oyster tissues on appropriate media, but they are normally regarded as saprobes but controlled experimental work is required to test their true role.

9.5.4   Nephromyces *Giard*

Johnson and Sparrow (1961) included this genus as an 'excluded, imperfectly known or doubtful taxon'. Four species have been described under the genus *Nephromyces*. Of these, one, *Nephromyces piscinus* Plehn (1916) is from the kidney of a freshwater carp, and it seems unlikely that Plehn intended to refer it to *Nephromyces* Giard.

Nephromyces Giard (1888) contains three marine species all from the 'kidney' of ascidians of the family Molgulidae. They are:

> *Nephromyces molgularum* Giard in *Molgula manhattensis* (De Kay)
> *Nephromyces sorokini* Giard in *Molgula complanata* Alder et Hancock
> *Nephromyces roscovitanus* Giard in *Molgula occulta* Kupffer.

The 'kidney' of Giard, or renal organ in the Molgulidae, is a closed sac in close contact with the pericardium which secretes a fluid and solid particles into its lumen to form a concretion of uric acid and urates that is stored until the death of the organism (Berrill, 1950). Within the renal organ, Lacaze-Duthiers (1874) noted the presence of 'filaments confervoides' associated with the concretions. It is apparently these elements which have been variously described as *Nephromyces* (Giard, 1888; Harant, 1931). The descriptions given by these authors have been discussed by Johnson and Sparrow (1961) who regarded the organism as an 'open question'. Berrill (1950) who presents an exhaustive survey of tunicates, makes no mention of the presence of possible fungal material in Molgulid renal organs, and Millar (1971) in a similar survey also ignores *Nephromyces*. The illustrations given by Harant (1931) do not give confidence in the existence of *Nephromyces* nor do they agree with the illustrations of Lacaze-Duthiers (1874). *Nephromyces* Giard must be regarded as extremely doubtful unless new evidence becomes available.

9.5.5 Spongiophaga

The genus *Spongiophaga* was erected by Carter (1878) to describe filaments observed in sponges *(Hircinia)*. Similar filaments were observed by others as described in Johnson and Sparrow (1961).

In late 1938 and in 1939 a mass mortality of adult commercial sponges (*Spongia* and *Hippospongia*) took place on the coasts of the West Indies. From 60 to 90% of the population died. Galtsoff (1942) investigated the mortality and reported the presence of masses of fine aseptate hyphae growing on the dead and dying sponges. No isolations were made and the mycelium was tentatively referred to as *Spongiophaga*. The disease was reviewed by Johnson and Sparrow (1961) and no more recent information is available.

9.6 Spore Dispersal and Entry

Knowledge of the life cycles of the many marine pathogenic fungi is incomplete and therefore details of infection mechanisms are also incomplete. The majority of these fungi are zoosporic phycomycetes and it is generally assumed that the zoospores are the major infective entity in spreading disease to new hosts. However, proof of this is lacking except in the cases of *Lagenidium chthamalophilum* and *Labyrinthomyxa marina*. Johnson (1960) studied *L. chthamalophilum* (as described previously) showing the effects of temperature and salinity on the infective ability of the zoospores. Perkins and Menzel (1966), by placing zoosporulating material of *Labyrinthomyxa marina* in one container and healthy oysters in another connected by an inverted U-shaped seawater filled tube, showed that infection would occur and with the distances involved, some form of active locomotion—i.e. zoospores rather than hypnospores, must have been involved. However, with *L. marina* all stages of the fungus are potentially infective and it seems probable that vegetative stages of most other fungi will also act as infective agents. In the case of *L. marina* and other parasites of soft tissues, such vegetative stages will be liberated when, on the death of the host tissue, lysis and breakdown occurs. In *L. marina*, it seems possible that such lysis will play a part in inducing zoosporulation since Perkins and Menzel (1966) were only able to produce such zoosporulation by enzymic digestion of host tissues.

In the case of parasites of hard tissues, the breakdown of such tissues will not normally occur rapidly after the death of the host. In the case of the oyster shell disease fungus it has been shown that infection can take place by physical contact when a healthy shell touches a diseased one (Alderman and Jones, 1971). However, this is not the sole means of transmission; vegetative mycelium grows readily from the surface of the shell and is grazed by zooplankton producing short fragments of mycelium. Experiments with mucelium fragmented in a blender have shown that short fragments of the order of 10 μm are quite viable and grow rapidly on contact with suitable substrate. It seems possible that similar 'mechanisms' could be involved with other mycelial fungi.

The Ascomycetes and lichen fungi growing on shells of course achieve distribution by means of their ascospores in the normal manner, although again, the spread of mycelium will also be a factor.

Nothing is known for any of the marine zoosporic forms about mode of entry into the host. There is, as yet, little evidence of any chemotactic response to host tissues. The feeding currents of molluscs are highly efficient, and there is good evidence that the majority of infections start in the gills, the palps and the digestive tract—indeed, it is these regions which are normally inspected for parasites in routine histopathology. In the case of *Ostracocblabe implexa,* it has been observed that many infections are sited near the holes of shell boring oligochaetes—*Polydora* sp. which live in the outer layers of oyster shells. These worms are filter feeders and it seems probable that infective fragments are swept into the oyster shell in their feeding currents, lodge there and proceed to grow.

9.7   Prevention, Cost and Cure

The concluding section of this chapter involves what is both the most important and the most difficult aspect of marine diseases. Diseases of commercially important marine organisms can often involve large scale financial losses. This is particularly so in fisheries run on an intensive farming basis such as many European shellfisheries.

It is clear that in a medium like the sea where no control over population is possible, there is no way in which a disease can, in general terms, be prevented. In the case of sedentary organisms such as molluscs, some measures are possible—mainly the avoidance of overcrowding to prevent conditions under which an epizootic is likely to be encouraged. There are always micro-organisms present capable of facultative parasitism in poorly nourished, overcrowded populations. Shell disease is, perhaps, unique among marine disease in the measures of prevention that may be taken by removing foci of diseases in the form of infested shell and restocking. Korringa (1951) has also shown that dipping oysters in 2% mercuric chloride will reduce infestation. This technique, even when modified by dipping the limed tile collectors used to collect settling larvae, has obvious dangers. Dipped tiles contain no fungus and the oyster will thus not be infected so rapidly. However, the problem of mercury in the marine environment is severe.

With other molluscan diseases—*Labyrinthomyxa marina* for example, where known natural foci of disease are present—the possibility of selective dredging to eliminate the focus exists. The economics of such work, however, are very much dependent on the circumstances of the fishery involved.

The cost of diseases in aquaculture is undoubtedly high, but attempts to quantify these costs are difficult, particularly when more than one disease is implicated, and the other poorly determined ecological factors may or may not be involved. Consequently our knowledge of the real costs involved is very incomplete. Weight loss and mortality figures have been quoted for populations of oysters infected by *Labyrinthomyxa* and these were discussed by Johnson and Sparrow (1961). Cost can also be indicated by the extremes to which growers are forced to relieve conditions— as, for example, the extensive and expensive clearance dredging of oyster beds in the Oosterschelde to remove shell disease undertaken by the Dutch in the late 1940s.

Another example of the effect of disease—though not yet of proven fungal origin—is that of oyster gill disease. Until 1969 the French industry had annually imported tons of *Crassostrea angulata* for relaying in the spring from Portugal. The advent of this disease and associated mortalities were the prime cause of the present French ban on oysters from Portugal. Thus this trade, which had been highly profitable to both countries, has been completely halted.

Finally, the economic effect of a disease may not be direct. Sindermann (1970) points out that the mass mortalities of *Eurytemora hirudenoides* infected with *Leptolegnia baltica* Höhnk et Vallin, besides clogging and fouling fishing nets may well have had an effect on herring *(Clupea harengus)* populations for which the copepod is an important food.

With more mobile organisms such as Crustaceans, little of practical value can be done except in terms of holding conditions where these apply. When it is the practice to hold animals for periods between fishing and sale in keeping ponds, regular cleansing of such ponds to eliminate dead animals and detritus will help to remove a potential reservoir of fungal and other pathogens. Similar simple hygienic procedures are obviously essential in the crowded rearing conditions in larval production.

In the case of marine fish, there seem to be no possible steps for prevention or cure of disease situation which are economically and technically practicable.

Whilst prevention and cure of disease remains a difficult problem, there are at least distinct actions that can be taken to prevent the spread of disease to new areas. Carefully designed limitations should be on the import, export and transfer of marine organisms from one area to another, particularly in the case where disease risks are known to exist. These, whilst being restrictive on the freedom of fishermen's actions, could significantly affect the distribution of diseases, or at least, delay their spread.

Acknowledgements

I wish to thank the following for their assistance, without which this chapter would not have been possible in this form: Dr. Charles Bland and *Mycologia* for permission to reproduce photomicrographs of *Lagenidium chthamilophilum* (Figs. 9.33-9.50), for making his paper available whilst still in the press, and for additional unpublished information.

Figures 9.8-9.24 are reproduced from Fishery Investigation 26 (8) with the permission of the Ministry of Agriculture, Fisheries and Food.

Dr. F. O. Perkins for supplying living and prepared material of *Labyrinthomyxa marina,* together with much additional information. The Keeper of the Herbarium, The Royal Botanic Gardens, Kew, for allowing access to type material of Dr. Atkins' marine fungi. Mr. J. Buchanan for the loan of material of *Ichthyophonus.*

Thanks are also due to Mrs. S. Martin and Miss S. Hopkins for photographic assistance.

References

ALDERMAN, D. J. (1971). 'Shellfish disease in the United Kingdom 1970-71'. I.C.E.S. C.M. 1971/K:19.

ALDERMAN, D. J., and JONES, E. B. G. (1971). 'Shell disease of oysters'. *Fishery Investigations,* London. Ser. II, Vol. 26 (8), 1-18.

ALEEM, A. A., RUIVO, M., and THÉODORIDÈS, J. (1953). 'Un cas de maladie à Saprolegniale chez un *Atherina* des environs de Salses'. *Vie et Milieu* 3, 44-51.

ANDREWS, J. D. (1955). 'Notes on fungus parasites of bivalve molluscs in Chesapeake Bay' *Proc. natn Shellfish. Assoc.* 45, 157-163.

ANDREWS, J. D. (1965). 'Infection experiments in nature with *Dermocystidium marinum* in Chesapeake Bay'. *Chesapeake Sci.,* 6, 60-7.

ANDREWS, J. D., and HEWATT, W. G. (1957). 'Oyster mortality studies in Virginia. II. The fungus disease caused by *Dermocystidium marinum* in oysters of Chesapeake Bay'. *Ecol. Monogr.,* 27, 1-25.

APSTEIN, C. (1910). '*Cyclopterus lumpus* der Seehase. Seine fischeri und sein wageninhalt'. *Mitteil. deutsch. Seefischerei-Vereins,* 26, 450-465.

APSTEIN, C. (1911). '*Synchaetophagus balticus,* ein in *Synchaeta* lebender Pilz'. *Wissenschaftlicht Meeresuntersuchungen, Abt. Kiel (N.S.),* 12, 163-166.

ARONSON, J. M., and FULLER, M. S. (1969). 'Cell wall structure of the marine fungus *Atkinsiella dubia'. Arch. Microbiol.,* 68, 295-305.

ATKINS, D. (1955 a). '*Pythium thalassium* sp. nov. infecting the egg-mass of the pea crab, *Pinnotheres pisum'. Trans. Br. mycol. Soc.,* 38, 31-46.

ATKINS, D. (1955 b). '*Pythium thalassium* n. sp. infecting the egg-mass of the pea-crab, *Pinnotheres pisum.' J. mar. biol. Ass. U.K.,* 34, 649 (Abstract).

BERRILL, N. J. (1950). 'The Tunicata with an account of the British species'. *Ray Society.* pp. 26-29, 242-267.

BLAND, C. E., and AMERSON, H. V. (1973). 'Observations on *Lagenidium callinectes:* Isolation and sporangial development'. *Mycologia,* 65, 310-320.

BONAR, L. (1936). 'An unusual Ascomycete in the shells of marine animals'. *Univ. Calif. Publs. Bot.,* 19, 187-194.

BORNET, E. (1891). 'Note sur l'*Ostracoblabe implexa* Born. et Flah.' *J. Bot.,* 5, 397-400.

BORNET, E., and FLAHAULT, C. (1889). 'Sur quelques plantes vivant dans le test calcaire des mollusques'. *Bull. Soc. bot. Fr.* Ser. 2, 11, pp. CXLVII-CLXXVI. (Congrès de Botanique Tenu à Paris en aôut 1889).

CARPENTER, W. P. (1843). 'General results of microscopic inquiries into the minute structure of the skeletons of Mollusca, Crustacea and Echinodermata.' *Am. Mag. nat. Hist.,* 12, No. 79, pp. 377-390.

CARTER, H. J. (1878). 'Parasites of the Spongida.' *Ann. and Mag. nat. Hist.,* 2, 157-172.

CAULLERY, M. J. G. C., and MESNIL, F. (1905). 'Recherches sur les haplo-sporidies'. *Archs. Zool. exp. gén.,* 4, 101-181.

COMPS, M. (1969). 'Observations relatives à l'affection branchiale des huîtres portugaises (*Crassostrea angulata* Lmk.)'. *Rev. Trav. Inst. Pêches Marit.,* 33, 151-160.

COUCH, J. N. (1942). 'A new fungus on crab eggs'. *J. Elisha Mitchell scient. Soc.,* 58, 158-162.

DAVIS, H. C., LOOSANOFF, V. L., WESTON, W. H., and MARTIN, C. (1954). 'A fungus disease in clam and oyster larvae'. *Science,* 120, 36-38.

DE MONTAUGE frères, (1878). 'Études practiques sur les ennemis et les maladies de l'huître dans le bassin d'Arcachon'. *Actes. Soc. Linne. Bordeaux,* 32, Ser. II. 217-245.

DICK, M. W. (1971). 'Leptolegniellaceae'. *Trans. Br. mycol. Soc.,* 57, 417-425.

DOLLFUS, R. F. (1921). 'Resumé de nos principales connaissances practiques sur les maladies et les ennemis d'huître'. *Notes Mem. Off. scient. tech. Pêch. Marit.* No. 7 46 pp.

DORIER, A., and DEGRANGE, C. (1960). 'L'évolution de l'*Ichthyosporidium (Ichthyophonus) hoferi* Plehn and Mulsow chez les salmonides d'élèvage (Truite arc en ciel et saumon de fontaine)'. *Trav. Lab. Hydrobiologique, Grenoble,* 52/3, 7-94.

DUNCAN, P. M. (1876). 'On some Thallophytes parasitic within recent *Madreporaria'. Proc. Roy. Soc.,* 25, 238-257.

DURVE, V. S., and BAL, D. V. (1960). 'Shell disease in *Crassostrea gryphoides* Sindermann'. *Curr. Sci.,* 29, 489-490.

FELDMAN, J. (1937). 'Sur les gonidies de quelques *Arthopyrenia* marins' *Revue bryol. lichen.,* (N.S.), 10, 64-73.

FELDMAN, J. (1954). 'Inventaire de la flore marine de Roscoff'. Supp. 6, *Trav. Stn. biol. Roscoff,* 152 pp. Prieur and Robin, Paris.

FISH, F. W. (1934). 'A fungus disease of fishes in the Gulf of Maine'. *Parasitology,* 26, 1-16.

FORSTER, R. P. (1941). 'The present status of the systemic fungus disease in herring of the Gulf of Maine'. *Bull. Mt. Desert Island Biol. Lab.,* 1941 33-35.

FRANC, A., and ARVY, L. (1969). 'Sur *Thanatostrea polymorpha* n. gen. et sp. agent de destruction des branchies et palpes de l'huître portugaise'. *C. r. hebd. Séanc. Acad. Sc.* Paris, 268, 3189-90.

FRANC, A., and ARVY, L. (1970). 'Données sur l'évolution de la "maladie des branchies" chez les huîtres et sur son agent causal: *Thanatostrea polymorpha* Franc et Arvy'. *Bull. biol.* 104, 3-19.

FULLER, M. S., FOWLES, B. E., and McLAUGHLIN, D. J. (1964). 'Isolation and pure culture study of marine phycomycetes'. *Mycologia* 56, 745-56.

GALTSOFF, P. S. (1942). 'Wasting disease causing mortality of sponges in the West Indies and Gulf of Mexico'. *Proc. 8th American Sci. Cong., 1940,* 3, 411-421.

GALTSOFF, P. S. (1964). 'The American oyster *Crassostrea virginica* Gmelin'. *Fishery Bull. Fish. Wildl. Serv. U.S.* 64, 1-480.

GIARD, A. (1888). 'Sur les *Nephromyces,* genre nouveau de champignons parasites du rein des Molgulidées'. *C. r. hebd., Séanc. Acad. Sci., Paris,* 106, 1180-1182.

GIRANT, H. (1936). 'Note appended to BONAR, L., (1936). An unusual Ascomycete in the shells of animals'. *Univ. Calif. Publs. Bot.,* 19, 187-194.

GOLDSTEIN, S., and MORIBER, L. (1966). 'Biology of a problematic marine fungus *Dermocystidium* sp. 1. Development and cytology'. *Arch. Mikrobiol.,* 53, 1-11.

GORDON, I. (1966). 'Parasites and diseases of Crustacea'. *Mem. Inst. Fondam. Afrique Noire.* No. 77, 27-86.

HARANT, H. (1931). 'Contribution à l'histoire naturelle des ascides et de leurs parasites. 2. Chytridinées.' *Ann. Inst. Oceanogr., Monaco,* 8, 349-352.

HENDRICKS, J. (1972). 'Two new host species for the parasitic fungus *Ichthyophonus hoferi* in the Northwest Atlantic. *J. Fish. Res. Bd. Can.,* 29, 1776-1777.

HERRICK, F. H. (1895). 'The American lobster, a study of its habits and development'. *Bull. U.S. Fish. Commn.,* 15, 1-252.

HERRICK, F. H. (1911). 'Natural history of the American lobster'. *U.S. Bur. Fish. Bull.,* 29, 149-408.

HOEK, P. P. C. (1902). 'Rapport over de oorzaken van den achteruitgang in hoedanigheid van de Zeeuwsche oester'. s'*Gravenhage, Ministerie van Waterstaat, Handel en Nijverheid,* 82-83.

JOHNSON, T. W. (1958). 'A fungus parasite in ova of the barnacle *Chthamalus fragilis denticulata'. Biol. Bull. Mar. biol. Lab., Woods Hole,* 114, 205-214.

JOHNSON, T. W. (1960). 'Infection potential and growth of *Lagenidium chthamalophilum'. Am. J. Bot.,* 47, 383-385.

JOHNSON, T. W. (1970). 'Fungi in marine Crustaceans'. In *A symposium on diseases of fishes and shellfishes.* Special publication 5., American Fisheries Society, Washington, D. C. 405-407.

JOHNSON, T. W. and BONNER, R. R. (1960). *Lagenidium callinectes* Couch in barnacle ova. *J. Elisha Mitchell scient. Soc.,* 76, 147-9.

JOHNSON, T. W., and ANDERSON, W. R. (1962). 'A fungus in *Anomia simplex* shell'. *J. Elisha Mitchell scient. Soc.,* 78, 43-47.

JOHNSON, T. W., and SPARROW, F. K. (1961). *Fungi in Oceans and Estuaries* J. Cramer, Weinheim. 688 pp.

KOHLMEYER, J. (1970). 'A new Ascomycete on Hydrozoa from the South Atlantic'. *Ber. dt. bot. Ges.,* 83, 505-509.

KOLLIKER, A. (1859). 'On the frequent occurrence of vegetable parasites in the hard structures of animals.' *Ann, Mag. nat. Hist. (Natur).,* 4, 300-303.

KOLLIKER, A. (1860). 'On the frequent occurrence of vegetable parasites in the hard tissues of the lower animals'. *Q. Jl. microsc. Sci.,* 8, 171-188.

KORRINGA, P. (1951). 'Investigations on shell disease in the oyster, *Ostrea edulis,* L.' *Rapports et Procès-verbaux, Conseil Permanent Internat. l'Exploration de la Mer,* 128, 50-54.

KORRINGA, P. (1952). 'Recent advances in oyster biology'. *Q. Rev. Biol.,* 27, 266-308, 339-365.

LACAZE-DUTHIERS, H. de (1874). 'Les Ascides simples des côtes de France'. *Archs. Zool. exp. gén.,* 3, 119-174, 257-330, 531-656.

MACKIN, J. G. (1951). 'Histopathology of infection of *Crassostrea virginica* (Gmelin) by *Dermocystidium marinum,* Mackin, Owen and Collier'. *Bull. mar. Sci. Gulf Caribb.,* 1, 72-87.

MACKIN, J. G. (1956). '*Dermocystidium marinum* and salinity'. *Proc. natn. Shellfish Assoc.,* 45, 116-128.

MACKIN, J. G. (1962). 'Oyster disease caused by *Dermocystidium marinum* and other microorganisms in Louisiana.' *Publ. Inst. mar. Sci., Univ. Texas,* 7, 132-229.

MACKIN, J. G., and BOSWELL, J. L. (1956). 'The life cycle and relationships of *Dermocystidium marinum'. Proc. natn. Shellfish. Assoc.,* 46, 112-115.

MACKIN, J. G., and RAY, S. M. (1966). 'The taxonomic relationships of *Dermocystidium marinum,* Mackin, Owen and Collier'. *J. Invert. Path.,* 8, 544-545.

MACKIN, J. G., OWEN, H. M., and COLLIER, A. (1950). 'Preliminary note on the occurrence of a new protistan parasite; *Dermocystidium marinum* n. sp. in *Crassostrea virginica* (Gmelin)'. *Science,* 111, 328-29.

MANN, H., and PIEPLOW, U. (1938). 'XI Die brandfleckenkrankheit bie krebsen und itare erreger'. *Z. Fisch.,* 38, 225-240.

MILLAR, R. H. (1971). 'The biology of ascidians'. In *Advances in Marine Biology,* (Eds. F. S. Russell and M. Yonge) 9. Academic Press, London and N. York. 47-54.

PAULEY, G. B., and SPARKS, A. K. (1965). 'Preliminary observations on the acute inflammatory reaction in the Pacific oyster *Crassostrea gigas* (Thunberg)'. *J. Invert. Path.,* 7, 248-256.

PEREZ, C. (1908). 'Rectification de nomenclature à propos de *Dermocystis pusula'. C. r. Séanc. Soc. Biol.* 64, 738.

PERKINS, F. P. (1966). 'Life history studies of *Dermocystidium marinum* an oyster pathogen'. Doctoral dissertation, 272 pp. Florida State University, Tallahassee, Fla. *Dissertation Abstracts* 66-9078.

PERKINS, F. O. (1969). 'Ultrastructure of vegetative stages in *Labyrinthomyxa marina (Dermocystidium marinum)* a commercially significant oyster pathogen'. *J. Invert. Path.,* 13, 199-222.

PERKINS, F. O. (1972). 'The ultrastructure of holdfasts, "rhizoids" and "slime tracks" in Thraustochytriaceous fungi and *Labyrinthula* spp'. *Arch. Mikrobiol.,* 84, 95-118.

PERKINS, F. O., and MENZEL, R. W. (1966). 'Morphological and cultural studies of a motile stage in the life cycle of *Dermocystidium marinum'. Proc. natn. Shellfish. Assoc.,* 56, 23-30.

PERKINS, F. O., and MENZEL, R. W. (1967). 'Ultrastructure of sporulation in the oyster pathogen *Dermocystidium marinum'. J. Invert. Path.,* 9, 205-229.

PLEHN, M. (1916). 'Pathogene schimmelpilze in der fischniere'. *Z. Fisch.,* 18, 51-54.

PLEHN, M., and MULSOW, K. (1911). 'Der erreger der "taumelkrankheit" der salmoniden'. *Centralblatt Bakt, Parasitenk. und Infektionskr,* 59, 63-68.

PORTER, C. L., and ZEBROWSKI, G. (1937). 'Lime-loving molds from Australian sands'. *Mycologia,* 29, 252-257.

POYTON, R. O. (1970). 'The characterisation of *Hyalochlorella marina* gen. et sp. nov., a new colourless counterpart of *Chlorella'. J. gen. Microbiol.,* 6, 171-188.

QUEKETT, J. (1852). '*Lectures on Histology.* Elementary tissues of plants and animals, skeleton of mollusca—conchifera'. Vol. 2. Lecture 166, 276-278.

QUICK, J. A. (1972). 'A new Thraustochytridiaceous fungus endoparasitic in the American oyster *Crassostrea virginica* Gmelin in Florida'. Abstract in *Soc. Invert. Pathol. Newsletter* IV (3), 13.

QUICK, J. A., and MACKIN, J. G. (1971). 'Oyster parasitism by *Labyrinthomyxa marina* in Florida'. *Fla. Dept. Nat. Res. Mar. Research Lab.,* professional papers Ser. No. 13, 53 pp.

RANSON, G. (1943). '*La vie des huîtres'.* Gallimard, Paris, 240 pp.

RAY, S. M. (1952 a). 'A culture technique for the diagnosis of infections with *Dermocystidium marinum,* Mackin, Owen and Collier in oysters'. *Science,* 116, 360-361.

RAY, S. M. (1952 b). 'A culture technique for the diagnosis of infection with *Dermocystidium marinum* in oysters'. *Nat. Shellfish. Assoc., 1952 Convention Addresses,* pp. 9-13.

RAY, S. M. (1966 a). 'Notes on the occurrence of *Dermocystidium marinum* on the Gulf of Mexico during 1961 and 1962'. *Proc. natn. Shellfish. Assoc.,* 54, 45-54.

RAY, S. M. (1966 b). 'A review of the culture method for detecting *Dermocystidium marinum,* with suggested modifications and precautions. *Proc. natn. Shellfish. Assoc.,* 54, 55-69.

RAY, S. M., MACKIN, J. G., and BOSWELL, J. L. (1953). 'Quantitative measurement of the effect on oysters of disease caused by *Dermocystidium marinum'. Bull. mar. Sci. Gulf Caribb.,* 3, 6-24.

REICHENBACH-KLINKE, H. H. (1954). 'Pilze in tumoren bei fischen. *Verhandl deutsch. Zool. Gesell,* Tubingen, 1954 351-357.

REICHENBACH-KLINKE, H. H. (1955). 'Untersuchungen uber die bei fischen durch parasiten hervorgerufenen zysten und deren wirkung auf den wirtskorper'. *Fischerei und deren Hilfswissenschaften,* 3, 565-636.

REICHENBACH-KLINKE, H. H. (1956 a). 'Die vermehrungsformer des zoophagen pilzes *Ichthyosporidium hoferi* (Plehn and Mulsow) (Fungi, Phycomycetes) in wirt'. *Veroff. Inst. Meeresforsch, Bremerh.,* 4, 214-219.

REICHENBACH-KLINKE, H. H. (1956 b). 'Ueber einige bischer unbekannte Hyphomycetin bei verschiedenen suβwasser-und meeresfischen'. *Mycopath. Mycol. appl.,* 7, 333-347.

ROGERS-TALBERT, R. (1948). 'The fungus *Lagenidium callinectes* Couch (1942) on eggs of the blue crab in Chesapeake Bay'. *Biol. Bull. mar. biol. Lab., Woods Hole,* 95, 214-228.

ROSE, C. B. (1855). 'On the discovery of parasitic borings in fossil fish-scales'. *Trans. Microsc. Soc., Lond.,* 7-9.

ROSEN, B. (1970). 'Shell disease of aquatic crustaceans'. In *A symposium on diseases of fishes and shellfishes.* Special Publ. No. 5. American Fisheries Soc., Washington, D. C. pp. 409-414.

ROSENFIELD, A. (1969). 'Oyster diseases in North America and some methods for their control'. *Proc. Conf. on Artificial Propagation of Commercially Valuable Shellfish—oysters.* University of Delaware. pp. 67-78.

SANDOZ, M., ROGERS, R. and NEWCOME, C. L. (1944). 'Fungus infection of the eggs of the blue crab *Callinectes sapidus* Rathbun'. *Science* 99, 124-5.

SANTESSON, R. (1939). 'Amphibious Pyrenolichens I.' *Ark. Bot.,* 29A, 1-67.

SCHAPERCLAUS, W. (1954). *'Fischrankheiten'.* 3rd. edition, Akademie Verlag, Berlin. 708 pp.

SCHLICHT, F. G. (1969). 'The populations and distribution of the oyster pathogen *Labyrinthomyxa marina* (Mackin Owen and Collier) and the relation of these populations to the pathogen of oysters, the Aransas Bay *Labyrinthomyxa'.* Ph.D. Thesis Texas A & M University, 94 pp.

SINDERMANN, C. J. (1963). 'Disease in marine populations'. *Trans. North Am. Wildlife Conf.,* 28, 336-356.

SINDERMANN, C. J. (1970). *'Principal Diseases of Marine Fish and Shellfish'.* Academic Press, New York and London. 369 pp.

SINDERMANN, C. J., and SCATTERGOOD, L. W. (1954). 'Diseases of fishes of western North Atlantic. II. *Ichthyosporidium* disease of the sea herring *(Clupea harengus)'. Maine Dept. Sea Shore Fish., Res. Bull.* No. 19, 1-40.

SORDI, M. (1958). 'Microsi dei crostacei decapodi marini'. *Riv. Parasitol.,* 19, 131-137.

SPRAGUE, V. (1965). *'Ichthyosporidium* Caullery and Mesnil, 1905, the name of a genus of fungi or a genus of sporozoans?' *Syst. Zool.,* 14, 110-114.

SPRAGUE, V. (1972). 'Diseases of oysters'. *A. Rev. Microbiol.,* 25, 211-230.

SPROSTON, N. (1944). *'Ichthyosporidium hoferi* (Plehn and Mulsow, 1911) an internal fungoid parasite of the mackerel'. *J. mar. biol. Ass. U.K.,* 26, 72-98.

STIRRUP, M. (1872). 'On shells of mollusca showing so-called fungoid growths'. *Proc. Lit. phil. Soc. Manchester,* 2 (session 1871-72) 137-138.

TOPSENT, E. (1887 a). 'Sur les pretendus prolongement periphériques des cliones'. *C. r. hebd. Séanc. Acad. Sci.,* Paris, 105, p. 1188.

TOPSENT, E. (1887 b). 'Notes sur les Thallophytes marins perforants'. *Mem. de la Soc. Linneene de Normandie,* 1887, p. 297.

VALLIN, S. (1951). 'Plankton mortality in the northern Baltic caused by a parasitic water-mould'. Rept. No. 32, *Inst. Freshwater Res. Drottningholm,* pp. 139-148.

VALUILIS, G. A., and MACKIN, J. G. (1969). 'Formation of sporangia and zoospores by *Labyrinthomyxa* sp. parasitic in the clam *Macoma balthica.' J. Invert. Pathol.,* 14, 268-70.

VISHNIAC, H. (1955). 'The morphology and nutrition of a new species of *Sirolpidium'. Mycologia,* 47, 633-645.

VISHNIAC, H. (1958). 'A new marine phycomycete'. *Mycologia,* 50, 66-79.

WEDL, C. (1859). 'Uber die bedeutung der in den schalen acephalen und gasteropoden vorkommenden canale'. *Sber. Akad. Wiss Wien,* 33, 451-472.

YONGE, C. M. (1960). *Oysters.* Collins New Naturalist Monographs 18, London. 209 pp.

10 Physiology of Marine Phycomycetes

E. B. GARETH JONES and J. L. HARRISON

10.1 Introduction

The ability to isolate phycomycetes and their growth in axenic culture has enabled mycologists to investigate their physiology and biochemistry. This has probably been the most significant contribution to the study of the lower fungi over the last decade. To Vishniac (1955 a, 1956) must go the credit for showing us how readily these organisms can be isolated from the sea, but the pioneer work of Höhnk (1939, 1953, 1956) must not go unrecorded. According to Johnson (Chapter 7) there are some 70 species of marine phycomycetes, and of these, members of the Thraustochytriaceae are the most frequently isolated. It is not surprising that these have been studied more intensively than members of the Chytridiomycetes, Hyphochytridiomycetes and Plasmodiophoromycetes. Some of the chytrids studied by Barr (1969; 1970 a, b, c, 1971) are also to be found in brackish waters, but his results are better discussed in Chapter 21.

10.2 Temperature

From Table 10.1 it can be seen that most of the fungi tested had their optimum growth within the temperature range 20-25°C and few grew well below 10°C. *Ostracoblabe implexa* Bornet et Flahault grew slowly at 5°C and this has obvious significance in view of the usual winter temperatures in British coastal waters. The two fungi studied by Alderman and Jones (1971) have very high temperature optima for growth, namely 30°C. Bremer (1974) has shown that out of 19 thraustochytrid fungi studied, 12 had optimum growth at 30°C and the remaining seven at 25°C. Of the five isolates of *Thraustochytrium roseum* Goldstein he tested, four grew best at 30°C, the fifth with optimum growth at 25°C. This shows there is some variation between different isolates in their physiological requirements.

The 30°C optima displayed by some of these fungi is surprising for aquatic fungi in temperate latitudes and as Bremer (1974) points out, such temperatures would probably only be achieved in summer months in situations such as shallow tidal waters and rock pools.

TABLE 10.1   The effect of temperature (°C) on the growth of some marine Phycomycetes.

Fungus		Maximal growth (in brackets)	No growth	Further observations
Althornia crouchii Alderman et Jones	Alderman and Jones (1971)	(30)	35	
Dermocystidium sp. *sensu* Goldstein *et al.*	Goldstein, Belsky Chosak (1969)	(19)	25	growth poor below 4
Haliphthoros milfordensis Vishniac	Ulken (1968)	(20)		
	Vishniac (1958)	15-30		
Ostracoblabe implexa Bornet et Flahault	Alderman and Jones (1971)	(30)	35	
Phlyctochytrium mangrovii Ulken	Ulken (1972)	(25)		
Schizochytrium aggregatum Goldstein et Belsky	Goldstein and Belsky (1964)	20-25	37	
	Schneider (1969 a)	(20)		
	Ulken (1968)	5-10		
Thraustochytrium aureum Goldstein	Goldstein (1963 c)	(20)	37	growth poor at 4
T. motivum Goldstein	Goldstein (1963 b)	12(20)25	37	growth poor at 4
T. multirudimentale Goldstein		12(20)25	37	growth poor at 4
T. roseum Goldstein	Goldstein (1963 a)	15(25)30	37	growth poor at 4

Species	Reference			
T. kinnei Gaertner	Bremer (1974)	15-(30)	35	growth poor below 10
T. aureum		15-(30)	35	growth poor below 10
T. visurgense Ulken		20(25)30	35	growth poor below 10
T. striatum Schneider		20(25)30	35	growth poor below 15
T. multirudimentale		15-(30)	35	growth poor below 10
T. roseum		15-(30)	35	growth poor below 10
Japonochytrium sp?		15-(30)	35	growth poor below 10
Sirolpidium zoophthorum Vishniac	Vishniac (1956)	20-30	36	growth poor below 10

Gaertner (1967) showed there was some correlation between the number of fungi isolated and water temperature in the German Bay, the maximum number occurring at 10°C. Ulken (1966) baited water samples taken from the Atlantic with pollen and incubated these at temperatures between 5 and 30°C. The results show that more pollen grains were infected between 20 and 30°C than at lower temperatures. Johnson (1960) suggests that the infection of *Chthamalus* egg masses by *Lagenidium chthamalophilum* Johnson is dependent on the combined influences of temperature and salinity. The higher the incubation temperature the greater was the percentage infection at high salinities.

10.3 Light

The effect of light on the growth of marine phycomycetes has received little attention. Alderman and Jones (1971) have shown that continuous light of 40 000 lux inhibits the growth of *Althornia crouchii* Jones et Alderman and *Ostracoblabe implexa*. Ulken (1972) has shown that light, at an intensity of 750 lux, also inhibits the growth of *Phlyctochytrium mangrovii* Ulken.

However, the growth of *Thraustochytrium roseum,* a pigmented form, is stimulated by light (Goldstein, 1963 c). Sporangia grown in light have thick sporangial walls which are gelatinous and easily deformed by pressure. An albino mutant obtained by exposure to ultra-violet irradiation did not respond to light or dark. Bremer (1974) examined the response of five isolates of *T. roseum* to continuous light of 20 000 lux. The growth of one isolate, Ho 20, was markedly stimulated but three other isolates, identical in morphology and pigmentation, showed no response to light (Table 10.2).

Alderman and Harrison (unpublished observations) have shown that the degree of pigmentation of thraustochytrid cultures is affected by age of the culture, degree of desiccation of the medium and by light.

10.4 Hydrogen Ion Concentration

Vishniac (1955 a) has shown that *Sirolpidium zoophthorum* Vishniac requires a pH of 6.7 to 7.5 for good growth and will not develop at an initial pH of 6.5. After a few days, growth tends to bring the pH of the medium to neutrality. *Haliphthoros milfordensis* Vishniac produced gemmae when the final pH of the culture was between 7.0 and 8.0 (Vishniac, 1958). The pH of the cultures was dependent on the carbon sources supplied. If there was an excess of glucose, the initial pH of 7.5 dropped to 5.8, while an excess of glutamate produced a final pH of 8.0.

Phlyctochytrium mangrovii was isolated by Ulken (1972) from mangrove swamps near Cananéia, Brazil, which were acidic (pH 6.3). However, in laboratory experiments, the fungus produced no growth at pH of 5.4 (or below), began to grow at 6.2 and grew well within the range 7.4 to 8.2.

The pH requirement of a number of species of *Labyrinthula* has been examined. Watson (1951) showed that pH levels below 7.5 inhibited growth of his *Labyrinthula* spp., while *Labyrinthula macrocystis* var. *atlantica* Vishniac et Watson and *L. vitellina* var. *pacifica* Watson had growth maxima at pH 7.5 and *L. minuta* Watson et Raper at 6.6 (Vishniac, 1955 b). Young (1943) showed that the *Labyrinthula* he was working with could grow over the range of pH 4 to 9.

TABLE 10.2 Growth of isolates of *T. roseum* in YPI/ASW* for four days at 20°C. Light grown flasks illuminated 20 000 lux (after Bremer, 1974).

Isolate	Light grown								Dark grown								Hours
	12	24	36	48	60	72	84	96	12	24	36	48	60	72	84	96	
HO20	6	9	12	30	39	50	76	90	4	6	10	16	19	23	41	53	
SF25	2	12	16	28	35	37	50	52	2	12	15	24	33	40	48	51	
SF22	4	6	10	17	21	36	44	55	3	8	11	18	24	33	47	54	
Q5	5	7	12	23	35	38	41	45	4	6	14	20	33	39	43	49	
T. roseum (Goldstein isolate)	7	9	15	32	37	50	66	80	6	10	13	18	24	36	44	57	

* YPI/ASW: Yeast peptone artificial seawater broth. Growth measured turbidometrically.

10.5   Oxygenation

Thraustochytrium motivum Goldstein, *T. multirudimentale* Goldstein and *T. roseum* have all been isolated by Goldstein (1963 a, b) from polluted waters (unspecified). However, they do not tolerate anaerobic conditions and are regarded as obligately aerobic. Goldstein and Belsky (1964) have shown that *Schizochytrium aggregatum* Goldstein et Belsky failed to grow in the absence of oxygen. Goldstein *et al.* (1969) have shown that oxygen consumption by unstarved thalli of *Dermocystidium* sp. (≡ *Hyallochlorella marina,* Poyton) increases in the presence of glucose. This stimulatory effect is accentuated by depriving cells of glucose for 24 hours. The fungus can survive seven days without a carbon source, but oxygen consumption does not fall to less than one quarter of that observed with unstarved cultures. They regard its ability to survive extensive periods of starvation and its rapid recovery response to substrate as of an adaptive value.

Phlyctochytrium mangrovii grew better in non-aerated cultures (50.0 μg dey wt.) than aerated cultures (17.3 μg). Ulken (1972) regards this as an adaptation to the habitat it was isolated from, namely a mangrove swamp deficient in oxygen due to anaerobic decomposition of materials by bacteria. However, there is no evidence that the fungus is wholly anaerobic, as has been shown for the freshwater phycomycete *Aqualinderella fermentans* Emerson et Weston (Emerson and Held, 1969).

10.6   Salinity

There is a great deal of information available concerning the ecology of Phycomycetes in relation to salinity. The early work of Höhnk (1939, 1952 a, b, 1953, 1956, 1957) has been fully discussed by Johnson and Sparrow (1961). Ulken (1970) has reported *Rhizophydium* sp. and *R. keratinophilum* Karling from samples collected from mangrove swamps in Brazil where the salinity ranged between 13 and 20°/oo and later (Ulken, 1972) described *Phlyctochytrium mangrovii* from the same locality. The extensive work of Booth (1969, 1971 a, b, c,) on chytrids recovered from sediments of varying saline conditions is summarized in Table 10.3. In these investigations, soil samples were taken from areas varying between those of constant saline conditions to those which are only periodically saline.

TABLE 10.3   Chytridiaceous fungi recovered by Booth (1969, 1971 a, b) from saline soils.

	1	2	3
No. of sites investigated	115	55	128

Fungus	No. of sites from which fungi were isolated			Recorded presence in freshwater
Blyttiomyces aureus	1	—	4	
Chytridium citriforme	1	—	—	

266

Fungus	No. of sites from which fungi were isolated			Recorded presence in freshwater
Chytridium megastomum	—	—	1	
Chytridium sp.	3	—	—	
Chytriomyces hyalinus	3	9	27	*
C. poculatus	1	—	19	
C. appendiculatus	—	—	2	*
Entophlyctis confervae-glomeratae	—	—	1	*
Entophlyctis sp.	—	8	3	
Karlingiomyces granulatus	—	—	2	*
Nowakowskiella elegans	—	—	3	
Olpidium gregarium	—	—	1	*
O. luxurians	—	—	2	
O. longicollum	8	—	—	
O. pendulum	26	—	50	
Phlyctidium marinum	10	—	—	
P. megastomum	—	—	2	*
Phlyctochytrium africanum	7	10	3	
P. chaetiferum	1	—	6	*
P. dichotomum	2	—	—	
P. kniepii	—	2	1	
P. irregulare	10	—	—	*
P. mucronatum	—	—	1	
P. palustre	5	4	4	
P. punctatum	—	6	2	
P. reinboldtae	5	—	1	
P. semiglobiferum	5	1	3	
P. spectabile	2	—	1	
Phlyctochytrium unidentified spp.	—	—	5	
Rhizidium laevis	—	—	1	
R. richmondense	2	—	—	
R. varians	—	—	1	
R. verrucosum	—	—	1	
Rhizidium sp.	—	—	1	
Rhizophylctis harderi	9	4	16	*
R. hyalina	—	—	1	*
R. rosea	3	—	4	*
Rhizophydium ampullaceum	—	—	2	*
R. angulosum	1	—	—	
R. carpophilum	—	—	12	*
R. chitinophilum	—	—	5	*
R. chytriomycetis	1	—	9	
R. coronum	—	—	1	
R. gibbosum	—	—	1	*
R. minutum	—	—	2	*٠

Fungus	No. of sites from which fungi were isolated			Recorded presence in freshwater
R. nodulosum	—	—	3	*
R. pollinis-pini	7	—	3	*
R. racemosum	6	—	4	
R. sphaerotheca	18	8	44	
R. sphaerocarpum	—	—	10	*
R. stipitatum	—	—	1	
R. transversum	—	—	1	*
R. utriculare	6	5	1	
Rhizophydium, unidentified spp.	1	—	28	

1 Saline soils collected around the Strait of Georgia and the interior desert regions of British Columbia.

2. Soils collected from Arctic and Western North America (1971 a).

3. Soils collected from Hibben and Moresby Islands, Queen Charlotte Islands (1971 b).

Members of the Thraustochytriaceae have been repeatedly isolated from waters and sediments ranging in salinity from 12 to 30°/oo (Schneider, 1971). A more detailed account of their ecology is to be found in Chapter 12.

Booth (1971 a) has studied the ecotypic responses of chytridiaceous fungi to combinations of salinity (up to 15°/oo) and temperature (under laboratory conditions). Fifty-seven taxa belonging to the Chytridiales and Blastocladiales were isolated from soils from a variety of habitats (see Table 10.3). He showed that the responses of the fungi isolated to salinity and temperatures may provide a means for recognizing ecotypes. For example, the four isolates of Phlyctochytrium palustre Gaertner (Nos. 21-24) may constitute two ecotypes. Isolates 21 and 22, which grew significantly better at 20°C than at 10 or 30°C and equally well in all salinities, were from a non-marine 'steppe' site. Isolates 23 and 24, however, grew better in 0°/oo and 5°/oo than in 15°/oo at 20° and 30°C. These isolates from the same 'beach-riser' site, suggest a constant species response of several isolates from a single collection site.

Table 10.4 presents observations on the salinity tolerances of a number of marine phycomycetes. All the fungi listed are obligately marine, requiring some level of sodium chloride in order to grow and develop normally. However, it is interesting to note the wide tolerance to salinity by these organisms. Many of these have been described as stenohaline, for example: Schizochytrium aggregatum (Goldstein and Belsky, 1964), Thraustochytrium motivum and Thraustochytrium multirudimentale Goldstein, 1963 b). From the results, however, all these organisms can be considered as being euryhaline, although their optimum salinities for growth lie within the stenohaline range (20-35°/oo). The wide range of salinities tolerated by these organisms is exemplified by Thraustochytrium sp. I (Schneider, 1969) which is reported to grow and develop normally in salinities of 1°/oo and up to 80-100°/oo NaCl. Goldstein (1963 a) recorded growth of T. roseum in 5-7°/oo. Table 10.5 summarizes the responses of some fungi tested by Bremer (1974); Harrison (1972),

TABLE 10.4   The response to salinity displayed by members of the
Thraustochytriaceae and other biflagellate marine fungi.

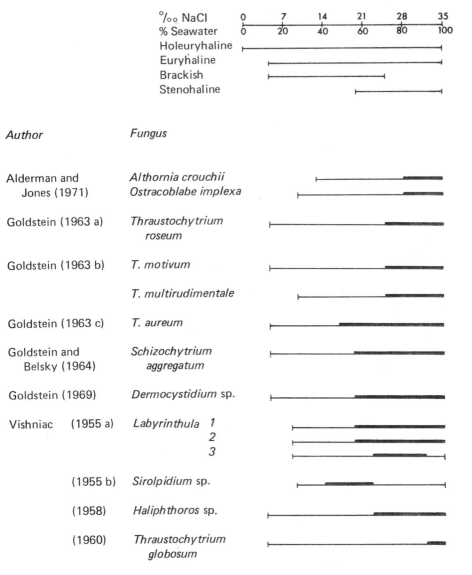

Author	Fungus
Alderman and Jones (1971)	*Althornia crouchii*
	Ostracoblabe implexa
Goldstein (1963 a)	*Thraustochytrium roseum*
Goldstein (1963 b)	*T. motivum*
	T. multirudimentale
Goldstein (1963 c)	*T. aureum*
Goldstein and Belsky (1964)	*Schizochytrium aggregatum*
Goldstein (1969)	*Dermocystidium* sp.
Vishniac (1955 a)	*Labyrinthula* 1
	2
	3
(1955 b)	*Sirolpidium* sp.
(1958)	*Haliphthoros* sp.
(1960)	*Thraustochytrium globosum*

Schneider (1969) and Ulken (1968, 1972). The most striking feature of these results
is the wide range of salinities at which growth and normal development will occur. No
growth was observed in distilled water and abnormal sporangia were observed at
$7^{\circ}/oo$ in *T. striatum* Schneider (Bremer, 1974). Alderman and Jones (1971) working
with *Althornia crouchii* report that in 30% ($10.5^{\circ}/oo$) and 40% ($14.0^{\circ}/oo$) seawater,
the lowest salinities at which this organism grew, the sporangia remained immature and
did not release zoospores. Harrison (1972) reports an 'all or nothing' response in the

269

isolates he tested. That is, even at the lowest salinities where the fungi grew, development was normal, with the inoculated zoospores producing mature sporangia which in turn dehisced releasing motile stages.

TABLE 10.5   Salinity tolerance of some marine phycomycetes (optimum range in brackets).

Fungus	Author	Range: $^o/oo$ seawater
Phlychtochytrium mangrovii	Ulken (1972)	5 (10-15) 25
Dermocystidium sp.	Ulken (1968)	(15-35)
Schizochytrium aggregatum		(15-35)
S. aggregatum	Schneider (1969 a)	(3.8-27)
Thraustochytrium striatum		4-80
T. spec. 1		1-60 (80-100)
T. spec. 137		2-60 (80)
T. kinnei		4-40
T. kinnei	Bremer (1974)	7(14-49) 63
T. aureum		7(21-56) 70
T. visurgense		7(14-56) 70
T. striatum		7(21-56) 70
T. multirudimentale		7(14-56) 63
T. roseum		(7-49) 70
S. aggregatum		7(14-56) 70
Ho20 *(T.roseum* type)		7(14-49) 56
Q5 *(T. roseum* type)		7(28-42) 56
SF25 *(T. roseum* type)		7(21-56) 63
SF22 *(T. roseum* type)		7(14-42) 56
FM19		(7-56) 70
S13 *(T. motivum-aureum* type)		7(21-42) 63
Z1		7(14-56) 63
Q1 *(T. aureum* type)		(7-56) 70
T4 *(T. kinnei* type)		7(21-56) 63
L1 *(Japonochytrium* sp.)		7(21-56) 70
BA 312 *(T. motivum-aureum* type)		7(14-49) 70
BD 107 *(T. motivum-aureum* type)		7(21-56) 63
W2 *(T. motivum-aureum* type)	Harrison (1972)	7(24.5-35)
L3 *(T. motivum-aureum* type)		7(21.0-35)
BD 114 *(T. motivum-aureum* type)		7(35)
BD 110 *(Dermocystidium* type)		3.5(7-35)
L1537 *(Dermocystidium* type)		3.5(17.5-35)

The quality of growth recorded for these organisms in low salinities is extremely variable and suggests the complete exploitation of available sodium chloride as a nutritional requirement. Siegenthaler *et al.* (1967) have shown that phosphate uptake by *T. roseum* varies linearly with increase in the concentration of sodium chloride up to 200 mM, with no marked increase over the range 200-400mM. This range corresponds to the concentration of sodium chloride encountered in littoral waters. They also showed that the effectiveness of sodium chloride for phosphate transport extends beyond its osmotic function and can be attributed specifically to sodium.

These observations on salinity tolerances suggest that a wider variety of marine phycomycetes may be found in natural waters of lower salinities than full seawater. For instance isolate Bd 110 *(Hyallochlorella marina)* has a marked tolerance of low salinities and was isolated from the Fleet, Weymouth, England, where the water had a salinity of 17°/oo NaCl. Similar results have been obtained by Ulken (1972) for *P. mangrovii;* Ulken (1965) for *T. visurgense* Ulken and *T. aggregatum* Ulken and by Schneider (1969) for *S. aggregatum.*

10.7   Cation and Anion Requirements

A number of marine phycomycetes will not grow in the absence of sodium chloride in the medium; for example; *Dermocystidium* sp. (Goldstein *et al.,* 1969); *Thraustochytrium motivum, T. multirudimentale, T. roseum, T. aureum* (Goldstein, 1963 a-c), *Althornia crouchii, Ostracoblabe implexa* (Alderman and Jones, 1971), *Schizochytrium aggregatum* (Goldstein and Belsky, 1964), *Haliphthoros milfordensis* and *Sirolpidium zoophthorum* (Vishniac, 1955, 1958). In none of the fungi tested could potassium chloride or calcium chloride substitute for sodium chloride. Alderman and Jones (1971) showed that magnesium chloride did have an effect on the growth of *A. crouchii* but only in the presence of sodium chloride.

TABLE 10.6   The effect of varying concentrations of $NaHCO_3$ on the growth of isolate Ho 20 (after Bremer, 1974).

$NaHCO_3$ (g/litre)	Mean turbidity	pH
0	0	7.2
0.096	54	7.0
0.192	77	6.8
0.384	75	6.8

Vishniac (1960), Alderman and Jones (1971) and Bremer (1974) have all shown that varying the bicarbonate ($NaHCO_3$) level in the medium had a marked effect on growth (Table 10.6). Vishniac (1960) reported that in 25 isolates of non-filamentous marine fungi she investigated there was a stimulation of growth by the addition of low levels of sodium bicarbonate to the medium. Alderman and Jones (1971) report a similar effect for *A. crouchii* and were able to show that the amount of bicarbonate added (0.0192%) had no significant effect on the final pH of the medium. They suggest that the effect of bicarbonate and the utilization of malate by the fungus might be connected, since carbon dioxide fixation is closely linked to malate metabolism (Cantino and Horenstein, 1959) in *Blastocladiella.*

Siegenthaler *et al.* (1967) have shown that phosphate uptake in *T. roseum* is maximally stimulated by sodium chloride in a range of concentrations $0.2 - 0.4$ molar. There was no phosphate uptake with monovalent cations (Li^+, K^+, Rb^+) other than sodium. Calcium chloride had no effect on phosphate uptake but magnesium chloride was approximately 40% as effective as sodium chloride. Combinations of NaCl and $MgCl_2$ and of NaCl and $CaCl_2$ did not produce any synergistic effects with respect to phosphate uptake. They were able to show that the stimulatory effect of sodium chloride was due to sodium, although sodium nitrate and sodium sulphate were less effective than the halides.

10.8 Nutrition

10.8.1 Carbon Requirements

Glucose, maltose and soluble starch supported the growth of all the fungi tested with the exception of *Ostracoblabe implexa* and *Althornia crouchii* (Table 10.7). Cellobiose, galactose and glycerol were able to support the growth of a few fungi while mannose was used by *Dermocystidium* sp. and *Thraustochytrium multirudimentale.* Fructose was also used by *Dermocystidium* sp. Only weak growth of one or two fungi occurred in xylose, ribose, lactose, sucrose, melobiose, trehalose, urea and ethanol, while raffinose and arabinose were not utilized by any of the fungi tested. The thraustochytrid species tested were not able to assimilate the sodium salts of gluconic, glucuronic, fumaric, oxalacetic, malic, pyruvic, lactic, acetic and formic acids at pH 7.4 or 6.1 (Goldstein, 1963 a-c).

Belsky and Goldstein (1964) have shown that, in *T. roseum,* 85% of the respiratory CO_2 was derived from endogenous reserves and 15% by exogenous glucose. They were able to show that the major pathway for glucose utilization was by the hexose monophosphate shunt while the presence of several enzymes of the Embden-Meyerhof and glyoxylate pathways and the tricarboxylic acid cycle were demonstrated.

Ellenbogen *et al.* (1969) have shown that *T. aureum, T. roseum, Schizochytrium aggregatum* and *Dermocystidium* sp. can synthesize polyunsaturated fatty acids of the w6 (linoleic) and the w3 (α-linoleic) groups. All the fungi contained large quantities of C_{20} and C_{22} polyunsaturated fatty acids which are unusual in fungi. These observations may be significant when considering the phylogeny of this group.

Of the fungi tested *A. crouchii* and *O. implexa* appear to be the most fastidious and good growth was only obtained when they were grown on a medium containing peptone and yeast extract. *A. crouchii* produced normal sporangia and zoospores on glycogen, D-trehalose or cellobiose. The addition of sodium malate to a weak yeast extract/peptone medium also permitted good growth but without zoospore production. *O. implexa* was stimulated by the simultaneous addition of sodium malate, aspartic acid and sodium glutamate. Most other carbohydrates and fatty acids tested either did not support growth, or were inhibitory (Alderman and Jones, 1971).

10.8.2 Nitrogen Requirements

Sodium glutamate supported the growth of all the fungi tested (Table 10.8) while they were unable to utilize potassium nitrate. *Thraustochytrium aureum* was able to utilize a range of nitrogen sources while in *T. motivum* good growth was only obtained with glutamate and poor growth with glutamine, L-aspartic acid and L-asparagine. Urea was not utilized by members of the Thraustochytriaceae despite the fact that it is a by product presumably present in the organically rich (polluted) waters from which they have been isolated (Goldstein, 1963 a-c).

10.8.3 Vitamin Requirements

Haliphthoros milfordensis has no requirement for thiamine while Vishniac (1955 a, b, 1958) has shown that *Sirolpidium zoophthorum, Labyrinthula* sp., isolate M and 39

Carbon source	Althornia crouchii Alderman and Jones (1971)	Ostracoblabe implexa Alderman and Jones (1971)	Dermocystidium sp. Goldstein et al. (1969)	Haliphthoros milfordensis Vishniac (1958)	Phlyctochytrium mangrovii Ulken (1972)	Schizochytrium aggregatum Goldstein and Belsky (1964)	Thraustochytrium aureum Goldstein (1963 c)	T. motivum Goldstein (1963 b)	T. multirudimentale Goldstein (1963 b)	T. roseum Goldstein (1963 a)	Sirolpidium zoophthorum Vishniac (1955)	Total No. fungi utilizing substrate
NaH glutamate	-	*	-	-	-	*p	*	0	0	*	-	4
D-glucose	*p	0	*	*	*	*	*	*	*	*	*	10
D-fructose	0	0	*	*p	*p	0	0	0	0	*p	0	4
D-mannose	0	*p	*	-	-	0	0	0	*	0	-	3
D-galactose	*	0	*	-	*p	*	0	0	*	0	0	5
D-xylose	*p	0	0	-	0	0	0	0	0	0	0	1p
L-arabinose	0	0	0	-	-	0	0	0	0	0	0	0
D-ribose	*p	0	0	*p	-	0	0	0	0	0	*p	3p
Lactose	0	0	0	*p	-	0	0	0	0	0	0	1p
Sucrose	0	0	0	*p	0	0	0	0	0	*p	*p	3p
Maltose	0	0	*	-	*	*	*	*	*	*	*p	8
Cellobiose	*p	0	-	-	-	*	*	*	*	*	0	6
D-melibiose	*p	0	0	-	-	0	0	0	0	0	-	1p
D-trehalose	*p	0	0	-	-	0	0	0	0	0	-	1p
D-raffinose	-	*p	0	-	-	0	0	0	0	0	-	0
Soluble starch	*p	-	-	*	*	*	*	*	*	*	*	10
Glycerol	-	-	0	*	0	*	*	0	0	*p	0	5
Urea	-	-	-	-	-	-	*	0	0	*p	-	2
Ethanol	-	-	0	0	-	*p	-	-	-	-	*p	2

*: Good growth.   *p: Poor Growth.   0: No growth.   –: Not tested.

273

TABLE 10.8. The effect of various nitrogen sources on the growth of some marine phycomycetes.

Nitrogen Source	Althornia crouchii Alderman and Jones (1971)	Dermocystidium sp. Goldstein et al. (1969)	Haliphthoros milfordensis Vishniac (1958)	Phlyctochytrium mangrovii Ulken (1972)	Schizochytrium aggregatum Goldstein and Belsky (1964)	Thraustochytrium aureum Goldstein (1963 c).	T. motivum Goldstein (1963 b).	T. multirudimentale Goldstein (1963 b)	T. roseum Goldstein (1963 a).	Sirolpidium zoophthorum Vishniac (1955)
KNO$_3$	0	0	–	0	0	0	0	0	0	–
(NH$_4$)$_2$SO$_4$	0	–	–	0	*p	*	0	0	*p	–
NaH glutamate	*	*	*	–p	*	*	*	*	0	*
Glutamine	–	*p	–	*p	*	*	*p	*p	*p	–
L-arginine	–p	0	–	–	*	*	0	*	*	–
L-aspartic acid	*p	*p	–	–p	*	*	*p	*p	*p	*
L-asparagine	–	*p	–	*p	*p	*	*p	*p	*	–
DL-alphaalanine	–	*p	*	0	*p	*	0	*p	*	–
DL-phenylalanine	–	*p	–	0	*	*	0	0	*	–
Urea	–	*p	–	–	0	*	0	0	*p	–
Cystine	–	0	–	0	0	0	0	0	0	–
Glycine	–	0	–	–	–	–	0	–	–	–
Histidine	–	*p	–	–	–	–	–	–	–	–
Proline	–	*p	–	–	–	–	–	–	–	–
Threonine	–	0	–	–	–	–	–	–	–	–
Valine	–	*p	–	–	–	–	–	–	–	–

*: Good growth.   *p: Poor growth.   0: No growth.   –: Not tested.

274

isolates of non-filamentous phycomycetes all require thiamine for growth. Vishniac (1961) used isolate S-3 (unidentified non-filamentous phycomycete) as a biological assay for thiamine in seawater. She found that this assay was sensitive to 25 μg/ml thiamine. Adair and Vishniac (1958) have shown that *Thraustochytrium globosum* Kobayashi et Ookubo requires cobalamin and B_{12}. Isolate S-3 is also sensitive to cobalamin.

Goldstein (1963 a-c) has tested the effect of indole-3-acetic acid on the growth of *T. aureum, T. motivum, T. multirudimentale* and *T. roseum.* IAA at 3 ppm and 10 ppm had no detectable effect on their morphology or yield.

10.8.4. Steroid Requirements

Vishniac (1955 b) and Vishniac and Watson (1953) have shown that *Labyrinthula vitellina* var *pacifica* requires a steroid as a growth factor. They showed that cholesterol, Δ, 4-cholestenone, fucosterol and B-sitosterol were all active.

10.9 Zoospore Production

Members of the Thraustochytriaceae form zoospores readily when compared with some freshwater phycomycetes (Emerson, 1958). The presence of seawater is essential, otherwise amoeboid spores or aplanospores may be formed. However in *Sirolpidium zoophthorum* sporulation is more critical and resistant cells or gemmae may be formed. Three to four day old cultures, to which 90% seawater has been added, usually result in sporangial formation. In *Haliphthoros milfordensis* sporulation can be stimulated by placing 1 ml of a stock culture into a petri dish containing 10 ml of sterile seawater, and washing with seawater every second or third day. Zoospores were formed by day 7.

Fuller, et al., (1964) were able to produce zoospores in *Lagenidium callinectes* Couch by the transfer of mycelium from a liquid medium to sterile seawater. Sporulation occurred after eight hours. They were able to obtain copious zoospore release in *Haliphthoros milfordensis* after it had been grown for 5 days at 22°C on a rotary shaker then washed three times in sterile seawater and placed in sterile seawater in a crystallizing dish for eight hours when sporulation occurred. Sporulation in *Atkinsiella dubia* (Atkins) Vishniac was induced by macerating an agar culture in a Waring Blender with 50 ml seawater for 15 seconds. After 3 days' growth on a liquid medium containing liver extract, glucose yeast extract, gelatin hydrolysate, the fungus was washed three times with sterile seawater and then left in 100 ml of sterile seawater in a crystallizing dish. Zoospores were released after about 12 hours.

Perkins and Menzel (1966) have succeeded in inducing sporulation in *Labyrinthomyxa marina* (Mackin, Owen et Collier) Mackin et Ray by placing cells in fluid thioglycollate medium for 48 hours and then digested in 0.25% trypsin for 6-8 hours. This suspension was then poured through six to eight thicknesses of cheesecloth to remove the larger clumps of cells and tissue debris. The suspension was then centrifuged at 340g for 2 minutes and four washings made. Following the washings, the cells were placed in seawater which contained antibiotics to retard bacterial growth. They were incubated at 30°C on a shaker. The first cleavage stages were observed at 24 hours and zoospores released after 3-4 days.

Marine phycomycetes are an interesting group, yet only members of the Thraustochytriaceae have had their physiology and biochemistry studied. Other fungi remain to be studied, especially species parasitic on micro-algae. The role of marine phycomycetes in the productivity of estuaries and oceans remains to be determined. It would appear that few of them are involved in the primary breakdown of materials but they may well be important in subsequent breakdown, as many of them are able to utilize cellobiose. However, Anastasiou and Churchland (1969) have shown that *Phytophthora vesicula* Anastasiou et Churchland and *Nowakowskiella elegans* (Nowak.) Schroeter are active in the degradation of leaves placed in the sea. Therefore, the role of these fungi in the breakdown of materials in natural waters cannot be totally ignored.

References

ADAIR, E. J., and VISHNIAC, H. S. (1958). 'Marine fungus requiring vitamin B_{12}' *Science,* 127, 147-148.

ALDERMAN, D. J., and JONES, E. B. G. (1971). 'Physiological requirements of two marine Phycomycetes, *Althornia crouchii* and *Ostracoblabe implexa.' Trans. Br. mycol. Soc.,* 57, 213-225.

ANASTASIOU, C. J., and CHURCHLAND, L. M. (1969). 'Fungi on decaying leaves in marine habitats.' *Can. J. Bot.,* 47, 251-257.

BARR, D. J. S. (1969). 'Studies on *Rhizophydium* and *Phlyctochytrium* (Chytridiales). II Comparative physiology'. *Can. J. Bot.,* 47, 999-1005.

BARR, D. J. S. (1970a). *'Phlyctochytrium arcticum* n.sp (Chytridiales); morphology and physiology.' *Can. J. Bot.,* 48, 2279-2283.

BARR, D. J. S. (1970b). *'Phlyctochytrium reinboldtae* (Chytridiales); morphology and physiology.' *Can. J. Bot.,* 48, 479-484.

BARR, D. J. S. (1907c). *'Hyphochytrium catenoides:* a morphological and physiological study of North American isolates.' *Mycologia,* 57, 492-503.

BARR, D. J. S. (1971). *'Entophlyctis confervae-glomeratae* (Chytridiales); physiology' *Can. J. Bot.,* 49, 2223-2225.

BELSKY, M. M., and GOLDSTEIN, S. (1964). 'Glucose metabolism of *Thraustochytrium roseum* a non-filamentous marine Phycomycete.' *Arch. Mikrobiol.,* 49, 375-382.

BREMER, G. B. (1974). 'Physiological responses of some Thraustochytrid fungi' Veröff. Inst. Meeresforsch., Bremerh., Suppl. 5, 237-250.

BOOTH, T. (1969). 'Marine fungi from British Columbia: monocentric chytrids and chytridiaceous species from coastal and interior halomorphic soils.' *Syesis,* 2, 141-161.

BOOTH, T. (1971a). 'Ecotypic responses of chytrid and chytridiaceous species to various salinity and temperature combinations.' *Can. J. Bot.,* 49, 1757-1767.

BOOTH, T. (1971b). 'Occurrence and distribution of some zoosporic fungi from soils of Hibben and Moresby Islands, Queen Charlotte Islands.' *Can. J. Bot.,* 49, 951-965.

BOOTH, T. (1971c). 'Occurrence and distribution of chytrids, chytridiaceous fungi, and some Actinomycetales from soils of Oregon, California and Nevada.' *Can. J. Bot.,* 49, 939-949.

CANTINO, E. G., and HORENSTEIN, E. A. (1959). 'The stimulatory effect of light upon growth and CO_2 fixation in *Blastocladiella* 3. Further studies in vivo and vitro.' *Plant Physiol.*, 12, 251-263.

ELLENBOGEN, B. B., AARONSON, S., GOLDSTEIN, S., and BELSKY, M. M. (1969). 'Polyunsaturated fatty acids of aquatic fungi: possible phylogenetic significance.' *Comp. Biochem. Physiol.*, 29, 805-811.

EMERSON, R. (1958). 'Mycological organisation' *Mycolgia*, 50, 589-621.

EMERSON, R., and HELD A. A. (1969). *'Aqualinderella fermentans* gen. et sp. n., a phycomycete adapted to stagnant waters. II Isolation, cultural characteristics and gas relations.' *Am. J. Bot.*, 56, 1103-1120.

FULLER, M. S., FOWLES, B. E. and McLAUGHLIN, D. J. (1964). 'Isolation and pure culture study of marine phycomycetes.' *Mycologia*, 56, 745-756.

GAERTNER, A. (1967). 'Neiderer mit pollen köderbarer Pilze in der sudlichen Nordsee.' *Veröff. Inst. Meeresforsch. Bremerh.*, 10, 159-165.

GOLDSTEIN, S.(1963 a). 'Studies of a new species of *Thraustochytrium* that displays light stimulated growth.' *Mycologia*, 55, 799-811.

GOLDSTEIN, S. (1963 b). 'Development and nutrition of a new species of *Thraustochytrium.' Am. J. Bot.*, 50, 271-279.

GOLDSTEIN, S. (1963 c). 'Morphological variation and nutrition of a new monocentric marine fungus.' *Arch. Mikrobiol.*, 45, 101-110.

GOLDSTEIN, S., and BELSKY, M. M. (1964). 'Axenic culture studies of a new marine Phycomycete possessing an unusual type of asexual reproduction.' *Am. J. Bot.*, 51, 72-78.

GOLDSTEIN, S., and MORIBER, L. (1966). 'Biology of a problematic marine fungus, *Dermocystidium* sp., 1. Development and cytology.' *Arch. Mikrobiol.*, 53, 1-11.

GOLDSTEIN, S., BELSKY, M. M., and CHOSAK, R. (1969). 'Biology of a problematic marine fungus, *Dermocystidium* sp. II. Nutrition and respiration.' *Mycologia*, 61, 468-472.

HARDER, R., and UEBELMESSER, E. (1955). 'Uber marine saprophytische Chytridiales und einige andere Pilze vom Meerestrand.' *Arch. Mikrobiol.*, 22, 87-114.

HARRISON, J. L. (1972). 'The salinity tolerances of freshwater and marine zoosporic fungi, including some aspects of the ecology and ultrastructure of the Thraustochytriaceae.' *Ph.D. Thesis, Univ. London.*

HÖHNK, W. (1939). 'Ein Beitrag zur Kenntnis der Phycomyceten des Brackwassers.' *Kieler Meeresforsch.*, 3, 337-361.

HÖHNK, W. (1952 a). 'Studien zur Brack — und Seewassermykologie I.' *Veröff. Inst. Meeresforsch. Bremerh.*, 1, 115-125.

HÖHNK, W. (1952 b). 'Studien zur Brack — und Seewassermykologie II. Oömycetes: Erster Teil.' *Veröff. Inst. Meeresforsch. Bremerh.*, 1, 247-278.

HÖHNK, W. (1953). 'Studien zur Brack — und Seewassermykologie III. Oömycetes: Zweiter Teil.' *Veröff. Inst. Meeresforsch. Bremerh.*, 2, 52-108.

HÖHNK, W. (1955). 'Niedere Pilze vom Watt und Meeresgrund (Chytridiales und Thraustochytriaceae).' *Naturwissenschaften*, 11, 348-349.

HÖHNK, W. (1956). 'Studien zur Brack — und Seewassermykologie VI. Uber die pilzeliche Besiedlung verschieden salziger submerser Standorte.' *Veröff. Inst. Meeresforsch., Bremerh.*, 4, 195-213.

HÖHNK, W. (1957). 'Fortschritte der marinen Mykologie in Jüngster Zeit'. *Naturw., Rdsch. Stuttg.*,2, 39-44.

JOHNSON, T. W. Jr. (1960). 'Infection potential and growth of *Lagenidium chthamalophilum.' Am. J. Bot.*, 47, 383-385.

JOHNSON, T. W. Jr., and SPARROW, F. K. Jr. (1961). 'Fungi in oceans and estuaries.' Weinheim: Cramer, J., 668 pp.

PERKINS, F. O. and MENZEL, R. W. (1966). 'Morphological and cultural studies of a motile stage in the life cycle of *Dermocystidium marinum.*' *Proc. natn. Shellfish Assoc.* 56, 23-30.

SCHNEIDER, J. (1969). 'Zur Taxonomie, verbreitung und Okologie einiger mariner Phycomyceten.' *Kieler Meeresforsch.*, 25, 316-327.

SCHNEIDER, J. (1971). 'Niedere pilze aus bodenproben des brack — und meerwassers der englischen west küste'. *Kieler Meeresforsch.*, 27, 94-101.

SIEGENTHALER, P. A., BELSKY, M. M., and GOLDSTEIN, S. (1967). 'Phosphate uptake in an obligately marine fungus: a specific requirement for sodium'. *Science*, 155, 93-94.

ULKEN, A. M. (1965). 'Zwei neue Thraustochytrien aus der Aubenweser.' *Veröff. Inst. Meeresforsch. Bremerh.*, 10, 289-294.

ULKEN, A. (1966). 'Untersuchungen uber marine pilze in äquatorialen Atlantik vor der Küste Brasiliens.' *Veröff. Inst. Meeresforsch. Bremerh.*, 10, 107-116.

ULKEN, A. (1968). 'Über zwei marine niedere pilze vom meeresboden der Nordsee.' *Veröff. Inst. Meeresforsch. Bremerh.*, 3, 71-74.

ULKEN, A. (1970). 'Phycomyceten aus der Mangrove bei Cananéia (Sao Paulo, Brasilien).' *Veröff. Inst. Meeresforsch. Bremerh.*, 12, 313-319.

ULKEN, A. (1972). 'Physiological studies on a Phycomycete from a mangrove swamp at Cananéia, Sao Paulo, Brasil' *Veröff. Inst. Meeresforsch. Bremerh.*, 13, 217-230.

VISHNIAC, H. S. (1955 a). 'The morphology and nutrition of a new species of *Sirolpidium.*' *Mycologia,* 47, 633-645.

VISHNIAC, H. S. (1955 b). 'The nutritional requirements of isolates of *Labyrinthula* spp.' *J. gen. Microbiol.*, 12, 455-463.

VISHNIAC, H. S. (1956). 'On the ecology of the lower marine fungi.' *Biol. Bull., mar. biol. Lab., Woods Hole*, 111, 410-414.

VISHNIAC, H. S. (1958). 'A new marine Phycomycete.' *Mycologia,* 50, 66-79.

VISHNIAC, H. S. (1960). 'Salt requirements of marine phycomycetes.' *Limol. Oceanogr.*, 5, 362-365.

VISHNIAC, H. S. (1961). 'A biological assay for thiamine in sea water.' *Limnol. Oceanogr.*, 6, 31-35.

VISHNIAC, H. S., and WATSON, S. W. (1953). 'The steroid requirements of *Labyrinthula vitellina* var. *pacifica.*' *J. gen. Microbiol.*, 8, 248-225.

WATSON, S. W. (1951). 'Studies on *Labyrinthula.*' M.Sc. Dissertation, Univ. Washington, Seattle.

YOUNG, E. L. (1943). 'Studies on *Labyrinthula.* The etiologic agent of the wasting disease of eel-grass.' *Am. J. Bot.*, 30, 586-593.

11 Fine Structure of Lower Marine and Estuarine Fungi*†

FRANK O. PERKINS

11.1 Introduction

There are only a few species of lower fungi which can be characterized as marine or estuarine micro-organisms to the satisfaction of most workers; however, despite the small number of presently known species, there is a considerable amount of information available on their ultrastructure. 'Lower fungi' are defined herein as being those eucaryotic, achlorophyllous organisms which are encompassed by the Myxomycota, Mastigomycotina, and Zygomycotina as defined by Ainsworth (1966). This does not imply acceptance of all subdivisions of Ainsworth's classification; however, the scheme is useful in defining the 'lower fungi'. With the many different taxonomic schemes which exist to accommodate the slime moulds, Plasmodiophorales, and Labyrinthulales (Honigberg et al., 1964; Kudo, 1966; Ainsworth, 1966; Pokorny, 1967; Olive, 1970) their classification can not be considered a settled issue.

In addition to Myxomycota, Mastigomycotina, and Zygomycotina, *Dermocystidium* spp. (except *Dermocystidium* sp., Goldstein and Moriber, 1966) are also considered herein to be members of the lower fungi, although their affinities are uncertain (Perkins, 1974). Members of the genus have many characteristics similar to the biflagellate Oömycetes and none which could definitely exclude them from the group. They are holocarpic species which form fungus-like walls around all cells except zoospores, have no photosynthetic apparatus, form biflagellate zoospores from sporangia, and have zoospores with mastigonemes along the anterior flagellum. *Dermocystidium* sp. sensu Goldstein and Moriber is excluded from this presentation, because Poyton (1970) has presented evidence that it is a colourless alga closely related to *Chlorella*. The labyrinthulids (species of *Labyrinthula, Labyrinthuloides,* and *Labyrinthomyxa*) are also questionable fungi; however, they are included because there is evidence that they are related to the Thraustochytriaceae (Perkins, 1972, 1974), currently members of the Saprolegniales (Oömycetes). The chief evidence lies in the

*Contribution No. 662, Virginia Institute of Marine Science, Gloucester Point, Virginia 23062.
†Supported in part by the Oceanography Section, National Science Foundation, NSF Grant GA-31014.

279

similarity of zoospore surface structure and the formation of ectoplasmic nets from specialized and unique organelles termed sagenogenetosomes (Perkins, 1972). Conversely these similarities may mean that the Thraustochytriaceae are not Oömycetes or even fungi; however, in the absence of convincing evidence and as a convenient measure, the thraustochytrids and labyrinthulids will be considered as fungi herein.

Mackin and Ray (1966) changed the name of the oyster pathogen *D. marinum* Mackin, Owen et Collier to *Labyrinthomyxa marina* (Mackin, Owen et Collier) Mackin et Ray, primarily because plasmodia, cells which glide on mucoid tracks, and diads, tetrads, and morula-like clumps of cells were observed on beef serum agar plates after inoculation with infected oyster blood. If the oyster pathogen does form gliding cells which use ectoplasmic nets (Perkins, 1972) to accomplish motility, then the placement would appear valid. Since I have not been able to induce the production of such cell types, I have chosen to utilize the name *D. marinum* until more information is available.

Among the organisms discussed herein none appears to possess structures which could be termed adaptive for existence in the marine or estuarine environment. Therefore, this information is probably of more interest to the worker curious about the biological characteristics of the species as fungi rather than as marine organisms. For example, most of the studies have significance in the area of phylogeny: to what degree are the lower fungi related to algae and Protozoa and to what groups? Other studies have importance in diverse areas such as organelle morphogenesis and virology.

The species considered in this presentation are listed in Table 11.1 with the pertinent literature citations and possible classifications.

11.2 Sporogenesis

11.2.1 Planospore Formation

Of the marine and estuarine Chytridiomycetes, only the fine structure of *Phlyctochytrium* sp. has been examined (Kazama, 1972 c). Growth was induced on artificial media *Bryopsis plumosa* (Hudson) Agardh. filaments, and grass leaves. After epibiotic encystment on the wall of a host cell, an unbranched germ tube is extended through the host wall (Fig. 11.1) followed by apophysis formation inside the wall. Branching of the rhizoid occurs inside the host cell from the distal end of the apophysis. The extensions of the encysted cell are true rhizoids in that they are delimited by a wall and contain cytoplasm and associated organelles such as mitochondria, ribosomes, membranes, and lipid droplets. Even the smallest subdivisions may contain organelles and inclusions (Kazama, personal communication). Rhizoids are markedly different from the ectoplasmic nets or 'rhizoids' of thraustochytriaceous organisms which are discussed below.

In his isolate of *Phlyctochytrium,* Kazama (1972 c) noted that considerable variability exists in whether or not apophyses are formed. Formation of the rhizoidal swelling may be a function of whether a restrictive structure such as a host cell wall is penetrated by the germ tube. Under those conditions the germ tube within the cell wall would be prevented from expanding and merging with the sporangium as they both enlarge. When cells are grown on nutrient agar medium a single germ tube is extended, forms branches on the distal end, and then enlarges as the cell increases in diameter. A pyriform cell results which becomes spherical as the cell mass increases and the germ tube is incorporated into the cell body. Apophyses are, therefore, not usually formed. If they are formed they are transient, being incorporated into the cell as it enlarges.

TABLE 11.1 List of lower fungi from marine and estuarine habitats which have been studied by electron microscopy.

Class or order	Species	References
Chytridiales	*Phlyctochytrium* sp. (isolate 71-1-E)	Kazama (1972 c, 1972 d)
Labyrinthulales	*Labyrinthula coenocystis* Schmoller	Bartsch (1971); Klie and Mach (1968); Stey (1968, 1969)
Labyrinthulales	*Labyrinthula* sp.	Hohl (1966)
Labyrinthulales	*Labyrinthula* sp. L65-8	Porter (1969, 1972)
Labyrinthulales	*L. algeriensis* Hollande et Enjumet	Amon and Perkins (1968); Moens and Perkins (1969); Perkins (1970, 1972, 1973 a, 1974); Perkins and Amon (1969)
Labyrinthulales	*L. vitellina* Cienkowski	Porter (1974)
Labyrinthulales	*L. minuta* Watson et Raper	Perkins (1972, 1973 a)
Labyrinthulales	*Labyrinthuloides yorkensis* Perkins	Perkins (1972, 1973 b)
Unknown	*Thraustochytrium* sp.	Gaertner (1964)
Unknown	*T. aureum* Goldstein	Goldstein *et al.* (1964)
Unknown	*Thraustochytrium* sp.	Kazama (1972 a, 1972 b, 1973); Kazama and Schornstein (1972, 1973)
Unknown	*Schizochytrium aggregatum* Goldstein et Belsky	Darley and Fuller (1970); Darley *et al.* (1973); Perkins (1974); Porter (1974)
Saprolegniales	*Atkinsiella dubia* (Atkins) Vishniac	Aronson and Fuller (1969)
Peronosporales	*Pythium marinum* Sparrow	Kazama and Fuller (1970)
Lagenidiales	*Lagenidium callinectes* Couch	Amerson and Bland (1973)
Unknown	*Althornia crouchii* Jones et Alderman	Jones and Alderman (1971)
Unknown	*Dermocystidium marinum* (= *Labyrinthomyxa marina*)	Perkins (1968, 1969); Perkins and Menzel (1966, 1967)

Phlyctochytrium sp. zoosporulation proceeds by enlargement of an uninucleate cell and proliferation of its rhizoidal complex followed by cross-wall formation at the base of the main trunk rhizoid where it merges with the cell. Progressive cleavage (repeated karyokineses followed by cytokinesis) occurs to delimit the zoospores, then 1-10 discharge papillae are formed. A secondary sporangial wall is formed within the original wall at the site of papilla formation after which electron-opaque plug material accumulates beneath the secondary wall to form a globe of material. The walls overlying the plug disintegrate and then the plug erodes peripherally. Internal pressure appears to in-

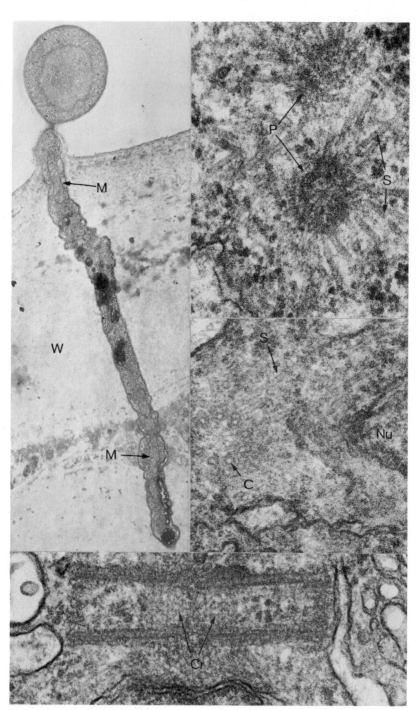

crease as evidenced by flattening of the formerly convex inner surface of the plug. Continued erosion leads to dissolution of the plug and formation of a pore through which the zoospores escape.

Kazama's studies of *Phlyctochytrium* sp. grown on three different substrates underlined the weaknesses inherent in taxonomic schemes based on numbers of discharge papillae, presence or absence of apophyses, degree of rhizoid branching, and sporangial size. However, there are so few structures which can be used as taxonomic markers that the above characteristics may need to be retained. Possibly a solution to the problem can be found in utilizing a 'standard' natural substrate such as *Bryopsis plumosa*. This approach has been championed by Goldstein (1963) and Gaertner (1972) in dealing with the difficult problems of classification within the Thraustochytriaceae. They used pine pollen as a substrate. Whereas natural substrates cannot be standardized to the degree that one can control a chemically defined medium, they can be standardized to cell type and species. This may prove to be adequate in identifying species in spite of the biochemical variability present in the natural substrates. Careful observations of many pure cultures grown on such substrates need to be made in the future where structural variability is a problem in fungal taxonomy.

Natural substrates are awkward to use; however, they may be necessary unless alternate techniques can be developed such as the one devised by Alderman and Harrison (1971) where the cells are immersed in seawater and the ectoplasmic nets are embedded in an agar medium which contains denatured protein. The medium is designed to present the cells with a gradient of nutrients similar to those which exist when the cells grow epibiotically and to avoid the apparently anomalous results obtained when cells are grown on nutrient agar without a fluid overlay. Gaertner (1972) believes that species-significant characteristics are not stable in such media as the culture ages. Possibly future studies will resolve whether the technique has merit as a replacement for natural substrates.

Zoosporulation in at least one species of *Labyrinthula* is a meiotic process in which motile cells aggregate into irregular masses of cells, all delimited by a fibrillar wall (Perkins and Amon, 1969). The *L. algeriensis* cells become rounded and two fibrogranular aggregates, the protocentrioles, are formed together next to the nuclear envelope (Perkins, 1970) (Fig. 11.2). They then migrate to opposite sides of the nucleus and meiosis I becomes evident in the formation of nine synaptonemal complexes (Moens and Perkins, 1969). Each protocentriole, in the centre of which has been formed a cartwheel complex (see Fig. 11.12 for similar mitotic structure), is then transformed into two end-to-end centrioles (Fig. 11.4). The transformation is initiated by the formation of a ring of nine microtubules, each at the end of a cartwheel spoke (Fig. 11.3). Additional microtubules are added to form nine triplet blades in the usual centriole configuration. Binary fission of the bicentrioles occurs to yield one diplosome

---

Fig. 11.1 Five-hour-old germling of *Phlyctochytrium* sp. with germ tube penetrating wall (W) of *Bryopsis plumosa* cell. Germ tube is delimited by a wall and contains mitochondria (M) and other cytoplasmic organelles (x 16 000). [Reproduced by permission of the National Research Council of Canada from the *Canadian Journal of Botany,* 50, pp. 499-505 (1972).] **Figs. 11.2-11.4** Morphogenesis of *Labyrinthula algeriensis* centrioles during meiosis in zoosporulation. Fig. 11.2; two protocentrioles (P) in early prophase I sporangium. Spindle microtubules (S) (x 70 000) (from Perkins and Amon, 1969). **Fig. 11.3**: centriole (C) developing from protocentriole. A ring of nine singlet and doublet microtubules has been formed which is normally followed by addition of more microtubules to form nine triplet blades of a mature centriole. Spindle microtubules (S); nucleus (Nu) (x 66 000) (from Perkins, 1970). Fig. 11.4: Bicentriole consisting of two mature centrioles derived from differentiation of a single protocentriole and joined at the proximal ends. Cartwheel regions (Cr) (x 95 000) (from Perkins, 1970).

at each pole of the elongating metaphase nucleus. Partial nuclear envelope breakdown occurs followed by migration of the fragments to the meiotic spindle poles, then reorganization to form the daughter nuclei.

Meiosis II and one mitosis occur to yield eight zoospores. Prior to the second and third divisions centriole replication appears to occur by orthogonal budding from each of the pre-existing centrioles. Cytokinesis was described as occurring by invagination of the plasmalemma (Perkins and Amon, 1969); however, the process requires further study particularly since Stey (1969) and Porter (1972) both deduced that cytokinesis in spindle cell division occurs by linking of vesicles.

Prior to mitotic cytokinesis in the zoosporulation sequence of *L. algeriensis,* the centrioles migrate to the cell surface and become kinetosomes. Two of the microtubules of each triplet blade lengthen resulting in a flagellar bud which becomes the full length flagellum through further lengthening and addition of two centrally located microtubules. The latter are attached to a thick basal plate which is formed at the transition zone where the triplet microtubular blades become doublets. An electron-dense cylindrical granule is formed in the lumen of the kinetosome, possibly by budding from the basal plate (Perkins and Amon, 1969).

Throughout sporulation in *L. algeriensis,* but most prevalent in nearly mature zoospores, cytoplasmic vesicles were found containing fibres now believed to be mastigonemes in light of studies such as those of Heath *et al.,* (1970). The fibres are about 155 Å in diameter with an electron-dense cortex and electron-light medulla. They appear to arise in the perinuclear continuum and migrate to the base of the anterior flagellum where they appear as a tuft of fibres attached around the flagellar base and directed toward the flagellar tip. Presumably migration occurs along the flagellum followed by attachment in a bilateral array along the full length of the flagellum. Lengths and diameters of the fibres in cytoplasmic vesicles were comparable to mastigonemes attached to the flagellum (Perkins, unpublished data). Since the fibres were found in presporangia it appears that synthesis of the mastigonemes begins very early in sporulation prior to meiosis.

Labyrinthula minuta, a species which appears to belong in the new genus *Labyrinthuloides* (Perkins, 1973 b), forms planospores from a four-cell sporangium as a result of two successive bipartitions of the protoplast. The resulting daughter cells form walls around themselves, the mother cell wall is torn, and the cells glide away by means of ectoplasmic nets. No flagellated cells have been observed (Perkins, 1972; unpublished data) except those seen by Watson (1957).

Labyrinthuloides yorkensis is similar to *L. minuta* except that from four up to 64 motile, gliding cells may be formed as a result of successive bipartition or progressive cleavage (Perkins, 1973 b). Biflagellate zoospores are formed; however, the details of morphogenesis have not been elucidated. It is not known whether invagination of the plasmalemma or fusion of vesicles is the mechanism for formation of cleavage furrows. In sporogenesis nuclear size varies greatly. Uninucleate motile cells of about 3 to 6 μm longest axis have nuclei of 1.5 to 2.0 μm diameter, whereas nuclei increase to 6 or 7 μm in enlarged (15 to 25 μm diameter) cells prior to the first nuclear division. Successive karyokineses reduce the nuclear size of the released motile cells back to 1.5-2.0 μm diameter.

The American oyster pathogen, *Dermocystidium marinum,* also shows marked changes in nuclear size during sporogenesis, except that the changes occur in zoosporulation (Perkins and Menzel, 1966; 1967). Spheroidal or cuneiform, immature thalli enlarge by a factor up to 10 times the original diameter in fluid thioglycollate medium or, presumably, degenerating oyster tissue. A large eccentrically located vacuole is formed which results in a signet ring-like arrangement of the cytoplasm around the cell periphery. At this time of maximum enlargement the cell is a presporangium and will initiate zoosporulation when placed in seawater or a comparable saline solution. The nucleus is oval, 3 to 6 μm in longest axis, and the cytoplasm contains numerous lipoidal inclusions and membrane arrays. No clearly identifiable mitochondria or Golgi bodies are visible.

When zoosporulation commences, cytoplasmic inclusions are digested resulting in a more hyaline cytoplasm, the nucleus enlarges further by a factor of two or three along the shortest axis, and mitochondria are reformed from membrane whorls and parallel arrays of membranes. Similar stages of mitochondrial development were observed by Stey (1969) in *Labyrinthula coenocystis* spindle cells which were emerging from aggregation cysts. As *D. marinum* zoosporulation progresses, two additional wall layers are formed beneath the primary cell wall and the innermost one thickens in one region to form a plug of reticulofibrillar material. Erosion of the two wall layers overlying the plug occurs followed by extension of the plug material to form a delicate discharge tube (Perkins and Menzel, 1967). Considerable internal cell pressure is apparently generated as evidenced by the bulging of the wall in the region of erosion prior to wall rupture. The sequence of steps is remarkably similar to that followed by *Phlyctochytrium* sp. (Kazama, 1972 c).

As the sporangium of *D. marinum* approaches first cleavage, the protoplasm contracts, the large vacuole is subdivided in the cytoplasm, and much of the vacuolar fluid is emptied into the resulting region between the wall and plasmalemma. Subsequent bipartitioning occurs to yield motile zoospores which escape through the single discharge pore after dissolution of the plug. Each successive set of divisions results in a smaller size nucleus until the nucleus is reduced to an oval structure about 0.8 x 2 μm in motile zoospores. Centrioles with microtubular, triplet blade substructure are present before and throughout zoosporulation. A cylindrical, electron-opaque granule like the one found in *Labyrinthula algeriensis* zoospores is present in the centriole lumen.

11.2.2 Aplanospore Formation

Only in *D. marinum* have the details of aplanospore formation been described (Perkins, 1969). Uninucleate, immature thalli, which are spheroidal or cuneiform, enlarge from about 3 to about 10 μm in longest axis, then repeated karyokineses occur followed by cytokinesis. Division of the cytoplasm appears to occur by invagination of the plasmalemma and not by linking of rows of vesicles. The resulting sporangia may contain 4, 8, 16, 32, or, rarely, 64 immature thalli, all with walls formed before rupture of the sporangial wall. Two-cell stages are observed, but it is uncertain whether they represent simple cell division or a stage in successive bipartition. A pair of typical microtubular centrioles, each with an electron-opaque cylindrical granule, are found embedded in depressions of the envelope of interphase nuclei. They are oriented in a parallel, not orthogonal configuration. The ultrastructure of mitosis has not been observed.

Numerous lomasomes are found beneath the walls of cells in all stages. They consist of tubular evaginations of the cytoplasm arranged in convoluted masses. There is no strong indication of lomasome participation in cell wall formation; although lomasome tubules are found to be extracted in some cells. It is suggested that wall deposition occurs by fusion of small vesicles to the plasmalemma and addition of their contents to the wall. No definite Golgi bodies were noted; the endoplasmic reticulum appears to be the source of the presumptive wall vesicles.

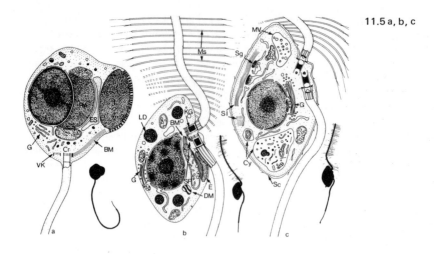

11.5 a, b, c

Figs. 11.5 Diagrams of zoospores described herein. Fig. 11.5 a *Phlyctochytrium* sp.; Fig. 11.5 b *Labyrinthula algeriensis*; Fig. 11.5 c *Thraustochytrium* sp.; Fig. 11.5 d *Schizochytrium aggregatum*; Fig. 11.5 e *Althornia crouchii*; Fig. 11.5 f *Dermocystidium marinum*. Zoospore silhouette drawings are presented on the right of each respective zoospore. Details of kinetosome and mastigoneme structure in *A. crouchii* were drawn from micrographs of Jones and Alderman (1971) and are the author's interpretations of available data. Future studies will probably reveal two mastigoneme extensions in *A. crouchii*, not one. Bundle of microtubules (BM); conoid-like apparatus (Co); cartwheel complexes (Cr); cytolysomes (Cy); developing mastigonemes (DM); eyespot (E); para-nuclear endoplasmic reticulum with swollen cisternae (ER); electron-opaque sac (ES); Golgi body (G); inclusion body (Ic); kinetosome granule (KG); lipoid body or eyespot? (L); lipid drop-let (LD); mastigonemes (Ms); microtubule (Mt); multivesicular body (MV); ribosomal aggregate (RA); membrane-limited sac (Sa); scales (Sc); striated fibre apparatus (SF); sagenogenetosome (Sg); striated inclusions (SI); vacuole (V); vestigial kinetosome (VK). (all figures x 7000).

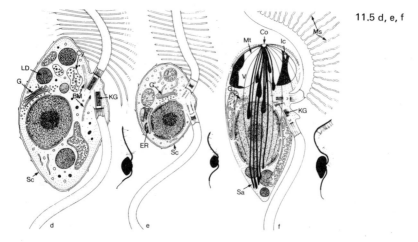

11.5 d, e, f

11.3   Zoospore Structure

Possibly because of the significance attached to the zoospore in fungal phylogeny, it has been extensively studied in marine and estuarine fungi as in other lower fungi (Fuller, 1966). Thus far, knowledge of its structure and mode of formation has been useful in helping to determine affinities. In Fig. 11.5 I have diagrammatically summarized known zoospore structure of the species discussed herein.

Phlyctochytrium sp. zoospores (Fig. 11.5a) are uninucleate cells with a whiplash flagellum, ribosomal cap, and large lipid droplet complex (Kazama, 1972 d). The functional kinetosome has a vestigial kinetosome oriented nearly parallel to it. A group of about four microtubules, oriented approximately parallel to each other, are attached to an electron-dense granular aggregate near the functional kinetosome and extend to the large lipid body. A dictyosome-like grouping of flattened vesicles is found next to the nucleus. Two or more mitochondria are clustered around an aggregate of ribosomes which are situated on one side of the nucleus. The aggregate is partially delimited by a double membrane, several mitochondria, and the nucleus. Aggregations of ribosomes organized into nuclear caps are typical of many uniflagellate fungal zoospores.

The large lipid body complex consists of a flattened sac containing electron-dense material, located between an obvate lipid droplet, and the ribosomal aggregate. Along the surface facing the plasmalemma are periodically arranged membranous tubes extending from the droplet face and packed together into hexagonal arrays. Since the zoospores are positively phototactic, Kazama (1972 d) suggested that the lipid body complex may serve as a photo-receptive organelle.

L. algeriensis zoospores (Fig. 11.5b) are uninucleate and biflagellate with an anteriorly directed pantoneme flagellum (mastigonemes along both sides of flagellum as seen in profile; Pitelka, 1963) and a posteriorly directed acroneme or whiplash flagellum (Amon and Perkins, 1968). Mastigonemes are 1.3-1.6 μm long and divided into two parts, a basal portion of uniform thickness and one or two thin distal extensions (Fig. 11.5b). The shorter extension may not be retained on many mastigonemes during specimen preparation, which would account for those with only one extension. This problem in specimen preservation applies to the other zoospores with pantoneme flagella (Figs. 11.5 b-11.5 e). Although two extensions have not always been reported, there is reason to suspect that they exist in the thraustochytrids and labyrinthulids (Kazama, personal communication).

The posterior flagellum contains a paraflagellar 'rod' about 0.7 μm long situated in a swelling at the base of the flagellum and overlying an eyespot which consists of an electron-opaque, rod-shaped granule or row of granules embedded in the cell body slightly beneath the plasmalemma (Perkins and Amon, 1969). The 'rod' consists of a crecent-shaped bar with a lattice substructure of 130-140 Å and 230-260 Å periodicities. Along the proximal face of the eyespot is found a single row of 17-21 microtubules which converge on the anterior kinetosome. Structure and arrangement of the flagellar swelling, eyespot, and microtubules are remarkably similar to many algal planonts (Leedale, 1967; Dodge, 1969; Hibberd, 1970). A single long mitochondrion lies parallel and proximal to the eyespot and is separated from it by a deep invagination of the cell surface (not shown in Fig. 11.5 b).

The kinetosomes which are almost in an orthogonal orientation are joined by an ellipsoidal striated, fibrous body similar to some green algal planonts (Ringo, 1967; Peterfi and Manton, 1968). A large cylindrical granule, typical of the labyrinthulids and thraustochytrids, is found in the lumen of each kinetosome. About five tiers of

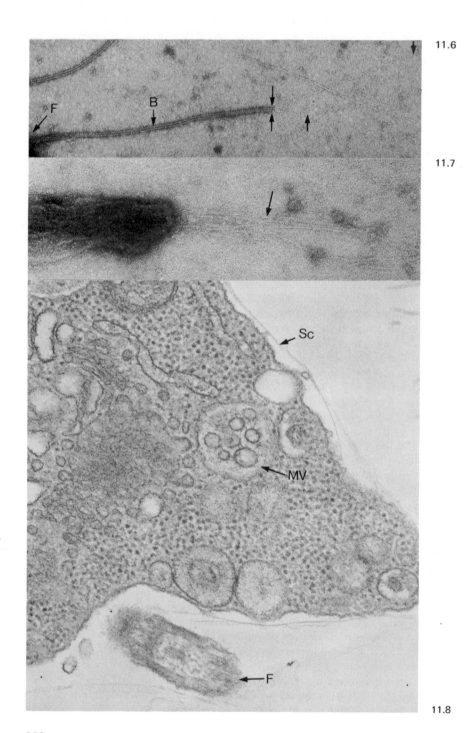

11.6

11.7

11.8

cartwheels are present at the proximal end of the kinetosome and a thick basal plate delimits the distal end.

A Golgi body is found along the nuclear surface opposed to the kinetosomes. Scattered mitochondria, membrane-free ribosomes, electron-dense inclusions, and endoplasmic reticulum cisternae are included in the rest of the cell structure.

Porter (1974) presented a brief description of *Labyrinthula vitellina* zoospores in which he found basically the same surface morphology and flagellar swelling-eyespot relationship as in *L. algeriensis.* The orange eyespot was observed with associated microtubules extending to the anterior kinetosome.

Thraustochytrium sp. zoospores (Fig. 11.5 c) have been described by Gaertner (1964) and Kazama (1972 a, b; 1973). Gaertner noted that the cells have an anteriorly directed pantoneme and a posteriorly directed whiplash flagellum. In working with another isolate of *Thraustochytrium*, probably *T. motivum*, Kazama (unpublished data) observed that each mastigoneme consists of a thick basal portion, about 0.78 μm long and hollow through part of its length, with two thin terminal extensions, about 0.57 μm and 0.12 μm long (Fig. 11.6). The whiplash flagellum was found to have several 34 Å diameter threads extending from its distal end (Figs. 11.5 c and 11.7). The surface of motile zoospores was found to be covered with thin scales which formed a thin 'wall' around the cell body with openings for the flagella (Kazama, unpublished data; Fig. 11.8). See Fig. 11.10 for whole mount view of comparable scales.

Internally *Thraustochytrium* sp. zoospores contain kinetosomes with complex substructure consisting of a proximal granule in the lumen and a medially located ringlet of nine electron-opaque rods which appear in longitudinal sections of the kinetosome as an electron-dense cylinder with convex ends (Kazama, 1972 a) (Fig. 11.5 c). In the transition zone between the triplet microtubules of the kinetosome and the doublets of the flagellum is found a curved electon-dense disc. Distal to the disc is a terminal plate with a cone attached to the plate and facing the disc. Thus the kinetosome lumen contains several electron-dense structures, not a single cylinder as in *L. algeriensis* or, as will be described below, in *D. marinum* and *S. aggregatum.*

Striated inclusion bodies up to 0.63 μm wide and 2.90 μm long are found scattered in the cytoplasm of *Thraustochytrium* sp. zoospores (Kazama, 1972 b). The bodies consist of parallel arrays of filaments, 36 Å in diameter, situated 52 Å apart. They are often found associated with sagenogenetosomes (see Section 11.5.2) in which case the electron-opaque granular aggregate is found closest to the inclusions and the endoplasmic reticulum portion is on the opposite side. Sagenogenetosomes have been shown to participate in ectoplasmic net formation; therefore, it is interesting to note that the zoospores, which have no nets, possess the generative organelles. Kazama (1972 b) suggested that the sagenogenetosomes (= bothrosomes) synthesize or assemble the inclusions and implied that the organelles might utilize the inclusions in net formation after the zoospore encysts (Fig. 11.27).

Fig. 11.6 Mastigoneme of *Thraustochytrium* sp. zoospore. Note the thicker basal portion (B) which is hollow and the two thin terminal extensions (limits indicated by arrows). Flagellum (F). (x 60 000) (micrograph by F. Kazama). **Fig. 11.7** *Thraustochytrium* sp. whiplash flagellum with thin filaments (arrow) extending from tip. (x 114 000) (micrograph supplied by F. Kazama, Virginia Institute Marine Science). **Fig. 11.8** *Thraustochytrium* sp. zoospore with 1 or 2 layers of scales (Sc) on cell surface. The layers are discontinuous where the flagellum (F) emerges from the cell body and the flagellum is naked. Multivesicular body (MV) (x 78 000) (micrograph by F. Kazama, Virginia Institute Marine Science).

Kazama (1973) presented evidence that zoospores of *Thraustochytrium* sp. auto-phagocytoze their cytoplasm. Using localization techniques for acid phosphatase at the fine structure level, he found that vesicles which contain the enzyme encircle and en-close portions of the cytoplasm in a vesicle consisting of two concentric, delimiting membranes. This results in degeneration of the vesicle contents after the inner mem-brane of the enzyme-containing vesicle degenerates. Many of these smaller cytoly-somes may fuse to form large ones where digestion presumably is completed. Multi-vesicular bodies also appeared to develop into large cytolysomes (Fig. 11.9). The fate of the large autophagic vesicles was not determined although it was suggested that dilution and distribution of the contents into zoospores occurred during asexual re-production.

The zoospore surface structure of *Schizochytrium aggregatum* closely resembles *Thraustochytrium* sp. zoospores (Fig. 11.5 d). Perkins (1974) noted that the anterior flagellum has mastigonemes, bilaterally arranged, with one or two thin terminal extensions. The posterior flagellum was described as naked, but has subse-quently been shown to have thin threads extending from the distal end of the pos-terior flagellum as in *Thraustochytrium* sp. zoospores (Perkins and Kazama, unpub-lished data). Kazama (unpublished data) also observed thin threads extending from the distal end of the anterior flagellum (Fig. 11.5 d). As can be seen in both sections and whole mounts, round and oval scales, about 30 to 50 Å thick and 0.9 μm in longest axis, cover the cell body, but not the flagella (Fig. 11.10) (Perkins, unpublish-ed data). Darley *et al.* (1973) did not find scales on zoospores in their isolate of *S. aggregatum.*

Kinetosomes of *S. aggregatum* resemble those of *L. algeriensis* with a cylindrical inclusion in the lumen and a single basal plate (Perkins, 1974). It is not known whether cartwheels are present at the proximal end. Multivesicular bodies, vesicles resembling the cytolysomes of *Thraustochytrium* sp., a Golgi body, and lipoid droplets are also present in the cytoplasm. As in the other zoospores rough endoplas-mic reticulum is not present.

Althornia crouchii was reported to form two types of biflagellate zoospores as a result of diplanetism (Jones and Alderman, 1971). A reappraisal of the organism has led the authors (personal communication) to believe that diplanetism is not present in the life cycle but rather that cell shape changes of individual zoospores occur during their swimming phase. Fig. 11.5 e has been drawn from their description of the 'secondary' zoospore using flagella and cell body dimensions obtained from Plate 3, Figs. 2 and 4 of Jones and Alderman (1971). Zoospore cell bodies are covered with thin oval or round scales about 1 μm in longest axis (measurements from Jones and Alderman, 1971; Figs. 3 and 4). Mastigonemes are present on the anterior flagellum in a pantoneme configuration with one or more thin terminal extensions (Alderman, personal communication). The cell body is unusually short being about 2 μm long, and the flagella are about 4 μm long (see Table 11.2 for comparative list of zoospore sizes). The posterior flagellum is of the whiplash type.

Fig. 11.9 *Thraustochytrium* sp. zoospore showing presumed sequence of development (A → D) from multivesicular body (MV) to cytolysome (Cy). Wall scales (Sc) (x 53 000 X) (from Kazama, 1973). **Fig. 11.10** Whole mount of *Schizochytrium aggregatum* zoospore shadowed with platinum and palladium. Scales (Sc) were dislodged from cell body (x 15 000). **Fig. 11.11** Protocentriole of *Labyrinthula* sp. from mitotic spindle cell. Centre of the fibrogranular aggregate has differ-entiated into a nine-fold cartwheel complex (Cr). No microtubular elements are present in the protocentriole (x 100 000) (from Porter, 1972). **Fig. 11.12** Protocentriole of *Labyrinthula algeriensis* in mitotic spindle cell. Cartwheel complex (Cr); microtubule of mitotic spindle (S) (x 86 000) (from Perkins, 1970).

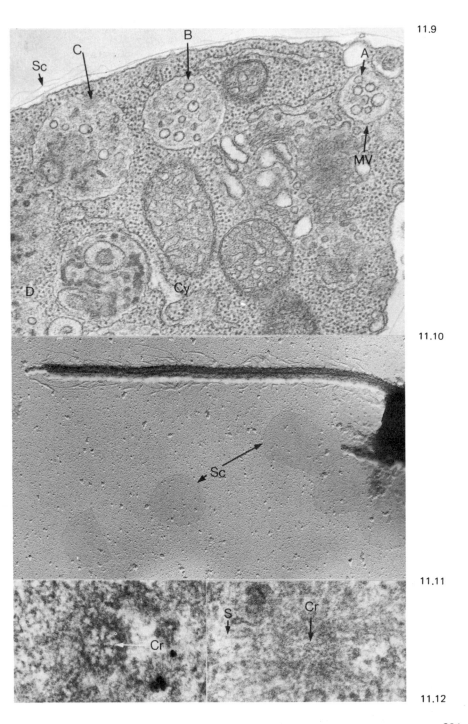

11.9

11.10

11.11

11.12

TABLE 11.2 Cell body and flagellum sizes (in microns) of zoospores considered herein. Figures in parentheses are averages.

Organisms	Cell body length	width	Anterior flagellum length	Posterior flagellum length	Reference
Phlyctochytrium sp.	2.5-5.0 (3.6)	2.5-3.5 (2.7)	—	21.2-27.5 (23.8)	Kazama (1972 c)
Labyrinthula algeriensis	3-5	2-3	13-15	6-10	Amon and Perkins (1968)
Thraustochytrium sp.	4.8-6.9 (5.3)	2.1-3.7 (2.9)	8.7-18.0 (11.8)	4.5-12.0 (7.3)	Kazama (unpublished data)
Schizochytrium aggregatum	3.5-5.0 (4.3)	2.0-4.0 (3.0)	5.0-13.0 (7.8)	4.0-7.0 (5.7)	Perkins (unpublished data)
Schizochytrium aggregatum	4.0-7.5	2.5-4.0	—	—	Goldstein and Belsky (1964)
Althornia crouchii	1-2	?	3-4	3-4	Jones and Alderman (1971)
Dermocystidium marinum	4-6	2-3	9-16	6-10	Perkins and Menzel (1966)

Internally the zoospore of *A. crouchii* contains a Golgi body, one nucleus, and numerous small vesicles. The kinetosome resembles that of *Thraustochytrium* sp. (Kazama, 1972 a) around the basal plate region and in the lumen (compare Plate 4, Fig. 1 of Jones and Alderman, 1971 with Fig. 1 of Kazama, 1972 a). Next to the nucleus of *A. crouchii* is a convoluted mass of inflated cisternae presumably of the endoplasmic reticulum (Fig. 11.2 6). Such configurations were also found in the sporangia of *A. crouchii* and in all cellular stages of *Labyrinthuloides yorkensis* (Perkins, 1973 b).

Zoospores of *D. marinum* from American oysters (*Crassostrea virginica* Gmelin) have a stichoneme, anteriorly directed flagellum with 1.2-1.5 μm long mastigonemes along one side of the flagellum (Perkins and Menzel, 1967). The zoospores of *Dermocystidium* sp. found in clams (*Macoma balthica* L.) are similar (Perkins, 1968). Mastigonemes are thinner than those described above and do not appear to have thin terminal extensions. The posterior flagellum is a whiplash. There are no scales on the cell body and contrary to what was originally reported (Perkins and Menzel, 1967), the cell body and flagellum are delimited by a single unit membrane, not two. Fibrillar material covers the plasmalemma of glutaraldehyde- and osmium tetroxide-fixed cells and appears to be the material which, in permanganate and osmium tetroxide fixations, led to the false interpretation of a second membrane (see Fig. 21; Perkins and Menzel, 1967).

Internally the zoospores contain a single nucleus, one or two small Golgi bodies, a cluster of lipid droplets at the posterior end of the cell and one mitochondrion (Fig. 11.5 f). Anteriorly there are two large vacuoles with electron-opaque, amorphous inclusions which are attached to the vacuole membrane. The inclusions and vacuoles resemble the vacuoplast-forming vacuoles of vegetative cells (Perkins, 1969; Figs. 12a and b). There are numerous membrane-limited, tubular and sac-like cisternae oriented parallel to each other and extending as much as the full length of the cell. They contain electron-dense material and have been previously termed the paranuclear body (Perkins and Menzel, 1967). Anteriorly they all converge on a tube of electron-dense material from which radiate microtubules. The latter lie a short distance beneath the plasmalemma and extend at least to the mid-region of the cell (Perkins, unpublished data). The tube, cisternae, and microtubules form a complex remarkably similar to the apical complex or penetration organelle of Sporozoa such as *Sarcocystis tenella* Railliet, *Toxoplasma gondii* Nicolle et Manceaux (Sénaud, 1967), and *Eimeria stiedae* Lindemann (Heller, 1972). If similar, the tube of *D. marinum* would be equivalent to a conoid of the Sporozoa.

11.4   Cell Division and Developmental Morphology

Cell division in spindle cells of *Labyrinthula* spp. has been studied by Stey (1969; *L. coenocystis*), Perkins (1970; *L. algeriensis*), and Porter (1972; *Labyrinthula* sp.). Non-mitotic cells are uninucleate and around the nucleus there are no structures resembling centrioles, microtubule organizing centres (Pickett-Heaps, 1969) or spindle pole bodies (Aist and Williams, 1972). Upon initiation of mitosis two fibrogranular aggregates appear at opposite sides of the nucleus (Perkins, 1970). Microtubules radiate from each aggregate and a cartwheel complex is formed in each aggregate centre. The cartwheel may be obvious with little fibrogranular material around it (Fig. 11.11) (Stey, 1969; Porter, 1972) or barely detectable (Fig. 11.12) (Perkins, 1970) depending on the species or possibly the stage of differentiation. No microtubules appear in ordered, nine-fold array around the cartwheel, and at the end of mitosis the cartwheel and aggregate disappear. Perkins (1970) termed the fibrogranular aggregates *protocentrioles* since in meiosis of *L. algeriensis* identical structures are formed which differentiate into true, microtubular centrioles with nine-fold symmetry (see Section 11.2.1). Porter (1972) suggested that the fibrogranular material around the protocentriole may act as a microtubule organizing centre as postulated by Pickett-Heaps (1969) for similar aggregates in other organisms.

Cytokinesis occurs transversely as a result of vesicles linking together then with the plasmalemma (Stey, 1969; Porter, 1972). Resulting daughter cells are uninucleate and subconical. Longitudinal and diagonal cleavage planes reported by many workers for *Labyrinthula* are probably only stages of cell elongation which follow cytokinesis to yield two spindle-shaped cells. Porter (1972) postulated that formation of a new set of microtubules from the region of the protocentriole causes cellular elongation after cytokinesis.

In studying the developmental morphology of the crab egg parasite *Lagenidium callinectes,* Amerson and Bland (1973) obtained evidence that meiosis may occur just before zoospore encystment. Polycomplexes or synaptonemal-like complexes (SLCs) were found in nuclei of encysting zoospores (Fig. 11.13). The fungus structures are structurally similar to synaptonemal complexes (SCs), but occur in stacked lamellae thus differing from SCs which occur in unstacked, ribbon-like arrays (Wettstein and Sotelo, 1971). Although meiosis apparently does not occur during germination, it may occur in zoosporulation. Previously SLCs have been found only in gametocytes of arthropods not in somatic cells, with the questionable exception of nurse cells in Diptera species (Wettstein and Sotelo, 1971); thus SLCs are found

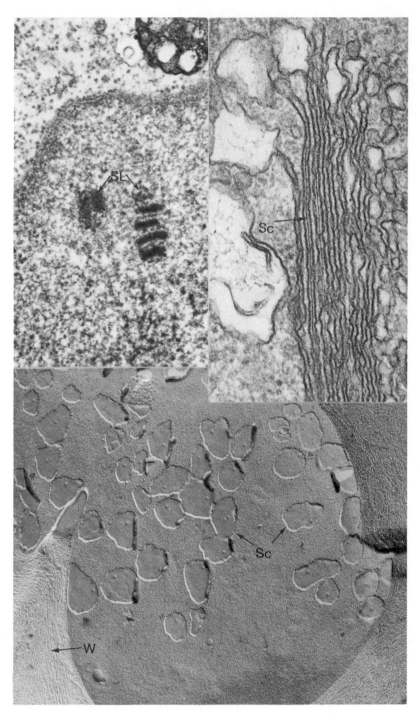

closely associated with meiosis. The closest preceding series of karyokineses in *L. callinectes* are those of zoosporulation, thus meiosis may occur there. It is unlikely that the SLCs would be carried to the encysted zoospore from an earlier stage. There are no reports of SLCs being found shortly before meiosis in any organism. Amerson and Bland's (1973) observations further emphasize the potential usefulness of fine structure studies of protists in efforts to elucidate their life cycles, particularly where chromosome counts and genetic information are lacking. Further efforts may determine the time of prophase I through identification of SCs in *L. callinectes,* and if required the haploid chromosome number may be determined as was accomplished with *L. algeriensis* (Moens and Perkins, 1969).

11.5 Cell Surfaces

11.5.1 Cell Walls

Ultrastructurally the walls of the organisms considered herein can be grouped into (1) those which are fungal-like in that they have a predictable, nearly uniform thickness, are compact, and consist of small granular, fibrogranular, or fibrillar subunits, and (2) those which are not fungal-like and consist of sheets or scales of electron-dense material loosely or compactly layered depending on the cell type and age.

Although no details were given in his publications, Kazama (personal communication) confirms that *Phlyctochytrium* sp. (Kazama, 1972 c) and *Pythium marinum* (Kazama and Fuller, 1970) have fungal-like walls as defined above. Walls of *L. callinectes* (Bland, personal communication) are also fungal-like. When fixed in glutaraldehyde and osmium tetroxide, fibrogranular walls are found around all of the vegetative cells of *Dermocystidium marinum* (Perkins, 1969) and fibrillar walls around the zoosporangia (Perkins, 1974). *Dermocystidium* sp. from salmon have fibrogranular walls (Perkins, unpublished data). *Atkinsiella dubia* walls have microfibrillar and amorphous regions as seen in mechanically isolated and shadowed walls (Aronson and Fuller, 1969); The microfibrils are more evident in chemically isolated walls due to extraction of the amorphous material. Both mechanically and chemically isolated walls of *A. dubia* contained large amounts of β-1 → 3 and β-1 → 6 linked glucan along with a small amount of cellulose thereby resembling the chemical composition of other Oömycete walls.

Walls of the thraustochytrids and labyrinthulids are structurally the same consisting of scales or plates of thin (20-50 Å) electron-dense material about 1 μm in diameter applied to the cell surface. In all species examined the plates appear to arise in Golgi vesicles.

Labyrinthula spp. spindle cells are apparently surrounded by one or two layers of overlapping plates which lie between the plasmalemma and ectoplasmic net with discontinuities where the net element is continuous with the plasmalemma (Perkins, 1972). Shadowed preparations of the plates have not yet been obtained to prove their

---

Fig. 11.13 Synaptonemal-like complexes (SL) in encysting zoospore nucleus of *Lagenidium callinectes* (x 54 000) (micrograph supplied by C. Bland, East Carolina University). Fig. 11.14 Golgi body of *Labyrinthuloides yorkensis* presporangium. The thin, electron-dense bands in the flattened vesicles are believed to represent forming wall scales (Sc) (x 86 000) (from Perkins, 1973 b). Fig. 11.15 Freeze-etch replica of *S. aggregatum* cell showing plasmalemma viewed from outside the cell. Circular depressions (Sc) in the plasmalemma are believed to represent scales emerging from the cytoplasm. Note laminar wall (W) which consists of layers of scales (x 18 000) (from Darley *et al.,* 1973).

existence, but sectioned material shows evidence of overlapping of lamellar units. Golgi vesicles may contain sheets of similar material with comparable thickness in both spindle cells and sporangia (Porter, 1974; Perkins, unpublished data). It is unlikely that the cell's spindle shape is maintained by the ectoplasmic net element surrounding the cell. One would expect a cell about 4 x 10 μm to be spherical or amoeboid unless a wall were present to alter the shape. It does not appear that the ectoplasmic net has enough tensile strength to maintain the spindle shape.

In *L. minuta* (Fig. 11.23), *L. yorkensis* (Fig. 11.22), *Thraustochytrium* sp., *S. aggregatum* (Figs. 11.18 and 11.29), and *A. crouchii* (Fig. 11.26) the walls are similar except that more plates are present (Perkins, 1972; Jones and Alderman, 1971; Perkins, 1973 b; Darley *et al.*, 1973). Material resembling the thinner sub-units of the walls has been found in Golgi vesicles of all species except *A. crouchii* (Perkins, 1973 b; Porter, 1974; Darley *et al.*, 1973; Perkins, unpublished data) (Fig. 11.14). Although it has not been observed, presumably the vesicles fuse with the plasmalemma and thus deposit the plates on the cell surface. Evidence for this is seen in the freeze-etch micrographs of *S. aggregatum* (Darley *et al.*, 1973) and *L. yorkensis* (Perkins, unpublished data) where circular depressions and raised plaques are observed in the plasmalemma (Fig. 11.15). It has not been determined, however, whether the circular profiles represent fracture patterns unrelated to plate deposition. In *S. aggregatum* they are smaller (0.25 to 0.60 μm) than the 0.5 to 1.1 μm scales seen in whole mounts (Darley *et al.*, 1973). In *L. yorkensis* they are 0.44 to 0.66 μm and the scales are 0.8 to 1.1 μm (Perkins, unpublished data).

In shadowed zoospore whole mounts of *Thraustochytrium* sp., *S. aggregatum*, and *A. crouchii*, the plates are easily dislodged from the cell and are detected as oval or round discs (Fig. 11.10) (Kazama and Perkins, unpublished data; Jones and Alderman, 1971). With the exception of *A. crouchii* (Fig. 11.26; see also Fig. 7.4, Jones and Alderman, 1971), the plates are not easily dislodged from non-flagellated vegetative cells, but have been demonstrated in *S. aggregatum* and *Thraustochytrium* sp. after sonication of the cells (Porter, 1974; Darley *et al.*, 1973). Plates adhere tightly to the cells of *L. minuta* and *L. yorkensis* and are not obvious in whole mount preparations unless the cells are grown on formvar rafts and allowed to proceed through several cell cycles. Plates can then be seen in the sporangial walls remaining after daughter cell dispersal. This technique also reveals the plates of *S. aggregatum* and *Thraustochytrium* sp. (Perkins, unpublished data).

11.5.2 Ectoplasmic Nets

As noted by Perkins (1972; 1973 a) the 'rhizoids' and 'slimeways' of the labyrinthulids and thraustochytrids are similar structures consisting of nets of ectoplasm (Fig. 11.27). They differ from the true rhizoids of *Phlyctochytrium* sp. and other chytrids, where the cell extensions are delimited by a wall, may contain any organelles except the

---

Figs. 11.16-11.17 Sagenogenetosomes (Sg) of *Labyrinthula coenocystis* showing continuity between plasmalemma (Pl) and inner membrane of ectoplasmic net (In) along an interconnecting isthmus (I) of ectoplasm. Continuity between cytoplasm and isthmus ectoplasm can be seen in Fig. 11.17 interrupted only by electron-dense granular band of the sagenogenetosome (arrow). Internal membranes (IM) in tubular configuration; wall (W); outer membrane of ectoplasmic net (Ot); endoplasmic reticulum cisternae (ER). (Fig. 11.16 x 115 000); (Fig. 11.17 x 80 000), (micrographs supplied by H. Schwab-Stey, University of Saarlandes). **Figs. 11.18-11.19** Two consecutive sections of *S. aggregatum* sagenogenetosome. Internal membranes (IM) of net element are in continuity with endoplasmic reticulum cisternae (ER), and plasmalemma (Pl) is continuous with membrane which delimits net element (NM). Wall (W) (both figures x 80 000) (from Perkins, 1972).

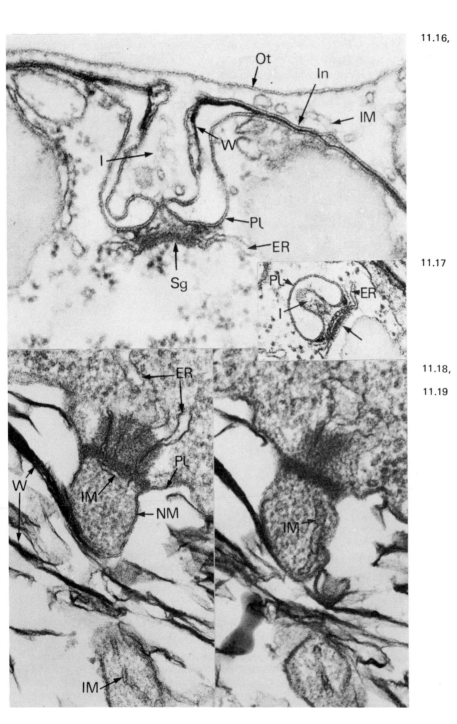

nucleus, are continuous with the cell body cytoplasm, and are not organized into nets (Kazama, 1972 c; personal communication). Cytoplasm of the chytrid extensions is continuous with the cell body cytoplasm (Fig. 11.1).

Ectoplasmic net elements arise from specialized organelles, termed sagenogeneto- somes by Perkins (1972), or in *Labyrinthula* spp. termed bothrosomes by Porter (1969). The elements are delimited by a membrane which is an extension of the plasmalemma (Figs. 11.16-11.19) and do not contain cytoplasmic organelles only vesicles or simple tubular or complex anastomosing membrane arrays. Spindle cells of *Labyrinthula* spp. (exception: *L. minuta*) are embedded in the net elements (Fig. 11.20) and many cells share common nets, whereas the cells of *L. minuta, L. yorkensis, S. aggregatum,* and *Thraustochytrium* spp. form one net per cell and are not enrobed by the net elements (Figs. 11.21, 11.27, and 11.28). In *Thraustochytrium* spp., one or two main trunk ele- ments of the net arise from clusters of 15 or more sagenogenetosomes, one cluster per

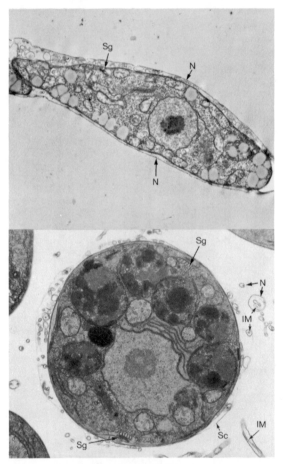

11.20

11.21

Fig. 11.20 *Labyrinthula* sp. spindle cell enrobed in ectoplasmic net element (N) through which the cell glides. Sagenogenetosome (Sg) (x 6400) (from Porter, 1969). **Fig. 11.21** *L. yorkensis* thallus show ectoplasmic net elements (N) used in motility by the cell. Elements radiate from cell and do not enrobe it. They arise from sagenogenetosomes (Sg) scattered in cell cortex. Internal membranes (IM) of net elements. Wall scale (Sc) (x 12 500).

trunk (Fig. 11.28), and from the trunk the lesser elements branch to form a net (Fig. 11.27). The wall partially covers the trunk element, but not the lesser elements (Fig. 11.28) (Harrison, 1972; Perkins, 1973 a). In *L. minuta, L. yorkensis,* and *S. aggregatum* there is also one net per cell, but it arises from as many as nine sagenogenetosomes scattered over the cell surface, not clustered together. Nets have been observed to be used in motility only by *Labyrinthula* spp. and *L. yorkensis,* but all species apparently use the nets to deliver lytic enzymes to substrates and absorb dissolved nutrients (Perkins, 1972, 1973 a). In studies of fixed and sectioned cells of *Labyrinthula* spp., Porter (1969) and Perkins (1972) found 10-20 sagenogenetosomes in each spindle cell; however, in a freeze etch study Schwab-Stey and Schwab (1973) deduced that only 5-8 are present per cell of *L. coenocystis.* The small number of net-forming organelles and their random distribution led the latter authors to suggest that synthesis of membranes from the generative sites must be supplemented by some other process in order to induce gliding movement.

In the formation of nets it appears that cisternae of the endoplasmic reticulum contribute small vesicles to an area at the base of the basal net element which is marked by an electron-dense granular aggregate (Figs. 11.21-11.23). Reaggregation of the vesicles leads to formation of the internal membrane complexes of the net elements. The membranes are organized into straight or anastomosing tubular (Figs. 11.18, 11.19, 11.22, and 11.23) or fenestrated complexes which appear to proliferate when the cells are grown on natural rather than artificial substrates (Perkins, 1973 a). Obviously the limits of the sagenogenetosome are not well defined; however, a working definition was proposed by Perkins (1972) in which the limits become the proximal and lateral edges of the electron-dense aggregate, the plasmalemma overlying the aggregate, and the unit membrane delimiting the isthmus up to the level of the cell surface.

Apparently the granular aggregate of the sagenogenetosome prevents movement of ribosomes and larger sized structures into the net elements. There is no membrane barrier between the cytoplasm and the contents of the net elements, thus the reason for calling the nets ectoplasmic (Perkins, 1972). Earlier Stey (1969) concluded that the 'slimeways' of *Labyrinthula coenocystis* are ectoplasm, also because no membrane barrier was observed in sectioned material. She demonstrated, in a freeze fracture study (Schwab-Stey and Schwab, 1973) that the isthmus (Perkins, 1972), or connection, between ectoplasmic net and cell body, cross-fractured as one would expect if there was continuity between cell and net element contents (Figs. 11.24 and 11.25). Membranes delimiting the net elements are apparently similar in permeability characteristics to the cell membrane as evidenced by net element swelling and rupture when placed in distilled water (Porter, 1973).

In light microscope studies, working with species of *Labyrinthula* and *Labyrinthomyxa,* Schmoller (1966; 1971) concluded that the 'slimeways' are ectoplasm and the spindle cells are endoplasm. He observed that myxamoebae of *Labyrinthomyxa* spp. metamorphose into gliding spindle cells, presumably by direct conversion of ectoplasm into 'slimeway' material. Spindle cells, embedded in 'slimeways', rounded and formed cysts in which the cyst walls were derived from the 'slimeway'. Upon encystment the cells became either spindle cells embedded in 'slimeways' or active amoebae, leaving no cyst wall behind. In either case the wall was transformed into ectoplasm of the amoebae or 'slimeway' material. If amoebae encystment occurred, the amoebae ectoplasm became the wall of the cyst.

Porter (1972) believes that the 'slimeway' is extracellular material, because it lacks many characteristics of ectoplasm, not because of resemblance to any known

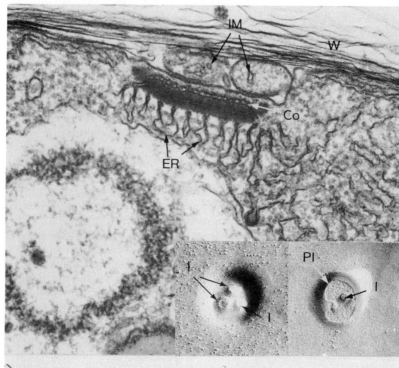

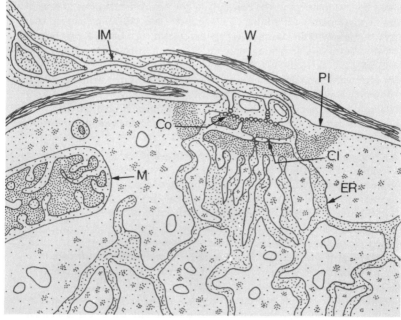

cell secretions. He argues that the spindle cells do not retract the 'slimeways' like ectoplasmic filopodia, but rather leave the material behind and it soom disintegrates. Granular flow, typical of ectoplasmic filopodia, is not observed. He states that branching and formation of *Labyrinthula* nets could be accomplished by extracellular material as is seen with myelin figures. Bubbles of matrix material may bleb off the edge of a *Labyrinthula* colony then fuse with the network when it advances to the bubble. This was not considered to be a likely characteristic of living protoplasm. Physical isolation of the matrix from spindle cells does not result in death of the cell as one would expect if the matrix were ectoplasm.

It does not appear that the issue of ectoplasm *vs.* extra-cellular material can be settled with present knowledge. A fine structure examination of amoebae-spindle cell interconversions in *Labyrinthomyxa* spp. may be enlightening, since the ectoplasm of the amoebae can be identified as a reference structure. Other questions must be answered, such as, whether an electrical potential difference exists between the medium and the ectoplasmic net interior and between the net and cell interiors. If there is a difference, does its maintenance depend on energy expenditure by the cell? Since the ectoplasmic nets of the other labyrinthulids and the thraustochytrids are structurally similar, the answers to these questions will presumably also apply to those species.

11.6 Viruses and Virus-Like Particles

Kazama and Schornstein (1972; 1973) found a herpes-like virus in *Thraustochytrium* sp. (resembling *T. motivum*). It is the first non-vertebrate herpes or herpes-like virus reported and one of the few reports of viruses in the lower fungi. Identical or very similar particles have been found in *S. aggregatum* (Perkins, unpublished data). Their development is similar to that observed in *Thraustochytrium* sp., except that large numbers of the virus particles may accumulate in the fungus, followed by lysis of the host (Fig. 11.29). In *Thraustochytrium* sp. assembly of nucleocapsids occurs in the nucleus, followed by passage through the nuclear envelope and temporary envelopment by the two membranes (Fig. 11.30). In the cytoplasm the nuclear membranes are degraded and the nucleocapsids become coated with fibrillar material (Fig. 11.31). Movement into cytoplasmic vacuoles or Golgi vesicles results in final envelopment by a single membrane (Fig. 11.32). Cell-free particles are elongate (280 nm long) and the capsids (130 nm diameter) are eccentrically located in the envelopes.

By starvation, cells were induced to become more productive for the viruses. Since non-integrated or highly integrated viral states can be induced in *Thraustochytrium* sp. and since it is unicellular and easily cloned, the fungus provides an excellent

---

Fig. 11.22 Sagenogenetosome of *Labyrinthuloides yorkensis.* Periodically arranged cisternae of endoplasmic reticulum (ER) contribute small beaded vesicles (CO) which coalesce to form internal membranes (IM) of net elements. Note laminated wall (W) consisting of layers of scales (x 68 000). **Fig. 11.23** Diagram of *L. minuta* sagenogenetosome and associated structures. Periodically arranged cisternae of endoplasmic reticulum (ER) showing continuity with inner cisternae (CI) and layer of small vesicles (CO). Internal membranes (IM) of net element; cell wall (W); mitochondrion (M); and plasmalemma (PI). **Figs. 11.24-11.25** Freeze etch replicas of *L. coenocystis* sagenogenetosomes cross-fractured at the isthmuses (I). Replica view is from outside the cell in Fig. 11.24 and inside the cell in Fig. 11.25. Cross-fractured plasmalemma (PI); cross-fractured isthmuses (I). Internal membranes and plasmalemma are not visible in either figure and plasmalemma is not cross-fractured in Fig. 11.24. (both figures are x 50 000). (from Schwab-Stey and Schwab, 1973).

301

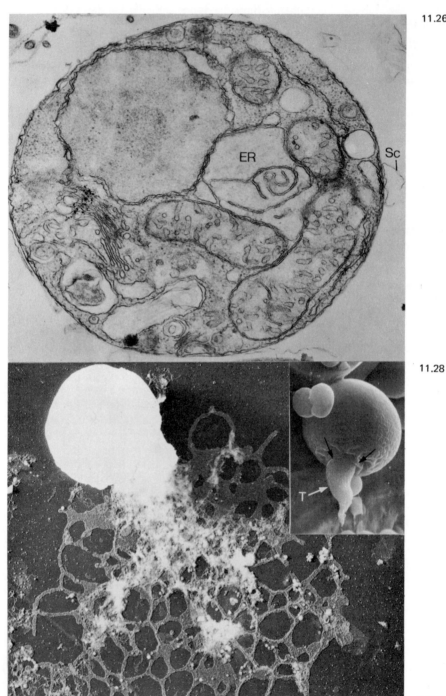

11.26

ER

Sc

11.28

T

11.27

system for studying a herpes-like virus in a cellular system phylogenetically different from the vertebrate systems previously studied.

Perkins (1969) observed 46.0 to 53.0 nm diameter virus-like particles in the nucleoplasm and cytoplasm of *D. marinum* thalli from Virginia but not Florida oysters. In addition to their size they are considered to be virus-like, because (1) in sections they have six- and five-fold rotational symmetry (thus thye could be icosahedra), (2) crystalline arrays have been found in the nucleoplasm (Perkins, unpublished data), and (3) their structure resembles some known viruses like the arboviruses (Davis *et al.*, 1968).

11.7 Phylogeny

Establishment of *Phlyctochytrium* sp. in the Chytridiomycetes and *Lagenidium callinectes, Atkinsiella dubia,* and *Pythium marinum* in the Oömycetes is generally agreed upon by mycologists; however, thraustochytrids and labyrinthulids present formidable problems in classification, particularly at the higher taxa levels (Perkins, 1974; Porter, 1974). At the core of this taxonomic problem lies our need for a greater knowledge of eucaryotic protist phylogeny.

Many schemes have been offered for classification of the labyrinthulids, all centring around placement in a special group of fungi or in the rhizopodean Protozoa (see for examples: Pokorny, 1967; Honigberg *et al.*, 1964; Kudo, 1966; Ainsworth, 1966). None of these schemes has been acceptable to all students of the groups. Classification with the Rhizopodea is not attractive, because other members of the class, unlike the labyrinthulids, do not form biflagellated cells with eyespots, a posterior whiplash flagellum, and an anterior pantoneme flagellum. Species of *Labyrinthomyxa* have replicating amoebae in their life cycles which are holozoic and which form pseudopodia like rhizopodean Protozoa; however, since replicating amoebae are found in the life cycles of algae (Pascher, 1939), the presence of amoebae in the labyrinthulids does not appear to necessarily indicate affinities with the Rhizopodea. In addition, the zoospore structure appears to be unlike that of flagellated cells in the Rhizopodea (Grell, 1968; Swale, 1969 a; Furtado and Olive, 1970) where mastigonemes and eyespots are noticeably lacking.

Although the zoospores of labyrinthulids have surface structures similar to the biflagellate Oömycetes, that is about the only similarity with the true fungi. The pigmented eyespots, method of motility, absence of a fungus-like wall, and cleavage of the zoosporangium by successive bipartition are all decidedly not fungus-like. This assumes that the thraustochytrids are not fungi, an assumption which appears valid. Thraustochytrid wall structure consisting of scales preformed in Golgi vesicles and chemical composition with high galactose and protein levels is unlike the biflagellate Oömycetes (Darley *et al.*, 1973). Formation of ectoplasmic nets is unlike fungi, resembling only the labyrinthulids. Although zoospore surface structure is generally

---

Fig. 11.26 Young sporangium of *Althornia crouchii* showing inflated cisternae of endoplasmic reticulum (ER) and wall scales (Sc) (x 16 000) (from Jones and Alderman, 1971). **Fig. 11.27** Shadowed (platinum and palladium) whole mount of encysted *Thraustochytrium* sp. zoospore shortly after initiation of net formation. Cell was grown on formvar raft in a drop of nutrient medium. Net emerges from one area of the cell as seen in Fig. 11.28 (x 6300). **Fig. 11.28** Scanning electron micrograph of *Thraustochytrium kinnei* sporangium showing main trunk element (T) of ectoplasmic net. Small subdivisions which form the net meshwork are missing. Wall does not cover the trunk. Wall termination (arrows) (x 11 000) (micrograph provided by J. L. Harrison, Portsmouth Polytechnic).

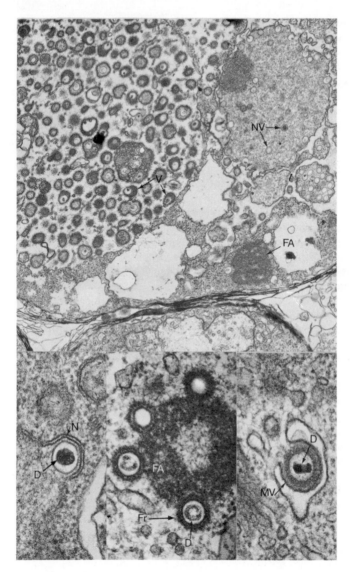

Fig. 11.29 Particles in *S. aggregatum* sporangium believed to be herpes-like viruses on basis of studies by Kazama and Schornstein (1973). Particles are associated with extensive cell damage in *S. aggregatum*. Cores (NV) appear to be formed in nucleoplasm and migrate to cytoplasm where coats of fibrogranular material are added in or around an aggregate of similar fibrogranular material (FA; see Fig. 11.31). Mature particles (V) accumulate in large cytoplasmic vesicles and are released upon rupture of the cell (x 22 000). **Figs. 11.30-11.32** Presumed ontogeny of herpes-like viruses in *Thraustochytrium* sp. Core is formed in nucleoblasm and acquires two enveloping membranes when passing through nuclear envelope (N; Fig. 11.30). In the cytoplasm the two membranes are lost and the cores are coated with fibrogranular material (Fr) while in association with an aggregate of similar material (FA; Fig. 11.31). The coated virions then migrate into cytoplasmic vesicles and acquire a delimiting membrane, contributed by the vesicle membrane as (MV; Fig. 11.32). DNase-extractable portion of the core (D) (Fig. 11.30: x 86 000; Fig. 11.31: x 81 000; Fig. 11.32: x 90 000) (from Kazama and Schornstein, 1973).

consistent with the biflagellate Oömycetes, it is not distinctive since the chrysophycean, xanthophycean, and phaeophycean algae all form zoospores with similar structure.

Similarities between the labyrinthulids and thraustochytrids are particularly striking. Ectoplasmic nets formed from sagenogenetosomes, wall scales formed in Golgi vesicles, biflagellated zoospores with a pantoneme and a whiplash flagellum, successive bipartition of the protoplast during sporulation, and kinetosomes with large electron-dense granules, are all characteristics common to both groups. Differences between the two groups include, (1) gliding motility by means of ectoplasmic nets only in the labyrinthulids, and (2) eyespots and associated flagellar swellings only in zoospores of the labyrinthulids. The molecular weights of the heavy ribosomal RNA sub-units suggest that those species, not enrobed by ectoplasmic nets (*L. yorkensis, S. aggregatum,* and *Thraustochytrium* sp.; all = 1.30-1.33 x 10^6 M.W.), constitute a group distinct from those which are enrobed in ectoplasmic nets (*L. vitellina,* 1.19 x 10^6 M.W. and *Labyrinthula* sp., type LX, 1.25 x 10^6 M.W.) (Porter, 1974). *Labyrinthula* sp., (a Vishniac strain) is believed to be more like *L. yorkensis* than species of *Labyrinthula* thus its molecular weight of 1.30 x 10^6 is not unexpected.

The differences mentioned above do not appear to this author to be significant enough to separate the labyrinthulids and thraustochytrids into different major taxa. The lack of gliding motility in the thraustochytrids appears less significant when one considers the cytological similarities between the gliding species *L. yorkensis* Perkins (1973 b) and the non-gliding species *S. aggregatum* Goldstein and Belsky (1964). Structurally, *S. aggregatum* appears to be equipped to accomplish gliding motility except that it has only one or two sagenogenetosomes, not 4-9 scattered over the cell surface, resulting in the formation of a less extensive ectoplasmic net. The lack of eyespots in the zoospore of the thraustochytrids may not pose a taxonomic problem, because within other groups such as the Chrysophyceae (Swale, 1969 b; Hibberd, 1971) not all species have eyespots. The RNA data indicate that the labyrinthulids and thraustochytrids are similar except for those species of *Labyrinthula* which enrobe themselves in ectoplasmic nets. Whether this difference is real and of fundamental importance is uncertain. More species and isolates should be examined. The studies of Loening (1968) and Lovett and Haselby (1971) indicate that RNA molecular weights are significant evolutionary indicators. If true, then the differences could be significant in any attempts to combine the thraustochytrids and labyrinthulids in one taxon at the familial or possibly ordinal level (Porter, 1974).

There are also differences between the species of *Labyrinthula* and *L. yorkensis* which may indicate a greater degree of heterogeneity within the labyrinthulids than I have assumed in this discussion; therefore, they should be noted. Species of *Labyrinthula* other than *L. minuta* form centrioles only during zoosporulation (Perkins, 1970; Porter, 1972), whereas *L. yorkensis* has centrioles or kinetosomes in all stages of the life cycle (Perkins, 1973 b; unpublished data) thus resembling the thraustochytrids. Whether or not centrioles are formed in *L. minuta* has not been determined. At present, only species of *Labyrinthula* have been shown to form zoospores as a result of meiosis. In all species of thraustochytrids zoosporulation appears to be a mitotic process. Zoosporulation in *L. yorkensis* has not been elucidated.

Phylogenetically, the Chrysophyceae or Haptophyceae appear to be most similar to the labyrinthulids and thraustochytrids (assuming they are a single group). Formation of wall scales in Golgi vesicles, followed by deposition on the cell surface, has been found in two phytoflagellates of those groups (Brown, 1969; Manton, 1967). Their substructure is more complex than the scales of the labyrinthulids and thraustochtrids; however, thin oval scales 0.6 to 1 μm in diameter have been observed on other phytoflagellates (Belcher and Swale, 1967; 1971). The chrysophycean flagellates also frequently have large electron-dense granules in the kinetosome lumen (Belcher and Swale, 1971; Hibberd, 1971), pigmented eyespots associated with a flagellar swelling (Belcher, 1969; Hibberd, 1970), and two rows of mastigonemes along one of two flagella (Hibberd, 1970, 1971; Belcher and Swale, 1971; 1972). Many species form filopodial-like structures (Belcher and Swale, 1971, 1972; Belcher, 1969; Hibberd, 1971), but sagenogenetosomes have not been reported. The significance of the large kineto-some granule as a phylogenetic marker becomes questionable when one considers that some ciliates also form similar structures (Allen, 1969); however, it must be remember-ed that the granules have been found only in the ciliates and the fungal and algal groups mentioned herein.

Construction of an adequate taxonomic framework for the thraustochytrids and labyrinthulids appears to be closer than it was only a few years ago; however, there still does not appear to be an order, or even a class, which can be used to accommo-date the organisms. Possibly further studies of the Chrysophyceae may reveal stronger similarities and they can be placed there, as was first suggested by Hollande and Enjumet (1955). They appear to have more structures which are similar to the Chrysophyceae than any group of fungi, Protozoa, or other group of algae. It will be particularly interesting if ectoplasmic nets and sagenogenetosomes are found in the Chrysophyceae. It may be that no combination of structures will prove to be ade-quate to indicate their phylogenetic affinities, in which case a complement of bio-chemical, physiological, and morphological data may be required as indicated by Porter (1974).

Althornia crouchii appears to be a thraustochytrid since, (1) it is a monocentric, achlorophyllous, coccoid micro-organism, (2) numerous 1.0 μm diameter, thin scales form walls on the zoospores and thalli, (3) diplanetism does not appear to exist as was originally believed, and (4) zoospores are formed which are laterally biflagel-lated with an anterior pantoneme and a posterior acroneme flagellum. *A. crouchii* appears to differ from the thraustochytrids in that ectoplasmic nets and sageno-genetosomes were not observed. Possibly, growth in different culture media and a re-examination of the fine structure will reveal the structures if they exist.

Dermocystidium marinum remains a taxonomic enigma. The stichoneme anterior flagellum of the zoospores, lack of ectoplasmic nets in the life cycle and formation of consolidated, non-laminar walls all indicate that the pathogen is not related to the labyrinthulids and thraustochytrids. The absence of an eyespot, the lack of wall scales, and the formation of a stichoneme flagellum do not indicate affinities with the Haptophyceae, Xanthophyceae, Chrysophyceae, or Phaeophyceae. Zoospore structure is unlike that of any of the chlorococcalean algae. The fact that the zoospores are formed makes it different from the colourless Chlorellid *Hyalochlorella marina* (Poyton, 1970) (=*Dermocystidium* sp. *sensu stricto* Goldstein and Moriber, 1966). Euglenoid flagellates (Leedale, 1967) and dinoflagellates (Leadbeater and Dodge, 1967) have stichoneme flagella; however, the similarity with *D. marinum* ends there.

If gliding motility by means of ectoplasmic nets can be demonstrated in the life cycle of the oyster pathogen then suggested affinities with the labyrinthulids (Mackin and Ray, 1966) must be reconsidered. There are some structural similarities in that both have electron-dense granules in the kinetosome and divide the zoosporangium protoplast by successive bipartition. In both, the zoospores are biflagellated with lateral insertion of flagella, and the anterior flagellum is longer than the posterior one.

Although the name *D. marinum* has been used herein for convenience the similarities with other species of *Dermocystidium,* such as *Dermocystidium* sp. from salmon (Pauley, 1967) are uncertain, primarily because little is known about the developmental morphology of the cyst-forming species. Plasmodia or uninucleate, spherical cells with a large eccentric vacuole and vacuoplast are the dominant cell types found in the many species examined (see for examples Jirovec, 1939; Sterba and Naumann, 1970). Other cellular stages have not been useful in determining developmental sequences. No species has been established in culture. About the only known similarity between the oyster pathogen and other species of *Dermocystidium* are the mature thalli each with a large eccentric vacuole and vacuoplast. The walls of *D. granulosum* Sterba et Naumann (Sterba and Naumann, 1970), *D. marinum,* and *Dermocystidium* sp. from salmon (Perkins, 1974) are similar having non-laminate fibrogranular substructure. Otherwise, morphological information which could be used to determine affinities is lacking.

11.8   Future Studies

Many of the interesting fine structure studies which can be pursued in the future centre around determining the phylogenetic affinities of the labyrinthulids, thraustochytrids, and *Dermocystidium* spp. The organisms are readily available for any visitor to the oceans and estuaries and most can be easily cultured. The first two groups are known to be worldwide in distribution and very common in plant and animal materials as well as sediments (Porter, 1967; Perkins, 1973a; Sparrow, 1968). *Dermocystidium* spp. are also widespread. All of those observed in marine waters have been found in molluscs and, possibly, a few polychaetes (Mackin, 1962) of shallow Atlantic Ocean and Caribbean Sea waters.

A more comprehensive knowledge is needed of the range of organisms which form ectoplasmic nets from sagenogenetosomes and which form walls comprised of unsculptured scales. Once the uniqueness of the structures is determined, their phylogenetic significance may be determined. Since zoospore structure is considered to be of major evolutionary significance, efforts should be expended to catalogue zoospore morphology for as many species as possible. Only then can informed determinations be made as to the phylogenetic significance of various structures. Zoospore surface structure and flagella lengths and insertion points appear to be useful indicators at this time, but the sum total of all zoospore morphology must be considered.

In efforts to elucidate life cycles of marine fungi, meiosis can be detected in the form of synaptonemal complexes. Serial sections of prophase I nuclei can be made and the haploid chromosome number determined by counting numbers of complexes. If the number is consistent for a given species, then the possibility of improperly identifying prophase I is eliminated. Polycomplexes or other synaptonemal-like complexes can be confusing, but their number in the nuclei of a given species will vary, unlike synaptonemal complexes. Synaptonemal-like complexes can, however, be used as indicators that meiosis has occurred in a recent stage of the life cycle.

From studies such as those of Bryant and Howard (1969) and Howard and Moore (1970) it is apparent that even those species such as *Saprolegnia* spp. which have been extensively studied, misconceptions had arisen as to where meiosis occurs in the life cycle. Life cycles of organisms such as *Labyrinthula algeriensis,* which have no cell types identifiable as differentiated sexual structures, are even more difficult to elucidate. Their chromosomes are too small to use as indicators of meiosis at the light microscope level. For those reasons synaptonemal complexes were used in *L. algeriensis* to identify the time of meiosis and chromosome number (Perkins and Amon, 1969; Moens and Perkins, 1969).

In studies of the ultrastructure of photoreceptors, the chytrids may provide particularly interesting organelles with which to work. The lipoid bodies (Koch, 1958) of many chytrid zoospores may prove to be photoreceptor complexes. In virology the marine and estuarine fungi may provide useful eucaryotic systems to study. Of the few species which have been investigated three isolates of three species are known to have virus-like particles (see Section 11.6).

Acknowledgements

I wish to thank Joseph Gilley for preparation of the drawings, Mrs Rita Tetterton for typing the manuscript, and Mrs. Diane Stallard and Mrs. Lynda Keating for laboratory assistance. Dr. David Porter is thanked for his helpful suggestions in reviewing the manuscript.

References

AINSWORTH, G. C. (1966). 'A general purpose classification of fungi'. *Bibliography System. Mycol.,* 1-4, Commonwealth Mycological Institute, Kew, Surrey.

AIST, J. R., and WILLIAMS, P. H. (1972). 'Ultrastructure and time course of mitosis in the fungus *Fusarium oxysporum.' J. Cell Biol.,* 55, 368-389.

ALDERMAN, D. J., and HARRISON, J. L. (1971). 'Observations on some British marine biflagellate fungi. 1st Internat. Mycol. Congress, Section: "The biflagellate Phycomycetes, are they a natural group?",' Exeter, 1971.

ALLEN, R. D. (1969). 'The morphogenesis of basal bodies and accessory structures of the cortex of the ciliated protozoan *Tetrahymena pyriformis.' J. Cell Biol.,* 40, 716-733.

AMERSON, H. V. and BLAND, C. E. (1973). 'The occurrence of poly-complexes in the nucleus of encysting spores of *Lagenidium callinectes,* a marine phycomycete.' *Mycologia,* 65, 966-970.

AMON, J. P., and PERKINS; F. O. (1968). 'Structure of *Labyrinthula* sp. zoospores.' *J. Protozool.,* 15, 543-546.

ARONSON, J. M., and FULLER, M. S. (1969). 'Cell wall structure of the marine fungus, *Atkinsiella dubia.' Arch. Mikrobiol.,* 68, 295-305.

BARTSCH, G. (1971). 'Cytologische Beobachtungen an *Labyrinthula coenocystis* Schmoller bie verschiedenen Kulturbedingungen.' *Z. allg. Mikrobiol.,* 11, 79-90.

BELCHER, J. H. (1969). 'A morphological study of the phytoflagellate *Chrysococcus rufescens* Kelbs in culture.' *Br. phycol. J.,* 4, 105-117.

BELCHER, J. H., and SWALE, E. M. F. (1967). '*Chromulina placentula* sp. nov. (Chrysophyceae), a freshwater nannoplankton flagellate.' *Br. phycol. Bull.,* 3, 257-267.

BELCHER, J. H., and SWALE, E. M. F. (1971). 'The microanatomy of *Phaeaster pascheri* Scherffel (Chrysophyceae).' *Br. phycol. J.,* 6, 157-169.

BELCHER, J. H., and SWALE, E. M. F. (1972). 'Some features of the microanatomy of *Chrysococcus cordiformis* Naumann.' *Br. phycol. J.,* 7, 53-59.

BROWN, R. M. (1969). 'Observations on the relationship of the Golgi apparatus to wall formation in the marine Chrysophycean alga, *Pleurochrysis scherffelii* Pringsheim.' *J. Cell Biol.,* 41, 109-123.

BRYANT, T. R., and HOWARD, K. L. (1969). 'Meiosis in the Oömycetes: I. A microspectrophotometric analysis of nuclear deoxyribonucleic acid in *Saprolegnia terrestris.' Am. J. Bot.,* 56, 1075-1083.

DARLEY, W. M., and FULLER, M. S. (1970). 'Cell wall chemistry and taxonomic position of *Schizochytrium.' Am. J. Bot.,* 57, 761 (Abstr.).

DARLEY, W. M., PORTER, D., and FULLER, M. S. (1973). 'Cell wall composition and synthesis via Golgi-directed scale formation in the marine eucaryote *Schizochytrium aggregatum,* with a note on *Thraustochytrium* sp.' *Arch. Mikrobiol.,* 90, 89-106.

DAVIS, B. D., DULBECCO, R., EISEN, H. N., GINSBERG, H. S., and WOOD, W. B. (1968). *Microbiology.* Harper and Row Publ., New York, 1376-1394.

DODGE, J. D. (1969). 'A review of algal eyespots'. *Br. phycol. J.,* 4, 199-210.

FULLER, M. S. (1966). 'Structure of the uniflagellate zoospores of aquatic Phycomycetes'. In *The Fungus Spore.* (Ed. M. F. Madelin) Butterworths, London, 67-84.

FURTADO, J. S., and OLIVE, L. S. (1970). 'Ultrastructural studies of proto-stelids: the amoeba-flagellate stage'. *Cytobiologie,* 2, 200-219.

GAERTNER, A. (1964). 'Elektronenmikroskopische Untersuchungen zur Struktur der Geisseln von *Thraustochytrium* spec.' *Veröff. Inst. Meeresforsch., Bremerh.,* 9, 25-30.

GAERTNER, A. (1972). 'Characters used in the classification of thrausto-chytriaceous fungi'. *Veröff. Inst. Meeresforsch. Bermerh.,* 13, 183-194.

GOLDSTEIN, S. (1963). 'Development and nutrition of new species of *Thraustochytrium'. Am. J. Bot.,* 50, 271-279.

GOLDSTEIN, S., and BELSKY, M. (1964). 'Axenic culture of a new marine phycomy-cete possessing an unusual type of asexual reproduction'. *Am. J. Bot.,* 51, 72-78.

GOLDSTEIN, S., and MORIBER, L. (1966). 'Biology of a problematic marine fungus, *Dermocystidium* spec. I. Development and cytology.' *Arch. Mikrobiol.,* 53, 1-11.

GOLDSTEIN, S., MORIBER, L., and HERSHENOV, B. (1964). 'Ultrastructure of *Thraustochytrium aureum,* a biflagellate marine phycomycete,' *Mycologia,* 56, 897-904.

GRELL, K. G. (1968). *Protozoologie.* Springer-Verlag, Berlin., 511 pp.

HARRISON, J. L. (1972). 'The salinity tolerances of freshwater and marine zoosporic fungi, including some aspects of the ecology and ultrastructure of the Thrausto-chytriaceae' Ph. D. Thesis, University of London.

HEATH, I. B., GREENWOOD, A. D., and GRIFFITHS, H. B. (1970). 'The origin of flimmer in *Saprolegnia, Dictyuchus, Synura,* and *Cryptomonas.' J. Cell Sci.,* 7, 445-461.

HELLER, G. (1972). 'Elektronenmikroskopische Untersuchung zur Bilding und Struktur von Conoid, Rhoptrien und Mikronemen bei *Eimeria stiedae* (Sporozoa, Coccidia).' *Protistologica,* 8, 43-51.

HIBBERD, D. J. (1970). 'Observations on the cytology and ultrastructure of *Ochromonas tuberculatus* sp. nov. (Chrysophyceae), with special reference to the discobolocysts.' *Brit. phycol. J.,* 5, 119-143.

HIBBERD, D. J. (1971). 'Obervations on the cytology and ultrastructure of *Chrysamoeba radians* Klebs (Chrysophyceae).' *Br. phycol. J.,* 6, 207-223.

HOHL, H. R. (1966). 'The fine structure of the slimeways in *Labyrinthula.' J. Proto-zool.,* 13, 41-43.

HOLLANDE, A. and ENJUMET, M. (1955). 'Sur l'évolution et la systématique des Labyrinthulidae; Étude de *Labyrinthula algeriensis* nov. sp.' *Ann. Sci. Nat., Zool.* IIme ser., 17, 357-368.

HONIGBERG, B. M., BALAMUTH, W., BOVEE, E. C., CORLISS, J. O., GOJDICS, M., HALL, R. P., KUDO, R. R., LEVINE, N. D., LOEBLICH, A. R., WEISER, J., and WENRICH, D. H. (1964). 'A revised classification of the phylum Protozoa.' *J. Protozool.,* 11, 7-20.

HOWARD, K. L., and MOORE, R. T. (1970). 'Ultrastructure of oögensis in *Saprolegnia terrestris.' Bot. Gaz.,* 131, 311-336.

JIROVEC, O. (1939). '*Dermocystidium vejdovskyi* n. sp., ein neuer Parasit des Hechtes, nebst einer Bemerkung über *Dermocystidium daphniae* (Rühberg).' *Arch, Protistenk.,* 92, 137-146.

JONES, E. B. G., and ALDERMAN, D. J. (1971). '*Althornia crouchii* gen. et sp. nov., a marine biflagellate fungus.' *Nova Hedwigia,* 21, 381-399.

KAZAMA, F. (1972 a). 'Ultrastructure of *Thraustochytrium* sp. zoospores. I. Kineto-some.' *Arch. Mikrobiol.,* 83, 179-188.

KAMAZA, F. (1972 b). 'Ultrastructure of *Thraustochytrium* sp. zoospores. II. Striated inclusions.' *J. Ultrastruct. Res.,* 41, 60-66.

KAZAMA, F. (1972 c). 'Development and morphology of a chytrid isolated from *Bryopsis plumosa.' Can. J. Bot.,* 50, 499-505.

KAZAMA, F. (1972 d). 'Ultrastructure and phototaxis of the zoospores of *Phlycto-chytrium* sp., an estuarine chytrid, *J. gen. Microbiol.,* 71, 555-566.

KAZAMA, F. (1973). 'Ultrastructure of *Thraustochytrium* sp. zoospores, III. Cytoly-somes and acid phosphatase distribution'. *Arch. Mikrobiol.* 89, 95-104.

KAZAMA, F., and FULLER, M. S. (1970). 'Ultrastructure of *Porphyra perforata* infected with *Pythium marinum,* a marine fungus.' *Can. J. Bot.,* 48, 2103-2107.

KAZAMA, F., and SCHORNSTEIN, K. L. (1972). 'Herpes-type virus particles associa-ted with a fungus.' *Science,* 177, 696-697.

KAZAMA, F., and SCHORNSTEIN, K. L. (1973). 'Ultrastructure of a fungus herpes-type virus.' *Virology,* 52, 478-487.

KLIE, H., and MACH, F. (1968). 'Licht-und elektronenmikroskopische Untersuchun-gen über die Wirkung von *Labyrinthula*-Enzymen auf Bakterien-und Hefezellen.' *Z. allg. Mikrobiol.,* 8, 385-395.

KOCH, W. J. (1958). 'Studies of the motile cells of chytrids. II. Internal structure of the body observed with light microscopy.' *Am. J. Bot.,* 45, 59-72.

KUDO, R. R. (1966). *Protozoology.* Charles C. Thomas Publ., Springfield, III. 1174 pp.

LEADBEATER, B., and DODGE, J. D. (1967). 'An electron microscope study of dinoflagellate flagella.' *J. gen. Microbiol.,* 46, 305-314.

LEEDALE, G. F. (1967). *Euglenoid flagellates.* Prentice-Hall, Inc., Englewood Cliffs, N. J., 242 pp.

LOENING, U. E. (1968). 'Molecular weights of ribosomal RNA in relation to evolu-tion.' *J. molec. Biol.,* 38, 355-365;

LOVETT, J. S., and HASELBY, J. A. (1971). 'Molecular weights of the ribosomal ribonucleic acid of fungi.' *Arch. Mikrobiol.,* 80, 191-204.

MACKIN, J. G. (1962). 'Oyster disease caused by *Dermocystidium marinum* and other microorganisms in Louisiana.' *Publ. Inst. Mar. Sci., Univ. Texas,* 7, 132-229.

MACKIN, J. G., and RAY, S. M. (1966). 'The taxonomic relationships of *Dermocystidium marinum* Mackin, Owen, and Collier.' *J. Invert. Pathol.*, 8, 544-545.

MANTON, I. (1967). 'Further observations on the fine structure of *Chrysochromulina chiton* with special reference to the haptonema, 'peculiar' Golgi structure and scale production.' *J. Cell Sci.*, 2, 265-272.

MOENS, P. B., and PERKINS, F. O. (1969). 'Chromosome number of a small protist: accurate determination.' *Science,* 166, 1289-1291.

OLIVE, L. S. (1970). 'The Mycetozoa: a revised classification.' *Bot. Rev.*, 36, 59-89.

PASCHER, A. (1939). *'Heterokontae'* In *Rabenhorst's Kryptogamen–Flora von Deutschland, Osterreich und der Schweiz.* Akad. Verlag, Leipzig. 1092 pp.

PAULEY, G. B. (1967). 'Prespawning adult salmon mortality associated with a fungus of the genus *Dermocystidium.' J. Fish. Res. Bd. Can.,* 24, 843-848.

PERKINS, F. O. (1968). 'Fine structure of zoospores from *Labyrinthomyxa* sp. parasitizing the clam *Macoma balthica.' Ches. Sci.,* 9, 198-202.

PERKINS, F. O. (1969). 'Ultrastructure of vegetative stages in *Labyrinthomyxa marina* (=*Dermocystidium marinum*), a commercially significant oyster pathogen.' *J. Invert. Pathol.,* 13, 199-222.

PERKINS, F. O. (1970). 'Formation of centriole and centriole-like structures during meiosis and mitosis in *Labyrinthula* sp. (Rhizopodea, Labyrinthulida). An electron microscope study.' *J. Cell Sci.,* 6, 629-653.

PERKINS, F. O. (1972). 'The ultrastructure of holdfasts, "rhizoids", and "slime tracks" in thraustochytriaceous fungi and *Labyrinthula* spp.' *Arch. Mikrobiol.,* 84, 95-118.

PERKINS, F. O. (1973 a). 'Observations of thraustochytriaceous (Phycomycetes) and labyrinthulid (Rhizopodea) ectoplasmic nets on natural and artificial substrates—an electron microscope study.' *Can. J. Bot.,* 51, 485-491.

PERKINS, F. O. (1973 b). 'A new species of marine labyrinthulid *Labyrinthuloides yorkensis* gen. nov. spec. nov.—cytology and fine structure.' *Arch. Mikrobiol.,* 90, 1-17.

PERKINS, F. O. (1974). 'Phylogenetic considerations of the problematic thraustochytriaceous-labyrinthulid-*Dermocystidium* complex based on observations of fine structure.' *Veröff. Inst. Meeresforsch. Bremerh.,* Suppl. 5, 45-63.

PERKINS, F. O., and AMON, J. P. (1969). 'Zoosporulation in *Labyrinthula* sp.; an electron microscope study.' *J. Protozool.,* 16, 235-257.

PERKINS, F. O., and MENZEL, R. W. (1966). 'Morphological and cultural studies of a motile stage in the life cycle of *Dermocystidium marinum.' Proc. natn. Shellfish. Assoc.,* 56, 23-30.

PERKINS, F. O., and MENZEL, R. W. (1967). 'Ultrastructure of sporulation in the oyster pathogen *Dermocystidium marinum.' J. Invert. Pathol.,* 9, 205-229.

PETERFI, L. S., and MANTON, I. (1968). 'Observations with the electron microscope on *Asteromonas gracilis* Artari emend. (*Stephanoptera gracilis* Artari wisl.), with comparative observations on *Dunaliella* sp.' *Br. phycol. Bull.,* 3, 423-440.

PICKETT-HEAPS, J. D. (1969). 'The evolution of the mitotic apparatus: an attempt at comparative ultrastructural cytology in dividing plant cells.' *Cytobios,* 1, 257-280.

PITELKA, D. R. (1963). *Electron-microscope structure of Protozoa,* International Series of Mongraphs on Pure and Applied Biology. Pergamon Press, New York, vol. 13, 269 pp.

POKORNY, K. S. (1967). *'Labyrinthula.' J. Protozool.,* 14, 697-708.

PORTER, D. (1967). 'Observations on the cytology and motility of *Labyrinthula.*' Ph. D. Thesis, University of Washington.

PORTER, D. (1969). 'Ultrastructure of *Labyrinthula.*' *Protoplasma,* 67, 1-19.

PORTER, D. (1972). 'Cell division in the marine slime mold, *Labyrinthula* sp., and the role of the bothrosome in extracellular membrane production.' *Protoplasma, 74,* 427-448.

PORTER, D. (1974). 'Phylogenetic considerations of the Thraustochytriaceae and Labyrinthulaceae.' *Veröff. Inst. Meeresforsch. Bremerh.,* Suppl. 5, 19-44.

POYTON, R. O. (1970). 'The characterization of *Hyalochlorella marina* gen. et sp. nov. a new colorless counterpart of *Chlorella.*' *J. gen. Microbiol.,* 62, 171-188.

RINGO, D. L. (1967). 'Flagellar motion and fine structure of the flagellar apparatus in *Chlamydomonas.*' *J. Cell Biol.,* 36, 329-339.

SCHMOLLER, H. (1966). 'Beitrag zur Kenntnis der Labyrinthulen-Entwicklung.' *Arch. Protistenk.,* 109, 226-244.

SCHMOLLER, H. (1971). 'Die Labyrinthulen und ihre Beziehung zu den Amöben.' *Naturwissenshaften,* 58, 142-146.

SCHWAB-STEY, H., and SCHWAB, D. (1973). 'Über die Feinstruktur von *Labyrinthula coenocystis* Schmoller nach Gefrierätzung.' *Protoplasma, 76,* 455-464.

SÉNAUD, J. (1967). 'Contribution a l'étude des sarcosporidies et des toxoplasmes (Toxoplasmea).' *Protistologica, 3,* 167-232.

SPARROW, F. K. (1968). 'Remarks on the Thraustochytriaceae.' *Veröff. Inst. Meeresforsch., Bremerh.,* Suppl. 3, 7-17.

STERBA, G., and NAUMANN, W. (1970). 'Untersuchungen über *Dermocystidium granulosum* n. sp. bei *Tetraodon palembengensis* (Bleeker 1852).' *Arch. Protistenk.,* 112, 106-118.

STEY, H. (1968). 'Nachweis eines bisher unbekannten Organells bei *Labyrinthula.*' *Z. Naturf.,* 23b, 566-567.

STEY, H. (1969). 'Elektronenmikroskopische Untersuchung an *Labyrinthula coenocystis* Schmoller,' *Z. Zellforsch.,* 102, 387-418.

SWALE, E. M. F. (1969 a). 'The fine structure of a species of the amoeboflagellate *Pseudospora* Cienk.' *Arch. Mikrobiol.,* 67, 71-90.

SWALE, E. M. F. (1969 b). 'A study of the nannoplankton flagellate *Pedinella hexacostata* Vysotskii by light and electron microscopy.' *Br. phycol. J.,* 4, 65-86.

WATSON, S. W. (1957). 'Culture and cytological studies on species of *Labyrinthula.*' Ph.D. Thesis, Univ. Washington.

WETTSTEIN, R., and SOTELO, J. R. (1971). 'The molecular architecture of synatonemal complexes.' In *Advances in Cell and Molecular Biology* (Ed. E. J. DuPraw), Academic Press, New York, vol. I, 109-152.

12 The Ecology of Marine Lower Fungi

G. B. BREMER

12.1 Introduction

The pioneer work on the ecology of the marine lower fungi was carried out by Dr. W. Höhnk. In a series of papers published between 1939 and 1957 he gave an account of the occurrence and distribution of lower fungi in coastal waters. The results of his extensive investigations are summarized by Johnson and Sparrow (1961).

Subsequent studies have indicated that one group of fungi, the Thraustochytriales, are the most consistently occurring lower fungi in the marine environment. Unfortunately very little has been revealed of their role in the ecosystem.

12.2 Methods

The methods of obtaining samples of plankton, marine sediments and water for investigation are reviewed by Höhnk (1972). 'Baiting' techniques are a well established method for the analysis of such samples for lower fungi and have continued to be extensively used. Pollen 'baits' particularly of *Pinus* species are the most commonly used, while the larvae of *Artemia salina* L. have been used with equal success (Bahnweg, personal communication). Cellophane and more exotic baits such as 'blond baby hair' (Booth 1971 a) have also been found effective.

Flooded nutrient agar plates as described by Fuller *et al.* (1964) have also been successfully employed. This method is particularly useful for isolating forms lacking rhizoids, e.g. *Hyalochlorella marina* Poyton.

Miller (1967) described a technique whereby water samples were filtered through Millipore filters, the filters were then placed on nutrient agar plates reinforced with antibiotics, and the growth of colonies on the filters observed. Bahnweg (1973) employed this technique for isolating lower fungi from Antarctic, subAntarctic and tropical waters.

While all the previously mentioned methods are excellent for isolating and therefore recording the occurrence of lower fungi, they have serious shortcomings in providing quantitative data. Gaertner (1968 a) described a pollen baiting method which attempted to overcome these shortcomings.

For the analysis of fungal propagules in seawater, a set of bottles containing various dilutions of the sample, baited with a constant volume of *Pinus* sp. pollen, is set up (Table 12.1). The bottles are incubated at circa 15°C for 14 days and then examined for fungi growing on the pollen grains. The calculation of the 'lowest sure number' of propagules in the original sample is made as follows:

where, a = sample size in the last dilution giving a positive result.

b = number of replicates at that dilution.

n = number of bottles yielding fungi at that dilution.

the number of fungi/ml = $\dfrac{n}{a \times b}$

∴ number of fungi/1000 ml = $\dfrac{n \times 1000}{a \times b}$

Sediment samples are analysed by incorporating successively halved volumes of sediment using specially deisgned quantitative forceps.

Gaertner (1968 a) uses the ten replicates solely as a means of increasing the sample volume, thus subsequent statistical analyses of the results are not easily carried out. The bulk of glassware required, would however make extensive replication extremely cumbersome.

Tables 12. 1. Contents and arrangement of culture bottles for quantitative determination of fungal propagules (from Gaertner, 1968 a).

Series	1	2	3	4	5	6	7	8	9
Sterile sea-water (ml)	—	—	—	12.5	19.75	21.875	23.44	24.22	24.61
Water sample (ml)	100	50	25	12.5	5.25	3.125	1.56	0.78	0.39
Number of bottles	10	10	10	10	10	10	10	10	10

12.3   Thraustochytriales

The morphological characteristics and taxonomic affinities of these fungi are discussed by Johnson (Chapter 7), Sparrow (Chapter 8), and Perkins (Chapter 11). Thraustochytrid fungi can be easily isolated from a wide variety of marine substrates and habitats. Table 12.2 gives an indication of their cosmopolitan occurrence. The importance of a fungal group with such a widespread and consistent occurrence, has become increasingly recognized in the past decade, with current research on the marine lower fungi focused on the Thraustochytriales.

12.3.1   Sediments and Water Samples

The bulk of the quantitative data on the distribution of Thraustochytrid fungi is provided by the work of Gaertner (1967 a, b; 1968 a, b, c; 1969) carried out from a research vessel cruising in the North Atlantic Ocean and the North Sea. Table 12.3 shows some of the findings of the 1968 b study in the North

TABLE 12.2   Geographical locations of some of the recorded isolations of thraustochytriaceous fungi (modified after Harrison, 1972).

Author	Substrate	Geographical Position
Gaertner (1967 a)	Water and sediment	North Sea
Gaertner (1967 b)	Water and sediment	Heligoland
Schneider (1967)	Algae and sediments	Baltic and North Sea
Gaertner (1968 b)	Water and sediments	North Atlantic
Gaertner (1968 c)	Water and sediments	German Bay
Schneider (1968, 1969)	Algae and sediments	West and Mid-Baltic
Booth and Miller (1968)	Algae	Coast of Maine, USA
Booth (1969)	Halomorphic soils	British Columbia
Konno (1969)	Algae	Tokyo Bay
Sparrow (1969)	Water and sediments	Pacific, NW Coast
Ulken (1970)	Sediments	Mangrove Swamp, Brazil
Clokie (1970)	Algae	Inverness Coast, Scotland
Alderman and Harrison (1971)	Algae	Southern England and Wales
Booth (1971 a)	Soils and sediments	NW America
Booth (1971 b)	Soils and sediments	Queen Charlotte Island
Artemchuk (1972)	Shore sediments	White Sea, USSR
Bahnweg and Sparrow (1972)	Water	Southern Indian Ocean
Sparrow and Dogma (1973)	Sand and algae	Dominican Republic

TABLE 12.3   Summary of range of types isolated from sediment and water samples by Gaertner (1968 b) and their frequency of occurrence.*

	No. of recordings from water samples at 16 sites	No. of recordings from sediment samples at 7 sites
Thraustochytrium kinnei	1	—
T. aggregatum	2	1
T. pachydermum	1	—
T. multirudimentale	1	—
T. 'Kreis hyaliner Formen'	12	1
T. grosse Cluster grossen Sporen	4	1
T. kleine runde Form	6	3
T. rund mit kompakten Oltropfen	1	—
T. sp	6	—
Schizochytrium aggregatum	1	1
Dermocystidium (?) sp.	11	7
Dermocystidium (?) 'Kreis hyalines Formen'	7	7

*The author's grouping and terminology have been used.

Atlantic. Recognizable forms are apparently only a small part of the mycoflora, 'Thraustochytrium kreis hyaliner formen' is recorded from 12 out of 16 water samples and *Dermocystidium* (?) = *Hyalochlorella marina* is predominant in sediment samples.

Gaertner (1968 b) also showed that lower fungi are present in far greater numbers in sediments than in the open sea. Table 12.4 illustrates this point, for example at station 229 there were 18 500 propagules/litre of sediment compared with only 710 propagules/litre in seawater. Of the recognizable species, only *Schizochytrium aggregatum* Goldstein et Belsky occurred in large numbers (126 fungi/litre). *Thraustochytrium* species formed only a small part of the mycoflora.

TABLE 12.4 Quantitative analysis of number of propagules in sediment and water samples* (modified after Gaertner, 1968 b).

Site	Temp. (°C)	Depth (m)	No. propagules per litre seawater	No. propagules per litre sediment
224	11.5	100	10	
225	10.25	300	525	
226	10.5	1500	75	2000
227	10.5	1000	710	5000
228	10.5	500	750	
229	10.0	500	710	18500
230	10.0	450	775	
231	10.5	300	50	16000
232	11.25	500	710	
233	11.5	500	710	14000
234	12.0	1000	710	
235	12.5	1200	710	
236	12.5	1500	710	10000
237	12.25	20000	710	
238	12.5	2400	710	1000
239	12.0	7100	50	

*All water samples taken at a depth of 3 metres.

Gaertner (1968 c) recorded far higher figures for lower fungi in sediments than in his 1968 b study. For example 88 800 fungi/litre were recorded at one station in the German Bay (Table 12.5). Such a concentration of lower fungi has not been reported by other workers using the same method (Schneider, 1968; Bahnweg, personal communication). The only comparable figures in terms of numbers of fungi, are for yeasts in marsh sediments (Meyers, *et al.* 1970) and for fungi in sewage sludge (Cooke, Chapter 15). Both of these environments are far richer in nutrients than offshore bottom sediments. It therefore seems probable, that the very large numbers of fungi recorded by Gaertner, represent 'freak' results, since his 'lowest sure number' technique does not allow for the computation of either mean or variance figures.

The studies of Schneider (1967, 1968, 1969 a, b) are also centred on coastal waters of Germany, principally the Baltic and North Sea coasts of Schleswig-Holstein. Using *Pinus* sp. pollen as 'bait', Schneider (1968 a) achieved a high re-

TABLE 12.5   Numbers of lower fungi present in sediment samples taken from three sites in the German Bay (adapted from Gaertner 1968c).

Date	Station Tonne K	Station Tonne D	Station N. W. Tonne Nathurn
10. 3.66	20 400	8 180	—
14. 3.66	20 400	2 040	—
4. 4.66	16 300	8 180	6 120
18. 4.66	12 300	2 020	—
2. 5.66	550	<230	4 070
16. 5.66	<230	2 020	505
31. 5.66	230	<230	<230
13. 6.66	4 040	6 120	8 170
29. 8.66	16 300	4 080	—
12. 9.66	12 300	12 300	18 400
19. 9.66	14 300	14 300	14 300
3.10.66	14 300	—	—
6.10.66	12 200	4 080	—
20.10.66	51 100	1 008	10 200
7.11.66	14 600	6 140	4 060
17.11.66	58 300	6 140	20 400
15.12.66	32 000	5 140	19 600

covery rate of 129 samples out of 181 water and sediment samples yielding thraustochytrid fungi. A more detailed account of these investigations is given by Schneider (1969 a, b). Table 12.6 summarizes some of Schneider's (1969 b) findings. *Schizochytrium aggregatum* was the most abundant fungus, occurring at all the sampling sites and even in H_2S sediments. *S. aggregatum* and two species of *Thraustochytrium* were also found in polluted areas of Kiel and Flensburg Harbour.

The use of thraustochytrid fungi as pollution indicators was further examined by Schneider (1972). Salts of mercury, cadmium, zinc, nickel, cobalt, copper and manganese were tested for their toxicity, using *Thraustochytrium striatum* Schneider as a test organism. Mercury and cadmium salts were found to be most toxic, with zinc and nickel yielding intermediate effects. Thraustochytrid fungi are ideal subjects for such pollution studies since synchronous cultures are easily established and growth response quickly assayed, by the methods of Alderman and Jones (1971) and Bremer (1972).

Ecophysiological studies have shown that the Thraustochytriales can be firmly categorized as euryhaline euthermic organisms (Jones and Harrison, Chapter 10). One aspect of their ecology in the sea has, however, not been extensively investigated, and that is the occurrence of the fungi relative to ocean depth. The findings of Schneider (1968 b) and Bahnweg (1973) indicate that the frequency of occurrence of marine lower fungi in the sea decreases with increasing depth (Table 12.7 and Fig. 12.1). Whether this is due to a decrease in supply of nutrients from the photic zone, or to the increase in hydrostatic pressure has not been resolved, but it is an aspect to which more detailed attention should be paid.

TABLE 12.6 The occurrence of thraustochytrid fungi at various stations in the Baltic and North Seas (from Schneider, 1969b).

Fungus	North Sea	Kiel and Lübecker Bight	Kiel Fjord	Schlei Fjord	Flensburger Fjord	Western sites	Sites polluted by sewage	Other locations
Schizochytrium aggregatum	*	*	*	*	*	Bornholm Bay	Bulk, Kiel Harbour, Flensburg Harbour	Also in H$_2$S sediments
Thraustochytrium multirudimentale	*	*	*	As far as Lindaunis	As Far as Glücksburg	Arcona Basin		
Thraustochytrium kinnei	*	*	*	As far as Rabelsund		Fehmarn Belt	Kiel Harbour	
Thraustochytrium striatum	*	*	*			Kiel Bight		
Thraustochytrium sp. Type 1	*	*		*	*	Darsser Skelf	Flensburger Harbour	
Thraustochytrium sp. Type 137	*	*				Kiel Bight		
Thruastochytrium sp. Type 148	*	*				Kiel Bight		

TABLE 12.7 Occurrence of phycomycetes at various depths in water samples from Kiel Bay (from Schneider, 1968).

Station	Depth (metres)	Phycomycetes per litre	Yeasts per litre	Bacteria per litre
Feuerschiff Kiel	5	79	23	5080
November 1965	10	49	6	3240
	15	43	5	1910
Boknis Eck	5	920	41	6060
February 1966	10	540	52	5100
	15	140	65	5300
Schlei-Olpenitz	5	1000	—	—
July 1966	10	—	—	—
	25	33	—	—
Schlei-Olpenitz	5	6000	—	—
September 1966	10	1000	—	—
	25	260	—	—
Breitgrund	5	1000	2	1030
July 1966	25	30	0	570

Valuable data on the occurrence of lower fungi in Arctic and subAntarctic waters are provided by Bahnweg (1973). The results were obtained during two cruises, Numbers 46 and 51 of the US Research Vessel *Eltanin*. The course of the cruises and the quantitative distribution of lower fungi obtained are shown in Figs. 12.2 and 12.3. Bahnweg found the distribution of marine lower fungi to be patchy. They were present at all stations in subtropical and subAntarctic regions. South of the Antarctic convergence, they occurred at some stations in the northernmost Antarctic surface waters and in waters adjacent to the Ross Ice

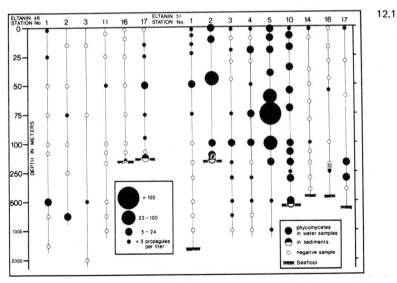

Fig.12.1. The occurrence of lower phycomycetes in water and sediment samples at varying depths, (from Bahnweg 1973) (geographical locations of numbered sites are shown by Fig.12.2 and 12.3).

319

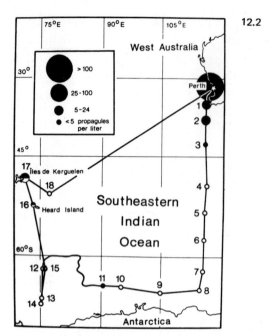

Fig. 12.2. Occurrence of lower phycomycetes at stations on *Eltanin* Cruise 46 (from Bahnweg, 1973).

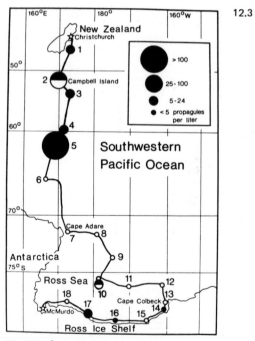

Fig. 12.3. Occurrence of lower phycomycetes at stations on *Eltanin* Cruise 51 (from Bahnweg, 1973).

Shelf (Figs. 12.1, 12.2 and 12.3). Substantial populations of fungi were found in waters at temperatures near and below 0°C.

The distribution of the fungi did not appear to be restricted by any particular water mass, for instance; at Station 10, Cruise 51 (Fig. 12.3) there was a uniform distribution throughout the water column, despite three water masses; Antarctic surface water, modified circumpolar deep water, and Ross Sea shelf water, being present.

The marine saprophytic phycomycetes are generally considered characteristic of coastal waters, with their numbers decreasing with increasing distance from land masses. Bahnweg found this generalization held true in subtropical and sub-Antarctic water, but not in Arctic waters. No increase in numbers of propagules was found at stations 6 (Bellamy Islands), 7 and 13 of cruise 51 (Fig. 12.1). All three stations are adjacent to land masses.

Bahnweg isolated four new species of *Thraustochytrium* from samples taken during the two cruises. At least one of these, *Thraustochytrium antarcticum* Bahnweg et Sparrow, has a lower temperature optimum (circa 10°C) than related forms from temperate waters.

12.3.2   Saline and Beach Soils

The studies of Booth (1971 a, c) provide data on the occurrence of thraustochytriaceous fungi in soils. *Schizochytrium aggregatum* and *Thraustochytrium roseum* Goldstein were found to be the most abundant fungi and occurred over the widest range of habitats (Table 12.7 from Booth, 1971 c).

Booth (1971 a) also relates the occurrence of these two species to physical and chemical parameters in the environment. The results (Fig. 12.4 a, b) indicate that the occurrence of *S. aggregatum* and *T. roseum* is highest in soils of high

TABLE 12.8   Summary of soil sampling sites on Queen Charlotte Islands, yielding Thraustochytrid fungi (from Booth, 1971 c).

Species	Habitats	Total no. of isolations.
Schizochytrium aggregatum	1, 2, 3, 4, 5, 6, 7, 8	21
Thraustochytrium aggregatum	1, 3, 6, 7	5
Thraustochytrium motivum aureum complex	1, 3, 6, 7	5
Thraustochytrium multi-rudimentale	1, 8	2
Thraustochytrium pachy-dermum	5, 6. 7	3
Thraustochytrium proliferum	1, 5	2
Thraustochytrium roseum	1, 2, 3, 5, 6, 7, 8, 9	24

Key to habitats	5 Marine beach.
1 Beach intertidal.	6 Tide marsh.
2 Coastal.	7 Tide affected stream.
3 Tidal edge sites.	8 Stream bank.
4 Headland.	9 Beach river.

salinity and osmolarity. The distribution of *S. aggregatum* appears to be more affected by salinity than that of *T. roseum*. Booth defined both fungi as 'obligately marine'. The findings of these field investigations on these soil inhabiting forms correlates well with responses recorded under controlled laboratory conditions (Jones and Harrison, Chapter 10).

12.3.3 Periodicity

Gaertner (1968 c) published the results of a two year (1965, 1966) investigation into the fluctuation of marine lower phycomycetes in sediment and water samples in the German Bay. Figure 12.5 shows the results for seawater samples at station Tonne K. The numbers of fungi for 1965 show maxima at months 1 and 7 which are not attained in 1966. Far less fungi are recorded throughout 1966 compared with the preceding year.

The numbers of fungi in sediments at three stations during 1966 are shown in Table 12.5 (from Gaertner, 1968 c). The numbers of fungi at the three sites on the same date are often quite similar. All sites show a drop in fungal populations during May and have maxima in the early spring and winter months. Gaertner found the sediment in May was very fine in texture, correlating with figures of less than 230 fungi/litre. There was, however, no correlation between the periodicity of the fungi and that of the phytoplankton at Heligoland.

Schneider (1969 b) recorded the fluctuation in the numbers of lower fungi in the Western Baltic. There was a minimum of 46 fungi/litre in winter and a maximum of 1500-6000 fungi/litre in summer. Schneider obtained population

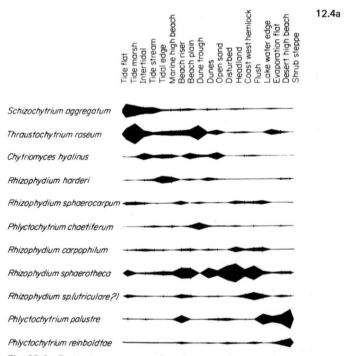

Fig. 12.4a. Derived density index (DDI) of chytrids and chytridiaceous species over 19 habitats. Blackened areas equal 25 DDI units per vertical millimetre (from Booth, 1971 c).

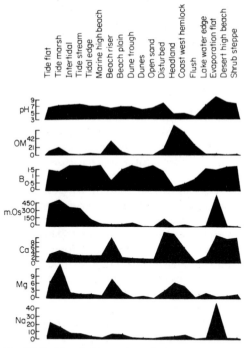

Fig. 12.4b. Mean habitat values of pH, organic matter (OM) bulk density (B), osmolarity (m. Os), Ca^{2+}, Mg^{2+}, and Na in 19 habitats.

peaks in May and September at Keil Bay, but only one summer peak at Rabel-sund. Schneider was unable to establish any relationship between the fluctuations observed and biotic or physical factors.

Newell in his account of the mycoflora of Red Mangrove seedlings (Chapter 2) records the fluctuation in frequency of occurrence of *Thraustochytrium* sp.

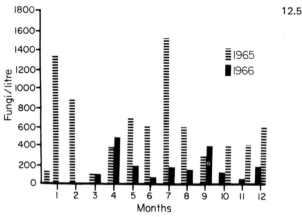

Fig. 12.5. Seasonal fluctuation of lower phycomycetes in seawater samples taken at station Tonne K, German Bay during 1965 and 1966 (from Gaertner, 1968 c).

associated with the seedlings (Table 2.4). The fungi show a seasonal occurrence pattern, being most abundant in December 1970 and 1971.

Clearly, more work is required to elucidate this facet of the ecology of the thraustochytrid fungi.

12.3.4   Substrate Relationships

As mentioned in Section 12.3.1, the marine lower phycomycetes are thought to be dependent on substrates of terrestrial origins. Clokie (1970) and Alderman and Harrison (1971) isolated a wide range of coccoid marine fungi from fragments of diverse species of littoral algae from British coastal waters. However, Goldstein (1963) and Goldstein and Belsky (1964) carried out inoculation experiments using *S. aggregatum* and *T. roseum* and found that these fungi grew poorly or not at all on a variety of living or dead algae. In contrast, luxuriant growths were achieved on pollen and Angiosperm leaves. Newell (Chapter 2) reports that *Thraustochytrium* is an active member of the mycoflora of dead Red Mangrove seedlings. Further evidence of the invasive ability of thraustochytrid fungi is given by Perkins (1973). Using electron microscopy, Perkins observed that the fungi were able to 'dissolve' the walls of pollen grains and yeast cells and extend ectoplasmic net elements into the interior, mingling with cellular organelles. A similar activity was also recorded with regard to animal tissues.

Bremer (unpublished data) has also used electron microscopy to investigate substrate relationships. Inoculations of zoospores of *Thraustochytrium kinnei* Gaertner were made onto dead adult brine shrimps (*Artemia salina* L.). Figures 12.6 a, b show sections through zoospores of the fungus recently settled on the exoskeleton of the shrimp. There are prominent electron-dense areas (Li), possibly stored lipids which are not observed when the fungus is grown in liquid culture media (*cf* Fig. 7.2). The extracellular material (Ad) is consistently observed and superficially resembles the adhesive produced by settling spores of the brown alga *Pylaiella* sp. (Chamberlain, personal communication). This 'adhesive' is apparently produced prior to the development of the ectoplasmic net system and possibly provides the initial anchorage of the zoospore to the substrate. Fig. 12.6 b shows the base of a settled zoospore, the cuticle (Cu) of the *Artemia* has been eroded and an area of muscle and connective tissue beneath has also been digested away. Elements of the ectoplasmic net system (Ect.) are visible within the eroded area.

Apparently thraustochytrid fungi have potent lytic properties which would befit them for a role as decomposers of moribund material derived from terrestrial sources, or the photic zone. Organic substrates were not found by Bahnweg (1973) in the vicinity of Arctic and Antarctic islands, yet substantial populations of phycomycetes were found in this area.

The assumed relationships between marine lower fungi and organic substrates is therefore more complicated than may appear at first glance. Bahnweg (1973) suggests that whereas marine yeasts and bacteria were found to be associated in large numbers with dissolved organic carbon, the phycomycetes favour high concentrations of particulate organic carbon. Particulate organic carbon was found to decrease with increasing depth. A tenuous link between the distribution of phycomycetes and the availability of particulate organic carbon in the sea can therefore be proposed.

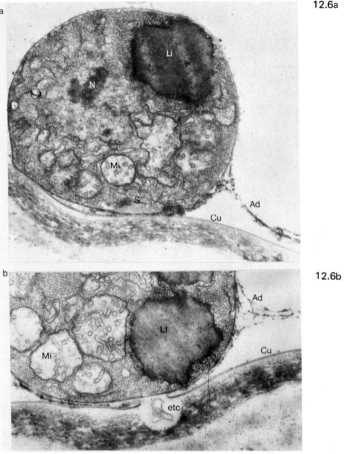

Fig.12.6a. Electron micrograph of section through young sporangium of *T. kinnei* Gaertner, attached to exoskeleton of *Artemia salina* L. (x 30 000 approx.) (photograph G. B. Bremer). **Fig.12.6b.** Electron micrograph of section through base of young sporangium of *T. kinnei,* attached to exoskeleton of *Artemia* showing erosion of cuticle and underlying tissues by the fungus (x 26 000 approx.) (photo. G. B. Bremer). N, nucleus; Li, possible lipid; Ad, possible adhesive material; Ect, ectoplasmic net system; Mi, mitochondrion; S, sagenogenetosome; Cu, cuticle.

12.4 Chytridiales

Although thought of by many as being predominantly freshwater and soil fungi, there are many genera of chytrids well represented in estuarine and marine environments.

Harder and Uebelmesser (1955) gave the first major account of chytrids in saline habitats. Their investigation failed to reveal any marked morphological differences between marine isolated chytrids and related forms isolated from non-saline environments.

Subsequent to the latter study, the most important contribution to our knowledge of the ecology of chytrids in saline influenced habitats, has been made by Booth

(1969, 1971 a, b, c, d). The 1969 study concerned the distribution of chytrids in homoio- and poikilo-halomorphic soils. His results are considered by Johnson (Chapter 7) and Jones and Harrison (Chapter 10). The occurrence of a given species was found to be widespread and habitat type was considered to be of little taxonomic value.

Later studies by Booth (1971 c, d) attempt to relate the distribution of chytridiaceous fungi, to physical and chemical parameters in the environment. A study of 11 species of lower fungi occurring in 19 habitats is summarized in Figs. 12.4 a, b (taken from Booth 1971 c). Correlations between density distribution index (DDI) of the fungi and environmental factors were proposed. From the results obtained, Booth divided the 11 species into four groups:

(1) Obligately marine:
     Schizochytrium aggregatum Goldstein et Belsky
(2) Marine:
     Thraustochytrium roseum Goldstein
(3) Facultatively marine:
     Chytriomyces hyalinus Karling
     Rhizophydium harderi Uebelmesser
     Rhizophydium carpophilum (Zopf) Fischer
     Rhizophydium sphaerotheca Zopf
     Phlyctochytrium chaetiferum Karling
     Rhizophydium sp. *(utriculare?)*
(4) Marine occasionals:
     Phlyctochytrium palustre Gaertner
     Phlyctochytrium reinboldtae Persiel

This study only indicated trends and related the density of the organisms in habitats which encompass within them individual sites with widely differing environmental parameters.

The results of the work of Harrison (1972) on the salinity tolerance in controlled cultural conditions of seven species of chytridiaceous fungi, reinforce the results in the field described by Booth (1971 c). The fungi tested by Harrison showed a variable response from species to species (Table 12.9), *Phylctochytrium californicum* Barr and *Phlyctochytrium semiglobiferum* Uebelmesser being quite halotolerant, while *Rhizophlyctis rosea* (de Bary et Woronin) Fischer was very intolerant of salinity, with cytoplasmic cleavage disrupted by 30% sea water concentrations.

Booth (1971 d) used controlled experimental conditions to investigate the temperature and salinity responses of 57 isolates of the Blastocladiales and the Chytridiales obtained from a variety of marine influenced habitats. Booth's data indicate that controlled variations in salinity (up to 15°/oo) and temperature, may be a convenient means for recognizing ecotypes. For example; Booth divided the four isolates of *Phlyctochytrium palustre* Gaertner into two ecotypes. The first ecotype comprises isolates 21 and 22 from steppe sites. This ecotype grew well at 20°C in salinities from 0 to 15°/oo. Better growth was observed at 20°C than at 30 or 10°C. The other ecotype includes isolates 23 and 24, from a beach riser. These isolates grew better at 5°/oo than at 0 or 15°/oo salinity.

For each isolate of each species that could be grouped into ecotypes, site values for certain parameters were plotted (Fig.12.). The environmental parameters tend to be similar over isolates of the same ecotypes, e.g. *Chytriomyces hyalinus* ecotype 1 occurred at sites of lower Na$^+$ concentration than those of ecotype 3 which in turn occupied

326

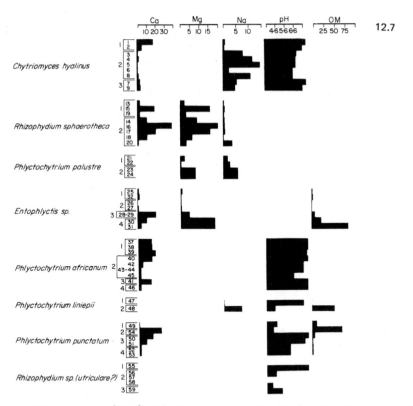

Fig. 12.7. Levels of Ca^{2+} Mg^{2+}, Na$^+$, pH and organic matter (OM) of sites of isolate recovery. Isolates are grouped into ecotypes indicated by large numerals (from Booth 1971 d).

TABLE 12.9   Response of seven chytridiaceous fungi to salinity variations in controlled culture conditions (from Harrison, 1972).

Fungus	Optimum salinity for growth % SW	Growth in DW as percentage of optimum	Growth in SW as percentage of optimum	Percentage increase or decrease in SW compared to DW
Rhizophlyctis rosea	0	100	0	−100 (70%)*
Rhizophydium sphaerotheca	10-20	64.1	30.4	−52.6
Rhizophydium sp.	10	33.3	3.7	−89.9
Chytridium olla	0	100	0	−100 (50%)
Phlyctochytrium acuminatum	0	100	0	−100 (50%)*
Phlyctochytrium californicum	40	29.11	37.9	+30.2
Phlyctochytrium semiglobiferum	40	75.6	37.0	−51.1

*   Salinity at which no growth was recorded.

327

sites lower in Na$^+$ than ecotype 2. Ecotypes of other species show the same trend, with the exception of isolates 15 and 40 which are anomalous.

Ulken (1972) also provided evidence for physiological adaptation in chytridiaceous fungi. *Phlycochytrium mangrovii* Ulken was isolated from swamp water with a salinity varying between 10 and 15°/oo, and with a mean temperature above 20°C. Under controlled conditions, Miss Ulken found the salinity optimum of the fungus to be 15°/oo and the temperature optimum 25°C. From further observation of occurrence relative to environmental factors, Miss Ulken concluded that salinity was the overriding factor influencing the distribution of the fungus.

Within the Chytridiales there appears to be a much more variable response to environmental factors and more adaptation to the factors operating at the source of isolation than has been recognized for the Thraustochytriales.

12.5 Other Taxa

Besides the two major taxa discussed in Sections 12.3 and 12.4, there are marine representatives of the Hyphochytriales, Plasmodiophorales, Lagenidiales, Saprolegniales and Peronosporales. Coherent ecological data on these groups in the marine environment

TABLE 12.10   The effects of salinity upon the asexual reproduction of saprolegniaceous fungi (from Harrison, 1972).

| Fungus | Salinity (% seawater) | | | | |
	0	10	20	30	40
Achlya bisexualis	****	****	**	*	0
A. flagellata	***(*)	**	*	0	0
A. diffusa	****	**	*	0	0
A. americana	****	**(**)	*	0	0
A. klebsiana	****	0	0	0	0
A. racemosa	****	***	**	0	0
A. crenulata	****	***(*)	*	0	0
Isoachlya toruloides	****	***	*	*	0
I. eccentrica	****	***	**	*	0
I. intermedia	****	***	**	**	*
Protachlya paradoxa	****	****	*	*	0
Thraustocheca clavata	****	****	**(*)	*	0
Saprolegnia mixta	****	****	**	*	*
S. diclina	****	**(**)	**	*	0
Saprolegnia sp	****	****	**	*	0
S. ferax	****	****	*	0	0
S. parasitica	****	****	***	**	*

****:Normal zoospore production.   ***: Some cleavage or gemmae.
**:   Gemmae.   *:   Very small asexual structures.
0:    Vegetative growth only.   ( ): Variable response.

are sparse. Some are parasitic forms, with obscure life cycles and taxonomic affinities and are dealt with elsewhere (Johnson, Chapter 7; Alderman, Chapter 9).

12.5.1 Saprolegniaceae

Although extremely common as freshwater moulds, there are only two marine members of this family. They are both species of *Leptolegnia*, parasitic in marine animals (see Alderman, Chapter 9).

Te Strake (1959), in an ecological investigation of the estuary of the River Neuse in North Carolina, found that the highest salinity at which saprolegniaceous fungi occurred was $2.8^\circ/oo$. This fact indicated that salinity was the limiting factor affecting their distribution. However, *Dictyuchus monosporus* Leitgeb under controlled conditions, growing on hempseeds, produced oospores at $7^\circ/oo$ salinity. Te Strake suggested that nutritional factors and not solely hydrographic ones limit the estuarine distribution of saprolegniaceous fungi. The findings of Harrison and Jones (1971) and Harrison (1972) support this view. *Saprolegnia parasitica* Coker grows well in glucose/yeast broth in up to 70% seawater concentrations. But, on solid agar media there were only small amounts of growth at 70% seawater. No growth occurred on hemp seeds at 70% seawater.

Vegetative growth alone is not a reliable parameter for assessing the salinity responses of a fungus. The organism must obviously reproduce in salinities found in saline habitats to be a successful marine fungus. Tables 12.10 and 12.11 show some of results of experiments by Harrison (1972) on the effect of salinity on the reproduction of 17 members of the Saprolegniaceae. Harrison concluded that although for some species, vegetative growth was good in high salinities, none of the organisms tested was able to reproduce normally at salinities above $7.5^\circ/oo$ NaCl. In fact, only *Protoachlya paradoxa* Coker and *Achlya flagellata* Coker formed sexual stages in 20% seawater. None of the organisms produced zoospores in salinities above 10% seawater concentrations. These findings tend to corroborate the known ecological distribution of members of the Saprolegniaceae. The Pythiaceae appear to be less restricted by salinity than saprolegniaceous forms, since Höhnk (1953) found several species of *Pythium* reproducing asexually and sexually in a wide range of salinities.

12.5.2   Hyalochlorella marina *Poyton*

This organism was first described as *Dermocystidium* sp. by Goldstein and Moriber (1966). It is a coccoid organism lacking rhizoids and producing aplanospores. Its taxonomic position is problematical and its possible affinities are reviewed by Johnson (Chapter 7). Organisms resembling *Hyalochlorella* have been reported by Gaertner (1968 b, 1969), Ulken (1968) and Alderman and Harrison (1971). Since this organism lacks rhizoids it will not be recovered using pollen baiting techniques and therefore possibly occurs in larger numbers than present results indicate. Alderman (personal communication) has found *H. marina* to be abundant in association with marine algae, but that its occurrence tends to be localized. Poyton (1970) found no correlation between the occurrence of *H. marina* and salinity fluctuations. However, Bremer (unpublished data) finds that Goldstein's original isolate (L1S37) is more widely tolerant of salinity than species of *Thraustochytrium*. Good growth is observed from 7 to $35^\circ/oo$ salinity under cultural conditions.

It is difficult to envisage a quantitative method for determining the frequency of occurrence of this organism, yet it is a species that should be borne in mind when considering investigations into the mycoflora of estuarine and marine environments.

TABLE 12.11   The effects of salinity upon the sexual reproduction of saprolegniaceous fungi (from Harrison, 1972).

Fungus	Salinity % Seawater				
	0	10	20	30	40
Achlya bisexualis	—	***(*)a	***a	**	0
A. flagellata	***(*)	***(*)a	**(*)a	0	0
A. diffusa	****a	****a	**a	0	0
A. americana	****a	****a	**(*)a	0	0
A. klebsiana	****a	****a	***	0	0
A. racemosa	****a	****a	***a	*	0
A. crenulata	****	****	0	0	0
Isoachlya toruloides	****	**	**	**	*
I. eccentrica	****	**(**)	*	*	*
I. intermedia	****a	****a	*	0	0
Protoachlya paradoxa	—	****a	****a	*	*
Thraustotheca clavata	****a	***a	**	*	0
Saprolegnia mixta	****a	***a	**	*	0
S. diclina	****a	****a	***a	*	0
Saprolegnia sp.	****a	****a	***a	*	0
S. ferax	****a	***a	**	0	0

****:Normal oöspheres.
**:   No cleavage.
a: Antheridia present.
( ): Variable response.

***: Aborting oöspheres or imperfect cleavage.
*:   Oogonial initials remain very small.
0:    Vegetative growth only.

12.6 Evaluation

From the work described in this chapter, a faint picture emerges of the ecology of the marine lower fungi. The Thraustochytriales are the dominant group in marine environments. They have been shown to be truly marine in nature, with a widespread and abundant occurrence.

The Chytridiales show a wide variety of responses to physio-ecological parameters, but overall their tolerance of high salinities is far lower than that of the Thraustochytriales. Although Höhnk (1955), presented numerical evidence to show that chytrids occur in marine sediments of up to $34^{\circ}/oo$ salinity Johnson (1967) found only two chytrids; *Rhizophydium* and *Olpidium* occurring at $34^{\circ}/oo$ salinity in estuaries. It can be postulated that the role of chytrids is possibly more important in brackish waters and that their importance in waters above $15^{\circ}/oo$ salinity is minor. Ulken (1969) found that chytrids in the Bassin d'Arcachon disappeared during the increased salinity experienced in the summer months, but infection with chytrids occurred in the spring, when the basin is flooded with freshwater. In contrast, thraustochytrid fungi have been shown by Schneider (1971) to have a decreasing occurrence with decreasing salinity and to occur in very small numbers in brackish water situations.

Besides establishing the truly marine nature of the Thraustochytriales, the past decade has revealed little else about their role in nature. These fungi appear to have remarkable abilities to penetrate solid material and a unique ectoplasmic net system to aid in the adsorption and transfer of nutrients. Although the numbers of thraustochytrids are small (250/litre) in water compared with yeasts and bacteria, it may be that instead of being saprophytically competitive with bacteria and yeasts, the thraustochytrids decompose material indigestible to the bacteria and yeasts. Yet this remains pure supposition, we still lack an effective tool for quantitative assay of the stock of marine lower fungi and although our knowledge of their occurrence has increased greatly in the past ten years, there remains a very great deal to be learnt about this enigmatic group of fungi.

Acknowledgements

I should like to thank Dr. G. Bahnweg for allowing me to read and refer to his unpublished results and for permission to reproduce Figs. 12.1-12.3.

References

ALDERMAN, D. J., and HARRISON, J. L. (1971). 'Some observations on British marine monocentric fungi'. Abstract. *1st. Internat. Mycol. Congress,* Exeter 1971.

ALDERMAN, D. J., and JONES, E. B. G. (1972). 'Physiological requirements of two marine Phycomycetes, *Althornia crouchii* and *Ostracoblabe implexa'. Trans. Br. mycol. Soc.,* 57, 213-225.

ARTEMCHUK, N. J. (1972). 'The fungi of the White sea. III. New Phycomycetes, discovered in the Great Salma Strait of the Kandalakshial Bay'. *Veröff. Inst. Meeresforch. Bremerh.,* 13, 231-237.

BAHNWEG, G. (1973). 'The occurrence, distribution and taxonomy of fungi: in particular lower phycomycetes, in the Subantarctic and Antarctic marine ecosystems.' Ph.D. Thesis. University of Michigan, Ann Arbor.

BAHNWEG, G. and SPARROW, F. K. (1971). 'Marine fungi: occurrence in the southern Indian Ocean'. *Antarctic J.,* 6, 155.

BREMER, G. B. (1972). 'The physiology of some thraustochytrid fungi'. *Veröff. Inst. Meeresforsch. Bremerh.* Suppl. 5, 237-250.

BOOTH, T. (1969). 'Marine fungi from British Columbia: monocentric chytrids and chytridiaceous species from coastal and interior halomorphic soils'. *Syesis,* 2, 141-161.

BOOTH, T. (1971a). 'Occurrence and distribution of some zoosporic fungi from soils of Hibben and Moresby Islands, Queen Charlotte Islands'. *Can. J. Bot.,* 49, 951-965.

BOOTH, T. (1971b). 'Occurrence and distribution of chytrids, chytridiaceous fungi, and some Actinomycetales from soils of Oregon, California and Nevada'. *Can. J. Bot.,* 49, 939-949.

BOOTH, T. (1971c). 'Distribution of certain soil inhabiting chytrid and chytridiaceous species related to some physical and chemical factors'. *Can. J Bot.,* 49, 1743-1755.

BOOTH, T. (1971d). 'Ecotypic responses of chytrid and chytridiaceous species to various salinity and temperature combinations'. *Can. J. Bot.,* 49, 1757-1767.

BOOTH, T., 'and MILLER, C. E. (1968). 'Some substrate relationships of the family Thraustochytriaceae'. *Veröff. Inst. Meeresforsch. Bremerh.,* 12, 329-351.

CLOKIE, J. (1970). 'Some substrate relationships of the family Thraustochytriaceae'. *Veröff. Inst. Meeresforsch. Bremerh.,* 12, 329-351.

FULLER, M. S., FOWLES, B. E., and McLAUGHLIN, D. J. (1964). 'Isolation and pure culture of marine phycomycetes'. *Mycologia,* 56, 745-56.

GAERTNER, A. (1967a). 'Niedere mit Pollen Köderbarer Pilze in der sudlichen Nordsee'. *Veröff. Inst. Meeresforsch. Bremerh.,* 10, 159-165.

GAERTNER, A. (1967b). 'Ökologische Untersuchungen an einem marinen Pilz aus der umgebung von Helgoland'. *Helgolander. Wiss. Meeresunters.,* 15, 181-192.

GAERTNER, A. (1968a). 'Eine Methode des quantitaven Nachweises niederer, mit Pollen Köderbarer Pilze im Meerwasser und im Sediment'. *Veröff. Inst. Meeresforsch. Bremerh.,* 3, 75-92.

GAERTNER, A. (1968b). 'Niedere, mit Pollen Köderbare marine Pilze diessiets und jenseits des Island-Färöer-Rückens im Oberflächenwasser und im Sediment'. *Veröff. Inst. Meeresforsch. Bremerh.,* 11, 65-82.

GAERTNER, A. (1968c). 'Die Flucktuationen Mariner niederer Pilz in der Deutschen Bucht 1965 and 1966.' *Veröff. Inst. Meeresforsch. Bremerh.,* 3, 105-120.

GAERTNER, A. (1969). 'Marine niedere Pilze in Nordsee und Nordatlantik'. *Ber. dt. bot. Ges.,* 82, 287-306.

GOLDSTEIN, S. (1963). 'Morphological variation and nutrition of a new monocentric marine fungus'. *Arch. Mikrobiol.,* 45, 101-110.

GOLDSTEIN, S., and BELSKY, M. (1964). 'Axenic culture of a new marine phyco-mycete possessing an unusual type of asexual reproduction'. *Am. J. Bot.,* 51, 72-78.

GOLDSTEIN, S., and MORIBER, L. (1966). 'Biology of a problematic marine fungus, *Dermocystidium* sp. I. Development and cytology'. *Arch. Mikrobiol.,* 53, 1-11.

HARDER, R., and UEBELMESSER, E. (1955). 'Uber marine saprophytische, Chytri-diales und einege andere Pilze vom Meeresboden und Meerestrans.' *Arch. Mikrobiol.,* 22, 87-114.

HARRISON, J. L. (1972). 'The salinity tolerance of freshwater and marine zoosporic fungi, including some aspects of the ecology and ultrastructure of the Thraustochy-triaceae, Ph.D. Thesis. University of London.

HARRISON, J. L., and JONES, E. B. G. (1971). 'Salinity tolerance of *Saprolegnia parasitica* Coker'. *Mycopath. Mycol. appl.,* 43, 297-307.

HÖHNK, W. (1953), 'Studien zur Brack-und Seewassermykologie II. Oömycetes: Erster Teil'. *Veröff. Inst. Meeresforsch. Bremerh.,* 1, 247-278.

HÖHNK, W. (1955). 'Niedere pilze im watt und meeresgrund (Chytridiales und Thraustochytriaceae). *Naturwissenschaften,* 11, 348-349.

HÖHNK, W. (1972). 'Analysis of the stock. E. Fungi'. In *Research Methods in Marine Biology.* (Ed. C. Schlieper) Sidgwick and Jackson, London, 142-155.

JOHNSON, T. W. (1967), 'The estuarine mycoflora'. In *Estuaries,* American Asso-ciation for the advancement of Science. 303-305.

JOHNSON, T. W., and SPARROW, F. K. (1961). *Fungi in Oceans and Estuaries.* J. Cramer, Weinheim, 688p.

KONNO, K. (1969). 'Studies on Japanese lower aquatic phycomycetes, II. On *Thraustochytrium* isolated from seaweed'. *Trans. mycol. Soc. Japan,* 10, 9-13.

MEYERS, S. P., NICHOLSON, M. L., RHEE, J., MILES, P. and AHEARN, D. G.

(1970). 'Mycological studies in Barataria Bay, Louisiana, and biodegredation of oyster grass, *Spartina alterniflora'. Coastal Studies Bulletin,* 5, 111-124.

MILLER, C. E. (1967). 'Isolation and pure culture of acquatic phycomycetes by membrane filtration'. *Mycologia,* 51, 524-527.

PERKINS, F. O. (1973). 'Observations of thraustochytriaceous (Phycomycetes) and labyrinthulid (Rhizopodea) ectoplasmic nets on natural and artificial substrates —an electron microscope study'. *Can. J. Bot.,* 51. 485-491.

POYNTON, R. O. (1970). 'The isolation and occurrence of *Hyalochlorella marina'. J. gen. Microbiol.,* 621, 189-194

SCHNEIDER, J. (1967). 'Ein neuer mariner Phycomycet aus der Kieler Bucht. *(Thraustochytrium striatum* spec. nov.)'. *Kieler Meeresforsch.,* 23, 16-20.

SCHNEIDER, J. (1968). 'Über Niedere Phycomyceten der westlichen Ostee'. *Veröff. Inst. Meeresforsch. Bremerh.,* 3, 93-104.

SCHNEIDER, J. (1969a). 'Über Nieder Pilze der westlichen Ostsee'. *Ber. dt. bot. Ges.,* 81, 369-74.

SCHNEIDER, J. (1969b). 'Zur Taxonomie, Verbreitung und Ökologie einiger mariner Phycomyceten'. *Kieler Meeresforsch.,* 25, 316-327.

SCHNEIDER, J. (1971). 'Niedere Pilze aus Bodenproben des Brack und Meervassers der Englischen Westkuste'. *Kieler Meeresforsch.,* 27, 94-101.

SCHNEIDER, J. (1972). 'Niedere Pilze al Testorganismen für Schadstaffe in Brackwasser Die Wirkung von Schwermetallverbindunger und Phenol auf *Thraustochytrium striatum.' Marine Biology,* 16, 214-225.

SPARROW, F. K. (1969). 'Zoosporic fungi from the Pacific Northwest (USA)'. *Arch. Mikrobiol.,* 66, 129-146.

SPARROW, F. K., and DOGMA, I. J. (1973). 'Zoosporic phycomycetes from Hispaniola'. *Arch. Mikrobiol.,* 89, 177-204.

Te STRAKE, D. (1959). 'Estuarine distribution and saline tolerance of some Saprolegniaceae'. *Phyton. Internat. J. Exp. Bot.,* 12, 147-152.

ULKEN, A. (1968). 'Über zwei marine niedere Pilze vom Meeresboden der Nordsee'. *Veröff. Inst. Meeresforsch. Bremerh.,* 3, 71-74.

ULKEN, A. (1969). 'Über das Vorkommen niederer saprophytischen Phycomyceten (Chytridiales) im Bassin d'Arcachon (Frankreich)'. *Veröff. Inst. Meeresforch. Bremerh.,* 11, 303-308.

ULKEN, A. (1970). 'Phycomyceten aus Mangrove bei Cananèia. (Sao Paulo, Brasilien)'. *Veröff. Inst. Meeresforsch. Bremerh.,* 12, 313-319.

ULKEN, A. (1972). 'Physiological studies on a Phycomycete from a mangrove swamp at Cananèia, Sao Paulo, Brazil'. *Veröff. Inst. Meeresforsch. Bremerh.,* 13, 217-230.

SECTION II: FRESHWATER FUNGI

A. Ascomycetes, Fungi Imperfecti and Basidiomycetes

13 The Morphology and Biology of Freshwater Fungi Excluding Phycomycetes

C. T. INGOLD

13.1 Introduction

It is difficult to characterize an aquatic fungus and indeed to define the aquatic environment itself. Almost any fungus can be grown in submerged shaken culture; it is potentially aquatic. Further, there are, as it were, micro-aquatic habitats such as the aqueous phase between soil particles, slime fluxes of trees, nectaries of flowers and films of sugary solution on the surface of ripe fruit. Each of these has its fungal flora. In this chapter, however, the view is taken that aquatic fungi are those normally completely submerged in large volumes of free water such as streams and rivers, ponds and lakes. It is to be noted that this limitation excludes such species as *Mitrula phalloides* Pers. ex Fr. in which the mycelium is usually submerged in a shallow pond but the sporophore projects into the air, and the aero-aquatic hyphomycetes which are considered in chapter 27 of this book.

In considering a large assemblage of living organisms, it is difficult to avoid speculation about their evolution, but in the fungi, where the fossil record is so imperfect, this is a particularly dangerous process. Nevertheless, it is probably fairly safe to assume that aquatic fungi reproducing by zoospores have had their evolutionary history in the aquatic environment. On the other hand, so far as the Ascomycetes and Fungi Imperfecti now found growing submerged in water are concerned, it is quite likely that their more immediate ancestors were essentially terrestrial organisms. Taking the story far enough back into the past, Ascomycetes seem likely to have had an aquatic origin and, in this connection, many mycologists have cast eyes on the red seaweeds (Florideae). However, the Ascomycetes of today form essentially a group of terrestrial fungi and aquatic Ascomycetes seem such a motley throng that it is easier to regard them as re-migrants from the land than as allied directly to a central stock of aquatic proto-Ascomycetes from which present day land species may also have arisen.

It might seem logical to include in this survey the aquatic lichens since these are essentially fungal. However, the biology of lichen-forming fungi is very different from that of other types, so aquatic lichens have been excluded.

13.2 Ascomycetes

Aquatic Ascomycetes are abundant in freshwaters (In gold 1951, 1954, 1955; Ingold and Chapman, 1952). In the sea, some Ascomycetes are rather harmless parasites of larger seaweeds. The only parallel on the freshwater side is *Leptosphaeria lemaneae,* (Cohn et Woron.) Sacc., a fairly common fungus endophytic in *Lemanea* (Ingold, 1955) sometimes described as a 'green, freshwater, red seaweed'. *L. lemaneae* (Figs 13.1 and 13.2) has minute perithecia (pseudothecia) embedded in the thallus and the bitunicate asci discharge their spores in a perfectly normal manner (Ingold, 1955).

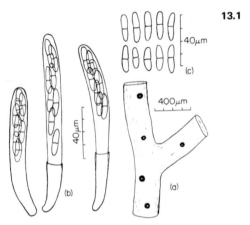

13.1

Fig. 13.1 *Leptosphaeria lemanea.* (a) part of a thallus of *Lemanea mammillosa* bearing five pseudothecia. (b) three asci two of which have expanded. (c) freshly discharged spores.

In lakes the richest sources of aquatic Ascomycetes are the submerged, dead but often *in situ,* stalks of reed swamp plants such as *Phragmites communis* trin, *Schoenoplectus lacustris* (L.) Palla, *Typha latifolia* L. and *Equisetum fluviatile* L. These nearly always bear ascocarps of various species. Both Discomycetes and Pyrenomycetes occur, in contrast to the marine situation where, although Pyrenomycetes abound, the apothecial types appear to be lacking. The other chief substratum for these fungi is submerged wood mainly in the form of waterlogged sticks of various kinds of trees.

This submerged aquatic Ascomycete flora is very considerable and not well known, so that it seems highly likely that large numbers of species remain to be described. Comparatively few studies have been made of this flora, possibly because the taxonomy of the organisms involved is of considerable difficulty.

Many species found in lakes and rivers are aquatic species of well known terrestrial genera, such as *Leptosphaeria,* and appear little, if at all, modified in relation to the aquatic environment. Thus the operculate *Psilopezia babingtonii* Berk., with sessile apothecia up to 1 cm in diameter, is quite common on submerged sticks in the English Lake District. However, this has all the features normal for a terrestrial cup fungus. It has oval spores having rather thick walls, like its humariaceous allies of dry land. It should be emphasized that in most submerged Ascomycetes the ascus is explosive, bursting apically to liberate its spores into the water. By contrast with *P. babingtonii* there are some aquatic cup fungi that seem to have become modified in relation to the aquatic environment. This is especially true of those with long thread-like spores. It will be argued later, in connection with aquatic hyphomycetes, that such spores have a special significance in the aquatic environment. So far as Discomycetes are concerned,

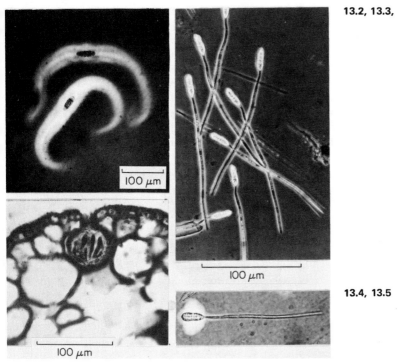

Fig. 13.2. *Leptosphaeria lemanea:* part of T.S. thallus of *Lemanea mammillosa* Kutz. including a median section through a pseudothecium of the fungus which is about the size of the larger cells of the host pseudoparenchyma. **Fig. 13.3.** *Pleospora scirpicola:* two freshly liberated ascospores mounted in indian ink to show the mucilage associated with them. **Figs. 13.4 and 13.5.** *Loramyces macrospora.* **Fig. 13.4.** Eight spores of a single ascus (part of which appears near bottom left); the eighth spore is just escaping; photographed with phase contrast. **Fig. 13.5.** Spore mounted in dilute indian ink to show mucilage around 'head' of the spore.

Apostemidium can be taken in illustration of a well defined genus of essentially aquatic fungi. *A. guernisaci* (Crouan) Boud. has ascospores 200 – 300 μm long and only 2 – 3 μm wide. These beg comparison with the long, thread-like pollen grains of the marine flowering plant *Zostera*. Both can be related biologically to the aquatic environment and the problem of underwater impaction.

Amongst Pyrenomycete types, *Pleospora scripicola* (DC) Karst. is interesting. The successive liberation of spores from the bitunicate ascus of this fungus was figured over 100 years ago by Pringsheim (1858), who, however, did not note that following liberation the mucilage sheath of the large muriform ascospore swells enormously to produce a long slug-like structure probably of real significance in relation to impaction on the underwater stalk of a reed (Fig. 13.3).

Another elegant example is the aquatic genus *Loramyces* with two known species: *L. junciola* Weston and *L. macrospora* Ingold et Chapman on submerged, dead, reed swamp plants (Ingold and Chapman, 1952). The perithecium is unusual in being superficial, not immersed in the substratum as are other aquatic flask fungi. In a squash preparation of a living perithecium the individual unitunicate asci readily dehisce, the eight spores of an ascus gliding out successively through an apical orifice (Ingold, 1968). Dehiscence of the ascus seems to result from the swelling of mucilage associated with the spores. Each emerging spore has a 2-celled oval 'head', encased in a large ellipsoid of

337

mucilage (Figs. 13.4 and 13.5). The lower cell of the spore is prolonged backwards as a filamentous 'tail'. In a water current, or settling under gravity in still conditions, the spore seems to glide through the water and, on contact with a solid object, impacts 'head' first. This places the spore in a strategic position, for it is from the apex of the upper cell that the germ tube always develops (Weston, 1929).

Another example of an aquatic Ascomycete with mucilaginous appendages that can be interpreted in relation to impaction is *Ceriospora caudae-suis* Ingold (Fig. 13.6j) which has a two-celled ascospore with polar appendages (Ingold, 1951). It may be remarked that the presence of appendages of this kind is common in marine Pyrenomycetes, but parallel examples from freshwater are few and far between.

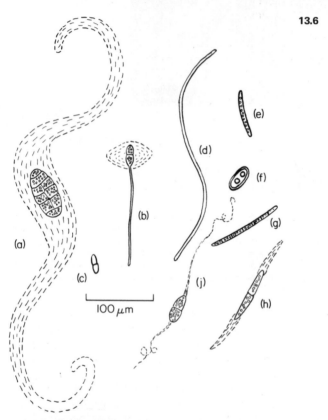

13.6

Fig. 13.6. Ascospores of some aquatic Ascomycetes: (a), *Pleospora scirpicola;* (b) *Loramyces macrospora;* (c) *Leptosphaeria lemaneae;* (d) *Apostemidium guernisaci;* (e) *Hypoderma scirpinum* DC; (f) *Psilopezia babingtonii;* (g) *Belanopsis excelsior* (Karst.) Rhem; (h) *Wettsteinina niesslii* Müller; (j) *Ceriospora caudae-suis.*

There will be more to say about Ascomycetes when considering the 'perfect' stages of aquatic hyphomycetes. However, it should be emphasized at this point that the chief feature of the study of aquatic Ascomycetes is lack of knowledge. Their taxonomy needs much fuller attention. Quantitative studies on their occurrence and distribution in lakes and rivers is needed if their ecology is to be put on a firm basis. Again, studies of spore liberation, of the occurrence of the ascospores in the natural aquatic spora, and experimental work on impaction are all most desirable.

Perhaps whilst discussing Ascomycetes something should be said about yeasts. No doubt there are many freshwater aquatic yeasts. Indeed, any isolation of fungi, by a poured plate method, from lake water, or from decaying debris taken from an aquatic habitat, yields colonies of yeasts as well as growths of such common mould genera as *Penicillium, Cladosporium,* and *Mucor.* The difficulty here is that there can be no certainty that these fungi really belong to the submerged environment, since all bodies of water receive a continual rain of spores from the air, and these are likely to remain viable for a considerable time.

However, mention may be made of one interesting and truly aquatic yeast. This is *Candida aquatica* Jones et Slooff. In water scum, where it was first discovered (Jones and Slooff, 1966), and when grown in shake culture in the laboratory, this produces striking tetraradiate cell groups which beg comparison with the tetraradiate propagules of other aquatic fungi to which reference is made below (Fig. 13.7).

13.7

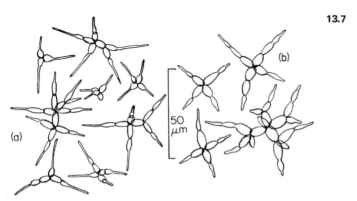

Fig. 13.7. *Candida aquatica.* (a) Cell groups seen in a sample of foam from a torrent in the Braemore area, West Scotland. (b) Jones and Slooff's original isolate from Malham Tarn, Yorkshire, England; drawn from culture streaked on plain agar.

13.3 Fungi Imperfecti

During the past 30 years it has been recognized that there is a vast flora of aquatic hyphomycetes (Fig. 13.8) growing on submerged decaying leaves and twigs of broad leaved trees and shrubs in well aerated waters (Ingold, 1942, 1943 a,b,c, 1944,1952, 1966). Although some of these fungi had been earlier recognized by de Wildeman (1893, 1894, 1895), the existence of a characteristic flora was not appreciated until much later (Ingold, 1942). Useful taxonomic summaries have recently been made by Peterson (1962, 1963 a,b) and by Nilsson (1964). These fungi are so widespread and so abundant that they may be regarded as the dominant type of aquatic fungi in freshwaters. Judging from the enormous concentrations of their spores that build up in tree lined streams during the autumn and early winter, in contrast to the rarity of spores of other aquatic species, the biomass of these fungi in the aquatic environment probably far outweighs that of all other kinds.

Aquatic hyphomycetes occur on submerged dead leaves of a great range of dicotyledonous trees such as alder *(Alnus),* willow *(Salix),* oak *(Quercus),* sycamore *(Acer),* ash *(Fraxinus)* and even holly *(Ilex).* They are seen to a much lesser extent on the herbaceous leaves of rushes, sedges and grasses. They seem to be absent from coniferous leaves. They are to be found on twigs and some, for example *Actinospora megalospora* Ingold and *Flagellospora* sp. (Archer and Willoughby, 1969) seem limited to submerged wood.

If an alder or oak leaf that is brown and beginning to skeletonize is collected from a well aerated stream in the autumn, washed and then just covered with water in a petri dish, abundant conidiophores develop in a day or two. These can readily be seen, on examining the leaf in the dish under the low power of the microscope, often forming miniature forests mainly associated with the petioles and larger veins. A single leaf frequently bears a number of distinct species readily identifiable at this magnification. Further, on the bottom of the dish there is soon an accumulation of liberated conidia which, because of their distinctive form, can usually be identified specifically. These are for the most part not of the nondescript spherical, ovoid or shortly elongate forms characteristic of aerial species. They are either branched with filamentous arms, or are long, and even thread-like, with a curvature lying in more than one plane (Fig. 13.8).

13.3.1 Development of Conidia

Amongst those species with branched conidia, the majority have a conidium consisting of four arms diverging from a common point. A striking feature of these tetraradiate conidia is that their mode of development differs so much that clearly quite distinct genera are involved. We may pause at this stage to consider these tetraradiate aquatic conidia with special reference to the various ways in which the form is achieved (Fig. 13.9).

Students of hyphomycetes now recognize a number of fundamentally different types of conidia.* Two of the most clearly contrasted are phialoconidia and thalloconidia. The former are produced, all at approximately the same level, in succession from a phialide which normally tapers towards its apex. Further the conidium is separated from its phialide by a septum only when it is fully formed. On the other hand the thalloconidium is cut off by a cross wall from the conidiophore at an early stage in its development; and after its liberation, a new one is not normally produced from the end of the old conidiophore. If, however, this does happen, there is further growth and the next conidium is at a higher level than the first.

The tetraradiate aquatic conidium is, in some genera, attached to the conidiophore by the tip of one of the four 'arms'; in others the attachment is near the point from which the four arms diverge. These two arrangements will be considered in turn.

In *Clavariopsis aquatica* de Wild. (Fig. 13.9g), the conidiophore projects from the substratum into the water and its tip swells to form a narrowly conical or clavate structure delimited basally by a cross wall. From the blunt apex of this primordium three little buds arise simultaneously and grow out as long, straight, and narrow hyphae. Meanwhile the original conical axis becomes two-celled. As soon as the spore is fully grown, it separates from its conidiophore by disarticulation at the cross wall. It is a feature of aquatic hyphomycetes generally that conidia are set free as soon as they are fully grown. In *C. aquatica,* a second conidium does not normally develop immediately, although occasionally the vacated conidiophore may continue to grow and produce a condium at a higher level. The developmental pattern clearly indicates that the spore of *C. aquatica* is a terminal thalloconidium.

*I have been influenced to some extent by *Taxonomy of Fungi Imperfecti* (1971) edited by B. Kendrick. I have tried to use 'conidium' in place of 'spore' throughout. However, as an alternative to 'aleuriospore' I am inclined to use 'terminal thalloconidium', in spite of the fact that 'arthroconidium' had a narrow win over 'thalloconidium' at Kananaskis.

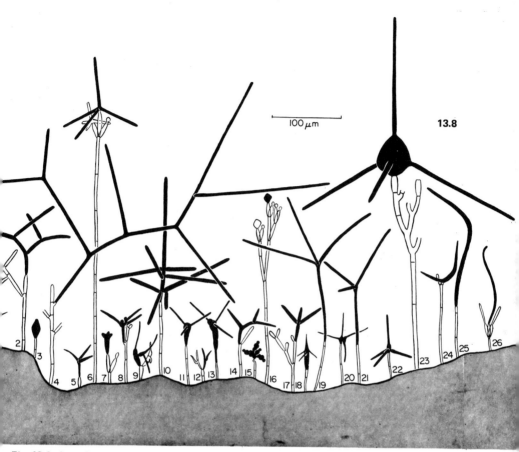

Fig. 13.8. Aquatic hyphomycetes belonging to 26 genera. In each case a conidiophore is shown and a single mature conidium is indicated in black. The substratum (dead leaf or dead wood) is stippled. 1 *Clavatospora longibrachiata* (Ingold) Nilsson; 2 *Varicosporium elodeae* Kegel; 3 *Dactylella aquatica* (Ingold) Ranzoni; 4 *Polycladium equeseti* Ingold; 5 *Alatospora acuminata* Ingold; 6 *Lemonniera aquatica* de Wild.; 7 *Heliscus lugdunensis* Sacc. et Therry; 8 *Tetracladium marchalianum* de Wild.; 9 *Gyoerffyella tricapillata* (Ingold) Marvanová; 10 *Dendrospora erecta* Ingold; 11 *Clavariopsis aquatica* de Wild.; 12 *Volucrispora graminea* Ingold, McDougall et Dann; 13 *Culicidospora aquatica* R.H. Petersen; 14 *Tricladium angulatum* Ingold; 15 *Pyramidospora constricta* Singh; 16 *Margaritispora aquatica* Ingold; 17 *Articulospora tetracladia* Ingold; 18 *Jaculispora submersa* Hudson et Ingold; 19 *Tetrachaetum elegans* Ingold; 20 *Campylospora chaetocladia* Ranzoni; 21 *Geniculospora inflata* (Ingold) Nilsson; 22 *Triscelophorus monosporus* Ingold; 23 *Actinospora megalospora* Ingold; 24 *Lunulospora curvula* Ingold; 25 *Anguillospora longissima* (de Wild.) Ingold; 26 *Flagellospora curvula* Ingold.

In the genus *Clavatospora,* of which there are three clearly defined species, there is a close similarity with *Clavariopsis.* The first formed arm of the conidium is narrowly conical, the other three, thinner ones developing subsequently and simultaneously from its crown (Fig. 13.9c). However, only when it is fully formed is it delimited basally by a cross wall and after its liberation a new phialoconidium is formed at the same level as the first.

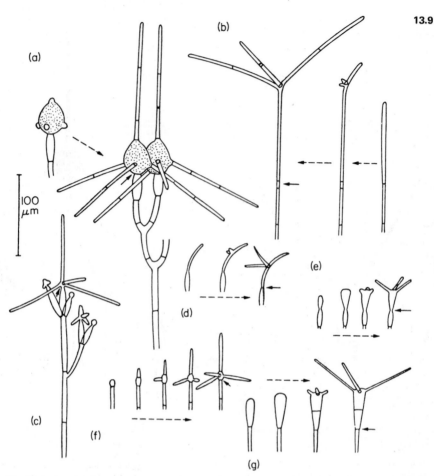

Fig. 13.9. Aquatic hyphomycetes. Some patterns of development in species with tetraradiate conidia. Arrows with interrupted shafts indicate development sequences. Arrows with short continuous shafts indicate where conidia separate from their conidiophores. The species are: (a) *Actinospora megalospora,* (b) *Tetrachaetum elegans,* (c) *Lemonniera aquatica,* (d) *Alatospora acuminata,* (e) *Clavatospora longibrachiata,* (f) *Triscelophorus monosporus,* and (g) *Clavariopsis aquatica.*

It is to be noted that the conidium of *Acaulopage tetraceros* Drescher, has the same basic structure as that of *Clavariopsis* and *Clavatospora.* This has usually been considered to be a phycomcycete and placed in the Zoopagaceae, although Tubaki (1958) is inclined to consider it rather as an imperfect fungus.

In *Tetrachaetum elegans* Ingold, the conidial primordium is a straight hypha delimited from the conidiophore by a septum. When it has grown to a certain length, two small lateral growing points appear just behind the extending apex. The development of these has the effect of changing the direction of growth of the apex. All three growing points continue to add to the conidium which, when mature, consists of four arms: two formed by the bending in the middle of the main axis, and the other two by the laterals. Whilst the conidium has thus been maturing, a small separating cell has become delimited at the end of the conidiophore and it is by the breakdown of this cell that the conidium is set free. Here again a typical thalloronidium is involved (Fig. 13.9b).

Alatospora acuminata Ingold is, as it were, the phialoconidium equivalent of *Tetrachaetum,* since the conidium consists of a main axis, bent in the middle, and two laterals which arise at the same level and develop together (Fig. 13.9d).

Amongst types in which the conidium is attached to the conidiophore by the tip of one of the four arms, there are several cases where a thalloconidial genus has no phialoconidial equivalent. In *Articulospora tetracladia* Ingold, the four arms of the conidium arise in strict succession. In *Tetracladium* this is also true, but in addition to the arms there are two little knobs (in *T. marchalianum* de Wild.) or three finger-like processes (in *T. setigerum* (Grove) Ingold). In the genus *Tricladium,* two of the arms are contributed by the main axis, as in *Tetrachaetum,* but the two laterals arise at different levels and in succession.

Consideration may now be given to genera in which the conidium is attached to its conidiophore near the point of divergence of the four arms.

Lemonniera aquatica de Wild., very common in Britain, is an outstanding example. The conidiophore has a main axis that is usually branched towards its free end, each branch ending in a typical phialide. The conidium starts at the end of this as a spherical primordium which soon becomes tetrahedral, and then the corners grow out simultaneously into long straight hyphae. As soon as the phialoconidium is fully grown it becomes delimited by a basal septum and is set free, a new conidium developing at once from the vacated phialide (Fig. 13.9e).

Actinospora megalospora Ingold, a worldwide species, but apparently commoner in warmer countries that in Britain, can be considered as a close thalloconidial equivalent of *L. aquatica* (Ingold, 1952). The fungus has large conidia, individually visible with a hand lens. Each starts as a more or less spherical primordium delimited by a septum from an ultimate cell, not a phialide, of the branched conidiophore. From this spherical centre four equally spaced protuberances appear which grow out simultaneously to form the four arms of the conidium (Fig. 13.9a).

Another example with thalloconidia is *Triscelophorus monosporus* Ingold. This again is a fungus which, though somewhat rare in Britain, is abundant on dead leaves in subtropical and tropical countries. The conidiophore is normally unbranched. The conidial primordium, delimited by a basal cross wall, is at first spherical but soon elongates and becomes two-celled. This is essentially the first formed arm of the conidium. Later arms develop in succession from the lower cell of the first arm to give the tetraradiate spore (Fig. 13.9f). When this fungus was first discovered (Ingold, 1943, c) it was heralded as a thalloconidial parallel of *Lemonniera,* except that the arms arise in succession and not together. It was only subsequently, with the discovery of *Actinospora* (Ingold, 1952), that an even closer parallel was revealed.

A further thalloconidial type in which the tetraradiate conidium is attached to its conidiophore near the point of divergence of the four arms is *Campylospora chaetocladia* Ranzoni. This fungus, though very rare in Britain, is one of the most abundant species in tropical countries. The conidial primordium is a small cell at the end of the simple conidiophore. This cell bends forward on itself, rather like a campylotropous ovule. The extreme tip goes on growing to form one arm of the conidium and the other three are produced as lateral branches of the bent primordium. The final result is a conidium with an extraordinary lack of symmetry.

The examples given so far do not exhaust the various modes of origin of tetraradiate conidia in aquatic hyphomycetes, but they serve to make the point that this kind of conidium has probably evolved independently along a number of separate lines in the aquatic habitat. It must be emphasized, however, that tetraradiate conidia are by no means limited to that environment. A well known example is the dematiaceous genus *Tetraploa,* with *T. aristata* Berk. et Br. as the commonest species. This fungus grows on the aerial parts of marsh plants and its spores may become incorporated in the air spora. Indeed, in India a study has been made of the daily periodicity of conidia of this species in the air (Sreeramula and Ramalingam, 1962). However, it is also capable of living and sporulating below water, and occasional conidia are often to be seen, associated with the much more numerous hyaline spores of aquatic hyphomycetes, in the foam of tree lined streams in autumn. Such conidia may, of course, have had either an aquatic or an aerial origin. Again it has been found recently (Bretton and Faurel, 1967, 1970) that a number of coprophilous imperfect fungi belonging to Sphaerop-sidales have tetraradiate conidia (e.g. *Pseusoneottiospora cunicularia* Faurel et Schotter; *Monodia elegans* Breton et Faurel, *Pullospora tetrachaeta* Faurel et Schotter. However, this does not invalidate the generalization that tetraradiate conidia are a special feature of the spora of well aerated freshwaters, especially streams and rivers.

Although amongst the branched conidia of the freshwater spora tetraradiate types predominate, there are branched conidia of other kinds. *Casaresia sphagnorum* Fragoso, *Polycladium equiseti* Ingold and *Dendrospora erecta* Ingold may be cited as conspicuous examples (Fig.13.10).

13.10

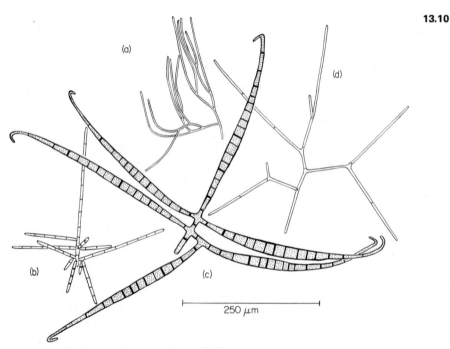

Fig. 13.10. Aquatic Hyphomycetes. Types of branched conidia other than tetraradiate. The species figured are; (a) *Varicosporium delicatum* Iqbal; (b) *Dendrospora erecta* Ingold; (c) *Casaresia phagnorum* Fragoso; (d) *Polycladium equiseti* Ingold.

Apart from branched conidia, mostly hyaline, greatly elongated curved conidia, often sigmoid, and with the curvature in more than one plane, are a feature of the freshwater spora of running water. As with the tetraradiate conidia, some of these are phialoconidia, although most are thalloconidia. As an example of the former *Flagellospora curvula* Ingold, extremely abundant in the spora of British streams and rivers, may be cited, and of the latter *Anguillospora longissima* (de Wild.) Ingold which is almost equally common. Other examples are the beautiful *Lunulospora curvula* Ingold common in Britain in the warmer months and extremely abundant in tropical waters; and *Centrospora acerina* (Hart.) Newhall, a frequent freshwater species which also causes a disease of carrots.

In addition to aquatic hyphomycetes with conidia of a somewhat unusual shape, there are relatively few species where the conidium is of a form more usually encountered in the air spora. Examples are the common *Dactylella aquatica* (Ingold) Ranzoni, and certain less frequently encountered species such as *Dimorphospora foliicola* Tubaki and *Margaritispora aquatica* Ingold (Fig. 13.8).

13.3.2   Liberation, Transportation and Impaction of Conidia

In aquatic hyphomycetes the branched, septate mycelium is in the dead leaf, mainly the petioles and veins, the conidiophores projecting into the water but rarely to the extent of more than a fraction of a millimetre. Thus to the naked eye, submerged decaying leaves do not exhibit a growth of fungus comparable with the readily visible fringe of saprolegniaceous mould around a floating dead fish in a lake or canal. In these hyphomycetes the whole story (apart from long distance dispersal) involving conidium production, liberation and transport occurs below water. In this connection the possible biological significance of the form of the conidium of aquatic hyphomycetes needs some consideration, especially in relation to the tetraradiate structure. Since this appears to have been developed along a considerable number of separate lines of evolution, it is natural to see in such a conidium some biological value in the particular habitat involved. Two plausible theories have been advanced. The first suggests that conidia of this kind are likely to remain longer in suspension in water than oval or spherical ones of the same mass, and thus achieve a wider dispersal. This theory is suggested by the long arms and spines so often seen in planktonic algae, for these are usually interpreted as of value in reducing the rate of sedimentation from the well illuminated layers of a body of water. However, in a river or stream, sedimentation of any fungal spores is very slow compared with movement of the water itself. Indeed, if tetraradiate conidia were to have this kind of value, it might be expected rather to find them developed in relation to aerial dispersal, for sedimentation rates are so much greater in air than in water. Put crudely, if the tetraradiate form is of little value to aerial spores in relation to remaining in suspension, how much less would it be significant in the aquatic environment.

The second theory is that the tetraradiate conidium is related to impaction on an underwater object; in other words that it may be regarded as a microscopic anchor. In the dispersal story of any fungus there tend to be three major episodes: liberation, transport and landing. In a stream or a river the arrest of a conidium on a suitable substratum such as a submerged leaf or twig may be a very real problem.

This problem of impaction of conidia on an object in a current of water has been studied experimentally by Webster (1959 a). He measured the efficiency of impaction of conidia on vertical cylinders using a set-up essentially like that employed by Gregory (1951) in his work on deposition of conidia on cylinders in an air tunnel. Water containing known concentrations of conidia was caused to flow at a defined rate through a horizontal tube in which a vertical glass rod was inserted. Later this rod was removed and deposition of conidia measured on the surface facing the current by appropriate counts under the microscope. Trapping efficiency was not much affected by variation of rates of water flow between 15 cm/s and 35 cm/s, but was greatest for tetraradiate conidia. Next came elongated conidia and the values for these were higher than for conidia of more conventional form, such as those of *Dactylella aquatica* (Table 13.1)

Any student of aquatic hyphomycetes soon becomes aware of the high concentrations of conidia found in the foam of a stream especially during the autumn. Particularly after heavy rain, when the water is very turbulent, cakes of foam accumulate below the rapids and waterfalls. If the foam is collected in a jar and allowed to break down into free water; and if a drop of this is placed on a microscope and slide, covered and examined, a rich collection of conidia is normally to be seen, and these represent

TABLE 13.1   Trapping efficiency (%) of some conidia of aquatic hyphomycetes at three water speeds. Each figure is the mean of three experiments. Extracted from a much larger table by Webster (1959 a).

	15 cm/sec	25 cm/sec	35 cm/sec	Mean
Articulospora tetracladia	0.35	0.51	0.33	0.40
Tetracladium marchalianum	0.28	0.37	0.27	0.31
Clavariopsis aquatica	0.3	0.4	0.3	0.33
Lemonniera aquatica	0.35	0.13	0.04	0.17
Anguillospora longissima	0.11	0.1	0.1	0.10
Flagellospora curvula	0.06	0.14	0.14	0.11
Heliscus lugdunensis	0.004	0.009	0.007	0.007
Dactylella aquatica	0.004	0.009	0.008	0.007

the principal element of solid material present. Further, since most of them can be specifically identified, a list of the species occurring in the stream or river can be quickly compiled. As a specific example Fig 13.11 illustrates the conidia present in a single sample of foam collected on 11th November 1972 just below an artificial waterfall in the Bourne near Plaxtol in Kent. The Bourne is a stream which is a tributary of the Medway.

It seems that air bubbles, as they move through the water, trap the conidia and these are retained in the foam. They are slightly denser than water but, once incorporated in foam or scum, are held firmly by surface-tension forces.

This trapping has been studied experimentally by Iqbal and Webster (1973). Using a number of contrasting types of aquatic hyphomycetes, suspensions of conidia of known concentrations were prepared from pure cultures, and they aerated these suspensions from below with a stream of air bubbles of measured size. The concentration of conidia remaining in the general body of water following aeration was determined. The stream of bubbles, each around 2 mm diameter, removed a large proportion of conidia from suspension, particularly during the first few minutes with a flow of 40 ml/min rising through a vertical column of water 20 cm high. The results showed clearly that not all kinds of conidia were trapped by bubbles with equal efficiency. Tetraradiate conidia were much more readily collected than were elongated conidia. The bubbles were enormously less effective in trapping yeast cells. It was of special interest that in *Varicosporium elodeae* Kegel, in which there is a considerable range in the degree of branching of the conidia, the more complex ones were more readily caught by the bubbles.

From this work it is reasonable to suppose that, although the examination of foam may reveal an exact picture of the mycoflora of a stream, the quantitative study of its composition may give a false impression of the relative abundance of species in the water spora.

An interesting and biological important feature of the conidia of aquatic hyphomycetes is that, while suspended in water or trapped in foam, they show little tendency to germinate. However, on coming to rest on a solid surface, such as glass, germination occurs in an hour or two, usually with a germ-tube developing from the tip of each arm of the conidium in contact with substratum. Iqbal and Webster (1973) have further shown that conidia may remain in aqueous suspension without germinating, but still viable, for weeks on end. The actual time varies with the species and with the temperature. Suspended conidia of *Articulospora tetracladia* showed a 91% germination at the end of a month with the temperature kept at 13°C, and 66% when it was maintained at 18°C.

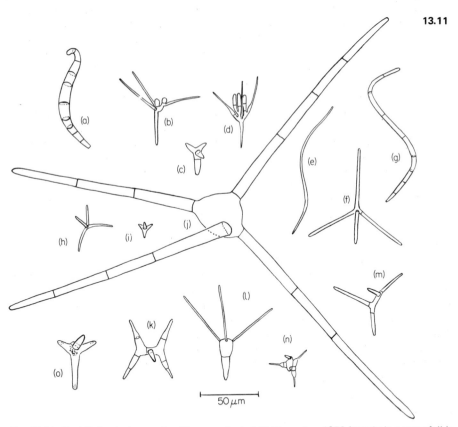

13.11

Fig. 13.11. Conidia in single sample of foam, collected 11 November 1972 from below waterfall in Bourne Stream near Plaxtol, Kent. All types of conidia present are figured. (a) *Anguillospora crassa;* (b) *Tetracladium marchalianum;* (c) *Heliscus lugdunensis;* (d) *Tetracladium setigerum;* (e) *Flagellospora curvula;* (f) *Lemonniera aquatica;* (g) *Anguillospora longissima;* (h) *Alatospora acuminata;* (i) *Clavatospora stellata;* (j) *Actinospora megalospora;* (k) unknown; (l) *Clavariopsis aquatica;* (m) *Tricladium angulatum;* (n) *Campylospora parvula* Kuzuha; (o) (?) rhizopod cyst.

13.3.3 Imperfect/Perfect Stages

Where hyphomycetes and other 'imperfect' fungi are concerned, mycologists are continually on the look out for the 'perfect' stage. If this exists, it is, on discovery, usually found to be an Ascomycete. There are, therefore, two obvious approaches in the search for the perfect stages of aquatic hyphomycetes: first, to attempt to induce the ascigerous stage in pure culture; and secondly, to culture aquatic Ascomycetes in the hope that a conidial stage corresponding to a known aquatic species may be produced. Both approaches have been tried.

Ranzoni (1956) found that certain cultures of *Flagellospora penicillioides* Ingold produced a perfect stage referable to *Nectria,* and later Webster (1959), in studying *Heliscus lugdunensis* Sacc. et Therry, also discovered that cultures sometimes formed perithecia of a species of *Nectria.* More recently Archer (1971) has found the same perfect stage *(Nectria lugdunensis* Webster) produced at low temperature (6°C) by damp incubation for six weeks or more of twigs, from a beck in the English Lake District, bearing pustules of *Heliscus ludgunensis.*

Webster found (1965) that colonies derived from ascospores of a Pyrenomycete on decorticated branches and roots of alder *(Alnus glutinosa)* from a stream gave rise to cultures which, when submerged, produced the typical conidia of *Dactylella aquatica.* He described this Ascomycete as *Massarina aquatica* Webster. Willoughby and Archer (1973) have found a species of *Massarina,* almost indistinguishable from *M. aquatica,* on twigs of alder, ash, oak and willow exposed in a Lake District beck for several months and later subjected to incubation under cold damp conditions for long periods. Ascospores from the perithecia gave pure cultures, and when strips of these were immersed in water, the well known aquatic hyphomycete *Anguillospora longissima* was produced. Further, if a perithecium (really a pseudothecium) of the *Massarina* was dissected from its substratum and immersed in sterile water, spores of *A. longissima* were formed from its surface overnight. It is rather surprising that another abundant species of *Anguillospora, A. crassa* Ingold, should form a perfect stage referable to the Discomycete genus *Mollisia.* Webster (1961) found that a multispore isolate of *A. crassa* produced small globose hyaline phialospores (microconidia) and also coiled hyphae resembling ascogonia but without trichogynes. He flooded a colony with water and kept it under observation for about five weeks, by which time the white apothecia had developed.

The fact that, of two species of *Anguillospora,* one forms a perithecial (pseudothecial) and the other an apothecial stage, calls for comment. It probably means that, as at the present defined, the genus *Anguillospora* is an unnatural one. Probably *A. longissima,* in which the spore is liberated by the breakdown of a small separating cell at the end of the conidiophore, and *A. crassa,* in which liberation is due to disarticulation at a cross wall, should be placed in different 'imperfect' genera.

From Japan, Tubaki (1966) has described an aquatic or semi-aquatic Discomycete, *Hymenoscyphus varicosporoides* that produces a conidial stage of branched septate spores referable to *Varicosporium.*

Attention has been drawn to the fact (Ingold *et al.,* 1968) that in *Tripospermum camelopardus* Ingold, Dann et McDougall what look like protoperithecia are formed, from which long hyphae resembling trichogynes project. Further, there are minute phialospores (2-3 μm diameter) which seem to be incapable of germination but which, in liquid culture, adhere to and fuse with the trichogynes. No perithecia of this species have yet been discovered. Very likely the species is self-incompatible.

In those few cases where a connection between a hyphomycete and an ascigerous stage has been established, the ascospore does not appear to be adapted in any way to the aquatic habitat. So far the one possible exception to this statement is *Corollospora pulchella* (Shearer and Crane, 1971) which is, perhaps, hardly to be regarded as a freshwater fungus although the type material was derived from brackish water with a salinity of 0.82%, seawater being 3.5%. In this fungus, the thalloconidium is tetraradiate and referable to *Clavariopsis,* while the septate ascospore has polar and equatorial appendages. The form of both (condium and ascospore) can be interpreted in biological terms as adapted in relation to impaction on a submerged substratum.

13.3.4   Aquatic Sphaeropsidales

Some reference should be made to the aquatic Sphaeropsidales which are probably not uncommon on submerged, dead, reed swamp plants. Their taxonomy is in need of careful study. Two examples may be noted. Cunnell (1958) described *Robillarda phragmitis* Cunnell on submerged dead stems of *Phragmites communis* L. The conidia are essentially tetraradiate, and are quite commonly encountered in the spora of streams both in temperate and in tropical regions. Another aquatic species with conidia having long appendages is *Chaetospermum chaetosporum* (Pat.) A. L. Smith et Ramsb., which de Fonseka (1960) found on a submerged decaying leaf of alder. Not too much significance should, however, be attached to the morphology of these conidia, for, as already remarked, certain coprophilous members of the Sphaeropsidales also have conidia of a form more usually associated with an aquatic habitat.

13.3.5   World Distribution and Abundance

There can now be little doubt about the great abundance of aquatic fungi classified in the Fungi Imperfecti (especially hyphomycetes) and Ascomycetes. This becomes apparent when the distribution of these fungi over the world is considered and when their detailed ecology is studied. These two aspects will now be reviewed in relation to the hyphomycetes.

So far as world distribution is concerned, it is only aquatic hyphomycetes that have been sufficiently studied to allow a tentative picture to be drawn. During the past 30 years, studies of these fungi have been made in many and well scattered parts of the world, and there are extensive species lists from quite a number of countries. The fact that such lists can so easily be constructed simply by microscopic examination of foam from streams has helped to give comprehensive information about the distribution of aquatic hyphomycetes.

At a rough estimate, 40 genera and 80 species of these organisms have been described as far, and these figures may well be doubled by further research. In the past mycologists have thought of saprolegniaceous types as the typical water moulds. It is almost impossible to get objective information on the relative abundance or biomass of fungi in nature, but anyone who studies the aquatic hyphomycetes is soon convinced that they represent the great bulk of fungus life in the well aerated waters of streams and rivers, if not of lakes and ponds.

Table 13.2 indicates the present records of the distribution of some of the more outstanding species in the various continents. In all probability most of the apparent gaps, which occur particularly in the records for South America and Australia, will be filled by further study. It is thus clear that these fungi, like submerged aquatic plants generally, tend to have a worldwide distribution.

TABLE 13.2 Aquatic hyphomycetes — world distribution†

	Europe	Asia	Africa	Australia	N.America	S.America
Actinospora megalospora Ingold	*	*	*	0	*	0
Anguillospora longissima (de Wild.) Ingold	*	*	*	0	*	*
Articulospora tetracladia Ingold	*	*	*	0	*	*
Campylospora chaetocladia Ranzoni	*	*	*	*	*	0
Clavariopsis aquatica de Wild.	*	*	*	*	*	*
Dendrospora erecta Ingold	*	*	0	0	*	0
Flagellospora penicillioides Ingold	*	*	*	*	*	0
Heliscus lugdunensis Sacc. et Therry	*	*	*	*	*	0
Lemonniera aquatica de Wild.	*	*	*	*	*	0
Tetrachaetum elegans Ingold	*	*	*	*	*	0
Tetracladium marchalianum de Wild.	*	*	*	*	*	*
Tricladium angulatum Ingold	*	0	*	0	*	0
T. splendens Ingold	*	*	*	0	*	0
Triscelophorus monosporus Ingold	*	*	*	*	*	*
Varicosporium elodeae Kegel	*	*	0	0	*	0

† Slightly modified from Crane (1968). The Asian records are mainly from Japan. Little collecting has been done in S. America.
*: Present   0: Absent

This raises an important issue in relation to dispersal. In the aquatic hyphomycetes the conidia, in any one water system, are no doubt normally dispersed through the water. Most are hyaline and rather thin-walled. They are unlikely to become airborne and, if they did, it is improbable that they would survive desiccation during aerial transport. There is thus the question of the spread from one isolated freshwater habitat to another, perhaps several hundreds of miles away. Although direct evidence is not available, it seems likely that dispersal is by water fowl. However, in this connection the units of dispersal are, perhaps, more likely to be decaying leaves or leaf fragments permeated by mycelium rather than individual conidia. In culture many of these fungi form thick-walled cells, some almost chlamydospores, and sclerotia which would seem capable of remaining alive during long distance dispersal by birds.

Modern ecology demands a quantitative approach. With green plants and animals there are difficulties, but in both, biomass in a restricted area can usually be estimated. However, with fungi the vegetative part, the mycelium, is so intimately associated with its organic substratum that estimation of the amount present is almost impossible. Further, although most fungi can be cultivated and their physiological potential assessed, it is extremely difficult to obtain meaningful estimates of their acitivity in nature. Thus, much of fungal ecology still consists of compiling species lists from different habitats.

So far as aquatic Ascomycetes are concerned, their ecology has not yet advanced beyond the simplest descriptive stage and even that is very incomplete because the basic taxonomy has not yet been established.

For the hyphomycetes the position is a little better. Their taxonomy is in a much more satisfactory condition and there is a growing body of information relating to their seasonal occurrence and particularly to the abundance of their conidia in the water of streams and rivers during the course of the year. What is basically lacking is any quantitative estimate of the part these fungi play in the decay of submerged organic matter and, indeed, it is not easy to see a satisfactory approach to this important problem.

Aquatic hyphomycetes appear to be the regular colonizers of dead leaves of broad leaved trees and shrubs in well aerated freshwater. Further, these leaves often represent a very considerable element in the annual addition of organic matter to a stream or river and thus may have a key position in the whole ecosystem. This aspect is further considered in chapter 16.

It has already been noted that several species of aquatic hyphomycetes may occur on a single submerged leaf. This may be illustrated by some results obtained by the writer during his very early studies of these fungi.

Samples of submerged alder leaves that had become brown, soft and were just starting to skeletonize were collected at roughly fortnightly intervals during the course of a summer. On each occasion 10 leaves were selected by eye from the bed of the stream at a certain place, washed well and separately placed in petri dishes of water. For the next few days each leaf in its dish was scanned under the low power of the microscope and the species present were recorded. The results are set out in Table 13.3. Of the 70 leaves examined all but one bore aquatic hyphomycetes, the average number of species developing per leaf being five. Later experience has shown that the state of affairs revealed in Table 13.3 is entirely representative.

Iqbal (1972) has made a thorough ecological investigation of the aquatic hyphomycetes in certain rivers of Devonshire in southern England. He studied, for example, the Creedy (a tributary of the Exe) which in its upper reaches is a fast flowing river of moderate size lined by alders (*Alnus glutinosa*). On individual days

TABLE 13.3 Aquatic hyphomycetes on decaying leaves of *Alnus* from a stream at Cropstone, Leicestershire. Number of leaves (out of 10) on which each species occurred on indicated date.

	30 June	11 July	26 July	9 August	25 August	4 September	20 September	Total occurrence
Tetracladium marchalianum de Wild.	9	10	10	10	10	5	7	61
Clavariopsis aquatica de Wild.	4	8	9	9	6	5	6	47
Lemonniera aquatica de Wild.	8	8	10	8	9	1	1	45
Flagellospora curvula Ingold	2	1	6	5	2	1	0	17
Anguillospora longissima (de Wild.) Ingold	5	8	10	6	8	3	2	42
Lunulospora curvula Ingold	3	4	8	9	10	9	10	53
Alatospora acuminata Ingold	1	4	6	0	2	3	2	18
Clavatospora longibrachiata (Ingold) Nilsson	3	7	4	3	4	5	5	31
Tricladium angulatum Ingold	2	4	2	0	4	1	1	14
Tetracladium setigerum (Grove) Ingold	0	0	1	1	1	0	0	3
Margaritispora aquatica Ingold	0	0	2	3	3	1	1	10
Tetrachaetum elegans Ingold	0	0	0	2	1	0	1	4
Varicosporium elodeae Kegel	0	0	0	1	0	0	0	1
Heliscus lugdunensis Sacc. et Therry	0	0	0	1	0	0	0	1
Tricladium splendens Ingold	0	0	0	1	2	0	0	3
Mean number species per leaf	3.7	5.4	6.8	5.9	6.2	3.4	3.6	

(normally a week apart) throughout the year the concentration of conidia of aquatic hyphomycetes was found by a standard procedure. In this a known volume of water was drawn through a millipore filter (8 μm pore size) and the conidia retained on it counted and identified. This was possible by direct microscopic examination of the filter membrane after appropriate preparation. Thus not only was the total number per litre determined, but also the concentration of individual species of the water spora. A method of estimating the leaf litter of the stream bed was also developed and data were collected of the water temperature for each sampling day.

Conidia of aquatic hyphomycetes occurred throughout the year in the Creedy, but during the summer months their numbers fell greatly as did also the number of species recorded (Fig. 13.12). During this period leaf litter was virtually absent from the river bed, and the low conidial counts can reasonably be related to a shortage of the principal substratum for the growth of these fungi. This general picture was closely reproduced in the other rivers and streams that were studied.

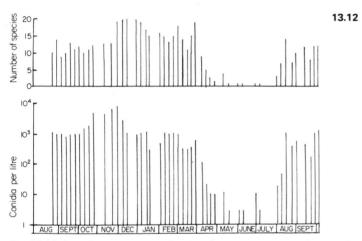

Fig. 13.12. Aquatic hyphomycetes in River Creedy, Devon, UK. Each vertical line represents the analysis of a sample taken on the indicated date. Above: number of species recorded on each sampling occasion. Below: number of conidia per litre of river water. Observations spread over 13 months; first observation towards end of August. Slightly modified after Iqbal (1972).

In the River Creedy the periodicity picture for some individual species was very similar to that for the whole water spora (e.g. *Clavariopsis aquatica,* Fig. 13.13). However, *Tricladium chaetocladium* Ingold was practically confined to the winter months and *Lunulospora curvula* Ingold was almost absent during the late winter and spring as well as during early summer (Fig. 13.13). This behaviour of *Lunulospora* is in keeping with my own considerable experience of this organism since its discovery 30 years ago (Ingold, 1942). It always seems to be absent in a sporulating condition from streams in the really cold months of the year when many of the other aquatic hyphomycetes are abundant. Further, this species is one of the most characteristic of these fungi in warmer countries, and is only rarely so abundant in British waters.

Conidia in the river often reached a concentration of over 10^3 per litre and occasionally the values rose to over 10^4. These are very high figures when compared with what aeromycologists have found in the air where values as high as 10^2 per litre are rare. It is interesting also to compare these with those of Willoughby (1962) for the propagules of saprolegniaceous fungi in Windermere. Using an indirect method of estimation, he found

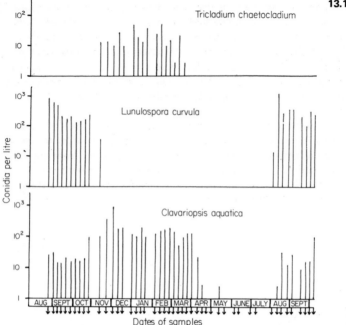

Fig. 13.13. Number of conidia per litre of three aquatic hyphomycetes in water of River Creedy, Devon, UK. sampled throughout year on dates indicated by arrows at the base of the diagram. Slightly modified after Iqbal (1972).

concentrations of over 10^3 propagules, probably representing zoospores, per litre at the margin of the lake, although values were usually much lower in the middle of the lake. Higher concentrations were obtained in the autumn, but in spring and summer they were low, seldom exceeding 10^2.

13.4 Basidiomycetes

Although Ascomycetes, and conidial fungi likely to be or have been connected with them, are well represented in the aquatic habitat, both freshwater and marine, Basidiomycetes are virtually absent. In the sea the outstanding exceptions are two lignicolous fungi: the hymenomycete *Digitatispora marina* Doguet and the gasteromycete *Nia vibrissa* Moore et Meyers. Both these remarkable fungi have basidiospores with four or five long divergent arms recalling vividly the tetraradiate conidia of aquatic hyphomycetes (see Chapter 1). However, no corresponding organisms have yet been found in freshwater. Nevertheless, some years ago in scum from a Nigerian stream (Ingold, 1959), tetraradiate conidia with clamp connections at the septa were observed. Later another branched type with clamps, consisting of a main axis and several laterals, was also discovered in Nigeria (Ingold, 1961). Recently the same fungus has been isolated and described from a stream in Queensland, Australia (Shaw, 1972). This organism, *Ingoldiella hamata* Shaw, seems to produce both types of spore reported from Nigeria. The cells of the mycelium and of the conidia are dikaryotic, and it seems likely that the fungus is essentially a Basidiomycete in which, as yet, only an imperfect (conidial) stage is known. Further, the conidia appear to be produced just above the surface of the water, so that *I. hamata* is probably best regarded as an aero-aquatic species.

References

ARCHER, J. F. (1971). 'Perithecium formation by *Nectria lugdunensis* on natural material.' *Trans. Br. mycol. Soc.,* 56, 475-477.

ARCHER, J. F., and WILLOUGHBY, L. G. (1969). 'Wood as the growth substrate for a freshwater foam spore.' *Trans. Br. mycol. Soc.,* 53, 484-486.

BRETON, A., and FAUREL, L. (1967). 'Etude de la sporogenèse chez *Pseudoneottiospora cunicularia* et remarques sur les genres *Neottiospora, Pseudoneottiospora* et *Robillarda.' Revue mycol.,* 32,108-121.

BRETON, A., and FAUREL, L. (1970) 'Etude comparative des *Monodia elegans* nov. gen., nov. sp. et *Pullospora tetrachaeta* Faur. et Schott., Sphaeropsidales coprophiles.' *Revue mycol.,* 35, 22-40.

CRANE, J.L. (1968). 'Freshwater hyphomycetes of the Northern Appalachian Highland including New England and three coastal plain states.' *Am. J. Bot.,* 55, 996-1002.

CUNNELL, G. J. (1958). 'On *Robillarda phragmitis* sp. nov.' *Trans. Br. mycol. Soc.,* 41, 405-412.

de FONSEKA, R.N. (1960). 'The morphology of *Chaetospermum chaetosporium.' Trans. Br. mycol. Soc.,* 43, 631-636.

GREGORY, P. H. (1951). 'Deposition of air-borne *Lycopodium* spores on cylinders.' *Ann. appl. Biol.,* 38, 357-376.

INGOLD, C.T. (1942). 'Aquatic hyphomycetes of decaying alder leaves.' *Trans. Br. mycol. Soc.,* 25, 339-417.

INGOLD, C.T. (1943a). 'Further observation on aquatic hyphomycetes of decaying leaves.' *Trans. Br. mycol. Soc.,* 26, 114-115.

INGOLD, C.T. (1943b). 'On the distribution of aquatic hyphomycetes saprophytic on submerged decaying leaves.' *New Phytol.,* 42, 139-143.

INGOLD, C.T. (1943c). *'Triscelophorus monosporus* n. gen., n. sp., an aquatic hyphomycete.' *Trans. Br. mycol. Soc.,* 26, 148-152.

INGOLD, C.T. (1944). 'Some new aquatic hyphomycetes.' *Trans. Br. mycol. Soc.,* 28, 35-43.

INGOLD, C.T. (1951). 'Aquatic Ascomycetes: *Ceriospora caudae-suis* n. sp. and *Ophiobolus typhae.' Trans. Br. mycol. Soc.,* 34, 210-215.

INGOLD, C.T. (1952). *'Actinospora megalospora* n. sp., an aquatic hyphomycete.' *Trans. Br. mycol. Soc.,* 35, 66-70.

INGOLD, C.T. (1954). 'Aquatic Ascomycetes: Discomycetes from lakes.' *Trans. Br. mycol. Soc.,* 37, 1-18

INGOLD, C.T. (1955). 'Aquatic Ascomycetes: further species from the English Lake District.' *Trans. Br. mycol. Soc.,* 38, 157-168.

INGOLD, C.T. (1959). 'Aquatic spora of Omo Forest, Nigeria.' *Trans. Br. mycol. Soc.,* 42, 479-485.

INGOLD, C.T. (1961). 'Another aquatic spore-type with clamp connexions.' *Trans. Br. mycol. Soc.,* 44, 27-30.

INGOLD, C.T. (1966). 'The tetraradiate aquatic fungal spore.' *Mycologia,* 58, 43-56.

INGOLD,C.T. (1968). 'Spore liberation in *Loramyces'. Trans. Br. mycol. Soc.,* 51, 323-325.

INGOLD, C.T., and CHAPMAN, B. (1952). 'Aquatic Ascomycetes: *Loramyces juncicola* Weston and *L. macrospora* n. sp.' *Trans. Br. mycol. Soc.,* 35, 268-272.

INGOLD, C.T., DANN, V. and McDOUGALL, P.J. (1968). *'Tripospermum camelopardus* sp. nov.' *Trans. Br. mycol. Soc.,* 51, 51-56.

IQBAL, S.H. (1972). 'Studies on aquatic hyphomycetes and Ascomycetes.' Ph. D. Thesis University of Exeter.

IQBAL, S.H. and WEBSTER, J. (1973). 'The trapping of aquatic hyphomycetes spores by air bubbles.' *Trans. Br. mycol. Soc.,* 60, 37-48.

JONES, E.B.G., and SLOOFF, W.C., (1965). *'Candida aquatica* sp. nov. isolated from water scums.' *Antonie van Leeuwenhoek,* 32, 223-228.

KENDRICK, B. Ed. (1971). *Taxonomy of Fungi Imperfecti.* University of Toronto Press Press.

NILSSON, S. 1964. 'Freshwater hyphomycetes. Taxonomy, morphology and ecology' *Symb. bot. upsal.,* 18, 1-130.

PETERSEN, R.H. (1962). 'Aquatic hyphomycetes from North America. I. Aleuriosporae (Part I) and key to genera.' *Mycologia,* 54, 117-151.

PETERSEN, R.H. (1963a). 'Aquatic hyphomycetes from North America II. Aleuriosporae (Part 2), and Blastosporae.' *Mycologia,* 55, 18-29.

PETERSEN, R.H. (1963b). 'Aquatic hyphomycetes from North America III. Phialosporae and miscellaneous species.' *Mycologia,* 55, 570-581.

PRINGSHEIM, N. (1858). 'Uber das Austreten der Sporen von *Sphaeria scirpi* aus ihren schlauchen.' *Jb. wiss. Bot.,* 1, 189-192

RANZONI, F.V. (1956). 'The perfect stage of *Flagellospora penicillioides.'* Am. J. Bot., 43, 13-17.

SHAW, D.E. (1972). *'Ingoldiella hamata* gen. et sp. nov., a fungus with clamp connexion from a stream in North Queensland.' *Trans. Br. mycol. Soc.,* 59, 255-259.

SHEARER, C.A., and CRANE, J.L. (1971). 'Fungi of the Chesapeake Bay and its tributaries. I. Patuxent River.' *Mycologia,* 63, 237-260.

SREERAMULU, T., and RAMALINGAM, A. (1962). 'Notes on air-borne *Tetraploa* spores.' *Curr. Sci.,* 31, 121-122.

TUBAKI, K. (1958). 'Studies on the Japanese hyphomycetes (IV) miscellaneous group.' *Bot. Mag. Tokyo,* 71, 131-137.

TUBAKI, D. (1966). 'An undescribed species of *Hymenoscyphus,* a perfect stage of *Varicosporium.'* *Trans. Br. mycol. Soc.,* 49, 345-349.

WEBSTER, J. (1959a). 'Experiments with spores of aquatic hyphomycetes. I. Sedimentation and impaction on smooth surfaces.' *Ann. Bot.,* 23, 595-611.

WEBSTER, J. (1959). *'Nectria lugdunensis,* sp. nov., the perfect stage of *Heliscus lugdunensis.'* *Trans. Br. mycol. Soc.,* 42, 322-327.

WEBSTER, J. (1961). 'The *Mollisia* perfect stage of *Anguillospora crassa.'* *Trans. Br. mycol. Soc.,* 44, 559-564.

WEBSTER, J. (1965). 'The perfect stage of *Pyricularia aquatica.'* *Trans. Br. mycol. Soc.,* 48, 449-452.

WESTON, W.H. (1929). 'Observations on *Loramyces,* an undescribed aquatic Ascomycete.' *Mycologia,* 21, 55-76.

de WILDEMAN, E. (1893). 'Notes mycologiques. Fascicle 2.' *Ann. Soc. belge Micr.,* 17, 35-68.

de WILDEMAN, (1894). 'Notes mycologiques. Fascicle 3.' *Ann. Soc. belge Micr.,* 18, 135-161.

de WILDEMAN, E. (1895). 'Notes mycologiques. Fascicle 6.' *Ann. Soc. belge Micr.,* 19, 191-232.

WILLOUGHBY, L.G. (1962). 'The occurrence and distribution of reproductive spores of Saprolegniales in fresh water.' *J. Ecol.,* 50, 733-759.

WILLOUGHBY, L.G., and ARCHER, J.F. (1973). 'The fungal spora of a freshwater stream and its colonization pattern on wood.' *Freshwat. Biol.,* 3, 219-239.

14 Cooling Tower Fungi

R. A. EATON

14.1 Introduction

The presence of fungi in water cooling towers is associated with the problems of cooling efficiency in the system. These may take two forms — the presence of fungi in the cooling water associated with slime formation, or the biodeterioration of timber within the cooling tower. Of major interest to cooling tower operators is prevention and treatment of these problems for efficient maintenance of cooling tower operation. A vast amount of information has now been accumulated on this subject, but the emphasis for research is still on methods of application of this knowledge. Close examination of the causative organisms and the factors which influence their successful growth in cooling towers still remains of minor interest. This chapter will deal with both the preventive and remedial treatments of problems in cooling towers and the fungi which cause many of these problems.

14.2 Cooling Tower Design and Function

Cooling towers are built to one of two basic designs — natural draught or mechanical draught (Fig. 14.1). The cooling towers shown in Fig. 14.1 are all 'wet' cooling towers. In 'dry' cooling towers, the cooling water flows through a closed system of tubes and does not come into direct contact with air. Heat loss from the cooling water is maintained by air movement around the tubes. Dry cooling towers which are found least frequently are more expensive to build and are most useful in regions where supplies of water are very limited.

In 'wet' cooling towers, warm cooling water pumped to the top of the towers is sprayed over the packing within the tower. The function of the packing in all cooling towers is to increase the surface area of cooling water in contact with the cold air passing through the packing. This is achieved by breaking up the water into fine droplets as it falls over a system of splash-bars, slats or louvres, or by allowing the water to trickle as a thin film over corrugated material. Air movement within the

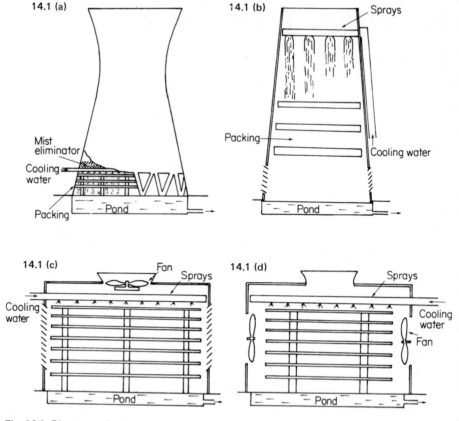

Fig. 14.1. Diagrammatic representations of water cooling tower design. (a) Concrete hyperbolic natural draught cooling tower. (b) Wooden natural draught cooling tower. (c) Mechanical induced draught cooling tower. (d) Mechanical forced draught cooling tower.

packing may be counter-flow in a vertically upward direction, or cross-flow in a lateral direction through the descending water spray. Transfer of heat from the water to the air is achieved, and the water is collected in a pond at the bottom of the tower and recycled to the condensers of the industrial plant.

Mechanical draught 'wet' cooling towers operate by maintaining a continuous flow of cold air through the inside of the tower. In many cooling towers electrically driven fans are positioned at the sides forcing air into the fill or packing of the tower (Fig. 14.1d), whilst induced draught flow towers draw air in through louvres at the sides of the tower, pass it through the packing and expel it through the fan at the top of the tower (Fig. 14.1c). The design of these towers is discussed by Gruber (1959).

Natural draught cooling towers were first constructed wholly of wood. A rectangular wooden shell with a louvred wall at the base and an open chimney at the top allows movement of air into the tower (Fig. 14.1b). Cooling water is pumped to the top of the tower, up to 40 metres high and sprayed over a loosely arranged packing within the cooling tower. Concrete 'hyperbolic' natural draught cooling towers operate on the same principle of air movement drawn upwards through the packing at the base of the tower. These cooling towers can be up to 150 metres high and 100 metres in diameter at the base. They consist of a massive reinforced concrete chimney which is built on stilts (Fig. 14.1a). The packing is positioned at the base of the tower only, and may be 10-15 metres in height covering the whole basal area of the tower or only its perimeter.

The temperature of cooling water entering the tower can be as high as 55°C but is generally maintained between 25° and 35°C. The concrete natural draught towers in Britain maintain an average 7-8°C drop in cooling water temperature from the inlet to the outlet points. The draught induced by fans and occurring naturally in natural draught towers is sufficient to cause considerable loss of cooling water mainly through evaporation and also drift (which is carriage of water droplets out of the tower in the air flow). In most towers, slats or mist eliminators are positioned above the packing to prevent excessive drift. Up to 1% of the cooling water may be lost through evaporation for every 10°F of cooling and 0.2% loss through drift (Woodson, 1971). In addition, bleed off of part of the cooling water in order to maintain an acceptable level of dissolved solids in the cooling water is necessary for efficient operation of the cooling system. The water which is replenished is called 'make-up', and at large electricity generating stations may amount to several million gallons per day. Cooling towers must therefore be built at sites with a large, available and permanent source of water close at hand.

The types of cooling tower used in different parts of the world vary with the size of unit required and the industry in which they are employed. Heavy industrial processes, particularly electricity generation, gas and petroleum production, petrochemical and iron and steel processes require large amounts of cooling water. In North America the mechanical draught towers are the most popular design despite high operating costs. Separate cooling cells are usually grouped together to form long rectangular structures up to 100 metres long, 25 metres wide and 30 metres high. In Europe, economy on available land, labour and electric power for fans has resulted in a preference for the hyperbolic natural draught towers. This trend is now becoming a feature of the more densely populated parts of eastern USA.

The appearance of typical cooling towers is shown in Fig. 14.2.

14.3 Cooling Tower Packing Materials and Their Degrade

The design of the cooling tower packing, the material used and its resistance to deterioration over many years are major considerations for economic design and efficient operation. The most commonly used material for cooling tower packing has been wood, but in recent years plastics, metals, asbestos, cement and concrete have been employed. In many instances these new materials have been used as film packing since they allow the moulding of new shapes over which cooling water may trickle in a thin film. So far, no evidence of biological deterioration of these materials has been reported.

The majority of towers employ the wooden splash bar type of packing (Fig. 14.3). Timber is a most serviceable material for cooling tower packing due to its low cost, ease of handling in construction and its strength (Ross and Wood, 1957). Cooling tower packing is built around a framework of vertical upright columns made of timber or concrete which support horizontal bearers also made of timber or concrete. The timber packing consists of slats, laths or louvres which are positioned horizontally and supported by the framework. All the timber in the packing is saturated whilst the tower is in operation. Above the distribution zone in most towers are the mist eliminators which usually consist of two layers of louvres positioned to prevent the upward dispersal of water droplets caught in the cooling tower draught. Mist eliminator timber remains very damp during cooling tower operation.

14.2 (a)   14.2 (b)

14.2 (c)   14.2 (d)

Fig. 14.2. Cooling tower design. (a) Concrete natural draught cooling towers. (b) Wooden natural draught cooling tower. (c) Mechanical induced draught cooling towers. (d) Mechanical forced draught cooling tower.

In 1946, the collapse of timber packing in a cooling tower in the United Kingdom after only seven years' service precipitated an extensive examination of the durability of timber packing. Similar observations of cooling tower timber deterioration in the USA were also made at this time. At first, chemical deterioration was suspected (Baker, 1962). Delignification of packing timber was related to high levels of carbonate and bicarbonate in the cooling water and excessive chlorination (Baechler *et al.*, 1961; Hurst, 1956). Water of high pH inhibits corrosion of steel heat exchangers and condensers. Chlorination prevents slime growth on the tubes of heat exchangers and excessive growth of algae in the tower packing. Balanced control of cooling water pH and chlorine addition has been recommended to inhibit chemical deterioration (Anon, 1966; Comeaux, 1953; Waldrop *et al.*, 1957). Controlled use of chemicals in water treatment was necessary as chemical deterioration also enhanced the effectiveness of fungal entry into wood resulting in biological deterioration.

In the early stages of investigation the causes of biological attack of the packing timber were thought to be due to Basidiomycete fungi especially in the mist eliminator part of the towers (Baker, 1951). This was a view expressed by workers in the USA. In the UK, Findlay and Savory (1950) were studying the importance of microfungi (Ascomycetes and Fungi Imperfecti) in the deterioration of water cooling tower timber. Savory (1954 a, b) described decay of cooling tower packing timber by microfungi as soft rot. The extensive use of softwoods as cooling tower packing is most appropriate since Savory (1954 a) observed that hardwoods were less resistant to soft rot attack. In addition, Walters (personal communication) has observed that European beech treated with a preservative which is most effective in pine gave no protection in cooling tower

14.3 (a)

14.3 (b)

Fig. 14.3. Timber packing in natural draught cooling towers. (a) The base of a concrete natural draught cooling tower showing horizontal slats. (b) Close-up view of the edge of the packing.

exposure. The characteristics of soft rot attack and the fungi associated with it will be dealt with later.

In addition to surface soft rot of the packing timber, internal attack of timbers by Basidiomycetes was also a problem (Shema, 1959). This type of decay is rarely found in the packing or flooded areas of the tower but occurs usually in the support timbers, mist eliminators, fan housings, decks, cell partitions and doors.

An investigation to determine the primary causes of cooling tower timber failure with a view to establishing preventive measures for its control was undertaken using timber from 103 cooling towers in the USA (C.T.I., 1963; Willa, 1959). The results state that proper treatment of the circulating water is effective in reducing both chemical and biological surface attacks of cooling tower timber, but that biological internal attack could not be related to water conditioning. The data indicated that proper water conditioning is a more effective safeguard against biological surface attack than is wood preservative treatments.

The following recommendations were put forward for cooling water treatment to produce minimal chemical and biological surface attack:

(1) Maintenance of pH between 6.0 and 7.0, minimal carbonates and bicarbonates
(2) Non-oxidizing biocides should be used in preference to chlorine.
(3) If chlorine is used, it should be only on an intermittent basis with the residual maintained below 1 ppm measured in the hot water.
(4) The use of high chlorine residuals and high pH simultaneously should be avoided since this combination produces accelerated attack more damaging than the effect of either alone.
(5) Chromate addition assists prevention of biological surface attack and low pH chromate treatment assists prevention of chemical surface attack.
(6) Minor constituents in the water have little effect on deterioration.

Where proper water treatment is not carried out, preservative treatment of the wood is necessary.

14.4 Preservation of Cooling Tower Timber Packing

The types of preservatives available for timber treatment are numerous but the abnormally rigorous conditions found within cooling towers require a treatment which is not only toxic but is sufficiently leach-resistant to remain within the wood for long periods of time. Since the 1950s the value of using treated packing timber has become established so that creosote and waterborne preservatives are now extensively used, although some operators are still reluctant to use treated wood.

In 1957, Ross and Wood observed soft rot attack in packing timber of all but a few of the British power station cooling towers they examined. Tests using creosote and waterborne salts containing high amounts of copper showed no attack of timber after 6 months. A new formulation of copper-chrome-arsenic preservative (Tanalith C.) was developed containing higher proportions of toxic constituents than Ascu or Greensalt (related waterborne preservatives). A new specification provided for adequate treatment of sapwood and heartwood of Baltic redwood (Ross and Wood, 1957). Both copper-chrome (Celcure) and copper-chrome-arsenic (Tanalith C.) preservatives were accepted by the electricity generating authority in Britain to be used at a solution strength of 5% to give a dry salt retention of not less than 1.25 lb/ft³ assuming that Baltic redwood for cooling tower packing would consist of 50% sapwood. Baltic redwood treated under this new specification is considered to have a life expectancy of 25 years or more. This specification is taken as a guideline by other users of cooling towers in heavy industry as a suitable pre-treatment for packing timber.

Copper-chrome-arsenic treated timber placed in nine British cooling towers showed no selective or progressive leaching of the preservative salts exposed for up to 36 000 hours' service. Although no precise figures for percentage loss of salts from treated cooling tower packings over a given period of time could be calculated, it was felt

364

that an assurance of 30 years' protection for timber in cooling towers using non-saline water could be given (Anon, 1965). Dunbar (1962) came to a similar conclusion following tests on copper-chrome and copper-chrome-arsenic preservatives and suggested that timber in cooling towers using seawater and estuarine make-up water may need replacing after 15 — 20 years. Marine microfungi were implicated as agents of decay in these towers.

More recent work indicates that cooling towers using non-saline water may also be prone to loss of copper chrome-arsenic preservative components (Irvine et al., 1972). The amounts of each component leached varied between the sites tested and was greater in 2.5% than 5% treatment concentrations. Despite the fact that most of the treated wood was sound after 40 weeks, fungi were found colonizing it. Walters (1970) reporting the results of 10 year exposure trials of test panels has also noted marked variation between cooling towers in Australia. He compared different untreated timbers with CCA treated radiata pine sapwood. Of the timbers commonly used in cooling towers in Australia, only Californian redwood remained in reasonable condition. Douglas fir, western red cedar and Scots pine showed considerable deterioration, whilst untreated radiata pine sapwood was degraded even more. The treated radiata pine sapwood remained in good condition after 10 years' exposure. Copper-chrome, copper-chrome-arsenic and copper-chrome-boron preservatives were found to be very effective against soft rot attack whilst certain creosotes and pentachlorophenol also performed well.

In the USA untreated southern pine and Douglas fir show little resistance to soft rot attack in cooling towers, and, although Californian redwood has a high natural durability, along with Douglas fir it is an unsuitable timber for preservative penetration (Baechler et al., 1961). The principal wood preservatives used in USA are creosote, acid copper chromate (Celcure), copper-chrome-arsenic (Erdalith or Greensalt) and ammoniacal copper arsenite (Chemonite). The use of creosoted timber in many British cooling towers is limited, as engineers fear contamination of the cooling water leading to loss of efficiency in the heat exchangers and risks of pollution when the cooling system is purged. Appreciable loss of creosote from pressure treated slats has been reported, but the retention of sufficient creosote after 7 years' exposure is considered adequate for long term exposure (Betts and Spranklin, 1972). Operators in the USA have found no problems in this respect. However, the arrest of decay in towers already built with untreated timber has required either fungicide spraying within the tower (e.g. polychlorophenates — Willa, 1965), addition of a fungicide to the cooling water, or double diffusion treatment. Double diffusion treatment involves spraying the wet packing with chemical solutions one after another. These combine within the wood to produce fungicidal compounds of low solubility (Baechler et al., 1961).

A range of timber preservatives and methods of treatment is therefore available to the builders and operators of cooling towers, but their effectiveness may be reduced in some towers. This is determined by the operating conditions which vary greatly in different towers (Irvine et al., 1972; Walters, 1970). The chief variable is the nature of the cooling water, for instance dissolved solids, suspended solids, pH, water treatment and temperature. Walters (1970) observed that high concentrations of dissolved solids are usually associated with severe soft rot attack and slime formation. Increased soft rot activity has also been observed in British cooling towers where high total conductivity readings of the water have been recorded (Eaton and Jones, 1971 a; Irvine et al., 1972). Frequent purging of the water can control the concentrating effect of cooling water evaporation during the cooling process, but is not always carried out. Although Gjovik *et al.* (1972) observed that timbers treated with waterborne preservatives resist leaching more than creosote and pentachlorophenol, their work was carried out at one tower operating under optimal conditions, and details of cooling water composition were not specified. It would seem that cooling towers operating with cooling water of low conductivity and where careful water treatment is maintained offer conditions of low hazard to preservative leaching, fungal colonization and decay of timbers.

14.5 Fungi in Slime Formation and Cooling Water Treatments

Treatment by addition of chemicals to the cooling water is carried out (1) to inhibit corrosion of the heat exchangers and condensers, (2) to inhibit the growth of algae and bryophytes in the cooling tower, (3) to inhibit the growth of slime-forming bacteria and fungi in the cooling system and (4) in some instances to arrest fungal degrade of the packing timber.

Chromate and phosphate addition is commonly carried out to reduce corrosion (Ross and Wood, 1957; Carlson, 1963; Hurst, 1955), but other compounds are also used to control this problem (Cook, 1956). Continual use of biocides is necessary to prevent excessive algal and bryophyte growth accumulating in the most illuminated parts of the tower packing. Blockages in the cooling system can result from plant material falling into the cooling water. In addition, biocidal treatment is necessary to inhibit slime formation in condenser tubes. Chlorine is a most commonly used and most effective biocide, but strict control in its application is needed to prevent chemical deterioration of the cooling tower packing. Bromine treatment may also be satisfactory in slime control, but serious hazards in handling preclude its widespread use in cooling water systems (Maguire, 1956).

The use of non-oxidizing biocides alone or with chlorine to improve slime control and prevent excessive attack of wood by chlorine has been recommended (Anon, 1966). The non-oxidizing biocides include quaternary ammonium compounds, amines, chlorinated phenols, organometallic compounds and sulphur organic compound which are effective against bacteria, fungi and algae in cooling systems. However, effluent problems and adverse interaction with corrosion inhibitors can be disadvantageous aspects of non-oxidizing biocide use (Mennie, 1971). Regular and necessary application requires strict monitoring of the microbial population dynamics in cooling water. This can assist operators in adjusting or supplementing biocide dosages to maintain effective microbiological control (Trautenberg and Askew, 1964). Examples of biocidal treatment of cooling systems are numerous (Beecher and Trautenberg, 1964; Carlson, 1961; Donohue and Woods, 1968; Fitzgerald, 1964; Dost, 1969; Himsley, 1959; Kelly, 1965). In Czechoslovakia, modern organic compound or mixtures with biocidal properties have to be imported. Tests on more easily available compounds from waste products of industry had limited biocidal effects and experiments are now under way to assess the effectiveness of hydrogen peroxide treatment (Sládečková, 1969).

The causal organisms involved in slime formation are rarely identified and little documented as the majority of investigations centre around prevention of their growth. Wise (1950) divided the microfungi found in cooling water systems into moulds and yeast-like forms. The most common moulds were species of *Aspergillus, Cephalosporium, Paecilomyces, Penicillium* and *Trichoderma,* whilst the most common yeast-like types were *Torula, Oidium* and *Monilia.* Bacteria and algae may be considered to be the greatest problem in cooling water slime, but fungi are extremely resistant to killing with normal chemical treatment. The toxic effectiveness of sodium pentachlorophenate, a frequently used biocide in cooling systems, against seven test fungi was investigated (Williams, 1953). The fungi used were *Poria incrassata* (Berk. et Curt.) Burt, *Trametes serialis* Fr., *Lenzites trabea* (Pers.) Fr., *Hormiscium gelatinosum* Hedge, *Chaetomium globosum* Kunze, *Aspergillus niger* van Tiegh, and *Rhizopus nigricans* Ehrenb., but no mention is made of where the organisms were isolated from. Eighty parts per million of the biocide were needed to produce total inbibition of growth of *Aspergillus niger,* the most resistant fungus to the treatment, but the fungi generally showed greater tolerance to the biocide than the bacteria, algae and protozoa tested. Maguire (1956) tested other chlorinated phenols against *Aspergillus niger* and *Penicillium expansum* Link, and found that many compounds required much greater concentrations to inhibit the growth of *Aspergillus niger* than did the test bacteria *Aerobacter aerogenes* (Kruse) Beijerinck and *Bacillus mycoides* Flugge. Tests on a range of quaternary ammonium compounds also revealed that both fungi were very resistant to these compounds except when mercury was present in the molecule.

The importance of fungi in slime formation is probably not significant, although Kaye (1965) observed a positive correlation between slime accumulation and fungal infestation of packing timber in a cooling tower. However, the use of water treatments may affect the activity of fungi growing on the timber in the packing. The concentration of chlorine in cooling water passing over the packing is not high enough to inhibit fungal growth and the addition of water soluble preservatives can be restrictive in cost and hazardous to local human, livestock and fish populations due to drift and purging of the cooling system. However, untreated timbers exposed for 10 years in a tower operating under carefully controlled cooling water conditions were recovered in sound condition. Water treatment in the tower included a chromium-phosphate mixture to inhibit corrosion which maintained a chromium residual of 6-9 ppm. High absorption of chromium by the wood is believed to have contributed to the resistance to decay shown by these untreated timbers (Gjovik *et al.,* 1972).

14.6 Fungal Decay of Cooling Tower Timber

14.6.1 Biological Internal Attack

This type of attack is brought about by Basidiomycetes which decay the internal regions of wooden structural members of the packing. They are also observed growing on wood in the mist eliminator region of towers. Basidiomycete attack in cooling towers produces white rot and brown rot. Brown rot fungi utilize the cellulose but little of the lignin in the wood, so that on drying the wood breaks up into brown cubical pieces. White rot fungi attack both the cellulose and lignin leaving the wood bleached in appearance and pocketed, fibrous or spongy in texture.

Basidiomycete attack is rarely observed in the slats of the packing although white rot has been found on occasions (author's personal observation; Duncan, 1960 b). The high moisture content of these timbers excludes the presence of Basidiomycetes which occur in the less saturated structural timbers or the warm, moist, non-flooded regions of the towers. The attack is internal and no evidence of decay is observed on the timber surface. Failure is commonly observed when the supporting timbers of the packing slats collapse or the mist eliminator slats and supports decay and collapse.

At the microscopic level, Basidiomycete hyphae proliferate through the wood in longitudinal and transverse directions. Entry of the hyphae into the wood probably occurs through the end grain. Penetration hyphae pass through the cell walls via the pits and by producing bore holes. The lignified cell walls are degraded by enlargement of bore holes and erosion of the inner surface of the cells walls by cellulase enzymes produced by the hyphae. Modes of Basidiomycete attack of wood are extensively reviewed by Liese (1970).

The instances of Basidiomycete attack of cooling tower timber which have been documented are numerous, but the number of identifications of causal organisms is limited. Duncan (1960 a, b) records the isolation of *Poria nigrescens* Bres. and *Peniophora mollis* (Bres.) Bourd et Galz, two white rot fungi and the brown rot fungus *Poria oleraceae* Davidson et Lombard. Three other brown rot isolates were unidentified. *Poria nigrescens* is the most frequently isolated Basidiomycete from cooling tower timber (Shema, 1959; Baker, 1962). Baechler *et al.* (1961) also found *P. oleraceae* frequently in the USA. In Britain, *P. nigrescens*, *P. oleraceae* *P. oleraceae* and *Lentinus cyathiformis* Schaef. (= *L. degener* Kalchbr.) are sometimes found in cooling tower packing (Ross and Wood, 1957). Duncan and Lombard (1965) compiled a list of Basidiomycetes causing decay of wood products in the USA and included *Odontia* sp. A., *Lenzites trabea*, *Polyporus versicolor* L. Fr., *Polyporus* sp. A and *Schizophyllum commune* Fr. recorded from cooling tower timbers.

14.6.2 Biological Surface Attack

Extensive biodeterioration of the timber slats of cooling tower packing is now attributed to decay by soft rot fungi. This group of fungi are Ascomycetes and Fungi Imperfecti which attack the surface layers of wood with a high moisture content. In the packing, the wood is saturated with warm water and dissolved oxygen concentrations are reduced. This does not inhibit the growth of microfungi on the surface of flooded timber, but the occurrence of Basidiomycetes is restricted.

Microfungi are also found on other timbers in the packing which are not continuously flooded. Like the brown rot Basidiomycete fungi, the soft rot fungi utilize the cellulose component of the wood most efficiently and leave a surface layer of brown, amorphous residue which is soft and soapy to the touch when wet. On drying, the decayed surface layers have a cracked and commonly cross-checked appearance (Fig. 14.4). The erosive force of the falling cooling water undoubtedly assists in removing this rotten surface layer contributing to the decrease in thickness of the slats. Switching the cooling tower off and allowing the wood to dry out will result in cracking of the rotten surface, exposing sound wood below to more rapid infection. Continued wetting and drying of the timber may therefore accelerate the rate of soft rot decay.

Initial infection of the wood by soft rot fungi is via the wood ray cells. Hyphae in the rays enter the wood tracheids and fibres through the pits and grow within the lumina of the cells. Lateral branches emerge from the hyphae which penetrate transversely into the inner surface layers of the cell wall to the secondary wall. Penetration hyphae may continue to penetrate through the cell wall into the lumen of an adjacent cell but in many instances on reaching the secondary wall the hyphae turn at right angles and follow the longitudinal helical orientation of the cellulose microfibrils in the S_2 layer of the secondary wall (Levy, 1965). Characteristic diamond-shaped cavities or cylindrical cavities with tapered ends are produced by cellulase activity as the hyphae maintain a helical passage through the S_2 layer of the

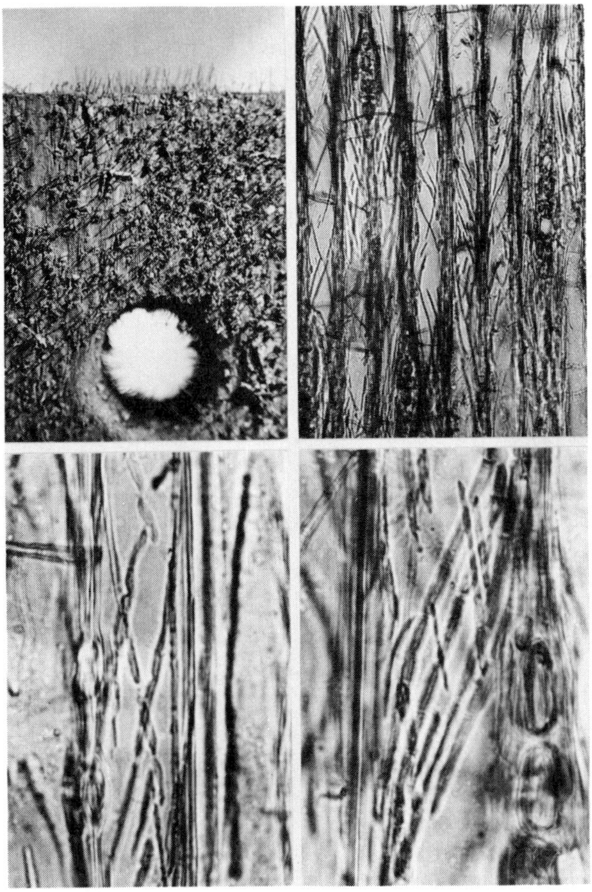

Fig. 14.4. Soft rot attack of wood. (a) Perithecial necks of *Sillia ferruginea* on the surface of beech test block exposed in cooling tower packing (x 1½). (b) Soft rot cavities in Scots pine tracheids (x 125). (c) and (d) Helically orientated soft rot cavities in Scots pine (x 375 and x 560).

secondary cell wall. In longitudinal section, early stages of soft rot attack are recognized by these cavities (Fig. 14.4) which in transverse section appear as small bore holes within the cell wall. The cavities become more numerous and gradually join up, first longitudinally and then laterally, until most of the S_2 and secondary wall is degraded. Continued production of cellulases by the hyphae degrades the primary and tertiary cell walls causing eventual collapse of the cell wall. In the early stages of attack, active decay is concentrated in the early or spring wood regions, which on drying produces a corrugated effect on the surface due to the greater shrinkage of these more decayed regions.

14.7 Soft Rot Fungi Recorded From Cooling Towers

In comparison to Basidiomycete decay in cooling tower timber, the causal organisms of soft rot attack are numerous and well documented. Several accounts listing isolations and identifications of Ascomycetes and Fungi Imperfecti able to cause soft rot and observed on wood from cooling towers have emerged from the USA, Britain, Germany,, the USSR and Australia (Duncan 1960 a, b; Baechler *et al.*, 1961; Eaton and Jones, 1971 a, b; Eaton, 1972; Courtois, 1963; Vakin *et al.*, 1968; Da Costa and Kerruish, 1963). A total list of microfungi from cooling towers is given in Table 14.

TABLE 14.1 A list of soft rot fungi recorded from timber exposed in water cooling towers. *For sources (numbers in parentheses) see page 374.*

Ascomycetes

Ceratocystis sp. (2)
Ceratosphaeria lampadophora (Berkeley et Broome) Niessl (5)
Chaetomium cochliodes Palliser (1).
Chaetomium elatum Kunze ex Fries (5)
Chaetomium funicolum Cooke (1)
Chaetomium globosum Kunze ex Fries (2) (5)
Chaetomium sp. (9)
Coniochaeta discospora (Auerswald) Cain (5)
Delitschia bispora Eaton et Jones (5)
Didymosphaeria sp. (5)
Eurotium sp. (5)
Griphosphaeria corticola (Fuckel) von Hohnel (5)
Leptosphaeria sp. (5)
Melogramma sp. (5)
Microthelia sp. (5)
Nectria ochroleuca (Schw.) Berk. (7)
Orbicula parietina (Schrader ex Fries) Hughes (6)
Phaeonectriella lignicola Eaton et Jones (5)
Phaeosphaeria eustoma (Fuckel) Holm (5)
Podospora setosa (Winter) Neissl. (5)
Pseudoeurotium multisporum (Saito et Minoura) Stolk (5)
Savoryella lignicola Jones et Eaton (5)
Sillia ferruginea (Persoon ex Fries) Karsten (5)
Sporormia leporina Niessl (2)
Sporormia minima Auerswald (5)
Trematosphaeria pertusa (Persoon ex Fries) Fuckel (5)
Unidentified Ascomycete 2 (5)
Unidentified Ascomycete 3 (5)
Unidentified Ascomycete 4 (5)
Xylaria sp. (1)

Marine Ascomycetes

Corollospora maritima Werdermann (5)
Haligena elaterophora Kohlmeyer (5)
Halosphaeria appendiculata Linder (5)
Halosphaeria mediosetigera Cribb et Cribb (5)
Halosphaeria tubulifera Kohlmeyer (5)

370

Table 14.1 *(contd.)*

Lulworthia floridana Meyers (5)
Microthelia maritima (Linder) Kohlmeyer (5)
Nais inornata Kohlmeyer (5)
Remispora maritima Linder (5) (Now *Halosphaeria maritima* (Linder) Kohlm.)
Remispora stellata Kohlmeyer (5) (Now *Halosphaeria stellata* (Kohlm.) Kohlm.)

Moniliales

Acremoniella sp. (3)
Alternaria sp. (1) (9)
Alternaria tenuis Nees (2)
Aspergillus niger von Tiegh (2) (9)
Aspergillus ochraceus Wilhelm (9)
Bactrodesmium sp. (5)
Bispora pusilla Sacc. (6)
Bisporomyces lignicola Mangenot (2)
Botryotrichium sp. (2)
Botrytis sp. (9)
Cadophora sp. (9)
Cephalosporium sp. (5) (9)
Chaetopsis sp. (5)
Chalaropsis/Pullularia sp. (1)
Cladosporium sp. (9)
Clasterosporium caricinum Schweinitz (5)
Codinea parva Hughes et Kendrick (5)
Coniella sp. (5)
Cytosporella sp. (1)
Dactylella sp. (5)
Dendryphion fumosum (Corda) Fr. (5)
Dicoccum asperum Corda (5)
Discula sp. (9)
Doratomyces microsporus (Sacc.) Morton et Smith (5)
Doratomyces purpureofuscus (Fries) Morton et Smith (5)
Doratomyces stemonitis (Pers. ex Fries) Morton et Smith (5)
Fusarium sp. (5) (9)
Fusarium solani (Martius) Appel et Wollenweber (7)
Graphium sp. (5)
Helicoon sessile Morgan (5)
Helminthosporium sp. (1)
Hormiscium sp. (1)
Humicola alopallonella Meyers et Moore (5)
Humicola sp. (5)
Leptographium sp. (9)
Macrosporium sp. (9)
Mammaria echinobotryoides Cesati (5)
Monodictys putredinis (Wallr.) Hughes (5)
Nematogonium sp. (1)
Paecilomyces sp. (2)

Table 14.1 *(contd.)*

Paecilomyces farinosus (Dicks ex Fr.) Brown et Smith (2)
Papularia arundinis Corda (2)
Papularia sphaerosperma (Persoon) von Hohnel (2)
Penicillium sp. (2) (9)
Phaeoscopulariopsis sp. (3)
Phaeostoma sp. (2)
Phialophora sp. (5) (9)
Phialophora richardsiae (Nannf.) Conant (1)
Pleurophragmium sp. (5)
Pullularia sp. (9)
Rhizoctonia crocorum Pers. (2)
Scytalidium lignicola Pesante (8)
Septonema sp. 1 (5)
Septonema sp. 2 (5)
Spicaria divaricata (Thom) Gilman et Abbot (5)
Sporocybe/Acremonium sp. (1)
Sporocybe/Haplochalara sp. (1)
Sporocybe sp. (1)
Stachybotrys atra Corda (5)
Stemphylium dendriticum Souza da Camara (2) (4)
Sterigmatobotrys macrocarpa (Corda) Hughes (5)
Trichoderma koningii Oudaggr. (5)
Trichoderma lignorum (Tode) Harz (9)
Trichoderma viride Pers. ex Fries (2)
Trichothecium sp. (9)
Tricladium splendens Ingold (5)
Tricladium varium Jones et Stewart (10)
Torula herbarum Pers. ex Fries (5)
Verticillium candelabrum Bonorden (5)
Verticillium sp. (5)

Sphaeropsidales

Ascochyta sp. (5)
Asteromella sp. (5)
Coniothyrium sp. (5)
Coniothyrium/Sporocybe/Acremonium sp. (1)
Phoma sp. (9)
Phoma sp. A (5)
Phoma sp. C (5)
Phoma sp. D (5)
Phoma/Cytosporella sp. (1)
Phyllostictina sp. (5)
Pleurophomella sp. (5)
Pyrenochaeta sp. (5)
Staganospora sp. (5)

372

Table 14.1 *(contd.)*

Marine Deuteromycetes

Cirrenalia macrocephala (Kohlm.) Meyers et Moore (5)
Culcitalna achraspora Meyers et Moore (5)
Dictyosporium pelagicum (Linder) Hughes G.C. (5)
Zalerion maritimum (Linder) Anastrasiou (5)

1   Duncan (1960 a, b) (USA).
2   Courtois (1963) (Germany).
3   Da Costa and Kerruish (1963) (Australia).
4   Rosch and Liese (1968) (Germany).
5   Eaton and Jones (1971 a, b) (UK).
6   Forest Products Research Laboratory, Princes Risborough, UK.
7   CMI, Kew, UK.
8   German unknown source.
9   Vakin *et al.* (1968) (USSR).
10 Jones and Stewart (1972) (UK).

This list of species, which totals 127, includes a large number of marine fungi, found only on wood in towers using brackish or seawater make-up. The majority of these marine species are Ascomycetes and all but one have been recorded previously on wood in British coastal waters (Jones, 1968). *Halosphaeria tubulifera* Kohlm. has been found only in the USA and German coastal waters but was also recorded on wood in a British cooling tower (Eaton, 1972). It is evident that marine fungi show a wide tolerance to temperature and salinity variations and it is interesting to note that a greater number of species were found on wood in brackish water rather than seawater cooling towers.

An extensive investigation by Shearer (1971) of the fungi growing on balsa wood in the estuarine reaches of the Patuxent River also revealed that many marine species occurred at salinities of less than 50% seawater concentration. Fungi Imperfecti were dominant in the freshwater sampling areas whilst Ascomycetes were found more frequently as the concentration of salt water increased. The influence of warm water effluent from a power station on the fungi recorded showed that high temperatures may induce the production of the perfect state. In addition, *Corollospora pulchella* Kohlm., Schmidt et Nair was found only in the effluent canal, and this fungus is a rare marine species found particularly in warm waters. Temperatures ranging from 26 to 35°C were recorded in the effluent canal during the summer months when the test was in progress, and fewer species were collected in the effluent channel than the inlet point. Nevertheless, marine fungi predominated on blocks in the effluent although maximum salinity readings were only 40% seawater.

These observations relate closely to the situation found in cooling towers where temperature and water type are crucial in determining the inoculum present and the growth potential of infective organisms. Small seasonal fluctuations in temperature are recorded in most cooling towers and frequent variations in water type can occur. Changes of this sort may affect the fungal population of a cooling tower which cannot be considered as being static. Table 14.1 lists all the fungi recorded from timber in cooling towers but in no way presupposes that they are all typical cooling tower fungi. The local operational conditions, the siting of the tower and the wood species of the packing determine the occurrence of the fungi, but it is interesting to note the high fre-

TABLE 14.2 Weight loss tests on fungi isolated from cooling tower timbers.

| | | Weight loss of substrates (%) | | | | | | | | | |
| | | No nutrient added | | | | | Nutrient added to wood | | | | |
Ascomycetes	Source	B	SP	SS	SPS	RH	B	SP	SS	SPS	RH
Chaetomium funicolum	1	–	–	34	0	0	–	–	36	0	0
Chaetomium globosum	5	–	–	–	–	–	28	7	–	–	–
Chaetomium globosum	3	–	–	–	–	–	34	4	–	–	–
Chaetomium globosum	4	26	–	–	–	–	25	–	–	–	–
Chaetomium globosum	2	52	46	–	–	–	–	–	–	–	–
Melogramma sp.	5	–	–	–	–	–	15	0	–	–	–
Nais inornata	5	–	–	–	–	–	9	–	–	–	–
Phaeosphaeria eustoma	5	–	–	–	–	–	14	–	–	–	–
Pseudeurotium multisporum	5	–	–	–	–	–	20	–	–	–	–
Savoryella lignicola	5	–	–	–	–	–	14	4	–	–	–
Sillia ferruginea	5	–	–	–	–	–	8	1	–	–	–
Sporormia leporina	2	23	1	–	–	–	–	–	–	–	–
Sporormia minima	5	–	–	–	–	–	21	–	–	–	–
Xylaria sp.	1	–	–	50	12	0	–	–	58	18	0
Deuteromycetes											
Acremoniella sp.	3	–	–	–	–	–	14	–	–	–	–
Alternaria sp.	1	–	–	6	0	0	–	–	4	0	0
Alternaria tenuis	2	–	2	–	–	–	–	–	–	–	–
Aspergillus niger	2	–	2	–	–	–	–	–	–	–	–
Asteromella sp.	5	–	–	–	–	–	25	–	–	–	–
Bisporomyces lignicola	2	20	1	–	–	–	–	–	–	–	–

Species	1	2	3	4	5	6	7	8	9	10	11
Botryotrichum sp.	2	18	–	–	–	–	–	–	–	–	–
Cephalosporium sp.	5	–	–	–	–	–	18	–	–	–	–
Cephalosporium sp.	1	–	–	10	10	0	–	–	64	2	0
Cephalosporium sp.	1	–	–	34	6	0	–	–	32	14	0
Chalaropsis/Pullularia sp.	1	–	–	28	–	–	–	–	–	8	0
Coniothyrium sp.	5	–	–	–	–	–	12	–	–	–	–
Coniothyrium, Sporocybe, Acremonium sp.	1	–	–	16	4	0	–	–	–	–	–
Cytosporella sp.	1	–	–	16	6	0	–	–	18	8	0
Cytosporella sp.	1	–	–	22	4	0	–	–	20	4	0
Cytosporella sp.	1	–	–	22	6	0	–	–	24	6	0
Cytosporella sp.	1	–	–	16	6	0	–	–	28	4	0
Cytosporella sp.	1	–	–	–	0	0	–	–	22	4	0
Cytosporella sp.	1	–	–	20	0	0	–	–	30	0	0
Cytosporella sp.	1	–	–	27	0	0	–	–	34	0	0
Cytosporella sp.	1	–	–	22	6	0	–	–	30	0	0
Cytosporella/Phoma sp.	1	–	–	20	0	0	–	–	20	4	0
Cytosporella/Phoma sp.	1	–	–	18	4	0	–	–	24	0	0
Cytosporella/Phoma sp.	1	–	–	–	–	–	–	–	30	8	0
Doratomyces microsporus	5	–	–	–	–	–	15	–	–	–	–
Doratomyces purpureofuscus	5	–	–	–	–	–	15	–	–	–	–
Fusarium sp.	5	–	–	–	–	–	17	9	–	–	–
Graphium sp.	5	–	–	–	–	–	20	–	–	–	–
Hormiscium sp.	1	–	–	6	6	0	11	–	6	4	0
Humicola alopallonella	5	1	–	–	–	–	29	1	–	–	–
Mucor sp.	2	1	0	–	12	0	–	–	–	12	0
Nematogonium sp.	1	–	–	24	–	–	–	–	28	12	–
Paecilomyces farinosus	2	21	2	–	–	–	–	–	–	–	–
Paecilomyces sp.	2	46	3	–	–	–	–	–	–	–	–
Papularia arundinis	2	22	3	–	–	–	–	–	–	–	–
Papularia sphaerosperma	2	11	2	–	–	–	–	–	–	–	–
Penicillium luteum	2	3	2	–	–	–	–	–	–	–	–

Table 14.2 (contd.)

Species										
Phaeostoma sp.	2	2	1	—	—	—	—	—	—	—
Phialophora richardsiae	1	—	—	18	4	0	—	—	36	6
Phialophora richardsiae	1	—	—	12	0	0	—	—	26	0
Phialophora richardsiae	1	—	—	14	6	0	—	—	42	4
Phialophora richardsiae	1	—	—	16	0	0	—	—	30	0
Phialophora richardsiae	1	—	—	16	0	0	—	—	36	0
Phialophora richardsiae	1	—	—	20	0	0	—	—	26	0
Phialophora richardsiae	1	—	—	—	0	0	—	—	28	0
Phialophora richardsiae	1	—	—	20	0	0	—	—	42	0
Phialophora richardsiae	1	—	—	—	0	0	—	—	28	0
Phialophora richardsiae	1	—	—	18	0	0	—	—	28	0
Phialophora sp.	1	—	—	16	0	0	—	—	28	0
Phialophora sp.	1	—	—	44	6	0	—	—	28	4
Phialophora sp.	1	—	—	16	0	0	—	—	20	0
Phialophora sp.	1	—	—	26	0	0	—	—	26	0
Phyllostictina sp.	5	—	—	—	—	—	11	—	—	—
Pyrenochaeta sp.	5	—	—	—	—	—	13	—	—	—
Rhizoctonia crocorum	2	15	1	—	—	—	20	—	—	—
Rhizopus nigricans	2	1	1	—	—	—	—	—	—	—
Septonema sp. 1.	5	—	—	—	—	—	3	—	—	—
Septonema sp. 2	5	—	—	—	—	—	5	2	—	—
Sporocybe sp.	1	—	—	32	8	0	—	—	44	8
Sporocybe/Haplochalara sp.	1	—	—	34	0	0	—	—	56	0
Sporocybe/Acremonium sp.	1	—	—	6	6	0	—	—	28	8
Sporocybe/Acremonium sp.	1	—	—	32	10	0	—	—	40	14
Sporocybe/Acremonium sp.	1	—	—	34	12	0	—	—	42	18
Sporocybe/Acremonium sp.	1	—	—	12	0	0	—	—	16	0
Sporocybe/Acremonium sp.	1	—	—	34	10	0	—	—	38	10
Sporocybe/Acremonium sp.	1	—	—	58	0	0	—	—	36	0

	Source											
Sporocybe/Acremonium sp.	1	—	—	36	12	0	—	—	—	40	12	0
Sporotrichum sp.	2	1	1	—	—	—	—	—	—	—	—	—
Stemphylium dendriticum	2	5	1	—	—	—	—	—	—	—	—	—
Trichoderma viride	2	1	0	—	—	—	—	9	—	—	—	—
Torula herbarum	5	—	—	—	—	—	—	—	—	—	—	—

Sources:

1   Duncan (1960a).
2   Courtois (1963).
3   Da Costa and Kerruish (1963).
4   Rosch and Liese (1968).
5   Eaton and Jones (1971a).

B: Beech.
SP: Scots pine.
SS: Sweetgum sapwood.
SPS: Southern pine sapwood.
RH: Redwood heartwood.

quency with which certain fungi are consistently recorded from different cooling towers. This aspect will be dealt with in more detail later in this chapter.

A large number of the fungi isolated from timber in cooling towers are able to cause significant decay of wood in pure culture (Table 14.2). No standard test procedure for soft rot capability has been adopted by workers, but the results presented show that most isolates were able to produce soft rot attack which in some cases was very extensive. A large number of Deuteromycetes have been tested for their soft rot ability, but it is unfortunate that many of these fungi have only been tentatively identified. The majority of these fungi may be considered to be terrestrial species. The evidence so far accumulated indicates that many fungi which grow on lignicolous substrates in natural hatitats are able to grow on wood in cooling towers.

14.7.1 Ecological Aspects

Very little work has been carried out on the patterns of colonization of cooling tower timbers by fungi. Most investigations have been restricted to records of presence or absence of fungi on packing timbers removed from cooling towers, followed up by an examination of the wood rotting ability of these fungi. A detailed comparative investigation of the patterns of appearance of fungi on test blocks placed in two cooling towers using freshwater and brackish water (Ince and Connah's Quay) has been carried out (Eaton and Jones, 1971 a). Test blocks were exposed over three test periods each lasting approximately one year. The test blocks (15x7.5x2 cm) were untreated Scots pine *(Pinus sylvestris* L.) and Scots pine treated with a copper-chrome-arsenic preservative, plus untreated beech (*Fagus sylvatica* L.) and greenheart (*Octotea rodiaei* (Schomb.) Mez. Test blocks were removed from the packing at regular six-weekly intervals during the course of each testing period.

The appearance of fungi on test blocks at both sites varied with the species of wood and preservative treatment applied. Some fungi only grew on beech, e.g. *Doratomyces* spp. *Phyllostictina* sp. and *Trematosphaeria pertusa* (Persoon ex Fr.) Fuckel, whilst others were found only on untreated Scots pine, e.g. *Griphosphaeria corticola* (Fuckel) von Hohnel, *Halosphaeria mediosetigera* Cribb et Cribb and *Sterigmatobotrys macrocarp* (Corda) Hughes. In addition, many species were found to have a clear preference for either beech or Scots pine. Soft rot fungi degrade hardwoods more readily than softwood in laboratory tests (Savory, 1954; Courtois, 1963), but under natural conditions, Scots pine was decayed at the same rate as beech (Eaton and Jones, 1971 a).

Fewer fungi grew on the more resistant tropical greenheart wood than the native wood species. This was not the case with preservative treated Scots pine blocks. The number of fungi present on treated Scots pine was only slightly fewer than on untreated Scots pine, but these fungi were recorded less frequently. The fruit bodies of several fungi e.g. *Melogramma* sp., *Septonema* spp., took longer to emerge on treated wood. This suggests that over a period of time these fungi develop a resistance to the impregnated toxic compounds in the wood, or that preservative components are gradually leached from the surface layers of the test blocks allowing the fungi to invade the wood and fruit. Levi (1969) has suggested that certain Basidiomycetes may bring about the dissolution and detoxification of the components of a water borne preservative provided that a sufficiently large inoculum and nutrient source is available. The resistance of many soft rot fungi to preserved wood in the aquatic environment requires more extensive study.

The fungi recorded from the two cooling towers investigated were placed into three major groups. The first group of fungi were present on test blocks during the initial stages of each test period. Some of these fungi disappeared during the course of the tests, e.g. *Chaetomium globosum* Kunze et Fries and *Graphium* sp., whilst others remained on the wood throughout, e.g. *Monodictys putredinis* (Wallr.) Hughes. Fungi in this group may be considered as a primary colonizing saprophytic phase (Hudson, 1968) growing rapidly and utilizing available soluble carbohydrates. Their continued persistence on the wood is determined by their ability to utilize cellulose at a later stage.

Group 2 fungi appeared several weeks after commencement of the tests and most of them remained on the wood until the end of the test. Fruiting bodies of these fungi emerged as certain group 1 members were disappearing from the wood. Those fungi which were only occasionally recorded during the tests were placed in group 3.

Soft rot capability tests carried out in the laboratory on those fungi which were isolated showed that single cultures of fungi in groups 1 and 2 were able to produce soft rot cavities and in many cases cause appreciable weight loss of small beech and Scots pine test blocks (Table 14.2). Of 24 fungi tested, only one did not produce soft rot cavities.

Despite differences between the two cooling towers, the basic fungal flora on wood from each site was similar and composed of Ascomycetes and Fungi Imperfecti. Marine fungi were recorded from the brackish water tower but their frequency of occurrence was related to the amount of seawater in the make-up. In addition, some fungi were found on wood from only one tower or the other; for instance single species of the genera *Doratomyces* and *Septonema* were recorded at each site (*D. microsporus* (Sacc.) Morton et Smith and *Septonema* sp. 1 at Ince; *D. purpureofuscus* (Fr.) Morton et Smith and *Septonema* sp.2 at Connah's Quay). A few fungi were therefore site specific but many of the frequently appearing fungi grew well in both situations.

Using similar test procedures, the fungi growing on test blocks in 16 other cooling towers have been listed (Eaton, 1972). Untreated beech and Scots pine blocks, acting as baits, were removed at 3-montly intervals over a 9 month test period. The cooling towers investigated were carefully selected to include a range of water types from fresh river water, polluted river water, sewage effluent, brackish and seawater. It was evident that the source of make-up water was a crucial factor in determining the fungi which appeared on the test blocks. Marine fungi appeared on wood removed from towers using brackish and seawaters, whilst a cooling tower (Elland) using fresh river water make-up provided an inoculum which included fungi found typically in natural freshwater situations e.g. *Tricladium splendens* Ingold, *Helicoon sessile* Morgan and *Delitschia bispora* Eaton et Jones. These fungi were absent on wood from other cooling towers. Treated timber which had been in service for 10 years at Elland cooling tower showed no evidence of soft rot attack. Service timber from the other towers investigated showed evidence of soft rot decay which in some instances was extensive. The source and chemical composition of the cooling water is important in determining not only those fungi which colonize the timber, but may also affect the activity of these organisms in decaying the wood (Liese, 1969).

The seawater-influenced towers showed some degree of exclusion of species. At Stella North, a brackish water tower, active growth of marine fungi was observed and only six species found on wood from inland towers were recorded. At Fleetwood, a cooling tower using seawater, only marine fungi colonized the wood, apart from *Monodictys putredinis* which was found regularly at all the cooling towers tested. The majority of other towers exhibited a fungal flora which was similar to that found at Connah's Quay and Ince and is typified by the most frequently recorded fungi listed in Table 14.3. This list includes newly described genera growing on wood from cooling towers (Jones and Eaton, 1969; Eaton and Jones, 1970). The regularity of occurrence of these fungi indicates that they form the core of a cooling tower fungal flora, whilst local operating conditions influence the occurrence of additional species. Although the majority of fungi found on wood from cooling towers at inland sites have been previously reported from terrestrial or freshwater habitats, they are unlike those communities of microfungi observed on wood in terrestrial situations.

TABLE 14.3   The most frequently occurring fungi growing on beech, Scots pine and treated service timber from 16 British cooling towers (Eaton, 1972).

Ascomycetes	No of sites reported	Deuteromycetes	No. of sites reported
Chaetomium globosum	10	Monodictys putredinis	16
Savoryella lignicola	8	Asteromella sp.	10
Melogramma sp.	6	Fusarium sp.	9
Ceratosphaeria lampadophora	5	Graphium sp.	9
Unidentified Ascomycete 1.*	4	Humicola alopallonella	9
Phaeonectriella lignicola	4	Septonema spp.	9
Trematosphaeria pertusa	4	Doratomyces microsporus	7
		Sterigmatobotrys macrocarpa	7

* Tentatively identified as Sillia ferruginea

14.7.2. Source of Fungal Inoculum

Fungal propagules may enter a cooling system in the make-up water, in the air passing continuously through the packing, or at the time of construction, if infected timber is used. The spasmodic appearance of marine fungi in the Connah's Quay cooling tower when the make-up contains a high concentration of seawater indicates that this is an important source of fresh inoculum. However, a comparison of the fungi inhabiting test blocks in a cooling tower pond at Ince and test blocks submerged in the River Dee, the source of make-up water some miles away, showed noticeable differences. Several fungi, including the aquatic hyphomycetes Heliscus lugdunensis Sacc. et Therry, Tricladium splendens, and Anguillospora longissima (Sacc. et Syd.) Ingold found on wood in the River Dee were absent on wood in the Ince cooling system. Similarly, many fungi commonly occurring on wood in the Ince cooling system, e.g. Chaetomium globosum, Doratomyces microsporus, Melogramma sp. were absent on wood in the River Dee. The contrasting temperature and chemical composition of the water were considered to be important in controlling the emergence of fungal species at each site. Although spores of 'cooling tower' fungi may be present in the make-up water, some species may not be stimulated into germination and development except in the cooling system habitat (Eaton and Jones, 1971 b). Temperature optima and aeration requirements of fungi growing on cooling tower timbers are considered later, but competitive physiological advantage may be achieved by aquatic hyphomycetes growing at low temperatures (Thornton, 1963) leading to the exclusion of 'cooling tower' fungi on wood in a river water environment.

14.7.3 Conditions for Growth

The factors which influence the growth of fungi generally remain stable for long periods of time in individual cooling towers but vary in different towers depending on local operating conditions. Liese (1969) undertook an extensive examination of 17 cooling towers in Germany in order to determine those factors influencing the breakdown of timber. Test samples of unimpregnated pine, spruce, larch and oak as well as service timbers were carefully examined. He was able to pinpoint those factors of greatest significance but found that the multiplicity of factors operating in cooling towers precludes objective determination of the process of wood decay.

Analysis of cooling water indicated that high Cl^-, SO_4^{2-}, PO_4^{4-} concentrations, increased hardness of the water and pH determinations of 8-8.8 encouraged growth of the fungi and was associated with extensive decay of the test panels and the tower lathwork. Similarly, the weight losses of untreated Scots pine test samples in seven British cooling towers showed a ten-fold variation between sites, the lowest weight losses being recorded in a freshwater tower, the highest in a brackish water tower (Irvine et al., 1972). The concentrations of individual ions or combinations of ions in the cooling water appear to influence the activity of fungi growing on wood in the packing.

Soft rot fungi isolated from a range of wood substrates showed higher temperature optima for growth on agar medium than Basidiomycetes (Duncan, 1960 a). Many of the cooling tower isolates had high temperature tolerances, and Duncan (1961) suggested that the cooling tower fungi, including the Basidiomycetes isolated, may represent an ecological group able to grow rapidly at temperatures above 30°C. In addition, the use of high cooling water temperatures (up to 55°C at the inlet point) leads to increased wood loss caused by structural alterations within the wood, facilitating fungal attack (Liese, 1969).

Soft rot fungi from cooling tower packing are known to be more tolerant of poor aeration than Basidiomycetes (Duncan, 1961). The operation of low density precipitation in some towers is associated with greater wood loss and may be related to the availability of oxygen reaching the fungi in the surface layers of the wood (Liese, 1969). The reduced availability of oxygen in the warm water on the surface of packing timbers explains the prevalence of soft rot attack and the absence of Basidiomycetes in the flooded areas of the tower.

From the operational standpoint, the factor of greatest importance is the efficiency of wood preservatives in the packing timber and the tolerance of fungi to these compounds. Duncan (1960 a) tested the tolerance of 41 soft rot and Basidiomycete isolates against a range of toxic compounds including creosote, sodium pentachlorophenate and the separate components of inorganic wood preservatives. Growth was measured in agar medium and up to one quarter of the soft rot isolates were more tolerant than Basidiomycetes to most of the toxic compounds. However, among the soft rot isolates tolerances varied considerably, although *Helminthosporium* and *Cytosporella* (cooling tower isolates) showed noticeable tolerances to most of the chemicals tested. Work by Da Costa and Kerruish (1963) also showed that soft rot isolates from cooling tower timber in Australia were tolerant to a range of wood preservatives. These tests were carried out using pure cultures on agar media but further work showed that decay of sweetgum and pine sapwood treated with creosote, pentachlorophenol and inorganic preservatives was greater when inoculation of the fungus was preceded by exposure of the blocks to another fungal isolate. The first fungus is believed to render the preservative ineffective without causing appreciable decay of the wood (Duncan and Deverall, 1964).

Soft rot fungi and Basidiomycetes are known to grow on preserved wood in many natural situations both terrestrial (Butcher, 1972) and aquatic (Jones, 1972), and many microfungi are able to degrade a wide range of wood preservatives (Russel, 1955; Madhosingh, 1961; Duncan and Deverall, 1964; Cserjesi, 1967; Unligil, 1968). The high hazard conditions encountered within the cooling tower environment make this situation ideal for the examination of preservative efficiency in aquatic habitats.

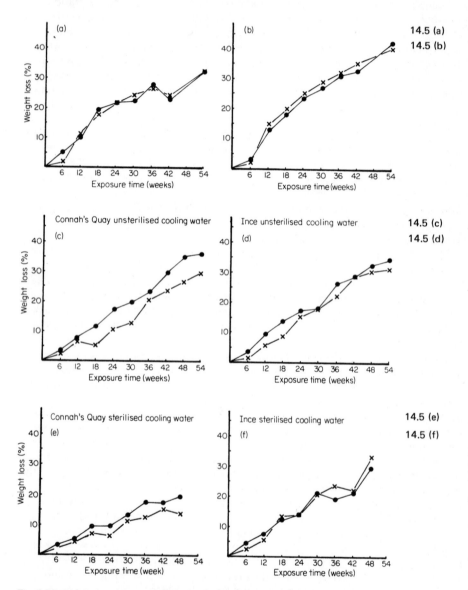

Fig. 14.5. Weight loss of untreated beech ●—● and untreated Scots pine x—x test blocks (5x2.5x0.5 c exposed in Connah's Quay cooling tower (a) and Ince cooling tower (b). Test blocks exposed in laboratory water circulating systems are shown in (c) — (f).

14.7.4. Decay Test Methods

The methods for assessing preservative effectiveness against soft rot fungi have been reviewed (Savory and Bravery, 1970 a) and limitations of procedure in laboratory test methodology are discussed. *Chaetomium globosum,* a widely used test organism, was found unsuitable in pure culture on pine whilst mixed culture testing of natural soil microflora proved to be more useful (Savory and Bravery, 1970 b). Current test methods do not reproduce comparable cooling tower conditions for assessing the decay ability of individual or groups of fungi on wooden test blocks. Similar misgivings have been expressed with regard to the evaluation of slimicides in cooling towers (Wolfson and Song, 1964) and a water circulating apparatus for evaluating slime control was constructed. More recently, experiments to simulate the environment within cooling tower packing were successful in inducing rapid decay of small wooden test samples (Eaton and Irvine, 1972). Circulating water systems constructed in the laboratory were charged with small test blocks, and cooling water from two cooling towers was introduced into the systems. Two systems were operated using sterilized cooling water from each source with a fungal population artificially introduced into each laboratory system. The fungal cultures were previously isolated off timbers from these cooling towers. Two other systems using unsterilized cooling water were also put into operation.

Examination of the test blocks removed from each system showed noticeable decay. The fungi which emerged on the surface of these blocks were those which had previously been recorded on wood from the towers under examination. Exposure of the same size test blocks in these cooling towers produced weight loss measurements comparable to those in the circulating water systems Fig. 14.5). Mixed culture systems were found to be more effective at producing rapid decay than single culture systems previously attempted (Lloyd, 1960; Corbett, 1963).

The value of the model system for the further study of biodeterioration and the ecology of its causative agents has been described by Walsh (1968). The construction of simulated cooling tower systems provided an environment as conducive to severe deterioration of untreated wood by the same fungal flora as was observed in water cooling towers. Simulation testing of the operating conditions to be expected in new cooling towers at proposed sites would therefore provide information for operators to predict the decay potential of micro-organisms in cooling towers yet to be erected.

With developing economic and industrial growth in all countries of the world, the requirement for water cooling towers will increase. The gathering awareness of problems created by thermal pollution of natural waters by industrial processes expedites the need for careful examination of the biological problems encountered in cooling towers.

References

ANON. (1965). 'C.E.G.B. research into the probable service life of "Tanalised" cooling tower fills.' *Hickson's Timber Impregnation Co. (G.B.) Ltd. Monograph* No. 215, pp. 9.

ANON. (1966). 'Slime control with chlorine and non-oxidising biocides.' *Mat. Prot.,* 5, 30-31.

BAECHLER, R.H., BLEW, J.O., and DUNCAN, C.G. (1961). 'Causes and prevention of decay of wood in cooling towers.' *Am. Soc.Mech. Eng.,* No. 61, 1-13

BAKER, D.R. (1951). 'Wood deterioration in cooling towers.' *Petrol Eng.,* 23, C76-80.

BAKER, D.R. (1962). 'Durability of wood in cooling tower service.' *Marley Company Tech. Bull.,* R-62-W-1, pp. 40.

BEECHER, J.S., and TRAUTENBERG, G.A. (1964). 'Control biological growths in open circulating cooling-water systems.' *Power,* 108, 80-82.

BETTS, W.D., and SPRANKLIN, D.H. (1972). 'Creosote as a preservative for timber in cooling towers.' *Brit. Wood Pres. Ann. Conv. Rec.,* 91-107.

BUTCHER, J.A. (1972). 'Colonisation by fungi of *Pinus radiata* sapwood treated with a copper-chrome-arsenate preservative.' *J. Inst. Wood Sci.,* 5, 16-25.

C.T.I. (1963). 'Wood maintenance for water cooling towers.' *Cooling Tower Inst. Bull.,* W.M.S. -104, pp. 16.

CARLSON, C.D. (1961). 'Field tests and evaluation of polychlorophenates in cooling tower preservation.' *Cooling Tower Inst. Bull.,* TPR-120.

CARLSON, C.D. (1963). 'Combating biological attack on the Gulf Coast', *Brit. Wood Pres. Ann. Conv. Rec.,* 17-36

CHANDRA, A., WILLEITNER, H., and LIESE, W. (1972). 'Investigations on the protection of Indian timber species in cooling towers.' *J. T.D.A. of India,* No. 2, 1-9.

COMEAUX, R.V. (1953). 'Redwood cooling towers – a look at causes of deterioration and methods of maintenance.' *Oil Gas J., 52,* 343-7.

COOK, C.H. (1956). 'Corrosion and deposit control in cooling water systems'. *Corrosion, 27,* 53-56.

CORBETT, N.H. (1963). 'Anatomical, ecological and physiological studies on microfungi associated with decaying wood.' Ph.D. Thesis, University of London.

COURTOIS, H. (1963). 'Beitrag zur Frag holzabbauender Ascomyceten und Fungi Imperfecti.' *Holzforschung,* 17, 176-183.

CSERJESI, A.J. (1967). 'The adaptation of fungi to pentachlorophenol and its biodegradation.' *Can. J. Microbiol.,* 13, 1243-1249.

DA COSTA, E.W.B., and KERRUISH, R.M. (1963). 'Laboratory evaluation of chromated metallic preservatives against soft rot fungi in beech.' *Holzforschung,* 17, 12-18.

DONOHUE, J.M., and WOODS, G.A. (1968). 'On-stream desludging of cooling systems.' *Mat. Prot.,* 7, 15-18.

DOST, W.A. (1959). 'Certification of redwood and effect of oxidising agents on redwood in cooling tower service.' *Proc. 20th Ann. Water Conf. Eng. Soc. of W. Pennsyl.,* 77-83.

DUNBAR, J. (1962). 'The fixation of water-borne preservatives in cooling tower timber.' *Brit. Wood Pres. Ann. Conv. Rec.,* 25-39.

DUNCAN, C.G. (1960a). 'Wood attacking capacities and physiology of soft rot fungi.' *F.P.L. Report 2173* U.S. Dept. of Agriculture, p. 28.

DUNCAN, C.G. (1960b). 'Soft rot in wood and toxicity studies of causal fungi.' *Am. Wood Pres. Ass. Proc.,* 56, 27-37.

DUNCAN, C.G. (1961). 'Relative aeration requirements by soft rot and Basidiomycete wood destroying fungi.' *F.P.L. Report 2218,* U.S. Dept. of Agriculture, p. 6.

DUNCAN, C.G., and DEVERALL, F.J. (1964). 'Degradation of wood preservatives by fungi.' *Appl. Microbiol.,* 12, 57-62.

DUNCAN, C.G., and LOMBARD, F.F. (1965). 'Fungi associated with principal decays in wood products in the USA'. *US Forest Service Res. Paper,* WO-4.

EATON, R.A. (1972). 'Fungi growing on wood in water cooling towers.' *Int. Biodetn. Bull.,* 8, 39-48.

EATON, R.A., and IRVINE, J. (1972). 'Decay of untreated wood by cooling tower fungi.' *In Biodeterioration of Materials* (Eds. A.H. Walters and E.H. Heuck-van der Plas) Applied Science. Vol.2. 192-200.

EATON, R.A., and JONES, E.B.G. (1970). 'New fungi on timber from water-cooling towers.' *Nova Hedwigia,* 19, 779-786.

EATON, R.A., and JONES, E.B.G. (1971a). 'The biodeterioration of timber in water cooling towers. I. Fungal ecology and the decay of wood at Connah's Quay and Ince.' *Material u. Organismen,* 6, 51-80.

EATON, R.A., and JONES, E.B.G. (1971b). 'The biodeterioration of timber in water cooling towers II. Fungi growing on wood in different positions in a water cooling system.' *Material u. Organismen,* 6, 31-92.

FINDLAY, W.P.K., and SAVORY, J.G. (1950). 'Breakdown of timber in water cooling towers.' *Proc. VII. Int. Bot. Cong.,* 7, 315-316.

FITZGERALD, G.P. (1964). 'Evaluation of potassium permanganate as an algicide for water cooling towers.' *Ind. Eng. Chem.,* 3, 82-85.

GJOVIK, L.R., BENDTSEN, B.A., and ROTH, H.G. (1972). 'Condition of preservative-treated cooling tower slats after 10-year service.' *For. Prod. J.,* 22, 35-40.

GRUBER, M.V. (1959). 'The function and design of industrial cooling towers.' *Proc. 20th Ann. Water Conf. Eng. Soc. of W. Pennsyl.,* 65-69.

HIMSLEY, A. (1959). 'Treatment of cooling waters in England.' *Proc. 20th Ann. Water Conf. Eng. Soc. of W. Pennsyl.,* 133-137.

HUDSON, H.J. (1968). 'The ecology of fungi on plant remains above the soil.' *New Phytol.,* 67, 837-874.

HURST, E.H. (1955). 'Factors other than mineral content which influence the corrosiveness of cooling water.' *Nalco Chemical Co. Reprint,* No. 51.

HURST, E.H. (1956). 'Why cooling towers decay.' *Petrol Eng.,* 28.

IRVINE, J., EATON, R.A., and JONES, E.B.G. (1972). 'The effect of water of different ionic composition on the leaching of a water borne preservative from timber placed in cooling towers and in the sea.' *Material u. Organismen,* 7, 45-71.

JONES, E.B.G. (1968). 'The distribution of marine fungi on wood submerged in the sea.' In *Biodeterioration of Materials* (Eds. A.H. Walters and J.J. Elphick). Elsevier, vol. 1, 460-485.

JONES, E.B.G. (1972). 'The decay of timber in aquatic environments.' *Brit. Wood Pres. Ann. Conv. Rec.,* 31-49.

JONES, E.B.G., and EATON, R.A. (1969). *'Savoryella lignicola* gen. et. sp. nov. from water-cooling towers.' *Trans. Br. mycol. Soc.* 52, 161-165.

JONES, E.B.G. and STEWART, R.J. (1972), *'Tricladium varium,* an aquatic hypho-mycete on wood in water cooling towers.' *Trans. Br. mycol. Soc.,* 59, 163-167.

KAYE, S. (1965). 'Slime/decay studies of cooling tower timbers.' *Int. Pest Control,* 7, 22-25.

KELLY, B.J. (1965). 'New chemical formulation will control micro-organisms in hydrocarbon contaminated cooling water systems.' *Mat. Prot.,* 4, 62-64, 67.

LEVI, M.P. (1969). 'The mechanism of action of copper-chrome-arsenate preservatives against wood destroying fungi.' *Brit. Wood Pres. Ann. Conv. Rec.,* 113-127.

LEVY, J.F. (1965). 'The soft rot fungi: their mode of action and significance in the degradation of wood.' In *Advances in Botanical Research.* (Ed. R.D. Preston) Academic Press, 2, 323-357.

LIESE, W. (1969). 'Untersuchungen uber die Ursachen der Holzzerstörung in Kuhltürmen.' *Forschungsberichte des Landes Nordrhein-Westfalen,* 2026, pp. 42.

LIESE, W. (1970). 'Ultrastructural aspects of wood tissue disintegration.' *A. Rev. Phytopath.,* 8, 231-258.

LLOYD, F.J. (1960). 'Studies in timber mycology.' D.I.C. Thesis, Imperial College, London.

MADHOSINGH, C. (1961). 'The metabolic detoxification of 2-4 dinitrophenol by *Fusarium oxysporum.' Can. J. Microbiol.,* 7, 553-567.

MAGUIRE, J.J. (1956). 'Biological fouling in recirculating cooling water systems.' *Ind. Eng. Chem.,* 48, 2161-2167.

MENNIE, A. (1971). 'Biocides in cooling systems.' *Process Biochem.* 6, 21-22 and 38.

ROSCH, R., and LIESE, W. (1968). 'Preservation of wood. Research programme 1. Biological questions. List of fungi tested for soft rot activity.' O.E.C.D. work Doc. No. 27/DAS/CSI/M/559, 65 pp.

ROSS, F.F., and WOOD, M.J. (1957). 'The preservation of timber in water cooling towers.' *Brit. Wood Pres. Ann. Conv. Rec.,* 171-197.

RUSSELL, P. (1955). 'Inactivation of phenyl mercuric acetate in ground wood pulp by a mercury-resistant strain of *Penicillium roquefortii* Thorn.' *Nature,* 176, 1123-4.

SAVORY, J.G. (1954a). 'Breakdown of timber by Ascomycetes and Fungi Imperfecti.' *Ann. appl. Biol.,* 41, 336-347.

SAVORY, J.G. (1954b). 'Damage to wood caused by micro-organisms.' *J. appl. Bact.,* 17, 213-218.

SAVORY, J.G., and BRAVERY, A.F. (1970a). 'Observations on methods of determining the effectiveness of wood preservatives against soft rot fungi.' Paper presented at German Society for Wood Research meeting, Munich, June 1970.

SAVORY, J.G., and BRAVERY, A.F. (1970b). 'Collaborative experiments in testing the toxicity of wood preservatives to soft rot fungi.' *Material u. Organismen,* 5, 59-80.

SHEARER, C.A. (1971). 'A study of the ecology, taxonomy and physiology of some wood-inhabiting Ascomycetes and Fungi Imperfectii from the Patuxent River.' Ph.D. Dissertation, University of Maryland.

SHEMA, B.F. (1959). 'Classification of cooling tower wood deterioration.' *Proc. 20th Ann. Water Conf. Eng. Soc. of W. Pennsyl.*

SLÁDEČKOVÁ, A. (1969). 'Control of slimes and algae in cooling systems.' *Verh. Internat. Verein. Limnol.,* 17, 532-538.

THORNTON, D.R. (1963). 'The physiology and nutrition of some aquatic Hyphomycetes.' *J. gen. Microbiol.,* 33, 23-31.

TRAUTENBERG, G.A., and ASKEW, A.C. (1964). 'Microbiological control to prevent corrosion in recirculating water systems.' *Mat. Prot.* 3, 26-28, 30.

UNLIGIL, H.H. (1968). 'Depletion of pentachlorophenol by fungi.' *Forest Prod. J.,* 18, 45-50.

VAKIN, A.T., SOKOLOV, D.V., PRIKOT, N.G., TARKHANOVA, R.Yu., MALINOVSKAY, K.V., SOLOVBEV, V.A., and TRANINA, N. (1968). 'Compound (fungal and bacterial) rot of wood in cooling towers of power stations and measures for controlling it.' *Nauchnye Trudy Leningr. Lesotekh. Akad.,* 110, 91-100.

WALDROP, F.B., DAY, J.R., and KITE, H.T. (1957). 'The deterioration of redwood cooling tower lumber.' US Atomic Energy Commission Technical Information Service, Oak Ridge, Tenn. Res. and Dev. Report *Y-1156,* 38.

WALSH, J.H. (1968). 'Ecological considerations of biodeterioration.' *Int. Biodetn. Bull.,* 4, 1-10.

WALTERS, N.E.M. (1970). 'Current results from cooling tower tests.' *C.S.I.R.O. F.P. Newsletter,* 374, 1-3.

WILLA, J.L. (1959). 'Report on field wood preservation studies.' *Proc. 20th Water Conf. Eng. Soc. of W. Pennsyl.,* 83-96.

WILLA, J.L. (1965). 'White pocket rot, a disease of cooling tower lumber can be combated by direct application of fungicides.' *Ind. Water Eng.* (March) 10, 11, 35, 37.

WILLIAMS, A.E. (1953). 'Control of slime and algae in cooling water systems.' *Cheap Steam,* 37, 74-75.

WISE, R.B. (1950). 'Cooling water slime.' *Oil and Gas. J.,* 48, 170, 173, 177-178.

WOLFSON, L.L., and SONG, P. (1964). 'A simulated cooling tower for evaluating slime control.' *Mat. Prot.,* 3, 14-17.

WOODSON, R.D. (1971). 'Cooling towers.' *Sci. American,* 224, 70-78.

15 Fungi in Sewage

W. BRIDGE COOKE

15.1 General

That literature available to the writer, published prior to 1954, has been reviewed (Cooke, 1954 a). At least one paper missed at that time is noted briefly here. Some general references will be noted here but papers dealing with streams and sewage treatment systems will be considered for each process type. In general, it will be noted, the fungi have been ignored, considered as nuisances, or treated as inferior in value to the bacteria. It is hoped that the potential for usefulness of fungi in waste treatment of all types will be demonstrated in this review.

Holtje (1943) briefly summarized the biological components of slimes in sewage sprinkling filters in a New Jersey sewage treatment plant. *Fusarium* and *Leptomitus* were mentioned and illustrated. Holtje was of the opinion that fungi and bacteria are in continual struggle for dominance, with the fungi predominant in the winter, and their film sloughing off in the spring.

Wurtz (1957), in a report on fungi, bacteria and algae in polluted waters in France, discussed *Leptomitus lacteus* (Rothert) Agardh. at length, and gave additional information on the distribution of *Saprolegnia, Mucor, Fusarium,* and other moulds and yeasts in the streams of that country. A key was presented for the identification of these fungi.

In Sweden, Stjerna-Pooth (1957) found that *Achlya prolifera* Wees was important in sewage polluted streams. The occurrence and ecology of this fungus were discussed at length.

Coudert and Sáez (1958) at Lyon, France, found several kinds of fungi in public fountains, medical laboratories, apartments, and in industrial wastes. Species found were listed and their habitats discussed briefly.

Branco (1962) in Brazil, based a brief note on the occurrence of fungi in polluted water and sewage on work done largely in North America.

Hynes (1960) recognized the presence of fungi in polluted stream water, but to him these were of little importance, apparently, unless they bloomed out into more or less massive growths indicating a large amount of organic pollution entering the stream in the vicinity.

McKinney (1962) published a text describing the microbiology of sewage treatment. The book is largely a survey of the biochemistry of degradative processes necessary to the removal of organic matter from sewage polluted waters. Introductory chapters summarize information on different kinds of micro-organisms present in sewage treatment systems. Data on each group are highly simplified, assuming that, within bacteria, algae, fungi and protozoa, each species is potentially as important as another, and that each answers the same basic definition of a cell system. In the biochemical process section it is assumed that only certain transformations basic to certain bacterial types are represented. The bases of statements such as that of Bu'loch (used in a discussion abstracted in 1964), to the effect that if one wants a lot of cells produced by relatively uninteresting processes one should go to species like *Escherischia coli* (Migula) Castellani et Chalmers, while if a large number of exciting processes are required one should go to the fungi, are ignored. It is unfortunate that there is still more than a grain of truth in McKinney's statement regarding the 'art' of mycology, but he should remember that a favourite expression of the chemist, the chemical engineer, and the sanitary engineer, used in summarizing information on any chemical or engineering process, is 'state of the art'. The mycologist, likewise, should take McKinney's statement as a goad to increased effort rather than as adverse criticism which may not have been intended.

15.2   Recent Trends in Research on Pollution Fungi

15.2.1   Aquatic Fungi

Few studies have been published in which a definite attempt has been made to correlate the occurrence of aquatic fungi with various levels of pollution in streams. In Europe, Höhnk and Bock (1954), and Höhnk (1956, 1958) surveyed the fungal populations of streams draining small communities in northern Germany. One technique which was introduced was the making of small bags of coarsely woven nylon cloth into which hemp seeds and other baits were placed. These bags were placed in streams and returned to the laboratory after appropriate lengths of exposure. The hemp seeds were transferred to dishes with fresh hemp seeds and the resulting populations of aquatic phycomycetes listed. Except for the work by Suzuki in Japan mentioned by Willoughby (1962), these authors are the only ones found to date who list significant populations of zoosporic fungi from polluted waters.

Harvey (1952) sampled a number of streams in the Little Miami Valley, Ohio, for aquatic fungi. His observations were restricted to Oömycetes recovered by bringing samples of stream water and stream bed materials to the laboratory where they were baited with hemp seed. He found that in streams with no pollution sources good populations of these fungi were recovered. As pollution loads increased, fewer and fewer Oömycetes were recovered. Where pollution consisted of domestic sewage or farmyard drainage, few, if any, Oömycetes were recovered.

Beneke and Schmitt (1961) and Schmitt and Beneke (1962) surveyed populations of uniflagellate and biflagellate phycomycetes off Lower Bass Island, Ohio, in Lake Erie. The list of species recovered did not mention a relationship between this population and the occurrence of polluting materials in Lake Erie.

Cooke and Bartsch (1959, 1960) sampled streams in the Great Miami and Little Miami Valleys, Ohio. Techniques used included bringing samples to the laboratory and baiting with hemp seed, taking hemp seed baits to the stream where they were floated in 'Höhnk nylon bags', or in aluminium tea balls, or exposing a series of baits in the water. These baits were impinged on a wire dowell in a cork stopper in a cylinder of hardware cloth. The baits included a piece of raw beef, a piece of apple, a whole date, and a rose hip in each sampler. It was found that if these samplers are used in an area of relatively high population density some may be disturbed beyond usefulness before they can be returned to the laboratory for replating with new hempseed. No quantitative data were gathered using these techniques. Again, as in the case of Harvey's work, it was found that recovery of aquatic phycomycetes, especially of Oömycetes (chytrids were not studied), was poor in streams carrying organic pollution, but good in streams sampled above the points of introduction of polluting effluents.

Willoughby (1962) studied the occurrence and distribution of saprolegniaceous fungi in freshwater lakes in the Lake District of England. Five or ten aliquots, 1-4 ml each, were incorporated in oatmeal agar, the hardened agar was divided into sectors each of which was placed in a dish of sterile distilled water. During incubation a fringe of growth developed around the margin of the agar sector. A quantitative estimate of the number of zoospores present in the original sample, thus in a litre of sampled water, was obtained. Using this technique it was estimated that at the margin of Windermere Lake were fewer than 25 to 5200 zoospores per litre, at the centre of Windermere Lake there were never more than 100 zoospores per litre with a mean of 11 per litre in the sampling period, and at Wraymires Fish Hatchery estimation figures varied from 400 to 4600 per litre. Seasonal distributions varied. The sampling technique appeared to report zoospores rather than gemmae or oospores. Of the genera found, *Saprolegnia* was the more common.

15.2.2   Geofungi and Aquatic Fungi

Most of the species of fungi assigned to groups of aquatic fungi have zoospores or gametes or both which bear flagella (Kole, 1965). Depending on the type of flagellation they are assigned to three classes. It is estimated (Ingold, 1971) that these species comprise only 2% of the 100 000 species of known fungi.

Cooke's statements (1959 a, 1962 a, 1972), concerning the use of fungi in sewage polluted waters, were developed as a result of studies made on various types of habitats, including streams, and such sewage treatment processes as trickling filters, activated sludge units, and waste stabilization ponds. Physiological studies helped elucidate the ability of some of the fungi found to survive and grow in the presence of selected known factors related to the pollution habitat.

The geofungi (Cooke, 1961 a, 1970 a), more familiarly known as the soil fungi, are without special organs of dissemination (flagella) capable of searching out a special food supply, or without special organs on the spores to aid in anchoring the disseminules or to resist the movement of water. In fact, the principal obvious distinction between true aquatic fungi and geofungi, which have returned to organically enriched waters, is the presence of flagella in the reproductive cells. These fungi reproduce, but poorly, by means of spores in an aquatic environment. Pieces of mycelium as such are not readily identifiable without culturing, and the spore producing structures, as a result of having been developed in an aquatic habitat, are so atypical that the available keys for identification provide little assistance. If the spores of these fungi become embedded in accumulated natural foams, they would be readily overlooked, usually on the basis of size and recognizability.

As the disseminules of these species reach the water of any pond, lake, or stream, especially if a relatively rich nutrient solution formed by organic pollutants is present, growth may take place and the fungus may be added to the biota of the concerned body of water. A number of filamentous geofungi have been isolated from organically enriched streams.

Some filamentous fungi have apparently returned to the aquatic habitat. These fungi rarely exhibit a sexual state and are known as 'aquatic hyphomycetes'. Their spores are adjusted to aquatic production and dispersal (Ranzoni, 1953; Nilsson, 1964; Ingold, 1959, 1971) by shape or by characteristic branching patterns.

According to Garrett (1956) the life cycle of a saprobic fungus living in the soil is as follows: a piece of dead organic matter such as a root, a leaf or stem, etc., comes to rest near a spore of a fungus. Activated in some way by the presence of this nutrient, the fungus spore germinates, the mycelium uses that fraction of the dead organic matter available to it, goes into a resting condition by producing a large number of spores, and the cycle is complete. In any body of water, two types of nutrients are available to the fungi. The first is in the form of solid organic matter in suspension or settling out onto the bottom. Here, if such a fragment and a spore capable of using it are brought together, the cycle described above will become operative. However, dissolved in the water are other nutrients some of which will be readily available to the fungus. Upon germination of the spore, the fungus continues to grow indefinitely in the presence of this continual bath of nutrient materials, no matter how dilute. Depending on the supply of nutrients, and the ability of the fungus to grow indefinitely, a small to large mass of mycelium may develop. Occasionally, this mycelium may sporulate, but such spore production may be atypical. In periods of flood, scouring action of inert materials in the stream bed results in the removal of much, if not all, of this growth. That not completely removed may be used to produce a new mycelial mat, that washed away may come to rest as a single mass or as many small fragments in other parts of the stream bed or on the bank, above the influence of the water. Depending on its ability to adjust to the new conditions of its existence, the mycelium may die, may go into a resting stage, or may continue to live, growing at the expense of dissolved, colloidal, or solid suspended organic matter in the water.

Techniques for the isolation and study of these fungi have been described in the author's Laboratory Guide (Cooke, 1963 a). Other writers have described techniques they have used in their studies.

Within the literature of the aquatic fungi one frequently finds the statement that the habitat is aerobic, and that the concerned fungi require oxygen. However, Tabak and Cooke (1968) have shown that at least 13 species of geofungi (selected at random and including all strains selected) can survive and even grow in the absence of oxygen, in a reduced medium in an atmosphere of prepurified nitrogen gas. Insufficient culture work has been done with the aquatic hyphomycetes to make a statement concerning their oxygen requirements, although it is noted in the literature that at least two species are always associated with anaerobic conditions in their habitat. However, spores are not produced until the substratum in which spores are expected is exposed to the air for a period of time. It is generally assumed that the aquatic hyphomycetes, as well as the aquatic phycomycetes, require well oxygenated habitats.

In relation to oxygen requirements of aquatic phycomycetes, of which members of the Chytridiomycetes and the Oōmycetes have been recovered from sewage polluted waters, specific information is available only for *Aqualinderella fermentans* Emerson et Weston (Emerson and Weston, 1967; Emerson and Held, 1969) which has been isolated from waters carrying high loads of natural organic pollutants. Until recently, the presence of geofungi in bodies of water has been considered an artefact. Students of aquatic mycology have considered geofungi contaminants of the habitat and therefore of their cultures.

Isolations made at regular intervals from a variety of streams and other bodies of water have shown that geofungi can tolerate high levels of organic pollution, low levels of oxygen concentration, or sometimes both. The presence of these geofungi in the aquatic environment may be considered another manifestation of the statement 'Nature abhors a vaccuum' (Spinoza, 1677). A habitat exists in which an apparently adaptable group of organisms does not become established, but this habitat is settled by another group of organisms capable of aggressive and persistent adaptation and colonization. The physiological processes of the geofungi are sufficiently varied and adaptable that an exceedingly wide series of habitats can be successfully colonized.

15.2.3 Streams

Following a description of geofungal populations, isolated from 12 sets of monthly samples taken from four points at each of eight stations on Lytle Creek, Clinton Co., Ohio, a concluding paragraph from Cooke (1961 a) is quoted here: 'Given the proper techniques for sorting out the individual organisms, the different groups of organisms, and the organisms with highly specialized requirements for nutrients or tolerances for microenvironments, each organism can be placed in its proper niche in the picture of the ecology of a stream. Until such techniques are available for geofungi, information can be developed in the laboratory concerning the role of each strain or group of strains in the environment. On this basis we may say that geofungi isolated from the water and stream bed samples from Lytle Creek are contributing to the reduction of organic pollutants in that stream, and that they are probably contributing to the food supplies of larger organisms or of organisms higher in the food chain which may ingest them accidentally or intentionally.'

Plating techniques used for Lytle Creek samples were described by Cooke (1954 b, 1961 a), as were the several types of physical and chemical data taken in the field and laboratory. During the year, a total of 127 species of fungi were isolated. These were distributed according to Table 15.1. It may be of interest to note that the larger number of species were represented by few colonies per species on the isolation plates.

The Bear River, in its cultivated reaches, flows through the Cache Valley of southeastern Idaho and northeastern Utah (Cooke, 1967 a). In addition to the wastes of several small communities, it receives the wastes from a sugar beet processing plant and several canning factories. Two sets of samples from most stations were supplemented by one set of samples from auxiliary stations. Of the 109 species of fungi recovered from all samples, 15 were present in all five major habitat types. Of the others, 41 species were found only once in any of the sampling locations. At the obvious sources of pollution near the head of the valley the number of species recorded from the streams sampled was 40, and only 35 species were recovered from points below the outfall of waste waters in the valley. However, at stations on streams in the valley, after pollution loads had been absorbed, 77 species were recovered. This contrasts with the 44 species recovered from stations above the pollution sources. In general, where larger numbers of species occurred, fewer colonies of any species were found on the primary isolation

Table 15.1   Distribution of fungal species in Lytle Creek, Ohio.

Station*	Pollution status	Number of species
8.7	upper clean water zone	71
7.6	above the sewage treatment plant, below a break in the trunk sewer; upper recovery zone	74
7.2	point of outfall of effluent from the primary-type sewage treatment plant; septic zone	61
6.5	lower septic zone	65
5.2	upper part of lower recovery zone; in warmer seasons supporting a blanket of *Sphaerotilus natans*	60
4.2	middle of lower recovery zone	65
2.8	lower end of recovery zone	75
1.0	lower clean water zone	80
Total number of fungal species:		127

* In miles above mouth of Lytle Creek at Todd's Fork of the Little Miami River.

Twelve sets of samples, taken at monthly intervals; each set from each station included separate samples of: (1) Water, (2) Pool sediments, (3) Riffle sediments, and (4) Bank soil, always moist.

plates. The Bear River flows into the Great Salt Lake, and no samples were collected to determine the lower limits of the effect of polluting substances.

The Cache la Poudre River (Cooke, 1968) flows out of the Rocky Mountains in northern Colorado and joins the South Platte River near Greeley. Two sets of samples on the lower portion, and one set from the mountain portion of the river were tested. The samples yielded 128 species of yeasts and moulds. Stations on relatively undisturbed reaches of the stream, including Poudre Lake, its source at 10 750 ft (3590 m) in the Rocky Mountains in Rocky Mountain National Park, yielded 32 species at its head, and 37 species at its outfall. At two stations on the lower portions of the river, 29 and 37 species were recovered. As the stream left the mountains at Bellvue, it yielded only 37 species of fungi. However, below the Fort Collins sewage treatment plant, and below a sugar beet plant near Greeley, four stations yielded 62, 55, 68, and 64 species. The fact that two sets of samples were tested for the last five stations is not considered to have affected their value significantly.

Stations on three river systems in Ohio and West Virginia carrying acid mine drainage (Cooke, 1967 b) were sampled in three seasons; a total of 196 aquatic phycomycetes, filamentous fungi, and yeasts were recovered. That fungi can readily adapt to a variety of habitat factors, reducing the element of man's surprise at finding species in a wide variety of river bank, soil and sewage samples, is attested to by daily contact in the laboratory. Everyone is familiar with the fact that stock solutions of chemicals are occasionally contaminated by fungus growths, in spite of the presumption that these stock solutions are prepared, stored, and used with the greatest of care for chemical cleanliness. Thus it should not be surprising that a number of fungi have become acclimatised to the acid mine-drainage habitat and that viable cells can be recovered in considerable numbers from water (Fjerdingstad, 1958; Weaver and Nash, 1968), stream bottom sediments, and stream bank soils that have received precipitates and sediments from such waters. Because these waters are continually receiving varying quantities of acids from upstream sources as a result of oxidative processes with or without the aid of bacterial action on the mineral contents of opened coal measures, it is most likely that the fungi themselves can only tolerate the environment rather than decrease the acidity to any great extent by their metabolic activities. Apparently, true fungi are not directly involved in transformations leading to the type of pollution referred to as 'acid mine-drainage', or to reduction of acidity of the habitat in which they can survive and grow.

It should be noted that throughout this review an attempt has been made to rely on Mason and Langenheim's (1957) definition of environment: The environment of any organism is the class composed of the sum of those phenomena that enter a reaction system of the organism or otherwise directly impinge upon it to affect its mode of life at any time throughout its life cycle as ordered by the demands of the ontogeny of the organism or as ordered by any other condition of the organism that alters its environmental demands.' When the word 'environment' is 'employed without qualification it can only mean operational environment as referring to those environmental phenomena that actually enter or have entered a reaction' as usually demonstrable by direct observation or laboratory experimentation.

15.2.4   Trickling Filters

The communities of organisms similar to those occurring on trickling filters have been referred to by Cooke (1956 a) as 'the binding, free-living, and grazing or scouring organisms on trickling filter stone which form three interdependent communities within the periphyton of the Aufwuchs biocoenose of the benthos, and they include both true benthic and facultative benthic-planktonic organisms which may be sessile or sessile attached to the substratum. Those that are sessile attached are true lithobionts, lithophytes or lithozoons, depending on the type of organism under consideration.' In the same paper various methods were described for sampling such populations by exposing artificial bare areas for colonization.

Information on trickling filter populations is limited. Stanbridge (1954, 1955) has discussed the information available to him regarding the development of trickling filter films. These films include such organisms as algae, fungi, bacteria, protozoa and metazoa. Becker and Shaw (1955) observed fungi in decreasing numbers in the effluents of successive processes in sewage treatment plants at Moscow, Idaho and Pullman, Washington. Filter bed slimes were sampled once; from the negative results of microscopic observations and platings it appeared unnecessary to sample this habitat further. Feldman (1955) has listed several fungi from experimental filters at Lawrence, Massachusetts.

Heukelekian and Crosby (1956) made a series of tests to determine rate of slime accumulation on various surfaces under a variety of conditions in sewage carrying channels and in the laboratory. It was observed that the nature and texture of a surface had no ultimate effect on the amount of slime growth, but initially smooth surfaces were less effective than rough. More growth occurred under aerobic than anaerobic conditions. The nature and concentration of food materials affected the production of slime: when food was reduced by artificial dilution or by removal and oxidation, growth increased; growth also increased when glucose and peptone were added. The velocity of the current increased the eventual amount of the attached growth, but inhibited it during the primary period. The slime growth was cyclic: there was an initial lag, a rapid accumulation, a sudden decrease from sloughing, followed by rapid accumulation, and more sloughing.

Moisture, ash and nitrogen content of accumulated slimes corresponded to those of solids collected by settling raw sewage. It was considered that the one percent nitrogen obtained from the growth was too low to be accounted for by cell substance alone, and, therefore, sewage solids were probably embedded in the slimes. In considering the biological characteristics of the slimes, only bacteria and protozoa were emphasized. Flagellates were the most abundant organisms present in the anaerobic exposures, whereas a wide variety of organisms were present under aerobic conditions. Protozoans were dominant in all types of submergence. This type of analysis indicated that only organisms recognizable to an observer through a microscope, or in routine bacterio-logical tests, were considered important.

Various devices have been developed since 1915 for sampling selected portions of complex populations. In a techniques described by Tomlinson (1941), five glass microscope slides 1 x 3.5 in were mounted side by side in photographic frames. These frames were laid on the bed of a stream, and held fast by anchored brass chains. The results from four slides were examined quantitatively for accumulated weight; the fifth was used for identification and enumeration of organisms.

The trickling filter is an ecological tool of the sanitary engineer in the treatment and purification of domestic sewage and industrial wastes. The biota of the trickling filter has received little attention as a working population unit, although various segments of that unit have been described (Cooke, 1959 c), as have types of fungal populations in other parts of the sewage treatment plant (Cooke, 1959 b). In addition, a semiquanti-tative technique for describing yeast populations has been suggested (Cooke, 1965 a).

Each of the 20 filters at the Dayton, Ohio, sewage treatment plant supports a separate community or biocoenose of macro- and micro-organisms. Each of these biocoenoses is independent of the other, except for common sources of inoculum and food materials received separately. Filter sloughings, which become filter sludge, are settled out of the filter effluent in the final basin and returned to the pre-aeration chambers.

For a study to determine the rate of development, and the fungal and algal com-ponents of the slimes on a high-rate and a low-rate trickling filter at the Dayton, Ohio, sewage treatment plant, the technique of slide exposure, modified from that of Tomlinson (1941, 1946), has been presented by Cooke (1956 a, 1958) and by Cooke and Hirsch (1958). It is of interest to note that in Prague the Sládečeks (1963 a, b) compared Cooke's technique of obtaining air dry weights of a slime with a technique of obtaining oven-dry weights of accumulated slimes. They found the two methods to yield statistically comparable results.

The surface film of the high-rate filters under consideration reached a maximum thickness of 2-3 mm during the 57 weeks of observation. This film was teeming with life of many types. It was continuously irrigated by spray from the nozzles of the rotary distributor. If the arms came to a stop or were slowed, as in the case of the low-rate filters on weekends or in periods of light flow, the surface film dried, and then flaked off with the rush of new flow, becoming part of the filter bed effluent.

The community of organisms comprising this film is built up without interference or disturbance from man, except for the manual removal of undesirable elements, such as mosses which may grow around the edge of the filter (Cooke, 1953), flushing or drowning for control of the insect larvae whose adult stages become nuisances, or for major shutdowns.

The community of organisms on any one filter is made up of many types of micro-organisms and a few macroscopic species. These micro-organisms include colonies and filaments of bacteria, colonies of yeasts, filaments of fungi, and colonies and filaments of algae. Moving about through this complex community are a number of different protozoa (of which some may be stalked and thus sessile attached), and nematodes. The larvae of several types of insects, as well as worms and snails which feed upon the slime, complete the population.

The trickling filter supports a man made ecosystem, and few man made ecosystems are truly self sufficient. The trickling filter is built for one purpose, the treatment of sewage by the action of the members of a biota upon it. This biota is independent only as long as sewage is applied to the filter. The development of such a biota is relatively rapid. Its members are derived from populations of surrounding soils, waters, or habitats in which decaying or decomposable materials are present, as well as from sewage.

As a result of fungal colony counts (Fig. 15.1) made from revived growths, a logistic curve (Fig. 15.2) has been developed to describe the rate of development of the population. The more rapid and steeper rise of the curve on a low-rate than on a high-rate filter, is more apparent than real since the same curve is obtained in plotting the lower values of the two curves in parallel, so that no actual difference was noted between the two types of filter.

The functional, factorial description (Major, 1951) of a community can be used to describe the biota of a trickling filter. Climate is relatively uniform for a single filter except in periods of excessive precipitation or run-off. The biotic effects within the community are limited to replacement phenomena, should an organism be unable to

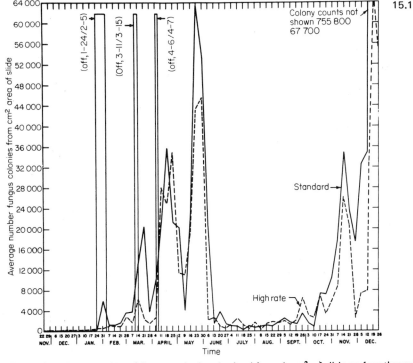

Fig. 15.1. Average number of fungus colonies obtained from 1 cm² of slide surface throughout the study period (from *Sewage and Indust. Wastes,* 30, 138-156, 1958, by permission).

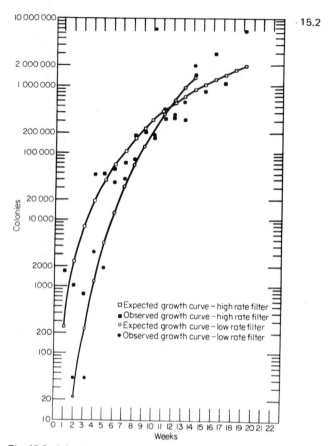

Colonies

Weeks

Fig. 15.2. Colony counts observed and expected under fitted logistic curve (from *Ecology,* 40, 273-291, 1959, by permission).

meet competition, and to the fact that grazing organisms tend to control the rate of population growth. Operational conditions of a specific filter, man's effect on a filter as operator and controller of the process, and the physicochemical nature of the applied sewage would be effective in time, but at the end of a study of samples cumulative up to one year (Fig. 15.3) the effect of time itself had not been completely discerned.

Filter bed populations are effective in removing a large percentage of solid, colloidal and dissolved matter in settled sewage, thus reducing the BOD (biochemical oxygen demand) of that sewage. This removal is not by metabolic processes alone, but by adsorption on the film as well.

Growth on the stones of the filter develops rapidly at first but slows down as the film matures. Points at which such slowing was most noticeable coincided with periods in which the filters were shut down for repair. No correlation between surface growth rate and total weekly precipitation, average weekly air temperature, and average monthly sewage temperature, was noted. Surface growth was not correlated with differences between settled and filtered sewage of ammonia nitrogen, organic nitrogen, chlorides or suspended solids. However, a slight correlation was noted in the case of BOD removal.

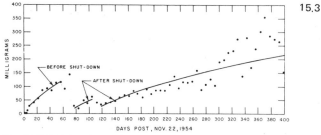

Fig. 15.3. Weight of cumulative growth on frames showing influence of shut downs, and rate of development (from *Ecology*, 40, 273-291, 1959, by permission).

On the whole, the habitat is alpha-mesosaprobic. However, different component organisms vary in their ability to tolerate the conditions to which they are exposed. Species represented most abundantly are lymaphiles (see page 405). Many species, represented by few individuals, are lymaxenes, while the one lymabiont has not been noted elsewhere than on trickling filters. Lymaphobes are not expected in this habitat, although an occasional spore or resting body may be observed.

Surface films on trickling filters or in areas of trickling filters receiving a continuous flow of sewage, appear to have a definite structure (Fig. 15.4). Underlying the mat, and at least partially embedded in the interstices of the porous slag rock, is a layer of fungus mycelium, bacterial cells, algal cells, or bases of filaments and holdfasts, and protozoa including sessile stalked species attached to the stone. From this fundamental

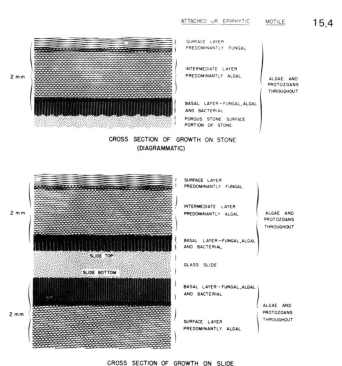

Fig. 15.4. Cross section of growth on stone and slide (from *Sewage and Indust. Wastes* 30, 138-156, 1959, by permission).

layer arises a mass of tissue including fungal and algal filaments, clusters of bacterial cells, fungi, algae, and free-swimming protozoans and nematodes. Overlying this mass of material is another layer of fungal cells through which algae rarely penetrate, but in which bacteria, yeasts and protozoa are found.

In Cooke's experience, the total ecosystem (Fig. 15.5) includes a few photosynthetic algae, but mostly the primary organisms present are dependent on preformed organic matter. Primary decomposers use such materials as food supplies, and may be acted upon by herbivores or carnivores, or may be parasitized. At death, all organisms in the system may be attacked by scavengers or saprobes which act as secondary decomposers whose products are transformed into mineralized nutrients which may re-enter the metabolic system. On the other hand, the populations described by Hawkes (1963) have a somewhat different orientation of the major groups of organisms.

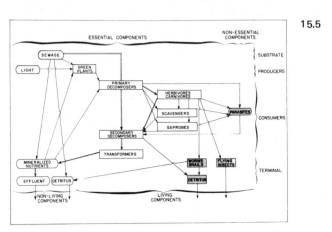

Fig. 15.5. Principal steps and components in the trickling filter ecosystem (from *Ecology*, 40, 273-291, 1959, by permission).

15.2.5   *Activated Sludge*

The organisms in a trickling filter film constitute a fortuitous combination of strains of species which can tolerate the habitat. The same is true of groups of organisms which develop as a community in any sewage treatment system. These organisms may be presumed to be present in the natural environment, or they may be introduced with the polluting substances. The ecosystem, defined by Billings (1964) as the 'energy driven complex of a community of organisms and its controlling environment', develops in response to a drastically modified environment although under certain circumstances the modification may be gradual. Where it develops in response to an especially constructed habitat, such as a sewage treatment system, it may be considered a 'synthetic ecosytem' since the environment is maintained in a constant condition to which the organisms present will remain in adjustment, and the organisms which are continually added may become adjusted quickly if they are to withstand the pressures of competition built up within the existing system. It has been thought by some that a 'starter' is required to get the system going in a new installation. McKinney (1953), and McKinney and Poliakoff (1953) have shown that this is unnecessary.

It has been noted that within the activated sludge treatment system (Cooke, 1970 b), as well as in the pre-aeration tanks of those systems using this device, the walls and other exposed surfaces form a location on which a slime film may develop. Within this

400

film the same organisms are present and active as in a film on a trickling filter. However, this film is insufficient to do an effective job in sewage treatment. In the activated sludge the introduction of air keeps the liquid primary settled sewage continually churned up as it flows through the tanks. The churning process affects the inorganic as well as the organic particles which are present. This brings into suspension, and actively keeps it there, any particulate matter to which organisms which require attachment to a substratum may become adherent.

Within the aquatic habitat are two principal groups of organism: the plankton and the benthos. The *plankton* includes those free-living organisms which float or swim in the water. These organisms occur in oceans, lakes, ponds, streams and other bodies of water. The *benthos* includes those organisms which occur on the bottom of the same types of bodies of water. It is usually attached or dependent upon attached organisms. It may be considered to be extended up the side of structures placed in the water, or on stems or leaves of organisms growing on the bottom of the pond, stream, lake or ocean, and reaching up to the surface, or well above the floor of the body of water. This type of growth is also referred to as Aufwuchs (Cooke, 1956 a). A variety of techniques are available for its study (Sládečková, 1962). By an extension of the meaning of terms, related to an introduced habitat factor, related to the artificial environment developed by man for promotion of the production of an artificial ecosystem, the activated sludge system, so far as the fungi are concerned, may be considered organisms of the benthos, attached to the bottom sediments which would, without the introduction of air streams, remain on the bottom of the tank in which treatment was to take place (Cooke, 1971).

Cooke and Pipes (1970), and Cooke (1970 b, c, 1971), have described populations of fungi which occur in activated sludge. Within limits developed by agitation of the settled sewage, there is little difference between populations found in activated sludge (moving submacroscopic or microscopic inorganic or organic surfaces of particulate matter) and those found on trickling filters (stationary macroscopic stone surfaces).

15.2.6 Waste Stabilization Ponds

The waste stabilization ponds described by Cooke and Matsuura (1969) formed a planned installation designed to treat the sewage and laundry wastes of a small community. Sewage entering the system carried a high load of solids, colloids and dissolved materials exerting a high BOD and carrying a low DO (dissolved oxygen). During the period that the sewage flowed through the ponds it lost 70-80% of its BOD, regaining, especially during the day in the presence of algae, some of its DO (Horning *et al.*, 1964). The solids, colloids and dissolved materials in this sewage constituted an organic enrichment of the habitat. These can act on the fungal cells or spores in the soil as well as those already forming part of the sewage.

Fungi, including filamentous moulds and yeasts, were abundantly present in the waters, sludges and soils of this system, as demonstrated by a number of isolation techniques at least one of which was semiquantitative. Data derived from the use of this technique showed that, depending on the season, the fungi increased as the habitat was enriched with organic wastes. This increase was accompanied by a decrease in BOD, since these organisms used only preformed organic matter as food materials.

It is assumed that the original fungal population of the pond system was derived from that already present in the soil. Cells, spores and hyphae were added regularly with the sewage, and other spores and cells were added regularly by the laundry wastes from the daily washing of farm labourers' uniforms. In addition, spores and

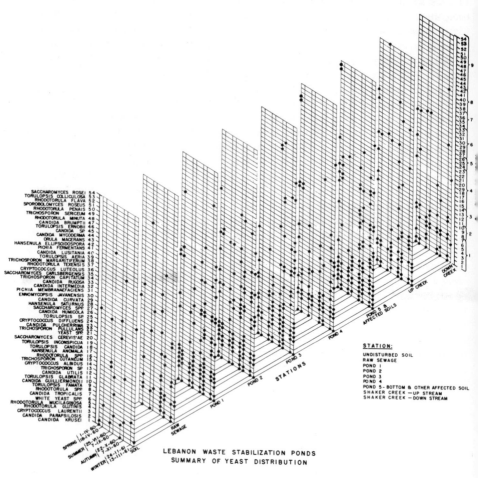

Fig. 15.6. Summary of distribution of yeast species, Lebanon, Ohio, waste stabilization pond system (from *Protoplasma*, 57, 163-187, 1963, by permission).

disseminules from the normal air spora fallout were probably added to these populations.

A population of slightly more than 5000 cells/g dry weight in the subsoil forming the bottom of the ponds was present before sewage was added. Following the initial trials this population was built up to about 24 000 viable cells per gram dry weight of the pond sediments. Following a quiescent period, in which the bottoms of the ponds were designed to hold water more effectively, sewage was regularly added and population studies initiated. In the spring sampling, an average of 250 000 cells of fungi per gram dry weight of sludges and liquids was present; in the summer sampling period this increased to 265 000 cells; by autumn this value decreased to 100 000 cells; and by the following March it had built up again to 990 000 cells. These cells represented at the beginning of the study some 40 species, by the end of the study this number had increased to 212.

Aside from indicating that potentially initial populations of the area, represented by undisturbed soil and raw sewage, are different, and that populations found on the two stations on Shaker Creek are different from each other and from populations in the main stabilization pond area, similarity coefficient analyses yielded no significant information. This is partially because of insufficient sampling, partly because of the nature of the basic food materials (sewage), and the nature of the introduced populations accompanying the sewage.

Although fungal populations were obviously active in all parts of the system, it is not obvious in what life form these organisms occurred. Yeasts (Fig. 15.6) were probably present as colonies or separate cells, just as were many of the bacteria. The filamentous fungi, including more of the species occurring in semiquantitative studies, were probably present as filaments of fungus tissue. In a mass of sludge, the filaments can grow onto a second food source as the first one becomes exhausted. While bacteria and probably yeasts are present in the waters and possibly the sludges in large numbers, there is no indication of the relative amount of food supplies each organism in each habitat is able to remove from that habitat.

Cooke et al. (1956) showed that at the pH levels found in the ponds fungi alone utilize weak nutrients (300 ppm glucose-glutamic acid) more slowly than do sewage seed, or a mixture of fungal cells and sewage seed (which includes fungal cells), as measured by the decrease of BOD in a 10 day laboratory culture. Since fungal growth occurred in both types of culture to which fungi were added, problems of competitive advantage were probably overcome by the nature of the groups of organisms involved. In the waste stabilization ponds, except for November when adverse conditions of undetermined nature (possibly related to wastes added to the ponds) reduced the fungal populations, the numbers of viable cells indicate a favourable habitat for fungi. On this basis, it appears that fungi can be counted among those saprobic organisms that play a part in the degradation, and thus the removal, of organic wastes from the waters of waste stabilization ponds.

15.2.7   Fungi in Sludge Digestion

Fungi, including yeasts and moulds, are present (Cooke, 1966) in the process of the digestion of sludges in sewage treatment systems. These organisms can be demonstrated by their culture from samples of sludges in a variety of media. The approximate minimal number of cells present in digesting sludges can be determined (Fig. 15.7). After three complete turnovers of digesting sludges, with a retention time of 16 days for each turnover, the yeasts and moulds still present in considerable numbers in draw-out samples indicate that they may be taking part in the digestion process to the extent of obtaining nutrients for growth, rather than being merely present in a quiescent state.

Following the development of a stable sludge digestion system, many yeasts and moulds are present. The use of sterile and non-sterile fishmeal, as a substitute for sewage solids, furnished an adequate substrate for the growth of filamentous fungi and for maintenance of a sludge, which was still adequately digesting after more than seven complete turnovers.

The presence of large numbers of viable cells at the end of more than seven complete turnovers (Fig. 15.8), even though the total initial population was reduced by a factor of about 3000, indicates that filamentous fungi can grow and multiply in an anaerobic digester. The extent of their importance in sludge digestion has not been determined. However, it has been demonstrated that more fungal activity occurs in sludge digestion than has been suspected by sanitary engineers, chemists and microbiologists.

Since a sludge digester has no measurable oxygen, and thus is presumably anaerobic,

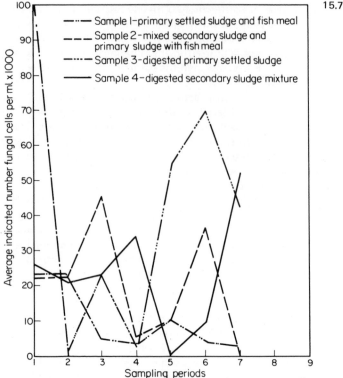

Fig. 15.7. Average minimal number of cells based on indicated number of fungus cells (including yeasts) in YNB-glucose broth, by inspection, for each sampling period during three complete turnovers, per ml (x 1000). Experiment 1 (from 20th Purdue Industrial Wastes Conference, 6-17, 1966, by permission).

and since fungi are thought to be strict aerobes, Tabak and Cooke (1968) tested the ability of 13 species of filamentous fungi and yeasts to grow in a reduced medium in an atmosphere of 100% prepurified N_2 gas. At the end of four weeks, all cultures tested had added weight as determined by oven dry weights of mycelium, and all used carbon from sugars in the medium.

15.3 Saprobic Valency of Fungi

The language of decay or deterioration is not a completely satisfactory one. However, in discussing aspects of deterioration related to pollution, certain words have become used to the extent that their meaning has become traditionalized in the thinking of those who deal with the populations of polluted waters and sewage. According to *Webster's Third International Dictionary,* 'saprobic' or 'saprophytic' means 'living in or being in an environment rich in organic matter and relatively free from oxygen (e.g. organisms living in sewage)'. If one thinks only of the faecal portion of sewage he could substitute 'lyma-' for 'sapro-' as the prefix in either word, or if one thinks of an organism living on or in dung he could substitute the prefix 'copro-'. For a long time the term 'saprophyte', or its more recent form 'saprobe' has been in use for those organisms such as fungi and nonchlorophyllous vascular plants, which live in and

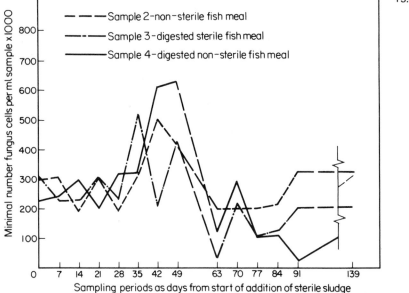

Fig. 15.8. Minimal number of cells of all fungi per ml sample based on indicated number in shaken flask culture in YNB-glucose broth (x 1000). Experiment 2 (from 20th Purdue Industrial Wastes Conference, 6-17, 1966, by permission).

produce decay of wood and leaves of the forest floor. While many of the same fungi, as well as a few others, live on and produce decay in sewage and polluted waters, the habitat is much more restrictive. In presenting the list of fungi known from sewage and polluted waters (Cooke, 1957 a) saprobic valency evaluations were included for each of the 147 species of fungi listed from 891 samples tested up to that time.

The original work on the saprobic system for describing the ecology of plants and animals in streams was published by Kolkwitz and Marsson (1908). It was summarized briefly and brought up to date by Kolkwitz (1950). Four species of fungi are included among the alpha-mesosaprobes, together with fair lists of bacteria, and lengthy lists of algae for all saprobic classes in the latter work.

An organism can become adapted to one set of environmental conditions or another (Cooke, 1957 d). In some cases the adaptation may be complete, so that the organism cannot tolerate any other condition, but more often various degrees of adaptation may be attained by an organism. A set of suffixes proposed by Moser (1949) for fungi growing in burned areas has been adopted for this use. Since 'copro-' has been used commonly in the combination 'coprophilous' for a fungus growing on dung, it might be confusing to use it in the set of terms wanted. The Greek word 'lyma' means 'filth'. *Lymabiont* species will grow on or in the presence of faecal materials; *lymaphilous* species will grow commonly on such materials but will also grow on other materials; *lymaxenous* species will grow commonly on other materials but will tolerate faecal materials; while *lymaphobous* species will not grow on or in the presence of faecal materials. The emphasis here is on nutrition tolerances or requirements, rather than on habitat types or tolerances as is the emphasis on the Kolkwitz (1950) system. It should be noted that the *lyma-* terms have been extended to

405

cover, at least in some instances, habitats rich in organic matter, usually added by man.

To equate this set of terms with those of Kolkwitz (1950), and Kolkwitz and Marsson (1908), the following parallels are suggested. Polysaprobes would include both lymabionts and lymaphiles. For use in connection with fungi, polysaprobe would be confusing since it implies the ability to live saprobically on any substrate. Alpha (or strong) mesosaprobes would include lymaphiles primarily, but lymabionts and lymaxenes could be expected to be found. Beta (or weak) mesosaprobes would include lymaphiles but lymaxenes could be found more frequently than in the preceding categories. Oligosaprobes would include the lymaphobes and probably some lymaxenes and lymaphiles.

Sládeček (1963) in Prague listed and illustrated 830 limnosaprobic plants and animals. Limnosaprobity classes for sewage polluted waters were the same as those established by Kolkwitz and Marsson, except that the cleanest water was separated out of oligosaprobity and referred to as xenosaprobity. According to the Standard Methods devised for the Council for Mutual Economic Assistance countries (Anon, 1968), numerical values can be derived from stream biota and pollution data for the determination of degrees of saprobity of sites being studied. These were refined (Sládeček, 1966, 1969) and, on the basis of criteria used, 13 degrees of saprobity were recognized. Where applicable, numerical bases for determining the values for assignment were suggested. Katharobity refers only to those waters falling under 'standard methods' definitions of potable water. Three types of radiosaprobity are recognized and their definition is left to specialized laboratories. Antisaprobity refers to toxicity in the strict sense, conditions which inactivate or kill all members of a biota. Cryptosaprobity refers to the action of various physical properties of the water. These three types of saprobity are grouped under the general term transsaprobity which contrasts with limnosaprobity and eusaprobity. Five degrees of limnosaprobity, in decreasing order of quality, include xenosaprobity, the cleanest natural water, oligosaprobity, relatively clean water, alpha-mesosaprobity, beta-mesosaprobity, and polysaprobity, including increasing degrees of pollution as also understood in the Kolkwitz and Marsson system. Four categories of eusaprobity refer more to industrial wastes than to domestic sewage pollution. These include isosaprobity, dominated by ciliates, metasaprobity, dominated by flagellates, hypersaprobity referred to by Fjerdingstad as the coprozoic zone and dominated by bacteria and fungi, and ultrasaprobity, an abiotic (but not related to toxicity) zone. The saprobity index is based on a scale of abundance values and can be plotted for the nine types of saprobity considered in limnosaprobity and eusaprobity. These can then be compared with other numerical indices such as the 5-day BOD, the coliform index, and the psychrophilic bacteria index. It should be noted that in this case psychrophilic bacteria are those cultured at $20°C$, apparently in contrast with those cultured usually at $37°C$.

Fjerdingstad (1960, 1964) surveyed the literature referring to different systems for classification of micro- and macro-organisms, as well as their aquatic habitats, with special reference to benthic communities. In his final evaluation (Fjerdingstad, 1964, 1971) of the available terms based on their usefulness for the description of populations and habitats of rivers in Denmark, he chose the following groups of terms: saprobiontic organisms occurring only in the most heavily polluted waters; saprophilic organisms, generally found in polluted waters, but also within other biotopes and consequently, within certain limits, indifferent; saproxenic organisms generally found in other, non-polluted biotopes, but which may thrive even in the presence of pollution; saprophobic organisms, which cannot live in polluted water. Note that to include fungi in a system using some of these terms involves a contradiction since only the most obligate parasite would be saprophobic.

Two zones were recognized for industrial pollution, the chemotoxic zone where chemicals toxic to all organisms occur, and the chemobiontic zone with special types of populations dependent on the types of organisms present and their response to the particular organic or inorganic chemical pollution found.

Communities can be described on the basis of dominant or subdominant species, and these species can be considered without necessarily referring to other species present.

The habitat can be described according to the Kolkwitz and Marsson system but with additional zones which seem to be needed at least for Danish streams: I the coprozoic zone comprising undiluted faecal matter as well as domestic sewage before entering a treatment plant; II, III and IV, the alpha-, beta- and gamma-mesosaprobic zones; VIII the oligosaprobic zone; and IX the katharobic zone.

Fjerdingstad (1965) listed 182 species of bacteria, algae (all classes), and fungi (three species), which he had studied in the waters of Denmark. For each species he gave a thorough review of the habitats from which they were reported in North America and Europe, and he concluded the discussion of each species with a statement concerning its saprobic valency.

The determination of to which organisms the terms proposed by Cooke (1957 a) should be applied is still highly subjective. One technique is to adopt a system similar to the one of Sládeček (1969), or one proposed by Palmer (1969) for the algae. Following Palmer, a series of literature citations is used in which fungi have been reported from a variety of habitats, all of which have been modified in one way or another by the addition of organic wastes. Of course, the basic group of papers is a

Table 15.2 Numbers of species of fungi recovered from sewage and polluted waters by observation number.

Observation number	Number of species
1	412
2	106
3	55
4	32
5	29
6	22
7	25
8	20
9	22
10	10
11-100	165
101-2022	52
Total	950

series of 39 by the writer and his colleagues which were brought together in a volume entitled *Our Mouldy Earth* (Cooke, 1970 a).

The number of times a colony of a species appeared on primary isolation plates, or in primary isolation flasks, in Cooke's studies, together with the number of times the species was reported in the literature, including, where possible, colony counts, or numerical estimates of importance, is a value which is called the 'observation number'. No attempt has been made to correct identifications published by others except to correlate synonymies where obvious discrepancies occurred. The resulting list includes the numbers given in Table 15.2.

There is no problem in deciding that *Subbaromyces splendens* Hesseltine is a lymabiont since it has never been reported except from slimes on trickling filters. However, it is represented by only 25 observation numbers. This does not mean that all species represented by 25 or more observation numbers are lymabionts. Likewise it is not difficult to decide that all species not represented on this list of 950 species of fungi are lymaphobes, and that probably 412 of them, those represented to date by only one observation number, fall into this category. As time goes on and more and more isolations are made, more species will appear on the list, some of these 412 species will advance to other positions in the list, and other species will also advance in the list. In advancing, some species will be overtaken, none will be replaced unless the lower limit for lymaphiles and lymaxenes is modified.

For present purposes, subject to change as additional observations are made, and lists are prepared and published, lymaxenes are considered to be those species with observation numbers between and including 2 and 10. Thus all those species having been observed and reported more than 10 times, as well as possibly a few others, are considered to be lymaphiles, fungi preferring a polluted or organically enriched habitat. Many other fungi could be added to this list, such as all those fungi commonly associated with agricultural soils, as contrasted with unfertilized natural or wild soils, and those fungi commonly associated with the deterioration of organic matter represented by products of man's industry in the areas of textiles, building materials, foods and related products. At present no qualitative statement concerning distribution reported in the systematic monographic literature is considered in this analysis.

A list of these lymabiont and lymaphile fungi, arranged alphabetically according to classes, is presented in Table 15.3, together with brief notes on distribution. Observation numbers, the basis for inclusion of the fungi in the list, are given for each species.

Park (1972 a, b) has added another dimension to the study of geofungi occurring in stream bottom materials. Following an assessment of techniques for the study of this habitat, he develops a classification of heterotrophic micro-organisms resident in water. Those species appearing as 'permanent' residents are 'indwellers' while the others are 'immigrants'. If an organism demonstrates a regular pattern of movement from aquatic to non-aquatic habitats it is 'migrant' with 'periodic' presence in water: if the pattern of movement is 'irregular' the organism is considered a 'versatile'. Four levels of activity are suggested. 'Transients' demonstrate 'no activity'. 'Residents' demonstrate one or more of the remaining three levels: versatiles have only 'sporadic' activity, migrants may have 'periodic' or 'sporadic' activity, and indwellers have, in addition to these two, 'constant' activity. Substrate activity, nutrition and site relationships are important areas for study to clarify these habitat relationships. Problems of succession and periodicity are important and may be developed as populations and the activities of their component species become better understood.

Table 15.3   Lymabiont and lymaphile fungi in sewage and polluted waters

Observation number	Species	Distribution in pollution reports	Reported species distribution
	Chytridiomycetes		
30	Chytridium spp.	Europe	Europe, Africa, Manchuria
65	Olpidium luxurians (Tomaschek) Fischer	Europe	Europe, Africa, Manchuria
82	Olpidium pendulum Zopf	Europe	U.S., Europe, Africa
25	Phlyctochytrium spp.	Europe	
19	Phlyctochytrium biporosum Couch	Europe	U.S., Europe, Africa
39	Phlyctochytrium equale Atkinson	Europe	U.S.
90	Phlyctochytrium hallii Couch	Europe	U.S., Japam
11	Phlyctochytrium laterale Sparrow	Europe	Europe
25	Phlyctochytrium vernale (Zopf) de Wildman	Europe	Europe
27	Rhizophidium spp.	U.S., Europe	
13	Rhizophidium gibbosum (Zopf) Fischer	Europe	U.S., Europe
73	Rhizophidium globosum (Braun) Rabenhorst	Europe	U.S., Europe, Africa, Japan
40	Rhizophidium pollinis-pini (Braun) Zopf	Europe	U.S., South America, Cuba, Europe
15	Rhizophidium sphaerotheca Zopf	Europe	U.S., South America, Europe, Africa
22	Synchytrium spp.	Europe	
	Oömycetes		
32	Achlya spp.	U.S., Europe, Japan	
20	Achlya americana Humphrey	U.S.	U.S., Europe, Japan
19	Achlya klebsiana Pieters	U.S., Europe	U.S., Europe
11	Aphanomyces spp.	Europe, Japan	
13	Brevilegnia diclina J. V. Harvey	U.S., Europe	U.S., Europe
57	Dictyuchus spp.	U.S., Europe	
12	Dictyuchus monosporus Leitgeb.	U.S., Europe	U.S., Europe, Japan

Table 15.3 Lymabiont and lymaphile fungi in sewage and polluted waters—contd.

Observation number	Species	Distribution in pollution reports	Reported species distribution
27	*Leptomitus lacteus* (Rothert) Agardh	U.S., Europe, Japan	cosmopolitan
233	*Pythium* spp.	U.S., Europe, Japan	
17	*Pythium debaryanum* Hesse	U.S., Europe	cosmopolitan
16	*Pythium elongatum* Matthews	Europe	U.S.
51	*Pythium inflatum* Matthews	Europe	U.S.
56	*Pythium monospermum* Pringsheim	Europe	U.S., Europe, Japan, Java, India
28	*Pythium proliferum* de Bary	Europe	U.S., Europe, Australia
23	*Pythium pulchrum* von Minden	Europe	U.S., Europe
15	*Pythium ultimum* Trow	U.S., Europe	cosmopolitan
48	*Saprolegnia ferax* (Gruithausen) Thöret	U.S., Europe	cosmopolitan
11	*Saprolegnia littoralis* Coker	U.S.	U.S., Europe
11	*Thaustotheca clavata* (de Bary) Humphrey	U.S., Europe	U.S., Europe, Japan
	Zygomycetes		
13	*Absidia glauca* Hagem	U.S., Europe	U.S., Canada, Central America, Europe, Israel, Australia
17	*Absidia spinosa* Lendner var. *spinosa*	U.S.	widespread
21	*Cunninghamella elegans* Lendner	U.S.	North America, Europe, Japan, Israel, India, Nigeria
20	*Gongronella butleri* (Lendner) Peyronel et Dal Vasco		widespread
14	*Mortierella* spp.	U.S.	
11	*Mortierella minutissima* van Tieghem	U.S.	Mexico, Europe, Japan
450	*Mucor* spp.	U.S., Europe	
80	*Mucor alternans* van Tieghem	U.S.	U.S., Europe, Japan, India, Israel
32	*Mucor angulisporus* Naumov	U.S.	Mexico, Europe, Japan
332	*Mucor fragilis* Bainier	U.S., Japan	U.S., Canada, Europe, India, Iraq, Tunis,

No.	Species		
353	*Mucor hiemalis* Wehmer	U.S., Europe	cosmopolitan
91	*Mucor plumbeus* Bonorden	U.S.	cosmopolitan
30	*Mucor racemosus* Fresenius	U.S., Europe	cosmopolitan
25	*Mucor ramannianus* A. Möller	U.S.	widespread
293	*Rhizopus* spp.	U.S.	
46	*Rhizopus arrhizus* Fischer	U.S.	widespread
21	*Rhizopus nigricans* Ehrenberg	U.S., Europe, Japan	cosmopolitan
29	*Syncephalastrum racemosum* (Cohn) Schröter	U.S.	U.S., Central America, Europe, Japan, Java, India
189	*Zygorhynchus moelleri* Vuillemin	U.S., Europe	widespread
	Ascomycetes		
16	*Hansenula californica* (Lodder) Wickerham	U.S.	U.S., Canada, Mexico, Europe, Japan, New Zealand, Australia
19	*Metschnikowia pulcherrima* Pitt et Miller *Candida pulcherrima* (Lindner) Windisch	U.S., Canada	United States, South America, Europe, Japan
78	*Saccharomyces cerevisiae* (Meyen ex Reess) Hansen	U.S., Canada, Europe	cosmopolitan
63	*Chaetomium funicola* M. C. Cooke	U.S., Japan	U.S., Canada, Europe, Japan, India, Africa
11	*Emericellopsis humicola* (Cain) Gilman	U.S., Central America	Canada, Central America
41	*Eupenicillium javanicum* (Beyma) Stolk et Scott	U.S.	Central America, South America, Japan, Java, India
82	*Penicillium javanicum* Beyma *Eurotium amstelodami* Mangin *Aspergillus amstelodami* (Mangin) Thom et Church	U.S.	U.S., South America, Europe, Japan, India, Africa

Table 15.3 Lymabiont and lymaphile fungi in sewage and polluted waters—contd.

Observation number	Species	Distribution in pollution reports	Reported species distribution
91	*Eurotium chevalieri* Mangin *Aspergillus chevalieri* (Mangin) Thom et Church	U.S.	U.S., Brazil, Europe, Japan, Africa
38	*Petriellidium boydii* (Shear) Malloch *Allescheria boydii* Shear *Monosporium apiospermum* Saccardo *Scedosporium apiospermum* (Saccardo) Vuillemin	U.S.	widespread
548	*Sartorya fumigata* (Fresenius) Vuillemin *Aspergillus fumigatus* Fresenius	U.S., Europe	cosmopolitan
25	*Subbaromyces splendens* Hesseltine	U.S.	U.S.
13	*Talaromyces stipitatus* (Thom) C. R. Benjamin *Penicillium stipitatum* Thom	U.S.	U.S., Europe, Japan, Iraq
	Fungi Imperfecti		
	Sphaeropsidales		
56	*Coniothyrium* spp.	U.S., Europe	
17	*Coniothyrium fuckelii* Saccardo	U.S.	U.S., Canada, Europe
434	*Phoma* spp.	U.S., Canada	
110	*Phoma herbarum* Westendorp	U.S.	cosmopolitan
	Moniliales (Imperfect Yeasts)		
183	*Candida* spp.	U.S., Europe	
17	*Candida catenulata* Diddens et Lodder	U.S.	Puerto Rico
75	*Candida curvata* (Diddens et Lodder) Lodder et Kreger-van Rij	U.S.	U.S., Europe

	Species		
130	*Candida guilliermondii* (Castellani) Langeron et Guerra var. *guilliermondii*	U.S., Canada	U.S., South America, Europe, Japan, Mozambique
59	*Candida humicola* (Daszewska) Diddens et Lodder	U.S.	U.S., Europe, Japan
75	*Candida intermedia* (Ciferri et Ashford) Langeron et Guerra	U.S.	Puerto Rico, Europe, South Africa
480	*Candida krusei* (Castellani) Berkhout	U.S.	U.S., South America, Europe, Japan, Africa
11	*Candida lambica* (Lindner et Genoud) van Uden et Buckley	U.S.	United States, Europe, Japan
11	*Candida melinii* Diddens et Lodder	U.S.	Europe, Japan
290	*Candida parapsilosis* (Ashford) Langeron et Talice	U.S.	U.S., Puerto Rico, Dominican Republic, Europe
17	*Candida rugosa* (Anderson) Diddens et Lodder	U.S.	U.S., Europe, Japan, New Zealand
153	*Candida tropicalis* (Castellani) Berkhout	U.S., Canada	United States, Europe, Japan, Ceylon
34	*Candida utilis* (Henneberg) Lodder et Kreger-van Rij	U.S.	U.S., Europe
62	*Cryptococcus albidus* (Saito) Skinner var. *albidus*	U.S., Canada	U.S., Canada, Europe, Antarctica, Japan, Chile, Mauritius
35	var. *aerius* (Saito) Phaff et Fell	U.S.	Japan, New Zealand
44	var. *diffluens* (Zaxk) Phaff et Fell	U.S.	U.S., Canada, Europe
93	*Cryptococcus laurentii* (Keufferath) Skinner var. *laurentii*	U.S.	widespread
34	*Cryptococcus luteolus* (Saito) Skinner	U.S.	Bahamas, Japan, New Guinea
20	*Kloeckera apiculata* (Reess em. Kloecker) Janke	U.S.	U.S., Europe, Japan
779	*Rhodotorula* spp.	U.S., Europe	
234	*Rhodotorula glutinis* (Fresenius) Harrison var. *glutinis*	U.S., Canada	U.S., Canada, Europe, Japan, Antarctica

413

Table 15.3 Lymabiont and lymaphile fungi in sewage and polluted waters—contd.

Observation number	Species	Distribution in pollution reports	Reported species distribution
15	*Rhodotorula minuta* (Saito) Harrison		
15	var. *minuta*	U.S., Canada	U.S., Europe, Japan, Antarctica, Bahamas
59	var. *texensis* (Phaff. Mrak et Williams) Phaff et Ahearn	U.S.	U.S., Europe, Japan, Bahamas, South Africa
505	*Rhodotorula rubra* (Demme) Lodder	U.S., Canada	United States, Canada, Europe, Japan, Madagascar
54	*Torulopsis* spp.	U.S.	
331	*Torulopsis candida* (Saito) Lodder	U.S., Canada	Europe, Japan, Australia
22	*Torulopsis dattila* (Kluyver) Lodder	U.S.	Europe
103	*Torulopsis glabrata* (Anderson) Lodder et de Vries	U.S., Canada	U.S., Europe, Japan, India, South America
16	*Torulopsis holmii* (Joergensen) Lodder	U.S.	U.S., Europe
25	*Torulopsis versatilis* (Etchells et Bill) Lodder et Kreger-van Rij	U.S.	
303	*Trichosporon* spp.	U.S.	
54	*Trichosporon capitatum* Diddens et Lodder	U.S., Europe, South Africa	Europe, South Africa
183	*Trichosporon cutaneum* (de Buermann, Gougerot et Vaucher) Ota var. *cutaneum*	U.S., Canada, Europe	U.S., Europe, Indonesia, Korea, Puerto Rico, Dominican Rep.
25	*Trichosporon pullulans* (Lindner) Diddens et Lodder	United States	Europe, Japan, Antarctica, Australia
	Moniliales (Filamentous fungi)		
684	*Alternaria alternata* (Fries) Keissler	U.S., Europe	cosmopolitan
165	*Aspergillus* spp.	U.S., Europe	
54	*Aspergillus candidus* Link ex Thom et Church	U.S. Europe	South America, Europe, Japan, Africa

(82)	*Aspergillus amstelodami*—see *Eurotium amstelodami*	
(91)	*Aspergillus chevalieri*—see *Eurotium chevalieri*	
19	*Aspergillus carneus* (van Tieghem) Blochwitz ex Thom et Church	U.S., South America
43	*Aspergillus clavatus* Desmazières	U.S.
99	*Aspergillus flavipes* (Bainier et Sartory) Thom et Church	U.S.
405	*Aspergillus flavus* Link ex Link	U.S., Europe
(548)	*Aspergillus fumigatus*—see *Sartorya fumigata*	
635	*Aspergillus niger* van Tieghem	U.S., Europe
293	*Aspergillus ochraceus* Wilhelm	U.S., Europe
32	*Aspergillus restrictus* G. Smith	U.S.
199	*Aspergillus sydowii* (Banier et Sartory) Thom et Church	U.S.
26	*Aspergillus tamarii* Kita	U.S.
82	*Aspergillus terreus* Thom var. *terreus*	U.S.
86	*Aspergillus ustus* (Bainier) Thom et Church var. *ustus*	U.S.
446	*Aspergillus versicolor* (Vuillemin) Tiroboschi	U.S.
21	*Aspergillus wentii* Wehmer	U.S., Europe
838	*Aureobasidium pullulans* (de Bary) Arnaud	U.S., Canada, Europe
23	*Beauvaria bassiana* (Balsano) Vuillemin	U.S.
14	*Botryotrichum piluliferum* Saccardo et Marchal	U.S.
11	*Botrytis cinerea* Persoon ex Fries	U.S., Europe
601	*Cephalosporium* spp.	U.S., Canada, Europe
24	*Chrysosporium pannorum* (Link) Hughes	U.S.

U.S, Cuba, Central America, Europe, India, Africa, New Zealand	
cosmopolitan	
cosmopolitan	
cosmopolitan	
cosmopolitan	
widespread	
U.S., Europe, Japan, Malaya, Africa, Java	
cosmopolitan	
North and South America, Europe, Japan, China, India, Africa, New Guinea	
cosmopolitan	
cosmopolitan	
cosmopolitan	
cosmopolitan	
cosmopolitan	
widespread	
U.S., Canada, Europe, Egypt, Japan	
U.S., Canada, Europe, Japan, India, Africa	
probably ubiquitous	

Table 15.3 Lymabiont and lymaphile fungi in sewage and polluted waters—contd.

Observation number	Species	Distribution in pollution reports	Reported species distribution
1142	*Cladosporium cladosporioides* (Fresenius) de Vries	U.S.	cosmopolitan
59	*Cladosporium herbarum* (Persoon) Link	U.S., Europe	cosmopolitan
23	*Colletotrichum destructivum* O'Gara	U.S.	cosmopolitan
13	*Curvularia geniculata* (Tracy et Earle) Boedijn	U.S.	widespread
93	*Curvularia lunata* (Wakker) Boedijn	U.S.	cosmopolitan
29	*Doratomyces stemonitis* (Persoon ex Fries) Morton et Smith	U.S., South America, Europe, Japan	North and South America, Europe, Japan
212	*Epicoccum purpurascens* Ehrenberg ex Schlechtendahl	U.S., Europe	cosmopolitan
194	*Fusarium* spp.	U.S., Europe	
25	*Fusarium acuminatum* Ellis et Everhart	U.S.	widespread
857	*Fusarium aquaeductuum* Lagerheim var. *medium* Wollenweber	U.S., Europe, Japan	U.S., Bermuda, Europe
16	*Fusarium herbarum* (Corda) Fries	Europe	Europe
16	*Fusarium moniliforme* Sheldon var. *moniliforme*	U.S., Europe	widespread
529	*Fusarium oxysporum* Schlechtendahl	U.S., Europe	worldwide
96	*Fusarium roseum* Link ex Fries em. Synder et Hansen		
122	*Fusarium solani* (Martius) Appel et Wollenweber	U.S.	widespread
2015	*Geotrichum candidum* Link ex Persoon	U.S., Europe	worldwide
19	*Gilmaniella humicola* Barron	U.S., Europe, Japan	cosmopolitan
59	*Gliocladium* spp.	U.S.	cosmopolitan
71	*Gliocladium catenulatum* Gilman et Abbott	U.S.	U.S., Canada, Central America, Europe, India, Australia

55	*Gliocladium deliquescens* Sopp	U.S.	U.S., Europe, Japan, Pakistan, Australia
46	*Gliocladium fimbriatum* Gilman et Abbott	U.S.	U.S., Europe, China, Pakistan, Ceylon
340	*Gliocladium roseum* (Link) Bainier	U.S., Europe	U.S., Canada, Europe, Japan, Australia
67	*Gliomastix murorum* (Corda) Hughes var. *felina* (Marchal) Hughes	U.S.	widespread
34	*Graphium* spp.	U.S.	
22	*Humicola grisea* Traaen	U.S.	cosmopolitan
14	*Monilia sitophila* (Montagne) Saccardo	U.S., Europe	U.S., Canada, Europe, Japan
132	*Myrothecium verrucaria* (Albertini et Schweinitz Ditmars et Fries	U.S., Europe	U.S., Canada, Europe, China, Iraq
12	*Nigrospora sphaerica* (Saccardo) Mason	U.S., Japan	cosmopolitan
15	*Oidiodendron cerealis* (Thümen) Barron	U.S.	Canada, Europe
124	*Paecilomyces* spp.	U.S.	
17	*Paecilomyces elegans* (Corda) Mason et Hughes in Hughes	U.S.	U.S., Europe, Japan, Malaya, Africa
43	*Paecilomyces marquandii* (Mason) Hughes	U.S.	U.S., Europe, Japan, Ceylon
169	*Paecilomyces varioti* Bainier	U.S., Europe	cosmopolitan
2022	*Penicillium* spp.	U.S., Canada, Europe, Japan	
13	*Penicillium canescens* Sopp	U.S.	U.S., Europe, Japan
25	*Penicillium charlesii* Smith	U.S.	cosmopolitan
161	*Penicillium chrysogenum* Thom	U.S.	worldwide
41	*Penicillium commune* Thom	U.S.	U.S., Europe, Japan
16	*Penicillium corylophilum* Dierckx	U.S.	widely distributed
29	*Penicillium corymbiferum* Westling	U.S.	U.S., Europe, Japan, Africa
11	*Penicillium crustosum* Thom	U.S.	worldwide
23	*Penicillium cyclopium* Westling var. cyclopium	U.S.	
25	*Penicillium decumbens* Thom	U.S., Europe	worldwide
66	*Penicillium expansum* Link ex Thom	U.S., Europe	probably worldwide
18	*Penicillium fellutanum* Biourge	U.S., Europe	worldwide
18	*Penicillium fellutanum* Biourge	U.S.	cosmopolitan
34	*Penicillium frequentens* Westling	U.S., Europe	cosmopolitan

417

Table 15.3   Lymabiont and lymaphile fungi in sewage and polluted waters—contd.

Observation number	Species	Distribution in pollution reports	Reported species distribution
608	*Penicillium funiculosum* Thom	U.S.	worldwide
84	*Penicillium herquei* Bainier et Sartory	U.S.	widely distributed
19	*Penicillium implicatum* Biourge	U.S.	cosmopolitan
261	*Penicillium janthinellum* Biourge	U.S., Europe	cosmopolitan
(41)	*Penicillium javanicum—see Eupenicillium javanicum*		
23	*Penicillium kapuscinskii* Zaleski	U.S., Europe	U.S., Europe
25	*Penicillium lanosum* Westling	U.S.	widespread
1411	*Penicillium lilacinum* Thom	U.S., Europe	cosmopolitan
91	*Penicillium martensii* Biourge	U.S., Europe	worldwide
78	*Penicillium nigricans* (Bainier) Thom	U.S., Europe	cosmopolitan
517	*Penicillium ochro-chloron* Biourge	U.S., Europe	cosmopolitan
185	*Penicillium oxalicum* Currie et Thom	U.S., Europe	cosmopolitan
13	*Penicillium palitans* Westling	U.S.	U.S., Canada, Europe, Japan, New Zealand
27	*Penicillium puberulum* Bainier	U.S., Europe	U.S., Europe
12	*Penicillium pulvillorum* Turfitt	U.S.	U.S., Central America, Europe
90	*Penicillium purpureogenum* Stoll var. *purpureogenum*	U.S.	widespread
11	*Penicillium raistrickii* G. Smith	U.S.	U.S., Europe
51	*Penicillium rubrum* Stoll	U.S.	widespread
14	*Penicillium sclerotiorum* Beyma	U.S.	U.S., Java, Africa
18	*Penicillium simplicissimum* (Oudemans) Thom	U.S., Europe	cosmopolitan
(13)	*Penicillium stipitatum—see Talaromyces stipitatum*		
82	*Penicillium thomii* Maire	U.S.	U.S., Europe, Japan, Africa
212	*Penicillium variabile* Sopp	U.S., Europe	widespread

46	*Penicillium velutinum* Beyma	U.S.	U.S., Europe, Japan, Java
15	*Pestalotia heterocornis* Guba	U.S.	U.S., South America, China
17	*Phialophora fastigiata* (Lagerberg et Melin) Conant	U.S., Canada, Europe	U.S., Canada, Europe
1533	*Rhinocladiella mansonii* (Castellani) Schol-Schwarz	U.S., Canada, Europe	cosmopolitan
(38)	*Scedosporium apiospermum*—see *Petriellidium boydii*		
19	*Scopulariopsis brevicaulis* Bainier	U.S., Europe	U.S., Canada, Europe, Japan, China, India, Africa
45	*Sepedonium* spp.	U.S., Europe	U.S., Europe
26	*Sporotrichum* spp.	U.S., Canada, Europe	
113	*Stachybotrys chartarum* (Ehrenberg ex Link) Hughes	U.S.	cosmopolitan
47	*Stemphylium* spp.		
12	*Stilbella* sp.		
20	*Trichoderma hamatum* (Bonorden) Bainier	U.S.	U.S., Europe, Ceylon, India, Indonesia, Australia, N. Zealand
58	*Trichoderma harzianum* Rifai	U.S.	U.S., Europe
19	*Trichoderma koningii* Oudemans	U.S., Europe, Japan	U.S., Europe
50	*Trichoderma polysporum* (Link ex Persoon) Rifai	U.S.	U.S., Europe, Australia
1349	*Trichoderma viride* Persoon ex S. F. Gray *sensu latissimo*	U.S., Europe	cosmopolitan
21	*Ulocladium consortiale* (Thümen) Simmons	U.S.	U.S., Europe, Japan
55	*Verticillium* spp.	U.S., Europe	
105	*Verticillium lateritium* Berkeley	U.S., Europe	U.S., Europe

15.4 Future Problems

15.4.1 Confirmatory Studies

Among the more important questions to be answered in relation to the occurrence of fungi in sewage and polluted waters are questions related to the credibility of the material presented above. Many people have isolated a few kinds of fungi from habitats of various sorts, but only a few people have isolated a large number of different kinds of filamentous geofungi and yeasts from sewage polluted waters and processes in sewage treatment systems. Confirmatory work needs to be carried out not only on the validity of these observations, but also in the type of physiological processes of which these fungi are capable which would make them useful members of the sewage treatment biota.

15.4.2 Ultimate Treatment

With the development of the use of fungi in sewage treatment processes, beyond mere reliance on existing populations, that is, with the addition to any one process of an inoculum of fungi of types which could be expected to become established and to aid in the treatment process, should come the regular blending of process products for more efficient use of the organisms. Composts formed of mixtures of solid wastes, sewage sludge and possibly other relatively dry organic matter such as excess sawdust, waste paper, etc., could form a basis for mycological activity designed not only to reduce the amounts of wastes, but to convert them to other types of materials such as edible fungal proteins. Experimentation should go beyond the attempt to discover the fate of presumed pathogens such as *Candida albicans* (Robin) Berkh., which in Cooke's experience is not present in sewage sludge, by addition of an inoculum (Shell and Boyd, 1969) to a composting mixture of solid wastes and sewage sludge. It may be noted that this yeast-like fungus is found rarely in nature (Winner and Hurley, 1964), and that its best survival record is in relatively warm marine waters where few competing organisms occur (Madri *et al.*, 1966). The work of Church *et al.* (1972) has pioneered the production of fungal proteins from a corn canning waste stream.

15.4.3 Fungal Groups

Information is needed concerning special groups of fungi which occur in sewage and polluted water. It should not be assumed that all species in each group are equally capable of carrying out the same reactions or series of reactions. Each species may be capable of a number of similar reactions, for example see Lodder (1971), but each species may be responsible for one or more highly specialized reactions. Organism groups which come to mind include human and animal pathogens, predators and yeasts. Other groups are probably also involved and worthy of study.

Pathogens   Cooke (1956 b), Cooke and Kabler (1957), and Cole *et al.* (1969) have presented some information concerning plant pathogens, but many questions remain unanswered. Cooke and Kabler (1953) have demonstrated survival of *Histoplasma capsulatum* Darling, and Cooke and Kabler (1955) have reported on the presence of human and animal pathogens in sewage and polluted waters. Work needs to be done, especially in the tropics, on sewage and polluted waters as sources of inoculum for these and other types of fungi which can cause disease in man. Yeasts in particular need some attention in this regard. The control of such fungi in sewage systems and sewage treatment plant effluents has been mentioned briefly by Cooke (1971). Work such as that by Chambers (1961) needs extension with special reference to fungi.

Predators   At least five species of predacious fungi have been recovered from activated sludges and from waters from the surfaces of settling basins. *Zoophagus insidians* Sommerstorff has been described by Cooke and Ludzack (1958), and by Pipes (1966). In addition, Pipes (1966) has noted that four species of nematode trapping fungi have been recovered from activated sludge. The biological relationships of these fungi need further elucidation. The *Zoophagus* has been found in other cultures in areas well isolated from Ohio and California and additional information about its biology and control in each occurrence could be useful.

Yeasts   Cooke *et al.* (1960) listed yeasts which had been identified from isolations from sewage and polluted waters. Later Cooke (1965 b) reported on temperature studies, and Cooke and Matsuura (1963 b) reported on the distribution of nearly 60 species of yeasts in the Lebanon, Ohio, waste stabilization ponds. Spencer *et al.* (1970) have reported on a polluted reach of the South Saskatchewan River, and Hedrick, and associates (Hedrick and Soyugenc, 1965, 1967, Hedrick *et al.*, 1964, 1966, 1968; Wollett and Hedrick, 1970; Wollett *et al.*, 1970) have discussed the occurrence of yeasts in the Great Lakes. Yeasts are an important segment of the biota in any organically enriched habitat where water forms an important part of the environment, although this was not apparent to Heukelekian (1942) who added *Saccharomyces cerevisiae* (Meyen ex Reess) Hansen to a digesting sludge unsuccessfully. The extent to which yeast populations, as well as those of filamentous fungi, can be affected by thermal pollution has not been investigated; the results of such a study should prove to be interesting and useful. The extent to which certain species could be used advantageously in treatment processes needs exploration. Within limits, yeasts are relatively easy to grow, and at least two species are known to have been used for feeds and foods. The extent to which other species could be used in the conversion of waste organic matter to useful proteinaceous materials needs intensive study. At least one species has potential as an indicator of paper mill wastes; *Candida lambica* (Lindner et Genoud) van Uden et Buckley can readily use pentose sugars.

15.4.4   Bottom Feeder Food

Investigators in Poland (Pieczynska, 1970 a, b), New York (Harman, 1972) and probably elsewhere are beginning to take notice of the fact that benthos or Aufwuchs growth forms part of the diet of animals which graze on the bottom of streams or other bodies of water, or on the growth which develops on plant stems or erect emplacements in such bodies of water. So far, the phenomenon noted has been general, with no indication that there is selective grazing on one area or another representing one type of growth or another. As work on this problem develops it might be well to take a hint from other organisms. For instance, Scheerpeltz and Höfler (1948) have shown that certain beetles prefer certain fleshy fungi as food. It is well known in mycology that slugs and snails feed on fleshy fungus fruit bodies. Is it not possible that grazing organisms eat one type of growth rather than another and that this could be related to a flavour factor not presently known to us? Is it possible that such information could aid in the development of a sewage treatment biota whose activity levels would be higher than those known today?

15.4.5 Physiological Studies

It has been noted above that the fungi are capable of a wide variety of transformations as a result of individual species being able to produce unique or unusual enzyme systems. Cooke (1957 c) has recorded the results of nutritional studies with nine common species of filamentous fungi, and the identification of yeasts (Lodder, 1971) is based on the ability of species to use or ferment a variety of carbon sources. Information of this type is needed for most, if not all, of the species listed in Table 15.3. McCallan (1958) has given techniques for determining volumes and thus surface areas of fungus cells, and Emerson (1950), and Marshall and Alexander (1960) have discussed growth rates of filamentous organisms as compared with bacteria, and probably yeasts. These types of work, as well as studies related to techniques of nutrient translocation (Schütte, 1956) within the cell under different habitat conditions related to different types of sewage treatment processes, need extension with the idea of developing techniques useful in engineering practice for the more efficient utilization of organisms naturally adaptable to sewage treatment processes and goals. Fractions of the content of waste streams available to fungi have been considered, including cellulose (Cooke and Busch, 1957), ABS (alkyl benzyl sulfonate) (Cooke and Matsuura, 1963 a), oil refinery wastes (Dotson *et al.,* 1971), and lignin by Cooke (1957 b, 1961 b, 1963 b).

15.4.6 Population Sort

The biota of a trickling filter film, an activated sludge floc, a digesting sludge or a waste stabilization pond, is a highly complex assemblage of a variety of types of organisms. For some, the working of the whole is incomprehensible, unless the activity of each component is understood. However, without that of its neighbour, the activity of one or another member of the population has little meaning. Within any one system, or within each system, the activities of the component members should be determined. The sum of these parts will never equal the whole, but it will go a long way towards explaining some of the activities of the mass. It should be remembered that each species in the complex will have a different series of reactions even though it may occur in the same genus, family, order, class or phylum with another.

15.5 Addendum: Some Japanese Literature

From 1960 to 1964, the student of mycology and mycologist, Shizimo Suzuki, and his colleagues, worked extensively on clean and polluted waters in the vicinity of Tokyo, Japan, studying the distribution of bacteria and fungi with relation to different types of clean water lakes, and different types of pollutants added to river waters. A total of 42 papers were published on the basis of this work. Work with clean waters from areas of volcanic activity was largely related to studies of aquatic phycomycetes, aquatic hyphomycetes, other filamentous fungi, and bacteria, found in individual lakes or groups of lakes. This work includes natural pollution, that is, clean waters carrying large amounts of minerals making them more or less comparable to North American streams carrying 'glacial milk', and naturally occurring acid mine drainage.

So far as I am aware, this is the first series of papers in which a quantitative method has been applied to the occurrence of zoospore-producing aquatic phycomycetes in any type of water. The technique was based on the assumption that each hypha arising in a colony of fungi developing on a hemp seed was produced from the colonization of that hemp seed by one zoospore. Therefore, the numbers of the hyphae on the hemp seed represent the numbers of zoospores in the tested unit of water brought from a particular body of water to the laboratory, but not necessarily tested directly in the field beside or within the body of water. Obviously, the technique cannot be used if the bait is placed directly in the body of water. When waters from various depths in lakes or rivers were tested, samples from several levels in the body of water were removed with the Eckmann apparatus. In most cases, chemical and physical analyses of the waters tested for micro-organisms were reported. The populations of bacteria and fungi were used as supplemental characteristics in the description of the tested bodies of water.

Ten species of aquatic phycomycetes were isolated from waters of Senshun-ike Pond, Tokyo (Suzuki, 1960 h). Maximum yields of zoospores produced 91 1/10 ml in spring and autumn, minimum yields were 32/10 ml in summer and winter. Water temperature was thought to play an important role in zoospore production as well as the increase and decline of lacustrine bacterial populations.

In Lake Nakanuma (Suzuki, 1960 i, 1961 j), sampled at monthly intervals in 1957 and 1958, it was found that seven species of aquatic phycomycetes were present, with a maximum of 65 zoospores per 10 ml water in early winter. A homogeneous distribution of zoospores occurred during the lake's circulation period, a stratum type during the stagnation period of the lake. Zoospore production was affected by water temperature and by lacustrine bacteria. In Lake Shinseiko (Suzuki, 1960 g) there was an increase in number of zoospores in spring and autumn, with a decrease in summer and winter. Following a survey of 68 lakes in Japan (Suzuki, 1961 c), was able to record three species of Achlya, of which two were rare, A. racemosa Hildebrand appearing only in the winter, and A. americana Humphrey only in the summer. A. flagellata Coker was common, widely distributed, appeared throughout the year, and in all types of lakes sampled.

It was found that the genus Pythium (Suzuki, 1961 f) is widely distributed in Japanese lakes. A seasonal fluctuation is shown with a maximum production in winter, the minimum coming in summer. Distribution was related to lake type, the species being more common in harmonic lakes, rare in dystrophic and acidotrophic lakes. The genus Aphanomyces (Suzuki, 1961 a) was found to be widely distributed in Japanese lakes. It occurred in bottom muds as well as in water. Seasonal fluctuation varied with each species. The distribution of the genus was also related to lake types: species were abundant in harmonic and dystrophic lakes, very abundant in eutrophic lakes, but rare in mesotrophic or oligotrophic lakes.

Diurnal distribution of zoospores of aquatic fungi (Suzuki, 1961 b) in a shallow lake was related to oxygen supplies and light. In spring and autumn, distribution was concentrated in winter layers rich in oxygen. On a clear day zoospores were most abundant in the bottom layer, on a cloudy day in the surface layer, and on a rainy day they were distributed homogeneously throughout the water of the lake. The vertical distribution of fungus zoospores (Suzuki, 1961 l; Suzuki and Nimura, 1961 f) was of two main types: homogeneous distribution occurred during the circulation period of the lake, stratum distribution during the stagnation period. All species were found in the epilimnion during the stagnation period, while variations according to genus were found during the circulation period. While the optimum temperature (Suzuki, 1963) for zoospore production of aquatic fungi collected in Japanese lakes lay between 16 and 20 °C, the critical temperatures below or above which zoospores were produced differed for each species observed. Studies made between August and November, 1957, in the mesotrophic Lake Tamanakoko showed (Suzuki and

Hatakeyama, 1961) that representatives of three genera of aquatic fungi were present. Maximum numbers of zoospores were present in mid-autumn, minimum numbers occurring in summer and late autumn samples. *Aphanomyces* was more abundant in the summer, *Saprolegnia* in the autumn, while *Pythium* species were present regardless of season. While zoospores were present only in the upper epilimnion in the summer, in the autumn they were generally present at all depths tested. Bottom muds were rich in species in autumn, but *Pythium* was preponderant regardless of season.

In a group of inorganic acidotrophic lakes (Suzuki, 1961 c) with pH ranges from 1.9 to 5.8, with high quantities of minerals, five aquatic phycomycetes were found. Zoospores to a number of 0-1800/10 ml were found in increasing numbers in increasing degrees of acidity. Fungi were rare or absent in bottom muds. The number of species increased with decreasing pH values.

On the slopes of the Volcano Bondai (Suzuki, 1960 d; Suzuki and Nimura, 1960 a, 1961 c, d) six of the groups of freshwater lakes were studied from the points of view of mineral content, certain physicochemical factors, and the fungal populations. Certain fungi were found to be restricted to lakes of varying degrees of acidity or mineral content. Most of the lakes fell into such categories as acidotrophic, ferrotrophic (with large amounts of iron), dystrophic, and harmonic. Larger numbers of fungi were found in harmonic lakes whose reactions ranged around neutral. Some aquatic phycomycetes and hyphomycetes were found to be restricted to acidotrophic lakes, others could not survive in more acid conditions than those found in harmonic lakes. Similar conditions were found in the lakes of Volcano Nikko (Suzuki, 1961 e), and the lakes of the Shiga Volcano (Suzuki and Hatakayama, 1960; Suzuki and Nimura, 1961 a).

Suzuki (1961 g) studied the bacteria and fungi of Lake Katanuma in the Katanuma Volcano. The water in this lake has a pH of 1.9 because of the quantity of sulphuric acid present. *Penicillium citrinum* Thom was the only fungus found. In the laboratory, spores of this fungus were found to survive at least seven months' exposure to water of this acidity, while other fungi, including members of the Mucorales, died within a few days.

The aquatic fungus *Saprolegnia monoica* Pringsheim var. *acidamica* has been found (Suzuki, 1961 i) to occur in highly acid waters which also carry heavy loads of mineral ions. It was found only in acidotrophic lakes and seems to be more adapted to lower water temperatures than most water fungi.

Aquatic hyphomycetes (Suzuki and Nimura, 1961 e) were found to follow a distribution pattern similar to that of aquatic phycomycetes. While most species were confined to dystrophic and harmonic lake types, a few species grew in acidotrophic lakes. Those species which grew in harmonic lakes could not sporulate in water of acidotrophic lakes.

Although absent from two, it was found (Suzuki and Nimura, 1962) that six species of aquatic hyphomycetes were found in inorganic acidotrophic lakes in Japan. The amounts of iron and pH values form the major restrictions on distribution of these fungi according to laboratory experiments.

As a result of numerous surveys of lakes and streams in Japan (Nimura and Suzuki, 1962), a list of 21 species, including one variety, belonging in 16 genera, of aquatic hyphomycetes has been developed.

In a stream polluted by municipal sewage wastes, aquatic fungi (Suzuki, 1960 a) were found in both polluted and unpolluted reaches. Species of *Saprolegnia* and *Achlya* were found below the sewage outfall, *Aphanomyces* and *Pythium* were restricted to the cleaner reaches of the stream above the outfall.

424

In the Kiryugawa River receiving sewage from Kiryu City (Suzuki, 1960 f), it was found that the rate of build-up of bacteria is higher in undiluted sewage than in that diluted by river water. Above the sewage outfall *Aphanomyces* was a common organism, while at the outfall *Monilia* sp. was a dominant fungus, and below the outfall a number of organisms occurred. Among the bacteria, *Beggiatoa* sp. and *Sphaerotilus natans* Kützing; among the aquatic phycomycetes, *Leptomitus lacteus* (Roth) Agardh; and among the filamentous fungi, *Monilia* sp., were common organisms in the 50-150 m reach of the river below the sewage outfall.

Larger numbers of bacteria were found downstream from the sewage outfall in the stream carrying domestic wastes from Fujisawa City (Suzuki and Nimura, 1961 b). Fungi were abundant at each sewage outfall point. Of the aquatic phycomycetes, *Aphanomyces* sp. was common in clean water, while *Pythium* sp. was common in the sewage polluted water. Among the abundant micro-organisms in sewage polluted water were *Beggiatoa* sp. amd *Sphaerotilus natans,* among the bacteria, and among the fungi, *Mucor fragilis* Bainier, *Monilia* sp. and *Trichoderma koningii* Oudemans.

A study of the Arakawa River (Suzuki, 1960 b) showed that in the upper reaches aquatic phycomycetes were rare but increased in number downstream especially in the vicinity of Kumagaya whose domestic and industrial wastes are dumped in the river. These organisms decrease downstream as urban and industrial pollution increase. The zoospores varied in quantity, the maximum occurred in winter, the minimum in summer. Seasonal fluctuations occurred according to species. Zoospores were distributed uniformly vertically, but spores of *Saprolegnia monoica* were found mostly in surface water, with *Leptomitus lacteus* mostly on the bottom.

In waters of a river polluted by candy factory wastes (Suzuki, 1961 d; Suzuki *et al.,* 1960) large numbers of fungi were found at the effluent point where the aquatic fungi *Saprolegnia* sp. and *Pythium* sp. were common and the filamentous fungi, *Monilia* sp. and *Mucor fragilis* were abundant. In the river bottom 50-80 m below the outfall, *Sphaerotilus natans* was dominant; a few colonies of *Monilia* sp. and *Mucor fragilis* also appeared here.

Studies were made in a river receiving paper mill wastes near Tokyo (Suzuki and Suzuki, 1961). Larger numbers of fungi occurred above the point of waste outfall from the mill than at or below that point. There were no aquatic phycomycetes associated with these wastes and the dominant, if not the only, organisms were *Sphaerotilus natans* and *Trichoderma koningii.* Physiological studies indicate that, for fungi, organic nitrogen is preferred in a medium based on Czapek's agar. The toxicity of the wastes from the mill was determined by the IC_{50} method developed by Suzuki. This technique demonstrates the 'inhibiting concentration for micro-organisms', the concentration at which half the micro-organisms are inhibited (or killed?). In the case of the paper mill wastes outfall the IC_{50} was found to be 1/8.

A study of the pollution in rivers entering Tokyo Bay has been carried out by S. Suzuki. The principal interest in this study was in the occurrence and distribution of general bacteria, specialized bacteria, filamentous fungi and aquatic fungi. In general, in the cleaner upstream area, fewer individuals and species of organisms were found. As pollutants from paper mills, candy and other factories, and as municipal sewage entered the river, colony counts and numbers of species increased and these dropped off again at the mouths of the rivers where they entered Tokyo Bay and blended with salt water. More kinds and numbers of fungi were found in water on the surface of the streams than in shore waters and bottom muds although some species were restricted in activities to these locations. For growth, the fungi found require nitrogen-bearing compounds. In summarizing early work done on the occurrence of fungi in polluted water and sewage in Japan (Suzuki and Suzuki, 1962), it was noted that *Leptomitus lacteus* had been isolated four times, *Mucor fragilis* 14 times, *Geotrichum candidum* Link ex Persoon 28 times, *Trichoderma koningii* 12 times, and *Fusarium aquaeductuum* Lagerhein three times. These isolations were made from waste streams from candy, paper and alcohol plants, as well as from municipal sewage and sewage treatment plants.

In the waters of 14 wells in Tokyo and its suburbs (Suzuki, 1961 h), were found relatively large numbers of bacteria, aquatic phycomycetes, and filamentous fungi. Bacteria isolated from water from some of the wells were inoculated in waters from all of the wells and showed a rate of increase at $30°C$ after 24 hours of 6-780. It is indicated that there are adaptable bacteria in each well. *Pythium* sp. and *Saprolegnia* sp. were dominant among the aquatic phycomycetes; *Mucor* and *Penicillium* species among the filamentous fungi.

Physiological studies were made (Suzuki, 1961 k) on *Monilia* sp. Best conditions for growth of the fungus, of which 19 strains were isolated from sewage polluted streams, industrial wastes, sewage, and seawater, were described for temperature, carbon and nitrogen sources.

Because of its prevalence in activated sludge, *Geotrichum candidum* was studied by Drs. S. Suzuki and T. Tatsuno. The authors found that under the conditions of their experiments, the ability of this fungus to break down organic matter was not as strong as under other experimental conditions. They thought that it did not play an important role in the activated sludge process.

Aluminium sulphate is used as a coagulant for particulate matter in raw water entering certain industrial processes and in water treatment plants. In one situation it was found that aluminium sulphate slurries were infected with *Trichoderma koningii,* a common organism of clean and polluted streams. The addition of copper chloride or other disinfectants effective against this organism was recommended.

References

ANON. (1968). 'Standard methods for the water quality examination for the member countries for the Council for Mutual Economic Assistance'. Ministry for Forestry and Water Management in cooperation with the Hydraulic Research Institute, Prague, Czechoslovakia. Selected Passages.

BECKER, J. G., and SHAW, C. G. (1955). 'Fungi in domestic sewage treatment plants.' *Appl. Microbiol.,* 3, 173-180.

BENEKE, E. S., and SCHMITT, J. A. (1961). 'Aquatic fungi from South Bass and neighboring islands in western Lake Erie. I. Uniflagellate and biflagellate Phycomycetes.' *Ohio J. Sci.,* 61, 283-285.

BILLINGS, W. D. (1964). *Plants and the Ecosystem.* Wadsworth Publ. Co., Belmont, Calif., 154 pp.

BRANCO, W. (1962). 'Fungos em asgoto e aguas poluidas.' *Revista D.A.E.,* 44, 2-3.

BU'LOCH, J. D. (1964). 'General conspectus of fungal metabolic products.' Tenth International Botanical Congress, Edinburgh. Abstract, p. 54.

CHAMBERS, C. W. (1961). 'The germicidal efficiency of silver, iodine, and quaternary ammonium compounds.' *Proc. 3rd. Sanit. Engineering Congress, Disinfection and Chemical Oxidation in Water and Waste Treatment, Cir.,* 71, 29-42.

CHURCH, B. D., NASH, H. A., and BROSZ, W. (1972). 'Use of Fungi Imperfecti in treating food processing wastes.' *Devl. Inds. Microbiol.,* 13, 30-46.

COLE, H., MERRILL, W., LUKEZIC, F. L., and BLOOM, J. R. (1969). 'Effects on vegetation of irrigation with waste treatment effluents and possible plant pathogen-irrigation interactions.' *Phytopathology, 59*, 1181-1191.

COOKE, W. B. (1953). 'Mosses in a sewage treatment plant.' *The Bryologist, 56*, 143-145.

COOKE, W. B. (1954 a). 'Fungi in sewage and polluted water. I. Literature review.' *Sewage and Indust. Wastes, 26*, 539-549.

COOKE, W. B. (1954 b). 'Fungi in sewage and polluted water. II. Isolation technique.' *Sewage and Indust. Wastes, 26*, 661-674.

COOKE, W. B. (1956 a). 'Colonization of artificial bare areas by microorganisms.' *Bot. Rev., 22*, 613-638.

COOKE, W. B. (1956 b). 'Potential plant pathogenic fungi in sewage and polluted water.' *Pl. Dis. Reptr., 40*, 681-687.

COOKE, W. B. (1957 a). 'Check list of fungi isolated from polluted water and sewage.' *Sydowia, 11*, 146-175.

COOKE, W. B. (1957 b). 'Natural and induced fungal degradation of lignin.' *TAPPI, 40*, 301-306.

COOKE, W. B. (1957 c). 'Nutritional requirements of nine common sewage fungi.' *Sewage and Indust. Wastes, 29*, 1243-1251.

COOKE, W. B. (1957 d). 'Use and value of fungi as biological indicators of pollution.' *Trans. Seminar on Biological Problems in Water Pollution.* R. A. Taft San. Engr. Center, Cincinnati, 1956, 23-27.

COOKE, W. B. (1958). 'Continuous sampling of trickling filter populations.' *Sewage and Indust. Wastes, 30*, 21-27.

COOKE, W. B. (1959 a). 'Are fungi important in sewage treatment?' *Public Works, 90*, Jan., 113-114.

COOKE, W. B. (1959 b). 'Fungi in polluted water and sewage. IV. The occurrence of fungi in a trickling filter-type sewage treatment plant.' *Proc. 13th. Ind. Wastes Conf., Purdue Univ. Engr. Bull., 43*, 3, 26-45.

COOKE, W. B. (1959 c). 'Trickling filter ecology'. *Ecology, 40*, 273-291.

COOKE, W. B. (1961 a). 'Pollution effects on the fungus population of a stream.' *Ecology, 42*, 1-18.

COOKE, W. B. (1961 b). 'Some effects of spray disposal of spent sulphite liquor on soil mold populations.' *Proc. 15th. Ind. Wastes Conf., Purdue Univ. Engr. Bull., 45*, 35-48.

COOKE, W. B. (1962 a). 'The role of fungi in environmental sanitation.' *Devl. Indus. Microbiol., 3*, 313-318.

COOKE, W. B. (1963 a). 'A laboratory guide to fungi in polluted waters, sewage, and sewage treatment systems.' *Public Health Service Publ.,* Cincinnati. 999-WP-1, 132 pp.

COOKE, W. B. (1963 b). 'Fungi associated with spent sulphite liquor disposal in a natural sand bed.' *TAPPI, 46*, 573-578.

COOKE, W. B. (1965 a). 'The enumeration of yeast populations in a sewage treatment plant.' *Mycologia, 57*, 696-703.

COOKE, W. B. (1965 b). 'The growth of yeasts at 37°C.' *Mycopath. Mycol. appl., 25*, 195-200.

COOKE, W. B. (1966). 'Fungi in sludge digesters.' *Proc. 20th. Ind. Wastes Conf., Purdue Univ. Engr. Bull., 50*, 6-17.

COOKE, W. B. (1967 a). 'Fungal populations in relation to pollution of the Bear River, Utah-Idaho.' *Proc. Utah Acad. Sci., Arts and Letters, 44*, 298-315.

COOKE, W. B. (1967 b). 'Fungi in streams carrying acid mine-drainage. *Proc. 21st. Ind. Wastes Conf., Purdue Univ. Engr. Bull.,* 50, 258-274.

COOKE, W. B. (1968). 'Some fungi of the Cache la Poudre River, Colorado.' *Mycopath. Mycol. appl.,* 35, 361-372.

COOKE, W. B. (1970 a). *Our Mouldy Earth.* F.W.P.C.A. Res. Contract Ser., Publ. Nr. CWR-., 533 pp.

COOKE, W. B. (1970 b). 'Fungi associated with the activated sludge process of sewage treatment at the Lebanon, Ohio, sewage treatment plant.' *Ohio J. Sci.,* 70, 129-146.

COOKE, W. B. (1970 c). 'Fungi in the Lebanon sewage treatment plants and in Turtle Creek, Warren Co., Ohio.' *Mycopath. Mycol. appl.,* 42, 89-111.

COOKE, W. B. (1971). 'The role of fungi in waste treatment.' *CRC Critical Reviews in Environmental Control,* 1, 581-619.

COOKE, W. B. (1972). 'Use of deterioration fungi in polluted water.' *Mycopath. Mycol. appl.* (in press).

COOKE, W. B., and BARTSCH, A. F. (1959). 'Aquatic fungi in water with high waste loads.' *Sewage and Indust. Wastes,* 31, 1316-1322.

COOKE, W. B., and BARTSCH, A. F. (1960). 'Aquatic fungi in some Ohio streams.' *Ohio J. Sci.,* 60, 144-148.

COOKE, W. B., and BUSCH, K. A. (1957). 'Activity of cellulose-decomposing fungi isolated from sewage polluted water.' *Sewage and Indust. Wastes,* 29, 210-217.

COOKE, W. B., and FOURNELLE, H. T. (1960). 'Some soil fungi from an Alaska tundra area.' *Arctic,* 13, 266-270.

COOKE, W. B., and HIRSCH, A. (1958). 'Continuous sampling of trickling filter populations. II. Populations.' *Sewage and Indust. Wastes,* 30, 138-156.

COOKE, W. B., and KABLER, P. W. (1953). 'The survival of *Histoplasma capsulatum* in water.' *Lloydia,* 16, 252-256.

COOKE, W. B., and KABLER, P. W. (1955). 'Isolation of potentially pathogenic fungi from polluted water and sewage. *Publ. Hlth. Rep.,* 70, 689-694.

COOKE, W. B., and KABLER, P. W. (1957). 'Plant disease fungi in sewage and polluted water.' *Publ. Hlth. Rep.,* 72, 651-654.

COOKE, W. B., and LUDZACK, F. J. (1958). 'Predacious fungus behavior in activated sludge systems.' *Sewage and Indust. Wastes,* 30, 1490-1495.

COOKE, W. B., and MATSUURA, G. S. (1963 a). 'Removal of ABS from solutions by a common fungus of sewage.' *Mycopath. Mycol. appl.,* 19, 295-297.

COOKE, W. B., and MATSUURA, G. S. (1963 b). 'A study of yeast populations in a waste stabilization pond system.' *Protoplasma,* 57, 163-187.

COOKE, W. B., and MATSUURA, G. S. (1969). 'Distribution of fungi in a waste stabilization pond system.' *Ecology,* 50, 689-694.

COOKE, W. B., MOORE, W. A., and KABLER, P. W. (1956). 'B.O.D. satisfaction by fungi.' *Sewage and Indust. Wastes,* 28, 1075-1086.

COOKE, W. B., PHAFF, H. J., MILLER, W., SHIFRINE, M., and KNAPP, E. P. (1960). 'Yeasts in polluted water and sewage.' *Mycologia,* 52, 210-230.

COOKE, W. B., and PIPES, W. O. (1970). 'The occurrence of fungi in activated sludge.' *Mycopath. Mycol. appl.,* 40, 249-270.

COUDERT, J., and SÄEZ, H. (1958). 'Micromycètes de l'eau de Lyon.' *Bull. Mens. Soc. Linn., Lyon,* 27, 181-183.

DOTSON, G. K., DEAN, R. B., COOKE, W. B., and KENNER, B. A. (1971). 'Land spreading, a conserving and non-polluting method of disposing of oily wastes.' *Proc. 5th. Int. Water Poll. Res. Conf.,* reprint pagination II—36-1-15.

EMERSON, R., and HELD, A. A. (1969). '*Aqualinderella fermentans* gen. et sp. nov., a Phycomycete adapted to stagnant waters. II. Isolation, cultural characterisitics, and gas relations.' *Am. J. Bot.,* 56, 1103-1120.

EMERSON, R., and WESTON, W. H. (1967). '*Aqualinerella fermentans* gen. et sp. nov., a Phycomycete adapted to stagnant waters. I. Morphology and occurrence in nature.' *Am. J. Bot.,* 54, 702-719.

EMERSON, S. (1950). 'The growth phase in *Neurospora* corresponding to the logarithmic phase in unicellular organisms.' *J. Bact.,* 60, 221-223.

FELDMAN, A. E. (1955). 'Fungi from trickling filters.' *Sewage and Indust. Wastes,* 27, 1243-1244.

FJERDINGSTAD, E. (1958). 'Untersgelse af Timå 1948-1953. (Timå a stream polluted by the discharge of drainage water from a lignite pit.)' *The Sewage Committee of the Institute of Danish Civil Engineers, Publ.,* Copenhagen. 12, 1-52.

FJERDINGSTAD, E. (1960). 'Forurening of vandløb biologisk bedømt.' *Norsk Hygienisk Tidskrift,* 41, 149-196.

FJERDINGSTAD, E. (1964). 'Pollution of streams estimated by benthal phytomicroorganisms. I. A saprobic system based on communities of organisms and ecological factors.' *Int. Rev ges. Hydrobiol. Hydrogr.,* 49, 63-131.

FJERDINGSTAD, E. (1965). 'Taxonomy and saprobic valency of benthic phytomicroorganisms.' *Int. Rev. ges. Hydrobiol. Hydrogr.,* 50, 475-604.

FJERDINGSTAD, E. (1971). 'Microbial criteria of environment qualities.' *A. Rev. Microbiol.,* 25, 563-582.

GARRETT, S. D. (1956). *The Biology of Root-Infecting Fungi.* Cambridge University Press, England. 293 pp.

HARMAN, W. N. (1972). 'Benthic substrates: their effect on freshwater mollusca.' *Ecology,* 53, 271-277.

HARVEY, J. V. (1952). 'Relationship of aquatic fungi to water pollution.' *Sewage and Indust. Wastes,* 24, 1159-1164.

HAWKES, H. A. (1963). *The Ecology of Waste Water Treatment.* Pergamon Press, The MacMillan Co., New York. 203 pp.

HEDRICK, L. R., COOKE, W., and WOOLLETT, L. (1968). 'Yeasts and molds in Lake Superior water and some of its tributaries.' *Proc. 11th. Conf. Great Lakes Res.,* 1968, 538-543.

HEDRICK, L. R., and SOYUGENC, M. (1965). 'Yeasts recovered in mud samples from Lake Michigan.' *Univ. of Michigan, Great Lakes Res. Div., Publ.,* 13, 69-76.

HEDRICK, L. R., and SOYUGENC, M. (1967). 'Yeasts and molds in waters and sediments of Lake Ontario.' *Proc. 10th. Conf. on Great Lakes Research* pp. 10-30.

HEDRICK, L. R., SOYUGENC, M., DUPONT, P., and AMBROSINI, R. (1964). 'Yeasts in Lake Michigan and Lake Erie.' *Univ. of Michigan, Great Lakes Res. Div. Publ.,* 11, 77-83.

HEDRICK, L. R., SOYUGENC, M., and LARSEN, L. (1966). 'Yeasts in sediment core samples from Lake Michigan.' *Univ. of Michigan, Great Lakes Res. Div., Publ.* 15, 27-37.

HEUKELEKIAN, H. (1942). 'Effect of yeast on the stabilization of sewage and sludge digestion.' *Public Works,* 73, 9, 17.

HEUKELEKIAN, H., and CROSBY, E. S. (1956). 'Slime formation in sewage. III. Nature and composition of slimes.' *Sewage and Indust. Wastes,* 28, 206-210.

HÖHNK, W. (1956). 'Mykologische Abwasserstudie I.' *Veröff. Inst. Meeresforsch. Bremerh.,* 4, 67-110.

429

HÖHNK,W. (1958). 'Mykologische Abwasserstudie II.' *Veröff. Inst. Meeresforsch. Bremerh.*, 5, 211-256.

HÖHNK, W., and BOCK, K. J. (1954). 'Ein Beitrag zur Okologie der saprophytischen Wasserpilze.' *Veröff. Inst. Meeresforsch. Bremerh.*, 3, 9-26.

HÖLTJE, R. J. (1943). 'The biology of sewage sprinkling filters'. *Sewage Works J.*, 15, 14-29.

HORNING, W. B., PORGES, R., CLARK, H. F., and COOKE, W. B. (1964). 'Waste stabilization pond study, Lebanon, Ohio.' *Public Health Service Publ.*, 999-WP-16, 1-48.

HYNES, H. B. N. (1960). *The Biology of Polluted Waters.* Liverpool University Press, Liverpool, England, 202 pp.

INGOLD, C. T. (1959). 'Submerged aquatic hyphomycetes.' *Jour. Queckett Microscopical Club, Series* 4, 5, 115-130.

INGOLD, C. T. (1971). *Fungal Spores, Their Liberation and Dispersal.* Clarendon Press, Oxford, England, 302 pp.

KOLE, A. P. (1965). 'Flagella.' In *The Fungi* (Eds. G. C. Ainsworth and A. S. Sussman), Academic Press, New York, vol. 1, 77-93.

KOLKWITZ, R. (1950). 'Oekologie der Saprobien'. *Schriftenreihe des Vereins für Wasser-, Boden-, und Luft-hygiene*, 1, 1-64.

KOLKWITZ, R., and MARSSON, M. (1908). 'Ökologie der pflanzenlichen Saprobien.' *Ber. dt. bot. Ges.*, 26a, 505-519.

LODDER, J. (Ed.) (1971). *The Yeasts, A Taxonomic Study* (2nd revised and enlarged edition). North-Holland Publishing Co., Amsterdam, 1385 pp.

MADRI, P. P., CLAUS, G. and MOSS, E. E. (1966). 'Infectivity of pathogenic fungi in a simulated marine environment.' *Revista de Biologia*, 5, 371-381.

MAJOR, J. (1951). 'A functional, factorial approach to plant ecology.' *Ecology*, 32, 392-412.

MARSHALL, K. C., and ALEXANDER, M. (1960). 'Growth characteristics of fungi and Actinomycetes.' *J. Bact.*, 80, 412-416.

MASON, H.L., and LANGENHEIM, J. (1957). 'Language analysis and the concept Environment.' *Ecology*, 38, 325-340.

MCCALLAN, S. E. A. (1958). 'Determination of individual fungus spore volumes and their size distribution.' *Contrib. Boyce Thompson Inst.*, 19, 303-320.

MCKINNEY, R. E. (1953). 'Biocatalysts and waste disposal. I. Fundamental biochemistry of waste disposal.' *Sewage and Indust. Wastes*, 25, 1129.

MCKINNEY, R. E. (1962). *Microbiology for Sanitary Engineers.* McGraw-Hill Book Co., New York, 293 pp.

MCKINNEY, R. E., and POLIAKOF, L. (1953). 'Biocatalysts and waste disposal. II. Effect on activated sludge.' *Sewage and Indust. Wastes*, 25, 1268.

MOSER, M. (1949). 'Untersuchungen über den Einfluss von Waldbranden auf die Pilzvegetation. I,' *Sydowia*, 3, 336-383.

NILSSON, S. (1964). 'Freshwater hyphomycetes. taxonomy, morphology, and ecology'. *Symb. bot. Upsal.*, 18, 1-130.

NIMURA, H., and SUZUKI, S. (1962). 'A list of the aquatic hyphomycetes in Japan.' *J. Jap. Bot.*, 37, 30-32.

PALMER, C. M. (1969). 'A composite rating of algae tolerating organic pollution.' *J. Phycol.*, 5, 78-82.

PARK, D. (1972 a). 'Methods of detecting fungi in organic detritus in water.' *Trans. Br. mycol. Soc.*, 58, 281-290.

PARK, D. (1972 b). 'On the ecology of heterotrophic microorganisms in fresh water.' *Trans. Br. mycol. Soc.*, 58, 291-299.

PIECZYNSKA, E. (1970 a). 'Periphyton as food of aquatic animals.' *Wiadomosci Ekologiczne*, 16, 133-144.

PIECZYNSKA, E. (1970 b). 'Periphyton in the tropic structure of freshwater ecosystems.' *Pol. Arch. Hydrobiol.*, 17, 141-147.

PIPES, W. O. (1966). 'Carnivorous plants in activated sludge.' *Proc. 20th. Ind. Wastes Conf., Purdue Univ. Engr. Bull.*, 50, 647-656.

RANZONI, F. V. (1953). 'The aquatic hyphomycetes of California.' *Farlowia*, 4, 353-398.

SCHEERPELTZ, O., and HÖFLER, K. (1948). *Käfer und Pilze.* Verlag für Jugend und Volk, Wien, 351 pp.

SCHMITT, J. A., and BENEKE, E. S. (1962). 'Aquatic fungi from South Bass Island and neighboring islands in western Lake Erie. II. Additional biflagellate and uniflagellate Phycomycetes.' *Ohio J. Sci.*, 62, 11-12.

SCHÜTTE, K. H. (1956). 'Translocation in the fungi'. *New Phytol.*, 55, 164-182.

SHELL, G. L., and BOYD, J. L. (1969). 'Composting dewatered sewage sludge.' *Public Health Service Publ.* 1936, 28 pp.

SEIPMANN, R. (1957). 'Ein Beitrag zur Saprophytischen Pilzflora des Wattes der Wesermündung. Inaugural Dissertation Ph.D. Christian-Albrechts-Universität, Kiel, Germany.

SLÁDEČKOVÁ, A. (1962). 'Limnological investigation methods for the periphyton ("Aufwuchs") community.' *Bot. Rev.*, 28, 286.

SLÁDEČEK, V., and SLÁDEČKOVÁ, A. (1963 a). 'Limnological study of the reservoir Sedlice near Zeliv. XXIII. Periphyton production.' *Scientific Papers, Inst. Chem. Techn. (Prague). Technology of Water*, 7, 77-133.

SLÁDEČEK, V., and SLÁDEČKOVÁ, A. (1963 b). 'Relationship between wet weight and dry weight of the periphyton.' *Limnol. Oceanogr.*, 8, 309-311.

SLÁDEČEK, V. (1963). 'A guide to limnosaprobical organisms.' *Scientific Papers, Inst. Chem. Tech. (Prague)*, 7, 543-612.

SLÁDEČEK, V. (1966). 'Water quality system.' *Verh. internat. Verein. Limnol.*, 16, 809-816.

SLÁDEČEK, V. (1969). 'The measure of saprobity.' *Verh. internat. Verein. Limnol.*, 17, 546-559.

SPENCER, J. F. T., GORIN, P. A. J., and GARDNER, N. R. (1970). 'Yeasts isolated from the South Saskatchewan, a polluted river.' *Can. J. Microbiol.*, 16, 1051-1057.

SPINOZA, B. (1677). *Ethics.* Part I, Prop. XV, Note.

STANBRIDGE, H. H. (1954, 1955). 'The development of biological filtration.' *Water and Sanitary Eng.*, 4, 297, 300, 326; 5, 213, 252, 308.

STJERNA-POOTH, I. (1957). '*Achlya prolifera* als Abwasserpilz in einem mittelschwedischer Wasserlauf.' *Institute of Fresh Water Research, Drottingholm*, 38, 247-266.

SUZUKI, S. (1960 a). 'Distribution of aquatic Phycomycetes in a river polluted by municipal wastes.' *J. Water Works and Sewage Assoc. (Japan)*, 35, 51-54;

SUZUKI, S. (1960 b). 'Ecological studies in the aquatic fungi in the Arakawa River.' *J. Limnology (Japan)*, 21, 25-31.

SUZUKI, S. (1960 c). 'Ecological studies on the genus *Aphanomyces* (Aquatic Fungi) in Japanese lakes.' *J. Limnology (Japan)*, 21, 17-24.

SUZUKI, S. (1960 d). 'The microbiological studies on the lakes of Volcano Bandai. I. Ecological studies of aquatic Phycomycetes of the Goshikunuma Lake group.' *Jap. J. Ecol.,* 10, 172-176.

SUZUKI, S. (1960 e). 'Microbiological studies on the lakes of Volcano Bondai. IV. The lacustrine bacteria in the Goshikunuma Lake group.' *J. Limnology (Japan),* 21, 58-63.

SUZUKI, S. (1960 f). 'Microbiological studies of sewage polluted water: aquatic fungi and bacteria in the Kiryugawa River.' *J. Water Works and Sewage Assoc. (Japan),* 35, 74-76.

SUZUKI, S. (1960 g). 'Seasonal variations in the amount of zoospores of aquatic Phycomycetes in Lake Shinseiko.' *Bot. Mag., Tokyo,* 73, 483-486.

SUZUKI, S. (1960 h). 'The seasonal variation of aquatic fungi in Senshun-ike Pond.' *J. Limnology (Japan),* 21, 271-278.

SUZUKI, S. (1960 i). 'The seasonal variation of aquatic Phycomycetes in Lake Nakanuma.' *Jap. J. Ecol.,* 10, 215-218.

SUZUKI, S. (1961 a). 'Distribution of aquatic Phycomycetes in some inorganic, acidotrophic lakes of Japan.' *Bot. Mag., Tokyo,* 74, 317-320.

SUZUKI, S. (1961 b). 'The diurnal migration of zoospores of aquatic fungi in a shallow lake.' *Bot. Mag., Tokyo,* 74, 138-141.

SUZUKI, S. (1961 c). 'Ecological specificity of *Achlya,* a genus of aquatic fungi in Japanese lakes.' *J. Jap. Bot.,* 36, 11-15.

SUZUKI, S. (1961 d). 'Ecological studies on aquatic fungi in polluted waters.' *Water Supply and Wastes (Japan),* 3, 55-58.

SUZUKI, S. (1961 e). 'Ecological studies on aquatic fungi in the lakes of Volcano Nikko.' *Jap. J. Ecol.,* 11, 1-4.

SUZUKI, S. (1961 f). 'Ecological studies on the genus *Pythium* (aquatic fungi) in Japanese lakes.' *Jap. J. Ecol.,* 11, 91-93.

SUZUKI, S. (1961 g). 'The microbial populations in Lake Katanuma, a very strong acid water lake in Japan.' *Bot. Mag. Tokyo,* 22, 201-207.

SUZUKI, S. (1961 h). 'On microorganisms in well water.' *J. Water Works and Sewage Assoc. (Japan),* 36, 53-54.

SUZUKI, S. (1961 i). 'On the ecological specificity of *Saprolegnia monoica* var. *acidamica.'* *J. Jap. Bot.,* 36, 292-295.

SUZUKI, S. (1961 j). 'The seasonal changes of aquatic fungi in the lake bottom of Lake Nakanuma.' *Bot. Mag., Tokyo,* 74, 30-33.

SUZUKI, S. (1961 k). 'Some physiological characters of a sewage fungus, *Monilia* sp.' *J. Water Works and Sewage Assoc. (Japan),* No. 319, 36, 79-82.

SUZUKI, S. (1961). 'The vertical distribution of the zoospores of aquatic fungi during the circulation and the stagnation periods.' *Bot. Mag., Tokyo,* 74, 254-258.

SUZUKI, S. (1963). 'Relation between zoospore production of aquatic fungi and water temperature in lakes.' *Misc. Repts. of the Res. Inst. for Nat. Res.,* 60, 88-92.

SUZUKI, S., and HATAKEYAMA, H. (1960). 'Ecological studies on the aquatic fungi in the Shiga Lake group.' *J. Limnology (Japan),* 21, 64-72.

SUZUKI, S., and HATAKEYAMA, H. (1961). 'Ecological studies of the aquatic fungi of Lake Yamanakako.' *Jap. J. Ecol.,* 11, 173-175.

SUZUKI, S., and NIMURA, H. (1960 a). 'The microbiological studies in the lakes of the Volcano Bandai. II. Ecological study on aquatic hyphomycetes in the Goshikinuma and Akanuma Lake groups.' *Bot. Mag., Tokyo,* 73, 360-384.

SUZUKI, S., and NIMURA, H. (1960 b). 'The microbiological studies in the lakes

of Volcano Bandai. III. The microbial populations in the Sunuma Lake group.'
Jap. J. Ecol., 10, 189-193.
SUZUKI, S., and NIMURA, H. (1961 a). 'Aquatic hyphomycetes in the lakes of
Volcano Shiga.' *J. Jap. Bot.,* 36, 135-138.
SUZUKI, S., and NIMURA, H. (1961 b). 'Ecological studies of fungi and bacteria in a
polluted river.' *J. Water Works and Sewage Assoc. (Japan),* No. 316, 36, 81-83.
SUZUKI, S., and NIMURA, H. (1961 c). 'The microbiological studies in the lakes of
Volcano Bandai. VI. The microbial populations in the Akanuma Lake group.'
Jap. J. Ecol., 11, 59-62.
SUZUKI, S., and NIMURA, H. (1961 d). The microbiological studies of the lakes
of the Volcano Bandai. VII. The microbial populations of the Onagawa Lake
group.' *Jap. J. Ecol.,* 11, 140-142.
SUZUKI, S., and NIMURA, H. (1961 e). 'Relation between the distribution of
aquatic hyphomycetes in Japanese lakes and lake types.' *Bot. Mag., Tokyo,*
74, 51-55.
SUZUKI, S., and NIMURA, H. (1961 f). 'The vertical distribution of fungi and
bacteria in lakes during the circulation and stagnation periods.' *Trans. Jap.
Mycol. Soc.,* 2, 115-117.
SUZUKI, S., and NIMURA, H. (1962). 'Distribution of aquatic hyphomycetes
in the inorganic acidotrophic lakes of Japan.' *J. Water Works and Sewage Assoc.
(Japan),* 23, 107-112.
SUZUKI, S., NIMURA, H., and SUZUKI, S. (1960). 'Ecological studies on the
microorganisms in a river polluted by confectionary wastes.' *J. Water Works
and Sewage Assoc. (Japan),* 35, 85-88.
SUZUKI, S., and SUZUKI, S. (1961). 'Ecological studies on fungi and bacteria
in a river polluted by a paper mill.' *Water Supply and Wastes, Japan,* 3, 23-26.
SUZUKI, S., and SUZUKI, S. (1962). 'Fungi in polluted water and sewage.'
Waste Water Research 2, 145-148.
SUZUKI, S., TATSUNO, T., and UENO, H. (1964). 'Studies on a fungus growing
on a solution of aluminium sulphate.' 54, 39-41.
TABAK, H., and COOKE, W. B. (1968). 'Growth and metabolism of fungi in an
atmosphere of nitrogen.' *Mycologia,* 60, 115-140.
TOMLINSON, T. G. (1941). 'The treatment of settled sewage in percolating filters
in series with periodic change in the order of the filters.' *J. and Proc. Inst. of
Sewage Purif.,* 27.
TOMLINSON, T. G. (1946). 'Growth and distribution of film in percolating filters
treating sewage by single and alternating double filtration.' *J. and Proc. Inst.
Sewage Purif.,* 1.

WEAVER, R. H., and NASH, H. D. (1968). 'Ecological study of the effects of strip
mining on the microbiology of streams.' *Univ. of Ky., Water Res. Inst., Res. Rept.,*
18, 1-35.
WILLOUGHBY, L. G. (1962). 'The occurrence and distribution of reproductive
spores of Saprolegniaceae in fresh water.' *J. Ecol.,* 50, 733-759.
WINNER, H. I., and HURLEY, R. (1964). *Candida albicans.* Little, Brown and Co.,
Boston, 306 pp.
WOOLLETT, L. L., and HEDRICK, L. R. (1970). 'Ecology of yeasts in polluted
water.' *Antonie van Leeuwenhoek,* 36, 427-435.
WOOLLETT, L. L., HEDRICK, L. R., and TARVER, M.-G. (1970). 'A statistical
evaluation of the ecology of yeasts in polluted water.' *Antonie van Leeuwenhoek,*
36, 437-444.

WURTZ, A. (1957). 'Champignons, Bacteriés, et Algues des eaux polluées,' *Bull. Francaise de Pisiculture,* Noc. 182, 184, reprinted with continuous pagination, 1-52.

16 Hyphomycetes as Intermediaries of Energy Flow in Streams

FELIX BÄRLOCHER AND BRYCE KENDRICK

16.1   Introduction

Many streams are essentially heterotrophic. We can clarify this cryptic comment by explaining that most of the plant material which forms the basis of the food chain is not synthesized in the stream, but is derived from the adjacent terrestrial environment. Various authors have calculated that 50-99% of the energy available to streams is derived from such allochthonous material (Cummins *et al*., 1966; Fisher and Likens, 1972; Nelson and Scott, 1962; Teal, 1957). This material largely consists of autumn-shed tree leaves which are known to serve as food for many members of almost all important groups of benthic organisms (Hynes, 1970).

Only a small fraction of the energy represented by the leaf material can be directly exploited by animals. For example, Hargrave (1970) estimated that *Hyalella azteca* Saussure, a common freshwater amphipod, assimilates only 5% of the material it ingests when feeding on elm leaves. So its faeces are still energy-rich and available to any opportunist organisms able to degrade them. These faeces, together with partly broken-up plant material, constitute most of the organic fraction of river sediments, which represent large reservoirs of food for many aquatic animals (Hynes, 1970).

It is many years since micro-organisms were first suspected of being important intermediaries in this food chain. Baier (1935) assumed that in lakes most detritus feeders are nourished by detritus-decomposing bacteria rather than by the actual detritus they appear to be feeding on. The same hypothesis had been advanced for terrestrial environments as early as 1891 (Simroth, cited by Baier, 1935). Since then, many experiments and observations have been reported which amply confirm the importance of bacteria in the diet of detritus feeders, terrestrial and aquatic. Ivlev (1945) succeeded in rearing chironomid larvae on filter paper to which suitable bacterial cultures had been added. The filter feeding larvae of *Simulium* (blackfly) can develop from egg to adult on pure suspensions of bacteria no more concentrated than those commonly encountered in natural waters (Fredeen, 1964). In Lake Michigan, the occurrence of the amphipod *Pontoporeia affinis* Lindstrom was found to be positively correlated with bacterial concentration (Marzolf, 1965).

The fact that detritus feeders usually pass their food very rapidly through their guts (Brown, 1961) suggests that only a small, easily digestible fraction of the food, presumably mainly micro-organisms, is assimilated. The snail *Hydrobia ulvae* Pennant extracts the nitrogenous matter from its food while most of the organic carbon escapes unscathed. Renewed bacterial growth then replenishes the nitrogen content of the faeces while the carbon decreases, and the faeces can subsequently be used as food again (Newell, 1965). This cycle may be repeated several times before the substrate is finally exhausted.

Nelson and Scott (1962) found that the ratio of invertebrate herbivores to the living plant material they consume is smaller than that of detritus feeders to the detritus they eat. If the detritus feeders are, in fact, feeding directly on the plant material constituting the bulk of the detritus, there is no reason why they should be able to assimilate it more efficiently than the herbivores do the fresh plants. Nelson and Scott concluded that the detritus feeders must receive additional nourishment in the form of bacteria growing on the detritus. It appears, then, that much of the plant material entering streams is unavailable to animals but can readily be used by micro-organisms, which in turn are easily digested by animals. Hargrave (1970) estimates that *Hyalella azteca* assimilates 60-90% of the bacterial biomass it ingests.

But this niche is far from being the exclusive preserve of the bacteria. In terrestrial environments it is well established that fungi also take part in colonizing and degrading plant debris, their relative importance depending on environmental factors such as substrate, pH, oxygen concentration, etc. Many soil invertebrates can be reared on either bacterial or fungal diets (for reviews see Burges and Raw, 1967). In contrast, the ecological significance of fungi in the food chain in aquatic environments, especially streams, has been ignored until recently. This neglect is all the more surprising when one reflects that fungi are superior to bacteria in their ability to degrade cellulose and lignin (Müller and Loeffler, 1971; Schlegel, 1972); substances which, although they account for 34-65% of the dry weight of leaves (Daubenmire and Prusso, 1963; Hering, 1967; Saito, 1957), cannot be digested by most invertebrates[*] (Bjarnov, 1972; Hargrave, 1970; Nielsen, 1962). In addition, a large number of hyphomycetes with typically tetraradiate or sigmoid conidia, obviously adapted to dispersal in water, have been described from decaying leaves in streams all over the world (Ingold, 1942, 1966, see also chapter 13; Nilsson, 1964; Petersen, 1962, 1963a, b).

16.2   Recent Work on Fungi in Aquatic Environments

16.2.1   Fungi in Bogs

Sphagnum can account for up to 75% of total plant production in open bogs (Smirnov, 1958). In a living sphagnous cover, the fauna is dominated by springtails and spiders. By gut analysis, Smirnov (1958) found that fungi are an indispensable link in this simple food chain. Fungi were found in the alimentary tracts of *Tomocerus flavascens* Tullberg in 80% of animals examined; *Sphagnum* itself in only 50%. In 35% the

---

In many cases, even those which appear to be able to digest these substances are actually dependent on the activities of a microbial gut flora since they themselves lack appropriate enzymes (Buchner, 1965).

hyphae more than half filled the alimentary canal. Knight and Angel (1967) showed the *Tomocerus* preferentially feeds on fungi when litter and humus are also offered.

16.2.2 Fungi in Estuaries

In Georgia estuaries, the main primary producer is the grass, *Spartina alterniflora* Loisel (Odum and de la Cruz, 1963, 1967). Only a small portion of this plant is eaten while it is still alive. However, about 95% of all suspended particles in these Georgian estuaries are derived from *Spartina*. They are rapidly colonized by a microflora which is almost exclusively fungal in the early stages of decomposition, bacteria coming in later (Odum, personal communication). The combined growth of fungi and bacteria then leads to radical changes in the composition of *Spartina* detritus. While the protein content of the living plant is 10% of the ash-free weight, and 6% in the dead plant as it enters the water, it can climb to an impressive 24% in *Spartina* particles colonized by micro-organisms. This certainly improves their food value to invertebrates. Similar observations were made in estuarine waters of south Florida where mangrove leaves are a major source of energy. They support fungi and bacteria, then pass through the guts of detritus feeders, are again colonized by micro-organisms and ingested. This cycle is repeated until the nutrients of the substrate are exhausted (Odum, 1971). Similar observations can be made in running waters where the consumption of living higher plants is often negligible (Hynes, 1970). The 'detritus food chain' is more prevalent than the 'grazing food chain' (Odum, 1971).

16.2.3 Fungi in Streams

The ecological significance of fungi in streams was first clearly demonstrated only recently by Kaushik and Hynes (1968, 1971) and Triska (1970). Kaushik and Hynes found that the protein content of some autumn-shed leaves in streams more than

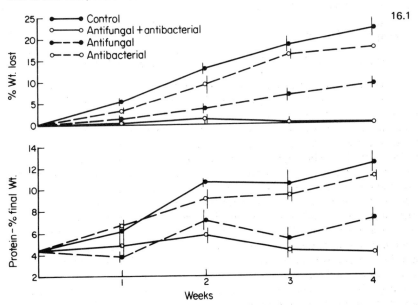

Fig. 16.1. Decomposition of elm leaves (after Kaushik and Hynes, 1971). Percentage weight loss and protein content of elm leaves kept at 10°C in stream water with different antibiotics. Mean values ± 95% confidence limits.

doubled. In artificial stream systems they compared decomposition rates and changes in protein content when antibacterial or antifungal, or both antibacterial and antifungal antibiotics were applied. Figure 16.1 shows the results obtained with elm leaves. Statistical analysis showed that in most cases the protein increases were not significantly influenced by the presence or absence of antibacterial antibiotics, but were significantly depressed by the application of antifungal antibiotics. Similarly, the loss of dry weight was usually high when only fungi were allowed to grow (use of antibacterial antibiotics) and low when fungal activity was prevented (antifungal antibiotics). Kaushik and Hynes (1968, 1971) concluded that fungi are far more successful than bacteria in the colonization and degradation of the leaves, at least in the early stages, and can bring about substantial protein increment. Triska (1970) took monthly samples of leaves from a stream. In the laboratory he compared respiration rates in systems to which antibacterial antibiotics had been added, and those prevailing in untreated controls. In almost every sample throughout the year the fungal share of total respiration was higher than the bacterial component, the difference being smallest in the warmer seasons. This again strongly suggests that fungi are more active than bacteria in the system investigated.

Kaushik and Hynes (1971) and Triska (1970) showed that several stream detritus feeders prefer to eat partly decomposed leaves with a rich microbial population rather than sterile or freshly fallen leaves. This behaviour confirms similar observations by woodland biologists who noted that fallen leaves are generally not eaten before they are colonized by micro-organisms (Minderman and Daniëls, 1966). Since the leaves may already bear inoculum of typical aquatic hyphomycetes when they enter the stream (Bandoni, 1972), and are in any case soon extensively colonized by these fungi (Nilsson, 1964), the food of leaf-eating invertebrates actually consists of two main components: leaf material and fungal mycelium. In our own experiments we have compared the relative merits of leaf and fungus in the diet of the amphipod *Gammarus pseudolimnaeus* Bousfield.

16.3   Experimental Work

16.3.1   *Assimilation of Fungus and Leaf by* Gammarus pseudolimnaeus

First we compared the efficiencies with which *Gammarus* converts different types of food into its own biomass. Body weight increase and daily food consumption were measured for different sets of animals which had as their sole food supply either maple or elm leaves, or mycelium of one of ten fungi (five terrestrial hyphomycetes, five aquatic hyphomycetes). Details of the experimental procedures are reported elsewhere (Bärlocher and Kendrick, 1973a, b). The results are given in Fig. 16.2. While the actual amount consumed in all-leaf diets was about ten times greater than in all-fungus diets, the highest weight increases were still found in those animals feeding on four of the fungi. This means that the fungi represent a form of nourishment which, from the animal's point of view, is more than ten times as concentrated as leaf substance. We calculated that the combined biomass of fungi and bacteria present on the leaves used in these experiments was only about 0.03% of the total dry weight. Even if our estimate is too low, it seems unlikely that the micro-organisms on the leaves represented a significant food supplement. Animals on an all-elm leaf diet grew twice as much as animals on the all-maple leaf diet with approximately the same daily consumption and microbial population. It seems, therefore, that fungi may not be an obligate component in the diet of *Gammarus*, though we cannot exclude the possibility that small populations of micro-organisms are needed to supply minute

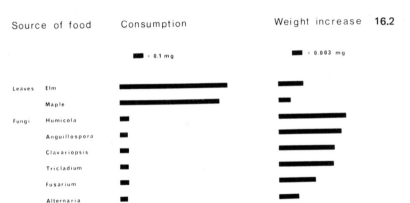

■ = 0.1 mg   ■ = 0.003 mg

Leaves	Elm
	Maple
Fungi	Humicola
	Anguillospora
	Clavariopsis
	Tricladium
	Fusarium
	Alternaria
	Cladosporium
	Flagellospora
	Aspergillus
	Tetracladium

Fig. 16.2. Assimilation of fungus and leaf by *Gammarus.* All values milligrams dry weight per animal per day.

amounts of some vital substances, e.g. vitamins. More significantly, we can confidently assert that good fungal growth on the leaves will very substantially improve their food value to the invertebrate stream fauna.

16.3.2   Food Selection

We have used the same ten fungi and three leaf species (ash, maple, oak) in food selection experiments, which will be fully reported elsewhere. All fungi are eaten in preference to maple leaves. This is shown in Fig. 16.3, where the animals had a choice between maple leaf discs and mycelium of *Tricladium angulatum* Ingold. All animals fed on the fungus during the entire experimental period of two hours. By contrast, the preference for fungus was least pronounced with *Tetracladium marchalianum* de Wild.

16.3

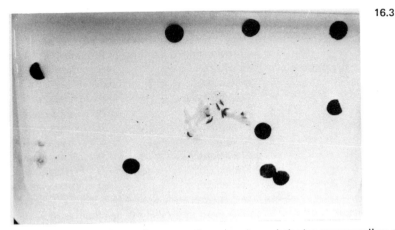

Fig. 16.3. Food selection by *Gammarus. Gammarus* has a choice between mycelium of *Tricladium* and maple leaf discs (diameter 1.2 cm). All animals are feeding on the fungus while the leaves are completely ignored.

Here, about 30% of observations found animals feeding on the leaves, 40% found them on the fungal mycelium, and 30% found them swimming around. If only leaves without fungal growth are offered, *Gammarus* likes ash best, followed by maple and finally oak. Such strict segregation of leaf and fungus is unlikely in nature, and we must emphasize that the normal feeding mechanism of *Gammarus* involves ingestion of the leaf together with the fungal population it bears.

This led us to investigate how individual fungi influence the palatability of leaves. Sets of leaf discs were differentiated by a system of notches and holes, sterilized, provided with nutrient solution, inoculated with a pure culture of the chosen fungus and incubated for 14 days. Then *Gammarus* was given a choice between several combinations of each particular leaf and various fungi. For three leaf species, Table 16.1 shows the whole sequence, from the fungus which improved the palatability most, to that with the least effect. The fungi which increased the palatability of leaves most were *Anguillospora* for maple and oak, and *Humicola* for ash. That with the smallest effect was *Tetracladium* for all three leaf species. Armed with this information, we set up an experiment in which *Gammarus* could choose between ash discs inoculated with *Humicola,* ash with *Tetracladium,* maple with *Tetracladium* and with *Anguillospora,* oak with *Anguillospora,* and oak with *Tetracladium.* After this experiment the combination most preferred (ash with *Humicola*) was deleted and a second experiment was done with the remaining five treatments. This procedure was repeated until the exact order of preference was established. The condition of the leaf discs at the end of the experiments is shown in Fig. 16.4. In each experiment, the leaf-fungus combination which had lost most weight through the feeding activity of *Gammarus* also showed the highest degree of skeletonization and could thus be picked out visually. The experiments show that the normal order of preference can, in fact, be changed or even reversed by an appropriate choice of fungal inoculum. For example, oak, normally the least popular leaf is chosen over maple and even ash, as long as the oak bears *Anguillospora* and the other leaf species bear *Tetracladium* (see Fig. 16.4). This clearly demonstrates the decisive influence

TABLE 16.1   Influence of fungi on palatability of three leaf species.

Ash		Maple		Oak	
1	Humicola	1	Anguillospora	1	Anguillospora
2	Fusarium	2	Fusarium	2	Humicola
3	Anguillospora*	3	Humicola	3	Alternaria
4	Alternaria	4	Cladosporium	4	Fusarium
5	Flagellospora*	5	Alternaria	5	Clavariopsis
6	Cladosporium	6	Flagellospora	6	Flagellospora
7	Aspergillus	7	Aspergillus	7	Cladosporium
8	Clavariopsis*	8	Clavariopsis	8	Aspergillus
9	Tricladium*	9	Tricladium	9	Tricladium
10	Tetracladium*	10	Tetracladium	10	Tetracladium

Humicola, Anguillospora and *Anguillospora* most improved the palatability of ash, maple and oak leaves respectively; *Tetracladium* had the least effect on all three leaf species. The leaves had been incubated for 14 days at 17°C in sterilized stream water with 10 mg $(NH_4)_2SO_4$ and 2.5 mg KH_2PO_4 added per litre. (* = aquatic fungi).

Leaf	Inoculum	Exp. 1	2	3	4	5
Ash	Humicola					
Maple	Anguillospora					
Oak	Anguillospora					
Ash	Tetracladium					
Maple	Tetracladium					
Oak	Tetracladium					

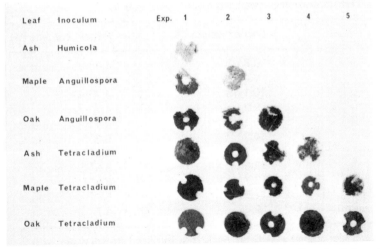

Fig. 16.4. Combined effect of leaf and fungus on food selection. Exp. 1: all six combinations were offered. Exp. 2: the most preferred combination of Exp. 1 was deleted. Exp. 3: the most preferred combination of Exp. 2 was also deleted etc.

which the fungal population of the leaves can have on food selection by *Gammarus*, and presumably other stream invertebrates, thereby potentially controlling and directing the turnover of leaf detritus. This information, combined with the various clearly defined preferences we have outlined above, suggests that the various leaf-fungus substrates fall along a graduate scale, from those which are eagerly eaten by the animals as soon as they become available, to those which are tardily and reluctantly consumed. This suggests a natural rationing or regulatory process which may help the large winter populations of benthic organisms to survive by spreading out their consumption of available food over a longer period than would be dictated by their natural appetites if all food materials were equally palatable.

16.3.3 Effect of Temperature

Most leaves which fall into streams do so in autumn or winter, when, at least in Canada, the water temperature is close to $0°C$, and they almost certainly support the high wintertime populations of benthos which occur in some streams (Hynes, 1970). If the fungi are to be of any major consequence they must be able to grow at this low temperature. Of the ten species which we used for feeding experiments, only the five aquatic species caused significant losses of dry weight and protein increases in sterilized leaves exposed to them at $0°C$ (see Table 16.2). Similarly, only they had any influence on the palatability of the leaves at this low temperature. Many more experiments with other species yielded comparable results, although the difference was not in all cases as absolute (unpublished data). Thornton (1963) working with pure cultures of aquatic hyphomycetes found them to be psychrotolerant. It seems safe to suggest that the aquatic hyphomycetes as a group are much less inhibited by very low temperatures than are many terrestrial fungi.

16.4 Conclusion and Prospects

The digestion of higher plant remains by animals is in most cases mediated by microorganisms. This is often an absolute necessity, since most invertebrates lack cellulases

TABLE 16.2   Decomposition of sterilized maple leaves at 0°C.

Inoculum	Loss of weight (%)	Protein content (%)
Aspergillus	9.8 n.s.	4.4 n.s.
Humicola	9.4 n.s.	4.8 n.s.
Fusarium	10.1 n.s.	4.7 n.s.
Cladosporium	9.2 n.s.	4.7 n.s.
Alternaria	10.1 n.s.	4.4 n.s.
Tricladium	14.3**	6.2**
Tetracladium	12.1**	6.0**
Anguillospora	13.9**	6.5**
Clavariopsis	13.7**	6.0**
Flagellospora	11.7*	5.6*
Control (no inoculum)	9.6	4.7

Sterilized leaves were incubated at 0°C for 14 days in sterilized stream water with 10 mg $(NH_4)_2SO_4$ and 2.5 mg KH_2PO_4 added per litre. Results of Duncan's Multiple Range Test:
n.s.: not significantly different from control;
*: significantly different at 5% level;
**: significantly different at 1% level.

and ligninases. In any case, the micro-organisms fulfil two important functions: they can be a major source of nutrients (proteins, fats, carbohydrates) or they can correct growth substance deficiences in the diet. The detritus feeders have evolved at least three mechanisms for exploiting these micro-organisms. They may, on the one hand, actually cultivate micro-organisms on the substrate (fungus gardens of ants, termites and beetles: Buchner, 1965) or they may have a gut microflora, often in specialized 'fermentation chambers', which digests natural polymers for them (Buchner, 1965); on the other hand they may simply ensure a supply of microbial substances by preferentially feeding on detritus which is already colonized by micro-organisms (Kaushik and Hynes, 1971; Minderman and Daniëls, 1966; Triska, 1970). We are concerned with this last strategy.

It appears that the fungi as a group have a definite edge over bacteria in initiating the breakdown of solid plant material, partly because of their superior enzymatic equipment, partly because their filamentous growth allows them to penetrate solid substrates (Harley, 1971), whereas the growth of bacteria may be more or less restricted to surfaces. Much of the bacterial activity depends directly on previous or concurrent presence of fungi. The bacteria decompose fungal hyphae (Tribe, 1961), and also take advantage of the fact that fungal hydrolysis of the substrate often releases an excess of soluble carbohydrates (Harley, 1971; Saitô, 1965). Fungal and bacterial growth then attracts animals, whose feeding breaks down the substrate into smaller particles, thereby increasing the surface area, and probably stimulating bacterial growth (Parr et al., 1967). The fungi obviously play a pivotal role at the very beginning of the breakdown.

We have shown that one aquatic detritus feeder's choice of food can be decisively influenced by the composition of the fungal flora present on the leaves. Because they can grow at very low water temperatures, and possibly also because of other as yet undetermined factors, the aquatic hyphomycetes seem to be the most important group in streams. Which factors, then, regulate their occurrence?

They are most abundant in clean, well aerated streams; less common in lakes and ponds, where they are concentrated on shores exposed to constant wave action; and rare or absent in dystrophic waters, characterized by low pH and large amounts of humic substances (Nilsson, 1964). Suzuki and Nimura (1961) report that they are more common and grow better in harmonic than in acid lakes.

They usually grow on leaves of deciduous trees, but may also colonize other substrates such as wood, paper or even glass (Nilsson, 1964). Ingold (1966), summing up over 20 years of observations on this group, mentions that he never found them on conifer needles.

These reports are too general to allow any definite statements about their requirements. It does appear that they are highly aerobic, and that they may be sensitive to acid conditions. Can these observed or suspected properties be related to factors which regulate the breakdown of vegetable matter in natural streams and consequently the composition of the fauna? In the Belgian Ardennes, afforestation with spruce of large areas originally supporting deciduous forests or heath resulted in a drastic reduction of the aquatic fauna, invertebrates and vertebrates, in nearby streams, and a lowering of the pH of the water (Huet, 1951). It was suggested that these effects were due to the release of toxins from the conifer needles and to shading of the streams which prevented the growth of algae which originally served as food for invertebrates. The tough conifer needles apparently made poor substitutes. The decay of conifer needles in terrestrial habitats has been the subject of several studies (Kendrick and Burges, 1962; Hayes, 1965; Gremmen, 1960), but a full investigation of their breakdown in aquatic habitats is clearly long overdue.

Egglishaw (1968) and Egglishaw and Morgan (1965), found in nine streams in Scotland that the rate of disintegration of plant material depended on the concentration of Ca^{++} and HCO_3^- ions. The higher their concentration, and consequently the higher the pH, the faster was the dead plant material decomposed, and the larger were the standing stocks of many benthic invertebrates.

It is tempting to suggest that in both cases part of the observed effect was caused by diminished activity of the aquatic hyphomycetes, mitigated by the absence of suitable substrate or by the lowered pH. But it must be remembered that bacteria are usually much more inhibited by acid conditions than fungi, and there is no doubt that they can decisively influence the trophic structures of natural waters. Still, it appears that a careful study of preferences and tolerances of aquatic hyphomycetes for various concentrations of Ca^{++}, HCO_3^- and pH ranges combined with observations of their natural occurrence in waters of different qualities would prove extremely enlightening.

As mentioned before, the growth of some fungi can double the protein content of some leaf species in a short time. This figure may be used to represent the 'standing crop' of fungal biomass; it is the resultant of fungal growth and the feeding activity of invertebrates (which can be assumed to ingest preferentially those parts with highest fungal concentration). The real production of protein by fungi during the residence of leaves in the stream may be considerably higher. It can be assumed that fungi convert their substrate into their own biomass with an efficiency of 40-70% (Harley, 1971). Even if this percentage is only approached, the amount of fungal biomass produced each year will still be impressive. Hynes (1970) estimates that a stream in a wooded valley received at least a kilogram of leaves per metre of its length per year.

Our own experiments and other reports have clearly demonstrated that the fungi, especially the typical freshwater hyphomycetes, are invaluable members of the stream community and can no longer be neglected in any comprehensive account of life in running waters. They play a key role in unlocking and distributing a major source of energy in streams. This is a very new and wide open field; we look forward to an extremely productive period, and we hope that this summary of current research will encourage more ecologically oriented mycologists to 'get their feet wet'.

References

BAIER, R. G. (1935). 'Studien zur Hydrobakteriologie stehender Binnengewässer.' *Arch. Hydrobiol.*, 29, 183-264.

BANDONI, R. J. (1972). 'Terrestrial occurrence of some aquatic hyphomycetes.' *Can. J. Bot.* 50, 2283-2288.

BÄRLOCHER, F., and KENDRICK, B. (1973a). 'Fungi in the diet of *Gammarus pseudolimnaeus.' Oikos*, 24, 295-300.

BÄRLOCHER, F., and KENDRICK, B. (1973 b). 'Fungi and food preferences of *Gammarus pseudolimnaeus.' Arch. Hydrobiol.*, 72, 501-506.

BJARNOV, N. (1972). 'Carbohydrases in *Chironomus, Gammarus* and some *Trichoptera* larvae.' *Oikos* 23, 261-263

BROWN, D. S. (1961). 'The food of the larvae of *Chloeon dipterum* L. and *Baetis rhodani* (Pictet) (Insecta, Ephemeroptera).' *J. Anim. Ecol.*, 30, 55-75.

BUCHNER, P. (1965). *Endosymbiosis of Animals with Plant Microorganisms.* John Wiley and Sons, New York, 909 pp.

BURGES, A., and RAW, F. (1967). *Soil Biology.* Academic Press, London and New York. 532 pp.

CUMMINS, K. W., COFFMAN, W. P., and ROFF, P. A. (1966). 'Trophic relations in a small woodland stream.' *Verh. int. Verein. theor. angew. Limnol.*, 16, 627-638.

DAUBENMIRE, R., and PRUSSO. D. C. (1963). 'Studies of the decomposition rates of tree litter.' *Ecology*, 44, 589-592.

EGGLISHAW, H. J. (1968). 'The quantitative relationship between bottom fauna and plant detritus in streams of different calcium concentration.' *J. appl. Ecol.*, 5, 731-740.

EGGLISHAW, H. J., and MORGAN, N. C. (1965). 'A survey of the bottom fauna of streams in the Scottish Highlands. Part II: The relationship of the fauna to the chemical and geological conditions. '*Hydrobiologia*, 26, 173-183.

FISHER, S. G., and LIKENS, G. E. (1972). 'Stream ecosystem: organic energy budget.' *Bioscience*, 22, 33-35.

FREDEEN, F. J. H. (1964). 'Bacteria as food for blackfly larvae (Diptera: Simuliidae) in laboratory cultures and in natural streams.' *Can. J. Zool.*, 42, 527-538.

GREMMEN, J. (1960). 'A contribution to the mycoflora of the pine forests in the Netherlands.' *Nova Hedwigia*, 1, 251-288.

HARGRAVE, B. T. (1970). 'The utilization of benthic microflora by *Hyalella azteca* (Amphipoda).' *J. Anim. Ecol.*, 39, 427-437.

HARLEY, J. L. (1971). 'Fungi in ecosystems.' *J. appl. Ecol.*, 8, 627-642.

HAYES, A. J. (1965). 'Studies on the decomposition of coniferous leaf litter. II. Changes in external features and succession of microfungi.' *J. Soil Sci.*, 16, 242-257.

HERING, H. T. (1967). 'Fungal decomposition of oak leaf litter.' *Trans. Br. mycol. Soc.*, 50, 267-273.

HUET, M. (1951). 'Novicité des boisements en Epicéas *(Picea excelsa* Link.)' *Verh. int. Verein. Theor. angew. Limnol.,* 11, 189-200.

HYNES, H. B. N. (1970). *The Ecology of Running Waters.* University of Toronto Press. 555 pp.

INGOLD, C. T. (1942). 'Aquatic hyphomycetes of decaying alder leaves.' *Trans. Br. mycol. Soc.,* 25, 339-417.

INGOLD, C. T. (1966). 'The tetraradiate aquatic fungal spore.' *Mycologia,* 58, 43-56.

IVLEV, V. S. (1945). 'The biological productivity of waters' (Russian, translated W. E. Ricker, 1966, *J. Fish. Res. Bd. Can.,* 23, 1727-1759.)

KAUSHIK, N. K., and HYNES, H. B. N. (1968). 'Experimental study on the role of autumn-shed leaves in aquatic environments.' *J. Ecol.,* 56, 229-243.

KAUSHIK, N. K., and HYNES, H. B. N. (1971). 'The fate of the dead leaves that fall into streams.' *Arch. Hydrobiol.,* 68, 465-515.

KENDRICK, W. B., and BURGES, A. (1962). 'Biological aspects of the decay of *Pinus silvestris* leaf litter.' *Nova Hedwigia,* 4, 313-342.

KNIGHT, C. B., and ANGEL, R. A. (1967). 'A preliminary study of the dietary requirements of *Tomocerus* (Collembola).' *Am. Midl. Nat.,* 77, 510-517.

MARZOLF, R. G. (1965). 'Substrate relations of the burrowing amphipod *Pontoporeia affinis* in Lake Michigan.' *Ecology,* 46, 579-592.

MINDERMAN, G., and DANIËLS, L. (1966). 'Colonization of newly fallen leaves by micro-organisms.' In *Progress in Soil Biology* (Eds. O. Graff and J. E. Satchell), North-Holland Publishing Company, Amsterdam. 3-9.

MÜLLER, E., and LOEFFLER, W. (1971). *Mykologie,* Georg Thieme Verlag, Stuttgart. 340 pp.

NELSON, D. J., and SCOTT. D. C. (1962). 'Role of detritus in the productivity of a rock-outcrop community in a Piedmont stream.' *Limnol. Oceanogr.,* 7, 396-413.

NEWELL, R. (1965). 'The role of detritus in the nutrition of two marine deposit feeders, the Prosobranch *Hydrobia ulvae* and the bivalve *Macoma balthiea.'* *Proc. zool. Soc. Lond.,* 144, 25-45.

NIELSEN, C. O. (1962). 'Carbohydrases in soil and litter invertrebrates.' *Oikos,* 13, 200-215.

NILSSON, S. (1964). 'Freshwater hyphomycetes.' *Symb. bot. Upsal.,* 18, 1-130.

ODUM, E. P. (1971). *Fundamentals of Ecology.* W. B. Saunders, Philadelphia. 574 pp.

ODUM, E. P., and DE LA CRUZ, A. (1963). 'Detritus as a major component of ecosystems.' *AIBS Bulletin* (now *Bioscience*), 13, 39-40.

ODUM, E. P., and DE LA CRUZ, A. (1967). 'Particulate organic detritus in a Georgian salt marsh-estuarine ecosystem.' In *Estuaries* (Ed. G. Lauff) Amer. Assoc. Adv. Sci. Publ., 83, 383-388.

PARR, J. F., PARKINSON, D., and NORMAN, A. G. (1967). 'Growth and activity of soil microorganisms in glass micro-beads: II. Oxygen uptake and direct observations.' *Soil Sci.,* 103, 303-310.

PETERSEN, R. H. (1962). 'Aquatic hyphomycetes from North America. I. Aleuriosporae (Part I) and key to the genera.' *Mycologia,* 54, 117-151,

PETERSEN, R. H. (1963 a). 'Aquatic hyphomycetes from North America. II. Aleuriosporae (Part 2), and blastosporae.' *Mycologia,* 55, 18-29.

PETERSEN, R. H. (1963 b). 'Aquatic hyphomycetes from North America. III. Phialosporae and miscellaneous species.' *Mycologia,* 55, 570-581.

SAITÔ, T. (1957). 'Chemical changes in beech litter under microbiological decomposition.' *Ecol. Rev.,* 14, 209-216.

SAITO, T. (1965). 'Coactions between litter-decomposing hymenomycetes and their associated microorganisms during decomposition of beech litter.' *Sci. Rep. Tohoku. Univ. Ser. IV. (Biol.),* 31, 255-273.

SCHLEGEL, H. G. (1972). *Allgemeine Microbiologie.* Georg Thieme Verlag, Stuttgart. 461 pp.

SIMROTH, H. (1891). *Die Entstehung der Landtiere.* Leipzig.

SMIRNOV, N. N. (1958). 'Some data about the food consumption of plant production of bogs and fens by animals.' *Verh. int. Venein. Theor. angew. Limnol.,* 13, 363-368

SUZUKI, S., and NIMURA, H. (1961). 'Relation between the distribution of aquatic hyphomycetes in Japanese lake types.' *Bot. Mag. Tokyo,* 74, 51-55.

TEAL, J. M. (1957). 'Community metabolism in a temperate cold spring.' *Ecol. Monogr.,* 27, 283-302.

THORNTON, D. R. (1963). 'The physiology and nutrition of some aquatic hyphomycetes.' *J. gen. Microbiol.,* 33, 23-31.

TRIBE, H. T. (1961). 'Microbiology of cellulose decomposition in soil.' *Soil Sci.,* 92, 61-77.

TRISKA, F. J. (1970). 'Seasonal distribution of aquatic hyphomycetes in relation to the disappearance of leaf litter from a woodland stream'. Ph. D. Thesis, University of Pittsburgh.

17 Interactions between Aquatic Fungi and DDT

MADELINE HODKINSON

17.1 Introduction

The synthetic chlorinated hydrocarbon compound, dichloro-diphenyl-trichloroethane (DDT), has been used extensively to control insect pests in agriculture, horticulture, silviculture, industry and public health (Edwards and Heath, 1964; Martin, 1965; Busvine, 1966). The principal constituents of commercial DDT are 1, 1, 1-trichloro-2, 2-bis(p-chlorophenyl) ethane (p, p'-DDT) and 1, 1, 1-trichloro-2-0-chlorophenyl-2-p-chlorophenylethane (o, p'-DDT). Löfroth (1968) estimates that about a million

$p, p'-DDT$ $o, p'-DDT$

metric tons of the insecticide have been used since large-scale production began in 1942. DDT has been detected in regions far removed from treated areas and is now considered to have a worldwide distribution (George and Frear, 1966; Sladen, et al., 1966; Tatton and Ruzicka, 1967; Holden and Marsden, 1967; Woodwell et al., 1971).

DDT, like other pesticides, is an economic poison distributed for the purpose of inducing population changes in the target species (Dustman and Stickel, 1966). It has been shown that pollution of aquatic and terrestrial ecosystems by DDT and other pesticides produces serious biological effects in non-target organism. These compounds may cause (1) death from acute or chronic toxicity; (2) reproductive impairment; (3) disruption of species balance; and (4) behavioural alteration (Dustman and Stickel, 1966).

In ecological systems, the reciprocal interaction in which the biota affects the fate of the pesticide is equally important. Cope (1965) suggests this might involve (1) the trapping of the pesticide on the surface of an organism; (2) the accumulation of the pesticide within an organism; (3) the degradation of the pesticide; and (4) the excretion of the pesticide or its metabolites. Thus, biological processes might influence environmental contamination by effecting removal, inactivation or destruction of DDT. Alternatively, they might encourage its persistence and accumulation. Pesticides can also be altered biologically to yield products that are either more toxic to the target species, or toxic to other organisms (Alexander, 1967).

Recognition of the seriousness of these problems has led to the introduction of legislation to restrict DDT usage in several countries (Walker, 1971; Woodwell et al., 1971; Gillette, 1972). This legislation is unlikely to have immediate effect because DDT is one of the most persistent insecticides (Alexander, 1965; Edwards, 1966). The persistence of DDT in natural ecosystems has stimulated research into the effects of the insecticide on microbial activity and the ability of micro-organisms to metabolize it. Interactions between soil populations and pesticides have been reviewed by Bollen (1961), Alexander (1964), Edwards (1966) and Martin (1966). More recently the interaction of pesticides with various groups of aquatic micro-organisms has been investigated (Ware and Roan, 1970). In this chapter the *in vitro* interactions between aquatic fungi and DDT are considered. The environmental implications of this work are discussed.

17.2   Aquatic Fungi

Ainsworth and Bisby (1963) define aquatic fungi as fungi living in water. The aquatic fungal populations in freshwater and seawater consist of representatives of the phycomycetes, Fungi Imperfecti, Ascomycetes and the Basidiomycetes (Sparrow, 1968; Johnson, 1968). A submerged aquatic mycoflora which produces non-motile spores has been described by Ingold (1954, 1959, 1961), Nilsson (1964) and others. In the majority of species the spores are branched and the commonest type is composed of four arms diverging from or near a common point (Ingold, 1966). These tetra-radiate spores occur in all the main groups of fungi, save the phycomycetes, although most belong to the Fungi Imperfecti. In a number of other aquatic species the spores are sigmoid or crescent-shaped. Few aquatic species have spherical or ovoid spores, the commonest spore shape of sub-aerial species (Ingold, 1959). Amongst the phycomycetes, the aquatic species produce motile zoospores (Sparrow, 1960).

From the heterotrophic nature of fungi, it seems their role in the aquatic environment is concerned with the utilization and transformation of organic matter (Sparrow, 1968). Various groups of saprophytic fungi attack many kinds of submerged plant and animal debris (Johnson, 1968; Sparrow, 1968), but there is little information concerning the precise function of individual species. However, some aquatic fungi appear to be physiologically specialized for the destruction of specific substrates, for example, lignin, cellulose, chitin and keratin. Other aquatic fungi, through parasitism, exercise an important influence on biological productivity (Sparrow, 1960). In addition, fungi which are not normally considered part of the aquatic biota, are found in aquatic habitats (Johnson and Sparrow, 1961; Willoughby and Collins, 1966; Anastasiou and Churchland, 1969; Bridge-Cooke, 1968; Newton and Hodkinson, 1971; Pugh and Mulder, 1971). Although of terrestrial origin, many of these fungi are associated with decaying plant material in water. In this chapter zoosporic phycomycetes and imperfect fungi with branched spores (ref. Ingold) are described as aquatic, but reference is also made to other groups of fungi.

17.3 DDT Pollution of the Aquatic Environment

According to Walker (1971), 'Pesticides are pollutants when they, their metabolites, or their degradation products remain in the environment after the desired purpose has been accomplished or when they reach some part of the environment other than the intended target'. On the basis of this definition DDT may be described as an environmental pollutant.

DDT pollution of the aquatic environment arises from (1) measures taken to control the waterborne stages of insect vectors of animal diseases (Simmons, 1959); (2) accidental spillage (Nicholson, et al., 1962; Marth, 1965; Westlake and Gunther, 1966); (3) airborne drift and drainage from DDT-treated land and water masses (Cope, 1961; Briedenbach and Lichtenberg, 1963; Grzenda, et al., 1964; Grzenda and Nicholson, 1965; Terriere et al., 1966; Hindin et al., 1966; Lichtenstein et al., 1966; Briedenbach et al., 1967); (4) the sedimentation of wind blown contaminated dust particles (West, 1964; Antommarria et al., 1965; Tabor, 1965; Abbott et al., 1965, 1966); and (5) the precipitation of the insecticide by rainwater (Wheatley and Hardman, 1965; Cohen and Pinkerton, 1966; Risebrough et al., 1968).

DDT has been detected in the surface waters or bottom sediments of (1) springs (Terriere et al., 1966); (2) wells (Hindin et al., 1964); (3) sewage effluents (Holden and Marsden, 1966); (4) irrigation canals (Hindin et al., 1964, 1966); (5) ponds (Bridges et al., 1963); (6) lakes (Middleton and Lichtenberg, 1960; Mack et al., 1964; Hindin et al., 1964); (7) streams (Cope, 1961; Welch and Spindler, 1964; Grzenda et al., 1964; Grzenda and Nicholson, 1965; Holden and Marsden, 1966; Cole, et al., 1967); (8) rivers (Middleton and Lichtenberg, 1960; Briedenbach and Lichtenberg, 1963; Hindin et al., 1964; Barthel et al., 1966; Sparr et al., 1966); (9) river estuaries (Weaver et al., 1965; Butler, 1966; Briedenbach et al., 1967); (10) tidal marshes (Croker and Wilson, 1965); and (11) melt waters of Antarctic snows (Peterle, 1969).

The concentration of DDT in waters which receive direct applications of the insecticide are usually greater than 10 parts in 10^{12} (ppb) (Bridges et al., 1963; Welch and Spindler, 1964; Cole et al., 1967). Concentrations in the range 0.001 to 1 ppb have been recorded in water which received the DDT indirectly (Grzenda and Nicholson, 1965; Terriere et al., 1966; Briedenbach et al., 1967). The insecticide is not held long in solution as it has a low aqueous solubility of 1 to 10 ppb (Biggar et al., 1967). Most of the DDT entering natural waters is rapidly adsorbed by suspended particles (Lasher and Applegate, 1966) and aquatic organisms (Bridges et al., 1963). In non-turbulent conditions, DDT-laden particles sediment quickly. If the flow of water is turbulent,

TABLE 17.1 DDT (ppm)* in components of aquatic ecosystems.

Author	Water	Sediment	Vegetation	Animals
Cope (1961)	0.03		2.3	14
Bridges et al. (1963)	0.08	2.4	30	2.5
Mack et al. (1964)	0.00033	0.07	0.01	38.4
Grzenda and Nicholson (1965)	9 (ppt)	4.62	2.94	

*: Except where stated otherwise.
ppt: parts per trillion.
Values are the maximum quoted by each author.

the DDT remains in suspension and may be transported several miles before it settles (Cope, 1961). The concentration of DDT in aquatic sediments is much higher than in water (Sparr et al., 1966; Bridges et al., 1963; Hindin et al., 1964; Mack et al., 1964; Grzenda and Nicholson, 1965). Even greater concentrations are found in aquatic plants and animals compared with the surrounding water (Table 17.1).

17.4   Effects of DDT on Fungi

The evaluation of DDT toxicity to fungi has usually involved measuring the effect of different concentrations of the insecticide on the growth of pure cultures. Depending on whether liquid or solid media are used, the amounts of dried mycelium or the colony diameters are measured, respectively. Other direct effects of DDT have been determined by studying the metabolic, respirometric and reproductive responses of fungi and the factors which influence them.

17.4.1   Influence of DDT on Fungal Growth

Dalton et al. (1970) found that the aquatic hyphomycete, Heliscus submersus Hudson exhibits an enhanced rate of growth in liquid medium containing 0.1 to 60 parts per million (ppm) of DDT. At concentrations greater than 2 ppm, the growth of Tetracladium setigerum (Grove) Ingold, Varicosporium elodeae Kegel and Clavariopsis aquatica de Wild is also enhanced. Hodkinson and Dalton (1973) later demonstrated that DDT stimulates the growth of the aquatic phycomycetes, Isoachlya sp., I. monilifera (de Barry) Kauffman, Saprolegnia sp. and Pythium sp. Terrestrial fungi isolated from aquatic habitats, Aureobasidium pullulans (de Barry) Arnaud, Cephalosporium acremonium Corda, Cladosporium cladosporioides (Fres.) de Vries and Cylindrocarpon orthosporium (Sacc.) Wollenw. are similarly affected. The growth rates of the fungi increase with increasing DDT concentration. A linear relationship exists between the growth of H. submersus and DDT concentrations up to about 35 ppm (Dalton and Smith, 1971). Only three of the 12 fungi respond readily to 2 ppm of DDT; but half the species tested show no reaction at this concentration.

Richardson and Miller (1960) described a dosage/response relationship for a variety of Rhizoctonia solani Kühn pathogenic to peas. In this case the DDT is fungitoxic. The percentage inhibition of mycelial growth increases with increasing DDT concentration from 0.2 to 100 ppm. The dosage response curve is bimodal and the shape is determined by two physical properties of the DDT; solubility in water and vapour pressure. Ramaraje Urs et al. (1967) also found that DDT has an inhibitory effect on the entomogenous fungi Beauveria bassiana Vuill. and Metarrhizium anisopliae (Metsch.) Sorokin. Growth retardation is caused by 40, 50, 60 and 100 ppm of DDT. Under certain conditions 100 ppm of DDT is completely inhibitory to B. bassiana. The insecticide also delays the onset of sporulation at DDT concentrations up to 50 ppm. At 60 and 100 ppm, spore production is prevented.

Other in vitro studies involving soil isolates have shown that DDT has no effect upon their growth. Ko and Lockwood (1968a, b) found that Aphanomyces eutreiches Dreschler, Fusarium solani (Martius) Aprel et Wollenweber, Penicillium frequentans Westling, Pythium ultimum Trow., Trichoderma viride Pers. Gray, Verticillium alboatrum Reinke et Berthold, Helminthosporium victoriae Meehan et Murphy, Glomerella cingulata (Stonem.) Spauld. et v. Shrenck, Mucor ramannianus Möller and Rhizoctonia solani are unaffected by up to 100 ppm of DDT.

17.4.2 Factors affecting the Growth Response.

A number of environmental conditions affect the growth responses of fungi to DDT. In particular, the nutritional status of the environment in which fungi and DDT interact determines the nature of the growth response. Dalton and Smith (1971) reported that the growth rate of *Heliscus submersus,* which is enhanced by DDT in basal medium, is retarded when either maltose, sucrose, lactose or arabinose is provided as the main carbon source. The insecticide impairs the efficient utilization of the carbohydrates as data in Table 17.2 illustrate. Since there is an increase in the acidity of the culture media, which is associated with the accumulation of pyruvate, the DDT possibly inhibits acetyl Co-A formation. When glucose or fructose is used, there is no change in fungal growth rate or substrate utilization. Richardson and Miller (1960) found that the growth of *Rhizoctonia solani* on Czapek-Dox agar is inhibited by 100 ppm of DDT. No change in growth rate was recorded by Ko and Lockwood (1968) when the fungus was cultured on nutrient agar containing a similar quantity of insecticide.

TABLE 17.2   Effect of DDT on the growth of *Heliscus submersus* in medium containing different carbohydrates.

Basal medium + 0.0117M carbohydrate	Molar growth yield* (mg/m. mole)		pH of medium	
	Control	DDT (25 ppm)	Control	DDT (25 ppm)
Glucose	73	73	5.1	5.1
Fructose	78	77	4.9	4.8
Maltose	72	56	4.8	4.1
Sucrose	72	52	4.7	4.1
Lactose	71	46	5.1	3.8
Arabinose	77	53	5.3	4.2

$$* \quad \text{Molar growth yield} = \frac{\text{Dry weight of culture (mg)}}{\text{Weight of substrate utilized (m. mole)}}$$

The chemical environment also influences the degree to which fungal growth is affected by DDT. Hodkinson and Dalton (1973) found that DDT increases the growth rates of *H. submersus, Isoachlya* sp. and *Cladosporium cladosporioides* in a variety of media. The percentage increases in growth in water and mineral medium are much greater than in media enriched with yeast extract, but the mycelial yields are smaller (Tables 17.3 and 17.4). They suggested that the insecticide provides the fungi with a source of carbon and energy which is more efficiently utilized in the presence of accessory growth factors. Anderson and Lichtenstein (1971) reported that DDT does not support the growth of spores and mycelium of *Mucor alternans* van Tieghem when no other carbon source is present.

The reactions of fungi to DDT are dependent to some extent on physical culture conditions. Because DDT is poorly soluble in water, it is usually added to aqueous media in an organic solvent such as acetone. The insecticide separates out from solution to produce a fine precipitate in the medium. As the DDT concentration is increased, heavier precipitates are formed. Dalton and Smith (1971) estimate that up

TABLE 17.3   Percentage increase in fungal growth in different media containing 60 ppm of DDT*.

Fungus	20°C				5°C			
	DW	MS	YE	BM	DW	MS	YE	BM
Isoachlya sp.	500	300	40	33	1000	575	37	24
H. submersus	600	240	94	45	600	250	19	38
C. cladosporioides	100	160	40	45	100	128	20	36

*Growth determined after 100 hours' at 20°C and 400 hours' incubation at 5°C
DW: distilled water.
YE: yeast extract.
MS: mineral salts.
BM: basal medium.

TABLE 17.4   Mycelial yields in different media containing 60 ppm of DDT.

Fungus	Mycelial yield (mg) at							
	20°C				5°C			
	DW	MS	YE	BM	DW	MS	YE	BM
Isoachlya sp.	3	6	16	18	5	6	18	21
H. submersus	7	9	24	30	3	5	22	28
C. cladosporioides	5	9	26	30	3	7	24	29

Growth determined after 100 hours' at 20°C and 400 hours' incubation at 5°C
DW: distilled water.
YE: yeast extract.
MS: mineral salts.
BM: basal medium.

to 20% of the increased growth of *H. submersus*, *Isoachlya* sp. and *C. cladosporioides* in DDT media is associated with insecticide particles providing more or larger loci for growth. When the insecticide is incorporated into agar rather than liquid media, the fungal growth response is different. Ramaraje Urs *et al.* (1967) found that 100 ppm of DDT completely inhibits the growth of *Beauveria bassiana* in a liquid medium, but growth occurs when the medium contains 2% agar. The difference in growth is perhaps related to a concentration effect. The low aqueous solubility of DDT must restrict its diffusion through the gel and thus limit its availability to the fungus. Adsorption onto the gel might further diminish the amount of available insecticide.

17.4.3   Influence of DDT on Fungal Respiration

Dalton and Smith (1971) found that DDT has no detectable effect on the respiration of *Heliscus submersus* during the early stages of incubation when the fungus has had

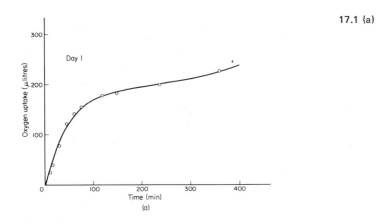

17.1 (a)

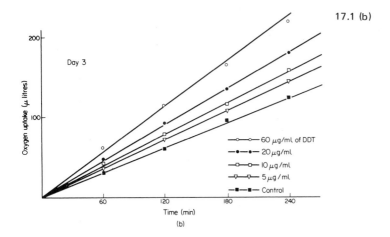

17.1 (b)

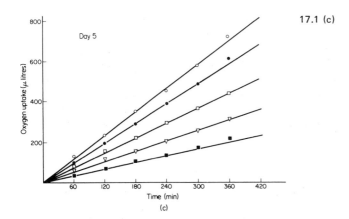

17.1 (c)

Figure 17.1. Oxygen uptake by *Heliscus submersus* in the presence of DDT. (a) Day 1. (b) Day 3. (c) Day 5.

no previous contact with DDT. As the incubation period proceeds, the insecticide stimulates the respiration rate (Fig. 17.1). This suggests the fungus requires a period of preconditioning before DDT affects metabolism. If mycelium which has been pregrown in DDT medium is used, there is no lag phase and fungal respiration is stimulated immediately. The respiration rate increases with increasing DDT concentration and a linear relationship exists between oxygen consumption and DDT concentration up to about 35 ppm. However, there is an upper limiting DDT concentration above which no further stimulation of fungal metabolism occurs. An investigation of the effect of DDT on carbohydrate metabolism revealed that the insecticide increases the respiratory quotients of various sugars (Table 17.5). This indicates that DDT inhibits the normal aerobic oxidation of sugars and correspondingly increases the anaerobic fermentation process.

TABLE 17.5   The effect of DDT on the respiration of sugars by *Heliscus submersus.*

| Phosphate buffer + 0.0017M carbohydrate | Respiratory quotient* | |
	Control culture without DDT	Culture + 20 ppm of DDT
Glucose	0.99	1.16
Fructose	1.01	1.17
Maltose	1.03	1.17
Sucrose	1.07	1.19
Lactose	0.99	1.33
Arabinose	1.01	1.23

* Respiratory quotient = $\dfrac{\text{volume of } CO_2 \text{ liberated}}{\text{volume of } O_2 \text{ consumed}}$

17.5 Effects of Fungi on the Fate of DDT

The effects of fungi on DDT persistence have been investigated by examining the ability of fungi to accumulate the insecticide or to degrade it. The uptake of DDT has been studied by measuring the rate at which the insecticide is either lost from a medium or is concentrated by fungal cells. Radiotracer techniques, using carbon[14] -DDT, have been used for this purpose. Evidence for the decomposition of the insecticide has been sought using the techniques of thin layer chromatography (TLC), gas-liquid chromatography (GLC), infrared spectroscopy (IRS) and mass spectrometry (MS). Various fractions of fungal and culture medium extracts have been analysed for DDT metabolites by these methods.

17.5.1   Accumulation of DDT by Fungi

The biological accumulation of DDT is rapidly achieved by both actively metabolizing and dead fungi. Dalton and Smith (1971) investigated the persistence of C^{14}–DDT in a medium to which living and ethylene oxide killed mycelia of *Heliscus submersus, Isoachlya* sp. and *Cladosporium cladosporioides* were added. Between 62 and 83% of the insecticide was lost from the medium within 15 minutes. The loss increased over a

454

period of 24 hours to between 71 and 95%. Most of the DDT was recovered from the fungal mycelia and the percentage uptake increased with prolonged exposure. Both the living and dead fungi accumulated the insecticide, but after 24 hours the live cultures contained up to 5% more DDT/mg of mycelium. The rate of accumulation also decreased with increased mycelial age. Kallman and Andrews (1963) found that living cultures of *Saccharomyces cerevisiae* Hausen accumulate much more insecticide than controls containing boiled cells.

The ability to accumulate DDT is common to a variety of fungi under different environmental conditions (Table 17.6). The results obtained by Ko and Lockwood (1968) indicate that species differ in their capacity to concentrate DDT. However, it is not possible to compare the abilities of other fungi to accumulate DDT since either different amounts of the various mycelia were used, or insufficient data were reported. The quantity of mycelium affects the rate of DDT accumulation. Barry (1968) found that the rate at which DDT is taken up by *Tetracladium setigerum* increases with increasing amounts of mycelium. The rate of accumulation is also affected by the pH of the medium. Chacko and Lockwood (1967) recorded that *Trichoderma viride* accumulates 90 to 100% of available DDT at pH 3.0, 5.5 and 8.0 in 24 hours. At pH 11.0 only 52% of the DDT is taken up.

TABLE 17.6 Accumulation of DDT by fungal mycelium.

Author	Fungus	Experimental details	Uptake	
Chacko and Lockwood (1967)	*Mucor ramannianus* *Glomerella cingulata* *Trichoderma viride*	Incubation for 4 hours in water containing 0.1 to 1 ppm of DDT.	83 ⎞ 77 ⎬ 60 ⎠	% of the available DDT.
Ko and Lockwood (1968)	*Pythium ultimum* *Rhizoctonia solani* *Aphanomyces eutreiches* *Fusarium solani*	Incubation of 50 mg of wet mycelium for 24 hours in soil containing 42 μg of DDT/g of moist soil.	9 ⎞ 8 ⎪ 6 ⎬ 4 ⎠	μg of DDT per gram of wet mycelium
Dalton (1971)	*Cladosporium cladosporioides* *Isoachlya* sp. *Heliscus submersus*	Incubation for 24 hours in medium containing 20 ppm of DDT.	86 ⎞ 85 ⎬ 79 ⎠	% of the available DDT

17.5.2 Decomposition of DDT by Fungi

A number of fungi have been found which partially degrade DDT *in vitro*. Dalton and Smith (1971) analysed hexane extracts of the culture filtrates and mycelia of aquatic hyphomycetes by GLC. *Tetracladium setigerum* and *Varicosporium elodeae* failed to decompose the insecticide but *Clavariopsis aquatica* converted 6% of the DDT to its metabolites, 1, 1-dichloro-2, 2-bis (p-chlorophenyl) ethane (TDE or DDD) and 1, 1-dichloro-2, 2-bis(p-chlorophenyl)ethylene (DDE). *Heliscus submersus* exhibited a greater capacity to degrade the insecticide. About 35% was converted to DDD (27%) and DDE (8%) in 330 hours. The aquatic phycomycete, *Isoachlya* sp. and the hyphomycete, *Cladosporium cladosporioides* similarly metabolise DDT. Initially DDE is produced at a faster rate than DDD, but with time, the rate of DDD formation increases rapidly and DDE production levels off (Fig. 17.2). In the presence of lactose in stand-

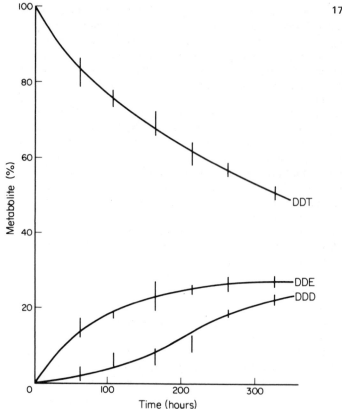

Figure 17.2. Breakdown of DDT in basal medium by *Heliscus submersus.*

ing culture, *H. submersus* also produces 4-chlorocatechol. Kallman and Andrews (1963) found that commercial yeast, *Saccharomyces cerevisiae,* rapidly converts over 50% of available DDT to DDD in 50 hours.

Fungi vary in their ability to decompose DDT. Dalton and Smith (1971) recorded the highest percentage conversion of DDT with *H. submersus* and the lowest with *Isoachlya* sp., after 100 hours incubation. Engst *et al.* (1967) found that five fungal isolates from carrot purée degrade DDT to DDD and DDE, but the most active isolate was *Fusarium solani.* Another metabolite, 4, 4' − dichlorobenzophenone (DBP) was also identified in extracts of this fungus. Matsumura and Boush (1968) tested 18 strains of *Trichoderma viride* for DDT decomposition and found one strain which converts 89% in 3 days. The main metabolite was 1-bis(p-chlorophenyl) ethane (DDNS or dicofol). Eight strains produced DDD and dicofol, three produced only DDD and one produced DDE and DDD. Six strains did not degrade the insecticide.

Unidentified metabolites have been detected in cultures of *Mucor alternans* (Anderson *et al.,* (1970). The insecticide is partially degraded in 2 to 4 days to three hexane soluble and two water soluble products. Anderson and Lichtenstein (1972) examined the effects of a wider range of fungi on C^{14}-DDT persistence. Of *M. alternans, Aspergillus flavus* Link ex Link, *Aspergillus niger* van Tiegham, *Aspergillus fumigatus* Fresenius, *Fusarium oxysporum* Schlechtendahl, *Mucor mucedo* Fr., *Penicillium notatum* Westling, *Rhizoctonia solani* and *T.viride,* only *M. alternans* and *M. mucedo* produced water soluble metabolites after 5 days' incubation. Chacko *et al.* (1966) found that *A. niger, Fusarium solani, Fusarium solani* (Mart.) Sacc. f. *phaseoli* (Burkh) Snyder et Hansen, *Glomerella cingulata, Helminthosporium victoriae, Mucor ramannianus, Myrothecium verrucaria* (Al. and Sch.) Ditmars ex Fries, *Penicillium frequentans* and *T. viride* do not decompose the insecticide when cultured in a medium containing 5 to 10 ppm of DDT.

17.5.3 Factors affecting DDT Decomposition

A number of environmental conditions affect the decomposition of DDT by fungi. Dalton and Smith (1971) found that the type of carbohydrate affects the percentage conversion of DDT to its metabolites. In media containing lactose, maltose, arabinose or sucrose, *Heliscus submersus* converted 64, 50, 49 and 41%, respectively, of the available DDT. Fructose and glucose restricted DDT conversion to 15 and 14%, respectively. When *H. submersus, Isoachlya* sp. and *Cladosporium cladosporioides* were cultured in media containing 60 ppm of DDT, a higher percentage of the insecticide was decomposed in an aqueous solution of yeast extract and a mineral salts solution containing yeast extract, than in water or the salts solution. Anderson and Lichtenstein (1971) obtained a greater quantity of DDT metabolites in cultures of *Mucor alternans* when the glucose concentration was increased from 1 to 2.5g/litre. The largest quantity of metabolities was obtained when glucose was the carbon source and ammonium nitrate the nitrogen source. Six out of the eight sugars and seven out of the nine nitrogen sources they tested produced over 30% reduction in metabolites. When the DDT concentration was increased, they found that the quantity of metabolites increased. However, when the metabolites are expressed as a percentage of the initial DDT concentration, an increase in the amount of DDT induces a relative decrease in metabolite production. At 10 ppm of DDT, the metabolic system of *M. alternans* appears to reach saturation since an increase to 20 ppm results in only a small increase in metabolites.

The ability of *M. alternans* to degrade DDT is greatly affected by cell free extracts of other fungi. Extracts of *Penicillium notatum* produced a 35% increase in metabolites; *Aspergillus niger* and *Fusarium oxysporum* extracts have no effect; *Aspergillus fumigatus* and *Rhizoctonia solani* cause a 26 to 49% decrease in metabolites; *Aspergillus fumigatus* more or less inhibits degradation and *Mucor mucedo* completely suppresses DDT decomposition by *M. alternans* (Anderson and Lichtenstein, 1972).

The availability of oxygen may also be an important factor which influences the rate of DDT breakdown. Dalton and Smith (1971) obtained 4-chlorocatechol from standing and shake cultures of *H. submersus,* but the metabolite was 50 times more concentrated in standing cultures. This was thought to be associated with the development of anaerobic conditions.

17.5.4 Mechanism of DDT Breakdown

Little is known about the fungal mechanisms involved in the conversion of DDT to its metabolites. Indications are that it is an enzymic process. Dalton and Smith (1971) reported that cell free extracts of *Heliscus submersus,* which had been grown in a medium containing DDT, convert 17.4 ± 3.7% of the insecticide to DDD (10.2 ± 1.6%) and DDE (7.2 ± 2.9%). No metabolites were produced when extracts were obtained from mycelium grown in the absence of DDT. Kallman and Andrews (1963) found that up to 88% of the radioactivity (C^{14}-DDT) in extracts of live yeast cells is distributed as DDD. The corresponding extract from boiled yeast cells gives a figure of 3%. Anderson *et al.* (1970) used living and autoclaved mycelium of *Mucor alternans* to investigate DDT breakdown. After 2 days' incubation only 42% of the insecticide was recovered from live cultures whereas 90 to 100% was recovered from the dead cultures. The disappearance of the insecticide was attributed to the activity of fungal enzymes. Hexane and water soluble metabolites were obtained only with the living fungus. Engst and Kujawa (1967) demonstrated that enzyme-containing preparations of *Fusarium solani* also decompose DDT.

Few mechanistic studies of the partial dechlorination of DDT by fungi have been carried out. One objective of these investigations is to determine whether DDD and DDE arise from the same metabolic pathway or by independent processes. Kallman and Andrews (1963) found that *Saccharomyces cerevisiae* produces DDD from DDT but not from DDE. The reductive dechlorination of DDT to DDD (Ott and Gunther, 1965) does not, therefore, require the intermediate formation of DDE. Smith (1970) investigated the production of DDE by *H. submersus.* The fungus was grown in a medium containing 50 ppm of either DDT or DDD. Although DDE was detected in both media, a much lower percentage of DDD than DDT was converted to DDE. It was concluded that the dehydrogenation of DDD to DDE is of minor importance in the degradation of DDT. The main pathway of DDT metabolism in *H. submersus* is thought to be the reductive dechlorination of DDT to DDD. Further investigations to determine whether the breakdown of DDT to 4-chlorocatechol proceeds via the formation of intermediates such as m-chlorophenol, p-chlorophenol or 2, 2-bis(p-chlorophenyl)acetate (DDA) were carried out. Experiments based on the theory of simultaneous adaptation (Stanier, 1947) indicated that growth of *H. submersus* in DDT adapts the fungus to DDA (Fig. 17.3). When the fungus is grown in a medium containing 50 ppm of DDA, 4-chlorocatechol accumulates. This indicates that DDA is a possible intermediate metabolite of DDT. The complete oxidation of C^{14}-DDT to carbon dioxide was not detected. Focht (1972) reported that an isolate of *Fusarium* from sewage effluent converts to carbon dioxide, water and hydrochloric acid, chlorinated products which result from bacterial metabolism of bis(p-chlorophenyl) methane (DDM) and p-chlorophenylacetic acid (PCPA). PCPA is formed from DDM (Focht and

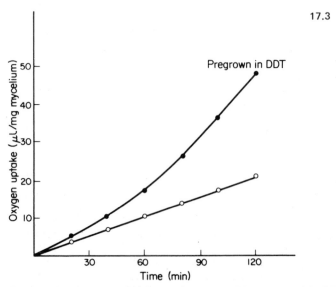

Figure 17.3. Adaptation of *Heliscus submersus* to DDA by growth in DDT.

Alexander, 1971) which is a degradation product of DDT. The generation of PCPA results from the cleavage of one of the rings of a DDT metabolite (Pfaender and Alexander, 1972). Metabolism of PCPA produces cleavage of both benzene rings (Focht and Alexander, 1971) and it is these ring fission products which *Fusarium* dehalogenates.

17.6 Discussion

As DDT is a widely distributed environmental pollutant, and fungi are an important component of the aquatic ecosystem, it is interesting to speculate on the possible ecological implications of their *in vitro* interactions. In doing so it is acknowledged that laboratory investigations have obvious limitations in the study of field problems. However, it is generally accepted that pure culture studies have the advantage of separating the responses of one species in defined conditions from the interactions of many organisms in a complex environment.

In natural waters the concentration of DDT rarely exceeds 2 ppm. Dalton *et al.* (1970) found that with one exception, the growth rates of aquatic fungi were not affected at concentrations below this value. The selective stimulation of an organism exposed to a low level of environmental contamination might thus affect the species balance in natural communities. At concentrations equivalent to those accumulated in bottom sediments and aquatic plants and animals (Table 17.1), DDT affects a wide range of fungi. It alters the sugar utilization, growth, respiration and reproduction of a number of species (Richardson and Miller, 1960; Ramaraje Urs *et al.*, 1967; Dalton *et al.*, 1970; Dalton and Smith, 1971; Hodkinson and Dalton, 1973). These reactions are modified further by a variety of physical and chemical conditions (Ramaraje Urs *et al.*, 1967; Dalton and Smith, 1971; Hodkinson and Dalton, 1973). Thus, the potential exists for DDT contamination of fungal habitats to interfere with the propagation, dispersal, competition and survival of fungi. The long term accumulation of DDT on fungal substrates could amplify and prolong its ecological effects, since dose response relationships have been described for a number of species (Richardson and Miller, 1960; Dalton *et al.*, 1970; Dalton and Smith, 1971; Hodkinson and Dalton, 1973). Ultimately this might alter the rate of organic decay and thereby change the quality of the environment. DDT inhibition of metabolism and growth in bacteria (Collins and Langlois, 1968; McBride and Wolfe, 1971; Trudgill *et al.*, 1971; Sutter, *et al.*, 1971) and microscopic algae (Ware and Roan, 1970; Dekoning and Mortimer, 1971; Batterton *et al.*, 1972) indicates even wider repercussions of environmental pollution by DDT.

The persistence of DDT in natural ecosystems has been attributed to the inability of micro-organisms to degrade the chlorinated hydrocarbon molecule (Pfaender and Alexander, 1972). Organic pollutants which remain unchanged because of the fallibility of microbes have been described as recalcitrant (Alexander, 1965). Fungi may contribute to the retention and concentration of DDT in the aquatic environment as fungal cultures rapidly accumulate the insecticide under various conditions (Kallman and Andrews, 1963; Chacko and Lockwood, 1967; Dalton and Smith, 1971). Metabolic activity and cell surface properties appear to be involved in this process because living fungi take up more insecticide than dead cultures (Kallman and Andrews, 1963; Dalton and Smith, 1971). Species differences in the rates of DDT accumulation may be related to the metabolism, surface area, cell wall composition and lipid content of the various fungi. The quantity of fungal lipids may be particularly important as the lipid solubility of DDT is about 100g/litre (Södergren, 1968).

The biological magnification of DDT in individual organisms is often parallelled by its accumulation and recycling in communities via links in food webs (Risebrough et al., 1967; Woodwell et al., 1971). In this context, the rapid adsorption of DDT by species of bacteria, Actinomycetes, zooplankton and phytoplankton is particularly important (Södergren, 1968; Ware and Roan, 1970; Cox, 1970; Dekoning and Mortimer, 1971). The amounts of accumulated DDT increase at the higher trophic levels and minute amounts of insecticide may be accumulated a thousand fold in this manner. Hunt and Bischoff (1960) consider there is no safe level for DDT in water where food chain build-up can occur.

Despite the apparent stability of DDT, the metabolites DDD and DDE have been detected in the aquatic environment (Hindin et al., 1964; Grzenda and Nicholson, 1965; Weaver et al., 1965; Barthel et al., 1966; Holden and Marsden, 1966; Sparr et al., 1966; Terriere et al., 1966). Laboratory investigations show that a wide range of fungi can partially degrade, if not fully catabolize, DDT and its metabolites (Kallman and Andrews, 1963; Engst et al., 1967; Matsumura and Boush, 1968; Anderson et al., 1970; Anderson and Lichtenstein, 1971; Dalton and Smith, 1971; Focht, 1972). The rate and extent of DDT conversion is greatly affected by the strain or species of fungus, the availability of sugars and growth factors, the gaseous environment and other micro-organisms (Dalton and Smith, 1971; Anderson and Lichtenstein, 1971; Focht, 1972). In addition, several species of Actinomycetes (Chacko, et al., 1966) and bacteria reductively dechlorinate DDT (Barker et al., 1965; Stenersen, 1965; Johnson et al., 1967; Wedemeyer, 1967 a, b; Mendel et al., 1967; Langlois and Collins, 1967; Plimmer 1968; Braunberg and Beck, 1968; French and Hoopingarner, 1970; Ware and Roan, 1970; Pfaender and Alexander, 1972). Dehydrochlorination of DDT has also been achieved using cultures of bacteria (Stenersen, 1965; Wedemeyer, 1967; Braunberg and Beck, 1968) and diatoms (Keil and Priester, 1969; Miyazaki and Thorsteinson, 1972). Further steps in DDT metabolism have been noted with a few fungi (Engst and Kujawa, 1967; Dalton and Smith, 1971), but so far the most detailed pathway of breakdown has been resolved using bacteria. Wedemeyer (1967 a) suggests that discrete enzymes are involved in the following stepwise degradation of DDT; DDT → DDD → 1, chloro-2, 2-bis(p-chlorophenyl)ethylene (DDMU) → 1-chloro-2, 2-bis(p-chlorophenyl) ethane (DDMS) → unsymbis(p-chlorophenyl)ethylene (DDNU) → DDA → DBP, or DDT → DDE Further intermediates in the conversion of DDA to DBP are dichlorophenylmethane (DPM) and dichlorobenzhydrol (DBH) (Wedemeyer, 1967 b). Although most evidence for microbial decomposition of DDT has been obtained using pure cultures, transformations of the insecticide have been recorded in samples of sewage, lake water and freshwater sediments containing heterogeneous microbial populations (Miskus et al., 1965; Hill and McCarty, 1967; Halvorson et al., 1971; Pfaender and Alexander, 1972). Different micro-organisms in pure culture also interact to produce extensive biodegradation of DDT (Pfaender and Alexander, 1972; Focht, 1972). Anaerobic conditions markedly increase the yield of metabolites in the conversion of DDT to DBP (Stenersen, 1965; Wedemeyer, 1966, 1967; Johnson et al., 1967; Braunberg and Beck, 1968; French and Hoopingarner, 1970; Pfaender and Alexander, 1972). Further degradation occurs under aerobic conditions to form PCPA through ring cleavage (Pfaender and Alexander, 1972). The PCPA is converted aerobically to p-chlorophenylglycolaldehyde and PCPA metabolites are dehalogenated to carbon dioxide, water and hydrochloric acid (Focht, 1972).

In view of the extensive biodegradation of DDT *in vitro*, a number of ideas have been advanced to account for the persistence of DDT in natural ecosystems. One hypo-

460

thesis is that complete destruction of DDT requires both anaerobiosis and subsequent aerobiosis (Pfaender and Alexander, 1972). Such fluctuations in oxygen concentration may be infrequent in some habitats. In the aquatic environment, low concentrations of readily available nutrients might also contribute to DDT persistence. A number of micro-organisms are unable to utilize DDT, or its metabolites, when provided as the only source of carbon and energy but decompose these compounds in rich media (Wedemeyer, 1967 a; Anderson and Lichtenstein, 1971). Hence, there would be no selective advantage to such organisms in environments containing DDT and they would not proliferate. Degradation would be achieved only by those species that could compete with other micro-organisms for alternative carbon sources. Observations that the rate of DDT metabolism is increased in media enriched with sugars and growth factors (Dalton and Smith, 1971; Anderson and Lichtenstein, 1971) supports this idea. So far, extensive decomposition of DDT has only been demonstrated *in vitro* when different micro-organisms are used to perform specific transformations (Focht, 1972; Pfaender and Alexander, 1972). Their occupation of similar habitats would therefore seem an essential prerequisite for environmental decontamination. Furthermore, there are many micro-organisms which have failed to decompose DDT *in vitro* (Chacko *et al.*, 1966; Engst *et al.*, 1967; Matsumura and Boush, 1968; Anderson and Lichtenstein, 1971b; Dalton and Smith, 1971), and some are inhibited by DDT metabolites (Ko and Lockwood, 1968). For biodegradation to occur, Alexander (1967) lists the following as necessary conditions: (1) an organism with the requisite catabolic systems must be present in the environment; (2) the compound must be available in a form which permits degradation to proceed and is accessible to micro-organisms; (3) the environmental conditions should be suitable for microbial proliferation and induction of the appropriate enzymes to bring about the desired reaction. Perhaps this combination of factors is rarely achieved in nature.

References

ABBOTT, D. C., HARRISON, R. B., TATTON, J. O. G., and THOMSON, J. (1965). 'Organochlorine pesticides in the atmospheric environment'. *Nature,* 208, 1317.

ABBOTT, D. C., HARRISON, R. B., TATTON, J. O. G., and THOMSON, J. (1966). 'Organochlorine pesticides in the atmosphere'. *Nature,* 211, 259-261.

AINSWORTH, G. C., and BISBY, G. R. (1963). *Dictionary of Fungi.* (5th Edition), Commonwealth Mycological Institute, Kew, Surrey.

ALEXANDER, M. (1964). 'Microbiology of pesticides and related hydrocarbons.' In *Principles and Applications in Aquatic Microbiology. Proc. Rudolfs Research Conf. Rugers,* N. J., Wiley, New York.

ALEXANDER, M. (1965). 'Persistence and biological reactions of pesticides in soils.' *Soil Sci. Soc. Am.,* 29, 1-7.

ALEXANDER, M. (1967). 'The breakdown of pesticides in soil.' *Publ. Amer. Ass. Advan. Sci.,* 85, 331-342.

ANASTASIOU, C. J., and CHURCHLAND, L. M. (1969). 'Fungi on decaying leaves in marine habitats'. *Can. J. Bot.,* 47, 251-257.

ANDERSON, J. P. E., and LICHTENSTEIN, E. P. (1971). 'Effect of nutritional factors on DDT-degradation by *Mucor alternans.' Can. J. Microbiol.,* 17, 1291-1298.

ANDERSON, J. P. E., and LICHTENSTEIN, E. P. (1972). 'Effects of various soil fungi and insecticides on the capacity of *Mucor alternans* to degrade DDT.' *Can. J. Microbiol.,* 18, 553-560.

ANDERSON, J. P. E., LICHTENSTEIN, E. P., and WHITTINGHAM, W. F. (1970). 'Effect of *Mucor alternans* on the persistence of DDT and Dieldrin in culture and in soil.' *J. econ. Ent.,* 63, 1595-1599.

ANTOMMARIA, P., CORN, M. and DEMAIO, L. (1965). 'Airborne particles in Pittsburgh: association with p,p'-DDT.' *Science,* 150, 1476-1477.

BARKER, P. S., MORRISON, F. O., and WHITAKER, R. S. (1965). 'Conversion of DDT to DDD by *Proteus vulgaris,* a bacterium isolated from the intestinal flora of a mouse.' *Nature,* 205, 621-622.

BARRY, A. L. (1968). The accumulation of C^{14}-DDT by aquatic fungi. M.Sc. Thesis, University of Salford.

BARTHEL, W. F., PARSONS, D. A., McDOWELL, L. L., and GRISSINGER, E. M. (1966). 'Surface hydrology and pesticides.' In *Pesticides and Their Effects on Soils and Water.* (Ed. M. E. Bloodworth *et al.*) Symp. Soil Sci. Soc. Amer. A.S.A. Special Publication, 8, 128-144.

BATTERTON, J. C., BOUSH, G. M., and MATSUMURA, F. (1972). 'DDT: Inhibition of sodium chloride tolerance by the blue-green alga *Anacystis nidulans.*' *Science,* 176, 1141-1143.

BIGGAR, J. W., DUTH, G. R., and RIGGS, R. L. (1967). 'Predicting and measuring the solubility of p,p'-DDT in water.' *Bull. Environ. Contam. Toxicol.,* 2, 90-100.

BOLLEN, W. B. (1961). 'Interactions between pesticides and soil micro-organisms.' *A. Rev. Microbiol.,* 15, 69-92.

BRAUNBERG, R. C., and BECK, V. (1968). 'Interaction of DDT and the gastro-intestinal microflora of the rat.' *J. agric. Fd. Chem.,* 16, 451-453.

BRIDGES, W. R., KALLMAN, B. J., and ANDREWS, A. K. (1963). 'Persistence of DDT and its metabolites in a farm pond.' *Trans. Am. Fish. Soc.,* 92, 421-427.

BRIEDENBACH, A. W., and LICHTENBERG, J. J. (1963). 'DDT and Dieldrin in rivers: a report of the national water quality network.' *Science,* 141, 899-901.

BRIEDENBACH, A. W., GUNNERSON, C. G., KAWAHARA, F. K., LICHTENBERG, J.J., and GREEN, R. S. (1967). 'Chlorinated hydrocarbon pesticides in major river basins 1957-1965.' *Publ. Hlth Rep.,* 82, 139-156.

BUSVINE, J. R. (1966). *Insects and Hygiene.* Methuen. 467pp.

BUTLER, P. A. (1966). 'The problem of pesticides in estuaries.' *Amer. Fish. Soc., Special Publication,* 3, 110-115.

CHACKO, C. I., and LOCKWOOD, J. L. (1967). 'Accumulation of DDT and Dieldrin by micro-organisms.' *Can. J. Microbiol.,* 13, 1123-1126.

CHACKO, C. I., LOCKWOOD, J. L., and ZABIK, M. (1966). 'Chlorinated hydro-carbon pesticides: degradation by microbes.' *Science,* 154, 893-895.

COHEN, J. M., and PINKERTON, C. (1966). 'Widespread translocation of pesticides by air transport and rain-out.' In *Organic Pesticides in the Environment* (Ed. R. F. Gould). Advances in Chemistry, Series 60. Am. Chem. Soc., 163-176.

COLE, H., BARRY, D., and FREAR, D. E. H. (1967). 'DDT levels in fish, streams, stream sediments and soil before and after DDT aerial spray applications for fall cankerworm in northern Pennsylvania.' *Bull. Environ. Contam. Toxicol.,* 2, 127-146.

COLLINS, J. A., and LANGLOIS, B. E. (1968). 'Effect of DDT, Dieldrin and Heptachlor on the growth of selected bacteria.' *Appl. Microbiol.,* 16, 799-800.

COOKE, W. B. (1968). 'Some fungi of the Cache La Poudre River, Colorado.'
Mycopath. Mycol. appl., 35, 361-372.

COPE, O. B. (1961). 'Effects of DDT spraying for spruce budworm on fish in the
Yellowstone River system.' *Trans. Am. Fish. Soc.,* 90, 239-251.

COPE, O. B. (1965). 'Agricultural chemicals and freshwater ecological systems.'
In *Research in Pesticides,* (Ed. C. O. Chichester). Proceedings of the conference
on research needs and approaches to the use of agricultural chemicals from a
public health viewpoint. Academic Press, 115-127.

COX, J. L. (1970). 'Low ambient level uptake of C^{14}-DDT by three species of
marine phytoplankton.' *Bull. Environ. Contam. Toxicol.,* 5, 218-221.

CROKER, R. A., and WILSON, A. J. (1965). 'Kinetics and effects of DDT in a tidal
marsh ditch.' *Trans. Am. Fish. Soc.,* 94, 152-159.

DALTON, S. A., HODKINSON, M., and SMITH, K. A. (1970). 'Interactions between
DDT and river fungi. I. Effects of p,p'-DDT on the growth of aquatic hyphomycetes.' *Appl. Microbiol.,* 20, 662-666.

DALTON, S. A. (1971). Uptake of C^{14}-DDT by river fungi and the effect of DDT
on their growth and respiration. Ph.D. Thesis. University of Salford.

DALTON, S. A., and SMITH, K. A. (1971). 'DDT and river fungi.' Proc. First Int.
Mycol. Cong., *Trans. Br. mycol. Soc.,* 58, Supplement, 28.

DEKONING, H. W., and MORTIMER, D. C. (1971). 'DDT uptake and growth of
Euglena gracilis.' Bull. Environ. Contam. Toxicol., 6, 244-248.

DUSTMAN, E. H., and STICKEL, L. F. (1966). 'Pesticide residues in the ecosystem.'
In *Pesticides and Their Effects on Soils and Water* (Ed. M. E. Bloodworth *et al.*)
Symp. Soil Sci. Soc. Amer. A.S.A. Special Publication, 8, 109-121.

EDWARDS, C. A., and HEATH, G. W. (1964). *The Principles of Agricultural Ento-
mology.* Chapman and Hall, 418 pp.

EDWARDS, C. A. (1966). 'Insecticide residues in soils.' *Residue Rev.,* 13, 83-132.

ENGST, R., and KUJAWA, M. (1967). 'Enzymatischer Abbau des DDT durch
Schimmelpilze. (2) Mittreactionsuerlauf des enzymatischen DDT-Abbaues.'
Die Nahrüng, 11, 751-760.

ENGST, R., KUJAWA, M., and MÜLLER, G. (1967). 'Enzymatischer Abbau des
DDT durch Schimmelpilze (1). Mitt Isolierung und Identifizierung eines DDT
abbauenden Schimmelpilzes.' *Die Nahrüng,* 11, 401-403.

FOCHT, D. D. (1972). 'Microbial degradation of DDT metabolites to carbon
dioxide, water and chloride.' *Bull. Environ. Contam. Toxicol.,* 7, 52-56.

FOCHT, D. D., and ALEXANDER, M. (1971). 'Aerobic cometabolism of DDT analo-
gues by *Hydrogenomonas* sp.' *J. agr. Fd. Chem.,* 19, 20-22.

FRENCH, A. L., and HOOPINGARNER, R. A. (1970). 'Dechlorination of DDT
by membranes isolated from *Escherichia coli.' J. econ. Ent.,* 63, 756-759.

GEORGE, J. L., and FREAR, D. E. H. (1966). 'Pesticides in the Antarctic.' In
Pesticides in the Environment and Their Effects on Wildlife (Ed. N. W. Moore)
J. appl. Ecol., Supplement, 3, 155-167.

GILLETTE, R. (1972). 'DDT: Its days are numbered except perhaps in pepper
fields.' *Science,* 176, 1313-1314.

GRZENDA, A. R., NICHOLSON, H. P., TEASLEY, J. I., and PATRIC, J. H. (1964).
'DDT residues in mountain stream water as influenced by treatment practices.'
J. econ. Ent., 57, 615-618.

GRZENDA, A. R., and NICHOLSON, H. P. (1965). 'The distribution and magnitude
of insecticide residues among various components of a stream system.' *Proc. 14th
Southern Water Resources Pollution Control Conf.,* 165-174.

HALVORSON, H., ISHAQUE, M., SOLOMON, J., and GRUSSENDORF, O. W. (1971). 'A biodegradability test for insecticides. ' *Can. J. Microbiol.,* 17, 585-591.

HILL, D. W., and McCARTY, P. L. (1967). 'Anaerobic degradation of selected chlorinated hydrocarbon pesticides.' *J. Water Pollution Contr. Fed.,* 39, 1259.

HINDIN, E., MAY, D. S., and DUNSTAN, G. H. (1964). 'Collection and analysis of synthetic organic pesticides from surface and ground water.' *Residue Rev.,* 7, 130-156.

HINDIN, E., MAY, D. S., and DUNSTAN, G. H. (1966). 'Distribution of insecticides sprayed by airplane on an irrigated corn plot.' In *Organic Pesticides in the Environment* (Ed. C. H. van Middelem). Symp. 150th Meeting Amer. Chem. Soc., 132-145.

HODKINSON, M., and DALTON, S. A. (1973). 'Interactions between DDT and river fungi. II Influence of culture conditions on the compatibility of fungi, and p.p'-DDT.' *Bull. Environ. Contam. Toxicol.,* 10, 356-359.

HOLDEN, A. V. (1965). 'Contamination of freshwater by persistent insecticides and their effects on fish.' *Ann. appl. Biol.,* 55, 332-335.

HOLDEN, A. V., and MARSDEN, K. (1966). 'The examination of surface waters and sewage effluents for organochlorine pesticides.' *J. Proc. Inst. Sewage Purif.,* 3, 295-299.

HOLDEN, A. V., and MARSDEN, K. (1967). 'Organochlorine pesticides in seals and porpoises. *Nature,* 216, 1274-1276.

HUNT, E. G., and BISCHOFF, A. I. (1960). 'Inimical effects on wildlife of periodic DDD applications to Clear Lake.' *Calif. Fish Game,* 46, 91-106.

INGOLD, C. T. (1954). 'Aquatic Ascomycetes: Discomycetes from lakes.' *Trans. Br. mycol. Soc.,* 37, 1-18.

INGOLD, C. T. (1959). 'Submerged aquatic hyphomycetes.' *J. Queckett microsc. Club* (Series 4), 5, 115-130.

INGOLD, C. T. (1961). 'Another aquatic spore type with clamp connections.' *Trans. Br. mycol. Soc.,* 44, 27-30.

INGOLD, C. T. (1966). 'The tetraradiate aquatic fungal spore.' *Mycologia,* 58, 43-56.

JOHNSON, T. W., and SPARROW, F. K. (1961). *Fungi in Oceans and Estuaries.* Cramer, Weinhein, 668 pp.

JOHNSON, T. W. (1968). 'Saprobic marine fungi.' In *The Fungi* (Ed. G. C. Ainsworth and A. S. Sussman) Academic Press, New York, vol. 3, 95-104.

JOHNSON, B. T., GOODMAN, R. N., and GOLDBERG, R. S. (1967). 'Conversion of DDT to DDD by pathogenic and saprophytic bacteria associated with plants.' *Science,* 157, 560-561.

KALLMAN, B. J., and ANDREWS, A. K. (1963). 'Reductive dechlorination of DDT to DDD by yeast.' *Science,* 141, 1050-1051.

KO, W. H., and LOCKWOOD, J. L. (1968 a). 'Conversion of DDT to DDD in soil and the effect of these compounds on soil micro-organisms.' *Can. J. Microbiol.,* 14, 1069-1073.

KO, W. H., and LOCKWOOD, J. L. (1968 b). 'Accumulation and concentration of chlorinated hydrocarbon pesticides by micro-organisms in soil.' *Can. J. Microbiol.,* 14, 1075-1078.

KEIL, J. E., and PRIESTER, L. E. (1969). 'DDT uptake and metabolism by a marine diatom.' *Bull. Environ. Contam. Toxicol.,* 4, 169.

LANGLOIS, B. E., and COLLINS, J. A. (1967). 'Reductive dechlorination of p,p'-DDT by *Escherichia coli.' J. Dairy Sci.,* 50, 946-947.

LASHER, C., and APPLEGATE, H. G. (1966). 'Pesticides at Presidio III. Soil and water.' *Texas J. Sci.,* 18, 385-395.

LICHTENSTEIN, E. P., SCHULZ, K. R., SKRENTNY, R. F., and TSUKANO, Y. (1966). 'Toxicity and fate of insecticide residues in water.' *Arch. Environ. Health,* 12, 199-212.

LÖFROTH, G. (1968). 'Pesticides and catastrophe.' *New Scientist,* 40, 567-568.

MACK, G. L., CORCORAN, S. M., GIBBS, S. D., GUTEMAN, W. H., RECKAHN, J. A., and LISK, D. J. (1964). 'The DDT content of some fishes and surface waters of New York State.' *NY Fish Game J.,* 11, 148-153.

MARTIN, H. (1965). *Insecticide and Fungicide Handbook for Crop Protection.* Blackwell, Oxford, 326 pp.

MARTIN, J. P. (1966). 'Influence of pesticides on soil microbes and soil properties.' In *Pesticides and Their Effects on Soils and Water* (Ed. M. E. Bloodworth *et al.)* Symp. Soil Sci. Soc. Amer. A.S.A. Special Publication, 8, 98-108.

MARTH, E. H. (1965). 'Residues and some effects of chlorinated hydrocarbon insecticides in biological material.' *Residue Rev.,* 9, 1-89.

MATSUMURA, F., and BOUSH, G. M. (1968). 'Degradation of insecticides by a soil fungus, *Trichoderma viride.' J. econ. Ent.,* 61, 610-612.

MENDEL, J. L., KLEIN, K. A., CHEN, J. F., and WALTON, M. S. (1967). 'Metabolism of DDT and some other chlorinated organic compounds by *Aerobacter aerogenes.'* *J. Ass. Offic. Anal. Chem.,* 50, 897-903.

MIDDLETON, F. M., and LICHTENBERG, J. J. (1960). 'Measurement of organic contaminants in the nation's rivers.' *Ind. Eng. Chem.,* 52, 73A-76A.

MISKUS, R. P., BLAIR, D. P., and CASIDA, J. E. (1965). 'Conversion of DDT to DDD by bovine rumen fluid, lake water and reduced porphyrins.' *J. agr. Fd. Chem.,* 13, 481-483.

MIYAZAKI, S., and THORSTEINSON, A. J. (1972). 'Metabolism of DDT by fresh water diatoms.' *Bull. Environ. Contam. Toxicol.,* 8, 81-83.

McBRIDE, B. C., and WOLFE, R. S. (1971). 'Inhibition of methanogenesis by DDT.' *Nature,* 234, 551-552.

NEWTON, J. A., and HODKINSON, M. (1971). 'Leaf decomposition in a river environment.' Proc. First Int. Mycol. Cong., *Trans. Br. Mycol. Soc.,* 58, Supplement, 29.

NICHOLSON, H. P., WEBB, H. J., LAUER, G. J., O'BRIEN, R. E., GRZENDA, A. R., and SHANKLIN, D. W. (1962). 'Insecticide contamination in a farm pond.' *Trans. Am. Fish. Soc.,* 91, 213-217.

NILSSON, S. (1964). 'Freshwater hyphomycetes; taxonomy, morphology and ecology.' *Symb. Bot. Upsal.,* 18, 1-130.

OTT, D. E., and GUNTHER, F. A. (1965). 'DDD as a decomposition product of DDT.' *Residue Rev.,* 10, 70-84.

PETERLE, T. J. (1969). 'DDT in Antarctic snow.' *Nature,* 224, 620.

PFAENDER, F. K., and ALEXANDER, M. (1972). 'Extensive microbiol degradation of DDT *in vitro* and DDT metabolism by natural communities.' *J. agr. Fd. Chem.,* 20, 842-846.

PLIMMER, J. R., KEARNEY, P. C., and VON ENDT, D. W. (1968). 'Mechanism of conversion of DDT to DDD by *Aerobacter aerogenes.' J. agr. Fd., Chem.,* 16, 594-597.

PUGH, G. J. F., and MULDER, J. L. (1971). 'Mycoflora associated with *Typha latifolia.' Trans. Br. mycol. Soc.,* 57, 273-282.

RAMARAJE URS, N. V., GOVINDU, H. C., and SHIVASHANKARA SHASTRY, K. S. (1967). 'The effect of certain insecticides on the entomogenous fungi *Beauveria bassiana* and *Metarrhizium anisopliae'. J. Inv. Path., 9,* 398-403.

RICHARDSON, L. T., and MILLER, D. M. (1960). 'Fungitoxicity of chlorinated hydrocarbon insecticides in relation to water solubility and vapour pressure.' *Can. J. Bot.,* 38, 163-175.

RISEBROUGH, R. W., MENZEL, D. B., MARTIN, D. J., and OLCOTT, H. S. (1967). 'DDT residues in Pacific sea birds: a persistent insecticide in marine food chains.' *Nature,* 216, 589-591.

RISEBROUGH, R. W., HUGGETT, R. J., GRIFFIN, R. J., and GOLDBERG, E. D. (1968). 'Pesticides: Transatlantic movements in the Northeast Trades.' *Science,* 159, 1233-1236.

SIMMONS, S. W. (1959) Ed. *DDT Insecticides, Vol. II-Human and Veterinary Medicine.* Hirkhauser Verlag, Basel und Stuttgart, 570 pp.

SLADEN, W. J. L., MENZIE, C. M., and REICHEL, W. L. (1966). 'DDT residues in Adelie penguins and a crabeater seal from Antarctica.' *Nature,* 210, 670-673.

SMITH, K. A. (1970). The effect of DDT on *Heliscus submersus* an aquatic hyphomycete. Ph.D. Thesis. University of Salford.

SÖDERGREN, A. (1968). 'Uptake and accumulation of C^{14}-DDT by *Chlorella* sp. (Chlorophyceae).' *Oikos,* 19, 126-138.

SPARR, B. I., APPLEBY, W. G., DEVRIES, D. M., OSMUN, J. V., McBRIDE, J. M., and POSTER, G. L. (1966). 'Insecticide residues in waterways from agricultural use.' In *Organic pesticides in the environment* (Ed. C. H. van Middelem). Symp. 150th Meeting Am. Chem. Soc., 146-162.

SPARROW, F. K. (1960). *Aquatic Phycomycetes* (2nd Revised Edition). Ann Arbor, University of Michigan Press, 1187 pp.

SPARROW, F. K. (1968). 'Ecology of freshwater fungi.' In *The Fungi* (Eds. G. C. Ainsworth and A. S. Sussman), Academic Press, London. Vol. 3, 41-93.

STANIER, R. Y. (1947). 'Simultaneous adaptation: A new technique for the study of metabolic pathways.' *J. Bact.,* 54, 339-348.

STENERSEN, J. H. V. (1965). 'DDT-metabolism in resistant and susceptible stable flies and in bacteria.' *Nature,* 207, 660-661.

SUTTER, G. R., ABRAHAMSON, M. D., HAMILTON, E. W., and VICK, I. D. (1971). 'Compatibility of *Bacillus thuringiensis* var. *thuringiensis* and chemical insecticides. I Effect of insecticide doses on bacterial replication rate.' *J. econ. Ent.,* 64, 1348-1350.

TABOR, E. C. (1965). 'Pesticides in urban atmospheres.' *J. Air Poll. Control Assoc.,* 15, 415-418.

TATTON, J. O. G., and RUZICKA, J. H. A. (1967). 'Organochlorine pesticides in Antarctica.' *Nature,* 215, 346-348.

TERRIERE, L. C., KIIGEMAGI, U., ZWICK, R. W., and WESTIGARD, P. H. (1966). 'The persistence of pesticides in orchards and orchard soils; a twenty year study.' In *Organic Pesticides in the Environment.* (Ed. C. H. van Middelem). Symp. 150th Meeting Am. Chem. Soc., 263-270.

TRUDGILL, P. W., WIDDUS, R., and REES, J. S. (1971). 'Effects of organo-chlorine insecticides on bacterial growth, respiration and viability.' *J. gen. Microbiol.,* 69, 1-13.

WALKER, K. C. (1971). 'The role of pesticides in pollution management.' *Residue Rev.,* 34, 163-172.

WARE, G. W., and ROAN, C. C. (1970). 'Interaction of pesticides with aquatic micro-organisms and plankton.' *Residue Rev.,* 33, 15-45.

WEAVER, L., GUNNERSON, C. G., BRIEDENBACH, A. W., and LICHTENBERG, J. J. (1965). 'Chlorinated hydrocarbon pesticides in major U.S. river basins.' *Publ. Hlth. Rep.,* 80, 481-493.

WEDEMEYER, G. (1966). 'Dechlorination of DDT by *Aerobacter aerogenes.' Science,* 152, 647.

WEDEMEYER, G. (1967 a). 'Dechlorination of 1,1,1-trichloro-2,2-bis(p-chlorophenyl) ethane by *Aerobacter aerogenes.' Appl. Microbiol.,* 15, 569-574.

WEDEMEYER, G. (1967 b). 'Biodegradation of dichlorodiphenyl trichloroethane: Intermediates in dechlorodiphenylacetic acid metabolism by *Aerobacter aerogenes.' Appl. Microbiol.,* 15, 1494-1495.

WELCH, E. B., and SPINDLER, J. C. (1964). 'DDT persistence and its effect on aquatic insects and fish after an aerial application.' *J. Water Poll. Control Fed.,* 36, 1285-1292.

WEST, I. (1964). 'Pesticides as contaminants.' *Arch. Environ. Health,* 9, 626-633.

WESTLAKE, W. E., and GUNTHER, F. A. (1966). 'Occurrence and mode of introduction of pesticides in the environment.' In *Organic Pesticides in the Environment.* (Ed. C. H. van.Middelem). Symp. 150th Meeting Am. Chem. Soc., 110-121.

WHEATLEY, G. A., and HARDMAN, J. A. (1965). 'Presence of organochlorine insecticides in rainwater in central England.' *Nature,* 207, 486-487.

WILLOUGHBY, L. G., and COLLINS, V. G. (1966). 'A study of the distribution of fungal spores and bacteria in Blelham Tarn and its associated streams.' *Nova Hedwigia,* 12, 150-171.

WOODWELL, G. M., CRAIG, P. P., and JOHNSON, H. A. (1971). 'DDT in the biosphere: Where does it go?' *Science,* 174, 1101-1107.

SECTION II: FRESHWATER FUNGI
B. Lower Fungi

18 Substrate–Influenced Morphological Variations and Taxonomic Problems in Freshwater, Posteriorly Uniflagellate Phycomycetes

CHARLES E.MILLER

18.1   Introduction

Classical chytridial taxonomy relies heavily on morphological characteristics of asexual and sexual or presumed sexual reproductive structures as taxonomic criteria in taxon delineation. Chytridial fungi are relatively simple in structure and have few diagnostic, morphological characters. These circumstances have led to the erection of poorly defined taxa, and chytridiologists have, generally, not faced up to the problems of intraspecific variability in morphological characters. Few studies are concerned with the establishment of parameters relating to morphological variability. There is no agreement among workers of the significance to descriptive taxonomy of various morphological characteristics. The 'rule-of-thumb' appears to be to erect a new taxon if a single morphological characteristic of a chytrid isolate is shown to differ, however so slightly, from a previously described taxon. Whether such an apparent difference is environmentally or genetically caused is usually not determined; whether such a difference is variable or stable and useful as a reliable descriptive taxonomic marker is only rarely determined. Many eucarpic chytrids have been described directly from original collections on added baits or on naturally occurring substrates. The erection of new taxa based on studies from gross cultures has probably caused the mixing of life cycles of two or more organisms. There has been shown a lack of concern for the non-reproducible influences of gross culture environments on variability in morphological characteristics. Chytridial taxa have often been based on too few specimens or collections and frequently on limited samples of preserved specimens.

Morphological characteristics frequently used to distinguish taxa include the following: *(sporangial characters)* general pre- and post-discharge shapes and dimensions; wall thickness; absence, presence and numbers, shapes, dimensions, locations and kinds of enations or ornamentations; discharge pore types (operculate, inoperculate or intermediate); numbers, dimensions, shapes, locations, and forms of discharge papillae or tubes; epi-, endo- or interbiotic nature; *(rhizoidal characters)* absence or presence, extent, dimensions, locations, shapes and wall thicknesses of apophyses; branching nature of rhizoidal system; number of sites of origin on sporangium; epi-, endo- or interbiotic nature of rhizoidal system; *(zoospore characters)* body dimensions and shapes; numbers, dimensions, locations and shapes of lipoid bodies or absence; ratio between lipoid body and zoospore body; flagellar length; ratio of flagellar length to body size; whiplash length. In addition, the presumable parasitic habit and living host on which they were found have been used as taxonomic characters for epibiotic chytrids, as have also the various substrates (chitin, keratin, cellulose, pollen, etc.) for those living as saprobes.

`The editor has instructed the author of this chapter to review morphological and taxonomic works of freshwater uniflagellate fungi since approximately 1960 onwards, so that such works may be brought together in one volume. This is not to suggest, of course, that works prior to 1960 have no bearing on our considerations today. We are fortunate to have the very valuable monograph of Sparrow (1960) who has catalogued and discussed significant morphological and taxonomic contributions from the very beginnings of aquatic mycology. Sparrow has set the stage for these discussions by stating the problem: 'Characters which appear from the original description of a species to be fixed, well marked, and distinctive are usually found, upon careful investigation of a great many individuals, to be subject to wide variation.'

18.2 Early Experimental Taxonomy in the Chytridiales

After indicating that this discussion will consider work done since 1960 onwards, the first paper to be discussed here was done in 1957 by Koch. In this work, perhaps the beginning of experimental taxonomy in the lower phycomycetous fungi, Koch (1957) described two new chytrids from pure or axenic agar culture. He compared certain morphological characteristics of *Phlyctochytrium punctatum* Koch and *P. irregulare* Koch in axenic agar culture with morphological characteristics of these same isolates growing on pollen. Koch had difficulty in applying the usual diagnostic morphological characteristics as taxonomic markers because of extreme morphological variability of these species in pollen and agar cultures. In some isolates, apophyses were present or absent; the rhizoidal system was sessile or stalked and epibiotic, endobiotic and interbiotic; and the ornamentation (punctations, 'hairs') and colour of the sporangium varied with culture conditions. *Phlyctochytrium punctatum* on agar culture parasitized itself, and the parasitic sporangia were often elongated and irregular. Sporangial shape varied with the substrate and was especially variable in axenic culture.

Zoospore body shapes were spherical, subspherical or irregularly elongated in water; in liquid film on the agar surfaces they were irregularly elongated, thinly rod-shaped and occasionally subspherical. A rather startling discovery by Koch was that zoospores of *Phlyctochytrium punctatum* were larger when they came from pollen-grown sporangia [5.5(3.6-6.1)μm] than from sporangia which were grown on K-1 agar cultures [3.7(2.6-4.8)μm], and that zoospores from pollen cultures had a greater number of lipoid bodies, with the conspicuous lipoid body being larger [1.0(0.3-1.7)μm *vs.* 4.3(1.8-5.1)μm respectively]. Flagellar lengths were found to be constant, whether from pollen or agar cultures [19.7(16.9-21.4)μm *vs.* 19.5(18.4-21.4)μm respectively].

Koch (1957) reported larger sporangia for *Phlyctochytrium irregulare* growing on agar culture media than on pollen. The sporangial wall lost its reddish-brown colour (apparent in the original collection on pollen) as it was subsequently cultured on pollen, but regained wall colour when grown on pollen in distilled water to which dead oak leaves had been added. Koch also reported variation in vesicular discharge and operculation; the vesicule was found to originate at times from the sporangium wall and at other times from the discharge plug. *Phlyctochytrium irregular,* a supposedly inoperculate chytrid, occasionally formed a hinged papillar cap which could be interpreted as a true operculum. Thus, are introduced the concepts of 'predominantly inoperculate' or 'predominantly operculate'. As discussed by Miller (1968) in reference to Koch's observations 'the instability exhibited by these taxonomic characters strikes at the very heart of chytridiaceous classification'.

Changes in the morphology of the swimming zoospore body were reported for *Phlyctochytrium punctatum* and, in general, for motile cells of posteriorly uniflagellated phycomycetes (Koch, 1957, 1961). In *P. punctatum,* Koch (1957) reported that the flagellum is 'apparently never truly posterior in attachment'. The flagellum was found attached sub-basally on zoospores with spherical or subspherical body shapes, attached laterally or subapically on zoospores with irregularly elongated bodies, and attached apically on zoospores with thinly rod-shaped zoospores. In 1961, Koch found for several species that zoospore body shapes changed little when the zoospores were placed in methocel from water; the spore body remained spherical to subspherical and the flagellum remained basally attached. In water, the spore bodies of other species were spherical with a sub-basally attached flagellum or had sub-basally to laterally attached flagella, when body shapes were subspherical to irregularly elongated. In methocel, the flagella were laterally attached at various positions and zoospore bodies were subspherically to irregularly elongated. On agar surfaces, most zoospore body shapes were very irregularly elongated and the flagella were laterally attached; some were thinly rod-shaped and the flagella were attached apically.

Register (1959) studied morphological variations in *Phlyctochytrium* sp. isolated from soil collections from the top of Whiteside Mountain, N. C. Axenic cultures were used to inoculate all experimental cultures from which data were taken. Experimental substrates used included pollen of *Liquidambar styraciflua* L. (sweetgum) in distilled water, sweetgum pollen in soil water, sweetgum pollen in glucose-peptone water, boiled *Achlya flagellata* Coker in distilled water, boiled *Spirogyra* in distilled water, cellophane in distilled water, and malt-peptone agar. Except for malt-peptone agar, experimental cultures from which measurements of morphological characteristics were made were apparently not axenic cultures. This point is not clear in the thesis, but the use of unsterilized sweetgum pollen would certainly introduce other microorganisms into the experimental cultures. The results (Table 18.1) indicated that sporangial size was substrate dependent, the number of papillae and/or discharge tubes were associated with sporangial size, the length of papillae and tubes varied from 0.3μm on malt-peptone agar to 12.0μm on pollen in distilled water, discharge pore diameter varied depending on substrate, zoospore body diameter was relatively stable on various substrates, the conspicuous lipoid body ranged from a low of 0.5 to 2.0μm and flagellar length appeared not to be substrate dependent. Sporangial wall thickness (not included in Table 18.1) was not substrate dependent and measured 1μm on all substrates, and sporangial walls were smooth on all substrates except on pollen in glucose-peptone water when the walls formed many simple and branched hairs. Register further reported that the rhizoidal system was highly branched, very variable in nature and with or without an apophysis. Apophyses were usually formed when thalli grew on *Spirogyra, Achlya* and cellophane, and occurred only occasionally on pollen and rarely on agar-grown thalli.

TABLE 18.1 Sporangial and zoospore characteristics of *Phlyctochytrium* sp. modified from Register (1959).

SPORANGIUM				ZOOSPORE			
Substrate	Size (μm)	Number of papillae or tubes	Length of papillae or tubes (μm)	Pore diam. (μm)	Body diam. (μm)	Lipoid body diam. (μm)	Flagellum length (μm)
Pollen[b] + DW[c]	11.0-30.0	1-16	0.4-12.0 S + B[a]	0.9-4.0	2.0-3.5	0.5-1.0	13.0-15.6
Pollen + SW[d]	20.0-39.6	1-11	0.4-4.0 S	0.9-5.0	2.0-3.5	0.5-2.0	13.0-15.0
Pollen + GPW[e]	22.0-50.4	1-23	0.4-7.5 S + B[a]	0.9-5.2	2.0-3.9	0.5-1.0	13.0-15.0
Boiled *Achlya flagellata* + DW	17.5-30.0	1-9	0.4-7.0 S + B[a]	0.9-3.2	2.0-3.7	0.7-1.3	13.0-15.0
Boiled *Spirogyra* + DW	15.0-27.5	1-4	up to 6.0 S[a]	—	2.0-3.5	0.7-1.5	13.0-15.0
Cellophane + DW.	7.2-20.8	1-4	0.5-5.0 S[a]	0.4-3.0	2.0-3.0	0.5-1.5	13.0-15.0
Malt Peptone Agar	12.0-32.5	1-16	0.3-3.5 S[a]	0.4-3.0	2.0-3.7	0.5-1.5	13.0-16.3

a: S + B = simple and branched: S = simple.
b: *Liquidambar styraciflua* (sweetgum).
c: DW = distilled water.
d: SW = soil water.
e: GPW = glucose-peptone water.

18.3 Some Examples of Substrate Influenced Morphological Variations in the Chytridiales

In 1967, I isolated into single spore, axenic culture a chytrid with varying numbers of papillae and/or discharge tubes per sporangium from a pond on the Ohio University campus. This isolate rarely produced what I recognized as an apophysis. I tentatively identified this isolate as a new species of *Rhizophydium* (Miller, 1969). Personal communication with W. J. Koch led to the realization that my *Rhizophydium* and Register's *Phlyctochytrium* belonged to the same species. Both Register's isolate and mine occasionally formed very atypical apophyses, or lacked apophyses. Chytridiologists have never agreed on what constitutes an apophysis; however, *Phlyctochytrium* and *Rhizophydium* are distinguished solely on the basis of the presence or absence of an apophysis. Lacking guidelines, workers have emphasized or ignored the presence of occasional atypical apophyses. I did not stress the occasional occurrence of an apophysis-like swelling in my isolate, referring it to the genus *Rhizophydium*. Register, on the other hand, chose to emphasize the atypical apophysis and referred his isolate to the genus *Phlyctochytrium*. This is an example of the confusion which may result when taxa are erected following the *laissez faire* measures in vogue in chytridial taxonomy (Miller, 1968).

In the work of Paterson (1963) on observations of two species of *Rhizophydium*, we find an example to emulate regarding the presumed parasitic nature of epibiotic chytrids. Paterson found the green alga *Pediastrum* sp. infested by two species of *Rhizophydium*. His first examinations seemed to indicate that these chytrids were parasites. Evidence for this conclusion included the observations that the appearance of the algal protoplasm was changing, chloroplasts were degenerating and plasmolysis was occurring, apparently as a result of the chytridial infestation. Host range studies on several algal species indicated at the end of a two week period that neither species of *Rhizophydium* would grow on healthy and actively growing algae. As some of the test algae became moribund during the third week of the experiment, the two chytrids began to grow on them. Luxuriant growth of the chytrids also occurred when boiled algae and non-viable pollen grains were offered them as substrates. Had Paterson not investigated the parasitic nature of the two species of *Rhizophydium*, but hastily described them as one or two new parasitic species on *Pediastrum*, additional 'arte-factual' taxa would have been incorporated into the literature. Workers must ascertain the parasitic nature of epibiotic chytrids with host range and substrate studies.

Paterson established unifungal cultures of the two species of *Rhizophydium*, one with a single apical pore, the other with 2-5 pores. These unifungal cultures were used as inocula in experiments on various non-living or dead (killed by boiling) substrates, including eight species of algae, *Allomyces javanicus* Kniep, two species of nematodes and non-viable pollen of *Pinus resinosa* Ait. Both species were also grown on YpSs, one in axenic culture the other in unifungal culture. Paterson found that the sizes of both sporangia and the rhizoids of one species varied in direct proportion to the sizes of the non-living or killed substrates on which they were grown. 'Sporangial sizes of *Rhizophydium* were smallest (6-15μm) on the smallest substrates, largest (19-33μm) on the largest substrates and intermediate (6-26μm) on the intermediate sized substrates.' Paterson also found that the rhizoids of *Rhizophydium* sp. were very variable. On agar, the rhizoids were much branched and arose from many places at the base of the sporangium; on pollen, the many branched rhizoids arose from a single main axis. Thalli growing on killed substrates formed endobiotic parts as found on pollen and agar as well as 'a much branched rhizoidal system arising directly from the tip of the original germ tube just inside the cell wall of the dead host'. Paterson reported no influence of substrate on the shape and size of zoospores, shape of sporangia, number of discharge pores and the manner of sporangial discharge. Paterson concluded that 'the amount of nutrients available may be a function of size of sporangia'. Paterson's study supports the work of Koch (1957), and Register (1959) summarized above. All three studies would have been more valuable if the methods of sampling, the total numbers of measurements in each category, and the means and ranges for all characteristics studied had been reported.

Johns (1964) found that sporangial size and shape of *Polyphagus* was influenced by different algal hosts as well as the amount of host available to the parasite. *Polyphagus starrii* Johns, parasitic on *Eudorina elegans* Ehrenb., formed sporangia through the third or fourth generation which averaged 30 x 44μm, with each sporangium producing more than 30 zoospores. Dwarf sporangia measuring 8.6 x 10.7μm, producing only one zoospore per sporangium and parasitizing a single host cell, were found after one week. The addition of host coenobia to cultures producing only dwarf sporangia resulted in renewed development of average-size sporangia. Johns also reported that the size and shape of sporangia of *P. starrii* were influenced by different hosts. On four different algal hosts *(Eudorina elegans, Pandorina morum* (Müll.) Barry, *Chlamydomonas monadina* Stein, *Volvulina pringsheimii* Starr), *P. starrii* varied as follows: mean prosporangial diameter decreased from 34.4 to 26.0 to 24.5 to 20.8 μm respectively; mean sporangial size decreased from 29.8 x 44.0 to 27.0 x 35.5 to 27.0 x 32.4 to 26.0 x 33.8μm respectively; mean zoospore number per sporangium decreased from 32 to 17 to 15 to 14 respectively; the mean diameter decreased from 23.5 to 23.0 to 23.1 to 22.5μm respectively. Sporangial shapes changed from cylindrical and broadly clavate to increasingly obovoid; zoospore size was not host substrate dependent, the zoospores on all four hosts measuring 8 x 13μm. Johns also found that *Polyphagus starrii* could parasitize 21 algal hosts. He rightly points out that so large a susceptible host spectrum by one parasite suggests that the use of host specificity as a taxonomic character is of dubious value without extensive host range studies.

Barr and Hickman (1967) studied morphological variation in *Rhizophydium sphaerocarpum* (Zopf) Fischer and *R. karlingii* Sparrow. While methods of sampling and measuring, total numbers measured, means and ranges for morphological characteristics studied were not included, the results reported further stress the need to recognise the influence of substrate on morphological characteristics and its importance to taxonomy These workers reported that *R. karlingii* expressed a wide range of substrate influenced morphological variations that were difficult to relate to its original description. Sporang varied in size from 5-9μm in diameter on moribund or damaged cells of *Netrium digitus* (Ehrenb.) Itzigs. et Rothe. and *Cladophora glomerata* (L.) Kütz. to 16.25μm in diamete on non-viable pine pollen. Sporangia in the original description of *R. karlingii,* a parasite o *Ulothrix zonata* Kütz., measured 9-18μm (13.5μm) in diameter. The rhizoid was found to be extremely variable (very much different from its original description) taking the form of: a single, slender unbranched rhizoid; an extensively branched rhizoid; a variably sized, frequently slightly forked knob-like apophysis; a multiple rhizoid system having more than one point of origin on the sporangium and an interbiotic network frequently exhibiting a 'polyphagus behavior . . . in pollen grain cultures'. Under no circumstances were the authors able to induce *R. karlingii,* originally described as an algal parasite, to infest any living alga tested. It grew, however, on non-viable pine pollen and a wide range of heat-killed algae. The authors stressed the value 'of experimental work in determing biological and morphological relationships amongst these fung

Koch (1968) compared flagellar lengths, body sizes and lipoid body sizes of zoospores from sporangia of several chytrid isolates growing on agar media with those growing on pollen of *Liquidambar styraciflua*. All isolates were from axenic agar cultures. It is not clear, however, from the methods given whether the pollen had been sterilized prior to its use in pollen cultures, how much inoculum was added to agar and pollen cultures and, in some experiments, how many measurements were made for each characteristic studied. All cultures were grown at room temperature. The methods used would 'easily meet the standards currently in use, and the data should have greater accuracy than the taxonomists of the group have heretofore demanded'.

Zoospore flagella of one isolate each of *Phlyctochytrium irregulare* and *Entophlyctis* sp. and two isolates each of *Phlyctochytrium punctatum* and *Chytriomyces hyalinus* Karling were measured following Koch's 'wet' method. Zoospores in a drop of water on a microscope slide were killed with fumes of 1% osmic acid, stained darkly with crystal violet, and covered with a coverslip. The mounted coverslip was blotted to remove as much water as possible and ringed with wax to inhibit drying. Camera lucida drawings were made of flagella. Ten to twenty camera lucida drawings were measured for each isolate studied.

Flagellar lengths (first of two figures given from agar; second of two figures from pollen; averages given first; ranges in parentheses) on agar compared with pollen were as follows: *Phlyctochytrium irregulare* 21.7 : 22.2μm (20.6-22.5μm) : (20.4-23.5μm); *Entophlyctis* sp. 20.6 : 20.5μm (19.4-21.5μm) : (18.9-21.6μm); *Phlyctochytrium punctatum* (Lucas isolate) 19.7 : 19.5μm (16.9-21.4μm); *P. punctatum* (La 6b isolate) 22.0 : 22.4μm (20.9-23.5μm) : (21.4-24.5μm); *Chytriomyces hyalinus* (CH-106 isolate) 29.6 : 28.6μm (25.5-33.2μm) : (25.5-29.1μm); *C. hyalinus* (La-1 isolate) 29.3 : 28.1μm (26.5-30.6μm) : (22.1-33.7μm). Koch concluded that flagellar length was about the same on agar as on pollen, suggesting that the slight differences in the averages on agar and pollen were not significant. Such a conclusion would have been more valid if supported by a larger number of measurements and an exact report of total measurements for each isolate. Seemingly minor differences in measurements might have proven significant if tested with statistical analysis. Differences in the ranges of flagellar length on the two substrates are apparent and a larger sample might have influenced the average. Koch used his 'dry' method, which assured that flagella were in one plane, in measuring flagellar lengths of two isolates of *Phlyctochytrium punctatum*. The slide containing the stained and killed zoospores was dried and covered with a #1 coverslip and a permanent mounting medium. Measurements were made using camera lucida drawings. In addition, the experimental thalli were grown in agar and pollen cultures made with triple distilled water. Zoospores were no older than 15 minutes when measured. The cultures were maintained under constant fluorescent light at 25°C. A total of approximately 300 measurements were randomly made for each of the four test cultures. Standard deviations and means were determined. Isolate MF 101 had the same ranges of flagellar lengths (9.0-22.5μm) on agar media and pollen. The mean, however, on agar (14.4μm ± 0.34μm) was 0.6μm less than on pollen (15.0μm ± 1.79μm). The differences in the means, even though the ranges are the same, stress the need for making counts large enough to include a representative expression of the range. Flagella of isolate R17 ranged from 10.0 to 25.3μm long on agar and 9.5-23.0μm long on pollen. The mean on agar was 16.8μm (± 2.95μm) and 16.5μm (± 2.94μm) on pollen.

Koch (1968) studied the ratio of average flagellar length to average spore body size. He found no correlation in any species between the size of the spore body and the length of the flagellum. He suggested that the common practice in taxonomic diagnoses of expressing flagellar length as so many times the lengths of the spore body or as a ratio of the zoospore body length to the length of the flagellum is less accurate than measurements of the flagellum alone. Koch also presented data on zoospore body measurements for four species (13 isolates) of chytrids: *Entophlyctis* sp., *Phlyctochytrium irregulare*, *P. punctatum* and *Chytriomyces hyalinus.* He compared zoospore body sizes of these fungi growing on various agar media with those growing on sweetgum pollen. Koch concluded that zoospore body size is 'fairly constant' but 'may vary with the substratum on which the fungus is growing'. Differences in zoospore body sizes were apparent in mean sizes as well as size ranges in isolates growing on agar and pollen cultures.

Koch (1968) studied variation in lipoid bodies of zoospores as influenced by substrate. He determined the average number and range of numbers of lipoid bodies per zoospore body, the percentage of zoospores having only one lipoid body per zoospore, the average and range sizes of the single lipoid body or the conspicuously largest lipoid body and the ratio of the diameter of lipoid body to the spore body size. Prior to this work nothing was known concerning the value of the lipoid body as a taxonomic character. Regardless of this fact, taxonomists have relied heavily on the lipoid body in distinguishing taxa, describing its presence, absence and number; colour, centricity or eccentricity; percentage of zoospore body occupied and its general location in the zoospore body. He offered examples of taxa distinguished solely on the basis of lipoid body morphology. Koch found that the conspicuous lipoid body usually filled more than one half the zoospore body when the zoospore came from various agar media. The lipoid body was usually larger in pollen grown cultures than agar grown cultures,while the zoospore body itself—in these same cultures—was larger, smaller or remained the same. Thus, the ratio of lipoid body diameter to zoospore body size was influenced in various ways. Chytrid species have usually been described as having a single, refractive lipoid body in the zoospore body. Koch found considerable substrate influence regarding the percentage of the time that only one lipoid body was present in the zoospore body. *Phlyctochytrium punctatum* (Lucas isolate) growing on agar had one lipoid body 76% of the time. The same chytrid on pollen never had only one lipoid body. *Phlyctochytrium punctatum* (La 6b isolate), on the other hand, was found to have one lipoid body 92 and 98% of the time on agar and pollen, respectively. Other isolates in this study showed considerable variability in response to influence of substrate on this morphological characteristic. The average number and ranges of lipoid bodies were also found to be substrate dependent. In *P. punctatum* (Lucas isolate) on agar, the average number of lipoid bodies was 1.6 (0-6) while on pollen it was 5.9 (2-11). *Entophlyctis* was 1.1 (0-5) and 1.3 (1-8) on two different agar media and 3.1 (1-15) on pollen. No isolate had the same number of lipoid bodies per zoospore on agar and pollen. Koch's experiments with lipoid bodies and zoosoore body sizes have indicated that caution must be exercised in the use of these substrate influenced morphological characteristics in taxonomy.

Bernstein (1968) compared the zoospore body diameters and numbers of lipoid bodies per zoospore body in eight isolates of *Rhizophlyctis rosea* (deBary et Woronin) Fischer on two substrates, Stainer's defined agar medium and leaves of *Paspalum dilatatum* Poir. in dilute salt solution of Machlis and Ossia (1953). She reaffirmed the importance of substrate influence on two morphological characteristics, zoospore body size and number of lipoid bodies. She also reported that substrate induced variation was more evident on agar medium than on *Paspalum* leaves in dilute salt solution. Her data are presented in such a way as to be confusing and difficult to read, at least to the writer. Apparently mean zoospore body diameters ranged from a low of approximately 3.7μm to a high of approximately 5.2μm on agar medium. On *Paspalum* leaves, mean zoospore body diameters ranged from approximately 4 to 4.3μm. Actually, except for two of the eight isolates, the means in both experimental cultures were close. In almost all isolates, there was, however, a larger number of smaller zoospore bodies within the ranges on agar than on *Paspalum*. Such data provide us with an understanding of the population-size make-up within a range. Insufficient, non-random counts might lead to incorrect conclusions, because one size-group within the range of the species might be emphasized. My interpretation of her data for the number of lipoid bodies per zoospore suggests no great difference between cultures on agar or grass. Some isolates on grass produced more lipoid globules per zoospore, while other isolates produced more when grown in agar culture. The mean numbers of lipoid bodies per zoospore from agar ranged from a low of approximately four to a high of approximately seven. On grass, the range in the means was approximately 3-6. The ranges on both substrates were also similar, approximately 1-16 lipoid bodies per zoospore on agar and approximately 1-17 on grass. Bernstein interpreted a correlation of sample means of diameter of zoospore bodies and number of lipoid bodies per zoospore, as a tendency for larger zoospore bodies to have fewer lipoid bodies, the converse also occuring to some extent.

Bernstein (1968) also reported on observations of sporangial size differences within isolates as well as among the eight isolates. On agar, six isolates had similar sporangial dimensions. Two of the isolates produced much larger sporangia. She only presented data for one isolate producing large sporangia (isolate BJ-1; mean 131.3μm; range 90-200μm) and two isolates producing small sporangia (isolate 127-1; mean 62.1μm; range 47-100μm: isolate 47-41; mean 88.2μm; range 60-145μm). Bernstein observed in agar cultures, morphological characteristics which showed 'a consistent constellation of features accompanying the two quantitative characters of the zoospore' presented in this study (zoospore body size and number of lipoid bodies per zoospore). Thus in six of the eight isolates, relatively small zoospores were associated with a relatively large number of lipoid bodies per zoospore body, small sporangia, long exit papillae, a non-clumping habit of sporangial growth and narrow rhizoids with many branches. The remaining two isolates expressed the opposite morphological features: large zoospore bodies, few lipoid bodies per zoospore body, large sporangia, short exit papillae, clumping growth habit of sporangia and thick, contorted rhizoids. Bernstein considers *Karlingia spinosa* Karling [=*Rhizophlyctis spinosa* (Karling) Sparrow] as possibly an invalid species. *Karlingia spinosa* was erected primarily upon at least two characteristics presumed to differ from *Rhizophlyctis rosea* (zoospore body size and number of lipoid bodies in the zoospore body), both of which she has shown in this work to be well within the ranges of morphological variability of these characteristics in *R. rosea*.

Bostick (1968) carried on experiments to investigate the effects of inoculum size, amount of food available, temperature, motion and aeration on some morphological characteristics of *Chytriomyces hyalinus*. Zoospore suspensions obtained from axenic cultures were added as experiments required to apparently unsterilized, but known weights of, sweetgum pollen or purified shrimp chitin in sterile distilled water. Reisert's defined medium was used for experiments on the effects of motion and aeration. Sporangial size and size range were influenced by the amount of food available in the pollen cultures. With a limited amount of pollen, 11-13 mg per dish, more sporangia were found in fewer size ranges, and sporangia in general were smaller (10-50μm). With an abundance of food available, 45-48 mg of pollen per dish, fewer sporangia were generally found in a particular size range, but the size range was considerably larger

477

(10-80μm). The amount of inoculum added to the experimental dishes affected the sizes and size ranges of sporangia. Inoculation with zoospore suspensions of 0.1 ml produced sporangial sizes and size ranges very similar to inocula ten times as large (1.0 ml of zoospore suspension). More sporangia were found in fewer ranges and sporangia were smaller (10-30 μm). Inoculations with zoospore suspensions of 10.0 ml, however, produced fewer sporangia per size range, but more sporangia were larger, as was also the size range, 20-65 μm. Differences noted in these experiments were found to be significant when subjected to a 't' test. One hundred sporangia were measured per dish.

Bostick also studied the effects of temperature and substrate on sporangial size. Cultures of *C. hyalinus* on purified shrimp chitin (43-50 mg per experimental dish) and sweetgum pollen (45-48 mg per dish) were grown at 10, 20, 25 and 30°C under constant fluorescent illumination (160 f.c.). Sporangia were larger on chitin than on pollen except at 10°C (chitin 5.0-19 μm x 20 μm: pollen 5.0-31 μm x 35 μm). No growth was found on pollen at 30°C, but sporangia growing on chitin were 12.5-44.0 μm at this temperature. The largest sporangia on both substrates were found at 25°C (chitin 15.0-75.0 μm: pollen 5.0-47.5 μm). At 20°C sporangia on chitin were 5.0-45 μm x 47 μm and on pollen 5.0-31μm x 35 μm. Growth was generally unfavourable for *C. hyalinus* at 10 and 30°C. Temperature was also found to influence the production of resting 'sporangia'. (From her discussion, it is apparent that Bostick was referring to resting bodies. These may be found to act as sporangia at germination.) Resting bodies were produced on chitin at all temperatures tested (10, 20, 25, 30°C), but were found on pollen at 20 and 25°C only. Resting body formation in *C. hyalinus* has been found to result from rhizoidal fusions (Moore and Miller, 1971, 1973).

Cultures of *C. hyalinus* in Reisert's medium were grown on a wrist action shaker, a swirl action shaker and without agitation. Half of the still cultures were aerated by bubbling with filtered compressed air. All information concerning methods and results of these experiments are not presented or are unclearly presented. There are no data indicating sporangial size ranges, means or total counts. Bostick's use of 'aerated' leads to confusion, since one is not certain if it is restricted to still cultures supplied with air or includes cultures agitated by wrist and swirl action shakers as well. Apparently, it is restricted to still cultures supplied with air. The largest sporangia were found in cultures agitated by swirl action, and the smallest sporangia were found in cultures agitated by the wrist action shaker. Abnormal zoospore discharge was found in cultures 'agitated frequently'. Resting bodies were not produced in still cultures and occurred earlier in wrist action cultures than in swirl action cultures. Aerated (still cultures?) produced larger sporangia than non-aerated sporangia.

Miller (1968) presented observations and discussions concerning the taxonomic validity of some morphological characters used in taxon delineation in chytrid taxonomy. Taxonomists have failed, generally, to consider variation of morphological characteristics used in taxonomy as influenced by substrate differences. Few taxonomic descriptions have been preceded by experimentation with several substrates or based on single spore axenic or unifungal cultures. Most chytrid taxa have been erected from gross cultures left standing at room temperatures for days. Chytrid taxonomists have generally failed to distinguish variation within a taxon from variation between taxa. Thus, many chytrid taxa have been erected with descriptions based on host ranges and morphological characteristics, whose stability has not been studied and remains unknown. Miller (1968) also offered an example of the difficulties inherent in using some morphological characteristics in taxon identification in the

Rhizophydium-Phlyctochytrium complex, specifically a dentiferous isolate and its similarity to both *Rhizophydium aureliae* Ajello and *Phlyctochytrium mucronatum* Canter.

Barr (1969) isolated a large number of soil chytrids into single spore axenic culture. He compared the morphology of eight of these isolates on pollens of *Pinus sylvestris* L., *P. nigra* Arnold, *P. resinosa* Ait., on a mixture of these three pollens and on yeast–peptone–dextrose medium (YPD). Barr established these eight isolates as four new species and proposed one isolate as neotype material for *Rhizophydium sphaerptheca* Zopf. Isolate no. 6 was designated *Rhizophydium capillaceum* Barr; nos. 15 and 68 *Phlyctochytrium californicum* Barr; nos. 33 and 39 *Phlyctochytrium plurigibbosum* Barr and nos. 62 and 7 as *Phlyctochytrium acuminatum* Barr. Barr reported that chytrid isolates in pollen cultures after 10-15 days (with increased bacterial populations) became almost indistinguishable from each other, resembling the appearance of chytrids in gross cultures from initial collections. The author (1971) and his students (Lwanga, 1969; Balaguru, 1972) have emphasized the need to use sterilized pollen for comparative morphological studies, to make morphological measurements on first generation individuals only and to use synchronous cultures (inoculated with zoospores of approximately the same age). Barr found that all species grew more uniformly in axenic culture in YPD than on pollen. Barr measured sporangial size and number of discharge pores of sporangia growing on pollen and YPD. At least 100 measurements of sporangial size and 50 counts of pore frequency were made for each isolate studied. Barr found 'that these characteristics are highly variable and of only limited use in taxonomy'. He also concluded that the number of discharge pores was related directly to sporangial size. Zoospore body sizes and flagellar lengths were studied, but measurements were not associated with a specific substrate, and one has found it difficult to evaluate their meanings.

Barr's (1969) erection of four new species has not helped the taxonomic chaos in the *Rhizophydium-Phlyctochytrium* complex. This is especially pertinent when one considers Barr's admission that 'among the morphological characteristics available in the fungi reported here, the rhizoidal system is the main distinguishing feature seen with the light microscope'. The rhizoidal system traditionally has been considered to be the least constant of all morphological characteristics. One has not had the advantage of studying these different rhizoidal types advanced by Barr, but one wonders how consistently they are formed and how they are modified by substrate. It would, perhaps, have been less damaging to have allied *Rhizophydium capillaceum* with his neotype material of *R. sphaerotheca.* The three species of *Phlyctochytrium* based upon Barr's useful arbitrary separation of *Rhizophydium* and *Phlyctochytrium* ('tubular rhizoids appearing hollow, adjacent to the sporangium in pure culture = *Phlyctochytrium;* thread-like rhizoids <1.0 μm in diameter = *Rhizophydium'*) could have been included as one species, since the only admitted differences among these taxa were stated to be rhizoidal swellings, a very variable feature. These species might also have been allied with existing similar species as discussed by Barr. *Rhizophydium capillaceum* essentially differs from *R. sphaerotheca* (Barr's neotype material) in that the rhizoidal system in the former arises from *one* to several closely situated points, while in the latter the rhizoidal system arises from a single point (always?). One would appreciate having quantitative data relating to the frequency of the rhizoidal phenomenon in all of Barr's species.

In the descriptions of Barr's four new species and of the neotype material of *R. sphaerotheca,* all taxa are said to be saprophytic on pine pollen and grass leaves. Quantitative data describing sporangial size, number of papillae, rhizoidal morphology, zoospore body sizes and flagellar lengths are included in each description. No mention is made in the descriptions of new taxa of the morphological characteristics on YPD. Yet, the quantitative data included in Tables I and II (Barr, 1969) comparing sporangial diameters and papillae number on pollen and YPD, are used in the descriptions. Barr's table III gives zoospore characteristics but offers no indication of the substrate on which these spores are produced. No quantitative data are included in the paper regarding morphological characteristics on the grass leaves referred to in the descriptions as a substratum.

Barr (1970 a) studied morphological variations of a single-sporangium isolate identified by him as *Phlyctochytrium reinboldtae* Persiel in unifungal pollen culture. He found that the epibiotic sporangium was sessile on the pollen grain, extended above the pollen grain on an apophysis or thickened rhizoidal stalk, attached interbiotically to more than one pollen grain by rhizoids extending from a branched apophysis stalk, or growing free from attachment to the pollen substrate. Sporangia growing on a single pollen grain measured 8-32 μm in diameter, but reached 40 μm in diameter if they were growing interbiotically on two pollen grains. In axenic culture on YPD, sporangia measured 36-70 μm in diameter. Papillae of *P. reinboldtae* most frequently measured 1.5-2.0 μm long by 2.5-3.0 μm in diameter. Barr found that approximately 10% of papillae in unifungal culture on pine pollen (bacteria present) were up to 5 μm long and 4-6 μm in diameter. In original collection cultures, *P. reinboldtae* growing on pollen under the influence of many micro-organisms, produced long and wide papillae much more frequently.

Rhizoids were found to be quite variable. In pine pollen, the apophysis was spherical to elongated, bearing a network of densely branched rhizoids. On YPD, the rhizoids were non-apophysate or the subsporangial swelling was elongated, pyriform or subspherical. The branching habit of the rhizoids also varied with pH, appearing not as open at pH 5.2 as at pH 6.5 in YPD. Barr also reported no size differences in flagellar lengths, numbers or sizes of lipoid bodies or shapes of zoospore bodies from pine-pollen culture or culture on YpSs. It is obvious from Barr's work (1970 a), that culture differences (unifungal, multi-organismal and axenic) influence morphological characteristics. More complete explanations of culture methods used (type of pine pollen) and the total numbers, ranges and means of measurements made would have been appreciated. The nutritional data on *P. reinboldtae* are interesting, but any comparison with physiological results of *P. punctatum* (Goldstein, 1960) may be meaningless unless methods of both studies were exactly similar. One must assume that variation in physiological phenomena influenced by culture methods will be as great as or greater than known variation in morphology influenced by culture and substrate.

Barr (1970 b) studied the nutritional requirements of two isolates of *Rhizophydium sphaerocarpum.* One was isolated from *Spirogyra* by Barr and Hickman (1967), the other by Paterson (1963) from moribund *Pediastrum.* Paterson's isolate grew on various non-living or dead (killed by boiling) substrates: eight species of algae, *Allomyces javanicus* Kniep, two species of nematodes, non-viable pollen of *Pinus resinosa* and in axenic culture on YpSs. This same isolate was found by Edwards (1966) to grow on killed and non-killed cells of *Staurastrum.* Edwards (1966) concluded that 'the ability of this fungus to grow better on killed than on non-killed algal cells indicated that it is a saprophyte rather than a parasite on algae'. Barr's isolate of *R. sphaerocarpum* 'failed to grow on heat-killed algae (including *Spirogyra*) or on pine pollen, although it grew on nutrient media in pure culture'. Barr found that these two isolates were 'virtually identical', both morphologically and physiologically. They differed morphologically in sporangial size and pigment formation on algae; physiologically in temperature optima and one isolate used 'nitrogen as ammonium chloride, ammonium nitrate and sodium nitrate when the inoculum is dense and contains actively growing thalli'.

Barr rightfully concluded that there was no justification for describing them as separate species. One wishes Barr would have stopped there. He, however, emphasizing substrate-host differences, erected two varieties: *R. sphaerocarpum* var. *sphaerocarpum* for Paterson's isolate and var. *spirogyrae* for the isolate of Barr and Hickman. The former variety is described as a saprophyte on algae, nematodes, pine pollen and producing whitish growth on YpSs agar; the latter, a parasite of *Spirogyra* spp. producing yellowish growth on YpSs agar. Since what is now Barr's new var. *sphaerocarpum* was found by Edwards (1966) to grow on non-killed cells of *Straurastrum,* what is the logic in considering it a saprophyte only? Would it not have been satisfactory to modify the description or concept of *R. sphaerocarpum* to include all its known substrates, including killed and non-killed *Spirogyra* spp. and *Straurastrum*?

As I pointed out earlier in this chapter, and in (Miller, 1968), it is essential that workers prove the parasitic nature of epibiotic chytrids before establishing new taxa at any level. Many problems in chytridial taxonomy have been caused by emphasizing the assumed parasitic or non-parasitic nature of chytrids in delineating taxa. Johns (1964) pointed out that host specificity as a taxonomic character was of dubious value without extensive host range studies, and he was referring to holocarpic endobiotic chytrids and not epibiotic, eucarpic forms!

Hasija and Miller (1971) studied the nutrition of two isolates (CR and CH) of *Chytriomyces hyalinus* and one isolate of *C. aureus* Karling and its influence on morphological characteristics. Sporangial size was influenced by temperature, pH, vitamins, carbohydrates and nitrogen sources. Rhizoidal characteristics were influenced also. Zoospore body sizes and number or sizes of lipoid bodies in zoospore bodies were not apparently affected. Sporangial diameter of *C. hyalinus* (isolate CH) averaged larger in media lacking calcium pantothenate or pyridoxine. Cultures minus para-amino-benzoic acid produced larger sporangia in *C. hyalinus* (CR) and *C. aureus.* Isolate CR also formed larger sporangia in media minus inositol, pyridoxine or riboflavin. Sporangia of *C. aureus* were also smaller when riboflavin was omitted. An external supply of thiamine was required by all isolates. Except for somewhat larger sporangia in isolate CR, temperature had little influence on sporangial size. Sporangia tended to average smaller diameters at lower (5.0 μm) or higher (8.0 μm) pHs. Sporangial sizes were little, if at all, affected by various carbon and nitrogen combinations. Rhizoids were poorly developed at concentrations of 1 g C + 0.1 g N and 4 g C + 1 g N; were long, slender and vigorously branched at a concentration of 1 g C + 0.2 g N; formed long and slender axes at a concentration of 2 g C + 0.1 g N.

Hasija and Miller further reported that isolate CH averaged smaller sized sporangia (48 μm) when grown on maltose as a carbon source. Sporangial diameter of isolate CR were smallest (94 μm) on fructose and largest (122 μm) when grown on cellobiose. *Chytriomyces aureus* produced larger sporangia on mannose (average 42 μm) and smallest (26 μm) on starch as the carbohydrate. The rhizoids of both isolates of *C. hyalinus* tended to be shorter on maltose, cellobiose and starch. Sporangial diameters in isolate CH ranged from 16-56 μm with averages ranging from 24 to 36 μm on various nitrogen sources. Isolate CH averaged smallest (24 μm) on l-aspartic acid and l-leucine and largest (36 μm) on ammonium nitrate. Isolate CR ranged from 20-140 μm in diameter with averages from 30 to 112 μm; smallest sporangia of CR isolates (30 μm) were produced on l-aspartic acid and l-leucine, while those grown on l-glutamine as the nitrogen source averaged largest (112 μm in diameter). Sporangial diameters in *C. aureus* ranged from 10 to 52 μm, with averages ranging from 30 to 34 μm on various nitrogen sources. Sporangial diameter of *C. aureus* averaged largest (34 μm) from media with peptone as the nitrogen source. Other nitrogen sources produced sporangia in *C. aureus* averaging 30-32 μm in diameter.

Booth (1971) discussed the ill-defined, highly variable and unstable morphological characters commonly employed in distinguishing taxa in the Chytridiales. Examples of substrate and environmental variation of several morphological characters used in identification of taxa are illustrated with the results of morphological and developmental studies on ten single-spore isolates of *Entophlyctis* species. The *Entophlyctis* isolates from several widely separated collection sites from California, Nevada and British Columbia were grown and studied on sterilized *Pinus sylvestris* L. pollen and MHU nutrient agar medium (0.3% malt extract, 0.3% peptone, 0.1% dextrose, 1.1% agar in 1 litre water of 0 to 7% salinity with 0.03% streptomycin sulphate, 774 μg/mg, and 0.03% penicillin G, 4 x 10^6 units.) Booth found considerable variation in morphological and developmental characteristics in *Entophlyctis:* when the germ tube on MHU medium did not expand, the first rhizoidal axis developed into the sporangium; on both substrates, the cyst rather than the germ tube expanded to form the sporangium; on pollen, an endobiotic-epibiotic thallus developed when both the cyst and the germ tube expanded concurrently; also on pollen, *Entophlyctis* was endobiotic, epibiotic or interbiotic; zoospores escaped through tubes, zoospore cysts or infrequently from sporangia via a split in the sporangial walls; complex, forked, irregular, simple or strap-like discharge tubes were formed; and sporangia and their zoospores were usually smaller when growing on pollen than on MHU medium.

Booth (1971) concluded that morphological and developmental variations in his ten isolates of *Entophlyctis* indicated that such taxonomic characters as zoospore size, lipoid body size and colour, cyst presence and function, presence or absence of discharge tube, coarseness and branching of rhizoidal axis, place of origin and number of rhizoidal axes, and sporangium size and shape were of little or questionable value in species delineation. Booth further concluded, since these isolates were grown on MHU medium and sterilized pollen grains, that the substrate and especially the 'saprophytic' versus 'parasitic' natures were questionable characters by which to distinguish these fungi. Resting spore features remained as the only characters useful in distinguishing species of *Entophlyctis*. Booth suggested that only three (E. *apiculata* (Braun) Fisher, *E. reticulospora* Cook and *E. crenata* Karling) of 17 species be recognized as valid and useful taxa. Booth also reported that the variability found in his comparative study related *Entophlyctis* to five other genera in one subfamily and four families.

Barr (1971) in an excellent study on the morphology and taxonomy of *Entophlyctis confervae-glomeratae* (Cienkowski) Sparrow, and having also the results of an almost concurrent and similar study by Booth (1971), proposed to recognize as valid only eight species in *Entophlyctis* of the previously described 17 species (four imperfectly known) and one form. The re-evaluation of the taxonomic characters of *Entophlyctis* was based on morphological studies of single-spore isolates in axenic culture by both Barr (1971) and Booth (1971). Barr used a variety of sterilized substrates and fungal substrates from axenic cultures. He also kept uninoculated control cultures of alga substrates as checks for the presence of other chytrids, when algal substrates were collected locally and inoculated fresh. Barr reported morphological variation in *E. confervae-glomeratae* so marked that many of the morphological characteristics were found valueless as taxonomic criteria. Sporangial sizes and shapes varied according to substrate. Substrate influenced the origin and number of rhizoids on the sporangium. Depending upon substrate, rhizoids arose from all sides of the sporangia or from one to four axes at the bases or sides of the sporangia. Rhizoids were extensively branched, simply branched or unbranched.

The number, location, length and type of discharge mechanisms (tubes of cysts) were also influenced by substrate. Discharge tube number correlated with sporangial size. The sporangia were able to originate from expansion of the zoospore cyst or of the germ tube and to grow endobiotically, epibiotically or interbiotically. The role of the cyst in sporangial discharge was of no consequence in separating taxa of *Entophlyctis,* and resting-spore colour and pigmentation of the lipoid globule were only used in separating taxa after extensive investigations of substrate influence on colour. Barr (1971) also found the fine rhizoids of *Entophlyctis* evanescent and apt to disintegrate by the time of sporangial maturity. In pine pollen, such mature sporangia were indistinguishable from *Olpidium,* even when the pollen grain was ruptured freeing the thallus of *Entophlyctis.* This fact causes Barr to question whether the species of *Olpidium* reported to be saprophytic in pine pollen exist, and if there is a saprophytic *Olpidium.*

Miller *et al.* (1973) examined under environmentally controlled, axenic culture conditions, the influence of several pollen grains and other substrates on sporangial sizes, sporangial wall thicknesses, numbers of discharge pores per sporangia, discharge pore diameters, structures of apophyses, zoospore body sizes, lipoid body sizes and flagellar lengths of single-spore cultures of *Rhizophydium* sp. and *Phlyctochytrium punctatum.* Both nonsynchronous and synchronous experimental cultures were used. Nonsynchronous cultures simulated 'natural conditions' when more than one zoospore generation of a particular experimental inoculum was permitted to reinfest the same substrate. Synchronous cultures were inoculated with zoospores of the same age and only this generation was permitted to develop in the test plates. Experimental synchronous cultures were measured after 45-55 hours and before second generation sporangia developed. This precaution was essential, because as the nutrients in experimental cultures were gradually depleted by first generation zoospores, sporangial size and other morphological characteristics of second generation zoospores were influenced.

Sporangial diameters of *Rhizophydium* sp. ranged from 4.0 to 13.8μm growing on onion epidermis; 5.6 to 17.6μm growing on human epidermis peelings; 5.0 to 32.7μm growing on sweetgum *(Liquidambar styraciflua)* pollen; and 12.6 to 44.1μm on 1/2YpSs agar medium, an overall range of 4.0 to 44.1μm. Mean sporangial sizes dramatically express the influence of substrate on sporangial size; sporangial mean sizes appear as four unrelated groups: 27.1μm ($\pm$ 7.5μm) on 1/2YpSs, 16.0μm($\pm$ 6.4μm) on sweetgum pollen, 11.1μm ($\pm$ 3.0μm) on human epidermis and 8.2μm ($\pm$ 1.8μm) on onion epidermis. Miller *et al.* (1973) suggest that following the usual practices in chytridial taxonomy of describing a new taxon on only one substrate and measuring only a few sporangia, a strong possibility exists that these morphological growth responses to different substrates might be described as separate taxa. Such a bias might be especially supported if the investigator only sampled a small expression of the taxon. For instance, considering sporangial size in *Rhizophydium* species, approximately 25% of the sporangia on onion epidermis were 7-9μm in diameter, while none was as small as that on 1/2YpSs. Also, 10% of sporangia on 1/2YpSs were 30μm wide, while no sporangia on human or onion epidermis and only 1% of sporangia on sweetgum pollen grew so large. The number of discharge tubes per sporangia was substrate dependent varying from a minimal functional low of 1 to a high of 19 (1/2YpSs,

range 3-19: mean 8; pollen, range 1-9: mean 8; human epidermis, range 1-4: mean 2; onion epidermis, range 1-5: mean 2). Discharge tube diameter ranged from 1.8 to 4μm wide on all four substrates with mean sizes ranging from 2.6 to 3.2μm wide. Both the number and diameter of discharge tubes were apparently directly related to sporangial size. Fifty measurements each of all sporangial and zoospore morphological characteristics studied on each of the four substrates were made.
Zoospore body diameter of *Rhizophydium* sp. varied from a low of 2.5-4.0μm. Lipoid body diameter varied only slightly on the different substrates, from 0.9 to 2.1μm. Flagellar length ranged from a low of 15.1μm to a high of 16.9μm. An analysis of the make-up of flagellar length range on particular substrates indicated that 16% of the zoospores from sporangia on 1/2YpSs had flagella measuring 15.1μm, while 46% of zoospores from onion epidermis had flagella measuring 15.1μm. Also, approximately 54% of zoospores from 1/2YpSs had flagella 16.3μm long while only 23% on human epidermis, 34% on sweetgum pollen and 38% on onion epidermis had flagella that length.

Miller *et al.* (1973) also studied morphological characteristics of *Phlyctochytrium punctatum* on nine different pollen grains, 1/2YpSs and a chemically defined medium (CDM) in axenic, nonsynchronous and synchronous cultures. In nonsynchronous pollen cultures, 160-260 measurements of sporangial and zoospore characteristics per substrate were studied from 3-4 day old cultures. Sporangial diameter ranged from a low of 8 μm on pollens of alder, *Alnus rugosa* (Du Roi) Spreng, and sweetgum to a high of 50 μm on spruce, *Picea abies* L., pollen. The mean sporangial diameters varied from 18.6 μm on *Carpinus caroliniana* Walt (ironwood) pollen to 30.3 μm on spruce pollen. There was a clinal increase in mean sporangial diameters from pollens of ironwood (18.6 μm); water oak, *Quercus nigra* L., (18.8 μm); alder (19.3 μm); wax myrtle, *Myrica cerifera* L., (19.9 μm); sweetgum (19.9 μm); white pine, *Pinus strobus* L., (24.1 μm); beech, *Fagus grandifolia* Ehrh., (29.5 μm); and spruce (30.3 μm). Substrate influences on distributional patterns within the size ranges were also noted. Sporangial wall thicknesses ranged from 1 to 4 μm thick. Mean wall thicknesses varied from a low of 1.8 μm for water oak pollen to a high of 2.6 μm on beech pollen. Generally, larger sporangia—produced on pollens of white pine, beech and spruce—had thicker walls, while smaller sporangia tended to have thinner walls (pollens of water oak, wax myrtle and alder). The number of discharge pores per sporangium, also influenced by substrate, ranged from 1 to 9. The distribution of pore number within a range was studied and its importance for taxonomic considerations discussed. On ironwood pollen, for instance, 82% of sporangia had one or two pores and only 4% of 260 counted had four pores. On beech pollen, 50% of the sporangia had one or two pores, but only five and two sporangia out of 290 had five and six pores respectively. On spruce pollen 45% of 260 sporangia had two pores each, while 17 had five, 10 and six, five had seven and two had nine pores. The number of discharge pores per sporangium was directly related to sporangial size.

Zoospore body diameters of *P. punctatum* growing in nonsynchronous, axenic pollen cultures ranged from a low of 3.0 μm on sweetgum pollen to a high of 7.0 μm in diameter on white pine and spruce pollens. Mean zoospore body diameters were 4.4 μm on pollen of sweetgum, 4.6 μm on beech and alnus, 4.7 μm on ironwood and wax myrtle, 4.8 μm on water oak, 5.0 μm on white pine and 5.2 μm on spruce pollen. Diameters of conspicuous lipoid bodies varied from a low of 0.8 μm in zoospores from sporangia growing on spruce pollen to a high of 6.0 μm in diameter on water oak pollen. Flagella ranged in length on various pollen substrates from a low of 11 μm on zoospores from sporangia growing on sweetgum pollen to a high of 22 μm from sporangia growing on pollens of ironwood, white pine and spruce. Mean flagellar lengths were 15.2 μm ($\pm$ 2.2 μm) on sweetgum, 16.2 μm ($\pm$ 1.0 μm) on wax myrtle, 16.3 μm ($\pm$ 0.9 μm) on beech, 16.7 μm ($\pm$ 1.1 μm) on alder, 16.9 μm ($\pm$ 1.4 μm) on spruce, 17.0 μm ($\pm$ 1.2 μm) on ironwood, 17.3 μm ($\pm$ 1.2 μm) on water oak and 17.3 μm ($\pm$ 1.7 μm) on white pine pollens. These data, along with similar data presented from synchronous cultures, suggested that flagellar length was also influenced by substrate.

Miller *et al.* (1973) studied the same sporangial and zoospore characteristics from synchronous cultures of *P. punctatum* on ironwood, sweetgum, alder, spruce, mugo pine (*Pinus mugo* Turra) and white pine pollens and on two synthetic agar media, 1/2 YpSs and a chemically defined medium (CDM). Each sporangial characteristic was studied on 200-300 sporangia per pollen substrate and on 100 sporangia per agar medium; each zoospore characteristic was studied on 50-100 zoospores from all eight substrates. All data were subjected to statistical analyses, and correlation coefficients were calculated for three characters: sporangial diameter, discharge pore number per sporangium and discharge pore diameter. The results were similar to results reported for nonsynchronous pollen cultures.

Mean sporangial size differences (means ranged from 18.4 to 36.0 μm) on all pollen and agar substrates except alder and CDM were significant at the 1 or 5% levels. Mean sporangial wall thickness as influenced by substrate fell into three groups. Group one, with a mean wall thickness of 1.0 μm, included sporangia from alder and spruce pollens, CDM and 1/2 YpSs. Group two with a mean wall thickness of 1.1 μm included sporangia growing on pollens of ironwood, mugo pine and white pine. Sweetgum pollen-grown sporangia with a mean wall thickness of 1.2 μm comprised the third group. Mean differences among the three groups were statistically significant at the 1% level, while within each group, no statistical differences were found. The number of discharge pores per sporangium was influenced by substrate. Except for mean number of discharge pores per sporangia between ironwood and alder pollens or between spruce pollen and CDM, all other substrates had mean values significantly different at the 1 or 5% levels. The number of discharge pores per sporangium ranged from a low of one to a high of 14; the means varied from three to nine pores per sporangium, as influenced by different substrates. Variation in number of discharge pores was directly related to sporangial size. Larger sporangia had more discharge pores, and a high, positive correlation between sporangial size and discharge pore number, significant at the 1% level, was found. Discharge pore diameter varied from 2 μm, a minimum found on all substrates except 1/2 YpSs to a maximum of 6 μm on spruce pollen. The mean values for discharge pore diameter on sweetgum, ironwood, mugo pine and white pine pollens were not significantly different from each other. Other mean values for discharge pore diameter on the remaining substrates were significantly different at the 1 or 5% levels. Correlation coefficient values between sporangial diameter and discharge pore diameter revealed a correlation at the 1% level of significance. Thus, the larger sporangia had larger discharge pores. Morphological characteristics of sporangia were more varied on pollen substrates than on synthetic media. Sporangial wall thickness and discharge pore diameter were influenced less by substrate than was sporangial diameter and number of discharge pores. Statistical analyses indicated that differences among the correlation coefficient values recorded on various substrates are significantly different and related to substrate.

Zoospore morphological characteristics of *P. punctatum* were also studied under synchronous, axenic culture conditions. Zoospore body sizes ranged from a low of

3 μm on all substrates to a high of 6 μm on ironwood, sweetgum and mugo pine pollens. The means ranged from a low of 3.8 μm on white pine pollen and 1/2 YpSs to a high of 4.7 μm on mugo pine pollen. Mean values of zoospore body sizes for sweetgum and mugo pine pollen-grown zoospores were significantly different from all other values at the 1% level. Zoospore body sizes from pine pollen and 1/2 YpSs were significantly different from sweetgum pollen grown zoospores at the 5% level. Substrate influenced lipoid body sizes of zoospores from sporangia growing on several pollens at the 1 or 5% level of significance. Mean lipoid body sizes ranged from 1.3 μm (CDM), 1.4 μm (spruce pollen), 1.6 μm (mugo pine pollens), 1.8 μm (alder and white pine pollens), 2.0 μm (sweetgum) and 2.2 μm (ironwood). No conspicuous lipoid bodies were found in zoospores from 1/2 YpSs cultures. Substrate influence on flagellar length was reported here for all three studies included in this paper (Miller *et al.,* 1973). This report was supported by statistical analysis only in the experiments using synchronous cultures of *P. punctatum,* and was the first report of marked substrate influence of flagellar length. Flagella varied from a low of 12 μm on CDM to a high of 43 μm on sweetgum pollen. Mean flagellar lengths were 14.9 μm (± 1.7 μm) on CDM, 19.0 μm (± 3.5 μm) on 1/2 YpSs, 19.6 μm (± 3.0 μm) on alder pollen, 20.6 μm (± 3.0 μm) on ironwood pollen, 21.5 μm (± 3.6 μm) on white pine pollen, 21.7 μm (± 4.7 μm) on spruce pollen, 25.4 μm (± 6.3 μm) on mugo pine pollen and 30.3 μm (± 7.0 μm) on sweetgum pollen. Mean flagellar sizes on CDM, sweetgum and mugo pine pollens were significantly different at the 1% level from all other mean values. Flagellar lengths from 1/2 YpSs were also significant at the 1% level from all other mean values except that recorded for alder, and only at the 5% level for ironwood pollen. The remaining mean flagellar lengths were not significantly different from each other.

Miller *et al.* (1973) concluded that all sporangial and zoospore morphological characteristics studied were substrate influenced and that variation caused by substrate must be considered in distinguishing future chytridial taxa.

References

BALAGURU, S. (1972). 'Influence of substrate on morphological characteristics of *Phlyctochytrium punctatum.'* M. S. Thesis, Ohio University, Athens.

BARR, D. J. S. (1969). 'Studies on *Rhizophydium* and *Phlyctochytrium* (Chytridiales). I. Comparative morphology.' *Can. J. Bot.,* 47, 991-997.

BARR, D. J. S. (1970 a). *'Phlyctochytrium reinboldtae* (Chytridiales): morphology and physiology.' *Can. J. Bot.,* 48, 479-484.

BARR, D. J. S. (1970 b). 'Two varieties of *Rhizophydium sphaerocarpum* (Chytridiales).' *Can. J. Bot.,* 48, 1067-1071.

BARR, D. J. S. (1971). 'Morphology and taxonomy of *Entophlyctis confervae-glomeratae* (Chytridiales) and related species.' *Can. J. Bot.,* 49, 2215-2222.

BARR, D. J. S., and HICKMAN, C. J. (1967). 'Chytrids and Algae. I. Host-substrate range, and morphological variation, of species of *Rhizophydium.'* *Can. J. Bot.,* 45, 423-430.

BERNSTEIN, L. B. (1968). 'A biosystematic study of *Rhizophlyctis rosea* with emphasis on zoospore variability.' *J. Elisha Mitchell scient. Soc.,* 84, 84-93.

BOOTH, T. (1971). 'Problematical taxonomic criteria in the Chytridiales: comparative morphology of 10 *Entophlyctis* sp. isolates.' *Can. J. Bot.,* 49, 977-987.

BOSTICK, L. R. (1968). 'Studies of the morphology of *Chytriomyces hyalinus.'* *J. Elisha Mitchell scient. Soc.,* 84, 94-99.

EDWARDS, B. H. (1966). 'Some aspects of the physiology and nutrition of three aquatic Phycomycetes.' Ph.D. Dissertation, University of Maryland, College Park.

GOLDSTEIN, S. (1960). 'Physiology of aquatic fungi. I. Nutrition.' *J. Bact.,* 80, 701-707.

HASIJA, S. K., and MILLER, C. E. (1971). 'Nutrition of *Chytriomyces* and its influence on morphology.' *Am. J. Bot.,* 58, 939-944.

JOHNS, R. M. (1964). 'A new *Polyphagus* in algal culture.' *Mycologia,* 56, 441-451.

KOCH, W. J. (1957). 'Two new chytrids in pure culture, *Phlyctochytrium punctatum* and *Phlyctochytrium irregulare.'* *J. Elisha Mitchell scient. Soc.,* 73, 108-122.

KOCH, W. J. (1961). 'The motile cell in posteriorly uniflagellate Phycomycetes.' In *Recent Advances in Botany,* The University of Toronto Press, 335-339.

KOCH, W. J. (1968). 'Studies of the motile cells of chytrids. IV. Planonts in the experimental taxonomy of aquatic Phycomycetes.' *J. Elisha Mitchell scient. Soc.,* 84, 69-83.

LWANGA, K. J. M. (1969). 'A study of character variation in *Phlyctochytrium punctatum* Koch.' M. S. Thesis, Ohio University, Athens.

MACHLIS, L., and OSSIA, E. (1953). 'Maturation of the meiosporangia of Euallomyces. I. The effect of cultural conditions.' *Am. J. Bot.,* 40, 358-365.

MILLER, C. E. (1968). 'Observations concerning taxonomic characteristics in chytridiaceous fungi.' *J. Elisha Mitchell scient. Soc.,* 84, 100-107.

MILLER, C. E. (1969). 'Variation in taxonomic characters of *Rhizophydium,* a chytridial fungus, as influenced by substratum.' In *Abstracts XI International Botanical Congress,* Seattle, 260 pp.

MILLER, C. E. (1971). 'Substrate-influenced variations in some taxonomic characters of *Phlyctochytrium punctatum,* a chytridial fungus.' In *Abstracts First International Mycological Congress* (Eds. G. C. Ainsworth and J. Webster), The Gresham Press, Surrey, England, 113 pp.

MILLER, C. E., BALAGURU, S., and LWANGA, K. J. M. (1973). 'Experimental taxonomy in chytridiales: substrate-influenced variation in *Rhizophydium* sp. and *Phlyctochytrium punctatum.'* In *Proceedings International Symposium on Taxonomy of Fungi* (Ed. C. V. Subramanian) Madras, India (in press).

MOORE, E. D., and MILLER, C. E. (1971). 'Observations on sexual fusions in *Chytriomyces.'* *Am. J. Bot.,* 48, 474-475 (abstract).

MOORE, E. D. and MILLER, C. E. (1973). 'Resting body formation by rhizoidal fusion in *Chytriomyces hyalinus.'* *Mycologia,* 65, 145-154.

PATERSON, R. A. (1963). 'Observations on two species of *Rhizophydium* from northern Michigan.' *Trans. Br. mycol. Soc.,* 46, 530-536.

REGISTER, T. E. (1959). 'Morphological variation in a new species of *Phlyctochytrium.'* M. S. Thesis, University of North Carolina, Chapel Hill.

SPARROW, F. K. (1960). *Aquatic Phycomycetes* (2nd Edition), University of Michigan Press, Ann Arbor, 1187 pp.

19 Freshwater Phycomycetes on Algae

MARGARET J. MASTERS

19.1 Introduction

The bulk of the literature on fungus parasites on algal hosts consists of taxonomic description. As new papers continue to appear it becomes increasingly apparent that these parasites can occur wherever suitable algal hosts are found. Geitler (1965), for example, described *Dangeardia sporapiculata* var. *minor* Geitler which attacked the alga *Heleocharis pallida* Koršikov growing on constantly moist wood of farm buildings in the eastern Alps. Stein and Amundsen (1967) and Kol (1970) found chytrid sporangia on *Chlamydomonas* cells in red snow. The majority of freshwater algal parasites described have been members of the order Chytridiales but a few belong to the order Lagenidiales. Canter and Willoughby (1964) however, described a species of *Blastocladiella* (order Blastocladiales) parasitic on the blue-green alga *Anabaena flos-aquae* (Lyngb.) Bréb. Several of the newly described fungi have been parasites of motile algae. Most of these fungi, however, attack the algae at a stage in which the host is immotile. *Rhizophydium fugax* Canter (1968 a) attacks a quiescent stage of the cryptomond *Cryptomonas*, *R. nobile* Canter (1968 b) attacks resting spores of the dinoflagellate *Ceratium hirundinella* O. F. Müll, *Pseudopileum unum* Canter (1963) attacks cysts of the chrysophyte *Mallomonas,* while *Dangeardia sporapiculata* Geitler (1962) attacks a palmella stage of the green alga *Chlamydomonas.*

Increasingly the study of algal pathology is becoming more complex. Not only a wide variety of aquatic fungi are able to attack and kill algal cells but also a startling variety of other micro-organisms. Certain dinoflagellates are able to attack and kill other algal cells. *Myxodinium pipiens* Cachon, Cachon et Bouquaheux (1969), for example, is an ectoparasite of the green alga *Halosphaera* spp., common in the phytoplankton of the Mediterranean Sea. Taylor (1968) described the attack of another dinoflagellate, the endoparasite *Amoebophrya ceratii* (Koeppen) Cachon on a dinoflagellate host *Gonyaulax catenella* Whedon et Koford.

Certain heterotrophic myxobacteria, aflagellate, aerobic, Gram-negative rods, have been found with remarkable abilities to inhibit and lyse a wide variety of algae. *Cytophaga* N-5 for example, isolated from sewage (Stewart and Brown, 1969) was able to lyse a wide variety of blue-green algae and kill without lysis a wide variety of green algae. Killing or lysis occurred within one day to two weeks. A variety of eubacteria, both Gram-negative and Gram-positive were also susceptible. Lysis of algae by pathogenic bacteria was extracellular. The bacterial cells apparently had to be in contact with the alga for lysis to occur and only growing bacterial cultures, not bacteria free filtrates, were effective (Daft and Stewart, 1971). These algal pathogens were unusual in their wide host spectrum. Moreover the fact that they could grow adequately as heterotrophs enabled them to be present in bodies of water even when suitable hosts were not present.

Virus pathogens infecting blue-green algae and comprising several morphological types, have been isolated from freshwaters. It is primarily from ponds with a high organic load, such as oxidation ponds, that such viruses have been isolated. A survey by Shane (1971), however, found LPP viruses in natural lakes, rivers and ponds where the water was not too oligotrophic. Their incidence appeared higher in rivers flowing through populated areas. One suspected lysogenic strain of the blue-green *Plectonema boryanum* Gomont has been found to carry virus strain LPP-1D (Cannon *et al.*, 1971). Other *Plectonoma boryanum* strains have been found, some of which are sensitive to LPP-1 and LPP-1D virus. Since these viruses are widespread in nature they must have some effect on host population numbers.

The remarkable ability of the planktonic protozoon *Pseudospora* to decimate colonial green algal populations was documented by Canter and Lund (1968). Reductions in algal numbers of over 90% were generally observed within one to two weeks, and most commonly the population was decreased by over 99%. Infestations were most common in spring and summer when the colonial green algae were most abundant. The free swimming protozoon had two anteriorly attached flagella. It became amoeboid inside an algal colony and the flagella remained passive while the organism moved around inside the mucilage ingesting algal contents through a pseudopodium which penetrated the host cell wall.

Gromov and Mamkaeva (1969, 1970 a, b) studied endoparasitic protozoons. They investigated the sensitivity of different *Scenedesmus* strains to *Amoeboaphelidium* (Gromov and Mamkaeva, 1969) and also the ultrastructure of the organism inside *Scenedesmus* cells (Gromov and Mamkaeva, 1970 a). Unlike fungi, these organisms digested the host cell contents by phagocytosis. Another endoparasitic protozoon *Aphelidium chlorococcarum f. majus* Gromov et Mamkaeva was observed to infect *Kirchneriella* and *Ankistrodesmus* species (Gromov and Mamkaeva, 1970 b). These parasitic organisms were in general quite specific. Each was able to infect only a small group of closely related species within the order Chlorococcales.

19.2 Taxonomy

19.2.1 Variation Within Species

The paucity of cultures of aquatic fungal parasites and saprophytes which grow on algae has meant that information on variation within species is very limited. The dilemma remains, then, whether to name a new species on the basis of substratum differences and small differences in morphology, or to identify the fungus with a similar one already described. Pongratz (1966), for example, observed a virulent attack of *Zygorhizidium planktonicum* Canter on *Synedra* in Lake Geneva. *Asterionella formosa* Hass, upon which the chytrid was also described by Canter and Lund (1953) was not infected upon the occasion which Pongratz described. The previous summer, however, a massive attack by a fungus not morphologically different from

Z. planktonicum was observed on *Asterionella formosa.* Pongratz delimited a new species, *Zygorhizidium asterionellae* Pongratz. Its distinguishing characteristics were its virulent attack on *Asterionella* and the fact that it was not seen on *Synedra* at the same time. This is a dubious practice. The fact that the fungus attacked one host at a time probably was the result of environmental factors which favoured growth on one host under certain conditions and on the other host under other conditions. At the time of attack on *Synedra acus* var. *angustissima* (Kütz) Hustedt this alga was common in the plankton while *Asterionella formosa* was rare. When *Asterionella* was attacked it was extremely abundant and few *Synedra* cells were present.

The study of chytrid parasites on a mass culture of *Scenedesmus* (Soeder and Maiweg, 1969) was another instance in which a taxon was delimited perhaps unnecessarily. The mass culture was first set up with *Scenedesmus acutus* f. *alternans* Hortb. (= *S. obliquus* (Turp.) Kütz). A contaminant species, *Scenedesmus armatus* (Chodat) Smith appeared in the culture. Both were attacked by a chytrid strongly resembling *Phlyctidium scenedesmi* Fott. This fungus has been described by Fott (1967) from mass cultures of *Scenedesmus quadricauda* (Turp.) Bréb. In Soeder and Maiwegi's culture only one host species was attacked at a time. Since the fungus looked slightly different on the two hosts, they designated the fungus on *S. acutus* f. *alternans* as a new variety.

The chytrid described by Fott was represented by subspherical or oval sporangia at maturity 4.6—8.0 μm diameter. Its endobiotic apophysis was 2 μm, the zoospore 2 μm diameter and the resting spore (size not quoted) appeared in the figures to range up to 8 μm in diameter. The cytoplasm of the sporangium, granular at first, became dotted with refractive globules and a small papilla, usually apical, indicated where sporangium dehiscence would occur.

The fungus which Soeder and Maiweg observed on *S. armatus,* fits Fott's description closely. The sporangium ranged from 5.0 to 7.5 μm diameter, and the apophysis was about 2 μm diameter. The zoospore measured 1.5 μm diameter. The sporangia on this host were observed to have granular cytoplasm and a very obvious papilla at maturity. The sporangium wall appeared thinner in the papilla region. These authors decided that the chytrid on *S. acutus* f. *alternans* must be a new variety on the basis of smaller size (sporangia 4.1—4.8 μm diameter, zoospore 1.0—1.2 μm diameter). No apophyses were drawn nor were they mentioned in connection with sporangia on this host. The cytoplasm contained larger refractive globules and the dehiscence papilla was larger. There was no difference in wall structure, moreover, in the papilla region. Empty sporangia showed a much larger aperture than was evident in sporangia on *Scenedesmus armatus* or in Fott's *S. quadricauda* figures. Lukavský (1970 a) also observed *P. scenedesmi* on *S. obliquus* (= *S. acutus* f. *alternans*) in the same cascade platform from which Fott had originally described the fungus. *Phlyctidium* in this instance closely fits Fott's description in the appearance of discharge papilla and discharge pore size.

Masters (1971 d) observed *Phlyctidium scenedesmi* on *Pediastrum boryanum* (Turpin) Meneghini and *Scenedesmus quadricauda* in the Delta Marsh, Manitoba. The fungus fit Fott's description well except that the sporangia were smaller on *Pediastrum* than on *S. quadricauda.* The sporangia on *Pediastrum* ranged from 3.0 to 7.0 μm diameter and the apophysis measured 2.0—3.5 μm. Zoospore cysts were 1.5 μm diameter and resting spores, observed upon only one occasion, varied from 5.0 to 6.5 μm. On *S. quadricauda* zoospore cysts measured 1.5—2.0 μm and sporangia varied from 4.5 to 8.5 μm. On both hosts empty sporangia resembled Fott's figures with small discharge pores.

Soeder and Maiweg claimed that separation of the fungus on *S. acutus* f. *alternans* from that on *S. armatus* was valid since size differences in sporangia on the different hosts were statistically significant. Conditions in the culture were similar during blooms of the fungi on each host so this was not a factor contributing to size differences. Studies of *Chytridium deltanum* Masters (1971 b), however, have shown that the same fungus can occur simultaneously on two host species and can be significantly smaller on one host species than on the other. Moreover *C. deltanum* developed sporangia significantly smaller on the host *Oocystis crassa* Wittrock during one summer than had been noted on the same host in the previous summer. Size is therefore not a valid criterion for separation. Nor do the other minor variations in thallus morphology seem to warrant the setting up of a new taxon. It seems possible that *Scenedesmus armatus* is resistant when it is present in low numbers and becomes more susceptible as its density increases. The same could hold for *S. acutus* f. *alternans*. This would account for the fact that only one host species was found infected at one time.

Study of morphology of *Chytridium deltanum* (*Diplochytridium* according to Karling, 1971) on *Oocystis* spp. is very interesting since this fungus simultaneously attacked several species. The fungus parasitized *Oocystis crassa, O. lacustris* Chodat, *O. submarina* Lagerheim and *O. parva* West in Lake Manitoba and the Delta Marsh (Masters, 1971 b). Interestingly the fungus did not attack *Oocystis eremosphaeria* G. M. Smith which was also occasionally observed. Positive identification of the fungus on these hosts was made on the basis of the resting spore and the sexual production of this spore. Variation in asexual morphology was often considerable. Although size ranges on different hosts overlapped slightly, sporangium size was significantly larger on *Oocystis crassa* in 1965 than on *O. lacustris* and those on *O. lacustris* were significantly larger than on *O. submarina* in the same year. Moreover sporangia on *O. crassa* were significantly larger in 1965 than those on the same host in 1966. Resting spore size varied too. Resting spores on *O. crassa* in 1965 were significantly larger than those on *O. lacustris* during the years 1965 and 1967 (pooled data). Another characteristic which varied with the host and the year was the amount of germ tube between zoospore cyst and the host cell which developed into the sporangium. If only the part nearest the cyst developed, then the sporangium was stalked. On *Oocystis lacustris* in 1965 all sporangia counted were sessile. In 1967 there were more sporangia with a stalk than there were sporangia which were sessile.

Another fungus which showed considerable variation in asexual characteristics, and which was identified largely on the basis of its sexual method of spore production was *Rhizophydium couchii* Sparrow. This fungus was first described by Couch (1932) under the name *R. globosum,* on *Spirogyra* sp. and *Mougeotia* sp. He called the fungus a parasite but noted that infection was most abundant while *Spirogyra* was undergoing conjugation. It was moreover the reproductive cells which appeared most susceptible. The mature sporangium 18—30 μm in diameter had 1—3 obvious discharge papillae and the rhizoidal system was very robust. Some sporangia had one main rhizoidal axis but others had many rhizoid axes emerging from the sporangium wall. The mature sporangia which Sparrow observed on *Spirogyra* sp. (1933) had only one discharge papilla. Both Sparrow and Couch observed resting spores in the size range 10—14 μm in diameter and Sparrow noted that the adherent male cell was 5 μm in diameter.

A fungus parasitic on desmids in Lake Windermere, England, was identified by Canter and Lund (1969) as *Rhizophydium couchii.* The sporangia were at first globose, but later became more broadly ovate. They varied from 5 to 34 μm in diameter. The robust rhizoidal system originated from a single axis. Mature sporangia differed from those of Sparrow and Couch in that there was no protruding papilla. Empty sporangia had only one discharge pore. The resting spore was similar to those of Couch and Sparrow and varied from 7 to 18 μm in diameter.

A fungus closely resembling Sparrow's species was observed growing on coenobia of *Pediastrum duplex* Meyen varieties *clathratum* A. Braun and *reticulatum* Lagerheim in Lake Manitoba (Masters, 1970). The fungus was considered to be a saprophyte since all cells in the coenobium appeared senescent, not just those supporting chytrid thalli. The fungus was identified as *Rhizophydium couchii* on the basis of its smooth-walled resting spores (5.5—8.5 μm diameter) with adherent male gametangia (2.5—3.0 μm diameter) and its globose sporangia with 1—3 protruding papillae at maturity (Fig. 19.1). The sporangia ranged from 2 to 11 μm in diameter. The rhizoidal system of the fungus, while growing on *Pediastrum* cells was sparse and consisted of a single axis which branched once near its tip. In culture, however, this same fungus showed a robust rhizoidal system attached to a single axis.

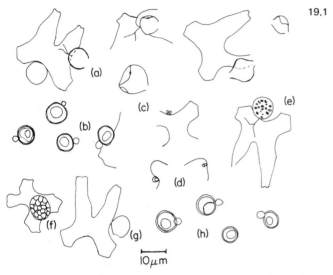

19.1

Fig. 19.1. *Rhizophydium couchii*, on *Pediastrum duplex* var. *clathratum* (a and b) and on *P. duplex* var. *reticulatum* (c—h). (a) empty sporangia, note endobiotic rhizoids and slight thickening on wall of two sporangia; (b) resting spores with attached male thalli; (c) adjacent cysts, possibly incipient gametangia; (d) zoospore cysts or developing sporangia; (e) immature sporangium; (f) mature sporangium; (g) empty sporangium; (h) resting spores (x 500).

The range of variation observed in this chytrid species then included virulence of attack: weakly parasitic on *Spirogyra* sp. (Couch), parasitic on desmids (Canter and Lund) and saprophytic on *Pediastrum duplex* varieties (Masters). The sporangia were always observed to have robust rhizoids except when growing on *Pediastrum duplex* varieties. Protruding discharge papillae were always observed except on the desmids. Sparrow, and Canter and Lund found only sporangia with a single discharge pore. Couch and Masters observed discharge pores varying from one to three. Only the appearance of the resting spores was constant although there was variation in sizes quoted.

Of course the most reliable way to establish range of variation within a species is with inoculation experiments. Paterson (1963) found a correlation between substratum size and sporangial size in *Rhizophydium globosum* (Braun) Rabenhorst. He noted considerable variation in the rhizoidal system but the spherical shape and the number of discharge pores in the sporangia remained constant as did zoospore diameter. This fungus was saprophytic on algae, nematodes and pine pollen as was another isolate *R. sphaerocarpum* (Zopf) Fischer. In this latter isolate only sporangium size varied on the various substrata. Barr and Hickman (1967 a) isolated a clone of *R. sphaerocarpum* from *Spirogyra*. They found that their isolate was a parasite which could attack only *Spirogyra* spp. The virulence of the attack varied with the host species. Paterson's saprophytic isolate and Barr and Hickman's parasitic one were compared by Barr (1970). The two cultures were very similar in morphology. The macroscopic appearance of the cultures differed, however, in that the saprophyte had a drab white crusty texture whereas the parasite varied from pale to bright, shiny yellow depending on the age of the culture. With the exception of different temperature optima, the two cultures showed very similar physiological requirements. Both needed an exogenous supply of thiamine; both had a similar pH range; and neither could grow on inorganic nitrogen when the inoculum was small. The saprophyte, however, did show some degree of growth on an inorganic nitrogen medium if the inoculum were large and actively growing. Despite their overall morphological and physiological similarity, then, the two isolates could be distinguished. For this reason Barr designated Paterson's saprophytic isolate *R. sphaerocarpum* var. *sphaerocarpum* and Barr and Hickman's isolate *R. sphaerocarpum* var. *spirogyrae* var. nov.

Johns (1964) also carried out a study on morphological variation within a chytrid parasitic on different algal hosts. He found that the fungus *Polyphagus starrii* Johns, showed variation in prosporangial and sporangial size depending upon the specific host. The shape of the sporangium also varied. Zoospore size, however, and resting spore size were similar on all hosts tested. Johns concluded that unless extensive inoculation experiments have been undertaken, the use of host specificity as a taxonomic character is of dubious value. He stated, moreover, that the observation of a fungus on a single host might lead to a limited view of its morphology.

Cook (1963) also managed successfully to culture parasitic aquatic fungi on their algal hosts. He investigated the ability of each parasite to infect a variety of closely related desmid species. The most important factor determining the ability of a fungus to attack a certain host, was the ability to germinate on the host cell wall or on the surrounding mucilage. Even a large inoculum would be ineffective if the zoospore cysts were unable to germinate. After germination had occurred some fungal isolates were unable to penetrate the thick walls of mature desmid cells. In this case, infections were found mainly on immature semicells. One method of resistance on the part of the desmid cells was the forming of refractive plugs against the invasion of the fungus germ tube. This defence method was often effective if the level of inoculum was low. A given algal species was not able to form resistant plugs against all parasite species. The reaction occurred only for certain host–parasite combinations, but to other fungal species the alga might well succumb. Usually normal development of the fungus followed the successful invasion of a host cell.

19.2.2 Effect of Electronmicrographs on Taxonomy

Fine structure studies are beginning to appear now that cultures of aquatic fungi growing on algae are becoming more common. These studies are showing themselves to be important tools in the study of taxonomic criteria. They are also important in elucidating relationships between a fungus and its algal substrate.

A study of the ultrastructure of *Phlyctidium scenedesmi* from a mass culture of

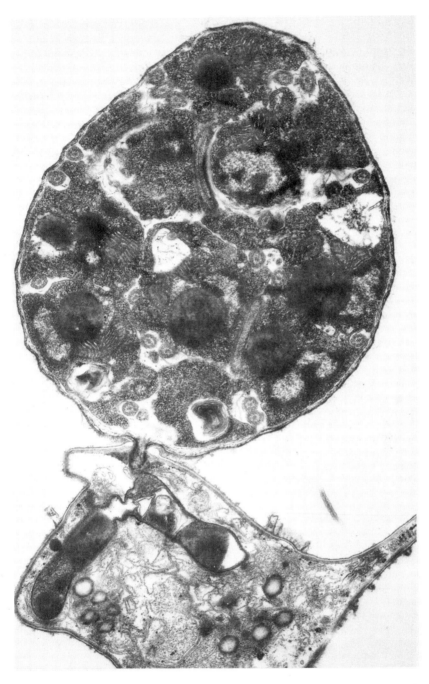

Fig. 19.2. Sporangium with newly formed zoospores, plasma residue in the haustorium and an operculum at the apex. The host plasma has degenerated. [Plate kindly provided by Prof. Dr. E. Schnepf with the permission of Springer-Verlag]

Scenedesmus armatus (Schnepf *et al.,* 1971) revealed that the fungus had been incorrectly named. Fott (1967) made the original description of the species. With a light microscope, he observed an endobiotic apophysis, a sporangium which appeared to be inoperculate, and epibiotic resting spores. Thus he included this fungus in the genus *Phlyctidium.* Soeder and Maiweg (1969) saw the sporangial stage of the fungus and they also described it as inoperculate. Masters (1971 d) saw both sporangial and resting spore stages, but did not observe an operculum. Schnepf *et al.* (1971) found opercula under the light microscope after electronmicrographs (Fig. 19.2) suggested their presence. Apparently, too, Kraut and Meffert (1966) had seen the same fungus and had described the operculum from light microscope studies. Electronmicrographs of *Phlyctidium scenedesmi* (Schnepf *et al.,* 1971) also revealed some ramification of the endobiotic structure. This characteristic alone would have meant the elimination of the fungus from the genus *Phlyctidium* had not the operculate character of the sporangium already signified that a change was necessary.

Method of sporangium discharge has been regarded as an important taxonomic criterion in the Chytridiales (Sparrow, 1960). Karling suggests (1967) that the separation of genera on the basis of this one criterion may be a case of undue emphasis on one characteristic. In view of the present emphasis on the method of zoospore discharge, the question as to how many chytrid species have been incorrectly described as inoperculate, is very important. Schnepf *et al.* (1971) suggest that *Phlyctidium scenedesmi* tentatively be regarded as *Chytridium* sp. until they find resting spores in their culture. However, since resting spores have been seen in related studies and have been found to be epibiotic, the correct genus would be *Chytriomyces.*

The ultrastructural study of *Phlyctidium scenedesmi* by Schnepf *et al.* (1971) is also interesting in its elucidation of the chytrid parasite–algal host relationship. The zoospore cyst is flattened against the host wall and bound to it by a flaky, net-like material. The cyst develops a tube which penetrates the host wall at an arbitrary point (Fig. 19.3), not through a pore in the host cell wall. Electron dense material

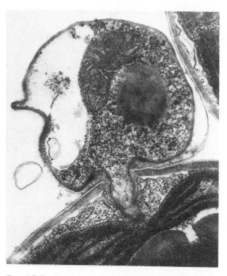

19.3

Fig. 19.3. Zoospore cyst whose germ tube has penetrated the host cell wall. In the cyst can be seen a large lipid drop, mitochondrion and vacuole. [Plate kindly provided by Prof. Dr. E. Schnepf with permission of Springer-Verlag]

from the host surrounds the germ tube but usually there is not enough to produce a callus. In cases where the host does form a wall around the invading germ tube, the fungus dies. Usually the host plasmalemma comes to lie very close to the haustorium wall. Should the haustorium encounter the algal chloroplast, it proliferates in this direction but never actually invades the organelle. The matrix of the host cytoplasm and chloroplast become increasingly spongy and finally even the membranes degenerate. The host plasmalemma around the haustorium eventually disappears. A uninucleate sporangium meanwhile has been developing from the body of the cyst. When the sporangium has fully developed, mitosis occurs. At this stage a plug of wall material cuts off the haustorium from the sporangium above. Cytokinesis now occurs in the mature sporangium. An operculum differentiates and as it is released the zoospores escape. Clearly the fungus causes the degeneration of the host cells. It is a parasite as observations from the mass culture (Soeder and Maiweg, 1969) suggested.

19.3 Ecology

19.3.1 Ecology of Saprophytic Fungi on Algae

In 1960, Paterson produced the first account of environmental conditions under which a chytridiaceous fungus *Amphicypellus elegans* Ingold, was able to grow on dead algal cells. Paterson maintained, and the observations of Ingold (1944) and Canter (1961) concur, that the fungus was saprophytic in its growth on *Ceratium hirundinella* O. F. Müll since it was observed only on dead thecae. In Paterson's study no correlation was found between numbers of dead *Ceratium* cells and times when high numbers of fungal thalli were observed. It is possible that such a correlation was not detected at the 0.5 and 1.5 m sampling levels in Frains Lake, Michigan because of the rapid rate at which dead cells tend to sink in the water column. The *Amphicypellus* blooms of early June and of July 1955, and June 1956, did not appear to be affected by varying pH or alkalinity values, but the temperature at the time of the three observed saprophyte maxima lay within the range 19.2-21.5 °C. Dissolved oxygen levels were observed to be falling on each occasion of an *Amphicypellus* maximum, but the actual oxygen levels differed widely (5.2–10.3 ppm). It is therefore unlikely that falling oxygen levels were an important factor favouring the development of *Amphicypellus elegans* on dead *Ceratium* thecae.

Pongratz (1966) observed *Ceratium hirundinella* populations in Lake Geneva, particularly the shallow Petit-lac area. Typically *Ceratium* became very abundant between July and October. In a ten year period he observed a bloom of *A. elegans* on *Ceratium* only once, in October 1965, at a time when the surface water temperature was 13.7 °C. Pongratz called the fungus a parasite, and attributed the algal cells, disorganized appearance to the effect of the fungus. It is probable that in October the alga was about the decline and the cells showing disorganised contents were already dead or dying before the development of the fungus on them. Also present in low numbers in the phytoplankton at that time were two other dinoflagellate species, *Peridinium willei* (Huitf). Kaas and *Peridinium cinctum* Ehrenb. No trace of *Amphicypellus* was noted on these organisms.

The apparently healthy appearance of an algal substratum at the time of zoospore encystment and germination usually leads an observer to conclude that the fungus is a parasite. The subsequently unhealthy appearance of the alga would then be due to the fungus. Paterson (1963) observed two *Rhizophydium* spp. growing on *Pediastrum* sp. in Carp Lake, Michigan. After isolating the two chytrid species and successfully growing them on agar media, he attempted to infect a variety of green algae, all Chlorococcales, with these fungi. The chytrids failed to grow. Nevertheless on boiled organisms including *Pediastrum boryanum, P. duplex, Hydrodictyon, Oedogonium,* the fungus *Allomyces javonicus* Kniep and the nematode *Ditylenchus dipsaci* (Kühn), *Rhizophydium* sp. 1 grew well. The other isolate also grew on a wide range of boiled organisms although it was not able to exploit as many algal species.

Yet another saprophyte was identified on *Pediastrum* sp. in Lake Manitoba, Canac (Masters, 1970). Cell contents appeared disorganized in coenobia of *Pediastrum duple* varieties *clathratum* and *reticulatum* upon which *Rhizophydium couchii* was growing. This suggested that the fungus was a saprophyte. Moreover the greatest numbers of chytrid thalli were noted at times when *Pediastrum dupex* numbers were falling (Fig. 19.4). No distinction was made between healthy and dying *Pediastrum* coenobia. It is probable therefore that the number of healthy coenobia had declined even more than Fig. 19.4 shows. In general, coenobia of the *clathratum* variety seemed to support more chytrid thalli, and the duration of the attack on this variety was more sustained than on the *reticulatum* variety. It is possible that there were more senescent *clathratum* than *reticulatum* coenobia in the phytoplankton during the summer months. Resting spores were found only in 1967. Several were noted on August 1 and August 21. *Pediastrum boryanum* was also found in Lake Manitoba at this time, in higher numbers than the *P. duplex* varieties. *P. boryanum* did not support growth of *Rhizophydium couchii* but a polyphagous fungus similar to *Podochytrium* was sometimes observed in coenobia of this species.

19.4

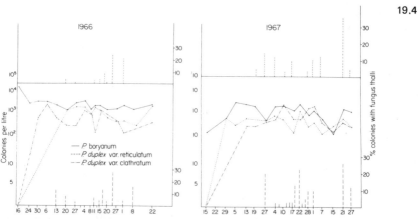

Fig. 19.4. Population levels of *Pediastrum boryanum P. duplex* var. *reticulatum* and *P. duplex* var. *clathratum* in Lake Manitoba in 1966 and 1967. The percentage of coenobia bearing thalli of *Rhizophydium couchii* are indicated by matching histograms. The sampling period was from mid-May to the end of August each year.

In preliminary experiments with unialgal *Pediastrum duplex* var. *clathratum* cultures, it was found that the alga grew best at 20-22 °C and its growth was much reduced at 25 and 30 °C. A culture of *Rhizophydium couchii* isolated from *P. duplex* var. *clathratum* did not grow on live coenobia of the alga at any temperature. Nevertheless, on steam-killed coenobia it grew not at all at 15, poorly at 20, and very well at 22, 25 and 30 °C. The alga showed best growth at pH 9.0. Again the chytrid did not grow on live colonies of the alga but on steam-killed coenobia a few chytrid thalli were observed at pH 7.0, many at pH 8.0 and very few at pH 8.5. Thus in culture experiments *R. couchii* grew best on dead colonies of *P. duplex* var. *clathratum* in the temperature range 22–30 °C and pH 8.0. In Lake Manitoba this fungus was observed most frequently in the temperature range 24–25 °C, but it did occur as low as 12.6 °C. The pH levels observed in nature during blooms of this fungus were, however, far higher than the organism was able to withstand in culture. The fungus was observed at pH values varying from 8.2 to 8.7, but at high levels of fungus occurrence the pH was most frequently noted in the range 8.6–8.8. Thus temperature appeared to exert a determining effect on the appearance of the fungus but the importance of pH was less obvious.

Saprophytes are usually associated with declining algal populations but a study in the Delta Marsh, Manitoba revealed that this is not always so (Masters, 1971 c). *Chytridium (Diplochytridium) marylandicum* Paterson was observed to colonize *Botryococcus braunii* Kütz as the algal population approached its maximum. A marked correlation was found between algal numbers and chytrid thalli colonizing them. Neither the alga nor fungus showed correlations with pH. Both, however, showed correlations with temperature and with conductivity. That *C. marylandicum* should occur only on healthy *Botryococcus* colonies is remarkable since the fungus is a saprophyte. It does not exploit cell contents, however, but only the copious extracellular mucilage which surrounds the *Botryococcus* cells. Unlike many saprophytes *C. marylandicum* appears to be highly specific. It has not been observed on other substrata. Moreover the fungus was almost never observed growing on the bright red, resting state colonies which were occasionally observed. Interestingly, the chemical composition of the mucilage in red, resting state colonies consists largely of a highly branched hydrocarbon molecule called botryococcene (Brown *et al.*, 1969). This compound disappears almost entirely when the colonies become green and actively growing. One might assume then that the mucilage of actively growing *Botryococcus* colonies provides nutrients more suitable for growth than does the high hydrocarbon content of resting state mucilage.

19.3.2   Ecology of Parasitic Fungi on Algae

Pongratz (1966) and Miller (1968) both stated that they knew of no generally acceptable criterion to measure parasitism of aquatic fungi on algae. How could one determine without experiments involving fungus cultures whether the alga was healthy or senescent at the time of zoospore encystment? Canter and Lund (1948) suggested that ecological data provide a very acceptable method of determining the nature of the host–fungus relationship. Chytrid attack on a rapidly growing host population is unquestionably parasitic in nature. Exploitation of a host population which is about to decline is also parasitic, particularly when the fungus blooms and disappears at a rate different from the decline of the alga. In this case the appearance of the fungus is definitely not a function of an increasing concentration of moribund cells. A good understanding of the nature of fungus attack on an alga, then, presupposes knowledge of growth rate or decline of the alga before, during and after such an attack. One must also know the number of fungal thalli able to grow successfully on algal cells during the course of the epidemic.

The 20 years of observations by Canter and Lund (1969) from Lake Windermere, England, confirm that one can detect parasitism and can make good estimates of the effects of such an attack. Their data on parasitic attacks on desmids showed in general that during years when the desmids were most numerous, fungus attack was more frequent and its results more severe. They noted that the parasites which attacked desmids were more frequently biflagellate (Lagenidiales) than uniflagellate

(Chytridiales). Unfortunately, the ecological data did not include accounts of which parasites were involved during any one epidemic. One of the summers in which desmid numbers were high and in which fungal attack was heavy was 1952. Seven desmid species were present in numbers high enough to permit counting. Of these at least 30% of the cells of six species were infected by fungus parasites at some time during the summer. The desmid species showed little or no decline in growth rates before the onset of fungus attack. In the case of *Staurastrum cingulum* (W. et G. S. West) G. M. Smith the population continued to increase despite levels of attack as high as 12% (Fig. 19.5). Counts of numbers of dividing cells showed that losses due to parasitism were more than offset by the host growth rate. It was only when the numbers of dividing cells declined that the host population fell drastically. The parasites disappeared before the host population had entirely disappeared, suggesting that they were not able to exploit cells which were too senescent. It was observed with all six desmid species parasitized in 1952 that increase in the number of dead cells closely paralleled severity of parasitism. This suggested that parasitism and not unfavourable environmental conditions was the main cause, initially, of desmid decline.

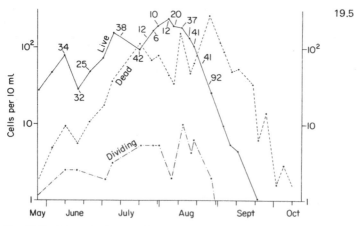

Fig. 19.5. Changes in the abundance of *Staurastrum cingulum* in Lake Windermere during the summer of 1952. Percentages of cells bearing parasites are indicated by numbers against the graph. (Permission to print this figure kindly provided by Dr. H. M. Canter-Lund).

Another long term study of the effects of fungal parasites on algae was that of Pongratz (1966). This paper reported the results of ten years' study on Lake Geneva and especially a shallow area called Petit-lac. The observations are interesting, but how reliable the conclusions are is questionable. If algal numbers were regularly counted, this paper gave no hint of it. Dates of occurrences of fungus blooms were given, but without host concentrations and often without an estimate of the percentage of host cells infected. Among other algae, Pongratz noted a pelagic filamentous green alga, *Mougeotia gracillima* (Hass) Wittrock present in Lake Geneva water throughout the year. It could produce problem blooms from early summer to late autumn. In November 1965 a *Rhizophydium* species attacked *Mougeotia* while the alga was still clearly dominant in the plankton. Within a month only limited numbers of the alga were observed. Again from February to May 1966 the chytrid was observed attacking *Mougeotia*. Pongratz named the chytrid *R. mougeotiae*. His account

500

however appeared to fit Sparrow's (1960) description of *Rhizophydium sphaero-carpum* (Zopf) Fischer. It would appear that cold weather, possibly less favourable to the alga, allowed *Rhizophydium* to grow on the *Mougeotia* population.

One chytrid parasite which has been much studied recently but is still little understood, is *Phlyctidium scenedesmi* Fott. When Fott described this fungus in 1967 he stated that it was a virulent parasite on *Scenedesmus quadricauda*. The fungus had heavily attacked a mass culture of *S. quadricauda* in a cascade platform near Třeboň, Czechoslovakia. The problem was so great that the culture had to be closed down for disinfection. The fungus flourished in the well aerated water of the cascade platform but tended to form mostly resting spores when subcultures *in vitro* were attempted. Preliminary results suggested that the fungus was unable to grow in water which contained only inorganic nitrogen. The nutrient medium used for the mass cultures contained urea which possibly promoted development of the parasite. Fott suggested too that the cold rainy summer, during which the fungus was observed to attack *S. quadricauda,* was an important factor favouring attack by the parasite. This has been discounted, however, by the studies of Soeder and Maiweg (1969) and Masters (1971. e).

Soeder and Maiweg (1969) described an ideal situation for studying the ecology of chytrid attack on an algal species. This was a mass culture of *Scenedesmus acutus* f. *alternans* in an open basin 16 m in diameter containing a volume of 34 m^3. Qualitative observations in the summer of 1967 were confirmed by a quantitative study in 1968. Both in 1967 and 1968 the basin contained only a unialgal culture of *S. acutus* f. *alternans* until the beginning of June. As the temperature grew warmer at the beginning of June a few *S. armatus* appeared. Their numbers made up a maximum 1% of the total *Scenedesmus* population. Within a few days *S. acutus* f. *alternans* (the dominant) was attacked by *Phlyctidium scenedesmi.* The authors described the chytrid on this host as *P. scenedesmi* var. *acuti. S. armatus,* the alga present in low numbers, was not attacked. The effect of the parasite on the dominant alga was so severe that the grass green colour of the mass culture had shifted to olive green by the second day. Later it turned golden brown. The dry weight of the suspension fell drastically and infected coenobia tended to clump in macroscopic flakes. The bacterial count climbed rapidly as the culture dry weight fell.

As *Scenedesmus acutus* f. *alternans* numbers fell, the *S. armatus* population rapidly increased. The authors suggested that high levels of dissolved organic matter contributed to mixotrophic growth of *S. armatus.* Soon this species comprised 98% of the algal population. Concomitant with the intensive growth of *S. armatus* was a sharp increase in dry weight. Five days after *S. armatus* had achieved a maximum however, it was attacked by *Phlyctidium scenedesmi.* The phenomena noted in the *Phlyctidium* attack on *S. acutus* f. *alternans* were repeated. These included loss in suspension dry weight, clumping of coenobia, change in suspension colour and increase in bacterial numbers. Now *S. acutus* f. *alternans,* free of fungus attack, rapidly increased to 98% of the population and at this point it was again attacked by *Phlyctidium.* Thus it declined again in favour of *S. armatus.* Fungicide was added at this point and the culture was returned to production research with a different *Scenedesmus* species from the original one.

Soeder and Maiweg implied that it was *Phlyctidium* which produced these shifts from one dominant to the other. Until *Phlyctidium* attacked *S. acutus* f. *alternans,* *S. armatus* did not increase above 1% of the total population. Soeder and Maiweg admitted that the factors which favoured fungus attack were unknown. Unfortunately the data presented were vague in terms of sampling dates, actual host cell numbers and changes in the fungus population with time. This made comparisons with other studies difficult. It was noteworthy, however, that these attacks by *Phlyctidium* took place in warm weather, not cold rainy weather, as Fott had postulated to favour such an attack.

Ultrastructural studies (Schnepf *et al.,* 1971) revealed that during the latter stages of a *Phlyctidium* bloom on *Scenedesmus armatus* there were many abnormal sporangia. The disturbance of the fungus cytoplasm appeared to be due to bacteria-like organisms inside the sporangia. Whether these organisms were responsible for the decline of the fungus parasite or a symptom of a decrease in vigour of the fungus population, the authors were not entirely certain. Yet another explanation would envisage no decrease in vigour by fungus parasite or alga but a virulent attack by the 'bacterium' on the fungus population. Thus the fungus would decline.

Soeder and Maiweg (1969) hypothesized that there were two fungus populations each capable of attacking one algal host species. The hyperparasite was a possible explanation for the decline of a fungus population as the numbers of its host were decimated. Alternatively if one were to assume only one fungus population capable of attacking both algal species, the role of the hyperparasite would be quite different. It might be that an algal species was susceptible to fungus attack when the density of the alga in the culture medium was great. The alga would decline due to fungus attack. The other alga would then increase but it would not be attacked because its density was not great enough as yet to produce decreased vigour in the population. When that point was reached the fungus could then attack the new dominant *Scenedesmus* species. The presence of a hyperparasite on the fungus population would then be incidental.

A virulent attack by *Phlyctidium scenedesmi* was also observed in the Delta Marsh, Manitoba (Masters, 1971 d). Here *Phlyctidium* was observed to attack two different host species simultaneously, but one, *Pediastrum boryanum* was attacked more successfully than was *Scenedesmus quadricauda.* The former host, *Pediastrum,* was obviously growing very rapidly as *Phlyctidium* bloomed at its expense. Daughter coenobia just released from parent cells were very numerous in the phytoplankton. The host population did not quite double however during this two week period, probably because of the heavy attack by the parasite. At the height of the epidemic 43% of *Pediastrum* coenobia bore chytrid thalli. At 46% coenobia infected on the same date, the level of attack on *Scenedesmus* by *Phlyctidium,* was comparable. Nevertheless few of the zoospore cysts on *Scenedesmus* completed their development. During the two week height of the epidemic, the percentage of chytrid thalli still in the zoospore cyst stage on *Pediastrum* fell from 94 to 42%. The percentage of developing sporangia increased in the same period from 5 to 52%. The percentage of zoospore cysts on *Scenedesmus* during the same period fell from 98 to only 81% and developing sporangia increased from 2 to only 13% of fungus thalli on that host.

No clue as to what factors favoured growth of *Phlyctidium scenedesmi* on *Pediastrum* or *Scenedesmus* could be found. While the first summer was warm, the next one was cold and rainy. *Pediastrum* and *Scenedesmus* populations were small and *Phlyctidium* was rare in its occurrence. The following summer was again a warm one. Both *Pediastrum* and *Scenedesmus* achieved unusually large maxima of 12.1×10^3 and 14.5×10^3 coenobia per litre respectively. In 1966 at the time of heavy *Phlyctidium* attack the maxima for these species had been 2.7×10^3 and 7.4×10^3 respectively. Apparently size of a host population was not in itself a factor which favoured the successful attack by *Phlyctidium scenedesmi,* since *Phlyctidium* was rarely seen on either host in 1968. Moreover none of the environmental parameters studied, including pH, temperature and conductivity, appeared to be correlated with fungus blooms or with algal maxima.

Studies of fungus parasitism on algal populations have brought to light some interesting fungus–alga interactions not previously elucidated. Among such interesting interactions were the several instances of differential attack by a fungus on two or more host growth forms, varieties or species. Koob (1966) for example documented the occurrence of five distinct populations of *Asterionella formosa* in the Rawah Wild Area, Colorado. His separation of the populations was based on distinct size classes in frustule length. The β population was important in both spring and fall blooms. It differed from the other populations in that it succumbed to attack by *Rhizophydium planktonicum* Canter, while they remained free.

Two lakes, Upper Twin and Sugarbowl, were compared. In Upper Twin in 1958 the β population constitued the total *Asterionella formosa* population. This alga was growing exponentially in mid-July when *Rhizophydium* first appeared on it. The alga continued to grow exponentially for a month and during that time the percentage of parasitized cells increased to about 25%. In the latter part of August, *Asterionella* numbers fell sharply and the percentage of parasitized cells increased to 40%. In early September the β populations increased very rapidly while *Rhizophydium* maintained itself on 40% of the cells. A different pattern was seen in Sugarbowl Lake where the β population formed only a small percentage of the total *Asterionella* population. *Rhizophydium* appeared on the β population at the beginning of August. Host numbers were at their maximum and they declined as *Rhizophydium* increased rapidly to about 35% algal cells infected. Early in September the algal population began to grow rapidly and *Rhizophydium* maintained itself on the host population and even increased to about 49% cells infected within 10 days.

Koob's study is interesting in that one group of *Asterionella formosa* cells, distinguishable on the basis of frustule size, was susceptible to *Rhizophydium* attack, while larger and smaller size classes were not. The chytrid was certainly a parasite, since it was able to attack and multiply successfully on a population which was growing rapidly, as well as on one that was declining. The fungus appeared to have no marked effect on the algal population since the host increased or decreased in numbers whether the parasite was present or not.

The pattern of attack by *Phlyctidium bumilleriae* Couch on *Staurastrum pinque* Teiling was full of paradoxes (Masters, 1971 e). A three-radiate form of *S. pinque,* a four-radiate form, and an intermediate form with three processes on one semicell and four on the other, were always found together in the summer phytoplankton of Lake Manitoba. In rare instances cells were found with five processes on one semicell and four on the other. Both in 1966 and 1967 there were more than twice as many three-radiate as four-radiate cells present in the phytoplankton during July. In 1968 the situation was reversed. In all three summers the two growth forms achieved their maxima simultaneously and declined together as well.

In July 1966 it was the less common four-radiate form of *Staurastrum* which was most heavily attacked by *Phlyctidium*. The maximum percentage of infected cells was 20.7% on the four-radiate form, 2.1% on the three-radiate form and 28.6% on the intermediate form. In 1967, *Phlyctidium* was very scarce although host cell numbers were similar to the year before. It was observed at its maximum on 2.7% of the four-radiate cells and 0.7% of the three-radiate cells. It was not observed on any intermediate cells. In July 1968 the four-radiate form was more numerous than the three-radiate form. Nevertheless the four-radiate form was still preferentially attacked. The maximum level of attack was 26.5% of the four-radiate cells, 2.2%

of the three-radiate cells and 25.0% of the intermediate cells. Other *Staurastrum* spp. observed occasionally in Lake Manitoba included *S. muticum, S. cuspidatum* var. *divergens* and a small species usually noted as a two-radiate form, *S. chaetoceros.* These species also on rare occasions were observed to bear *Phlyctidium bumilleriae* sporangia.

Phlyctidium then, attacked one growth form of *Staurastrum* much more severely than the other, whether the susceptible form was more common or less common than the resistant form. This meant that even when conditions favoured the susceptible form it was still more heavily parasitized than the resistant form. The phenomenon of differential attack on the two growth forms is more remarkable when one considers that the three-radiate and four-radiate populations were probably derived one from the other. The common occurrence of intermediate cells with three radii on one semicell and four on the other bears testimony to this suggestion. Whether the intermediate cells were shifting from three-radiate to four-radiate, or vice-versa, is not known. However the intermediate cells resembled the four-radiate form in their susceptibility to *Phlyctidium.* One might postulate that the resistance of the three-radiate form is cytoplasmic in nature since the genetic constitution of the two forms was almost certainly the same. Indeed, self-duplicating units in the cytoplasm have been postulated to be the cause of shifts from biradiate to triradiate clones of another desmid (Tews, 1969). It is interesting that this fungus, which attacked one growth form of *S. pinque* almost to the exclusion of the other, was nevertheless able to attack several other *Staurastrum* species.

Another fungus, *Chytridium (Diplochytridium) deltanum* Masters was observed to attack several *Oocystis* spp. simultaneously but the level of attack on different hosts varied considerably (Masters, 1971 a). The genus *Oocystis* although found in low numbers relative to the dominants was represented in Lake Manitoba by five species. Of these, by far the most successful were *O. crassa* and *O. lacustris.*

In 1966, *C. deltanum* attacked *O. crassa* during the first week of July at the time of the host maximum. Within two weeks the fungus had increased so that 12% of the *O. crassa* cells were parasitized (Fig. 19.6). *C. deltanum* maintained itself at this level for two more weeks and then started to decline in early August. *Oocystis crassa* counts were rather erratic during this month and a half period but the population did not appear to decline until the second week of August by which time *C. deltanum* had largely disappeared. Low levels of attack by *Chytridium oocystidis* Huber-Pestalozzi and a polyphagous chytrid were occasionally noted on *O. crassa* throughout July and August 1966.

Oocystis lacustris achieved its maximum, which was about four times the size of the *O. crassa* maximum, at the end of the first week in July 1966. Two days before the alga had reached its maximum, *Chytridium oocystidis* attacked (Fig. 19.6). Within two days of the maximum, *O. lacustris* numbers had declined drastically, but this decline was probably not due to the relatively low level of fungus attack. Meanwhile *C. oocystidis* increased on the greatly reduced *O. lacustris* population to a maximum on 13 July of 28% algal cells infected. On 8 July, on the reduced *O. lacustris* population *C. deltanum* also appeared. It rapidly increased to a maximum of 26% cells infected by 15 July (two days after the *C. oocystidis* maximum on the same host). *C. deltanum* now rapidly declined and had disappeared entirely within 10 days of its maximum. *C. oocystidis,* which showed a decline at the *C. deltanum* maximum, increased again briefly to 17% cells infected on 20 July. By the end of the month *C. oocystidis* too had disappeared. A polyphagous interbiotic fungus was occasionally also noted on *Oocystis lacustris* during July. The alga continued in low numbers in the plankton during August after the chytrids had disappeared.

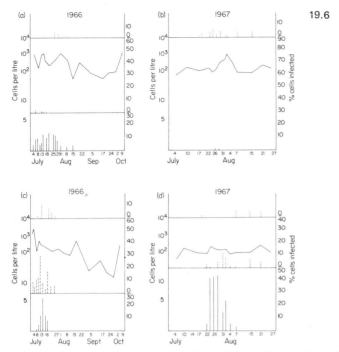

Fig. 19.6. *Oocystis crassa* cells per litre (a) and (b); and *Oocystis lacustris* (c) and (d); during the summers of 1966 and 1967 in Lake Manitoba. Solid line histogram indicates percentage of cells infected by *Chytridium deltanum* and the broken line indicates percentage of cells infected by *C. oocystidis.* *

During 1967 the appearance of chytrids on *O. crassa* was rare and consisted mainly of a robust saprophyte which was probably able to exploit the low percentage of moribund cells found even in the healthiest *O. crassa* populations. The maximum of this alga was comparable in size to the previous year but was achieved a month later, on 1 August. The situation on *Oocystis lacustris* at this time was very different from that on *O. crassa.* On 22 July *C. deltanum* and *C. oocystidis* simultaneously appeared on low numbers of *O. lacustris* cells. The latter fungus remained for a month in low numbers on the algal population. Its maximum attack was 12% cells infected on 31 July. *C. deltanum* on the other hand, within two days of its first appearance, had developed on 42% of the *O. lacustris* cells. The host population did not decline but at least doubled during the subsequent four days as the fungus continued on 43-44% of the host cells. During the next week *C. deltanum* declined and disappeared. The host remained in numbers comparable to the level present at the time when the two *Chytridium* spp. first attacked. A polyphagous interbiotic fungus was occasionally also observed on *O. lacustris* during July and August. During July 1968 both *O. crassa* and *O. lacustris* were present in numbers comparable to previous years but the level of chytrid attack was for the most part, insignificant.

That *C. deltanum* is a virulent parasite is particularly evident from the 1967 data on *Oocystis lacustris.* The alga not only maintained its numbers, but increased slightly, during a four day period when 42–44% of its cells were parasitized, and thus doomed to die. Had the algal growth rate not been very rapid in this period, host numbers would have fallen drastically. Instead they increased slightly. Thus in 1967 a situation obtained in which one potential host was heavily parasitized while another host remained almost free of attack.

The sudden explosion of *C. deltanum* on *O. lacustris* in 1967 raises the question of sources of inoculum. The fungus was not observed on any substrate in the phytoplankton, alga or detritus, as late as 20 July. Nevertheless by 22 July it had attacked 3% of *Oocystis lacustris* cells in a host population of about 110 cells per litre clumped into 45 colonies per litre. Two days later 42% of the 340 host cells per litre, clumped into 70 colonies per litre, had succumbed to fungus attack. Lund (1957) discussed the problem of inoculum sources necessary to produce sudden heavy chytrid attack on an algal population. He suggested residual populations of the fungus present in the phytoplankton`or germination of resting spores. In both cases, however, mathematics suggested that the fungus would need to grow on a suitable substrate for several weeks in order to produce enough inoculum to infect a host population to epidemic proportions. In 1967 in Lake Manitoba the dramatic appearance of the fungus could not be explained in terms of residual infection since careful searching failed to discover any. Resting spore production in *C. deltanum,* too, was very sparse. However, germination of these spores seems to be the only possible source of inoculum. All that can be said with certainty is that the inoculum, whatever its source, can appear rapidly and in heavy concentrations.

Study of changes with time in the composition of a fungus population on an alga can help to explain continued success or rapid disappearance of a chytrid from an algal host. In 1966, *C. deltanum* maintained itself for about six weeks on *Oocystis crassa.* The progress of the epidemic appeared to be cyclical with a marked increase in the percentage of germinated zoospore cysts approximately every 7–9 days (Fig. 19.7). The increase in percentage of developing sporangia was generally the opposite of the encysted zoospore cycle. Dehisced sporangia remained at a relatively high level, from 50 to 80% of the fungus population. Despite continued successful encystment and germination of zoospores on *O. crassa,* the period in which they were able to encyst on *O. lacustris* was very brief. On 11 July, 65.5% of the *C. deltanum* thalli on *O. lacustris* consisted of germinated zoospore cysts. Four days later this had declined to 28.2% as the percentage of developing and empty sporangia increased. By 18 July germinated zoospore cysts comprised 4.3% of the population, and their germ tubes grew in a random direction nowhere near the host cells. Thereafter zoospore cysts of *C. deltanum* were not seen on *O. lacustris.*

During 1967 *C. deltanum* zoospores successfully encysted on *O. lacustris,* but only during a brief two day period (Fig. 19.7). Attack on the other potential host, *O. crassa,* was negligible. On *O. lacustris* the percentage of zoospore cysts steadily declined from 72.6% on 24 July to 28.6% two days later, 11.9% on 1 August, to no zoospore cysts on 4 August. These data suggest that a period of two days favourable to zoospore encystment is sufficient to produce a brief but devastating epidemic. The range of conditions favourable to chytrid parasites would thus appear to be very narrow. Environmental conditions which obtain during the course of an epidemic may not be useful indicators of factors favouring the onset of an epidemic, but only those factors which obtain during heavy zoospore encystment. Resting spore production was generally sparse. Only on one occasion in 1966 were resting spores observed in *O. crassa* cells. Nevertheless, they occurred in *O. lacustris* both in 1966 to a maximum of 8.8% and in 1967 to a maximum of 50.0% of the fungus thalli.

Examination of the 1966 and 1967 data from Lake Manitoba suggested that temperature was important in the appearance of *C. deltanum* in the phytoplankton. The slower warming of the water in 1967 was the possible cause of the three week delay

Composition of fungus population on–

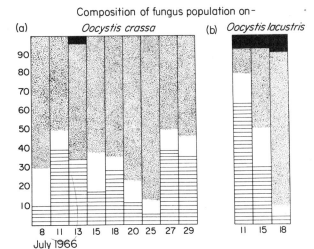

(a) *Oocystis crassa*   (b) *Oocystis lacustris*

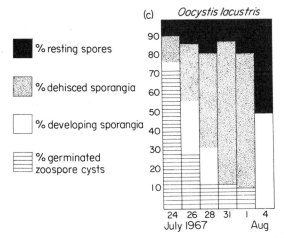

(c) *Oocystis lacustris*

■ % resting spores

▨ % dehisced sporangia

□ % developing sporangia

≡ % germinated
   zoospore cysts

Fig. 19.7. Composition of *Chytridium deltanum* population (a) on *Oocystis crassa* in July 1966, (b) on *O. lacustris* in July 1966, and (c) on *O. lacustris* in July 1967.

in the appearance of the fungus. Once the fungus had appeared it was observed to attack *O. lacustris* in the range 20–26 °C, but most of the infection occurred in the range 22–26 °C. Interestingly the temperature optimum of a Lake Manitoba isolate of *O. lacustris* was found in preliminary experiments to be 20–22 °C. Thus the chytrid attacked mostly at temperatures above the algal optimum. A similar pattern was noted for *O. crassa,* where the majority of infections occurred in the range 20-26 °C and the optimum for a local isolate of this alga was 20 °C.

An experimental study of factors favouring the onset of a chytrid epidemic was carried out by Barr and Hickman (1967). An isolate of *Rhizophydium sphaero-carpum* (Zopf) Fischer was studied for its ability to attack *Spirogyra* isolates. It was found that susceptible species grew poorly or not at all at 30 °C, the optimum for the chytrid. Resistant species grew well at 30 °C. Thus the most effective epidemics occurred in situations where the temperature was favourable for the fungus but above the optimum of the alga. Other factors slightly unfavourable to the alga were also found to promote fungus attack. Decreasing the nutrient level of the culture medium also produced less healthy, and therefore more susceptible, *Spirogyra* cultures. The algal isolates appeared to tolerate a wide range of hydrogen ion concentrations, whereas the fungus showed a narrower tolerance. One would not then expect pH to be a factor favouring the growth of *Rhizophydium* on *Spirogyra*. Another factor which affected infection levels was a period of darkness. The longer the dark period which *Spirogyra* had to undergo the greater would be the depletion of its energy reserves. A dark period of from 12 to 72 hours immediately preceding inoculation enhanced infection levels. However, conditions which reduced the algal filaments to a very moribund condition, such as long periods of darkness before and after inoculation, led to very reduced levels of parasite attack.

Despite the occasional severity of fungus attack on a given algal host, the overall impact of these fungi on the phytoplankton community is often small. The effect of a parasitic attack on an algal species may be only to depress the size of the algal maximum, or to hasten the decline of the host population. Canter and Lund (1948) observed virulent attacks on dominant diatom species in the English Lake District, but Masters (1970) was surprised at how seldom during the summer months the dominant algae of the Lake Manitoba–Delta Marsh area were attacked by aquatic fungi. There the dominants were diatoms in the early summer and blue-greens later in the summer. Only in one small bay of the marsh were dominants occasionally heavily attacked by parasites. These dominants were the green algae *Pediastrum* and *Scenedesmus*.

Very seldom has a fungus parasite been observed to bring about the complete elimination of a host from the phytoplankton. The more usual situation is for a parasite to disappear as the host numbers decline drastically (Canter and Lund, 1969). Often the alga then remains in low numbers in the phytoplankton. Canter and Lund, however, documented instances such as the summer of 1965 in Lake Windermere where the desmid population resumed growth as the parasites declined. They pointed out that an increase of 100% in a host population is equivalent to one synchronous division of all cells in that species in a week. In a hypothetical situation where 90 out of 100 cells were parasitized, favourable growth condtions could result in the population returning to its previous level within three weeks. Faster growth rates than this, of course, frequently occur in nature.

One of the most obvious characteristics of algal parasites is their sporadic occurrence. A fungus parasite may effect a virulent attack on an alga one summer, and show only a negligible level of attack the next. Such was the case for *Phlyctidium scenedesmi* in the Delta Marsh (Masters, 1971 d). Pongratz (1966) mentioned several parasites which occurred only two or three times in his ten year survey of Lake Geneva. Studies with fungus and algal cultures such as that of Barr and Hickman (1967 a, b) suggest that while an alga can perform fairly well over a broad range of environmental conditions, the fungus parasite may have a much narrower tolerance range. The data from successful zoospore encystment on *Oocystis lacustris* in Lake Manitoba (Masters, 1971 a) similarly suggest very narrow ranges of factors favourable to fungus attack on an alga.

Just as their algal hosts are not uniformly distributed throughout a body of water, so fungus parasites may be clumped in their distribution. Paterson (1967) observed different populations of fungus parasites on diatom species at different levels in the water column of Grand Traverse Bay, Lake Michigan. Pongratz (1966) maintained that fungus populations on algae were much greater in shallow water up to about 5 m than in the deep open areas of Lake Geneva. Lukavský (1970 b) documented the distribution of *Chlamydomonas braunii* and the occurrence of *Rhizophydium acuforme* (Zopf)

Fischer on it in a reservoir in Czechoslovakia. All samples were collected within a few hours of one another (personal communication). The first samples were collected at 6 a.m. near the inlet and the last ones, near the outlet, had been collected by noon. His sampling was both vertical and horizontal in a reservoir which became progressively deeper from the inflow to the outflow. At the inflow *Chlamydomonas* levels were very low, less than 100 cells/ml, but at the next sampling point surface numbers were over 500 cells/ml, and about 100 cells/ml at 6 m. At the next sampling point algal numbers had declined to just over 200 cells/ml at the surface but at 6 m there were about 400 cells/ml. Surface levels remained near 200 cells/ml from this point right up to the outlet, and 6 m levels declined to a similar level. At 9 m the population was a fairly constant 100–200 cells/ml throughout the reservoir. From a depth of less than a metre at the inlet, the reservoir gradually got deeper, but at a depth of 12 m to the maximum 39 m, *Chlamydomonas* levels were consistently very low. The percentage of *Chlamydomonas* cells parasitized by *Rhizophydium* was calculated from pooled data from the entire water column at each sampling point. About 33% of the host cells were parasitized at the inlet. At the next point, where algal numbers were very high, the fungus was found on approximately 5% of the cells. As algal numbers declined further along in the reservoir, chytrid numbers were found on approximately 20, 40, 50 and 60% of the *Chlamydomonas* population. Chytrid numbers varied with depth as well as with horizontal sampling point in the reservoir. There were generally more cells bearing *Rhizophydium* thalli at 3 and 6 m depths than at the surface. From 12 m down, chytrid numbers were very low or not found at all.

It would seem that studies on aquatic fungi and their attacks on algae are still in a pioneer stage. Our understanding of the factors which enable them to multiply at the expense of an algal host are very sketchy indeed. Each additional study, however, provides new data, so that useful comparisons can be made. Experimental studies are of course essential in the elucidation of the questions raised from field studies.

One simplifying assumption which may well have to be discarded in the near future is the idea that all individuals in a host population are equally susceptible. The success of a fungus parasite may depend not only on favourable environmental conditions but also on the number of susceptible individuals in that population. A hint that this may be the case comes from a study by Gromov and Mamkaeva (1969) on the susceptibility of *Scenedesmus* strains to an endoparasitic protozoon *Amoeboaphelidium*. They isolated four strains of *A. protococcarum* Gromov et Mamkaeva and tested their pathogenicity on a wide range of *Scenedesmus* species isolated from a local pond. They found that the four strains of the pathogen differed in their ability to infect the various isolates. They also found, however, that host sensitivity was a genetically stable character. Moreover, even in the local population of one morphological species, several physiological races were found. Some were susceptible to all pathogen strains, others only to some or none of the strains.

Until recent times the economic significance of parasitic aquatic fungi has been almost nil. This situation is changing, however, as more countries start to investigate the potential of open air mass algal cultures as a cheap source of high quality protein. The appearance of aquatic fungi in these cultures not only increases interest in these organisms but also provides ideal conditions in which to study their biology. Our understanding of aquatic fungi in their attacks on algae may well expand greatly in the near future.

References

BARR, D. J. S. (1970). 'Two varieties of *Rhizophydium sphaerocarpum* (Chytridiales)'. *Can. J. Bot.,* 48, 1067-1071.

BARR, D. J. S., and HICKMAN, C. J. (1967 a). 'Chytrids and algae. I. Host-substrate range, and morphological variation of species of *Rhizophydium.' Can. J. Bot.,* 45, 423-430.

BARR, D. J. S., and HICKMAN, C. J. (1967 b). 'Chytrids and algae. II. Factors influencing parasitism of *Rhizophydium sphaerocarpum* on *Spirogyra.' Can. J. Bot.,* 45, 431-440.

BROWN, A. C., KNIGHTS, B. A. and CONWAY, E. (1969). 'Hydrocarbon content and its relationship to physiological state in the green alga *Botryococcus braunii.' Phytochemistry,* 8, 543-547.

CACHON, J., CACHON, M., and BOUQUAHEUX, F. (1969). *'Myxodinium pipiens* gen. nov., sp. nov., péridinien parasite d'*Halosphaera.' Phycologia,* 8, 157-164.

CANNON, R. E., SHANE, M. S., and BUSH, V. N. (1971). 'Lysogeny of a blue-green alga, *Plectonema boryanum.' Virology,* 45, 149-153.

CANTER, H. M. (1961). 'Studies on British chytrids. XVIII. Further observations on species invading planktonic algae.' *Nova Hedwigia,* 3, 73-78.

CANTER, H. M. (1963). 'Studies on British chytrids. XXIII. New species on Chrysophycean algae.' *Trans. Br. mycol. Soc.,* 46, 305-320.

CANTER, H. M. (1968 a). 'Studies on British chytrids. XXVII. *Rhizophydium fugax* sp. nov., a parasite of planktonic cryptomonads with additional notes and records of planktonic fungi.' *Trans. Br. mycol. Soc.,* 51, 699-705.

CANTER, H. M. (1968 b). 'Studies on British chytrids. XXVIII. *Rhizophydium nobile* sp. nov., parasitic on the resting spore of *Ceratium hirundinella* O. F. Müll. from the plankton.' *Proc. Linn. Soc. Lond.,* 179, 197-201.

CANTER, H. M., and LUND, J. W. G. (1948). 'Studies on plankton parasites. I. Fluctuations in the numbers of *Asterionella formosa* Hass. in relation to fungal epidemics.' *New Phytol.,* 47, 238-261.

CANTER, H. M., and LUND, J. W. G. (1953). 'Studies on plankton parasites. II. The parasitism of diatoms with special reference to lakes in the English Lake District.' *Trans. Br. mycol. Soc.,* 36, 13-37.

CANTER, H. M., and LUND, J. W. G. (1968). 'The importance of Protozoa in controlling the abundance of planktonic algae in lakes. *'Proc. Linn. Soc. Lond.,* 179, 203-219.

CANTER, H. M., and LUND, J. W. G. (1969). 'The parasitism of planktonic desmids by fungi.' *Öst. bot. Z.,* 116, 351-377.

CANTER, H. M., and WILLOUGHBY, L. G. (1964). 'A parasitic *Blastocladiella* from Windermere plankton'. *J. Roy. microsc. Soc.,* 83, 365-372.

COOK, P. W. (1963). 'Host range studies of certain Phycomycetes parasitic on desmids.' *Am. J. Bot.,* 50, 580-588.

COUCH, J. N. (1932). '*Rhizophidium, Phlyctochytrium* and *Phlyctidium* in the United States'. *J. Elisha Mitchell scient. Soc.,* 47, 245-260.

DAFT, M. J., and STEWART, W. D. P. (1971). 'Bacterial pathogens of freshwater blue-green algae.' *New Phytol.,* 70, 819-829.

FOTT, B. (1967). *'Phlyctidium scenedesmi* spec. nova, a new chytrid destroying mass cultures of algae.' *Z. allg. Mikrobiol.,* 7, 97-102.

GEITLER, L. (1962). *'Dangeardia sporapiculata* n. sp., der Begriff "Apikulus" und die Gattungsabgrenzung bei ienigen Chytridialen.' *Sydowia,* 16, 324-330.

GEITLER, L. (1965). 'Notizen über einige wenig bekannte Grünalgan und eine neue Chytridiale.' *Öst. bot. Z.*, 112, 603-609.

GROMOV, B. V., and MAMKAEVA, K. A. (1969). 'Sensitivity of different *Scenedesmus* strains to the endoparasitic microorganism *Amoeboaphelidium.*' *Phycologia*, 7, 19-23.

GROMOV, B. V., and MAMKAEVA, K. A. (1970 a). 'The fine structure of *Amoeboaphelidium proctococcarum* Gromov and Mamkaeva—an endoparasite of green alga *Scenedesmus.*' *Arch. Hydrobiol.*, 67, 452-459.

GROMOV, B. V. and MAMKAEVA, K. A. (1970b). 'The culture of *Aphelidium chlorococcarum* Fott f. *majus* f. nova.' *Acta Protozoologica*, 7, 263-267.

INGOLD, C. T. (1944). 'Studies on British chytrids. II. A new chytrid on *Ceratium* and *Peridinium.*' *Trans Br. mycol. Soc.*, 27, 93-96.

JOHNS, R. M. (1964). 'A new *Polyphagus* in algal culture.' *Mycologia*, 56, 441-451.

KARLING, J. S. (1967). 'Some zoosporic fungi of New Zealand. VI. *Entophlyctis, Diplophylyctis, Nephrochytrium* and *Endochytrium.*' *Sydowia*, 20, 109-118.

KARLING, J. S. (1971). 'On *Chytridium* Braun, *Diplochytridium* N. G., and *Canteria* N. G. (Chytridiales).' *Arch. Mikrobiol.*, 76, 126-131.

KOL, E. (1970). 'Vom roten Schnee der Tiroler Alpen.' *Annales Historico-Naturales Musei Nationalis Hungarici*, 62, 129-135.

KOOB, D. D. (1966). 'Parasitism of *Asterionella formosa* Hass. by a chytrid in two lakes of the Rawah Wild Area of Colorado.' *J. Phycol.*, 2, 41-45.

KRAUT, H., and MEFFERT, M.-E. (1966). 'Über unsterile Grosskulturen von *Scenedesmus obliquus.*' *Forsch. d. Landes Nordrhein-Westfalen*, Nr. 1648. Westd. *Verl., Köln u. Opladen.* 1-61.

LUKAVSKÝ, J. (1970 a). '*Phlyctidium scenedesmi,* a chytrid destroying an outdoor mass culture of *Scenedesmus obliquus.*' *Nova Hedwigia*, 19, 775-777.

LUKAVSKÝ, J. (1970 b). 'Observations on some parasitic Chytridiomycetes.' *Arch. Protistenk.*, 112, 138-144.

LUND, J. W. G. (1957). 'Fungal diseases of plankton algae.' In *Biological Aspects of the Transmission of Disease,*(Ed. C. Horton-Smith) Oliver and Boyd, London, 19-23.

MASTERS, M. J. (1970). 'Chytrid parasitism of phytoplankton in the Delta Marsh, Manitoba.' Ph.D. Thesis, University of Western Ontario.

MASTERS, M. J. (1971 a). 'The ecology of *Chytridium deltanum* and other fungus parasites on *Oocystis* spp.' *Can. J. Bot.*, 49, 75-87.

MASTERS, M. J. (1971 b). '*Chytridium deltanum* n. sp. and other Phycomycetes on *Oocystis* spp. in the Delta Marsh, Manitoba.' *Can. J. Bot.*, 49, 471-481.

MASTERS, M. J. (1971 c). 'The occurrence of *Chytridium marylandicum* on *Botryococcus braunii* in School Bay of the Delta Marsh.' *Can. J. Bot.*, 49, 1479-1485.

MASTERS, M. J. (1971 d). 'The occurrence of *Phlyctidium scenedesmi* on *Pediastrum boryanum* and *Scenedesmus quadricauda* in School Bay of the Delta Marsh'. *Can. J. Bot.*, 49, 1605-1608.

MASTERS, M. J. (1971 e). 'The occurrence of *Phlyctidium bumilleriae* on two growth forms of *Staurastrum pinque* and other *Staurastrum* spp., in Lake Manitoba.' *Can. J. Bot.*, 49, 1637-1641.

MILLER, C. E. (1968). 'Observations concerning taxonomic characteristics in chytridiaceous fungi.' *J. Elisha Mitchell scient. Soc.*, 84, 100-107.

PATERSON, R. A. (1960). 'Infestation of chytridiaceous fungi on phytoplankton in relation to certain environmental factors.' *Ecology*, 41, 416-424.

PATERSON, R. A. (1963). 'Observations on two species of *Rhizophydium* from Northern Michigan.' *Trans. Br. mycol. Soc.*, 46, 530-536.

PATERSON, R. A. (1967). 'Benthic and planktonic Phycomycetes from northern Michigan.' *Mycologia* 59, 405-416.

PONGRATZ, E. (1966). 'De quelques champignons parasites d'organismes planctoniques du Léman.' *Schweiz. Z. Hydrologie Rev. Suisse d'Hydrologie,* 28, 104-132.

SCHNEPF, E., DEICHGRÄBER, G., HEGEWALD, E., and SOEDER, C. -J. (1971). 'Elektronenmikroskopische Beobachtungen an Parasiten aus *Scenedesmus*-Massenkulturen. 3. *Chytridium* sp.' *Arch. Mikrobiol.,* 75, 230-245.

SHANE, M. S. (1971). 'Distribution of blue-green algal viruses in various types of natural waters.' *Water Res.* 5, 711-716.

SOEDER, C. -J., and MAIWEG, D. (1969). 'Einfluss pilzlicher parasiten auf unsterile massenkulturen von *Scenedesmus.' Arch. Hydrobiol.,* 66, 48-55.

SPARROW, F. K. (1933). 'Inoperculate chytridiaceous organisms collected in the vicinity of Ithaca, NY, with notes on other aquatic fungi.' *Mycologia,* 25, 513-535.

SPARROW, F. K. (1960). *Aquatic Phycomycetes* (2nd Edition), University of Michigan Press, Ann Arbor, 1187 pp.

STEIN, J. R., and AMUNDSEN, C. C. (1967). 'Studies on snow algae and fungi from the front range of Colorado.' *Can. J. Bot.,* 45, 2033-2045.

STEWART, J. R., and BROWN, R. M. (1969). '*Cytophaga* that kills or lyses algae.' *Science,* 164, 1523-1524.

TAYLOR, F. J. R. (1968). 'Parasitism of the toxin-producing dinoflagellate *Gonyaulax catenella* by the endoparasitic dinoflagellate *Amoebophrya ceratii.' J. Fish. Res. Bd. Canada,* 25, 2241-2245.

TEWS, L. L. (1969). 'Dimorphism in *Cosmarium botrytis* var. *depressum.' J. Phycol.,* 5, 270-271.

20 The Ecology of Aquatic Phycomycetes

M. W. DICK

20.1 Introduction

Fungi contribute to the energy flow and productivity of aquatic ecosystems by their existence as a source of carbon as well as by their active metabolism on suitable substrates. In the natural environment, substrate degradation is achieved by associations and successions of taxonomically unrelated fungi and other organisms adapted to, or tolerant of, the special environmental conditions associated with the fluid medium. These associated conditions include the rates of diffusion of oxygen and carbon dioxide and the effect of dissolved substances, including carbon dioxide, on the pH of the medium. Oxygen availability, pH and temperature are important parameters regulating the efficiency of the enzyme system of a fungus. In aquatic environments these factors may change rapidly. The facility with which certain fungi can mobilize adaptive enzyme systems to these changing conditions is therefore important in understanding their ecology.

The efficiency of energy conversion from substrate to fungal protoplasm depends on the interaction between the environmental matrix, the biochemical resources of the organism and the type of carbon source available in the substrate. The relative inefficiency of fermentative pathways compared with aerobic respiration constitutes a force in favour of the latter when oxygen is present and the carbon source is limiting; this in turn requires a high degree of internal cytoplasmic differentiation and high endogenous respiration. However, in the aquatic environment, oxygen diffusion is relatively slow, and unless there is turbulence or an immediately adjacent input of oxygen from photosynthesis, there will be a tendency for an oxygen deficit to develop, thus impairing efficiency. Organisms adapted to oxidative respiration in the aquatic environment could therefore be expected to show trends towards either a low metabolic growth rate on a restricted range of carbon sources, or a short-lived vegetative cycle on substrates in which the carbon source rapidly becomes limiting, as would be the case with holocarpic organisms which are known to be frequent in aquatic environments.

This chapter is dedicated to Professor Frederick K. Sparrow, Jr. in the year of his retirement as Professor of Botany at the University of Michigan, and in honour of his distinguished service to the field of mycology.

It is also well known that an abundance of rapidly fermentable sugars tends to impair the machinery for aerobic respiration even under aerobic conditions. (This shift to a fermentative pathway normally operates through the adaptive enzyme fumarate reductase.) If such nutrient sources were less liable to rapid total degradation because of structural barriers to non-intrusive competitors, and if these nutrient sources were of regular or periodic availability, one might predict the evolution of organisms with an enzyme system more geared to fermentation even in partially aerobic conditions. This interaction between the aquatic environment, the substrate and the biochemical capabilities of the fungus is utilized in the classic baiting with rosaceous fruits or oranges for the collection of Rhipidiaceae and Blastocladiaceae.

It is thus conceivable that a complex natural substrate may at the same time support different fungi, some of which may be respiring aerobically while others use fermentative pathways. In these circumstances it would be difficult to correlate overall respiratory quotients with estimations of fungal propagule numbers and/or mycelial mass to give a generalized equation for fungal productivity, unless the composition of the fungus population was well established. Thus the first requirement is an understanding of the composition of fungus population.

The ecology of aquatic fungi is developing as a series of specialized studies made necessary by the requirements for taxonomic identification in certain fungal groups, and by the techniques associated with the examination of particular substrates. However, the description of defined fungus/substrate relationships must not be allowed to obscure the fact that the same fungus population, or elements of it, may also be active in other ecological relationships; nor must it be assumed that particular substrates are only degraded by one section of the fungus community. This chapter considers only that section of the fungus community known as the 'aquatic phycomycetes'.

The aquatic phycomycetes span a number of classes between which the relationships are for the most part obscure or non-existent. The slime fungi, including the Labyrinthulales and associated genera, are not commonly regarded as aquatic phycomycetes: there would appear to be grounds for considering some of these fungi to be distantly related to the Oömycetes*, but few of these fungi has been recorded from freshwater. Therefore this group will be excluded from the following account. The classes and orders containing fungi which ecologically constitute the freshwater aquatic phycomycetes are:

Oömycetes	Saprolegniales
	Leptomitales
	Lagenidiales
	Peronosporales
Hyphochytridiomycetes	Hyphochytriales
Chytridiomycetes	Chytridiales
	Blastocladiales
	Monoblepharidales
Zygomycetes	Mucorales
	Entomophthorales
Trichomycetes	Amoebidiales
	Harpellales
	Eccrinales
	Asellariales

* See appendix

514

No ecological facts are known for the Hyphochytridiomycetes beyond incidental comments in taxonomic works. Thus most of the following account will be confined to three fungal groups, the heterokont biflagellate fungi, the uniflagellate fungi and the Zygomycotina. Even within these three better known groups the balance of ecological work has been very uneven.

Fungi have been isolated within an aquatic ecosystem which comprises rivers, their tributaries and upper estuarine reaches; lakes and ponds; bogs and marshes; and temporary puddles, pools and paddy fields. In locations or seasons in which the lateral flow of water is of paramount influence, the environment may be described as *lotic;* but in more static water bodies (*lentic* environments) vertical changes may predominate resulting in the production of a thermocline at the physicochemical level, or diurnal migrations at the biotic level. Small relatively shallow lentic environments may become lotic environments at certain seasons of high rainfall. Thus all of these general descriptive terms are arbitrary and approximate and must be used accordingly.

In all of these environments it is helpful to recognize four possible zones; the free water, the water/air interface, the water/bottom interface and the littoral zone. These habitats are linked only by the presence of free surface and interstitial water. Differences are to be expected from the interaction of climate and season with this water, affecting directly or indirectly oxygen and carbon dioxide tensions, leaching and solubilization of minerals, and substrate availability.

The aquatic environment also embraces a range of substrate relationships. For example there are:

(1) Small particulate substrates (including pollen grains, small seeds, plankton, exuviae and cadavers of small insects, etc.) freely suspended in the water column and characterized by the highly ephemeral and separate nature of any one unit of the substrate;

(2) Substrates lying upon or anchored within the aquatic system (including bottom detritus, epiphytes and parasites of growing higher plant stems, leaves and roots, and superficial saprophytes and parasites of larger animals) in which change is more gradual and replacement successional;

(3) Enclosed saprophytes in animal guts in which adaptation to the ecological niche is equivalent to that of obligate internal parasites and in which the direct influence of the aquatic environment on the vegetative fungal growth is minimal.

This hierarchy is simply expressed in Fig. 20.1.

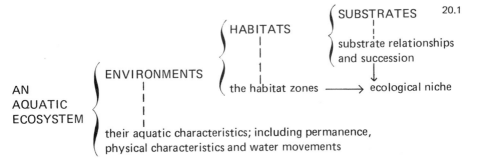

Fig. 20.1. Hierarchy of ecological terms used in this chapter.

Water is important in the aquatic environment as a vehicle for transport of both fungus and substrate, but must not necessarily be regarded as the exclusive agent. The function of zoospore motility must be assessed and the role of air movements is obviously important in relation to pollen-substrate transport and spore movements of fungi such as *Ancylistes.* Transport by water may involve either wave action, which is essentially redistributional within a given aquatic system, or scouring, which may involve transfer to and from other aquatic and non-aquatic systems in addition to redistribution.

Consideration of the ecology of fungi of freshwater involves the interaction of the origin and movement of the water body, the origin and timing of colonization of the substrate and the origin of the fungus. Further discussion of the origin and movement of the water is outside the scope of this chapter. The majority of studies reviewed below are concerned with the origin of the fungus and the availability of substrates.

20.2   Ecology

Ecological studies of 'aquatic phycomycetes' may be discussed under the headings of distribution, occurrence and activity. As yet there have been no attempts to estimate by biochemical techniques the total productivity of fungi in any aquatic ecosystem.

Data on distribution are accumulated from the identification of isolates from particular sites with subsequent qualitative comparison of sites either on a global or local scale. Such studies may include the evaluation of sampling techniques, and sometimes comparisons with non-mycological methods of characterizing sites have been made. Occurrence is mainly concerned with quantitative or semi-quantitative estimations of propagule numbers and fluctuations in these numbers for given species at particular localities. Under this heading it is appropriate to consider also the significance of these estimations as a measure of activity. Studies of activity aim to investigate the periods of vegetative growth, including the length of life of any single thallus, the types of substrate and substrate specificity, and the production and role of spores.

20.2.1   Methods

Before discussing the detailed results obtained in ecological studies under these different headings, it is advisable to review the entire range of methods which have been used and to assess their inherent shortcomings.

The methods employed in studying the ecology of aquatic phycomycetes are in almost every case derived from selective techniques designed primarily to isolate these fungi for taxonomic purposes. The variety of baiting, trapping and plating procedures recommended for collecting particular phycomycetes are well known (Couch, 1939; Sparrow, 1960, 1968) and their effectiveness, compared with more standard mycological practices, is made obvious by the almost total absence in such records for flagellate fungi. Although the mycelial Zygomycotina can be collected using standard procedures, there is no study which specifically relates to their occurrence in natural waters.

One of the principal requirements in an ecological study is the replication of samples to provide an adequate statistical basis for subsequent conclusions. The need to use a wide variety of different particulate substrates makes it impossible to achieve both a comprehensive treatment and a reliable statistical framework at the same time. (This is true for species within a single family, e.g. Saprolegniaceae (Dick, 1966) let alone members of orders such as the Chytridiales.) It is therefore necessary to consider separately those methods which attempt to delimit different communities of phycomycetes and those methods which attempt to provide measures of abundance. Although the former may purport to provide the latter, the bases for the conclusions drawn are often weak.

Community methods involve combinations of (1) the collection and incubation of naturally occurring particulate organic material, including the hosts of obligate parasites, (2) the direct suspension of possible substrates in traps in the aquatic environment, (3) the collection of natural waters and substrate samples followed by baiting, and (4) dilution or particle plating on nutrient agar.

The first two methods have been used notably by Sparrow (1943, 1960), Johnson (1951, 1956), Dayal and Ji (1966), and Perrott (1960), particularly for Monoblepharidales and Blastocladiales but also for other groups. Specialist studies of parasites must also include direct sampling of hosts (Canter and Lund, 1969; Masters, 1971; Scott and Warren, 1964; Unestam and Weiss, 1970). In general, it is very difficult to make any deductions concerning abundance because of the problems in standardizing collection and data recording procedure (e.g. size and age of twigs used, the counting of colonies on rotting submerged fruits etc.). The elimination of factors associated with the ecological origin of the naturally occurring substrate and the duration of its exposure in that particular habitat prior to collection is also difficult. These methods omit to consider the fact pointed out by Dick (1968 a) that the presence of a germinating spore or growing mycelium is no guarantee of its generation in that locality. Furthermore, major problems, which have also been ignored, will almost certainly be presented by the position effect of any trap and the disturbance to the environment caused by positioning the trap.

The range of substrates collected or put in traps is, naturally, vast, and the choice depends much upon the idiosyncrasies of the research worker. Favoured substrates range from rosaceous fruits (Sparrow 1960, 1968), oranges (Emerson, 1958; Emerson and Held, 1969) and oak twigs (Perrott, 1960), to ant pupae stuck on to waxed paper (Stoll, 1936; Johannes 1957). Regrettably there have been no controlled experiments in this sphere.

For the Chytridiales and Saprolegniales, baiting techniques have provided the most reliable data on species distribution in particular habitats (Alabi, 1971; Apinis, 1960, 1964; Dayal and Ji, 1966; Dick, 1966, 1968; Dick and Newby, 1961; Gaertner and Sparrow, 1966; Hughes, 1962; Moruzi and Toma, 1968 a, b; Roberts, 1963; Willoughby, 1961; 1962). They have involved the use of a wide variety of substrates ranging from seeds (*Cannabis,* Dick and Newby, 1961; *Crotalaria,* Alabi, 1971; *Brassica,* Park, 1972 a) grass leaves and cellophane (Willoughby, 1962), pollen (Gaertner and Sparrow, 1966), snakeskin (Willoughby, 1962; Dick, 1966), and chitin (Willoughby, 1962), but only in Dick (1966) are there any objective data from which one can assess the relative efficiency of different types of bait: rich plant and animal substrates proved to be equally effective for most species of Saprolegniaceae but snakeskin was the more effective bait in a few cases (Table 20.1).

Plating techniques have been utilized for qualitative assessments, but are better considered with those methods principally concerned with abundance.

Measurements of abundance may be divided into those which are primarily analytical and designed to give numerical estimates, and those which are primarily relative and aim to measure abundance on an arbitrary scale. The former basically sample a known amount of water or mud and this is then subjected to a standard dilution procedure. They range from straightforward dilution plating on nutrient agar (Park, 1972 a) through combined dilution plating and baiting (Willoughby, 1962;

Dick, 1966) to controlled baiting (Ulken and Sparrow, 1968) and particle plating (Park, 1972 a). The first and last of these methods have been used for the Mucorales and for the Peronosporales in soil.

TABLE 20.1   Relative efficiency of different types of bait for isolating Saprolegniaceae.

Cumulative data from three soil samples 4 m apart, with ten replicates from each core. (Data from Dick (1966), and reproduced with the permission of the Society for General Microbiology.)

Species	Bait		
	Hemp seed	Ant pupae	Snake skin
Pythiopsis cymosa de Bary	28	30	11
Aplanopsis terrestris Höhnk	2	–	6
Aplanopsis spinosa Dick	30	29	1
Saprolegnia terrestris Cookson	22	21	21
Saprolegnia subterranea (Dissmann) Seymour	6	7	–
Saprolegnia monilifera de Bary	4	2	–
Saprolegnia megasperma Coker	1	3	2
Aphanomyces sp.	–	–	26

Park (1972 a) found that more reproducible results were obtained when the dilution was spread over cooled agar rather than the more usual technique of incorporating the dilution in cool molten agar. For aquatic fungi it may also be important to use very recently poured plates since some Oömycetes do not establish readily on 'dried' plates. The depth of agar used is not important for purposes of calculation but it must be remembered that the depth of solidified agar may be a barrier to diffusion, especially of dissolved oxygen. Park (1972 a) has further noted that particle plating may be preferable for fast-growing fungi. However, particle plating and dilution plates are not suitable for Saprolegniaceae either because of competition factors or the dilutions required, nor are they suitable for monocentric Chytridiales. Willoughby (1962) devised an agar sector technique in which the dilution plate was sectored and the pieces put into water. The fungi were identified as they sporulated on the margins of the agar sectors. The weak nutrient supply led to attenuated sporulation and was accompanied by considerable bacterial contamination. To overcome the former, Dick (in Willoughby, 1962) suggested the addition of particulate nutrient sources. The method has been used by Collins and Willoughby (1962), Willoughby (1965), Willoughby and Collins (1966) and Dayal and Ji (1966). The fungus is required to make considerable vegetative growth (30-50 mm) before sporulation and the propagule may be an equivalent distance from any added rich nutrient source. Selection of a suitable agar is therefore important. Willoughby (1962) used an agar containing potassium tellurite as a bacteriostatic agent. However, this substance can depress sporulation in Saprolegniaceae. For these reasons Dick (1966) proposed a modification using corn meal agar without any antibiotic agents. This method was suitable for mud as well as water samples and increased the number of poss ble replicates. Even so, it was noted that some germlings—notably a leptomitaceous fungus—failed to establish on the baits and would have been missed in routine sampling. This inability of Lepto-mitaceae to compete in culture has also been noted by Park (1972 a).

The most probable number (MPN) method provides an alternative, but indirect, assay for propagules which do not readily establish themselves on semi-solid media. So far it has only been used in freshwater for chytrids growing on pollen (Ulken and Sparrow, 1968), though it has been used previously in marine studies. The principal problems with this method are the selection of suitable particulate nutrient sources and the assessment of the optimum density of such nutrient particles for any particular fungus.

All of these methods may be criticized on the grounds of selectivity in the nutrient source, and much more work needs to be carried out before we can have confidence of the percentage efficiency of establishment of propagules of individual species. Nevertheless, these methods still provide the best information available on absolute numbers of discrete viable fungal units in the aquatic ecosystem.

It is important to realize that, valuable as the above methods are, they tend to record spores, the mycelial or vegetative state probably representing only a minor frac-tion of the total isolates. The type of spore isolated is also important. Asexual spores are thought to constitute most of the records for water samples using Willoughby's technique, while sexual spores incorporated in particulate matter formed the larger part of the counts made by Dick. It is thus difficult to relate the numbers of spores to the energy required to form them and their inoculum potential. These quotients will be different for different species and only detailed autecological studies can there-fore provide any estimate of productivity, in the sense of the role of the fungus in the ecosystem.

Relative measures of abundance have also been used in aquatic fungal ecology. These are based on the ratio: number of fungi found/number of samples examined. Modifications of this method of assessment have been used by Apinis (1960, 1964), Dick and Newby (1961), Gaertner and Sparrow (1966) and Dick (1966, 1971). The principal difficulty in judging the value of this method rests in the selection and definition of a sample. It is further confused when numerical counts for different fungi are added together and the total expressed as a percentage.

This method can only be used when sufficient true replicates have been made to enable statistical analysis to be carried out. In some of the work cited above, there is no control test on sample equivalence, the replicates are too few and the data have been expressed in percentage terms without an accompanying analysis of variance. Without reworking the raw data it is not possible to place any confidence in some of the conclusions drawn from such work. Other authors (e.g. Roberts, 1963) were aware of this problem and have been content to express abundance on a non-numerical and perhaps less objective scale. Dick and Newby (1961) were able partially to overcome this criticism of the use of numbers by repeated examination of permanently marked sites in soils and muds. Sufficient statistical analysis using true replicates was made by Dick (1966).

Dick (1966) has also shown that a ten-fold difference in dilution is unlikely to have any effect on estimates of relative abundance and that a hundred-fold difference (using as little as 0.1 ml of slurry per petri dish) may have little effect on qualitative estimates. Therefore in any baiting technique for estimations of relative abundance of Saprolegniaceae the amount of soil or mud plated out is not critical and likely always to be in excess of requirements. On the other hand, comparisons of adjacent sites

(Dick, 1963, 1966, 1968) show considerable differences in relative abundance, even when the species lists are similar. Thus, within the limits imposed by a selective technique and provided that procedures are standardized, considerable reliance may be placed on relative abundance.

Such relative methods do not provide any measure of productivity. They do not distinguish between the hypothetical extremes of the low total productivity from a species-rich fungus flora with many co-dominants and the high total productivity of a single dominant species. However, they can be used to assess fluctuations in the ease and availability of isolation (which may not be the same as the number of propagules!) for given species and they can enable comparisons to be made of several sites in a single locality over a relatively short period of time.

20.2.2 Distribution

Distribution may be considered at the global, regional and local levels. At the global level there is little evidence for marked geographically based species differences (Sparrow, 1968), though Hughes (1962) has suggested that the eccentric *Achlya* species may be more frequent in warm temperate or tropical climates. There are also suggestions that *Saprolegnia* species (nearly all of which are centric or subcentric) are absent from warm temperate and tropical waters (Alabi, 1971; Dr. S. D. Patil, personal communication with reference to south India). *Allomyces* has generally been considered as a warm temperate fungus but its occurrence in regions subject to winter cold (e.g. Michigan, USA, unpublished data) or arctic conditions (e.g. Devon Island, Canada, Booth and Barrett, 1971), suggests that other factors may be more important. For example, one could suggest a possible relationship to seasonal temporary pools (Ji, 1970; Jeffrey and Willoughby, 1964) since irregular periods of moist conditions could deplete the potential inoculum derived from meiosporangia. The Rhipidiaceae are also apparently more easily found in warmer climates and again highly specialized environmental conditions may be responsible (Emerson and Held, 1969). Studies of the Coelomomycetaceae (Couch, 1972; Umphlett, 1968) may indicate that these obligate parasites of mosquito larvae are warm temperate, since they seem adapted to a purely vegetative life cycle dependent upon a permanent population of mosquito larvae. Other apparently continental differences suggestive of endemism are found in the genus *Achlya*. *Achlya radiosa* Maurizio is common in Europe, absent in North America and with a single record (Milanez, 1969) in South America. It is possible that in South America this species, *Achlya pseudoradiosa* Rogers et Beneke (Rogers and Beneke, 1962) and *Achlya echinulata* Beroqui (Beroqui, 1969 a) may be conspecific. This example, and also those of *Achlya oviparvula* Rogers et Beneke (Beneke and Rogers, 1962) with *Achlya caroliniana* Coker and *Achlya curvicollis* Beroqui (Beroqui, 1969 b) with *Achlya apiculata* de Bary illustrate one of the major problems in this type of discussion: the ecological data are weak and there are reasons to doubt the validity of the taxonomy (Dick, 1969 a, b, 1972; Green and Dick, 1972). It is nevertheless true to say that the majority of all three groups of aquatic phycomycetes is world-wide in distribution. While most work has been concentrated in North America and Europe, studies such as those of Karling and others in India, New Zealand and the Pacific (Karling, 1964 a-d, 1965, 1966, 1967 a-j, 1968 a-e; Srivastava, 1964, 1966, 1967 a; Srivastava and Bhargava, 1963; Singh and Pavgi, 1971; Elliott, 1967, 1968 and unpublished data for Queensland, Australia) and the South American studies (Beneke and Rogers, 1962, 1970; Beroqui 1969 a, b; Carvalho 1965; Furtado, 1965; Milanez, 1965 a, b, 1968, 1969, 1970; Milanez and Val, 1969; Rogers and Beneke, 1962; Rogers *et al.*,

1970) help to fill in some gaps in our knowledge of global distributions even though they include very little strictly ecological information.

At the regional level one may consider distribution in relation to entire watersheds. Apart from early work on the Bremen by Höhnk (1935) reviewed by Sparrow (1968) recent work is confined to that of Willoughby and Collins (1966) on a small short stream in the English Lake District and some unpublished work on Cambridgeshire rivers by Mrs. R. E. Hunter (née Roberts). Neither the above studies on Saprolegniaceae, nor the study by Park (1972 a) on microfungi in general from rivers in Northern Ireland, provide data which are strictly comparable, but in all cases an often considerable percentage of isolations could be attributed to leaching. Willoughby and Collins (1966) noted that while the effect of sewage effluent greatly increased propagule counts of *Saprolegnia* at the outfall, its effect was recognizable, though diluted, at lower stations. In the larger river system studied by Mrs. Hunter, differences were on the whole quantitative rather than qualitative, but an effect due to flooding over marginal land was noted. Park's study extended the range of species studied, including the Mucorales, but no conclusions were drawn concerning distribution in relation to the river system as a whole. The relationship between rates of flow, numbers of propagules and productivity has been discussed by Park and seems likely to be complex. In lotic environments the origins and mobility of both inocula and substrates become critical when conclusions are based on data of spore availability rather than mycelial activity. As these origins have not been satisfactorily determined it is not possible to draw any conclusions concerning the distribution of vegetatively active fungi as opposed to potential inoculum in lotic environments.

Local site variations are difficult to assess in open water because of the uncertainty attached to inoculum origin. For this reason most work on distribution patterns at the local level has been carried out on marginal muds and marshy soils in which inoculum movements are more easily monitored. Again, comparisons between data from different workers are difficult because of differences in aim, method and quantity of supporting data.

Distribution in relation to wet soils and marshes has been studied by Apinis (1964) and Dick (1963). Apinis has drawn attention to correlations with angiosperm vegetation types and soil profiles. Closely related species of Chytridiomycetes, Oömycetes and Mucorales were found to vary in the degree to which they were restricted to particular ranges of the vegetation types studied. In the absence of statistical analysis, some reservations might be attached to the method of calculating abundance which was employed, but the qualitative observations are of considerable value. Similar data are provided for soil profiles. Dick (1963) provided further data for determining communities of Saprolegniaceae in relation to water content and pH rather than vegetation type.

Evidence for patterns of distribution, supported by statistical analysis, has been provided by Dick (1962, 1966). It has been shown that several orders of mosaic pattern may be superimposed upon a more widespread zonation related to topography (Fig. 20.2). The demonstration that differences in relative counts depend on small spatial site differences of an order of less than 1 metre, rather than the size of the sample, which could vary by a volume factor of 10 without affecting relative counts, means that considerable caution must be employed when discussing the quantitative data from once-sampled sites. Nevertheless, it was determined (Dick, 1962) that mosaic patterns within 1 m^2 were persistent for more than a year and probably represent differences in microhabitats not apparent when using angiosperm cover as an index of site character. It may therefore be advisable to mix two or three cores a few centi-

521

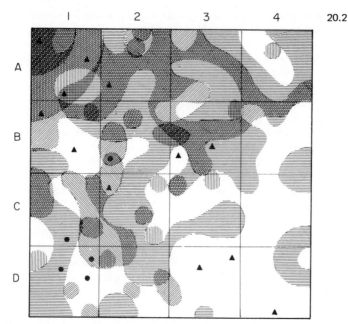

Fig. 20.2 (after Dick, 1962). Distribution, in a quadrat of approximately 1 m², of the six most frequently isolated species of Saprolegniaceae. Ten samples were taken from each of the 16 subdivisions on one occasion in November 1957. *Saprolegnia litoralis* Coker▓▓ from 88 samples. *Achlya racemosa* Hildebrand▨▨ from 42 samples. *Saprolegnia turfosa* (Minden)▐▌ from 19 samples. *Achlya colorata* Gäumann Pringsheim▚▚ from 15 samples. *Pythiopsis cymosa* de Bary ▲ from 12 samples. *Saprolegnia eccentrica* (Coker) Seymour ● from 5 samples. Seven other species accounted for a further 20 records: none of these was from C3, C4 or D2 and only three were from D3 and D4.

From this diagram it is cleár that although some of the more abundant species have different distributions*, there is a general decrease in frequency of isolations in the part of the quadrat represented towards the lower right hand. Competition cannot be considered an important factor since the average number of species per sample ranges from 2.5 in A1 to 0.4 in D4.

* 66% of the samples yielding *Achlya racemosa* (the second most abundant species) also possessed the most abundant species *(Saprolegnia litoralis)*. However, only 20% of the *Achlya colorata*
records were accompanied by *A. racemosa* and only 26% by *S. litoralis*; none was accompanied
by both these species yet only 20% of the records for *A. colorata* were unaccompanied by any
other Saprolegniaceae.

metres apart to provide the site sample when the sampling site is visited once only.

One must also recognize that when counts are presumed to be derived from germinating spores, then the predominant type of sporulation, which is a character of the
individual species, will vary from species to species. This in turn affects the type of
pattern revealed. Such a difference in sporulation behaviour is thought to be responsible for the different local patterns of distribution found for *Thraustotheca clavata*
(de Bary) Humphrey and *Aplanopsis spinosa* Dick (Dick, 1968 b), zoospore clumps
of the former species resulting in greater fluctuations in observed relative abundance,
assessed by dilution methods, than the naturally dispersed oöspores of the latter
species.

It is more difficult to obtain distributional data of fungi within a body of open
water and in its benthic deposits, if only because of the imprecision in positioning

Fig. 20.3. *Achlya americana* Humphrey

Month	M	J	J	A	S	O	N	D	J	F	M	A	M	J	J	A	S	O
number of subdivisions / in which this species occurred	A2 C1 C2	A1 B1 B3	A2	C3 D1 D2	B1	A1 C3	D2	A1	D1	C1 C2 D1	C2 D1 D3	C2 D2 D3	C2 D4	A1 A2 C1 D1 D2	A2 C2 C4	D2	A1 A2 B1 C3 D1	E1 C1 C4

	1	2	3	4
A	5	5	.	.
B	4	.	1	.
C	4	6	3	2
D	6	5	2	1

Achlya apiculata de Bary

Month	M	J	J	A	S	O	N	D	J	F	M	A	M	J	J	A	S	O
number of subdivisions / in which this species occurred	B2 C1 D4			B2 C3 D4		B2 C3 D2		C1	B2	B2 C4 D3	D3 D4	C1	B3 D1 D3	D3	D3 D4		C1 C3	

	1	2	3	4
A	.	.	.	.
B	.	5	1	.
C	4	.	3	1
D	1	1	4	4

Achlya radiosa Maurizio

Month	M	J	J	A	S	O	N	D	J	F	M	A	M	J	J	A	S	O
number of subdivisions / in which this species occurred	B3 C2	B1 B3		A1 A3 B1 B3 C1 C4	A1 A2 A4 B1 B2	A3 A4 C2 C4	C4	A2 A3	A1 A2 A3 C1 C4 D1	A2 B2 B4 D2 D4		A3 C4		A4			C1 C2 D1	

	1	2	3	4
A	3	3	5	2
B	3	2	3	2
C	3	3	.	5
D	2	1	.	1

Fig. 20.3. The distribution of three species of *Achlya* in 16 subdivisions of a marked quadrat over a period of 18 months, 1957–1958.

20.4

Month	M	J	J	A	S	O	N	D	J	F	M	A	M
Numbers of subdivisions without Saprolegniaceae	A1 B1 D4	A2 A3	A1 A2 A3 B1 B2 C1	A1 A2 A4 B1 B2	A1 A2 A3 C1	A1 A2 B2	A1 A2	A1 A2 A3	A1 A2 B2 C4	A1	A1 B1	A1 C1	A1 B1

	1	2	3	4
A	138	4	1	
B	65	1	.	
C	3	.	.	1
D	.	.	.	1

Fig. 20.4. The distribution of samples negative for any Saprolegniaceae in 16 subdivisions of another marked quadrat over a period of 13 months 1957–1958.

the collecting apparatus and the time necessary to obtain sufficient samples for statistical analysis.

In open water, Willoughby (1962) and Collins and Willoughby (1962) have found aquatic phycomycete spores to be most readily collected in the upper water layers. Their frequency was found to decrease as one moved away from the shoreline. These authors concluded that much of the spore population was related to leaching by rainfall, and thus the distributions recorded were largely of transitory alien spores. Paterson (1967) using a trap procedure at various depths away from the shore in a small Michigan Lake (Douglas Lake) and in a bay of Lake Michigan itself, found that many substrates normally colonized by flagellate fungi in shallow water remained uncolonized over periods extending to 7 weeks. The efficiency of the traps in very shallow waters was not assessed, but the inference to be made is that propagule numbers were low in deep water away from the shore. Dick (1970) has studied the Saprolegniaceae occurring on insect exuviae, most of which are cast at the water/air interface of open water. This small community of species and its pattern of propagule frequency is closely tied to diurnal patterns of substrate availability. For this reason this study will be considered more fully below in relation to activity, but it is worth noting here that the time of sampling may be critical when determining distribution patterns of propagules in open water. In studies such as these, in which propagule numbers are thought to be low, the chance establishment of alien spores becomes important and cannot easily be estimated when all the fungi recovered are also known from neighbouring habitats.

Benthic muds have been randomly sampled by Willoughby (1965) and Dick (1971). An alternative approach has been to make both quantitative and qualitative comparisons along a transect line which embraces soil, marginal sites and lentic environments. Willoughby (1961) has made comparisons of three arbitrary zones, depending upon their liability to inundation, and he has been able to show that these zones have correspondingly different chytridiaceous floras (Fig. 20.5). As might be expected, the littoral zone had most elements from both adjoining zones, but there was little overlap between the terrestrial and lentic communities. When a species occurred in two adjacent zones, its relative dominance in the total flora of each zone was different.

Dick (1966, 1971) has used transects across the lake margin as well as arbitrary zone categories to determine the distribution of Saprolegniaceae. Compared with the Chytridiomycetes, a rather more complex picture has emerged from both methods, although a similar general trend can be seen. A formula for site correlation (Oosting, 1956) was used in an attempt to determine floristic patterns in the analysis of both sets of data. As might be anticipated from the above description of mozaic patterns in soil, correlations between emergent sites were low in random sampling, but higher in the repeatedly sampled transect sites.

In the marginal zone the number of species was high; there were more propagules, as evidenced by the reciprocal curve of negative samples; qualitatively there was fairly high correlation for species between the emergent and submerged littoral sites, but when abundance was taken into consideration, correlations were at their lowest between these same sites. This complex relationship (Fig. 20.6) between the emergent and submerged littoral zones was also found in the data from singly sampled sites in which two categories could be discerned:

(1) those with good internal correlation plus correlation with a section of emergent littoral sites,

(2)   those not correlating internally, but collectively showing some correlation
       with certain emergent littoral sites (Fig. 20.7).

Taken as a whole the combined data suggest that two distribution patterns are
overlapping. On the one hand there is a group of species (including *Saprolegnia* species
and *Achlya* section 2b-racemose) predominantly of the emergent littoral, but which
shows an outwash of propagules to the submerged littoral, and on the other hand,
another group of species (characterized by *Achlya* section 2c-subcentric) probably
located in the submerged littoral but with propagules carried up into the normally
emergent zone, by, for example, animals, flooding or wave action. If this interpretation is correct then the datum for each site is derived partly from propagules of inhabitants and partly from alien spores.

Both sets of data also show a discrete benthic community dominated by non-
sexual *Achlya*. This community is most clearly defined in deposits found below 1 m
depth of water. Negative samples and within site lack of homogeneity in the species
lists recorded were greatest in deposits at a distance from the shore exceeding 1 m and
in water less than 1 m deep. It is in this zone that one would expect a transition
from the essentially littoral elements to the benthic moiety of the aquatic species.
However, unlike the rich cross dissemination of the littoral transition zone, these data
suggest that this second transition zone is more likely to be barren. Willoughby (1961,
1965) and Dick (1966, 1971) conclude that the bottom muds of lakes do not form a
prominent reservoir of Saprolegniaceous spores, although this may not be true for
other aquatic phycomycetes such as the Mucorales.

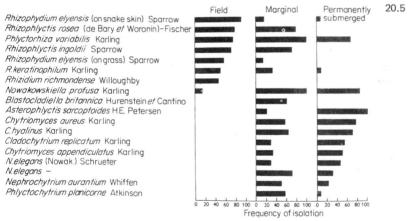

Fig. 20.5 (from Willoughby, 1962). Comparison of the chytridaceous floras from three arbitrary
zones distinguished on their liability to inundation from Esthwaite Water (English Lake District).
The field zone was above the highest recorded lake level, the marginal zone was subject to periodic
inundation and the submerged zone was at c.2 m in *Littorella* beds.

Fourteen collections were made in each zone, species being recorded on an absolute basis for
each collection. The sum of these qualitative records for each species was then converted to a percentage.

Thirty-six species were recorded. Of the 18 species having a frequency of isolation greater
than 40% in any zone, only one *(Phlyctorhiza variabilis)* occurred frequently in all three zones,
and in this case it was noticed that presence was based on relatively far fewer thalli in the submerged zone.

From this comparison it was concluded that a distinct and limited terrestrial flora co-existed
with a more species-rich aquatic flora in the marginal zone.

While most of the data for aquatic phycomycetes suggest that marginal and littoral sites contain the widest variety of species, this primary relationship with water is not simply a topographical one, since other sites away from lake margins, but having similar water relations and soil textures, provide similar distribution patterns (Dick 1963, 1966, 1971). Moreover, the pH of the environment is also important, for Roberts (1963), Srivastava (1967 b) and Dick (1963, 1971) have shown a clear association of species characteristic of highly acid environments.

The importance of the marginal zone and the influence of other undetermined environmental factors may account for differences in distribution recorded in studies of a number of pools and ponds by Dayal and Tandon (1962) and Dayal and Ji (1966). The latter authors found temporary pools to have the larger species list while the former study showed greater numbers of species from artificial ponds. How far planting and maintenance affect species diversity in artificial ponds is unknown, and it is surprising that only one study has ever been made of aquatic phycomycetes in ponds of botanic gardens, with their diversity of physical conditions, such as temperature (Moruzi and Toma, 1968 b).

The permanence and dynamics of distribution patterns have hardly been studied and there are no mycological equivalents to the studies on agents of algal distribution (Stewart and Schlichting, 1966; Proctor *et al.,* 1967; Atkinson, 1970, 1971).

20.2.3   Occurrence

The mere isolation of a species from a particular site provides no evidence of its origin or potential activity in relation to that site. Records of vegetatively growing fungi are occasional and hence statistically insignificant. Most collections either do not distinguish between mycelium and spores, or presume that a spore inoculum has been sampled. When discussing occurrence we are concerned with the establishment of a probability that the fungus in question is or has been growing vegetatively at that spot.

Most *in situ* trapping procedures initially isolate naturally occurring spores, but they may result in the production of an enormous increase in potential inoculum which cannot be distinguished from the initial inoculum. For how long does the effect of this trap-induced inoculum persist? The removal of a sample may not only disturb and change the site but may remove potential inoculum. Examination of the site for *in situ* vegetative growth is seldom practicable and is not likely to lead to statistically acceptable evidence. Of these possibilities, the second poses the least evil, since repeated sampling over an extended period of time will either have no effect or will deplete an inactive inoculum. Repeated isolation of a species from a given site may reflect (1) a highly persistent inactive inoculum in which the spore population has a long half-life, (2) a continually replenished inactive inoculum, or (3) an inhabitant either in an active or inactive phase. There are very little factual data for the majority of aquatic phycomycetes in this respect and no controlled experiments have been carried out. It has been argued by Dick and Newby (1961) and Dick (1962) that the continuity of a potential inoculum over periods of up to 2 years (or 10 years for *Scoliolegnia subeccentrica* Dick (Dick, 1969 b) coupled with a mozaic distribution and seasonal fluctuations, constitute occurrence as defined above. This is probable but not proven. However, this somewhat unsatisfactory state of knowledge for the Saprolegniaceae is better than any available information for Zygomycetes or Chytridiomycetes.

Any discussion of occurrence must be based on absolute or at least relative numbers. This numerical information may be derived from asexual spores, sexual spores or

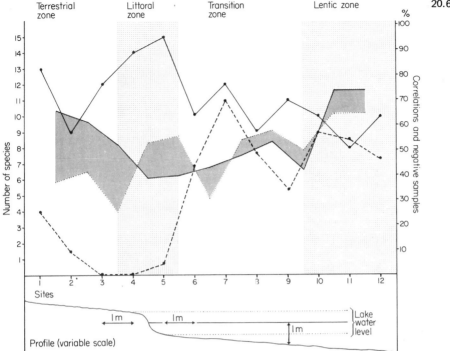

Fig. 20.6 (after Dick, 1971). Results from two transects each sampled four times between September and October 1969. Ten replicates were made of each sample giving a total plate count of 80 for each site. The total number of species recorded at each site is given ●—●. The percentage of negative samples is given ●- - -●. Percentage correlations between adjacent sites according to the formula $2w/a + b \times 100$ are given —— and the contiguous stippled area represents the difference between this coefficient and one based on species presence or absence only.

In the terrestrial zone the number of individuals is fairly low but quantitative comparisons provide a higher degree of correlation. A continuum of well defined communities compatible with mosaic patterns of distribution and relatively low propagule numbers at any one time may be presumed.

Numbers of species and propagules increase towards the littoral zone and this diversity is reflected in somewhat lower, but similar correlation coefficients. In the littoral zone maximum numbers of individuals and greatest diversity of species are found. Although qualitative correlation is high, quantitative correlation is lower. It would appear that propagules from adjacent communities, the predominantly supralittoral (sites 3 and 4) and the predominantly sublittoral (sites 5 and 6) are disseminated over the entire littoral zone by fluctuating water levels.

In the submerged transition zone negative samples rapidly increase to a peak at site 7, and numbers of species show a progressive decline into the lentic zone. The two correlation levels are inverted between sites 6 and 7 possibly due to the preponderant influence of a sublittoral community in the shallow water. On this basis, coupled with the peak of negative samples, one can subdivide this zone into two: a shallow transition zone with distinctive flora and a deeper transition zone in which a considerable proportion of isolations are the result of fortuitous dissemination of propagules, still viable but without a continuous substrate.

In the lentic zone negative samples are still high, but the number of species falls to the lowest recorded. Nevertheless both quantitative and qualitative correlations between adjacent sites are high indicating the existence of a distinct lentic community.

527

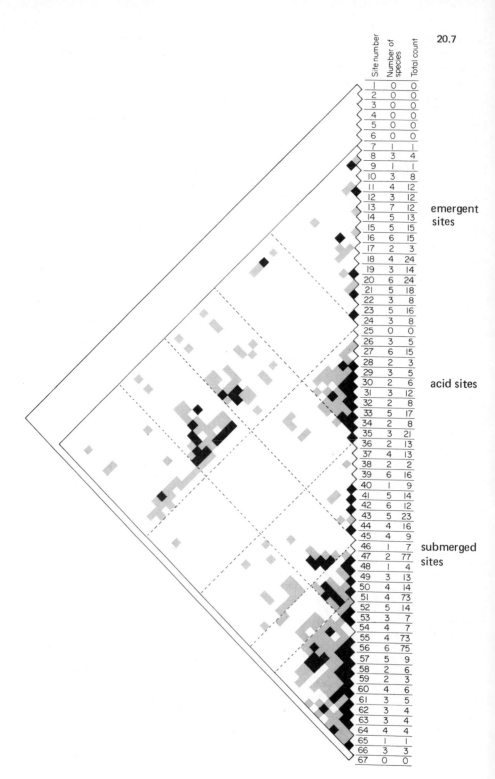

20.7

Site number	Number of species	Total count	
1	0	0	
2	0	0	
3	0	0	
4	0	0	
5	0	0	
6	0	0	
7	1	1	
8	3	4	
9	1	1	
10	3	8	
11	4	12	
12	3	12	
13	7	12	emergent
14	5	13	sites
15	5	15	
16	6	15	
17	2	3	
18	4	24	
19	3	14	
20	6	24	
21	5	18	
22	3	8	
23	5	16	
24	3	8	
25	0	0	
26	3	5	
27	6	15	
28	2	3	
29	3	5	
30	2	6	acid sites
31	3	12	
32	2	8	
33	5	17	
34	2	8	
35	3	21	
36	2	13	
37	4	13	
38	2	2	
39	6	16	
40	1	9	
41	5	14	
42	6	12	
43	5	23	
44	4	16	
45	4	9	
46	1	7	submerged
47	2	77	sites
48	1	4	
49	3	13	
50	4	14	
51	4	73	
52	5	14	
53	3	7	
54	4	7	
55	4	73	
56	6	75	
57	5	9	
58	2	6	
59	2	3	
60	4	6	
61	3	5	
62	3	4	
63	3	4	
64	4	4	
65	1	1	
66	3	3	
67	0	0	

mycelium, or combinations of these. It will be immediately obvious that unless the type of inoculum is known, any fluctuations in counts for a species cannot be taken as indicating activity. Zoospores may have a life span of less than 24 hours in lake water (Clausz, 1971), but they may remain viable in the laboratory for much longer. Oöspores may require a period of after-ripening and maturation before being capable of germination (Ziegler, 1948), thus maximum counts based on oöspores may reflect a period of activity much earlier than that determined by zoospore counts. The period of greatest vegetative activity may occur when neither type of spore is being produced. Therefore, while interesting, the data on seasonal periodicity in the Saprolegniaceae (Dick, 1962; Hughes, 1962; Roberts, 1963; Clausz, 1971) are very difficult to interpret. It is unlikely, given the methods used, that a high proportion of the counts is due to mycelium. Water samples, provided they contain little suspended detritus, are most likely to provide zoospore inocula (Willoughby, 1962), but mud and soil sample counts are likely to be derived from oöspores (Dick, 1966).

With the above reservations to be borne in mind, it is possible to consider data for occurrence of Saprolegniaceae. There is close agreement between Dick and Newby (1961), Hughes (1962), Roberts (1963), Milanez (1967), Srivastava (1967 b) and Alabi (1971) that different patterns of observed periodicity are found for the centric/subcentric and eccentric oöspore types. The former group tends to fluctuate with season, being most readily isolated in spring and autumn in temperature zones and in rainy seasons in tropical countries. This may reflect a potential period of activity when oöspores are more readily germinated (Dayal and Tandon, 1962), or it may reflect a leaching factor. Willoughby (1962), working with zoospore counts mostly referable to *Saprolegnia,* has also recorded spring and autumn maxima. On the other hand those species with eccentric oöspores tend to be relatively more abundant in summer or dry seasons. But this relative abundance may be an artefact arising from the fact that most of these species are distributed principally in the submerged littoral and lentic environments. Roberts (1963 and unpublished work: Mrs. Hunter, personal communication) and Alabi (1971) also distinguish a third group of 'constant' species, but this is difficult to justify on relative abundance alone. Mrs. Hunter has suggested that these three groups, while showing apparent correlation with various meteorological conditions, may only be indirectly linked to these conditions through their affect on the availability of particular substrates. It must also be noted that some species do not fit any of these patterns of occurrence precisely, for example *Pythiopsis cymosa* (Dick and Newby, 1961; Mrs. Hunter, personal communication) has only a winter to spring maximum

---

Fig. 20.7 (after Dick, 1971). Table of correlations between 67 singly sampled sites, each with ten replicates, from emergent and submerged sites around a north temperate lake (Marion Lake, B.C. Canada). Correlations of 25-44% stippled, correlations of over 45% in black. Sites 1-6 and 67 had no Saprolegniaceae.

It will be noted that good internal correlation was found between the 'acid' sites (25-35), but that these sites did not correlate with either the emergent or submerged sites. Internal correlation between the emergent sites was poor, as would be predicted with mozaic distributions.

The relationships between the submerged sites was more complex. At least two and possibly three groups could be distinguished. There was a lentic group of sites, having good internal correlation, but with little relation to any other group of sites; there were also the submerged marginal sites, one group with good internal correlation *and* correlation with certain terrestrial sites, and another group with poor internal correlation, but better correlation with a slightly different spectrum of terrestrial sites.

It is suggested that this pattern of correlations reflects a cross contamination, through water movements, of propagules derived from primarily supralittoral and primarily sublittoral communities.

while *Isoachlya toruloides* Kauffman ex Coker (Dick and Newby, 1961) was never recorded in the winter months and was most abundant in August.

Perrott (1960) has reported two periods in the year when Monoblepharidales are most readily isolated. These were also autumn (October-November) and spring (March-May) but some differences within these periods were noted for different species.

For Chytridiomycetes, Willoughby (1960, 1961) has found that isolations of zoospores were confined to spring and autumn for soil and submerged sites and that zoospores were most rapidly detected in these seasons from the littoral zone.

The seasonal changes in abundance of Trichomycete thalli in insect guts (Moss, 1972) appear to have a complex explanation more appropriately discussed under the heading of activity.

There are no data for occurrence of Mucorales in aquatic habitats.

Thus the fluctuations in the occurrence of flagellate fungi are inextricably mixed with the problems associated with the identification of propagule types and the relationship between the site and time of origin and the site of isolation of these propagules. Although it appears likely that littorally distributed species show spring and autumn maxima in the number of propagules available, there remains some doubt as to whether this can be used as a measure of activity, since zoospore isolations could be assumed to represent an immediately precursive vegetative phase, whilst counts due to oöspore germination may indicate a potential inoculum which could herald a future active phase.

20.2.4 Activity

Apart from the incidental references made above to presumed periods of activity, very little is known about the active phase of aquatic phycomycetes. The only sector in which some information exists on activity is that of fungus/insect relationships in lentic environments. Three sets of data need to be considered here: these are the studies on *Coelomomyces*, the colonization of insect exuviae by Saprolegniaceae and the occurrence of Trichomycetes in the guts of aquatic insects.

Coelomomyces parasitizes the body cavity of mosquitoes, with the production of large numbers of thin-walled or thick-walled sporangia. The life cycle has not been fully worked out, but appears to depend largely on an asexual reinfection of larval stages. Adult insects are rarely infected but may nevertheless be responsible for distribution of the parasite from one locality to another (Umphlett, 1968). Sporangial germination occurs above 10 °C with an optimum at 25 °C (Couch, 1968; Pillai and O'Loughlin, 1972), thus the genus appears to be adapted to permanent pools in warmer climates in which continuous infection of larvae may occur (Couch, 1968; Pillai, 1971; Pillai and O'Loughlin, 1972). Higher temperatures (23-28 °C) are required to induce sporangial germination from dead infected larvae, and a low oxygen concentration is probably necessary to induce resting sporangia to germinate (Umphlett, 1968). First instar larvae are not infected, but the population of fourth instar larvae is likely to be heavily infected, and death of the host probably occurs before completion of the pupal stage. The activity of *Coelomomyces* appears to correlate with an increase in the population of the host and the percentage of fourth instar larvae. However, it is interesting to note that a year by year survey (Umphlett, 1970) of one population has shown a progressive decline in the overall incidence of infection from about 36 to 10%. Couch (1972) has noted that optimum infection occurs at the second instar and he has pointed out that optimum conditions for control of larvae by massive inoculations of such larvae by zoospores results in death by the third instar, before the fungus has matured to produce a new crop of zoosporangia. This element of 'overkill' means that to provide adequate control of mosquito activity by the parasite, one cannot rely on natural regeneration of the fungus inoculum. This will only occur at a lower incidence of percentage diseased individuals which is probably below that regarded as desirable for biological control.

The colonization of insect exuviae by Chytridiomycetes and Oömycetes is well known, but only one study, in a north temperate lake, has been made of the ecology of this substrate relationship. Dick (1970) was able to demonstrate that this substrate supported a surprisingly limited saprolegniaceous flora comprised of two principal species, a *Saprolegnia* of the *diclina* group and *Aphanomyces laevis* de Bary. Investigation of the colonization of the small exuviae of chironomid flies revealed that almost all the exuviae in shallow water were colonized within 24 hours (74% of exuviae not more than 48 hours old taken at 0.5 m depth showed hyphal outgrowths within 3 hours of collection). In deep water (4.5 m) there was relatively little colonization (3% at 3 hours) and in all stations further incubation increased the colonization count by only about 12%. This suggested that colonization occurred only within a few hours of the exuviae becoming available. If it is recalled that most exuviae become available at one period in the day; that the zoospores of these fungi remain viable for less than 24 hours (Clausz, 1971) and given that on such small substrata these fungi tend to be holocarpic producing zoospores in about a day, then it is apparent that a diurnal periodicity of fungal zoospores could be expected. Moreover, since this substrate becomes available at the air/water interface, and the zoospores respond to high levels of oxygenation of the water, a distinct distribution of zoospores with respect to depth would also be expected.

It can thus be seen that there is considerable harmony between substrate availability and propagule production. The life cycle of the fungus is to be seen as an essentially asexual one in which both the vegetative and asexual phases are ephemeral. However, the continuous supply of substrates and spores especially in shallow water, will mean that there will be considerable conversion of energy resources by the activity of these fungi. It must also be noted that possibly approaching 200 generations of the asexual cycles will occur in a season. A tendency to holocarpy means that nearly every one of the 100 or more nuclei produced in each vegetative phase represents a possible germ-line. If this is coupled with the diploid nature of these nuclei then it can be seen that heterozygous mutant nuclei will accumulate. With the onset of less favourable climatic conditions a limited amount of resting spore production may take place, possibly when a longer vegetative phase occurs on whole dead insects. Oöspores so produced not only serve a function as propagules but they may also provide an essential mechanism for filtering out excessive undesirable mutations in the fungus. Given the rapid exponential increase in asexual propagules that this pattern of activity represents, only a very few oöspores are required as potential inoculum in the ecosystem, and even decimation of the oöspore numbers will only delay the development of the sequential repetitive asexual life cycle by a few days.

This study also provides some slight evidence of the activity of flagellate fungal parasites of Oömycetes. These would appear to be confined to host fungi occurring on substrates supporting a longer vegetative phase than are represented by insect exuviae, since the collective incidence of these parasites even on larger exuviae was less than 10%. Support for this view also comes from the account of parasitism by *Aphanomyces parasiticus* Coker on Saprolegniaceae (Dick, 1964, 1966).

The third study of fungal activity in relation to aquatic insects concerns the gut-inhabiting Trichomycetes. Data from many taxonomic and morphological accounts

(Moss, 1972) have shown that endozoic Trichomycetes are confined to the larval stages of herbivorous mandibulate arthropods. As far as the aquatic insects are concerned, host specificity was known to be variable: the Harpellaceae are confined to the mid-guts of dipterous larvae while the Genistellaceae are restricted to the hind-guts of Diptera, Ephemeroptera and Plecoptera.

Using a species of *Stachylina* (Harpellaceae), Moss has been able to demonstrate that both natural and artificial cross-infection were confined to herbivorous, tubicolous hosts. The method employed was to provide a starvation diet, so that faecal material from infected hosts was ingested by test hosts. Infection could not be induced in the carnivorous chironomid larvae.

No infection was found in the non-feeding, dispersal stage, first instar larvae, and relatively little infection was noted at the second instar, but between 60 and 80% of the third and fourth instar larvae were infected.

An interesting relationship was discovered between thallus density and season in the heavily infected fourth instar larvae. Incidence was high from November to May, dropped sharply in June and rose again during September. This has been explained on the basis of the interaction between the feeding activity of the host and spore liberation by the fungus. During the cold weather overwintering fourth instars feed little, but peristaltic activity recirculates material in the mid-gut. Spore production by the fungus is confined to the rear portion of the mid-gut. Fungus spores produced in cold weather are recirculated within the gut and become attached at the anterior part of the mid-gut lining. The mid-gut lining of these insects is continually produced at the anterior end and is sloughed off in the hind-gut, the rate of production being geared to the metabolic activity of the insect. Thus in cold weather high incidence of fungal thalli occurs as a result of internal inoculation, while in warmer weather a lower incidence of fungal thalli occurs as a result of inoculum ingested with food. In this example, therefore, incidence of vegetative thalli does not have a direct relationship either with activity, or with spore production.

These three widely differing studies on different groups of aquatic phycomycetes have two major points of similarity: there is the overriding importance of the asexual cycle, even in those instances where a sexual cycle is thought to exist; secondly the incidence of propagule numbers can only be meaningfully discussed in relation to the fluctuations in the host or substrate availability. They differ in that the parasitic and commensal relationships have a longer active vegetative phase than that of the saprophytic relationship.

20.3 Models

In any discussion of the ecology of aquatic phycomycetes, the role of these fungi in the ecosystem must be placed in context with the roles of other fungi. For this purpose it is necessary to erect hypotheses or models of the system in order to define those parts which must be subjected to scientific analysis.

Dick (1971) and Park (1972 b) have independently produced fundamentally similar hypotheses based respectively upon their work in lakes and rivers. Both workers have stressed that there may be many different patterns of behaviour. Park has chosen to emphasize a classificatory approach in which the types of substrate are listed and in which the fungi are placed according to the form ('active' or 'inactive') from which development, if any, proceeds. The fungi are also categorized in terms of their ecological niches ('indwellers', 'migrant immigrants', 'versatile immigrants' and 'transients'). On the other hand, Dick has selected fewer, broader terms ('inhabitants', 'active aliens' and 'inactive aliens') emphasizing the potential versatility of any particular individual. This has the result that ecological classifications may sometimes refer to entire populations of a species, sometimes to clones and sometimes only to certain phases of the life cycle of a species. Such a system corresponds only approximately to specific identifications.

There is close equivalence between the 'indwellers' of Park and the 'inhabitants' of Dick. There is also considerable overlap between the 'immigrants' of Park and the 'active aliens' of Dick, but here the theoretical concepts have different bases. Park envisages a regular ('migrant immigrant') or haphazard ('versatile immigrant') alternation between aquatic and non-aquatic habitats occupied by a fungus species, while Dick regards the alien individual, although capable of differing and possibly considerable degrees of active growth in the aquatic environment, as essentially unable to maintain a potential inoculum in that environment. Park's concept is thus cyclic rather than unidirectional. There is also some possible confusion in terminology, since 'resident' as used by Park includes species whose principal habitat is extra-aquatic. The term 'transient' may also be misinterpreted as it is defined on the basis of 'occurrence without ecological significance'. Inactive 'aliens' which contribute organic carbon to the detritus are transient in time but not in space. They are thus neither fully transient nor without ecological significance.

Park also considers the questions of succession and periodicity. While his comments are of a very general nature and not in dispute, the relationships between occurrence and activity discussed above may well present problems in practice.

Figure 20.8 summarizes my hypothesis (Dick, 1971), and it is valuable to give one or two examples to indicate how it applies.

In the littoral zone, the interaction between the emergent and submerged communities immediately provides support for the concept of the 'active alien' unable to maintain a permanent potential inoculum in the alternate community, but nevertheless capable of growth and sporulation. The relatively high numbers of *Aplanopsis spinosa* recorded from submerged muds (Willoughby, 1965) despite indications from relative abundances (Dick, 1966) that this is not the principal ecological niche for this fungus, suggests that these counts may represent an 'alien' deposit in benthic muds. It may also be significant that littoral and lentic species which apparently depend upon more ephemeral spore forms were not recorded as frequently as expected (Willoughby, 1965). It is open to question whether the records of Zygomycetes (Willoughby, 1965; Dick, 1966) should also be placed in this category. Unfortunately there are no estimates for the gross mass of fungus material in the upper layer of benthic deposits from which one could estimate the passive ecological role of 'inactive aliens'.

In the lentic environment it has been possible to determine a number of separate types of 'inhabitant' and to suggest mechanisms by which sufficient potential inoculum is maintained, as with those 'inhabitants' associated in one way or another with insects.

Another type of model is that concerned with life form and life cycle. Dick (1968 b) illustrated a scheme, relating these factors with ecology, which has been supported by subsequent ecological studies (Dick, 1970, 1971). Recent cytogenetic considerations (Dick, 1972) have also lent weight to these relationships. For the lentic communities, the zoospore is the principal progagule, being produced in large numbers with minimal energy expenditure and capable of active dissemination. Many asexual cycles accompanied only infrequently by sexual cycles will be characteristic. In the littoral environment large oögonia with many oöspores are characteristic. The vegetative phase will tend to be longer on more substantial food bases. The larger detritus bound oögonia

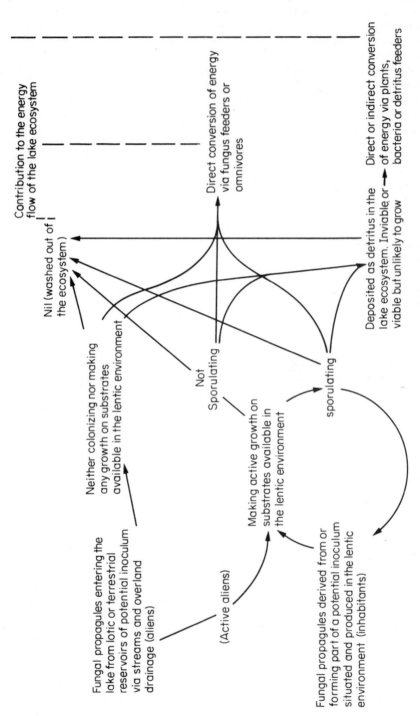

Fig. 20.8 (from Dick, 1971). Diagram summarizing the possible origins and roles of fungi in a lake ecosystem.

are not readily moved and the oöspores are essential for maintaining viability during adverse conditions (not only or necessarily lack of water). Zoospore production is more limited than in lentic environments and zoospores are important in magnifying the inoculum potential of the oöspores as the latter germinate. Because of the longer vegetative phase and variation in oöspore germination, the numbers of zoospores are unlikely to show diurnal fluctuations in this environment. The vegetative phase is more likely to culminate in oöspore formation.

In terrestrial environments the life form will change again to a limited, often more slender and shorter lived vegetative phase with a tendency to produce larger numbers of smaller resistant spores (either small oöspores or resistant encysted zoospores). The life cycle is found to show signs of conserving resources for resistant spores, such as a diminution in the capacity to produce zoospores and a tendency to agamospermous oöspore production.

These trends all indicate that morphologically similar life cycles must be considered in an ecological context in order to appreciate the relative significance of the different phases.

20.4   Conclusions

Our knowledge of the ecology of aquatic phycomycetes is incomplete. Many of the problems require solutions. Many of the problems still await adequate definition.

An interest in aquatic fungi can be traced back to early investigations of strange forms with flagellate spores. Gradually, annotated lists from local water systems began to be produced, and from such studies has come a knowledge of the fungi present. Such lists provide ecological information that is not only very difficult to collate, but is also of doubtful value for a general account since it provides more exceptions than rules. The advantage of this type of approach is that a lot of ground can be covered with relatively little labour. Unfortunately, ecological procedures require much labour and may still yield equivocal data.

It must be admitted that difficulties associated with the selection of methods are one of the sources of equivocal data. Of necessity, much of the work on aquatic fungal ecology has been descriptive and with some groups, notably the Mucorales in the Zygomycetes, much remains to be done. However, this group illustrates very well the central problem of methods of approach: how can data derived from spores be evaluated for ecological purposes? It is precisely this question which has also restricted advance in soil fungal ecology.

Descriptive ecology has been both qualitative and quantitative. While patterns of distribution have been described and confirmed, there is little understanding of the basic causes of this distribution. Is it related to higher plant root systems, to rhizospheres or pockets of microbiological activity? Or is it a random distribution inadequately analysed? Or is it a remnant of past activity of little relevance to any future vegetative growth? Likewise, fluctuations in numbers have been recorded, and while it is tempting to relate these to climatic conditions there are very few solid scientific data to support what amounts to more or less inspired guesswork. Always one returns to the ecological significance of the spore. On which species should one do germination studies? On which species should one study dormancy?

The work on correlations with physical factors has been thoroughly reviewed by Sparrow (1968) and there is little to add, except to emphasize that differences in the pH of the environment can have an overriding effect on distribution.

Ultimately, one must return to the identification of the mycelial state, its occurrence and its persistence in nature. Such studies must be autecological because of the time factors involved. A few such specialized studies have been carried out and these have revealed the need to understand the significance of every stage in the life cycle of the organism being investigated.

Models may summarize our current concepts of the ecology of aquatic fungi, but the balance between an opportunity and an individual, and the genotypic adaptation of a species to particular substrates is hard to gauge.

Until there is confidence in the significance of particular aspects of descriptive studies there can be only limited approaches to experimental ecology. For such studies to be worthwhile and successful, it is essential to possess a convenient quantitative method, a knowledge of the natural life form being sampled, a knowledge of the ecological life cycle, a knowledge of the natural substrates and a knowledge of the likely origin of both substrate and fungus. Without such information that environment cannot usefully be manipulated.

20.5   Appendix

I hereby propose a new subdivision of the fungi, the Heterokontimycotina to contain those fungi possessing, or thought to be derived from organisms which once possessed heterokont flagellation at some stage in their life cycle.

In this respect this subdivision corresponds directly, and may share common ancestry with, the heterokont algae (Phaeophyta, Xanthophyta, Chrysophyta and Bacillariophyta).

Heterokontimycotina
Subdivisionova fungorum flagellis heterokontis
included classes, orders and type families:

Oŏmycetes:	Saprolegniales, Saprolegniaceae
	Leptomitales, Leptomitaceae
	Peronosporales, Peronosporaceae
	Lagenidiales, Lagenidiaceae
	Labyrinthulales, Labyrinthulaceae
	Thraustochytriales, Thraustochytriaceae
Hyphochytriomycetes:	Hyphochytriales, Hyphochytriaceae

Acknowledgements

Acknowledgement is made to Blackwell Scientific Publications Limited, Cambridge University Press and the British Mycological Society for permission to reproduce previously published material by Dr. L. G. Willoughby and myself.

References

ALABI, R. O. (1971). 'Seasonal periodicity of Saprolegniaceae at Ibadan, Nigeria.' *Trans. Br. mycol. Soc.,* 56, 337-341.

APINIS, A. E. (1960). 'Über das Vorkommen niederer Pilze in alluvialen Boden bestimmter Pflanzengesellschaften.' *Mitt. Floristisch. Arbeitsgemeinschaft N.F.,* 8, 110-117.

APINIS, A. E. (1964). 'Concerning occurrence of phycomycetes in alluvial soils of certain pastures, marshes and swamps.' *Nova Hedwigia,* 8, 103-126.

ATKINSON, K. M. (1970). 'Dispersal of phytoplankton by ducks'. *Wildfowl,* 21, 110-111.

ATKINSON, K. M. (1971). 'Further experiments in dispersal of phytoplankton by birds.' *Wildfowl,* 22, 98-99.

BENEKE, E. S., and ROGERS, A. L. (1962). 'Aquatic phycomycetes isolated in the states of Minas Gerais, Sao Paulo, and Paraná, Brazil.' *Rickia,* Sao Paulo, 1, 181-193.

BENEKE, E. S., and ROGERS, A. L. (1970). 'Aquatic fungi of Parque Nacional do Itatiaia in the state of Rio de Janiero.' *Rickia,* Sao Paulo, 5, 51-64.

BEROQUI, M. E. (1969 a). 'Dos especies nuevas del género *Achlya* (Phycomycetes-Saprolegniales) de la Argentina.' *Darwiniana,* 15, 9-13.

BEROQUI, M. E. (1969 b). 'Una nueva especie de *Achlya* (Saprolegniales Phycomycetes).' *Kurtziana,* 5, 95-99.

BOOTH, T., and BARRETT, P. (1971). 'Occurrence and distribution of zoosporic fungi from Devon Island, Canadian Eastern Arctic.' *Can. J. Bot.,* 49, 359-369.

CANTER, H. M., and LUND, J. W. G. (1969). 'The parasitism of planktonic desmids by fungi.' *Öst. bot. Z.,* 116, 351-377.

CARVALHO, P. C. T. (1965). 'Ocorrência no Brasil de algumas espécies de *Pythium* Pringsheim de intrêsse à olericultura.' *Rickia,* Sao Paulo, 2, 89-106.

CLAUSZ, J. C. (1971). 'Periods of water mold activity in a lake.' *Abstracts, First International Mycological Congress,* Exeter. 16.

COLLINS, V. G., and WILLOUGHBY, L. G. (1962). 'The distribution of bacteria and fungal spores in Blelham Tarn with particular reference to an experimental overturn.' *Arch. Mikrobiol.,* 43, 294-307.

COUCH, J. N. (1939). 'Technic for collection, isolation and culture of chytrids.' *J. Elisha Mitchell scient. Soc.,* 55, 208-214.

COUCH, J. N. (1968). 'Sporangial germination of *Coelomomyces punctatus* and the conditions favoring the infection of *Anopheles quadrimaculatus* under laboratory conditions.' *Proceedings of the Joint U.S.–Japan Seminar on Microbial Control of Insect Pests,* Fukuoka, April 21-23, 1967, pp. 93-105.

COUCH, J. N. (1972). 'Mass production of *Coelomomyces,* a fungus that kills mosquitoes.' *Proc. Nat. Acad. USA,* 69, 2043-2047.

DAYAL, R., and JI, T. (1966). 'The occurrence and distribution of aquatic fungi in certain ponds of Varanasi.' *Hydrobiologia,* 27, 548-558.

DAYAL, R., and TANDON, R. N. (1962). 'Ecological studies of some aquatic phycomycetes.' *Hydrobiologia,* 20, 121-127.

DICK, M. W. (1962). 'The occurrence and distribution of Saprolegniaceae in certain soils of south-east England. II. Distribution within defined areas.' *J. Ecol.,* 50, 119-127.

DICK, M. W. (1963). 'The occurrence and distribution of Saprolegniaceae in certain soils of South-East England. III. Distribution in relation to pH and water content.' *J. Ecol.,* 51, 75-81.

DICK, M. W. (1964). 'A note on the occurrence and host range of *Aphanomyces parasiticus.'* *Trans. Br. mycol. Soc.,* 47, 627-628.

DICK, M. W. (1966). 'The Saprolegniaceae of the environs of Blelham Tarn: sampling techniques and the estimation of propagule numbers.' *J. gen. Microbiol.,* 42, 257-282.

DICK, M. W. (1968 a). *'Saprolegnia parasitica* Coker in estuaries.' *Nature,* 217; 875.

DICK, M. W. (1968 b). 'Considerations of the role of water on the taxonomy and ecology of the filamentous biflagellate fungi in littoral zones.' *Veröff. Inst. Meeresforsch. Bremerh.,* 3, 27-28.

DICK, M. W; (1969 a). 'Morphology and Taxonomy of the Oomycetes, with special reference to Saprolegniaceae, Leptomitaceae and Pythiaceae. I. Sexual reproduction.' *New Phytol.,* 68, 751-775.

DICK, M. W. (1969 b). 'The *Scoliolegnia asterophora* aggregate, formerly *Saprolegnia asterophora* de Bary (Oömycetes).' *J. Linn. Soc. Bot.,* 62, 255-266.

DICK, M. W. (1970). 'Saprolegniaceae on insect exuviae.' *Trans Br. mycol. Soc.,* 55, 449-458.

DICK, M. W. (1971). 'The ecology of Saprolegniaceae in lentic and littoral muds with a general theory of fungi in the lake ecosystem.' *J. gen. Microbiol.,* 65, 325-337.

DICK, M. W. (1972). 'Morphology and taxonomy of the Oömycetes, with special reference to Saprolegniaceae, Leptomitaceae and Pythiaceae. II. Cytogenetic systems.' *New Phytol.,* 71, 1151-1159.

DICK, M. W., and NEWBY, H. V. (1961). 'The occurrence and distribution of Saprolegniaceae in certain soils of south-east England. I. Occurrence.' *J. Ecol.,* 49, 403-419.

ELLIOTT, R. F. (1967). 'Morphological variation in New Zealand Saprolegniaceae 1. *Achlya caroliniana* Coker and *A. flagellata* Coker.' *NZ J. Bot.* 5, 418-423.

ELLIOTT, R. F. (1968). 'Morphological variation in New Zealand Saprolegniaceae 2. *Saprolegnia terrestris* Cookson and *S. australis* sp. nov.' *NZ J. Bot.,* 6, 94-105.

EMERSON, R. (1958). 'Mycological organisation.' *Mycologia,* 50, 589-621.

EMERSON, R., and HELD, A. A. (1969). *'Aqualinderella fermentans* gen. et sp. n., a phycomycete adapted to stagnant waters. II. Isolation, cultural characteristics, and gas relations.' *Am. J. Bot.,* 56, 1103-1120.

FURTADO, J. S. (1965). 'A new aquatic fungus, *Achlya benekei* sp. nov.' *Rickia,* Sao Paulo, 2, 121-128.

GAERTNER, A. M., and SPARROW, F. K. (1966). 'A preliminary study of aquatic phycomycetes in the lakes of the Huron Mountains, Michigan.' *Veröff. Inst. Meeresforsch. Bremerh.,* 10, 93-106.

GREEN, B. R., and DICK, M. W. (1972). 'DNA base composition and the taxonomy of oömycetes.' *Can. J. Microbiol.,* 18, 963-968.

HÖHNK, W. (1935). 'Saprolegniales und Monoblepharidales aus der umgebung Bremens, mit besonderer Berücksichtigung der Oekologie der Saprolegniaceae.' *Abh. Naturwiss. vereins Bremen,* 29, 207-237.

HUGHES, G. C. (1962). 'Seasonal periodicity of the Saprolegniaceae in the south-eastern United States.' *Trans. Br. mycol. Soc.,* 45, 519-531.

JEFFREY, J. M., and WILLOUGHBY, L. G. (1964). 'A note on the distribution of *Allomyces* in Australia.' *Nova Hedwigia,* 7, 507-515.

JI, T. (1970). 'Studies in aquatic fungi of Varanasi VI. Taxonomy and distribution of some peculiar isolated species of *Allomyces.'* *Acta Mycologica,* 6, 59-69.

JI, T., and DAYAL, R. (1966). 'The occurrence and distribution of reproductive spores of Saprolegniales in certain ponds of Varanasi.' *Nova Hedwigia,* 12, 509-517.

JOHANNES, H. (1957). 'Zur Ökologie der Saprolegniaceen.' *Mitt. thüring. bot. Gesellsch.*, 1, 90-111.

JOHNSON, T. W. (1951). 'A new *Mindeniella* from submerged rosaceous fruits.' *Am. J. Bot.* 38, 74-78.

JOHNSON, T. W. (1956). '*The genus* Achlya: *Morphology and Taxonomy.*' University of Michigan Press. Ann Arbor. 180 pp.

KARLING, J. S. (1964 a). 'Indian anisochytrids.' *Sydowia,* 17, 193-196.

KARLING, J. S. (1964 b). 'Indian chytrids I. Eucarpic monocentric species.' *Sydowia,* 17, 285-296.

KARLING, J. S. (1964 c). 'Indian chytrids II. *Olpidium indianum* sp. nov.' *Sydowia,* 17, 302-307.

KARLING, J. S. (1964 d). 'Indian chytrids III. Species of *Rhizophlyctis* isolated on human fibrin film.' *Mycopath. Mycol. appl.,* 23, 215-222.

KARLING, J. S. (1965). 'Some zoosporic fungi of New Zealand. 1.' *Sydowia,* 19, 213-226.

KARLING, J. S. (1966). 'The chytrids of India with a supplement of other zoosporic fungi.' *Beih. Sydowia,* 6, 1-125.

KARLING, J. S. (1967 a). 'Some zoosporic fungi of New Zealand. II. Synchytriaceae.' *Sydowia,* 20, 51-66.

KARLING, J. S. (1967 b). 'Some zoosporic fungi of New Zealand. III. *Phlyctidium, Rhizophydium, Septosperma,* and *Podochytrium.*' *Sydowia,* 20, 74-85.

KARLING, J. S. (1967 c). 'Some zoosporic fungi of New Zealand. IV. *Polyphlyctis* gen. nov., *Phlyctochytrium* and *Rhizophidium.*' *Sydowia,* 20, 86-95.

KARLING, J. S. (1967 d). 'Some zoosporic fungi of New Zealand. V. Species of *Asterophlyctis, Obelidium, Rhizoclosmatium, Siphonaria* and *Rhizophlyctis.*' *Sydowia,* 20, 96-108.

KARLING, J. S. (1967 e). 'Some zoosporic fungi of New Zealand. VI. *Entophlyctis, Diplophlyctis, Nephrochytrium* and *Endochytrium.*' *Sydowia,* 20, 109-118.

KARLING, J. S. (1967 f). 'Some zoosporic fungi of New Zealand. VII. Additional monocentric operculate species.' *Sydowia,* 20, 119-128.

KARLING, J. S. (1967 g). 'Some zoosporic fungi of New Zealand. VIII. Cladochytriaceae and Physodermataceae.' *Sydowia,* 20, 129-136.

KARLING, J. S. (1967 h). 'Some zoosporic fungi of New Zealand. IX. Hyphochytridiales or Anisochytridiales.' *Sydowia,* 20, 137-143.

KARLING, J. S. (1967 i). 'Some zoosporic fungi of New Zealand. X. Blastocladiales.' *Sydowia,* 20, 144-150.

KARLING, J. S. (1967 j). 'Some zoosporic fungi of New Zealand. XI. Plasmodiophorales.' *Sydowia,* 20, 151-156.

KARLING, J. S. (1968 a). 'Some zoosporic fungi of New Zealand. XII. Olpidiopsidaceae, Sirolpidiaceae and Lagenidiaceae.' *Sydowia,* 20, 190-199.

KARLING, J. S. (1968 b). 'Some zoosporic fungi of New Zealand. XIII. Thraustochytriaceae, Saprolegniaceae and Pythiaceae.' *Sydowia,* 20, 226-234.

KARLING, J. S. (1968 c). 'Zoosporic fungi of Oceania. I. Hyphochytriaceae.' *J. Elisha Mitchell scient. Soc.,* 84, 166-178.

KARLING, J. S. (1968 d). 'Zoosporic fungi of Oceania. II. Two saprophytic species of *Aphanomycopsis.*' *Mycologia,* 60, 271-284.

KARLING, J. S. (1968 e). 'Zoosporic fungi of Oceania. III. Monocentric chytrids.' *Arch. Mikrobiol.,* 61, 112-127.

KARLING, J. S. (1969). 'Zoosporic fungi of Oceania. IV. Additional Monocentric chytrids.' *Mycopath. Mycol. appl.,* 36, 165-178.

KARLING, J. S. (1970). 'Some zoosporic fungi of New Zealand. XIV. Additional species.' *Arch. Mikrobiol.*, 70, 266-287.

MASTERS, M. J. (1971). 'The ecology of *Chytridium deltanum* and other fungus parasites on *Oocystis* spp.' *Can. J. Bot.*, 49, 75-87.

MILANEZ, A. I. (1965 a). *'Myzocytium megastomum* de Wild. in Sâo Paulo, Brazil.' *Rickia,* Sâo Paulo, 2, 153-158.

MILANEZ, A. I. (1965 b). *'Achlya braziliensis,* a new species from Brazil.' *Rickia,* Sâo Paulo, 2, 183-189.

MILANEZ, A. I. (1967). 'A study of the aquatic "phycomycetes" of the Gull Lake area in Michigan.' *Dissert. Abstr.,* 28.

MILANEZ, A. I. (1968). 'Aquatic fungi of the "cerrado" region of Sâo Paulo state. I. First results.' *Rickia,* Sâo Paulo, 3, 97-109.

MILANEZ, A. I. (1969). 'Occurrence of *Achlya radiosa* in the Americas.' *Rickia,* Sâo Paulo, 4, 41-46.

MILANEZ, A. I. (1970). 'Contributions to the knowledge of aquatic phycomycetes of Sâo Paulo state. I. Oömycetes from west region.' *Rickia,* Sâo Paulo, 5, 23-43.

MILANEZ, A. I., and VAL, F. (1969). 'Occurrence of *Petersenia irregulare* (H. E. Petersen) Sparrow in Brazil.' *Rickia,* Sâo Paulo, 4, 75-82.

MORUZI, C., and TOMA, N. (1968 a). 'Contributii la studiul micoflorei acvatice din complexul lacustru crapina—Jijila.' *Microbiologia,* 1, 407-413.

MORUZI, C., and TOMA, N. (1968 b). 'Contribution à la connaissance des Saprolégniées des bassins aquatiques du Jardin botanique de Bucarest.' *Rev. Roum. Biologie-Botanique,* 13.

MOSS, S. T. (1972). 'Occurrence, cell structure and taxonomy of the Trichomycetes, with special reference to electron microscope studies of *Stachylina.'* Ph.D. Thesis, University of Reading.

OOSTING, H. J. (1956). *'The study of Plant Communities: An Introduction to Plant Ecology.'* San Francisco, California; Freeman.

PARK, D. (1972 a). 'Methods of detecting fungi in organic detritus in water.' *Trans. Br. mycol. Soc.,* 58, 281-290.

PARK, D. (1972 b). 'On the ecology of heterotrophic micro-organisms in freshwater.' *Trans. Br. mycol. Soc.,* 58, 291-299.

PATERSON, R. A. (1967). 'Benthic and planktonic phycomycetes from Northern Michigan.' *Mycologia,* 59, 405-416.

PERROTT, P. E. (1960). 'The ecology of some aquatic phycomycetes.' *Trans. Br. mycol. Soc.,* 43, 19-30.

PILLAI, J. S. (1971). *'Coelomomyces opifexi* Pillai et Smith. Coelomomycetaceae: Blastocladiales. I. Its distribution and the ecology of infection pools in New Zealand.' *Hydrobiologia,* 38, 425-436.

PILLAI, J. S., and O 'LOUGHLIN, I. H. (1972). *'Coclomomyces opifexi* Pillai et Smith. Coelomomycetaceae: Blastocladiales. II. Experiments in sporangial germination.' *Hydrobiologia,* 40, 77-86.

PROCTOR, V. W., MALONE, C. R., and DEVLAMING, V. L. (1967). 'Dispersal of aquatic organisms: viability of disseminules recovered from the intestinal tract of captive killdeer.' *Ecology,* 48, 672-676.

ROGERS, A. L., and BENEKE, E. S. (1962). 'Two new species of *Achlya* in Brazil.' *Rickia,* Sâo Paulo, 1, 243-249.

ROGERS, A. L., MILANEZ, A. I., and BENEKE, E. S. (1970). 'Additional aquatic fungi from Sâo Paulo State.' *Rickia,* Sâo Paulo, 5, 93-110.

ROBERTS, R. E. (1963). 'A study of the distribution of certain members of the Saprolegniales.' *Trans. Br. mycol. Soc.,* 46, 213-224.

SCOTT, W. W., and WARREN, C. O. (1964). 'Studies of the host range and chemical control of fungi associated with diseased tropical fish.' *Va. Agri. Exp. Sta. Bulletin,* 171, 1-24.

SINGH, U. P., and PAVGI, M. S. (1971). 'A new species of *Cladochytrium* from India.' *Hydrobiologia,* 37, 565-568.

SPARROW, F. K. (1943). *The aquatic Phycomycetes, exclusive of the Saprolegniaceae and* Pythium. University of Michigan Press. Ann Arbor. 785 pp.

SPARROW, F. K. (1960). *'Aquatic Phycomycetes* (2nd revised edition).' University of Michigan Press. Ann Arbor. 1187 pp.

SPARROW, F. K. (1968). 'Ecology of Freshwater Fungi.' In *'The Fungi, an Advanced Treatise.'* (Eds. G. C. Ainsworth and A. S. Sussman) Academic Press, London and New York, vol. 3, 41-93.

SRIVASTAVA, G. C. (1964). 'Observations on Indian aquatic fungi. II. Occurrence of *Olpidiopsis varians* Shanor at Gorakhpur.' *Indian Phytopathol.,* 17, 249-253.

SRIVASTAVA, G. C. (1966). 'The host range of four species of *Olpidiopsis.'* *Trans. Br. mycol. Soc.,* 49, 69-72.

SRIVASTAVA, G. C. (1967 a). 'Some species of Saprolegniaceae collected from Gorakhpur, India.' *Hydrobiologia,* 30, 281-292.

SRIVASTAVA, G. C. (1967 b). 'Ecological studies on some aquatic fungi of Gorakhpur, India.' *Hydrobiologia,* 30, 385-404.

SRIVASTAVA, G. C., and BHARGAVA, K. S. (1963). 'Observations on Indian aquatic fungi I. Three species of *Olpidiopsis* from Gorakhpur.' *Indian Phytopathol.,* 16, 271-274.

STEWART, K. W., and SCHLICHTING, H. E. (1966). 'Dispersal of algae and protozoa by selected aquatic insects.' *J. Ecol.,* 54, 551-562.

STOLL, K. (1936). 'Saprolegniineen aus der Umgebung von Greifswald.' *Mitt. Naturw. Ver Neuvorpommern und Rügen,* 63, 20-40.

ULKEN, A., and SPARROW, F. K. (1968). 'Estimation of Chytrid Propagules in Douglas Lake by the MPN = Pollen grain method.' *Veröff. Inst. Meeresforsch. Bremerh.,* 11, 83-88.

UNESTAM, T., and WEISS, D. W. (1970). 'The host—parasite relationship between freshwater crayfish and crayfish disease fungus *Aphanomyces astaci*: Responses to infection by a susceptible and a resistant species.' *J. gen. Microbiol.,* 60, 77-90.

UMPHLETT, C. J. (1968). 'Ecology of *Coelomomyces* infections of mosquito larvae.' *J. Elisha Mitchell scient. Soc.,* 84, 108-114.

UMPHLETT, C. J. (1970). 'Infection levels of *Coelomomyces punctatus,* an aquatic fungus parasite, in a natural population of the common malaria mosquito, *Anopheles quadrimaculatus.'* *J. Invert. Pathology,* 15, 299-305.

WILLOUGHBY, L. G. (1960). 'The occurrence of some lower fungi (Chytridiales) in lake muds and soil, with special reference to a site at Esthwaite.' In *The Ecology of Soil Fungi* (Eds. D. S. Parkinson and J. S. Waid) University of Liverpool Press, 29-32.

WILLOUGHBY, L. G. (1961). 'The ecology of some lower fungi at Esthwaite Water.' *Trans. Br. mycol. Soc.,* 44, 305-332.

WILLOUGHBY, L. G. (1962). 'The occurrence and distribution of reproductive spores of Saprolegniales in fresh water.' *J. Ecol.,* 50, 733-759.

WILLOUGHBY, L. G. (1965). 'Some observations on the location of sites of fungal activity at Blelham Tarn.' *Hydrobiologia,* 25, 352-356.

WILLOUGHBY, L. G., and COLLINS, V. G. (1966). 'A study of the distribution of fungal spores and bacteria in Blelham Tarn and its associated streams.' *Nova Hedwigia,* 12, 150-171.

ZIEGLER, A. W. (1948). 'A comparative study of zygote germination in the Saprolegniaceae.' *J. Elisha Mitchell scient. Soc.,* 64, 13-40.

21 The Physiology of the Lower Freshwater Fungi

FRANK GLEASON

21.1 Introduction

The lower fungi include a very heterogeneous array of micro-organisms, and very little is known about the physiology of the vast majority of them. These fungi are mostly saprophytes, although a large number of them are parasites on plant, animal or microbial hosts. In general they can be grown readily in axenic culture in the laboratory and are therefore quite suitable for experimentation. However, most of the recent physiological investigations have concentrated on only a few genera, such as *Allomyces*, *Blastocladiella*, *Achlya*, *Pythium* and *Phytophthora*.

This chapter will be restricted to selected research topics on the physiology of freshwater members of the Chrytridiomycetes and Oömycetes. The general topics to be discussed are (1) catabolism, (2) anabolism, (3) the cell wall and (4) growth and development.

21.2 Catabolism

21.2.1 Nutrition

Nutrition has been a very popular subject for investigation in water moulds for a long time. The early literature was reviewed thoroughly by Cantino (1950, 1955) and more recent literature by Cantino (1966) and Cantino and Turian (1959). Among the main considerations in these papers was the significance of certain nutritional parameters to phylogeny. Some of their general statements concerning the physiology of water moulds have been corroborated by numerous investigations during the past decade

---

During the past two decades the physiology of aquatic fungi has indeed come of age and research in this area has become very fashionable. Most of the background necessary for recent physiological investigations was established prior to 1950, and the importance of these early experiments should not be ignored (see Cantino, 1950 and Emerson, 1950).

while others need slight modification. A brief attempt to give the reader a general view of nutritional capacities of Chytridiomycetes and Oömycetes will be made in this review.

Vitamin Requirements   Most aquatic fungi are autotrophic for vitamins or require only thiamin. There can often be considerable variation in the requirements for thiamin in closely related fungi. The usefulness of the thiamin requirement in classification has been discussed by Ridings *et al.* (1969). Rarely other vitamins may be necessary, for example: biotin, *p*-amino benzoate and nicotinamide (Cantino, 1955; Unestam, 1966a).

Nitrogen Requirements   The commonly used nitrogen sources can be subdivided into three groups for simplification: amino nitrogen, ammonium nitrogen and nitrate nitrogen. The requirements vary considerably in both Chytridiomycetes and Oömycetes. Some members of the Chytridiales (Goldstein, 1960 a, 1961; Willoughby, 1962; Murray and Lovett, 1966; Barr, 1969, 1970), Monoblepharidales (Unestam, 1966 a) and Peronosporales (Roncadori, 1965; Kraft and Erwin, 1967) can utilize ammonium and nitrate nitrogen. Some members of the latter orders and the Blastocladiales (Nolan, 1969), Saprolegniales (Papavizas and Davey, 1960 a; Dayal, 1961 a; Unestam, 1965; Cantino, 1955) and Leptomitales (Gleason, 1968 a; Gleason and Stuart, 1970) can utilize ammonium but not nitrate nitrogen. Some aquatic fungi cannot use any known source of inorganic nitrogen for example, *Catenaria* (Blastocladiales) (Nolan, 1969) and *Sapromyces* (Leptomitales) (Golueke, 1957; Gleason and Stuart, 1970). Glutamic acid or asparagine are very often selected as sources of amino nitrogen, but a number of other amino acids can also be adequate nitrogen sources (Nolan, 1969; Golueke, 1957). It is interesting to note that addition of lysine stimulated the growth of *Catenaria* when asparagine was the only other nitrogen source (Nolan, 1969). Usually glutamic acid or asparagine permit more rapid growth than inorganic sources of nitrogen.

Sulphur Requirements   Inorganic sulphur, usually sulphate, provides an adequate source of sulphur for the Chytridiales (Cantino, 1955), Monoblepharidales (Unestam, 1966 a), Leptomitales (Gleason, 1968 a), and Peronosporales (Fothergill and Hide, 1962; Cantino, 1955). Cantino (1950, 1955) and Cantino and Turian (1959) stated that all members of the Blastocladiales and Saprolegniales cannot utilize sulphate as a source of sulphur. The recent studies of Nolan (1970 a), Dayal (1961 b), Papavizas and Davey (1960 a), and Unestam (1965) substantiate this generalization. Methionine is the most commonly employed sulphur source for fungi in the latter two orders. Cysteine and elemental sulphur have been shown to be effective sulphur sources for *Aphanomyces* (Papavizas and Davey, 1960 a; Unestam, 1965) and a variety of reduced sulphur sources will support the growth of *Catenaria* (Nolan, 1970 a).

Carbon Requirements   The fact that there is enormous variation in the range of substrates utilized by water moulds is borne out by numerous recent investigations (Barksdale, 1962; Barr, 1969, 1970; Faro, 1971; Gleason, 1968 a; Gleason *et al.*, 1970 a, b; Goldstein, 1960 a, b, 1961; Held, 1970; Nolan, 1970 b; Papavizas and Ayers, 1964; Powell *et al.*, 1972; Roncadori, 1965; Unestam, 1965, 1966 a; Willoughby, 1962, 1969; and Zehender and Böck, 1964). Some fungi such as *Saprolegnia* can use a large number of carbon sources (Gleason *et al.*, 1970 a) while other fungi such as *Aphanomyces astaci* Schikora (Unestam, 1965) and *Karlingia* (Murray and Lovett, 1966) can use only a very few. A number of substrates which are known to support growth of one or more aquatic fungi as single sources of carbon and energy are listed below. There are undoubtedly numerous others which have not been reported.

Carbohydrates: glucose, fructose, mannose, galactose, xylose, arabinose, maltose, sucrose, cellobiose, lactose, trehalose, melibiose, starch, glycogen, dextrin, cellulose, chitin, glycerol, sorbitol, arabitol and inositol.
Acids: acetate, pyruvate, succinate, malate, fumarate, lactate, butyrate and valate.
Amino acids: alanine, glutamate, glutamine, leucine, proline, hydroxyproline, ornithine, arginine, aspartate, asparagine, phenylalanine, serine and lysine.
Proteins: gelatin, casein and keratin.

Other Growth Factors   Emerson and Weston (1967), Emerson and Held (1969), and Held (1970) demonstrated the requirement for a high level of atmospheric carbon dioxide (5 to 20%) for good growth of *Aqualinderella fermentans* Emerson and Weston. Also the growth of *Blastocladia* is markedly stimulated by a high level of atmospheric carbon dioxide (Held *et al.,* 1969). These are the only well documented cases of water moulds which require carbon dioxide for growth. However, Lynch and Calvin (1952) and Cantino and Horenstein (1956) have shown that *Allomyces, Blastocladia* and *Blastocladiella* fix carbon dioxide. The requirement for carbon dioxide in *Aqualinderella* can be partially replaced by organic acids, such as succinate (Emerson and Held, 1969; Held, 1970). *Aqualinderella* also has a lipid requirement (Held, 1970). The complex mixture of lipids in wheat germ oil and yeast extract normally added to the growth media could be replaced by cholesterol and oleic acid. Finally, a requirement for *N*-acetyl glucosamine for growth of *Karlingia asterocysta* Karling an obligate chitinophile, on glucose was discovered by Murray and Lovett (1966). Glucose plus *N*-acetyl glucosamine or chitin seemed to be the only possible substrates for this fungus.

Requirement for Oxygen   Fungi generally are thought to be highly aerobic, but in both the Chytridiomycetes—and Oomycetes there are a number which are able to ferment sugars to lactic acid (Cantino, 1955; Gleason and Price, 1969) and which contain high levels of activity of lactate dehydrogenase in their cytoplasm. D(-)lactate dehydrogenase activity has been detected in *Allomyces, Blastocladia, Blastocladiella, Achlya, Apodachlya, Aphanomyces, Araiospora, Aqualinderella, Pythium, Phytophthora, Rhipidium, Saprolegnia, Sapromyces and Thraustotheca* (Gleason, 1972; Bianchi *et al.,* 1971; Lé John, 1971; Gleason and Price, 1969). The machinery for production of energy by lactic acid fermentation in the absence of oxygen is therefore present in certain members of the Chytridiomycetes and Oömycetes. Since it is possible for these fungi to synthesize ATP in the absence of oxygen, one might expect growth under those conditions; and yet only two aquatic fungi, *Blastocladia ramosa* Thaxter and *Aqualinderella fermentans,* grow well under anaerobic conditions (Held *et al.,* 1969). *Sapromyces elongatus* (Cornu) Coker and *Mindeniella spinospora* Kanouse grow slowly under anaerobic conditions (Gleason, 1968 a). In contrast *Leptomitus lacteus* (Roth) Agardh requires efficient aeration and is unable to ferment sugars (Gleason, 1968 a). The rest of the Chytridiomycetes and Oomycetes span the range from obligately aerobic to facultatively fermentative at quite low oxygen tensions. One possible explanation for these phenomena is as follows, but it remains to be substantiated. Although many aquatic fungi can satisfy their energy requirements by lactic acid fermentation, oxygen is necessary for the synthesis of many constituents of the cell, such as unsaturated fatty acids and steroids. Normally the plasma membrane is impermeable to these constituents so that they cannot be supplied from the growth medium under anaerobic conditions. The membranes of *Aqualinderella fermentans* and *Blastocladiella ramosa* have become more permeable during the course of evolution in order to adapt to an anaerobic environment.

The primary purpose of most nutritional studies has been to develop synthetic media for optimal growth which are relatively easy to prepare. However, some significant work has been done with mixtures of substrates. In nature, fungi are confronted with complex mixtures of utilizable substrates in the media, not just a single substrate for carbon and energy. The growth of *Phytophthora* on vegetable oils and other lipids has recently been investigated by Hendrix *et al.* (1966) and Hendrix and Apple (1964). *Leptomitus* (Gleason, 1968 a) and *Saprolegnia* (Gleason, 1973) grow well on mixtures of amino acids. The effect of one component of a mixture on growth of a second component has been the subject of several investigations. In *Allomyces,* Sistrom and Machlis (1955) observed that small amounts of glucose added to the growth medium stimulated utilization of fructose and mannose by cutting the length of the lag phase. Machlis (1957) found that the amino acids asparagine, arginine, citruline, ornithine, glutamic acid and proline also stimulated mannose utilization by *Allomyces.* Papavizas and Ayers (1964) studied the growth of *Aphanomyces* on mixtures of glucose, mannose and galactose. Good growth is observed with glucose as a single course of carbon and poor growth with either mannose or galactose. The growth obtained on mixtures of mannose and galactose, mannose and glucose, and galactose and glucose was comparable to that on glucose with the same total amount of sugar in each mixture. In *Apodachlya* small amounts of methionine inhibited growth on medium containing glutamic acid as a carbon source (Gleason and Stuart, 1970). Finally, a mixture of leucine and glucose permits better growth than either of these two carbon sources used singly by *Leptomitus* (Gleason, 1968 a).

Most nutritional studies are concerned with growth of the vegetative cells. However, Faro (1971) and Barksdale (1962) have shown that some of the substrates which support vegetative growth do not permit sexual reproduction in *Achlya.* Child *et al.* (1969 a) tested a number of carbon and nitrogen sources for their ability to support both growth and sexual reproduction in *Pythium*, and reached the same conclusions as Faro (1971) and Barksdale (1962). Child *et al.* (1969 a) also varied the carbon-nitrogen ratio. Furthermore, Leal *et al.* (1967) were concerned with the relation of the carbon-nitrogen ratio in the medium to sexual reproduction in *Phytophthora.* The effect of different nitrogen and sulphur sources on formation of oögonia was investigated by Papavizas and Davey (1960 b) and Davey and Papavizas (1962) in *Aphanomyces euteiches* Dreschler. The role of sterols in sexual reproduction in the Peronosporales will be discussed later.

Finally there has been some work on catabolism of substrates by zoospores. Motile and germinating zoospores of *Phytophthora* catabolized C^{14}-labelled glucose, acetate, serine, glutamate and asparagine (Barash *et al.,* 1965).

Many water moulds are able to hydrolyse soluble and insoluble macromolecules such as starch, glycogen, cellulose, chitin, pectins, gelatin, casein and keratin (Cantino, 1950, 1955) by excreting extracellular enzymes. The ability to excrete proteases, chitinases, cellulases and pectinases can be detected on agar media (Gleason, 1968 a; Unestam, 1966 b). Not much is known about the chemical and physical properties of these enzymes in general. Recently, two extracellular enzymes, endopolygalacturonase (Ayers *et al.,* 1969) and chitinase (Unestam, 1968), have been partially characterized from *Aphanomyces.* The cellulase found in *Achlya* by Thomas and Mullins (1969) appears to act on the cell wall rather than on extracellular cellulose. *Pythium* also can synthesize cellulase (Sietsma and Haskins, 1968).

21.2.2 Respiration and Intermediary Metabolism

As previously mentioned, many Chytridiomycetes and Oömycetes ferment sugars to lactic acid. The isomer of lactic acid produced is D(-) (Gleason and Price, 1969). D(-) lactate dehydrogenases from *Pythium* (Lê John, 1971), *Sapromyces* (Gleason, 1972; Gleason and Price, 1969) and *Allomyces* (Purohit and Turian, 1972; Bianchi *et al.,* 1971) have been isolated and compared with lactate dehydrogenases from other sources. There are considerable differences in chemical, physical and kinetic properties of the lactate dehydrogenases from Oömycetes (Gleason, 1972, Lé John, 1971). In batch culture, *Blastocladiella* and *Sapromyces* convert glucose to lactic acid and then reassimilate the lactic acid (Cantino, 1965; Gleason, 1968 a). *Mindeniella* lacks the enzymatic machinery to reassimilate lactic acid once it is released into the medium (Gleason, 1968 a). The rate of production of lactic acid depends upon the aeration (Kobr and Turian, 1967; Gleason, 1968 a) since aeration decreases the rate of glycolysis. It also depends upon the stage of development (Kobr and Turian, 1967; Cantino and Lovett, 1960). In *Allomyces* differentiation requires adequate aeration; furthermore, aeration promotes differentiation, i.e. the formation of gametangia (Kobr and Turian, 1967). In unaerated cultures where no differentiation occurs, the lactate dehydrogenase activity is much higher than in aerated cultures (Bianchi *et al.,* 1971). Sexual reproduction is accompanied by a shift in respiratory pattern from a glycolytic to an oxidative one in *Allomyces*. It is interesting that the activity of lactate dehydrogenase in the male differentiated strain is twice that in the female differentiated strain in aerated cultures (Bianchi *et al.,* 1971). Also the male differentiated strain produces more lactic acid than the female strain (Turian, 1960). Finally, the rate of production of lactic acid undoubtedly is influenced by sugar concentration in water moulds.

Sugars can also be catabolized by the Embden-Meyerhof-Parmas pathway and the tricarboxylic acid cycle with the uptake of oxygen. Bonner and Machlis (1957) and Cantino and Horenstein (1956) demonstrated the presence of the tricarboxylic acid pathway using C^{14}-labelled glucose in *Allomyces* and *Blastocladiella* respectively. Enzymes from these pathways were found to be active in *Achlya* (Warren and Mullins, 1969) and in *Blastocladiella* (Cantino and Hyatt, 1953; Cantino, 1956). The acids of the tricarboxylic acid cycle can serve as substrates for respiration in isolated mitochondria from *Allomyces* (Bonner and Machlis, 1957) and *Saprolegnia* (Gleason, unpublished data). Normally one would expect to find an active tricarboxylic cycle in aerobic aquatic fungi. However, the activities of certain of the enzymes of the tricarboxylic acid cycle are repressed during formation of resistant sporangia in *Blastocladiella* (Cantino and Horenstein, 1955). Cantino and Hyatt (1953) isolated a mutant of *Blastocladiella* which lacks two enzymes in the tricarboxylic acid cycle. One enzyme closely associated with the tricarboxylic acid cycle, glutamate dehydrogenase, has been the subject of investigations on regulation (Lé John, 1968; Lé John and Stevenson, 1970; Lé John *et al.,* 1969; Price and Gleason, 1972; Sanner, 1971, 1972). The activity of glutamic dehydrogenase is controlled by allosteric effectors (ATP, GTP, *p*-enolpyruvate, etc.). Induction of glutamate dehydrogenase was studied by Price and Gleason (1972) in *Apodachlya*. With glucose as the sole carbon source, the synthesis of this enzyme was repressed; whereas glutamate, proline, alanine or ornithine plus aspartate as sole carbon sources induced synthesis.

The endogenous respiration rate of many fungi is considered to be quite high due to catabolism of stored substrates. In Chytridiomycetes and Oömycetes the Q_{O_2} is commonly between 20 and 30. However, the endogenous respiration rate is a function of age (Warren and Mullins, 1969; Hine, 1965; Cantino and Lovett, 1960; McCurdy and Cantino, 1960; Turian and Chordat, 1959; Bonner and Machlis, 1957). It is also a function of the state of development (Cantino and Lovett, 1960; Turian and Chordat, 1959). In *Allomyces,* for example, the respiratory activity increases during cleavage of gametangia into gametes. The respiratory activity of the sporophyte is 50% greater than the gametophyte (Turian and Chodat, 1959). In *Blastocladiella* the Q_{O_2} of the OC plants is much greater than that of RS plants (Cantino and Lovett, 1960; McCurdy and Cantino, 1960). The respiratory activity of a zoospore is usually very high and as the mycelium which develops from it ages, the activity decreases. The endogenous respiration rate may not change with addition of exogenous substances, but in starved cells the rate is often greatly stimulated (Unestam and Gleason, 1968; Hine, 1965; Bonner and Machlis, 1957). The respiration rate of many lower fungi is inhibited by sodium fluoroacetate, diphenylamine, dinitrophenol, antimycin A, cyanide and azide (Gleason and Unestam, 1968 a; Unestam and Gleason, 1968). One exception to the rule is *Saprolegnia* sp. Young mycelium is sensitive to antimycin A and cyanide, while old mycelium is completely insenstive to these inhibitors (Gleason, 1974; Unestam and Gleason, 1968).

The cytochrome systems of Chytridiomycetes and Oömycetes were examined by means of reduced-minus-oxidized difference spectra (Gleason, 1968 b; Gleason and Unestam, 1968 a and b; Unestam and Gleason, 1968). All of these fungi have a c-type cytochrome with an absorption maximum at 551 mμ and a b-type cytochrome at 564 mμ. Additional b-type cytochromes are found at approximately 560 mμ in the Chytridiomycetes and at 557 mμ in the Oömycetes. The Chytridiomycetes have a-type cytochromes at 606 mμ (Blastocladiales) or at 609 mμ (Monoblepharidales), and the Oomycetes have an a-type cytochrome at 605 mμ. Horgen and Griffin (1969) found cytochrome oxidase present in all developmental stages of *Blastocladiella* examined; zoospores, OC plants, and RS plants. Factors which may stimulate fermentation such as poor aeration, high partial pressure of carbon dioxide, and high levels of sugar in the growth medium may also cause the repression of synthesis of the machinery for oxidative energy production. These correlations need to be clarified.

Turian et al. (1969) isolated acridine treated male strains of *Allomyces arbusculus* Butler which were respiratory deficient; i.e. the rate of endogenous respiration and activities of succinate dehydrogenase and cytochrome oxidase were reduced. The mitochondria from one acridine treated male strain were poorly developed. Respiratory function is also altered when *Pythium ultimum* Trow is grown in the presence of chloramphenicol (Marchant and Smith, 1968). The effects of chloramphenicol and a wide range of other antibiotics on *Allomyces* and *Blastocladiella* were investigated by Matsumae and Cantino (1971).

Blastocladia and *Aqualinderella* have evolved an obligately fermentative type of energy yielding metabolism. The cells of both fungi lack the cristate mitochondria and typical cytochromes found in aerobic fungi (Held et al., 1969). The facts that *Blastocladia* can utilize glycerol (Cantino, 1949), has some capacity for oxygen uptake, contains some b-type cytochrome, and contains double membraned vesicles in the cytoplasm (Held et al., 1969) suggest some capacity for oxidative energy generation. There is no evidence for oxidative energy generation in *Aqualinderella* (Held et al., 1969). A third water mould, *Mindeniella,* appears to have restricted capacity for oxidative energy generation. The latter fungus has a reduced rate of endogenous respiration, reduced amount of cytochrome, and a density of mitochondria lower than expected of highly aerobic fungi (Gleason and Unestam, 1968). These three fungi have a metabolism which is restricted to the fermentation of a few sugars.

The typical water mould has the capacity for lactic acid fermentation when the supply of oxygen is limited and the capacity for oxidative modes of catabolism when the supply of oxygen is in excess. It can utilize a wide range of substances released by enzymatic digestion of natural substrates.

21.3 Anabolism

21.3.1 Chemistry of the Cell

DNA   Two approaches have been followed in comparative studies on DNA from Chytridiomycetes and Oömycetes: base composition and hybridization of DNAs isolated from different sources. In the Chytridiomycetes DNA has been isolated from *Blastocladiella emersonii* Cantino et Hyatt by Comb *et al.* (1964) and Myers and Cantino (1971). Comb *et al.* (1964) found two types of DNA with different buoyant densities: a DNA (1.725 g cm^{-3}, 66% GC) in chromatin and nuclear fractions and β DNA (1.710) g cm^{-3}, 51% GC) in only the chromatin fraction. They proposed that the chromatin was the site of messenger RNA synthesis and that the nucleolus was the site of ribosomal RNA synthesis. Myers and Cantino (1971) identified four types of DNA from zoospores of the same fungus with different buoyant densities and provided some evidence for their localization within the cell: species I (1.731 g cm^{-3}, 72% GC) in the nucleus; species II (1.715 g cm^{-3}, 56% GC) in the nucleolus; species III (1.705 g cm^{-3}, 45% GC) in mitochondria, and species IV (1.687 g cm^{-3}, 28% GC) in γ-particles. The γ-particle may contain genetic information, i.e. factors controlling phenotype expression. In the Oömycetes, DNA has been isolated from *Saprolegnia* (Clark-Walker and Gleason, 1973) and from *Achlya* (Jaworski and Horgen, 1973). Clark-Walker and Gleason (1973) found three components of different buoyant densities in *Saprolegnia* 1.717 g cm^{-3}, 59% GC; 1.707 g cm^{-3}, 48% GC, and 1.685 g cm^{-3}, 25.5% GC. The 1.685 g cm^{-3} fraction was composed of close circles 14 μm in circumference and was probably mitochondrial in origin. Jaworski and Horgen (1973) isolated two components from *Achlya:* one nuclear in origin (1.697 g cm^{-3}, 37% GC) and one mitochondrial in origin (1.685 g cm^{-3}, 25.5% GC). Their data indicated the presence of a third component also. Cytoplasmic ribosomal RNA hybridized with nuclear DNA but not with mitochondrial DNA in *Achlya* (Jaworski and Horgen, 1973).

Green and Dick (1972) and Storck and Alexopoulos (1970) found a wide range in buoyant densities of DNAs isolated from Oömycetes. Their survey was restricted to the Saprolegniales and Peronosporales. Unpublished data from Clark-Walker and Gleason and from Mandel and Gleason provided buoyant density values for various members of the Leptomitales. Data from the previously cited studies are given in Table 21.1. The range in GC content is 40.5 to 62 for the Saprolegniales, 29 to 52 for the Leptomitales and 49 to 58 for the Peronosporales. The significance of the wide range in values in the Saprolegniales and Leptomitales is not known. Green and Dick (1972) have discussed the correlation of GC content with morphological characters.

TABLE 21.1   Base compositions of DNAs isolated from Oömycetes.

	GC content	Reference
Saprolegniales		
Achlya ambisexualis Raper	54.5	S+A
A. benekei Furtado	62	S+A
A. colorata Pringsheim	52	G+D
A. flagellata Coker	55	S+A
A. inflata Coker	42	G+D
A. klebsiana Pieters	44.5	S+A
A. oviparvula Rogers et Beecke	46.5	S+A
A. ramosa	52	G+D
A. sparrowii Reischer	51	G+D
Aphanomyces laevis de Barry	43	G+D
Dictyuchus pseudoachlyoides Beecke	40.5	S+A
Isoachlya subterranea Dissmann	61.5	S+A
Protoachlya paradoxa Coker	60.5	S+A
Saprolegnia sp.	59, 48	C+G
S. diclina (average of three isolates)	58.5, 48	G+D
S. ferax (Gruith.) Thur.	49.5	S+A
S. hypogyna Pringsheim	55.5	S+A
S. parasitica Coker	60.5	S+A
	59,51	G+D
Thraustotheca primoachlya Coker et Couch	45.5	S+A
Leptomitales		
Apodachlya punctata Minden	38	M+G
Leptomitus lacteus (Roth.) Ag.	52	C+G
Mindeniella spinospora Raciborski	41.5	M+G
Rhipidium sp.	41	M+G
Sapromyces elongatus	29	M+G
Peronosporales		
Phytophthora boehmeriae Sawada	52.5	S+A
P. cactovorum Lebert et Cohn	53.5	S+A
P. calocasiae	58	S+A
P. cinnamoni Rands	57	S+A
(four isolates)	52	
	49	
	57	
P. cryptogea Pethybridge et Lafferty	52	S+A
P. dreschleri Tucker	50	M+G
P. fragariae Hickman	54	S+A
P. heveae Thompson	55	S+A
P. infestans (Montagne) de Barry	54	S+A
P. palmivora (Butler) Butler	53	S+A

TABLE 21.1 (continued).

P. parasitica Dastur	50.5	S+A
P. parasitica-nicotianae (Van Breda de Haan) Tucker	49	S+A
Pythium pulchrum Minden	51.5	S+A
Pythium ultimum Trow	53.5	M+G

S+A: Storck and Alexopoulos (1970).
G+D: Green and Dick (1972).
C+G: Clark-Walker and Gleason (unpublished data).
M+G: Mandel and Gleason (unpublished data).

The values given are for the dominant species of DNA which is nuclear DNA in origin.
No attempt was made to include the minor satellite DNA values, some of which are
presumably mitochondrial in origin. Note that two DNA species are found in some
isolates of *Saprolegnia*. Density values of the DNAs were obtained in caesium chloride
density gradients.

RNA Studies on RNA in water moulds began with measurement of the RNA nucleo-
tide composition in *Blastocladiella emersonii* by Cantino (1961). He found that the
percentage composition of RNA nucleotides in the cell changed during differentiation
and that these changes could be related to developmental stages. Subsequently research
in this area has concentrated on ribosomal RNA.

The nuclear cap is an interesting organelle which is restricted to zoospores and
gametes of Chytridiomycetes, and it contains all of the cytoplasmic ribosomes of the
zoospore or gamete (Lovett, 1963). Normally ribosomes are freely distributed throughout the cytoplasm but they become closely packed within a cytoplasmic double membrane during formation of zoospores and then disperse again during germination. The
83s cytoplasmic ribosomes of *Blastocladiella* (Chytridiomycetes) consisted of 63%
RNA and 37% protein (Lovett, 1963). The ribosomal RNA of *Blastocladiella* contained two components of 1.32×10^6 (25s) and 0.73×10^6 (18s) molecular weight
(Lovett and Leaver, 1969). Lovett and Haselby (1971) compared the molecular weights
of ribosomal RNAs from six water moulds by electrophoresis in polyacrylamide
gel. The molecular weights of the 18s RNAs were nearly identical. The molecular
weights of the 25s RNAs from four Chytridiomycetes *(Allomyces, Blastocladiella,
Entophlyctis* and *Rhizophlyctis)* were smaller than those from two Oömycetes
Achlya and *Phytophthora).* Thus there is a difference in size between 25s RNA cistrons
of Chytridiomycetes and those of Oömycetes. Lovett and Haselby (1971) also provided evidence that suggests considerable base sequence homology between the 18s and
25s RNAs.

Lipids. Bowman and Mumma (1967), Haskins et al., (1964) and Shaw (1965) determined the fatty acid composition of three species of *Pythium.* Also the fatty acid compositions of two other water moulds have been examined: *Saprolegnia* (Shaw, 1965)
and *Blastocladiella* (Sumner, 1970). In *Pythium* both age and temperature influenced
the fatty acid composition (Bowman and Mumma, 1967). The significance of the
variation in fatty acid composition between species cannot yet be appreciated because
of the small number of species studied. The fact that γ-linolenic acid is present in all
of the above fungi whilst a-linolenic acid is present only in *Blastocladiella* has led to
some speculation on evolution of fatty acid synthesis (Sumner, 1970; Shaw, 1965).

Law and Burton (1973) partially characterized a fatty acid synthetase in *Pythium* which is capable of catalysing the *de novo* synthesis of long chain fatty acids, particularly palmitic and stearic, from acetyl CoA, malonyl CoA and NADPH. Steroids are not synthesized by the fungi in the Peronosporales (Hendrix, 1970). The concentrations of four sterols have been measured in various members of the Saprolegniales and Leptomitales: cholesterol, desmosterol, 24-methylenecholesterol, and fucosterol (McCorkindale *et al.*, 1969). A number of carotenoids, especially γ-carotene, and melanin can be synthesized by Chytridiomycetes (Cantino, 1965).

Proteins   With the exception of a few enzymes which have previously been discussed not much is known about proteins in water moulds. Recently, taxonomists have attempted to use proteins as a tool in classification. For example, Hall *et al.* (1969) subjected proteins in extracts from a number of isolates of *Phytophthora* to electrophoresis in polyacrylamide gel, and the patterns after electrophoresis were compared. Gleason (1972) and Gleason and Price (1969) found charge differences in lactate dehydrogenases from six Oömycetes using the technique of electrophoresis in starch gel. A third avenue of investigation has involved the use of proteins as a tool in developmental biology. Cantino and Goldstein (1962) fractionated on DEAE cellulose proteins extracted from cells of *Blastocladiella* at different stages of development. They observed that quantitative changes in various components of the soluble protein pool could be correlated with ontogeny. Furthermore, Pandhi and Cantino (1966) were able to correlate changes in isozyme patterns of glucose-6-phosphate dehydrogenase with development in the same fungus. Fourthly, there has been some investigation of histones, basic proteins associated with chromosomal DNA. It is interesting that *Allomyces* lacks histones (Stumm and van Went, 1968). P. A. Horgen (personal communication) found histones in *Achlya* but not in *Blastocladiella*. Perhaps histones are present in Oömycetes but not in the Chytridiomycetes.

Carbohydrates   Most of the recent work on carbohydrates in water moulds has concerned the cell wall which will be considered later. There has also been research on carbohydrate storage products. In the Chytridiomycete, *Blastocladiella* the major storage product is glycogen (Camargo *et al.*, 1969). Glycogen synthesis is regulated in a major way by glucose-6-phosphate concentration, because glucose-6-phosphate activates the enzyme glycogen synthetase. In actively growing cells the rate of accumulation of glycogen and the rate of growth are similar. Soluble β-$(1\rightarrow3)$ glucan appears to be an important storage product in *Achlya, Dictyuchus, Isoachlya, Saprolegnia, Thraustotheca, Phytophthora* and *Pythium* (Oömycetes) (Faro, 1972 a, b; Zevenhuizen and Bartnicki-Garcia, 1969, 1970). In *Pythium* it accumulates when the mycelium is grown in a medium rich in glucose and disappears when glucose is removed (Zevenhuizen and Bartnicki-Garcia, 1970). β-$(1\rightarrow3)$ glucan in the cytoplasm is consumed by *Achlya* during formation of sexual organs and during starvation (Faro, 1972 a).

Biosynthesis of amino acids   The pathways for biosynthesis of lysine and tryptophan have been investigated in water moulds. Using radioactively labelled precursors, Vogel (1960, 1964) found that *Phlyctochytrium, Rhizophlyctis, Allomyces* and *Monoblepharella* (Chytridiomycetes) synthesize lysine by the α aminoadipic acid pathway; while *Achlya, Thraustotheca, Sapromyces, Sirolpidium* and *Pythium* (Oömycetes) and two Hyphocytridiomycetes synthesize lysine by the α, ε diaminopimelic acid pathway. Five biosynthetic reactions are involved in tryptophan synthesis. Hütter and De Moss (1967) compared the differential precipitation with ammonium sulphate and the sedimentation pattern after zone centrifugation of enzymes catalysing these reactions. The sedimentation behaviour in *Rhizophlyctis* and *Allomyces* (Chytridiomycetes) is quite different from that in *Saprolegnia* and *Pythium* (Oömycetes). These data suggest the polyphyletic origin of lower fungi (Hütter and De Moss, 1967; Vogel, 1964).

RNA and protein synthesis   RNA and protein synthesis have been studied in three Chytridiomycetes *(Rhizophlyctis, Allomyces* and *Blastocladiella)* and in one Oömycete *(Achlya),* and the work with these four fungi will be discussed below.

In *Rhizophlyctis* Lé John and Lovett (1966) detected only very low rates of RNA and protein synthesis in zoospores. Turian (1963) measured the ratios of DNA, RNA and protein during differentiation of gametangia in the haploid life cycle of *Allomyces.* He observed a sharp increase in RNA synthesis associated with the formation of the nuclear caps of the future female gametes in the female strain. Only a slight increase in RNA synthesis was detected in the male strain.

Olson and Fuller (1971) employed the leucine-lysine synchronization technique to study various biosynthetic and morphological events during germination of mitospores and early development of germlings in the diploid life cycle of *Allomyces.* DNA replication, nuclear cap breakdown, early protein synthesis and morphogenetic development appeared to occur prior to RNA synthesis. These data suggest that the early processes of germination are under the control of pre-existing messenger RNA. All of these processes were underway before nuclear division began.

Burke *et al.* (1972) were concerned with protein and RNA synthesis in the diploid life cycle of *Allomyces.* They divided the life cycle arbitrarily into five phases for investigation: mitospore induction, mitospore encystment, mitospore germination and outgrowth, vegetative growth, and mitosporangium formation. Induction, encystment, germination and mitosporangium formation were not inhibited whilst vegetative growth was inhibited by Actinomycin D. Induction, germination, vegetative growth and mitosporangium formation were inhibited, whilst encystment was not inhibited by cycloheximide. They concluded that RNA synthesis is required only during vegetative growth and that protein synthesis is necessary during the entire life cycle except during cyst formation. A sharp increase in rate of synthesis of both RNA and protein occurred during germination suggesting activation of the genome. These data further suggest that at particular stages in its life cycle *Allomyces* contains stable messenger RNA. The messenger RNA necessary for mitosporangial formation accumulates early in vegetative growth.

Asexual reproduction in *Blastocladiella* provides an excellent system for the study of regulation of ribonucleic acid and protein synthesis. After the transfer of plants from a rich medium to a dilute salt medium, a number of biochemical processes are initiated leading to the differentiation and release of zoospores. RNA and protein synthesis cease during this period of development (Murphy and Lovett, 1966). If the zoospores are returned to a rich medium, they encyst and germinate, and RNA and protein synthesis begin again during germination (Lovett, 1968). During the process of zoospore formation, Murphy and Lovett (1966) observed that the rate of incorporation of uracil into RNA decreased first, indicating cessation of ribosomal and transfer RNA synthesis. At this stage, messenger RNA synthesis was still necessary for papilla formation, cleavage of zoospores and other processes; but just prior to completion of the nuclear cap, the cells become insensitive to Actinomycin D and messenger RNA synthesis is no longer needed. Then incorporation of leucine into protein, and thus protein synthesis, ceased; and finally the zoospores were released. Mature zoospores are motile and display a high endogenous respiratory rate but do not synthesize RNA or protein in detectable amounts. The processes of encystment and subsequent germination involve loss of motility, withdrawal of the flagellum, rounding of the cell, nuclear cap disorganization, cell wall synthesis and formation of a germ tube. Lovett (1968) recorded a sharp rise in rates of precursor incorporation into RNA and protein during encystment and germination. Actinomycin D inhibits RNA synthesis but not protein synthesis in the early stages because protein synthesis depends upon messenger RNA and ribosomes already present in the zoospore before germination. Soll and Sonneborn (1971) presented evidence that the very early events of zoospore germination in *Blastocladiella* are not dependent upon concomitant protein synthesis because they are not inhibited by cycloheximide.

The mechanisms of control of RNA and protein synthesis have been the subject of recent investigations. Three RNA polymerases are present in both vegetative plants and zoospores of *Blastocladiella* (Horgen, 1971 Horgen and Griffith, 1971 a, b). Polymerase I is located in the nucleolus, is responsible for ribosomal RNA synthesis, and is inhibited by cycloheximide. Polymerase II is located in the nonnucleolar nucleoplasm, is responsible for synthesis of DNA like RNA, and is inhibited by alphaamanitin. Polymerase III is located in the mitochondria and is inhibited by rifampicin. No inhibitors of these polymerases are known to be present in the cytoplasm of zoospores (Horgen, 1971). Charged transfer RNA and aminoacyl-transfer RNA synthetases were found inside the nuclear cap and in the cytoplasm of *Blastocladiella* zoospores (Schmoyer and Lovett, 1969). In fact, all components of the machinery for protein synthesis were present in the double membrane bound nuclear cap including a low level of messenger RNA; but an unidentified inhibitor of protein synthesis was discovered in the cytoplasm which bound to nuclear cap ribosomes. This inhibitor bound reversibly to the ribosomes and blocked their function. *Allomyces arbuscula* also has three RNA polymerases (Cain and Nester, 1973). Polymerase II is inhibited by α-aminitin, but none of the three polymerases are inhibited by cycloheximide or rifampicin.

Ribonucleic acid synthesis has not been totally neglected in Oömycetes. Griffin and Breuker (1969) studied the role of RNA synthesis in the development of sporangia in *Achlya*. Under the starvation conditions imposed for the differentiation of sporangia and the release of zoospores, net DNA, RNA and protein synthesis ceased. However, the machinery for RNA synthesis remained in an active state, since incorporation of radioactive precursors continued at a low level during the period of differentiation. Actinomycin D inhibited all stages of the sporulation process as well as incorporation of precursors. Therefore DNA-dependent RNA synthesis is required for differentiation. The total RNA content did not increase, perhaps due to turnover of RNA. During formation of sporangia a new class of RNA not found in vegetative cells was synthesized.

Finally Timberlake *et al.* (1973) investigated the rate of protein synthesis during differentiation of sporangia in *Achlya*. In the absense of added nutrients *Achlya* actively synthesized new protein. This new protein, however, was built from amino acids derived from degradation of pre-existing protein. They observed a considerable incease in the rate of protein synthesis and in the activity of intracellular proteolytic enzymes after the initiation of the sporulation sequence. During this sequence inhibition of protein synthesis by cycloheximide completely prevented further differentiation. The process of differentiation was paralleled by a slight decrease in total protein content.

554

21.4 The Cell Wall

The fungal cell wall is a complicated structure consisting mainly of polysaccharides, 80 to 90% and lesser amounts of protein, lipid and minerals. Based upon early cytochemical techniques it was thought that the major components of the cell wall were cellulose and chitin. Studies on the distribution of cellulose and chitin in fungi led to the conclusion that the major structural component of the cell wall was cellulose in Oömycetes and chitin in Chytridiomycetes. The cell wall of Hyphochytridiomycetes contained both cellulose and chitin. Aronson (1965) and Bartnicki-Garcia (1968, 1969) have thoroughly reviewed the early literature and have considered the significance of these conclusions to the classification and phylogeny of fungi. Recently cell walls have been purified, and subsequent chemical analyses have provided data which have substantially altered the early concepts of the nature of the fungal cell wall.

24.4.1 Chytridiomycetes

Analysis of the cell walls of *Allomyces* by Aronson and Machlis (1959) revealed a chemical composition of approximately 60% chitin, 15% glucan, 10% protein and 10% ash. Using the technique of X ray diffraction Aronson and Preston (1960 a, b) demonstrated the presence of chitin in five members of the Chytridiomycetes: *Allomyces, Chytridium, Rhizophydium, Monoblepharella* and *Gonopodya.* They examined cell wall preparations of the same five fungi in the electron microscope and found microfibrils 150 to 200 Å in width. Aronson (1962) later detected chitin in *Monoblepharis*, a sixth member of Chytridiomycetes. Skucas (1967) studied the multilayered cell wall of the resistant sporangium of *Allomyces*. Hydrolysis of the wall released two monosaccharides, glucose from glucan and glucosamine from chitin. The wall also contained 4% protein, 9% lipid and melanin. Both Skucas (1967) and Dodge and Lawes (1969) observed microfibrils and pits in the outer layer of the resistant sporangium. Using immunofluorescent techniques Fultz and Sussmann (1966) showed differences in surface components on hyphae and rhizoids of *Allomyces*. Fultz and Woolf (1972) also observed some differences in the surface of the cell wall in different stages of *Alloymces* in the electron microscope. The physical state of the cell wall of Chytridiomycetes is poorly understood. However, the presence of chitin, noncellulosic glucan, protein and lipid in the cell wall of some Chytridiomycetes has been clearly established.

21.4.2 Oömycetes

The cell walls of *Saprolegnia, Achlya, Brevilegnia* and *Dictyuchus* were studied by Parker *et al.* (1963). Noncellulosic polysaccharides constituted approximately 85% of the total weight of the wall. Weakly crystalline cellulose and a trace of glucosamine were detected. They concluded that the cellulose microfibrils were somewhat obscured by amorphous noncellulosic polysaccharide. Based upon investigations on *Atkinsiella, Achlya, Pythium* and *Phytophthora*, Aronson *et al.* (1967) stated that the cell walls of Oömycetes are composed primarily of glucans with a relatively small proportion of cellulose. The noncellulosic polysaccharides (glucans) contained β- (1→3) and β- (1→6) linkages. Bartnicki-Garcia (1966) detected poorly crystalline cellulose with β- (1→4) linkages which accounted for only about 25% and amorphous glucan with β-(1→3) and β- (1→6) linkages which accounted for 63% of the total polysaccharide in *Phytophthora*. The protein fraction contained 19 amino acids including hydroxyproline. The hyphal wall composition was 90% polysaccharide, 3 to 5% protein, 1 to 3% lipid and small amounts of mannose, glucosamine and minerals. Cell walls isolated from *Pythium* by Cooper and Aronson (1967) contained 82% polysaccharide, 8% protein and 2% ash. The lipid content was not measured. The polysaccharide fraction contained crystalline cellulose I which was microfibrillar and glucans with β- (1→3) and β- (1→6) linkages. Trace amounts of hexosamine and mannose but no chitin were detected. Manocha and Colvin (1968) could not confirm the presence of cellulose in *Pythium* cell walls with X-ray diffraction, but they did observe a microfibrillar phase and an amorphous matrix. The microfibrillar phase consisted of two layers: an outer layer with randomly oriented fibrils and an inner layer with fibrils oriented parallel to the hyphal axis. Composition studies on cell walls of *Phytophthora, Pythium* and *Saprolegnia* by Novaes-Ledieu and Jiménez-Martínez (1967, 1968) gave results very similar to those of Bartnicki-Garcia (1966) and Cooper and Aronson (1967). Poorly crystalline cellulose I and microfibrils were also found in the cell walls of a marine Oömycete, *Atkinsiella,* by Aronson and Fuller (1969) and in *Sapromyces* by Pao and Aronson (1970). Aronson and Fuller (1969) and Pao and Aronson (1970) measured the amino acid composition of cell wall protein. *Atkinsiella* cell wall protein consists of 18 amino acids while that of *Sapromyces* consists of 17 amino acids. Hydroxyproline is present in both. Sietsma *et al.* (1969) measured the fatty acid composition in the cell wall lipid fractions and the ratios of β- (1→4) glucan, branched β- (1→3) glucan and linear β- (1→3) glucan to total carbohydrate in *Apodachlya, Dictyuchus, Saprolegnia* and *Pythium.* From the data mentioned thus far, one must conclude that cellulose, protein and lipid appear to be minor components and noncellulosic glucan a major component of the cell wall of Oömycetes.

Chitin was not found in the previously mentioned studies. However, Parker *et al.,* (1963), Bartnicki-Garcia (1966), Cooper and Aronson (1967), Novaes-Ledieu *et al.,* (1967), Aronson and Fuller (1969) and Pao and Aronson (1970) all detected small amounts of hexosamine in the cell wall fractions. Investigations by Lin and Aronson (1970) revealed a high hexosamine content in cell walls of *Apodachlya.* Subsequent X-ray diffraction studies showed the presence of both chitin and cellulose in *Apodachlya.* Thus, like *Rhizidiomyces* (Hyphochytridiomycetes) *Apodachlya* (Oömycetes) contains both chitin and cellulose in the cell wall (Lin and Aronson, 1970; Fuller, 1960; Fuller and Barshad, 1960).

An extracellular enzyme prepared from *Streptomyces* sp. has cellulose, exolaminarase and endolaminarase activity (Bartnicki-Garcia and Lippman, 1967; Sietsma *et al.,* 1969). Digestion of cellulose and glucan with this preparation results in a wide range of fragments including glucose and three β-linked glucose disaccharides: cellobiose, laminaribiose and gentiobiose. This preparation can be used to make protoplasts from hyphae of *Phytophthora, Apodachlya, Dictyuchus, Pythium* and *Saprolegnia* (Bartnicki-Garcia and Lippman, 1966, 1967; Sietsma *et al.,* 1969). It can also be used to detect the presence of cellulose and glucan and the ratio of these components in the cell wall (Bartnicki-Garcia and Lippman, 1967; Sietsma *et al.,* 1969).

It is interesting that in addition to the insoluble glucan in the cell wall a soluble glucan was detected by Zevenhuizen and Bartnicki-Garcia (1969, 1970) in the cytoplasm of *Phytophthora.* This glucan is an important cellular reserve material.

Cellular differentiation in *Phytophthora* is accompanied by textural and structural changes in the cell wall, for example: surface texture, susceptibility to attack by enzymes, proportion of β- (1→3), 1→6), and (1→4) linkages and protein content (Tokunaga and Barnicki-Garcia, 1971).

The physical state of the cell wall of Oömycetes, like that of Chytridiomycetes, is poorly understood. The presence of cellulose, noncellulosic glucans, protein and lipid has been documented in most of the Oömycetes studied. At least one member of the Oömycetes, namely *Apodachlya,* has chitin in the cell wall. It has been shown that cellulose and chitin are present in microfibrils (Aronson, 1965). The precise function of noncellulosic glucans in unknown, and yet they make up major proportion of the cell walls of many Oömycetes. 'Noncellulosic glucans and proteins in the matrix possibly could cement the structural components, the microfibrils, together. The role of the cell wall lipids is also unknown.

21.4.3   De Novo Cell Wall Synthesis During Germination of Zoospores

De Novo cell wall synthesis has been investigated during encystment and germination of zoospores in *Blastocladiella* (Cantino and Myers, 1972) and in *Phytophthora* (Tokunaga and Bartnicki-Garcia, 1971). Zoospores of both fungi lack cell walls, and cell wall synthesis commences during encystment. The enzymes for synthesis of the cell wall polysaccharides are, however, present in the motile zoospores of both fungi before encystment begins. In *Blastocladiella* Camargo *et al.* (1967) detected chitin synthesis in both spores and vegative cells. This enzyme is activated by acetyl glucosamine (Camargo *et al.,* 1967) and is confined inside γ particles (Cantino and Myers, 1972). During encystment in *Blastocladiella,* the γ particles disintegrate releasing chitin synthetase, and then chitin synthesis proceeds and the cyst wall is formed. Not much is known at present about the cyst wall glucan synthetase in *Phytophthora.* Zoospore encystment in *Phytophthora* takes place without need for exogenous nutrients (Barash *et al.,* 1965). Cyst wall polysaccharide, which is mainly insoluble β- $(1 \rightarrow 3)$ glucan and which is outside the plasma membrane, is synthesized from a cytoplasmic storage product, which is soluble β- $(1 \rightarrow 3)$ glucan.

21.5   Growth and Development

The literature on growth and development of water moulds is very extensive, and therefore only certain topics can be included here. The effects of certain physical and chemical factors on growth and development will be considered; these are light, sex hormones and chemotaxis, steroids, and carbon dioxide. Morphological and ultrastructural aspects of growth and development have been reviewed previously by Cantino (1966), Cantino *et al.* (1968), Truesdell and Cantino (1971) and also Heath (Chapter 23).

21.5.1   Light

The general subject of photobiology of fungi was reviewed by Carlile (1965). Light affects a number of developmental processes in water moulds.

In *Blastocladiella emersonii,* light caused higher rates of growth, glucose consumption and carbon dioxide fixation, increased the volume of mature plants and extended the generation time (Cantino and Horenstein, 1956, 1957). Addition of succinate plus glyoxylate to the growth medium completely replaced the light requirement (Cantino and Horenstein, 1959). The effective wavelengths were at the blue end of the spectrum (Cantino and Horenstein, 1959). Goldstein and Cantino (1962) found that light stimulated synthesis of soluble protein and soluble carbohydrate and increased the dry weight. Furthermore, the encystment of zoospores of dark grown plants is induced by light (Cantino and Myers, 1972; Cantino and Truesdell, 1971). In another species of *Blastocladiella, B. brittanica* Horenstein and

Cantino, colourless, thin-walled sporangia are formed in the light, while brown, pitted, thick-walled sporangia are formed in the dark (Horenstein and Cantino, 1964). In the latter fungus, the capacity for glucose uptake in the dark exceeds that in the light.

The zoospores of at least two members of the Chytridiomycetes are highly positively phototactic: species of *Phlyctochytrium* (Kazama, 1972) and *Allomyces* (Robertson, 1972). The action spectrum of phototaxis in *Allomyces* indicated a broad peak in the region of 470 to 525 mμ (Robertson, 1972).

The effect of light on formation of sporangia and oöspores has been studied in Oömycetes. In *Phytophthora* light favoured production of sporangia, while darkness favoured production of oospores (Harnish, 1965; Brasier, 1969). Aragaki and Hine (1963) observed an enormous increase in the number of sporangia produced in blue light as opposed to the number in the dark. According to Leal and Gomez-Miranda (1965) oöspores must have a period of darkness for maturation; and then afterwards upon illumination, germination is stimulated and zoosporangia are produced from the oögonia. Hendrix (1967) observed a difference in morphology between light and dark grown sporangia of *Phytophthora*. The effect of light upon formation of oögonia and oöspores has also been studied in *Saprolegnia* (Szaniszlo, 1965).

Nothing is known about the nature of the light receptor in water moulds.

21.5.2   Sex hormones and chemotaxis

Sex hormones   The literature on sex hormones in fungi has been reviewed by Machlis (1966, 1972) and by Barksdale (1969). With the exception of a preliminary study on sex hormones in *Dictyuchus* (Sherwood, 1966), recent investigations have concentrated on *Allomyces* and *Achlya*. A short summary is given here.

In *Allomyces,* sirenin is produced during female gametogenesis (cleavage and release of female gametes), and this hormone attracts the male gametes to the female gametes. Machlis (1958 a) described a procedure for the bioassay of sirenin in liquid media based upon the phenomenon of attraction of motile male gametes by the hormone. Aggregation of male gametes at the source of sirenin results from direct approach of gametes brought about by a concentration gradient. The range of sirenin concentration effective in attraction of male gametes is 10^{-10} to 10^{-4} molar (Carlile and Machlis, 1965 a). If the sirenin concentration is too high, the chemoreceptors become saturated. Carlile and Machlis (1965 a) observed that male gametes inactivate sirenin. Machlis and co-workers developed methods for extraction and purification of sirenin and determined its chemical structure (Machlis, 1958 b; Machlis *et al.,* 1966; Machlis *et al.,* 1968). Sirenin is an oxygenated sesquiterpene.

In *Achlya* hormone A is secreted by the thallus which produces oögonia and acts upon the thallus which produces antheridia to cause the formation of antheridial branches. In addition to induction of production of antheridial branches, hormone A also functions to attract the antheridial branches to the oögonial initials and to bring about the formation of the antheridia delimited by crosswalls (Barksdale, 1963 b). Barksdale (1963 a) described a procedure for the bioassay of the hormone in liquid media based upon the phenomenon of induction of antheridial branches. The antheridia producing hyphae inactivated hormone A (Barksdale, 1963 b). Barksdale and co-workers developed methods for extraction and purification of hormone A and determined its chemical structure (Barksdale, 1963 a; McMorris and Barksdale, 1967; Arsenault *et al.,* 1968). Hormone A, now called antheridiol, is a steroid similar to stigmasterol. Male strains produce about one tenth the antheridiol produced by female strains. A supply of nitrogen, carbon and energy is required for induction of branching by antheridiol. The level of nutrients determines whether branches initiated will be vegetative or sexual, and the concentrations of hormone and nutrients together determine the number of branches produced (Barksdale, 1970). Antheridiol elicits a rise in cellulase activitiy which is dependent upon protein synthesis in hyphae of *Achlya* (Thomas and Mullins, 1967). Branching in general is always accompanied by increased cellulase activity. Increased branching and cellulase activity can be induced by either antheridiol or casein hydrolysate (Thomas and Mullins,1969).

Barksdale *et al.* (1965) found no reaction with sirenin in the bioassay for antheridial branching in *Achlya* and no reaction with hormone A in the bioassay for attraction of male gametes in *Allomyces*. Within the genus *Allomyces* there are strain differences in the ability of gametes to react to sirenin (Machlis, 1968). The sexual hormones are products of highly evolved creatures.

Chemotaxis. The response of male gametes in *Allomyces* to sirenin is one type of chemotaxis. There are five kinds of motile cells in *Allomyces* (male gametes, female gametes, zygotes, mitospores and meiospores), but only the male gametes respond to sirenin. However, zygotes, mitospores, and meiospores respond positively to casein hydrolysate (Carlile and Machlis, 1965 b), and this is a second type of chemotaxis. Neither the male nor female gametes is attracted by casein hydrolysate, but the chemotactic response is established quickly after fertilization (Machlis, 1969 b). In careful experiments with mixtures of amino acids, Machlis (1969 b) attributed this chemotactic response of zygotes, mitospores and meiospores to two or possibly three amino acids. Equimolar mixtures of L-leucine and L-lysine (2×10^{-4} M) attracted the motile swarmers, and the addition of proline enhanced the response somewhat (Machlis, 1969 a, b). Dill and Fuller (1971) found that a 0.2M mixture of leucine and lysine immobilized mitospores of *Allomyces* by stopping flagellar motion. This provided a good method for synchronous encystment and germination if the encysted cells were placed in a medium for growth (Olson and Fuller, 1971). Casein hydrolysate and amino acids are effective in causing positive chemotaxis of zoospores of *Pythium* (Royle and Hickman, 1964) and positive chemotropism of hyphae of *Saprolegnia* (Fischer and Werner, 1955).

21.5.3 Steroids

Since Hendrix (1970) has recently reviewed in depth the role of sterols in the growth and reproduction of fungi, the effects of steroids on water moulds will only be considered briefly here. One steroid mediated phenomenon, the attraction of antheridial hyphae by antheridiol in *Achlya,* was previously discussed. Exogenous sterols are apparently essential for the formation of oöspores and zoosporangia in *Pythium* and *Phytophthora*. The sterol requirement was first discovered independently by Elliot *et al.* (1964), Haskins *et al.* (1964), Hendrix (1964) and Leal *et al.* (1964), and further studies have confirmed their initial discovery (Child and Haskins, 1971; Child *et al.,* 1969 a; Elliot, 1972; Hendrix, 1965). The growth rate is also increased by the addition of sterols to the medium (Child *et al.,* 1969 a; Elliot *et al.,* 1964, 1966; Schlösser and Gottlieb, 1968). The range of sterols satisfying the requirement has been investigated by Elliot (1972), Elliot *et al.* (1966), and Child and Haskins (1971). The activities of eight sterols on oöspore production by *Phytophthora* were measured by Elliott (1972) and are arranged here in order of decreasing activity: β sitosterol = Δ^5-avenasterol = fucosterol = stigmasterol > cholesterol = 7-dehydrocholesterol > ergosterol > cholestanol. Certain sterols, for example cholestanol and estradiol, can inhibit the oöspore production induced by other sterols (Elliott, 1968; Hendrix and Guttman, 1968, 1969). Some polyene antibiotics inhibit sterol induced sexual reproduction in *Pythium* (Child *et al.*, 1969b; Hendrix and Lauder, 1966; Schlösser and Gottlieb, 1966). There is also inhibition of growth in sterol-free media in some cases, thus the functions of sterols are somewhat unresolved at present.

Pythium and *Phytophthora* (Peronosporales) are apparently incapable of synthesizing sterols, with the exception of squalene, an intermediate in sterol synthesis (Hendrix, 1966; Sietsma and Haskins, 1967; Schlösser *et al.*, 1969). Fungi in the Saprolegniales and Leptomitales on the other hand can synthesize sterols (McCorkindale *et al.*, 1969). Sietsma and Haskins (1967) observed uptake but not catabolism of C^{14}- labelled cholesterol in *Pythium*. However, Gain (1972) reported esterification of C^{14}-labelled cholesterol by saturated and unsaturated fatty acids in *Phytophthora*, and Hendrix *et al.* (1970) reported two metabolites from C^{14}-labelled cholesterol in *Pythium*, one of which was an ester. The major portion of the cholesterol taken into the cell became incorporated into the plasma membrane and a lesser portion into intracellular membranes in *Pythium* (Sietsma and Haskins, 1968). Child *et al.* (1969 b), Sietsma and Haskins (1968) and Schlösser and Gottlieb (1966) proposed that cholesterol incorporation into the plasma membrane decreases the rate of leakage of low molecular weight constituents from the cell by altering permeability. The integrity and structure of the plasma membrane is improved by the addition of sterols. Polyene antibiotics interfere in some way with the action of sterols, perhaps by their incorporation into the membrane. These inhibitors increase leakage from *Pythium* cells grown in the presence of cholesterol.

The role of sterols in sexual reproduction in the Peronosporales is not thoroughly understood. It appears that these fungi cannot synthesize and do not require sterols for vegetative growth, although growth is stimulated by the addition of sterols to the medium. However, sterols are necessary for unknown biochemical processes in sexual reproduction.

21.5.4 Carbon dioxide

There are many examples of the effects of carbon dioxide on the morphology of fungi, and perhaps one of the most studied effects is the control of sporangium differentiation in the Blastocladiales (Cantino, 1966). Two types of sporangium can be formed in the Blastocladiales: a brown, pitted, thick-walled, resistant sporangium (RS) and a colourless, thin-walled sporangium (OC). The resistant sporangium can tide the fungus over unfavourable environmental conditions. Elevated concentrations of carbon dioxide can induce resistant sporangium formation in *Blastocladia* and in *Blastocladiella* (Emerson and Cantino, 1948; Cantino, 1951). Careful control of the pH must be maintained, however.

The biochemical events in the formation of the two types of sporangia in *Blastocladiella emersonii* have been intensively investigated by Cantino and his associates (see Cantino, 1966). Carbon dioxide causes a pronounced change in the function of the tricarboxylic acid cycle, a directional shift in the operation of isocitrate dehydrogenase from oxidative decarboxylation of isocitrate to reductive carboxylation of a-ketoglutarate. Isocitrate is converted to glyoxylate and succinate by isocitrate lyase and then glyoxylate to glycine by glycine-alanine transaminase. Cantino and his associates reported that carbon dioxide caused increased activities of isocitrate dehydrogenase, isocitrate lyase, glycine-alanine transaminase, glucose-6-phosphate dehydrogenase and glucosamine synthetase, but decreased activity of a-ketoglutarate dehydrogenase, growth rate and rate of endogenous respiration (Cantino, 1966; Cantino and Horenstein, 1956, 1959; Cantino and Lovett, 1960; Lovett and Cantino, 1961; McCurdy and Cantino 1960) . C^{14}-labelled bicarbonate was incorporated into acids of the tricarboxylic acid cycle (Cantino and Horenstein, 1956). Carbon dioxide or bicarbonate seems to interfere with oxidative decarboxylations, and the flow of intermediates along the tricarboxylic acid cycle is reversed (Cantino, 1966). *Blastocladiella* obtains the bulk of its energy from lactic acid fermentation according to Cantino's data (1966). *De novo* synthesis of melanin and carotene, increased synthesis of chitin and lipids, and a magnitude of other events follow.

Using recently developed techniques for the continuous culture of micro-organisms, Griffin (1965) also studied the effect of carbon dioxide on the formation of resistant sporangia in *Blastocladiella emersonii*. However, Griffin's conclusions about the environmental factors influencing morphogenesis disagreed with those of Cantino and his associates. First, under the particular conditions of nutrition and aeration employed by Griffin, the metabolism of *Blastocladiella* was largely oxidative rather than largely fermentative. This fungus is therefore capable of generating its energy by oxidative machinery. Second, morphogenesis was dependent upon potassium, bicarbonate and carbonate ion concentrations and was independent of partial pressure of carbon dioxide and pH.

The mechanism of action of carbon dioxide on morphogenesis in sporangium formation is not known. Is resistant sporangium formation a reaction to conditions of environmental stress? The introduction of continuous culture and synchronized culture techniques represents a giant step forward in sophistication of experimentation on morphogenesis in water moulds.

Concluding Remarks

Research during the past two decades has contributed much information on the physiology of aquatic fungi but we are only beginning to understand a few of the fundamental physiological processes essential to their way of life. Perhaps the most exciting avenues of research on water moulds deal with developmental problems such as sporangium formation and spore germination. By combining biochemical, cytological and culture techniques, future investigations will undoubtedly greatly increase our knowledge of the processes of cellular differentiation.

Acknowledgements

The author is extremely grateful to Professor Ralph Emerson for his inspiration and guidance during the early portion of the author's career and wishes to thank Professor Denis J. Carr for providing a visiting fellowship for one year during which this manuscript was written.

References

ARAGAKI, M., and HINE, R. B. (1963). 'Effect of radiation on sporangial production of *Phytophthora parasitica* on artificial media and detached papaya fruit.' *Phytopathology*, 53, 854-856.
ARONSON, J. M. (1962). 'Hyphal wall structure in *Monoblepharis*.' *Am. J. Bot.*, 49, 665.

ARONSON, J. M. (1965). 'The cell wall.' In *The Fungi*, (Eds. G. C. Ainsworth and A. S. Sussman) Academic Press. Vol. 1, 48-76.

ARONSON, J. M., and FULLER, M. S. (1969. 'Cell wall structure of the marine fungus *Atkinsiella dubia*.' *Arch. Mikrobiol.*, 68, 295-305.

ARONSON, J. M., and MACHLIS, L. (1959). 'The chemical composition of the hyphal walls of the fungus *Allomyces*.' *Am. J. Bot.*, 46, 292-300.

ARONSON, J. M., and PRESTON, R. D. (1960 a). 'The microfibrillar structure of the cell walls of the filamentous fungus *Allomyces*.' *J. Biophys. Biochem. Cytol.*, 8, 247-256.

ARONSON, J. M., and PRESTON, R. D. (1960 b). 'An electron microscopic and X-ray analysis of the walls of selected lower Phycomycetes.' *Proc. Roy. Soc.*, London. B152, 364-352.

ARONSON, J. M., COOPER, B. A., and FULLER, M. S. (1967). 'Glucans of oomycete cell walls.' *Science,* 155, 332-335.

ARSENAULT, G. P., BIEMANN, K., BARKSDALE, A. W., and McMORRIS, T. C., (1968). 'The structure of antheridiol, a sex hormone in *Achlya bisexualis*.' *J. Am. Chem. Soc.*, 90, 5635-5636.

AYERS, W. A., PAPAVIZAS, G. C., and LUMSDEN, R. D. (1969). 'Purification and properties of the endopolygalacuronase of *Aphanomyces euteiches*'. *Phytopathology,* 59, 925-930.

BARASH, I., KLISIEWICZ, J. M., and KOSUGE, T. (1965). 'Utilization of carbon compounds by zoospores of *Phytophthora drechsleri* and their effect on motility and germination.' *Phytopathology,* 55, 1257-1261.

BARKSDALE, A. W. (1962). 'Effect of nutritional deficiency on growth and sexual reproduction of *Achlya ambisexualis*.' *Am. J. Bot.*, 49, 633-638.

BARKSDALE, A. W. (1963 a). 'The uptake of exogenous hormone A by certain strains of *Achlya*.' *Mycologia,* 55, 164-171.

BARKSDALE, A. W. (1963 b). 'The role of hormone A during sexual conjugation in *Achlya ambisexualis*.' *Mycologia,* 55, 627-632.

BARKSDALE, A. W. (1969). 'Sexual hormones of *Achlya* and other fungi.' *Science,* 166, 831-837.

BARKSDALE, A. W. (1970). 'Nutrition and antheridiol-induced branching in *Achlya ambisexualis*.' *Mycologia,* 62, 411-420.

BARKSDALE, A. W., CARLILE, M. J., and MACHLIS, L. (1965). 'A comparative study of hormone A and sirenin.' *Mycologia,* 57, 138-140.

BARR, D. J. S. (1969). 'Studies on *Rhizophydium* and *Phlyctochytrium* (Chytridiales). II. Comparative physiology.' *Can. J. Bot.*, 47, 999-1005.

BARR, D. J. S. (1970). '*Phlyctochytrium reinboldtae* (Chytridiales): morphology and physiology.' *Can. J. Bot.*, 48, 479-484.

BARTNICKI-GARCIA, S. (1966). 'Chemistry of hyphal walls of *Phytophthora*.' *J. gen. Microbiol.*, 42, 57-69.

BARTNICKI-GARCIA, S. (1968). 'Cell wall chemistry, morphogenesis, and taxonomy of fungi.' *A. Rev. Microbiol.*, 22, 87-108.

BARTNICKI-GARCIA, S. (1969). 'Cell wall differentiation in the Phycomycetes.' *Phytopathology,* 59, 1065-1071.

BARTNICKI-GARCIA, S., and LIPPMAN, E. (1966). 'Liberation of protoplasts from the mycelium of *Phytophthora*.' *J. gen. Microbiol.*, 42, 411-416.

BARTNICKI-GARCIA, S., and LIPPMAN, E. (1967). 'Enzymic digestion and glucan structure of hyphal walls of *Phytophthora cinnamoni*.' *Biochim. biophys. Acta,* 136, 533-543.

BIANCHI, D. E., PUROHIT, K. and TURIAN, G. (1971). 'Lactate dehydrogenase activity and cellular localization of several dehydrogenases in *Neurospora* and *Allomyces.*' *Arch. Mikrobiol.,* 75, 163-170.

BOWMAN, R. D., and MUMMA, R. O. (1967). 'The lipids of *Pythium ultimum.*' *Biochim. biophys. Acta,* 144, 501-510.

BONNER, B. A., and MACHLIS, L. (1957). 'Respiration of the mycelia and mitochondria of the filamentous watermold *Allomyces macrogynus.*' *Pl. Physiol.,* 32, 291-301.

BRASIER, C. M. (1969). 'The effect of light and temperature on reproduction in vitro in two tropical species of *Phytophthora.*' *Trans. Br. mycol. Soc.,* 52, 105-113.

BURKE, D. J., SEALE, T. W., and MCCARTHY, B. J. (1972). 'Protein and ribonucleic acid synthesis during the diploid life cycle of *Allomyces arbuscula.*' *J. Bact.,* 110, 1065-1072.

CAIN, A. K., and NESTER, E. W. (1973). 'Ribonucleic acid polymerase in *Allomyces arbuscula.*' *J. Bact.,* 115, 769-776.

CAMARGO, E. P., DIETRICH, C. P., SONNEBORN, D. and STROMINGER, J. L. (1967). 'Biosynthesis of chitin in spores and growing cells of *Blastocladiella emersonii.*' *J. Biol. Chem.,* 242, 3121-3128.

CAMARGO, E. P., MEUSER, R., and SONNEBORN, D. (1969). 'Kinetic analyses of the regulation of glycogen synthetase activity in zoospores and growing cells of the water mold, *Blastocladiella emersonii.*' *J. Biol. Chem.,* 244, 5910-5919.

CANTINO, E. C. (1949). 'The physiology of the aquatic phycomycete, *Blastocladiella pringsheimii,* with emphasis on its nutrition and metabolism.' *Am. J. Bot.,* 36, 95-112.

CANTINO, E. C. (1950). 'The nutrition and phylogeny in the water molds.' *Q. Rev. Biol.,* 25, 269-277.

CANTINO, E. C. (1951). 'Metabolism and morphogenesis in a new *Blastocladiella.*' *Antonie van Leeuwenhoek,* 17, 325-362.

CANTINO, E. C. (1955). 'Physiology and phylogeny in the water molds—a reevaluation.' *Q. Rev. Biol.,* 30, 138-149.

CANTINO, E. C. (1956). 'The relation between cellular metabolism and morphogenesis in *Blastocladiella.*' *Mycologia,* 48, 225-240.

CANTINO, E. C. (1961). 'Transitional states of ribonucleic acid and morphogenesis in synchronous single generations of *Blastocladiella emersonii.*' *Phytochemistry,* 1, 107-124.

CANTINO, E. C. (1965). 'Intracellular distribution of C^{14} during sporogenesis in *Blastocladiella emersonii.* Effect of light on hemoprotein.' *Arch. Mikrobiol,* 51, 42-59.

CANTINO, E. C. (1966). 'Morphogenesis in fungi.' In *The Fungi,* (Eds. G. C. Ainsworth and A. S. Sussman). Academic Press, vol. 2, pp. 283-337.

CANTINO, E. C., GOLDSTEIN, A. (1962). 'Protein changes during morphological differentiation and its reversal in synchronized single generations of *Blastocladiella emersonii.*' *Am. J. Bot.,* 49, 642-646.

CANTINO, E. C., and HORENSTEIN, E. A. (1955). 'The role of ketoglutarate and polyphenol oxidase in the synthesis of melanin during morphogenesis in *Blastocladiella emersonii.*' *Physiologia Pl.,* 8, 189-221.

CANTINO, E. C., and HORENSTEIN, E. A. (1956). 'The stimulatory effect of light upon growth and carbon dioxide fixation in *Blastocladiella.* I. The S.K.I. cycle.' *Mycologia,* 48, 777-799.

CANTINO, E. C., and HORENSTEIN, E. A. (1957). 'The stimulatory effect of light upon growth and carbon dioxide fixation in *Blastocladiella*. II. Mechanism at an organismal level of integration.' *Mycologia, 49,* 892-894.

CANTINO, E. C., and HORENSTEIN, E. A. (1959). 'The stimulatory effect of light upon growth and carbon dioxide fixation in *Blastocladiella*. III. Further studies, in vivo and in vitro.' *Physiologia Pl., 12,* 251-263.

CANTINO, E. C., and HYATT, M. T. (1953). 'Further evidence for the role of the tricarboxylic acid cycle in morphogenesis in *Blastocladiella emersonii.*' *J. Bact., 66,* 712-720.

CANTINO, E. C., and LOVETT, J. S. (1960). 'Respiration of *Blastocladiella* during bicarbonate-induced morphogenesis in synchronous culture.' *Physiologia Pl., 13,* 450-458.

CANTINO, E. C., and MYERS, R. B. (1972). 'Concurrent effect of visible light on γ-particles, chitin synthetase, and encystment capacity in zoospores of *Blastocladiella emersonii.*' *Arch. Mikrobiol., 83,* 203-215.

CANTINO, E. C., and TURIAN, G. F. (1959). 'Physiology and development of lower fungi (Phycomycetes).' *A. Rev. Microbiol., 13,* 97-124.

CANTINO, E. C., TRUESDELL, L. C. and SHAW, D. S. (1968). 'Life history of the motile spore of *Blastocladiella emersonii:* a study in cell differentiation.' *J. Elisha Mitchell scient. Soc., 84,* 125-146.

CANTINO, E. C., and TRUESDELL, L. C. (1971). 'Light-induced encystment of *Blastocladiella emersonia zoospores.*' *J. gen. Microbiol., 69,* 199-204.

CARLILE, M. J. (1965). 'The photobiology of fungi.' *A. Rev. Plant Physiol., 16,* 175-202.

CARLILE, M. J., and MACHLIS, L. (1965 a). 'The response of male gametes of *Allomyces* to the sexual hormone sirenin.' *Am. J. Bot., 52,* 478-483.

CARLILE, M. J., and MACHLIS, L. (1965 b). 'A comparative study of the chemotaxis of the motile phases of *Allomyces.*' *Am. J. Bot., 52,* 484-486.

CHILD, J. J., and HASKINS, R. H. (1971). 'Induction of sexuality in hetero-thallic *Pythium* spp. by cholesterol.' *Can. J. Bot., 49,* 329-332.

CHILD, J. J., DÉFAGO, G., and HASKINS, R. H. (1969 a). 'The influence of carbon and nitrogen nutrition on growth and sterol-induced sexuality of *Pythium* sp. PRL 2142.' *Mycologia, 61,* 1096-1105.

CHILD, J. J., DÉFAGO, G., and HASKINS, R. H. (1969 b). 'The effect of cholesterol and polyene antibiotics on the permeability of the protoplasmic membrane of *Pythium* PRL 2142.' *Can. J. Microbiol., 15,* 599-603.

CLARK-WALKER, G. D., and GLEASON, F. H. (1973). 'Circular DNA from the water mold *Saprolegnia.*' *Arch. Mikrobiol., 92,* 209-216.

COMB, D. G., BROWN, R., and KATZ, S. (1964). 'The nuclear DNA and RNA components of the aquatic fungus *Blastocladiella emersonii.*' *J. molec. Biol., 8,* 781-799.

COOPER, B. A., and ARONSON, J. M. (1967). 'Cell wall structure of *Pythium debaryanum.*' *Mycologia, 59,* 658-670.

DAVEY, C. B., and PAPAVIZAS, G. C. (1962). 'Growth and sexual reproduc-tion of *Aphanomyces euteiches* as affected by the oxidation state of sulfur.' *Am. J. Bot., 49,* 400-404.

DAYAL, R. (1961 a). 'Nitrogen requirements of some members of the family Saprolegniaceae.' *Proc. natn. Acad. Sci., India,* B31, 332-336.

DAYAL, R. (1961 b). 'Sulfur requirements of some members of the family Sapro-legniaceae.' *Proc. natn. Acad. Sci., India,* B31, 399-401.

DILL, B. C., and FULLER, M. S. (1971). 'Amino acid immobilization of fungal motile cells.' *Arch. Mikrobiol.,* 78, 92-98.

DODGE, J. D., and LAWES, G. B. (1969). 'The arrangement of microfibrils in sporangial walls of *Allomyces.' Planta,* 84, 134-140.

ELLIOT, C. G. (1968). 'Competition and synergism between cholesterol and cholestanol in oospore formation in *Phytophthora cactorum.' J. gen. Microbiol.,* 51, 137-143.

ELLIOT, C. G. (1972). 'Sterols and the production of oospores by *Phytophthora cactorum.' J. gen. Microbiol.,* 72, 321-327.

ELLIOTT, C. G., HENDRIE, M. R., and KNIGHTS, B. A. (1966). 'The sterol requirement of *Phytophthora cactorum.' J. gen. Microbiol.,* 42, 425-435.

ELLIOTT, C. G., HENDRIE, M. E., KNIGHTS, B. A. and PARKER, W. (1964). 'A steroid growth factor requirement in a fungus.' *Nature,* London, 203, 427-428.

EMERSON, R. (1950). 'Current trends of experimental research on the aquatic phycomycetes.' *A. Rev. Microbiol.,* 4, 169-200.

EMERSON, R., and CANTINO, E. C. (1948). 'The isolation, growth and metabolism of *Blastocladia* in pure culture.' *Am. J. Bot.,* 35, 157-171.

EMERSON, R., and HELD, A. A. (1969). *'Aqualinderella fermentans gen. et sp. nov.* a phycomycete adapted to stagnant waters II. Isolation, cultural characteristics, and gas relations.' *Am. J. Bot.,* 56, 1103-1120.

EMERSON, R., and WESTON, W. H. (1967). *'Aqualinderella fermentans gen. et sp. nov.,* a phycomycete adapted to stagnant waters. I. Morphology and occurrence in nature.' *Am. J. Bot.,* 54, 702-719.

FARO, S. (1971). 'Utilization of certain amino acids and carbohydrates as carbon sources by *Achlya heterosexualis.' Mycologia,* 63, 1234-1237.

FARO, S. (1972 a). 'The role of a cytoplasmic glucan during morphogenesis of sex organs of *Achlya.' Am. J. Bot.,* 59, 919-923.

FARO, S. (1972 b). 'A soluble β-1, 3-glucan found in selected genera of oomycetes.' *J. gen. Microbiol.,* 72, 393-394.

FISCHER, F. G., and WERNER, G. (1955). 'Eine analyse des chemotropismus einiger pilze, insbesondere der Saprolegniaceen.' *Hoppe-Seyler's Z. Physiol. Chem.,* 300, 211-236.

FOTHERGILL, P. G., and HIDE, D. (1962). 'Comparative nutritional studies of *Pythium* spp.' *J. gen. Microbiol.,* 29, 325-334.

FULLER, M. S. (1960). 'Biochemical and microchemical study of the cell walls of *Rhizidiomyces* sp.' *Am. J. Bot.,* 47, 838-842.

FULLER, M. S., and BARSHAD, I. (1960). 'Chitin and cellulose in the cell walls of *Rhizidiomyces* sp.' *Am. J. Bot.,* 47, 105-109.

FULTZ, S. A., and SUSSMAN, A. S. (1966). 'Antigenic differences in the surfaces of hyphae and rhizoids in *Allomyces.' Science,* 152, 785-787.

FULTZ, S. A., and WOOLF, R. A. (1962). 'Surface structure in *Allomyces* during germination and growth.' *Mycologia,* 64, 212-218.

GAIN, R. E. (1972). 'Esterification of 4 [14] C cholesterol by *Phytophthora cactorum.' Mycologia,* 64, 198-199.

GLEASON, F. H. (1968 a). 'Nutritional comparisons in the Leptomitales.' *Am. J. Bot.,* 55, 1003-1010.

GLEASON, F. H. (1968 b). 'Respiratory electron transport systems of aquatic fungi. I. *Leptomitus lacteus* and *Apodachlya punctata.' Pl. Physiol.,* 43, 597-605.

GLEASON, F. H. (1972). 'Lactate dehydrogenase in oomycetes.' *Mycologia, 64,* 663-666.

GLEASON, F. H. (1973). 'Uptake of amino acids by *Saprolegnia.' Mycologia, 65,* 465-468.

GLEASON, F. H., and PRICE, J. S. (1969). 'Lactic acid fermentation in lower fungi.' *Mycologia, 61,* 945-956.

GLEASON, F. H., and STUART, T. D. (1970). 'Nitrogen and sulfur requirements in the Leptomitales.' *Mycologia, 62,* 1212-1214.

GLEASON, F. H., and UNESTAM, T. (1968 a). 'Cytochromes of aquatic fungi.' *J. Bact.,* 95, 1599-1603.

GLEASON, F. H., and UNESTAM, T. (1968 b). 'Comparative physiology of respiration in aquatic fungi I. The Leptomitales.' *Physiologia Pl.,* 21, 556-572.

GLEASON, F. H., RUDOLPH, C. R., and PRICE, J. S. (1970 a). 'Growth of certain aquatic oomycetes on amino acids I. *Saprolegnia, Achlya, Leptolegnia,* and *Dictyuchus.' Physiologia Pl.,* 23, 513-516.

GLEASON, F. H., STUART, T. D., PRICE, J. S., and NELBACH, E. T. (1970 b). 'Growth of certain aquatic oomycetes on amino acids. II. *Apodachlya, Aphanomyces,* and *Pythium.' Physiologia Pl.,* 23, 769-774.

GOLDSTEIN, S. (1960 a). 'Physiology of aquatic fungi. I. Nutrition of two monocentric chytrids.' *J. Bact.,* 80, 701-707.

GOLDSTEIN, S. (1960 b). 'Factors affecting the growth and pigmentation of *Cladochytrium replicatum.' Mycologia,* 52, 490-498.

GOLDSTEIN, S. (1961). 'Studies of two polycentric chytrids in pure culture.' *Am. J. Bot.,* 48, 294-298.

GOLDSTEIN, A., and CANTINO, E. C. (1962). 'Light-stimulated polysaccharide and protein synthesis by synchronized, single generations of *Blastocladiella emersonii.' J. gen. Microbiol.,* 28, 689-699.

GOLUEKE, C. G. (1957). 'Comparative studies of the physiology of *Sapromyces* and related genera.' *J. Bact.,* 74, 337-343.

GREEN, B. R., and DICK, M. W. (1972). 'DNA base composition and taxonomy of the Oomycetes.' *Can. J. Microbiol.,* 18, 963-968.

GRIFFIN, D. H. (1965). 'The interaction of hydrogen ion, carbon dioxide and potassium ion in controlling the formation of resistant sporangia in *Blastocladiella emersonii.' J. gen. Microbiol.,* 40, 13-28.

GRIFFIN, D. H., and BREUKER, C. (1969). 'Ribonucleic acid synthesis during the differentiation of sprogania in the water mold *Achlya.' J. Bact.,* 98, 689-696.

HALL, R., ZENTMYER, G. A., and ERWIN, D. C. (1969). 'Approach to taxonomy of *Phytophthora* through acrylamide gel-electrophoresis of proteins.' *Phytopathology,* 59, 770-774.

HARNISH, W. N. (1965). 'Effect of light on production of oospores and sporangia in species of *Phytophthora.' Mycologia,* 57, 85-90.

HASKINS, R. H., TULLOCH, A. P., and MICETICH, R. G. (1964). 'Steroids and the stimulation of sexual reproduction of a species of *Pythium.' Can. J. Microbiol.,* 10, 187-195.

HELD, A. A. (1970). 'Nutrition and fermentative energy metabolism of the watermold *Aqualinderella fermentans.' Mycologia,* 62, 339-358.

HELD, A. A., EMERSON, R., FULLER, M. S., and GLEASON, F. H. (1969). '*Blastocladia* and *Aqualinderella:* Fermentative water molds with high carbon dioxide optima.' *Science,* 165, 706-709.

HENDRIX, J. W. (1964). 'Sterol induction of reproduction and stimulation of growth of *Pythium* and *Phytophthora.'* *Science,* 144, 1028-1029.

HENDRIX, J. W. (1965). 'Influence of sterols on growth and reproduction of *Pythium* and *Phytophthora* spp.' *Phytopathology,* 55, 790-797.

HENDRIX, J. W. (1966). 'Inability of *Pythium aphanidermatum* and *Phytophthora palmivora* to incorporate acetate into digitonin-precipitable sterols.' *Mycologia,* 58, 307-312.

HENDRIX, J. W. (1967). 'Light-cholesterol relationships in morphogenesis of *Phytophthora palmivora* and *P. capsici* sporangia.' *Mycologia,* 59, 1107-1111.

HENDRIX, J. W. (1970). 'Sterols in growth and reproduction of fungi.' *A. Rev. Phytopathol.,* 8, 111-130.

HENDRIX, J. W., and APPLE, J. L. (1964). 'Fats and fatty acid derivatives as growth stimulants and carbon sources for *Phytophthora parasitica* var. *nicotianae.'* *Phytopathology,* 54, 987-994.

HENDRIX, J. W., BENNETT, R. D., and HEFTMANN, E. (1970). 'Metabolism of cholesterol by *Pythium periplocum.'* *Microbios,* 5, 11-15.

HENDRIX, J. W., and GUTTMAN, S.-M. (1968). 'Annulment of sterol-induced sexual reproduction by estradiol in *Pythium periplocum.'* *Science,* 161, 1252.

HENDRIX, J. W., and GUTTMAN, S.-M. (1969). 'Resistance to oestradiol in species of *Pythium* and *Phytophthora.'* *Microbios,* 2, 137-143.

HENDRIX, J. W., and LAUDER, D. K. (1966). 'Effects of polyene antibiotics on growth and sterol-induction of oospore formation by *Pythium periplocum.'* *J. gen. Microbiol.,* 44, 115-120.

HENDRIX, J. W., NORMAN, C., and APPLE, J. L. (1966). 'Chemical and physical factors influencing growth of *Phytophthora parasitica* var. *nicotianae* on vegetable oils.' *Physiologia Pl.,* 19, 159-166.

HINE, R. B. (1965). 'The influence of age, starvation, and nutrition on endogenous respiration of mycelium of *Pythium aphanidermatum.'* *Mycologia,* 57, 36-72.

HORENSTEIN, E. A., and CANTINO, E. C. (1964). 'An effect of light on glucose uptake by the fungus *Blastocladiella brittannica.'* *J. gen. Microbiol.,* 37, 59-65.

HORGEN, P. A. (1971). 'In vitro ribonucleic acid synthesis in the zoospores of the aquatic fungus *Blastocladiella emersonii.'* *J. Bact.,* 106, 281-282.

HORGEN, P. A., and GRIFFIN, D. H. (1969). 'Cytochrome oxidase activity in *Blastocladiella emersonii.'* *Pl. Physiol.,* 44, 1590-1593.

HORGEN, P. A., and GRIFFIN, D. H. (1971 b). 'RNA polymerase III of *Blastocladiella emersonii* is mitochondrial.' *Nature New Biology,* 234, 17-18.

HORGEN, P. A., and GRIFFIN, D. H. (1971 a). 'Specific inhibitors of the three RNA polymerases from the aquatic fungus, *Blastocladiella emersonii.'* *Proc. natn. Acad. Sci.,* 68, 338-341.

HÜTTER, R., and DE MOSS, J. A. (1967). 'Organization of the tryptophan pathway: Phylogenetic study of the fungi.' *J. Bact.,* 94, 1896-1907.

JAWORSKI, A. J., and HORGEN, P. A. (1973). 'The ribosomal cistrons of the water mold *Achlya bisexualis.'* *Arch. Biochem. Biophys.,* 157, 260-267.

KAZAMA, F. Y. (1972). 'Ultrastructure and phototaxis of zoospores of *Phlyctochytrium* sp. an estuarine chytrid.' *J. gen. Microbiol.,* 71, 555-566.

KOBR, M. J., and TURIAN, G. (1967). 'Metabolic changes during sexual differentiation in *Allomyces.'* *Arch. Mikrobiol.,* 57, 271-279.

KRAFT, J. M., and ERWIN, D. C. (1967). 'Effects of nitrogen sources on growth of *Pythium aphanidermatum* and *Pythium ultimum.'Phytopathology,* 57, 374-376.

LAW, S. W. T., and BURTON, D. N. (1973). 'Fatty acid synthetase from *Pythium debaryanum.' Can. J. Biochem.,* 51, 241-248.

LEAL, J. A., and GOMEZ-MIRANDA, B. (1965). 'The effect of the light and darkness on the germination of the oospores of certain species of *Phytophthora* on some synthetic media.' *Trans. Br. mycol. Soc.,* 48, 491-494.

LEAL, J. A., FRIEND, J., and HOLLIDAY, P. (1964). 'A factor controlling sexual reproduction in *Phytophthora.' Nature,* 203, 545-546.

LEAL, J. A., GALLEGLY, M. E. and LILLY, V. G. (1967). 'The relation of the carbon-nitrogen ratio in the basal medium to sexual reproduction in species of *Phytophthora.' Mycologia,* 59, 953-964.

LÊ JOHN, H. B. (1968). 'Unidirectional inhibition of glutamate dehydrogenase by metabolities.' *J. biol. Chem.,* 243, 5126-5131.

LÊ JOHN, H. B. (1971). 'D(-)lactate dehydrogenase in fungi. Kinetics and allosteric inhibition by guanosine triphosphate.' *J. biol. Chem.,* 246, 2116-2126.

LÊ JOHN, H. B., and LOVETT, J. S. (1966). 'Ribonucleic acid and protein synthesis in *Rhizophlyctis rosea* zoospores.' *J. Bact.,* 91, 709-717.

LÊ JOHN, H. B., JACKSON, S. G., KLASSEN, G. R., and SAWULA, R. V. (1969). 'Regulation of mitochondrial glutamic dehydrogenase by divalent metals, nucleotides, and α-ketoglutarate.' *J. biol. Chem.,* 244, 5346-5356.

LÊ JOHN, H. B., and STEVENSON, R. M. (1970). 'Multiple regulatory processes in nicotinamide adenine dinucleotide-specific glutamic dehydrogenases.' *J. biol. Chem.,* 245, 3890-3900.

LIN, C. C., and ARONSON, J. M. (1970). 'Chitin and cellulose in the cell walls of the oomycete, *Apodachlya* sp.' *Arch. Mikrobiol.,* 72, 111-114.

LOVETT, J. S. (1963). 'Chemical and physical characterization of "nuclear caps" isolated from *Blastocladiella* zoospores.' *J. Bact.,* 85, 1235-1246.

LOVETT, J. S. (1968). 'Reactivation of ribonucleic acid and protein synthesis during germination of *Blastocladiella* zoospores and the role of the ribosomal nuclear cap.' *J. Bact.,* 96, 962-969.

LOVETT, J. S., and CANTINO, E. C. (1961). 'Reversible bicarbonate-induced enzyme activity and the point of no return during morphogenesis in *Blastocladiella.' J. gen. Microbiol.,* 24, 87-93.

LOVETT, J. S., and HASELBY, J. A. (1971). 'Molecular weights of the ribosomal ribonucleic acid of fungi.' *Arch. Mikrobiol.,* 80, 191-204.

LOVETT, J. S., and LEAVER, C. J. (1969). 'High-molecular weight artifacts in RNA extracted from *Blastocladiella* at elevated temperatures.' *Biochim. biophys. Acta,* 195, 319-327.

LYNCH, V. H., and CALVIN, M. (1952). 'Carbon dioxide fixation by microorganisms.' *J. Bact.,* 63, 525-531.

MACHLIS, L. (1957). 'Effect of certain organic acids on the utilization of mannose and fructose by the filamentous watermold, *Allomyces macrogynous.' J. Bact.,* 73, 627-631.

MACHLIS, L. (1958 a). 'Evidence for a sexual hormone in *Allomyces.' Physiologia Pl.,* 11, 181-192.

MACHLIS, L. (1958 b). 'A study of sirenin, the chemotactic sexual hormone from the watermold *Allomyces.' Physiologia Pl.,* 11, 845-854.

MACHLIS, L. (1966). 'Sex hormones in fungi.' In *The Fungi* (Eds. G. C. Ainsworth and A. S. Sussman), Academic Press, vol. 2, 415-433.

MACHLIS, L. (1968). 'The response of wild type male gametes of *Allomyces* to sirenin.' *Pl. Physiol.,* 43, 1319-1320.

MACHLIS, L. (1969 a). 'Zoospore chemotaxis in the watermold *Allomyces.'* *Physiologia Pl.,* 22, 126-139.

MACHLIS, L. (1969 b). 'Fertilization-induced chemotaxis in the zygotes of the watermold *Allomyces.'* *Physiologia Pl.,* 22, 392-400.

MACHLIS, L. (1972). 'The coming of age of sex hormones in plants.' *Mycologia,* 64, 235-247.

MACHLIS, L., NUTTING, W. H., WILLIAMS, M. W., and RAPAPORT, H., (1966). Production, isolation and characterization of sirenin.'*Biochemistry,* 5, 2147-2152.

MACHLIS, L., NUTTING, W. H., and RAPAPORT, H. (1968). 'The structure of sirenin.' *J. Am. chem. Soc.,* 90, 1674-1676.

MANOCHA, M. S., and COLVIN, J. R. (1968). 'Structure of the cell wall of *Pythium debaryanum.'* *J. Bact.,* 95, 1140-1152.

MARCHANT, R., and SMITH, D. G. (1968). 'The effect of chloramphenicol on growth and mitochondrial structure of *Pythium ultimum.'* *J. gen. Microbiol.,* 50, 391-397.

MATSUMAE, A., and CANTINO, E. C. (1971). 'Sensitivity of the spores of *Blastocladiella emersonii* and related fungi to antibiotics and some other drugs.' *J. Antibiotics,* 24, 77-84.

MCCORKINDALE, N. J., HUTCHENSON, S. A., PURSEY, B. A., SCOTT, W. T., and WHEELER, R. (1969). 'A comparison of the types of sterol found in species of Saprolegniales and Leptomitales with those found in some other Phycomycetes.' *Phytochemistry,* 8, 861-867.

MCCURDY, H. D., and CANTINO, E. C. (1960). 'Isocitritase, glycine-alanine transaminase and development in *Blastocladiella emersonii.'* *Pl. Physiol.,* 35, 463-476.

MCMORRIS, T. C., and BARKSDALE, A. W. (1967). 'Isolation of a sex hormone from the water mould *Achlya bisexualis.'* *Nature,* 215, 320-321.

MURRAY, C. L., and LOVETT, J. S. (1966). 'Nutritional requirements of the chytrid *Karlingia asterocysta,* an obligate chitinophile.' *Am. J. Bot.,* 53, 469-476.

MURPHY, M. N., and LOVETT, J. S. (1966). 'RNA and protein synthesis during zoospore differentiation in synchronized cultures of *Blastocladiella.'* *Devl. Biol.,* 14, 68-95.

MYERS, R. B., and CANTINO, E. C. (1971). 'DNA profile of the spore of *Blastocladiella emersonii:* evidence for γ-particle DNA.' *Arch. Mikrobiol.,* 78, 252-267.

NOLAN, R. A. (1969). 'Nutritional requirements for species of *Allomyces.'* *Mycologia,* 61, 641-644.

NOLAN, R. A. (1970 a). 'Sulfur source and vitamin requirements of the aquatic phycomycete, *Catenaria anguillulae.'* *Mycologia,* 62, 568-577.

NOLAN, R. A. (1970 b). 'Carbon source and micronutrient requirements of the aquatic phycomycete, *Catenaria anguillulae* Sorokin.' *Ann. Bot.,* 34, 927-939.

NOVAES-LEDIEU, M., JIMÉNEZ-MARTÍNEZ A., and VILLANUEVA, J. R. (1967). Chemical composition of hyphal wall of Phycomycetes.' *J. gen. Microbiol.,* 47, 237-245.

NOVAES-LEDIEU, M., and JIMÉNEZ-MARTÍNEZ, A. (1968). 'The structure of cell walls of Phycomycetes.' *J. gen. Microbiol.,* 54, 407-415.

OLSON, L. W., and FULLER, M. S. (1971). 'Leucine-lysine synchronization of *Allomyces* germlings.' *Arch. Mikrobiol.,* 78, 76-91.

PANDHI, P. N., and CANTINO, E. C. (1966). 'Differentiation of glucose-6-phosphate dehydrogenase isozymes and morphogenesis in *Blastocladiella emersonii.'* *Arch. Mikrobiol.,* 55, 226-244.

PAPAVIZAS, G. C., and AYERS, W. A. (1964). 'Effect of various carbon sources on growth and sexual reproduction of *Aphanomyces euteiches.*' *Mycologia,* 56, 816-830.

PAPAVIZAS, G. C., and DAVEY, C. B. (1960 a). 'Some factors affecting growth of *Aphanomyces euteiches* in synthetic media.' *Am. J. Bot.,* 47, 758-765.

PAPAVIZAS, G. C., and DAVEY, C. B. (1960 b). 'Some factors affecting sexual reproduction of *Aphanomyces euteiches.*' *Am. J. Bot.,* 47, 884-889.

PAO, V. M., and ARONSON, J. M. (1970). 'Cell wall structure of *Sapromyces elongatus.*' *Mycologia,* 62, 531-541.

PARKER, B. C., PRESTON, R. D. and FOGG, G. E. (1963). 'Studies of the structure and chemical composition of the cell walls of Vaucheriaceae and Saprolegniaceae.' *Proc. Roy. Soc.,* London, B158, 435-445.

POWELL, J. R., SCOTT, W. W., and KRIEG, N. R. (1972). 'Physiological parameters of growth in *Saprolegnia parasitica* Coker.' *Mycopath. Mycol. appl.,* 47, 1-40.

PRICE, J. S., and GLEASON, F. H. (1972). 'Glutamate dehydrogenase from *Apodachlya* (Oomycetes).' *Pl. Physiol.,* 49, 87-90.

PUROHIT, K., and TURIAN, G. (1972). 'D(-)lactate dehydrogenase from *Allomyces.* Partial purification and allosteric properties.' *Arch. Mikrobiol.,* 84, 287-300.

RIDINGS, W. H., GALLEGLY, M. E., and LILLY, V. G. (1969). 'Thiamine requirements helpful in distinguishing isolates of *Pythium* from those of *Phytophthora.*' *Phytopathology,* 59, 737-742.

ROBERTSON, J. A. (1972). 'Phototaxis in a new *Allomyces.*' *Arch. Mikrobiol.,* 85, 259-266.

RONCADORI, R. W. (1965). 'A nutritional comparison of some species of *Phytophthora.*' *Phytopathology,* 55, 595-599.

ROYLE, D. J., and HICKMAN, C. J. (1964). 'Analysis of factors governing in vitro accumulation of zoospores of *Pythium aphanidermatum* on roots. II Substances causing response.' *Can. J. Microbiol.,* 10, 201-219.

SANNER, T. (1971). 'Activation of glutamate dehydrogenase from *Blastocladiella emersonii* by AMP.' *Biochim. biophys. Acta.,* 250, 297-305.

SANNER, T. (1972). 'The unidirectional inhibition of glutamate dehydrogenase from *Blastocladiella emersonii.*' *Biochim. biophys. Acta,* 258, 689-700.

SCHLÖSSER, E., and GOTTLIEB, D. (1966). 'Sterols and the sensitivity of *Pythium* species to filipin.' *J. Bact.,* 91, 1080-1084.

SCHLÖSSER, E., and GOTTLIEB, D. (1968). 'The effect of sterols on metabolism of *Pythium* species.' *Arch. Mikrobiol.,* 61, 246-253.

SCHLÖSSER, E., SHAW, P. D., and GOTTLIEB, D. (1969). 'Sterols in species of *Pythium.*' *Arch. Mikrobiol.,* 66, 147-153.

SCHMOYER, I. R., and LOVETT, J. S. (1969). 'Regulation of protein synthesis in zoospores of *Blastocladiella.*' *J. Bact.,* 100, 854-864.

SHAW, R. (1965). 'The occurrence of γ linolenic acid in fungi.' *Biochim. biophys. Acta,* 98, 230-237.

SHERWOOD, W. A. (1966). 'Evidence for a sexual hormone in the water mold *Dictyuchus.*' *Mycologia,* 58, 215-220.

SIETSMA, J. H., EVELEIGH, D. E., and HASKINS, R. H. (1969). 'Cell wall composition and protoplast formation of some oomycete species.' *Biochim. biophys. Acta,* 184, 306-317.

SIETSMA, J. H., and HASKINS, R. H. (1967). 'Further studies on sterol reproduction in *Pythium.' Can. J. Microbiol.,* 13, 361-367.

SIETSMA, J. H., and HASKINS, R. H. (1968). 'The incorporation of cholesterol by *Pythium* sp. PRL 2142, and some of its effects on cell metabolism.' *Can. J. Biochem.,* 46, 813-818.

SISTROM, D. E., and MACHLIS, L. (1955). 'The effect of d-glucose on the utilization of d-mannose and d-fructose by a filamentous fungus.' *J. Bact.,* 70, 50-55.

SKUCAS, G. P. (1967). 'Structure and composition of the resistant sporangial wall in the fungus *Allomyces.' Am. J. Bot.,* 54, 1152-1158.

SOLL, D. R., and SONNEBORN, D. R. (1971). 'Zoospore germination in *Blastocladiella emersonii:* cell differentiation with protein synthesis.' *Proc. natn. Acad. Sci.,* 68, 459-463.

STORCK, R., and ALEXOPOULOS, C. J. (1970). 'Deoxyribonucleic acid of fungi.' *Bact. Rev.,* 34, 126-154.

STUMM, C., and VAN WENT, J. L. (1968). 'Histone bei dem Phycomyceten *allomyces arbuscula* (Butl.).' *Experientia,* 24, 1112-1113.

SUMNER, J. L. (1970). 'The fatty acid composition of *Blastocladiella emersonii.' Can. J. Microbiol.,* 16, 1161-1164.

SZANISZLO, P. J. (1965). 'A study of the effect of light and temperature on the formation of oogonia and oospores in *Saprolegnia diclina.' J. Elisha Mitchell. scient. Soc.,* 81, 10-15.

THOMAS, D. des S., and MULLINS, J. T. (1967). 'Role of enzymatic wall-softening in plant morphogenesis: hormonal induction in *Achlya.' Science,* 156, 84-85.

THOMAS, D. des S., and MULLINS, J. T. (1969). 'Cellulase induction and wall extension in the water mold *Achlya ambisexualis.' Physiologia Pl.,* 22, 347-353.

TIMBERLAKE, W. E., MCDOWELL, L., CHENEY, J., and GRIFFIN, D. H. (1973). 'Protein synthesis during the differentiation of sporangia in the water mold *Achlya.' J. Bact.,* 116, 67-73.

TOKUNAGA, J., and BARTNICKI-GARCIA, S. (1971). 'Structure and differentiation of the cell wall of *Phytophthora palmivora:* cysts, hyphae and sporangia.' *Arch. Mikrobiol.,* 79, 293-310.

TRUESDELL, L. C., and CANTINO, E. C. (1971). 'The induction and early events of germination in the zoospore of *Blastocladiella emersonii.'* In *Current Topics in Developmental Biology* (Eds. A. A. Moscona and A. Monroy), Academic Press, 1-44.

TURIAN, G. (1960). 'Déficiences du métabolisme oxydatif et différenciation sexuelle chez *Allomyces* et *Neorospora.* Activité d'une DPN-deshydrogénase lactique chez *Allomyces.' Path. Microbiol.,* 23, 687-699.

TURIAN, G. (1963). 'Synthèse différentielle d'acide ribonucléique et différenciation sexuelle chez l'*Allomyces.' Devl. Biol.,* 6, 61-72.

TURIAN, G., and CHODAT, F. (1959). 'Recherches comparatives sur la respiration ses phases gamétophytique et sporophytique du développement chez *Allomyces.' Physiologia Pl.,* 12, 70-81.

TURIAN, G., OJHA, M. N., SCHEPS, R., and OULEVEY, N. (1969). 'Oxidative deficiencies and some ultrastructural features of acridine-induced male strains of *Allomyces arbusculus.' Arch. Mikrobiol.,* 69, 92-100.

UNESTAM, T. (1965). 'Studies on the crayfish plague fungus *Aphanomyces astaci* I. Some factors affecting growth in vitro.' *Physiologia Pl.,* 18, 483-505.

UNESTAM, T. (1966 a). 'Studies on the physiology of *Monoblepharis'. Physiologia Pl.,* 19, 1-14.

UNESTAM, T. (1966 b). 'Chitinolytic, cellulolytic and pectinolytic activity in vitro of some parasitic and saprophytic oomycetes.' *Physiologia Pl.,* 19, 15-30.

UNESTAM, T. (1968). 'Some properties of unpurified chitinase from the crayfish plague fungus, *Aphanomyces astaci.' Physiologia Pl.,* 21, 137-147.

UNESTAM, T., and GLEASON, F. H. (1968). 'Comparative physiology of respiration in aquatic fungi. II. The Saprolegniaceae, especially *Aphanomyces astaci.' Physiologia Pl.,* 21, 573-588.

VOGEL, N. J. (1960). 'Two modes of lysine synthesis among lower fungi: evolutionary significance.' *Biochim. biophys. Acta,* 41, 172-173.

VOGEL, H. J. (1964). 'Distribution of lysine pathways among fungi: evolutionary implications.' *Am. Naturalist,* 98, 435-446.

WARREN, C. O., and MULLINS, J. T. (1969). 'Respiratory metabolism, in *Achlya ambisexualis.' Am. J. Bot.,* 56, 1135-1142.

WILLOUGHBY, L. G. (1962). 'The fruiting behaviour and nutrition of *Cladochytrium replicatum* Karling.' *Ann. Bot.,* 26, 13-26.

WILLOUGHBY, L. G. (1969). 'Pure culture studies on the aquatic Phycomycete, *Lagenidium giganteum.' Trans. Br. mycol. Soc.,* 52, 393-410.

ZEHENDER, C., and BÖCK, A. (1964). 'Wachstums—und Ernahrungsbedingungen des Abwasserpilzes *Leptomitus lacteus* Ag.' *Zbl. Bakt. Abt. II Bd.,* 117, 399-411.

ZEVENHUIZEN, L. P. T. M., and BARTNICKI-GARCIA, S. (1969). 'Chemical structure of the insoluble hyphal wall glucan of *Phytophthora cinnamoni.' Biochemistry,* 8, 1496-1501.

ZEVENHUIZEN, L. P. T. M., and BARTNICKI-GARCIA, S. (1970). 'Structure and role of a soluble cytoplasmic glucan from *Phytophthora cinnamomi.' J. gen. Microbiol.,* 61, 183-188.

22 Immunological Aspects of Fungal Disease in Fish

J. G. M. WILSON

22.1 Fungal Diseases of Freshwater Fish

22.1.1 Introduction

Fungal disease in fish may arise as a primary infection, with the fungus as the initial pathogen, or as a secondary invasion of tissue already damaged by viral, bacterial or mechanical agencies.

All fungal parasites, with the notable exception of *Ichthyophonus hoferi* Plehn et Mulsow are facultative. They occur naturally, living on nitrogenous organic matter derived from decaying plants and animals and are easy to culture *in vitro* (Willoughby and Collins, 1966).

They are a constant and ubiquitous component of the environment, subjecting fish to a continuous challenge. For example, Willoughby (1969 and personal communication) found *Saprolegnia* present throughout the year in the hatchery at Windermere at a concentration of 400 zoospores/litre; smaller numbers were present in the lake (6-17/litre) and in a stream feeding the lake (200/litre); while the highest concentration (4000/litre) was recorded in sewage effluent.

Thus, the host lives with the parasite in an equilibrium governed by the environment; however, this equilibrium may be upset and the resulting stress and reduced physiological competence concomitant with lowered resistance gives rise to the outbreak of disease.

22.1.2 Fungi Associated with Fish Disease

Saprolegnia is the most important fungal parasite of fish, but a number of other species have been involved in disease. A valuable contribution to this subject was made by Scott (1964) who not only isolated and identified fungi infesting fish but also carried out inoculation experiments with live fish to test their virulence. He found that *Saprolegnia parasitica* Coker, *S. ferax* (Gruith.) Thuret, *S. delica* Coker, *S. monoica* Pringsheim, *Achlya bisexualis* Coker et A. Couch and all isolates of *Saprolegnia* species would grow on wounded platyfish kept under controlled laboratory conditions. *S. ferax* killed non-wounded fish within 24 hours. *Pythium, Aphanomyces, Allomyces* and *Leptomitus* were observed growing on fish eggs but no conclusion could be drawn as to their pathogenicity. However, Vishniac and Nigrelli (1957) succeeded in inducing *Aphanomyces laevis* de Bary to grow on wounded platyfish, and further work may clarify the status of these fungi which are outside the genus *Saprolegnia*. It would be particularly desirable to test each fungus on the host species from which it was isolated, under conditions known to be most favourable for zoospore germination and successful colonization.

Secondary mycoses deriving from an initial bacterial aetiology are common and have been investigated in young perch (Willoughby, 1970), eels (Egusa and Nishikawa, 1965) and salmon (Hume Patterson, 1903). In the eel study *Aeromonas liquefaciens* Beijerinck was consistently isolated from the skin lesions and/or the viscera of the diseased fish. Healthy fish inoculated intramuscularly with the bacterium became easily infected with *Saprolegnia parasitica* and there was a parallel between the severity of haemorrhagic septicaemia and the extent of fungal infestation. Hume Patterson's efforts to infect salmon with pure cultures of the fungus were unsuccessful, but when the fish were rubbed with sandpaper, causing slight abrasions, and pure cultures of *Aeromonas liquefaciens* had been introduced to the water, the fungus grew rapidly on the abraded areas. It was concluded that the bacterium was the primary causative agent and was necessary to induce the fungal growth.

The spectrum of fungal species in an outbreak of disease may be broad, or it may be extremely narrow. The study of disease in young perch, for example, yielded a variety of fungi (Willoughby, 1970). These included *Aphanomyces* sp., *Achlya* sp., *Leptolegnia caudata* de Bary, *Leptomitus lacteus* Agardh., and *Saprolegnia diclina* Humphrey, of which *Achlya* and *Leptolegnia* tended to be predominant on the fish. These different forms occurred on separate lesions on the same fish or even together in a single lesion. This was in striking contrast to the recent outbreak of ulcerative dermal necrosis (UDN) in Atlantic salmon (Roberts, 1972) in which the fungal involvement is consistently and exclusively confined to a single species, *Saprolegnia* type I (Willoughby, 1968) (Figs. 22.1 to 22.4). The disease is confined initially to the unscaled areas of the head where the epithelial architecture is destroyed; the causative agent is not yet known, although the way in which the disease has spread and can be transmitted favours a viral origin.

Primary mycoses are often in the form of a delicate ring of fungus enclosing clean areas of the body surface and not associated with any tissue damage (Willoughby, 1972) and this is illustrated in Figs. 22.5 and 22.6. Secondary mycoses, on the other hand, assume a circular colony spreading from a focal lesion (Figs. 22.7 and 22.8). The way in which rings of fungus arise is not yet fully understood.

Non-oögonial forms of *Saprolegnia* are traditionally associated with isolations from fish. The oögonia produced by *Saprolegnia parasitica* in contaminated cultures or when kept at $10°C$ on dry cholesterol agar were meagre and notable for the small size of the oöspores (Fig. 22.4); these were present in generally small numbers, frequently with only two (Fig. 22.2). All six *Achlya* strains isolated from diseased perch (Willoughby, 1970) proved to be male and this striking observation provokes the enquiry whether the sexually sterile *Saprolegnia* strains found in UDN might also represent

574

mating strains of heterothallic species which lack suitable partners in a restricted environment.

Table 22.1 lists some of the fungi known to parasitize freshwater fish.

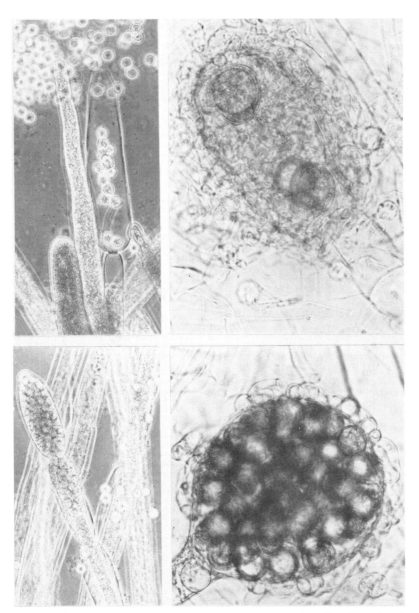

Fig. 22.1. *Saprolegnia* type I, dehiscence and zoospore release. Fig. 22.2. Oögonium showing abortive oöspores, a condition which occurs frequently in *Saprolegnia* type 1. Fig. 22.3. *Saprolegnia* type I. Two connected sporangia at the hyphal apex mature simultaneously. Fig. 22.4. *Saprolegnia* type I oögonium showing its close investment by antheridial hyphae. Oögonia only appear very sparsely in culture.

22.5

22.6

Fig. 22.5. Windermere char *Salvelinus alpinus* infected with *Saprolegnia* sp. Note delicate ring conformation in the upper fish, which become filled in at a later stage as in the lower fish (Photograph kindly supplied by Dr. L. G. Willoughby D.Sc.). **Fig. 22.6.** Windermere char *Salvelinus alpinus* infected with *Saprolegnia* sp. showing the delicate ring formation of the fungus in greater detail than Fig. 22.5.

22.7

Fig. 22.7. Fungus on the head and pectoral fin of a male grilse *Salmo salar* (December, 1905) from *'Life History and Habits of the Salmon, Sea Trout and Other Freshwater Fish'* by P. D. Mallock (Adam and Charles Black, 1912).

576

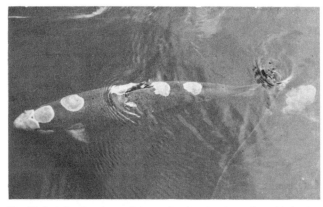

Fig. 22.8. Atlantic salmon *Salmo salar* showing dense fungal infection of Saprolegnia type I (Willoughby, 1968) in an outbreak of ulcerative dermal necrosis. (Photograph kindly supplied by Dr. L. G. Willoughby D.Sc.)

TABLE 22.1   Fungi parasitic on fish: host range

Species	Host	Authority
Saprolegnia type I	Atlantic salmon (*Salmo salar* L.)	Willoughby (1968)
	Sea trout (*Salmo trutta* L.)	Willoughby (1968)
	Brown trout (*Salmo trutta* L.)	Willoughby (1972)
	Windermere charr (*Salvelinus alpinus* L.)	Willoughby (1972)
Saprolegnia parasitica	Eel (*Anguilla japonica*)	Hoshina *et al.* (1960)
	Channel catfish (*Ictalurus punctatus* Rafinesque)	Scott and O'Bier (1962)
	Golden shiner (*Notemigonus crysoleucas* Mitchill)	
	Bluegill (*Lepomis macrochirus* Rafinesque)	
	Rainbow trout (*Salmo gairdneri* L.)	
	Rainbow trout eggs	
	Common shiner (*Notropis cornutus* Mitchill)	
	Spotfin shiner (*Notropis spilopterus* Cope)	
	Blacknose dace (*Rhinichthys atratulus* Hermann)	
	Brook trout (*Salvelinus fontinalis* Mitchill)	

TABLE 22.1 (cont.)

Species	Host	Authority
	Carp	Graff (1928)
	(Cyprinus carpio L.*)*	
	Leuciscus	Lund (1934)
	Very low resistance (highly susceptible)	Tiffney
	(Siluridae)	(1939 a, b)
	Coker catfish	
	(Ameiurus nebulosus Le Sueur)	
	(Catostomidae)	
	Lake chubsucker	
	(Erimyzon sucetta Lacepede)	
	(Salmonidae)	
	Landlocked Atlantic salmon	
	(Salmo sevago Girard)	
	Rainbow trout	
	(Salmo irideus gairdneri Gibbons)	
	Brown trout	
	(Salmo fario (trutta) L.)	
	(Esocidae)	
	Grass pickerel	
	(Esox americanus reticulatus Le Sueur*)*	
	Greater resistance	
	(Cyprinidae)	
	Creek chub	
	(Semotilus atromaculatus Mitchill)	
	(Centrarchidae)	
	Crappie	
	(Pomoxis sparoides Lacepede)	
	(Eupomotis gibbosus L.)	
	(Percidae)	
	Yellow perch	
	(Perca flavescens Mitchill)	
	(Poecilidae)	
	Mummichog	
	(Fundulus heteroclitus L.)	
	(Serranidae)	
	White perch	
	(Morone americana Gmelin)	
	Immune	
	Eel.	
	(Anguilla chrysypa Rafinesque)	
	High resistance	
	(Cyprinidae)	
	Goldfish	
	(Carassius auratus L.)	
	(Poecilidae)	

Species	Host	Authority
	(*Lebisters reticulatus* Peters) *(Centrarchidae)* Large mouth bass (*Micropterus salmoides* Lacepede)	
Saprolegnia ferax	Goldfish *(Carassius auratus)*	Knight (1885)
	Sunfish (*Lepomis macrochirus* Rafinesque)	Lockwood (1890)
	Perch *(Perca fluviatilis* L.)	Nolard-Tintigner (1970)
	Atlantic salmon (*Salmo salar* L.)	Drew (1909)
	Brown trout (*Salmo trutta* L.)	
	Eel (*Anguilla anguilla* L.)	
	Brook trout eggs (*Salvelinus fontinalis* Mitchill)	Scott (1964)
	Platyfish *(Platypoecilus maculatus)*	
	Fish eggs (unspecified)	Berkley (1864)
	Pike (*Esox lucius* L.)	Blanc (1888)
	Salmon (*Salmo salar* L.)	Murray (1885)
	Pickerel *(Esox americanus vermiculatus)*	Schnetzler (1887) Collins (1920)
	Trout	Smith (1878)
	Eels Lampreys Flounders Minnows	Agersborg (1933)
	Salmon (*Salmo salar* L.)	Huxley (1882) Hardy (1910)
	Salmon *(Salmo salar)*	Stirling (1880)
	Badly diseased Black bass (adult) (*Micropterus dolomieu* Lacepede) White bass *(Roccus chrysops* Rafinesque) Yellow bass Calico bass (*Pomoxis nigromaculatus* Le Sueur)	Clinton (1894)

TABLE 22.1 (cont.)

Species	Host	Authority
	Yellow perch	
	(*Perca flavescens* Mitchill)	
	Grayling	
	(*Thymallus thymallus*)	
	Pike	
	(*Esox lucius* L.)	
	Pike perch	
	(*Stizostedion incioperca* L.)	
	Sheepshead	
	(*Aplodinotus grunniens* Rafinesque)	
	Sand pike	
	(*Stizostedion canadense* Smith)	
	Bream	
	(*Notemigonus crysoleucas* Mitchill)	
	Blue sunfish	
	(*Lepomis macrochirus* Rafinesque)	
	Warmouth	
	Sucker	
	(*Catostomas commersonii* Lacepede)	
	Redhorse	
	(*Moxostoma* sp.)	

Somewhat affected
Small-mouthed black bass
  (*Micropterus dolomieu* Lacepede)
Rock-bass
  (*Ambloplites rupestris* Rafinesque)
Brook trout (adults)
  (*Salvelinus fontinalis* Mitchill)
Yellow catfish
  (*Ictalurus* sp.)
Spotted catfish
  (*Ictalurus* sp.)
Buffalo
  (*Ictiobus cyprinellus* Valenciennes)
Dogfish or Common Bowfin
  (*Amia calva.*)
Mooneye
  (*Hiodon tergisus* Le Sueur)
Long-nosed gar
  (*Lepisosteus osseus* L.)
Short-nosed gar
  (*Lepisosteus oculatus* Winchell)
Redhorse
  (*Moxostoma* sp.)
Suckers
  (*Catostomas* sp.)

Species	Host	Authority
	Practically free from attack	
	Sturgeon	
	(*Acipenser sturio* L.)	
	Burbot	
	(*Lota lota* L.)	
	Mud catfish	
	(*Ictalurus* sp.)	
	Mississippi catfish	
	(*Ictalurus* sp.)	
	Carp	
	(*Cyprinus carpio*)	
	Tench	
	(*Tinca tinca* L.)	
	Goldfish	
	(*Carassius auratus* L.)	
	Golden ide	
	(*Idus* sp.)	
	Brook trout (young)	
	(*Salvelinus fontinalis*)	
	Brown trout (young)	
	(*Salmo trutta* L.)	
	Black bass (young)	
	(*Micropterus dolomieu* Lacepede)	
Saprolegnia diclina	Roach	Nolard-Tintigner (1970)
	(*Rutilus rutilus* L.)	
	Perch (young)	Willoughby (1970)
	(*Perca fluviatilis* L.)	
(syn. *S. delica*)	Rainbow trout and eggs	Scott (1964); Scott and O'Bier (1962)
	(*Salmo gairdneri* Richardson)	
	Cisco	
	(*Coregonus artedi* Le Sueur)	
	Northern pike and eggs	
	(*Esox lucius* L.)	
	Brown trout and eggs	
	(*Salmo trutta* L.)	
	Cutthroat trout	
	(*Salmo clarkii*)	
Saprolegnia monoica	Rainbow trout and eggs	Scott and O'Bier (1962)
	(*Salmo gairdneri* Mitchill)	
	Bluegill	
	(*Lepomis macrochirus* Rafinesque)	
	Brown trout eggs	
	(*Salmo trutta* L.)	
		Fischer (1892)

TABLE 22.1 (cont.)

Species	Host	Authority
	Carp (*Cyprinus carpio* L.)	Walentowicz (1885)
Saprolegnia mixta de Bary	Sick fish (unspecified)	De Bary (1888) Clinton (1894)
Saprolegnia invaderis Davis and Lazar*	Trout	Davis and Lazar (1940)
Saprolegnia torulosa de Bary†	Salmon (*Salmo salar* L.)	Huxley (1882)
Saprolegnia sp.	Brown trout (*Salmo trutta* L.) Largemouth bass and eggs (*Micropterus salmoides* Lacepede) Bluegill (*Lepomis macrochirus* Rafinesque) Green sunfish (*Lepomis cyanellus* Rafinesque) Brook trout fingerlings (*Salvelinus fontinalis* Mitchill) Common shiner (*Notropis cornutus* Mitchill) Northern pike and eggs (*Esox lucius* L.) Minnows (*Fundulus* sp.) Brook trout (*Salvelinus fontinalis* Mitchill) Golden trout (*Salmo aquabonita*) Golden shiner (*Notemigonus crysoleucas* Mitchill)	Scott and O'Bier (1962)
	Goldfish (*Carassius auratus* L.)	Bennett (1842)
	Carp (*Cyprinus carpio* L.)	Chiapelli (1933)
	Salmon (*Salmo salar* L.)	Hume-Patterson (1903)
Fish mould (unspecified)	Salmon fry (*Salmo salar* L.)	Robinson (1896)

* An aberrant form of *Saprolegnia ferax*   † Doubtful taxon

Species	Host	Authority
	Brook trout (*Salvelinus fontinalis* Mitchill)	Rosenberg (1908)
	Shad (*Alosa sapidissima* Wilson)	Ryder (1883)
	Roach (*Rutilus rutilus* L.)	Stirling (1880)
	Dace (*Leuciscus leuciscus* L.)	
	Gudgeon (*Gobio gobio* L.)	
	Pike (*Esox lucius* L.)	
	Perch (*Perca fluviatilis* L.)	
	Salmon (*Salmo salar* L.)	
	Brown Bullhead (*Ictalurus nebulosus*)	Unger (1843)
Achlya americana Humphrey	Bluegill (*Lepomis macrochirus* Rafinesque)	Scott and O'Bier (1962)
Achlya bisexualis Coker and A. Couch	*Betta* sp. (*Betta splendens*) Zebra danio (*Brachydanio rerio*) Platyfish (*Platypoecilus maculatus*) Dwarf gourami (*Colisa lalia*) Rosy barb (*Puntius conchonius*)	Scott and O'Bier (1962)
Achlya prolifera (Nees) de Bary	Pike (*Esox lucius* L.)	Schnetzler (1887) Blanc (1888) Robin (1863)
Achlya sp.	Goldfish (*Carassius auratus* L.) Perch (0+) (*Perca fluviatilis* L.)	Cohn (1968) Willoughby (1970) Tiffney (1939 b)
Achlya flagellata Coker	Trout (unspecified—serious epidemic) Chub (*Fundulus heteroclitus* L.) Mummichog (inoculated)	Tiffney and Wolf 1937

TABLE 22.1 (cont.)

Species	Host	Authority
Achlya nowickii Raciborski*	Carp (*Cyprinus carpio* L.)	Walentowicz (1885)
A. racemosa Hildebrand	Trout eggs (unspecified)	Humphrey (1893) Hine (1878-79)
A. polyandra Hildebrand		Hine (1878-79)
Aphanomyces laevis	Rainbow trout and eggs (*Salmo gairdneri* Mitchill)	Scott and O'Bier (1962)
Aphanomyces	Perch (0+) (*Perca fluviatilis* L.)	Willoughby (1970)
	Betta and eggs (*Betta splendens*) Rainbow trout eggs (*Salmo gairdneri* Mitchill) Platyfish (*Platypoecilus maculatus*) Angel Fish (*Pterophyllum scalare*)	Scott and O'Bier (1962)
Leptolegnia caudata de Bary	Perch (0+) (*Perca fluviatilis* L.)	Willoughby (1970)
Leptomitus lacteus	Perch (0+) (*Perca fluviatilis* L.)	Willoughby (1970)
	Rainbow trout eggs (*Salmo gairdneri* Mitchill) Northern pike eggs (*Esox lucius* L.)	Scott and O'Bier (1962)
Allomyces anomalus Emerson	*Betta* eggs (*Betta splendens*)	Scott and O'Bier (1962)
Pythium ultimum Trow.	Bluegill (*Lepomis macrochirus* Rafinesque)	Scott and O'Bier (1962)
Pythium sp.	*Betta* and eggs (*Betta splendens*) Brook trout eggs (*Salvelinus fontinalis*) Bluegill (*Lepomis macrochirus* Rafinesque) Bumblebee (*Brachygobius doriae*)	Scott and O'Bier (1962)

* Doubtful taxon

Species	Host	Authority
	Brown trout eggs (*Salmo trutta* L.)	
Dictyuchus monosporus Leitgeb	Green newt *(Triturus viridescens)*	Tiffney (1939 a)

22.1.3 Ulcerative Dermal Necrosis (UDN)

Ulcerative dermal necrosis (UDN) is a disease of the skin of mature salmonid fish, characteristically occurring as they enter freshwater on their spawning migration from the sea. The lesion takes the form of a progressive cytolytic necrosis at specific sites on the integument of the head, which rapidly becomes secondarily infected with *Saprolegnia parasitica* (Roberts, 1972; Roberts *et al.,* 1970 a, b; 1971; 1972) (Figs. 22.7, 22.8). Once this occurs the fish usually succumb, death being due to circulatory failure resulting from osmotic haemodilution, often complicated by bacterial infection.

The present epidemic started in 1964 in South West Ireland (Jensen, 1965; Carbery, 1968) and has now spread to almost all British rivers (Elson, 1968; Munro, 1970; Stevenson, 1970). In 1968 the condition was observed in France (De Kinkelin and Le Turdu, 1971). The same disease broke out in Britain in 1877, and during the following decade it caused heavy losses on many rivers (Report of the Inspector of Salmon Fisheries (England and Wales) 1881 and 1882; Grimble, 1899). The disease, then known as salmon disease, precipitated a spate of research which led to the conclusion that *Saprolegnia ferax* was the causative agent (Smith, 1878; Stirling, 1978, 1880 a, b; Brook, 1879; Buckland *et al.,* 1880; Huxley, 1882; Murray, 1885; Swan, 1889). Hume Patterson (1903), however, disputed the importance of the fungus and reduced its status to that of a secondary invader of wounds caused by a bacterium *Bacillus salmonis pestis*. This culture has been shown to consist of a mixture of two facultative pathogens *Aeromonas liquefaciens* and *Pseudomonas fluorescens* Migula which are ubiquitous in freshwater (Bisset, 1946). The bacteriological aspect was further investigated in the present epidemic and a cold water form of Columnaris disease was suggested, but not substantiated (Jensen, 1965; Brown and Collins, 1966; Carbery and Strickland, 1968; Elson, 1968).

The role of the fungus *Saprolegnia parasitica* has proved controversial (Stuart and Fuller, 1968; Harrison and Jones, 1971). Positive identification on the basis of sexual structures was made by Willoughby (1968) who has continued to investigate the fungal aspect (Willoughby, 1969, 1971, 1972).

Carbery and Strickland (1968) succeeded in transmitting the disease from infected to healthy salmon by simple siphoning techniques between tanks, as well as by inoculation of membrane filtered tissue homogenates. However, attempts to isolate or demonstrate a virus from diseased fish have failed so far (Carbery and Strickland, 1968; De Kinkelin and Le Turdu, 1971), but until this can be done the theory of a viral aetiology remains an attractive but elusive hypothesis.

22.1.4 Fungal Serology

Serological analysis of the antigens of fungi has been concerned with two major aspects. Firstly as an aid to diagnosis and prognosis of fungal diseases in man and his animals, and secondly in the elucidation of taxonomic relationships between fungi.

Serological tests have become firmly established as useful and reliable in the study of several mycotic infections. Patients suffering from fungal diseases exhibit characteristic antibodies in their serum (Longbottom and Pepys, 1964); the serum may further be classified according to the number of precipitin lines produced ('reactivity') and the number of antigenic extracts with which the serum reacts ('range') (English and Henderson, 1967). The intensity of the precipitin reaction is also of value in diagnosis (Amos, 1970).

The application of immunological analysis to fungal taxonomy was made practicable by the development of gel-diffusion methods, both by the Ouchterlony (1949) technique and by electrophoresis. This latter method has made a bigger impact on fungal taxonomy than any other technique of molecular analysis. These techniques rely on the antibody forming mechanism of animals to distinguish between molecules which express a direct reflection of the genetic code. Different strains and species possess different molecules and therefore a distinction can be drawn between them. This subject has been reviewed by Seeliger (1960) and Hall (1969).

Differences between strains was first reported by Chang *et al.* (1962) who found that each of four wild *Neurospora* strains, as well as a mutant strain of *N. crassa* Shear and Dodge had a distinctive protein complement. Antigenic strain differences were noted by Riddell *et al.* (1968) in a study of malt workers, and these differences have been further documented in the study of enzymes, especially esterase in different strains of *Phytophthora* (Hall *et al.*, 1968, 1969) and *Fusarium* (Meyer *et al.*, 1964; Hall, 1967).

Species differences based on general proteins were shown to be vallid in *Pythium* (Clare, 1963; Clare, *et al.*, 1968) *Phytophthora* (Clare *et al.*, 1968) *Neurospora* (Chang *et al.*, 1962) *Septoria* (Durbin, 1966) *Candida* (Shechter *et al.*, 1968) *Ceratocystis* (Stipes, 1967) *Colletotrichum* and *Glomerella* (McCombs and Winstead, 1963) and *Penicillium* (Bent, 1967). The ability to differentiate between pathogenic and nonpathogenic fungi can be extremely valuable. Identification of fungi with few useful or reliable morphological characters becomes a reality. Precipitin lines specific to the isolate of each species were obtained and serological comparison of three *Fusarium* species (Madhosingh, 1964) and three *Ascochyta* species (Madhosingh and Wallen, 1967). Antiserum to crude extracts of mycelia or spores also revealed species specific antigens in *Ceratocystis* (Burrell *et al.*, 1965; Amos and Burrell, 1967; Morton and Dukes, 1967; Suerth and Varney, 1968). A refinement of this technique using antiserum specific for a single antigen is often more valuable and has, for example, been applied successfully in determining serological groups among various species of the yeast genus *Kloeckera* (Tsuchiya *et al.*, 1966).

22.2 Introduction to Immunological Aspects of Fungal Disease

Resistance to infectious diseases may be innate or specifically acquired. Innate resistance is largely nonspecific and based on physiological and anatomical features which can act as physical barriers to the invasion of organisms (e.g. the skin), or chemical barriers, where substances such as lysozyme or interferon inhibit the growth and reproduction of micro-organisms after penetration, or inactivate toxins. Specifically acquired resistance in vertebrates is a host response to initial exposure or challenge from an invading foreign organism or its metabolites by (1) the production of antibodies, (2) the development of immune memory as measured by an enhanced response to a secondary exposure to an antigen, (3) the proliferation of cells concerned with recognition and neutralization and (4) the rejection of foreign tissue graft from an unrelated donor of the same species.

22.3 Mechanisms of Innate Resistance

22.3.1 The Skin

In fish, the skin is composed of two regions, the epidermis and dermis, separated by a basement membrane. The outer layer, which is continuous over the scales, is the epidermis and consists of several layers of stratified epithelial cells which become progressively more flattened and fibrillar as they approach the surface (Jimbo *et al.*, 1963). Abundant mucous cells are normally dispersed throughout this zone as they migrate to the surface.

The dermis is composed of densely arranged fibrous connective tissue in which the scales are embedded. This is backed by loosely dispersed connective tissue fibres, and pigment cells occur below and parallel to the basement membrane.

The protective role of the epidermis is evident whenever fish suffer abrasion. Almost invariably the site of cell damage is a focus of invasion. In UDN following the loss of the epidermal cells the lesion is invaded by *Saprolegnia parasitica*. The most important factor governing fungal invasion would appear to be the integrity of the basement membrane. Fungal infections were not seen when this was intact, although the epithelial architecture was completely destroyed (Roberts *et al.*, 1970). However, it should be noted that fin clipping, when marking fish, did not lead to infection. Damage to the epidermis would result in stress and a reduced potential for mucus production: both these factors have been implicated in fish disease.

Sexual dimorphism has been observed in the skin structure of migratory sea trout, *Salmo trutta* L. by Stoklosowa (1966). He described the epidermis of an adult spawning male sea trout as thin, consisting of one irregular layer of small epithelial cells lacking in mucous cells. Not only had it lost most of its regular structure but it appeared to have a tendency to be moulted. In contrast, the epidermis of female sea trout was thick and was formed by many layers of distinct epithelial cells accompanied by many mucoid cells full of mucus. The observed incidence of fungal infection at the spawning stage in the life history, especially among male salmonids, may be due to the changes in the structure and pigmentation of the skin, which occur at that time. However, the sexual differences noted in trout migrating to sea were not as obvious in non-migrating lake trout. The deficiencies in male sea trout skin structure have not been evident in spawning male salmon *Salmo salar* L. which have also migrated to the sea (J. E. Harris, personal communication).

22.3.2 The Mucus

Fish secrete mucus externally, where its viscosity acts as a protection against mechanical damage, and in enhancing swimming ability (Jakowska, 1963; Rosen and Cornford, 1971). The constant secretion of mucus might tend to prevent some parasites from settling; fish challenged with dense suspensions of zoospores did not take any onto the body surface (Willoughby, 1971), thus suggesting a mechanical barrier.

Glycoproteins account for about 90% of the dry weight of the nondiffusible material in mucus (Fletcher and Grant, 1969) and their physical nature produces a highly viscous film covering the body surface. Furthermore, the mucus in lungfish has been shown to have remarkable powers of coagulating and precipitating particles in suspension (Van Oosten, 1957). The flagella of *Saprolegnia* zoospores cease to beat immediately on contact with trout mucus (Willoughby, 1972); however, germination then ensues and immobility may therefore be the first stage in this process and not the result of inhibition!

Mucus is synthesized in the goblet cells of the epidermis which begin to differentiate initially near the basement membrane. The endoplasmic reticulum and Golgi apparatus are extensively developed, suggesting that both these organelles are involved in the formation of mucus, which is deposited as clear vesicles increasing in number as the cells reach the periphery. The plasma membrane of mature goblet cells, distended with mucus vesicles, ruptures as they reach the epidermal surface, releasing their contents.

A. D. Pickering (personal communication) studied the distribution of goblet cells in the epidermis of brown trout and char and found significantly more cells on the body than on the fins. This was confirmed by measuring the sialic acid concentration of the epidermis. It is interesting to note that in outbreaks of *Saprolegnia* in hatcheries, infected fish frequently develop fungal patches on the fins before the rest of the body is affected.

In view of the accumulating evidence that mucus production is under the control of the endocrine system (Ogawa and Johanson, 1967; Ogawa, 1970; Olivereau and Lemoine, 1971; Mattheij and Stroband, 1971) further work must be directed towards the study of changes in mucus production resulting from environmental or endocrine influences. The significance of the role of mucus production in fungal infection may then be assessed in terms of the noted differences between the sexes, especially at maturity, and at different water temperatures. The incidence of fungal disease is especially high in winter.

Mucus carries a variety of biologically active molecules. Skarnes and Watson (1957) have provided a very detailed summary of the 14 kinds of antimicrobial factors reported in vertebrates, including lysozyme. Lysozyme is an enzyme, which by cleaving the bonds between the muramic acid and N-acetylglucosamuric constituents of certain bacterial cell walls, can destroy their integrity. Lysozyme activity has been demonstrated in the mucus of plaice *Pleuronectes platessa* L. (Fletcher and Grant, 1969) and salmon *Salmo salar* L. (J. E. Harris, personal communication). The lysozyme isolated from the plaice also exhibited weak chitinase activity (Fletcher and White, 1973 a). Other nonspecific bacteriostats causing bacteriolysis, e.g. properdin, have not yet been detected in fish mucus but occur in the serum (Vladimirov, 1968). Interferon production following a virus infection has been demonstrated *in vivo* in Rainbow trout (*Salmo gairdneri* (De Kinkelin and Dorson, 1973)).

Willoughby (1972) took mucus from a variety of hatchery trout and char and examined it for signs of fungus. In the case of sexually immature trout, fungal mycelium was completely absent from the freshly collected mucus, and, in addition, germlings derived from zoospores were never seen in it following overnight incubation. However, when mucus was taken from an ostensibly clean ripe female trout, it was found to contain mycelium, and the fish died four days later, heavily infected. The presence in mucus of an inhibitory factor which is impaired at sexual maturity was further suggested when the mucus from a clean spent male char was examined. No mycelium was found in the mucus, but it was shown that viable zoospores were present in it after overnight incubation. During the following ten days the fish remained outwardly clean, but mycelium was observed in the mucus, although some of the mycelium was dead and autolysed. Predictably, this fish died 11 days later with heavy fungal infection.

22.3.3 Cellular Mechanisms

Cellular aspects of immunity, which include phagocytosis and encapsulation, are the most active contributing factors to native resistance in mammals, but their importance in resisting fungal infection in fish is uncertain.

Encapsulation of the spores takes place in systemic infections of *Ichthyophonus hoferi*. Concentric layers of fibroblast-like cells wall off the parasites but the disease is rarely arrested completely, and death occurs in most fish within six months (Sindermann, 1956, 1970).

A marked leucocyte response against secondary invaders has been observed in advanced lesions of UDN (Roberts *et al.*, 1970). These phagocytes are cells with a system of digestive vacuoles capable of removing and digesting most foreign matter. Teleosts have been shown to have a family of lymphocytes, but it is difficult to imagine how they would effectively resist fungal infection.

22.4 Mechanisms of Acquired Immunity

22.4.1 Serum Antibodies

Antibodies are produced in the serum as a response to antigenic challenge. These antibodies may act in different ways: precipitins precipitate soluble antigens (e.g. enzymes and endotoxins); agglutinins immobilize foreign cells and particulate antigens by causing them to clump together; opsonins interact with the bacterial surface making it more vulnerable to phagocytosis; and lysins effect the dissolution or lysis of cells.

Adaptive immune responses are well developed in teleosts. High levels of specifically acquired humoral antibodies have been demonstrated against a wide variety of antigens both particulate and soluble, by artificial immunization (Ridgway *et al.*, 1966). A more rapid response with larger amounts of antibody is produced on secondary stimulation. Naturally acquired precipitating antibodies against fungal antigens have been detected in the serum of Atlantic salmon *Salmo salar* (Hodkinson and Hunter, 1970). Many other species of freshwater and marine teleosts have recently been shown to possess naturally occurring serum precipitins, which react with both mycelial extracts and culture filtrates of a variety of fungi. These fungi are not only strains of *Saprolegnia* isolated from diseased fish, but also species which are neither parasitic on fish nor naturally occurring in water. These include *Armillaria mellea* L., *Trichoderma* sp., *Fusarium avenaceum* (Fr.) Sacc., *Botrytis cinerea* De Bary, and *Penicillium claviforme,* L. The nature of this reaction suggests the presence of antigens common to different fungal species. Seeliger (1960) states that serological reactions with fungal antigens and antisera are not absolutely specific and cross-reactions are quite frequent. Antigenic relationships are known to exist between fungi and bacteria and even human blood cells (Neill *et al.*, 1955; Davis *et al.*, 1968). Until specific fungal antigens are used, the interpretation of precipitin reactions in sera must be of limited value. At least six precipitin lines are produced in double diffusion-in-gel reactions between salmon sera and fungal antigens; no clear relation was found between the number of lines and the extent of disease in these fish (Figs. 22.9, 22.10). The serum of some fish with extensive and dense fungal colonization produced a strong precipitin reaction showing several lines, and therefore the protective value of serum antibodies must be doubtful at least; their diagnostic and prognostic value has yet to be assessed. However, in an experiment, mature brown trout maintained in a hatchery from October to December and tested at intervals for the presence of serum antibodies against fungal antigens, showed substantial reductions in the quantity of antibody when the fish developed fungal infections. This period is characterized by a drop in the water temperature and by spawning stress which together are thought to result in an increase in the incidence of fungal disease. Of the fish which survived, both showed a comparable reduction in the quantity of serum antibody without becoming diseased. It should be borne in mind that the serum antibody measured only represents free antibody and not necessarily the total amount produced. Nevertheless, it is difficult to ascribe a defensive function to a serum antibody when the site of infection is external.

The major sites of humoral antibody production in the teleosts are the anterior kidney and the spleen (Smith *et al.*, 1967; Chiller *et al.*, 1969).

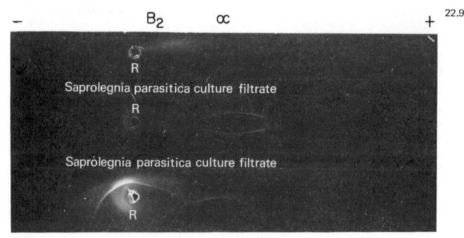

Fig. 22.9. Immuno-electrophoresis of the serum from rainbow trout *(Salmo gairdneri)* to show the electrophoretic mobility of the precipitins against fungal antigens.

22.4.2 Mucus Antibodies

Fungal infection rarely extends beyond the dermis, and it is at the external body surface that the parasitic zoospores are encountered in their efforts to germinate and establish themselves. Clearly, the possible presence of protective antibodies at this surface would be of direct practical value to the wellbeing and survival of the fish.

Local antibody production at mucous surfaces is well established in mammals (Pierce, 1959); the secretory immunoglobulin IgA, is synthesized locally and independently of the serum (Rossen *et al.*, 1968). Precipitating antibody was detected in the intestinal mucus in chub, *Leuciscus cephalus* L. in response to natural and experimental infections with an acanthocephalan helminth parasite (Harris, 1972). Agglutinating antibody was present in both epithelial and intestinal mucus of plaice *Pleuronectes platessa* L. following oral and parenteral immunization with bacterial antigens (Fletcher and White, 1973 b). Both these types of antibody resembled IgM

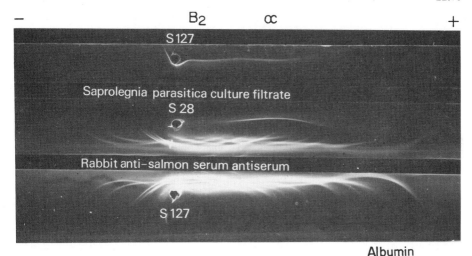

Fig. 22.10. Immuno-electrophoresis of the serum from two different Atlantic salmon *(Salmo salar)* to show the electrophoretic mobility of the precipitins against fungal antigens in relation to the total serum proteins (0.1 M Barbitone buffer pH 8.6).

in mammals. As yet, no muco-antibodies have been detected to fungi in fish. South *et al.* (1966) concluded that the biosynthesis of IgA has evolved at a comparatively recent stage in the phylogenetic sequence. IgA has now been tentatively described in the Amphibia (Yamaguchi *et al.,* 1973). Local synthesis of IgM in patients lacking an IgA system has been reported by Brandtzaeg *et al.* (1968) and this supports the possibility of local synthesis of IgM in fish also lacking an IgA system. In man, at least, the plasma cells are predominantly IgA producers. Good *et al.* (1966) stated that plasma cells were absent from the lamina propria in fish, but it is possible that the antibody producing cells in the skin have not yet been recognized.

Secretory antibodies were produced in plaice in response to oral immunization, often in the almost complete absence of circulating antibody (Fletcher and White, 1973 b). Parenteral administration of antigen, however, resulted in the production of high titre serum antibodies and low levels in the epithelial secretions. It is therefore possible that both local synthesis and transudation operate to protect the mucous surfaces, the dominant mechanism being determined by the route by which the antigen enters the fish.

Fryer *et al.* (1972 and personal cummunication) give evidence of an acquired immunity in the complete absence of serum antibody in chinook salmon orally immunized with a lyophilized sonicate prepared from cells of *Vibrio anguillarum,* and Nigrelli (1937) demonstrated an acquired immunity to an external monogenean trematode; the parasite did not survive in the mucus from fish which had acquired immunity, although it could live for longer periods in the mucus from susceptible fish. In a study of young perch *Perca fluviatilis* L., Willoughby (1970) cultured a variety of fungi from diseased fish. The complete absence of *Saprolegnia ferax*, a weak known pathogen which was present to the greatest extent in the lake water, might be considered as evidence for a specific immune response to this species of fungus which has been previously reported from perch (Nolard-Tintigner, 1970). This does not, however, preclude an innate physiological factor.

It has been suggested by Hildemann (1962) that the newly hatched fry of the Amazon discus fish obtain protection against important pathogens from antibodies in the parental male mucus on which they live exclusively for the first five weeks of their lives. In the absence of this parent, the young fish die, although abundant food may be available. The fry, however, survived when broad spectrum antibiotics were added to the water.

22.5   Immunochemistry of Teleost Antibodies

The serum of Atlantic salmon *Salmo salar* contains natural precipitins against fungal antigens. These precipitins are of at least two types.

Firstly, a macroglobulin, with a sedimentation coefficient of 14S, which migrates as a β_2 globulin on immuno-electrophoresis and is sensitive to 2-merceptoethanol reduction (Figs. 22.11 and 22.12). This corresponds to the tetrameric immunoglobulin induced in the giant grouper *Epinephelus itaira* (Clem, 1971) and in rainbow trout *Salmo gairdneri* (Dorson, 1972). Immunoglobulins resembling mammalian IgM have been demonstrated in birds, reptiles, amphibia and elasmobranchs (sharks and rays) and these have a pentameric structure with a sedimentation coefficient of 19S (Feinstein and Munn, 1969). IgM is characteristic of the primary immune response, and functionally it is most effective as an agglutinin. This β_2 macroglobulin has not been found in all fish tested.

22.11

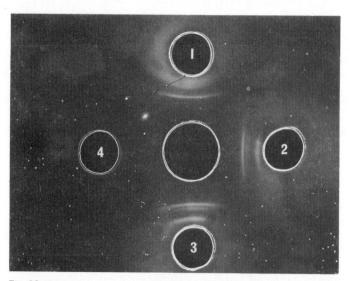

Fig. 22.11. Ouchterlony double diffusion-in-gel between sera from different salmon and fungal antigens. Centre well: *Saprolegnia parasitica* isolate P41 from diseased brown trout (culture filtrate); Well 1: Salmon A; Wells 2 and 3: Salmon B; Well 4: normal saline control.

Secondly, a 7S, 2-mercaptoethanol insensitive precipitin which migrates towards the anode on electrophoresis ($\alpha-1$ mobility). No antibody with these physical characteristics has been induced in teleosts even after repeated and prolonged immunization, nor has an 'antibody shift' from 'heavy' to 'light' antibody been observed in rainbow trout (Hodgins *et al.*, 1967) or in the margate *Haemulon albium* (Sigel and

Clem, 1965). For these reasons it must be doubtful whether the 7S precipitin found universally in salmon and other fish is an antibody, although it is antigenically related to the 14S precipitin (D. H. Davies, personal communication).

A protein in normal nurse shark reacts specifically with fructosans (Harisdangkul *et al.,* 1972), and there is an eel antihuman blood group H (O) serum protein which precipitates specifically with monosaccharides (Springer and Desai, 1971); these are other examples of serum precipitins which cannot be considered as true antibodies although they may be functionally related.

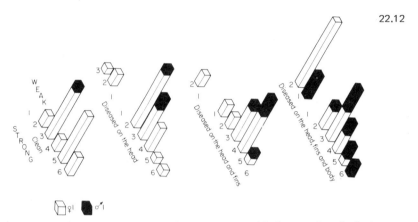

22.12

Fig. 22.12. To show the 'reactivity' (number of precipitin lines produced) of salmon sera in double diffusion-in-gel against the culture filtrate of *Saprolegnia* type I (Willoughby, 1969), according to the extent of fungal infection on the fish. N.B. The reactivity of the serum of heavily diseased fish did not differ markedly from that of clean or lightly diseased fish. Proportionately more males than females were heavily diseased.

22.6   Factors Affecting the Immune Response

22.6.1   Temperature

Antibody production in poikilotherms, as with other metabolic processes, closely relates to the temperature of the animal, which in turn reflects the environmental temperature of the animal's normal habitat; thus, detectable agglutinins were produced after 27 days at 5 °C in the sable fish *Anoplopoma fimbria* Pallas which inhabits the colder regions of the North Pacific (Ridgway, 1962) and precipitating antibody has been detected in the serum of chub *Leuciscus cephalus* L. (Harris, 1972) and salmon taken from the river at temperatures of 4 °C and less, but it could not be induced in dace *Leuciscus leuciscus* L. at 2 °C although haemagglutins were produced at that temperature, in response to intra-peritoneal injections of a human Rh +, 0 erythrocyte suspension (Harris, 1973).

Optimum antibody response takes place at the optimum temperature for the fish, and lower temperatures slow down the process. The primary response induction period is especially vulnerable to low temperatures, because it takes much longer than a secondary response. Carp immunized with bovine serum albumin at 25 °C, and kept at that temperature for 8 days before a change to 12 °C, showed a rising titre of antibody. The rising titre occurred even although they were transferred to the lower temperature before the appearance of the first circulating antibody. In contrast, no circulating antibody was detectable in carp kept at 12 °C for the same period of time. The ability to produce antibody at low temperature is thus demonstrated, but it is dependent on immune memory, and in consequence the primary response is very much slower (Avtalion, 1969).

The long induction period at low temperatures in poikilotherms argues for a defence system which does not require initial stimulation. In addition to the innate mechanisms of immunity which have been discussed earlier, the precipitins recently discovered in the serum of the nurse shark, eels and salmon would fulfil this requirement.

22.6.2 Sex and Sexual Maturity

Sexual differences have been noted in the serum precipitins against fungal antigens in salmon, rainbow trout and brown trout. In the author's experience, no natural β_2 precipitins have been detected in mature male fish, although they occur in some female fish. This may be reflected in a reduced competence in resisting infection. Jones (1959) states that almost all of the salmon kelts which survive spawning are females. Klontz (1967) failed to obtain antibodies from immunized spawning salmon even though the temperature was 9-14 °C. High mortalities from fungal infection have been noted among spawning fish, although immature fish in the same water were unaffected.

22.6.3 Social Behaviour

Social behaviour represented by the 'peck' order apparently influences the response to trypanosome infection in tench *Tinca tinca* L. Only the dominant fish was able to eliminate its infection; and it is noteworth that this was also the only fish which fed (Barrow, 1955). Stress significantly reduces the antibody response to immunization in mammals (Solomon, 1969) and it is thought to be a major factor in the incidence of disease in fish.

Acknowledgements

I would like especially to thank Professor W. E. Kershaw CMG, VRD, DSc, MD in whose department my own contribution was carried out. I am also deeply indebted to Dr. L. G. Willoughby DSc, Dr. T. C. Fletcher, and Dr. J. E. Harris for their invaluable help and advice not only during the course of this study but also in preparing the manuscript.

References

AGERSBORG, H. P. K. (1933). 'Salient problems in the artificial rearing of salmonid fishes, with special reference to intestinal fungisitosis and the cause of white-spot disease.' *Trans. Am. Fish. Soc.,* 63, 240-250.

AMOS, W. M. G. (1970). 'The extraction of fungal antigens and their use in serological tests as an aid to the diagnosis of bronchial disorders'. *J. med. Lab. Technol.,* 27, 18-32.

AMOS, R. E., and BURRELL, R. G. (1967). 'Serological differentiation in *Cerato-cystis.'* Phytopathology, 5, 32-34.

AVTALION, R. R. (1969). 'Influence de la température ambiante sur la production des anticorps chez la carpe'. *Verh. Internat. Verein. Limnol.,* 17, 630-635.

BARROW, J. W. (1955). 'Social behaviour in fresh-water fish and its effect on resistance to trypanosomes.' *Proc. natn. Acad. Sci.* USA, 41, 676-679.

BENNETT, J. H. (1842). 'On the parasitic fungi growing on living animals.' *Trans. R. Soc.,* Edinburgh, 15, 18.

BENT, K. J. (1967). 'Electrophoresis of proteins of 3 *Penicillium* species on acrylamide gels.' *J. gen. Microbiol.,* 49, 195-200.

BERKLEY, M. J. (1864). 'Egg parasites and their relations.' *The Intellectual Observer,* 5, 147-153.

BISSET, K. A. (1946). 'The effect of temperature on non-specific infections of fish.' *J. Path. Bact.,* 58, 251-258.

BLANC, H. (1888). 'Notice sur une mortalité exceptionelle des brochets.' *Bull. Soc. Vaud. Sci. Nat., Lausanne,* 23, 33-37.

BRANTZAEG, P., FJELLANGER, I., and GJERULDSEN, S. T. (1968). 'Immunoglobulin M: Local synthesis and selective secretion in patients with Immunoglobulin A deficiency.' *Science,* 160, 789-791.

BROOK, G. (1879). 'Notes of the salmon disease in the Esk and Eden.' *Trans. Proc. bot. Soc. Edin.,* 13, 389-394.

BROWN, M. E. and COLLINS, V. G. (1966). 'Irish salmon disease– an interim report.' *Salm. Trout. Mag.,* 178, 180-188.

BUCKLAND, F., WALPOLE, S., and YOUNG, A. (1880). 'Report on the disease which has recently prevailed among the Salmon on the Tweed, Eden and other rivers in England and Scotland.' HMSO.

BURRELL, R. G., CLAYTON, C. W., GALLEGLY, M. E., and LILLY, V. G. (1965). 'Factors affecting the antigenicity of the mycelium of three species of *Phytophthora.'* *Phytopathology,* 55, 1052-1053.

CARBÉRY, J. T. (1968). 'UDN of salmon; description, aetiology and differential diagnosis.' *Bull. Off. int. Epizoot,* 69, 1401-1410.

CARBERY, J. T., and STRICKLAND, K. L. (1968). 'Resistance of rainbow trout to ulcerative dermal necrosis.' *Nature,* 217, 1158.

CHANG, L. O., SRB, A. M., and STEWARD, F. C. (1962). 'Electrophoretic separations of the soluble proteins of *Neurospora.'* *Nature,* 193, 756-759.

CHIAPELLI, R. (1933). 'Indagini sperimentali sulle cause d'infezione di dermatocomicosi Saprolegniacea nella carpa.' *Giorn. di. Risicolt.,* 23, 169-173.

CHILLER, J. M., HODGINS, H. O., and WEISER, R. S. (1969). 'Antibody response in rainbow trout *(Salmo gairdneri)* II. Studies on the kinetics of development of antibody-producing cells and on complement and natural hemolysin.' *J. Immunol.,* 102, 1202-1207.

CLARE, B. G. (1963). 'Starch-gel electrophoresis of proteins as an aid in identifying fungi.' *Nature,* 200, 803-804.

CLARE, B. G., FLENTJE, N. T., and ATKINSON, M. R. (1968). 'Electrophoretic patterns of oxidoreductases and other proteins as criteria in fungal taxonomy.' *Aust. J. biol. Sci.,* 21, 275-295.

CLINTON, G. P. (1894). 'Observations and experiments on *Saprolegnia* infesting fish.' *Bull. US Fish Comm.* 13, 163-172.

CLEM, L. W. (1971). 'Phylogeny of immunoglobulin structure and function IV. Immunoglobulins of the giant grouper *Epinephelus itaira.'* *J. biol. Chem.,* 246, 9-15.

COLLINS, M. I. (1920). 'Note on certain variations of the sporocyst in a species of *Saprolegnia.' Proc. Linn. Soc. NSW,* 45, 277.

DAVIS, B. D., DULBECCO, R., GINSBERG, H. S., EISEN, H. N., and WOOD, W. B. (Eds) (1968). *'Principles of Microbiology and Immunology.'* New York, Harper and Row.

DAVIS, H. S., and LAZAR, E. C. (1940). 'A new fungus of trout.' *Trans. Am. Fish. Soc.,* 70, 264-271.

DE BARY, H. A. (1888). 'Species der Saprolegnieen.' *Bot. Ztg.,* 46, 617.

DE KINKELIN, P., and DORSON, M. (1973). 'Interferon production in rainbow trout *(Salmo gairdneri)* experimentally infected with egtved virus.' *J. gen. Virol.,* 19, 125-127.

DE KINKELIN, P., and TURDU, Y. LE. (1971). 'L'enzootie d' "Ulcerative Dermal Necrosis" du saumon (*Salmo salar* L1766) en Bretagne.' *Bull. Fr. Pisciculture,* 43, 115-125.

DORSON, M. (1972). 'Some characteristics of antibodies in the primary immune response of rainbow trout *(Salmo gairdneri).'* In *Diseases of Fish* (Ed. L. E. Mawdsley-Thomas) Symp. Zool. Soc. London, No. 30, 129-140.

DREW, G. H. (1909). 'Some notes on parasitic and other diseases of fishes'. *Parasitology,* 2, 193-201.

DURBIN, R. D. (1966). 'Comparative gel-electrophoretic investigation of the protein patterns of *Septoria* species.' *Nature,* 210, 1186-1187.

EGUSA, S., and NISHIKAWA, T. (1965). 'Studies of a primary infectious disease in the so-called fungus disease of eels.' *Bull. Jap. Soc. Scient. Fish.,* 31, 804-813.

ELSON, K. G. R. (1968). 'Salmon disease in Scotland.' *Salmon Net,* 4, 9-17.

ENGLISH, M. P., and HENDERSON, A. H. (1967). 'Significance and interpretation of laboratory tests in pulmonary aspergillosis.' *J. clin. Path.,* 20, 832-834.

FEINSTEIN, A. and MUNN, E. A. (1969). 'Conformation of the free and antigen-bound IgM antibody molecules.' *Nature,* 224, 1307.

FISCHER, A. (1892). 'Phycomycetes Die Pilze Deutschlands, Oesterreichs und der Schweiz.' *Rabenhorst. kryptogamen-Fl.,* 1, 490 pp. Leipzig.

FLETCHER, T. C., and GRANT, P. T. (1969). 'Immunoglobulins in the serum and mucus of plaice, *Pleuronectes platessa.' Biochem. J.,* 115, 65.

FLETCHER, T. C., and WHITE, A. (1973 a). 'Lysozyme activity in the plaice (*Pleuronectes platessa* L.).' *Experientia,* 29, 1283-1285.

FLETCHER, T. C., and WHITE, A. (1973 b). 'Antibody production in the plaice (*Pleuronectes platessa* L.) after oral and parenteral immunisation with *Vibrio anguillarum* antigens.' *Aquaculture,* 1, 417-428.

FRYER, J. L., NELSON, J. S., and GARRISON, R. L. (1972). 'Vibriosis in fish.' *Prog. Fish Food Sci.,* 5, 129-133.

GOOD, R. A., FINSTAD, J., POLLARA, B. and GABRIELSEN, A. E. (1966). 'Morphologic studies on the evolution of lymphoid tissues among the lower vertebrates.' In *Phylogeny of Immunity* (Eds. R. J. Smith, P. A. Miescher, and R. A. Good) University of Florida Press, Gainesville, 149-168.

GRAFF, P. (1928). 'Contributions to our knowledge of Western Montana fungi II. Phycomycetes.' *Mycologia,* 20, 158-179.

GRIMBLE, A. (1899). *'The Salmon Rivers of England and Wales.'* A. Kegan Paul, Trench, Trubner, London.

HALL, R. (1967). 'Proteins and catalase isoenzymes from *Fusarium solani* and their taxonomic significance.' *Aust. J. biol. Sci.,* 20, 419-428.

HALL, R. (1969). 'Molecular approaches to taxonomy of fungi.' *Bot. Rev.,* 35, 285-304.

HALL, R., ZENTMYER, G. A. and ERWIN, D. C. (1968). 'Acrylamide gel electrophoresis of proteins and taxonomy of *Phytophthora.' Phytopathology,* 58, 1052.

HALL, R., ZENTMYER, G. A., and ERWIN, D. C. (1969). 'Approach to taxonomy of *Phytophthora* through acrylamide gel-electrophoresis of proteins.' *Phytopathology,* 59, 770-774.

HARDY, A. D. (1910). 'Association of alga and fungus in salmon disease *(Myxonema and Saprolegnia).' Proc. Roy. Soc. Vict.,* 23, 27-32.

HARISDANGKUL, V., KABAT, E. A., MCDONOUGH, R. J., and SIGEL, M. M. (1972). 'A protein in normal nurse shark serum which reacts specifically with fructosans. 1. purification and immunochemical characterization.' *J. Immunol.,* 108, 1244-1258.

HARRIS, J. E. (1972). 'The immune response of a cyprinid fish to infections of the acanthocephala *Pomphorhynchus laevis.' Int. J. Parasitol.,* 2, 459-469.

HARRIS, J. E. (1973). 'The immune response of dace *Leuciscus Leuciscus* (L.) to injected antigenic materials.' *J. Fish Biol.,* 5, 261-276.

HARRISON, J. L., and JONES, E. B. G. (1971). 'Salinity tolerance of *Saprolegnia parasitica.* Coker.' *Mycopath. Mycol. appl.,* 43, 297-307.

HILDEMANN, W. H. (1962). 'Immunogenetic studies of poikilothermic animals.' *Am. Nat.,* 96, 195-204.

HINE, F. B. (1878-79). 'Observations on several forms of *Saprolegnia.' Am. Q. Mic. J.,* 1, 18-24.

HODGINS, H. O., WEISER, R. S. and RIDGWAY, G. J. (1967). 'The nature of antibodies and the immune response in rainbow trout *(Salmo gairdneri).' J. Immunol.,* 99, 534-544.

HODKINSON, M., and HUNTER, A. (1970). 'Immune response of UDN—infected salmon to *Saprolegnia.' J. Fish Biol.,* 2, 305-311.

HOSHINA, T., SANO, T., and SUNAMAYA, M. (1960). 'Studies on the saprolegniosis of eel.' *J. Tokyo Univ. Fish.,* 47,59-79.

HUME PATTERSON, J. (1903). 'On the course of the salmon disease— A bacteriological—investigation.' Edinburgh. H.M.S.O.

HUMPHREY, J. E. (1893). 'The Saprolegniaceae of the United States, with notes on other species.' *Trans. Am. Phil. Soc.,* 17, 63-148.

HUXLEY, T. H. (1882). *'Saprolegnia* in relation to salmon disease.' *Q. J. Mic. Soc.,* 22, 311-333.

JAKOWSKA, S. (1963). 'Mucus secretion in fish: A note.' *Ann. NY Acad. Sci.,* 106, 458-462.

JAKUBOWSKI, K. (1960). 'The structure and vascularization of the skin of the leather carp (*Cyprinus carpio* L. var. *nuda*) and flounder *(Pleuronectes flesus Inscus Pall).' Acta Biol. Cracoviensia,* 3, 139-147.

JENSEN, M. H. (1965). 'Disease among salmon in Irish Rivers 1964-5.' Report to the Department of Agriculture and Fisheries, Dublin.

JIMBO, SHIBUTAWA, G. T., KOBAYASHI, K., SODA, K., and KIMURA, K. (1963). 'Electron microscopic observation on epidermis of teleost *Salmo irideus.' Bull. Yamaguchi Med. Sch.,* 10, 49-52.

JONES, J. W. (1959). *The Salmon,* Collins.

KLONTZ, G. (1967). 'Immunopathology' In *Progress in Sport Fishery Research.* Resource publ. 39, Bur. Sport. Fish. Wildl., 1966, 81-82.

KNIGHT, (1885). *Bull. Torrey bot. Club.*, 12, 56.

LOCKWOOD, (1890). *J. NY Micr. Soc.*, 1, 67.

LONGBOTTOM, J., and PEPYS, J. (1964). 'Pulmonary aspergillosis: diagnostic and immunological significance of antigens and C-substance in *A. fumigatus.' J. Path. Bact.*, 88, 141.

LUND, A. (1934). 'Studies on Danish fresh-water phycomycetes.' *Mem. Acad. R. Sci.*, 97.

McCOMBS, C. L., and WINSTEAD, N. N. (1963). 'Mycelial protein comparisons of isolates of cucurbit anthracnose fungi.' *Phytopathology*, 53, 882.

MADHOSINGH, C. (1964). 'A serological comparison of three *Fusarium* species.' *Can. J. Bot.*, 42, 1143-1146.

MADHOSINGH, C., and WALLEN, V. R. (1968). 'Serological differentiation of the *Ascochyta* species on peas.' *Can. J. Microbiol.*, 14,449-451.

MATTHEIJ, J. A. M., and STROBAND, H. W. J. (1971). 'The effects of osmotic experiments and prolactin on the mucous cells in the skin and the ionocytes in the gills of the teleost *Chichlasome biocellatum.' Z. Zellforsch. mikrosk. Anat.*, 121, 93-101.

MEYER, J. A., GARBER, E. D., and SHAEFFER, S. C. (1964). 'Genetics of phytopathogenic fungi XII. Detection of esterases and phosphatases in culture filtrates of *Fusarium oxysporium* and *F. xylarioides* by starch-gel zone electrophoresis.' *Bot. Gaz.*, 125, 298-300.

MORTON, D. J., and DUKES, P. D. (1967). 'Serological differentiation of *Pythium aphanidermatum* from *Phytophthora parasitica* var. *nicotianae* and *Ph. parasitica.' Nature*, 213, 923-925.

MUNRO, A. L. S. (1970). 'Ulcerative dermal necrosis, a disease of migratory salmonid fishes in the rivers of the British Isles.' *Biol. Conservation*, 2, 129-132.

MURRAY, G. (1885). 'Notes on the inoculation of fishes with *Saprolegnia ferax.' J. Bot.*, 23, 302-308.

NEILL, J. M. (1963). 'Immunological relationships between pneumococci and various species of fungi.' Third International Congress of Microbiology Abstracts of communications 807-8. International Association of Microbiologists Part 9.

NEILL, J. M., CASTILLO, C. G., and PINKES, A. H. (1955). 'Serological reactions between fungi and bacteria I. Cross-reactions of *Sporotrichum schenkiii* with pneumococci.' *J. Immun.*, 74, 120-125.

NIGRELLI, R. J. (1937). 'Further studies on the susceptibility and acquired immunity of marine fishes to *Epibdella melleni* a monogenetic trematode.' *Zoologica*, 22, 185-191.

NOLAND-TINTIGNER, N. (1970). Deux epidemies de *Saprolegniose* des poissons par *Saprolegnia ferax* (Smith) et par *Saprolegnia declina* (Humphrey).' *A. Parasit.* (Paris), 45, 761-770.

OGAWA, M. (1970). 'Effects of prolactin on the epidermal mucous cells of the goldfish *Carassius auratus* L.' *Can. J. Zool.*, 48, 501-503.

OGAWA, M., and JOHANSEN, P. H. (1967). 'A note on the effects of hypophysectomy on the mucous cells of the goldfish *Carassius auratus* L.' *Can. J. Zool.*, 45, 885-886.

OLIVEREAU, M., and LEMOINE, A. M. (1971). 'Action de la prolactive chez l'anguille intacte et hypophysectomisee VII. Effet sur la tenent en acide sialique (n-acetyl-neuraminique) de la peau.' *Z. vergl. Physiol.*, 73, 34-43.

OUCHTERLONY, O. (1949). 'Antigen-antibody reactions in gels.' *Ark. Kemi, Min. Geol.*, B26, 1-9.

PIERCE, A. E. (1959). 'Specific antibodies at mucous surfaces.' *Vet. Rev.*, 5, 17-33.

REPORT OF THE INSPECTOR OF SALMON FISHERIES. (England and Wales) (1882). Twenty-first Report HMSO London. C3217. 10-13, 22-25.

REPORT OF THE INSPECTOR OF SALMON FISHERIES. (England and Wales) (1883). Twenty-second report HMSO. London C3656. 23-26.

RIDDELL, H. F. V., CHANNELL, S., BLYTH, W., WEIR, D. M., LLOYD, M., AMOS, W. M. G., and GRANT, I. W. B. (1968). 'Allergic alveolitis in a maltworker.' *Thorax*, 23, 271.

RIDGWAY, G. J. (1962). 'The application of some special immunological methods to marine population problems.' *Am. Nat.*, 96, 219-224.

RIDGWAY, G. J., HODGINS, H. O., and KLONTZ, G. W. (1966). 'The immune response in teleosts.' In *Phylogeny of Immunity*' (Eds. R. T. Smith, P. A. Meischer, and R. A. Good) University of Florida Press, Gainesville, 199-207.

ROBERTS, R. J. (1972). 'Ulcerative dermal necrosis (UDN) of salmon (*Salmo salar* L).' In *Diseases of Fish* (Ed. L. E. Mawdesley-Thomas). Symp. Zool. Soc. London, No. 30, 53-81.

ROBERTS, R. J., BALL, H. J., MUNRO, A. L. S., and SHEARER, W. M. (1971). 'Studies on ulcerative dermal necrosis of salmonids III. The healing process in fish maintained under experimental conditions.' *J. Fish. Biol.*, 3, 221-224.

ROBERTS, R. J., SHEARER, W. M., ELSON, K. G. R., MUNRO, A. L. S. (1970 a). 'Studies on ulcerative dermal necrosis of salmonids. 1. The skin of the normal salmon head.' *J. Fish Biol.*, 2, 223-229.

ROBERTS, R. J., SHEARER, W. M., MUNRO, A. L. S. (1972). 'Studies on ulcerative dermal necrosis of salmonids IV. Failure to detect epithelial auto antibodies in sera from diseased fish.' *J. Fish. Biol.*, 4, 21-25.

ROBERTS, R. J., SHEARER, W. M., MUNRO, A. L. S., and ELSON, K. G. R. (1970 b). 'Studies on ulcerative dermal necrosis of salmonids. II. The sequential pathology of the lesions.' *J. Fish. Biol.*, 2, 373-378.

ROBIN, C. (1863). *'Histoire Naturelle des Vegetaux-Parasites, etc., qui Croissent sur l'Homme et sur les Animaux Vivants.* B. Bailliere, Paris.

ROBINSON, E. M. (1896). 'Fungus and parasites on salmon fry.' *Rep. US Fish. Com.* p 60.

ROSEN, M. W., and CORNFORD, N. E. (1971). 'Fluid friction of fish slimes., *Nature*, 234, 49-51.

ROSEN, R. D., MORGAN, C., HSU, K. C., BUTLER, W. T., and ROSE, H. M. (1968). 'Localization of external secretory IgA by immunofluorescence in tissues lining the oral and resporatory passages in man.' *J. Immunol.*, 100, 706-717.

ROSENBERG, A. (1908). 'Experience in abating disease among brook trout.' *Bull. Bur. Fish.*, 28, 943-945.

RYDER, J. A. (1883). 'Cause of the non-development of fungus on the eggs hatched in the MacDonald jar.' *Bull US Fish. Com.*, 2, 188.

SCHNETZLER, J. B. (1887). 'Infection dune larve de grenouille par *Saprolegnia ferax.*' Arch. Sci. Phys. Nat. *Geneve*, 18, 492.

SCOTT, W. W. (1964). 'Fungi associated with fish diseases.' *Devl. Indust. Microbiol.*, 5, 109-123.

SCOTT, W. W., and O'BIER, A. H. (1962). 'Aquatic fungi associated with diseased fish and fish eggs.' *Progve. Fish Cult.*, 24, 3-15.

SEELINGER, H. P. R. (1960). 'Advances in the serology of fungi.' *Trans. Br. mycol. Soc.*, 43, 543-555.

SHANOR, L., and SASLOW, H. B. (1944). *'Aphanomyces* as a fish parasite.' *Mycologia*, 36, 413-415.

SHECHTER, Y., LANDAU, J. W., DABROWA, N., and NEWCOMER, V. D. (1968). 'Comparative disc electrophoresis of proteins from *Candida* species.' *Bact. Proc.,* 89.

SIGEL, M. M., and CLEM, L. W. (1965). 'Antibody response of fish to viral antigens.' *Ann. NY Acad. Sci.,* 126, 662-677.

SINDERMANN, C. J. (1956). 'Diseases of fishes in the western North Atlantic IV. Fungus disease and resultant mortalities of herring in the Gulf of St. Lawrence in 1955.' *Maine Dept. Sea Shore Fish. Res. Bull.,* 25, 1-23.

SINDERMANN, C. J. (1970). *Principal Diseases of Marine Fish and Shellfish.* Academic Press. New York and London.

SKARNES, R. C., and WATSON, D. W. (1957). 'Antimicrobial factors of normal tissues and fluids.' *Bact. Rev.,* 21, 273-294.

SMITH, A. M., POTTER, M., and MERCHANT, E. B. (1967). 'Antibody-forming cells in the pronephros of the teleost *Lepomis macrochirus.' J. Immun.,* 699, 876-882.

SMITH, W. G. (1878). 'The salmon disease.' *The Gardners' Chronicle.* 9, 560-562.

SOLOMON, G. F. (1969). 'Stress and antibody response in rats.' *Int. Archs. Allergy appl. Immun.,* 35, 97.

SOUTH, M. A., COOPER, M. D., WOLLHEIM, F. A., HONG, R., and GOOD, R. A. (1966). 'The IgA system 1. Studies of the transport and immunochemistry.' *J. Exp. Med.,* 123, 615.

SPRINGER, G. F., and DESAI, P. R. (1971). 'Monosaccharides as specific precipitinogens of eel anti-human blood group H(O) antibody.' *Biochemistry,* 10, 3749-3760.

STEVENSON, J. P. (1970). 'Scourge of the salmon.' *New Scientist,* 45, 353-354.

STIPES, R. J. (1967). 'Disc electrophoresis of mycelial proteins from *Ceratocystis* species.' *Phytopathology,* 57, 832.

STIRLING, A. B. (1878). 'Notes on the fungus disease affecting salmon.' *Proc. Roy. Soc. Edin.,* 9, 726-732.

STIRLING, A. B. (1880 a). 'Additional observations on fungus disease of salmon and other fish.' *Proc. Roy. Soc. Edin.* 10, 232-250.

STIRLING, A. B. (1880 b). 'Additional observations on the fungus disease affecting salmon and other fish. *Proc. Roy. Soc. Edin.* 10, 370-378.

STOKLOSOWA, S. (1970). 'Further observations on the sexual dimorphism in the skin of *Salmo trutta* in relation to sexual maturity.' *Copeia,* 2, 332-339.

STUART, M. R., and FULLER, H. T. (1968). 'Mycological aspects of diseased Atlantic salmon.' *Nature,* 217, 90-92.

SUERTH, C. J., and VARNEY, E. H. (1968). 'Serological investigations of races 1-8 of *Phytophthora fragariae.' Phytopathology,* 58, 403.

SWAN, A. P. (1889). 'The fungus of salmon disease: its life and function.' *Belfast Nat. Hist. Soc. Rep. Proc.,* 1888-9, 54-85.

TIFFNEY, W. N. (1939 a). 'The identity of certain species of the Saprolegniaceae parasitic to fish.' *J. Elisha Mitchell scient. Soc.,* 55, 134-151.

TIFFNEY, W. N. (1939 b). 'The host range of *Saprolegnia parasitica.' Mycologia,* 31, 310-321.

TIFFNEY, W. N., and WOLF, F. T. (1937). '*Achlya flagellata* as a fish parasite.' *J. Elisha Mitchell scient. Soc.,* 53, 298.

TSUCHIYA, T., KAWAKITA, S., IMAI, M., and MIYAGAWA, K. (1966). 'Serological classification of the genera *Kloeckera* and *Hanseniaspora.' Jap. J. exp. Med.,* 36, 555-562.

UNGAR, F. (1843). 'Eigiges zur Lebensgeschichte d. *Achlya prolifera.' Linnaea,* 17, 129.

VAN OOSTEN, J. (1957). In *Physiology of Fishes,* (Ed. M. E. Brown) Academic Press, New York. Vol. 1, p. 207.

VISHNIAC, H. S., and NIGRELLI, R. F. (1957). 'The ability of the Saprolegniaceae to parasitize platyfish.' *Zoologica,* 42, 131-134.

VLADIMIROV, V. L. (1968). 'Immunity in fish.' *Bull. Off. int. Epizoot.,* 69, 1365-1372.

WALENTOWICZ, A. (1885). 'Karpfenfest in Kaniow.' *Oesterreich vierteljahresoschrift wissensch. Veterinärk,* Wien, 64, 193-200.

WILLOUGHBY, L. G. (1968). 'Atlantic salmon disease fungus.' *Nature,* 217, 872-873.

WILLOUGHBY, L. G. (1969). 'Salmon disease in Windermere and the River Leven: the fungal aspect.' *Salmon and Trout Magazine,* 186, 124-130.

WILLOUGHBY, L. G. (1970). 'Mycological aspects of disease of young perch in Windermere.' *J. Fish. Biol.,* 2, 113-116.

WILLOUGHBY, L. G. (1971). 'Observations on fungal parasites of Lake District salmonids.' *Salmon and Trout Magazine,* 192, 152-158.

WILLOUGHBY, L. G. (1972). 'UDN of Lake District trout and char; outward signs of infection and defence barriers examined further.' *Salmon and Trout Magazine,* 195, 149-58.

WILLOUGHBY, L. G., and COLLINS, V. G. (1966). 'A study of the distribution of fungal spores and bacteria in Blelham Tarn and its associated streams.' *Nova Hedwigia,* 12, 149.

YAMAGUCHI, N., KURASHIGE, S., and MITSUHASHI, S. (1973). 'Immune response in *Xenopus laevis* and immunochemical properties of the serum antibodies.' *Immunology,* 24, 109-118.

23 Ultrastructure of Freshwater Phycomycetes

I. BRENT HEATH

23.1 Introduction

This chapter aims to examine recent ultrastructural work from a correlated structure and function viewpoint. In keeping with this approach, information will be discussed in the context of functional problems as opposed to the more traditional taxonomic arrangement. The selection of organisms based on habitat presents problems because much of the relevant ultrastructural work has been performed on taxonomically and functionally closely related organisms, some of which are aquatic whilst others are terrestrial. The functional approach indicated that the most useful selection procedure should be to include taxa which are predominantly aquatic, include observations on closely related terrestrial species which are not correlated specifically with the environment, and exclude observations which are environmental adaptations, e.g. haustoria of *Phytophthora* species. If it helps to clarify a point, analogy will be made with other organisms outside this defined sphere of interest. Taxonomic terminology will follow Alexopoulos (1962).

In fields such as cell ultrastructure it is inevitable that rapidly improving technology has resulted in observations which are no longer considered technically valid. For the sake of clarity such observations will be omitted when more valid data are available. Similarly, there is a considerable problem of preparation artefacts, even in the most recent work. The policy adopted here will be only to present information which in the author's experience, is not negated by preparation problems.

23.2 Vegetative Structures

23.2.1 Cell Walls and Morphogenesis

It is now well established that fungal hyphae elongate by tip growth, with the main site of wall synthesis located at the extreme apex, e.g. Gooday (1971). Hyphal morphology is apparently the result of an interaction between the osmotic pressure of the cytoplasm and the rate of setting of the newly synthesized plastic wall (Robertson, 1968). However, once set, the subapical, slightly elastic, wall may again become locally plastic to allow the formation of branches, zoosporangia, antheridia, etc. The search for ultrastructural information correlated with these localized changes has focused on two main questions: what changes occur in the structure of the wall itself and what structures occur in the underlying cytoplasm which may be involved in cell wall metabolism? Because much of the relevant work has been performed on aquatic fungi, and there is as yet little reason to believe that the basic processes differ between different fungi, the following is a general analysis of the problems and is not necessarily confined to the aquatic groups.

Fungal cell walls are typically composed of three major components: fibrillar polysaccharide, amorphous polysaccharide and protein. Using auto-radiographic techniques, Gooday (1971) has shown that both fibrillar and amorphous components of a number of genera are synthesized at the hyphal apex. The site of addition of the protein components is uncertain, but at least some appears to be added to the apex (Hunsley and Burnett, 1970). With chemical and enzymatic dissection followed by whole mount microscopy, Hunsley and Burnett (1970) and Tokunaga and Bartnicki-Garcia (1971 b) have shown that the cell walls of *Phytophthora* species have an outer amorphous layer of β-1, 3 and β-1, 6 glucans which encloses a randomly arranged network of fibrils (composed in part of cellulose 1) surrounded by a small amount of protein. All three components appear to enclose the hyphal apices as well as the older subapical regions, although there is less protein at the apex (Hunsley and Burnett, 1970). The only qualitative difference detected between the apex and subapical walls is a gradual increase in fibril diameter away from the apex (Hunsley and Burnett, 1968). Where branches arise there is no detected differentiation of the fibrillar components, the random network of the main hyphae merges with that of the branches (Heath, unpublished observations on *Saprolegnia*). Before considering the functional implications of these observations, it must be pointed out that there is no proof that the apex shaped fragments (thus termed apices) examined by the above authors were in fact actively growing at the time of death prior to preparation. The following discussion is valid only if this assumption is made.

If hyphal morphology is the product of a balance between turgour pressure and setting of the newly formed wall, then some 'setting factor' or factors must exist in the wall. Such a primary setting factor may also retain the shape of the older hyphal wall, or there may be additional factors involved. Because all observed wall components apparently enclose the apex, then the addition of any one *per se* cannot be the 'setting factor'. Thus one must look for 'cross links' between one or more of the components. Such cross links must be labile to allow branch formation, etc. Hunsley and Burnett (1970) have shown that each wall component (fibrillar, amorphous and protein) can retain the shape of the original hypha independently of the other two. Thus each must have significant independent cross links. The observation of copious cellulase production during branch initiation in *Achlya* (Thomas and Mullins, 1967) and the essential role of cellulose in protoplast production of various Oömycetes (Sietsma *et al.,* 1969) suggest that cellulase fibrils, or cross links between them, are morphogenetically important. This suggestion is supported by the work of Katz and Rosenberger (1970) on an *Aspergillus* mutant which lacks chitin (and thus fibrils). They noted that this mutant is unable to grow in a normal medium due to lack of strength in the cell walls. However, if the organism was grown in a medium with a high osmotic pressure it grew 'normally' indicating weak but significant setting factors in either the protein or amorphous polysaccharide components. A mutant additionally lacking either of the latter should be interesting! The involvement of the protein component in cell wall morphogenesis is predicted by analogy to the extensin hypothesis in which Lamport (1965, 1969) suggests that proteinaceous bonds, possibly including disulphide bonds, between polysaccharide fibrils are important in higher plant morphogenesis. This hypothesis is supported in the aquatic fungi by the observation of hyphal tip swelling in *Saprolegnia* when disulphide bond formation was disrupted by dithiothreitol (Heath, 1970). However, the complexity of the search of setting factors is indicated by the necessity of β-1,3 glucanase and lipase for protoplast formation in several Oömycetes (Sietsma *et al.,* 1969). (But see also Bartnicki-Garcia, 1973.)

In additon to studies of the hyphal apex system, information on wall mechanics can be obtained from observations of the cysts formed by the asexual 'phycomycete' zoospores when they cease to be motile. The cysts of *Phytophthora palmivora* Butler and the secondary cysts of *Saprolegnia ferax* (Gruith.) Thuret. are composed almost exclusively of fibrillar polysaccharide (Tokunaga and Bartnicki-Garcia, 1971 b; Heath and Greenwood, 1970 a). The ability of these cysts to retain their shape supports the concept of a major cross link system associated with the fibrils, but the role of protein here is uncertain because pronase is without effect. When the cysts of *P. palmivora* germinate an amorphous polysaccharide layer is deposited outside the fibrils of the germ tube (Tokunaga and Bartnicki-Garcia, 1971 b). It is difficult to conceive a function for this layer in other than some aspect of hyphal morphogenesis.

Clearly, to date the ultrastructural analysis of fungal walls has produced little conclusive information relating to hyphal morphogenesis. Evidence for a morphogenic role for the fibrillar and proteinaceous components is better than for the amorphous polysaccharide but it seems almost certain that any 'cross link' or 'setting factor' is likely to be a combination of several factors.

The search for cytoplasmic structures involved in cell wall synthesis has been rather more conclusive. In all hyphal fungi, including aquatic 'phycomycetes', critically examined the cytoplasm of the hyphal apex contains a high concentration of single membrane bound vesicles which may be termed wall vesicles (Fig. 23.1). Wall vesicles typically occupy much of the apical 10 μm of cytoplasm to the exclusion of other major organelles (Hemmes and Hohl, 1969; Grove and Bracker, 1970; Grove *et al.,* 1970; Heath *et al.,* 1971; Hoch and Mitchell, 1972 b). Morphologically these vesicles range from spheres to irregular short tubules with diameters up to approximately 300 nm (Fig. 23.1). Part of the variability may be due to coalescence of the smaller vesicles (Grove *et al.,* 1970). Wall vesicles achieve their greatest concentration in the apical 5 μm but are also present at considerable distances behind the apex where they may be clustered at presumed incipient branch points (Grove *et al.,* 1970). The active movement of the vesicles towards the apex (Grove *et al.,* 1970) and their accumulation at the apical site of cell wall synthesis suggests a role in this process. This suggestion is supported by a number of lines of evidence.

(1)   The wall vesicle contents stain with the periodic acid silver hexamine (PASH) stain which indicates a high polysaccharide concentration (Heath *et al.,* 1971).

(2)   The membranes of the vesicles are similar to those of the cell membrane and profiles of vesicles apparently fusing with the cell membrane are observed. indicating that the vesicle contents are liberated to the cell wall (Grove *et al.,* 1970).

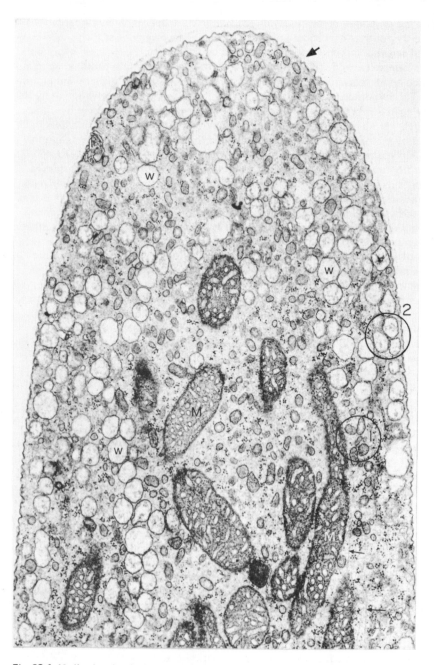

Fig. 23.1. Median longitudinal section of a hyphal apex of *Pythium aphanidermatum*. The cell wall is very thin and lightly stained (large arrow). Wall vesicles (w) are abundant and appear to be of two categories, the smaller ones (circle 1) possibly fusing or expanding to produce the larger ones (circle 2). Mitochondria (M) are excluded from the extreme apex as are other organelles. Note the lomasome or plasmalemmasome (L) and cytoplasmic microtubules (small arrows) (X 25 700) Glut/Os/Pb/UAc (from Grove and Bracker, 1970 with permission of the authors and the American Society for Microbiology).

(3)   When hyphal growth is stopped, the vesicles disappear, i.e. wall vesicles are
        only present when wall synthesis is occurring (Girbardt, 1969). This paper
        does not consider aquatic fungi but their wall vesicles are comparable with
        other groups. This paper also demonstrates that the vesicles undergo *reverse*
        pinocytosis, i.e. they are not derived from the cell membrane.

(4)   There is a close correlation between accumulations of wall vesicles and cell
        wall synthesis in various parts of the life cycle, for example they are associated
        with developing (and thus wall producing) but not mature, zoosporangia apical
        papillae, zoosporangia walls, oögonia and antheridia walls, and primary cyst walls
        (Heath and Greenwood, 1971; Heath *et al.,* 1971). The presence of such vesicles
        only, during the active part of a discontinuous sequence of wall production,
        suggests that they are involved in that process.

None of the above evidence is conclusive, but by weight of circumstantial evidence it
seems reasonable to conclude that the wall vesicles are indeed contributing material to
the cell wall. If, as seems probable, the contents of the vesicles are released by reverse
pinocytosis, then they must also add their membranes to the cell membrane. In an
extending hyphal apex this could conveniently supply the amount of membrane needed
to line the enlarged hypha. However, in such circumstances as the primary cyst walls of
Dictyuchus sterile Coker, vesicle fusion must add to a non-expanding cell membrane
(Heath *et al.,* 1971). Although formed initially, the vast excesses of cell membrane
expected do not persist; thus there must be some system capable of reabsorbing
'excess' membrane (Heath and Greenwood, 1970 b).
    By analogy with other plant systems the wall vesicles probably contain material
destined to become amorphous wall polysaccharide (Northcote, 1969). Comparable
vesicles in pollen tube tips have been isolated and shown to contain 'hemicelluloses'
and 'pectins' which appear to be chemically identical to these fractions of the cell
wall (Van der Woude *et al.,* 1971). However the material in the wall vesicles is probably less highly polymerized than in the mature wall (Van der Woude *et al.,* 1971;
Pickett-Heaps, 1968; Bonnett and Newcomb, 1966). The stronger PASH reactivity of
the cell walls relative to the wall vesicles, and the loss of wall vesicle PASH reactivity
in material fixed only in osmium tetroxide suggests that such a difference occurs in
Saprolegnia also (Heath *et al.,* 1971). Wang and Bartnicki-Garcia (1966) have shown
that cytoplasmically located UDP-glucose is a precursor for β-1, 3 and β-1, 6 glucans in
Phytophthora cell walls, and there is a possibility that such a precursor is contained in
the wall vesicles of *Saprolegnia* (Heath *et al.,* 1971).
    In addition to possible wall precursors it should be noted that the wall vesicles
probably also contain various enzymes. For example in other plant systems some
wall synthesizing enzymes appear to be located on the cell membrane (Preston and
Goodman, 1968; Villemez *et al.,* 1968; Robinson and Preston, 1972) which is derived
in part from the membranes of the wall vesicles. Brown *et al.* (1970) have demonstrated cellulose synthesis in vesicles ontogenetically comparable to wall vesicles. Thus
fungal wall vesicles should perhaps be assayed for cellulose or chitin synthetase as
appropriate. The possible enzyme complement may also extend to wall degrading
enzymes which could be important in morphogenesis, for example wall vesicles isolated from yeast contain glucanase (Cortat *et al.,* 1972) and branch initiation in
Achlya is associated with cellulase production (Thomas and Mullins, 1967) and by
analogy with *Pythium* is likely to involve wall vesicle accumulations (Grove *et al.,*
1970). Clearly the question of the contents of wall vesicles will be resolved only when

they have been isolated and chemically analysed. However, we now have pointers to the substances which should be assayed for.

The origin of the wall vesicles is now fairly clearly defined in some species. Based on morphology, staining reactions and analogy to other systems it seems certain that they are derived from Golgi bodies or dictyosomes in *Pythium, Phytophthora, Saprolegnia* and *Dictyuchus* (Grove et al., 1968; Hemmes and Hohl, 1969; Grove et al., 1970; Heath and Greenwood, 1970 b; and Heath et al., 1971). However, the possibility of an origin from direct evaginations of endoplasmic reticulum has not been ruled out.

Whilst there is evidence in a few species for Golgi derived vesicles contributing material to the cell wall, it should be noted that in many aquatic phycomycetes, for example the chytrids, the body of the plant enlarges and must undergo extensive wall synthesis, yet no evidence has been presented for the involvement of wall vesicles. In fact, despite an extensive search, wall vesicles are only reported in the rhizoids of *Blastocladiella* (Barstow and Lovett, 1974). These rhizoids grow by tip growth in a manner comparable to hyphae.

Whatever the contents of the wall vesicles, clearly the fibrillar component of the cell wall must be made external to the cell membrane. Preston and Goodman (1968) have recently reviewed Preston's original hypothesis of cell membrane bound enzyme 'granules' which synthesize cellulose, and Villemez et al. (1968) have shown evidence for cell membrane bound wall synthesizing enzymes in higher plants. Although freeze etch replicas of the cell membrane of *Saprolegnia* do show granules (Heath et al., 1971), there is no evidence for fungal wall fibril synthesis by membrane bound enzymes. In fact, Wang and Bartnicki-Garcia (1966) and McMurrough et al. (1971) claim that a β-1, 3 glucan synthetase in *Phytophthora cinnamomi* Rands (has β-1, 3 glucan fibrils in its wall) and chitin synthetase of *Mucor rouxii* Vuillemin are located in the cell wall. However, they do not give ultrastructural analyses of their supposed pure wall fractions, and in this author's experience comparably prepared wall fractions of *Saprolegnia ferax,* which appear clear of cytoplasmic contamination under the light microscope, do in fact contain depressingly high amounts of membrane material. Thus it is not possible to be sure whether their synthetase activities are truly in the cell wall or on contaminating membranes. Furthermore, lomasomes (see below) become trapped in cell walls, and if present would undoubtedly contaminate a wall fraction. However, when the secondary zoospores of *Saprolegnia ferax* and the zoospores of *Phytophthora palmivora* encyst, they rapidly produce a wall almost exclusively of fibrils (Heath and Greenwood, 1971; Tokunaga and Bartnicki-Garcia, 1971 b). Clearly the enzyme(s) responsible for the synthesis of these fibrils must be membrane bound, but that does not exclude the possibility of the enzyme continuing to function if it were detached and free in the cell wall at a later stage. Clearly the site of fibril synthesis in fungal walls remains an open question.

Lomasomes.   No review of fungal ultrastructure would be complete without some mention of lomasomes. These structures are basically composed of variously arranged, mainly vesicular or tubular, membranes lying exterior to the cell membrane, either protruding into the cytoplasm or embedded to various depths in the cell wall (Fig. 23.1). They are apparently derived from the cell membrane and in fact their membranes can be seen joined to the cell membrane (Heath and Greenwood, 1970 b). Comparable structures occur widely in diverse plant cells (see the reviews of Bracker (1967) and Marchant and Robards (1968)). Perhaps their major characteristic is their variability which is such that no attempts to date have successfully correlated their presence with any cellular function. For this, and other diverse reasons, it has been

608

suggested that they merely represent an imbalance between the amount of cell membrane produced relative to that needed to line the cell wall (Heath and Greenwood, 1970 b; Hemmes and Hohl, 1971). Such a hypothesis has the demerit that it is difficult to verify, but it does appear to be more compatible with all the reported observations than any other prepared to date. The implication of this hypothesis is that a lomasome would have no function beyond that attributable to a normal cell membrane.

23.2.2 Cytoplasmic Components

The functional requirements of the cytoplasmic constituents of vegetative aquatic fungi are essentially similar to those of other organisms. Thus they do not show great differences in structure to the typical descriptions in any recent cell biology text. For this reason this review will concentrate on the less well known points and those aspects which are peculiar to the aquatic fungi.

Mitochondria.   Phycomycete mitochondria are typically sausage shaped organelles bounded by two membranes, the innermost of which is increased in area by being projected into finger-like cristae typical of animal and higher plant mitochondria (Figs. 23.1 - 23.3). In the hyphal Oömycetes, the apical, presumably physiologically young, mitochondria have a diameter of about 0.5 μm and a length seldom exceeding 1 μm. However, this length increases to frequently in excess of 15 μm in older regions of the hyphae where Y-shaped profiles clearly show the existence of mitochondrial branching. The functional significance of such large mitochondria is obscure, but is a factor which must be considered in attempts at organelle fractionation. In this context it should also be remembered that structural continuity exists between outer mitochondrial membranes and endoplasmic reticulum (Bracker and Grove, 1971 a). Such a connection if it persists would certainly affect the sedimentation properties of the organelles. It also suggests that the outer mitochondrial membrane should be considered a part of the endomembrane system (see below).

The outer mitochondrial envelope of certain Oömycetes bears characteristic projections composed of regular lines of 5 - 8 nm diameter, 12 - 18 nm high tubules which are arranged in double columns parallel to the long axis of the mitochondria (Bracker and Grove, 1971b and Figs. 23.4, 23.5). Comparable structures have only been reported in *Pythium* spp., *Achlya* sp., *Phytophthora* sp. (Bracker and Grove, 1971 b) and *Apodachlya brachynema* (Hildb.) Pringsheim (Figs. 23.4, 23.5). Whilst such small structures could easily be overlooked, a specific search has failed to reveal them in *Lagenidium* sp., *Saprolegnia ferax, Dictyuchus sterile* and *Thraustotheca clavata* (de Bary) Humphrey (Heath, unpublished observations). Bracker and Grove (1971 b) have suggested a possible role in producing shape changes of these large mitochondria, but no behavioural differences have been demonstrated between mitochondria which do or do not bear such structures. Thus at present their function is unknown.

One feature of the Oömycete mitochondria is their easily observed motility which is independent of cytoplasmic streaming. The hyphal cytoplasm of many species is permeated by numerous longitudinally oriented microtubules (e.g. Fig. 23.1). In *Saprolegnia ferax* and *Thraustotheca clavata,* the mitochondria often appear to be closely associated with these microtubules (Fig. 23.3) in such a way that has led to the suggestion of a force producing interaction between the microtubules and the mitochondrial outer membrane (Heath and Greenwood, 1970 c, and Heath, unpublished

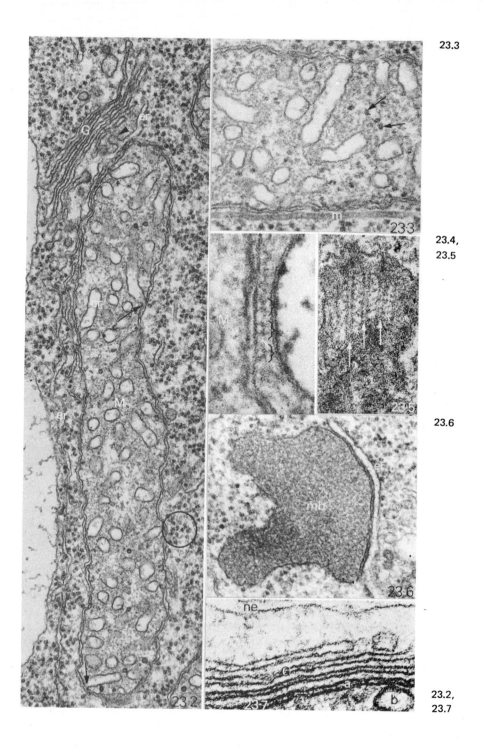

23.3

23.4,
23.5

23.6

23.2,
23.7

observations). Such an interaction is thought to be analagous to that discussed in connection with mitosis (see Section 23.3.2) and may be responsible for mitochondrial motility.

Microbodies. The term microbody is a morphological term used to describe single membrane bound, approximately spherical, organelles with a characteristic catalase rich content, often containing an osmiophilic granule or crystal (e.g. Frederick *et al.*, 1968). Following characterization of their enzyme complement, a microbody may be functionally termed a glyoxysome or peroxisome (e.g. Trelease *et al.*, 1971) indicating their involvement in higher plant lipid metabolism and photorespiration. Typical microbodies, frequently associated with a cisternum of endoplasmic reticulum (Fig. 23.6), are seen in a number of aquatic fungi, for example *Pythium aphanidermatum* (Edson) Fitzpatrick (Bracker and Grove, 1971 a), *Saprolegnia terrestris* Cookson (Howard and Moore, 1970), *Phytophthora capsici* Leonian (Williams and Webster, 1970), *Blastocladiella emersonii* Cantino et Hyatt (Barstow and Lovett, personal communication) and *Apodachlya* and *Lagenidium* sp. (Heath, unpublished; see also 'side bodies', Section 23. 3.2). In *Thraustotheca clavata* and *Saprolegnia ferax,* there are rather pleomorphic structures which could also be defined as microbodies but which contain small tubular structures of uncertain nature (Heath, unpublished). Comparable structures have not been reported elsewhere, and their identity remains uncertain. In the absence of isolation and enzyme studies, the functions of microbodies in the aquatic fungi remain uncertain although it is interesting to note that in *Saprolegnia terrestris* they do appear to be more abundant in the oögonia which are rich in lipid reserves (Howard and Moore, 1970) thus suggesting a role in subsequent lipid metabolism of the germinating oöspores.

Endomembrane system. The use of the term endomembrane system to refer to the Golgi apparatus and endoplasmic reticulum is in keeping with the current concepts of a functional continuity between these cellular componets (e.g. Morré *et al.*, 1971). The basic principle of this concept is that both membrane and luminal components originate in the endoplasmic reticulum, are modified or added to during transition through the Golgi apparatus, and are finally packaged in vesicles whose membranes are compatible with, and thus can fuse with, the cell membrane, thereby releasing the

---

Fig. 23.2. Portion of a vegetative hypha of *Saprolegnia ferax* showing a typical mitochondrion (M) with tubular cristae (cr) which are invaginations of the inner mitochondrial membrane (see arrows). Associated with the mitochondrion in a manner typical of this species is a cisternum of the endoplasmic reticulum (er) and a Golgi body (G). Note the 'fuzzy' vesicle (arrow head) which appears to be budding off from the endoplasmic reticulum. Cytoplasmic ribosomes are abundant (e.g. circle) (X 50 200) Glut/Os/Pb/UAc. **Fig. 23.3.** A mitochondrion (M) in a vegetative hypha of *Saprolegnia ferax* showing a typical association with a cytoplasmic microtubule (m). Note the mitochondrial ribosomes (arrows) (X 72 500) Glut/Os/Pb/UAc. **Fig. 23.4.** Portion of a mitochondrion (M) showing a transverse view of the double ranked elaborations of its outer membrane (brackets). Note how the tops of the projections appear to be fused to form a π like configuration. *Apodachlya* sp. (X 209 000) Glut/Os/Pb/UAc. **Fig. 23.5.** Surface view (arrows) of comparable structures to those shown in Fig. 23.4. Specimen and fixation as in Fig. 23.4 (X 135 000). **Fig. 23.6.** Typical microbody (mb) in a hypha of *Lagenidium* sp. Note characteristically associated cisternum of endoplasmic reticulum (er) (X 62 500) Glut/Os/Pb/UAc. **Fig. 23.7.** Nuclear envelope (ne) and associated Golgi body (G) in a vegetative hypha of *Pythium ultimum* showing increasing staining of the membranes from the lightly stained nuclear envelope to the very intensely stained secretory face cisternum (a) and secretory vesicle (b) membranes (X 135 000). Glut/Os/Ba(MnO$_4$)$_2$ (from Grove *et al.*, (1968) with permission of the authors. Copyright 1968 by the American Association for the Advancement of Science).

contents of the vesicles to the exterior of the cell (e.g. cell wall precursors, Section 23.2.1). Evidence for the operation of this flow system in aquatic fungi is seen in *Pythium ultimum* Trow, where, by observing the thickness, osmiophilia and clarity of the tripartite structure of the membranes (Fig. 23.7), Grove *et al.* (1968) were able to show a progression from endoplasmic reticulum, through adjacent Golgi cisternae, to secretory (Golgi derived) vesicles and cell membrane. Similarly, by observing increasing PASH staining (Heath and Greenwood, 1970 a) and lead staining (Heath *et al.*, 1971) a comparable progressive change in lumen contents has been shown in *Saprolegnia ferax*. However, there are features of the endomembrane system of the aquatic fungi which are unusual outside of the group.

All reported phycomycete Golgi bodies or dictyosomes are composed of approximately 2 - 5 cisternae (Fig. 23.2) each with fenestrated margins and dilated vesicles attached to their periphery (Fuller and Reichle, 1965; Gay and Greenwood, 1966; Shatla *et al.*, 1966; Grove *et al.*, 1967; Grove *et al.*, 1968; Bracker *et al.*, 1971; Heath and Greenwood, 1971; Reichle, 1972; Travland and Whisler, 1971; Elsner *et al.*, 1970; Williams and Webster, 1970; Chapman and Vujičić, 1965; Schnepf *et al.*, 1971). Each Golgi body is typically surrounded by a 'zone of exclusion' (Morré *et al.*, 1971) from which ribosomes are apparently excluded by some as yet unidentified material. Almost invariably the forming face is adjacent to either a cisternum of endoplasmic reticulum (Fig. 23.2) or the nuclear envelope, the intervening space being occupied by vesicles which appear to bud off the nuclear envelope or endoplasmic reticulum and fuse to form the cisternum of the forming face (e.g. Grove *et al.*, 1970; Heath and Greenwood, 1971). Rarely, direct membrane connections occur beyween the endoplasmic reticulum or nuclear envelope and the forming face cisternum (Bracker *et al.*, 1971) thus emphasizing the homology of these two membranes. To date, intercisternal rods as reported in higher organisms (Mollenhauer, 1965) are lacking in the phycomycetes.

In addition to the common association between the nuclear envelope or endoplasmic reticulum and Golgi bodies, in some of the Saprolegniales, approximately 80% of the hyphal Golgi bodies are found in a characteristic tripartite association with a cisternum of endoplasmic reticulum and a mitochondrion (Fig. 23.2 and Heath and Greenwood, 1971). The only previous report of such an association is in the alga *Vaucheria* (Greenwood, 1959). The significance of this triple association is uncertain; it may be phylogenetic but the loss of the association during zoosporogenesis (see Section 23.3.1) suggests a functional significance.

The appearance of the vesicles which are apparently budded off the margins of the Golgi cisternae apparently varies with the activity of the system. Vesicles containing presumed wall precursors tend to be relatively large with membranes undifferentiated from the cisternae from which they are derived (e.g. Grove and Bracker, 1970; Heath and Greenwood, 1970). However, some Golgi bodies have 'fuzzy' membraned vesicles attached to their cisternae (e.g. Morré *et al.*, 1971; Heath and Greenwood, 1971). In some cases such vesicles appear to be associated with the water expulsion vacuole of zoospores (Fig. 23.18 and Morré *et al.*, 1971) but their precise function remains obscure.

Whilst the above observations apply to most Oӧmycete and Hyphochytridiomycete fungi so far examined, a number of the Chytridiomycetes, for example, apparently lack typical stacking Golgi bodies (e.g. *Allomyces,* Fuller, personal communication; *Blastocladiella,* Lessie and Lovett, 1968). The lack of such Golgi bodies should not be taken to indicate the absence of functionally equivalent structures, because Morré *et al.* (1971) and McLaughlin (1972) have shown evidence for single cisternae of endoplasmic reticulum having comparable functions in higher fungi. In fact Temmink and

Campbell (1968) show a 'perinuclear membrane system' in *Olpidium brassicae* (Woro) Dang, and Barstow and Lovett (personal communication) show 'vesicular zones of exclusion' in *Blastocladiella emersonii,* both of which appear to be simple Golgi body equivalents. It seems probable that careful examination of most aquatic fungi will reveal functional Golgi bodies of one form or another.

The endoplasmic reticulum of the aquatic fungi reported on to date is quite unremarkable. It occurs as fenestrated sheets which are frequently connected to the nuclear envelope. Ribosomes, often arranged in spiral polyribosome configurations, adorn the surface of the membranes in most areas (Figs. 23.2 and 23.15) except those adjacent to Golgi bodies. Thus the normal functions in protein synthesis may be assumed.

23.2.3 Nuclear Division

Detailed ultrastructural studies of mitosis in aquatic fungi have been restricted to only three species to date: *Catenaria anguillulae* Sorokin (Ichida and Fuller, 1968), *Saprolegnia ferax* (Heath and Greenwood, 1969, 1970 c) and *Phlyctochytrium irregulare* Koch (McNitt, 1973). There is also some information available on *Blastocladiella emersonii* (Lessie and Lovett, 1968), *Phytophthora infestans* (Mont.) de Bary (Elsner *et al.,* 1970), *Aphanomyces euteiches* Dreschler (Hoch and Mitchell, 1972 b), *Allomyces arbusculus* Butler (Turian and Oulevey, 1971), *Albugo candida* (Pers.) Ktze. (Berlin and Bowen, 1964), *Rhizidiomyces apophysatus* Zopf. (Fuller and Reichle, 1965) and *Allomyces macrogynus* (Emerson) Emerson et Wilson (Robinow and Bakerspigel, 1965). The shortage of complete information makes any sort of phylogenetic review impossible. However, there are a number of points of comparison which can be made.

Interphase nuclei are typically enclosed by a nuclear envelope which is continuous with the endoplasmic reticulum. Although not always clear, nuclear pores (Fig. 23.14), in varying abundance, are probably universal. They are typically 'plugged' by osmiophilic material of unknown function (Fig. 23.14). In most aquatic fungi reported on to date, each interphase nucleus is accompanied by a pair of centrioles[*].

In some Oōmycetes, such as the Saprolegniales, the centrioles are approximately 0.2 μm long and are aligned end to end at 180° to each other (Fig. 23.13 and Heath and Greenwood, 1970 c), an arrangement also found in liverworts (Moser and Kreitner, 1970), *Labyrinthula* (Perkins, 1970) and *Nitella* (Turner, 1970) but otherwise unreported. However in various *Phytophthora* species and *Aphanomyces* the vegetative nuclei are reported to lack centrioles and instead are accompanied by fibrous bullet-shaped structures which are smaller than true centrioles and may be termed procentrioles (Williams and Webster, 1970; Hohl and Hammamoto, 1967; King and Butler, 1968; Hoch and Mitchell, 1972 a). In none of these cases is the procentriole well illustrated and only in *Aphanomyces* is mitosis described (Hoch and Mitchell, 1972 b). In this latter case true centrioles are found at the spindle poles in germinating cysts, thus raising the question of when reversion to procentrioles occurs. Similarily in the *Phytophthora* species 'normal' kinetosomes (see Section 23.3.1) are produced during zoosporogenesis, yet the transition is not documented. Further studies are needed to demonstrate clearly procentrioles, their role in mitosis, and their conversion to kinetosomes (Heath, 1974 a).

[*]In this review the term centriole will only be used for the 9 triplet tubule structure such as is shown in Figs. 23.11 and 23.13.

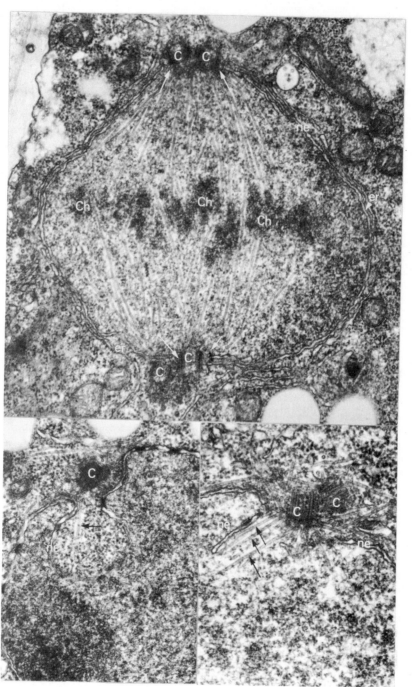

In the uniflagellate fungi, the centrioles are of comparable size but are arranged at right angles to each other, often with the one parallel to the nuclear envelope being somewhat shorter than the other (Renaud and Swift, 1964; Lessie and Lovett, 1968; Ichida and Fuller, 1968; see also Section 23.3.1). In all reported species the centrioles lie close to a differentiated 'pocket' (Heath and Greenwood, 1968) of the nuclear envelope (Figs 23.11, 23.12 and 23.13).

The first sign of incipient mitosis is normally centriole replication, a process which yields two pairs of centrioles each with their 'pockets' of nuclear envelope (Heath and Greenwood, 1970 c). The centriole pairs then begin to migrate away from each other (Heath and Greenwood, 1970 c; McNitt, 1973). Ichida and Fuller (1968) suggested that centriole replication occurred after migration in *Catenaria* but now concede that replication prior to migration probably occurs here also (Fuller, personal communication). In the Oömycetes, *Saprolegnia, Thraustotheca* and *Dictyuchus* (Heath and Greenwood, 1970 c; Heath, 1974 a, b) a small number of microtubules begins to develop from the 'pocket' regions of the nuclear envelope as soon as centriole migration starts. These microtubules constitute the detectable part of the mitotic spindle apparatus which continues to elongate as the centrioles continue to separate. Thus, in these organisms the spindle begins to form at the very start of centriole migration. However, in *Phlyctochytrium,* the centrioles migrate to opposite sides of the nucleus to their metaphase positions prior to any manifestation of spindle development (McNitt, personal communication). Only when centriole migration has ceased do spindle microtubules develop from the region of the centriole pairs. The tubules appear to push through the nuclear envelope (Fig. 23.9), thus creating polar fenestrae (Figs. 23.10 and 23.8), and continue to elongate to form the metaphase spindle (Fig. 23.8). Comparable details are lacking in the other fungi reported on to date. An interesting question arises from these observations; namely, what brings about centriole migration? In *Saprolegnia* the developing spindle could separate the centrioles, but such is clearly not the case in *Phlyctochytrium.* Thus an alternative motive agent is needed. There are two motive agents postulated to date: cytoplasmic microtubules (Heath and Greenwood, 1970 c) and localized membrane growth (McCully and Robinow, 1971. These authors studied the yeast *Schizosaccharomyces* which is comparable to the Oömycetes in having an intranuclear spindle.). Whilst rod-like microtubules seem intuitively more likely to be involved in force generation than a semifluid membrane, to date there are no facts which support either model strongly.

The central theme of mitosis is the equipartitioning of genetic material, and here little clear information is available on the detailed mechanics of the process. In the Oömycetes such as *Saprolegnia* (Heath and Greenwood, 1968, 1970 c) and *Thrausto-*

Fig. 23.8. Metaphase mitotic nucleus from *Phlyctochytrium irregulare* showing chromosomes (Ch) arranged in a metaphase plate on a microtubule containing spindle. The nuclear envelope (ne) is intact except for polar fenestrations (arrows) which are partially plugged by the centrioles (C) which lie in pairs at each pole. Note the distinct perinuclear cisternum of endoplasmic reticulum (er) which seems to be a consistent feature of this mitotic system (X 28 700) Glut/Os/Pb/UAc.
Fig. 23 9. A detail of the pole of a prophase mitotic nucleus of *P. irregulare* showing apparent spindle microtubule (arrow) which appears to be elongating from the region of the centriole (C) and causing an invagination of the nuclear envelope (ne). (X 31 500) Glut/Os/Pb/U Ac.
Fig. 23.10. A comparable region to that shown in Fig. 23.9 but at a later stage in mitosis. A number of the microtubules (arrows) have apparently ruptured the nuclear envelope and are elongating to form the spindle (X 37 500) Glut/Os/Pb/UAc. Figs. 23.8-23.10 were unpublished micrographs kindly supplied by Dr. R. E. McNitt formerly of the University of North Carolina, Chapel Hill (see McWitt, 1973).

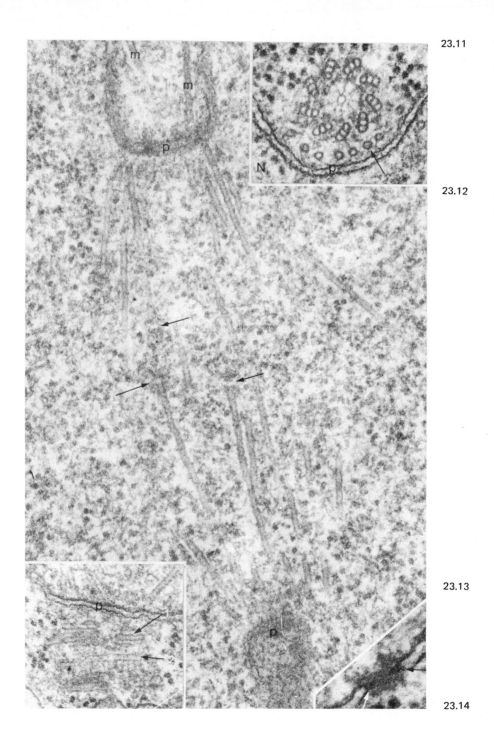

theca (Fig. 23.12) the chromatin does not stain well but kinetochore-like structures are present. Their behaviour is consistent with the hypothesis, supported by some light microscopists (e.g. Bakerspigel, 1960), that the chromatin is associated with the spindle tubules from the very beginning of centriole migration. A diffuse metaphase, with overlapping chromosomal spindle tubules to opposite poles, seems to occur while the spindle is still fairly short (Fig. 23.12), then an anaphase-like separation must occur because the spindle continues to elongate and the chromosomal tubules shorten (Heath and Greenwood, 1970 c). However, confirmation of this behaviour awaits superior preparative techniques for these species.

In contrast, the chromosomes of the uniflagellate species reported stain clearly and can be seen to form a well defined metaphase plate (Fig. 23.8) (Fuller and Reichle, 1965; Ichida and Fuller, 1968; McNitt, personal communication). The details of prometaphase are obscure in these organisms, thus the mode of development of the plate is unknown. However, kinetochores comparable to those described above for the Oömycetes are clearly seen in *Phlyctochytrium* (McNitt, 1973). Anaphase separation of chromosomes seems to vary with species, since Ichida and Fuller (1968) note only elongation of the pole to pole spindle tubules in *Catenaria,* whereas McNitt (personal communication) finds both pole to pole elongation and shortening of chromosomal spindle tubules in *Phlyctochytrium.* Whatever the mechanisms involved, at least the uniflagellate fungi, with the possible exception of *Blastocladiella* (Lessie and Lovett, 1968), do show clearly recognizable metaphase, anaphase and telophase configurations comparable to those of higher organisms.

A unifying feature of all 'phycomycetous' mitoses is the persistence of the intact nuclear envelope (with the exception of the localized polar fenestrae of *Phlyctochytrium,* Fig. 23.8). This feature necessitates the generation of forces to elongate and divide the nucleoplasm. In the uniflagellates, the poles of the spindle are coincident with the poles of the elongating anaphase-telophase nucleus, but in *Saprolegnia* this is not the case. Instead the nucleus projects beyond the end of the spindle in the form of pointed processes (Heath and Greenwood, 1968, 1970 c). During interphase as well as anaphase-telophase, the nuclear envelope of these processes is associated with cytoplasmic microtubules which radiate from the centriole regions (Fig. 23.12). The nature of this association has led to the suggestion that a force-producing mechanism exists in the association, and that this mechanism accounts for part of the forces needed for nuclear elongation during mitosis and also for nuclear motility during interphase (Heath and Greenwood, 1970 c; see also Sections 23.2.2 and 23.3.2. Heath and Heath (1971) have also noted apparent microtubule dependent

---

Fig. 23.11. Cross section of a typical phycomycete centriole (from *Thraustotheca clavata)* showing the nine triplet microtubules and the hub and spokes of the cartwheel. As is typical in the Oömycetes this centriole is located adjacent to a 'pocket' of the nuclear envelope (p). The single microtubules (e.g. arrow) are cytoplasmic or astral microtubules (X 100 000) Glut/Os/Pb/UAc. **Fig. 23.12.** Longitudinal section of a developing spindle of *T. clavata* showing the microtubules which converge to obliquely sectioned polar nuclear envelope pockets (p) in which pairs of centrioles were located in adjacent sections. There are cytoplasmic or astral microtubules (m) radiating back from the pocket region. The arrowed structures are shown by serial sections to be microtubule terminations which may be kinetochores. No attempts have succeeded in staining chromatin in this organism but it is presumed that the kinetochore-like structures are attached to the chromosomes (X 85 200) Glut/Os/Pb/UAc. **Fig. 23.13.** Median longitudinal section of a pair of *Saprolegnia ferax* centrioles showing the typical Oömycete 180° orientation. Note the triplet tubules (arrow 1) and cartwheel hubs (arrow 2) (X 70 080) Glut/Os/Pb/UAc (from Heath and Greenwood, 1970 c in the *Journal of General Microbiology).* **Fig. 23.14.** Cross section of a nuclear pore of *Thraustotheca clavata* showing the osmiophilic plug (arrowed) (X 166 500). Glut/Os/Pb/UAc.

nuclear motility in the rust *Uromyces.*). Morphological evidence supports this suggestion, but of course the association could not explain motility in those genera in which it is apparently absent, for example the uniflagellate fungi reported above. However, the need for such additional forces during mitosis may not exist in the uniflagellate fungi which typically have a much larger and presumably stronger spindle than the Oömycetes (compare Figs. 23.8 and 23.12). Whatever the mechanics of the process may be, at telophase there are typically two masses of chromatin at opposite ends of an elongated nucleus inside an intact nuclear envelope.

In *Saprolegnia* (Heath and Greenwood, 1968, 1970 c) and *Blastocladiella* (Lessie and Lovett, 1968) mitosis is apparently completed by a median constriction and fusion of the nuclear envelope. However in *Catenaria* (Ichida and Fuller, 1968) and *Phlyctochytrium* (McNitt, personal communication) the nuclear envelope constricts closely around each mass of chromatin and excludes the bulk of the nucleoplasm in the form of a cigar-shaped mass which soon degenerates. The significance of such a seemingly 'wasteful' process is totally obscure. In all reported organisms but the Saprolegniales (Heath and Greenwood, 1968; Heath, 1974 a, b), the nucleolus becomes undetectable by metaphase and apparently re-forms in the daughter nuclei, but in *Saprolegnia* it persists throughout mitosis, becoming constricted with the rest of the nucleus at telophase.

The aquatic fungi exhibit a number of features which are not comparable with the more classical mitoses, yet fulfil the same basic functions. The phylogenetic aspects of these variations promise to be very interesting, but with such a small sample examined to date, such comparisons are premature.

23.2.4 Parasitism

Although there have been a number of reports dealing with the ultrastructure of 'phycomycetous' parasites, only two can be considered as freshwater species as opposed to soil inhabitants. *Rozella allomycis* Foust. is a completely intracellular parasite of *Allomyces arbuscula* (Held, 1972 a), whereas *Chytridium* sp. parasitizes the alga *Scenedesmus* only by the insertion of haustoria (Schnepf *et al.,* 1971). In both cases host penetration is from encysted zoospores which attach to the host wall by means of some extracellular material, presumably secreted by the spore. Subsequent germination produces an infection peg which passes through the host wall. Penetration probably involves wall degrading enzymes, which may be secreted from small vesicles contained in the germ tube (Held, 1972 a) but the force needed for penetration seems to be provided by enlargement of a vacuole within the spore of both species. The host reaction to penetration is variable. In *Scenedesmus* a small amount of osmiophilic material is normally deposited around the penetration site, but in a few unsuccessful penetrations a large deposit, probably composed in part of callose (a 'callosity'), is apparently produced (Schnepf *et al.,* 1971). The host reaction of *Allomyces* is more difficult to describe due to sparse information, but the data can be interpreted as showing that usually a variable sized callosity is produced in response to penetration. Such is not the author's interpretation (Held, 1972 a), but is more consistent with the weight of evidence from higher plants where the production of a callosity is a common response to many types of cell damage (e.g. Heath and Heath, 1971). In *Allomyces* such a response is not always successful in resisting infection, but it can apparently work in the case of *Scenedesmus* (Schnepf *et al.,* 1971). The success of penetration probably lies in the balance between the rate of formation of the callosity and the rate of penetration of the fungus. However, before the role of the callosities can be unequivocally defined, a detailed serial section analysis of known stages of penetration must be undertaken.

Subsequent to penetration we have no information on the ultrastructure of the development of *Rozella,* but in *Chytridium* a branched haustorium develops. This haustorium is enclosed by fungal wall and surrounded by an invagination of the host cell membrane (Schnepf *et al.,* 1971). There are no obvious modifications of its structure which might be correlated with its probable role in nutrient absorption. However, as the host cytoplasm becomes progressively deranged, so eventually the spore body which remained outside the cell enlarges and develops into a zoosporangium which yields zoospores to repeat the cycle.

Clearly, the field of aquatic parasitic fungi is one which needs considerable development, and should yield results which will be of significance to the broader spectrum of host parasite interaction.

23.3 Asexual Reproduction

Apart from the obvious genetic aspects, the main objective of a reproductive system is the packaging of the minimal ingredients for producing a new organism in such a way as to ensure maximum longevity and dispersal. Aquatic fungi exhibit an economy of production. They develop large numbers of asexual spores which are not well protected but are designed for short range dispersal in favourable conditons and also produce fewer, well protected sexual spores which have greater potential for survival and long range dispersal in adverse conditions. Thus the objective of zoosporogenesis is to package the requirements for a new individual into an efficiently motile unit.

23.3.1 Zoospore Formation

In most studies controlled zoosporangium induction has been achieved by replacing the normal growth medium with a nutrient-poor solution such as water with traces of various salts. In such a system one can clearly differentiate between vegetative and zoosporogenesis events.

Cross walls. Zoosporogenesis typically involves an initial flow of cytoplasm and organelles into the developing sporangium, prior to the insertion of a cross wall (Lessie and Lovett, 1968; Gay and Greenwood, 1966). After the cross wall is inserted, the nuclei may undergo mitosis (Heath and Greenwood, 1970 c) and some nuclei may be degraded (Heath, 1969), but there is probably not a large change in the number of nuclei after cross wall formation. In *Blastocladiella* the cross wall seems to be formed by gradual localized centripetal growth so that is is essentially indistinguishable from the sporangium wall (Lessie and Lovett, 1968). However, a more specialized structure is found in some Oömycetes where cross wall insertion can occur within a few seconds. In both the cross walls of *Saprolegnia, Dictyuchus* and *Thraustotheca* (Heath and Greenwood, 1970 b; Heath, unpublished) and the analogous basal plugs of various *Phytophthora* species (e.g. Hohl and Hamamoto, 1967; Williams and Webster, 1970) the wall material contains various osmiophilic inclusions including membranes, ribosomes and other trapped cytoplasmic components. Such configurations are reminiscent of callosities (see Section 23.2.4) and may be a general feature of rapidly synthesized walls (Heath and Greenwood, 1970 b). The mode of deposition of these walls and plugs is unknown, however once inserted they can be added to by apposition of

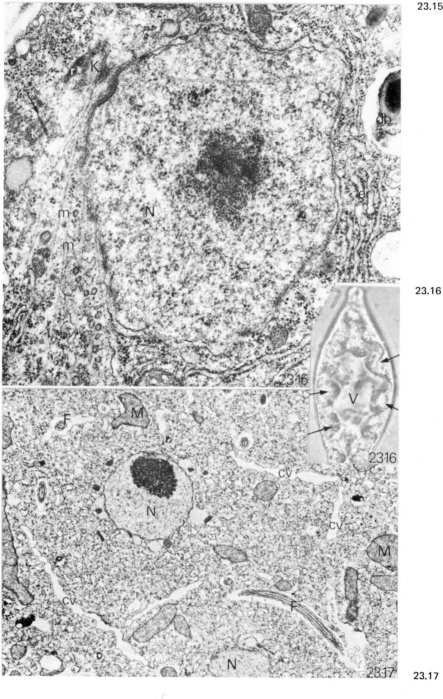

the same material which thickens the wall of the sporangium during its development (Chapman and Vujičić, 1965; Williams and Webster, 1970; Heath *et al.*, 1971). In *Saprolegnia* this additional material is apparently deposited in part from wall vesicles (Heath *et al.*, 1971) and contains a considerable amount of material which exhibits birefringence, probably cellulose fibrils (Heath, 1969). Little is known of the functional significance of these cross walls and their characteristics apart from the obvious intuitive ideas, but it should be noted that *Chytridium* apparently functions well in the absence of a basal cross wall (Schepf *et al.*, 1971).

Cytoplasmic cleavage.   The normal phycomycete zoospore is uninucleate, thus any cytoplasmic cleavage mechanism must have evolved a means of ensuring this nuclear distribution. There seem to be two basic mechanisms of cytoplasmic cleavage in the phycomycetes. Conceptually the simplest is found in *Saprolegnia* where the central vacuoles expand between uninucleate masses of cytoplasm (Fig. 23.16) until the vacuole and cell membranes fuse, thus producing zoospores which are clothed with a membrane derived in part from both the vacuole and cell membranes (Gay and Greenwood, 1966; Gay *et al.*, 1971). Since the sporangium does not normally expand significantly during this process, the vacuole must expand at the expense of the cytoplasm. Such expansion could easily result if the osmotic potential of the vacuole became higher than the cytoplasm, thus causing flow of water from cytoplasm to vacuole. Concomitantly, additional membrane synthesis is required to line the enlarging vacuole. It has been suggested that both processes are brought about by the fusion of the 'dense body' vesicles with the central vacuoles (Gay and Greenwood, 1966; Gay *et al.*, 1971). These vesicles are only produced on induction of sporulation, are apparently rich in phospholipids, and some do indeed appear to fuse with the cleaving central vacuoles (see Section 23.4.2 and Fig.23.31). Thus it is suggested that some of the phospholipids may be utilized for expansion of the vacuolar membrane, whilst some are degraded into smaller molecules which could increase the osmotic pressure of the vacuole. Phospholipase A and B and a diesterase might be predicted as suitable cleaving enzymes. At present this hypothesis rests entirely on circumstantial evidence and awaits detailed autoradiographic and enzyme localization investigations for confirmation.

The cleavage pattern in *Aphanomyces* is essentially similar to that in *Saprolegnia* but is simpler in that only one row of zoospores are produced (Hoch and Mitchell, 1972 a). Again vacuole expansion is the cleaving agent, but here the role of the dense bodies is less well documented, especially as they are present in this species before

---

Fig. 23.15. Portion of a zoosporangium of *Saprolegnia ferax* at an early stage in zoospore formation. The nucleus (N) has become pyriform with its apex directed towards the cell wall. The centrioles have become kinetosomes (K) which are sectioned obliquely, one of which shows a clear terminal plate (arrow). Interconnecting the kinetosomes is a fibrous root (r) and radiating from the base of the kinetosomes are numerous microtubular roots (m). Rough endoplasmic reticulum (er) and a dense body (db) are prominent (X 28 300) Glut/Os/Pb/UAc (from Heath and Greenwood, 1971 with permission of Springer-Verlag). **Fig. 23.16.** Light micrograph of a cleaving zoosporangium of *S. ferax* showing the central vacuole (V) which is enlarging and delimiting uninucleate masses of cytoplasm (arrows) (X 660) . Living specimen. Unpublished micrograph kindly supplied by Dr. J. L. Gay, Imperial College, London. **Fig. 23.17.** Portion of a zoosporangium of *Blastocladiella emersonii* midway through cleavage. The cleavage vesicles (cv) are aligned around uninucleate masses of cytoplasm. Flagella (F) are well developed within some of these vesicles. (X 8 000). Glut/Os/Pb/UAc. Unpublished micrograph kindly supplied by Drs. W. E. Barstow and J. S. Lovett, Purdue University, Lafayette.

zoospore induction. (For further information on the function of dense bodies see Sections 23.3.2, 23.3.3 and 23.4.2.)

In the Oömycetes such as various *Phytophthora* species (Hohl and Hamamoto, 1967; Elsner *et al.,* 1970) and *Thraustotheca* (Heath, unpublished) and all the uni-flagellate fungi studied to date, cytoplasmic cleavage is brought about by the alignment and subsequent fusion of a reticulum of small vesicles (Fig.23.17). The origin of these vesicles is uncertain; in *Phytophthora parasitica* (Hohl and Hamamoto, 1967), *Phytophthora infestans* (Elsner *et al.,* 1970) and *Harpochytrium* (Travland and Whisler, 1971) there is morphological evidence for a Golgi body origin, while in *Phytophthora capsici,* Williams and Webster (1970) suggest that some may be derived from the central vacuole. In *Allomyces,* Renaud and Swift (1964) claim that they may be budded off the cell membrane. Clearly, the problem will not be resolved satisfactorily until more specific morphological or histochemical markers are available. However, it is interesting to note that many of the cleavage vesicles are the ones into which the developing flagellum grows during cleavage (King and Butler, 1968; Williams and Webster, 1970; Elsner *et al.,* 1970; Schnepf *et al.,* 1971; Lessie and Lovett, 1968; Renaud and Swift, 1964). Thus final cleavage is brought about by fusion of the cleavage vesicles, flagellum containing vesicles, central vacuole (if present) and the cell membrane.

The important aspect of control of cleavage pattern so that only uninucleate spores are normally produced, is a problem on which essentially no information is available The only mechanism so far suggested (Heath and Greenwood, 1971) is found in the *Saprolegnia* cleavage system where the observed array of microtubular roots around each nucleus (Fig.23.15) may space the nuclei apart from each other and leave areas of relatively 'weaker' cytoplasm between nuclei along which the cleaving vacuole may preferentially expand. The micrographs of Hoch and Mitchell (1972 a) show that a comparable mechanism could function in *Aphanomyces* but such a system is clearly impossible in the uniflagellate type of cleavage where the root system frequently develops after cleavage and where the three dimensional arrangement is far more complex.

Flagellum development.   There are essentially two components to the flagellar apparatus of a zoospore, the flagella themselves and the components ('roots') which attach the flagella to the zoospore. The roots will be more conveniently discussed in the context of zoospore structure (Section 23.3.2), thus only the flagellum will be dealt with in this section. All fungal flagella develop from kinetosomes which are comparable to elongated centrioles (Figs.23.15 and 23.20). In *Saprolegnia, Dictyuchus* (Heath and Greenwood, 1971), *Thraustotheca* (Heath, unpublished), *Blasto-cladiella* (Lessie and Lovett, 1968), *Chytridium* (Schnepf *et al.,* 1971), *Rhizidio-myces* (Fuller and Reichle, 1965), *Olpidium* (Temmink and Campbell, 1968) and *Harpochytrium* (Travland and Whistler, 1971) the kinetosomes are produced by the direct elongation of the nine triplet microtubules of one or both of the centrioles which are present adjacent to each nucleus throughout interphase. Thus a structure composed of nine triple microtubules only 0.2 μm long would be a centriole, whereas a comparable structure approximately 0.7 μm long would be termed a kinetosome. In the uniflagellate fungi the centriole which lies at right angles to the nuclear envelope tends to be longer than the other. This is the one which develops into a kinetosome (Fig. 23.21). In the biflagellate fungi both centrioles reorientate from 180° to approximately 100° prior to becoming kinetosomes. Typically the kinetosomes, prior to flagellum development, have a terminal plate of osmiophilic material which at spore maturation comes to lie at the surface of the spore where the flagellum emerges from the spore (Fig.23.20). The second centriole of the uniflagellate fungi remains short and adjacent to the kinetosome for the life of the spore (Fig.23.21). The universal occurrence of a second short centriole or vestigial kinetosome in the uniflagellate fungi has been suggested as evidence for a biflagellate ancestry for this group (Olson and Fuller, 1968).

In the biflagellate species such as *Phytophthora infestans* (King and Butler, 1968), *Phytophthora parasitica* (Hohl and Hamamoto, 1967), *Phytophthora capsici* (Williams and Webster, 1970) and *Aphanomyces euteiches* (Hoch and Mitchell, 1972 a) true centrioles are reportedly lacking in the vegetative phase (see Section 23.2.3). Kinetosomes are reported to arise by an as yet unreported process from 'procentrioles' whose true structure awaits detailed elucidation.

Once formed the kinetosome may remain 'dormant' showing no further development until after cytoplasmic cleavage has occurred (as in *Saprolegnia, Thraustotheca, Aphanomyces, Harpochytrium, Olpidium*) or they may develop into flagella during the cleavage process. In either event the nine doublet microtubules of the flagellum axoneme develop as extensions of the doublets of the kinetosome (the third tubule of each group having terminated below the basal plate) and the typical central pair of tubules start just above the basal plate (Fig.23.21). In the organisms whose flagella develop after cleavage, the axoneme apparently 'stretches' the cell membrane to form the sheath of the flagellum, but in those species where flagellum development occurs before cleavage the axoneme grows into a sheath-like vesicle which is apparently enlarged by the coalescence of vesicles from an essentially unknown origin (see previous discussion on cytoplasmic cleavage) (Lessie and Lovett, 1968; Renaud and Swift, 1964; Williams and Webster, 1970; King and Butler, 1968). Thus in the latter system the flagellum sheath is derived from the membranes of the vesicles. In no fungi do we have any information regarding the origin of sub-units nor the mode of synthesis of the axonemal microtubules, although by analogy to the alga *Ochromonas* we may expect tip growth (Rosenbaum and Child, 1967). Heath and Greenwood (1971) speculated that Golgi bodies may be involved in microtubule synthesis in *Saprolegnia* but until autoradiographic investigations have been undertaken such speculation is not very valuable. Similarly, whilst the membrane needed for the flagellum sheath could come from the same source as the rest of the cleavage membranes in the vesicular cleavage system, the membrane needed for the developing flagellum in those species which develop after cleavage is quite substantial (approximately 1/10th of that needed to cover the spore) yet nothing is known concerning its origin.

Flimmer hairs. In the Oōmycetes and Hyphochytridiomycetes the zoospores bear Flimmer flagella, i.e. flagella which have characteristic Flimmer hairs or mastigonemes arranged in two opposing ranks along the sheath of the flagellum. Flimmer hairs are typically tripartite with a tapering solid basal region, a 1.5 μm long, 10 nm diameter tubular shaft and one or more solid hair-like tips. They are attached to the flagellum sheath by the tapering tip (Heath and Greenwood, 1971; Elsner *et al.,* 1970), although some undetected connection to the axoneme cannot be ruled out since Manton *et al.,* (1952) noted that in shadowed preparations of *Saprolegnia* the Flimmer hairs remained associated with the doublet microtubules even in the apparent absence of the sheath. The site of synthesis of the Flimmer hairs is now established in a number of species. They are produced within ribosome-studded cisternae of endoplasmic reticulum (Figs. 23.22 and 23.23) or dilations of the nuclear envelope (Reichle, 1969; Hoch and Mitchell, 1972 a, b; Heath *et al.,* 1970; see also reinterpretation of Fuller and Reichle,

1965 and Fuller, 1966). At least in *Pythium middletonii* Sparrow they are apparently transferred through Golgi bodies into Golgi vesicles prior to their release to the surface of the spore (Bracker *et al.,* 1970). The mode of release and mechanism of arrangement and attachment to the flagellum is obscure, although they appear to be added towards the end of flagellum development (Heath and Greenwood, 1971). The 'smooth' whip-lash flagellum of some Oömycetes also bears fine hairs attached to its sheath. These hairs are considerably smaller than Flimmer hairs, being only about 0.2-0.3 μm long by 3 nm thick (Reichle, 1969) and whilst they occur on a number of species (Manton *et al.,* 1952; Colhoun, 1966) their site of synthesis and function is unknown.

The above are only some of the changes which occur during zoospore formation. However the other changes will more easily be considered in the context of zoospore structure and function in the following sections. However there is one more impor-tant feature of zoosporangium development which should be considered here, the formation of structures which are associated with spore release. Typically some form of apical papillum develops and its subsequent rupture releases the zoospores. In one of the simplest cases, the papillum of *Saprolegnia* develops as a localized exten-sion of the sporangium wall (Heath *et al.,* 1971) and then the tip of the papillum breaks down due to enzymic activity (discussion following Gay and Greenwood, 1966). Since the breakdown occurs in the absence of adjacent cytoplasm (i.e. after cleavage) the enzymes must be located in the wall. The mechanism of enzyme control in such a case is an intriguing unsolved poblem. In *Chytridium* the 'papillum' is essentially an undifferentiated region of the sporangium wall which is not extended in the same way as *Saprolegnia* but is delimited by a clear circle of discontinuity along which rupture occurs at the time of spore release (Schnepf *et al.,* 1971). Most other organisms appear to synthesize a definite additional structure which is clearly differentiated from the sporangium wall. Thus the sporangium wall of *Blastocladiella* is degraded and a new plug-like layer is inserted (Lessie and Lovett, 1968). A pulley shaped plug of 'protopectin' is inserted in an aperture of the wall of *Allomyces* (Skucas, 1966). Again, spore release is achieved by apparent enzyme degradation of the plug. Perhaps the most spectacular apical plugs are developed in *Phytophthora* species (Williams and Webster, 1970; Elsner *et al.,* 1970; Hohl and Hamamoto, 1967; Hemmes and Hohl, 1969) and *Olpidium* (Temmink and Campbell, 1968), where a plug of unknown nature develops inside the papillum-like sporangial wall and may subsequently be pushed out (Hohl and Hamamoto, 1967) or dissolved (Temmink and Campbell, 1968), to release zoospores, or partially dissolved to permit the passage of a germ tube in direct germination (Hemmes and Hohl, 1969). The necessity for such a massive plug-like structure remains totally unexplained.

23.3.2 Zoospore Structure

There are more ultrastructural investigations of the zoospores than any other stage in the life cycle of the phycomycetes; consequently there is a wealth of detailed informa-tion, much of which is difficult to correlate with a known function. Whilst there is a general trend to increasing specialization of zoospore structure from the relatively simple primary Oömycete zoospore to the Blastocladiales spore, there are a number of irregularities so that a spore may be more 'advanced' on one feature but less 'advanced' on another. Thus for clarity this section will be based on variations of organelles through taxonomic groups rather than a repetitive description of each group.

Mitochondria. The least specialised arrangement of the mitochondria is found in both primary and secondary zoospores of the Oömycetes, in the Hyphochytridiomycetes and in the Monoblepharidales. The elongated mitochondria typical of vegetative hyphae are replaced by short, 2-3 μm long organelles (Figs. 23.18 and 23.21). The vegative association between mitochondria, endoplasmic reticulum and Golgi bodies and the elaboration of the outer membranes typical of various species are lost (see Section 23.2.2), but otherwise the mitochondria are distributed randomly throughout the cytoplasm of the spore with no obvious specialization of structure or arrangement. Examples of this condition are found in *Saprolegnia, Dictyuchus* (Heath and Greenwood, 1971), *Thraustotheca* (Heath, unpublished), *Aphanomyces* (Hoch and Mitchell, 1972 a, b), *Phytophthora* species (Reichle, 1969; Ho *et al.*, 1969), *Pythium* (Grove, 1970 a, b; Morré *et al.*, 1971), *Rhizidiomyces* (Fuller, 1966; Fuller and Reichle, 1965), *Harpochytrium* (Travland and Whisler, 1971), *Monoblepharella* (Fuller and Reichle, 1968; Reichle, 1972), *Oedogoniomyces* (Reichle, 1972) and *Rhizophydium* (Fuller, 1966). *Olpidium* (Temmink and Campbell, 1969 a) has essentially the same arrangement but tends to have one larger mitochondrion surrounding the point where the rhizoplast joins the nucleus. A comparable trend is seen in *Allomyces* (Fuller and Calhoun, 1968; Hill, 1969; Fuller and Olson, 1971) where the mitochondrion around the kinetosome is somewhat larger than that in *Olpidium* and in addition the smaller mitochondria tend to be closely appressed to the membrane of the nuclear cap (Fig.23.32). This association of mitochondria and nuclear cap (see below) membrane is also found in *Nowakowskiella* (Chambers *et al.*, 1967). The greatest specialization of mitochondrial arrangement seems to be in *Blastocladiella* (Cantino *et al.*, 1963; Reichle and Fuller, 1967; Lessie and Lovett, 1968) where the mitochondria fuse during development to produce one large mitochondrion per zoospore. This mitochondrion envelops the kinetosome and apex of the associated nucleus, and is penetrated by a short evagination of the nucleus, the function of which remains completely obscure (Cantino and Truesdell, 1970; Reichle and Fuller, 1967). *Chytridium* also only has one mitochondrion per spore but its organization is not clear at present (Schnepf *et al.*, 1971). This trend to concentrate the mitochondrion around the kinetosome may have functional significance both in placing the energy generating system close to the main source of energy utilization during motility and in increasing the size of material associated with the base of the flagellum, thus giving it a firmer base to absorb the reaction to its beating.

Golgi bodies. In those species which possess typical Golgi bodies in their vegetative cells, it is normal to find Golgi bodies in the Zoospores. Typically there are only one or two Golgi bodies per spore. They are usually arranged adjacent to the nuclear envelope along the sides of the apex of the nucleus as in *Saprolegnia* (Heath and Greenwood, 1971), *Aphanomyces* (Hoch and Mitchell, 1972 a, b), *Pythium* (Grove, 1970 b), *Phytophthora* (Ho *et al.*, 1968; Reichle, 1969), *Rhizidiomyces* (Fuller and Reichle, 1965), *Harpochytrium* (Travland and Whisler, 1971), or around the water expulsion vacuole (Morré *et al.*, 1971). Frequently the nuclear envelope appears to be producing vesicles which contribute to the Golgi bodies (e.g. Heath and Greenwood, 1971; see also Section 23.2.2) but the reason for this exclusive association and the clustering of the Golgi bodies around the apex of the nucleus and water expulsion vacuole remains obscure. Circumstantial evidence has led to suggestions of a role in contractile vacuole production in *Pythium* (Fig.23.18, Morré *et al.*, 1971) and flagellum formation in *Saprolegnia* (Heath and Greenwood, 1971). Clearly autoradiographic or histochemical work is needed for the resolution of these questions.

Dense Bodies and Lipid Droplets.   Dense bodies comparable to those described in the context of cytoplasmic cleavage (Section 23.3.1) occur widely in zoospores. For example, all the biflagellate zoospores examined, both primary and secondary, possess them (Figs.23.18 and 23.15; references above and Gay *et al.,* 1971), and comparable structures can be seen in *Monoblepharella* (Fuller, 1966, Fig.14). However, in general terms they are apparently rare or absent in the uniflagellate zoospores. Certainly no bodies with comparable striations have been seen in micrographs of uniflagellate zoospores. Since dense bodies were said to be involved in zoospore cleavage, it might be considered anomalous that so many should be present in the zoospores. There are two functions which might explain the apparent anomaly. As will be seen some dense bodies are involved in vacuole production during cyst germination (Gay *et al.,* 1971; Colt and Endo, 1972; see also Section 23.3.3), and Katsura (1970) has performed RQ measurements and microanalytical experiments to show that in *Phytophthora capsici* phosphatidyl choline is used as an energy source in the motile spore. Phosphatidyl choline is believed to be a major constituent of dense bodies (Gay *et al.,* 1971).

Any propagative structure which may need to be capable of dormancy needs an energy store. Dense bodies may fulfil this role in some species, but more probable, universal, energy reserves are the lipid droplets which seem to be a universal feature of zoospore ultrastructure (Figs. 23.18 and 23.21 and references cited above). Typically these lipid droplets are dispersed throughout the cytoplasm of the zoospore, but again in the highly specialized *Blastocladiella* the lipid droplets are clustered adjacent to the mitochondrion and enclosed by an extension of the nuclear cap membrane (see below and Reichle and Fuller, 1967; Lessie and Lovett, 1968). *Allomyces* is apparently closely related to *Blastocladiella* in this respect since, whilst most of the lipid droplets are dispersed in the cytoplasm, some are aggregated with other structures to form a 'side body' adjacent to the single posterior mitochondrion (Fuller and Olson, 1971). Perhaps *Chytridium* is one of the most specialized in this respect in only having one large lipid droplet which is associated with the mitochondrion (Schnepf *et al.,* 1971). Intuitively, it would seem logical to place the energy reserve next to the respiratory centre of the cell, but clearly more needs to be known of the biochemistry of the zoospore before the full functional significance of this association is certain.

Nuclei.   The typical configuration for the nucleus in virtually all zoospores is a pear shape with its apex closely adjacent to the kinetosome(s) (Figs.23.15, 23.18 and 23.32). The nucleolus may reside in the bulbous portion of the nucleoplasm as in *Aphanomyces* (Hoch and Mitchell, 1972 a), *Saprolegnia* (Heath and Greenwood, 1971), *Phytophthora* (Reichle, 1969; Ho *et al.,* 1968), *Rhizidiomyces* (Fuller and Reichle, 1965) and *Harpochytrium* (Travland and Whisler, 1971), or it may be located in the apex as in *Allomyces* (Fig. 23 32 and Fuller and Olson, 1971) or *Blastocladiella* (Reichle and Fuller, 1967; Lessie and Lovett, 1968). The marked exception to this general pyriform arrangement is seen in the Monoblepharidales type spores where the nucleus remains near the centre of the spore, is apparently only loosely, if at all, connected to the kinetosome, and retains an approximately spherical shape as shown in *Monoblepharella* (Fig.23 21 and Fuller and Reichle, 1968; Reichle, 1972) and *Oedogoniomyces* (Reichle, 1972). The significance of these arrangements will become more apparent in the context of flagellum anchorage.

Ribosomes and Nuclear Caps.   Apparently the simplest arrangment of ribosomes

626

is dispersion throughout the cytoplasm, or attachment to endoplasmic reticulum, as found in the biflagellates such as *Saprolegnia* (Heath and Greenwood, 1971), *Aphanomyces* (Hoch and Mitchell, 1972 a, b), *Phytophthora* (e.g. Reichle, 1969), *Pythium* (Fig.23.18 and Grove, 1970 b) and a few uniflagellates such as *Rhizophydium* (Fuller, 1966) and *Chytridium* (Schnepf *et al.*, 1971). However, in the uniflagellate zoospores there is a trend towards aggregation of the ribosomes into a membrane enclosed cap around the nucleus. Thus in *Rhizidiomyces* (Fuller and Reichle, 1965) the ribosomes form a loose cluster around the nucleus. They are more tightly clustered and are permeated by cisternae of endoplasmic reticulum in *Monoblepharella* and *Oedogoniomyces* (Fig.23.21 and Fuller and Reichle, 1968; Reichle, 1972). In *Harpochytrium* the cap becomes more prominent, is partially enclosed by membranes, presumably of endoplasmic reticulum origin, but is divided into two or three lobes (Travland and Whisler, 1971). The most highly organized caps reported are found in *Allomyces* and *Blastocladiella* where extensions of the nuclear envelope completely enclose the ribosomal complement of the cell into a cup-shaped mass around the bulbous part of the nucleus (Figs.23.32 and 23.33, and Hill,1969; Fuller and Olson, 1971; Reichle and Fuller, 1967; Lessie and Lovett, 1968; Fuller and Colhoun, 1968). In *Blastocladiella* and *Allomyces* these caps form towards the end of zoospore differentiation by aggregation of ribosomes, and their subsequent enclosure by vesicles, possibly of endoplasmic reticulum origin, which ultimately fuse with each other and the nuclear envelope in a continuous sheet (Lessie and Lovett, 1968; Blondel and Turian, 1960). The packaging of the *Blastocladiella* ribosomes into caps coincides with cessation of protein synthesis (Murphy and Lovett, 1966) although the actual mechanism of switching off the ribosomes seems to involve an inhibitor (Schmoyer and Lovett, 1969). Thus because packaging *per se* does not result in cessation of protein synthesis, some other function probably led to the evolution of such a system. Perhaps an increase in material closely attached to the flagellar roots, thus yielding a larger basal structure, is advantageous in dissipating the reaction to flagellar motion and hence producing more efficient motility. However, such a hypothesis is still pure speculation and hardly explains the apparently weak aggregation of ribosomes found in *Rhizidiomyces* for example.

Flagellar Roots.   Simple observation shows that a beating flagellum generates a lot of force relative to the size of a zoospore, and clearly if it were not firmly attached it would quickly tear itself from the spore. There is considerable variation in speed of zoospore movement (Couch, 1941), which presumably reflects variation in amount of propulsive force generated by the flagellum. Thus, one would predict that the most rapidly moving spores would have the most highly developed attachment system. The most competent swimmers seem to be the uniflagellate spores, followed by the secondary biflagellate spores, with the primary biflagellate spores being the least competent (Couch, 1941). As seen above, the mass to which the flagellum is apparently anchored (i.e. nucleus, nuclear cap, mitochondria, etc) is larger and more complex in the uniflagellates such as *Blastocladiella*. Similarly there is a parallel trend in complexity of the root system.

In the primary biflagellate zoospores such as *Saprolegnia,* the flagella are apparently anchored by a cone of approximately 100 single microtubules which radiate from around the base of the kinetosome, some passing into the cytoplasm and others closely associated with the nuclear envelope in a manner comparable to that discussed for mitosis in this genus (see Sections 23.2.3, Figs 23.15 and 23.18, and Heath and Greenwood, 1971). The pyriform shape of these spores is probably due to this arrange-

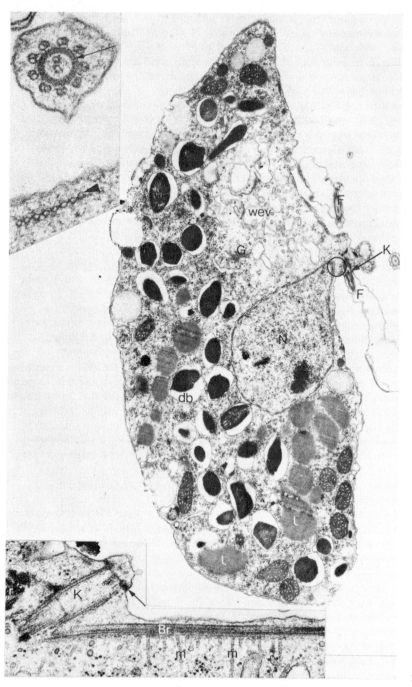

ment of roots. That the nucleus is strongly attached to the kinetosomes is clear from the observations of Manton et al., (1952) where it was noted that disintegrated spores of Saprolegnia retained a close association between nucleus and flagella. In addition to these roots there is a small striate fibre (Figs. 23.15 and 23.18) which interconnects the two kinetosomes and presumably functions to buttress them from moving relative to each other (Heath and Greenwood, 1971).

Whilst secondary zoospores of Saprolegnia have not been examined to date, spores with a comparable reniform shape have been examined in other genera of the Oömycetes. Since their shape is similar and there is a tendency in the group for suppression or loss of the primary spores, all reniform spores are probably comparable in root structure. In Aphanomyces (Hoch and Mitchell, 1972 b), Pythium (Grove, 1970) and Phytophthora (Reichle, 1969; Williams and Webster, 1970) the root system is composed of a backbone of 7-8 microtubules which are fused into a sheet with osmiophilic material and which run from the kinetosomes along the base of the groove (Ho et al., 1968) of the spore (Figs. 23.19, 23 20). This backbone is connected to the kinetosomes by a number of complex osmiophilic fibres (Hoch and Mitchell, 1972 b). Attached laterally to the backbone are a number of rib-like single microtubules (Fig. 23.20) which run along the sides of the zoospore close to the cell membrane (Hoch and Mitchell, 1972 b; Reichle, 1969; Grove, 1970). As in the primary spore there is a fibre interconnecting the kinetosomes (Fig.23.20) and single microtubules associated with the nuclear envelope (Fig.23.18). Apart from an obvious correlation with zoospore shape the mechanical advantage offered by this arrangement is uncertain, but since both root complexity and swimming ability are increased, it is presumably a more highly evolved structure.

The simplest uniflagellate spores described have a root system which is apparently comparable in simplicity to that of the primary biflagellate spores described above. Thus in Rhizidiomyces (Fuller and Reichle, 1965) and possibly also in Rhizophydium (Fuller, 1966) there is a cone of single microtubular roots. In Rhizidiomyces (anteriorly flagellate) these arch up from the kinetosome before passing posteriorly under the cell membrane, unassociated with the nucleus, whereas in Rhizophydium (posteriorly flagellate) they tend to pass directly anteriorly along the envelope of the pyriform nucleus. However, it should be noted that in Rhizidiomyces the nucleus is also pyriform and lies closely adjacent ot the kinetosomes. Clearly some as yet undefined attachment structures must exist.

The line of development of attaching the kinetosome to the nucleus reaches its peak in the Blastocladiales. In this group there are characteristically nine groups of triple microtubules (27 in all) which run from osmiophilic material at the base of

---

Fig. 23.18. Zoospore of Pythium aphanidermatum showing laterally inserted flagella (F) with microtubular roots (circled) adjacent to the pyriform nucleus (N). Note the ribosome free area which is associated with the water expulsion vacuole (wev) and the surrounding Golgi bodies (G). Numerous dense bodies (db) and lipid droplets (l) are present. The backbone root would run from the kinetosomes (K) vertically in the plane of the micrograph on adjacent sections. (X 11 500) Glut/Os/Pb/UAc. Fig. 23.19. Cross section of the transition region of a flagellum of P. aphanidermatum showing the nine doublets and central pair of microtubules and the prominent osmiophilic cylinder (arrow). The arrow head points to a cross section of the 'backbone' root composed of eight microtubules and associated osmiophilic material (X 75 000) Glut/Os/Pb/UAc. Fig. 23.20. A kinetosome (K) of P. aphanidermatum showing the way in which the terminal plate (arrow) is adjoining the cell membrane. The 'backbone' root (Br) is sectioned longitudinally to show the attached rib like microtubules (m). Note a portion of the fibrous root (r) which connects the kinetosomes. (X 40 000) Glut/Os/Pb/UAc. Figs. 23.18-23.20 are unpublished micrographs kindly supplied by Drs. S. N. Grove and C. E. Bracker.

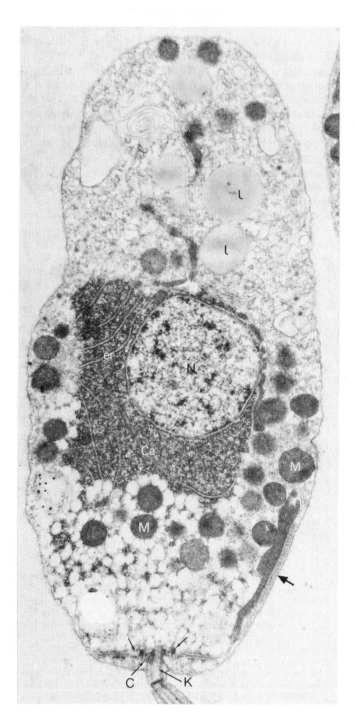

the kinetosome in an evenly spaced conical array along the surface of the nuclear envelope and nuclear cap membrane. These are the only microtubular roots present in these spores. Their close association with the membranes is strictly comparable with the association described above for *Saprolegnia*. This 9 triplet arrangement has so far been reported for *Allomyces, Blastocladia, Catenaria* and *Blastocladiella* (Fuller and Colhoun, 1968; Fuller and Olson, 1971) and may prove to be universal in this group. In addition to these microtubular roots there is commonly a striated ribbon-like rootlet associated with the kinetosomes. In *Allomyces* this is a relatively short structure which appears to be closely associated with the large mitochondrion (Fuller and Olson, 1971). In *Blastocladiella* there are two (Cantino *et al.,* 1963; Lessie and Lovett, 1968; Cantino and Truesdell, 1971) or clearly three (Reichle and Fuller, 1967) longer striated rootlets which run from the kinetosome through channels in the mitochondrion. The details of the interconnections between the striated rootlet and the various membranes and organelles in this region of the spore remain unclear and may vary from spore to spore (Reichle and Fuller, 1967).

In addition to the apparent trend of attachment of microtubular roots to the nucleus there are a number of other variations. For example in *Monoblepharella* and *Oedogoniomyces* (Fuller and Reichle, 1968; Reichle, 1972) the nucleus is located approximately centrally in the zoospore and is not closely associated with the kinetosome (Fig.23.21). Instead there is a large striated disc surrounding the kinetosome with a few single microtubules inserted in it at some distance from the kinetosome and radiating anteriorly to the nuclear cap (Fig. 23.21). There is no apparent association between the microtubular roots and any membranous components, presumably the large disc and cytoplasmic-microtubule interactions provide sufficient support.

Harpochytrium (Travland and Whisler, 1971) exhibits an alternative arrangement where there is a small striated rootlet, which is apparently connected to the rumposome (see below), from which single microtubules radiate into the nuclear cap. Again there is no apparent association with membranes. The tubular roots are embedded in the ribosomes of the cap which in this case is located adjacent to the kinetosome, as opposed to its central location in *Monoblepharella*.

Perhaps the zoospores with the most abnormal root system are those of *Olpidium* (Temmink and Campbell, 1969 a) where microtubular roots are apparently absent. Instead a large striated, strap-like, root connects the base of the kinetosome to the nucleus which is located centrally in the cell.

In addition to the assorted root-like structures cited above, there is typically some structural association between the transition zone of the flagellum axoneme (where the flagellum joins the kinetosome) and the cell membrane of this region. This may take the form of an expanded terminal plate whose edges are apparently fused to the cell membrane (e.g. Fig.23.20 and Heath and Greenwood, 1971; Reichle, 1969; King and Butler, 1968; Hoch and Mitchell, 1972 b; Fuller, 1966; etc.) or there may be special props which run from the doublets (or triplets depending on level) of the

Fig. 23.21. Median longitudinal section of a zoospore of *Monoblepharella* sp. The nucleus (N) is located in the centre of the cell and most of the ribosomes are aggregated into a loose cap (Ca) which is permeated by endoplasmic reticulum (er). Mitochondria (M) and lipid droplets (l) are dispersed. The rumposome with its backing cisternae is indicated by the large arrow. Note the striate disc (cut in cross section) (arrows), the kinetosome (K) and associated vestigial kinetosome or centriole (c). Microtubular roots (circled) run from the disc anteriorly through the spore (X 18 800) Glut/Os/Pb/UAc (from Fuller and Reichle, 1968 with permission of the authors and the National Research Council of Canada).

axoneme to the membrane as shown by Olson and Fuller (1968), Fuller and Reichle (1968), Travland and Whisler (1971) and Fuller and Olson (1971). The general trend seems to be props in the uniflagellate spores and plates in the biflagellates with the Hyphochytrid, *Rhizidiomyces* having a plate (Fuller and Reichle, 1965).

Clearly there is diversity in the details of flagellum anchorage but on the few examples studied to date there is at least some evidence for a coherent evolutionary trend which correlates with swimming proficiency.

Transition Zone of Flagella.   There is frequently a complex arrangement of structures in the region where the flagellum axoneme joins the kinetosome (e.g. Heath and Greenwood, 1971). This region may be defined as between the termination of the central pair of tubules of the flagellum and the termination of the third tubules of each triplet on the kinetosome. The structures in this region are apparently somewhat delicate in that they are not always strongly contrasted by normal fixation techniques. Thus, a detailed comparative survey of organisms fixed by different techniques is not very profitable. However, there are a few structures which are normally apparent. An osmiophilic terminal plate (Figs. 23.20 and 23.21) is universal, although not always well developed (e.g. in *Phlyctochytrium,* Olson and Fuller, 1968). Above the terminal plate the biflagellate Oömycetes typically have an osmiophilic concertina-like cylinder (Fig. 23.19) which is of variable length but basically extends from just above the plate to a little above the termination of the central pair of microtubules. This cylinder is clearly seen in various species of *Phytophthora* (Hemmes and Hohl, 1972; Williams and Webster, 1970; Reichle, 1969), *Aphanomyces* (Hoch and Mitchell, 1972 b), *Pythium* (Grove, 1970) and *Saprolegnia* (Heath and Greenwood, 1971). It has only been reported elsewhere in the alga *Sphaleromantis* (Manton and Harris, 1966), its functional or phylogenetic significance is completely obscure. This cylinder is lacking in the uniflagellate fungi which are typically devoid of any clear structures inside the axoneme at the transition zone apart from the above mentioned terminal plate.

Rumposomes and Side Bodies.   Chytridiomycete zoospores typically contain a complex organelle which is located in the posterior part of the cell adjacent to the kinetosome and appressed to the cell membrane. Undoubted intraspecific variability and interpretational disputes make generalizations difficult but there are clearly two basic types of organelle—the rumposome and the side body.

The term rumposome was coined by Fuller (1966) for the highly organised disc-like organelle found in *Monoblepharella* (Fig. 23.21). It characteristically is a 0.1 μm thick disc composed of three layers of interconnecting tubules which show a hexagonal array in surface view (Fuller, 1966; Fuller and Reichle, 1968). The outer face of the disc is closely appressed to the cell membrane whilst the inner face is subtended by two or three dense lamellae which extend through the cytoplasm to the nuclear cap. Comparable rumposomes are also found in *Oedogoniomyces* (Reichle, 1972), *Nowakowskiella* (Chambers *et al.,* 1967) and probably *Chytridium* (Schnepf *et al.,* 1971; Koch, 1956). Rumposomes are reminiscent of the eyespots of many algae but as noted by Fuller (1966) phototaxis is absent in *Monoblepharella.* However, the estuarine fungus *Phlyctochytrium* does have a rumposome and is phototactic (Kazama, 1972). Clearly, more work is needed to elucidate the functional and phylogenetic significance of rumposomes.

In the blastocladillan zoospores rumposomes are unreported but in a comparable position are the side bodies. A side body is somewhat pleomorphic (Cantino and Truesdell, 1970) but in both *Blastocladiella* (Reichle and Fuller, 1967; Lessie and Lovett, 1968; Cantino and Truesdell, 1970) and *Allomyces* (Fuller and Olson, 1971) it is composed of a double backing membrane which is an extension of the nuclear cap membrane. The backing membrane lies close to the cell membrane and forms a mantle which partially surrounds the kinetosome and envelops numerous lipid droplets and 'side body granules' so that they are trapped between the large mitochondrion and the backing membrane. The side body granules, also termed 'Stüben bodies' by Fuller and Olson (1971) are morphologically similar to microbodies. Barstow and Lovett (personal communication) have shown that in *Blastocladiella,* typical dispersed microbodies aggregate and apparently fuse to a certain extent during zoosporogenesis so that they become the side body granules of the side body. The functional significance of the side body is completely obscure.

Whilst side bodies and rumposomes typically occur in different species, Travland and Whisler (1971) have shown a clearly composite organelle in *Harpochytrium* where the rumposome honeycomb acts as a backing membrane for lipid droplets and side body granules.

Water expulsion vacuoles. To date, water expulsion or contractile vacuoles have only been reported in the biflagellate zoospores. In *Phytophthora* (Ho *et al.,* 1968; Reichle, 1969), *Pythium* (Grove, 1970 a, b; Morré *et al.,* 1971) and *Aphanomyces* (Hoch and Mitchell, 1972 b) the large water expulsion vacuole is surrounded by a 'zone of exclusion' (Morré *et al.,* 1971) which is populated by vesicles whose membranes have a characteristic fuzzy appearance (Fig. 23.18). A comparable membrane is found in places on the vacuole membrane and on Golgi vesicles associated with the Golgi bodies which tend to cluster around the water expulsion vacuole. This similarity of membrane morphology has led to the suggestion of Golgi derived contributions to the water expulsion vacuole (Grove, 1970), but the functional significance of this is unclear. It is assumed that the water expulsion vacuole is involved in zoospore osmoregulation as in many other cell types.

In all the studies of uniflagellate zoospores not only are there no reports of water expulsion vacuoles but there is rarely any indication of sufficient space in the spore to contain such a structure. These observations suggest that the uniflagellate series have evolved an alternative osmoregulatory system of, as yet, unknown nature.

Gamma Particles. Gamma particles have only been reported clearly in *Blastocladiella emersonii* (Cantino *et al.,* 1963; Reichle and Fuller, 1967; Cantino and Mack, 1969). They are small vesicles which enclose a cup shaped osmiophilic 0.5 μm diameter body surrounded by a nonstaining matrix. They may be formed during zoosporogenesis (Lessie and Lovett, 1968) and also from evaginations of the nuclear envelope during the motile life of the spore (Cantino and Mack, 1969). Based on a variety of morphological, histochemical and biochemical analysis observations it has been suggested that gamma bodies may be involved in cyst wall formation (Truesdell and Cantino, 1970) and cell membrane production (Truesdell and Cantino, 1969). They also apparently contain their own unique single stranded DNA and some RNA (Myers and Cantino, 1971). These observations attribute considerable complexity to such a morphologically simple organelle, and one wonders how closely related species perform these proposed functions in the absence of gamma bodies. Since all clearly identifiable gamma bodies have only been seen in one isolate of *B.emersonii,* it is conceivable that they are a type of infective agent, for example Kazama and Schornstein (1972) have shown a herpes type virus which is only detectable during zoosporogenesis in *Thraustochytrium* (see Figs. 11.29-11.32).

In addition to the structures discussed above there are a wide range of structures which occur specifically during the zoospore part of the life cycle in many different species. Each morphologically distinct unit has usually only been reported in one or two species with no indication of function or phylogenetic significance. A catalogue of such structures seems superfluous, hence the reader is referred to the various publications cited above for details.

23.3.3 *Zoospore Encystment and Germination*

The termination of the motile life of a zoospore and its subsequent germination into a new vegetative thallus is typically experimentally induced by replacing the nutrient poor sporulation medium with a rich medium. The transition which occurs can be divided into four basic processes: (1) flagellum loss, (2) cyst wall synthesis, (3) reversion of organelles to their vegetative structures and functions, and (4) production of a germ tube or thallus which is essentially the same as the mature vegetative structure.

Flagellum Loss.   In most genera the flagella axonemes are withdrawn into the spore body prior to encystment. This is clearly shown by the presence of naked axonemes in the cytoplasm of such species as *Rhizidiomyces* (Fuller and Reichle, 1965), *Blastocladiella* (Fuller, 1966; Reichle and Fuller, 1967; Soll and Sonneborn, 1971; Cantino et al., 1968), *Harpochytrium* (Travland and Whisler, 1971), *Allomyces* (Hill, 1969), *Monoblepharella* (Fuller and Reichle, 1968), *Olpidium* (Temmink and Campbell, 1969 b) and in the primary spores of *Saprolegnia* (Fig. 23.24, Heath and Greenwood, 1971). The mechanism of flagellum withdrawal is probably variable. Koch (1961) suggested a wrap-around mechanism whereby the intact flagellum wraps around the spore body and subsequent membrane fusion transfers the axoneme into the cytoplasm. Cantino et al. (1963) noted that nuclear rotation accompanied flagellum withdrawal in *Blastocladiella* and suggested a possible reeling-in mechanism with force generation by the rotating nucleus to which the axoneme was attached. Subsequently Cantino et al. (1968) suggested that membrane contraction produced the force and that nuclear rotation was passive. In the biflagellate *Saprolegnia*, Holloway and Heath (1974) have noted independent flagellum retraction, one of the pair shortening before the other, an observation which is difficult to explain other than by a depolymerization of axonemal microtubules.

Once withdrawn, the axoneme usually breaks down very rapidly to the level of the terminal plate of the kinetosome (e.g. Heath and Greenwood, 1971).   Such breakdown in *Blastocladiella* is apparently dependent on new protein synthesis (Soll and Sonneborn, 1971) and in *Allomyces* the sub-units of the microtubules are apparently utilized in subsequent mitoses of the germinating spore (Olson, 1972).

The time of reversion of the kinetosomes to centrioles is variable. In *Saprolegnia* kinetosomes are still present at least at the second mitosis of the germinating zoospore (Heath and Greenwood, 1971), whereas in *Aphanomyces* they have reverted 30 minutes after encystment, before cyst germination and mitosis (Hoch and Mitchell, 1972 b).

Flagellum withdrawal not only necessitates the degradation of the axoneme but also the dispersion of considerable quantities of membrane. Grove (oral presentation at AIBS—CBA   Meeting, Edmonton, 1971) has suggested that there are localized sites on the *Pythium* spore membrane from which membrane is withdrawn during encystment, but there is no evidence to differentiate between this and the concept of random removal of 'sub-units' throughout the membrane (see also Section 23.2.1).

The organisms which bear Flimmer flagella and withdraw their axonemes upon encystment typically leave the Flimmer hairs on the exterior of the cyst attached to the cyst wall (Meier and Webster, 1954; Fuller and Reichle, 1965; Heath and Greenwood, 1971).

In contrast to the above withdrawal system, the norm in the biflagellate secondary type zoospores is to shed the flagella, even when subsequent emergence of another flagellate spore is possible, e.g. *Phytophthora* (Hemmes and Hohl, 1971). Such a loss is very rapid, taking less than 30 seconds in *Aphanomyces* (Hoch and Mitchell, 1972 b), and usually involves the coiling of the axoneme inside the distorted membranous flagellum sheath (Colhoun, 1966; Ho *et al.,* 1967) with ultimate shedding of the ball-like, membrane bound, package. Since axonemal proteins can be re-utilized for subsequent mitoses (Olson, 1972) and since the primary type of zoospore has the ability to withdraw its flagella, it is difficult to understand why such a seemingly profligate system has evolved. Clearly, much more needs to be known about the cellular economics of these motile spores.

Cyst Wall Formation.   To date there is little information on cyst wall production in the uniflagellate fungi. Apparently a wall is laid down rapidly in *Blastocladiella* (Reichle and Fuller, 1967) but details of the process are unreported. In contrast there are a number of detailed studies available in the Oömycetes where there is typically a two step process, the rapid release of apparently prepolymerized material from vesicles in the zoospore followed by a gradual deposition of a chemically different inner wall layer which is comparable to the hyphal wall system. Thus in *Phytophthora palmivora* (originally erroneously named *P. parasitica,* see Tokunaga and Bartnicki-Garcia, 1971 a; Hemmes and Hohl, 1971) and *Pythium* (Grove, 1970 b) there is a loosely arranged, apparently amorphous, outer layer which is deposited by release of the contents of vesicles derived from the Golgi bodies during zoosporogenesis. This outer wall layer appears to be easily lost since no trace of it was detected in whole mounts of ultra-sonicated cysts of *P. palmivora* (Tokunaga and Bartnicki-Garcia, 1971 b). In *P. palmivora* the outer layer apparently functions as a 'stabilizing layer' since the cysts become less prone to fixation damage once it is formed (Hemmes and Hohl, 1971) but its precise role is far from clear.

In species of *Saprolegnia* and *Dictyuchus* a more compact, thinner osmiophilic outer cyst wall layer is laid down (Fig. 23.26). Attached to this layer of material are various spines (Figs. 23.25 and 23.26) whose structure varies with both spore type (primary *vs.* secondary) and species (Heath and Greenwood, 1970 a; Manton *et al.,* 1952; Meier and Webster, 1954). Both the osmiophilic wall layer and the spines are formed from an unknown source during spore cleavage and are packaged into vesicles termed bars (Fig. 23.27 and Gay and Greenwood, 1966) from which they are released by reverse pinocytosis at the time of encystment. In the primary spores of *Saprolegnia* and the secondary spores of *Dictyuchus* the osmiophilic outer layer is continuous, but on the secondary spore cysts of *Saprolegnia* it only forms plaques around each boat-hook shaped spine (Heath and Greenwood, 1970 a). This observation suggests that, although the deposition of the primary outer layer coincides with increased 'stability' of the cytoplasm as in *Phytophthora,* the function of the outer material may be dispensable to the encystment process itself and may rather act as a 'glue' for the attachment of the spines (Heath and Greenwood, 1970 a). The spines themselves

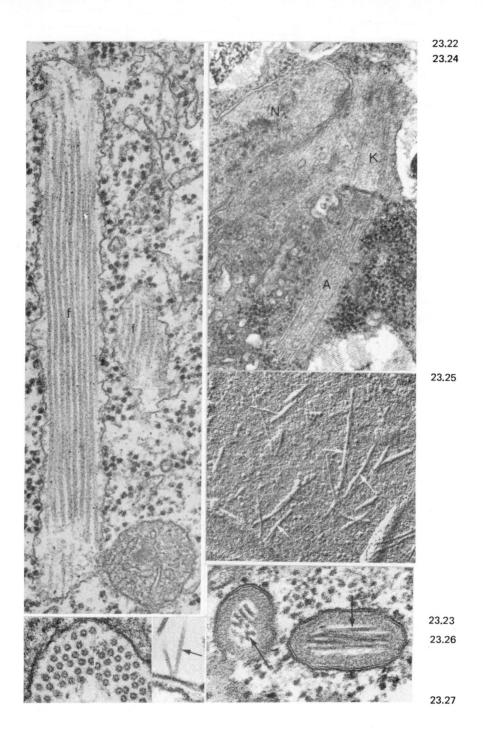

probably function as an obvious aid to cyst dispersal as originally suggested by Manton, *et al.,* (1952).

As in *Saprolegnia,* so *Aphanomyces* also produces a thin osmiophilic but spineless outer cyst wall layer, apparently also from characteristic bar-like vesicles, but in this organism this cyst layer shows a membrane-like tripartite structure which has led to the suggestion that the cyst wall is laid down underneath the cell membrane (Hoch and Mitchell, 1972 b). If such is proven, this will be a unique wall deposition system.

Subsequent to the formation of the initial cyst wall layer, a thick inner wall is gradually deposited. In *Phytophthora* and *Saprolegnia* this inner layer shows a pure fibrillar structure (Tokunaga and Bartnicki-Garcia, 1971 b; Heath and Greenwood, 1970 a) but probably does contain amorphous components since it is laid down with a contribution from Golgi derived vesicles (Hemmes and Hohl, 1971; Grove, 1970 b; Heath and Greenwood, 1970 a). In staining characteristics this inner wall is indistinguishable from that of the germ tube which develops as a simple extension of the inner cyst wall (see below).

Organelle Reversions.   One of the first 'organelles' to disappear after encystment is the flagellar root system. For example, within minutes the microtubular roots of *Blastocladiella* are lost, although the striated rootlets disappear later (Reichle and Fuller, 1967), and in *Aphanomyces* the pyriform nucleus reverts to a spherical shape within 30 minutes after initial encystment, presumably due to the loss of the microtubular roots (Hoch and Mitchell, 1972 b). If it is assumed that the root system of the zoospore is responsible for its morphology, then degradation of the roots must begin at the instant of encystment, when the spore rounds up, although final loss of the roots must occur later because the 'backbone' root of *Aphanomyces* can still be detected in the new cyst (Hoch and Mitchell, 1972 b). Loss of microtubular roots coincident with encystment probably explains Held's (1972 b) observations of induction of encystment by agents known to cause microtubule depolymerization. At present there are no critical studies using serial sections of synchronously encysting zoospores such as are needed to define in detail processes such as root degeneration.

As with root degeneration, so the time course of other organelle reversions is uncertain. In general terms, all organelles which underwent changes during zoosporogenesis revert to their vegetative configuration prior to germination of a cyst. Thus Golgi bodies tend to lose their exclusive paranuclear or paravacuolar arrangement and resume their vegetative positions, as for example in *Aphanomyces* (Hoch and Mitchell, 1972 b), *Phytophthora* (Hemmes and Hohl, 1971) and *Saprolegnia* (Heath and Greenwood, 1971). In *Harpochytrium,* Golgi bodies reappear (Travland and Whisler, 1971)

Fig. 23.22. Longitudinally sectioned Flimmer hairs (f) lying in a cisternum of ribosome studded endoplasmic reticulum in *Saprolegnia ferax* (X 73 700) Glut/Os/Pb/UAc. **Fig. 23.23.** Transversely sectioned Flimmer hairs (f) of *S. ferax* (X 120 600) Glut/Os/Pb/UAc. **(Figs. 23.22-23.23** from Heath *et al.,* 1970 with permission of the Company of Biologists Ltd). **Fig. 23.24.** Recently encysted primary zoospore of *S. ferax* showing the withdrawn flagellum axoneme (A) lying naked in the cytoplasm with the kinetosome (K) still associated with the nucleus (N) (X 30 700) Glut/Os/Pb/UAc (from Heath and Greenwood, 1971 with permission of Springer-Verlag). Fig. **23.25.** Whole mount of a primary cyst of *S. ferax* showing the amorphous outer wall and attached spines (e.g. arrows) (X 47 400) Material untreated except for drying and coating with evaporated gold-palladium alloy. **Fig. 23.26.** Section of a primary cyst of *S. ferax* showing osmiophilic outer wall layer and attached spines (arrow) (X 83 500) Glut/Os/Pb/UAc. **Fig. 23.27.** Transversely and longitudinally sectioned bars in the cytoplasm of a primary zoospore of *S. ferax* showing spines (arrows) surrounded by amorphous material which is presumed to become the osmiophilic outer cyst wall layer to which the spines are attached (X 91 600) Glut/Os/Pb/UAc. **Figs. 23.25-23.27** from Heath and Greenwood, 1970 a with permission of Springer-Verlag).

and in many species the nuclear cap disintegrates to produce dispersed ribosomes (e.g. Fuller and Reichle, 1965; Travland and Whisler, 1971) which, at least in *Blastocladiella,* become active in protein synthesis again (Lovett, 1968). Similarly, such specialized structures as rumposomes and side bodies fragment and the single large mitochondrion, when present, splits into smaller units typical of vegetative cells (e.g. Reichle and Fuller, 1967; Travland and Whisler, 1971). Such organelle changes seem to be excellent examples of correlated structural and functional changes which should provide interesting models if only the functional changes were understood fully.

Cyst Germination.   There are three interrelated processes essential to cyst germination; breaching the cyst wall, production of germ tube wall and production of turgour pressure to drive the germ tube forward. Morphologically, germ tube production involves the localized accumulation of wall vesicles (see Section 23.2.1) adjacent to the cyst wall and the subsequent localized extension of the inner cyst wall layer which ruptures the outer wall layer (Grove, 1970 a, b; Hemmes and Hohl, 1971; Hoch and Mitchell, 1972 b; Heath, 1969). In this case it is presumed that the wall vesicles contain cell wall precursors as in a normal hyphal apex, but the concomitant plasticizing of the cyst wall strongly suggests the presence of a possible wall, softening enzyme as found in the yeasts (Cortat *et al.,* 1972). In sectioned material the germ tube wall is indistinguishable from the inner cyst wall, but Tokunaga and Bartnicki-Garcia (1971 b) have shown the presence of an additional outer wall layer on the germ tube of *Phytophthora.* Thus wall synthesis is undoubtedly more complex than sectioned material suggests, but there is apparently no difference between a germ tube and an older hyphal apex.

Generation of the hyphal vacuole with presumed accompanying increase of turgor pressure of the cell seems to be the function of the dense bodies which have remained in the zoospores throughout their prior development. In *Pythium* (Colt and Endo, 1972; Grove, 1970 a, b), *Saprolegnia* (Gay *et al.,* 1971) and *Aphanomyces* (Hoch and Mitchell, 1972 b) the dense body vesicles enlarge and coalesce with concomitant shrinkage of the osmiophilic granules so that they form the vacuole of the germling. Such a function is, of course, comparable with their role in cytoplasmic cleavage discussed in Sections 23.3.1 and 23.4.3.

Considering the numerous studies of uniflagellate zoospore structure there are surprisingly few detailed studies of cyst germination in these groups. Germination of *Harpochytrium* (Travland and Whisler, 1971) seems to be comparable to the process found in the biflagellate group described above including the presence of dense body-like vesicles which generate vacuoles, but other organisms have received insufficient analysis for meaningful descriptions.

23.4   Sexual Reproduction

There is currently very little ultrastructural information available on any of the stages of sexual reproduction in the aquatic fungi. In part, this appears to be due to technical preparation difficulties, the sexual phases of the life cycle function as propagules which are adapted to survive adverse conditions and thus resist the penetration of obnoxious compounds such as fixatives and resins very successfully. However, in a few species we have information on at least the early stages of the sexual reproductive cycle as discussed below.

23.4.1 Meiosis

We only have ultrastructural observations on meiosis in the Oömycetes *Saprolegnia terrestris* (Howard and Moore, 1970) and *Thraustotheca clavata* (Heath, unpublished). In these Oömycetes, it now seems certain that meiosis is gametic, occurring during antheridium development prior to the entry of the fertilization tube into the oögonium, and in the oöspheres after cytoplasmic cleavage (Bryant and Howard, 1969; Howard and Moore, 1970; Heath, 1974 b). In the prophase I nuclei there are a number of osmiophilic structures (Fig. 23.30) which appear to be the equivalent of axial elements (Moses, 1968). In the absence of serial sections, Howard and Moore (1970) were unable to determine the detailed arrangment of these elements, but in *Thraustotheca* the similar axial element of each chromosome seems to be attached at each end to the nuclear envelope (Fig. 23.30) as in *Locusta* (Moens, 1969). Subsequent pairing of axial elements seems to occur (Howard and Moore, 1970) but typical well defined synaptinemal complexes characteristic of many other organisms are not detected.

In *Saprolegnia* (Howard and Moore, 1970) metaphase I and anaphase I are essentially comparable to mitosis in this genus (see Section 23.2.3), although the spindle appears to contain more microtubules, and the microtubule-nuclear envelope association has not been reported. Another point of difference is that the members of each centriole pair are more widely spaced from each other and are each enclosed in a cap of endoplasmic reticulum, the significance of which is unknown. The really unusual feature of this meiosis is that the spindles for meiosis II develop in the original nucleus at right angles to the former axis of the meiosis I spindle; thus there are two spindles within one nuclear envelope at metaphase II. Also each spindle only has a single centriole at each pole. After meiosis II is accomplished, still inside the original nuclear envelope, a curious clover leaf configuration is observed in which all four centrioles come close together at the centre of a four lobed nucleus. Presumably meiosis is completed by membrane fusions which yield four haploid nuclei each with only one accompanying centriole.

This author's study of *Thraustotheca* is less complete than that of Howard and Bryant (1970), but so far the data are consistent with the description given above. Whilst many more details in more species need to be elucidated, such a rare meiotic system must surely have phylogenetic, if not functional significance. The only other organisms with a comparable meiotic system are some yeasts such as *Saccharomyces* (Moens and Rapport, 1971).

23.4.2 Gametangium Fusion

The Oömycetes are characterized by a sexual system of gametangium fusion and subsequent nuclear fusion. As with meiosis, so we have little ultrastructural information on this process, but in *Saprolegnia* and *Phytophthora* the development of the gametangia appears to be essentially similar to zoosporangium development. Enlargement of the specialized hyphal branches into gametangia involves considerable cell wall synthesis which is accomplished in the presence of wall vesicles (see Section 23.2.1) (Heath *et al.*, 1971; Vujičić, 1971). Cytoplasm flows into these developing gametangia which are then delimited from the rest of the hyphae by cross walls comparable to those isolating the zoosporangia (Heath *et al.*, 1971; Vujičić, 1971). In the oögonia of *Saprolegnia* cytoplasmic cleavage involves dense body fusion with the central vacuole (Fig. 23.31) and subsequent fusion of the vacuole and cell membranes (Gay *et al.*, 1971). This process produces naked oöspheres within the oögonium. These oöspheres then rapidly synthesize a thick cell wall, again, at least in *Thrausto-*

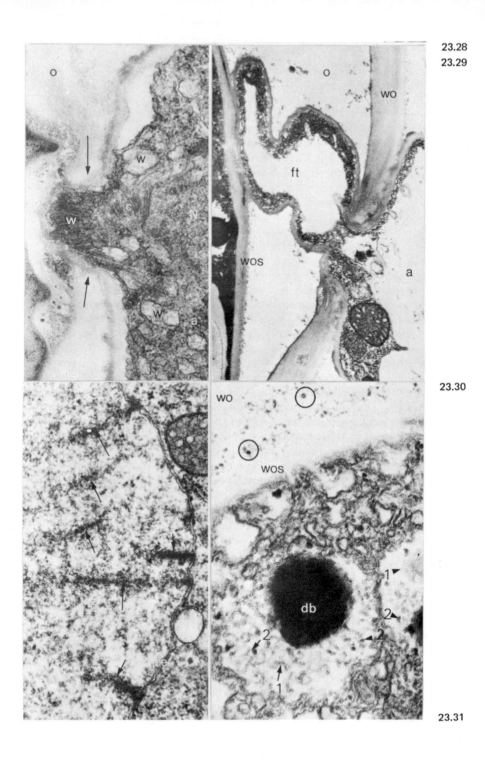

theca utilizating wall vesicles (Heath, unpublished). The antheridia at this stage produce fertilization tubes which apparently enzymatically penetrate the oögonium wall (Figs. 23.28 and 23.29), grow by tip growth into the oösphere (Fig. 23.29) and presumably penetrate the oösphere wall to enable nuclear migration to occur. In *Thraustotheca* (Heath, unpublished) oögonium wall penetration and fertilization tube growth involves apical accumulations of wall vesicles (Fig. 23.28), clearly the penetration state is another instance where wall vesicles may contain wall lytic enzymes. During oösphere development, lipid droplets become increasingly abundant and the remaining dense bodies apparently coalesce into larger units which are then termed the oöplast (Howard and Moore, 1970). The final arrangement of these presumed storage products is a useful taxonomic character (Howard and Moore, 1970) but its functional significance is unclear.

Vujičič (1971) reports that in *Phytophthora parasitica,* the above sequence of antheridia and oögonia development is rather different, claiming that the oögonium actually grows up through the preformed antheridium. Such a process is not documented in her paper and would appear to be an unnecessary complication to the more normal process whereby the antheridium grows to engulf the oögonium.

23.4.3 Gamete Fusion

Sexual reproduction by fusion of haploid motile gametes is the norm in many aquatic fungi, yet this system has only been studied at the ultrastructural level in *Allomyces.* In this genus, male and female uniflagellate gametes are produced in separate gametangia, with the females being considerably larger than the males (Fig. 23.33). In a brief study of the developing gametes, Turian and Oulevey (1971) indicated that gamete development is comparable to zoospore development in the chytrids (see Section 23.3.1). The only difference which they noted between male and female gametangia was more numerous mitochondria with more highly developed internal structure in the females as compared with the males. However in mature gametes Fuller (unpublished) has noted that, whilst the basic morphology of both gamete types is similar to that of the zoospores, the female gamete has a larger nucleus and nuclear cap and more mitochondria and lipid droplets when compared with the male. Clearly, more work is needed to explain the differential mechanisms of gamete production.

Gamete fusion first occurs by lateral contact of the gametes and subsequent fusion of the cell membranes to produce a biflagellate, binucleate motile unit (Fig. 23.33). Whilst retaining the flagella, fusion of the nuclear cap membrane and nuclear envelope (Fig. 23.33) occurs to yield a biflagellate uninucleate zygote. Bearing in mind the

---

Fig. 23.28. Portion of an antheridium (a) of *Thraustotheca clavata* showing penetration of the oögonium (o) wall. Serial sections verified that this is an early stage in penetration. The penetration 'peg' contains numerous wall vesicles (w) and a nucleus (N) with a single centriole (c) is close by as is typical for this stage. Penetration of the oögonial wall appears to be enzymatic as judged by the neatness of the hole (arrows) (X 33 800) Glut/Os/Pb/UAc. **Fig. 23.29.** A later stage in the fertilization process of *T. clavata* showing the penetrated oögonium wall (wo) and the fertilization tube (ft) appressed to the oösphere wall (was) (X 21 200) Glut/Os/Pb/UAc. **Fig. 23.30.** A prophase 1 meiotic nucleus in an antheridium of *T. clavata* showing axial cores (arrows), four of which are joined to the nuclear envelope (ne) (X 41 000) Glut/Os/Pb/UAc. **Fig. 23.31.** A recently cleaved oösphere of *Saprolegnia furcata* showing a dense body (db) containing myelin like configurations (arrows 1) and small granules (arrows 2). The granules are comparable with those (circled) lying between the oögonium wall (wo) and the oösphere wall (wos). Such locations would be consistent with the hypothesis of dense body participation in oösphere cleavage (X 58 000) Os/Pb/UAc (from Gay *et al.,* 1971 in the *Journal of General Microbiology).*

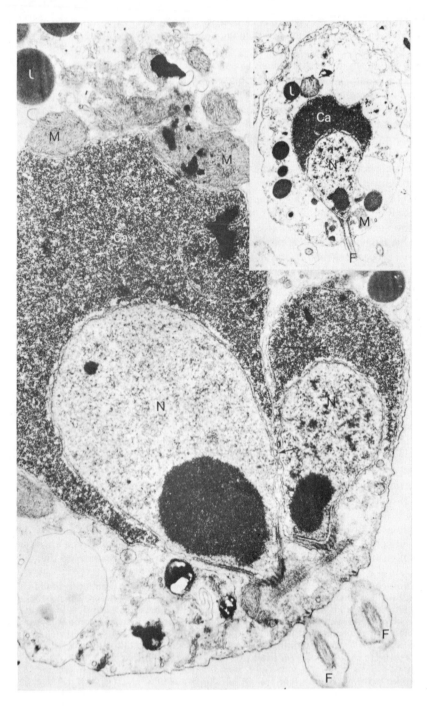

microtubular root systems of the gametes (see Section 23.3.1), clearly, considerable microtubule rearrangements must occur in addition to the membrane fusions. Subsequent events in the production of the non-motile zygote await elucidation.

In many respects our knowledge of fungal ultrastructure has raised more questions than it has answered, and clearly it is too fragmentary to allow broad generalizations to be made. However, it has shown a number of directions for future structural and biochemical inquiry and has also introduced a number of features which may prove to have phylogenetic and thus taxonomic value. Hopefully this brief review will help introduce some of the possibilities of ultrastructural investigations to the uninitiated and stimulate them to use this approach in their own investigations. If the review also stimulates other workers already in the field to disprove some of the generalizations and comments contained herein, it will have served an additional useful function.

Acknowledgements

The preparation of this review and some of the unpublished work described was supported by grants from the Brown-Hazen Grants Programme and the National Research Council of Canada, the receipt of which are gratefully acknowledged. I am also pleased to acknowledge the excellent secretarial assistance of Mrs. Dorothy Gunning.

References

ALEXOPOULOS, C. J. (1962). *Introductory Mycology* (2nd Edition) Wiley, New York and London.

BAKERSPIGEL, A. (1960). 'Nuclear structure and divisions in the vegetative mycelium of the Saprolegniaceae.' *Am. J. Bot.,* 47, 94-100.

BERLIN, J. D., and BOWEN, C. C. (1964). 'Centrioles in the fungus *Albugo candida.'* *Am. J. Bot.,* 51, 650-652.

BLONDEL, B., and TURIAN, G. (1960). 'Relation between basophilia and fine structure of cytoplasm in the fungus *Allomyces macrogynus* Em.' *J. biophys. biochem. Cytol.,* 7, 127-134.

BONNETT, H. T., and NEWCOMB, E. H. (1966). 'Coated vesicles and other cytoplasmic components of growing root hairs of radish.' *Protoplasma,* 62, 59-75.

BRACKER, C. E. (1967). 'Ultrastructure of fungi.' *A. Rev. Phytopathology,* 5, 343-374.

BRACKER, C. E., HEINTZ, C. E., and GROVE, S. N. (1970). 'Structural and

Fig. 23.32. A male gamete of *Allomyces macrogynus* showing posterior flagellum (F), nucleus (N) nuclear cap (Ca), mitochondria (M) and lipid droplets (I). A zoospore of this genus would look very similar (X 13 300) Glut/Os/Pb/UAc. **Fig. 23.33.** Male and female (larger) gametes of *A. macrogynus* after fusion, showing an early stage of nuclear fusion (arrow). The fusion process is variable, on other occasions the nuclear caps fuse before nuclear envelope fusion. Note two flagella (F) and root complex around the apices of each nucleus (X 23 900) Glut/Os/Pb/UAc.

Figs. 23.32-23.33 unpublished micrographs kindly supplied by Dr. M. S. Fuller, University of Georgia, Athens, USA.

functional continuity among endomembrane organelles in fungi.' In *Proc 7th International Congress of Electron Microscopy, Grenoble,* 103-104. Soc. Francaise de Microscopie Electronique, Paris.

BRACKER, C. E., and GROVE, S. N. (1971 a). 'Continuity between cytoplasmic endomembranes and outer mitochondrial membranes in fungi.' *Protoplasma,* 73, 15-34.

BRACKER, C. E., and GROVE, S. N. (1971 b). 'Surface structure on outer mitochondrial membranes of *Pythium ultimum.' Cytobiologie,* 3, 229-239.

BRACKER, C. E., GROVE, S. N., HEINTZ, C. E., and MORRÉ, D. J. (1971). 'Continuity between endomembrane components in hyphae of *Pythium* spp.' *Cytobiologie,* 4, 1-8.

BROWN, R. M., FRANKE, W. W., KLEINIG, H., FALK, H., and SITTE, P. (1970). 'Scale formation in chrysophycean algae. I. Cellulosic and non cellulosic wall components made by the Golgi apparatus.' *J. Cell Biol.,* 45, 246-271

BRYANT, T. R., and HOWARD, K. L. (1969). 'Meiosis in the oomycetes. I. A microspectrophotometric analysis of nuclear deoxyribonucleic acid in *Saprolegnia terrestris.' Am. J. Bot.,* 56, 1075-1083.

CANTINO, E. C., LOVETT, J. S., LEAK, L. V., and LYTHGOE, J. (1963). 'The single mitochondrion, fine structure, and germination of the spore of *Blastocladiella emersonii.' J. gen. Microbiol.,* 31, 393-404.

CANTINO, E. C., and MACK, J. P. (1969). 'Form and function in the zoospore of *Blastocladiella emersonii* I. The γ particle and satellite ribosome package.' *Nova Hedwigia,* 18, 115-148.

CANTINO, E. C., and TRUESDELL, L. C. (1970). 'Organization and fine structure of the side body and its lipid sac in the zoospore of *Blastocladiella emersonii.' Mycologia,* 62, 548-567.

CANTINO, E. C., and TRUESDELL, L. C. (1971). 'Cytoplasmic γ-like particles and other ultrastructural aspects of zoospores of *Blastocladiella britannica.' Trans. Br. mycol. Soc.,* 56, 169-179.

CANTINO, E. C., TRUESDELL, L. C., and SHAW, D. S. (1968). 'Life history of the motile spore of *Blastocladiella emersonii:* a study in cell differentiation.' *J. Elisha Mitchell scient. Soc.,* 84, 125-146.

CHAMBERS, T. C., MARKUS, K., and WILLOUGHBY, L. G. (1967). 'The fine structure of the mature zoosporangium of *Nowakowskiella profusa.' J. gen. Microbiol.,* 46, 135-141.

CHAPMAN, J. A., and VUJIČIČ, R. (1965). 'The fine structure of sporangia of *Phytophthora erythroseptica.' J. gen. Microbiol.,* 41, 275-282.

COLHOUN, J. (1966). 'The biflagellate zoospore in aquatic phycomycetes with particular reference to *Phytophthora* spp.' In *The Fungus Spore, Proc. Symp. Colston Res. Soc.* (Ed. M. F. Madelin), Butterworths, London, 18, 85-92.

COLT, W. M., and ENDO, R. M. (1972). 'Ultrastructural changes in *Pythium aphanidermatum* zoospores and cysts during encystment, germination and penetration of primary lettuce roots.' *Phytopathology,* 62, 751 (Abstr.).

CORTAT, M., MATILE, P., and WIEMKEN, A. (1972). 'Isolation of glucanase-containing vesicles from budding yeast.' *Arch. Mikrobiol.,* 82, 189-205.

COUCH, J. N. (1941). 'The structure and action of the cilia in some aquatic phycomycetes.' *Am. J. Bot.,* 28, 704-713.

ELSNER, P. R., VANDERMOLEN, G. E., HORTON, J. C., and BOWEN, C. C. (1970). 'Fine structure of *Phytophthora infestans* during sporangial differentiation and germination,' *Phytophathology,* 60, 1765-1772.

FREDERICK, S. W., NEWCOMB, E. H., VIGIL, E. L., and WERGIN, W. P. (1968). 'Fine-structural characterization of plant microbodies.' *Planta,* 81, 229-252,

FULLER, M. S. (1966). 'Structure of the uniflagellate zoospores of aquatic phycomycetes.' In *The Fungus Spore, Proc. Symp. Colston Res. Soc.* (Ed. M. F. Madelin), Butterworths, London, 18, 67-84.

FULLER, M. S. and CALHOUN, S. A. (1968). 'Microtubule-kinetosome relationships in the motile cells of the Blastocladiales.' *Z. Zellforsch mikrosk. Anat.,* 87, 526-533.

FULLER, M. S., and OLSON, L. W. (1971). 'The zoospore of *Allomyces.' J. gen. Microbiol.,* 66, 171-183.

FULLER, M. S., and REICHLE, R. E. (1965). 'The zoospores and early development of *Rhizidiomyces apophysatus.' Mycologia,* 57, 946-961.

FULLER, M. S., and REICHLE, R. E. (1968). 'The fine structure of *Monoblepharella* sp. zoospores.' *Can. J. Bot.,* 46, 279-283.

GAY, J. L., and GREENWOOD, A. D. (1966). 'Structural aspects of zoospore production in *Saprolegnia ferax* with particular reference to the cell and vacuolar membranes.' In *The Fungus Spore, Proc. Symp. Colston Res. Soc.* (Ed. M. F. Madelin), Butterworths, London, 18, 95-108.

GAY, J. L., GREENWOOD, A. D., and HEATH, I. B. (1971). 'The formation and behaviour of vacuoles (vesicles) during oosphere development and zoospore germination in *Saprolegnia.' J. gen. Microbiol.,* 65, 233-241.

GIRBARDT, M. (1969). 'Die Ultrastruktur der Apikalregion von Pilzhyphen.' *Protoplasma,* 67, 413-441.

GOODAY, G. W. (1971). 'An autoradiographic study of hyphal growth of some fungi.' *J. gen. Microbiol.,* 67, 125-133.

GREENWOOD, A. D. (1959). 'Observations on the structure of the zoospores of *Vaucheria,* II.' *J. exp. Bot.,* 10, 55-68.

GROVE, S. N. (1970a). 'Protoplasmic correlates of hyphal tip initiation and development in fungi.' Ph. D. Thesis, Purdue University.

GROVE, S. N. (1970 b). 'Fine structure of zoospore encystment and germination in *Pythium aphanidermatum.' Am. J. Bot.,* 57, 745a.

GROVE, S. N., and BRACKER, C. E. (1970). 'Protoplasmic organization of hyphal tips among fungi: vesicles and Spitzenkörper'. *J. Bact.,* 104, 989-1009.

GROVE, S. N., BRACKER, C. E., and MORRÉ, D. J. (1968). 'Cytomembrane differentiation in the endoplasmic reticulum—Golgi apparatus—vesicle complex.' *Science, NY.,* 161, 171-173.

GROVE, S. N., BRACKER, C. E., and MORRÉ, D. J. (1970). 'An ultrastructural basis for hyphal tip growth in *Pythium ultimum.' Am. J. Bot.,* 57, 245-266.

GROVE, S. N. MORRÉ, D. J., and BRACKER, C. E. (1967). 'Dictyosomes in vegetative hyphae of *Pythium ultimum.' Proc. Indiana Acad. Sci.,* 76, 210-214.

HEATH, I. B. (1969). 'Structural aspects of the growth and reproduction of *Saprolegnia* spp.' Ph.D. Thesis, Imperial College, University of London.

HEATH, I. B. (1970). 'Hyphal growth in *Saprolegnia.' Am. J. Bot.,* 57, 745a.

HEATH, I. B., GAY, J. L., and GREENWOOD, A. D. (1971). ' Cell wall formation in the Saprolegniales: cytoplasmic vesicles underlying developing walls.' *J. gen. Microbiol.,* 65, 225-232.

HEATH, I. B., and GREENWOOD, A. D. (1968). 'Electron microscopic observations of dividing somatic nuclei in *Saprolegnia.' J. gen. Microbiol.,* 53, 287-289.

HEATH, I. B., and GREENWOOD, A. D. (1970 a). 'Wall formation in the Saprolegniales II. Formation of cysts by the zoospores of *Saprolegnia* and *Dictyuchus.'* *Arch. Mikrobiol.,* 75, 67-79.

HEATH, I. B., and GREENWOOD, A. D. (1970 b). 'The structure and formation of lomasomes.' *J. gen. Microbiol.*, 62, 129-137.

HEATH, I. B., and GREENWOOD, A. D. (1970 c). 'Centriole replication and nuclear divisions in *Saprolegnia.' J. gen. Microbiol.*, 62, 139-148.

HEATH, I. B. and GREENWOOD, A.D. (1971). 'Ultrastructural observations on the kinetosomes and Golgi bodies during the asexual life cycle of *Saprolegnia.' Z. Zellforsch. mikrosk. Anat.*, 112, 371-389.

HEATH, I. B., GREENWOOD, A. D., and GRIFFITHS, H. B. (1970). 'The origin of flimmer in *Saprolegnia, Dictyuchus, Synura* and *Cryptomonas.' J. Cell Sci.*, 7, 445-461.

HEATH, M. C., and HEATH, I. B. (1971). 'Ultrastructure of an immune and a susceptible reaction of cowpea leaves to rust infection.' *Physiol. Pl. Path.*, 1, 277-287.

HELD, A. A. (1972 a). 'Host-parasite relations between *Allomyces* and *Rozella.' Arch. Mikrobiol.*, 82, 128-139.

HELD, A. A. (1972 b). 'Fungal zoospores are induced to encyst by treatments known to degrade cytoplasmic microtubules.' *Arch. Mikrobiol.*, 85, 209-224.

HEMMES, D. E., and HOHL, H. R. (1969). 'Ultrastructural changes in directly germinating sporangia of *Phytophthora parasitica.' Am. J. Bot.*, 56, 300-313.

HEMMES, D. E., and HOHL, H. R. (1971). 'Ultrastructural aspects of encystation and cyst-germination in *Phytophthora parasitica.' J. Cell Sci.*, 9, 175-191.

HEMMES, D. E., and HOHL, H. R. (1972). 'Flagellum degeneration in the fungus *Phytophthora palmivora* (formerly *Phytophthora parasitica)'. J. gen. Microbiol.*, 73, 345.

HILL, E. P. (1969). 'The fine structure of the zoospores and cysts of *Allomyces macrogynus.' J. gen. Microbiol.*, 56, 125-130.

HO, H. H., HICKMAN, C. J., and TELFORD, R. W. (1968). 'The morphology of zoospores of *Phytophthora megasperma* var. *sojae* and other phycomycetes.' *Can. J. Bot.*, 46, 88-89.

HO, H. H., ZACHARIAH, K. and HICKMAN, C. J. (1967). 'Anatomy of beads on flagella of zoospores of *Phytophthora megasperma* var. *sojae.' Can. J. Bot.*, 45, 1765-1766.

HO, H. H., ZACHARIAH, K., and HICKMAN, C. J. (1968). 'The ultrastructure of zoospores of *Phytophthora megasperma* var. *sojae.' Can. J. Bot.*, 46, 37-41.

HOCH, H. C., and MITCHELL, J. E. (1972 a). 'The ultrastructure of *Aphanomyces euteiches* during asexual spore formation.' *Phytopathology*, 62, 149-160.

HOCH, H. C., and MITCHELL, J. E. (1972 b). 'The ultrastructure of zoospores of *Aphanomyces euteiches* and their encystment and subsequent germination.' *Protoplasma*, 75, 113-138.

HOHL, H. R., and HAMAMOTO, S. T. (1967). 'Ultrastructural changes during zoospore formation in *Phytophthora parasitica.' Am. J. Bot.*, 54, 1131-1139.

HOWARD, K. L., and MOORE, R. T. (1970). 'Ultrastructure of oogenesis in *Saprolegnia terrestris.' Bot. Gaz.*, 131, 311-336.

HUNSLEY, D., and BURNETT, J. H. (1968). 'Dimensions of microfibrillar elements in fungal walls.' *Nature*, 218, 462-463.

HUNSLEY, D., and BURNETT, J. H. (1970). 'The ultrastructural architecture of the walls of some hyphal fungi.' *J. gen. Microbiol.*, 62, 203-218.

ICHIDA, A. A., and FULLER, M. S. (1968). 'Ultrastructure of mitosis in the aquatic fungus *Catenaria anguillulae.' Mycologia*, 60, 141-155.

KATSURA, K. (1970). 'Swimming behaviour of *Phytophthora capsici* zoospores.'

In *Morphological and Related Biochemical Events in Host-Parasite Interaction,* East-West Center, Honolulu, Hawaii, The United States–Japan Cooperative Science Program, pp.20-29.

KATZ, D., and ROSENBERGER, R. F. (1970). 'A mutation in *Aspergillus nidulans* producing hyphal walls which lack chitin.' *Biochim. biophys. Acta.,* 208, 452-460.

KAZAMA, F. Y. (1972). 'Ultrastructure and phototaxis of the zoospores of *Phlyctochytrium* sp., an estuarine chytrid.' *J. gen. Microbiol.,* 71, 555-566.

KAZAMA, F. Y., and SCHORNSTEIN, K. L. (1972). 'Herpes-type virus particles associated with a fungus.' *Science,* 177, 696-697.

KING, J. E., and BUTLER, R. D. (1968). 'Structure and development of flagella of *Phytophthora infestans.' Trans. Br. mycol. Soc.,* 51, 689-697.

KOCH, W. J. (1956). Studies of the motile cells of chytrids. I. Electron microscope observations of the flagellum, blepharoplast, and rhizoplast.' *Am. J. Bot.,* 43, 811-819.

KOCH, W. J. (1961). 'The motile cell in posteriorly uniflagellate Phycomycetes.' In *Recent Advances in Botany,* Proceedings 9th International Botanical Congress, University of Toronto Press, Toronto, 335-339.

LAMPORT, D. T. A. (1965). 'The protein component of primary cell walls.' In *Advances in Botanical Research* (Ed. R. D. Preston), Academic Press, London & New York, 151-218.

LAMPORT, D. T. A. (1969). 'The isolation and partial characterization of hydroxy-proline-rich glycopeptides obtained by enzymic degradation of primary cell walls.' *Biochemistry,* 8, 1155-1163.

LESSIE, P. E., and LOVETT, J. S. (1968). 'Ultrastructural changes during sporangium formation and zoospore differentiation in *Blastocladiella emersonii.' Am. J. Bot.,* 55, 220-236.

LOVETT, J. S. (1968). 'Reactivation of ribonucleic acid and protein synthesis during germination of *Blastocladiella* zoospores and the role of the ribosomal nuclear cap.' *J. Bact.,* 96, 962-969.

MANTON, I., CLARK, B., and GREENWOOD, A. D. (1951). 'Observations with the electron microscope on a species of *Saprolegnia.' J. exp. Bot.,* 2, 321-331.

MANTON, I., CLARKE, B., GREENWOOD, A. D. and FLINT, E. A. (1952). 'Further observations on the structure of plant cilia by a combination of visual and electron microscopy.' *J. exp. Bot.,* 3, 204-215.

MANTON, I., and HARRIS, K. (1966). 'Observations on the microanatomy of the brown flagellate *Sphaleromantis tetragona* Skuja with special reference to the flagellar apparatus and scales.' *J. Linn. Soc. (Bot.),* 59, 397-403.

MARCHANT, R., and ROBARDS, A. W. (1968). 'Membrane systems associated with the plasmalemma of plant cells.' *Ann. Bot.,* 32, 457-471.

McCULLY, E. K., and ROBINOW, C. F. (1971). 'Mitosis in the fission yeast *Schizosaccharomyces pombe:* A comparative study with light and electron microscopy.' *J. Cell. Sci.,* 9, 475-507.

McLAUGHLIN, D. J. (1972). 'Golgi apparatus in the postmeiotic basidium of *Coprinus lagopus.' J. Bact.,* 110, 739-742.

McMURROUGH, I., FLORES-CARREON, A., and BARTNICKI-GARCIA, S. (1971). 'Pathway of chitin synthesis and cellular localization of chitin synthetase in *Mucor rouxii.' J. biol. Chem.,* 246, 3999-4007.

MEIER, H., and WEBSTER, J. (1954). 'An electron microscope study of cysts in the Saprolegniaceae.' *J. exp. Bot.,* 5, 401-409.

MOENS, P. B. (1969). 'The fine structure of meiotic chromosome polarization and pairing in *Locusta migratoria* spermatocytes.' *Chromosoma, 28,* 1-25.

MOENS, P. B., and RAPPORT, E. (1971). 'Spindles, spindle plaques, and meiosis in the yeast *Saccharomyces cerevisiae* (Hansen).' *J. Cell Biol., 50,* 344-361.

MOLLENHAUER, H. H. (1965). 'An intercisternal structure in the Golgi apparatus.' *J. Cell Biol., 24,* 504-511.

MORRÉ, D. J. MOLLENHAUER, H. H., and BRACKER, C. E. (1971). 'Origin and continuity of Golgi apparatus.' In *Results and Problems in Cell Differentiation. II. Origin and Continuity of Cell Organelles* (Eds. T. Reinert and H. Ursprung), Springer-Verlag, Berlin, 82-126.

MOSER, J. W., and KREITNER, G. L. (1970). 'Centrosome structure in *Anthoceros laevis* and *Marchantia polymorpha.' J. Cell Biol., 44,* 454-458.

MOSES, M. J. (1968). 'Synaptinemal complex.' *A. Rev. Genetics, 2,* 363-412.

MURPHY, M. N., and LOVETT, J. S. (1966). 'RNA and protein synthesis during zoospore differentiation in synchronized cultures of *Blastocladiella.' Devl. Biol., 14,* 68-95.

MYERS, R. B., and CANTINO, E. C. (1971). 'DNA profile of the spore of *Blastocladiella emersonii:* evidence for γ particle DNA.' *Arch. Mikrobiol., 78,* 252-267.

NORTHCOTE, D. H. (1969). 'Fine structure of cytoplasm in relation to synthesis and secretion in plant cells.' *Proc. Roy. Soc. B., 173,* 21-30.

OLSON, L. W. (1972). 'Colchicine and the mitotic spindle of the aquatic phycomycete *Allomyces.' Arch. Mikrobiol., 84,* 327-338.

OLSON, L. W., and FULLER, M. S. (1968). 'Ultrastructural evidence for the biflagellate origin of the uniflagellate fungal zoospore.' *Arch. Mikrobiol., 62,* 237-250.

PERKINS, F. O. (1970). 'Formation of centriole and centriole-like structures during meiosis and mitosis in *Labyrinthula* sp. (Rhizopodea, Labyrinthulida). An electron microscope study. *J. Cell Sci., 6,* 629-653.

PICKETT-HEAPS, J. D. (1968). 'Further ultrastructural observations on polysaccharide localization in plant cells.' *J. Cell Sci., 3,* 55-64.

PRESTON, R. D., and GOODMAN, R. N. (1968). 'Structural aspects of cellulose microfibril biosynthesis.' *J. Roy. microsc. Soc., 88,* 513-528.

REICHLE, R. E. (1969). 'Fine structure of *Phytophthora parasitica* zoospores.' *Mycologia, 61,* 30-51.

REICHLE, R. E. (1972). 'Fine structure of *Oedogoniomyces* zoospores, with comparative observations on *Monoblepharella* zoospores.' *Can. J. Bot., 50,* 819-824.

REICHLE, R. E., and FULLER, M. S. (1967). 'The fine structure of *Blastocladiella emersonii* zoospores.' *Am. J. Bot., 51,* 81-92.

RENAUD, F. L., and SWIFT, H. (1964). 'The development of basal bodies and flagella in *Allomyces arbusculus.' J. Cell Biol., 23,* 339-354.

ROBERTSON, N. F. (1968). 'The growth process in fungi.' *A. Rev. Phytopath., 6,* 115-136.

ROBINOW, C. F., and BAKERSPIGEL, A. (1965). 'Somatic nuclei and forms of mitosis in fungi.' In *The Fungi, an Advanced Treatise. The Fungal Cell* (Eds. G.C. Ainsworth and A. S. Sussman), Academic Press, New York and London, Vol. 1. 119-142.

ROBINSON, D. G., and PRESTON, R. D. (1972). 'Polysaccharide synthesis in mung bean roots—an x-ray investigation.' *Biochim. biophys. Acta., 273,* 336-345.

ROSENBAUM, J. L., and CHILD, F. M. (1967). 'Flagellar regeneration in protozoan flagellates.' *J. Cell Biol., 34,* 345-364.

SCHMOYER, I. R., and LOVETT, J. S. (1969). 'Regulation of protein synthesis in zoospores of *Blastocladiella.' J. Bact., 100,* 854-864.

SCHNEPF, E., DEICHGRÄBER, G., HEGEWALD, E., and SOEDER, C.-J. (1971). 'Elektronenmikroskopische Beobachtungen an Parasiten aus *Scenedesmus*-Massenkulturen 3. *Chytridium* sp.' *Arch. Mikrobiol.,* 75, 230-245.

SHATLA, M. N., YANG, C.Y., and MITCHELL, J. E. (1966). 'Cytological and fine-structure studies of *Aphanomyces euteiches.' Phytopathology,* 56, 923-928.

SIETSMA, J. H., EVELEIGH, D. E., and HASKINS, R. H. (1969). 'Cell wall composition and protoplast formation of some oömycete species.' *Biochim. biophys. Acta.,* 184, 306-317.

SKUCAS, G. P. (1966). 'Structure and composition of zoosporangial discharge papillae in the fungus *Allomyces.' Am. J. Bot.,* 53, 1006-1011.

SOLL, D. R., and SONNEBORN, D. R. (1971). 'Zoospore germination in *Blastocladiella emersonii* III. Structural changes in relation to protein and RNA synthesis.' *J. Cell Sci.,* 9, 679-699.

TEMMINK, J. H. M., and CAMPBELL, R. N. (1968). 'The ultrastructure of *Olpidium brassicae.* I. Formation of sporangia.' *Can. J. Bot.,* 46, 951-956.

TEMMINK, J. H. M., and CAMPBELL, R. N. (1969 a). 'The ultrastructure of *Olpidium brassicae.* II. Zoospores.' *Can. J. Bot.,* 47, 227-231.

TEMMINK, J. H. M., and CAMPBELL, R. N. (1969 b). 'The ultrastructure of *Olpidium brassicae.* III. Infection of host roots.' *Can. J. Bot.,* 47, 421-424.

THOMAS, D. des S., and MULLINS, J. T. (1967). 'Role of enzymatic wall-softening in plant morphogenesis: hormonal induction in *Achlya.' Science,* 156, 84-85.

TOKUNAGA, J., and BARTNICKI-GARCIA, S. (1971 a). 'Cyst wall formation and endogenous carbohydrate utilization during synchronous encystment of *Phytophthora palmivora* zoospores.' *Arch. Mikrobiol.,* 79, 283-292.

TOKUNAGA, J., and BARTNICKI-GARCIA, S. (1971 b). 'Structure and differentiation of the cell wall of *Phytophthora palmivora:* cysts, hyphae and sporangia.' *Arch. Mikrobiol.,* 79, 293-310.

TRAVLAND, L. B., and WHISLER, H. C. (1971). 'Ultrastructure of *Harpochytrium hedinii.' Mycologia,* 63, 767-789.

TRELEASE, R. N., BECKER, W. M., GRUBER, P. J., and NEWCOMB, E. H. (1971). 'Microbodies (glyoxysomes and peroxisomes) in cucumber cotyledons.' *Pl. Physiol., Lancaster,* 48, 461-475.

TRUESDELL, L. C., and CANTINO, E. C. (1969). 'The gamma particle: membrane source for germination in the zoospore of *Blastocladiella emersonii.' J. Cell Biol.,* 43, 148 a.

TRUESDELL, L. C., and CANTINO, E. C. (1970). 'Decay of γ particles in germinating zoospores of *Blastocladiella emersonii.' Arch. Mikrobiol.,* 70, 378-392.

TURIAN, G., and OULEVEY, N. (1971). 'Nouveaux aspects ultrastructuraux de la morphogenese d'*Allomyces* (phase gamétophytique).' *Cytobiologie,* 4, 250-261.

TURNER, F. R. (1970). 'The effects of colchicine on spermatogenesis in *Nitella.' J. Cell Biol.,* 46, 220-234.

VAN DER WOUDE, W. J., MORRÉ, D. J., and BRACKER, C. E. (1971). 'Isolation and characterization of secretory vesicles in germinated pollen of *Lilium longiflorum.' J. Cell Sci.,* 8, 331-351.

VILLEMEZ, C. L., McNAB, J. M., and ALBERSHEIM, P. (1968). 'Formation of plant cell wall polysaccharides.' *Nature,* 218, 878-880.

VUJIČIĆ, R. (1971). 'An ultrastructural study of sexual reproduction in *Phytophthora palmivora.' Trans. Br. mycol. Soc.,* 57, 525-530.

WANG, M. C., and BARTNICKI-GARCIA, S. (1966). 'Biosynthesis of β-1, 3 and β-1, 6-linked glucan by *Phytophthora cinnamoni* hyphal walls.' *Biochem. biophys. Res. Commun.,* 24, 832-837.

WILLIAMS, W. J., and WEBSTER, R. K. (1970). 'Electron microscopy of the sporangium of *Phytophthora capsici.' Can. J. Bot.,* 48, 221-227.

Addendum

BARSTON, W. E., and LOVETT, J. S. (1974). *'Apical vesicles and microtubules in* rhizoids of *Blastocladiella emersonii:* effects of actinomycin D and cyclo-heximide on development during germination', *Protoplasma,* 82, 103-117.

BARTNICKI-GARCIA, S. (1973). 'Fundamental aspects of hyphal morpho-genesis', *Symp.Soc.Gen.Microbiol.* 23, 245-267.

HEATH, I. B. (1974 a). 'Centrioles and mitosis in some oömycetes', *Mycologia,* 66, 354-359.

HEATH, I. B. (1974 b). 'Mitosis in the fungus *Thraustotheca clavata', J. Cell. Biol.* 60, 204-220.

HOLLOWAY, S. H., and HEATH, I. B. (1974). 'Observations on the mechanism of flagellar retraction in *Saprolegnia terrestris', Can. J. Bot.* 52, 939-942.

McNITT, R. (1973). 'Mitosis in *Phlyctochytrium irregulare', Can. J. Bot.* 51, 2065-2074.

24 Trichomycetes

ROBERT W. LICHTWARDT

24.1 Occurrence and Distribution

The Trichomycetes live obligately within the digestive tract of arthropods, and are not usually thought of as aquatic fungi. Nevertheless, most known species are associated with freshwater or marine hosts and have morphological structures and physiological capabilities which insure their dissemination and success in aquatic ecosystems.

It has become evident in recent years that Trichomycetes are widely distributed. They have been found wherever experienced biologists have sought them, and are probably limited only by the distribution of their hosts. Most species have been discovered in Europe and North America. This certainly is a result of the location of investigators and is not indicative of the actual geographical distribution of the Trichomycetes. Published and unpublished research already has shown their distribution to include England and many parts of Europe, including regions north of the Arctic Circle; west and north Africa; Madagascar; Israel; India; all of the main islands of Japan; Taiwan and Southeast Asia; Hawaii; Greenland; North America from Alaska to the southern United States; Panama; the West Indies; and Brazil. Some species of Trichomycetes are believed to be distributed worldwide (e.g. *Amoebidium parasiticum* Cienkowski; *Harpella melusinae* Léger et Duboscq). Most have been found in more restricted regions of the world, but the known range of many species undoubtedly will increase as more collections are made. One can anticipate the discovery of many new taxa as well.

24.2 Systematics

The class Trichomycetes is generally considered to be a taxon of lower fungi, but whether or not this is a group of naturally related orders has not been resolved with any degree of satisfaction. The problem of relationships among the four orders has been discussed recently (Lichtwardt, 1973 a). Despite apparent disparities in morphology and reproductive processes, it has been suggested that basic similarities might exist among the orders. But differences such as cell wall composition, fine structure and presence or absence of sexuality make it evident that the relationships will be resolved only when additional studies have been completed.

TABLE 24.1   Trichomycetes

Order	Family	Genus	Habitats and hosts
Harpellales	Harpellaceae	*Carouxella* *Harpella* *Stachylina*	all in freshwater insect larvae (Diptera)
	Genistellaceae	*Genistella* *Genistellospora* *Glotzia* *Graminella* *Orphella* *Pennella* *Pteromaktron* *Simuliomyces* *Smittium* *Spartiella* *Stipella* *Trichozygospora*	all in freshwater insect larvae (Diptera, Ephemerida, or Plecoptera)
Asellariales	Asellariaceae	*Asellaria*	freshwater, marine and terrestrial isopods
		Orchesellaria	terrestrial insects (Collembola)
		Trichoceridium	terrestrial (humus) insect larvae (Tipulidae)
Eccrinales	Eccrinaceae	*Alacrinella*	marine isopods
		Arundinula	marine Crustacea (Anomura) and freshwater crayfish
		Astreptonema	freshwater and marine amphipods
		Eccrinidus	terrestrial millipeds (Diplopoda)
		Eccrinoides	mostly terrestrial millipeds and isopods; one marine isopod
		Enterobryus	freshwater insects (Hydrophilidae), marine decapods (Anomura and Brachyura), but mostly in terrestrial millipeds and beetles (adults and/or larvae)
		Enteromyces	marine decapods (Anomura and Brachyura)
		Paramacrinella	marine amphipods
		Ramacrinella	terrestrial amphipods
		Taeniella	marine decapods (crabs)
		Taeniellopsis	marine or terrestrial amphipods
	Palavasciaceae	*Palavascia*	marine isopods
	Parataeniellaceae	*Parataeniella*	terrestrial isopods

Order	Family	Genus	Habitats and hosts
		Lajassiella	terrestrial insect larvae (beetles)
Amoebidiales	Amoebidiaceae	*Amoebidium*	external on a variety of freshwater insects, crustacea and other arthropods
		Paramoebidium	all in freshwater insect larvae (Diptera, Ephemerida, Plecoptera)

The production of zygospores by many genera of Harpellales points to affinities with the Mucorales or Entomophthorales. It has been found that septa of the Harpellales are perforated and have a characteristic flared border around the pit within which a plug usually develops (Farr and Lichtwardt, 1967; Reichle and Lichtwardt, 1972; Moss, 1972). A very similar type of perforate septum has also been found in a species of merosporangiferous Mucorales, *Linderina pennispora* Raperet Fennell (Young, 1969). The similarity of these structures as well as evidence of some serological relationship between *Smittium* spp. (Harpellales) and two species of Kickxellaceae, *L. pennispora* and *Dipsacomyces acuminosporus* Benjamin, suggest a relationship between the Trichomycetes and Mucorales (Sangar *et al.,* 1972).

Table 24.1 classifies the currently recognized genera of Trichomycetes (Manier and Lichtwardt, 1968; Manier, 1969; Manier and Grizel, 1971; Lichtwardt, 1972) and the types of hosts that contain them. Twenty-eight of the 34 genera have at least some aquatic species. There are more than 50 known aquatic species plus others presently not described or not yet validly published. Two orders, the Harpellales and Amoebidiales, have only freshwater species. In the Eccrinales and Asellariales marine habitats are more common than freshwater, but several genera have species that are mostly or entirely terrestrial.

In this chapter both freshwater and marine species are considered together, because it is not practicable to treat them otherwise. A few genera (e.g. *Arundinula, Astreptonema*) have some species with hosts that live in freshwater and others in marine habitats. One species, *Asellaria ligiae* Tuzet et Manier, has been found in various parts of the world in 'marine' isopods of the genus *Ligia*. (Although *Ligia* spp. live in the splash zone, some species may immerse themselves in seawater and are capable of sustained immersion when properly aerated.) In Hawaii (Oahu), *Asellaria ligiae* occurs in *Ligia* on the seashore and also in an undetermined species of *Ligia* living some distance from the coast along a pure, freshwater stream. In general, however, freshwater species of Trichomycetes are distinct from those living in marine hosts.

Knowledge of the Trichomycetes is based predominantly upon material obtained directly from dissected hosts. Perhaps the most significant achievement in recent years has been the axenic cultivation of some of these fungi. This was first done by Whisler (1960) who obtained an isolate of *Amoebidium parasiticum,* which is the only Trichomycete growing on the external cuticle of its hosts. This accomplishment was soon followed by axenic isolation of two species of *Smittium* (*S. culicis* (Tuzet et Manier) Manier and *S. culisetae* Lichtwardt by Clark *et al.* (1963) from the guts of mosquito larvae. There now exist, in addition to several cultures of *A.*

parasiticum, more than 60 isolates of *Smittium* taken from larvae of mosquitoes, blackflies and midges in North America, Europe, Hawaii and Japan. These include *S. culicis, S. culisetae, S. simulii* Lichtwardt, *S. mucronatum* Manier et Mathiez ex Manier, and one or two undetermined species (Lichtwardt, unpublished). Recently isolates of a new monotypic genus of Harpellales, *Trichozygospora chironomidarum* Lichtwardt, were obtained by Lichtwardt (unpublished).

Physiological studies have been carried out on *Amoebidium parasiticum* and *Smittium culisetae* (Whisler, 1962; Farr and Lichtwardt, 1967; Williams and Lichtwardt, 1972 b; El-Buni, 1972), but no peculiarity in nutritional requirements has been discovered that might account for their obligate association with arthropod hosts. (The cultured species may not, in fact, be representative of other Trichomycetes which have remained unculturable to date.) Host specificity and developmental studies have also been possible using axenic cultures. An investigation (Sangar *et al.,* 1972) using immunoelectrophoretic methods on species of *Smittium* showed that serological relationships generally corresponded well with spore morphology, thus substantiating taxonomic criteria used at the species level. No serological relationships were found between species of *Smittium* and *A. parasiticum* using immunoelectrophoretic and immunodiffusion techniques.

Identification of described aquatic Trichomycetes can often be accomplished through identification of the host. This is the most practical approach, especially where faunas are known or invertebrate zoologists are available for consultation. Identification of the arthropod genus is usually sufficient, because Trichomycetes probably are not species specific, as discussed briefly in the next section. Some are known to infest different families or orders of hosts. It therefore follows that a Trichomycete discovered in an unreported host is not necessarily new. The current tendency among biologists working with Trichomycetes is to put less taxonomic emphasis than formerly on hosts and geographical distribution.

Determination of genera in most families of Trichomycetes is not difficult if sporulating material is available and the kind of host is known. Genera of Eccrinaceae, however, often present special identification problems because of the great morphological variation within some species and the need often to have more than one type of spore available. Approximately half of the aquatic genera of Trichomycetes are monotypic. No worldwide monograph on the Trichomycetes exists at the moment. The most useful single reference for descriptions of taxa is that published by Manier in 1969. Keys to genera have been published by Lichtwardt (1973 b).

24.3 Relationships with Arthropod Hosts

The geographical distribution and wide taxonomic variety of arthropod hosts, as well as the many morphological features which they have evolved, attest to the success of the Trichomycetes. The biological relationships are not clearly understood. It seems evident that the dependence of the fungi on their hosts is obligate, but the reverse does not appear to be true, because all populations of potential hosts are not infested with the fungi. Most of the early literature refers to the Trichomycetes as parasites. While this designation may be appropriate in the broad sense, at present there is no evidence that these fungi have deleterious effects on arthropods in nature. The heaviest infestation of Trichomycetes often is found in healthy, vigorous populations of hosts. It is perhaps best to refer to the Trichomycetes as *commensals* until such time as deleterious or beneficial effects are experimentally demonstrated.

It has been shown that first instar larvae of mosquitoes (*Aedes aegypti* Linn.) may be killed by growth of the Trichomycete, *Smittium culisetae,* after feeding them large numbers of spores from axenic cultures, but such death may not occur in natural situations (Williams and Lichtwardt, 1972 a). It is conceivable that Trichomycetes under certain conditions may play a beneficial—even a survival—role by providing arthropods in dense populations with organic micronutrients which may have become exhausted in the substrate. Experimental evidence to support or refute this relationship has not yet been obtained. Whatever the affect of the fungus on survival of hosts, one should seek to understand it better, because some of the hosts of Trichomycetes are vectors of disease (mosquitoes, blackflies) and others are destructive, such as the wood-boring isopods *(Limnoria).*

Most species of Trichomycetes are found in the hindgut of the host. A few genera of Eccrinales found in Crustacea may be restricted to the foregut or stomach (e.g. *Enteromyces*) or may occur in both the foregut and the hindgut *(Arundinula).* Genera of Harpellaceae are located on the peritrophic membrane that lines the midgut of dipteran larvae. *Amoebidium parasiticum* is the only species of Trichomycete that grows on the external surfaces of its hosts; despite its specific epithet it is a benign associate. All species of Trichomycetes produce a holdfast of one sort or another that allows them to maintain their position in or on the host. The endozoic species attach to the chitinous lining of the gut and obtain their nutrients from the contents of the gut lumen. They do not penetrate the host tissues. In some aquatic dipteran larvae, it is not uncommon to find more than one genus of Trichomycetes in the same gut (Lichtwardt, 1972). Occasionally one species will grow on another, as well as attach directly to the gut lining (e.g. *Simuliomyces*).

Moulting of the host is a critical process for these fungi. The chitinous linings of the gut normally are shed from the host together with the exoskeleton. In several genera there is evidence that ecdysis of the host affects morphogenesis of the fungus. This may involve the production of amoeboid cells *(Amoebidiales),* zygospores (e.g. *Genistella, Glotzia*), or thick-walled resting spores (e.g. *Taeniella*).

The degree of host specificity depends upon the taxon. It is doubtful that any Trichomycete will prove to be species specific so long as closely related species of hosts are extant. Some of the fungi appear to be restricted to certain genera of hosts (e.g. *Asellaria ligiae* in *Ligia* spp.), and many are characteristically found in particular families of hosts (*Harpella melusinae* in Simuliidae; *Stachylina* spp. in Chironomidae). *Enteromyces callianassae* Lichtwardt was once thought to grow only in shrimp-like crabs (Anomura), but now has been found also in several genera of true crabs (Brachyura). *Amoebidium parasiticum* has the widest host range; it can be found in ponds growing on various arthropods including Crustacea (Cladocera, Copepoda, Isopoda, Amphipoda) and several orders of insects.

Larvae of blackflies *(Simulium)* may grow on the same substrata in flowing streams as midge larvae (Chironomidae) and mayfly nymphs (Ephemerida). In such situations one finds *Harpella* only in the blackflies and *Stachylina* only in the midges. *Smittium simulii,* however, occurs in both dipteran families of hosts, but not in mayfly nymphs, which have their own Trichomycete genera. It is evident, therefore, that host specificity to some degree does exist even among arthropods in close physical association where one would expect occasional transmission of spores from one kind of arthropod to another.

Host specificity has been further substantiated by experimentally feeding larvae of *Aedes aegypti* with spores of several *Smittium* species axenically isolated from a variety of dipteran hosts. Species of *Smittium* that normally occur in mosquito larvae generally grew better in the experimental mosquito larvae than did isolates from chironomids or blackflies (Williams and Lichtwardt, 1972 a). Other genera of Harpellales appear to have an even more limited host preference, as judged by field collections. Perhaps they are more particular with respect to their growth requirements than cultured *Smittium* spp., which could account in part for the present lack of success in culturing the other genera.

Species of *Smittium* can be isolated and grown on a variety of mycological media. The two most commonly used have been dilute brain–heart infusion (Difco Laboratories) and a tryptone-glucose-salts medium (Lichtwardt, 1964). Hindguts of the host containing the attached fungus can be washed in several changes of distilled water containing penicillin and streptomycin and can then be transferred to small petri dishes containing an agar medium covered by a thin layer of distilled water with antibiotics. After growth is evident (usually in 2-5 days) and if contaminants are not present, the fungus can be transferred to fresh agar medium with an overlayer of distilled water without antibiotics. *Smittium* spp. have been maintained on agar medium slants to which a small amount (1-2 ml) of distilled water has been added prior to inoculation. The fungus is grown by intermittently rocking the slants for several days to allow some of the growth to adhere to the agar surface. After one week, such slants can be refrigerated and will often remain viable for 6 months or longer. For experimental studies, *Smittium* spp. grow well in shaken liquid media in flasks, reaching maximum dry weight in 3-5 days at 24 °C. Yields of more than 3 mg dry weight per millilitre of medium are possible. Spores of most isolates do not germinate *in vitro;* consequently it is necessary to use a fragmented mycelium inoculum.

24.4 Morphology

24.4.1 Harpellales

Species of Harpellales are restricted to aquatic larvae of insects, most of which are found in rapidly flowing freshwater streams, a few in ponds or pools. Those fungi attached to the peritrophic membrane of the midgut are unbranched (Harpellaceae), whereas the hindgut species are branched (Genistellaceae). Reproductively, the two families are indistinguishable.

TABLE 24.2 Trichomycetes

Order	Type of thallus	Reproduction	
		Asexual	Sexual
Harpellales	branched or unbranched; septate	trichospores	biconical zygospores
Asellariales	branched; septate	arthrospores	unknown
Eccrinales	unbranched; nonseptate	sporangiospores	unknown
Amoebidiales	unbranched; nonseptate	amoeboid cells or sporangiospores	unknown

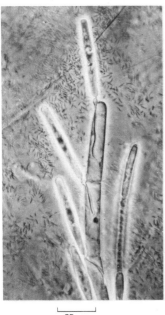

24.1

25 μm

Fig. 24.1. Apex of an unbranched *Stachylina grandispora* (Harpellaceae) thallus with trichospores, as seen through the peritrophic membrane of a dissected bloodworm (*Chironomus* sp.). The appendage within the generative cell at the base of each spore unfolds upon release of the spore.

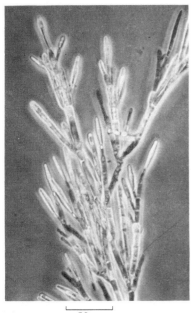

24.2

50 μm

Fig. 24.2. Part of a *Smittium mucronatum* (Genistellaceae) thallus from the hindgut lining of a midge larva (*Psectrocladius sordidellus* (Zett.) Edw.).

657

24.3

25 μm

Fig. 24.3. Released spore of *Smittium mucronatum* showing a single appendage attached to the spore inside a basal collar.

Harpellales (Table 24.2) produce 'trichospores' asexually from specialized generative cells. In the Harpellaceae the entire thallus is converted to spore production (Fig. 24.1), but in the Genistellaceae normally only the tips of branches form basipetalous generative cells (Fig. 24.2). The spores, upon release, bear at their bases one or more very fine, hair-like appendages (Fig. 24.3) which may help them to become attached to the substratum. In this way the spores may be more accessible to another host than if they were to float away in the water. Motility is not a function of the appendages, and electronmicrographs reveal no flagellum-like ultrastructure. Trichospores are ellipsoidal, ovoid, or cylindrical, and may be curved *(Orphella)* or even coiled *(Harpella).* Genera of Harpellales can be distinguished in most cases by the shape of the trichospore and the number of appendages, although other features, such as zygospore morphology and type of holdfast, may be useful or necessary.

Appendages form outside the plasmalemma of the generative cell by a process involving the transport of substances in vesicles which migrate from the central part of the cell to the plasmalemma. The vesicles then fuse with the plasmalemma in a sort of reverse pinocytosis (Reichle and Lichtwardt, 1972; Moss, 1972). In some genera the appendages are coiled next to the wall (e.g. *Harpella, Genistella*), but in others the appendage(s) is located near the centre of the generative cell. Moss (1972) has shown that in *Stachylina grandispora* Lichtwardt (Fig. 24.1) the plasmalemma invaginates to form a sacklike structure below the spore within which the folded single appendage forms. The generative cell at spore maturity becomes essentially empty and contains only the appendages and degenerated organelles. The fine structure of appendages has been seen in only a few genera, but additional ultrastructure studies are currently in progress. In *Harpella,* the appendages have periodic transverse banding (Reichle and Lichtwardt, 1972); in *Smittium* the appendage in cross section may have a series of more or less concentric electron-dense rings (Manier and Coste-Mathiez, 1968); and in other genera, such as *Stachylina* and *Genistellospora,* there is no special substructure (Moss, 1972; and unpublished).

Zygospores develop subsequent to conjugations. In most cases it appears that conjugations occur only between different thalli, suggesting heterothallism. This has not been tested experimentally, because it has not been possible to produce zygospores in axenic cultures. One genus, *Genistellospora,* is apparently homothallic, and zygospores form without conjugations. The nuclear behaviour during zygospore development has not been studied in any species, consequently it is only an assumption that this is a true sexual process. Unlike zygospores of the Mucorales and Entomophthorales, those of the Harpellales are biconical. In *Carouxella* (and also in a new genus of Genistellaceae, see first Addendum p. 671) zygospores are attached at one pole so that only the free end is pointed (Manier *et al.,* 1961). Several other types of zygospores are recognized. In *Genistellospora* and *Pennella,* zygospores are attached medially and are orientated parallel to the axis of the zygosporophore. In *Harpella, Simuliomyces, Stipella* and *Spartiella* they are perpendicular to the zygosporophore. And in other genera with zygospores *(Genistella, Glotzia, Smittium, Trichozygospora)* the angle is oblique and attachment is submedian. Zygospores of the latter type may have appendages like those on trichospores (Fig. 24.4).

Holdfast morphology in the Harpellales varies among the genera and species. In most species attachment is by a more or less prominent secreted holdfast at the base of the main cell of the thallus. In *Glotzia ephemeridarum* Lichtwardt, hold-fasts develop on many parts of the main cell (Lichtwardt, 1972). A more diffuse substance seems to cement thalli of *Pennella* spp. to the chitinous lining of the host gut. *Stachylina minuta* Gauthier thalli actually penetrate the peritrophic membrane and produce a slightly bulbous basal swelling beneath the membrane (Lichtwardt, 1973 a). *Harpella melusinae* has a more complicated holdfast than other Harpellales studied; electronmicrographs show that there are many finger-like structures arising from a short basal cell and that the cementing substance is secreted around these 'digits' (Reichle and Lichtwardt, 1972).

24.4

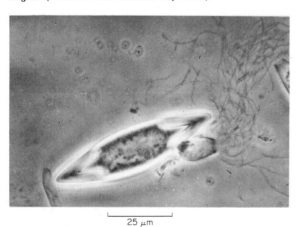

25 μm

Fig. 24.4. Released biconical zygospore of *Trichozygospora chironomidarum* (Genistellaceae) from the hindgut of a midge larva *(Orthocladius* sp.). This is one of several genera of Genistel-laceae whose zygospores are appendaged.

The perforate septum of the Harpellales probably will prove to have phylogenetic significance. It has been found in the Asellariales (Manier, 1973), and possibly in a modified form in the Eccrinales (Grizel, 1971; Moss, 1972). As mentioned previously, a similar septum occurs in the Kickxellaceae (Mucorales) (Young, 1969). Perforate septa of the Harpellales appear to occur not only throughout the vegetative parts of the thallus, but also at the bases of spores where they become delimited from the generative cell. Thus, like Ascomycetes and Basidiomycetes, the cells may be uninucleate but the thallus is functionally a coenocyte, at least until the plug develops in the pore of the septum.

24.4.2 Asellariales

The Asellariales, like the Genistellaceae, have branched, septate thalli (Fig. 24.5). Cells of branches break apart to form arthrospore-like bodies (Fig. 24.6). In *Asellaria ligiae* it has been observed that such cells germinate to produce a lateral spore-like cell morphologically similar to the modified trichospores of *Carouxella* (Harpellaceae). It has been suggested, in fact, that the arthrospores of *A. ligiae* may be generative cells that delay their production of 'spores' until after they disarticulate (Lichtwardt, 1973 a). Further studies are needed to determine whether or not the Asellariales and Harpellales are indeed related, and if the three genera currently included in the Asellariales have more than superficial morphological similarities.

Sexual reproduction is not known in the order, but in *A. ligiae* conjugations among branches have been observed, similar to those which precede zygospore formation in the Harpellales (Lichtwardt, 1973 a).

24.5

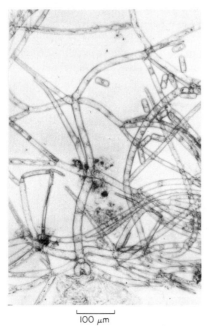

100 μm

Fig. 24.5. *Asellaria ligiae* (Asellariaceae) dissected from the marine isopod *Ligia italica* Fabricius. Note at the base the lobed holdfast cell attached to a piece of hindgut lining.

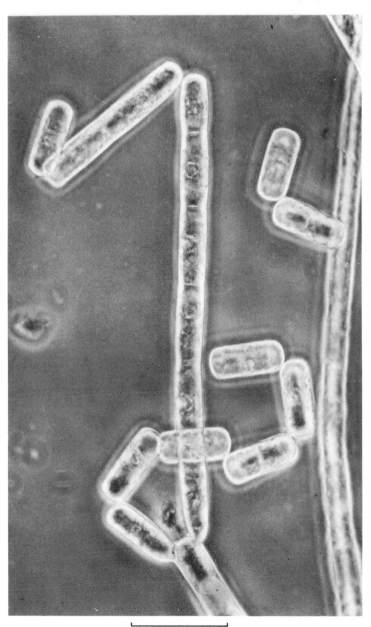

50 μm

Fig. 24.6. Arthrospore-like cells of *Asellaria ligiae*.

24.4.3 Eccrinales

This is the largest order in terms of number of species described, and it also presents the greatest variety of hosts and habitats. It is the most difficult order to discuss morphologically, because many of the species are insufficiently described and some show great variability in structure and reproduction.

Basically, the Eccrinales are those Trichomycetes with unbranched, nonseptate, thalli producing sporangiospores singly in basipetal series of sporangia (Fig. 24.7). Many kinds of sporangiospores have been described, some of which may be non-functional or merely morphological varieties of other basic types. There seem to be two principal spore types in the order. One is thin-walled, bi- or multinucleate, normally germinates within the gut where produced, and functions to increase in-festation of the gut endogenously (Fig. 24.8). Among all families of Trichomycetes, only the Eccrinaceae and Parataeniellaceae seem to produce spores that normally germinate in the gut where they differentiate. The second type of spore is usually uninucleate (although it may in some cases become bi- or multinucleate before release), is thin- or often thick-walled, frequently oval, and passes through the gut to the outside, later to be ingested by another host. Possibly these spores can withstand unfavourable conditions such as desiccation and freezing. Such conditions are known to occur periodically in habitats of some aquatic hosts, but no experimental work has been done on spore resistance.

24.7

250 μm

Fig. 24.7. *Enteromyces callianassae* (Eccrinaceae) from the stomach (foregut) of the red ghost shrimp, *Callianassa californiensis.* The unbranched, dimorphic thalli share a common multiple holdfast, thus grow in a cluster. Both kinds of thalli are producing sporangiospores. At the apex of some can be seen a bulbous structure which is the mother spore that gave rise to the thallus.

Species of Eccrinaceae produce both types of spores described above, in addition to some other types. The Palavasciaceae differ in that only one type of spore—that which passes from the gut—is produced (Fig. 24.9). In the Parataeniellaceae, species produce their binucleate spores singly in sporangia, but in other sporangia many uninucleate spores are produced, as in the Amoebidiales.

662

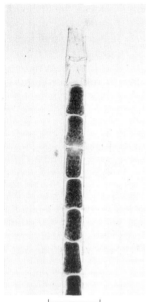

50 μm (2·75cm)

Fig. 24.8. Tip of an *Arundinula orconectis* Lichtwardt (Eccrinaceae) thallus bearing multinucleate sporangiospores, from the stomach of a crayfish (*Orconectis nais* (Faxon)). The terminal spores have been released through tears developed in the side of the sporangium. The empty sporangia subsequently disintegrate.

In recent years it has been discovered that several species of freshwater and marine Eccrinales produce thick-walled spores with appendages. They occur in *Arundinula, Taeniella, Astreptonema* and possibly *Palavascia* (Manier, 1969; Galt, 1971; Lichtwardt, 1973 a). Appendages may develop on one or both ends of the spore. At present it is not known whether these appendages are homologous with those of trichospores. Moss (1972) found that development of the single appendage at each

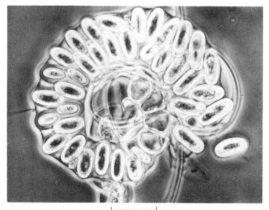

24.9

Fig. 24. 9. Sporulating tip of *Palavascia sphaeromae* (Palavasciaceae) which was projecting from the anus of the marine isopod, *Sphaeroma serratum* (Fabricius).

end of oval spores of *Astreptonema gammari* Léger et Duboscq involves the blebbing off of vesicles from dictyosomes located near the nucleus of the developing spores, and migration of these vesicles to the region of appendage formation. Further studies may reveal if this process is similar to appendage formation in the Harpellales. The function of eccrinid appendages, if any, is not known, but the fact that they seem to occur only in aquatic species suggests that they may be involved, like trichospores, in transmission from one host to another.

24.4.4   Amoebidiales

Paramoebidium spp. grow in the rectum of various aquatic insects (Fig. 24.10). Upon moulting of the host, large numbers of amoeboid cells are released into the water (Fig. 24.11). They are teardrop shaped with the narrow end trailing behind (Fig. 24.12) and move by a sort of rolling motion. Recent investigations indicate that they do not feed nor do they function as gametes. After moving over the substratum for an hour or less, they form a round cyst (Fig. 24.13). The cysts enlarge and eventually produce one to a dozen or more cystospores (Fig. 24.14) each within its own chamber. Later (presumably, under natural conditions, after being ingested) the cytospores pop out of the cyst and develop into new thalli.

24.10

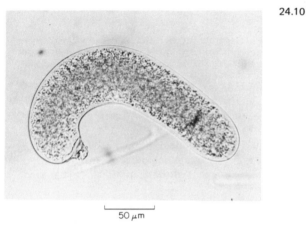

50 μm

Fig. 24.10. Thallus of *Paramoebidium* sp. (Amoebidiaceae) removed from the rectum of a blackfly larva (*Simulium vittatum* Zet.). The holdfast can be seen at the base of this sausage-shaped species.

Amoebidium growing on the surface of aquatic arthropods (Figs. 24.15, 24.16) produces amoeboid cells provided the host undergoes ecdysis or is injured. *Amoebidium* thalli on non-moulting and healthy hosts become filled with allantoid to lunate spores that eventually break through and protrude from the thallus (sporangium) wall and adhere to the exoskeleton of passing arthropods upon contact. Whisler and Fuller (1968) have shown that sporangiospores of *Amoebidium* have a series of small pits in the wall at each apex. Upon attachment to a substrate, a substance is secreted, presumably through the pits, to form the holdfast. They have found in the fine structure of developing sporangia no difference between amoeboid cells and sporangiospores, except that walls are laid down in the latter.

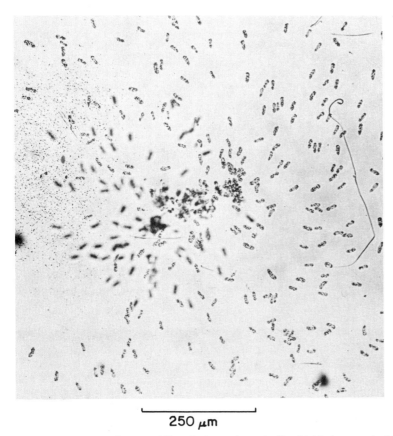

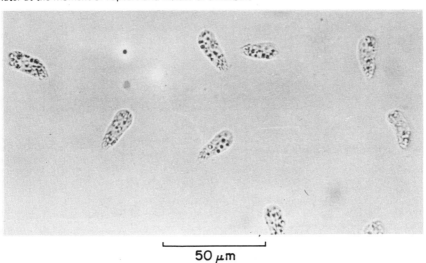

250 μm

Fig. 24.11. The same *Paramoebidium* thallus as shown in Fig. 24.10 photographed 2.5 hours later at the moment of rupture and release of amoebae.

50 μm

Fig. 24.12. Migrating amoebae of *Paramoebidium* sp. The posterior end is tapered.

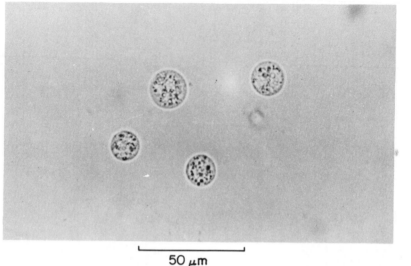

50 μm

Fig. 24.13. Encysting amoebae of *Paramoebidium* sp. These cysts eventually enlarge before forming cystospores.

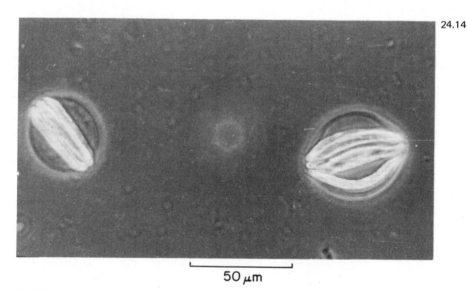

50 μm

Fig. 24.14. Cystospores of *Paramoebidium* sp.

24.5 Adaptive features

Infestation of arthropods by aquatic Trichomycetes is dependent upon several methods of spore transmission. It is not uncommon in some populations to find almost 100% of individuals infested with a particular species of fungus, whereas other geographical areas containing the same host-commensal combinations may reveal a much lower percentage of infestation, or a similar variation may occur in the same population at different times. The fact that infestation can be high in hosts that moult at frequent intervals indicates that successful mechanisms operate to reinfest individuals following moulting, which may occur even in rapid streams or shifting waters of intertidal zones.

24.15

100 μm

Fig. 24.15. *Amoebidium parasiticum* (Amoebidiaceae) attached to the antennae of a water flea (Cladocera). The smaller lunate cells are newly attached spores. The clusters of cells are thalli (sporangia) whose spores have burst through the wall. Such spores adhere to passing arthropods.

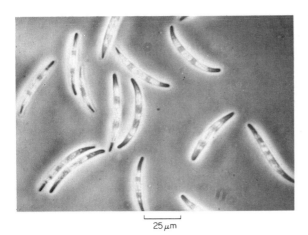

25 μm

Fig. 24.16. Free sporangiospores of *Amoebidium parasiticum* as they would appear in axenic culture.

Density of population is at least one reason for high infestation. Animals, such as blackfly and mosquito larvae, amphipods, isopods, mud crabs and others, may live in close contact with each other. Hosts that live in less dense natural populations sometimes have a lower percentage of infestation. It is sometimes possible in the laboratory to increase the percentage by crowding. In nature, changes in the environment may concentrate individuals: bodies of water may partially dry up or ebbing tides may temporarily reduce habitats to small tide pools or other restricted sites. The marine isopod, *Sphaeroma quadridentatum* Say, host of *Palavascia sphaeromae* Tuzet et Manier, lives in the intertidal zone (Lichtwardt, 1961). At low tide, to prevent desiccation and death, these small animals when seeking shelter congregate in barnacle shells, wood crevices, the undersurfaces of rocks, etc. This enforced aggregation probably is largely responsible for the very high incidence of infestation in some populations of *S. quadridentatum,* because the amount of spore production is relatively low in this fungus. Immature specimens can be found infested with many germinating spores and young thalli of *Palavascia* even though their intermoult period is too short for the thalli to mature and produce spores. The source of spores is primarily from older isopods. One explanation for the high infestation in the total population seems to be that small individuals are often found attached to the ventral abdomen of larger ones, among the pleopods near the anus; the sporulating tip of the fungus projects from the gut of the larger isopods (Fig. 24.9) and the spores are thus capable of being ingested directly by the young animals.

Some Crustacea and other arthropods may eat part of their moult (possibly to conserve calcium) and could conceivably become reinfested with the fungus by this method. However, it was not possible to demonstrate this experimentally with fiddler crabs: specimens of *Uca pugilator* (Bosc) were isolated upon moulting, to be certain that they were not infested with *Enterobryus* sp. After several days, hindgut linings with sporulating *Enterobryus* were taken from other crabs or from moults and were force-fed to the recently moulted crabs, but upon subsequent dissection no infestation was found. Possibly success was not achieved with these hosts because they were still in the postmoult stage prior to the complete hardening of the new gut lining.

With mosquito larvae, on the other hand, it is relatively easy to infest populations under laboratory conditions by the introduction of a few larvae containing *Smittium* or by adding fungus spores from cultures. It is perhaps significant that spores of *Smittium* spp. grown axenically usually do not have the ability to germinate under culture conditions. Only a small percentage of the existing cultures of *Smittium* have spores that can germinate *in vitro.* In fact, there is reason to believe that in some of these cultures there has been a selection for germinability through repeated transfers of stock cultures. In nature, however, one would expect germinability outside the host to be disadvantageous. Chapman (1966) and El-Buni (1972) tried many chemical and physical methods, including treatment with digestive enzymes, to induce *in vitro* germination of spores of several *Smittium* isolates that do not germinate in culture, but without success. Yet, it was shown that spores of those same isolates would germinate when fed to mosquito larvae (Williams and Lichtwardt, 1972 a; and unpublished). It is quite evident that passage of the spore through the gut somehow triggers germination so that the spore germinates and attaches at the proper time and place. It was found that germination and attachment of *Smittium culisetae* spores in *Aedes aegypti* larvae could occur within 30 minutes of ingestion (Williams and Lichtwardt, 1972 a), whereas spores of that species *in vitro* take at least 24 hours to germinate (El-Buni, 1972). Also, *S. culisetae* can grow and sporulate much faster *in vivo.* In first instar larvae, growth and sporulation of new thalli are possible within 22 hours of ingestion of spores (Williams and Lichtwardt, 1972 a). Under optimum conditions in the laboratory, *A. aegypti* larvae moult and begin the second instar stage at 23-30 hours, so it can be seen that the fungus is remarkably well adapted to the host cycle.

Aquatic Trichomycetes assimilating and developing within the gut are influenced by the osmoregulatory mechanisms of the host, but expelled spores are directly subjected to the osmotic forces of the external aquatic medium. Whether or not a

Trichomycete should be considered freshwater or marine is dependent upon the habit of the host, but even here a distinction cannot always be made, especially in brackish or estuarine waters where host tolerances and distribution vary. Several species of *Uca* live in the region of Beaufort, North Carolina, USA. *Uca pugilator* is more tolerant of higher salinity, whereas *Uca pugnax* (S. I. Smith) and *Uca minax* (La Conte) prefer waters of considerably lower salinity, such as those found in the North River. A species of *Enterobryus* occurs commonly in all three species of crabs and therefore can be found in a wide range of salt concentrations.

The same tolerance was not found in the freshwater Trichomycete, *Smittium (Rubetella) culicis,* that infests larvae of many mosquito genera. Larvae of *Aedes detritus* (Haliday), unlike most species of mosquitoes, are capable of living in a wide range of salinities. Tuzet *et al.* (1961) studied 16 natural populations of *A. detritus* in southern France in waters ranging from 0.1 to 46 grams per litre NaCl. No infestation by *S. culicis* occurred in salinities above 14 grams per litre. In an experiment, they place one group of infested third instar larvae in a container of spring water and another in lagoon water with 38 grams per litre NaCl. After moulting, all fourth instar larvae in the freshwater became reinfested, but none in the saltwater did. Presumably, spores were not successfully transmitted in water with high salinity.

The possible role of appendages in the transmission of trichospores of the Harpellales (which occur mostly in fast streams) has already been mentioned. *Paramoebidium* spp. likewise live mostly in hosts that inhabit running waters. *Amoebidium* usually is found in ponds or quiet pools, but the author has collected *A. parasiticum* several times on the bodies of bloodworms (*Chironomus* spp.) in rather fast flowing polluted ditches and streams. Amoebae in both genera of Amoebidiales are produced when the host moults or is wounded. Whisler (1965) studied amoebagenesis in axenic cultures of *A. parasiticum* in an attempt to understand the morphogenetic shift from sporangiospore to amoeba production that takes place. Axenic cultures of *Amoebidium* produce only sporangiospores under usual growth conditions. Whisler was able to induce amoeba formation in about 17% of the thalli by adding an extract of crushed hosts *(Daphnia)* to cultures whose development had been synchronized by 'starvation' in a dilute salt solution. Yet almost 100% of the thalli could be induced to form amoebae, instead of sporangiospores, when a dialysate of dried *Daphnia* extract was used. The inducing substance in the dialysate was heat stable, had a relatively small molecular size, and was not soluble in ether, acetone or chloroform. Subsequent work (Whisler, 1968) using Sephadex fractionation of the host extract showed that calcium, glucose and amino acids (especially histidine and methionine) are essential for amoebagenesis.

At present we are unable to account for the wide dissemination of many aquatic species of Trichomycetes. Marine habitats are essentially interconnected, for even though hosts are often restricted to particular ecological sites, they may be carried by floating materials or in other ways to new areas. Many freshwater habitats, however, are discontinuous. Larvae of mosquitoes containing *Smittium,* for instance, have been found in isolated bodies of water (tree holes, discarded bottles, etc.) Although rivers are interconnected, many dipteran larvae containing species of Harpellales and *Paramoebidium* have been collected repeatedly in the headwaters of streams in major mountain ranges. One would expect in time to find the fungi only in downstream hosts unless replenishment were constantly occurring upstream, for the larvae themselves cannot migrate any appreciable distance upstream. Spores of aquatic Trichomycetes do not appear to be carried by air currents as a regular means of dispersal, and the adult flying stages of insect hosts are not believed to carry spores, at least not internally.

Acknowledgement

The author acknowledges with appreciation support from National Science Foundation grants GB-7072X, GB-24947, and BMS 72-02380 for much of the research reported in this chapter.

References

CHAPMAN, M. E. (1966). 'Isolation and experimental studies on some Trichomycetes.' M.A. Thesis, University of Kansas.

CLARK, T. B., KELLEN, W. R., and LINDEGREN, J. E. (1963). 'Axenic culture of two Trichomycetes from Californian mosquitoes.' *Nature,* 197, 208-209.

EL-BUNI, A. M. (1972). 'Spore germination in axenic cultures of *Smittium* spp. (Trichomycetes).' M.A. Thesis, University of Kansas.

FARR, D. F., and LICHTWARDT, R. W. (1967). 'Some cultural and ultrastructural aspects of *Smittium culisetae* (Trichomycetes) from mosquito larvae.' *Mycologia,* 59, 172-182.

GALT, J. H. (1971). 'Studies on some protists associated with Crustacea: the Ellobiopsidae and the Trichomycetes.' M.S. Thesis, University of Washington.

GRIZEL, H. (1971). 'Le parasitisme chez les Amphipodes de la région de Montpellier.' Docteur de Spécialité (3ème cycle) Thesis, Université des Sciences et Techniques du Languedoc.

LICHTWARDT, R. W. (1961). 'A *Palavascia* (Eccrinales) from the marine isopod *Sphaeroma quadridentatum* Say.' *J. Elisha Mitchell scient. Soc.,* 77, 242-249.

LICHTWARDT, R. W. (1964). 'Axenic culture of two new species of branched Trichomycetes.' *Am. J. Bot.,* 51, 836-842.

LICHTWARDT, R. W. (1972). 'Undescribed genera and species of Harpellales (Trichomycetes) from the guts of aquatic insects.' *Mycologia,* 64, 167-197.

LICHTWARDT, R. W. (1973 a). 'The Trichomycetes: what are their relationships?' *Mycologia,* 65, 1-20.

LICHTWARDT, R. W. (1973 b). 'Trichomycetes.' In *The Fungi,* (Eds. G. C. Ainsworth, F. K. Sparrow, and A. S. Sussmann), Academic Press, New York, Vol. 4B, 237-243.

MANIER, J.-F. (1969). 'Trichomycètes de France.' *Annls. Sci. nat. (Bot.), Sér.* 12, 10, 565-650.

MANIER, J.-F., and COSTE-MATHIEZ, F. (1968). 'L'ultrastructure du filament de la spore de *Smittium mucronatum* Manier, Mathiez 1965 (Trichomycète, Harpellale). *C. r. hebd. Séanc. Acad. Sci., Paris,* 266, 341-342.

MANIER, J.-F., and GRIZEL, H. (1971). '*Paramacrinella microdeutopi* n.g., n. sp., Trichomycète parasite de *Microdeutopus anomalus* H. Rathke (Amphipode).' *Annls. Sci. nat. (Bot.), Sér. 12,* 12, 1-8.

MANIER, J.-F., and LICHTWARDT, R. W. (1968). 'Révision de la systématique des Trichomycètes.' *Annls. Sci. nat. (Bot.), Sér. 12,* 9, 519-532.

MANIER, J.-F., RIOUX, J. A. and WHISLER, H. C. (1961). '*Rubetella inopinata* n.sp. et *Carouxella scalaris* n.g., Trichomycètes parasites de *Dasyhelea lithotelmatica* Strenzke, 1951 (Diptera Ceratopogonidae).' *Naturalia Monspeliensia, Sér. Bot.,* 13, 25-38.

MOSS, S. T. (1972). 'Occurrence, cell structure and taxonomy of the Trichomycetes, with special reference to electron microscope studies of *Stachylina.*' Ph.D. Thesis, University of Reading.

REICHLE, R. E., and LICHTWARDT, R. W. (1972). 'Fine structure of the Trichomycete, *Harpella melusinae,* from black-fly guts.' *Arch. Mikrobiol.,* 81, 103-125.

SANGAR, V. K., LICHTWARDT, R. W., KIRSCH, J. A. W., and LESTER, R. N. (1972). 'Immunological studies on the fungal genus *Smittium* (Trichomycetes).' *Mycologia,* 64, 342-358.

TUZET, O., RIOUX, J. A. and MANIER, J.-F. (1961). *'Rubetella culicis* (Tuzet et Manier, 1947), Trichomycète rameux.parasite de l'ampoule rectales des larves de Culicides (morphologie et spécificité).' *Vie et Milieu,* 12, 167-187.

WHISLER, H. C. (1960). 'Pure culture of the Trichomycete, *Amoebidium parasiticum.' Nature,* 186, 732-733.

WHISLER, H. C. (1962). 'Culture and nutrition of *Amoebidium parasiticum.' Am. J. Bot.,* 49, 193-199.

WHISLER, H. C. (1965). 'Host-integrated development in the Amoebidiales.' *J. Protozool.,* 13, 183-188.

WHISLER, H. C. (1968). 'Developmental control of *Amoebidium parasiticum.' Devl. Biol.,* 17, 562-570.

WHISLER, H. C., and FULLER, M. S. (1968). 'Preliminary observations on the hold-fast of *Amoebidium parasiticum.' Mycologia,* 60, 1068-1079.

WILLIAMS, M. C., and LICHTWARDT, R. W. (1972 a). 'Infection of *Aedes aegypti* larvae by axenic cultures of the fungal genus *Smittium* (Trichomycetes).' *Am. J. Bot.,* 59, 189-193.

WILLIAMS, M. C., and LICHTWARDT, R. W. (1972 b). 'Physiological studies on the cultured Trichomycete, *Smittium culisetae.' Mycologia,* 64, 806-815.

YOUNG, T. W. K. (1969). 'Ultrastructure of aerial hyphae in *Linderina pennispora.' Ann. Bot.,* 33, 211-216.

Addenda

The unnamed genus referred to on page 659 is *Zygopolaris* Moss, Lichtwardt et Manier (1975 *'Zygopolaris,* a new genus of Trichomycetes, producing zygospores with polar attachment', *Mycologia,* 76, 120-127).

MANIER, J.-F. (1973). 'Quelques aspects ultrastructuraux du Trichomycète Asellariale, *Asellaria ligiae* Tuzet et Manier, 1950 ex Manier 1968'. *C. r. hebd. Séanc. Acad. Sci., Paris,* 276, 3429-3431.

25 Freshwater Actinomycetes

L. G. WILLOUGHBY

25.1 Introduction

The Actinomycetales constitute a fairly compact group of micro-organisms, finding a natural place between the fungi and the bacteria. The outstanding fungal characteristic is a morphological one, the possession of a true branching mycelium. It may be noted that as this characteristic tends to become transient or be lost, so does it apparently become controversial whether a strain should be considered as an Actinomycete or as a bacterium. Taxonomic entities now placed within the genera *Nocardia* and *Mycobacterium* frequently give cause for such a dilemma (Goodfellow, 1971). In addition to possessing mycelium, Actinomycetes may also show strong parallels with the true fungi in their production of sporangia (Figs. 25.4-25.11) and motile spores (Figs. 25.12-25.16), this being especially significant in the aquatic representatives. However, mycelium diameter and spore size is of a lower order of magnitude in the Actinomycetes as compared with the fungi, averaging 1 μm only. Several other Actinomycete characters are those of procaryotic rather than eucaryotic cells (Stanier and Van Niel, 1962) for example their lack of membrane-bounded organelles such as nuclei and mitochondria and their ready susceptibility to phage. Although further detailed discussion of Actinomycete affinity perhaps lies outside the scope of this contribution, and is to some extent academic, a point of considerable practical importance concerns the antibiotic sensitivity spectrum. This again relates the group to the bacteria rather than to the fungi. In isolating Actinomycetes from water it is a convenience that the antibiotic actidione (cycloheximide) prevents growth of the associated fungi, but an inconvenience that there is no known antibiotic which will serve to free the Actinomycetes completely from bacteria (Fig. 25.1). From an ecological point of view, Actinomycetes stand in an intermediate position between the fungi and the bacteria in terms of numerical frequency of occurrence in various biotypes. The aquatic biotype is not widely recognised as being an amenable one for Actinomycetes but it is the aim of this chapter to suggest that such a conclusion stems largely from lack of knowledge rather than any positive information.

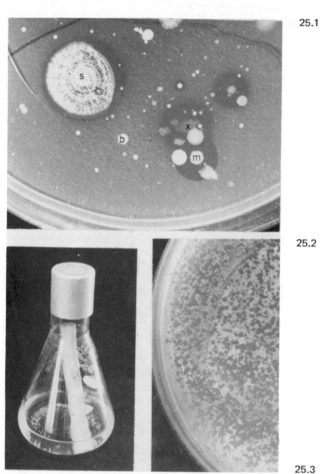

25.1

25.2

25.3

Fig. 25.1 Chitin-actidione growth medium for the isolation of Actinomycetes. A river water sample has been dried down and incubated. Growing colonies of *Streptomyces* (s) and *Micromonospora* (m) show hydrolysis zones, as also do myxobacteria (x). Other bacteria (b) are growing but not producing hydrolysis zones (X 3). **Fig. 25.2** Pure culture of *Actinoplanes* inoculated onto a decorticated ash twig in stream water. There is prolific growth as pellets in the liquid and on submerged portions of the twig (X 0.4). **Fig. 25.3** *Actinoplanes* phage from allochthonous leaf material in Windermere giving lysis of the host in the form of plaques on agar (X 2).

Fig. 25.4 *Actinoplanes* growth and sporangia on damp-incubated allochthonous leaf material from Windermere (X1000). **Fig. 25.5** *Actinoplanes* culture on agar in vertical section showing strongly marked palisade nature of the mycelium and sporangia forming at the surface only (X1000). **Fig. 25.6** *Actinoplanes* sporangia showing rounded off spores about to be released as motile cells (X1000). **Fig. 25.7** Accessory spore formation in conidia of *Actinoplanes* (X1000). **Fig. 25.8** *Streptosporangium* dehiscing to release chains of motile spores (X1000).

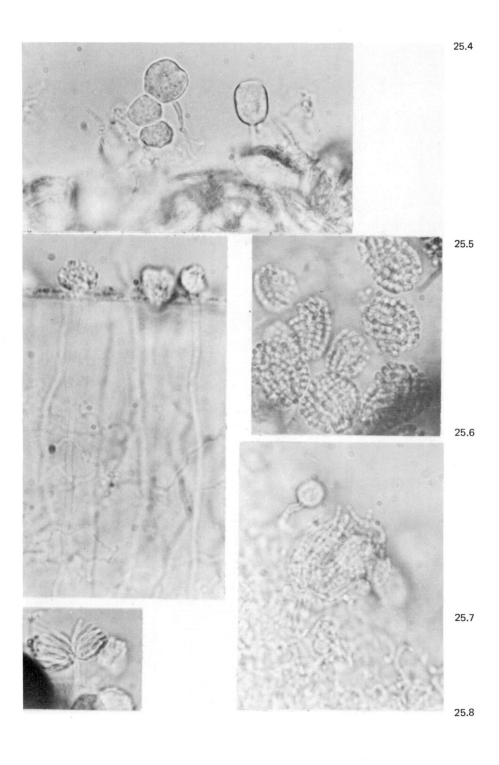

25.4

25.5

25.6

25.7

25.8

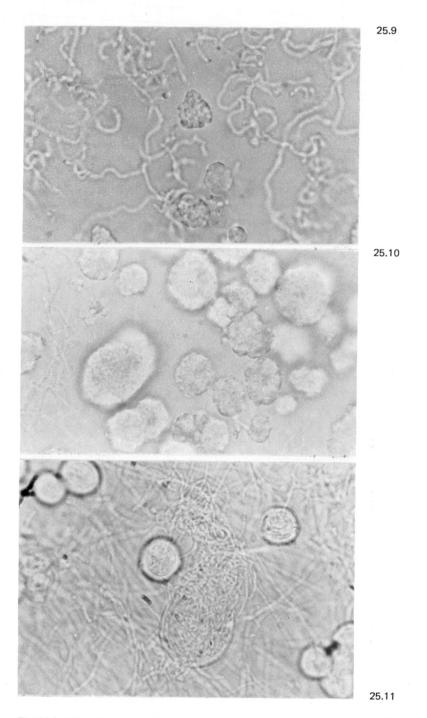

25.9

25.10

25.11

Fig. 25.9 *Actinoplanes* culture in surface view showing mycelium and sporangia (X1000). **Fig. 25.10** *Amorphosporangium* mature sporangia (X1000). **Fig. 25.11** *Spirillospora* dehiscing to release long filiform motile spores (X1000).

Records of direct observations made on aquatic Actinomycetes growing in their natural milieu are virtually non-existent so far. However, the author was able to find a few sporangia of *Actinoplanes missouriensis* Couch (Couch, 1963) on twigs left exposed in a stream for several weeks, encouraged by a very high recovery rate of this species in agar plated washings from parallel exposures. Moving to more indirect procedures the technique of damp incubation has potential, and using this on damp allochthonous leaf litter collected at the margin of Windermere it became possible to observe a variety of sporangial forms of the family Actinoplanaceae. Although *Actinoplanes* was the dominant recovery (Fig. 25.4), strains of *Spirillospora* (Fig. 25.11) and other unidentified genera were also present (Willoughby, 1969 a). Recourse to the classical microbiological method of plating water samples onto solidified nutrient agar has often been made and, although as mentioned above there is no antibiotic which will curb the growth of associated bacteria, several other associated procedures have been found helpful in this regard. Dr. N. P. Burman (personal communication) recommended a preliminary chlorination of the water sample before plating

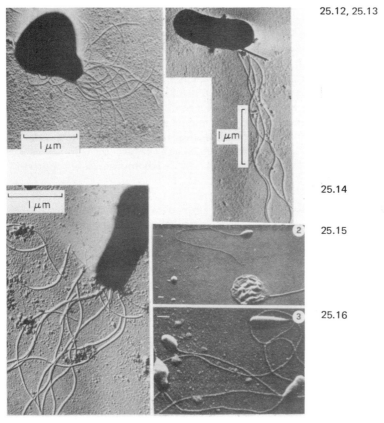

25.12, 25.13

25.14

25.15

25.16

Figs. 25.12-25.16 Electron-micrographs of Actinoplanaceae spores. **Fig. 25.12** *Actinoplanes,* showing polar tuft of flagella. **Fig. 25.13** *Spirillospora.* **Fig. 25.14** *Ampullariella.* **Fig. 25.15** *Actinoplanes* showing a single flagellum, just escaped from sporangium (bottom). **Fig. 25.16** Several *Actinoplanes* spores showing a single flagellum on each. **Figs. 25.12-25.14** from Higgins *et al.* (1967), Figs. 25.15, 25.16 from Locci and Petrolini Baldan (1971). In Figs. 25.15 and 25.16 the scale marks indicate 1μm.

and as applied by Willoughby (1969 b) the method was to treat with 4 ppm ammonia followed by 2 ppm chlorine as sodium hypochlorite for 30 minutes. At the end of this time the excess chlorine was neutralized with sodium thiosulphate, the correct amount of which had been calculated from titration of a duplicate sample. Unfortunately, although chlorination showed some effect in reducing bacterial competition, the evidence was that it had a strong differential action within the Actinomycetes also. Thus *Actinoplanes* recovery was reduced following chlorination but *Micromonospora* (Figs. 25.2, 25.24) recovery was seemingly greatly enhanced. Burman also reported (1968) that a preliminary heat treatment of a water sample before plating and even an elevated initial incubation temperature (30°C) could be helpful in reducing bacteria and obtaining correspondingly higher Actinomycete counts. However, the possibly selective nature of this procedure on the different Actinomycete genera has yet to be fully evaluated. More general benefit stems from the use of chitin-actidione (Lingappa and Lockwood, 1961; Willoughby, 1968) as the nutrient agar, a growth medium inhibitory to fungi and selective against many bacteria, although still allowing the myxobacteria to become troublesome on occasions (Fig. 25.1). The rationale for the use of chitin agar is that most Actinomycetes produce chitinase and hence can hydrolyse the colloidal carbon source supplied, but observation shows that some *Nocardia*-like forms which do not clear this medium will also grow well on it, on the first isolation plate. In these cases some soluble fraction produced in the autoclaving may perhaps be utilized. In his investigations of aquatic Actinomycetes, Masschelein (1966) has recommended the passage of water samples through a membrane filter which is incubated directly on a rather acid (pH 5—5.5) maltose-Sabouraud agar (Oxoid CM 41), with incorporated bromocresol green. Apparently the main objective in this system is to prevent the growth of troublesome aquatic bacteria such as *Pseudomonas fluorescens* Migula, but so far its possible advantages have not led to a widespread use. Rose bengal has also been recommended as a chemical agent to reduce bacteria in isolation procedures (Ottow, 1972), but only *Streptomyces* was encountered in this particular investigation,

So far then, methods for obtaining aquatic Actinomycetes have been adapted without much modification from those in use by water bacteriologists and mycologists or by students of soil Actinomycetes. However, the recent discovery of the peculiar motile-spored forms from littoral allochthonous leaf material (Figs. 25.17-25.22), and the difficulty experienced in observing and handling them, (Willoughby, 1969 a) has drawn attention to the possible limitations of current isolation methods for obtaining these micro-organisms from nature. Therefore, a future development in the study of aquatic Actinomycetes may well be the discovery of further novel and specialized forms, occupying particular micro-niches. Correspondingly specialized techniques may be necessary to obtain them. In this connection there are the observations of Shapiro *et al.* (1971) on what they consider to be free-living lacustrine forms, filtered out of the hypolimnion water of Lake Washington, and apparently associated with deposited iron on their mycelium. This may perhaps even imply a chemosynthetic habit, but it would be premature to speculate too far at present. From the knowledge currently available to us, aquatic Actinomycetes clearly have a role in the environment as heterotrophic decomposers. They have acquired a reputation for their capacity to taint water supplies, although the information presented here shows that there has been some equivocation over this, and the issue is still under active examination. With the increasing usage of 'second class' lowland supplies as potable waters and in the knowledge that the viable Actinomycete count of

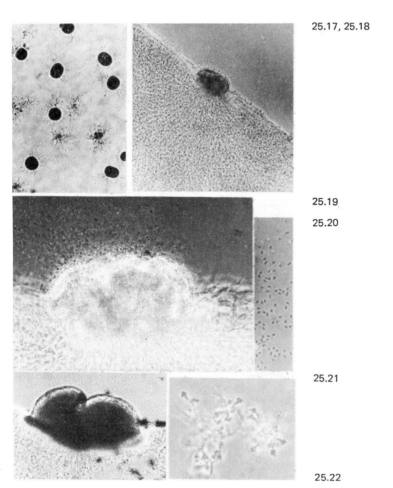

25.17, 25.18

25.19

25.20

25.21

25.22

Fig. 25.17 Young spore dome colonies in surface view on agar (X66). **Fig. 25.18** Vertical section of a spore dome colony on agar showing profuse radiating mycelium and spore release into the water (X66). **Fig. 25.19** A high power view of the central dome (X270). **Fig. 25.20** Motile spores from a spore dome (X666). **Fig. 25.21** Spore dome colony on chitin-yeast extract agar showing crustose sporing structure but little mycelium within the agar (X66). **Fig. 25.22** Spore head colony showing terminal aggregations of spores (X666).

a particular water seems to a great extent to be a function of the trophic status of its source, further studies on this aspect will certainly be warranted in the future.

Although the subject of this article is the Actinomycetes as they occur in the freshwater aquatic environment, the occurrence in marine situations may well be considered here briefly also. Early reports were that viable Actinomycetes only occurred in the sea in the littoral sediments, but it has been shown recently (Weyland, 1969 and personal communication) that they also occur in the benthic muds many miles from the nearest land mass; for example, on a Barents Sea and Norwegian Sea cruise of the *Anton Dohrn* in October 1969, they were found in situations from 150 to 200 miles from the mainland at depths of water of 100 to 1100 metres. There was a considerable variation in the recovery depending on the particular isolation agar used, chitin-peptone-yeast extract often being less productive than peptone-starch or sucrose nitrate, but figures of 100 viable units per milli-litre of wet sediment were not unusual. The numbers were such that it was con-cluded that these micro-organisms were not temporary survivors of terrestrial run-off, but part of the marine ecosystem.

25.2   Actinomycetes in Waters of Lakes and Reservoirs

The viable Actinomycete content of lake water has been examined by agar plating and seems generally to be rather low in Britain. Johnston (1972) found that of the English Lakes he examined in the summer all except Blelham Tarn usually had fewer than 10 viable Actinomycetes per millilitre and even after the autumnal overturn only this lake and Loweswater consistently gave figures greater than 20/ml. Willoughby (1969 a) also found very few Actinomycetes in certain lakes, for example only 5/ml in Thirlmere, the Manchester reservoir. Considering Blelham Tarn in more detail, Johnston's recorded numbers ranged from 3 (all *Micromonospora*)/ml to 61 (50 *Micromonospora*)/ml, and this compared with a slightly higher range recorded by Willoughby (1969 a) for the same lake, namely 60 to 125/ml. The total of 580 colonies obtained from water samples by Willoughby in his investigation at this lake comprised 442 *Micromonospora*, 34 *Streptomyces*, 29 *Nocardia* types, six *Actino-planes* and 69 sterile. The 307 colonies obtained by Johnston in a parallel investiga-tion on the same lake comprised 235 *Micromonospora*, 41 *Nocardia*, 23 *Streptomyces* and eight unidentified. Johnston found that when Buttermere, Derwentwater and Loweswater were sampled immediately after heavy rain in September 1969 there was a dramatic increase in *Nocardia* isolations, but only in the upper waters of the lake. In Loweswater at this time, the *Nocardia* content at 0, 5 and 10 metres was 24, 27 and 54/ml respectively, while it was only 1/ml at lower depths in the lake. On other sampling occasions *Nocardia* had only been recorded as 1-3/ml, irres-pective of depth. These results suggested that the spate of rainwater passing into the lake via the inflow streams was carrying a high *Nocardia* load into the position on the water profile which matched its own temperature and density. This position was probably in the epilimnion, just above the thermocline.

In a study of the vertical distribution of *Micromonospora* species in Blelham Tarn water, Cross and Collins (1966) noted an interesting situation in the month of October, just before the summer thermal stratification broke down completely at the onset of winter. At this time the temperature discontinuity in the lake was deep, at 9 metres, and at this depth and below down to the bottom mud at 13 metres there was a complete depletion of oxygen. Thus this lower portion of the lake was effectively isolated from the upper aerobic portion. *Micromonospora* numbers were low in the surface water and down to 9 metres depth, estimations ranging from 0 to 35/ml. At 9, 10, 11 and 12 metres, however, numbers were much higher and were 70, 100, 190 and 260/ml respectively. This is suggestive of considerable re-suspension of viable *Micromonospora* from the bottom mud of the lake at a time when this was anaerobic. Such field observations re-inforce others made in the laboratory that certain *Micromonospora* strains may be facultative anaerobes.

White (1962) examined the Actinomycete content of the water supplies of Welling-ton, New Zealand, by incubating samples on nutrient agars. Strains of *Micromono-spora globosa* Krassilnikov and of *Streptomyces* were isolated, but there were no representatives of *Nocardia*. Chlorinated water samples from the reservoirs were generally unproductive but a particular type of *Streptomyces* was consistently obtained from chlorinated water from the River Hutt. It was placed in the Hesseltine *et al.* (1954) classification scheme for *Streptomyces* in Group IV, characterized by an orange coloured vegetative mycelium and the absence of any soluble pigment on nutrient agars.

25.3   Actinomycetes in Waters of Streams and Rivers

There is evidence that the Actinomycete content of the waters of streams and rivers may generally be higher than that of the waters of lakes and reservoirs, and have a different specific composition. At Blelham Tarn, samplings were made in one day along the Tock How inflow stream and into the lake (Willoughby 1969 b). The total number of colonies recovered by plating was between five and six times as many in the stream as compared with the lake and the high Actinoplanaceae component of the stream water, including *Ampullariella* and *Streptosporangium* (Fig. 25.8) in addition to *Actinoplanes,* was almost unrepresented in the lake (Table 25.1). Similarly the *Streptomyces* and the *Nocardia*-type contents also showed a decline along the transect, but on the other hand *Micromonospora* maintained its level and even increased. Although the Tock How stream is notoriously polluted by chemical enrichment and hence may represent a special case, transect samplings on the same day at another and more natural inflow stream also gave an essentially similar picture. At this site the total number of colonies recovered was approximately three times as many in the stream as in the lake, with a similar pattern for the relative distribution of the genera as mentioned above. One possible explanation for the high Actinoplanaceae (especially *Actinoplanes*) content of streams and rivers may lie in the apparent predilection of these forms for decaying leaves and even wood (Willoughby, 1971) as growth substrata (Fig. 25.2) and the relatively greater abundance of these materials in such situations. The particularly high *Actinoplanes* content of Tock How Beck may perhaps also be a reflection of the capacity of this Actinomycete to draw on soluble nutrients (especially nitrogen and phosphorus) present in the water. Such a phenomenon has recently been described (Kaushik and Hynes, 1971; Willoughby and Redhead, 1973) for the aquatic fungi growing on cellulosic-type materials in lotic environments.

In the River Kent at Kendal in May 1969 there were high Actinomycete estimations from water samples, again with a well marked Actinoplanaceae component (Table 25.2). Sampling in relation to the entry of the town sewage effluent suggested that this had little effect downstream on the total micro-flora recovered. Only *Micromonospora* and *Streptomyces* were obtained from the actual treated effluent.

25.4   Actinomycetes in Lake Muds

As is the case with the waters of the English Lakes so also are the benthic muds beneath them dominated numerically by Actinomycetes of the three genera *Micromonospora, Nocardia* and *Streptomyces.* In American lakes also *Micromonospora* has been reported as a dominant Actinomycete genus in this situation (Umbreit and McCoy, 1941). However, there are some signs of the presence of a greater diversity of genera and species than that seen in lake water, and the persistent occurrence of *Streptosporangium* for example (Johnston, 1972; Willoughby, 1969 b), although always in relatively low numbers, is particularly intriguing. From a survey of the

TABLE 25.1 Actinomycetes at Blelham Tarn on 9 November 1967 sampled along a transect through the Tock How inflow stream and into the lake. Lake 1 is the point where the stream first mixed with lake water. Lake 2 is the surface water mid-way between this point and the lake centre, while Lake 3 is surface water at the lake centre. For each site Actinomycete numbers recorded are from a total water sample of 0.6 ml. Modified from Willoughby (1969 a).

	Actinoplanes	Other Actinoplanaceae	Micromonospora	Nocardia-types	Streptomyces	Sterile	Totals
Tock How Stream 1	8	49	13	64	88	71	293
Tock How Stream 2	13	52	13	14	42	105	239
Lake 1	15	43	15	15	25	79	192
Lake 2	0	0	35	1	4	13	53
Lake 3	2	0	40	0	5	12	59

TABLE 25.2 Actinomycetes at Watts Field, River Kent, Kendal on 8 May 1969. Sampling was in relation to the entry of the town sewage effluent (S), at stations immediately above (AS) and below (BS) this. Other sampling stations (100 AS and 100 BS) were 100 metres from the effluent entry.

	Temperature (°C)	O_2 % saturation	B.O.D. mg/litre (5 day)	Bacteria per ml ($\times 10^{-3}$)	Total Actinomycetes per ml	Actino-planaceae	Micro-monospora	Nocardia-types	Streptomyces
100AS	9.0	115	—	149	165	46	26	24	51
AS	9.0	112	—	150	219	39	31	33	53
S	13.0	60	23.0	1321	31	0	9	0	15
BS	12.7	63	19.8	1231	78	10	16	9	23
100 BS	9.3	98	—	184	333	87	91	33	86

Lake District lakes, Johnston examined 4987 colonies derived from benthic muds and of these he considered 2715 *Micromonospora,* 1322 *Streptomyces,* 691 *Nocardia,* 124 *Streptosporangium,* six *Actinomadura,* three *Dactylosporangium,* two *Microbispora,* two *Thermomonospora,* one *Actinoplanes* and 121 unidentified. The dominance of *Micromonospora* over *Streptomyces* was even more striking in the deeper muds; for example, at Blelham Tarn at 20 cm depth the isolates derived from one typical sampling comprised 120 *Micromonospora* and only three *Streptomyces,* two *Nocardia,* one *Streptosporangium* and three sterile. Johnston saw a correlation between the Actinomycete content of the surface benthic mud and the productivity status of the particular lake from which it was obtained. Thus, his calculated viable propagule numbers (x 10^{-4}) per gram dry weight of mud from Blelham Tarn, Coniston Water, Grasmere and Windermere S. basin were 277, 148, 134 and 68 respectively. These lakes are all productive and eutrophic. Parallel collections from the less productive and more oligotrophic lakes Buttermere, Wastwater, Thirlmere, Ennerdale Water and Devoke Water gave lower numbers of 46, 42, 39, 31 and 17 respectively. The recovery of large numbers of *Micromonospora, Nocardia* and *Streptomyces* strains by nutrient agar plating of surface mud of the Lake District lakes has provoked further enquiry. The question which arises is whether these Actinomycetes have an active role in decomposition in the benthic deposits, in which case they are likely to be present in the form of viable mycelium, or whether they have no active role but are merely present as viable but inert spores washed in from the surrounding soils. In an attempt to answer this question Johnston (1972) employed homogenization and ultrasonification techniques both on pure culture material and on freshly collected surface mud slurries (Fig. 25.28). In this work, pure *Micromonospora* spore suspensions were obtained from agar plates by flooding with sterile water and lightly abrading the surface spore layer with a glass tool. *Micromonospora* mycelium was obtained by growing cultures in agitated flasks of nutrient medium, but since there is sporulation in submerged culture it always contained at least some spores. When the suspensions of spores were homogenized and sampled at intervals up to 90 minutes, there was no change in the viable count. When the suspensions of mycelium and spores were homogenized, there was a large increase in the viable count after 5 and 10 minutes, but this was halved at 60 minutes and the count then remained constant. This pattern of results suggests that *Micromonospora* spores are not affected by homogenization but the mycelium is broken up, giving an initial increase in the viable count. With further homogenization the mycelium is so disrupted that non-viable units result and the total count from suspensions of mycelium plus spores is then attributed entirely to the presence of the latter. When surface mud from Windermere was homogenized and analysed for the presence of *Micromonospora,* it behaved as a mucelium-spore mixture in that the viable count showed an increase from the initial value and then a fall to a lower value which remained constant. On the other hand, analyses for *Nocardia* and *Steptomyces* showed smaller increases, or none at all, with increasing homogenization time. The conclusion was therefore made that surface lake mud contained *Micromonospora* both as mycelium and spores but contained *Nocardia* and *Streptomyces* predominantly as spores only. Ultrasonification also distinguishes spores from mycelium within the total viable count, its application to mixtures having no effect on the former but being lethal to the latter. When surface mud from Windermere was subjected to ultrasonification, analysis for the presence of *Micromonospora* again gave results suggesting occurrence both asmycelium and as spores also. The viable count fell with time from its initial value as ultrasonification proceeded. On the other hand, ultrasonification results for *Nocardia* and *Strepto-myces* again suggested that representatives of these genera occurred in lake mud predominantly as spores since they showed no fall in their viable counts as ultra-sonification proceeded. Johnston continued his investigation of the roles of the Actinomycetes in surface lake muds by introducing extraneous substrates to these in the laboratory and observing whether or not there was any resultant growth of the Actinomycetes. This was deemed to be measured, rather indirectly, by demonstrating an increase in the total viable plate count from the mud. When puri-fied cellulose plus chitin was introduced, such an increase was demonstrated in the *Micromonospora* count, but no such increase occurred for *Nocardia* or for *Strepto-myces*. Yet again, therefore, *Micromonospora* was seen as the active Actinomycete constituent of benthic lake mud, in marked contrast to the seeming inactivity of the other associated genera. Although these results of Johnston's are extremely interesting and provocative, it is important that they should not be regarded as having closed this issue entirely. In the growth experiments, for example, the possibility can be considered that Streptomycetes grew also but, since they did not sporulate in the system used, their activity did not produce any expression as an increased count from plating. Again, if competitive effects are considered, it may well be that the establishment of what amounts to enrichment conditions induced phage activity in the Streptomycetes but not in the *Micromonospora* strains. As we see the situation at present, *Streptomyces* phage seems likely to be active in the benthic muds while *Micro-monospora* phage has a more problematical activity. Its presence there has yet to be demonstrated.

Johnston sampled from a shallow lake near Silloth, Cumberland, where the water was very acid, having a pH of 4.9. The isolation of *Micromonospora* and *Strepto-myces* from the surface benthic mud there once again provoked the inquiry whether representatives of these genera could be active in such a situation, since low pH's are generally inhibitory to Actinomycetes in pure culture. There was the possibility that washed-in spores having a limited viability, but no possible potentiality for growth, accounted for all the isolations. Accordingly, surface mud dilutions were plated onto chitin agar with the pH adjusted to 4.5 or 5.0 and on both of these media, strains of both *Micromonospora* and *Streptomyces* were isolated. This suggested that some at least of the strains present in the mud did indeed have the potentiality to grow at the environmental pH, leaving open the possibility that they may be active even in a highly acid lake.

Johnston enlarged our conception of the 'wash-in' of Actinomycete spores by studying the distribution of *Thermoactinomyces vulgaris* Tsiklinsky in the English Lakes. Strains of *T. vulgaris* have definite morphological characteristics, but in addition they are strongly thermophilic and hence seem unlikely to be active in aquatic situations in Britain. Previous workers had employed an incubation tempera-ture of 60°C in making isolations but in this connection Johnston pointed out that there was some variation in temperature tolerance of the various strains recognized. Some had been isolated with a temperature as low as 40°C and were unable to grow above 50°C in subculture, while conversely others were isolated at 55°C and were unable to grow at 40°C. In view of the possibility that setting the isolation tempera-ture too high might lead to loss of some of the true *T. vulgaris* component, while setting it too low might confuse the results by giving too many marginal thermo-philes, Johnston made his incubations from nature at 50°C. Addition of cyclo-heximide and novobiocin to half-strength nutrient agar gave a highly selective growth medium and the only complication on the isolation dishes was the phenomenon of auto-inhibition, which occurred when the colonies were very crowded. In the laboratory, the isolates showed both their thermophilic nature and their potential longevity at normal temperatures. For example, strains which were incubated on agar for 2 years at 15, 20, 25 and 30°C showed no visible growth, but on re-incubation at 50°C typical colonies appeared. At Blelham Tarn, agar plating determined the numbers of *T. vulgaris* spores in 50 ml of water samples and these increased with depth from three at the surface to 65 at 6 metres and 110 at the maximum depth of 12 metres. At the lake mud surface at this depth there were 207 x 10^4 spores per gram dry weight. These surface mud figures compare with 309 x 10^4/g obtained from Windermere, 44 x 10^4/g from Wastwater, 13 x 10^4/g from Buttermere and only 10 x 10^4/g from Thirlmere. Since the origin of the *T. vulgaris* endospores is in composts, mouldy fodder and dungs, the disparity between these different figures is explained by the differing nature of the drainage basins of these lakes and their differing utilization for agriculture. The drainage basins of Blelham Tarn and Windermere include tracts of cultivated land and farms. In a farm in the Blelham Tarn basin, mouldy hay had 4.8 x 10^7 spores per gram dry weight of *T. vulgaris* and dung from cows eating it had 3.5 x 10^7 spores per gram. Wastwater and Buttermere lie in more mountainous regions and their drainage basins include bare rock and scree slopes with little low-lying level land suitable for cultivation, while Thirlmere is a reservoir, largely surrounded by coniferous plantations, with no farms allowed by the local authority. The longevity of *T. vulgaris* endospores washed into the aquatic environment was investigated further from the point of view of the sedimentary history. Using a Jenkin tube sample of the soft bottom deposits of Windermere, the *T. vulgaria* content was examined down to a depth of 20 cm, and although a steady decline in viability was apparent from the surface, down to this depth *T. vulgaris* was always recovered. Working from Tutin's (1955) published figures for the mean deposition rate for Windermere, 2.6 mm a year, the conclusion was reached that *T. vulgaris* endospores could survive there for at least 128 years. Such a time scale is comparable with the reported longevity of the species in dried soil.

25.5 The Status of *Micromonospora* and *Nocardia* Isolates from Freshwater

Johnston (1972) attempted to place the *Micromonospora* (Figs. 25.23 and 25.24) strains he obtained from lake mud into groups, based on colony morphology and pigment colours produced. In general, he found that the strains could be arranged into a spectrum or series of forms rather than in distinct groups representing species. However, he tentatively identified 64% of his strains as *Micromonospora chalcea* (Foulerton) Ørskov, 38% as *M. parva* Jensen and a few strains only as *M. purpurea* Luedemann et Brodsky.

Following much experience of isolating *Micromonospora* from various environments, Luedemann (1970) concluded that *M. chalcea, M. halophytica* Weinstein and strains matching ATCC 10026 were the most typical recoveries from aquatic situations. These forms also appeared to sporulate more readily and rapidly in an aqueous medium than *M. carbonacea* Luedemann et Brodsky and *M. echinospora* Luedemann et Brodsky. *Micromonospora* sp. ATCC 10026 and kindred strains produce the antibiotic micromonosporin, and were originally mis-identified as *M. fusca* Jensen. However, Luedemann has pointed out that *M. fusca* is predominantly a soil taxon and is characterized by the production of dark brown to black diffusible pigment on agar medium, whereas the isolates under discussion produce a yellow diffusible pigment which is fluorescent under ultra violet light.

685

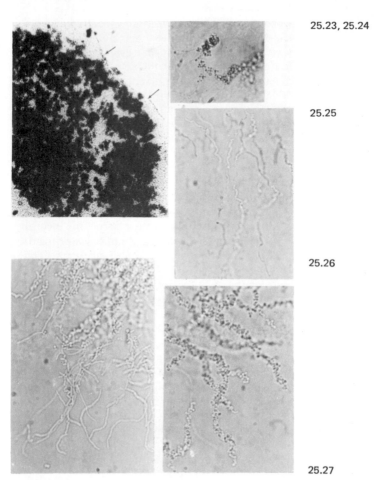

25.23, 25.24

25.25

25.26

25.27

Fig. 25.23 *Micromonospora* colony in vertical section on agar showing how the growth with dark spores is almost entirely below the surface (arrows) (X66). **Fig. 25.24** *Micromonospora* mycelium and spores (X666). **Fig. 25.25** *Nocardia* (Nt) colony on agar (X666). **Figs. 25.26, 25.27** *Nocardia* (Lspi) colonies on agar (X666).

In a study of *Nocardia* strains at Blelham Tarn, Willoughby (1969 b) distinguished distinct types on the grounds of morphology, chitinolytic activity and pigment production. So far, these cannot be related to species, and code designations are adopted. Nt (Fig. 25.25) occurred at three soil sites in the drainage basin, and on Blelham Tarn itself was relatively numerous in the inflow streams but less so in the outflow stream. On the other hand, it was barely represented in lake mud or in the lake water. These records are suggestive of a soil organism, the spores of which are readily washed into streams and rivers, but which do not develop there. Nt was the type of *Nocardia* which Johnston found to be washed into Buttermere, Derwentwater and Loweswater following rain, as described above. Lspi-type *Nocardia* (Figs. 25.26, and 25.27) was also recovered from the drainage basin soils but only if these were waterlogged. In the lake it was found in quantity in the bottom mud, and in the mud of the inflow streams it was even more prominent relatively, displacing *Micromonospora* in some numerical estimations. It is concluded that Lspi is a truly aquatic form. Goodfellow

(1971) in a study of the numerical taxonomy of numerous *Nocardia* strains placed four (of Lspi?) isolated by Dr. T. Cross from Blelham Tarn into his subgroup 14 G, with no specific epithet, and one in subgroup 1 B named as *N. asteroides* (Eppinger) Blanchard.

25.6 Specialized Actinomycete Taxa from Freshwater

The strongest evidence which could be produced to show that Actinomycetes have shown an evolutionary adaptation to life in freshwater would be the demonstration that there are distinct morphological or physiological ecotypes in the environment. In the case of the fungi the large tetraradiate spore of the aquatic hyphomycetes, presumably produced to aid attachment in flowing water, is a classical example of such a morphological adaptation. Physiological adaptation is seen in the tolerance of low oxygen regimes in the aquatic Blastocladiales, culminating in the evolution of the facultative anaerobe *Aqualinderella fermentans* Emerson et Weston in stagnant pools in South America. When the bacteria are considered, the potential range of morphological adaptation is less wide but we see for example specialized attachment devices in iron bacteria of the genus *Leptothrix*. At the physiological level we note the evolution of forms such as the sulphur oxidizing bacteria, *Achromatium* and *Beggiatoa,* with a requirement for free H_2S and only low levels of oxygen. In freshwater they find these conditions on the surface mud of stratified lakes just prior to the complete de-oxygenation of the hypolimnion water in early summer.

Turning to the Actinomycetes, the attention which the freshwater component has attracted has hardly been sufficient so far to provide the background for parallel findings. However, there is already some evidence that further and more detailed investigations may well be more productive in this respect. For example, according to Roach and Silvey (1958) there are specialized strains of aquatic Actinomycetes which may not only combine the morphological characters of both *Micromonospora* and *Streptomyces* but also exhibit an alternation of haplobiontic and diplobiontic thalli. The former, the primary mycelium, has hyphae 0.2-0.6 μm in diameter and liberates endo-fragments which eventually fuse as gametes. The zygotes so formed give rise to the secondary mycelium, which has wider hyphae of 0.6-1.2 μm in diameter and bears *Micromonospora*-type spores in lateral clusters. Later in its development the secondary mycelium also produces chains of *Streptomyces*-type spores. Both types of spore can give rise to the primary mycelium once more. It is not at all clear what biological advantage in freshwater might be conferred by such a life cycle, as compared with the normally accepted one for Actinomycetes which does not recognize the occurrence of any sexual stage or chromatic doubling.

In another study of life cycles by Higgins and Silvey (1966), two *Streptomyces* strains were grown under continuous observation in a slide culture system with control of the gaseous environment. These strains were odour producing and had been isolated from algal mats in a reservoir. On this occasion the secondary spore bearing hypha was found to originate from the primary hypha without any preliminary fusion. Furthermore, the secondary hypha, which always bore chains of spores in the orthodox *Streptomyces* fashion, could be borne on an isolated colony produced from a single spore. Thus the Roach and Silvey account of the life cycle observed previously was not substantiated on this occasion. However, this more recent investigation produced several interesting original observations. For example, it was found that when the culture system was anaerobic, spore germination and the development of the primary mycelium could occur, but not the secondary mycelium. Without formation of the secondary mycelium there was no odour or pigment production. However, when anaerobic conditions were applied late in the development of the primary mycelium, the secondary mycelium could occasionally grow as a faculta-tive anaerobe.

The examination of damp decaying allochthonous leaves at the margin of Windermere (Willoughby, 1969 a) suggests that this material provides a unique micro-habitat for certain Actinomycetes which are so far unknown elsewhere. At the present level of investigation they are distinguished on morphological grounds and are characterized by the possession of motile spores which are borne on hyphal apices of the mycelium.

Two types of mycelial organization are distinguished. 'Spore dome' colonies (Figs. 25.17-25.21) are small, without obvious pigment, and only 1-2 mm in diameter on chitin agar after 6 weeks' incubation of washings made from the leaves. The colonies are sterile except for a central projecting dome where the spore bearing phialides are massed together to form a sporodochium. Generally the spores are abstricted successively, but under certain circumstances septation of the whole length of the phialide to give spores may occur, and if the growth medium is enriched with yeast extract, crustose masses of spores usually develop (Fig. 25.21). The spores become motile only on the addition of free water, after a variable time lag. Motile spores have a single group of about five polar flagella.

'Spore head' colonies (Fig. 25.22) are also small, again only 1-2 mm in diameter after 6 weeks' incubation and usually entirely lacking in any kind of projection above the agar surface. Inflated phialides bearing one to several spores ('spore heads') are totally immersed in the agar, but spore motility has been induced by adding water to sections of the whole colony. As in *Micromonospora*, the occurrence of the growth and spores entirely within the thickness of the agar could imply a tolerance of low oxygen tensions. 'Spore head' isolates have so far not been subcultured satis-factorily on orthodox media, but the application of humic acids has shown some promise in this respect. Occasionally 'spore head' colonies show spore domes in addition, but these are rarely as described above and more usually are derived from highly complex aggregations of spherical groups of phialides, the phialides in each sphere radiating from a common point. An additional complication is that filiform sterile hyphae can also be present in the spheres. Presumably these may function as cohesive structures. In addition to the central mass of spheres comprising the dome, other single and subsidiary ones can also occur on the surface of the agar, grading down at the periphery of the colony to individual sporing phialides. In these mixed colonies, dome and head spores are similar in size and shape, with the former more readily becoming motile on mounting in water. Considering some individual samplings which yielded spore dome and spore head colonies, portions of one leaf from an Ash Landing, Windermere collection of August 1966 gave 155 colonies comprising 120 domed types, 33 *Actinoplanes* and two *Streptomyces*. Of these domed colonies, 102 were obtained from the first of four successive washes, implying a ready dislodgement from the substratum. Again, from Ash Landing and other sites, in March 1967, por-tions of eight separate leaves yielded 1004 Actinomycete colonies at the first wash, including 173 spore dome, 10 Actinoplanaceae, four *Streptomyces,* three spore head and a large number unidentified. On other occasions, however, fewer of these peculiar sporing colonies were obtained, for example in February 1967 portions of 32 leaves derived from four different sites at Esthwaite Water and Windermere gave 293 colonies including 56 *Streptomyces,* 25 Actinoplanaceae, three spore dome and two *Micromonospora.* It was noteworthy in all these leaf washes that *Micromonospora,* such a dominant genus in the water and mud samplings, was obtained rather rarely, as was *Streptomyces.* The evidence seems strong that the leaves tend to support the elements of a true endemic Actinomycete micro-flora and that viable but inert spores of extraneous species are not attracted physically to this material.

25.7   Environmental and Nutritional Requirements of Aquatic Actinomycetes

The Actinomycetes obtained from freshwater grow as aerobic micro-organisms. However, the recovery of *Micromonospora, Nocardia* and *Streptomyces* from the surface benthic mud of Blelham Tarn during the summer season, when the lake water was thermally stratified and depeleted of oxygen at its lower levels, suggests that at least partial anaerobiosis can be resisted. There was also some evidence from the same lake that a few *Micromonospora* and *Nocardia*-type Actinomycetes obtained from below the surface mud could actually grow as facultative anaerobes, but these seem to be a very small component of the total population (Willoughby, 1969 b).

In a study of cellulose decomposition by Actinomycetes, Jones and Bradley (1964) investigated 63 stains from various sources. These included a number of *Nocardia* and *Streptomyces* strains, and of these only *N. madurae* (Vincent) Blanchard and *S. violaceoruber* Waksman et Curtis were active. However, strains of the genera *Actinoplanes* and *Micromonospora,* representatives of which occur in freshwater as described above, were shown to be cellulose decomposers. Johnston (1972) studied numerous *Micromonospora* strains from lake mud and showed that these were able to utilize cellulose and chitin for growth. Other results of possible ecological significance were that the majority of strains could also utilize xylan and *p*-hydroxybenzoic acid. Xylan is an important component of the hemicelluloses associated with the plant cell wall and is the polysaccharide, following cellulose, which occurs most abundantly in nature. *p*-Hydroxybenzoic acid is one of the phenolic breakdown products of both humic acids and lignin. However, none of the strains investigated could utilize humic acids, and only a few were able to utilize vanillin or *p*-hydroxybenzaldehyde, which are also breakdown products of lignin. The significance of the production of chitinase by so many Actinomycete strains, including those isolated from water, is not properly understood at present. As in the case of the fungi (Unestam, 1966), it may not necessarily imply a predilection of these micro-organisms for chitinous substrates in nature.

A wide range of genera and species can be obtained on nutrient agars which lack growth factors such as vitamins, suggesting that the Actinomycetes are undemanding in this regard. However, in the experience of the author and other workers, it is not unusual for certain Actinomycetes, for example *Streptosporangium* representatives, to grow better on the initial isolation medium than on the same medium in subculture. In these instances the lack of accessory growth factors, possibly derived from the water sample in the first instance, may be responsible. It is noted that Nonomura and Ohara (1969) have reported B-vitamin requirements for strains of *Streptosporangium* they isolated from soil.

25.8   Sporulation Phenomena in the Aquatic Actinoplanaceae

Although representatives of the Actinoplanaceae, particularly *Actinoplanes,* can be obtained consistently from stream and river water they are probably considerably underestimated there at present. This is because their recognition for enumeration following agar plating of water samples depends on sporangium formation by the developing colony, and this may be a very capricious phenomenon. In the study on the Actinoplanaceae of allochthonous leaves (Willoughby, 1969 a), *Actinoplanes* strains usually formed sporangia readily on the chitin agar isolation medium but *Amorphosporangium* (Fig. 25.10) and *Ampullariella* strains did not. However, the colonies were recognized as presumptive Actinoplanaceae by their production of yellow and orange pigments and the lack of any aerial mycelium, and standard manipulations to induce sporangium formation in aquatic micro-organisms, such as cutting out small slivers into water, often gave success. When the leaf material from Ash Landing, Windermere was damp-incubated, sporangia of an unusual type, possibly related to *Pilimelia* Kane (1966), were observed directly and isolations were obtained. These isolations failed to form sporangia on chitin, chitin-yeast extract and starch-casein agars both dry and immersed in water. Furthermore, material first grown in liquid as pellets and then transferred to sterile filtered lake water, a classical method for sporangium induction in the aquatic phycomycetes, was also unproductive. Consequently, these *Pilimelia*-type strains were very challenging as far as sporangium induction *in vitro* was concerned. Some of the observations so far had hinted that certain of the Actinoplanaceae fruit better with a chemically refractory or impoverished growth medium than an enriched one. For example, some Actinoplanes isolates made from twigs left exposed in a stream actually formed sporangia readily on a plain agar-tellurite solidified growth medium, whereas they were sterile once again on more standard media (Willoughby, 1971). This is in contrast to *Streptosporangium,* which seems to require a yeast extract addition to oatmeal agar to fruit well (Johnston, 1972), and to the aquatic Actinomycetes of the 'spore dome' and 'spore head' type discussed above, where the addition of yeast extract again often produces a dramatic enhancement of sporulation. Chemically refractory components of the freshwater niche which the *Pilimelia*-type strains inhabit were therefore considered as possibly being of importance in the full growth cycle. In this connection it was decided to test humic acids as agents for sporangium induction (Willoughby *et al.,* 1968) as these occur both in the littoral leaf deposits and in the water lapping it where they are present as a part of the small (circa 2 ppm) dissoloved organic content. Humic acid samples from three separate sources were tested. The terrestrial source of humic acids was an acid blanket-bog peat. This was extracted with acetone and then with NaOH. The filtrate was acidified with HCl and the resulting precipitate centrifuged off and air-dried. The marginal source of humic acids consisted of compacted decomposing tree leaves (mainly oak and alder) collected from the shore of Windermere. The aquatic source of humic acids was sand-filtered water from Windermere. This was extracted with an anion-exchange resin and eluted with NaCl, then precipitated with HCl and treated as described above. In the experiment, a final concentration of 0.5% humic acids was used, the material being dissolved in dilute NaOH and incorporated into 2% agar, with a final pH of 7.0-7.3. In addition, plain agar (pH adjusted) was poured in control dishes. With the terrestrial sample of humic acids, growth was sparse but of a slightly greater density than that on the plain agar control dishes. This indicated only limited utilization of the added material. However, sporangium formation occurred in both of the two *Pilimelia*-type isolates tested, for the first time on a reproducible laboratory growth medium. The marginal sample of humic acids also gave sporangia, in one of the two isolates tested, but the sample of humic acids from Windermere water was quite ineffective. However, the latter sample was not toxic and in fact supported abundant sporangium production in a stock *Actinoplanes* isolate which had fruited readily on most standard Actinomycete media. Thus there is the suggestion from this work that complex organic materials which occur in nature may be available to Actinomycetes and have effects on their growth. There is also the suggestion that the biological effects of humic acids may be different, to parallel the different sources from which the latter are obtained. The possibility arises that the various humic acid fractions have different molecular sizes and that these determine the response of the micro-organism.

In an attempt to analyse further the Actinomycete sporulation factor in humic acids, these were subjected to simple degradative treatments using water and mineral acids (Willoughby and Baker, 1969). Humic acids (HA) are probably a heterogeneous mixture of macromolecules, the composition of which depends on the source and isolation technique. Boiling water removes polysaccharides, phenolic acids and bound amino acids (e.g. proteins, polypeptides). Boiling 0.5N HCl yields carbohydrates, phenols, amino acids, and iron. Boiling 50% (5 N) HCl yields phenols, amino acids, and iron. If the hot water extracts are acid boiled, black insoluble products are obtained (e.g. ABS/WBF). These are probably formed by the coupling of carbohydrates or their breakdown products (e.g. furfural) with themselves, phenols or other constituents. The parent humic acids (HA) were refluxed with distilled water and with 5 N HCl for 20 hours, after which the soluble products were removed from the residue by filtration. This gave a water boiled solid (WBS/HA), a water boiled filtrate (WBF/HA), an acid boiled solid (ABS/HA), and an acid boiled filtrate (ABF/HA). The water boiled products were then submitted to acid boiling procedures giving the solids ABS/WBS/HA and ABS/WBF/HA, also the filtrates ABF/WBS/HA and ABF/WBF/HA. Thus nine separate products (including the parent material) were available for test. In order to examine the growth effects of humic acid and its derivatives in a systematic way, test strains were grown under standard conditions in 0.1% solutions of these. The results from these liquid culture experiments using several Actinoplanaceae strains were that the total growth, as measured by the final dry weight of mycelium achieved, was very much a function of the nitrogen content of the particular HA preparation used. Thus the parent HA material, which had a nitrogen content of only 3.9%, gave combined yields of only 12 mg, which were no greater than those from the plain water controls. On the other hand ABF/HA, which had a nitrogen content of 9.9% and an amino acid content of 40%, gave much higher yields of 34 mg of mycelium. Again, WBS/HA, with a nitrogen content of 2.8%, gave combined yields of only 13 mg, while ABF/WBS/HA, with a nitrogen content of 10.5% and a high amino acid content, gave yields of 36 mg of mycelium.

To examine the sporangium induction effects of these HA preparations, they were incorporated into agar and inoculated with several different strains of the Actinoplanaceae which were known to be reluctant to fruit, and representing several different genera. In the case of HA, sporangia formed in 3-5 days in all the test strains, as they did on WBS/HA, and in no case was a derivative material more efficacious than the parent one. The derivative materials with low or no efficacy for sporangium induction were the filtrates, particularly ABF/WBS/HA, on which the sporangia did not form until 23 days had elapsed in one instance, and not at all in the most recalcitrant isolates. Thus, growth and fruiting effects of humic acids and their derivatives on the Actinoplanaceae are seen as mutually exclusive phenomena. If a preparation enhances growth through its ready availability of nutrients, it is unlikely to promote sporangium formation. Although the converse is true up to a point, and the central aromatic core of the humic acid macromolecule seems to hold the clue to the fruiting effect, it is noted that the latter could not be enhanced by stripping away the smaller peripheral molecules.

25.9 Actinomycete Virus in Freshwater

The occurrence of phage-type viruses of *Actinoplanes* and *Streptomyces* has been demonstrated in freshwater (Willoughby *et al.,* 1972), using the technique of host enrichment and exposure followed by testing for activity, as demonstrated by plaque formation (Fig. 25.3). The distribution of *Actinoplanes* phage in a lake system seems to correlate well with the known distribution of the host. Thus *Actinoplanes* had been isolated readily from the allochthonous leaf material lying on the shores of Lake District lakes but hardly ever from the actual lake water and not at all from the benthic lake mud. On the other hand, *Actinoplanes* was readily obtained also from the flowing water of streams and rivers as mentioned above. Correspondingly, *Actinoplanes* phage was equally readily obtained from the allochthonous leaves and the waters of local streams (1 viable unit per millilitre in Wilfin Beck, a Windermere inflow stream), less readily obtained from the waters of the lakes (1 viable unit per 25 ml in Blelham Tarn, and 1 per 100 ml in Windermere) and not obtained at all from the benthic lake muds. These results, arguing that viable phage only occurs where the host is active, with no suggestion of a wash-in effect, suggest that phage distribution might be a powerful tool to use in ecological studies. In particular, it might be expected to shed further light on the role of *Streptomyces* in freshwater. In the initial results reported, a *Streptomyces* phage from benthic lake mud lysed a *S. griseus* (Krainsky) Waksman et Henrici (?) isolated from there but did not lyse a soil *S. griseus.* This argued that distinct *Streptomyces* ecotypes existed in the mud. However, further testing of a large number of local soil isolates of *Streptomyces* has now shown that phage capable of attacking these often does occur in lake mud, and the simple initial working hypothesis is abandoned. Phage studies on *Streptomyces* are greatly complicated by the variety of strains and species which can be isolated locally and the polyvalent nature of the phages which attack them. The highly specific nature of the *Actinoplanes* phage obtained was demonstrated in cross-testing and the fine structure was also contributive in this direction. The contractile tail sheath which the *Actinoplanes* phage showed is unreported for the phages of *Dactylosporangium, Nocardia, Thermoactinomyces, Thermomonospora* or *Streptomyces.*

25.10 The Resistance of Actinomycetes to Chlorination in Freshwater

In view of the increasing use of chlorination to disinfect potable water, the resistance which waterborne Actinomycetes may show to this treatment has attracted some interest. An instance is cited by Popalisky and Pogge (1967) for the Kansas City water supply. As mentioned above this attribute has even been made use of in current isolating techniques, and evidence for a differential effect has been presented. Johnston (1972) investigated the effect of chlorination on lake mud, and once again he was able to control the contact time by neutralizing with sodium thiosulphate when this had expired. Using a contact time of 15 minutes, the non-actinomycete bacterial flora of the mud was reduced by 90-95% with 5 ppm chlorine.

Since the Actinomycetes were more resistant to chlorine at this level of addition, they benefited from reduced bacterial competition on the isolation dishes from which the numerical results were calculated, and all three of the dominant genera *Micromonospora*, *Nocardia* and *Streptomyces* showed an apparent increase over the initial estimation values. As was the case with water, the resistance of *Micromonospora* from lake mud to chlorine was particularly striking, and addition of higher chlorine doses, up to 15 ppm, gave an even greater apparent increase for this genus.

25.11   Actinomycetes and Tastes and Odours

A connection between the presence of Actinomycetes and the taste and odour tainting of water and the fish it may contain has been suspected for many years (Adams, 1929; Thaysen, 1936). In this regard most so-called tastes are, in fact, odours, the misconception arising because the odour is perceived when the water is in the observer's mouth. Because of the fugitive nature of many odours in water, however, and the essentially subjective nature of their recognition and detection, progress in their study has been rather slow. The Actinomycete connection also has been a matter of some controversy, one of the sources of confusion being that the monitoring of a water supply by means of Actinomycete counts has often failed to produce a clear relationship between these and the detectable odour intensity. One attempt to explain this was made by Silvey and Roach (1953) who reported that the Actinomycete contribution to odour in water is derived indirectly, through an algal association. They reported that in water from Lake Hefner, a part of the Oklahoma City water supply, tastes and odours which had previously been tentatively attributed to *Cladophora* were in fact more exactly ascribed to the Actinomycetes growing inside the decaying filaments of that alga. Plating of these filaments directly on nutrient agar did not demonstrate the Actinomycetes; the algae had first to be subjected to disruptive freezing or mechanical crushing before they could make contact with the nutrients and form colonies. Subsequently, samples of *Anabaena* and *Melosira* from other reservoirs with a history of odour production were also crushed and plated and these also yielded numerous Actinomycete colonies. Although no positive attributions were made to any specific Actinomycetes, it was stated that several genera were represented in the platings. Silvey ascribed a variety of water odours to the algal-Actinomycete association, these being described as aromatic, earthy, fishy, geranium, manurial, medicinal and even chemical.

In another contribution, Silvey (1953) examined the algal-Actinomycete association further by inoculating healthy *Chlorella* and *Cladophora* cells with spores of a *Streptomyces* strain which had been isolated from the parent clone of the latter alga. Twenty-four hours after introduction of the spores, motile 'micro-arthrospores' appeared inside the algal cells. Extractions from the culture fluid at this state yielded free methyl, dimethyl and butyl amines together with the amino acids glycine and alanine. Forty-eight hours after introduction of the spores, the algal cells showed slight signs of disintegration, and culture fluid extraction gave valeraldehyde and other undetermined short-chained aldehydes. These compounds in water in concentrations of 20-40 parts per billion gave musty, grassy and hay-like odours. When the algal-Actinomycete association was at the state of obvious destruction of the interior of the cells of the former partner, additional compounds were recovered from the culture fluid. These were saturated fatty acids such as butyric, isobutyric and valeric acids, which in concentrations of 10-40 parts per billion produced earthy

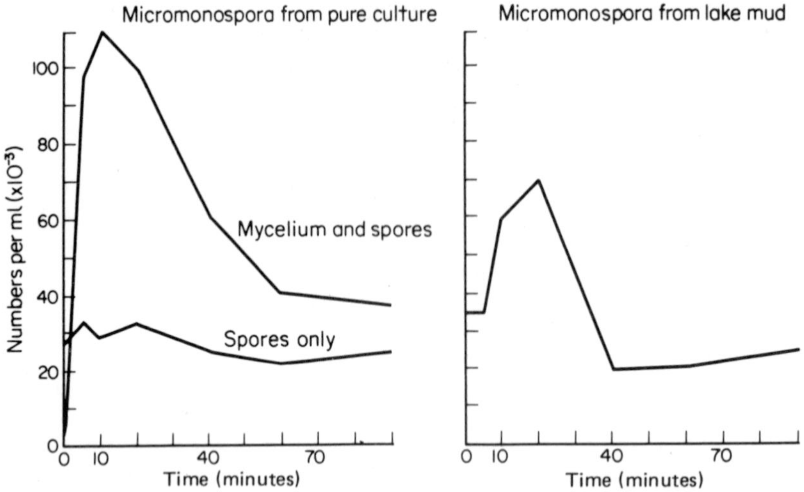

Fig. 25.28 A comparison of the effects of homogenization on *Micromonospora* in pure culture and on *Micromonospora* in lake mud from Windermere North Basin (after Johnston, 1972).

and musty odours. With the complete destruction of the alga, still other compounds were extracted from the medium, some of which were aromatic substances of unknown constitution, and these also were odoriferous.

Recent work by Gerber and Lechevalier (1965), by Gerber (1968) and by Rosen *et al.* (1970) has not followed the lines of Silvey's studies but rather has re-examined the possibility of a direct connection between the presence of Actinomycetes in water and the presence of a detectable odour. Their conclusions show a strong measure of agreement. Two strongly odoriferous organic compounds, namely geosmin and 2-methylisoborneol (Fig. 25.29) have been isolated both from water and from aquatic Actinomycetes in vitro, and their structural similarity suggests that additional odoriferous metabolites of similar structure again may yet remain to be discovered. Both compounds are aliphatic alcohols, geosmin being trans - 1,10-dimethyl-trans- 9- decalol and having a threshold odour concentration of 0.0002 mg/litre. Geosmin has also been obtained from the blue-green algae *Oscillatoria tenuis* Ag. and *Symploca muscorum* (Ag.) Gom. in addition to Actinomycetes, but 2- methylisoborneol is known only from representatives of the latter group so far. In the detection of 2 -methylisoborneol, Rosen *et al.* (1970) examined the musty odour in the Wabash River, Indiana and its headwater at Grand Lake, Ohio, the lake having a more constant and intense odour than the river. One highly odorous sample, of 1.5 litres, was extracted with ethyl ether and the combined extract concentrated to 1 ml and steam distilled. An ether extract of the steam distillate was analysed by gas chromatography. Three significant peaks occurred, these peaks being characterized by the interpolated boiling points of normal hydrocarbons with the same retention index. The peak with the lowest apparent boiling point (210°C) located the component containing all the characteristic odour of the water, although it constituted only 6% by weight of the total material volatilized in the steam. At the time of its examination, in March 1968, Grand Lake had an area of 7000 ha and an average depth of only 2.7 metres. Its shallow nature may have been responsible for its extremely high viable Actinomycete count which at 3200/ml was of a higher order of magnitude than any known to the author as being reported from Britain. Thirty-nine Actinomycetes were isolated from the lake for

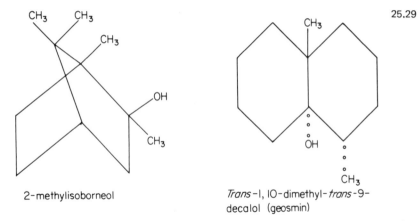

2-methylisoborneol

25.29

Trans-I, IO-dimethyl-*trans*-9-decalol (geosmin)

Fig. 25.29 Structural formulae of odoriferous organic compounds 2-methylisoborneol and Trans- 1, 10-dimethyl-trans-9-decalol (geosmin) (From Rosen *et al.* 1970).

tests, three of them yielding a musty odour, and from each of these the component with an apparent boiling point of 210°C was obtained again. Subsequently the musty component, 2 -methylisoborneol, was even obtained from a stock laboratory strain of *Streptomyces lavendulae* (Waksman et Curtis) Waksman et Henrici which had been isolated on a previous occasion, implying that it may be produced by a number of Streptomycetes. In order to confirm the presumptive presence of 2-methylisoborneol in Grand Lake water 3000 litre samples of water were filtered through carbon. The latter was extracted with chloroform, steam distilled, and extracted with ether. Of six extracts which were so worked up for examination, five gave 2 -methylisoborneol and one gave geosmin. In considering possible methods of control for the Actinomycete derived odours in water, the consensus opinion so far as that the actual odour, rather than the organism producing it, should be the target of attack. In this connection the high chemical stability of geosmin and 2-methylisoborneol has been noted, and indeed made use of, in the extraction procedure by steam distillation. Consequently oxidative treatments such as exposure to chlorine, ozone and permanganate have not been completely successful, as might be expected. Considering chemical methods, only adsorption onto activated carbon seems entirely effectual so far in removing these two compounds. Very recently a third terpenoid substance with odoriferous qualities has been isolated by Gerber (1972) from an Actinomycete, on this occasion *Streptomyces fradiae* (Waksman et Curtis) Waksman et Henrici. The substance, selina-4 (14), 7 (11) -diene-9-ol, had previously been known from hops.

Other odoriferous compounds derived from Actinomycetes which are believed to occur in water, namely mucidone (a carbonyl compound with the empirical formula $C_{12}H_{18}O_2$) and 5-methyl -3-heptanone are less stable than the terpenoids, and chemical treatment has more hope of success with them. It has been suggested (Bays *et al.,* 1970) that biological pre-treatment prior to coagulation in the water treatment plant might have some prospects of destroying the tainting materials by their metabolic utilization and transformation, with the appropriate micro-flora components for the reaction held on porous material such as pumice to increase the reaction. Work by Hoehn on Lake Hefner (reported in Bays *et al.,* 1970) suggests that *Bacillus cereus* Frankland et Frankland is a possible organism to utilize in this way. He found that water he examined lost its earthy or musty odour on standing and coincidentally there was an increase in its turbidity due to the presence of

Bacillus cereus. In trials on a lake, 9000 litres of *B. cereus* culture fluid, made cheaply using 0.5% tapioca dextrin, 0.5% low gluten cake flour and yeast extract, were added and showed some success in controlling the natural production of odour.

In summarizing the findings on the production of odoriferous compounds by Actinomycetes in freshwater, certain observations and discussions are of general interest. The importance of temperature is recognized. The prevalence of earthy and musty taints in the summer rather than the winter in the rivers and reservoirs of temperate countries is well known, and a temperature of 15-18°C or above generally seems to be a prerequisite for their production. Again, the water which gives 'vegetative', 'musty' or 'earthy' tastes in water supplies is usually derived from inland rivers and waterways rather than from wells. Thus there is the suggestion that the greater organic enrichment in river water may allow a more luxuriant Actinomycete growth and a metabolic expression of this in odour production.

Looking beyond the present there is the known trend towards increasing enrichment of lake and reservoir water due to multiple use, and to the application of fertilizers to the surrounding soils of the drainage basin. Consequently the problem of taste and odour in water supplies may become more pressing in the future. The possible correlation between organic enrichment of the water and Actinomycete odour parallels laboratory observations that in the Actinomycetes the nature of the substratum plays a great part in determining the nature of the odour produced. Thus on rich nitrogenous peptone media there is the production of 'barnyard' type odours due to the production of ammonia and amines. To consider the matter more critically, the actual direct evidence that Actinomycetes responsible for odours do grow in the water is rather slight. However, pointers in this direction are seen in the work of Bays *et al.* (1970) who sterilized large volumes of water from the River Severn water system and inoculated them with Actinomycetes. An increased count was obtained subsequently, suggesting that growth had occurred, and this was greater in reservoir and river water with a high degree of organic pollution than in water with only a low degree of organic pollution. As it is known that the bottom muds are a rich source of viable Actinomycetes (see above) there is the further possibility that the odoriferous compounds are produced there.

In Russian work by Issatchenko (1946), the release of odoriferous substances from muds into the water was investigated. It was suggested that the release was dependent not only on the number of Actinomycetes present, but also on the adsorbing capacity of the bottom material. Sandy muds liberated a marked odour whilst clay muds, being strongly adsorptive, released little odour to the overlying water. Another possibility is that the actual Actinomycete-derived odour is not produced in water at all but is washed in from the surrounding soil together with mycelium and spores of the organisms. In this connection Masschelein (1966) is of the opinion that, in certain circumstances, winter rather than summer conditions in a European climate regime may cause taste and odour problems, attributed on these occasions to melting snow carrying soil from the drainage basin into the water system. Again, the odoriferous metabolites may only be released from the Actinomycetes during lysis or their decomposition by other aquatic micro-organisms, after growth in freshwater or after being washed in from soil.

References

ADAMS, B. A. (1929). 'The *Cladothrix* dichotoma and allied organisms as a cause of an 'indeterminate' taste in chlorinated water.' *Wat. Wat. Engng.*, 31, 327-329.

BAYS, L. R., BURMAN, N. P., and LEWIS, W. M. (1970). 'Taste and odour in water supplies in Great Britain: a survey of the present position and problems for the future.' *Wat. Treat. Exam.* 19, 136-160.

BURMAN, N. P. (1968). 'Microfungi and actinomycetes in water.' *Rep. Results bact. chem. Exam. Lond. Wat.,* 43, 24-27.

CROSS, T., and COLLINS, V. G. (1966) '*Micromonospora* in an inland lake.' IX Int. Congr. Microbiol. Moscow, 11 pp. (cyclostyled). *Coll. Pap. Freshwat. biol. Ass.,* 639.

COUCH, J. N. (1963). 'Some new genera and species of the Actinoplanaceae.' *J. Elisha Mitchell scient. Soc.,* 79, 53-70.

GERBER, N. N. (1968). 'Geosmin, from micro-organisms, is Trans-1, 10—Dimethyl - Trans-9-Decalol.' *Tetrahedron Lett.,* 25, 2971-2974.

GERBER, N. N. (1972). 'Sesquiterpenoids from actinomycetes.' *Phytochemistry,* 11, 385-388.

GERBER, N. N., and LECHEVALIER, H. A. (1965). 'Geosmin, an earthy-smelling substance isolated from Actinomycetes.' *Appl. Microbiol.,* 13, 935.

GOODFELLOW, M. (1971). 'Numerical taxonomy of some nocardioform bacteria.' *J. gen. Microbiol.,* 69, 33-80.

HESSELTINE, C. W., BENEDICT, R. G., and PRIDHAM, T. G. (1954). 'Useful criteria for species differentiation in the genus *Streptomyces.*' *Ann. NY Acad. Sci.,* 60, 136-151.

HIGGINS, M. L., LECHEVALIER, M. P., and LECHEVALIER, H. A. (1967). 'Flagellated Actinomycetes.' *J. Bact.,* 93, 1446-1451.

HIGGINS, M. L., and SILVEY, J. K. G. (1966). 'Slide culture observations of two freshwater Actinomycetes.' *Trans. Am. microsc. Soc.,* 85, 390-398.

ISSATCHENKO, V. L. (1946). 'Flavors and tastes of water.' *Priroda Mosk.,* 3, 26-33.

JOHNSTON, D. W. (1972). 'Actinomycetes in aquatic habitats.' Ph. D. Thesis, University of Bradford.

JONES, L. A., and BRADLEY. S. G. (1964). 'Relationships among streptomycetes, nocardiae, mycobacteria and other Actinomycetes.' *Mycologia,* 56, 505-513.

KANE, W. D. (1966). 'A new genus of the Actinoplanaceae, *Pilimelia,* with a description of two species, *Pilimelia terevasa* and *Pilimelia anulata.*' *J. Elisha Mitchell scient. Soc.,* 82, 220-230.

KAUSHIK, N. K., and HYNES, H. B. N. (1971). 'The fate of the dead leaves that fall into streams.' *Arch. Hydrobiol.,* 68, 465-515.

LINGAPPA, Y., and LOCKWOOD, J. L. (1961). 'A chitin medium for isolation, growth and maintenance of actinomycetes.' *Nature,* 189, 158-159.

LOCCI, R., and PETROLINI BALDAN, B. (1971). 'On the spore formation process in actinomycetes. V. Scanning electron microscopy of some genera of Actinoplanaceae.' *Riv. Patol. veg. Padova,* Ser. 4, 7 (Suppl.), 81-96.

LUEDEMANN, G. (1970). '*Micromonospora* taxonomy. In *Advances in Applied Microbiology* (Ed. W. W. Umbreit) Academic Press Inc., New York. Vol. II., 101-133.

MASSCHELEIN, W. (1966). 'Mise au point du dénombrement des actinomycètes dans les eaux par l'emploi de membranes.' *Techqs. Sci. munic.,* 61, 95-98.

NONOMURA, H., and OHARA, Y. (1969). 'Distribution of actinomycetes in soil. (VI) A culture method effective for both preferential isolation and enumeration of *Microbispora* and *Streptosporangium* strains in soil (Part I).' *J. Ferment. Technol., Osaka,* 47, 463-469.

OTTOW, J. C. G. (1972). 'Rose bengal as a selective aid in the isolation of fungi and actinomycetes from natural sources.' *Mycologia,* 64, 304-315.

697

POPALISKY, J. R., and POGGE, F. (1967). 'Study of three-phase water treatment for Kansas City, Missouri. *J. Am. Wat. Wks Ass.,* 59, 1121-1133.

ROACH, A. W., and SILVEY, J. K. G. (1958). 'The morphology and life cycle of freshwater Actinomycetes.' *Trans. Am. micros. Soc.,* 77, 36-47.

ROSEN, A. A., MASHNI, C. I., and SAFFERMAN, R. S. (1970). 'Recent developments in the chemistry of odour in water: the cause of earthy/musty odour.' *Wat. Treat. Exam.,* 19, 106-119.

SHAPIRO, J., EDMONDSON, W. T., and ALLISON, D. E. (1971). 'Changes in the chemical composition of sediments of Lake Washington, 1958-1970.' *Limnol. Oceanogr.,* 16, 437-452.

SILVEY, J. K. G. (1953). 'Relation of irrigation runoff to tastes and odors.' *J. Am. Wat. Wks Ass.,* 45, 1179-1186.

SILVEY, J. K. G., and ROACH, A. W. (1953). 'Actinomycetes in the Oklahoma City water supply.' *J. Am. Wat. Wks Ass.,* 45, 409-416.

STANIER, R. Y., and VAN NIEL, C. B. (1962). 'The concept of a bacterium.' *Arch, Mikrobiol.,* 42, 17-35.

THAYSEN, A. C. (1936). 'The origin of an earthy or muddy taint in fish. I. The nature and isolation of the taint.' *Ann. appl. Biol.,* 23, 99-105.

TUTIN, W. (1955). 'Preliminary observations of a year's cycle of sedimentation in Windermere, England.' *Memorie Ist. ital. Idrobiol.,* 8, 467-484.

UMBREIT, W. W., and McCOY, E. (1941). 'The occurrence of actinomycetes of the genus *Micromonospora* in inland lakes.' In *A Symposium on Hydrobiology,* University of Wisconsin Press, 106-114.

UNESTAM, T. (1966). 'Chitinolytic, cellulolytic, and pectinolytic activity in vitro of some parasitic and saprophytic oomycetes.' *Physiologia Pl.,* 19, 15-30.

WEYLAND, H. (1969). 'Actinomycetes in North Sea and Atlantic Ocean sediments.' *Nature,* 223, 5208, 858.

WHITE, A. J. (1962). 'The occurrence of actinomycetes in Wellington water supplies.' *NZ Jl Sci.,* 5, 54-63.

WILLOUGHBY, L. G. (1968). 'Aquatic Actinomycetales with particular reference to the Actinoplanaceae.' *Veröff. Inst. Meeresforsch. Bremerh.,* 3, 19-26.

WILLOUGHBY, L. G. (1969 a). 'A study on aquatic actinomycetes—the allochthonous leaf component.' *Nova Hedwigia* 18, 45-113.

WILLOUGHBY, L. G. (1969 b). 'A study of the aquatic Actinomycetes of Blelham Tarn.' *Hydrobiologia,* 34, 465-483.

WILLOUGHBY, L. G. (1971). 'Observations on some aquatic Actinomycetes of streams and rivers.' *Freshwat. Biol.,* 1, 23-27.

WILLOUGHBY, L. G., and BAKER, C. D. (1969). 'Humic and fulvic acids and their derivatives as growth and sporulation media for aquatic Actinomycetes.' *Verh. int. Verein theor. angew. Limnol.,* 17, 795-801.

WILLOUGHBY, L. G., BAKER, C. D., and FOSTER, S. E. (1968). Sporangium formation in the Actinoplanaceae induced by humic acids.' *Experientia,* 24, 730-731.

WILLOUGHBY, L. G., and REDHEAD, K. (1973). 'Observations on the utilization of soluble nitrogen by aquatic fungi in nature.' *Trans. Br. mycol. Soc.,* 60, 598-601.

WILLOUGHBY, L. G., SMITH, S. M., and BRADSHAW, R. M. (1972). 'Actinomycete virus in freshwater'. *Freshwat. Biol.,* 2, 19-26.

26 A Reference List of Films on Aspects of Aquatic Fungi

G. B. BREMER

26.1   Introduction

For many mycologists the attraction to aquatic fungi lies in the varied and exciting
mechanisms of spore release and in observing motile stages in the life cycle of the
lower forms. Attempts to demonstrate these phenomena in words and pictures often
prove inadequate and an increasing number of workers are employing the medium
of film, both for teaching and demonstration, and for research documentation.

The following list is thought to include all films on topics of relevance to
aquatic mycology and the details of prices and distributors are correct at the time of
going to press (1975). The price of films is directly related to the price of photographic raw materials, which is continually rising. Prospective purchasers would
therefore be well advised to check on the current price before placing a firm order. A
list of the postal addresses of the distributors will be found after the following
summaries of the films.

26.2   Films Available

Labyrinthula coenocystis

Supervised by K. G. Grell, Tubingen, Germany. Produced by Institut für den Wissenschaftlichen Film. 1965/1966. The film illustrates the characteristic gliding motility
of the *Labyrinthula* cells and asexual reproduction by means of biflagellate zoospores.

16 mm, silent, black and white, 7 minutes. Available from Institut für den
Wissenschaftlichen Film. Catalogue No. E1172. Purchase price 132 DM. Hire 10.50
DM per week.

Motility in Labyrinthula

Made by D. Porter, University of Athens, Georgia, USA 1967. The film shows the
movement of cells of a *Labyrinthula* colony within the 'ectoplasmic net' system. The
branching and anastomosing of the individual filaments is shown. Subsequent sequences
show the movement of cells along artificial channels in the agar plate and the response
of *Labyrinthula* cells to the presence of yeast cells on which they feed.

16 mm, silent, black and white, 12 minutes. Available from Educational Services,
University of Washington Press. Details of price on application.

An introduction to the Marine Slime Mould Labyrinthula

Supervised by D. Porter, University of Athens, Georgia, USA. The movement of individual cells and colonies is shown. Deposition of the extracellular network in the cells move, cell division and the formation of crude cysts is illustrated. Electron micrographs demonstrate that the cells are encased in tubes of material of extracellular origin.

16 mm, sound and silent versions, colour, 9 minutes. Available from Media Department, Holt, Reinhart and Winston, New York. Purchase price: sound version $110, silent version $99.

Zoospores of Labyrinthula vitellina

A research record made by D. Porter, University of Athens, Georgia, USA. The film shows the biflagellate zoospores of this protist which can prove difficult to induce to sporulate in culture.

16 mm, silent, black and white, 5 minutes. Dr. Porter has kindly consented to make this film available at the cost of processing a copy. Details from him.

Motility of Labyrinthuloides yorkensis

A research film by D. Porter, University of Athens, Georgia, USA. The film records the unique motility of this estuarine fungus. The coccoid thallus is moved across the surface of the agar by extension and withdrawal of elements of the ectoplasmic net system.

16 mm, silent, black and white, 5 minutes. Available from Dr. Porter.

Sporulation in Thraustochytriaceae

Supervised by A. Gaertner, Institut für Meeresforschung, Bremerhaven. Produced by Institut für den Wissenschaftlichen Film, 1970. This film was made using interference phase microscopy and employs time lapse techniques. The development of a single sporangium is followed from zoospore encystment, through cleavage to zoospore release. The characteristic development of *T. kinnei, T. aureum, T. multirudimentale, T. striatum, T. aggregatum,* and *T. visurgense* is illustrated.

16 mm, sound (English translation supplied), black and white, 8 minutes. Available from Institut für Wissenschaftlichen Film. Cat. No. B. 107B. Prices on application. Available for hire in UK from British Film Institute Distribution Library. Fee £3.00.

Marine Biflagellates. I Aspects of the Thraustochytriaceae

Made by D. J. Alderman, Portsmouth Polytechnic, England, 1971. This film shows and compares the sporangial form and mode of zoospore release in proliferous and non-proliferous members of the Thraustochytriaceae. The species shown are *T. motivum, T. aureum, T. roseum* and *T. striatum.*

16 mm, sound, black and white, 14 minutes. Available from Dr. Alderman. Purchase price £20. Hire fee £3.00 plus delivery charges.

Thraustochytrium kinnei

Supervised by A. Gaertner. Institut für Meeresforschung, Bremerhaven. Produced by Institut für den Wissenschaftlichen Film, 1970. The development of a single sporangium on pine pollen grains is shown using time lapse photography and interference phase microscopy. The thallus is seen to enlarge, cleave and release leaving behind a basal rudiment which is then seen to proliferate into a new sporangium.

16 mm, sound (English translation supplied), black and white, 10½ mins. Available from Institut für den Wissenschaftlichen Film. Cat. No. E. 1664. Purchase price 532 DM. Hire 19 DM per week.

Marine Biflagellates. II Flagellar Movement

Made by D. J. Alderman, Portsmouth Polytechnic, 1972. The film explains by means of photomicrography, diagrams and electron micrographs the movements of the flagella of the zoospores of the marine fungus *Schizochytrium aggregatum* and the manner in which these movements effect the locomotion of the biflagellate zoospores.

16 mm, magnetic sound, black and white, 7½ minutes. Available from Dr. Alderman. Purchase price £18, hire £3.00 plus delivery charges.

Saprolegnia mixta. *Asexual*

Supervised by A. Gaertner, Institut für Meeresforschung, Bremerhaven. Produced by Institut für den Wissenschaftlichen Film 1961 and 1970. Using time lapse techniques the film shows the sequential development of the zoosporangia and the release of zoospores.

16 mm, sound (English translation supplied), black and white, 7 minutes. Available from Institut für den Wissenschaftlichen Film. Cat. No. C. 1080. Purchase price 188 DM. Hire 12.50 DM per week.

Saprolegnia mixta. *Sexual*

Supervised by A. Gaertner, Institut für Meeresforschung, Bremerhaven. Produced by Institut für den Wissenschaftlichen Film. 1961 and 1970. The formation of antheridia and oögonia is shown by time lapse photography. This is followed by sequences showing the fertilization of the egg, the separation of the oögonium from the hypha and the germination of the oöspore.

16 mm, sound (English translation supplied), black and white, 7 minutes. Available from Institut für den Wissenschaftlichen Film. Catalogue no. C. 1079. Purchase price 154 DM. Hire 10.50 DM per week. Available for hire in UK from British Film Institute Distribution Library. Hire charge £3.00.

Saprolegnia

Made by A. D. Greenwood, Imperial College, University of London. This film is concerned with asexual stages and employs 'stop-action' techniques to illustrate important features.

16 mm, silent, black and white, 20 minutes. Available from Mr. Greenwood. Purchase price £20.00 approx. Hire £1.00 plus delivery charges. Available in Canada from Dr. W. B. Kendrick details on application.

A Monoecious Water Mould Saprolegnia ferax

Made by R. A. Woodworth, Bennington College, Vermont, USA. The growth of the fungus on hempseeds and agar plates is shown. The development of the sporangium and zoospore release is depicted. Sexual stages shown include the formation of antheridia and oögonia on the same thallus.

16 mm, silent, black and white, 10 minutes. Available from Professor Woodworth. Purchase price approx. $90-100, plus delivery charges.

Pythium middletonii

Made by J. Webster, University of Exeter. Produced by Cinephoto Film Productions Ltd. The film illustrates the sequence of events leading to zoospore release. The formation of the vesicle, the flow of cytoplasm, cleavage of the cytoplasm and differentiation into zoospores are shown. Zoospore activity by rupture of the sporangial wall is clearly seen. A time lapse sequence of germination of the encysted zoospore concludes the film.

16 mm, silent, black and white, 8 minutes. Available from Professor Webster. Purchase price £14.50. Also available on loan.

Reproduction in Achlya ambisexualis

Made by R. A. Woodworth, Bennington College, Vermont, USA. The formation of primary, secondary and tertiary zoospores is seen. The film also illustrates the involvement of hormones in the sexual stages of the fungus.

16 mm, silent, black and white, 12 minutes. Available from Professor Woodworth. Purchase price $120 plus delivery charges.

Syngamy and Alternation of Generation in Allomyces

Made by A. T. Brice and R. Emerson. Produced by Phase Films Ltd.

16 mm, silent, black and white, 20 minutes. Available from Audiovisual Department, Sanoma State College. Purchase price approximately $100. For hire in UK from British Film Institute Distribution Library. Fee £2.50.

Alternation of Generations in Allomyces macrogynus

Made by R. H. Woodworth, Bennington College, Vermont, USA. Illustrating the formation and release of antheridia and oögonia, followed by the fertilization of the egg. The germination of the resultant diploid zygote is seen.

16 mm, silent, black and white, 12 minutes. Available from Professor Woodworth. Purchase price $90-100 plus delivery charges.

Rhizidiomyces

Made by M. S. Fuller, University of Athens, Georgia, USA. The film follows the development and discharge of the anteriorly uniflagellate zoospores of this fungus.

16 mm, silent, black and white, 10 minutes. Available on loan from Professor Fuller. In UK available from Dr. J. Gay.

Rhizophydium sphaerotheca

Made by G. B. Bremer, Portsmouth Polytechnic. The development of the fungus on nutrient agar is followed. The posteriorly uniflagellate zoospores are seen swimming, shortly followed by their encystment. The zoospore cyst enlarges and the rhizoidal system is seen to proliferate, discharge papillae develop, the cytoplasm differentiates into zoospores which are active within the sporangium. The final sequence shows the release of the zoospores through a discharge papilla.

16 mm, silent, black and white, 8 minutes. Available from G. B. Bremer. Purchase price £18. Hire charge £3.00 plus delivery charges.

Monoblepharis

Made by H. S. Whisler, University of Washington. The film illustrates the reproductive processes of this fungus, in which the male gamete is engulfed by the female gamete at fertilization.

16 mm, silent, black and white, 20 minutes. Available for purchase or hire from Dr. H. S. Whisler, prices on application. For sale to Canadian Universities for $200 from Dr. W. B. Kendrick.

Developmental Pathways of the Water Mould Blastocladiella emersonii

Supervised by E. C. Cantino, Michigan State University. Demonstrates that the fungus can develop along three pathways in response to environmental stimuli. Normally producing abundant zoospores, the fungus is induced by low nutrient levels to produce a single zoospore. In adverse conditions a resting stage is formed, remaining dormant until suitable conditions initiate zoospore production.

16 mm, sound, colour, 11 minutes. Available from Media Department, Holt Reinhart and Winston. Purchase price $150.

Lagenisma coscinodisci

Supervised by G. Drebes, Heligoland. Produced by Institut für den Wissenschaftlichen Film. 1967. The film illustrates the vegetative development of this fungus parasitic in the diatom Coscinodiscus granii.

16 mm, silent, black and white, 10½ minutes. Available from Institut für den Wissenschaftlichen Film. Catalogue No. E. 1398. Purchase price 202 DM. Hire 12.50 DM per week.

Polymyxa betae

Supervised by W. H. Fuchs, Gottingen. Produced by Institut für den Wissenschaftlichen Film. 1966. Showing the vegetative development of the fungus parasitic in the root hairs of the sugar beet.

16 mm silent, black and white, 11 minutes. Available from Institut für den Wissenschaftlichen Film. Cat. No. 1001. Purchase price 178 DM. Hire 12.50 DM per week.

Spore Discharge in Sillia ferruginea

Made by K. Fazzani, Portsmouth Polytechnic. This Ascomycete is prevalent in the packing timber of water cooling towers in the British Isles. The long necks of the perithecia can be seen protruding from the surface of the wood. In water the fungus discharges entire asci together with a mucilaginous matrix. A build up of asci within the perithecia causes 'pulsing' contractions of the perithecial neck, a phenomenon hitherto unreported.

16 mm, silent, black and white, 6 minutes. Available from K. Fazzani. Purchase price £16. Hire £3.00 plus delivery charges.

Motility

Made by M. Holwill, Queen Elizabeth College, University of London. Using high speed photography the film demonstrates the movement of the flagella of the gametes of *Blastocladiella emersonii* and *Allomyces.* Particular attention is paid to the function of the flagella when the direction of movement is changed.

16 mm, silent, black and white, 2 minutes. Available from Dr. Holwill. Purchase price £2.

26.3   Postal addresses of film distributors

Dr. D. J. Alderman
Department of Biological Sciences
Portsmouth Polytechnic
King Henry 1 Street
Portsmouth
Hants.
UK

Mr. G. B. Bremer
Department of Biological Sciences
Portsmouth Polytechnic
King Henry I Street
Portsmouth
Hants.
UK

British Film Institute
Distribution Library
42/3 Lower Marsh
London SE1
UK

Mr. K. Fazzani
Department of Biological Sciences
Portsmouth Polytechnic
King Henry 1 Street
Portsmouth
Hants.
UK

Prof. M. S. Fuller
Department of Botany
University of Athens
Athens
Georgia 30601
USA

Dr. J. Gay
Department of Botany
Imperial College of Science and Technology
Prince Consort Road
London
SW7 2BB
UK

Mr. A. D. Greenwood
Department of Botany
Imperial College of Science and Technology
Prince Consort Road
London SW7 2BB
UK

Holt, Reinhart and Winston
383 Madison Avenue
New York 10017
USA

Dr. M. E. J. Holwill
Department of Physics
Queen Elizabeth College
Campden Hill Road
London W8 7AH
UK

Institut für den Wissenschaftlichen Film
34 Gottingen
Nonnenstieg 72
BRD

Dr. W. B. Kendrick
Department of Biology
University of Waterloo
Ontario
Canada

Dr. D. Porter
Department of Botany
University of Athens
Athens
Georgia 30601
USA

Audiovisual Department
Sanoma State College
Sanoma
California 95476
USA

Prof. J. Webster
Department of Biological Sciences
University of Exeter
Exeter, Devon
EX4 4PS
UK

Dr. H. C. Whisler
Department of Botany
University of Washington
Seattle
Washington 98105
USA

Prof. R. H. Woodworth
Bennington College
Vermont 05201.802
USA

Education Services
University of Washington Press
Seattle
Washington 98105
USA

27 Topics of Further Interest

E. B. GARETH JONES

27.1 Introduction

The previous chapters in this volume have dealt with the major areas of research on aquatic fungi over the past 10–15 years. However, there are a number of topics which have not been discussed. For the most part they are subjects currently receiving little attention or only of marginal interest. It is the aim of this chapter briefly to review these subjects and indicate future lines of research in aquatic mycology.

27.2 Methods of Isolation and Growth Under Laboratory Conditions

Emerson (1958) and Jones (1971) have described a variety of techniques used for the isolation, maintenance and sporulation of freshwater and marine fungi. However, the search for novel methods for the growth and sporulation of aquatic fungi continues. Frequently the answer lies in the careful adjustment of environmental factors. For example, the isolation of aquatic fungi is frequently carried out at laboratory temperatures, despite the fact that the fungi concerned are rarely found in nature at these temperatures. Therefore it is not surprising that incubation at temperatures below $10\,^{\circ}$C has resulted in the isolation of a number of new and interesting fungi, e.g. *Thraustochytrium antarcticum* Bahnweg et Sparrow was isolated by Bahnweg and Sparrow (*Am.J.Bot.,* 61,754-766,1974). See also Bremer,Chapter 12. Similarly, a number of yeasts have also been isolated from waters at temperatures below 10°C (Fell, Chapter 3). The sexual stage of *Saprolegnia parasitica* Coker has also been observed by growing cultures at temperatures below $10\,^{\circ}$C.

A more fascinating example of control of environmental conditions has been the discovery by Emerson and Held (1969) that *Aqualinderella fermentans* Emerson et Weston would not grow in the presence of air. When grown in an atmosphere with high CO_2 content (by burning a candle in a sealed jar) growth and good sporulation occurred. *Aqualinderella fermentans* is now grown on a glucose yeast extract medium at pH 6.1-6.3 in flasks placed in a sealed cabinet or jar under 5% CO_2 in air. The fungus can also be grown in air on a succinate-containing medium.

In recent years, a number of yeasts have been shown to be heterobasidiomycetes (Fell, Chapter 3). They form large terminal or intercalary teliospores which germinate to produce a one to four celled promycelium with lateral and terminal sporidia. These stages are produced under a variety of conditions but in general cultures are grown at 12 °C on either malt agar (5% Fleischmann's diastatic dry diamalt, 2% agar in distilled water) or cornmeal agar (1.7% Difco cornmeal agar) plates. After 1-3 weeks teliospores are formed and pieces of the agar plus teliospores are removed from the plates and transferred to sterile distilled water incubated at 12 °C for 2-10 weeks. The teliospores are then streaked on 2% agar in distilled water plates and incubated at 5 or 12 °C. After one week, germination usually takes place (Fell et al., 1969; Newell and Fell, 1970; Newell and Hunter, 1970). In Leurosporidium scottii Fell, Statzell, Hunter et Phaff, the entire life cycle was observed on cornmeal agar at room temperature.

Few Trichomycetes have been grown successfully in culture. Exceptions are four species of Smittium and Amoebidium parasiticum Ciensk. Williams and Lichtwardt (1972) grew Smittium culisetae Lichtwardt on a tryptone glucose medium at temperatures of 24-26 °C (Difco tryptone, 20 g; glucose 5 g; KH_2PO_4, 0.28 g; K_2HPO_4, 0.35 g; $(NH_4)_2 SO_4$, 0.26 g; $MgCl_2 . 6H_2O$, 0.10 g; $CaCl_2 . 2H_2O$, 0.07 g; thiamine, 200 μg; biotine, 50 μg and glass distilled water to make 1 litre).

Members of the Lagenidiales are primarily regarded as parasitic. However, Willoughby (1969) has shown that Lagenidium giganteum Couch can be successfully grown in the laboratory on 1% Difco beef extract with 2% agar. This fungus was shown to utilize chitin and that calcium was conducive to zoospore dehiscence. Bland and Amerson (1973) were also able to grow Lagenidium callinectes Couch under laboratory conditions, on a peptone-yeast extract medium.

The use of pollen grains as baits for aquatic Phycomycetes is well established and they have been successfully used in the isolation of the thraustochytrids. Larvae of Artemia salina L. have also been used as baits for the isolation of these marine coccoid fungi. They have also been successfully grown on flooded media, especially modified vitamin B_1 agar (Fuller et al., 1964) and calf serum agar. Modified vitamin B_1 agar contains 5 g glucose, 1 g peptone (Oxoid), 1 g yeast extract, 12 g agar in 1.0 litre seawater. Calf serum agar contains 100 ml calf serum (Wellcome No. 1) and 9 g agar in 900 ml seawater. For isolation purposes antibiotics are also included in the media.

27.3 Terrestrial Occurrence of Some Aquatic Hyphomycetes

Freshwater aquatic hyphomycetes have been reported from decaying leaves (Ingold Chapter 13) and on twigs and timber submerged in streams and rivers (Jones and Oliver, 1964; Willoughby and Archer, 1973; Eaton, Chapter 14). However, Waid (1954), Webster (1961) and Price and Talbot (1966) have reported their occurrence in terrestrial habitats. Hudson and Sutton (1964) have also described two hyphomycetes with tetraradiate conidia growing on Acer pseudoplanatus L. and Saccharum officinarum leaves collected on land (Trisulcosporium acerinum Hudson et Sutton and Tetranacrium gramienum Hudson et Sutton).

TABLE 27.1 Freshwater hyphomycetes reported from terrestrial habitats.

	Scourfield (1940)	Waid (1954)	Tubaki (1960)	Webster (1961)	Hudson and Sutton (1964)	Bandoni (1972)
Tetracladium setigerum (Grove) Ingold	*	—	—	—	*	*
Alatospora acuminata Ingold	—	—	*	—	*	*
Articulospora tetracladia Ingold	—	—	*	—	—	*
Anguillospora crassa Ingold	—	—	*	*†	—	—
Heliscus lugdunensis Sacc. et Therry	—	—	—	*†	—	—
Varicosporium elodae Kegel	—	*	—	*	—	*
Flagellospora spp.	—	—	—	—	—	*
Ingoldia craginiformis Petersen	—	—	—	—	—	*
Tricladium splendens Ingold	—	—	—	—	—	*
Voluscrispora aurantica Haskins	—	—	—	—	—	*
V. graminae Ingold, McDougal et Dann	—	—	—	—	—	*
Campylospora sp. ⎫	—	—	—	—	—	*
Lunulospora sp. ⎪ Observed but	—	—	—	—	—	*
Tetraploa sp. ⎬ not cultured	—	—	—	—	—	*
Triposporium sp. ⎪ or identified	—	—	—	—	—	*
Tripospermum sp. ⎭ to species	—	—	—	—	—	*
Tricellula aquatica Webster	—	—	—	—	*	—
Tripospermum myrti (Lind.) Hughes	—	—	—	—	*	—

† as the perfect stage.

Bandoni (1972), in a more recent study, has recovered nine species from plant materials collected on the campus of the University of British Columbia. The collected material was placed in petri dishes, flooded with sterile distilled water and incubated at 10 °C. Table 27.1 lists some of the aquatic hyphomycetes reported from terrestrial habitats. Bandoni found these fungi to be extremely abundant in the winter and spring but few in number during the early summer. Conidia appeared to be present throughout the leaf carpet but the well decayed leaves from the lower leaf layers gave higher number of spores.

Bandoni (1972) reports that many of his isolates sporulated in the absence of a layer of water. A similar observation was made by Jones and Stewart (1972) for *Tricladium varium* Jones et Stewart, a fungus isolated from timber submerged in water cooling towers. However, Bandoni found that a greater number of spores were obtained from leaves if they were flooded with water. This raises the question are these hyphomycetes truly aquatic? Further work is obviously required to determine their distribution in the leaf mycoflora. The work of Jones

TABLE 27.2 Freshwater Lignicolous Fungi.

	Eaton and Jones (1971 b)		Shearer (1971)	Jones (unpublished)	Willoughby and Archer (1973)	Byrne (1971)	
	B 12	*Sp* 12	*Balsa* 15	*B* 5	*% occurrence on 52 twigs*	*B* 6	*Sp* 6
Ascomycetes							
Apostemidium quernisaci (Crouan) Boudier	—	—	—	—	*	—	—
Ceratosphaeria lampadophora (Ber. et Br.) Niessl	6	—	—	—	—	—	—
Ceratostomella sp.	—	—	—	—	*(22)	—	—
Chaetomium sp.	—	—	1	—	—	3	—
Coniochaeta sordaria	—	—	5†	—	—	—	—
Cudoniella clavus (Albertini et Schw.) Dennis	—	—	—	—	*(26)	—	—
Haligena elaterophora Kohlm.	3	1	—	—	—	—	—
Leptosphaeria spp.	—	—	5†	6	*(44)	—	—
Massarina sp.	—	—	—	—	*(18)	—	—
Mollisia sp.	—	—	—	—	*(9)	—	—
Nectria lugdunensis Webster	—	—	—	—	—	—	—
Pleospora vitalbe	—	—	—	—	—	4	—
Pleurage curvula (de Bary) Kuntz	—	—	—	—	—	4	1
Rosselinia sp.	—	—	10†	—	—	—	—
Trematosphaeria pertusa (Persoon ex Fries) Fuckel	8	1	—	—	—	—	—
Phycomycetes							
Mucor sp.	1	1	—	2	—	—	—

Fungi Imperfecti

Alatospora acuminata Ingold	—	—	—	5	*(23)	—	—
Alternaria sp.	—	—	7	—	—	1	—
Anguillospora longissima (Sacc. et Syd.) Ingold	2	—	—	—	*(58)	—	—
A. crassa Ingold	—	—	—	—	*(9)	—	—
Articulospora tetracladia Ingold	—	—	7	—	*(7)	—	—
Bispora fusca	—	—	—	—	—	—	—
Brachysporium sp.	—	—	—	—	*(16)	—	—
Centrospora acerina (Hart.) Newhall	—	—	—	—	*(3)	—	—
Cephalosporium sp.	1	2	—	—	—	1	1
Clasterosporium caricium Schw.	10	2	—	—	—	—	—
Clavariopsis aquatica de Wild.	—	—	—	4	*(49)	—	—
Clavatospora stellatacula Krik	—	—	—	—	—	—	—
Codinea gonytrichodes Shearer et Crane	—	—	4	—	—	—	—
Coniothyrium fuckelii Sacc.	—	—	18†	—	—	—	—
Conioscypha varia Shearer et Crane	—	—	24†	—	—	—	—
Dactyllela aquatica (Ingold) Ranzoni	—	—	—	—	*	—	—
Dictyosporium elegans (Linder) Hughes	—	—	6	—	—	—	—
D. toruloides (Corda) Guegen	—	—	—	—	*(7)	—	—
Dimorphospora foliicola Tubaki	—	—	—	—	*(21)	—	—
Endophragmia hyalosperma (Corda) Morgan-Jones et Cole	—	—	20†	—	—	—	—
Epicoccum nigrum Link	—	—	24+	—	—	2	2
Fusarium spp.	2	3	2	3	*(84)	—	—
Gonytrichum macrocladum (Sacc.) Hughes	—	—	6†	—	—	—	—
Helicomyces sp.	9	—	—	—	*(9)	—	—
Helicoon sessile Morgan	—	1	5	—	—	—	—
Heliosporium phragmites Hohnel	2	—	8	—	—	—	—
Heliscus lugdunensis Sacc. et Therry	2	2	—	—	*(84)	—	—
Humicola alopallonella Meyers et Moore	2	2	—	—	—	—	—
Lemmoniera aquatica de Wild.	—	—	—	1	*(41)	—	—

TABLE 27.2

	Eaton and Jones (1971 b)		Shearer (1971)	Jones (unpublished)	Willoughby and Archer (1973)	Byrne (1971)	
	B 12	Sp 12	Balsa 15	B 5	% occurrence on 52 twigs	B 6	Sp 6
L. terrestris Tubaki	—	—	—	—	*(6)	—	—
Mammaria echinobotryoides Cesati	3	—	*	—	*	—	—
Margaritispora aquatica Ingold	—	10	—	—	*	—	—
Monodictys putredinis Wallroth	6	—	—	—	—	—	—
Monodictys sp.	3	—	*	—	—	3	—
Neta patuxentica Shearer et Crane	—	—	7†	—	—	—	—
Penicillium sp.	1	—	—	4	—	—	—
Pithomyces chartarum (Berk. et Curt.) M. B. Ellis	—	—	10†	—	—	—	—
Phaeosaria clematidis (Fuckel) Hughes	—	—	6	—	—	—	—
Phoma spp.	—	—	—	8	—	9	7
Pyrenochaeta sp.	—	—	35†	—	—	—	—
Robillarda sp.	—	—	5	—	—	—	—
Sterigmatobotrys macrocarpa (Corda) Hughes	—	6	—	—	—	1	—

Species						
Tetrachaetum elegans Ingold	—	—	—	*(5)	—	—
Torula herbarum (Pers.) Link	—	—	8†	—	—	1
Triadelphia heterospora Shearer et Crane	—	—	5†	—	9	—
Tricladium splendens Ingold	6	—	—	*(14)	—	—
T. angulatum Ingold	—	—	—	*(5)	4	—
T. varium Jones et Stewart	—	—	6†	—	—	—
Trichocladium sp.	—	—	4†	—	—	—
Trichoderma sp.	—	—	—	—	—	—

B: beech.

Sp.: Scots pine.

†30 test samples taken.

713

and Oliver (1964), Eaton and Jones (1971a, b), Newton (1971), Willoughby and Archer (1973) and Kane (unpublished) shows that leaves, twigs and test panels submerged in streams and rivers soon become colonized by aquatic hyphomycetes. Table 27.2 lists some of the more frequently recorded species and shows that fungi other than the tetraradiate hyphomycetes are also present in significant numbers. Newton (1971) studied the fungi colonizing leaves of *Alnus glutinosa* (L.) Gaern., *Salix viminalis* L., *Ulmus glabara* Huds., *Fagus sylvatica* L. and *Quercus* sp. submerged in the River Lune below lower Halton Weir at Halton, Lancashire. She was able to show that the early fungal colonist (terrestrial) developing on the leaves was interrupted abruptly when placed in the river. An aquatic flora, dominated by species of the Pythiaceae, replaced them quickly. Early aquatic colonizers were *Phytophthora* sp. No. 4 and *Pythium ostracodes* (?) Dreschler. As the dominance of the Pythiaceae declined, they were replaced by *Dimorphospora foliicola* Tubaki, Oömycete species, *Heliscus lugdunensis* Sacc. et Therry, *Varicosporium elodeae* Kegel and *Helicodendron tubulosum* (Riess) Linder. Other aquatic fungi were also present. Clearly further work is required on the ecology of fungi occurring in freshwater habitats.

27.4 Aero-Aquatic Fungi

The late Miss Agatha van Beverwijk described a number of hyphomycetes that have been termed aero-aquatic fungi because of their mode of growth and sporulation. These fungi produce mycelium and condiophores on decaying leaves and wood submerged in water (often stagnant) while the conidia are developed above the water surface. Good collecting sites are bogs, ponds, ditches, fishponds, garden fountains and slow moving streams. Eaton and Jones (1971a) have also recovered these fungi from timber placed in the River Dee at Chester.

Aero-aquatic fungi frequently have large globose conidia which retain some air inside them that acts as a float. They can be grown in culture on a variety of agar media (Hennebert, 1968), to which water is added so that the mycelium is covered by a layer of water. Subcultures are easier to make if a spore suspension is made and poured on to fresh agar plates.

Shaw (1972) has described a fungus (*Ingoldiella hamata* Shaw) with clamped tetraradiate hooked spores from submerged decayed leaves from a stream in north Queensland. This fungus was first collected by Ingold (1961) in scums taken from three Nigerian streams. However, Dr. Shaw is of the opinion that *I. hamata* may be aero-aquatic rather than truly aquatic. Studies of these fungi have been largely taxonomic (Table 27.3) while little is known of their ecology, physiology and mode of spore dispersal.

27.5 Predacious Fungi in Aquatic Habitats

Cooke (Chapter 15) has already indicated that fungi capable of predation on nematodes, amoebae, radiolaria and rotifers occur in aquatic habitats. Table 27.4 lists some of the predacious fungi known to occur in aquatic environments.

Johnson and Autrey (1961) were the first to report a predacious fungus on

TABLE 27.3 Some aero-aquatic fungi

Fungus	Author	Substrate
Candelabrum spinuloseum van Beverwijk	van Beverwijk (1951 a)	*Betula, Castanea, Carpinus, Quercus* and *Alnus* leaves
Clathrosphaerina zalewskii van Beverwijk	van Beverwijk (1951 b)	various leaves
Helicoon pluriseptatum van Beverwijk	van Beverwijk (1954)	decaying leaves
Papulospora pulmonaria van Beverwijk	van Beverwijk (1954)	*Fagus* leaves
Spirosphaera floriforme van Beverwijk	van Beverwijk (1953)	*Betula, Quercus,* and *Rhododendron* leaves
Helococodendron giganteum Glen-Bott	Glen-Bott (1951)	*Betula* leaves
Helicodendron tubulosum (Riess) Linder	Glen-Bott (1955)	on a variety of decaying leaves
H. conglomeratum Glen-Bott	Glen-Bott (1955)	*Fagus* and *Quercus*
H. articulatum Glen-Bott	Glen-Bott (1955)	*Fagus*
H. luteo-album Glen-Bott	Glen-Bott (1955)	*Fagus, Salix and Quercus*
H. triglitziensis (Jaap) Linder	Glen-Bott (1955)	twigs and leaves
H. multicatenulatum van Beverwijk	Glen-Bott (1955)	on decaying leaves
H. westerdijkae van Beverwijk	Glen-Bott (1955)	on *Acer* leaves
?*H. paradoxum* Peyronel	Glen-Bott (1955)	grass leaves
Helicoon fuscosporum Linder	Glen-Bott (1955)	*Betula* leaves
S. beverwijkiana Hennebert	Hennebert (1968)	*Quercus, Betula, Fagus* and *Populus* leaves
S. minuta Hennebert	Hennebert (1968)	decaying leaves of *Quercus, Betula, Fagus, Populus* and *Corylus.*

wooden test panels submerged in brackish water. It is surprising that so few have been reported from the marine environment, especially as there appears to be a rich nematode population in the sea (Meyers and Hooper, 1967; Jones and Byrne, Chapter 5). J. Irvine and K. Fazzani (personal communication) have both reported the presence of these fungi on test panels placed in water cooling towers.

TABLE 27.4   Some predacious fungi found in aquatic habitats.

	Peach (1950)	Peach (1952)	Peach (1954)	Peach and Juniper (1955)	Jones (1959)	Cooke and Ludzack (1958)	Johnson and Autery (1961)
Acaulopage macrospora Drechsler	*	—	—	—	—	—	—
A. tetraceros Drechsler	*	—	—	—	—	—	—
A. tetraceros var. *longa* Jones et Peach	—	—	—	—	*	*	—
Arthrobotrys cladodes Drechsler var. *marcoides* Drechsler	—	—	*	—	—	—	—
A. dactyloides Drechsler *	—	—	—	—	—	—	*
A. superba Corda	—	—	*	—	—	—	—
Dactylaria brochopaga Drechsler	—	—	*	—	—	—	—
D. canida (Nees) Sacc.	*	—	—	—	—	—	—
D. scaphoides Peach	—	*	—	—	—	—	—
Dactylella heptameres Drechsler	—	*	—	—	—	—	—
D. reticulata Peach	*	—	—	—	—	—	—
D. spermatophaga Drechsler	—	—	*	—	—	—	—
Stylopage araea Drechsler var. *magna* Peach et Jones	—	—	—	*	—	—	—
S. lepte Drechsler	—	*	—	—	—	—	—
S. rhabdospora Drechsler	—	──	*	—	—	—	—
Zoopage pachyblasta Drechsler	—	*	—	—	—	—	—
Zoophagus insidians Sommerstoff †	—	—	—	—	—	*	—

* Brackish water.
† Activated sludge.

27.6   Higher Fungi in Marine Sediments

The role of the lower fungi in muds and sediments has already been considered by Bremer (Chapter 12) and Dick (Chapter 20).

A number of fungi have been reported from estuarine and oceanic sediments by Ritchie (1954), Siepmann (1959), Siepmann and Johnson (1960), Borut and Johnson (1962), Anastasiou (1963), Roth *et al.* (1964), Tubaki (1966) and Steele (1967), while Bayliss-Elliott (1930), Brown (1958), Pugh (1962), Pugh and Mathison (1962), Pugh *et al.* (1963) and Cowley (1973) have isolated fungi from salt marshes. The majority of these fungi were very similar to terrestrial soil species (mainly Fungi Imperfecti) rather than the fungi usually thought of as aquatic. The question that therefore arises is : are they active in aquatic habitats?

Cooke (1961, 1963 also Chapter 15) divides the fungi encountered in freshwater into two principal groups. The *hydrofungi*, which require the presence of water to complete their life cycle and are regarded as obligate aquatic fungi. The second group are *geofungi* or typical soil fungi, which are not specifically adapted to an aquatic existence, but nevertheless they may be found under water because of an adequate supply of nutrients. These, Cooke regards as facultative aquatic fungi or his lymaxenes.

At present, little work has been carried out to determine the activity of terrestrial type fungi in seawater. Are they to be considered marine or facultatively marine (the lymaxenes of Cooke—not tolerant of such a habitat but only passing through the system)? A similar problem has been found with fungi colonizing timber in cooling towers (Jones, 1972). Most of the species found growing and fruiting on the wood were not encountered when plating out techniques were used. Fungi appeared on the plates that were not observed on the test panels, but these were sporadic in their frequency of appearance. Are these fungi active in the degradation of wood or merely present as resting spores which germinate when plated out onto nutrient media?

Park (1972 a) has used plating and baiting techniques to try and characterize fungi present in organic detritus in freshwater. Baiting techniques yielded a number of fungi not recorded by the plating out method, but a feature of all such work is the high number of Fungi Imperfecti and Phycomycetes isolated and the low number of Ascomycetes recorded. However, this work emphasizes the need for the use of a variety of techniques and an increase in the number of baits. Dick (Chapter 20) has also discussed the activity of soil fungi in aquatic habitats.

27.7 Future Work

The study of aquatic fungi is at an exciting stage and in the next decade a number of the problems mentioned by various authors in this volume will undoubtedly receive attention. The foundation has been well established, and the mycologist interested in this group of organisms is fortunate in being able to identify accurately 95% of his fungi. However, a number of taxonomic problems remain, e.g. speciation within the genera *Lulworthia* and *Thraustochytrium*.

The various contributors to this volume have suggested topics inadequately researched and outlined areas for future research. Major topics for investigation for the next ten years will be ecology, physiology, biochemistry, ultrastructure and experimental work.

27.7.1 Methodology

Sporulating cultures of a large number of the higher marine fungi have not been obtained, and this aspect needs further investigation before future experimental, physiological and biochemical studies can proceed. Here the interrelationship of light, temperature and salinity should be considered.

A major topic that warrants attention is the enumeration of fungi in aquatic habitats. The methods currently available are inadequate, especially for the aquatic lignicolous fungi, and to a lesser extent the yeasts and phycomycetes in water and sediment samples. Iqbal and Webster (1973) have shown that the freshwater aquatic hyphomycetes can easily be counted using millipore filtration techniques. This has not proved successful for other aquatic fungi. There is room

TABLE 27.5 Some terrestrial fungi isolated from seawater.

Fungi	Eulittoral	Oceanic	Estuarine						Total
	Roth et al. (1964)		Ritchie (1954)	Siepmann and Johnson (1960)	Anastasiou (1963)	Tubaki (1966)	Steele (1967)	Borut and Johnson (1962)	
Alternaria tenuis Nees	*	*	—	—	*	—	*	*	5
A. sp.	*	*	—	—	*	*	*	*	6
Aspergillus spp.	12	8	*	—	—	*	20	11	6
Aureobasidium pullulans (de Bary) Arraud	*	*	—	*	—	—	—	—	3
Bipolaris sp.	—	*	—	—	—	—	—	—	1
Cephalosporium sp.	*	*	—	—	—	—	*	*	4
Cladosporium herbarum (Pers.) Link	*	—	—	—	—	*	*	*	4
C. sphaerospermum Penz.	*	*	—	—	—	—	*	—	3
C. spp.	*	*	—	—	—	—	*	*	4
Curvularia lunata (Walker) Boedijn	*	*	—	—	—	—	—	*	3
C. pallescens Boedijn	—	*	—	—	—	—	*	*	3
Epicoccum nigrum Link	*	*	—	—	—	—	*	*	4
Fusarium spp.	5	1	*	*	—	*	*	*	7
Geotrichum candidum Link	*	—	—	—	—	—	—	*	2
Gliocladium roseum (Link) Thom	*	*	—	—	—	—	—	—	2
Helminthosporium sp.	*	—	—	*	—	*	*	*	5
Hormodendron sp.	*	*	—	—	—	—	—	*	3
Humicola sp.	*	*	—	—	—	—	—	*	3
Monilia acremonium Delacroix	*	—	—	—	—	—	—	—	1

Species	1	2	3	4	5	6	7	No
M. implicata Gilman et Abbott	*	—	—	—	—	—	*	2
Mucor spp.	2	*	*	—	—	—	*	3
Nigrospora oryzae (Berk. et Br.) Petch	—	*	—	—	—	*	—	1
N. sphaerica (Sacc.) Mason	*	*	—	—	—	*	*	4
N. sacchari (Speg.) Mason	—	*	—	—	*	—	*	1
Pestalotia sp.	*	—	—	—	*	—	*	4
Penicillium spp.	15	6	—	—	*	20	37	5
Paecilomyces varioti Bainier	—	*	—	—	*	*	*	4
Pithomyces atro-olivaceus (Cooke et Harkness) Ellis	—	*	—	—	—	—	—	1
P. charatarum (Berk. et Curt.) Ellis	—	*	*	—	—	—	—	1
Phoma spp.	*	*	*	—	*	*	*	4
Scopulariopsis sp.	*	—	*	*	*	—	—	5
Stachybotrys atra Corda	—	—	—	*	*	—	—	2
Trichoderma sp.	*	*	—	—	—	*	*	5
Torula sp.	*	—	—	—	—	—	—	2

* present
— not recorded
No = Number of species

here for innovation as well as a reappraisal of methods already in use. Mycologists should be encouraged to use a variety of methods; visual and isolation techniques, the latter using a wide range of media. Park (1972 a, b) discussed this aspect, but even the range of media he used was inadequate for the enumeration of the total fungi present in any one aquatic habitat. In the marine and brackish water habitat, temperature, salinity and pH may also be important (see Section 27.2) as well as the vigorous aeration of the substrates. Kirk (1969) has shown that, by aerating wood samples, fungi like *Clavatospora stellatacula* Kirk and *Flagellospora* sp. could be detected. This degree of sampling is frequently impossible due to the work load involved. No ecological study of aquatic fungi to date has considered all the fungal groups present on the substratum. This clearly cannot continue if a serious attempt is to be made to understand the interrelationships of organisms present on a substratum.

27.7.2   Diseases of Aquatic Animals

This aspect has been discussed by Alderman (Chapter 9) and Wilson (Chapter 22) but the subject is not currently receiving much support. At present economically significant, and of future greater importance as man overcomes the technical problems of farming of the sea, it is imperative that mycologists study pathogenic fungi of commercial fish and shellfish. Many freshwater pathogenic fungi have been reported in the literature, but few have been isolated and adequately characterized. Little experimental work has been undertaken to reinfect the host animal with adequate control measures (Stevenson, 1970).

The incidence of ulcerative dermal necrosis (UDN) has drawn attention to the problem of fungal diseases in fish. However, a number of other aquatic animals are susceptible to fungal disease (Unestam, 1964, 1965, 1969) and further work is necessary.

27.7.3   Ultrastructure

There are a number of ultrastructural studies of both the marine and freshwater Phycomycetes (Perkins, Chapter 11; Heath, Chapter 23). These organisms lend themselves to such studies but there are frequently difficulties in the fixation of the higher fungi. Problems of interest include the spore structure of marine Ascomycetes and the development of the spore appendages.

27.7.4   Physiology and Biochemistry

Physiological and biochemical studies of the type outlined by Jones and Byrne (Chapter 5), Jones and Harrison (Chapter 10) and Gleason (Chapter 21) will continue as more aquatic fungi are isolated or discovered. Future lines of research of interest will be the search for new or novel secondary metabolites (Kirk, Chapter 6) and the production of fungal protein using substrates such as hydro-carbons and waste products, e.g. carob beans and effluents rich in organic matter. The role of marine fungi in the conditioning of wood for borer settlement has been inadequately investigated and offers scope for those interested in the inter-relationships of organisms. The work outlined by Bärlocher and Kendrick (Chapter 16) on feeding freshwater gammarids with mycelium is important when considering the productivity of aquatic ecosystems. This subject will undoubted-ly receive much attention over the next decade.

27.7.5   Experimental Work

The experimental work of Webster (1959) will undoubtedly stimulate other mycologists to study the impaction, settlement and germination of spores of aquatic fungi. Iqbal and Webster (1973) have also investigated the trapping efficiency of air bubbles and shown that branched spores are more readily removed from suspension than spores of conventional shape. Aquatic hyphomycetes have frequently been reported as sporulating only when aerated, and this aspect has recently been studied by Webster and Towfik (1972).

Similar studies to those mentioned above are in progress for marine fungi (see Fig. 1.2, Fazzani; Fig. 12.6, Bremer) but are only in their infancy.

Thornton (1971) has investigated the long range dispersal of aquatic Phycomycetes by birds, while birds have also been implicated in the introduction of marine fungi into the Salton Sea (Anastasiou, 1963).

This volume has attempted to draw together work carried out over the past decade on aquatic fungi. Much of the work is at the embryonic stage and clearly, there are many areas for continued research.

References

ANASTASIOU, C. J. (1963). 'Fungi from salt lakes. II Ascomycetes and Fungi Imperfecti from the Salton Sea.' *Nova Hedwigia,* 6, 243-276.

BANDONI, R. J. (1972). 'Terrestrial occurrence of some aquatic hyphomycetes.' *Can. J. Bot.,* 50, 2283-2288.

BAYLISS-ELLIOTT, J. S. (1930). 'The soil fungi of the Dovey salt marshes.' *Ann. appl. Biol.,* 17, 284-305.

VAN BEVERWIJK, A. L. (1951 a). *'Candelabrum spinulosum* a new fungus species.' *Antonie van Leeuwenhoek,* 17, 278-284.

VAN BEVERWIJK, A. L. (1951 b). 'Zalewski's *Clathrosphaera spiritera.'* *Trans. Br. mycol. Soc.,* 34, 280-290.

VAN BEVERWIJK, A. L. (1953). 'Helicosporus hyphomycetes. I.' *Trans. Br. mycol. Soc.,* 36, 111-124.

VAN BEVERWIJK, A. L. (1954). 'Three new fungi: *Helicoon pluriseptatum,* n. sp., *Papulaspora pulmonaria* n. sp. and *Tricellula inaequalis* n. gen. n. sp.' *Antonie van Leeuwenhoek,* 20, 1-16.

BLAND, C. E., and ANDERSON, H. V. (1973). 'Observations on *Lagenidium callinectis*; isolation and sporangial development.' *Mycologia,* 65, 310-320.

BORUT, S. Y., and JOHNSON, T. W. (1962). 'Some biological observations on fungi in estuarine sediments.' *Mycologia,* 54, 181-193.

BROWN, J. C. (1958). 'Soil fungi of some British sand dunes in relation to soil type and succession.' *J. Ecol.,* 46, 641-664.

BYRNE, P. (1971). 'The physiological responses of some marine, freshwater and terrestrial fungi to salinity.' Ph.D. Thesis, London University.

COOKE, W. B. (1961). 'Pollution effects on the fungus population of a stream.' *Ecology,* 42, 1-18.

COOKE, W. B. (1963). 'A laboratory guide to fungi in polluted waters, sewage and sewage treatments systems.' *Public Health Service Publ.,* Cincinnati, 999-WP-1, 132 pp.

COOKE, W. B., and LUDZACK, F. J. (1958). 'Predaceous fungus behaviour in activated sludge systems.' *Sewage and Indust. Wastes,* 30, 1490-1495.

COWLEY, G. T. (1973). 'Variations in soil fungus populations in a South Carolina salt marsh.' (in press).

EATON, R. A., and JONES, E. B. G. (1971 a). 'The biodeterioration of timber in water cooling towers. I. Fungal ecology and the decay of wood at Connah's Quay and Ince.' *Material u. Organismen,* 6, 51-80.

EATON, R. A., and JONES, E. B. G. (1971 b). 'The biodeterioration of wood in water cooling towers. II. Fungi growing on wood in different positions in a water cooling system.' *Material u. Organismen,* 6, 81-92.

EMERSON, R. (1958). 'Mycological organization.' *Mycologia,* 50, 589-621.

EMERSON, R., and HELD, A. A. (1969). *'Aqualinderella fermentans* gen. et sp. n., a phycomycete adapted to stagnant waters. II. Isolation, cultural characteristics and gas relations.' *Am. J. Bot.,* 56, 1103-1120.

FELL, J., STATZELL, A. C., HUNTER, I. L., and PHAFF, H. J. (1969). *'Leuco-sporidium* gen. n., the heterobasidiomycetous stage of several yeasts of the genus *Candida.'* *Antonie van Leeuwenhoek,* 35, 433-462.

FULLER, M. S., FOWLES, B. E., and MCLAUGHLIN, D. J. (1964). 'Isolation and pure culture study of marine Phycomycetes.' *Mycologia,* 56, 745-756.

GLEN-BOTT, J. I. (1951). *'Helicodendron giganteum* n. sp., and other aerial-sporing hyphomycetes of submerged dead leaves.' *Trans. Br. mycol. Soc.,* 34, 275-279.

GLEN-BOTT, J. I. (1955). 'On *Helicodendron tubulosum* and some similar species.' *Trans. Br. mycol. Soc.,* 38, 17-30.

HARRISON, J. L., and JONES, E. B. G. (1974). 'Zoospore discharge in *Thrausto-chytrium striatum* Schneider.' *Trans. Br. mycol. Soc.,* 62, 283-288.

HENNEBERT, G. L. (1968). 'New species of *Spirosphaera.'* *Trans. Br. mycol. Soc.,* 51, 13-24.

HUDSON, H. J., and SUTTON, B. C. (1964). *'Trisulcosporium* and *Tetranacrium,* two new genera of Fungi Imperfecti.' *Trans. Br. mycol. Soc.,* 47, 197-204.

INGOLD, C. T. (1961). 'Another aquatic spore-type with clamp connexions.' *Trans. Br. mycol. Soc.,* 44, 27-30.

IQBAL, S. H., and WEBSTER, J. (1973). 'The trapping of aquatic hyphomycete spores by air bubbles.' *Trans. Br. mycol. Soc.,* 60, 37-48.

JOHNSON, T. W., and AUTERY, C. L. (1961). 'An *Arthrobotrys* from brackish water.' *Mycologia,* 53, 432-433.

JONES, E. B. G. (1971). 'Aquatic fungi.' In *Methods in Microbiology* (Ed. C. Booth), Academic Press, London, vol. 4, 335-365.

JONES, E. B. G. (1972). 'The decay of timber in aquatic environments.' *Brit. Wood Preserving Assoc., Ann. Convention,* 31-49.

JONES, E. B. G., and OLIVER, A. C. (1964). 'Occurrence of aquatic hyphomycetes on wood submerged in fresh and brackish water.' *Trans. Br. mycol. Soc.,* 47, 45-48.

JONES, E. B. G., and STEWART, R. J. (1972). *'Tricladium varium,* an aquatic hyphomycete on wood in water cooling towers.' *Trans. Br. mycol. Soc.,* 59, 163-167.

JONES, F. R. (1958). 'Three Zoopagales from brackish water.' *Nature,* 181, 575-576.

JONES, F. R. (1959). 'Some Zoopagales from Kenya.' *Trans. Br. mycol. Soc.,* 42, 75-89.

JONES, F. R., and PEACH, M. (1959). *'Acaulopage tetraceros* Drechsler var. *longa* var. nov.' *Trans. Br. mycol. Soc.,* 42, 95-96.

KIRK, P. W. (1969). 'Aquatic hyphomycetes on wood in an estuary.' *Mycologia,* 61, 177-181.

MEYERS, S. P., and HOOPER, B. E. (1967). 'Attraction of the marine nematode *Metoncholaimus* sp., to fungal substrates.' *Bull. mar. Science,* 16, 142-150.

NEWELL, S. Y., and FELL, J. W. (1970). 'The perfect form of a marine-occurring yeast of the genus *Rhodotorula.' Mycologia,* 62, 272-281.

NEWELL, S. Y., and HUNTER, I. L. (1970). *'Rhodosporidium diobovatum* sp. n., the perfect form of an asporogenous yeast (*Rhodotorula* sp.).' *J. Bact.,* 104, 503-508.

NEWTON, J. A. (1971). 'A mycological study of decay in the leaves of deciduous trees on the bed of a river.' Ph.D. Thesis, University of Salford.

PARK, D. (1972 a). 'Methods of detecting fungi in organic detritus in water.' *Trans. Br. mycol. Soc.,* 58, 281-290.

PARK, D. (1972 b). 'On the ecology of heterotrophic micro-organisms in freshwater.' *Trans. Br. mycol. Soc.,* 58, 291-299.

PEACH, M. (1950). 'Aquatic predaceous fungi.' *Trans. Br. mycol. Soc.,* 33, 148-153.

PEACH, M. (1952). 'Aquatic predaceous fungi. II.' *Trans. Br. mycol. Soc.,* 35, 19-23.

PEACH, M. (1954). 'Aquatic predacious fungi. III.' *Trans. Br. mycol. Soc.,* 37, 240-247.

PEACH, M., and JUNIPER, A. J. (1955). *'Stylopage araea* Drechsler var *magna* var. nov.' *Trans. Br. mycol. Soc.,* 38, 431-434.

PRICE, I. P., and TALBOT, P. H. B. (1966). 'An aquatic hyphomycete in a lignicolous habitat.' *Aust. J. Bot.,* 14, 19-23.

PUGH, G. J. F. (1962). 'Studies on fungi in coastal soils. II. Fungal ecology in a developing salt marsh.' *Trans. Br. mycol. Soc.,* 45, 560-566.

PUGH, G. J. F., and MATHISON, G. E. (1962). 'Studies on fungi in coastal soils.' III. An ecological survey of keratinophilic fungi.' *Trans. Br. mycol. Soc.,* 45, 567-572.

PUGH, G. J. F., BLAKEMAN, J. P., MORGAN-JONES, G., and EGGINS, H. O. W. (1963). 'Studies on fungi in coastal soils. IV. Cellulose decomposing species in sand dunes.' *Trans. Br. mycol. Soc.,* 46, 565-571.

RITCHIE, D. (1954). 'A fungous flora of the sea.' *Science,* 120, 579.

ROTH, F. J., ORPURT, P. A., and AHEARN, D. G. (1964). 'Occurrence and distribution of fungi in a subtropical marine environment.' *Can. J. Bot.,* 42, 375-383.

SCOURFIELD, D. J. (1940). 'The microscopic life of the leaf carpet of woods and forests.' *Essex Nat.,* 26, 231-246.

SHAW, D. E. (1972). *'Ingoldiella hamata* gen. et sp. nov., a fungus with clamp connexions from a stream in north Queensland.' *Trans. Br. mycol. Soc.,* 59, 255-259.

SHEARER, C. A. (1971). 'A study of the ecology, taxonomy and physiology of some wood-inhabiting Ascomycetes and Fungi Imperfecti from the Patuxent River.' Ph.D. Thesis, University of Maryland.

SIEPMANN, R. (1959). 'Ein bietrag zue saprophytischen pilzflora des wattes der Wesermündung.' *Veröff. Inst. Meeresforsch. Bremerh.,* 6, 213-281, 283-301.

SIEPMANN, R., and JOHNSON, T. W. (1960). 'Isolation and culture of fungi from wood submerged in saline and freshwaters.' *J. Elisha Mitchell scient. Soc.,* 76, 150-154.

STEELE, C. W. (1967). 'Fungous populations in marine waters and coastal sands of the Hawaiian Line, and Phoenix Islands.' *Pacific Science,* 21, 317-331.

STEVENSON, J. P. (1970). 'Scourge of the salmon.' *New Scientist,* 45, 353-354.

THORNTON, M. L. (1971). 'Potential for long-range dispersal of aquatic phycomycetes by internal transport in birds.' *Trans. Br. mycol. Soc.* 57, 49-59.

TUBAKI, K. (1960). 'On the Japanese aquatic hyphomycetes. Scum and foam group, referrring to the preliminary survey of the snow group.' *Nagava,* 7, 15-29.

TUBAKI, K. (1966). 'Marine fungi from Japan. Lignicolous 1.' *Trans. mycol. Soc. Jap.,* 7, 73-87.

UNESTAM, T. (1964). 'The problem of the crayfish plague.' *Svensk Naturvet enskap,* 317-327.

UNESTAM, T. (1965). 'Studies on the crayfish plague fungus *Aphanomyces astaci* 1. Some factors affecting growth in vitro.' *Physiologia Pl.,* 18, 483-505.

UNESTAM, T. (1969). 'On the adaptation of *Aphanomyces astaci* as a parasite.' *Physiologia Pl.,* 22, 221-235.

WAID, J. S. (1954). 'Occurrence of aquatic hyphomycetes upon the root surfaces of beech grown in woodland soils.' *Trans. Br. mycol. Soc.,* 37, 420-421.

WEBSTER, J. (1959). 'Experiments with spores of aquatic hyphomycetes. I. Sedimentation and impaction on smooth surfaces.' *Ann. Bot.,* 23, 595-611.

WEBSTER, J. (1961). 'The *Mollisia* perfect state of *Anguillospora crassa.'* *Trans. Br. mycol. Soc.,* 44, 559-564.

WEBSTER, J., and TOWFIK, F. H. (1972). 'Sporulation of aquatic hyphomycetes in relation to aeration.' *Trans. Br. mycol. Soc.,* 59, 353-364.

WILLIAMS, M. C., and LICHTWARDT, R. W. (1972). 'Physiological studies on the cultured trichomycete, *Smittium culisetae.'* *Mycologia,* 64, 806-815.

WILLOUGHBY, G. L. (1969). 'Pure culture studies on the aquatic phycomycete *Lagenidium giganteum.'* *Trans. Br. mycol. Soc.,* 52, 393-410.

WILLOUGHBY, G. L. and ARCHER, J. F. (1973). 'The fungal spora of a freshwater stream and its colonization pattern on wood', *Freshwat. Biol.,* 3, 219-239.

Index

Note: Page references in italics indicate illustrations

sex hormones 557-8; *anomalus* 584; *arbusculus* 548, 613, 618; axonemes in 634; cell walls of 555; effect of light on 558; *javanicus* 473, 480, 498, 520; life cycle of 553; *macrogynus* 613, *642;* nuclear caps of 624, 627; nucleolus position 626; respiratory rate of 548

Alnus glutinosa 348, 351; *rugosa* 484

alpha-mesosaprobity 406

Altenaria 3, 33, 83, 148, 167, 371, 374, 440, 442, 711, 718; *alternata* 62, 65-6, 75-6, 78-9, 81, 414; *maritima* 4, 12, 14, 17, 19, 25, 30-1, 159; *tenuis* 81, 85, 371, 374, 718

Althornia 220; *crouchii 199-200,* 201, 262, 264, 269, 271-4, 281, *286,* 290, 292, 296, *302,* 306

amino-acids 554-6, 559, 693; biosynthesis of 552-3; for amoebagenesis 669; fungi-supporting 545-6; removal of 691

Ammophilia 30; *arenaria* 30

amoebae 299, 301, 303; fungi predatory on 714; holozoic 303

amoebagenesis 669

Amoebidiales 514, 653, 655-6, 662, 664, *664-6,* 669; holdfasts of 664

Amoebidiaceae 653, *664-7*

Amoebidium 653, 664, 669; *parasiticum* 651, 653-5, *667,* 669, 708; situation of 669

Amoeboaphelidium 490, 509; *protococcarum* 509

amoebid cells 656, 664; stages 196

Amoebophya ceratii 489

amorphosporangia *676,* 690

amphigynous antheridia 216

Amphicypellus elegans 497

amphipods, freshwater 435-6, 438

Amphisphaeria 34

Ampullariella 677, 681, 690

Amylocarpus 36; *encephaloides* 3, 34, 38-9

Anabaena 693; *flos-aquae* 489

anabolism 549-54

anaerobiosis, conditions of 460-1, 680, 687-8

angiosperms 521

Anguillospora 440, *441,* 442; *crassa 347,* 348, 350, 709, 711; *longissima 341,* 345-6, *347,* 348, 352, 380, 711

animals, annelid tubes 28, 30; and leaf material 435, 438-44, *439, 441;* balanid shells 28, 30; calcareous algae 28, 30; diseases of marine 223-60; faeces of 435; fungal interrelationships 166, 442, 531-2; hydrozoan tubes 28, 30; molluscan shells 28, 30; teredinid shells 28, 30

Ankistrodesmus 490

Anomia simplex 234

Antarctic and subantarctic water masses 102

antherida 330, 558, *575,* 604, 607; development of 639, *640,* 641; and cellulase activity 559

antibiotics, antibacterial 438, 673, 677; antifungal 438; broad spectrum 592; effect on

fungus cells 548; in isolations 708; polyene 559

antibodies, and fish survival 590; and mucus 590-2; humoral 589-90; serological 586-7, 589-94; teleost 592-3

antigens 586-7, 589; analysis of 586; bacterial 590-1; fungal 589-90, 590-2; 592, 594

antisaprobity 406

antisera 586, 589, *591*

Anthostomella 63, 75

Aphanodictyon 220

Aphanomyces 220, 409, 423-5, 518, 545-6, 584, 613, 623, 632-4, 637; and fish disease 574, 584; *astaci* 544-5; cleavage patterns in 621-2; *eutreiches* 450, 455, 546, 613, 623; flagella shedding by 635; Golgi bodies in 625, 638; *laevis* 531, 550, 574, 584; mitochondria in 625; nucleolus position in 626; on fish eggs 574; *parasiticus* 531; ribosomes in 627; root system of 629, 637; vacuole generation in 638

Aphanomycopsis 215, 220

Aphelenchoides 166

Aphelidium chlorococcarum 490

Aphyllophorales 41

Aplanochytrium 219-20; *kerguelensis* 206, *207*

Aplanopsis 220; *spinosa* 518, 522, 533; *terrestris* 518

aplanospore 285-7, 329

Apodachlya 215, 220, 545, 547, *610,* 611; *brachynema* 609; cell walls of 556-7; *punctata* 550

Apodachlyella 215, 220

apophyses 470-1, 473-4, 480; endobiotic 491, 496; influence of substrates on 483; spherical 480; wall thickness of 469

apothecia 348

Apostemidium 337; *quernisaci 337-8,* 710

appendages 2, 5-6, 338, 658-9, *658-9,* 663-4; eccrinid 664

Aqualinderella 216, 220, 545, 548; absence of growth in air of *fermentans* 707-8; *fermentans* 266, 392-3, 545-6, 687, 707-8

Araiospora 216, 545

arboviruses 303

Arbutus menziesii 29

arenicolous 1, 32-3

Armillaria mellea 589

Arthopyrenia 229, 233; *sublittoralis* 201, 234

arthropods, and Trichomycetes 532, 651, 654-5, 664, 666, *667;* ecdysis of 655, 664; moulting of 655, 664, 667-9

Artemia salina 313, 324, *325,* 708

Arthrobotrys cladodes 716; *dactyloides* 716; *superba* 716

arthrospores 656, 660, *661*

Articulospora tetracladia 341, 343, 346-7, 350, 709, 711

Arundinula 652-3, 655; *orconectis 663*

asci 336, *336-7;* deliquescing 39, 41; ectoascus

272, 274; oxygenation 266, 531; pH 139-41, 160, 264-5; potassium efflux 153; protein production 160; reproduction—*see* under reproduction—salinity 141-51, 160, 266-71; spore germination 138, 152-3; steroids 275; temperature 135-9, 160, 261-4; vegetative growth 141-7, 153; vitamin needs 161-2, 272

fungi—*see also* flagellates, fungal physiology, lignicolous fungi—aero-aquatic 714; aerobic 548-9; algicolous 1, 4, 37; and cooling towers 359-87, 709; and DDT 447-67; and fish 573-601; and geofungi 390; and leaf palatability 440-1, *441;* and pH values 424, 442; and plant debris 436, *534, 573, 674-5,* 577, 581, 717; and sex hormones 588-9; and timber 378; animal relationships 166; antigens of 586-7; aquatic 390-1, 440-1, 459, 489, 494, 499-509, 513-42, 612, 618, 708-14; asexual 492, 519, 530-2; as food 421, 438-44; attackers of algae 489-511; biflagellate 622-3, 627, 632; blooms of 492, 497, 499-500, 502-3; chytridial 469. 497; colonization patterns of 378-9, 437-8, 442-3, 524, 574, 717; colony counts of 397, *397-8;* contribution to energy flow 513-14, 531, 558-9, 561; composition of population of 514; density of 317-19, 321, 323; differences between strains 586; distribution of 4, 18-19, 314-21, 408-19, 459, 516, 520*ff, 522-3, 525, 527;* ecology of aquatic 513-42; effect on leaf protein 437-8; endomembrane system of aquatic 611-13; enumeration of 717, 720; enzyme efficiency of 509; estuarine 18. 279-312, 325, 329-30, 373, 437, 632, 716-17; evolution of 1, 39-41, 335; filamentous 78, 392, 394, 397, 401, 403, 414, 421-2, 425-6; flooding, effects of 521, 525; Floridean evolution, theory of 40-1; free-floating 1; freshwater 673-98; freshwater on algae 469-512; freshwater uniflagellate 469-87, 516*ff;* gardens of 442; growth and development of 557-61, 707-8; growth in cooling towers 380-2, 715; growth responses to pesticides 450-2, *453,* 458-9, *458;* gut inhabiting 531-2, 654*ff;* heterokont biflagellate 515; higher, in marine sediments 716-17; hydrocarbonoclastic 126-7; in bags 436-7; in sludge digestion 403-4, *404-5;* in waste stabilization ponds 401-3; *402,* 421-2; isolation of—*see* isolates—larvae-dwelling 651*ff;* light effect on 557-8; lower freshwater 543-72; marine 279-333, 373, 379-81, 423; metabolism of 454, 513; morphological adaptations of 687-9; mud 521, 525, 533, 679, 681, 683-5, 692, *694;* mutations in 531; nutrition of 543-7, 689; occurrence of 516-17, 519-24, *525,* 526, *527,* 528; oxygen needs of 392, *453,* 454, 545, 547; parasitic 489-512, 530-1, 543; perfect stages of 348-9, 709*n;* period-

icity of 322-4, 529, 717; pollution effects on 390-1; polyphagous 504-5; predacious 421, 714-16; productivity of 126, 513-14, 516, 519; protein production of 4; reproduction of saprolegniaceous 328-30, 391-2; resistance of 367, 381, 507, 692-3; respiration of 452, 454, 459, 513-14, 547-9; role of aquatic 448, 519, 532, *534;* saline soils 194-5, 266-71, 321-2, 325-8; salinity—*see* salinity—saprobic 404-19; saprophytic 25, 448, 479-81, 483, 490, 493-4, 497-9, *498,* 505, 515, 543; sexual reproduction in 638-43; sewage 316, 389-434, *404-5, 407,* 521; slime 514; soil 391, 401, 408, 518, 521, 716-7; substrate relationships of 324-8, *325, 327;* temperature effect on 135-9, 160, 164, 225, 233-4, 261-4, 275, 365, 373, 380-1, 441, 497-9, 506-8; terrestrial 1, 80, 379, 381, 448, 450, 708-14, 716-17; test blocks/panels for 373, 378-80, *382,* 383, 715, 717; trickling filter situation of 395-401, *397,* 408; uniflagellate 469-87, 515, 615, 617-8, 622-3, 632, 635; vegetative phases of 141-7, 153, 531-3, 535, 553, 623; vitamin needs of 161-2, 272, 544, 689; weight loss tests on 374-7, 379, 381, *382*

fungicides 501

Fungi Imperfecti 1, 3, 12-14, 16-17, 25, 28-9, 32-3, 37-8, 82, 136-7, 144-5, 147, 153, 159, 163-4, 166, 223, 262, 335, 339-57, 362, 368, 370, 373, 378-9, 412-19, 711-12, 717; aquatic 448; coprophilous 244, 349; evolution of 335; soil inhabiting 82, 85, 315, 321-2, 716

Furcellaria fastigiata 21

Fusarium 29, 62, 83, 85, 125, 145, 147, 371, 375, 380, 389, 416, 440, 442, 458, 586, 711, 718; *acuminatum* 416; *aquaeductum* 416, 426; *avenaceum* 589; esterification in 586; *herbarum* 416; *moniliforme* 416; *oxysporum* 416, 456; *roseum* 416; *solani* 371, 416, 450, 455-8

Gadus morhua 226

Galaxaura 20

gametangia 493, *493,* 547-8; differentiation of 553; fusion of 639-41

gametes 391, 548, 687; and sirenin 559; flagellate 391, *642;* fusion of 641, 643; motile 558, 641; of Chytridiomycetes 551; release of 558, 641, 643; RNA synthesis and 533; similarity to zoospores 641

gametogenesis 558

gamma particles 633-4

Gammarus pseudolimnaeus 438-41, *439;* assimilation of fungus etc by 438-40, *439;* vitamin needs of 438-9

Gasteromycetes 41, 82, 138

Gelasinospora retispora 144, 150, 152

gemmae 217, 328, 391

parasites 329, 336, 473-4, 481, 500, 543; and fish 573, 577-85, 589, 591; and fish mucus 587; attacks on insects by 530; biflagellate 499; crab eggs 215; ecology of fungal on algae 499-509; flagellate fungal 531; obligate 517, 520; on algal hosts 489-512; phycomycetous 618; source of protein 509; sporadic occurrence of 508; studies of 517; Trichomycetes as 654; ultrastructure of 618-19; uniflagellate 499

parasitism 448, 500, 503, 618-19

Parataeniella 652

Parataeniellaceae 652, 662

Paspalum dilatatum 476-7

pathogens 306, 420, 509, 573, 585, 591-2; algal 490; enzootic 225; epizootic 225; oyster 306-7; virus 490

Pediastrum 473, 480, 497-8, 502, 508; *boryanum* 491, 498, *498,* 502; *duplex* 493, *493,* 498-9, *498;* var. *clathratum* 493, *493,* 498-9. *498;* var. *reticulatum* 493, *493,* 498, *498*

Pelvetia 21, 24; *canaliculata* 21-5

penetration 618-19, 639, *640,* 641

Penicillium 82-4, 87, 125, 128, 339, 366, 372, 417, 426, 712, 719; *canescens* 417; *charlesii* 417; *chrysogenum* 417; *citrinum* 424; *claviforme* 589; *commune* 417; *corylophilum* 417; *corymbiferum* 417; *crustosum* 417; *cyclopium* 417; *decumbens* 417; *expansum* 367, 417; *fellutanum* 417; *frequentans* 417, 457; *funiculosum* 418; *herquei* 418; *implicatum* 418; *janthinellum* 146, 418; *javanicum* 411, 418; *kapuscinskii* 418; *lanosum* 418; *lilacinum* 418; *luteum* 375; *martensii* 418; *nigricans* 418; *notatum* 145, 147, 152, 456-7; *ochro-chloron* 418; *oxalicum* 418; *palitans* 418; *puberulum* 418; *pulvillorum* 418; *purpureogenum* 418; *raistrickii* 418; *roseopurpureum* 62, 66, 74, 76-7, 79-80, 82-4; *rubrum* 418; *sclerotiorum* 418; *simplicissimum* 418; *steckii* 62, 65-6, 76, 79; species differences in 586; *stipitatum* 412, 418; *thomii* 418; *variabile* 418; *velutinum* 419

Peniophora mollis 368

Pennella 652, 659

Periconia 52; *balani* 30; *prolifica* 52, 62, *236,* 237

Peridinium cinctum 497; *willei* 497

Peronospora 220, 328

Peronoplasmopara 220

Peronosporaceae 216, 218, 220

Peronosporacean galaxy 214-15, 220

Peronosporales 216, 220, 246, 251, 514, 518; isolations of DNA from 549-50; nutritional needs of 544; sterols in reproduction of 546, 560

Pestalotia 63-4, 67-8, *70,* 72, 74, 76, 78-81, 83, 87, 719; *heterocornis* 419

Pestalotiopsis westerdijkii 161

pesticides—*see also* Dichloro (DDT)—and aqua-

tic fungi 448*ff;* dechlorination of 458-9; degradation of 448, 454-6, *456;* degradations, products of 449; dehydrogenation of 458; effects of 447-8; influences on 448, 454-7, *456;* pollution from 447, 449-50; restrictions on using 448

Petersenia 218, 220

Petriellidium boydii 412

petroleum products 126

pH 139-41, 160, 164, 264, *323,* 362, 364-5, 381, 403, 424, 436, 442, 494, 499, 513, 684; and DDT accumulation 455; control of with carbon dioxide 560; effect on algae 498, 503, 508; influence of on fungi 480-1, 521, 527, 720

Phaeonectriella lignicola 370, 380

Phaeophyceae 306

Phaeosaria clematidis 712

Phaeoscopulariopsis 372

Phaeosphaeria ammophilae 30; *eustoma* 370, 374

Phaeostoma 372, 376

phagocytosis 589; digestion by 490

Pharcidia balani 30; *pelvetiae* 23

phialides 340, 343, 688

phialoconidia 340, 343, 345

Phialophora 372, 375; *fastigiata* 32, 419; *richardsiae* 372, 375

Phialophorophoma littoralis 136

phialospores 341, 348

Phlyctaena 63

Phlyctidium 195, 501-2; *bumillariae* 503-4; *marinum* 267; *megastomum* 267; *scenedesmi* 491, 494, 496, 501-2, 508

Phlyctochytrium 194-5, 198, 267, 280-1, *282,* 283, 285, *286,* 287, 292, 295, 303, 409, 471, 473, 479, 552, 615, 617-8, 632; *acuminatum 327,* 479; *africanum* 267, *327; bisporum* 409; *californicum* 326, *327,* 479; *chaetiferum* 267, 322, 326; characteristics of 472; *dichotomum* 267; effect of light on 558; *equale* 409; flagella shedding 635; *hallii* 409; *infestans* 613; *irregulare* 267, 470-1, 475-6, 613, 614; kinetochores in *616,* 617; *kniepii* 267; *laterale* 409; *liniepii 327;* *mangrovii* 87, 262, 264, 266, 270-1, 273-4, 328; *mucronatum* 267, 479; *palustre* 195, 267-8, 320, 326, *327; planicorne 525; plurigibbosum* 479; *punctatum* 267, *327,* 470-1, 475-6, 480, 483-6; *reinboldtae* 194, 267, 322, 326, 480; rumposomes in 632; *semiglobiferum* 195, 267, 326, *327; spectabile* 267; *vernale* 409

Phlyctorhiza variabilis 525

Phoma 11, 18, 29-32, 52, 63, 65, 67, 72, 86, 145-6, 226, 372, 412, 712; *herbarum* 145, 412; *cytosporella* 372, 375; *laminariae* 23; moniliales 412; *typharum* 85

Phomopsis 63

phospholipids 621

photoreceptors 308

Pontoporeia 3; *biturbinata* 31
pores, nuclear 613, *616*
Poria incrassata 367; *nigrescens* 368; *oleraceae* *368*
Porolithon onkodes 22
Portunus depusator 245-6
Prasiola 21-2
precipitin 589, 592-4; lines of 586, 589-90, *593;* mobility of *590-1;* reactions of in sera 589; sexual differences in 594
preservatives, timber 362-6, 378, 380-3, *382;* waterborne 364, 366, 378
primordia 342-3
procentrioles 283, 291, 293, 613, 623
productivity, and propagules 521, 531; in marine ecosystems 126, 513-14, 516
promycelium 708
propagules, and substrate 531-2; asexual 531-2; cross-contamination of *528,* 532; fungal 314, 316, 321, 353-4, 380, 514, 518-19, *534;* in life cycle 638-9; numbers of 516, 520-1, 524-5, *527,* 530, 533; tetra-radiate 339
protein, and cell walls 555-7, 604-5; complement of 586; degradation of 554; effect of light on 557; production of 100, 160; removal of 691; synthesis of 553-4, 559, 613, 627, 634, 638
proteins, fungi-supporting 545, in water moulds 552; shark serum 593
proteolytic activity 161
Protoachlya paradoxa 328-30, 550
protopectin 624
protoperithecia 348
protoplasm, fungal 513
protoplasts 306, 556; role of cellulase in 604
Protozoa 224, 306, 390, 396-7; endoparasitic 490, 509; on trickling filters 395-7, 399-400; planktonic 490; resistance to fungicide 367; rhizopodean 303
Prunus laurocerasus 29
Pseudoeurotium indicum 18; *multisporum* 370, 374
Pseudolithophyllum 20, 30; *expansum* 22
Pseudomonas fluorescens 585, 678
Pseudoneottiospora cunicularia 344
Pseudopileum unum 489
pseudopodia 303, 490
Pseudosphaerita 220
Pseudospora 490
pseudothecia 336-7, *336-7,* 348
Pseudotsuga 198
Psilopezia babingtonii 336, *338*
psychrophiles 121
Pteromaktron 652
Ptilonia australasica 20
Pullospora tetrachaeta 344
Pullularia 146, 371-2, 375
Purpura lapillus 228
Pylaiella 324
Pyramidospora constricta 341

Pyrenochaeta 372, 376, 712
Pyrenomycetes 2, 3, 25, 34, 39, 336-8, 348
Pyronema domesticum 144
pyruvate
Pythiaceae 216, 220, 246, 329, 714
Pythiella 220
Pythiogeton 216, 220; *utriforme* 64, 74-5
Pythiopsis 220; *cymosa* 518, *522,* 529
Pythium 145, 201, 215-17, 220, 329, 410, 423-6, 450, 543, 545, 547, 552-3, 559-60, 584, 609, 632-3, 635; and fish 574, 584; *aphanidermatum 606,* 611, *628;* cell walls of 555-6, *606,* 608; cholesterol in 560; *debaryanum* 410; *elongatum* 410; fatty acids in 551-2; Golgi bodies in 625-6; *inflatum* 410; *marinum* 281, 295, 303; *middletonii* 624; *monospermum* 410; *ostracodes* 714; *pulchrum* 410, 551; ribosomes in 627; root system of 629; species differences in 586; *thallassium 245,* 246; *ultimum* 146, 410, 450, 455, 548, 551, 584, *610,* 612; vacuole generation in 638

Rabenhorstia 63
radiolaria, fungi predatory on 714
radiosaprobity 406
Ramacrinella 652
Ramularia brachialis 237
red cedar 365
redwoods 364-5
Remispora 34, 36-7; *hamata* 12, 15, 18; *maritima* 12-13, 15, 18, 34, 371; *ornata* 184; *pilleata* 18; *stellata* 371
reproduction 147-9, 153, 162-6; and sterols 546, 560; asexual 553, 619, 656, 658; cells of 493; gamete fusion 641, 643; influence of substrate type on 546; morphological aspects of 469; pesticide effect on 447, 459; salinity effects on 147-51; spore-activated in water 138, 152-3, 391
respiration, aerobic 513-14; DDT and fungal 452, 454, 459, 547-9; endogenous 513, 548-9, 554, 561; lag phase in 454; oxidative 513
Rhinocladiella mansonii 419
Rhipidiaceae 216, 220, 514; distribution of 520
Rhipidium 216, 220, 545, 550
Rhizidiomyces 556; *apophystatus* 613; axonemes in 634; Golgi bodies in 625; kinetosomes in 622; mitochondria in 625; nucleolus position 626; ribosomal characteristics of 627; root system of 629, 632
Rhizidium 267; *laevis* 267; *richmondense* 267, *525; varians* 267; *verrucosum* 267
Rhizoctonia crocorum 372, 376; *solani* 450-1, 455-7
rhizoidal system 469-70, 479, 493-4; branched 470-1, 473-4; multiple 474; nature of 469-70

species imbalance, DDT 447
Spegazzinia 146
Sphaceloma cecidii 24
Sphaerella 11
Sphaeriaceae 3
Sphaeropsidales 61, 63, 67, 71, 75, 344, 349, 372, 412-19
Sphaerotilus natans 394, 425
Sphaerulina 3, 34; *albispiculata* 136; *codicola* 24; *orae-maris* 11; *pedicellata* 29-31
Sphagnum 436
Sphaleromantis 632
Spicaria 146; *divaricata* 372
spindles 613, *614,* 615, *616,* 617-18, 639
Spirillospora 677, *676-7*
Spirogyra 471-2, 480-1, 492-4, 507-8; susceptibility of 508
Spirosphaera floriform 715
Spongia 252
Spongiophaga 252
sporangia 199, 205, 207, *302, 325,* 469-70, 472, 489, 491-4, *493, 495,* 502, 554-5, *663,* 673, *675-7,* 690; abnormal 502; and carbon dioxide 560-1; colour variations in 470-1, 558; differentiation of 554; discharge method 496; dwarf 474; effect of light on 588; epibiotic 480; from rhizoidal axes 482, 493; globose 492-3; influence of cultures on 477-9, 481-5, 491-4, 502, 690; inoperculate 496; oval 491; ovate 492; papillae of 472-3, 477, 479-80, 492-3, 624; proliferation of 203-4, 218; resistant 560-1; resting 478, 530; sessile 492; stalked 492; substrate effect on size 471, 473-4; temperature effect on 478, 481, 530; time effect on 506; uninucleate 497; wall thickness of 469-71, 483-5, 491, *493,* 530, 560
sporangiospores 656, 662, *662-3,* 664, *667,* 669; attached to substrate 664
spore dispersal 391-2, 478, 483-4, 666; ascus explosion 336-7, *337;* asexual 619; pathogenic fungi 252-3
spore germination 38, 138, 152-3, 380, 392, 494, 506, 517, 522, 529-30, 535, 553-4, 557-9, 574, 588, 611, 634-8, 668, 687-8, 708; salinity effect 149-51; structure 182, 225; temperature effect on 138
spore liberation 1, 37-8, 338, 340, 624, *657, 679;* airborne 339; bitunicate asci 39; passing discharge 38; seasonal 532; unitunicate asci 38, 337
spores, alien 524-5; appendages to 658-9, *658-9,* 663-4, 669, 720; asexual 519, 526, 619; availability of 521; biflagellate 627, 629, 632; binucleate 662; branched 448, 558-9; chitin synthesis in 557; dome colonies of *679,* 688, 690; encapsulation of 589; filiform *676,* 688; head colonies of 688, 690; homogenization of 683; isolation of 519, *686;* maturation of 623; motile 626, 633, 635, 673, *676,* 678, *679,* 688; movement of

627; multinucleate 662, *663;* non-motile 448; ovoid 448; production of and DDT 450-1, pyriform 629; relation to leaching 524; reniform 629; resting 218, 482-3, 478, 489, 491-4, *493,* 496, 498, 501, 506, 531, *667;* root system of *628,* 629, *630,* 631; sedimentation of fungal 345; sexual production of 492, sigmoid 448; spherical 448; suspension of 683; tetra-radiate 343, 448, 687, 714; thick-walled 662-3; thin-walled 662, uniflagellate 627, 629, 632, 639; uninucleate 622, 662
spore settlement (impaction) 1, 37-8, 338-9
spore transportation 1, 37, 401-2
Sporidesmium 3; *salinum* 6, 13-14, 16, 38, 142, 153-4
sporidia 708
Sporobolomyces 97, 101, 129; *hispanicus* 101, 105; *odorus* 101, 105-6, 120; *pararoseus* 101, 117; *roseus* 101, 117-19, 402; *salmonicolor* 101, 106, 112-13, 117-18
Sporidiobolus 97; *johnsonii* 101
Sporobolus virginicus 87
Sporocybe 372, 376; */Acremonium* 372, 376-7; */Coniothyrium* 375; */Haplochalara* 372-3, 376
sporodochia 688
sporogenesis 280-6
Sporormia leporina 370, 374; *minima* 370, 374
Sporothrix 62
Sporotrichum 377, 419; *maritimum* 24
Sporozoa 293
sporulation 11, 305, 424, 518, *534,* 554, 621, *663,* 668, 685, 689-92, 707; effect of DDT on 450; varying 522; waterless 709
springs, pollution of 449
Stachybotrys 166-7; *atra* 144, 148, 152, 372, 719; *Chartarum* 419
Stachylina (Harpellaceae) 514, 532, 652-5, 659; *grandispora 657,* 658; *minuta* 659
Stagonospora 11, 372
Staurastrum 480-1, 504; *chaetoceros* 504; *cingulum* 500, *500;* *cuspidatum* 504—var. *divergens* 504—*muticum* 504; *pinque* 503-4
Stemphylium 3, 146, 419; *codii* 24; *dendriticum* 372, 377; *maritimum* 17, 31, 159; *triglochinicola* 30
Sterigmatobotrys macrocarpa 372, 378, 380, 712
Sterigmatomyces 101-2; *halophilus* 105, 137, 156-7; *indicus* 105
steroids/sterols 275, 552, 558-60; synthesis of 560
Stigmatea pelvetiae 24
Stilbella 419
Stipella 652, 659
streams, etc 435; Actinomycetes in 681, 689-90; allochthonous material in 435; artificial 438; energy available to 435-46; pollution of 449

748

GLASSBORO STATE COLLEGE